W9-AXZ-344

Less managing. More teaching. Greater learning.

INSTRUCTORS...

Would you like your **students** to show up for class **more prepared**?
(Let's face it, class is much more fun if everyone is engaged and prepared…)

Want an **easy way to assign** homework online and track student **progress**?
(Less time grading means more time teaching…)

Want an **instant view** of student or class performance?
(No more wondering if students understand…)

Need to **collect data and generate reports** required for administration or accreditation?
(Say goodbye to manually tracking student learning outcomes…)

Want to **record and post your lectures** for students to view online?
(The more students can see, hear, and experience class resources, the better they learn…)

With **McGraw-Hill's *Connect*,®**

INSTRUCTORS GET:

- Simple **assignment management**, allowing you to spend more time teaching.
- **Auto-graded** assignments, quizzes, and tests.
- **Detailed visual reporting** where student and section results can be viewed and analyzed.
- Sophisticated **online testing** capability.
- A **filtering and reporting** function that allows you to easily assign and report on materials that are correlated to learning objectives and Bloom's taxonomy.
- An easy-to-use **lecture capture** tool.
- The option to **upload course documents** for student access.

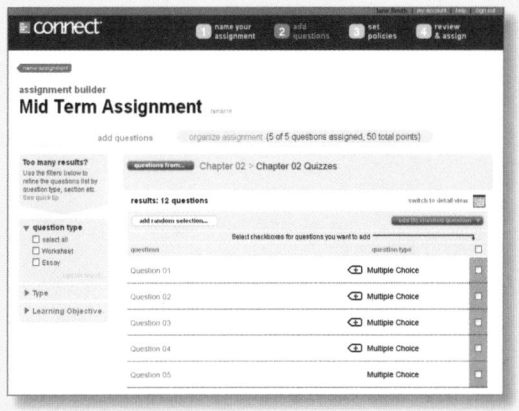

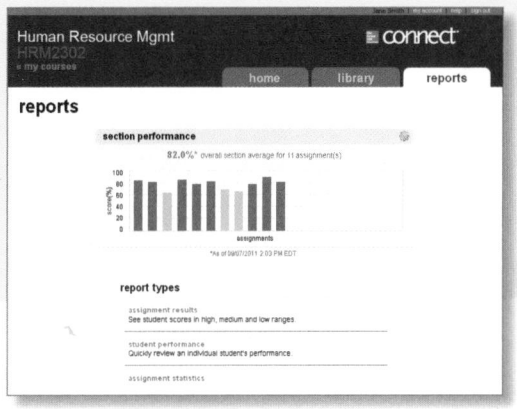

VOLUME **TWO**

INTERMEDIATE ACCOUNTING

SIXTH EDITION

Thomas H. Beechy
Schulich School of Business
York University

Joan E.D. Conrod
Faculty of Management
Dalhousie University

Elizabeth J. Farrell
Schulich School of Business
York University

Ingrid McLeod-Dick
Schulich School of Business
York University

McGraw-Hill Ryerson

McGraw-Hill Ryerson

Intermediate Accounting
Volume 2
Sixth Edition

Copyright © 2014, 2011, 2008, 2005, 2003, 2000 by McGraw-Hill Ryerson Limited. All rights reserved. No part of this publication may be reproduced or transmitted in any form or by any means, or stored in a data base or retrieval system, without the prior written permission of McGraw-Hill Ryerson Limited, or in the case of photocopying or other reprographic copying, a license from The Canadian Copyright Licensing Agency (Access Copyright). For an Access Copyright license, visit www.accesscopyright.ca or call toll free to 1-800-893-5777.

The Internet addresses listed in the text were accurate at the time of publication. The inclusion of a website does not indicate an endorsement by the authors or McGraw-Hill Ryerson, and McGraw-Hill Ryerson does not guarantee the accuracy of the information presented at these sites.

ISBN-13: 978-0-07-133882-0
ISBN-10: 0-07-133882-9

1 2 3 4 5 6 7 8 9 10 TCP 1 9 8 7 6 5 4

Printed and bound in Canada.

Care has been taken to trace ownership of copyright material contained in this text; however, the publisher will welcome any information that enables them to rectify any reference or credit for subsequent editions.

Director of Product Management: Rhondda McNabb
Product Manager: Keara Emmett
Executive Marketing Manager: Joy Armitage Taylor
Product Developers: Lindsay MacDonald and Chris Cullen
Senior Product Team Associate: Christine Lomas
Supervising Editor: Jessica Barnoski
Photo/Permissions Researcher: Steve Rouben, Photo Affairs, Inc.
Copy Editor: Karen Rolfe
Proofreader: Rohini Herbert
Plant Production Coordinator: Tammy Mavroudi
Manufacturing Production Coordinator: Lena Keating
Cover Design: Katherine Strain
Cover Images: Flag: Louis B. Wallach Inc./Getty Images RM; Graph: Saul Gravy/Getty Images (RM); Building: Shutterstock/Alex Saberi; Money: Vstock LLC/Getty RF.
Interior Design: Katherine Strain
Page Layout: Christopher Hudson
Printer: Transcontinental Printing Group

Library and Archives Canada Cataloguing in Publication

Beechy, Thomas H., 1937–, author
Intermediate accounting / Thomas H. Beechy, Schulich School of Business, York University, Joan E.D. Conrod, Faculty of Management, Dalhousie University, Elizabeth J. Farrell, Schulich School of Business, York University, Ingrid McLeod-Dick, Schulich School of Business, York University. — Sixth edition.

Includes index.

Revision of: Intermediate accounting / Thomas H. Beechy, Joan E.D. Conrod, Elizabeth J. Farrell. — 5th ed. — Toronto : McGraw-Hill Ryerson, c2011.

ISBN 978-0-07-133947-6 (v. 1 : bound).—ISBN 978-0-07-133882-0 (v. 2 : bound)

1. Accounting—Textbooks. I. Conrod, Joan E. D. (Joan Elizabeth Davison), 1956–, author II. Farrell, Elizabeth, author III. McLeod-Dick, Ingrid, author IV. Title.

HF5635.B466 2014 657'.044 C2013-905925-3

About the Authors

Thomas H. Beechy, York University

Thomas H. Beechy is a Professor Emeritus of Accounting at the Schulich School of Business, York University. He also is the Director of International Academic Development. Professor Beechy holds degrees from George Washington University (BA), Northwestern University (MBA), and Washington University (DBA). Before entering Canada in 1971, Professor Beechy taught for 10 years at Illinois Institute of Technology, after which he was employed at the Kellogg School of Business (Northwestern University) as a case writer. He has been active in research and publication for about 50 years, having published six books, including *Advanced Financial Accounting*, and numerous articles in accounting journals. Professor Beechy has been a leader in Canadian accounting education, emphasizing the importance of case analysis in developing students' professional judgement and accounting skills. He also has been an active researcher and advocate in both business and nonprofit financial reporting.

Joan E. D. Conrod, Dalhousie University

Joan E. D. Conrod is a Professor of Accounting in the Rowe School of Business at Dalhousie University. Her teaching excellence has been recognized through awards, such as the 2013 3M National Teaching Fellowship, the Dalhousie University Alumni Award for Teaching Excellence, and the AAU Distinguished Teacher award. She was awarded her FCA from the Nova Scotia Institute of Chartered Accountants in 1999. Joan is an active member of the University community and has served on the Dalhousie University Senate and the Board of Governors. She is a past president of the Canadian Academic Accounting Association. Joan has a lengthy history of involvement in professional accounting education. She has taught financial and managerial accounting courses to CA students across Canada, but particularly in Atlantic Canada, for 20 years. She has served on CA education committees at the local, regional, and national levels. Her publications include the text *Intermediate Accounting*, *Financial Accounting 3* for CGA-Canada, and a variety of case material and other publications.

Elizabeth J. Farrell, York University

Elizabeth J. Farrell is an adjunct professor and has taught at the Schulich School of Business for many years. She was awarded her FCPA, FCA from the Institute of Chartered Accountants of Ontario in 2013. In recognition of her excellence in teaching, she was awarded the Seymour Schulich Award for Teaching Excellence in 1999, 2003, and 2010 and was nominated for the award in 2004, 2005, 2006, 2007, 2008, and 2012. She was awarded the John Peace teaching faculty award in 2001 and 2012. She has taught financial accounting courses for over 20 years. Liz is assistant coordinator of the Institute of Chartered Accountants of Ontario's School of Accountancy, where she also has served as a seminar leader for many years. She has taught executive development courses for the Schulich Executive Education Centre (SEEC), as well as professional development courses for the ICAO and for CA firms. In addition to being a co-author of the *Intermediate Accounting*, she has also worked on an accounting case analysis software package; study guides; an IFRS Property, Plant, and Equipment, Intangible Assets and Impairment professional development course; *ASPE—A Comparison to IFRS*; *Guide to ASPE*; and a variety of case material and other publications.

Ingrid McLeod-Dick, York University

Ingrid McLeod-Dick is an adjunct professor and has taught at the Schulich School of Business for many years in its BBA, MBA, and EMBA programs. In recognition of her excellence in teaching, she received the John Peace part-time faculty teaching award in 2000 and was nominated for the Seymour Schulich Award for Teaching Excellence in 2000 to 2007 and 2012. She was awarded her FCA from the Ontario Institute of Chartered Accountants in 1994. Ingrid also served as a seminar leader for many years for the Institute of Chartered Accountants of Ontario's School of Accountancy. She currently teaches professional development courses for the ICAO. Her publications include the IFRS Financial Presentation and Disclosure course, and she is a contributing author to *Financial Reporting under IFRS* and *Guide to ASPE*, as well as a variety of case material.

Brief Table of Contents—Volume 2

Preface xi

Acknowledgements xvii

CHAPTER 12 Financial Liabilities and Provisions 715

CHAPTER 13 Financial Instruments: Long-Term Debt 771

CHAPTER 14 Shareholders' Equity 825

CHAPTER 15 Financial Instruments: Complex Debt and Equity 885

CHAPTER 16 Accounting for Corporate Income Tax 953

CHAPTER 17 Accounting for Tax Losses 1009

CHAPTER 18 Leases 1059

CHAPTER 19 Post-Employment Benefits 1131

CHAPTER 20 Earnings per Share 1189

CHAPTER 21 Accounting Changes 1249

CHAPTER 22 Financial Statement Analysis 1301

APPENDIX Statement of Cash Flows 1375

Compound Interest Tables and Formulae TA-1

Index IN-1

Table of Contents—Volume 2

Preface xi

Acknowledgements xvii

CHAPTER 12 FINANCIAL LIABILITIES AND PROVISIONS 715

Introduction 715
Liability Definition and Categories 716
Common Financial Liabilities 718
Foreign Currency Payables 723
Nonfinancial Liabilities: Provisions 724
Examples of Provisions 726
The Impact of Discounting 735
Classifying Liabilities 743
Disclosure and Statement of Cash Flows 745
Accounting Standards for Private Enterprises 748
Summary of Key Points 750
Key Terms 751
Review Problem 752
Questions 754
Cases 755
Technical Review 759
Assignments 760

CHAPTER 13 FINANCIAL INSTRUMENTS: LONG-TERM DEBT 771

Introduction 771
Sources of Financing 772
Debt Issuance and Interest Expense 777
Debt Denominated in a Foreign Currency 788
Capitalization of Borrowing Costs 790
Debt Retirement 792
Statement of Cash Flows and Disclosure 797
Accounting Standards for Private Enterprises 801
Summary of Key Points 803
Key Terms 804
Review Problem 804
Questions 806
Cases 807
Technical Review 813
Assignments 814

CHAPTER 14 SHAREHOLDERS' EQUITY 825

Introduction 825
The Corporate Form of Organization 826
Issuance of Share Capital 828
Retirement of Share Capital 832
Treasury Stock 835
Retained Earnings 837
Dividends 838
Stock Splits 848
Additional Contributed Capital 850
Reserves 851
Statement of Changes in Equity, Disclosure, and SCF 853
Accounting Standards for Private Enterprises 856
Summary of Key Points 857
Key Terms 858
Review Problem 859
Questions 861
Cases 862
Technical Review 867
Assignments 869

CHAPTER 15 FINANCIAL INSTRUMENTS: COMPLEX DEBT AND EQUITY 885

Introduction 885
Financial Instruments—Classification 886
Convertible Debt—Conversion at the Investor's Option 892
Convertible Debt—Conversion Mandatory 897
Stock Options 899
Warrants 901
Share-Based Payments 903
Derivatives 915
Statement of Cash Flows and Disclosure 919
Accounting Standards for Private Enterprises 922
Summary of Key Points 924
Key Terms 925
Review Problems 926
Questions 927
Cases 928
Technical Review 936
Assignments 937

CHAPTER 16 ACCOUNTING FOR CORPORATE INCOME TAX 953

Introduction 953
Income Tax Provision versus Expense 954

Interperiod Tax Allocation—Introduction 954
Conceptual Issues in Interperiod Tax Allocation 957
Approach to Income Tax Questions 962
Statement of Financial Position Elements 969
Disclosure 971
Shortcut Approach If Rates Have Not Changed 975
Statement of Cash Flows 977
Is Deferred Income Tax a Liability? 978
Accounting Standards for Private Enterprises 979
Summary of Key Points 980
Key Terms 981
Review Problem 981
Appendix: The Investment Tax Credit 984
Summary of Key Points 987
Questions 988
Cases 989
Technical Review 994
Assignments 996

CHAPTER 17 ACCOUNTING FOR TAX LOSSES 1009

Introduction 1009
Recognizing the Tax Benefits of a Loss 1010
Tax Loss Carrybacks 1010
Temporary and Permanent Differences in a Loss Year 1012
Tax Loss Carryforwards 1014
Using a Valuation Allowance 1020
Which Tax Rate? 1023
Basic Illustration 1024
Extended Illustration 1026
Disclosure 1034
Evaluation of Future Benefit Accounting 1034
International Consistency? 1035
Accounting Standards for Private Enterprises 1036
Summary of Key Points 1036
Key Terms 1037
Review Problem 1037
Questions 1040
Cases 1041
Technical Review 1045
Assignments 1047

CHAPTER 18 LEASES 1059

Introduction 1059
Definition of a Lease 1060
The Leasing Continuum 1060

Operating Leases 1061
Finance Leases 1064
Accounting for Finance Leases—Lessee 1068
Finance Lease Illustration—Basic Example 1068
Lessee Accounting—Basic Example 1069
Sale and Leaseback 1080
Lessee Disclosure 1084
Long-Term Leases: Pros and Cons 1085
Avoiding Lease Capitalization 1087
Lessor Accounting 1088
Leases in the Statement of Cash Flows 1097
Accounting Standards for Private Enterprises 1099
Lessees 1099
Lessors 1100
Summary of Key Points 1101
Key Terms 1102
Review Problems 1103
APPENDIX: Forthcoming Changes in Lease Accounting 1107
Overview 1107
Short-Term Leases 1107
Long-Term Leases—Lessee 1107
Other Issues 1111
Questions 1112
Cases 1113
Technical Review 1119
Assignments 1120

CHAPTER 19 **POST-EMPLOYMENT BENEFITS** **1131**

Introduction 1131
Types of Pension Plans 1132
Pension Terms 1132
Defined Contribution Plans 1135
Defined Benefit Plans—Introduction 1136
Defined Benefit Plan Pension Accounting—Three Elements 1141
Evaluation 1148
Spreadsheet Approach 1149
Other Post-Employment Benefits 1156
Statement of Cash Flows 1158
Disclosure Requirements 1159
Accounting Standards for Private Enterprises 1161
Summary of Key Points 1164
Key Terms 1166
Review Problem 1166
Questions 1168
Cases 1169

Technical Review 1172
Assignments 1173

CHAPTER 20 EARNINGS PER SHARE 1189

Introduction 1189
EPS Figures 1190
Interpreting EPS 1190
Basic Earnings per Share 1191
Diluted Earnings per Share 1199
Complicating Factors 1210
Comprehensive Illustration 1213
Restatement of Earnings per Share 1217
Subsequent Changes in Share Capital 1217
Required Disclosure 1218
Other per Share Amounts 1219
Accounting Standards for Private Enterprises 1220
Summary of Key Points 1220
Key Terms 1221
Review Problem 1222
Questions 1223
Cases 1225
Technical Review 1232
Assignments 1233

CHAPTER 21 ACCOUNTING CHANGES 1249

Introduction 1249
Types of Accounting Changes 1250
Changes in Accounting Estimates 1250
Changes in Accounting Policies 1253
Reporting Accounting Changes 1255
Retrospective Application 1256
Prospective Application 1262
Correction of a Prior-Period Error 1265
Summary of Approaches for Accounting Changes 1268
Statement of Cash Flows 1269
Accounting Standards for Private Enterprises 1271
Summary of Key Points 1272
Key Terms 1273
Review Problem 1273
Questions 1275
Cases 1276
Technical Review 1284
Assignments 1285

CHAPTER 22 FINANCIAL STATEMENT ANALYSIS 1301

Introduction 1301
Overview of Statement Analysis. 1302
Ratio Analysis 1307
Other Analytical Techniques 1335
Accounting Standards for Private Enterprises 1336
Summary of Key Points 1336
Key Terms 1337
Review Problem 1338
Appendix: Recasting Financial Statements—Demonstration Case. 1342
Questions. 1351
Cases. 1352
Technical Review 1360
Assignments 1361

APPENDIX STATEMENT OF CASH FLOWS 1375

Comprehensive Illustration 1375
Comprehensive SCF Example 1378
Accounting Standards for Private Enterprises 1388
Summary of Key Points 1389
Technical Review 1389
Assignments 1391

Compound Interest Tables and Formulae TA-1

Index IN-1

Preface

Welcome to the complex Canadian GAAP reporting environment! The vast majority of Canadian public companies prepare financial statements that comply with International Financial Reporting Standards (IFRS), as set by the International Accounting Standards Board (IASB) and contained in the *CPA Canada Handbook, Part I*. In contrast, Canadian private companies may choose to comply with either IFRS or Canadian Accounting Standards for Private Enterprise (ASPE), as contained in the *CPA Canada Handbook, Part II*. These two sets of GAAP are similar in many respects but quite different in other respects. This duality presents a huge challenge to accountants, managers, and financial statement users.

Clearly, accounting standards are ever expanding, and change is the norm; you might find the expanding universe of accounting knowledge to be intimidating. Intermediate accounting is the essential course for developing both the technical skills and the professional judgement that you need to succeed. We believe that neither technical knowledge nor professional judgement is sufficient on its own; it is the blend of the two that represents the value added by a professional accountant.

So that is what *Intermediate Accounting* will do for you: provide complete, appropriate technical knowledge while also developing your professional judgement. Both these elements are described in the broad range of topics in this text. We will clearly explain the standards, identify patterns, explore the impact of alternatives on users and uses of financial statements, and look forward to further changes that are on the horizon. Throughout this text, we stress the importance of ethical standards—an accountant must learn to recognize and respond appropriately in potentially challenging situations.

In selecting material to include in this book, we have assessed the realities of Canadian business practice and the choices that are currently available. We have a distinctly Canadian agenda, looking at the issues that matter in Canadian business. We are clear in our treatment of the body of knowledge. Our coverage does not get bogged down in the (sometimes twisted) past history of a given issue, nor does it speculate needlessly on what might or might not happen in the future. Our emphasis is on preparing you to apply the standards now in place, providing an overview of some expected changes, and moving to develop the necessary judgemental skills to apply those standards wisely and effectively. These same judgemental skills will serve you equally well even when standards change in the future, as they undoubtedly will.

After you master the contents of *Intermediate Accounting*, you will be able to account for the wide range of events and transactions found in this unique and challenging economic environment. We are proud that this text is now in its sixth edition. Many thousands of students have started their substantive study of the corporate reporting environment with this text. In addition, many people have supported the evolution of this book over the last 20 years, and we are very grateful for their encouragement and continued goodwill. In particular, Tom, Joan, and Liz are very pleased to welcome Ingrid McLeod-Dick to the author team for this edition; Ingrid is a great colleague who brings solid classroom experience and a history of expertise in professional accounting education.

IFRS AND ASPE

A Canadian agenda means that we all must master international standards. Every chapter is based first and foremost on IFRS. Differences between ASPE and IFRS are explained in a separate section, to provide clarity regarding one set of standards as compared with the other. Assignment material reflects both IFRS and ASPE so that applications reflect the dual GAAP environment.

TECHNICAL KNOWLEDGE

Accountants have to be able to account for things! There is a base level of expertise that must become part of every accountant's body of knowledge: how to record a receivable, capitalize a lease, account for a pension, or prepare a statement of cash flows. Some of the transactions that we must account for are very complex, and the specific rules must be mastered. An affinity for numbers is important.

PROFESSIONAL JUDGEMENT

Professional judgement, it is often said, is the hallmark of a profession. There are often different ways to account for the same transaction. Professional accountants must become expert at sizing up the circumstances and exercising judgement to determine the appropriate accounting policy for those circumstances.

Once an accounting policy has been established, management almost always must make accounting measurement estimates before the numbers can be recorded. Accounting estimates require the exercise of professional judgement.

Professional judgement is not acquired overnight. It is nurtured and slowly grows over a lifetime. In this book, we begin the development process by explicitly examining the variables that companies consider when evaluating their options, and the criteria that accountants use to make choices. Many opportunities to develop and improve judgement are provided in the case material.

ACCURACY

The text has been extensively reviewed and proofread prior to publication. Chapter material has been reviewed by professional accountants. All assignment materials have been solved independently by multiple individual "assignment checkers" in addition to the authors. Nevertheless, errors may remain, for which we accept full responsibility. If you find errors, please email the authors at **j.conrod@dal.ca**, **tbeechy@schulich.yorku.ca**, **efarrell@schulich.yorku.ca,** or **ing.mcleod@sympatico.ca**. Your help will be greatly appreciated.

TOPICAL REVIEW IDENTIFYING KEY CHANGES

Chapter 1

The book starts by exploring the multiple accounting frameworks in use in Canada for public companies and private companies—IFRS or U.S. standards for public companies, IFRS or ASPE or DBA for private companies. The chapter then explores the issue of international comparability and the difference between nations in their acceptance of IFRS—whether a nation adopts, adapts, or harmonizes with IFRS. While companies in different countries may use IFRS, the financial reports still imbed significant differences that arise from differences in nations' economic, business, and sometimes even religious practices.

After establishing the multiple GAAP frameworks, our attention turns to the basis of application of any framework. Before we can make judgements on choosing accounting policies and making accounting estimates, we must understand the many possible (and often conflicting) objectives underlying a company's financial reporting. Thus, the second major theme of the first chapter is how the many different factors and influences shape a company's financial reporting. This is fundamental material that supports professional judgement.

Chapter 1 has been extensively revised and rewritten for this edition, with new exhibits to further clarify the material.

Chapter 2

Chapter 2 has been completely rewritten in this edition. The primary focus is on the accounting choice process, emphasizing underlying assumptions, qualitative characteristics, and measurement methods. Having set the basic reporting framework in Chapter 1, Chapter 2 further develops the theme of professional judgement. This chapter explains the basic assumptions underlying financial reporting and then moves on to develop the qualitative characteristics that must be considered when developing professional approaches to accounting issues.

Ethical issues are strongly emphasized in this chapter, as they are throughout the book. After discussing the broad recognition issues for revenue and expense, the chapter then sets out the elements of financial reporting. The increased incidence of fair value measurement within IFRS requires that the traditional distinction between "revenue" and "gains" be modified, which is clarified both by discussion and by a revised exhibit.

By the end of Chapter 2, all of the factors and elements underlying the exercise of professional judgement have been laid out and clarified. These factors and elements underlie the professional judgements that students must make as they move through the text, particularly in the case material at the end of each chapter.

Chapter 3

Chapter 3 discusses the nature of income and the difference between the economic and accounting concepts of income. The statement of comprehensive income is explained, and a new section emphasizes the distinction between operating income and comprehensive income. The general presentation approach is explained, along with format variations that are accepted in practice.

In the previous edition, it was necessary to use non-Canadian examples in this chapter and the next. This was due to a lack of Canadian examples that illustrate the application of IFRS because Canadian companies had not yet switched to IFRS. In this edition, all financial statement examples in Chapters 3 and 4 (as well as the following chapters) are of Canadian companies.

Chapter 3 contains the book's primary discussion of asset disposals, discontinued operations, and restructuring. Discontinued operations is just one part of a broader issue of asset disposals. We have introduced asset disposals in this chapter to provide a clearer context for understanding discontinued operations. We discuss and provide examples of all forms of asset disposals, including abandonment, sales of individual assets, sale of asset groups, and discontinued operations. Because asset disposals are often connected with restructurings, we also present the criteria and reporting requirements for restructuring plans as well as the requirements for reporting constructive obligations that frequently accompany restructurings.

The chapter ends with a discussion of ASPE and the ways in which the reporting requirements for private enterprises using ASPE differ from enterprises reporting under IFRS.

Chapter 4

This chapter begins with a general discussion of the purpose and limitations of the statement of financial position. This discussion includes an explanation of the different ways in which the assets, liabilities, and shareholders' equity can be presented, depending on the individual regional practice.

Specific individual items on the statement are then discussed. IFRS requires certain items to be reported on the face of the statement but does not prescribe a specific format. In this edition, we have introduced rates-of-return analysis at this early stage in the book.

The next section discusses and illustrates the statement of changes in equity. We illustrate that the statement of changes in equity (SCE) includes not only the "normal" shareholder accounts (e.g., share equity and retained earnings) but also each of the various components of other comprehensive income.

In the fourth section, we have expanded the overview of accounting changes, including changes in estimate, changes in accounting policy, and error correction. Accounting changes are pervasive, and this section prepares students to understand accounting changes as they move through the specific topics that comprise the rest of the book. A full discussion of accounting changes is reserved for the end of the book, Chapter 21 (in Volume Two).

The final section is a discussion of disclosure notes. This section reflects the current disclosure requirements of IFRS, including related party transactions, segment reporting, contingencies, and guarantees. In this edition, we have expanded our discussion of segment reporting and provided a numerical illustration.

Chapter 5

The statement of cash flows (SCF) is dealt with in sequence, as a primary financial statement. The chapter deals with the mechanics of statement preparation, using both a format-free approach and the T-account method. The journal-entry-based worksheet approach is included in an appendix. Coverage is linked to the reporting example of International Forest Products, to emphasize IFRS presentation issues and judgemental presentation choices. Presentation of investment revenue cash flow, interest, and dividends paid is discussed and illustrated in a separate section later in the chapter. Statement of cash flows (SCF) issues are reviewed in every subsequent chapter of the text. And, new in this edition, there is a comprehensive SCF review at the end of Volume Two.

Chapter 6

Revenue is one of the most judgemental areas of accounting policy choice in the GAAP world. For the sixth edition of the book, we have more specifically outlined the five criteria required for revenue recognition. A consistent approach is used to apply these criteria to determine the appropriate revenue recognition for various types of transactions. Specifically, the chapter provides examples of revenue transactions, including sales with rights of return or warranty agreements, bill and hold arrangements, consignments, and licensing fees. Transactions involving multiple deliverables are explained, with examples of loyalty point programs and franchisee fees provided. Biological assets and agricultural produce are also discussed in the chapter.

In accounting for long-term contacts, we illustrate only the percentage-of-completion method, as this is the only method normally acceptable under IFRS. The completed-contract method is illustrated in the ASPE section at the end of the chapter. This separation helps students to better understand the difference between IFRS and ASPE as applied to long-term contracts. Barter transactions and exchanges of similar and dissimilar goods or services are important but challenging aspects of accounting. The chapter puts these transactions into a broader context and illustrates, based on IFRS, just how each of the various types of non-monetary exchanges should be measured and reported. Also new to this edition is the discussion of non-monetary transactions under ASPE.

New for the sixth edition is an Appendix that explains the details of the new standard on revenue recognition (effective for annual reporting periods beginning on or after 1 January 2017) and how it will be applied. There is also a supplemental chapter on Connect that goes into further detail, applying the new revenue recognition criteria to various types of revenue transactions. This supplement also includes some end-of-chapter questions related to this new standard.

Chapter 7

This chapter now deals with two important financial instruments: cash and receivables. Coverage of payables has been shifted to Volume Two. Classification and valuation decisions are central to the coverage of cash and receivables. Important topics, such as foreign currency translation (a must, in this age of globalization) and the IFRS rules governing the transfer of receivables, are incorporated. Material on bank reconciliations is in an appendix, and coverage of present- and future-value calculations is available online on Connect, as is a more extensive set of compound interest tables.

Chapter 8

This chapter conforms to the IFRS approach applying lower of cost or market valuation methods wherein the IFRS defines "market" as net realizable value. Also, we explain the process for writing inventory backup if NRV recovers before the inventory is sold. The allowance method of accounting for inventory writedowns is fully illustrated—the allowance method is the *only* feasible method when the LCNRV test is applied on a group basis.

Inventory valuation always raises the possibility of unethical behaviour. Therefore, the chapter includes discussion of the ethical issues surrounding inventory valuation and accounting.

Introductory accounting texts deal with inventory systems and the cost flow assumptions, and thus we present that more basic material in the Appendix, available for student review, if needed.

Chapters 9 and 10

Accounting for capital assets and intangible assets is challenging in the IFRS context. There are three possible models to consider depending on the type of asset: the fair value model, the revaluation model, and the cost model. Also, component accounting and depreciation add complexities to the accounting for capital assets. Impairment testing and reversals will create more volatility on the income statement using IFRS. These chapters systematically look at acquisition, amortization, impairment, and disposal considering both the IFRS standards and ASPE. The appendices cover the complexities related to investment property, government assistance, capital cost allowance, and the revaluation model.

Chapter 11

This chapter reflects coverage of IFRS 9, effective in 2015 but available for early adoption as a response from standard setters to the upheaval in financial markets. Accounting for amortized cost, fair value through profit and loss, fair value through other comprehensive income, cost, significant influence, and control investments is covered. Both policy and numeric issues are thoroughly explored. The chapter includes a number of helpful diagrams and figures to help clarify the roadmap through this complex territory. ASPE alternatives are very different in this area, and the choices are documented and described.

Volume One Appendix—Fundamentals: The Accounting Information Processing System

The Appendix reviews the accounting cycle from the original transaction to the journals, trial balance, and preparation of financial statements. Examples of adjusting journal entries are discussed as well as subsidiary ledgers and worksheet applications. Extensive examples are used to illustrate the accounting cycle.

Chapters 12 and 13

New in this edition, there are two chapters on liabilities to start Volume Two. Chapter 12 deals with operating payables, as well as notes payable and provisions. The chapter includes some examples of liability measurement that require discounting. We hope that this shorter chapter is a more appropriate way to start off a new term! This chapter fully reflects IFRS and ASPE standards in the area, and has complete case and problem material.

Chapter 13 delves into long-term debt, using bonds as an example. The chapter relies on discounted cash flow models for liability measurement, accompanied by the effective-interest method of amortization. Straight-line amortization is illustrated in the ASPE section. Various valuation and measurement complexities are covered, including the effect of upfront fees and derecognition scenarios. This chapter includes a section on the capitalization of borrowing costs.

Chapter 14

This chapter deals with straightforward shareholders' equity issues. Multicolumn presentation of the shareholders' equity statement, consistent with International Accounting Standard 1 (IAS 1), is completely incorporated. Classification and presentation of amounts in accumulated other comprehensive income, (e.g., from fair-value-through-other-comprehensive-income [FVTOCI] investments, and certain foreign currency gains/losses) is included, and is supported by assignment material. Summary charts have been incorporated, where appropriate.

Chapter 15

One major topic in this chapter is classification: debt versus equity, compound financial instruments, and the like. Classification is based on the substance of a financial instrument rather than its legal form. A major section covers the IFRS approach to share-based payments, emphasizing the estimates needed for measurement and forfeitures. Basic patterns for option accounting are established. Finally, the material on derivative instruments is included in this chapter. While many of the complexities of derivatives are appropriately left to advanced accounting courses, this introduction is vital. We think that the material is clear and understandable, at an appropriate level for Intermediate courses.

Chapters 16 and 17

Accounting for income tax remains two separate chapters, to acknowledge that many instructors prefer to spend two blocks of time on this most challenging area. The Chapter 16 material establishes a three-step process for typical situations. The focus of Chapter 17 remains accounting for the tax effect of losses—carrybacks and carryforwards. This is difficult material for students, but the Chapter 17 problems incorporate the prior-chapter material and allow solid reinforcement of the steps associated with tax accounting. The ASPE section explains the taxes payable or flow-through method that is available for private enterprises.

Chapter 18

The major change to this chapter is the introduction of IASB's new approach for lease accounting. The proposal requires all leases lasting longer than 12 months to be capitalized. At the time of writing this textbook, the proposed changes were still in Exposure Draft form and no effective implementation date had yet been specified. Although there is no doubt that a new standard will be issued, corporations will need at least three years to implement the change. A new standard cannot become effective before 2017. We present this new approach as an Appendix rather than in the main body of the text as the current standards will remain effective in the interim.

Chapter 19

Pensions and other post-retirement benefits are highly complex arrangements, with correspondingly complex accounting treatment. This chapter has been completely revamped to reflect up-to-date standards for defined benefit pension plans, both from IFRS and ASPE. We are pleased that the revised rules are easier to understand, but more importantly, the new standards result in better reflection of the economic position of such plans. The worksheet structure used is helpful to organize the material. This chapter also includes an example of accounting for other post-retirement benefits and appropriate coverage of defined contribution plans, since the latter are gaining in popularity.

Chapter 20

Earnings per share material includes an explanation of basic and diluted earnings per share (EPS). IFRS terminology is used throughout. The procedural steps associated with organizing a complex EPS question are emphasized to provide more comfort and support in this complicated area. There are a variety of useful summary figures and tables.

Chapter 21

Accounting policy changes and error corrections require restatement of one or more prior years' financial statements. Restatement is surely an important topic, given the number of fraud-based restatements reported in the public press in recent years. Also, the ongoing changes in accounting standards means that companies must often restate their accounts. This chapter deals with the theory and mechanics related to such restatement, reflecting current IFRS standards.

Chapter 22

The text concludes with a review of financial statement analysis and emphasizes the importance of accounting policy choice and disclosure in the analysis of published financial statements. New in the sixth edition is an in-depth discussion related to the type of information to gather specifically to assist with the analysis. Each of the ratios described in the chapter are calculated for the same sample company, and the results are analyzed, taking into consideration the entity's business and industry. There is an extensive case illustration, showing restatements, which demonstrates the importance of accounting policy choice.

Volume Two Appendix—Statement of Cash Flows

SCF topics have been explained in each chapter of the text, and students have had assignment material to reinforce each topic. However, some prefer to end the course with a comprehensive review of SCF topics, as review and reinforcement. This Appendix gathers material that will support this approach. The appendix is based on a T-account analysis, and has an appropriate range of assignment material.

ACKNOWLEDGEMENTS

Our initial draft of this text was reviewed by several colleagues with expertise in IFRS. Our manuscript benefitted significantly from the comments and suggestions from Judy Cumby, FCA, Ingrid McLeod-Dick, FCPA, FCA, and Marisa Morriello, CPA, CA. Many other reviewers had contributed valuable comments on the previous edition, which informed our decisions about coverage and approach for the sixth edition.

We are grateful to the team members who exhaustively checked the assignment material and the solutions, including Mike Lutes, CA; Andrew Bonner, CA; Borden Rhodes; James Rockwood; Chantelle Loucks; Alex Kogan, CPA, CA; Winnie Siu; Alex Fisher, CPA, CA; Marisa Morriello, CPA, CA; Marcella Augustina, CPA, CA; Susan Cohlmeyer, FCA; and Cara Chesney, CA. The residual errors are our responsibility, but these expert individuals have significantly improved our accuracy. A special thanks to Judy Cumby, FCA, Laura Cumming, CA, and Tammy Crowell, CA.

We appreciate the permissions granted by the following organizations to use their problem and case material:

- The Canadian Institute of Chartered Accountants
- The Certified General Accountants' Association of Canada
- The Ontario Institute of Chartered Accountants
- The Atlantic School of Chartered Accountancy
- The American Institute of Certified Public Accountants

We are grateful to the people at McGraw-Hill Ryerson who guided this manuscript through the development process. We appreciate the strong support of Keara Emmett, our Product Manager; Lindsay MacDonald and Chris Cullen, our Product Developers; and the production team, led by Margaret Henderson and including Jessica Barnoski and Tammy Mavroudi, who have all contributed in significant ways to this final product. And, of course, Karen Rolfe, copy editor, and Rohini Herbert, proofreader, have become welcome and active partners in this enterprise.

On a personal level, we would like to thank our friends and family members for their support and encouragement throughout the lengthy process of bringing this book to fruition, especially, in Toronto—Brian McBurney; in Halifax—Andrew, Yen, Meredith, and Daniel Conrod; in Richmond Hill—Ed Farrell, Catherine, Michael, and Megan Farrell; and in Collingwood—Michael Dick and Kenneth Dick.

Pedagogical Walkthrough

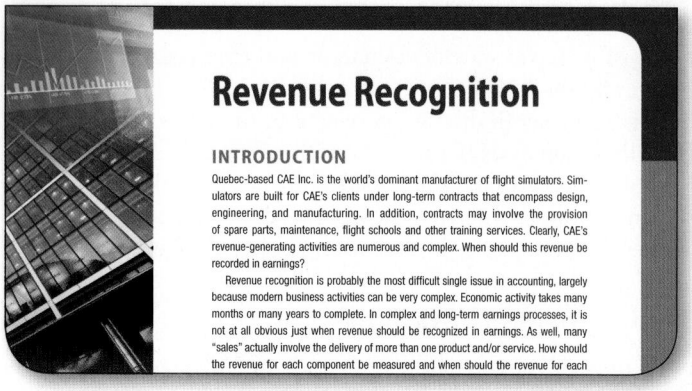

Revenue Recognition

INTRODUCTION

Quebec-based CAE Inc. is the world's dominant manufacturer of flight simulators. Simulators are built for CAE's clients under long-term contracts that encompass design, engineering, and manufacturing. In addition, contracts may involve the provision of spare parts, maintenance, flight schools and other training services. Clearly, CAE's revenue-generating activities are numerous and complex. When should this revenue be recorded in earnings?

Revenue recognition is probably the most difficult single issue in accounting, largely because modern business activities can be very complex. Economic activity takes many months or many years to complete. In complex and long-term earnings processes, it is not at all obvious just when revenue should be recognized in earnings. As well, many "sales" actually involve the delivery of more than one product and/or service. How should the revenue for each component be measured and when should the revenue for each

Introduction

Each chapter has an introduction that explains the objectives of the chapter in narrative form.

CONCEPT REVIEW

1. How is a *gain* different from a *revenue*?
2. List the five criteria that must be satisfied before revenue from the sale of goods can be recognized.
3. What measurement issues might arise in determining the amount of revenue to be recognized?

Concept Review

Throughout each chapter concept review questions are included. Students can stop and think through the answers to these basic questions, covering the previously explained material. This helps comprehension and focus! Answers to these questions can be found online on Connect.

EXHIBIT 3-6

DETERMINING IF A CONSTRUCTIVE OBLIGATION EXISTS

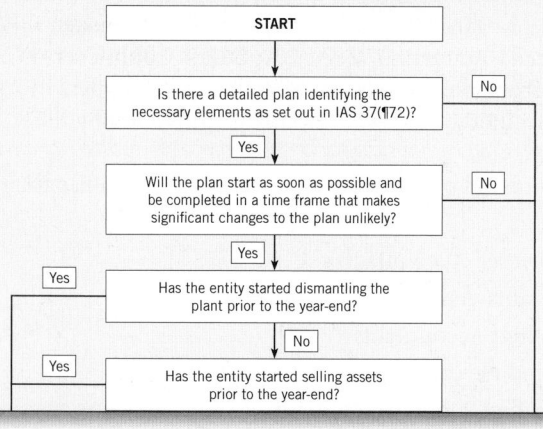

Figures and Tables

Where appropriate, chapter material is summarized in figures and tables to establish the patterns and help reinforce material.

ETHICAL ISSUES

The reason for the conditions for reclassifying an asset as held-for-sale is to prevent managers from reclassifying assets as "current" for a short period and then reversing that decision later. For example, a company may have a lending covenant that requires a minimum current ratio. If these restrictions were not in place, an unethical manager could temporarily reclassify a *noncurrent* asset to *current*, claiming that it is held-for-sale, just to meet the current ratio requirement, and then reclassify it back to noncurrent after the reporting date had passed. Clearly, there is an ethical issue involved in the "held-for-sale" classification.

Ethical Issues

Many chapters discuss accounting issues that raise ethical concerns. These concerns are highlighted in the chapter. Where ethical issues are particularly problematic, we have included a separate "Ethical Issues" section to help students focus on the ethical aspects of policy choice.

Ethics assignment material has also been incorporated into the case material. Essentially, when an accountant makes a recommendation on a contentious choice of accounting policy, ethics are tested. Students exercise true-to-life ethical judgement when they have to make a tough judgement call and recommend an accounting policy that is "good" for one group but "bad" for another. These ethical overtones are highlighted in the case solutions to help instructors draw them out in discussion and evaluation.

ACCOUNTING STANDARDS FOR PRIVATE ENTERPRISES

Comprehensive Income

There is no SCI in Canadian ASPE; only an income statement should be provided. The concept of *other comprehensive income* does not exist in ASPE. Instead:

- Net income after taxes is transferred directly from the income statement to retained earnings (or via the statement of changes in retained earnings, if a separate statement is prepared);
- Unrealized foreign exchange translation gains or losses related to a foreign subsidiary (a component of OCI under IFRS) are reported as a separate component of shareholders' equity; and
- Any other nonearnings items that affect shareholders' equity are reported in shareholders' equity, as appropriate.

Under ASPE, *consolidated* financial statements are not required. The statements of a private enterprise are not issued to the public, and users are presumed to be knowledgeable. If a user wants consolidated statements, he or she can request them (or insist on them, in the case of a major provider of capital, such as an institutional investor).

Format

- ASPE does not specify a format other than the obvious fact that it should begin with "revenue" and end with "net income." There is no requirement for basing the expense disclosure on "functional" versus "nature of expense" approach as required by IFRS.

Accounting Standards for Private Enterprises

At the end of each chapter, there is a section that expands on essential items to understand for Accounting Standards for Private Enterprise (ASPE) in Canada. These sections include numeric examples, where appropriate. The ASPE sections provide students and instructors with a detailed, but easy-to-use guide to these important standards.

Looking Forward

In November 2012, the IASB began looking into a wide range of issues on presentation, disclosure and measurement. Among the issues on the IASB's Conceptual Framework agenda are a re-examination of the definitions of elements, definitions of liabilities, recognition principles, measurement principles, the distincion between equity and liability instruments, and measurements other than cost and fair value. In coming years, the Board is likely to issue new guidance on the format and presentation of items on the SFP.

This is a long-term project. We are not likely to see a resolution of these many issues for quite a while.

Looking Forward

Standards are constantly evolving and changing! To help keep abreast of forthcoming probable changes, at the end of each chapter we provide a discussion of key anticipated changes in IFRS and/or ASPE standards.

RELEVANT STANDARDS

CPA Canada Handbook, Part I (IFRS):

- IAS 1, Presentation of Financial Statements
- IAS 8, Accounting Policies, Changes in Accounting Estimates and Errors
- IAS 37, Provisions, Contingent Liabilities and Contingent Assets
- IFRS 5, Non-current Assets Held-for-sale and Discontinued Operations

CPA Canada Handbook, Part II (ASPE):

- Section 1520, Income Statement
- Section 3475, Disposal of Long-lived Assets and Discontinued Operations

Relevant Standards

At the end of each chapter, we provide a comprehensive list of the IASB and ASPE standards that are relevant to the material in that chapter. We have not quoted the standards directly in chapter material, and we have not provided paragraph references to either the IASB publications or *CPA Canada Handbook*. This omission is intentional—the two sources are harmonized but may use different words. Also, the IASB makes "annual improvements" that change the wording of some standards. Our focus is on the application of standards, not the technicalities of the wording.

SUMMARY OF KEY POINTS

1. Public companies must report *comprehensive income*, which has two components: (1) profit or loss (i.e., net income), and (2) *other comprehensive income*. OCI generally includes value changes that have been recognized in the SFP but are excluded from periodic earnings, either temporarily or permanently.
2. Comprehensive income can be presented either in one continuous statement, or in two consecutive statements with net income as the final line of the profit or loss statement (i.e., income statement) and also as the first line of the SCI, which must follow immediately on the same page.
3. Companies can report expenses in the profit and loss section either by *nature of expense* or by *function*. Under either presentation approach, two compulsory expense disclosures are (1) depreciation and amortization expense and (2) the cost of employee benefits.
4. Both IFRS and ASPE require a subtotal for net earnings from continuing operations (net of income tax). IFRS encourages companies to provide information, headings, and other subtotals that will help the financial statement reader understand the company's financial performance.
5. Income taxes must be allocated over two dimensions: *intraperiod*, which is within the financial statements of a reporting period, and *interperiod*, which allocates the income tax burden to the current and future years.

Summary of Key Points

A summary of key points concludes each chapter. This provides a list of the key ideas and reinforces the chapter material.

KEY TERMS

abandoned asset
accounting income
basic EPS
cash-generating unit
comprehensive income
constructive obligation
diluted EPS
discontinued operation
disposal group
economic income
fair value less the cost to sell
flipping
held-for-sale
idle asset
income
interperiod tax allocation
intraperiod tax allocation
multiple-step statement
noncontrolling interest (NCI)
provision
recoverable amount
restructuring plan
single-step statement
statement of comprehensive income (SCI)
unusual items
weighted average number of shares

Key Terms

Each chapter concludes with a list of key terms used and explained in the chapter.

REVIEW PROBLEM 3-1

The following information is taken from the adjusted trial balance of Killian Corporation at 31 December 20X5, the end of Killian's fiscal year:

Account	Amount
Sales revenue	$1,000,000
Service revenue	200,000
Interest revenue	30,000
Gain on sale of capital asset	100,000
Cost of goods sold[1]	630,000
Selling, general, and administrative expense[2]	170,000
Interest expense	20,000
Loss on sale of long-term investment	10,000
Loss from earthquake damage	200,000
Loss on sale of assets of discontinued business segment	60,000
Loss on operations of discontinued business segment	10,000

[1]Consists of depreciation of $30,000, employee wages and benefits of $40,000, and $580,000 of merchandise purchases less $20,000 increase in inventory.
[2]Includes depreciation of $35,000 and employee wages and benefits of $90,000.

Review Problem

From Chapter 3 onward, we provide at least one self-study review problem, with the solution. This provides an opportunity to practise the primary aspects of that chapter's content.

CASE 3-1

DELUCA SOLUTIONS INC.

Deluca Solutions Inc. is an Ontario-based manufacturer. The company is listed on the TSX, but the family of founder David Deluca retains control through multiple-voting shares.

Cases

More than 60 cases are included in *Intermediate Accounting*, and there is at least one new case in every chapter in the sixth edition. The cases portray realistic situations, usually with multiple financial reporting implications. Students must put themselves into the situation and grapple with the facts to arrive at the most appropriate accounting policies for the circumstances. A blend of professional judgement and technical skills is needed to respond to a case. Case coverage is not limited to "one chapter" bites but often integrates material learned to date. For those trying to build a base of professionalism, the use of cases consistently over the term is highly recommended. Cases can be assigned for class debriefing, class presentations, or written assignments.

TECHNICAL REVIEW

connect

TR4-1 Financial Statement Classification: The first list below shows the financial statements normally included in a company's annual financial statements. The second list shows some amounts that often appear in those financial statements.

A. SFP
B. Statement of comprehensive income—profit and loss section
C. Statement of comprehensive income—other comprehensive income section
D. Statement of cash flows
E. Statement of changes in shareholders' equity

B, D, E 1. Net income
____ 2. Retained earnings (opening)
____ 3. Translation gain/loss on foreign subsidiaries
____ 4. Provision for restructuring costs
____ 5. Cumulative translation gain or loss
____ 6. Dividends declared, unpaid at year-end
____ 7. Appropriation for factory reorganization
____ 8. Loss on discontinued operation
____ 9. Non-controlling interest in subsidiaries
____ 10. Investment property held-for-sale
____ 11. Cumulative effect of change in accounting policy
____ 12. Proceeds from issuance of common shares
____ 13. Unrealized gains/losses on hedge derivatives
____ 14. Deferred pension cost

Required:
Use the letters given in the first list to indicate the financial statement on which each item in the second list will appear. Some letters may be used more than once or not at all. The first item is completed for you as an example.

Technical Review

In this edition, we have added Technical Review exercises at the end of each chapter, preceding the somewhat more demanding assignment material. These technical exercises are directive, brief, and quantitative and encourage students to ensure they understand the chapter's basic quantitative aspects. We have provided five such exercises in each chapter (except in the introductory chapters; these are more conceptual than numerical in nature, and technical review is not the focus.)

Assignment Material

There is an extensive range of assignment material at the end of each chapter. The assignments provide the opportunity to "learn by doing."

The technical review questions and many of the assignments are available online on Connect; the Connect logo identifies these questions. The Connect problems allow web-based iterations of the problem for assessment, immediate feedback, and extra practice.

★ Stars accompany each assignment to indicate length, with one star indicating a shorter assignment and three stars indicating a longer assignment.

To help students practise on their own, we have selected a few assignments from each chapter and put their solutions online. These selected assignments are highlighted by the icon in the margin.

Excel® templates for selected assignments provide an introduction to basic spreadsheet applications. These assignments are identified with the icon in the margin and are available online.

Integrative Problems

From time to time, we include integrative problems that formally deal with accounting topics covered in five or six chapters. These problems are a great pretest review!

SUPPLEMENTS

Connect

McGraw-Hill Connect™ is a web-based assignment and assessment platform that gives students the means to better connect with their coursework, with their instructors, and with the important concepts that they will need to know for success now and in the future. With Connect, instructors can deliver assignments, quizzes, and tests easily online. Students can practise important skills at their own pace and on their own schedule. With Connect, students also get 24/7 online access to an eBook—an online edition of the text—to aid them in successfully completing their work, wherever and whenever they choose.

LearnSmart

No two students are alike. Why should their learning paths be? LearnSmart uses revolutionary adaptive technology to build a learning experience unique to each student's individual needs. It starts by identifying the topics a student knows and does not know. As the student progresses, LearnSmart adapts and adjusts the content based on his or her individual strengths, weaknesses, and confidence, ensuring that every minute spent studying with LearnSmart is the most efficient and productive study time possible.

SmartBook

As the first and only adaptive reading experience, SmartBook is changing the way students read and learn. SmartBook creates a personalized reading experience by highlighting the most important concepts a student needs to learn at that moment in time. As a student engages with SmartBook, the reading experience continuously adapts by highlighting content based on what each student knows and does not know. This ensures that he or she is focused on the content needed to close specific knowledge gaps, while it simultaneously promotes long-term learning.

INSTRUCTOR RESOURCES

Instructor Resources

- Instructor's Manual
- Instructor's Solutions Manual
- Computerized Test Bank
- Microsoft® PowerPoint® Lecture Slides

SUPERIOR LEARNING SOLUTIONS AND SUPPORT

The McGraw-Hill Ryerson team is ready to help you assess and integrate any of our products, technology, and services into your course for optimal teaching and learning performance. Whether it is helping your students improve their grades or putting your entire course online, the McGraw-Hill Ryerson team is here to help you do it. Contact your Learning Solutions Consultant today to learn how to maximize all of McGraw-Hill Ryerson's resources!

For more information on the latest technology and Learning Solutions offered by McGraw-Hill Ryerson and its partners, please visit us online: www.mcgrawhill.ca/he/solutions.

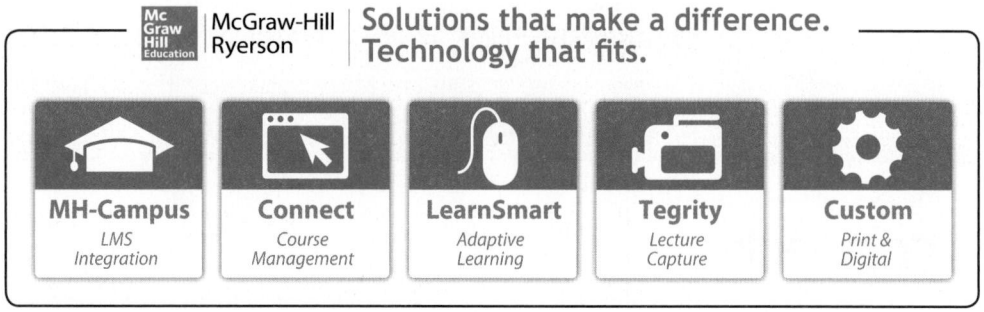

CHAPTER 12

Financial Liabilities and Provisions

INTRODUCTION

What is a liability? The answer might seem rather obvious: an amount owed from one entity to another. In fact, many liability situations, especially those related to financial liabilities, are straightforward from an accounting perspective. However, when liabilities are estimated or uncertain, they can present accounting challenges. For instance:

- Does a liability exist if there is no legal liability but the company has announced a particular commitment or plan of action?
- How is a liability measured if the obligation is for services, not a set amount of money?
- How can a liability be measured if the amount of cash to be paid is based on future events?

Liability financing is an integral part of the capital structure of many companies. For example, Canadian Tire Corporation Limited is a Canadian company that offers a range of general merchandise and also apparel, sporting goods, petroleum, and financial services to consumers. The company reported total assets of $13.2 billion in 2012. Of this amount, $4.8 billion, or 36%, was financed through shareholders' equity, with the balance, $8.4 billion, or 64%, provided by debt in various forms. A sizable portion of the debt represents deposits from the financial services segment ($2.4 billion, or 18% of total assets) and trade payables represent 12% of assets ($1.6 billion). There are also long-term loans of $2.3 billion, or 17% of total assets.

This chapter reviews common liabilities, including both financial liabilities and provisions. Financial statement classification and disclosure are reviewed. Long-term debt is covered in Chapter 13. Chapter 14 deals with accounting for share equity. Then, in Chapter 15, coverage returns to debt arrangements, those that have some attributes of debt and some attributes of equity. Innovative financial markets have introduced significant complexities into the accounting world!

LIABILITY DEFINITION AND CATEGORIES

According to the conceptual framework, a liability is defined as a *present obligation* of the entity *arising from past events*, the settlement of which is expected to result in an *outflow* of economic benefits. Settlement could be accomplished through *future transfer or use of assets, provision of services, or other yielding of economic benefits.* These characteristics can be simplified for practical purposes by remembering that a liability:

- Is an expected *future* sacrifice of assets or services;
- Constitutes a *present* obligation; and
- Is the result of a *past* transaction or event.

Note that there are three time elements in the definition: a *future* sacrifice, a *present* obligation, and a *past* event. All three elements are necessary for a liability to be recognized. It is not possible to create a liability from an anticipated future event, such as expected future operating losses. There must be some past transaction that is identifiable as an **obligating event**, which is an event that creates an obligation where there is no other realistic alternative but to settle the obligation.

Constructive Obligations Some liabilities are **legal obligations**, or liabilities that arise from contract or legislation. Most liabilities are legal obligations, including trade payables and borrowings. Other liabilities are **constructive obligations**, where a liability exists because there is a pattern of past practice or established policy. A company can create a constructive obligation if it makes a public statement that the company will accept certain responsibilities *because the statement creates a valid expectation that the company will honour those responsibilities.* Others rely on this representation. Thus, a liability can be created when a company reacts to moral or ethical factors.

ETHICAL ISSUES

A company has announced a voluntary product recall that will take several months to complete. Customers have been offered a replacement product or repair on the original unit. The recall was prompted by the company's code of ethics to support its product integrity and customer base. The recall is voluntary in that the defect is not covered by warranty, and no legislation exists to force the company to act. In this case, clear communication to another party establishes the obligation. A constructive liability exists and the *anticipated costs of the recall must be accrued.*

Categories of Liabilities

Accounting for liabilities depends on whether the liability fits into one of two categories:

- Financial liabilities; or
- Nonfinancial liabilities.

A **financial liability** is a *financial instrument.* A financial liability is a contract that gives rise to a financial liability of one party and a financial asset of another party. That is, one party has an account payable and the other party has an account receivable. Another example is a loan payable and a loan receivable. The two elements are mirror images of each other.

A **non-financial liability** can be defined by what it is *not*—any liability that is not a financial liability is a nonfinancial liability. A non-financial liability has no offsetting financial asset on the books of another party. **Provisions,** or liabilities that have uncertainty surrounding timing or amount, are a major category of non-financial liabilities.

Examples of non-financial liabilities include:

- Revenue received in the current period but not yet earned (i.e., unearned revenue); or

- Cash outflows that are expected to arise in the future but that are related to transactions, decisions, or events of the current period (e.g., a decommissioning obligation).

Categories of Financial Liabilities Financial liabilities themselves fall into two categories. *Classification determines the subsequent measurement of the financial liability.* Specifically, the alternatives can be summarized as follows:

Classification	Summarized Classification Criteria	Initial Valuation	Subsequent Valuation
1. "Other" financial liabilities	Most financial liabilities; all those except those in category 2, below	Fair value, which is the transaction value and establishes the cost of the financial instrument ADD Transaction costs, if any	Cost (Amortized cost)
2. Fair value through profit or loss (FVTPL)	May be FVTPL if: a. The liability will be sold in the short term; or b. Designated FVTPL by management to avoid an accounting mismatch (related/hedged financial instruments are FVTPL)	Fair value, which is the transaction value and establishes the cost of the financial instrument	Fair value; gains and losses in earnings

Most liabilities fall in the *other financial liabilities* category. The FVTPL liability category is meant primarily for liabilities that will be sold/transferred in the short term. In other circumstances, management may designate liabilities as FVTPL. This might be appropriate, for example, if various hedging strategies were in place and management wished to have both hedged asset and liability in the same category for valuation purposes.

Measurement of Other Financial Liabilities *Other financial liabilities* are initially measured as the fair value of the consideration received plus transaction costs and then carried at this value (which is cost), or amortized cost, over their lives. That is, the initial fair value is (generally) the stated amount of the transaction, or the transaction price.[1] For example, a company receives an invoice for the fair value of goods shipped by a supplier; the goods are the consideration, and their invoice price is the fair value of the liability.

Discounting Liabilities of all categories must be valued at the present value of cash flows—commonly called **discounting**—where the time value of money is material. The discount rate chosen must reflect the current market interest rate, specific to the risk level of the liability. Note, however, that if the amount and timing of cash flows is highly uncertain, then discounting is not possible and undiscounted amounts are recorded. When liabilities are discounted, interest expense on the discounted liability is recorded as time passes. Discounting will be illustrated later in the chapter.

Reporting Example Included in its significant accounting policy disclosure, Canadian Tire reports information about the valuation of financial liabilities. These liabilities are valued at

[1] The *stated amount* of the transaction might not be *fair value* if the transaction is a related party transaction.

amortized cost. Provisions, which are non-financial liabilities, are measured based on best estimate and are discounted, if the effect of discounting is material.

The company's ... financial liabilities are generally classified and measured as follows:

Asset/Liability	Category	Measurement
Bank indebtedness	Other liabilities	Amortized cost
Deposits	Other liabilities	Amortized cost
Trade and other payables	Other liabilities	Amortized cost
Short-term borrowings	Other liabilities	Amortized cost
Loans payable	Other liabilities	Amortized cost
Long-term debt	Other liabilities	Amortized cost

Provisions

A provision is recognized if, as a result of a past event, the Company has a present legal or constructive obligation that can be estimated reliably and it is probable that an outflow of economic benefits will be required to settle the obligation. The amount recognized as a provision is the best estimate of the consideration required to settle the present obligation at the end of the reporting period, taking into account risks and uncertainty of cash flows. Where the effect of discounting is material, provisions are determined by discounting the expected future cash flows at a pre-tax rate that reflects current market assessments of the time value of money and the risks specific to the liability.

...

Source: Canadian Tire Corporation Ltd. 2012 Annual Consolidated Financial Statements, www.sedar.com, posted 21 February 2013.

CONCEPT REVIEW

1. What are the three time periods inherent in the definition of a liability?
2. What are the two classifications of liabilities? The two possible classifications for financial liabilities?
3. When is a liability discounted?

COMMON FINANCIAL LIABILITIES

Common financial liabilities are reviewed in the section that follows. These financial liabilities are all classified as *other financial liabilities* and are initially measured as the fair value of the consideration received plus transaction costs, if any, and then are carried at this value (which is the transaction value) over their lives.

Accounts Payable

Accounts payable—more descriptively, **trade accounts payable**—are obligations to suppliers arising from the firm's ongoing operations, including the acquisition of merchandise, materials, supplies, and services used in the production and sale of goods or services. Current payables that are not trade accounts payable (e.g., income tax payable and the current portion of long-term debt) should be reported separately from accounts payable.

In determining the amount of the liability, it is necessary to adjust for purchase discounts, allowances, and returns, as is done for accounts receivable. Of course, a company does not record an allowance for anticipated nonpayment, since it is the payer!

Notes Payable

Notes payable often result from borrowing from a lender. Other notes payable are from suppliers, as part of the terms of a purchase agreement. Notes payable are a written promise to pay a specified amount at a specified future date (or a series of amounts over a series of payment dates). Some notes formalize **collateral security** for the lender, assets of the borrower that the secured lender can seize if the note goes into default.

The **stated interest rate** in a note may not equal the market rate prevailing on obligations involving similar credit rating or risk. The **market interest rate** is the rate accepted by two parties for loans of equal profile—identical amounts, with identical credit risk, terms, and conditions.

Notes may be categorized as **interest-bearing** or **non-interest-bearing** notes. Interest-bearing notes specify the interest rate to be applied to the face amount in computing interest payments. Non-interest-bearing notes do not state an interest rate but command interest through the difference between cash lent and (higher) cash repaid. Notes with stated interest rates below market rates may be used by suppliers as a sales incentive.

Notes payable are initially valued at fair value, which is often simply the loan amount. *If the note carries a stated interest rate equal to market interest rates or has a very short term, then valuation issues are immaterial and stated values are used.* If the stated and market interest rates are different, and term is more than a year (i.e., not short), then present value—discounting—must be used to establish initial fair value. When discounting is used, the *market interest rate is used to value the note and the transaction. The market rate is also used to measure interest expense.* Discounting is illustrated in a later section of this chapter.

Example: Interest-bearing note at market interest rate On 1 May 20X4, Sun Company borrowed $120,000 from Dominion Bank. The note has a two-year term, and requires that interest of 4% be paid each 30 April, with the principal payable on 30 April 20X6. *The stated and market interest rates are equal.* The entries over the life of the loan:

Initial entry:

Cash	120,000	
Notes payable		120,000

Interest is accrued at the 31 December year-end:

Interest expense ($120,000 × 4% × 8/12)	3,200	
Accrued interest payable		3,200

Interest is further recorded, and also paid, on 30 April:

Interest expense ($120,000 × 4% × 4/12)	1,600	
Accrued interest payable	3,200	
Cash		4,800

Identical interest entries are repeated for the second year of the loan and then the principal is repaid on 30 April 20X6.

Loan Guarantees

A loan guarantee requires the guarantor to pay the loan principal and interest if the borrower defaults. This is a *financial liability* of the guarantor. The financial instruments rules require that loan guarantees be recorded at their *fair value*. Assume that a loan guarantee for $500,000 is issued for a related company, but there is only a 10% chance that it will have to be honoured. The 10% probability means that the guarantee has a positive fair value of $50,000 ($500,000 × 10%) and must be recorded at this amount, with an expense recognized. Timing must be considered to evaluate the need for discounting. *Loan guarantees would not be recorded if there was a zero percent chance of payout.* Extensive disclosure of guarantees is also required, including the maximum potential future payment, the identity of the other party, and collateral, if any.

Cash Dividends Payable

Cash dividends declared but not yet paid are reported as a current liability if they are to be paid within the coming year or operating cycle. Declared dividends are reported as a liability between the date of declaration and payment because declaration gives rise to an enforceable contract.

Liabilities are not recognized for undeclared dividends in arrears on preferred shares or for any other dividends not formally declared by the Board of Directors. Dividends in arrears on cumulative preferred shares should be disclosed in the notes to the financial statements. These dividends must be paid before any common dividends can be paid.

Monetary Accrued Liabilities

Examples of monetary accrued liabilities include wages and benefits earned by employees, interest earned by creditors but not yet paid, and the costs of goods and services received but not yet invoiced by the supplier. Accrued liabilities are recorded in the accounts by making adjusting entries at the end of the accounting period.

Advances and Returnable Deposits

A company may receive advances or cash deposits from customers as guarantees for payment of future obligations or to guarantee performance on a contract or service. Deposits may also be made as guarantees in case of noncollection or for possible damage to property. For example, deposits required from customers by gas, water, electricity, and other public utilities are liabilities of such companies to their customers. Employees may also make returnable deposits to ensure the return of keys and other company property, for locker privileges, and for club memberships.

Advances from customers and deposits should be reported as current or long-term liabilities, depending on the time involved between date of deposit and expected termination of the relationship. If the advances or deposits are interest bearing, an annual adjusting entry is required to accrue interest expense and to increase the related liability.

Assume that Harcourt Limited receives $5,000 from a customer, as a deposit for merchandise with a retail value of $18,500. When the deposit is received:

Cash	5,000	
Customer deposit liability		5,000

When the sale takes place:

Cash ($18,500 – $5,000)	13,500	
Customer deposit liability	5,000	
Revenue		18,500

If for some reason the sale were to not be completed, the customer typically has recourse to the company for refund or alternative product arrangement. The terms of these arrangements are set by contract when the deposit is accepted.

Taxes

Provincial and federal laws require businesses to collect certain taxes from customers and employees for remittance to governmental agencies. These taxes include sales tax, income tax withheld from employee paycheques, property tax, and various payroll taxes. Similar collections are made on behalf of unions, insurance companies, and employee-sponsored activities. Collections made for third parties increase both cash and current liabilities. The collections represent liabilities that are settled when the funds are remitted to the designated parties. Common examples of such taxes follow.

Sales Taxes Companies are required to collect sales taxes from customers and remit them to the appropriate government agency. Taxes include the goods and services tax (GST) and, in most provinces, provincial sales taxes (PST), or both together, the harmonized sales tax (HST). Revenues are recorded net of GST/HST collected, and purchases of goods and services are recorded net of any GST/HST recoverable. Any GST/HST that is not recoverable are accounted for as a component of the cost of the goods or services to which it relates. On the other hand, *PST is never refundable*, and PST paid is part of the cost of whatever was bought: capital assets or inventory, for example.

GST/HST is remitted periodically, net of GST/HST paid on purchases. The *net amount* of GST/HST payable or receivable should be carried as a liability or asset, as appropriate. Typical entries, with 5% GST and assuming 8% provincial sales tax and $500,000 of sales, are as follows:

1. At date the tax is assessed (point of sale):		
Cash and accounts receivable	565,000	
Sales revenue		500,000
GST payable ($500,000 × 5%)		25,000
PST payable ($500,000 × 8%)		40,000

Assume that $300,000 of inventory was purchased, subject to GST and PST. *Note that PST is part of the cost of inventory, but GST is a recoverable amount.*

2. At inventory purchase:		
Inventory ($300,000 × 1.08)	324,000	
GST payable ($300,000 × 0.05)	15,000	
Cash or accounts payable ($300,000 × 1.13)		339,000

Taxes are remitted:

3. At date of remittance to taxing authority:		
GST payable ($25,000 – $15,000)*	10,000	
Cash		10,000
PST payable	40,000	
Cash		40,000

*GST remitted is reduced by GST paid on purchased goods and services.

If the company were in an HST jurisdiction, there would be no PST and all HST is accounted for exactly as for GST: The HST amount is a liability when collected, but HST paid on purchases reduces the subsequent remittance.

Payroll Taxes Employers act as a collection agent for certain taxes and payments. They withhold appropriate amounts from their employees and remit money to the appropriate party shortly thereafter; a liability exists in the meantime. Common withholdings include:

- *Personal income tax.* An employee's personal federal and provincial tax are deducted at source and remitted regularly (at least monthly) to the federal government. At the end of the year, the employee receives a record of deductions, and determines, on his or her annual tax return, who owes whom and how much.

- *Canada pension plan (CPP).* Employees have to pay a percentage of their salary to the CPP; employers have to match this amount dollar for dollar.
- *Employment insurance (EI).* Employees have to pay a percentage of their salary to secure EI benefits; the employer must pay 1.4 times the employees' contributions as its share.
- *Insurance premiums, pension plan payments, union dues, etc.* A variety of employee benefits, such as group insurance, medical insurance, and pension plans, require that employees pay all or a portion of the premiums; these are deducted at source. If stipulated in labour agreements, union dues are also deducted at source. Other deductions may include charitable donations and parking fees. All of these are remitted to the appropriate party after deduction.

Payroll deduction accounting is illustrated in Exhibit 12-1.

Property Taxes Property taxes paid directly by a company are based on the assessed value of real property. Unpaid taxes constitute a lien on the assessed property. Property taxes are based on the assessed value of the property, which may or may not correspond to market value, and the mill rate (tax rate per thousand dollars of assessed value).

EXHIBIT 12-1

ILLUSTRATION OF PAYROLL DEDUCTIONS

Thor Company reported the following payroll information for January 20X5:		
Gross wages		$100,000
Deductions:		
Income tax	$ 20,000	
Canada Pension Plan	2,250	
Employment Insurance	2,100	
Union dues	1,400	
Charitable contributions	1,600	27,350
Net pay		$ 72,650
To record salaries and employee deductions:		
Salary expense	100,000	
Employee income tax payable		20,000
CPP payable		2,250
EI payable		2,100
Union dues payable		1,400
Charitable contributions payable		1,600
Cash		72,650
To record payroll expenses payable by the employer:		
Salary expense	5,190	
CPP payable (matching payment)		2,250
EI payable ($2,100 × 1.4)		2,940
To record remittance of payroll deductions (composite entry):		
Employee income tax payable	20,000	
CPP payable	4,500	
EI payable	5,040	
Union dues payable	1,400	
Charitable contributions payable	1,600	
Cash		32,540

Estimates are needed for monthly property tax accruals because tax rates are usually set by the taxing authority partway through the fiscal year. When corrections are needed, prior fiscal years are *not* restated—changes in these estimates are lumped into the current year.

Conditional Payments

Some liabilities are established on the basis of a firm's periodic income. They are either legal liabilities or constructive liabilities, but their amount cannot be firmly established until year-end. However, order for monthly or quarterly financial statements to be complete, the liabilities must be estimated whenever interim statements are prepared. Until paid, they represent current liabilities of the organization.

Income Tax Payable Interim reports require a provision for both federal and provincial tax liabilities, so estimates are required. The estimated liability should be reported as a current liability based on the firm's best estimates. After year-end, the tax return is prepared and the estimate is adjusted for the year-end financial statements before the books are finally closed. Periodic installment payments are required. Accounting for corporate income tax is reviewed in Chapters 16 and 17.

Bonuses Many companies pay cash bonuses, which depend on earnings. These are estimated at interim periods, but calculated "for real" at the end of the fiscal year. Calculations must be made in accordance with established formulas or the authorization of the Board of Directors. Bonuses can be material—both to the company and to the employee, so it is important that they are properly approved and recorded. Compensation arrangements are covered in more depth in Chapter 15.

CONCEPT REVIEW

1. Why is a loan guarantee with only a 10% chance of payout recorded as a liability?
2. What is the cost of $100,000 inventory bought with $5,000 of PST and $8,000 of GST?
3. When an employer deducts income tax from employees' pay, why does this create a liability?

FOREIGN CURRENCY PAYABLES

If a company has accounts or notes that are payable in foreign currencies, they must be *restated to Canadian dollars* at the current exchange rate at the year-end date. When the payable is first recorded, the then-current exchange rate is used. For example, suppose that Talud Limited buys inventory from a supplier in England for €5,000 when the **spot rate** (current exchange rate) was €1 = Cdn$2.20. The purchase would be recorded as follows:

Inventory	11,000	
Accounts payable (€5,000 × Cdn$2.20)		11,000

The payable is stated (or *denominated*) in euros, not in dollars. The inventory is recorded at the Canadian dollar equivalent of the sales price. However, when Talud pays the account, it will pay €5,000, not Cdn$11,000. The cash payment must be recorded at the current exchange rate. Suppose that Talud pays when the exchange rate is €1 = Cdn$2.10. Talud will pay only Cdn$10,500 when it obtains €5,000. The exchange gain is recognized in earnings.

Accounts payable	11,000	
Foreign exchange gains and losses		500
Cash (€5,000 × Cdn$2.10)		10,500

Exchange Gain or Loss The difference between the Canadian equivalent of the payable and of the cash paid is recorded in an *exchange gain or loss* account. Exchange gains and losses are netted in this account over the period, and the net balance is reported in earnings. It is important to understand that changes in the exchange rate following the initial transaction *do not affect the amount initially charged to inventory.* In the Talud Limited example above, the Cdn$11,000 inventory amount is not affected by the subsequent exchange rate change. *Historical cost is determined by the exchange rate at the date of the purchase transaction.*

Year-End Assume instead that at Talud's year-end date, the payable (recorded at Cdn$11,000) is still outstanding. The payable must be translated at the then-current exchange rate. If the exchange rate at the year-end date is €1 = Cdn$2.25, the value of the account payable will be Cdn$11,250 (€5,000 × Cdn$2.25). The increase of $250 in the Canadian equivalent of the €5,000 balance would be recorded as follows:

Foreign exchange gains and losses	250	
Accounts payable (Cdn$11,250 – Cdn$11,000)		250

When the account payable is paid on its due date, a further exchange gain or loss is recorded if the exchange rate is no longer €1 = Cdn$2.25.

CONCEPT REVIEW

1. What is the recorded value of a capital asset costing €100,000 that is purchased by a Canadian company when the exchange rate is €1 = Cdn$2.10 and paid for when €1 = Cdn$1.95?
2. What total amount of exchange gain or loss is recorded in the transaction in question 1?

NON-FINANCIAL LIABILITIES: PROVISIONS

Provisions are the major category of nonfinancial liability. A provision is defined as *a liability of uncertain timing or amount.* Provisions can be caused by both legal and constructive obligations. Remember that since liabilities are "expected" outflows, some degree of uncertainty can exist.

Financial liabilities, such as payables and accruals, have a high degree of certainty. A liability that has *some uncertainty about the amount or the timing,* but is judged to be "more likely than not"—that is, the liability is probable but not completely certain—is recognized as a liability called a *provision.* A liability that is judged to have a lower degree of certainty and falls below the "likely" threshold—that is, a liability that is *not probable*—is called a **contingency** and is not recognized; information about contingencies is included in the disclosure notes. That is:

Degree of Certainty	Classification
Completely certain	Financial liabilities: Payables, accruals (recorded)
Probable	Provision (recorded)
Not probable	Contingency (disclosed)

Measurement of a Provision

When a liability is characterized by a degree of uncertainty, the uncertainty often is centred on the amount involved. A reasonable estimate must be obtained. The amount recognized as a provision is the *best estimate of the expenditure required to settle the present obligation* at the end of the reporting period.

First, to be recorded, there must be a *probable payout,* or a probability of payout must be more than 50%. Provisions are then recorded at the *best estimate.* This is the amount that would be rationally paid to settle the obligation at the reporting date, if such a payment were possible. The **most likely outcome** (highest probability alternative) should be considered. If there is a range of outcomes, the **expected value** (the sum of outcomes multiplied by their probability distribution) is also a factor to be considered.

For example, assume that there is a large population of items, each with a probability attached. *Expected value* should be used for valuation. A company might have 50 legal claims outstanding, each with a $10,000 potential claim. If 30% are judged to be likely to end with no cost to the company, and 70% end with a $10,000 payout, some payout is certain (>50%). The amount to be recorded is the *expected value* of $350,000 [(50 × 30% × $0) + (50 × 70% × $10,000)]. *Expected value is the best estimate for a large population scenario.*

If there is a small population, then the most likely outcome may be the best estimate. For example, assume that there are three legal claims outstanding against a company, each for $100,000. There is a 30% chance that the company will have to make a payment on one lawsuit, a 50% chance for two payouts, and a 20% chance for three payouts. Some payout is certain. The *most likely outcome* is two lawsuits because the probability of that outcome is highest, at 50%. This means that the company should accrue $200,000. The *expected value* is $190,000, which is close, and provides support for the $200,000 accrual [(30% × $100,000) + (50% × $200,000) + (20% × $300,000)]. *For a small population, the most likely outcome is often recorded as the best estimate.*

However, the *most likely outcome* is not always close to the *expected value,* especially in a small population. Assume now that there is a 40% chance that the company will have to make a payment on one lawsuit, a 30% chance for two payouts, and a 30% chance for three payouts. The most likely (40%) outcome is a $100,000 payment, but the expected value is $190,000 [(40% × $100,000) + (30% × $200,000) + (30% × $300,000)]. In this case, there are considerable odds (the cumulative probability is 60%) that either two or three lawsuits will have to be paid, and a $100,000 accrual is not enough. Therefore, $200,000 should be accrued; there is only a 40% chance that the payout would be less than this amount. *For a small population, the expected value can provide evidence to support an accrual of a particular outcome, even if it alone is not the most likely.*

Summary *A provision must be probable to be recorded.* Then the *best estimate* to record for a provision is:

Population	Best Estimate	Adjusted for
Large population	Expected value	Discounted for time value of money
Small population	Most likely outcome, with judgement, considering: 1. Expected value, and 2. Cumulative probabilities	Discounted for time value of money

Re-estimate Annually If a provision is estimated, then the amounts are re-estimated at each reporting date. The change in any recorded amount is expensed in the year. For example, if the estimate of a payout is originally $35,000, then this amount is recorded. If the estimate increases from $35,000 to $50,000 in a later year, an additional $15,000 of expense is recorded *in the year that the estimate changed.* On the other hand, if the estimated payment were to decline to $5,000, a *recovery* (negative expense) would be recorded in the period that the estimate changed.

Discounting Provisions must be discounted where the time value of money is material. The discount rate chosen must reflect current market interest rates, and the risk level specific to the liability. For a reporting example, refer again to the note disclosure provided by Canadian Tire, presented earlier in this chapter, where the company stated that discounting is used where material. Discounting is illustrated later in this chapter.

Exception If the amount and timing of cash flows is highly uncertain, *discounting cannot be accomplished in a meaningful fashion* and amounts are recorded on an undiscounted basis. Since provisions are by their nature uncertain amounts, discounting may often be impractical.

Contingency When a liability situation gives rise to a *contingency*, it is not recognized but instead is included in the disclosure notes. No financial statement liability element is recorded. In general, contingencies exist when:

- The obligation is possible but not probable;
- There is a present obligation but no economic resources are attached; or
- There is a present obligation but *rare circumstances* dictate that an estimate cannot be established.

Contingent Assets

While on the subject of contingencies, note that an asset is not recorded until a company is *virtually certain* of the related benefits to be obtained. *Virtual certainty* is a much higher degree of certainty than just *certainty*. *Contingent assets* are assets that arise from past events but whose existence must be confirmed by a future event that is not wholly in the control of management. If a company is suing a supplier, for instance, no amount is recorded for the claimed amount, even if it is likely that the company will win and the amount can be estimated. In fact, a winning court judgement would not be recorded until it seems virtually certain that the *amount will be paid*. Disclosure is the appropriate route.

Prohibited Practices

In the past, some companies have attempted to smooth earnings through the creation and reversal of provisions. For example, an expense and a liability might be recorded in years when earnings were high (e.g., "provision for future losses") just to lower earnings, and then reversed in a year when earnings was low to raise earnings. This practice is not permitted by accounting standards.

Finally, it is not permissible to use a provision set up for one purpose to offset expenditures for another purpose. For example, only environmental remediation expenditures can be used to reduce the environmental remediation provision.

CONCEPT REVIEW

1. What is a *provision* versus a *contingency*?
2. How is an expected value obtained for a provision?
3. Why might a multiyear, non-interest-bearing provision *not* be discounted?

EXAMPLES OF PROVISIONS

Lawsuits

If a company is being sued by another party, the company may be found guilty and ordered to pay money or otherwise make restitution to the plaintiff. Alternatively, the courts may find the company not guilty. Court decisions are subject to appeals, and the process may last for years. The defendant and the plaintiff may agree in the meantime to an out-of-court settlement.

Based on the certainty of payout, an unsettled court case may result in a provision (probable payout) or a contingency (not probable). Probability is assessed by the legal team, and the accountant and auditor may rely on the opinion of these experts. Note, though, that a constructive liability may be present if a company has announced that a settlement is being sought. A contingency may be present if there is a probable payout but the amount cannot be estimated; this inability to measure the payout should be rare. That is:

First:	Then, either/or:	
Ability to Measure Degree of Certainty	**Measurable**	**Not Measurable**
Certain (Probable)	Provision (recorded)	Contingency (disclosed) (rare situation)
Not certain (Not probable)	Contingency (disclosed)	Contingency (disclosed)

In general, defence teams are NOT often willing to admit that their clients are *likely to lose* a lawsuit, although obviously there is a loser and a winner in every case. Therefore, recorded provisions are relatively rare. Instead, disclosure of contingencies relating to lawsuits is common, despite accounting standards regarding probability and measurability.

ETHICAL ISSUES

Assume that a company is being sued by an ex-employee for $500,000 for wrongful dismissal. The company is defending itself actively but has privately admitted that a settlement of $200,000 would be acceptable. Should the $200,000 be recorded? Making it known would provide information to the plaintiff and possibly hurt the company's bargaining position in discussions to end the lawsuit. On the other hand, leaving the $200,000 out of the financial statements understates probable liabilities and overstates profits.

The company is ethically required to follow appropriate reporting but is equally ethically bound to serve its shareholders' best interests. Recording the $200,000 is appropriate. If disclosure is expected to prejudice the position of the company in a dispute with another company, the expense and the liability may be grouped with other items to avoid granting additional information to the plaintiff. The omission of disclosure must be explained.

Reporting Example The Nestlé Group has a recorded provision for outstanding lawsuits but also has contingencies. Information from the disclosure notes is as follows (in millions of Swiss francs (CHF); note that disclosure of litigation is restricted in the best interests of the company, and measurement is problematic:

Provision for Litigation	
At 31 December 2010	2,773
Currency retranslations	(39)
Provisions made in the period	194
Amounts used	(85)
Unused amounts reversed	(327)
Modification on the scope of consolidation	18
At 31 December 2011	2,534

continued on next page

Litigation

Litigation provisions have been set up to cover tax, legal and administrative proceedings that arise in the ordinary course of the business. These provisions cover numerous separate cases whose detailed disclosure could be detrimental to the Group interests. The Group does not believe that any of these litigation proceedings will have a material adverse impact on its financial position. The timing of outflows is uncertain as it depends upon the outcome of the proceedings. In that instance, these provisions are not discounted because their present value would not represent meaningful information. Group Management does not believe it is possible to make assumptions on the evolution of the cases beyond the balance sheet date.

...

12.2 Contingencies

The Group is exposed to contingent liabilities amounting to a maximum potential payment of CHF 1363 million (2010: CHF 1121 million) representing potential litigations of CHF 1344 million (2010: CHF 1110 million) and other items of CHF 19 million (2010: CHF 11 million). Potential litigations relate mainly to labour, civil and tax litigations in Latin America.

Contingent assets for litigation claims in favour of the Group amount to a maximum potential recoverable of CHF 281 million (2010: CHF 247 million).

Source: Nestlé Group, 2011 Consolidated Financial Statements, www.nestle.com, retrieved 11 July 2013.

Executory Contracts and Onerous Contracts

Companies often have contracts outstanding that require them to pay another party in the future, after the other party has performed some service or act. These contracts are known as **executory contracts** because they do not become liabilities until they have been *executed* by one party or the other. The contracts commit the enterprise to a future expenditure, but they are not *liabilities* until the other party has performed the service or act specified in the contract. Examples are employee contracts for future employment, contracts for future delivery of goods and services, and most unfilled purchase orders.

If the unavoidable costs of meeting the contract exceed the economic benefits under the contract, then the contract is classified an **onerous contract**. A *provision* must be recorded with respect to the onerous contract, for the net loss associated with the contract terms.

For example, assume that a company has agreed to purchase 10,000 kg of ore at a price of \$1.00 per kg. The price in today's market is \$0.80 per kg. A provision must be recorded for the expected loss of \$2,000 [10,000 kg × (\$1.00 – \$0.80)]:

Loss on purchase commitment	2,000	
Provision for loss on purchase commitment		2,000

If the ore is then purchased when the price is \$0.95 per kg, there is a partial loss recovery, and the inventory is recorded at its fair value:

Ore inventory	9,500	
Provision for loss on purchase commitment	2,000	
Loss recovery on purchase commitment		1,500
Accounts payable		10,000

Restructuring

A *provision for restructuring* is an estimate of the money that will be paid out in connection with a future restructuring program. A restructuring program is a plan of action that is planned and controlled by management, which materially changes the scope of the business undertaken by the entity, or the manner in which the business is conducted. Examples include the sale or termination of a line of the business, closure or relocation of operations in a country or region, change in management structure, and the like.

A liability will be recorded if the entity has a detailed formal plan for the restructuring *and* has started to implement the plan or otherwise announced the specifics of the plan to those who will be affected. An announcement that creates a provision must include major specific facts and details that raise valid expectations that the restructuring will take place.

Common elements of restructuring provisions are employee termination costs and costs to end contracts. A more detailed review of impairment implications, including any impairment of assets triggered by such a decision, is found in Chapters 3 and 10.

Warranty

This discussion deals with warranties that provide assurance that the product will operate as intended and meet specifications. The *cost deferral method* is used for these warranties.[2,3] A warranty is often a *legal liability*, specifically awarded to the customer in the sale contract as protection against damaged goods. Warranties may also be in force as *constructive obligations* based on a company's announced intentions.

Cost Deferral—Example To illustrate accounting for warranties, assume that Rollo Limited sells merchandise for $200,000 during 20X2. Rollo's merchandise carries a two-year unconditional warranty for parts and labour, and the cost deferral method is appropriate. Rollo's past experience has indicated that warranty costs will approximate 0.6% of sales. Payout is certain and the amount estimated is an expected value. The entry to record sales and the warranty obligation in 20X2 will be as follows:

Accounts receivable	200,000	
Sales revenue		200,000
Warranty expense	1,200	
Provision for warranty		1,200

If, in 20X3, Rollo incurs costs of $350 to repair or replace defective merchandise, the cash outflow is charged to the liability account:

Provision for warranty	350	
Cash (and other resources used)		350

The expense for the year *is not the amount paid*; the expense is the *total of all expected future claims*. The balance in the provision for warranty account will be $850, credit. The provision will be carried forward from year to year, adjusted each year for management's estimate of the future warranty costs. As is the case for all accounting estimates, the estimate of annual warranty cost and the outstanding liability may be changed in the light of new experience or as the result of changed product design.

---

[2] If warranties are sold as a separate service contract, the *revenue deferral method* is used. Refer to Chapter 6 for a discussion of these circumstances.

[3] When revenue recognition standards switch to a contract-based approach in 2017, the approach to accounting for warranties will be affected. The discussion in this chapter is based on existing, pre-2017 standards.

In 20X3, Rollo sells another $240,000 worth of merchandise. Rollo now plans to use an estimate of 0.4% of sales for warranties, and believes that it should have used this estimate in the prior year, as well. The current year expense is $560, which is $960 for this year ($240,000 × 0.4%), less a $400 adjustment to decrease last year's accrual [$200,000 × (0.6% – 0.4%)]. The $400 correction is made this year, and *changes the current year expense.* Correction is not done retrospectively. An amount of $500 is spent on claims in 20X3, some for product sold in 20X2 and some related to goods sold in 20X3. After these entries, the provision for warranty will have a credit balance of $910 ($850 + $560 – $500).

Accounts receivable	240,000	
Sales revenue		240,000
Warranty expense ($960 – $400)	560	
Provision for warranty		560

Provision for warranty	500	
Cash (and other resources used)		500

If, in any year, the charges to the provision for warranty work done are higher than the balance in the provision account, the provision account will *temporarily* go into a debit balance until the year-end adjustment is made. The temporary existence of a debit balance simply indicates that the expense has not yet been accrued. The ending provision for warranty must be reviewed for reasonableness, though. If costs are creeping up, the provision will have a low balance, and the estimate that is accrued each year may need upward revision. On the other hand, if the provision credit balance builds up over time, the rate should be revised downward. Sometimes, the "excess" in a particular year may not call for an increase in the regular estimate if it is a one-time occurrence.

The provision for warranty is a current liability if the warranty is for one year or less. If the warranty is for a longer period, the provision should be split between current and long-term portions and the need for discounting should be considered.

Warranty as a Constructive Liability A warranty obligation that provides assurance that the product will operate as intended and meet specifications may be a *constructive liability for repair or replacement because of actions or statements of the company.* For example, if a hazard is identified because of a product defect, a company may put a repair, replacement or refund program in place that exceeds its legal responsibilities. This may be done to preserve the company's reputation, or simply to avoid future court action. This constructive liability is recorded as a provision, along with an expense, when it arises—the announcement of the program. Expected value is used for valuation, and the provision must be regularly reviewed to ensure valuation is reasonable.

Restoration and Environmental Obligations

Provisions are often created with respect to environmental obligations, as discussed in Chapter 9. If there are legislative remediation requirements, then the cost of the required activities must be estimated and accrued. If legislative requirements are *pending,* the provision is accrued only if there is **virtual certainty** that the legislation will be enacted. On the other hand, the liability may be a constructive liability, which must be accrued absent legislative requirements. For example, if a company has a published policy concerning environmental cleanup activities, or otherwise accepts responsibility for remediation in a public forum, then a provision for expected costs must be recorded. Lengthy time periods are common in this area, and discounting is usually required. An example is included with the section on discounting later in the chapter.

Sales Returns and Refunds

A company may allow merchandise to be returned for a cash refund or a credit on account. This may be a legal obligation, in accordance with stated return policies, or a constructive obligation based on past practice. The obligation must be estimated and recorded at the time of the sale.[4] At any reporting date, the provision for sales returns must be reviewed for reasonableness, taking into account usage and recent transaction history.

Coupons, Refunds, and Gift Cards

Coupons are often used as sales incentives. A provision for outstanding coupons may be recorded, but only in limited circumstances. The key to a coupon offer is whether economic benefits are transferred. If the product is still sold at a profit, even after the coupon, then no economic benefits are deemed to transfer and the provision has no accounting value. If, on the other hand, retailers or customers are reimbursed in cash for coupons or if products are sold at a loss, then a provision is appropriate. Note also that if the company reserves the right to cancel the coupons at any time, then there is no enforceable obligation. A reliable measurement for the provision includes estimating the take-up rate for the coupons; the **breakage** (unused) rate can be estimated based on past history or other valid evidence.

For example, assume 1,000 customers buying an appliance are given a coupon for a $10 cash rebate if proof of purchase is submitted. A liability exists because of the promise to pay cash, and the liability is a provision because the amount must be estimated. Based on past experience, 40% of the coupons will be submitted. The amount recorded is an expected value of $4,000 ($10 refund × 40% take-up rate × 1,000 coupons). The following entry would be made when the sale of 1,000 units is recorded:

Sales discounts	4,000	
Provision for coupon refund		4,000

If 370 coupons are honoured, and the remainder expire:

Provision for coupon refund	4,000	
Cash (370 coupons × $10 refund)		3,700
(Recovery of) sales discounts		300

Many companies sell gift cards or service passes to customers. Issuance of these cards creates an unearned revenue liability. The cards usually have an unlimited life due to provincial legislation and thus represent an indefinite legal liability. However, if the entity believes that some cards will be unused and can gather evidence to estimate *breakage*, then the liability becomes an estimate and thus is a provision. Discounting might be appropriate if the time period is long.

Loyalty Programs

A common sales incentive is a customer loyalty program, where the customer is awarded loyalty points, which can then be used to obtain free (or discounted) goods or services. There are many ways that these programs can be structured.

A loyalty program is an example of a sales contract involving multiple deliverables, as we saw in Chapter 6. No separate expense is recognized—*the loyalty program is an allocation of original revenue*. That is, the sale transaction with the customer has multiple parts, and the value of the award credits is one such part. An *unearned revenue* account, sometimes called a *provision for rewards*, is created. This provision is measured according to the value of the awards to the customer, not the cost of the goods to the company.

For example, assume that a sale of $65,000 to customers carries with it loyalty points that allow acquisition of product with a fair value of $5,000. This $5,000 estimate assumes

[4] See also the Chapter 6 discussion of uncertainties associated with transactions that trigger revenue recognition.

some breakage of points awarded. The following entry would be made when the sale is recorded:

Cash	65,000	
Sales revenue		60,000
Provision for loyalty program rewards		5,000

The provision is reduced when the loyalty points are redeemed.

Reporting Example Shoppers Drug Mart offers loyalty points to shoppers and records a provision with respect to the program. This policy is described in Note 3, Significant accounting policies:

> When points are earned by Program members, the Company defers revenue equal to the fair value of the awards. The Program's deferred revenue is recognized within accounts payable and accrued liabilities in the Company's consolidated balance sheets. When awards are redeemed by Program members, the redemption value of the awards is charged against the deferred revenue balance and recognized as revenue.
>
> The estimated fair value per point is determined based on the expected weighted average redemption levels for future redemptions based on the program reward schedule, including special redemption events. The trends in redemption rates (points redeemed as a percentage of points issued) are reviewed on an ongoing basis and the estimated fair value per point is adjusted based upon expected future activity.
>
> Source: Shoppers Drug Mart Corporation 2011 Annual Financial Statements, www.sedar.com, posted 1 March 2012.

Repairs and Maintenance

Repairs and maintenance are expenses of the year in which the repair or maintenance activity occurs. Such costs are not accrued to smooth out earnings, even when they are "lumpy." For example, assume that a cargo vessel must be painted every five years. The cost of painting is simply an expense of year five. The company may *not* accrue one-fifth of the cost each year and establish a provision for maintenance. Essentially, no obligating event has taken place after one year or even four years; the decision to paint is still in the future.

As another example, assume that a company has a contractual obligation to overhaul a leased aircraft every five years. Again, no provision is set up prior to the overhaul because there has been no obligating event. After an obligating event, the end of the fifth year, the company has no ability to avoid the overhaul. Before the end of the fifth year, the company could avoid the overhaul by selling the aircraft. When the overhaul is done, the cost is capitalized and then depreciated over the next five years. Similarly, if a lease requires maintenance activity after 1,000 hours of use, no obligating event occurs until the 1,000th hour is clocked. Up to that point in time, management could decide to leave the asset idle to avoid the maintenance activity.

Self-Insurance

Companies may choose to self-insure for known risks. Many large companies self-insure for fire and theft losses, meaning that they carry no external insurance. The cost of claims is assumed to be lower, over time, than the cost of insurance and so the choice is a rational business decision. Self-insurance does, however, retain certain risks for the company.

A provision for estimated losses must be established for *events (fire and theft) taking place prior to the reporting date*, but also for *loss events that have happened during the year but are not yet known*, such as undiscovered damage. Such damage might be discovered after the year-end, and it must be accrued. This allows for a reasonable delay based on known events. The amount is a provision because it is estimated.

However, companies may not record a provision in excess of the cost of estimated incidents in the year. A company may wish to do this to smooth the expense between years with low losses and years with high losses. *A provision must be justified based on a loss event.* If there is no such event, no accrual can be made, even if the odds suggest that a future year will have heavier incidence of loss events.

Compensated-Absence Liabilities

The Canada Labour Code requires that employees receive paid vacations and holidays. The expense for salaries and wages paid during these absences from work is recognized in the current year. *When employees can carry over unused time to future years,* any expense due to compensated absences must be recognized (accrued) in the year in which it is earned. The accrual is based on the additional amount that the entity expects to pay as a result of the unused entitlement accumulated at the year-end date.

An adjusting entry must be made at the end of each fiscal year to accrue all of the compensation cost for the vacation and medical leave time that is carried over. An expense and a current liability are recorded. When the time is taken, the liability account may be debited at the time the employee is paid. Alternatively, the liability may be adjusted only at year-end. Either approach will recognize the cost of the compensated absences as an expense in the period earned rather than when taken.

For example, consider the carryover of vacation time of the Conway Company, which has 500 employees. Each employee is granted three weeks paid vacation time each year. Vacation time, up to a maximum accumulation of four weeks, may be carried over to subsequent years prior to termination of employment. At the end of 20X5, the end of the annual accounting period, personnel records revealed the following information concerning carryover vacation amounts:

Carryovers from 20X5*				
Number of Employees	**Weeks per Employee**	**Total Weeks**	**Salary per Week**	**Total Accrual**
10	2	20	$ 1,500	$30,000
3	1	3	2,000	6,000
				$36,000

*These are carryovers from 20X5 to future years.

Disregarding payroll taxes, which are excluded here to simplify the analysis, the indicated entries are as follows:

31 December 20X5—adjusting entry to accrue vacation salaries not yet taken or paid		
Salary expense	36,000	
Provision for compensated absences		36,000

During 20X6, vacation time carryover is taken and salaries paid (all employees took their carried-over vacation time, except for one person who still carried over two weeks, valued at $1,500 per week)

Provision for compensated absences	33,000	
Cash ($36,000 – $3,000)		33,000

The balance remaining in the liability account is $3,000: two weeks at $1,500 per week.

This illustration assumes that there was no change in the rate of pay from 20X5 to 20X6 (when the carryover was used) for those employees who had the carryover. If there were rate changes, the pay difference would be debited (if an increase) or credited (if a decrease) to salary expense during 20X6.

This item is a liability only if a company allows employees to *carry over vacation entitlements:* many do not, and no liability exists. Most financial institutions, for example, require employees to take all their vacation entitlements before the end of each calendar year; it is important to their internal control systems to have someone else go in and do the employee's job regularly so that the employee cannot hide suspicious activities indefinitely.

Summary

Refer to the following chart as a summary:

Possible Financial Statement Element—Provision	Record?
Lawsuits	Yes—if certain and measurable No—if not certain; classified as a contingency if not certain or if certain but not measurable (rare)
Executory contracts	No—wait and record only on delivery
Onerous contracts	Yes—record estimated loss
Restructuring	Yes—if formal plan that has been implemented or communicated
Warranty	Yes—accrue provision when the warranty contract provides a guarantee that the product will operate as intended and meet specifications. Yes—accrue provision if constructive liability (*Note:* In some circumstances, revenue deferral is used.)
Restoration and environmental	Yes—record if constructive or legislative; estimate must be made
Sales returns	Yes—record if constructive or contractual; estimate must be made
Coupons and gift cards	Yes—if distribution of economic benefits involved (cash or products issued at a loss); breakage rate to be estimated No—if cancellable or non-cash and represent a small discount so that products still sold at a profit
Loyalty programs	Yes—assign fair value and allocate unearned revenue on initial sale; breakage rate to be estimated Multiple deliverables approach used
Repairs and maintenance	No—normally accounted for in the year of the repair or maintenance activity Yes—if an obligating event (under contract) takes place
Self-insurance	Yes—for losses experienced and for expected losses where the incident has happened No—no general provision designed for smoothing permitted
Compensated absence	Yes—accrue for rights carried over to subsequent fiscal year

CONCEPT REVIEW

1. What is an onerous contract?
2. Why does selling a product with a warranty attached give rise to a provision?
3. When is a provision for coupons recorded?
4. When is a provision for self-insurance recorded?

THE IMPACT OF DISCOUNTING

Liabilities must be discounted where the time value of money is material. This will affect multiyear liabilities that bear no interest rate (i.e., are interest-free), or multiyear liabilities that have interest rates below market interest rates. Remember, though, the following:

- As a matter of convenience, and materiality, liabilities with an initial term of less than one year are not discounted.
- If the timing or amounts of liabilities are uncertain, then discounting is not practical and is not required.

Common examples of liabilities that must be discounted are low-interest loans, perhaps provided as sales incentives by suppliers, and environmental liabilities.

Calculation of Present Value

The **nominal interest rate** is the interest rate stated for a liability; the nominal rate might be zero. The **effective interest rate**, or **yield**, is the *market interest rate, for debt of similar term, security, and risk.* Using the effective interest rate as the discount rate, the discounted amount, or **present value**, (P) is calculated as:[5]

$$P = [I \times (P/A, i, n)] + [F \times (P/F, i, n)], \text{ where}$$

P = fair value of the loan; issuance proceeds on issuance date
I = dollar amount of each period's interest payment, if any, or
= nominal rate, if any, times the loan face value
F = maturity value of the loan
n = the number of periods to maturity
i = the market interest rate

That is, the maturity amount and the interest amount—the entire cash flow stream associated with the liability—must be discounted to present value using the market interest rate.

When a liability pays the effective market interest rate, the discounted amount is equal to the maturity amount and there is no need to discount. When the nominal and market interest rates are different, the discounted amount will differ from the maturity amount, and there are accounting implications.

Examples of liabilities that must be discounted follow.

Example 1: No-Interest Note Payable Assume that Radial Information Limited has purchased equipment and signed a note payable for $18,000. If Radial had agreed to pay $18,000 for the equipment in six months' time, with no additional interest, the liability and

[5] A review of present value calculations is included on Connect, if practice is needed.

the capital asset would be recorded at $18,000, with no discounting because the interest-free period is short.

Assume now that the note payable is due in three years' time, with no additional interest. Discounting is required because the time span is longer. Assume also that Radial could borrow a similar amount over three years from a financial institution at a 9% interest rate. Assuming annual compounding, the present value[6] of the liability is $13,900 [$18,000 × (P/F, 9%, 3)]. This is the value at which the equipment and the liability will be recorded. The liability will increase by 9% interest on the outstanding balance each year and be equal to $18,000 at maturity. The **effective interest method** is used to measure interest expense and the growth of the liability. This series of events and transactions is recorded as follows:

Equipment	13,900	
Note payable, net		13,900

In subsequent periods, interest expense is recorded, and then the liability is paid:

Year 1 interest:

Interest expense ($13,900 × 9%)	1,251	
Note payable, net		1,251

Year 2 interest:

Interest expense [($13,900 + $1,251 = $15,151) × 9%]	1,364	
Note payable, net		1,364

Year 3 interest and payment:

Interest expense [($15,151 + $1,364 = $16,515) × 9%]	1,485	
Note payable, net		1,485

Note payable ($16,515 + $1,485)	18,000	
Cash		18,000

The interest calculations may be organized in a table:

	(1) Opening Net Liability	(2) Interest Expense at Market Rate (1) × 9%	(3) Closing Net Liability (1) + (2)
Year 1	$13,900	$1,251	$15,151
Year 2	15,151	1,364	16,515
Year 3	16,515	1,485	18,000

[6] Present value tables are appended at the end of the text and illustrate the notation used throughout this text.

Use of a discount account When the discounted account is a formal note payable, with a specified maturity value, the note payable is usually recorded at its maturity value. A discount account is used to revalue the note to its discounted amount. The discount account is a contra account to the note payable, and is netted with the liability on the SFP. Interest is then recognized by **unwinding**—or reducing—the discount. Returning to Example 1 above, the entries, if a discount account were used:

Equipment	13,900	
Discount on note payable ($18,000 – $13,900)	4,100	
Note payable		18,000

As before, the liability is reported *net* on the SFP at $13,900 ($18,000 – $4,100). The presence or absence of a discount account does not change the net value reported on the statement of financial position (SFP).

Year 1 interest:

Interest expense	1,251	
Discount on note payable		1,251

The liability is reported on the SFP *net* at $15,151 [$18,000 – $2,849 ($4,100 – $1,251)]. This is the same amount as is reflected in the net method.

Year 2 interest:

Interest expense	1,364	
Discount on note payable		1,364

The liability is reported net on the SFP *net* at $16,515 [$18,000 – $1,485 ($2,849 – $1,364)]. Again, this is identical to the net method.

Year 3 interest and payment:

Interest expense	1,485	
Discount on note payable		1,485

Note payable	18,000	
Cash		18,000

There are no reporting or measurement implications that arise from use of a separate discount account. Use of a discount account is common practice for notes payable but is not used for (estimated) provisions, since provisions lack a specified maturity value.

Interest accrual If the fiscal year is different from the date of the note, accruals must be made at the year-end to record interest incurred. To illustrate this interest accrual, assume that the year-end is 31 December, or 9/12 of the year. The $1,251 interest that relates to the first twelve months of the loan is recorded as time progresses. The accrual entry for nine months of interest at the end of Year 1, using the gross method:

Interest expense ($1,251 × 9/12)	938	
Discount on note payable		938

Entry on loan anniversary date, 31 March:

Interest expense ($1,251 × 3/12)	313	
Discount on note payable		313

The entire first 12 months' interest of $1,251 must be recorded before interest is recalculated (i.e., before compounding), in order to correspond to compounding periods. Tracking the interest calculation with a table helps with the accuracy of the calculations.

Example 2: Note Payable with Different Market and Stated Rate. Assume that Baylor Company purchases inventory on 1 April 20X2 and agrees to pay the vendor $12,000 on 31 March 20X4, plus annual interest at 4% each 31 March. The market interest rate for similar term and security is 10%. Assume also that the inventory purchased does not have a readily determinable market value. To value the transaction, it is necessary to calculate the present value of the note, including both principal and interest:

Present value of maturity amount:	
$12,000(P/F, 10%, 2) =	$ 9,917
Present value of the nominal interest payments:	
$480(P/A, 10%, 2) =	833
Present value of the note at 10%	$10,750

The note may be recorded gross (with a discount) or net. The two methods are illustrated below.

1 April 20X2:	Gross		Net	
Inventory (1)	10,750		10,750	
Discount on note payable	1,250		—	
Note payable		12,000		10,750

(1) If the note were a cash loan, this debit would be to cash.

Under either method, the *net book value* of the note is $10,750, the present value.

The interest calculation may again be organized in a table, which now includes cash paid and the discount:

	(1) Opening Net Liability	(2) Interest Expense 10% Market Rate (1) × 10%	(3) Interest Paid 4% Stated Rate $12,000 × 4%	(4) Discount Amortization (2) – (3)	(5) Closing Net Liability (1) + (4)
Year 1	$10,750	$1,075	$480	$595	$11,345
Year 2	$11,345	1,135	480	655	12,000

The net notes payable balance—columns 1 and 5—*is always the present value of remaining payments.* For example, the $11,345 balance is the present value on 31 March 20X3 of the remaining payment (principal plus interest), a payment that is due on 31 March 20X4.

$12,480(P/F, 10%, 1) = $11,345

If the fiscal year corresponded with the dates of the note, the interest and payment information from this table would correspond directly to the interest entry, that is, for the first payment:

31 March 20X3:	Gross		Net	
Interest expense	1,075		1,075	
Discount on note payable		595		—
Note payable		—		595
Cash		480		480

For the second payment and principal repayment:

31 March 20X4:	Gross		Net	
Interest expense	1,135		1,135	
Discount on note payable		655		—
Note payable		—		655
Cash		480		480
Note payable	12,000		12,000	
Cash		12,000		12,000

Interest accrual If the fiscal year is different from the date of the note, accruals must be made that also include discount amortization. To illustrate, assume that the year-end is 31 December, or 9/12 of the year. The entry at the end of the fiscal year, using the gross method:

Interest expense ($1,075 × 9/12)	806	
Accrued interest payable ($480 × 9/12)		360
Discount on note payable ($595 × 9/12)		446

The accrual entry records a portion of the discount and the cash interest payable. The amounts recorded are 9/12 of each of the lines in the interest table that correspond to the first year.

The entry on cash payment, 31 March, picks up the elimination of interest payable, the remaining three months of interest expense, three months of discount amortization, and the cash payment:

Interest expense ($1,075 × 3/12)	269	
Accrued interest payable	360	
Discount on note payable ($595 × 3/12)		149
Cash		480

Example 3: Provision for Lawsuit Assume that a provision of $200,000 is recorded for a lawsuit, on the expectation that the amount will be paid in two years' time. Timing can be estimated with certainty. The company can borrow for general operating purposes over this term at an interest rate of 8%. The discounted amount represents the maturity amount only, since there is no interest. A discount account is not used; the provision is recorded net.

The discounted amount is $171,468 [$200,000 × (P/F, 8%, 2)], and is recorded as follows:

Loss on litigation	171,468	
Provision for litigation		171,468

In subsequent periods, interest expense is recorded, and then the liability is paid:

Year 1 interest:

Interest expense ($171,468 × 8%) Provision for litigation	13,717	13,717

Year 2 interest and payment:

Interest expense [($171,468 + $13,717) × 8%] Provision for litigation	14,815	14,815

Provision for litigation ($171,468 + $13,717 + $14,815) Cash	200,000	200,000

The calculations may be organized in a table:

	(1) Opening Net Liability	(2) Interest Expense at Market Rate (1) × 8%	(3) Closing Net Liability (1) + (2)
Year 1	$171,468	$13,717	$185,185
Year 2	$185,185	14,815	200,000

Example 4: Provision with Estimate Change Assume that on 2 January 20X5 HDL Limited purchases a transmission tower for $1,300,000, which it installs on the roof of its leased premises. This is recorded as an asset. HDL is required by the terms of the building lease to remove the tower at the end of six years. The estimated cost of removal is $50,000.

To recognize the liability, the $50,000 must be discounted at an interest rate for borrowing with similar term and security. This rate is assumed to be 6%:

$$P = \$50{,}000 \times (P/F, 6\%, 6) = \$35{,}248$$

The retirement obligation is added to the cost of the transmission tower, and a provision is recorded:

Transmission tower Decommissioning obligation	35,248	35,248

The cost of the transmission tower is the acquisition cost plus the decommissioning obligation amount, or $1,335,248. This asset will be depreciated over its six-year life. HDL must also accrue interest expense on the decommissioning obligation each year, using the 6% interest rate. For 20X5, the accrual will be:

Interest expense ($35,248 × 6%) Decommissioning obligation	2,115	2,115

At the end of 20X5, the book value of the obligation will be $35,248 + $2,115 = $37,363. As in other examples, a table can be used to organize the calculations:

	(1) Opening Net Liability	(2) Interest Expense at Market Rate (1) × 6%	(3) Closing Net Liability (1) + (2)
20X5	$35,248	$2,115	$37,363
20X6	37,363	2,242	39,605
20X7	39,605	2,376	41,981
20X8	41,981	2,519	44,500
20X9	44,500	2,670	47,170
20X10	47,170	2,830	50,000

Remeasurement HDL must adjust the amount of the obligation—and adjust the asset value—if there is:

- A change in the amount or timing of the expected retirement obligation cash flows; or
- A change in the discount rate to reflect current market rates.

In HDL's case, the timing could change if the lease term is extended. The estimated cost of removal is quite likely to change over time because of technology changes and cost component changes driven by increasing or decreasing prices.

When an estimate changes, *interest for the year is first recorded based on estimates in place at the beginning of the period.* Any adjustment caused by estimate changes is then recorded, but not to interest expense—this is an adjustment to the asset account.

Assume that the appropriate interest rate was revised to 5% at the end of 20X6. The other major assumptions—$50,000 amount to be paid, and the date of tower removal—have not changed.

First, 20X6 interest is recorded at the old rate of 6%:

Interest expense (see table above)	2,242	
Decommissioning obligation		2,242

The decommissioning obligation now has a balance of $39,605, per the table above.

Reflecting the new interest rate, the decommissioning obligation is recalculated as:

$$\$50{,}000 \times (P/F,\ 5\%,\ 4) = \$41{,}135$$

An increase of $1,530 ($41,135 – $39,605) is needed, reflecting the lower interest rate. *This is adjusted to the asset account.*

Transmission tower	1,530	
Decommissioning obligation		1,530

At the end of 20X6, HDL's decommissioning obligation is as follows:

Initial recognition, 2 January 20X5	$35,248
Interest, 31 December 20X5	2,115
Interest, 31 December 20X6	2,242
Balance of original estimated obligation	39,605
Adjustment, 20X6	1,530
Balance, 31 December 20X6	$41,135

Future years will reflect interest expense at the rate of 5%. The table is as follows:

	(1) Opening Net Liability	(2) Interest Expense at Market Rate (1) × 5%	(3) Closing Net Liability (1) + (2)
20X7	$41,135	$2,057	$43,192
20X8	43,192	2,160	45,352
20X9	45,352	2,268	47,620
20X10	47,620	2,380	50,000

Suppose that at the end of 20X7, HDL decides that the cost of removing the tower will be $45,000 and that the appropriate interest rate is now 7%. Following the same patterns as in 20X6, interest is first recorded using the 5% rate that was deemed appropriate in the prior year:

Interest expense (see table above)	2,057	
Decommissioning obligation		2,057

The decommissioning obligation now has a balance of $43,192, per the table above.

Reflecting the new cost estimate and interest rate, the decommissioning obligation is recalculated as:

$$\$45{,}000 \times (P/F,\ 7\%,\ 3) = \$36{,}734$$

A decrease of $6,458 ($36,734 – $43,192) is needed, reflecting the revised estimates. This is adjusted to the asset account. As a result, at the end of 20X7, HDL's decommissioning obligation has a balance of $36,734.

Decommissioning obligation	6,458	
Transmission tower		6,458

Changes to estimates and interest rates are common, and as result, changes to these liability accounts and the related assets are common. Annual depreciation on the transmission tower reflects these changing values!

Reporting Example International Forest Product Limited records a provision regarding its obligation to reforest areas harvested under various timber rights. The disclosure notes include detailed information about the change to the provision for the year, which grew from approximately $27 million to $32 million in 2011. The change in the provision includes $545 thousand of interest in 2011, unwinding the discount. Also included is an increase of $470 thousand for changes in estimate, less than 2% of the opening balance. Note that the $32 million is reported as a $14 million current liability and $18 million as a long-term liability, reflecting the timing of expenditures.

---

12. Reforestation liability:

The Company has an obligation to reforest areas harvested under various timber rights. The obligation is incurred as logging occurs and the fair value of the liability for reforestation is determined with reference to the present value of estimated future cash flows required to settle the obligation.

Changes in the reforestation liability for the years ended December 31 are as follows:

(Canadian dollars in thousands)	2011	2010
Reforestation liability, beginning of year	$27,110	$23,360
Reforestation expense on current logging and market logging agreements	12,998	8,663
Reforestation liability on acquisition of timber tenure	—	804
Reforestation expenditures	(9,225)	(6,260)
Unwind of discount	545	604
Changes in estimated future reforestation expenditures	470	(61)
	$31,898	$27,110
Consisting of:		
Current reforestation liability	$14,121	$ 9,785
Long term reforestation liability	17,777	17,325
	$31,898	$27,110

The total undiscounted amount of the estimated future expenditures required to settle the reforestation obligation at December 31, 2011, is $33,282,000 (2010—$29,490,000). The reforestation expenditures are expected to occur over the next one to fifteen years and have been discounted at the long term risk-free interest rate of 2%. Reforestation expense resulting from obligations arising from current logging are included in Production costs for the year and expense related to the unwinding of the discount is included in Finance costs.

Source: International Forest Products Ltd. 2011 Annual Financial Statements, www.sedar.com, posted 17 February 2012.

CONCEPT REVIEW

1. Why might an asset purchased for $20,000 but paid for in five years' time be recorded at a lower amount?
2. What is discounting? What does it mean to unwind a discount?
3. What interest rate must be used to discount a low-interest note payable?
4. If an estimate changes on a discounted provision for environmental cleanup for a resource property, what two accounts are affected?

CLASSIFYING LIABILITIES

Most companies segregate their liabilities using the current and long-term categories. Working capital, or current assets less current liabilities, is a traditional measure of short-term liquidity and is often the subject of loan covenants. For this reason, classification of liabilities is an important issue.

A **current liability** is one that will be settled *within the next operating cycle or the next 12 months.* The operating cycle is the time between acquisition of assets for processing and their realization in cash. If the operating cycle is not clearly identifiable, it is assumed to be 12 months. For most companies, the effective guiding time period is the 12-month requirement. A **long-term liability** has a due date past this time window.

Some companies lack a clearly defined operating cycle and thus do not use a current/non-current distinction. These companies are required to present liabilities (and assets) in order of liquidity but do not make a "cut" between current and long term. For example, financial institutions normally categorize their assets and liabilities according to order of liquidity but do not segregate financial statement elements on the basis of **maturity date**.

In North America, current liabilities normally are listed in descending order based on the strength of the creditors' claims. In other countries, this may be reversed. Either approach is acceptable.

Classification of Notes Payable

Notes payable may be long-term liabilities or current liabilities. Classification depends on the terms of the loan. Loans are current liabilities if:

1. *Loans are due on demand.* Demand loans are payable on demand, or after a short delay of 7 to 30 business days to arrange alternative financing. These loans are legally current liabilities and must be classified as such, even if a demand for payment within the current year is not expected.
2. *Loans are due within the next year.* If a loan has a due date within the next 12 months, it is a current liability, even if the company expects to renegotiate the loan. That is, a 20-year note payable will be long term until year 19, and then it will be a current liability. The liability is current even if the company plans to refinance in year 20 with a new long-term bond.

If debt is partially due within the next year, the current portion must be reclassified. For example, consider the classification of this $500,000 liability, of which $100,000 must be repaid in the year to come:

Current liabilities:	
Current portion of notes payable	$100,000
Long-term liabilities:	
Notes payable ($500,000 less current portion: $100,000)	$400,000

3. *Long-term debt is in violation of covenants and thus can be called by the lender at any time.* Since the lender could demand repayment, the loan is current. A company might be in arrears on loan terms, such as the requirement to pay interest on time, or may have violated covenants, such as the maximum debt-to-equity ratio on the financial statement date. If the lender has agreed *before year-end* to new terms, then the loan may remain as long term. The loan is also long term if the lender has agreed to a 12-month grace period, from the year-end date, to renegotiate the loan. However, if such agreements are reached *after year-end*, then the loan must reflect its *status at year-end* and would be classified as a current liability.

Short-Term Obligations with an Arrangement for Refinancing A company may wish to reclassify liabilities from current to long term to improve the reported working capital position. This reclassification is not to be taken lightly—a large reclassification has a material impact on the financial statements.

Intention to restructure a short-term loan as a long-term loan is not enough to justify reclassification. However, it may happen that a company enters into an arrangement for refinancing debt, prior to actually restructuring the obligation. A *contractual arrangement* may be relied on to support classification of short-term obligations as long-term debt, as long as it is, indeed, a legal contract with a reputable party. *This agreement must be in place at the year-end date.* An agreement entered into after this date cannot be used as a basis to reclassify. If a short-term obligation is to be excluded from current liabilities under a future financing agreement, note disclosure of the details would be appropriate.

Classification of Provisions

Provisions are classified as current or long term based on the timing of expected future cash flows. However, classification must be first based on the legal terms of the provision.

For example, assume that customers must make a deposit for containers, refundable 30 days after the container is returned. Most customers are continuing customers, and the deposits are "rolled over" from one shipment to the next, with the result that years go by with no refunds made. Regardless of the expected cash flow, the deposit liability is current because the customer has the right to a refund after 30 days.

DISCLOSURE AND STATEMENT OF CASH FLOWS

Disclosures for Financial Liabilities

Accounting standards require disclosure of information that will allow users to evaluate the significance of financial instruments in an evaluation of financial position and performance. Financial instrument disclosure is extensive; this recap provides the highlights only. Companies must disclose:

1. The *carrying amounts* for financial instruments in each category. For some categories, this is amortized cost or cost. For others, carrying value is fair value.
2. Regardless of what is used for carrying value, disclosure must be made of fair value, and a description of the methods used to estimate fair value. For many of the financial instruments in this chapter, cost and fair value are identical.
3. The important components of each financial statement category. For example, trade payables versus income tax payable must be shown separately, as must various notes payable.
4. Information related to the legal terms of the liability, including maturity date, interest rate, collateral, and so on.
5. Any defaults and breaches of notes payable, including any resolution of the default issues and the carrying amount of the related loan.
6. Various revenue and expense amounts, including interest expense.
7. Information on exposure to various sources of risk, as appropriate. Risks might include credit, risk, liquidity risk, and market risk. Objectives, policies, and processes for managing risk must be disclosed. Such disclosure is extensive and includes both qualitative and quantitative elements.
8. Accounting policy information is required as a matter of course for all financial statement elements.

Disclosures for Provisions and Contingencies

Provisions must be shown in a separate category from payables and accruals, and the nature of each recorded liability explained. In fact, extensive disclosure for each class of obligations is required to improve transparency in an area that is dominated by judgement. In particular, companies must disclose a reconciliation, or *a continuity schedule* (opening balance to closing balance), that explains the movement in each *class* of provisions. Unrecorded amounts, that is, contingencies, must be described completely, along with a discussion of their nature and an estimate of their financial effect, if practicable.

The continuity schedule for provisions of Canadian Tire Corporation is shown below. This schedule reports opening and closing balances for five provisions, as well as the source of changes during the year. Provisions are set up primarily for sales and warranty returns, site restoration and decommissioning, onerous contracts, and customer loyalty. Customer loyalty relates to the cash value of Canadian Tire "money" (coupons) between Canadian Tire and their dealers. Note that two provisions, sales and warranty returns and site restoration and decommissioning, are discounted; each of these reports "unwinding" of the discount. The site restoration and decommissioning provision has also been increased because of a change in the discount rate. The disclosure note also indicates the dollar value of provisions reported as current versus long term on the SFP.

21. PROVISIONS

The following table presents the changes to the Company's provisions:

	2012					
(Cdn dollars in millions)	Sales and warranty returns	Site restoration and decommissioning	Onerous contracts	Customer loyalty	Other	Total
Balance, beginning of year	$113.2	$26.8	$7.1	$ 68.1	$31.8	$247.0
Charges, net of reversals	242.8	11.5	0.4	112.8	1.0	368.5
Utilizations	(245.7)	(5.0)	(2.8)	(107.7)	(16.0)	(377.2)
Unwinding of discount	1.0	0.4	—	—	—	1.4
Change in discount rate	—	0.9	—	—	—	0.9
Balance, end of year	$111.3	$34.6	$4.7	$ 73.2	$16.8	$240.6
Less: Current provisions	108.6	7.3	1.5	66.1	2.3	185.8
Long-term provisions	$ 2.7	$27.3	$3.2	$ 7.1	$14.5	$ 54.8

Note: Comparative figures have been excluded.

Sales and warranty returns

The provision for sales and warranty returns relates to the Company's obligation to stores within its Dealer network for defective goods in their current inventories and defective goods sold to customers throughout its store operations that have yet to be returned, as well as after sales and service for replacement parts.

Site restoration and decommissioning

In the normal course of business, the Company leases property and has a legal or constructive obligation to return the sites to their original or agreed-upon state at the end of the lease term.

Onerous contracts

The Company recognizes a provision for onerous lease contracts on premises that are no longer being used due to store closures.

Customer loyalty

The Company maintains a provision related to its loyalty programs, including paper-based Canadian Tire "Money" issued at Petroleum gas bars and to Dealers and Electronic Canadian Tire "Money" on-the-Card issued whenever consumers make a Canadian Tire Options MasterCard purchase. In addition, the Company is testing a new loyalty program called Canadian Tire "Money" Advantage. All forms of loyalty can be redeemed only at the Canadian Tire Retail stores for merchandise at the option of the consumer.

An obligation arises from the above customer loyalty program when the Dealers pay the Company to acquire paper-based Canadian Tire "Money" because the Dealers retain the right to return Canadian Tire "Money" to the Company for refund in cash. An obligation also arises when the Company issues electronic-based Canadian Tire "Money" on-the-Card or Canadian Tire "Money" Advantage. These obligations are measured at fair value by reference to the fair value of the awards for which they could be redeemed based on the estimated probability of their redemption and are expensed to sales and marketing expenses in the consolidated statements of income.

Other

Other provisions include liabilities for severance under restructuring arrangements, the cost of legal issues that have not yet been settled and other claims. The amount and timing of when the Company expects to discharge these liabilities are uncertain and are based on the Company's best estimates.

Source: Canadian Tire Corporation, Ltd. 2012 Annual Consolidated Financial Statements, www.sedar.com, posted 21 February 2013.

Statement of Cash Flows

With respect to liabilities and the issues in this chapter, the following reporting must be observed when preparing statement of cash flows (SCF):

- Changes in liabilities and provisions that are related to earnings are adjusted in operating activities.
- Cash changes in borrowings, both new loans and repayments, are reported in financing activities.
- Non-cash changes in borrowings, such as notes payable issued for assets, are non-cash transactions and are excluded from the SCF. Non-cash transactions are described in disclosure notes.
- Interest that is represented by unwinding a discount is a non-cash expense and is added back in operating activities.
- Cash paid for interest can be reported either in operating activities or financing activities, and excludes any portion of interest caused by unwinding a discount.

Example As an example, consider the following liability accounts of Milo Resources Limited:

	20X5	20X4
Trade accounts payable	$1,706,300	$1,423,000
Provision for legal	260,000	—
Decommissioning obligation	245,000	210,000
Notes payable, 8%	200,000	—
Notes payable, net, 9%	68,500	—

Additional information:

- Provision for legal is based on three outstanding court cases. No cash was paid this year. The amount is not discounted due to uncertainty of timing of cash flows.
- The decommissioning obligation relates to a mining property. The $35,000 change in this account this year is due to interest ($17,000) and also due to a change in estimate ($18,000).
- The 8% notes payable were issued at market interest rates in early 20X5.
- The 9% note payable reflects market interest rates at issuance but is in fact a no-interest, five-year note payable arranged with a supplier in early 2X05, for a piece of equipment. The note was originally recorded at its discounted amount of $65,000. Interest of $3,500 was recorded in 20X5.

Milo Resources uses the indirect method of presentation in the operating activities section of the SCF, and classifies interest paid in the operating activities section.

As a result of these transactions, the SCF would report:

1. In operating activities, as an add-back, change in non-cash working capital, trade accounts payable, +$283,300.
2. In operating activities, as an add-back, non-cash expense for legal, +$260,000.
3. In operating activities, as an add-back, non-cash expense for interest on decommissioning obligation, +$17,000. The other $18,000 change in this account is not shown on the SCF, because it is a non-cash "acquisition"/addition to the mining property. Non-cash transactions are disclosed.
4. In financing, issuance of 8% notes payable, +$200,000

5. The $65,000 issuance of 9% notes payable is a non-cash acquisition of equipment and is not shown on the SCF. The transaction is described in a disclosure note.
6. The company would show, in operating activities, as an add-back, non-cash expense for interest 9% notes payable, +$3,500.
7. Cash paid for interest on the 8% note, $16,000 ($200,000 × 8%) is shown as an outflow in operating activities.

In operating activities, one must examine sources of revenue and expense that do not reflect the underlying cash flow, and make appropriate adjustments. This includes changes in current liability accounts, and interest expense that represents unwinding a discount. Finally, issuing notes payable for cash and repaying notes for cash are financing transactions.

LOOKING AHEAD

Definition—Proposed Change

As part of a review of the conceptual framework, the International Accounting Standards Board (IASB) is reconsidering the definition of financial elements, including the definition of a liability. The definition under consideration is that a liability is "a present obligation for which the entity is the obligor." This definition removes the requirement that the liability relates to a past event but retains the requirement that there be a *present obligation*. In particular, a present economic obligation exists when a company is committed to a specific action that is capable of resulting in cash outflows, and there is a mechanism to enforce the economic obligation against the entity. If such a change is made, there would be a ripple effect through reporting standards.

ACCOUNTING STANDARDS FOR PRIVATE ENTERPRISES

Accounting Standards for Private Enterprise (ASPE) and the International Financial Reporting Standards (IFRS) for financial liabilities are largely similar. Much of the similarity stems from the common financial instruments rules, which were developed as a joint project between the IASB, Canada, and the United States.

For non-financial liabilities, there is less direct alignment. In fact, ASPE contains no comprehensive standards governing accounting policy for non-financial liabilities. The term "provision" is not used under ASPE; IFRS standards use this term for liabilities that are *uncertain as to timing or amount*. Under ASPE, such estimated liabilities are recognized if they *meet the liability definition, if they are measurable, and if future economic sacrifices are probable*. The outcome of applying this approach is largely consistent with IFRS; for example, restructuring liabilities are recorded, expected losses on contracts (onerous contracts) are recorded when fair values decline and so on.

There are some differences with ASPE, where IFRS standards contain specific guidance for provisions, for example, with respect to measuring the amount to record (expected value versus most likely outcome) and choice of discount rate, if needed.

Constructive liabilities are not recorded under ASPE. Accordingly, in areas such as decommissioning obligations, only legal liabilities are recognized.

There are no standards for customer loyalty points under ASPE. The IFRS approach explained in this chapter may be adopted or not.

When comparing IFRS and ASPE, the term "contingent liabilities" has a different meaning. An ASPE contingent liability is one that will result in the outflow of resources only *if* another event happens. ASPE accounting treatment for contingencies follows the following grid:

Measurability: Probability:	Measurable	Not Measurable
Likely	Record (plus disclose if amount recorded is uncertain).	Disclose in the notes.
Undeterminable	Disclose in the notes.	Disclose in the notes.
Not Likely	Do not record or disclose unless material.	Do not record or disclose unless material.

Under ASPE, a *contingent liability is either recorded or disclosed*; under IFRS, the liability is deemed a contingency only if it is *disclosed and not recorded.* Under IFRS, the liability is a *provision* if it is recorded. This is a different use of the word "contingency."

Under both sets of standards, the general framework is the same—some situations result in only a disclosure note, and other situations in a recorded liability, depending on the likelihood and measurability of the outflow of economic resources. In addition, though, the specifics of the criteria established under IFRS and ASPE may dictate somewhat different results.

Straight-Line Discount Amortization Under ASPE, use of the effective-interest method is not required. The **straight-line method** can be used to amortize the discount and measure interest expense.

Example Return to the example in the chapter, where Baylor Company purchases inventory of 1 April 20X2 and agrees to pay the vendor $12,000 on 31 March 20X4, plus annual interest at 4% each 31 March. The present value of the note payable is $10,750, discounted at the market interest rate of 10%.

The interest calculation, based on straight-line amortization, reflects equal amounts of discount amortization in each year. The original discount is $1,250 ($12,000 – $10,750). This is $625 ($1,250 ÷ 2) per year, over the two-year term of the loan. Interest expense is then cash paid plus the discount amortization, or $1,105 ($625 + $480). The calculations can be organized in a table:

	(1) Opening Net Liability	(2) Interest Expense (3) + (4)	(3) Interest Paid 4% Stated Rate $12,000 × 4%	(4) Discount Amortization Straight-Line	(5) Closing Net Liability (1) + (4)
20X3	$10,750	$1,105	$480	$625	$11,375
20X4	$11,375	1,105	480	625	12,000

The straight-line method produces the same interest amount each period but shows a varying *rate* of interest period by period (i.e., "interest ÷ opening net liability" will vary). It is less accurate for this reason, and is not permitted under IFRS standards. However, it is much simpler and may yield results that are not materially different from the effective interest method.

Classification and disclosure A company may wish to reclassify liabilities from current to long term to improve the reported working capital position. If a long-term loan is coming due but is being renegotiated, IFRS requires that a legally enforceable agreement be in place *by the end of the fiscal year (the reporting date)* if the loan is to be classified as long term. Under ASPE, classification of such a loan as long term would be permitted if renegotiation resulted in agreement by the *date the financial statements are released.*

Finally, disclosure is less onerous in all areas under ASPE compared with IFRS. For example, no reconciliations or continuity schedules are required.

RELEVANT STANDARDS

CPA Canada Handbook, Part I (IASB):

- IAS 1, Presentation of Financial Statements
- IAS 21, The Effects of Changes in Foreign Exchange Rates
- IAS 37, Provisions, Contingent Liabilities and Contingent Assets
- IAS 32, Financial Instruments: Disclosure and Presentation
- IAS 39, Financial Instruments: Recognition and Measurement
- IFRS 9, Financial Instruments

CPA Canada Handbook, Part II (ASPE):

- Section 1651, Foreign Currency Translation
- Section 3210, Long-Term Debt
- Section 3280, Contractual Obligations
- Section 3290, Contingencies
- Section 3856, Financial Instruments
- Acg-14, Disclosure of Guarantees

SUMMARY OF KEY POINTS

1. Liabilities are present obligations of a company resulting from past events, the settlement of which is expected to result in the outflow of economic benefits. Liabilities may be non-financial or financial and may result from legal obligations or constructive obligations.
2. Accounts and notes payable are *financial liabilities* that are classified as *other payables*, and carried at amortized cost and discounted, if needed. In some circumstances, such financial liabilities are classified as FVTPL and carried at fair value.
3. Non-financial liabilities include provisions, which are liabilities of *uncertain timing or amount*. Provisions are recorded if there is a present obligation as a result of a past event, the outflow of resources is probable, and an estimate can be made. If the potential provision is *not probable or is not measurable*, then it is a *contingency* and is not recorded but is disclosed.
4. Common liabilities include accounts, notes, accruals, property taxes, cash dividends, taxes, bonuses, and other payables.
5. Transactions that are denominated in a foreign currency are recorded at the exchange rate that exists at the transaction date. Monetary balances (i.e., cash, receivables, and payables) are restated to the exchange rate that exists on the year-end date. Exchange gains and losses are recognized in earnings.
6. Provisions are recorded at the best estimate, discounted if needed, and are re-estimated each reporting period. Best estimate may be the expected value (large populations) or the most likely outcome informed by expected value and cumulative probability (small populations).

7. Examples of provisions include lawsuits, onerous contracts, restructuring, warranties, restoration and environmental obligations, sales returns, coupons, loyalty programs, repairs and maintenance, self-insurance, and compensated absences. Accounting policy for these elements is summarized in a chart in the chapter.
8. Discounting is required to value a liability if it is long term and is a non-interest-bearing liability or if it is interest-bearing but the interest rate is below the market interest rate. Subsequent interest expense is measured using the market interest rate and will involve unwinding the discount.
9. Using the effective-interest method as applied to a discounted liability, interest expense is the product of the market rate at issuance and the net discounted balance in the liability at the beginning of the period. Interest is accrued with the passage of time.
10. Common situations where discounting is required include non-interest-bearing notes payable, low-interest loans, and non-interest-bearing provisions.
11. Discounted notes payable may be recorded in the books net of the calculated discount, or the discount can be recorded using the gross method, where there is a separate contra account for the discount.
12. When a provision is discounted, interest is recognized as time passes. If estimates of future cash flows change in amount or timing, or the market interest rate changes, interest is accrued on the provision for the period and then the carrying value is adjusted to the revised present value.
13. Liabilities are current when they are due within the next operating cycle or 12 months; this includes the current portion of a long-term liability. If refinancing arrangements are in place before the end of the year, a liability to be refinanced may be classified as long term.
14. Extensive disclosure is required for financial liabilities, including carrying value, fair value, details of contractual requirements, and continuity schedules for provisions, in addition to information on credit risk, liquidity risk, and market risk. Disclosure for provisions includes a description of the provision, and a continuity schedule that shows how the liability changed over the fiscal year.
15. ASPE does not require that constructive liabilities be recorded and thus results in lower levels of liabilities in certain circumstances. ASPE also allows straight-line amortization of a discount. Other differences between IFRS and ASPE include the definition of the term "contingency," and details governing measurement and classification in specific situations.

KEY TERMS

breakage
collateral security
constructive obligation
contingency
current liability
discounting
effective interest method
effective interest rate
executory contracts
expected value
financial liability
interest-bearing
legal obligation
long-term liability
market interest rate
maturity date
most likely outcome
nominal interest rate
non-interest-bearing
nonfinancial liability
obligating event
onerous contract
present value
provision
stated interest rate
straight-line method
spot rate
trade accounts payable
unwinding
virtual certainty
yield

REVIEW PROBLEM 12-1

The following selected transactions and events of Oakland Ltd. were completed during the accounting year just ended, 31 December 20X5. Interest rates reflect market rates unless indicated.

a. On 1 June, the company borrowed $55,000 in cash from the bank on a demand basis. The interest rate was 6%, to be paid on the anniversary date of the loan.

b. Merchandise was purchased on account; a $30,000, one-year, 7% interest-bearing note, dated 1 April 20X5, was given to the supplier. Interest is paid when the amount is due on 1 April 20X6.

c. Merchandise was purchased on account; a two-year, $16,000, 1% note dated 1 February 20X5 was given to the supplier. Interest is due annually on 1 February. The going interest rate for this term and risk was 7%. Use the gross method to record the note payable.

d. A supplier delivered goods on account costing US$20,000. The exchange rate was US$1 = Cdn$0.98 at that time.

e. Oakland has been sued by a customer for $500,000. The legal team confidently believes that there is an 80% chance that Oakland will successfully defend itself.

f. New legislative requirements came into force at the beginning of this year regarding environmental remediation. Oakland believes it will have to pay $80,000 in eight years' time when the company vacates leased premises. The going interest rate for this term and risk was 7%.

g. Payroll records showed the following:

Employee				
Gross Wages	Income Tax	EI	CPP	Union Dues
$120,000	$32,000	$6,100	$5,500	$2,500

h. The employer portion of EI and CPP are recorded.

i. Remittances were income tax, $31,350; EI, $10,250; CPP, $9,720; union dues, $1,480.

j. Cash dividends declared but not yet paid were $22,500.

k. Accrue appropriate interest at 31 December, and adjust the foreign-denominated payable to the year-end rate, US$1 = Cdn$0.96.

Required:

1. Give the entry or entries for each of the above transactions and events, if needed.
2. Prepare a list (title and amount) of the liabilities of Oakland at 31 December 20X5.

REVIEW PROBLEM 12-1—SOLUTION

Requirement 1

a. Bank demand loan:

Cash	55,000	
Note (or loan) payable, 6%		55,000

b. Purchased merchandise (1 April 20X5):

Inventory	30,000	
Note payable, 7%		30,000

c. Purchased merchandise (1 February 20X5):

Inventory	14,264	
Discount on notes payable	1,736	
Note payable, 1%; yield 7%		16,000

$16,000 (P/F, 7%, 2) + $160 (P/A, 7%, 2) = $14,264

d. US-denominated liability:

Inventory	19,600	
Accounts payable ($20,000 × $0.98)		19,600

e. No entry. Small population and most likely outcome is no payout.

f. Decommissioning obligation:

Leased premises or other asset	46,561	
Decommissioning obligation		46,561
$80,000 (P/F, 7%, 8) = $46,561		

g. To record salaries and employee deductions:

Salary expense	120,000	
Employee income taxes payable		32,000
EI payable		6,100
CPP payable		5,500
Union dues payable		2,500
Cash		73,900

h. To record payroll expenses payable by the employer:

Salary expense	14,040	
CPP payable		5,500
EI payable ($6,100 × 1.4)		8,540

i. To record remittance of payroll deductions:

Employee income taxes payable	31,350	
EI payable	10,250	
CPP payable	9,720	
Union dues payable	1,480	
Cash		52,800

j. Cash dividends declared but not yet paid:

Retained earnings (or dividends)	22,500	
Cash dividends payable		22,500

k. Year-end adjustments:

Interest expense	1,925	
Interest payable		1,925
$55,000 × 0.06 × 7/12		
Interest expense ($30,000 × 0.07 × 9/12)	1,575	
Interest payable		1,575
Interest expense ($14,264 × 0.07 × 11/12)	915	
Discount on note payable		768
Interest payable ($160 × 11/12)		147
Accounts payable	400	
Exchange gain		400
($20,000 × $0.96) = $19,200 versus $19,600 recorded		
Interest expense	3,259	
Decommissioning obligation		3,259
($46,561 × 0.07)		

Requirement 2

Liabilities:

Note (loan) payable	$55,000
Accounts payable (US)	19,200
Interest payable ($1,575 + $1,925 + $147)	$ 3,647
Employee income tax payable	650
EI payable	4,390
CPP payable	1,280
Union dues payable	1,020
Cash dividends payable	22,500
Note payable ($16,000 – ($1,736 – $768)	15,032
Note payable, 7%	30,000
Decommissioning obligation ($46,561 + $3,259)	49,820

QUESTIONS

Q12-1 What three time elements are embedded in the definition of a liability?

Q12-2 What is a non-financial liability? Provide three examples, and explain how such liabilities are measured.

Q12-3 A firm has an environmental cleanup liability recorded as a decommissioning obligation. Under what circumstances would this have resulted from a constructive liability, and under what circumstances would it have been a legal liability?

Q12-4 Beacon Ltd. has guaranteed a $400,000 loan of Gerard Limited, a customer. There is security valued at $250,000—assets of Gerard—registered against the loan. Beacon estimates that there is a 30% chance that they will be required to step in and pay $150,000 on the loan this coming year. Calculate the liability Beacon must record, if any.

Q12-5 Inventory is purchased for $42,400 plus PST of 6% and GST of 8%. What value is recorded for inventory? Assume that there is a sale for $25,000, plus PST and GST, in the same period. What amount of GST must be remitted or refunded? PST?

Q12-6 A monthly payroll results in income tax of $8,200, EI of $5,000, and CPP of $3,000 deducted from employee wages. Including the employer portion, what dollar value must be remitted?

Q12-7 A company has an account payable to a U.S. company, a supplier of inventory, in the amount of US$75,000. The payable was incurred when the exchange rate was US$1 = Cdn$1.12. At year-end, the rate is $1.13. What amount of inventory is recorded? What amount of exchange gain or loss will the company report for the year?

Q12-8 A company has four legal claims outstanding, each for $25,000. There is a 75% chance that one claim will be paid out, a 10% chance that two will be paid out, a 5% chance for three, and a 10% chance for four payouts. Compare the most likely outcome with the expected value, and explain the amount that must be recorded.

Q12-9 A company has four legal claims outstanding, each for $25,000. There is a 40% chance that one claim will be paid out, a 25% chance that two will be paid out, a 30% chance for three, and a 5% chance for four payouts. Compare the most likely outcome with the expected value, and explain the amount that must be recorded.

Q12-10 A firm is being sued for $550,000 by an unhappy customer; the lawsuit is in its early stages, and the firm feels that it has a good case and is willing to defend itself. However, legal costs will be high, and the company, in all likelihood, will be prepared to settle with the ex-customer for $150,000. Why is liability recognition for this lawsuit complicated at this stage?

Q12-11 A company signs a purchase order for 5,000 cases of a product at $10 per case. The product will be delivered next year. Is a liability for $50,000 recorded? Under what conditions will some amount of liability be recognized? Explain.

Q12-12 A company sells a product in 20X3, with a warranty that the product will not be defective during 20X3 and 20X4. No warranty work is required in 20X3. Why will a warranty cost and provision be recorded in 20X3?

Q12-13 A company issues 10,000 coupons that allow a discount of $1 off the retail price of a $14 product. Will a provision be recorded? Explain.

Q12-14 The statement of financial position includes an obligation for insurance for a company that self-insures. How is this obligation measured? What is *not* included in this obligation?

Q12-15 What is a compensated absence? When should the expense related to compensated absences be recognized?

Q12-16 How is a note payable valued if it is (a) a no-interest note and (b) a low-interest note? Assume in all cases that the note had a term of two years. How would your answer change if the note had a term of two months?

Q12-17 Compute the present value of a $200,000 decommissioning obligation to be paid in 10 years. The estimate of cash outflow includes no interest, although 10% would be a realistic rate.

Q12-18 A decommissioning obligation has been discounted and recorded at an interest rate of 6%. In reviewing estimates at the end of the current fiscal year, the interest rate is re-estimated to be 8%. Will recorded interest expense in the current year reflect a rate of 6% or 8%? Explain.

Q12-19 A company has a short-term bank loan outstanding, due on demand. The loan has been outstanding for several years, and will not be repaid in the coming year. Can it be classified as a long-term loan?

Q12-20 Explain the primary difference between the two method to unwind, or amortize, a loan discount: effective interest (required under IFRS) and straight-line amortization (allowed as an alternative under ASPE).

CASE 12-1

PRESCRIPTIONS DEPOT LIMITED

Prescriptions Depot Limited (PDL) is a national chain of drug stores, some company owned and some operated as franchises. The company reported $5.4 billion in revenue in the most recent fiscal year, and net earnings of $295 million. Gross profit was in the range of 20% but is different for various product lines. Some products are essentially grocery items, and gross margin is minimal. Other products sell with a 30%–40% profit margin. Prescription drugs also generate a range of profit margins, but industry averages are 15%–25% gross margin. Company reporting objectives are focused around increasing earnings. PDL realizes, though, that many market analysts carefully look for trends in sales growth, particularly year-over-year same-store sales growth. The company is not public but wishes to comply with IFRS, since medium-term plans include a public offering.

You are a new analyst in the company's performance reporting department. You have been asked to review accounting policy for several issues.

PDL accepts vendor "cents off" coupons, which involve small discounts to the retail price of a given product. PDL records the sale to the customer at the net cash received. PDL remits the coupons to the vendor and reduces the amount otherwise owing to the vendor and the cost of inventory by the coupon amount. For example, assume that PDL has accepted 5,000, $1 coupons for shampoo. Sale of the shampoo has a retail value of $25,000, but PDL reports the sale at the $20,000 amount of cash collected from the customer ($25,000 less the $5,000 in coupons). If PDL owes the vendor $98,000, PDL then pays only $93,000, and PDL records $93,000 as the cost of the product.

PDL has also issued certain coupons for cash refunds, a cash payment directly to the end consumer from PDL and not through a vendor arrangement. For example, in one promotion, any customer who purchased $500 of home health care merchandise on a given weekend would, after filing the appropriate form and receipts, receive a $35 cash refund. A six-week period is provided for the documents to be filed, and then the offer expired. The volume of these refunds has been low, but PDL may be more active with these promotions in the future. The refund was recorded as a reduction to cash and a reduction to sales, when the refund was issued.

The company has a loyalty points program, wherein customers with membership cards earn five loyalty points for every dollar spent in the store. Higher points per dollar are assigned to prescription drug sales. Once points accumulate, customers can redeem the points at various levels/values for full or partial payment on merchandise purchases. At various times, sales incentives are offered, such as "double points" awarded to large one-time purchases. At other times, to trigger redemption, redeemed points are given bonus values. Some points are never redeemed, but the collection and redemption levels are healthy, and PDL is convinced that customer loyalty is significantly enhanced by the program.

When points are granted in conjunction with a sale transaction, the sale is recorded for the full amount of the sale. An estimate of the cost of goods to be obtained through point redemption is recorded at the same time. For example, a sale of $100 is recorded, along with its $75 cost of goods sold. Points are issued that are expected to be redeemed for goods with a retail price of $4 and a cost of $3. Accordingly, a $3 expense and liability is recorded at the same time as the sale. When points are redeemed, inventory is reduced, at its $3 cost, and the liability is reduced. The overall liability balance is carefully reviewed each quarter, and adjusted up or down for shifts in cost expectations, redemption levels, and changes to the percentages redeemed under "bonus" conditions.

PDL rents many of its premises, under three- to five-year lease contracts. Typically, the lessor undertakes renovations for PDL to make the premises suitable for occupancy as a retail drugstore. However, PDL itself installs certain behind-the-counter set up in the pharmacy area. This includes an area for secure drug storage, drug disposal, "sharps" (needle) disposal, and secure data transmission and storage devices. These are all designed to meet legislative or industry standards, and the set-up is built to exacting standards to ensure drug safety and patient confidentiality. PDL is then responsible for the removal of this set-up when and if it vacates at the end of a lease term.

Required:

As the analyst, prepare a report that identifies the accounting issues with your analysis and recommendations.

CASE 12-2

CAMANI CORPORATION

Camani Corporation (CC) is involved in the production, distribution and marketing of consumer products that encompass a broad range of items, from hair care products, to cosmetics and perfume, to vitamins and supplements. CC has been hard hit by the recent economic downturn, during which consumer spending has been curtailed. The financial results of the current year, 20X3, are critical for all stakeholders and will reflect on the viability of the existing strategic model. The executive team will receive a healthy "return to profitability" bonus if 20X3 earnings are positive, after two years of losses.

You are a member of the Board of Directors of CC and sit on the Audit Committee. You have a fair understanding of financial statements and take some pride in your technical proficiency. You have just left an Audit Committee meeting, where a 20X3 summarized draft SFP and a summarized draft statement of earnings has been presented (Exhibit 1). Earnings are positive. However, you are concerned that no SCF has yet been prepared. You also are concerned that some of the estimates and policy decisions made might have been affected by management's desire to show positive 20X3 earnings (Exhibit 2).

Therefore, you have decided to do some analysis of your own. First, you want to calculate cash flow from operating activities for the draft set of financial statements that have been presented. Second, you feel you could learn about the sensitivity of the results if you adjust the financial statements for estimates and policies that you believe are aggressive. Finally, you plan to recalculate cash from operating activities based on your revised financial statements. You know you will need to write a brief report around your analysis so that you can refer it on to the chair of the Audit Committee for discussion at your next meeting.

Required:

Prepare the suggested analysis and report. Note that CC includes dividend payments to its shareholders as an operating cash flow. There is no income tax.

EXHIBIT 1

CAMANI CORPORATION

Summarized Draft 20X3 Statement of Financial Position

At 31 December (in thousands)	20X3	20X2
Cash	$ 2,340	$ 1,680
Accounts receivable	16,780	13,040
Inventory	61,920	54,970
Prepaids	542	455
Land	5,860	5,860
Plant and equipment (net)	19,720	18,650
Other assets	650	290
Total debits	$107,812	$94,945
Liabilities		
Accounts payable and accrued liabilities	47,388	42,867
Long-term debt	53,527	46,200
Equity		
Common shares	5,640	5,235
Retained earnings	1,257	643
Total credits	$107,812	$94,945

Summarized Draft Statement of Earnings

For the year ended 31 December 20X3	
Sales revenue	$104,910
Cost of goods sold	(66,230)
Depreciation expense	(3,900)
Operating, administration, financing and marketing	(33,245)
Earnings and comprehensive income	$ 1,535

EXHIBIT 2

CAMANI CORPORATION

Policy and Estimate Information, 31 December 20X3

1. Legal issues
   In 20X3, as in prior years, CC is a defendant in a range of small lawsuits, primarily resulting from customer issues but also with several suppliers. These lawsuits are often settled out of court, and payments in prior years for individual cases have been in the $20,000 to $100,000 range. At the end of 20X3, an accrual of $830 was made based on expected value and the following "probability as recorded" (second column) assessment to determine expected value:

Total payment (in thousands)	Probability as Recorded	Alternative Probability
$ 100	10%	0%
500	30	20
700	30	30
1,200	20	30
2,200	10	20

   Another assessment of the probability might be as listed in the "alternative probability" column, above.

2. Depreciation policy
   CC reviewed estimates of useful life and residual values for depreciable assets in 20X3. Based on this review, the depreciation amount of $3,900 was recorded. If prior year estimates and amounts had been used, depreciation would have been in the range of $4,100.

3. Technology services
   CC had recorded $1,200 as an estimate for technology services rendered to date by a supplier. The supplier has a $4,000 contract, and CC estimated that this contract was 30% complete. Another suggestion is that the project is 45% complete.

4. Inventory valuation
   CC has significant inventory on hand at the end of 20X3. This inventory is valued after a writedown to lower of cost or market. The writedown in 20X3 was $2,350. This is the lowest writedown in the company's history, although it is justified by a thorough analysis of sales values and volumes. If percentage writedowns were similar to those in prior years, the writedown would have been in the range of $3,125.

5. Restructuring
   CC is contemplating the restructuring of its sales and marketing group, to improve efficiency and reduce costs. The tentative plan involves downsizing one group of sales people in 20X4; likely severance costs would be in the range of $500. No accrual has been made in the books because the program has not yet been approved or announced.

6. Environmental liability
   CC has an environmental liability for premises remediation at one rental location. When CC vacates this location, construction will be required to return the site to its previous condition. Accordingly, the $400 cost of this, at its present value of $306 (4 years, at 7%), was recorded as a long-term liability as of 1 January 20X3. Interest of $21 (a non-cash expense) was recorded in 20X3, along with straight-line depreciation over four years. Another estimate of the interest rate would be 5%.

Note: In all assignment material in this text, assume a 31 December fiscal year-end unless advised otherwise.

TECHNICAL REVIEW

connect

TR12-1 Provision—Measurement: Consider the following three cases:

Case 1 A company has four legal claims outstanding, each for $100,000. There is a 10% chance that one claim will be paid out, a 10% chance that two will be paid out, a 5% chance for three, and a 5% chance for four payouts.

Case 2 A company has four legal claims outstanding, each for $100,000. There is a 10% chance that one claim will be paid out, a 60% chance that two will be paid out, a 5% chance for three, and a 15% chance for four payouts.

Case 3 A company has four legal claims outstanding, each for $100,000. There is a 30% chance that one claim will be paid out, a 20% chance that two will be paid out, a 20% chance for three, and a 20% chance for four payouts.

Required:

For each case, decide if *some* payout is *likely* or *not likely*. Compare the most likely outcome with the expected value, and explain the amount that must be recorded.

connect

TR12-2 Provision—Warranty: Helpi Auto Parts Ltd. offers a six-month warranty on parts that the company has installed. This warranty ensures that parts are working as intended. The warranty covers the cost of parts, plus labour for repairs. Warranty costs are estimated to be 1.5% of sales for parts plus 3% of sales for labour. On 1 April, the warranty liability had a $16,400 credit balance. Warranty work in April consumed $8,700 of parts and $14,000 of labour. Sales amounted to $550,000 in April.

Required:

1. What amount of warranty expense should be recorded in April?
2. What is the balance in the warranty provision at the end of April?

connect

TR12-3 Note Payable: On 1 October 20X6, Halpern Company borrowed $120,000 from Canada Bank. The note has a two-year term, and requires that interest of 9% be paid each 30 September, with the principal payable 30 September 20X8.

Required:

Provide all entries for the note from 20X6 to 20X8.

connect

TR12-4 Discounting—Note Payable: Materials Limited purchases inventory on 1 April 20X7 and agrees to pay the vendor $250,000 on 31 March 20X9, plus annual interest at 2% each 31 March. The market interest rate for similar term and security is 7%. Assume also that the inventory does not have a readily determinable market value.

Required:

1. Calculate the present value of the note payable.
2. Prepare a table that shows the balance of the note payable and interest expense over the life of the note.

connect

TR12-5 Discounting—Provision: On 2 January 20X8, Keen Mining Limited commenced a mining operation. Keen is required by the terms of provincial legislation to remediate the mine site when mining is completed, likely in 10 years' time. This means that a provision for decommissioning must be recorded. Keen estimates that decommissioning will cost $420,000 in 10 years. A reasonable market interest rate is 6%.

Required:

1. Calculate the present value of the decommissioning obligation.
2. Prepare a table that shows the balance of the obligation for three years (only).
3. Assume that in 20X10, Keen estimates that the cost of remediation will be $490,000, and that interest rates are now in the range of 8%. Calculate the interest expense for 20X10, the new present value, and the adjustment to the obligation for the change in estimates.

ASSIGNMENTS

★ connect

A12-1 Common Financial Liabilities: Technology Management Limited engaged in various transactions during the month of September:

a. Bought $2,600 of office supplies on account.
b. Borrowed $15,000 for the Dominion Bank at the beginning of the month and agreed to pay the loan back in one year, plus interest at 12%. This is the market interest rate.
c. Bought inventory for resale with an invoice price of $71,500.
d. The September utilities bill for $1,300 arrived but is not due until October.
e. Declared a cash dividend of $2 per preferred share and $0.50 per common share, payable 16 October. There are 4,000 preferred shares and 10,000 common shares outstanding.
f. Returned goods with an invoice price of $17,600 to the supplier in (c).
g. Paid the supplier in (c) 50% the net amount owing.
h. Accrued interest on the bank loan at the end of the month.
i. Accrued monthly rent of $1,200 for September, to be paid in October.

Required:

1. Journalize each of the above transactions in general journal form. Use a general accounts payable account in journal entries except for loans, interest, and dividends payable.
2. List the liability accounts and amounts that result from your entries in requirement 1.

★★ connect

A12-2 Common Financial Liabilities—Taxes: Braybrooke Limited had the following transactions in February 20X8:

a. Recorded sales of $1,800,000, plus GST of 5%.
b. Recorded sales of $6,200,000, plus GST of 5%.
c. Bought equipment for $625,000, plus GST of 5%.
d. Recorded the bimonthly payroll of $85,800. CPP deductions were $1,200, EI deductions were $1,400, and income tax withheld amounted to $7,400. (Employer portions are recorded only at the end of the month.)
e. Recorded sales of $1,400,000, plus GST of 5%.
f. Bought inventory for $6,100,000, plus GST of 5%.
g. Recorded the bimonthly payroll. The amounts were identical to the prior bimonthly payroll.
h. Recorded the employer portion of payroll expenses for the entire month.
i. Remitted payroll taxes for the month.
j. Remitted net GST for the month.

Required:

Provide journal entries to record all transactions. Assume transactions with customers and suppliers were for cash.

★★ **A12-3 Common Financial Liabilities—Taxes:** Hoffman reported opening balances as at 1 June 20X8:

GST payable	$21,500 (cr.)
Income tax deductions payable	1,300 (cr.)
CPP payable	950 (cr.)
EI payable	400 (cr.)

The company had the following transactions in June 20X8:

a. Collected $354,000 of GST on sales to customers.
b. Recorded the bimonthly payroll, which included CPP deductions of $1,400, EI deductions of $1,200, and income tax withheld of $10,700.
c. Recorded the second bimonthly payroll. The payroll included CPP deductions of $1,500, EI deductions of $1,400, and income tax withheld of $11,700.
d. Bought capital assets of $960,000, plus GST of 5%.
e. Recorded the employer portion of payroll expenses for the entire month.
f. Paid $266,500 GST to the Receiver General for Canada.

Required:
Calculate the balances in the four accounts listed above as at 30 June 20X8. There were no payments on account during the month.

★ **A12-4 Foreign Currency Payables:** Golden Limited had the following transactions in 20X5:

a. Bought goods on 1 June from Brit Limited for 70,000 euros, with payment due in four months' time.
b. Bought goods from New York Sales Corp. on 15 June for US$150,000; payment was due in one month.
c. Bought goods from a London Limited on 15 July for 20,000 euros; settlement was to be in two months.
d. Paid New York Sales Corp. on 15 July.
e. Paid London Limited on 15 September.
f. Paid Brit Limited on 1 October.

EXCHANGE RATES:

Canadian Equivalencies	Euros	US$
1 June	2.11	1.07
15 June	2.19	1.11
15 July	2.13	1.17
15 September	2.20	1.03
1 October	2.17	1.06

Required:
Prepare journal entries for the above transactions.

★★ **A12-5 Common Financial Liabilities and Foreign Currency:** Data regarding Viran Corp. in March 20X9:

Selected opening balances:	GST payable	$31,400 (cr.)
	CPP payable	1,950 (cr.)
	EI payable	2,600 (cr.)
	Income tax deductions payable	8,160 (cr.)

a. Cash sales for the period, $490,000 plus 5% GST.
b. Monthly payroll, $58,500; less EI, $1,900; CPP, $1,100; income tax, $6,100. The employer portion of payroll taxes was also recorded.
c. Inventory purchases on account, $760,000 plus 5% GST.

d. Cash sales, $1,570,000, plus 5% GST.
e. Sales to U.S. customer on account, US$88,000. There was no GST on the sale. The U.S. dollar was worth Cdn$1.03 on this date.
f. The U.S. customer paid US$70,000 on account, when the U.S. dollar was worth $1.07. The remaining amount will be paid in June.
g. GST owing was remitted.
h. Sixty percent of the amount owing to suppliers in (c) was paid.
i. At the end of the month, the U.S. exchange rate was Cdn$1.06.

Required:

1. Journalize all transactions listed above.
2. List the accounts and amounts that would appear on the 31 March statement of financial position. Exclude cash and inventory.

★★ **A12-6 Provisions:** The following items pertain to possible provisions:

a. The ABC Mining Company has announced that it will restructure its Atlantic Canada operations and lay off 80% of workers in the area. The employees affected are informed and given six months' notice and promised generous severance packages at the end of six months.
b. Siam Services Limited has 500 coupons outstanding that allow customers a $10 cash rebate from a $120 purchase price for a computer monitor. Customers must submit documentation to prove cash purchase. Approximately 65% of the coupons will be submitted by customers for payment.
c. The Board of Directors for the Dillon Timber Company has decided to lay off 10% of its Canadian workforce. The plan is still in the proposal stage, and it is not clear which workers will be affected. The cost is likely to be in excess of $5 million.
d. The Sweet Mining Company has a legislative requirement for site environmental remediation in its northern Manitoba operations. This remediation must be performed when the mineral resources are depleted and the site is closed to active mining, likely in four years.
e. Ming Metals Limited has announced that it plans to perform site environmental remediation at its active Quebec mine site. This remediation is in excess of provincial legislative requirements and will be performed when the mineral resources are depleted and the site is closed to active mining, likely in four years.
f. Jackson Limited has signed a lease with another company to rent a facility for three years at a cost of $27,000 per year.
g. On the leased premises per (f), Jackson will erect a transmission tower, at its own expense, on the building roof. At the end of the lease term, Jackson must remove the tower under the terms of the lease, and removal is expected to cost $50,000.
h. A customer has sued the Kerman Company for $2 million. The company may lose but may well offer to settle the suit for $400,000 in the next six months. The customer may or may not accept the settlement. The amount would have a significant impact on the company's financial position.
i. A prior employee has sued Luong Limited for $500,000 for health-related issues that the employee claims were caused by working conditions. The company will likely successfully defend itself. However, the amount is material and if the lawsuit is successful, other employees will likely also sue.
j. The Y34 Company has guaranteed the $10 million loan of another company. This amount is material. The other company has a poor credit rating, and there is a 40% chance of having to make a $10 million payment under the guarantee.
k. The Week Company has been audited by Canada Revenue Agency, resulting in a tax assessment for $1.5 million, an amount that would have a significant impact on the company's financial position. The company has appealed the decision and feels it has a good case.

Required:

For each of the above items, indicate whether the appropriate accounting treatment is to record a liability in the statement of financial position and report a loss in earnings, or whether there is no liability to be recognized.

★★ **A12-7 Provisions:** The following items pertain to the 20X9 operations of Fillet Information Services Limited:

Solution

a. The company issued a purchase order for manufacturing equipment with an invoice price of $850,000, to be installed next year.
b. The company issued a purchase order for $200,000 of a commodity to be delivered next year. The price of this commodity subsequently declines to $160,000, but Fillet is committed to pay $200,000.
c. Fillet borrows $100,000 in US dollars when the exchange rate is US$1 = Cdn$1.10. At year-end, the exchange rate is US$1 = Cdn$1.05.
d. A lawsuit for $2 million was brought against Fillet by a customer for lost profits after an information system failure. Lawyers estimate that there is only a 5% chance that the lawsuit will result in a $2,000,000 payment, but there is a 65% chance that there will be a $500,000 payment, and a 30% chance that the lawsuit will be dismissed with no payment.
e. Fillet has guaranteed a $550,000 bank loan taken out by another company; there is only a 10% chance that Fillet would have to make a payment under this guarantee. If any payment were made, it would not be the full amount; it would be only $300,000 because of other security held for the loan.
f. Fillet has issued 1,000 coupons allowing customers to get a $100 cash rebate from Fillet when they purchase a $1,000 technology hardware and software bundle from a retailer. Based on past history, only 10% of these coupons will be used. The technology bundle will still sell at a profit.
g. Fillet participates in a "loyalty points" program, where customers with certain loyalty point levels may receive free merchandise from Fillet's regular product and service line.

Required:

Explain how each of these items will affect the financial statements of Fillet at year-end 20X9.

★★ **A12-8 Provisions:** The following items pertain to possible provisions:

a. A company uses milk powder imported from China in one of its products. Milk products in China have caused significant health concerns because of an alleged toxic additive. No product safety issues have been identified with the milk powder used, but further testing is underway. Meanwhile, the product has been removed from stores in Canada as part of a voluntary recall. The recall is 40% complete and has cost $520,000 to date. No health concerns linked to the company's product have yet been reported in Canada.
b. A company self-insures for fire hazards. That is, it pays no insurance but is liable to replace assets lost through fire or theft. No losses have been incurred this year, but there have been $100,000 of losses in most other years, and the company is concerned that there might well be $200,000 of losses next year, evening out the pattern.
c. A company offers a two-year guarantee over parts and labour for products sold to ensure that parts work as expected. There were no payments this year, and only 10% of products sold this year are expected to need repairs in the next year. The cost of this work would be in the range of $50,000.
d. A company has been sued by a supplier for $500,000. The company returned raw materials to the supplier that the company found to be of poor quality. The lawsuit from the supplier claims that the products met specifications and the return was without merit. The company's lawyer has indicated that there is a 20% chance that the company will lose the lawsuit.
e. A company is required by legislation to undertake environmental remediation for a mining site that is currently active. The site will not be cleaned up until the mine closes, which

is now scheduled for 2032. It is not certain how much the cleanup will cost at that time, or how long it will take.

Required:
In each of the above cases, indicate whether a liability is recorded or not. If recording is required, give the amount, or explain how it will be estimated.

★ **A12-9 Provision Measurement:** Delivery Company Limited is gathering evidence to support an accrual for legal claims. Three lawsuits are outstanding:

Claim 1 is a lawsuit from an employee for $500,000. According to the legal team, there is a 10% chance that it will have to be paid in full and a 90% chance that it will be dismissed.

Claim 2 is a lawsuit from a supplier for $10,000,000 for breach of contract. According to the legal team, there is a 70% chance that it will have to be paid out in full and a 30% chance that it will be dismissed.

Claim 3 is a lawsuit from a customer for $800,000. According to the legal team, there is only a 30% chance that it will be dismissed in court. Accordingly, the company has made a settlement offer of $500,000 to the plaintiff, but the plaintiff has not yet responded to the settlement offer. The legal team believes there is a 40% chance the settlement will be accepted. If it is not accepted, the action will go to court, with a 30% chance of dismissal and a 70% chance of an $800,000 payout.

Required:
For each case, indicate the amount that should be recorded as a liability for the lawsuit. Assume that the payment period is relatively short so that discounting is not needed.

★ **A12-10 Provision Measurement:** Fresh Products Limited is gathering evidence to support an accrual for warranty claims. The warranty is offered on three products sold to ensure that they operate as expected.

For Product 1, there are 75 warranty claims outstanding. One-third have a potential value of $1,000 each (90% of these will be paid, based on past history), one-third have a potential value of $5,000 each (70% of these will be paid), and one-third have a potential payout of $12,000 each (60% will be paid). The claims that are not paid are likely to be dismissed because of an expired warranty or incorrect statement of damages.

For Product 2, there are only nine claims outstanding; however, all are large, at $50,000 each. The experienced claims adjustor reviewing the files is completely confident that eight will be dismissed without any payment. For the remaining claim, there is a 60% chance that it will have to be paid in full and a 40% chance that it will be dismissed.

Product 3 has only one potential claim outstanding. The claim is for $1,000,000, and the adjustor believes that there is a 60% chance it will be dismissed, a 10% chance it will result in a payout of $1,000,000, and a 30% chance that there will be a payout of $200,000.

Required:
Indicate the amount that should be recorded as a warranty provision for each product.

★ **A12-11 Provisions—Compensated Absences:** Tunacliff Mowers allows each employee to earn 15 fully paid vacation days each year. Unused vacation time can be carried over to the next year; if not taken during the next year, it is lost. By the end of 20X5, all but 3 of the 30 employees had taken their earned vacation time; these 3 carried over to 20X6 a total of 20 vacation days. These 20 days represented total 20X5 salary of $6,000. During 20X6, each of these three used their 20X5 vacation carryover; none of them had received a pay rate change from 20X5 to the time they used their carryover. Total cash wages paid: 20X5, $700,000; 20X6, $740,000.

connect

Required:

1. Give the entries for Tunacliff related to vacations during 20X5 and 20X6. Disregard payroll taxes.
2. Compute the total amount of wage expense for 20X5 and 20X6. How would the vacation time carried over from 20X5 affect the 20X5 statement of financial position?

★ **A12-12 Provisions—Warranty:** Review the financial statement extract provided below:

(amounts in thousands)	Provision for warranty
Balance, 1 January 20X5	$ 531
Additional provision created	582
Utilized during the year	(345)
Unwinding of discount	40
Balance, 31 December 20X5	$ 808

Required:

1. In general, what is a provision?
2. The provision for warranty might be a legal liability or a constructive liability. What is the meaning of "constructive liability"?
3. What is the meaning of the $582 "additional provision created"?
4. How would the $582 be measured, assuming a large population of potential claims?
5. What is the meaning of the $345 "utilized during the year"?
6. What is the meaning of the $40 "unwinding of discount"?

★★ **A12-13 Provisions—Warranty:** Consumer Corp. sells dishwashers and washing machines that come with a two-year unlimited warranty on parts and labour for repairs. The warranty is intended to assure customers that the appliances will operate as advertised. The warranty is expected to cost 1% of sales in the first year and 6% of sales in the second year, for a total of 7%. The provision for warranty has a credit balance of $145,000 at the beginning of 20X5. The following events and decisions relate to the warranty:

connect

20X5	Sales revenue of $4,600,000 was generated from products covered by the warranty. Both the sale and the warranty provision must be recorded.
20X5	Warranty work consumed parts inventory with a cost of $9,000, and labour of $22,000.
20X6	Sales revenue from products covered by the warranty were $6,100,000. Both the sale and the warranty provision must be recorded.
20X6	Sales revenue of $6,100,000 was generated from products covered by the warranty.
	Warranty work consumed parts inventory with a cost of $126,000, and labour of $289,000
20X6	Year-end review indicated that the percentage used as an estimate for warranty work in 20X5 and 20X6 should have been a total of 9.5% of sales, rather than 7%.
20X6	Because of a specific prevalent defect to a seal discovered during repairs in 20X6, the company announced that it would cover repairs for this specific defect for a third year for all sales of product made in 20X5 and 20X6. The cost of this work was estimated to be 1.5% of sales. This is in excess of the percentage increase described above. Products were re-engineered to eliminate the defect starting in 20X7.

Required:

1. Prepare journal entries for the events listed above. Because of uncertainty of estimates, no discounting is to be applied.
2. Calculate the balance of the provision for warranty at 31 December 20X5 and 20X6.

★★ **A12-14 Provisions—Warranty:** Garage Hardware Ltd. provides a product warranty for defects on two major lines of items sold since the beginning of 20X5. Line A carries a two-year warranty for parts and service, while Line B carries a three-year warranty for parts and service. The warranty cannot be purchased separately, and is intended to provide assurance to customers that the products will operate in accordance with the specifications provided. Garage contracts with a local service company to service the warranty on Line A, at a cost of $75 per unit payable at the date of sale. Garage performs its own warranty work for Line B. On the basis of experience, Garage estimates that warranty work costs 3% of sales for parts and 7% for labour and overhead for the entire three years; this cost is expected to be incurred 25% in Year 1, 10% in Year 2, and 65% in Year 3.

Data is as follows:

	20X5	20X6	20X7
Sales in units, Line A	700	1,000	none
Sales price per unit, Line A	$ 610	$ 660	
Sales in units, Line B	600	800	none
Sales price per unit, Line B	$ 700	$ 750	
Actual warranty outlays, Line B			
Parts	$3,000	$ 9,600	$12,000
Labour and overhead	7,000	22,000	30,000

Required:

1. Prepare journal entries for annual sales, expense and warranty transactions for 20X5 to 20X7, inclusive. Because of uncertainty of estimates, no discounting is to be applied.
2. How much is warranty expense in each year from 20X5 to 20X7?
3. What is balance in the provision for warranty at 31 December 20X5, 20X6, and 20X7?
4. What warranty work is left to do? What is in the dollar value of the provision for this work?
5. Comment on the adequacy of the 20X7 provision. Have estimates for Line B been accurate? Comment.

★★ **A12-15 Discounting—No-Interest Note:** Bay Lake Mining Ltd. purchases earth-moving equipment on 1 August 20X6 and signs a three-year note with the supplier, agreeing to pay $425,000 on 31 July 20X9. There is no interest in the note. The equipment purchased does not have a readily determinable market value.

excel

connect

Required:

1. Does Bay Lake Mining Ltd. actually have a no-interest loan? Explain.
2. Calculate the present value of the note payable, using an interest rate of 6%.
3. Explain the factors that would be considered in determining the 6% discount rate.
4. Prepare a table that shows the balance of the note payable and interest expense over the life of the note.
5. Provide all entries for the note for 20X6 and 20X7. Record adjusting entries at the end of the fiscal year and on the anniversary date of the loan. Use the gross method.
6. Show the note payable (accounts and amounts) as it would be included on the statement of financial position at 31 December 20X6 and 20X7.

★ **A12-16 Discounting—Low-Interest Note:** Infinite Solutions Limited purchases inventory on 1 September 20X7 and signs a note with the supplier, agreeing to pay $90,000 on 31 August 20X9, plus annual interest at 2% each 31 August. The market interest rate for similar term and security is 8%. Assume also that the inventory purchased does not have a readily determinable market value.

Solution

Required:

1. Calculate the present value of the note payable.
2. Prepare a table that shows the balance of the note payable and interest expense over the life of the note using the effective-interest method.
3. Provide all entries for the note from 20X7 to 20X9. Use the gross method.

★ **A12-17 Discounting—Low-Interest Note:** On 1 January 20X9, a borrower signed a long-term note, face amount, $800,000; time to maturity, four years; stated rate of interest, 4%. The effective rate of interest of 6% determined the cash received by the borrower. The principal of the note will be paid at maturity; stated interest is due at the end of each year.

excel

connect

Required:

1. Compute the cash received by the borrower.
2. Give the required entries for the borrower for each of the four years. Use the effective-interest method.

★ **A12-18 Discounting—Provision:** In late September of 20X6, Moon Rock Developments established a provision of $310,000 for a legal matter. The company expects the amount will be paid in late September 20X8. Timing can be estimated with certainty.

excel

Required:

1. Why is discounting required?
2. Calculate the present value of the provision, using an interest rate of 8%.
3. Explain the factors that would be considered in determining the 8% discount rate.
4. Prepare a table that shows the balance of the provision and interest expense over the life of the liability.
5. Provide all entries for the provision for 20X6 through 20X8. Record adjusting entries at the end of the fiscal year and on the anniversary date of the provision. The estimated amount was paid to the plaintiff on 30 September 20X8.
6. Show the provision as it would be included on the statement of financial position at 31 December 20X6 and 20X7.
7. Explain how the accounting for this provision would change if the amounts and timing of cash outflows were highly uncertain.

★★ **A12-19 Discounting—Provision:** Silver Linings Ltd. commenced a mining operation in early 20X5. The company is required by the terms of provincial legislation to remediate the mine site when mining is completed, likely in five years' time. Silver Linings Ltd. estimates that this will cost $2,700,000. A reasonable market interest rate is 8%.

excel

connect

Required:

1. Calculate the present value of the decommissioning obligation.
2. Prepare a table that shows the balance of the provision and interest expense over the life of the liability.
3. Assume that at the end of 20X6, the company re-estimates that the cost of remediation at $3,400,000. Other assumptions are unchanged. Calculate the interest expense for 20X6, the new present value, and the adjustment to the obligation for the change in estimates. Also prepare a table that shows the balance of the provision and interest expense over the life of the liability.
4. Assume that at the end of 20X8, the company re-estimates that the cost of remediation at $2,900,000, and the market interest rate is now 7%. Calculate the interest expense for 20X8, the new present value, and the adjustment to the obligation for the change in estimates.
5. Calculate the balance of the decommissioning obligation at each 31 December, from 20X5 to 20X8.

★★ **A12-20 Discounting—Provision:** Homespun Resources Ltd was incorporated in 20X2 and is a mining operation operating in northern Alberta. The company is required by the terms of provincial legislation to remediate mine sites when mining is completed. The following events and decisions with respect to operations relate to Homespun's decommissioning obligations:

January 20X2	Commenced mining on Site #1; expected duration of operations is three years, and site remediation is expected to be $500,000 at that time. Decommissioning obligation is recorded. A reasonable interest rate is 7%.
30 September 20X2	Commenced mining on Site #2; expected duration of operations is five years, and site remediation is expected to be $1,200,000 at that time. Decommissioning obligation is recorded.
31 December 20X2	Interest on decommissioning obligation for Site 1 and Site 2 is recorded.
30 September 20X3	Interest on decommissioning obligation for Site 2 is recorded, on the anniversary date of the mine opening.
31 December 20X3	Interest on decommissioning obligation for Site 1 and Site 2 is recorded. Site 1 is now estimated to close in two years' time (rather than the one remaining year expected) and remediation costs are anticipated to increase by 30%.
30 September 20X4	Interest on decommissioning obligation for Site #2 is recorded, on the anniversary date of the mine opening. Site #2 is now estimated to close in two years (rather than the three remaining years expected) and remediation is now estimated at $900,000.
31 December 20X4	Interest on decommissioning obligation for Site 1 and Site 2 is recorded.

Required:

1. Prepare journal entries for the events listed above.
2. Calculate the balance of the decommissioning obligation at each 31 December, from 20X2 to 20X4.

★★ **A12-21 Classification and Statement of Cash Flows:** GYO Limited reports the following amounts on its statement of cash flows:

	20X5	20X4
Trade accounts payable	$1,706,300	$1,423,000
Dividends payable	50,000	—
Provision for restructuring	260,000	—
Provision for coupon refunds	45,000	10,000
Decommissioning obligation	52,500	46,500
Note payable, 8%	400,000	—
Note payable, net, 6%	68,500	—

Other information:

- The 8% note payable is a bank loan due in 20X6, but negotiations for its renewal are taking place. Interest of $32,000 was paid at year-end.
- The provision for restructuring is based on the company's plan to reduce its work force in 20X6, according to a plan approved by the Board of Directors. The provision for restructuring is the estimated severance amounts that will be paid to employees affected by the restructuring.

- The decommissioning obligation relates to a leased premises that must be remediated at the end of the lease term in 20X9. The change in this account this year is due to interest.
- The 6% note payable reflects market interest rates at issuance but is, in fact, a no-interest, five-year note payable arranged with a supplier, for a piece of equipment. The note was originally recorded at its discounted amount of $89,000. Interest of $4,000 was recorded in 20X5.
- Dividends of $140,000 were declared during the year.

GYO uses the indirect method of presentation in the operating activities section of the statement of cash flows and follows the policy of reporting dividends paid in financing activities. Interest paid is included in operating activities.

Required:

1. For each item above, indicate whether the balance would be reported as a current or a long-term liability. For the 8% note payable, what condition must be met by year-end to ensure that the note may be classified as long term?
2. List the items as they would appear on the statement of cash flows in 20X5. Include the amount, description and classification.

★★ **A12-22 Statement of Cash Flows:** Sing Imports Corp. reports the following amounts on its statement of cash flows:

connect

	20X2	20X1
Trade accounts payable	$506,300	$699,600
Dividends payable	10,000	25,000
Provision for litigation	260,000	100,000
Decommissioning obligation	112,700	106,000
Note payable, 5%	400,000	600,000
Note payable, net, 6%	66,500	62,100

Other information:

- Dividends of $100,000 were declared during the year.
- The provision for litigation is based on outstanding legal claims. The amount is not discounted because of uncertainty of cash flow amounts and timing. The provision was increased this year because of new lawsuits filed against the company.
- The decommissioning obligation relates to a leased premises that must be remediated at the end of the lease term. The change in this account this year is due to unwinding the discount.
- The 5% note payable is a bank loan at market interest rates. Interest of $30,000 was paid at year-end.
- The 6% note payable reflects market interest rates at issuance but is, in fact, a no-interest, multiyear liability associated with inventory purchase. The change in the account relates to unwinding the discount.

Sing uses the indirect method of presentation in the operating activities section of the statement of cash flows and follows the policy of reporting dividends paid in financing activities; interest paid is included in operating activities.

Required:

List the items as they would appear on the statement of cash flows in 20X2. Include the amount, description and classification.

★ **A12-23 Liabilities—ASPE:** Harmon Industries Ltd. has a $2,000,000 note payable outstanding. The terms of the note require repayment of principal on 30 June 20X2. The company is now finalizing the financial statements for the year ended 31 December 20X1. In January 20X2, before the financial statements are released, the company comes to an agreement with the lender to refinance the liability, with the new due date 30 June 20X5.

Harmon also has committed to donate $100,000 to a local community centre to support a new hockey rink. The rink will be named for Harmon and promote its commitment to the local community. No donation agreement has yet been signed, but a public announcement has been made, and the building committee has approved plans and called for tenders.

Required:

1. If Harmon complies with IFRS, will this note payable be classified as current or long-term liability as at 31 December 20X1?
2. If Harmon complies with IFRS, will the $100,000 amount be recorded as a liability? Explain.
3. Repeat requirements 1 and 2, assuming that Harmon complies with ASPE.

★★ **A12-24 Liabilities—ASPE:** Return to the facts of A12-16.

Solution

Required:

1. Repeat the assignment question, using straight-line amortization of the discount.
2. Which method of discount amortization provides the more accurate measure of interest expense? Why does ASPE allow use of straight-line amortization?

★★ **A12-25 Liabilities—ASPE:** Return to the facts of A12-17.

connect

Required:

1. Repeat the assignment question, using straight-line amortization of the discount.
2. Which method of discount amortization provides the more accurate measure of interest expense? Why does ASPE allow use of straight-line amortization?

connect LEARNSMART SMARTBOOK™

For more information on the resources available from McGraw-Hill Ryerson, go to www.mcgrawhill.ca/he/solutions.

CHAPTER 13

Financial Instruments: Long-Term Debt

INTRODUCTION

Long-term debt is a significant source of financing for many companies. The lender becomes a significant stakeholder in the company for a lengthy period of time. Obviously, the lender is an important user of the financial statements. The terms of these loans, including the requirement to pay not only interest and principal but also terms regarding security and covenants, are meant to limit, or at least define, the risks that the lender accepts. In all cases, some risk remains; lenders will use the financial statements as well as other information to evaluate the liquidity, solvency, and financial performance of the companies in which they have invested.

Hydro One Inc. is responsible for the transmission and distribution of electricity to customers in Ontario. The company reports over $18 billion in total assets and a massive $7.4 billion in long-term debt. It has 18 different financial instruments listed as long-term debt, with various interest rates, due dates, and conditions. Obviously, the company has a large group of lenders, and its financial statements are carefully scrutinized by all.

Reporting long-term debt in the financial statements requires appropriate accounting for issuance and retirement. In addition, derecognition prior to maturity can create major changes in the financial statements. Measurement of annual interest cost is critical, and there are some circumstances that require borrowing costs to be capitalized rather than expensed. Remember, debt transactions often involve millions of dollars at a time. As a result, in all accounting measurements and policies, the amounts are material, and the stakes are high.

This chapter reviews common sources of debt financing. The technical elements of accounting for long-term debt—issuance, interest measurement, and derecognition—are reviewed using bonds payable as a base. Chapter 14 moves on to equity transactions, but Chapter 15 returns to more complex debt arrangements that combine attributes of both debt and equity.

SOURCES OF FINANCING

The discussion that follows provides a review of common forms of financing, which are summarized in Exhibit 13-1.

Short-Term Financing

Trade Credit The most obvious source of short-term financing is through the trade credit extended by suppliers. Some corporations use trade creditor financing to its fullest extent as a source of "interest-free" financing, sometimes stretching the ethical boundaries of business practice. For example, large corporations may rely on their purchasing power and their "clout" as big customers of smaller suppliers to put off paying their trade accounts payable.

Some purchases are made by signing promissory notes that obligate the company to pay a supplier (or an intermediary, e.g., a financial institution) at or before a given date. Promissory notes are legally enforceable negotiable instruments. The notes may bear interest, or they may be non–interest bearing. The use of notes for trade purchases is particularly common in international trade, since the financial institutions that act as intermediaries are better placed to enforce payment.

Short-Term Bank Loans Like individuals, Canadian business entities borrow from chartered banks. Lending arrangements can be classified according to term and security.

Short-term loans to business entities usually take the form of **operating lines of credit**. These loans are granted to help finance working capital and typically are secured by a lien or charge on accounts receivable and inventory. There normally is a gap between the time that cash is paid to suppliers for inventory and the time that money is received from customers who, in the end, buy the inventory. Businesses can use equity funds to finance this cash flow, but receivables and inventories are reasonable collateral for loans, and it is typically cheaper to borrow for this purpose. The interest rate on bank lines of credit is usually flexible and is based on the cost of funds for the financial institution.

There is typically a limit on working capital loans, expressed as a percentage of the collateral base. For example, a business may have an operating line of credit (also called a **credit facility**) that allows the company to borrow up to 75% of the net realizable value of accounts

EXHIBIT 13-1

SOURCES OF FINANCING

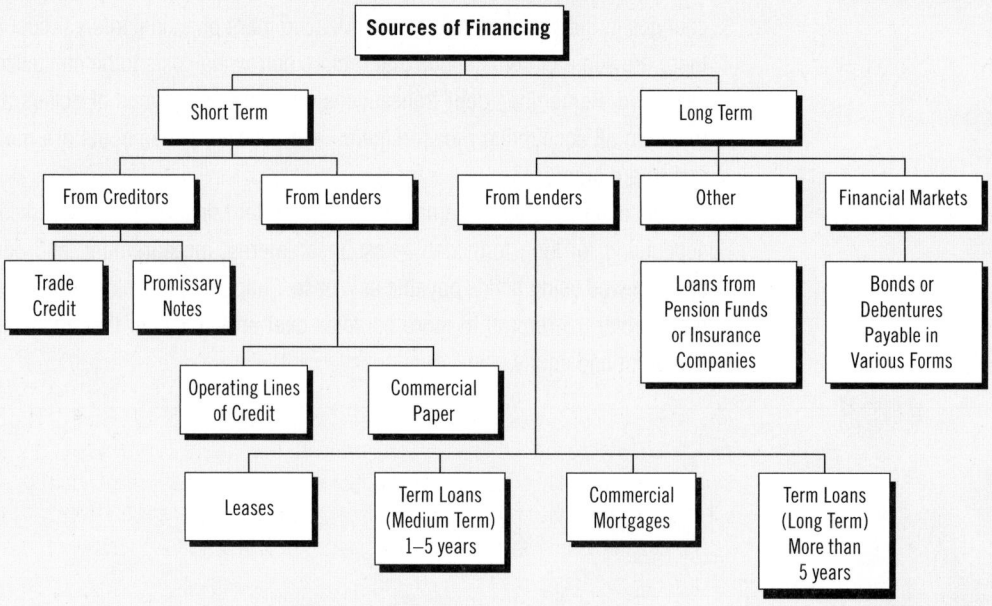

receivable and 50% of the book value of inventory. These loans will increase and decrease in seasonal businesses, following the ebb and flow of the business cycle.

Operating lines of credit are due on *demand*, which means that if the lender gives the borrower appropriate notice, usually a few business days, the loans must be repaid immediately. In practice, repayment is not normally demanded unless the amount of collateral declines or the company otherwise violates some aspect of the loan agreement.

Despite their "due on demand" status, lines of credit often are a permanent fixture in a company's financial structure. The credit facility may be attached to the business's current account (i.e., the business chequing account) and drawn on as an *overdraft*. Companies use such loans as part of their cash management strategies.

Large corporations that have good credit ratings can issue *commercial paper*, which is a type of short-term promissory note that is sold (through a financial intermediary, again usually a bank) in open markets. The issuer of commercial paper does not know who the purchaser is, and settlement at the due date is through the financial intermediary.

Commercial paper is meant to be issued by only very stable companies. In the liquidity crunch that spiked in 2007, some asset-backed commercial paper (ABCP) turned out to be highly risky because the issuers lacked liquid resources to repay the loans. Under a court-supervised restructuring program, ABCP obligations were replaced with notes payable of varying maturities, some reasonably long term. One of the criteria for issuing ABCP is an excellent credit rating; the credit rating agencies were severely criticized for their role in the ABCP episode because hindsight showed that the issuers were not as stable as needed.

A final type of short-term financing that merits mention is the sale or assignment of a company's receivables to a financial institution. This represents another way current assets can be used as a source of short-term financing.

Long-Term Financing

Long-term loans are often an attractive means of financing for the borrower compared with either short-term debt or equity. These loans are appealing because:

- Short-term financing may not be available from period to period, and the cost may be higher than for long-term debt;
- Long-term lenders are not shareholders, and do not acquire voting privileges over the borrower, so issuance of debt causes no ownership dilution;
- Debt capital is obtained more easily than equity capital for many companies, especially private companies;
- Interest expense, unlike dividends, is tax deductible; and
- A firm that earns a return on borrowed funds that exceeds the rate it must pay in interest is using debt to its advantage and is said to be successfully levered (or leveraged).

Leverage is risky. If sales or earnings decline, interest expense becomes an increasing percentage of earnings. Business failure may be the result of carrying high debt levels in expectation of high sales and profits. If sales and profits (and operating cash flows) do not materialize, overlevered companies soon find themselves in financial difficulty. Firms often attempt to restructure their debt by extending maturity dates or requesting a reduction in principal or interest.

Debt is an attractive investment for *investors (lenders)* because it provides legally enforceable debt payments, eventual return of principal, and a priority claim to assets if the corporation restructures its debt or if it goes into receivership or bankruptcy. Creditors can further reduce their risk by extending secured debt, where the obligation is contractually tied to specific assets that the creditor can seize in the event of the debtor's default.

Long-term debt can take a wide variety of forms, including:

- Bank loans;
- Notes payable;

- Mortgages;
- Other asset-backed loans;
- Publicly issued bonds, secured or unsecured; and
- Long-term leases.

Long-term leases are the subject of Chapter 18. Other forms of financing are discussed in this chapter. More inventive forms of financing that have at least some of the characteristics of long-term debt are discussed in Chapter 15.

Long-Term Bank Financing

Long-term loans could be *term loans* or *commercial mortgages*. **Term loans** might better be characterized as *medium-term* loans because they are usually for periods of 1.5 to 5 years. Banks will lend for this medium term if there is appropriate collateral, such as tangible capital assets (e.g., equipment, land, or buildings). Land and buildings would also qualify for longer-term loans. Security is lodged in the form of a claim on the property/plant/equipment. At the end of the loan term, after all the payments have been made, the security is released. The repayment terms of medium-term loans can be structured in either of two ways:

1. *Blended payments.* The interest rate is fixed at the beginning of the loan term, and regular equal annuity payments are made, which include both principal and interest. For example, a $1,000,000, five-year loan at an interest rate of 7% could be repaid in five annual instalments of $243,891 [$1,000,000 ÷ (P/A, 7%, 5)]. Each payment includes some interest and some principal.
2. *Designated monthly principal payments, plus accrued interest on the outstanding balance.* The interest rate may be *fixed* at the beginning of the loan term or may *float* with prime interest rates. The borrower makes an interest payment at the end of every month, based on the loan balance for that month and the interest rate in effect. In addition, the borrower and lender work out a repayment scheme for the principal that will fully repay the loan by the end of its term. The payment terms may require equal monthly, quarterly, or semi-annual principal payments (plus interest), or lump-sum payments following a busy season. Sometimes there is a large final lump-sum payment required; this is known as a *balloon payment.*

For accounting purposes, interest is accrued as time passes and is paid when due. If principal and interest payments are *blended*, the portion of each payment that represents principal is recorded as a reduction of the loan. Alternatively, if designated lump-sum principal payments are made, these are recorded as a direct reduction of the loan. Medium-term loans are classified as long term on the borrower's statement of financial position, although the principal portion due within one year or operating cycle is classified as a current liability.

Long-Term Loans Long-term loans, *in the eyes of the lenders*, are loans with repayment terms extending beyond five years. Financial institutions typically grant such loans as *asset-based financing* or as *commercial mortgages*. Commercial mortgages are secured against land and buildings and involve regular blended payments (e.g., monthly or bimonthly). The amortization period of such loans could be for as long as 25 years, but the term, or the lender's commitment to extending the loan at the given interest rate arrangement, is usually a shorter period. The term normally will not exceed five years and may be shorter. The lender is under no obligation to renew the loan at the end of the term if it is not satisfied with the creditworthiness of the borrower.

When a long-term loan is extended at a fixed interest rate, the interest rate is fixed only for the term of the loan, not for the entire amortization period. The interest rate is reset at the beginning of each term. For example, a business could arrange a 25-year (amortization period) mortgage with a five-year term. Blended payments would be devised to repay all principal after 25 years, but the interest rate would be reset after every five years. The blended payments would be recalculated and could go up if interest rates increased or down if rates decreased.

For example, assume that Medical Arts Building Limited reported a mortgage in its 30 September 20X9 disclosure notes as follows:

6.75% mortgage loan, repayable at $18,880 per month, including principal and interest, due 1 April 20X11	$2,213,335
Security for the mortgage consists of land and buildings, an assignment of insurance proceeds, and a general assignment of rents and leases.	

The end of the *term* is 1 April 20X11, but *the amortization period* is 25 years. The mortgage would not be fully repaid at the end of the *term*, since the $18,880 blended monthly payments are not high enough to achieve this. Repayment amounts and interest rates would be renegotiated at the end of each term.

Long-term loans with a floating interest rate can also be arranged. Floating-rate loans normally provide for an adjustment of the interest rate (and the monthly payment) at six-month intervals. The blended payments for the next six months are recalculated at that time. Like fixed-rate loans, the term of a floating-rate loan is limited so that the lender can periodically reassess the risk of the loan.

Other Sources of Long-Term Debt

For small and most medium-sized private companies, the chartered banks are the major source of financing. However, large companies (both public and private) have other sources of financing available. Larger corporations can arrange loans with life insurance companies or pension funds, which have money to invest for long periods of time.

Bonds or Debentures Payable

A bond (or **debenture**) is a debt security issued by a corporation or government to secure large amounts of capital on a long-term basis. A bond represents a formal promise by the issuing organization to pay principal and interest in return for the capital invested.

A formal bond agreement, known as a **bond indenture**, specifies the terms of the bond and the rights and duties of both the issuer and the bondholder. The indenture specifies any restrictions on the issuing company, the dollar amount authorized for issuance, the interest rate and payment dates, the maturity date, and any conversion and call privileges. An independent trustee is appointed to protect the interests of both the issuer and the investors. The trustee (usually a financial institution) maintains the necessary records and disburses interest and principal. The investors receive bond certificates, which represent the contractual obligations of the issuer to the investors.

Debt Covenants

Debt agreements often restrict the operations and financial structure of the borrower to reduce the risk of default. **Debt covenants** are restrictions placed on a corporation's activities as a condition of maintaining the loan. If the covenants are broken, the lender has the right to call the loan: The lender can demand immediate repayment of the principal. Bankers also refer to covenants as *maintenance tests*. Restrictions can be either accounting based or behavioural (restricted actions). Examples of each type are as follows:

Accounting-Based Covenants

- Maximum debt-to-equity ratio or debt-to-assets (often called debt-to-capitalization);
- Minimum current ratio; and
- Minimum interest coverage ratio, often based on **EBITDA** (Earnings before interest, tax, depreciation, and amortization).

Restricted Actions

- Limitations on the issuance of additional debt without the permission of the lender;
- Restrictions on dividend payments;
- Prohibition or restriction on the redemption or retirement of shares;

- Limitations on the ability of the company to pledge assets as security for other purposes;
- Requirement that current management or key employees remain in place; and
- Limitations on transfer of control.

Reporting Example

The following information has been extracted from the financial statements of AltaGas Ltd. These disclosures come from Note 9, Short-term Debt; Note 10, Long-term Debt; and Note 14, Capital Disclosures. These notes also include extensive disclosures, not repeated here, on the terms and condition of debt. Note the wide range of financing sources that the company uses, including short-term credit facilities, medium-term notes, and debentures. The company's debt covenants centre around the debt-to-capitalization ratio and a comparison of interest expense to EBITDA.

(amounts in thousands)

9. SHORT-TERM DEBT

	2011	2010
Bank indebtedness	$ 5,564	$4,528
$50 million demand operating facility	—	4,320
$25 million demand operating facility	11,260	—
$20 million demand operating facility	—	630
$1 million demand operating facility	—	—
	$16,824	$9,478

10. LONG-TERM DEBT

	December 31 2011	December 31 2010
Credit facilities	$ 30,966	$113,789
Medium-term notes	1,175,000	775,000
Debentures notes	87,376	—
Bankers acceptances	8,000	—
Loan from Province of Nova Scotia	4,815	4,535
Capital lease obligations	4,567	6,076
Promissory note	3,839	—
Other long-term debt	547	807
Unamortized deferred financing	(7,675)	(5,201)
	1,307,435	895,006
Less current portion	105,962	1,508
	$1,201,473	$893,498

14. CAPITAL DISCLOSURES

The following table summarizes the Corporation's debt covenants for all credit facilities as at December 31, 2011:

Ratios	Debt covenant requirements
Debt-to-capitalization	not greater than 60 percent
EBITDA-to-interest expense	not less than 2.5x
Debt-to-capitalization (Utility Group)	not greater than 67.5 percent

Source: AltaGas Ltd. 2011 Annual Financial Statements, www.sedar.com, posted 12 March 2012.

CONCEPT REVIEW

1. What assets are most commonly used as security for operating lines of credit?
2. What are the advantages of long-term debt over equity financing?
3. What is the difference between the *term* and *amortization period* for a commercial mortgage?
4. What is a debt covenant?

DEBT ISSUANCE AND INTEREST EXPENSE

Accounting for long-term debt will be illustrated in the context of bonds payable, since bonds are a common form of long-term debt.

Classification

Bonds payable are *financial instruments* and are classified as *other financial liabilities. A bond is initially valued at fair value,* which is the cash received, netted with transaction costs. A bond is then carried at this value (which is cost on the date of acquisition) and then *amortized cost* over its term. That is, the initial fair value is the cash received when the bond is issued, which is based on a present value model. Transaction costs, such as upfront fees, are netted with this amount. If this amount is not the par value, or maturity value, the difference is amortized and recorded over the life of the bond.

Bond Valuation

Fair value is established as the present value of all future cash payments discounted using the *effective interest rate,* also called the *market yield rate,* or the **incremental borrowing rate (IBR)**. The effective interest rate is *the borrower's interest rate for additional debt of similar term and risk.* Discounting was illustrated in Chapter 12 and is an important valuation model for long-term liabilities, such as bonds.

Remember that the *nominal interest rate* is the interest rate stated in the bond agreement. The **effective interest rate**, or **yield**, is the true cost of borrowing. The discounted amount, which is fair value and the proceeds on issuing a bond payable, is:

$$P = [I \times (P/A, i, n)] + [F \times (P/F, i, n)], \text{ where}$$

P = fair value of the bond payable; issuance proceeds on issuance date;
I = dollar amount of each period's interest payment, or
= nominal rate × the bond face value
F = maturity value of the bond
n = the number of periods to maturity
i = the market interest rate

When a bond pays the effective market interest rate, the bond will be issued for its par value, or maturity amount. When the nominal and market interest rates are different, price of the bond (issue proceeds) will be greater or less than the maturity amount, and a premium or discount will be recognized.

Fair Value after Issuance After issuance, the bond may be bought and sold between different investors. The bond will trade at its *current fair value.* This is a discounted amount, using a market yield rate that reflects updated assessment of both *company risk* and *market yield.* The number of interest periods, *n,* reflects the *remaining* life of the bond. If the yield rate, *i*, rises, the discounted amount will decline, and if the yield rate decreases, the discounted amount will be higher.

Measurement of Interest Expense

Accounting for long-term debt is straightforward if the effective interest rate and the nominal interest rate are the same. If these two rates are the same, the liability is issued at its maturity value. Interest is accrued as time passes, and interest payments are accounted for as cash is disbursed. Cash amounts correctly state the liability amount and interest expense.

If the nominal interest rate is *different* from the market interest rate at the time the note is issued, the *discount rate* is used to measure interest expense over the life of the liability. The initial discount or premium is reduced to zero, or *amortized to interest expense*, over the life of the liability. This is also called *unwinding* the discount or premium. The net liability is carried on the statement of financial position (SFP) at amortized cost or par value combined with the discount or premium.

Example

To illustrate accounting for bonds payable, assume that on 1 January 20X5, Gresham Limited, a calendar-year firm, issues $100,000 of 7% debentures dated 1 January 20X5, with interest paid each 31 December. The bonds mature on 31 December 20X9. Note the simplifying assumptions: This bond is for only a five-year term and pays interest *annually* at the end of Gresham's fiscal year.

1. The **face value** or *par value* (also called *maturity*, or *principal value*) of a bond is the amount payable when the bond is due ($100,000 for Gresham).
2. The **maturity date** is the end of the bond term and the due date for the face value (31 December 20X9, for Gresham).
3. The **nominal interest rate** (also called the *coupon, stated,* or *contractual rate*) is the rate that determines periodic interest payments. For Gresham, the nominal rate is 7%, paid annually.
4. The **interest payment dates** are the dates the periodic interest payments are due (31 December for Gresham). Gresham pays $7,000 interest on the $100,000 bond on each 31 December regardless of the issue price or market rate of interest at date of issue.
5. The **bond date** (authorization date) is the earliest date the bond can be issued and represents the planned issuance date of the bond issue (1 January 20X5 for Gresham).

Three situations will illustrate accounting for bonds, under different effective interest rate assumptions. (Always assume that the effective interest rate is quoted for compounding periods identical to those offered by the bond unless told otherwise.)

- Situation A: Effective interest rate = 7%
- Situation B: Effective interest rate = 6%
- Situation C: Effective interest rate = 8%

Situation A The bond will sell at face value because the market and stated interest rates are both 7%. The price of the bonds will be equal to the present value of the future cash flows at the market rate of 7%:

$$\begin{aligned}\text{Issue price} &= [\$100{,}000 \times (P/F, 7\%, 5)] + [(\$100{,}000 \times 7\%) \times (P/A, 7\%, 5)] \\ &= \$100{,}000\end{aligned}$$

When the bonds are issued, the issuer records a long-term liability, and interest is recorded as time passes. The bond is repaid at maturity.

1 January 20X5—issue bonds		
Cash	100,000	
Bonds payable		100,000
31 December each year, 20X5 through 20X9—interest payment		
Interest expense	7,000	
Cash ($100,000 × 7%)		7,000
31 December 20X9—bond maturity		
Bonds payable	100,000	
Cash		100,000

Interest expense for bonds issued at face value equals the amount of the interest payment. The book value of the bonds remains $100,000 to maturity. Changes in the fair market value of the bond, *caused by changes in the yield rate subsequent to the issuance date*, are not recognized in the financial statements but are disclosed.

Situation B The market rate of interest is 6%; the bonds sell at a premium.

Issue price = [$100,000 × (P/F, 6%, 5)] + [($100,000 × 7%) × (P/A, 6%, 5)]
= $104,213

The bonds sell at a *premium* because they pay a stated rate that exceeds the market rate on similar bonds. The initial $4,213 premium is recorded in an account titled *premium on bonds payable*, which is shown with the bonds payable account on the statement of financial position.[1] The following entry is made to record the issue:

1 January 20X5—issue bonds		
Cash	104,213	
Bonds payable		100,000
Premium on bonds payable		4,213

Total interest expense over the term of a bond is *not* equal to total cash interest when a bond is sold at a premium or discount. Instead, interest expense must equal the total cash payments required by the bond (face value and interest) less the aggregate issue price. Total interest expense is shown by this calculation:

Face value	$100,000
Total cash interest: 7% × $100,000 × 5 years	35,000
Total cash payments required by bond	135,000
Issue price	104,213
Total interest expense over bond term ($35,000 – $4,213)	$ 30,787

[1] If a premium or discount is recorded separately, recording follows the *gross method*. The premium or discount is shown with the bond on the SFP. Alternatively, the *net method* may be used. Under the net method, one account may be used for both the par value and the premium or discount, mimicking the financial reporting treatment in the general ledger. Text examples will reflect the gross method.

Gresham received $4,213 more than face value at issuance but will pay only face value at maturity. Therefore, the effective rate is less than the stated rate, and total interest expense for Gresham over the bond term is *less* than total interest paid.

Premium or Discount Recognition The premium or discount must be completely recognized (*unwound* or *amortized*), over the bond term using the *effective-interest method*, so that net book value equals face value at maturity. Amortized premium reduces periodic interest expense to an amount less than interest paid, and amortized discount increases interest expense over the cash interest paid. The net bond liability equals face value *plus* the remaining unamortized bond premium or *less* the remaining unamortized bond discount. The following entries illustrate unwinding a premium:

31 December 20X5		
Interest expense ($104,213 × 6%)	6,253	
Premium on bonds payable	747	
Cash ($100,000 × 7%)		7,000
The carrying value of the bond is now $103,466 ($104,213 – $747)		
31 December 20X6		
Interest expense ($103,466 × 6%)	6,208	
Premium on bonds payable	792	
Cash		7,000
The carrying value of the bond is now $102,674 ($103,466 – $792)		

Interest expense under the effective-interest method is the product of the effective interest rate (6%) and the net liability balance at the beginning of the period. In effect, the company returns part of the original "excess" proceeds with each interest payment. In 20X5, this amount is $747, which reduces the net bond liability at the beginning of 20X6. Consequently, 20X6 interest expense is less than that for 20X5.

The bonds are listed on the 31 December 20X6 SFP as a long-term liability:

Bonds payable	$100,000
Premium on bonds payable ($4,213 – $747 – $792)	2,674
Net book value of bonds payable	$102,674

Proof of Book Value The book value of the bonds at 31 December 20X6 is the present value of remaining cash flows *using the effective interest rate at the date of issuance:*

$$PV_{31/12/20X6} = [\$100{,}000 \times (P/F, 6\%, 3)] + [(\$100{,}000 \times 7\%) \times (P/A, 6\%, 3)]$$
$$= \$102{,}674$$

Amortization Table An amortization table is often prepared to support bond accounting. The table gives all the data necessary for journal entries over the term of the bond and each year's ending net liability balance. An amortization table is shown in Exhibit 13-2.

EXHIBIT 13-2

AMORTIZATION TABLE FOR GRESHAM LIMITED BONDS

Situation B—Bonds Sold at Premium; Effective-Interest Amortization

Date	Interest Payment at 7%	Interest Expense at 6%	Premium Amortization[1]	Unamortized Premium[2]	Net Bond Liability[3]
1 Jan. 20X5				$4,213	$104,213
31 Dec. 20X5	$ 7,000	$ 6,253	$ 747	3,466	103,466
31 Dec. 20X6	7,000	6,208	792	2,674	102,674
31 Dec. 20X7	7,000	6,160	840	1,834	101,834
31 Dec. 20X8	7,000	6,110	890	944	100,944
31 Dec. 20X9	7,000	6,056	944	0	100,000
	$35,000	$30,787	$4,213		

(1) Interest payment – Interest expense
(2) Previous unamortized premium – Current period's amortization
(3) $100,000 face value + Current unamortized premium

Situation C The market rate of interest is 8%; the bonds sell at a discount.

Issue price = [$100,000 × (P/F, 8%, 5)] + [($100,000 × 7%) × (P/A, 8%, 5)]
= $96,007

The Gresham bonds sell at a discount in this case because the stated rate is less than the yield rate on similar bonds. The discount is recorded in the discount on bonds payable account, a contra-liability valuation account, which is subtracted from bonds payable to yield the net liability. The entries for the first two years after the bond issuance follow, along with an amortization table (Exhibit 13-3) and the relevant portion of the SFP after two years.

Journal Entries:

1 January 20X5—issue bonds		
Cash	96,007	
Discount on bonds payable	3,993	
Bonds payable		100,000
31 December 20X5—interest expense		
Interest expense ($96,007 × 8%)	7,681	
Discount on bonds payable		681
Cash ($100,000 × 7%)		7,000
31 December 20X6—interest expense		
Interest expense [($96,007 + $681) × 8%]	7,735	
Discount on bonds payable		735
Cash ($100,000 × 7%)		7,000

SFP presentation:

31 December 20X6	
Bonds payable	$100,000
Discount on bonds payable	(2,577)
Net book value of bonds payable	$ 97,423

EXHIBIT 13-3

AMORTIZATION TABLE FOR GRESHAM LIMITED BONDS

Situation C—Bonds Sold at Discount: Effective-Interest Amortization

Date	Interest Payment at 7%	Interest Expense at 8%	Discount Amortization[1]	Unamortized Discount[2]	Net Bond Liability[3]
1 Jan. 20X5				$3,993	$ 96,007
31 Dec. 20X5	$ 7,000	$ 7,681	$ 681	3,312	96,688
31 Dec. 20X6	7,000	7,735	735	2,577	97,423
31 Dec. 20X7	7,000	7,794	794	1,783	98,217
31 Dec. 20X8	7,000	7,857	857	926	99,074
31 Dec. 20X9	7,000	7,926	926	0	100,000
	$35,000	$38,993	$3,993		

(1) Interest expense – Interest payment
(2) Previous unamortized discount – Current period's amortization
(3) $100,000 face value – Current unamortized discount

Summary

Exhibit 13-4 summarizes several aspects of bond accounting. The exhibit relates to bonds with semi-annual interest payments, which is the usual situation.

EXHIBIT 13-4

SUMMARY TABLE: ACCOUNTING FOR BONDS ASSUMING SEMI-ANNUAL INTEREST PAYMENTS

Fair value of bonds = Present value of the cash flow to the investor
= Discounted principal payments + Discounted interest payment annuity
= [(Face value) × (P/F, i, n)] + [(Face value × s) × (P/A, i, n)]

Where: i = effective interest rate *per six-month period*
n = number of semi-annual periods in bond term
s = stated (nominal) interest rate per six-month period

continued on next page

EXHIBIT 13-4 (*cont'd*)

Discount or premium =
When effective rate (*i*) exceeds stated rate (*s*):
Initial discount = Face value – Price of bond issue

When stated rate (*s*) exceeds effective rate (*i*):
Initial premium = Price of bond issue – Face value

Net book value of bonds = Face value *plus* unamortized premium or *minus* unamortized discount

As Maturity Approaches:	Premium	Discount
The unamortized amount	Declines	Declines
The net book value	Declines	Increases
Annual interest expense, using effective-interest method	Declines	Increases

Interest Measurement:

	Effective-Interest Method
Calculations:	
Calculation of interest expense	Effective rate × Net carrying value of bond
Calculation of discount or premium amortization	Difference between cash paid and expense
Patterns:	
Annual interest expense	Changes each year
Annual interest expense as a percentage of beginning *book value* of the bond (interest rate)	Constant over term

Interest Payment Dates Different from Statement Dates

In the preceding situations, all specified interest payment dates coincided with the fiscal year-end. However, this coincidence is not frequent in practice. When the end of a fiscal period falls between interest payment dates, it is necessary to accrue interest from the last (previous) interest payment date, and to bring the bond discount/premium amortization up to date.

For example, assume the facts for Situation C for Gresham Limited bonds, except that the fiscal year-end is 30 September. The bonds are issued on the bond date, 1 January 20X5, and interest is payable annually on 31 December. On 30 September 20X5, interest must be accrued and the discount amortized:

30 September 20X5—interest accrued		
Interest expense ($7,681 (first full year's expense) × 9/12)	5,761	
Accrued interest payable ($100,000 × 7% × 9/12)		5,250
Discount on bonds payable [$681 (first full year's amortization) × 9/12]		511

The amortization is derived from the table in Exhibit 13-3 and is allocated evenly over the period between interest dates. The loan balance is not recalculated and included in the table (i.e., not recompounded) because *compounding is tied to interest dates and not to reporting periods*. That is, the table is always based on the *bond's* dates and terms. Then it is necessary to adjust calculations to fit the fiscal year.

When the interest is paid on 31 December, the following entry is made, assuming that the interest accrual has not been reversed:

31 December 20X5—interest payment		
Interest expense ($7,681 × 3/12)	1,920	
Accrued interest payable	5,250	
Discount on bonds payable ($681 × 3/12)		170
Cash		7,000

Delayed Issuance and Issuance Between Interest Payment Dates

In the previous examples, bonds were issued on their original issue date, an assumption chosen to emphasize the accounting principles regarding effective interest rates and bond amortization. However, bonds are not necessarily issued on their initial issue date. Market conditions or company plans may change the issuance date away from the original intent. Bonds that are sold at some time later than their initial issue date are sold at a price that reflects the future cash flows discounted to the actual date of sale.

Delayed Issuance Suppose that the Gresham Limited bonds are sold on 1 January 20X6 instead of on their bond date of 1 January 20X5. This *is* an interest payment date, although one year late. The price of the bonds will be the present value of the future cash flows from interest ($7,000 per year for *four* years) and principal ($100,000 received *four* years hence). If the market rate of interest is 8% (Situation C), the price of the bonds will be:

$$\text{Issue price} = [\$100{,}000 \times (P/F, 8\%, 4)] + [(\$100{,}000 \times 7\%) \times (P/A, 8\%, 4)]$$
$$= \$96{,}688$$

This price can be verified by referring to the net bond liability shown in Exhibit 13-3 for 31 December 20X5. The discount will be amortized over the four years remaining until maturity.

Between Interest Dates The delayed issuance of a bond may not coincide with an interest date, and issuance may occur *between interest dates*. In this case, the bond issue price cannot be directly calculated as a present value figure, since the present value figure must be at a particular interest date. Instead, the present value of the bond must be calculated as of the two interest dates *around* the issuance date (one before, one after). The difference between these two values is then pro-rated to the issuance date. Alternatively, some calculators and spreadsheet models allow numbers other than whole numbers to be entered as n (e.g., n = 14.75; 14 years and 9 months.)

For example, if the Gresham bonds in Exhibit 13-3 were issued on 1 March 20X5 when the effective-interest rate was 8%, the proceeds would be $96,121. This is the $96,007 present value on 1 January 20X5 (n = 5) plus $114, which is 2/12 of the $681 difference between the present value of the bond on 1 January 20X5 and the $96,688 present value on 31 December 20X5 (n = 4). *The present value has to be calculated twice and the difference pro-rated.*

Accrued Interest When bonds are sold between interest dates, interest accrued since the last interest date is also collected in cash. Accrued interest is added to the price because the holder of the bonds on any interest date *receives the full amount of interest* since the last interest date, even if the investor held the bonds for a shorter period.

Example Assume that the Gresham Limited bonds are sold on 1 June 20X5, five months after the bond date but seven months before the next interest date. The holders of the bonds on 31 December 20X5 will receive the full 12-month interest payment of $7,000 despite the fact that they held the bonds for only 7 months. To compensate for the fact that they have earned only 7 months' interest but will receive 12 months' interest, they *pay the issuing company for interest for the five-month period that they did not hold the bonds.*

On 1 June 20X5, Gresham would receive net proceeds of $96,291 for the bond, plus accrued interest of $2,917. Note that:

- The $96,291 proceeds is calculated as $96,007 plus 5/12 of the $681 difference between the two surrounding present values; and
- Interest of $2,917 is five months' accrued interest ($100,000 × 7% × 5/12).

The bond issuance will be recorded by Gresham Limited as follows:

1 June 20X5—initial issuance of bonds		
Cash ($96,291 + $2,917)	99,208	
Discount on bonds payable ($100,000 – $96,291)	3,709	
Interest payable ($100,000 × 7% × 5/12)		2,917
Bonds payable		100,000

Initial Discount Amortization After a bond is issued between interest dates, the initial discount amortization recognized will be the amount needed to get the bond to the "end point" in the amortization schedule at the end of the relevant period. For this bond, the issuance proceeds were $96,291, and the 20X5 period ends with an amortized value of $96,688 in the table. Therefore, amortization of $397 is needed ($96,688 – $96,291).

When the company pays the $7,000 interest on 31 December 20X5, the entry to record the interest payment and the discount amortization will be as follows:

31 December 20X5—payment of interest and amortization of discount		
Interest expense	4,480	
Interest payable	2,917	
Cash		7,000
Discount on bonds payable ($96,291 – $96,688)		397

The $4,480 recorded as interest expense is seven months' expense.

Alternative Interest Expense Treatment When the bonds were issued, the accrued interest portion of the proceeds could have been credited to *interest expense* instead of interest payable; the debit for the payment of interest on 31 December would then be recorded entirely to interest expense. The result is still $4,480 in interest expense after the first payment (i.e., a debit of $7,397 and a credit of $2,917 equals $4,480.) The entries would appear as follows; they are identical to those shown above, except where highlighted.

1 June 20X5		
Cash	99,208	
Discount on bonds payable	3,709	
Interest expense		2,917
Bonds payable		100,000
31 December 20X5		
Interest expense	7,397	
Cash		7,000
Discount on bonds payable		397

The choice of approach is up to the company; the second entry is more straightforward under this approach, which is helpful. However, the credit to interest expense in the initial entry is counter-intuitive. The (temporary) credit balance in interest expense would have to be reclassified if financial statements were prepared in the period between issuance and first interest payment.

Observations on Bond Amortization

A bond discount or premium is unwound over the life of the bond to measure the "true" cost of debt. Remember that the cost of debt is a sensitive issue for many companies. However, premium and discount amortization represents an arbitrary allocation, departing (as all interperiod allocations do) from the underlying cash flow of the transaction.

This chapter has emphasized the use of the effective-interest method of amortization. The effective-interest method is the method required by accounting standards because it best reflects the underlying basis of valuation for long-term debt. It also is the method used in other major areas of long-term liability accounting, such as lease accounting (see Chapter 18) and pension accounting (see Chapter 19). The inherent advantage of the effective-interest method is that it provides a measure of interest expense (and liability valuation) that reflects the present value process by which the liability was originally valued and recorded. The effective-interest method of amortization achieves a constant *rate* of interest expense over the life of the bond.

The premium or discount can also be unwound using a *straight-line pattern.* This method is simpler and results in a constant *dollar amount* of interest expense each year. This interest expense represents a *different rate* each period (i.e., the interest expense divided by the liability balance is not constant.) This can be a troubling inconsistency when borrowing rates are sensitive.

Straight line may be used under ASPE and is acceptable in any case where the result is not materially different than the effective-interest method. The straight-line approach was illustrated in Chapter 12 and is illustrated again in this chapter in the ASPE section.

Remember also that accounting measurement is based on the *historical* interest rate and fair value as of the date of issuance. Amortization does not reflect *current* market interest rates or fair values.

Fair Value of the Bond

Bonds are an investment for lenders and may be sold before the maturity date. The bond will have a fair value that reflects a revised present value. Discounting uses *a revised yield rate* that reflects not only current market yield rates but also any new information about company risk. The number of interest periods used, *n*, reflects the *remaining* life of the bond.

Return to Situation C, where the Gresham 7% bond was issued to yield 8% in 20X5; proceeds were $96,007. After two years, on 31 December 20X6, it is reported on the SFP for $97,423 (refer to Exhibit 13-3). If the yield rates increase to 9%, the bond will have a fair value of $94,937:

$$\text{Fair value} = [\$100{,}000 \times (P/F, 9\%, 3)] + [(\$100{,}000 \times 7\%) \times (P/A, 9\%, 3)]$$
$$= \$94{,}937$$

Note that cash flows—principal and interest—have not changed. The term, *n*, is different, and is now three periods rather than five. The discount rate used is now the revised market yield rate, or 9%.

This is the value that one investor would pay another to purchase this bond. *This fair value is not recorded in Gresham's financial statements but must be disclosed.*

Debt Issuance Costs

Debt issuance costs include not only upfront fees, underwriting charges and commissions but also legal, accounting, engraving, printing, registration, and promotion costs. These costs are paid by the issuer and reduce the *net proceeds* from the debt issue. This increases the overall cost, or the effective interest rate, for the issuer.

Accounting standards require that debt issuance cost be recorded and amortized on an effective-interest basis, as is any debt discount.[2] The amount acts as an additional discount, or reduction of a premium. Unwinding this account results in additional interest expense. Alternatively, it may be included in "other financing expense." On the SFP, companies should present unamortized debt issuance cost as a contra account to long-term liabilities.

Example

Upfront fees and underwriting fees can be substantial. In effect, the fee increases the loan's effective-interest rate. For example, assume that a firm issues a $5 million dollar, 10-year 5% bond with annual interest payments. Underwriting costs, paid at the beginning of the loan term (up front) are $368,000. The bond sells at par, and the firm will receive the net proceeds, or $4,632,000 ($5,000,000 – $368,000), on issuance.

The effective interest rate inherent in the cash flow pattern, including the fee, has to be calculated, to determine the effective interest rate charged. The payments are $368,000 at the beginning of the loan, $250,000 at the end of each year, and then the principal after 10 years. That is,

$$\$5{,}000{,}000 = \$368{,}000 + [\$250{,}000 \times (P/A,\ i,\ 10)] + [\$5{,}000{,}000 \times (P/F,\ i,\ 10)]$$

The next step is to solve for *i*. Since the cash flow streams are uneven, this calculation must be done with a financial calculator or computer spreadsheet with the IRR function. The discount rate that will equate the cash flow streams to the principal amount of $5,000,000 is 6%.

Accounting for the transaction, for the first two years, is as follows:

On issuance		
Cash	4,632,000	
Deferred financing cost	368,000	
Bond payable		5,000,000
At the end of the first year, to record interest expense		
Interest expense ($4,632,000 × 6%)	277,920	
Deferred financing cost		27,920
Cash ($5,000,000 × 5%)		250,000
At the end of the second year, to record interest expense		
Interest expense [($4,632,000 + $27,920) × 6%]	279,595	
Deferred financing cost		29,595
Cash		250,000

Note that interest expense is measured using the effective-interest method. Subsequent years would follow this pattern, and, after the 10th interest payment, the balance in the deferred financing cost account is zero.

[2] The discussion relates to liabilities carried at amortized cost. If liabilities are classified as fair-value-through-profit-and-loss (FVTPL), these costs are expensed immediately.

CONCEPT REVIEW

1. For a bond to sell at par, what must be the relationship between the nominal rate and the effective rate of interest? At a discount? At a premium?
2. When a bond is issued at a discount, why is interest expense higher than cash paid?
3. What happens to the fair value of an issued, outstanding bond when the yield rate increases? Is this reflected in the financial statements?
4. When there are upfront fees charged as a result of the issuance of a bond payable, is there an immediate expense? What happens to the effective interest rate?

DEBT DENOMINATED IN A FOREIGN CURRENCY

Many Canadian companies borrow from foreign lenders; most commonly, from U.S. lenders. These transactions are channelled through U.S. banks and other financial institutions and through the U.S. bond markets. Corporations also borrow in other currencies, such as euros, Japanese yen, and so on.

Exchange Risk

The most obvious point about these loans is that the borrowing company has exchange risk, caused by exchange fluctuations. For example, if a company borrows US$100,000 when the exchange rate for US$1.00 is Cdn$1.05, the company will receive Cdn$105,000. If the exchange rate changes to US$1.00 = Cdn$1.12 by the time that the debt must be repaid, the company will have to pay Cdn$112,000 to buy US$100,000 dollars for debt principal repayment and thus will have to repay more than it borrowed. This $7,000 difference ($105,000 less $112,000) is called an *exchange loss*, and it is equal to the change in the exchange rates multiplied by the principal: ($1.05 – $1.12) × US$100,000.

Note that exchange rates can be expressed in U.S. dollar equivalencies, as shown above, where US$1.00 = Cdn$1.05, or can be described as Canadian dollar equivalencies, Cdn$1.00 = US$0.9524 (i.e., $1.00 ÷ $1.05). There are also differences between buying and selling exchange rates, as quoted by exchange brokers or banks; the brokers make an element of profit on the spread between the buying and selling rates. *Rates for buying exchange should be used for liabilities.*

Hedging Companies may take a number of actions to reduce their risk of losses (and gains) from changes in exchange rates. **Hedges** reduce risk and typically involve arranging equal and offsetting cash flows in the desired currency. Hedges are a protective measure. Hedging will be explored in Chapter 15.

Accounting for Exchange Rate Fluctuations

As we saw in Chapter 12, the basic principle underlying valuation of foreign currency monetary liabilities is that they should be reported on the SFP in the equivalent amount of reporting currency (normally, Canadian dollars for Canadian companies) at the **spot rate** on the *reporting date*. The loan principal is originally translated into Canadian dollars on the day it is borrowed at the current, or spot, exchange rate. At every subsequent reporting date, the loan is *remeasured* at the spot rate. If exchange rates have changed, an exchange gain or loss will result. This gain or loss is *unrealized. The exchange gain or loss is included in earnings in the year in which it arises.*

Exhibit 13-5 illustrates accounting for a long-term loan, whose Canadian dollar equivalent is $545,000 when borrowed and $565,000 when retired. When the Canadian dollar equivalent goes up during the life of the bond, a loss is recorded. When the Canadian dollar equivalent goes down, a gain is recorded.

EXHIBIT 13-5

EXCHANGE GAINS AND LOSSES ON LONG-TERM DEBT PRINCIPAL

Data:

Four-year term loan, US$500,000
Funds borrowed 1 January 20X6; due 31 December 20X9
Exchange rates:

1 January 20X6	US$1 = Cdn$1.09
31 December 20X6	US$1 = Cdn$1.10
31 December 20X7	US$1 = Cdn$1.12
31 December 20X8	US$1 = Cdn$1.08
31 December 20X9	US$1 = Cdn$1.13

Entries:

Note: Entries are for principal only.

1 January 20X6—to record receipt of loan proceeds		
Cash ($500,000 × $1.09)	545,000	
Long-term debt		545,000
31 December 20X6—to record adjustment to spot rate		
Exchange loss	5,000	
Long-term debt [$500,000 × ($1.09 – $1.10)]		5,000
31 December 20X7—to record adjustment to spot rate		
Exchange loss	10,000	
Long-term debt [$500,000 × ($1.10 – $1.12)]		10,000
31 December 20X8—to record adjustment to spot rate		
Long-term debt [$500,000 × ($1.12 – $1.08)]	20,000	
Exchange gain		20,000
31 December 20X9—to record adjustment to spot rate		
Exchange loss	25,000	
Long-term debt [$500,000 × ($1.08 – $1.13)]		25,000
31 December 20X9—to repay loan		
Long-term debt ($500,000 × $1.13)	565,000	
Cash		565,000

Summary:

Canadian dollar cash borrowed	$545,000
Canadian dollar cash repaid	565,000
Exchange loss over the life of the loan	$ 20,000

Accounting recognition of loss:

20X6	$ 5,000 (dr.)
20X7	10,000 (dr.)
20X8	20,000 (cr.)
20X9	25,000 (dr.)
Total	$20,000 (dr.)

The effect of an exchange fluctuation appears in earnings in the year of the change in rates. This makes it easier for financial statement users to determine the impact of an exchange rate fluctuation on the company's financial position. Of course, it also makes earnings fluctuate if exchange rates are volatile. Note the volatility year-by-year in Exhibit 13-5 for the exchange gain or loss. Sizable gains are followed by sizable losses.

Interest Expense Annual interest, also denominated in the foreign currency, is accrued using the exchange rate in effect during the period—the *average exchange rate.* When it is paid, cash outflows are measured at the exchange rate in effect on that day. The difference between the expense and the cash paid is also an exchange gain or loss.

For example, if the US$500,000 loan had an interest rate of 7%, and exchange rates were US$1.00 = Cdn$1.08 on average over the first year, the interest expense accrual would be recorded as follows:

Interest expense ($500,000 × 7% × $1.08)	37,800	
Interest payable		37,800

At year-end, the exchange rate is $1.10, and the interest is paid:

Interest payable	37,800	
Exchange loss	700	
Cash ($500,000 × 7% × $1.10)		38,500

If the interest is not due at year-end, the interest payable account is adjusted to the year-end spot rate, and again an exchange gain or loss is recognized.

CONCEPT REVIEW

1. A Canadian company borrows US$1,000,000 when the exchange rate is Cdn$1.03. The exchange rate is $0.99 at the end of the fiscal year. How much long-term debt is reported on the statement of financial position? How much is the exchange gain or loss?
2. A loan requires that US$10,000 be paid in interest annually, at the end of each fiscal year. The average exchange rate is US$1 = Cdn$1.02, and the year-end rate is US$1 = Cdn$0.99. How much interest expense and exchange gain is recorded?

CAPITALIZATION OF BORROWING COSTS

Borrowing costs are normally expensed. However, any such cost that is *directly attributable to the acquisition, construction, or production of a qualifying asset* forms part of the cost of that asset and *must be capitalized.* This is consistent with the general principal that all acquisition costs, including all costs of getting the asset ready to use, are appropriately part of its capital cost. Capitalization is limited, though, by the fair value cap imposed through impairment tests. That is, the maximum asset value is fair value regardless of the component costs.

Qualifying Assets Borrowing costs can be capitalized for **qualifying assets**, which are limited to non-financial assets, such as inventories, intangible assets, machinery, and office or manufacturing facilities. Borrowing costs cannot be capitalized on financial assets, such as investments.

Borrowing costs are to be capitalized if the assets take a substantial time to get ready for intended use or sale. There must be a time delay for construction, customization, or shipping.

For example, inventory that is manufactured over a short period of time is not eligible for borrowing cost capitalization. Also, if an asset is ready for its intended use (or resale) when it is acquired, no borrowing costs can be capitalized. If an asset is purchased and the shipping time is lengthy, then borrowing costs are capitalized for the shipping period.

Borrowing costs need not be capitalized on inventory if the inventory is carried at fair value (e.g., biological inventories), or if borrowing costs relate to inventories that are *manufactured in large quantities on a regular basis*. For these two cases, companies may choose whether to capitalize or not, depending on their reporting objectives and circumstances.

Borrowing Costs Defined Borrowing costs to be capitalized include interest, measured using the effective-interest method, plus any other cost that an entity incurs in connection with the borrowing of funds. This includes expensed upfront fees, and foreign currency adjustments. **Imputed interest** on equity is not eligible for capitalization.

Capitalized borrowing costs might be those that are specific to the acquisition transaction. If there is a specific loan in place to finance the acquisition, identifying borrowing costs is straightforward. If a qualifying asset is purchased from *general borrowings* rather than with a specific loan, then the calculations are more complex because it is harder to associate the borrowing with the acquisition. If this is the case, *the average borrowing rate is calculated on the total of general borrowings,* and this rate is applied to the specific expenditures made, for the time period involved.

Capitalization begins when the following three criteria are all met:

- When money is borrowed; *and*
- A payment is made on an asset; *and*
- Activities begin that will make the asset ready to use.

Capitalization ends when the asset is put into use or is ready for its intended purpose. If *substantially all* the activities to get the asset into use are completed, then capitalization should cease. Finally, capitalization stops if the work is not progressing—if work is stopped because of a strike or other delay, capitalization is not permitted for the idle period.

Capitalization Calculations Hercules Limited has purchased a custom piece of machinery overseas, with the following payments made:

1 February payment	$340,000	Hercules buys the equipment but contracts the supplier for customization. Customization work commences.
31 March payment	50,000	Customization is complete and equipment is shipped.
31 August final payment	40,000	Equipment arrives, is tested, and is accepted; the equipment is placed in use on this date.
Total cost	$430,000	

The company had no specific loan for this acquisition but paid for the equipment out of general borrowed money. The company's capital structure and borrowing costs for the year:

	Average Balance	Borrowing Cost
Operating line of credit	$ 500,000	$ 31,000
Term bank loan	2,300,000	119,000
Long-term loan	5,200,000	210,000
Mortgage loan for manufacturing facility	4,800,000	185,000
Equity financing	8,500,000	—

The capitalization rate is based on the general loans, *excluding the mortgage loan specific to the manufacturing facility* and excluding any (imputed) cost of capital for equity financing. The mortgage loan is excluded because it is not *general borrowing*, and its specific purpose is not related to the machinery.

This produces a rate of 4.5% ($31,000 + $119,000 + $210,000)/($500,000 + $2,300,000 + $5,200,000). This rate is then used to calculate the borrowing cost that can be capitalized for the months between purchase and first use of the asset:

Payment	Calculation	Capitalizable Borrowing Costs
1 February payment	$340,000 × 7/12 × 4.5% (1 February–31 August)	$8,925
31 March payment	$50,000 × 5/12 × 4.5% (31 March–31 August)	938
31 August final payment	$40,000 × 0/12 × 4.5% (31 August–31 August)	—
		$9,863

The capitalization period includes the shipping period, the installation period, and the testing period, and ends when the machinery is put in service.

If the interest had previously been expensed, the following adjusting entry would now be made:

Equipment	9,863	
Interest expense		9,863

Timing Depreciation for the equipment is based on its total cost, which now includes interest and accordingly is higher than if the interest had not been capitalized. In the end, interest is expensed either way—*up front* if no capitalization were appropriate, or *over time*, through depreciation after capitalization. With capitalization, though, the cost of the asset is more completely captured, and the cost of acquisition is reflected with more accuracy.

CONCEPT REVIEW

1. What kinds of assets are eligible for interest capitalization?
2. When an asset is paid for out of general borrowing, how is the borrowing rate calculated?

DEBT RETIREMENT

Derecognition

When debt is recorded in the accounts, it is *recognized*. When it is removed from the accounts, it is **derecognized** or *extinguished*. The vast majority of financial liabilities, both current and long term, are derecognized because the company *pays the amount of the liability* to the creditor or bond holder at maturity. Sometimes, debt is repaid and derecognized before its maturity, either by arrangement with the debt holder or through open-market transactions.

Derecognition at Maturity

Debt retirement at maturity is straightforward. By the time the debt reaches full maturity, all the related discount or premium is fully amortized, thereby making the carrying value of the debt equal to its face value. As well, any debt issue cost will be fully amortized.

For example, assume that a company pays the full amount of an outstanding $5,000,000 bond at maturity. The entry to record extinguishment of the debt is:

Bonds payable	5,000,000	
Cash		5,000,000

There are no gains or losses to be recorded. Any costs incurred to retire the bond (e.g., trustee management fees, clerical costs, or payment fees) will be charged immediately to expense.

Derecognition Prior to Maturity

Borrowers will sometimes retire debt before maturity. Retirement of debt may be motivated by a wish to improve the debt-to-equity ratio, facilitate future debt issuances, and eliminate debt covenants.

Bonds may be purchased on the open market at any time. In an open-market purchase of bonds, the issuer pays the fair value of the bond (which is the present value using current market interest rates), as would any investor buying the bonds. Alternatively, the terms for early retirement might be set out in the original bond indenture. Bonds may be **redeemable**, which means that the *borrower* may pay back the loan using a **call option** that sets a *specific price* at a specific time prior to maturity. *Investors can force repayment* of a bond if the bond is **retractable**.

If bonds carry a call privilege, the issuer may retire the debt by paying the call price, or redemption price, during a specified period. Typically, the **call price** exceeds face value by a certain percentage (e.g., 5%), which may decline each year of the bond term. If the call premium were 5%, a $100,000 bond would be redeemed for a payment of $105,000, plus accrued interest, if any.

Fair Value and the Gain or Loss A major factor in retiring bonds before maturity is the change in fair value that is caused when market yield rates change. Open market retirement prices are based on this fair value. When interest rates increase, the fair value of an existing liability will decline because the yield rate has increased. The fair value will then rest below book value. However, the only way to *record* this change in value is to repay the bond.

Examine the following cases, relating to a $500,000, 5% bond, originally sold to yield 6%, that pays interest semi-annually and has 18 periods left to maturity:

	Case 1 (Yield Rate Now 7%)	Case 2 (Yield Rate Now 4.5%)
Bond carrying value—amortized cost	$465,616	$465,616
Bond fair value—present value based on market interest rates	$434,052 (7% yield)	$518,335 (4.5% yield)
Retirement price	Fair value	Fair value
Gain or loss recorded	Gain of $31,564	Loss of $52,719

If market interest rates *increase* (causing bond prices to *fall*), firms could retire existing bonds by buying them on the open market, triggering a gain and immediate higher earnings. For example, in Case 1, market interest rates are now 7%, and this bond, with a book value of $465,616, can be retired on the open market for $434,052. A gain of $31,564 is recorded. Since a replacement bond will have the same fair value as the old bond, this *economic decision* is value-neutral. However, it has distinct *accounting implications* because the gain is recorded.

If interest rates *decrease* (causing bond prices to *rise*), firms would retire existing bonds at a loss, and earnings will fall in the retirement period. For example, in Case 2, market interest rates are now 4.5%, and a bond with a book value of $465,616 can be retired on the open market for $518,335. A loss of $52,719 is recorded.

In both cases, the retirement decision results in recording a gain or loss that *reflects the changed fair value of the bond.* Of course, *whether the retirement happens or not, the fair value of the bond has still changed,* which has a natural impact on the value of the firm as a whole.

Now, consider the impact of a call provision. A call provision at the company's option protects the company from a change in fair value caused by a decline in interest rates. If the $500,000 bond above specified that the company could call the bond for 102% of par, the highest value to be paid out would be $510,000. This fair value has an implicit yield rate of approximately 4.7% when $n = 18$ and caps the fair value of the liability at this level. If market rates fell below 4.7%, the company would have an economic, if not an accounting, incentive to retire. The real frustration is that retirement at $510,000 would still trigger an accounting loss; this is the result when the accounting system is based on amortized cost rather than fair value.

ETHICAL ISSUES

Some companies will enter into retirement transactions simply to trigger the gain or loss. Some might wish a boost to earnings in the current year (Case 1), while others will be looking to trigger a loss in the current year (Case 2). These companies may have various incentive contracts that provide motives for such activities. For example, a bonus based on earnings might trigger a repurchase as in Case 1. A company in a loss year, in which there will be no bonuses, may trigger a loss as in Case 2 to "clear the deck" for lower interest costs in the subsequent years and improve the chance of a bonus at that time.

Recording Derecognition Prior to Maturity

Accounting for debt retirement prior to maturity involves the following:

- Update interest expense to the retirement date, through recording interest payable, discount or premium amortization, and related debt-issue costs;
- Remove the liability accounts, including the appropriate portion of the unamortized premium or discount and bond issue costs;
- Record the transfer of cash, other resources, or the issuance of new debt securities; and
- Record a gain or loss.

Classification of the Gain or Loss A gain or loss on bond retirement is classified either as an *ordinary* gain and loss or as an *unusual* item, depending on its frequency and the circumstances surrounding the transaction. A gain or loss is *deferred and amortized* over the term of any "replacement" debt, *if* and *only if* the transaction is a *substitution or modification of debt.* This circumstance is explained later in this section.

Example As a basis for an example, Exhibit 13-6 repeats a portion of the amortization table for the Gresham bonds from Exhibit 13-2. Assume that interest rates have increased since the bonds were issued and that on 1 March 20X6, Gresham purchases 20% ($20,000 face value) of the bonds on the open market at 90. The price decline reflects increased market interest rates. Gresham has undertaken this transaction because the company has idle funds and wishes to improve (reduce) its debt-to-equity ratio.

EXHIBIT 13-6

OPEN-MARKET EXTINGUISHMENT

Gresham Limited Bonds

Data:

Issue date: 1 January 20X5
Stated (nominal) interest rate: 7% per annum
Interest payment date: 31 December
Maturity date: 31 December 20X9
Bond repurchase date: 1 March 20X6
Bond face value extinguished: $20,000

Total face value: $100,000
Bond date: 1 January 20X5
Yield rate at issuance: 6% per annum

Bond repurchase price: 90

Partial Amortization Table

Date	Interest Payment at 7%	Interest Expense at 6%	Premium Amortization	Unamortized Premium	Net Bond Liability
1 Jan. 20X5				$4,213	$104,213
31 Dec. 20X5	$7,000	$6,253	$747	3,466	103,466
31 Dec. 20X6	7,000	6,208	792	2,674	102,674

Entries:

1 March 20X6—update interest and premium amortization on portion retired

Interest expense (6% × $103,466 × 2/12 × 20% of the bond)	207	
Premium on bonds payable	26	
Interest payable ($20,000 bonds being redeemed × 7% × 2/12)		233

1 March 20X6—record purchase of bonds; eliminate relevant accounts and recognize gain

Bonds payable	20,000	
Premium on bonds payable ($3,466 unamortized bond premium × 20% redeemed) – $26 amortized in previous entry	667	
Interest payable	233	
Cash ($20,000 × 90% purchase price) + $233 interest payable		18,233
Gain on bond redemption		2,667

The $2,667 gain on bond retirement is the difference between the net book value of the bond and the cash paid on retirement. Brokerage fees and other costs of retiring the bonds decrease the gain or increase the loss.

Extinguishment does not affect the accounting for the remaining 80% of the bond issue; 80% of the values in the amortization table would be used for the remaining bond term.

Defeasance

A transaction called a **defeasance** may be used to engineer derecognition of a bond liability without formally repaying it; repayment is often not appealing to the investor. To set the stage for a defeasance, the original bond indenture will contain a provision that permits the corporation that issued the bonds to transfer investments into an irrevocable, trusteed fund. The trustee is then responsible for interest and principal payments on the debt, using money generated by the investments.

If and when such a trust is set up and fully funded according to terms in the bond indenture, accounting standards allow the liability to be derecognized.

The bonds still exist, but the trust assumes all responsibility for them, and the issuer has no further liability. Furthermore, the investor has consented to the transaction as part of the original bond indenture.

The entry to record a defeasance is a debit to the liability account and credit to cash or investments, with a gain or loss recorded for any difference in amounts.

Example Assume that a bond with a par value of $100,000 and remaining unamortized premium of $6,000 is *defeased* according to the terms of the bond indenture for $92,600. The $92,600 is the present value of the bond payments, discounted at market rates, or the investment required in interest-bearing securities that will yield interest and principal amounts sufficient to cover the required future cash flows for the bond.

Note that market yields must have increased to the extent that investments of $92,600 generate sufficient cash over time to both pay the bond interest and repay principal at maturity. The following entry would be made:

Bonds payable (par value)	100,000	
Premium on bonds payable (remaining balance)	6,000	
Cash		92,600
Gain on bond defeasance		13,400

Taking the liability off the books in essence nets the liability with the investments segregated for liability repayment. Netting is not allowed unless very stringent criteria are met, and an important criterion for netting is that the *borrower has a legal release from the creditor.* The agreement in the bond indenture establishes this release.

In-Substance Defeasance **In-substance defeasance** establishes a trust for bond interest and principal repayment, *even though the original bond indenture is silent on the possibility.* In essence, it establishes the trust without creditor permission (or perhaps without even creditor knowledge of the arrangement). In the past, an in-substance extinguishment would be recorded, derecognizing the bonds and recognizing a gain or loss, if certain criteria were met.

Under current accounting standards, this is no longer allowed because there is no legal release provided by the creditor. Accordingly, the company would record a separate investment account if funds were transferred to the trustee, and then would continue to report the liability and the separate investment.

The Concern about In-Substance Defeasance Standard setters had many reasons to be concerned about in-substance defeasance transactions recorded as extinguishments.

ETHICAL ISSUES

Companies demonstrated a tendency to set up an in-substance defeasance if interest rates increased. The increase in interest rates reduced the amount of investment needed to fully service the related debt, (i.e., reduced the fair value of the debt). This defeasance transaction resulted in a gain for the company. The transaction might have been used primarily to manipulate earnings.

Another concern of standard setters is that the borrowing company would have debt legally outstanding that is not reported on the SFP. This situation does not appeal to the basic *representational faithfulness* of financial reporting.

Standard setters were also concerned that something might go awry with the trust or the debt to make the in-substance defeasance economically or legally unsuccessful. For example, if the debt were subject to financial statement covenants, and the covenants were breached, then the debt might come due immediately. Alternatively, assets in the fund may lose value unexpectedly. If either of these things happened, the investments in the trusteed fund would not be sufficient to make all required payments.

For all these reasons, *debt may not be derecognized as a result of an in-substance defeasance.*

Substitution or Modification of Debt

A company may go to an existing lender, and essentially *repay a loan and reborrow in one transaction,* replacing an existing loan prior to its due date. As for an early retirement, the motive may be a desire to borrow at a different interest rate, record movement in fair value of the existing obligation, or to release a restrictive covenant. This is called a **substitution of debt** or **modification of debt**.

If the exchange results in significantly different terms, the company must record an extinguishment (loan retired at a gain or loss), and a new loan, with the two transactions accounted for independently. This will be the case as long as the present value of the new loan arrangement is at least 10% different than the present value of the old loan arrangement, including fees and transaction costs. The presence of a 10% difference implies that there has been a change in the *substance* of the agreement.

On the other hand, if there is less than a 10% difference in present value, no gain or loss on retirement is recorded. Balances of the old loan are rolled to the new loan. Any additional fees from such a substitution or modification may be amortized over the remaining term of the modified liability.

CONCEPT REVIEW

1. Under what circumstances is the change in the fair value of a bond liability recorded in the financial statements?
2. What is a retractable bond?
3. How is a gain or loss on retirement of bonds calculated?
4. What are the accounting implications of a defeasance transaction? An in-substance defeasance?

STATEMENT OF CASH FLOWS AND DISCLOSURE

Changes in long-term debt trigger disclosure on the statement of cash flows (SCF), and also require significant disclosure so that financial statement readers will appreciate the future cash flow implications as well as the agreed-upon terms and conditions.

Statement of Cash Flows

The SCF will reflect cash paid and cash received. The presence of multiple accounts related to a particular liability can complicate analysis in the area. For example, consider the accounts of Hilmon Limited:

	20X5	20X4
Bonds payable, 5%	$5,000,000	0
Discount on bonds payable	246,000	0
Interest payable	125,000	$ 25,000
Bonds payable, 4 1/2%	0	2,000,000
Discount on bonds payable	0	18,000

During the year, the 5% bonds were issued for $4,750,000. The 4½% bonds were retired for 102. Interest expense was $252,000, and a loss was reported on retiring the 4½% bond. Discount amortization was recorded during the period—$4,000 on the discount for the 5% bond and $2,000 on the discount for the 4½% bond before retirement.

These transactions would appear on the SCF as follows:

1. In the financing section, an inflow of cash from issuing the 5% bond, $4,750,000, is reported. The proceeds are reported at their actual cash amount, and par value is not separately reported.
2. In the financing section, an outflow of cash from retiring the 4½% bond, $2,040,000 ($2,000,000 × 102%), is reported. Again, the par value of the bond is irrelevant, as is the carrying value. It is the cash flow that is important. It is *not acceptable* to net an issuance with a disposal or lump several issuances and disposals together. Transactions are to be shown separately.
3. In the operating activities section, reported using the indirect method, the loss on the bond retirement must be added back to earnings. This loss is $56,000. (The carrying value of the bond on the day of retirement was $1,984,000, including the discount but after this year's $2,000 discount amortization. The cost of bond retirement was $2,040,000; the difference is the $56,000 loss.)
4. In the operating activities section, interest expense of $252,000 is added back.
5. On the SCF, interest paid can be classified as an operating activity or a financing activity. The cash paid for interest is $146,000 (the expense, $252,000 less $6,000 of discount amortization and also reduced for the increase in interest payable of $100,000).

Disclosures for Long-Term Liabilities

Most liabilities are financial instruments, and significant disclosure is required. This disclosure was reviewed in Chapter 12. Remember that, among many other elements of disclosure, a company must disclose accounting policies used for liabilities, the *fair value* of each class of financial liability, and the method used to establish fair value (discounted cash flow, most likely).

Required disclosure for long-term debt also includes information primarily related to the terms of the debt contract, security, and future cash flows. Some of the highlights are:

- The title of the issue, interest rate, interest expense on long-term debt in total, maturity date, amount outstanding, assets pledged as collateral, sinking fund, if any, and redemption or conversion privileges;
- The aggregate amount of payments required in the next five years to meet sinking fund or retirement provisions;
- If the debt is denominated in a foreign currency, then the currency in which the debt is to be repaid;
- Secured liabilities must be shown separately, and the fact that they are secured must be disclosed; and
- Details of any defaults of the company in principal, interest, sinking fund, or redemption provisions, carrying value of loans payable in default, and any remedy of the default that was undertaken by the financial statement completion date.

It is also interesting to note the requirement to disclose objectives, policies, and processes for managing risk and managing capital must be disclosed. Information must be disclosed to allow assessment of the significance of liabilities for the company's financial position and performance. Such disclosure is extensive, and includes both qualitative and quantitative elements.

Reporting Example Exhibit 13-7 includes *selected* disclosures related to capital disclosure and fair value of financial instruments for AltaGas Ltd.

Note that the company reports that it uses the effective-interest method in the accounting policy disclosure note. AltaGas defines the term " capital" under capital disclosures, and provides its target and actual debt-to-total capitalization ratios. The company also reports cost versus fair value of financial liabilities in a separate note. Long-term debt has an amortized cost of approximately $1.2 billion; this is also its fair value, which implies that interest rates have been stable. Discounting is used to establish the fair value of long-term debt.

EXHIBIT 13-7

SELECTED NOTE DISCLOSURE, ALTAGAS LTD.

2. SUMMARY OF SIGNIFICANT ACCOUNTING POLICIES

...

Financial Instruments

...

Other financial liabilities not classified as held-for-trading are recognized at amortized cost, using the effective interest method.

...

14. CAPITAL DISCLOSURE

AltaGas' objective for managing capital is to maintain its investment grade credit ratings and to maximize the profitability of its existing assets and grow its energy infrastructure to create long-term value and enhance returns for its investors. AltaGas considers shareholders' equity (including accumulated other comprehensive income), short-term and long-term debt (including current portion) less cash and cash equivalents comprise its capital structure.

The use of debt or equity funding is based on AltaGas' capital structure, which is determined by considering the norms and risks associated with each of its business segments. AltaGas' target debt-to-total capitalization ratio is approximately 50 percent. AltaGas' debt-to-total capitalization ratio as at December 31, 2011, was 49.3 percent (December 31, 2010—42.7 percent).

	December 31 2011	December 31 2010
Debt		
Short-term debt	$ 16,824	$ 9,478
Current portion of long-term debt	105,962	1,508
Long-term debt	1,201,473	893,498
Less cash and cash equivalents	(4,220)	(2,109)
	1,320,039	902,375
Shareholders' equity	1,356,714	1,211,031
Total capitalization	$2,676,753	$2,113,406
Debt-to-total capitalization ratio (%)	49.3	42.7

All of the borrowing facilities have covenants customary for these types of facilities that must be met at the end of each calendar quarter. AltaGas has been in compliance with these covenants each quarter since the issuance of the facilities.

continued on next page

EXHIBIT 13-7 (*cont'd*)

15. FINANCIAL INSTRUMENTS AND FINANCIAL RISK MANAGEMENT

Fair Values of Financial Instruments

...

The fair value of long-term debt has been estimated based on discounted future interest and principal payments using estimated interest rates.

...

Summary of Fair Values December 31, 2011	Held-for trading	Cash flow hedges	Loans and receivables	Available-for-sale	Other financial liabilities	Non-financial instruments	Total
Financial liabilities							
Accounts payable and accrued liabilities[1]	$ —	$ —	$ —	$ —	$ 79,316	$247,827	$ 327,143
Dividends payable	—	—	—	—	10,264	—	10,264
Short-term debt[1]	—	—	—	—	16,824	—	16,824
Current portion of long-term debt[2]					105,962		105,962
Customer deposits[1]	—	—	—	—	25,570	—	25,570
Risk management liabilities (current)	54,009	18,964	—	—	—	—	72,973
Other current liabilities[1]					1,717	9,597	11,314
Long-term debt[3]	—	—	—	—	1,201,473	—	1,201,473
Risk management liabilities (noncurrent)	20,250	358	—	—	—	—	20,608
Other long-term liabilities	—	—	—	—	10	28,800	28,810
	$ 74,259	$ 19,322	$ —	$ —	$1,441,136	$286,224	$1,820,941

(1) Due to the nature and/or short maturity of these financial instruments, the carrying amount approximates the fair value.

(2) Fair value of current portion of long-term debt is approximately $103.4 million

(3) Fair value of long-term debt excluding non-financial instruments is approximately $1,255.6 million.

Source: AltaGas Ltd. 2011 Annual Financial Statements, www.sedar.com, posted 12 March 2012.

LOOKING AHEAD

Recording Fair Value

Many *financial assets* are recorded at fair value in the financial statements. Fair values are felt to be highly relevant to users, because they reflect the realities of the company and its business environment. Why not extend fair values to liabilities, too? Fair value measurement of *financial liabilities* might be considered *reasonably determinable* in stable markets, since fair value is based on discounting contractually based (i.e., *certain)* cash flows.

The major estimation variable in the discounting model is the choice of an appropriate yield rate. This decision can be problematic. Of particular concern is the situation that arises if a company's financial condition deteriorates. Deterioration sharply increases the risk premium that a lender would expect, and the yield rate used for discounting would accordingly rise. With a higher discount rate, fair value declines, and a *gain* results. This is counter-intuitive when a company is in financial distress!

Standard setters are contemplating a change in standards, to give companies the *option* of recording *financial liabilities at fair value.* To avoid volatility in earnings, the suggestion is to record the changes in value of these liabilities in comprehensive income and then in accumulated other comprehensive income (OCI) on the SFP, effectively bypassing earnings. Others suggest that fair values are not appropriate because the financing arrangements are meant to be held to maturity, not traded. Standard setters continue to struggle with these issues.

ACCOUNTING STANDARDS FOR PRIVATE ENTERPRISES

ASPE and IFRS standards for long-term liabilities are similar. There are some differences in terminology and approach, but the impact of these differences is not significant in the bigger picture. Much of the similarity stems from the common financial instruments rules, which were developed as a joint project between the IASB, Canada, and the United States. Since these standards govern the accounting model for a significant section of the financial statements, the similarity of standards between these major jurisdictions provides a fair bit of common ground. There are several major differences, however.

Capitalization of Borrowing Costs Capitalization of borrowing costs *is not required* for private enterprises as it is under IFRS. Companies may choose to capitalize or not, although imputed interest on equity financing may *not* be capitalized. If companies follow a policy of capitalization, ASPE includes no guidelines governing the kinds of borrowing costs to be capitalized, commencement and completion dates, or determining the costs of general borrowing pools. Companies must disclose policy in the area and the extent of interest capitalized.

In this area, as in most other areas, disclosure is less onerous under ASPE compared with IFRS.

Straight-Line Amortization As we noted in Chapter 12, ASPE allows the use of the straight-line method to unwind a discount or premium. Straight-line amortization is also permitted for upfront costs. The effective-interest method *is permitted but is not required.*

Refer to Exhibit 13-8, which repeats the amortization table for Situation B for the Gresham bonds reviewed earlier in the chapter. These bonds sold at a premium of $4,213, reflecting the fact that the bonds paid interest at 7%, but the market yield was lower, at 6%. When straight-line amortization is used to unwind the premium, premium amortization is set at $843 per year. This is the premium divided by the five-period term of the bond. Interest expense is then the combination of interest paid, $7,000, less the premium amortization. The expense is the same amount each period.

EXHIBIT 13-8

AMORTIZATION TABLE FOR GRESHAM LIMITED BONDS

Situation B—Bonds Sold at Premium; Straight-Line Amortization

Date	Interest Payment at 7%	Interest Expense[1]	Premium Amortization[2]	Unamortized Premium[3]	Net Bond Liability[4]
1 Jan. 20X5				$4,213	$104,213
31 Dec. 20X5	$ 7,000	$ 6,157	$ 843	3,370	103,370
31 Dec. 20X6	7,000	6,157	843	2,527	102,527
31 Dec. 20X7	7,000	6,157	843	1,684	101,684
31 Dec. 20X8	7,000	6,158	842	842	100,842
31 Dec. 20X9	7,000	6,158	842	0	100,000
	$35,000	$30,787	$4,213		

(1) $7,000 – $843
(2) $4,213 ÷ 5 ; rounded
(3) Previous unamortized premium – Current period's amortization
(4) $100,000 face value + Current unamortized premium

Compared with the effective-interest method, interest expense is not as accurately measured. Interest expense should be 6% each period, reflecting the yield rate. However, for example, in 20X5 interest expense is $6,157, or 5.9% of the opening liability balance of $104,213. In 20X9, interest expense of $6,158 is 6.1% of the opening liability balance of $100,842. These measurement differences seem small, but may be significant in certain circumstances.

Exhibit 13-9 contrasts the two amortization methods.

EXHIBIT 13-9

COMPARISON OF STRAIGHT-LINE AND EFFECTIVE-INTEREST AMORTIZATION

	Effective Interest	Straight Line
Calculations:		
Calculation of interest expense	Effective rate × Net carrying value of bond	Cash paid + Discount amortization or – Premium amortization
Calculation of discount or premium amortization	Difference between cash paid and expense	Discount or premium ÷ Period that bond is outstanding
Patterns:		
Annual interest expense	Changes each year	Constant over term
Annual interest expense as a percentage of beginning book value (interest rate)	Constant over term	Changes each year

RELEVANT STANDARDS

CPA Canada Handbook, Part I (IASB):

- IAS 1, Presentation of Financial Statements
- IAS 21, The Effects of Changes in Foreign Exchange Rates
- IAS 23, Borrowing Costs
- IAS 32, Financial Instruments: Disclosure and Presentation
- IAS 39, Financial Instruments: Recognition and Measurement
- IFRS 9, Financial Instruments

CPA Canada Handbook, Part II (ASPE):

- Section 1651, Foreign Currency Translation
- Section 3210, Long-Term Debt
- Section 3856, Financial Instruments

SUMMARY OF KEY POINTS

1. Debt financing introduces financial leverage in a company's capital structure, and increases financial risk.
2. Short-term financing is available through trade credit, promissory notes, and short-term bank loans of various kinds.
3. Long-term financing can be sourced through financial institutions or capital markets. Common loan vehicles are term loans, commercial mortgages, and bonds.
4. Long-term debt often involves debt covenants to provide reassurance and recourse to lenders. Covenants include accounting-based covenants and restricted actions.
5. Long-term debt is usually classified as a financial liability, in the *other financial liabilities* category, and is carried at amortized cost. Bonds payable are a classic example of long-term debt instruments that specify the face value paid at maturity and the stated interest rate payable according to a fixed schedule.
6. The recorded value at date of issuance for long-term debt is the present value of all future cash flows discounted at the current market rate for debt securities of equivalent risk. The net book value of long-term debt at a reporting date is amortized cost, which is the present value of all remaining cash payments required, discounted at the market rate at issuance.
7. Using the effective-interest method, interest expense is the product of the market rate *at issuance* and the net balance the liability (including the premium or discount) at the beginning of the period. Interest is accrued with the passage of time.
8. The price of a bond at issuance is the present value of all future cash flows discounted at the current market rate of interest for bonds of similar risk. Bonds are sold at a premium if the stated rate exceeds the market rate and at a discount if the stated rate is less than the market rate. The price of a bond issued between interest dates is based on a pro-rata calculation of present values at interest dates.
9. Accrued interest is paid by the investor when a bond is issued between interest dates; the investor is then entitled to a full interest payment on the next interest payment date. The issuer records accrued interest received as a credit to interest payable, which is repaid on the next interest payment date.
10. Debt issue costs and upfront fees are sometimes involved in the issuance of debt. Such fees are a cost of borrowing and are charged to interest expense over the life of the loan. This increases the effective-interest cost of the loan.
11. Long-term loans may be denominated in a foreign currency, which causes exchange gains or losses when exchange rates fluctuate. Exchange gains and losses are reported in earnings.
12. Borrowing costs can be capitalized on eligible non-financial assets if there are costs relating to loans for the period of time to acquire, construct, or produce such an asset. Costs of specific loans or general borrowing can be capitalized, subject to a fair value cap.
13. Bonds retired, or derecognized, at maturity are recorded by reducing the liability and the asset given in repayment. No gain or loss arises. Bonds retired/derecognized before maturity, through call, redemption, or open market purchase, typically involve recognition of a gain or loss as the difference between the book value of the debt (including all related accounts, such as unamortized premium or discount, and upfront fees) and the consideration paid.
14. A defeasance is an arrangement whereby the debtor irrevocably places investments in a trust fund for the sole purpose of using those resources to pay interest and principal on specified debt. The creditor agrees to this and legal release is given. A defeasance is recognized on the books and results in derecognition of the liability.

15. If a bond is subject to a substitution or modification of terms, an extinguishment (with a gain or loss) must be recognized and a new loan recorded if the present value of the new arrangement is 10% different from the old arrangement.

16. Disclosures for long-term debt include significant disclosure related to accounting policy, nature and extent of risks, as well as fair value. Other disclosure relates to the terms of debt contracts, including the major conditions and cash flows agreed to in the loan contract.

KEY TERMS

bond date
bond indenture
call option
call price
credit facility
debenture
debt covenants
debt issuance costs
defeasance
derecognized
EBITDA
effective interest rate
face value
hedges
imputed interest
in-substance defeasance
incremental borrowing rate (IBR)
interest payment dates
long-term loans
maturity date
modification of debt
nominal interest rate
operating line of credit
qualifying asset
redeemable
retractable
spot rate
substitution of debt
term loan
yield

REVIEW PROBLEM 13-1

On 1 August 20X6, Pismo Corporation issued bonds with the following characteristics:

a. $50,000 total face value
b. 12% nominal rate
c. 16% yield rate
d. Interest dates are 1 February, 1 May, 1 August, and 1 November
e. Bond date is 31 October 20X5
f. Maturity date is 1 November 20X10

Required:

1. Provide all entries required for the bond issue through 1 February 20X7 using the effective-interest method. The company has a 31 December year-end.
2. On 1 June 20X8, Pismo retired $20,000 of bonds at 98 through an open market purchase. Provide the entries to update the bond accounts in 20X8 (entries have been completed through 1 May 20X8) for this portion of the bond and to retire the bonds.
3. Provide the entries required on 1 August 20X8.

REVIEW PROBLEM 13-1—SOLUTION

1. *1 August 20X6—issue bonds*

Cash	43,917[1]	
Discount on bonds payable ($50,000 – $43,917)	6,083	
Bonds payable		50,000

[1] Four and one-quarter years, or 17 quarters, remain in the bond term: $43,917 = [$50,000 × (P/F, 4%, 17)] + [($50,000 × 3%) × (P/A, 4%,17)]

1 November 20X6—interest payment date

Interest expense	1,757[1]	
Discount on bonds payable		257
Cash		1,500[2]

[1] $1,757 = $43,917 × 4%
[2] $1,500 = $50,000 × 3%

31 December 20X6—adjusting entry

Interest expense	1,178[1]	
Discount on bonds payable		178
Interest payable		1,000[2]

[1] $1,178 = ($43,917 + $257) × 4% × (2/3 of quarter)
[2] $1,000 = $1,500 × 2/3

1 February 20X7—interest payment date

Interest expense	589[1]	
Interest payable	1,000	
Discount on bonds payable		89
Cash		1,500

[1] $589 = ($43,917 + $257) × 4% × (1/3 of quarter)

2. On 1 May 20X8, the remaining term of the bonds is 2½ years, or 10 quarters, and the $20,000 of bonds to be retired have the following book value:

$18,378 = [$20,000 × (P/F, 4%,10)] + [($20,000 × 3%) × (P/A, 4%,10)]

On 1 May 20X8, the remaining discount on the portion of bonds to be retired is therefore $1,622 ($20,000 – $18,378).

1 June 20X8—update relevant bond accounts before retirement

Interest expense	245[1]	
Discount on bonds payable		45
Cash		200[2]

1 June 20X8—remove relevant bond accounts

Bonds payable	20,000	
Loss, bond extinguishment	1,177	
Discount on bonds payable		1,577[3]
Cash (.98 × $20,000)		19,600

[1] $245 = $18,378 × 4% × 1/3 (one month of the three-month period) (or 16% × 1/12)
[2] $200 = $20,000 × 3% × 1/3 (or 12% × 1/12)
[3] $1,577 = $1,622 – $45

3. On 1 May 20X8, the remaining term of the bonds is 2½ years, or 10 quarters, and the remaining $30,000 of bonds have the following book value:

$$\$27,567 = \$30,000\ (P/F,\ 4\%,\ 10) + [(\$30,000 \times 3\%) \times (P/A,\ 4\%,10)]$$

On 1 May 20X8, the remaining discount is therefore $2,433 (i.e., $30,000 – $27,567).

1 August 20X8—interest payment date

Interest expense	1,103[1]	
Discount on bonds payable		203
Cash		900[2]

[1] $1,103 = $27,567 × 4%
[2] $900 = $30,000 × 3%

QUESTIONS

Q13-1 What is the primary advantage of trade credit?

Q13-2 What type of bank loan is most frequently secured with accounts receivable and inventory? Land and buildings?

Q13-3 What are the advantages of long-term loans over equity financing?

Q13-4 Describe two different repayment patterns for a long-term loan.

Q13-5 What is the difference between an amortization period and term for a long-term loan?

Q13-6 Other than a financial institution, what entities might be willing to extend a long-term loan to a company?

Q13-7 Name two accounting covenants and two restricted actions that may be established in a bond indenture.

Q13-8 Distinguish between the par value and the issue price of a bond. When are they the same? When are they different? Explain. If a $5,000 bond is sold for 101, how much cash is paid/received?

Q13-9 A bond is issued at 98, and market yield rates decline after issuance. What happens to the fair value of the bond? Is this change reflected on the company's books?

Q13-10 Explain why and how a bond discount and bond premium affect (a) the statement of financial position and (b) earnings of the issuer of the bond.

Q13-11 When the end of the accounting period of the issuer is not on a bond interest date, adjusting entries must be made for (a) accrued interest and (b) discount or premium amortization. Explain in general terms what each adjustment amount represents.

Q13-12 When bonds are sold (or purchased) between interest dates, accrued interest must be recognized. Explain why.

Q13-13 How would the payment of a $5,000 upfront administration fee on a $50,000, 6%, five-year loan affect subsequent recognition of interest expense?

Q13-14 Assume that a Canadian company borrowed US$325,000, for five years, when US$1.00 = Cdn$1.01. If the exchange rate at the end of the first year is US$1.00 = Cdn$1.03, and at the end of the second year is US$1.00 = Cdn$0.98, how much exchange gain or loss would be shown in earnings in the second year?

Q13-15 When does capitalization of borrowing costs begin, if a company borrows money to finance the acquisition of capital assets that have a lengthy delivery period?

Q13-16 A company has a $2 million operating line of credit at an interest rate of 4% and (general use) long-term loans of $8 million at an interest rate of 7%. If general borrowings are used to finance inventory with a lengthy acquisition period, what average rate is used as the borrowing cost?

Q13-17 Under what circumstances will a gain or loss occur on the repayment of a bond payable?

Q13-18 When will a bond discount or premium be included in an entry to retire bonds? How is the amount calculated?

Q13-19 What is meant by *defeasance*? Can debt that is defeased be derecognized? Contrast this with *in-substance defeasance*.

Q13-20 Interest expense of $45,500 is recorded after discount amortization of $4,500. Interest payable has increased by $2,000 during the year. How much cash was paid for interest?

Q13-21 What is the primary conceptual difference between straight-line and effective-interest amortization? Why does ASPE allow straight-line, whereas IFRS requires effective interest?

CASE 13-1

HUY PUBLICATIONS LTD.

Huy Publications Ltd. (HPL) operates in the highly competitive printing business, a sector known for its high rate of business failures. While HPL has had some rough financial years in the past, it now owns state-of-the-art printing facilities—financed through government-guaranteed debt—that have stabilized the company's position. HPL is controlled by Jack Huy and his two sons, but there are several other shareholders who were brought into the company when additional share capital was necessary for survival.

In March 20X2, HPL Publications Ltd. completed negotiations for a 10-year, $14,600,000 loan. Senior management was meeting to evaluation the three alternatives:

1. A 10-year $14,600,000 long-term loan from the Canadian Bank. The loan has the following terms:
   a. The interest rate is 8.2%, compounded annually. The interest rate is fixed for the life of the loan and is paid at the end of each year.
   b. Principal is to be repaid in one lump sum at the end of 10 years.
   c. The bank will charge a $19,000 upfront administrative fee.
   d. HPL will be required to move all banking activities of the company to the Canadian Bank (from the Ottawa Bank, its current financial institution.) This will cost HPL $5,500 in fees, either at Canadian or Ottawa.
   e. HPL will agree to a maximum debt-to-equity ratio of 2-to-1 and pay no dividends in excess of 30% of reported earnings during the life of the loan. Ratios are based on audited financial statements.
   f. Loan security is a second mortgage on HPL's printing facilities and personal guarantees from the principal shareholders of HPL.
2. A 10-year $14,600,000 long-term loan from the Ottawa Bank. The loan has the following terms:
   a. The interest rate is 6.5%, compounded annually, for the first five years of the loan. The interest rate for the second five years is to be established at the beginning of the second five-year term based on prime interest rates at that time. Interest is due at the end of each year.
   b. The bank will charge a $110,000 upfront administration fee.
   c. HPL will agree to issue no new long-term debt over the life of the loan, without the express permission of Ottawa, and maintain dividend declarations to common shareholders at no more than current levels (approximately 10%–15% of earnings).
   d. The loan will be secured by a second mortgage on HPL's printing facilities and a floating charge on all corporate assets.
   e. Principal is due at the end of the loan term.
3. A 10-year, $14,600,000 bond payable from a pension fund. The bond has the following terms:
   a. The interest rate is fixed at 8%, compounded semi-annually over the life of the bond. Interest is due every six months.
   b. The bond is secured by the general credit rating of HPL.

c. HPL will agree to the following conditions:
   i. The current ratio will not go lower than 3-to-1.
   ii. The debt-to-equity ratio will not exceed 2.5-to-1.
   iii. No dividends will be paid to common shareholders unless the current ratio is 3.5 to 1 after declaration. (All ratios are based on audited financial statements.)
   iv. No common shares will be issued or repurchased without the written permission of the lender.
   v. No changes to management will take place without informing the lender.
   vi. The lender will be given a seat on the HPL Board of Directors for the life of the bond.
   vii. The bond will involve $227,500 in legal and other costs at inception, to be paid by HPL.

Required:
Prepare a preliminary evaluation of the financing decisions for senior management.

CASE 13-2

DRY CLEAN DEPOT LIMITED

"Kevin, it's such a relief to get this $2,000,000 of financing in place at a reasonable cost. We finally have the go-ahead for that new equipment! If we order now, we'll have it in place and operating next year this time, what with production, shipping, installation, and testing. We'll have to use some of our own money for this, but we'll now be able to pay for it." Max Benstead was excited as he called you, Kevin Mohammed, into his office.

Max is the CFO of Dry Clean Depot Limited (DCDL), a company with a chain of 40 dry cleaning stores in Southern Ontario. DCDL's retail stores are leased, under three- to five-year leases, in various malls and store-front locations. Each pod of retail outlets is served by one larger hub location where the dry-cleaning operation is performed; clothes are transported to and from the hub locations daily.

The new loan has the following terms:

Principal:	$2,000,000
Term:	Ten years; money to be advanced in one payment, immediately, net of upfront fees
Security:	First charge on machinery, inventory, and accounts receivable
Upfront fees:	$377,000
Interest:	$90,000 paid at the end of each year
Covenants:	No dividends in excess of $100,000 per annum; Maximum 2-to-1 debt-to-equity ratio; Minimum cash balance of $500,000 on deposit required at all times

You are a professional accountant, reporting to Max, and he has asked you to analyze any accounting implications of the new loan, along with some other issues in relation to accounting policies for the areas that Max has listed (Exhibit 1). He has requested a brief report on his desk tomorrow.

DCDL has revenues of approximately $7,000,000, and an average gross profit rate of 60%. Operating costs, including occupancy and labour, are high. The company complies with IFRS, despite being a private company. Max influenced this decision, knowing that the company might be part of a public offering in the future, but also because Max wished to develop expertise in IFRS applications to enhance his own personal skills profile.

Required:
Write the report.

EXHIBIT 1

DCDL

Additional Information

1. DCDL is a tenant at a retail location in Sudbury, one of its drop-off locations. Two years of the five-year lease will have expired as of the end of this fiscal period. DCDL has been disappointed with the sales volume at this location and has decided to vacate the premises at the end of this year, even though it will still be responsible for the $27,500 annual rent payments for a further three years. The landlord has been informed of this decision. After considerable effort, DCDL has located an acceptable alternate tenant for the premises, but rent terms reflect the downturn in rental markets. This subtenant has signed a contract with DCDL, agreeing to pay $5,000 for the first year of the remaining lease period, with second- and third-year rent equal to $5,000 plus 10% of sales reported by the subtenant in excess of $150,000.
2. Dry cleaning involves a cleaning process that uses an organic solvent, typically perchloroethylene (called "perc") rather than water. Perc is classified as a hazardous air contaminant and it must be handled as a hazardous waste. In particular, special precautions for storage, use, and disposal are required to prevent perc from getting into any underground drinking water supply system. The landlords housing dry cleaning operations, rather than drop-off depots, require premise inspections and core soil samples on surrounding property to be completed regularly. DCDL is responsible for site remediation in the event of contamination under the terms of all such leases. One of the eight operating sites under lease appears to have some contamination and may have to have remediation work performed. Additional tests are underway to determine the nature and extent of the issue. If there are indeed contamination issues, DCDL has agreed with the landlord that remediation will take place when the lease ends in two years' time, and DCDL will move its cleaning operation at that time. DCDL will not move if there is no contamination issue. The cost of remediation might be in the $250,000 to $500,000 range.
3. Starting in March of the current year, DCDL began offering customers the option of buying a prepaid card for dry cleaning services. The plastic cards can be loaded with "dry cleaning dollars" and offer a discount to encourage use. It costs $100 for a card that can be used for $120 of services. During the year, when a card is sold, a liability for $120 is recognized, and the $20 discount is entered in an account called *promotion expense.* The cards have no expiration date, in accordance with provincial legislation. To date, cards with a face value of $468,000 have been issued, and an expense of $78,000 has been recorded. Services with a retail value of $342,000 have been paid for through the cards. When the card is used, the retail value of the sale is transferred to revenue. Max is expecting that somewhere between 5% and 10% of the value on the cards will never be used, between cards that are lost or neglected, or with customers relocating.
4. DCDL is planning to purchase replacement dry cleaning equipment, with enhanced efficiency and perc recycling abilities. This equipment resembles a large front-load washing machine, and acts as both a washer and a dryer. New technology is capable of extracting 99.99% of perc for re-use, in half the time that the existing models use. This will increase efficiency, allowing either more volume or fewer operating locations. The invoice price of equipment is $2,450,000, all of which is due when the order is placed. Equipment is custom-made to exacting specifications that are unique for each case. After a six-month lead time for custom production, equipment will be shipped from the manufacturer in the Pacific Rim. Shipping will cost approximately $34,000. Shipping will take three months. Import duties will likely amount to 20% of invoice price. DCDL expects to pay $17,000 to have the equipment installed and another $21,000 for labour and supplies during the one-month testing phase.

CASE 13-3

DARCY LIMITED

You are a professional accountant in public practice. You have just left a meeting with Michel Lessard, a local entrepreneur, who is considering a potential acquisition. Mr. Lessard, with four others, is considering buying Darcy Ltd (DL), a company that is now the subsidiary of Micah Holdings Limited (MHL), a private investment holding company.

The group of potential investors is scheduled to meet later in the week to finalize an offer for DL. You have the financial statements prepared by the company (Exhibit 1) and a page of notes from your discussion with Mr. Lessard (Exhibit 2). While the group has hired a lawyer to investigate various issues and appropriate conditions for the purchase, they would like advice on the price to be offered in the first round of negotiations.

You generally understand that the potential investors would be willing to pay six times earnings, a common valuation rule of thumb in this industry. Another valuation norm in this industry is 1.2 times net tangible assets less liabilities. Mr. Lessard has asked that both valuation rules be applied, and he is hoping the two results will be in the same ballpark.

When earnings are used for valuation purposes, earnings must be "sustainable" or "continuing" earnings, excluding unusual and infrequent items, and, in valuation, elements must be measured at fair values, neither high nor low. Appropriate accounting polices must be used for this measurement of earnings and net assets, recognizing the purpose of the accounting measurements.

Required:

Evaluate the investment based on the information given, and provide a report that provides a range of valuation for the potential investors to discuss next week and any other issues you think are important. Your report must include an explanation of adjustments made.

EXHIBIT 1

DARCY LIMITED

Statement of Financial Position

As of 31 December (in thousands)

Assets	20X7	20X6
Current assets		
Cash	$ —	$ 1,400
Accounts receivable (less allowance of $270 in 20X7 and $420 in 20X6)	18,720	8,583
Inventory	2,680	3,200
Prepaid expenses and deposits	45	100
	21,445	13,283
Property, plant, and equipment (net)	19,800	16,600
Goodwill	400	350
	$41,645	$30,233

continued on next page

	20X7	20X6
Liabilities		
Current liabilities		
Operating loan	$ 8,045	$ —
Accounts payable and accrued liabilities	3,750	3,188
Deferred revenue	850	790
Warranty	75	545
	12,720	4,523
Long-term liabilities		
Note payable, 2%, due 1 October 20X12	2,600	—
Deferred tax	1,835	2,210
Shareholders' equity		
Share capital	20,700	20,700
Retained earnings	3,790	2,800
	24,490	23,500
	$41,645	$30,233

DARCY LIMITED

Statement of Comprehensive Income

For the year ended 31 December (in thousands)

	20X7	20X6
Revenue	$32,670	$44,960
Operating costs	24,180	32,970
	8,490	11,990
Other operating costs		
Selling general and administrative	3,580	3,980
Amortization	2,130	1,650
Research	120	350
Bad debts	60	120
Warranty	650	900
Gain on disposal of property	(80)	—
Gain on appreciation of goodwill	(50)	(50)
	6,410	6,950
Operating earnings	2,080	5,040
Financing		
Interest expense	430	410
Income before tax	1,650	4,630
Income tax	660	1,850
Net earnings and comprehensive income	990	2,780
Retained earnings, opening	2,800	20
Dividends	—	—
Retained earnings, closing	$ 3,790	$ 2,800

EXHIBIT 2

NOTES FROM MEETING WITH MICHEL LESSARD

(amounts in thousands)

1. The principal business activity of DL is the manufacturing of equipment for the oil and gas industry.
2. The note payable is a 2% loan offered as 100% financing by the equipment manufacturer, issued for new equipment bought on 1 October 20X7. The equipment has an eight-year life. Annual interest is paid on the anniversary date, and 2% interest for three months has been accrued in the financial statements as presented.
3. Goodwill has been written up by $50 each year based on management estimates of improved operations.
4. The pre-20X7 base of property, plant, and equipment includes land that is likely worth approximately 150% of its $7,000 cost. Other pre-20X7 property, plant, and equipment would likely have a replacement cost of 120% of net book value at the beginning of 20X7. Values have risen only slightly through 20X6 and 20X7.
5. For capital assets, straight-line amortization over periods ranging from four to eight years has been used. Amortization periods seem reasonable.
6. DL provides a three-year limited warranty on equipment sold that is meant to ensure that the equipment operates as intended. The warranty expense has been recorded based on 2% of sales revenue. Warranty claims history is as follows:

Year	Sales	Claims Paid re: Current-Year Sales	Claims Paid re: Sales of One Year Prior	Claims Paid re: Sales of Two Years Prior
20X4	$31,020	$260	$160	$500
20X5	37,810	190	320	420
20X6	44,960	230	325	460
20X7	32,670	190	300	630

7. Revenue is recognized on delivery. Unearned revenue arises because of pre-paid orders.
8. During 20X7, DL provided inventory, with a cost of $23 and list price of $31, to a customer. In return, the customer will do machining work for DL during 20X8. This machining work is for a second customer's special order, which DL does not have the expertise to complete. DL expensed the cost of inventory provided, $23, as part of operating costs and made no other entries. The machining work would be worth something in the range of $28–$30 if DL had to have it done by another party.
9. The allowance for doubtful accounts has historically been approximately 5% of outstanding accounts receivable. The year-end balance of accounts receivable is extremely high this year because of a single, $7,620 account receivable (US$7,000) with a foreign government. DL has stated, and Mr. Lessard agrees, that collection risk is minimal for this account.
10. The tax rate is 40% and market interest rates are in the range of 6%. The year-end exchange rate is US$1 = Cdn$1.12.

TECHNICAL REVIEW

connect

TR13-1 Debt Present Value: Prentice Limited was authorized to issue $5,000,000 of 10-year, 6% bonds payable on 1 August 20X2. The bonds are due on 31 July 20X12. Interest payments dates were 31 July and 31 January. The bond was sold to yield 8%.

Required:

1. Calculate the proceeds from issuance.
2. Calculate the proceeds from issuance if the yield rate is 5% and the bond is issued on 1 August 20X4, still with a maturity date of 31 July 20X12.
3. Calculate the proceeds from issuance if the yield rate is 8%, and the bond is issued between interest dates, on 1 October 20X2, still with a maturity date of 31 July 20X12. Exclude accrued interest.

connect

TR13-2 Interest Expense—Effective-Interest: Cumming Corp. issues a $6,000,000, 5% bond on 1 April 20X3. At this time, market interest rates are in the range of 6%. The bond had a 10-year life from 1 April 20X3, and paid interest semi-annually on 31 March and 30 September.

Required:

1. Calculate the proceeds that would be raised on bond issuance.
2. Prepare an amortization table using the effective-interest method of amortization. Complete the first four payments *only*.

connect

TR13-3 Debt Issuance Costs: Power Solutions Ltd. issues a $10,000,000, five-year, 4.5% bond with semi- annual interest payments. Underwriting costs, paid up front, are $640,000. The bond sells at par.

Required:

1. How much cash does Power receive when the bond is issued?
2. What is the effective interest rate on the bond (rounded)?
3. Prepare an amortization table using the effective-interest method of amortization. Complete the first four payments *only*.

connect

TR13-4 Borrowing Costs: Li Corp. purchased a container load of antiques for resale at an invoice cost of $1,200,000. The goods were paid for when they were shipped in early June. The container arrived in Canada at the end of August, and then at Li's location, by rail, at the end of September. The goods were then available for sale. Freight costs of $126,000 were paid in October. Li has recorded $174,000 of total interest expense from $2,900,000 of general borrowing over the year.

Required:

Prepare the adjusting journal entry to capitalize borrowing costs on inventory.

connect

TR13-5 Debt Retirement: On 31 December 20X7, a company has the following bond on the statement of financial position:

Bond payable, 7%, interest due semi-annually on 31 Dec. and 30 June; maturity date, 30 June 20X11	$10,000,000
Premium on bonds payable	84,000
	$10,084,000

On 28 February 20X8, 20% of the bond was retired for $2,200,000 plus accrued interest to 28 February. Interest was paid on this date only for the portion of the bonds that were retired. Premium amortization was recorded on this date in the amount of $800, representing amortization on the retired debt only.

Required:
Provide the entries to record the bond interest on 28 February and the bond retirement.

ASSIGNMENTS

★ **A13-1 Sources of Financing:** The following are possible sources of financing:

Operating line of credit
Commercial paper
Term loan
Commercial mortgage

Required:
Explain the circumstances under which each source of financing is a logical suggestion. (*Hint:* this is often based on the security required.)

★ **A13-2 Sources of Financing:** The following are possible sources of financing:

Operating line of credit
Commercial paper
Term loan
Commercial mortgage
Long-term bonds payable
Equity financing

Consider each of the following cases:

Case A The company's primary assets are land and buildings.
Case B The company is a large public company with significant tangible assets and a need for millions of dollars in long-term financing.
Case C The company's primary assets are intangible and earnings are erratic.
Case D The company requires short-term financing and has sizeable inventory and account receivable balances.

Required:
For each case, suggest a logical source of financing. Explain.

★ **A13-3 Sources of Financing:** The following are possible sources of financing:

Operating line of credit
Commercial paper
Term loan
Commercial mortgage
Long-term bonds payable
Equity financing

Consider each of the following cases:

Case A The company is a large public company with significant tangible assets, an excellent credit rating, and a need for short-term loans at low cost.

Case B The company has significant tangible assets that are all pledged as security for other loans, and the industry sector is very risky.
Case C The company's primary assets are machinery and equipment.
Case D The company's primary assets are accounts receivable.

Required:
For each case, suggest a logical source of financing. Explain.

★ **A13-4 Debt Issuance—Fair Value:** Quinn Limited issued $8,000,000 of bonds payable on 30 April 20X0. The bonds are due on 30 April 20X8, and bear interest at 4.5% per annum, payable every 30 October and 30 April. The bonds were issued to yield 5% per annum. Quinn's fiscal year ends on 31 December. Quinn uses the effective-interest method of amortization.

connect

Required:
1. Calculate the proceeds from issuance.
2. Calculate the proceeds from issuance if the yield rate is 4% and the bond is issued on 30 October 20X2, still with a maturity date of 30 April 20X8.
3. Calculate the proceeds from issuance if the yield rate is 8%, and the bond is issued on 30 April 20X1, still with a maturity date of 30 April 20X8.
4. Assume that on 30 October 20X5 the market rate of interest is 10% for notes of similar risk and maturity. Determine:
   a. The book value (including unamortized discount/premium) that will be shown on the statement of financial position at that date assuming the bond was issued as in requirement 1; and
   b. The fair value that will be disclosed in the notes.

★ **A13-5 Debt Issuance—Interest Expense:** Ma Transportation Corp. issued $40,000,000 of bonds payable on 1 June 20X5. The bonds are 20-year bonds, and bear interest at 5.5% per annum, payable semi-annually each 31 May and 30 November. The bonds were issued to yield 6% per annum.

Required:
1. Calculate the proceeds from issuance and interest expense and interest paid for the first six months that the bond is outstanding.
2. Calculate the proceeds from issuance if the yield rate is 8% and the bond is issued on 1 June 20X7, still with the original maturity date. Also calculate interest expense and interest paid for the first six months that the bond is outstanding.
3. Calculate the proceeds from issuance if the yield rate is 4% and the bond is issued on 30 November 20X9, still with the original maturity date. Also calculate interest expense and interest paid for the first six months that the bond is outstanding.
4. Explain why interest expense is different in requirements 1 to 3, even though interest paid is identical.

★★ **A13-6 Interest Expense:** ABC Company issues a $5,000,000, 8½% bond on 1 October 20X4. At this time, market interest rates are in the range of 8%. The bond had a 20-year life from 1 October 20X4, and paid interest semi-annually on 31 March and 30 September.

excel

connect

Required:
1. Calculate the proceeds that would be raised on bond issuance.
2. Prepare an amortization table using the effective-interest method of amortization. Complete the first four payments *only*.
3. Prepare journal entries for 20X4 and 20X5, using the effective-interest method. ABC has a 31 December fiscal year-end.

★★ **A13-7 Interest Expense:** On 30 September 20X1, Golf Mania Company issued $3 million face-value debentures. The bonds have a nominal interest rate of 10% per annum, payable semi-annually on 31 March and 30 September, and mature in 10 years, on 30 September 20X11. The bonds were issued at a price to yield 8%. Golf Mania Company's fiscal year ends on 30 September and the company uses the effective-interest method.

Solution

Required:

1. Determine the price at which the bonds were issued.
2. Prepare journal entries to record the issuance of the bonds, payment of interest, and all necessary adjustments for the first two years (i.e., through 30 September 20X3).
3. Compute the amount of unamortized bond premium remaining on 1 October 20X7 reflecting the effective-interest method, without preparing an amortization schedule. (*Note:* At any point in time, the book value of the bonds is equal to the present value of the remaining cash flows.)
4. Calculate the amount of premium amortization, for the six months ending 31 March 20X8.

★★ **A13-8 Interest Expense:** Taggart Ltd. (TL) issued $2,000,000 of 5% bonds payable on 1 September 20X9 to yield 4%. Interest on the bonds is paid semi-annually and is payable each 28 February and 31 August. The bonds were dated 1 March 20X8, and had an original term of five years. The accounting period ends on 31 December. The effective-interest method is used.

excel

connect

Required:

1. Determine the price at which the bonds were issued.
2. Prepare a bond amortization table for the life of the bond.
3. Prepare journal entries to record the issuance of the bonds, payment of interest, and all necessary adjustments through to the end of 20X10.
4. Calculate the interest expense that would be recorded in each of 20X9 and 20X10.
5. Show how the bond would be presented on the statement of financial position as of 31 December 20X9 and 20X10.

★★ **A13-9 Bond Issuance and Interest Expense:** The following partial amortization table was developed for a 5.4%, $800,000 5-year bond that pays interest each 30 September and 31 March. The table uses an effective interest rate of 5%. The bond was dated 1 April 20X1.

Amortization Schedule, Effective-Interest Method:

Interest Period	Cash Interest	Interest Expense	Premium Amortization	Balance Unamortized Premium	Carrying Amount of Bonds
Opening				$14,003	$814,003
1 (30 Sept. 20X1)	$21,600	$20,350	$1,250	12,753	812,753
2	21,600	20,319	1,281	11,472	811,472
3	21,600	20,287	1,313	10,159	810,159
4	21,600	20,254	1,346	8,813	808,813
5	21,600	20,220	1,380	7,433	807,433
6	21,600	20,186	1,414	6,019	806,019
7	21,600	20,150	1,450	4,569	804,569

Required:

1. Assume that the bond was issued on 1 April 20X1. Prepare all entries for 20X1 and 20X2. The fiscal year ends on 31 December.
2. Show how the bond would be reported on the statement of financial position as of 31 December 20X2 consistent with the entries in requirement 1.

★★ **A13-10 Bond Issued Between Interest Dates:** Randy Corporation issued $200,000 of 7.6% (payable each 28 February and 31 August), 4-year bonds. The bonds were dated 1 March 20X4, and mature on 28 February 20X8. The bonds were issued (to yield 8%) on 30 September 20X4, for appropriate proceeds plus accrued interest. The accounting period ends on 31 December.

Solution

Required:

1. Calculate the present value of the bond first assuming that it was issued on an interest date, 1 March 20X4.
2. Prepare an amortization schedule using the effective-interest method of amortization.
3. Calculate the proceeds of the bond reflecting the fact that it was actually issued on 30 September 20X4. Also calculate the accrued interest.
4. Give entries from the 30 September 20X4 date of issuance through 28 February 20X5. Base amortization on (2) above. Credit the accrued interest collected on 30 September 20X4 to interest payable in the initial journal entry.

★★ **A13-11 Bond Issued Between Interest Dates:** Return to the facts of A13-9. The bond is now issued on 1 August 20X1.

excel

connect

Required:

1. Calculate the issuance proceeds of the bond and accrued interest.
2. Record all entries associated with the bond for 20X1 and 20X2.
3. Calculate interest expense for 20X1 and determine the net balance of bonds payable as of 31 December 20X1.

★★ **A13-12 Bond Issued Between Interest Dates:** Radian Company issued $30,000 of three-year, 6% bonds dated 1 December 20X5. Interest is payable semi-annually on 31 May and 30 November. The bonds were issued on 1 February 20X6. The effective interest rate was 8%.

Required:

1. Calculate the present value of the bond assuming that it had been issued on 1 December 20X5.
2. Prepare a bond amortization schedule. Use the effective-interest method of amortization.
3. Calculate the proceeds of the bond reflecting the fact that it was issued on 1 February 20X6. Also calculate the accrued interest.
4. How much amortization is included in interest expense for the period ended 31 May 20X6?

★ **A13-13 Debt Issuance Costs:** A 3% loan was granted to Beacon Theraputics Limited in 20X2. The principal amount was $4,000,000 and the term was three years. Interest is paid at the end of each year. In addition, the lender charged an upfront fee of $217,860 for evaluating the loan application. Beacon plans to expense this as a financing fee in 20X2. Management was delighted to get a 3% loan because other financial institutions had bid a much higher interest rate for the same terms and security.

excel

Required:

1. Did Beacon get a 3% loan? Explain, and calculate the effective interest rate associated with the loan.
2. What is the appropriate accounting treatment of the upfront fee? When is it expensed?
3. Give the required entries for Beacon over the life of the loan.

★ **A13-14 Debt Issuance Costs:** On 1 January 20X8, a borrower arranged a $500,000 three-year 2% bond payable, with interest paid annually each 31 December. There was an upfront fee of $53,460, which was deducted from the cash proceeds of the loan on 1 January 20X8.

excel

connect

Required:

1. Calculate the effective interest rate associated with the loan. What net amount is received on 1 January 20X8?
2. Calculate the interest expense reported by the borrower for each year.

★ **A13-15 Foreign Currency:** On 1 May 20X9, All-Man Imports Limited (AML) obtained a five-year loan from a major New York bank. The loan is for US$20,000,000, bears interest at 6% per annum (paid annually on the loan anniversary date), and matures on 31 December 20X14. AML reports in Canadian dollars. At the date the note was issued, the exchange rate was US$1.00 = Cdn$0.99. On 31 December 20X9, the exchange rate was US$1.00 = Cdn$0.95, and the average exchange rate for the last 8 months of the year was US$1.00 = Cdn$0.98.

connect

Required:

1. Prepare the journal entry to record the loan on 1 May 20X9.
2. What amounts relating to the loan will appear on AML's statement of financial position on 31 December 20X9? What amounts are included in earnings for 20X9?

★ **A13-16 Foreign Currency:** In order to take advantage of lower U.S. interest rates, Zhang Limited borrowed $8 million from a U.S. bank on 1 May 20X2. Annual interest, at 7¼%, was due each subsequent 1 May, with lump-sum principal due on 1 May 20X5. Zhang Limited has a 31 December year-end. Exchange rates were as follows:

Solution

	US$1 =
1 May 20X2	Cdn$1.09
31 December 20X2	1.12
1 May 20X3	1.14
31 December 20X3	1.10
Average, 1 May 20X2 – 31 December 20X2	1.11
Average, 1 January 20X3 – 31 December 20X3	1.09

Required:

1. Calculate the loan principal that would appear on the 31 December 20X2 and 20X3 statement of financial position and the related exchange gain or loss in 20X2 and 20X3.
2. Calculate interest expense for the years ended 31 December 20X2 and 20X3. Why would there be an exchange gain or loss related to interest expense? Calculate this gain or loss for the year ended 31 December 20X2.

★ **A13-17 Borrowing Costs:** Compass Direction Limited has constructed a warehouse facility, paying $560,000 for land on 1 February 20X2, $500,000 to a contractor in late March 20X2, another $2,000,000 in late August 20X2, and finally $1,200,000 in late November 20X2. The warehouse was put into use in early December 20X2. The company had one construction loan, a note payable for $1,700,000. This money was borrowed in late August 20X2. The rest of the acquisition was financed through general borrowing. The company's capital structure and borrowing costs for the year:

	31 December Balance (stable over year)	Borrowing Cost for Year
Operating line of credit	$1,200,000	$ 84,000
Term bank loan	4,300,000	280,000
Long-term loan, warehouse facility (commencing in late August)	1,700,000 (from late August to year-end)	35,500
Mortgage loan for manufacturing building	2,500,000	125,000
Equity financing	3,500,000	—

Required:

1. Calculate the cost of general borrowing, and indicate when the capitalization period ends for borrowing costs.
2. Calculate the borrowing cost that is to be capitalized as part of the warehouse asset.

★★ **A13-18 Borrowing Costs:** Jerrow Corporation has recorded $520,000 of total interest expense from $9,500,000 of general borrowing, which consists of short-term bank debt of $1,500,000 and an $8,000,000 bond payable. Other financing for the company's $14 million operation was sourced through equity financing, which has an approximate cost of 18%.

In March 20X2, Jerrow acquired inventory for resale at an invoice cost of $730,000. The goods were paid for when they were shipped in early March. Due to delays in shipping, the goods arrived in late November and were then available for sale, although they were still unsold at 31 December, the year-end.

In June 20X2, the company contracted for construction of a storage facility, which was nearing completion by the end of 20X2. Payments on the facility were $500,000 in late July, $400,000 in late October, and $1,200,000 in early December. One final payment of $200,000 is expected sometime in January after final inspection is completed. The company borrowed $1,000,000 in early December for this project, at an annual interest rate of 7%. No interest on this loan had been paid or recorded at 31 December, the year-end. This project is financed through the specific loan and general cash balances.

Required:

1. What accounting policy must Jerrow adopt for borrowing costs related to inventory and the storage facility under construction?
2. Prepare the adjusting journal entry to capitalize borrowing costs on inventory and the storage facility at year-end.

★★ **A13-19 Borrowing Costs:** Early in 20X1, Nitro Demolition Limited borrowed money to partially finance the acquisition of a bulldozer. The loan was a five-year, $90,000 loan, secured by a first charge on the bulldozer and the guarantee of the company president. The interest rate was 2%, with interest paid annually at the end of each year. An upfront fee of $15,165 was charged on the loan.

The money was borrowed on 15 January, and the bulldozer was ordered and paid for on this date. It was delivered on 30 June 20X1. The invoice price of the equipment was $180,000. It was then customized at a cost of $15,000 in July. Staff training and testing on the equipment was completed in August at a cost of $10,000, and the machine was operational in early September 20X1.

In addition to the loan for this equipment, the company had the following capital structure and borrowing costs for the year:

	Average Balance	Borrowing Cost
Operating line of credit	$3,000,000	$160,000
Term bank loan	1,500,000	95,000
Mortgage loan for manufacturing facility	5,000,000	305,000
Equity financing	3,500,000	—

Required:

1. Provide journal entries to record the $90,000 loan on 15 January. What is the effective cost of this financing (round to the nearest whole percent)? How much cash is received?
2. Calculate the total cost of the equipment, including capitalized borrowing costs. Round the percentage cost of general borrowing to two decimal places.

★★ **A13-20 Debt Retirement—Open Market Purchase:** On 1 July 20X2, Buoy Metals Corporation issued $3,000,000 of 5% (payable each 30 June and 31 December), 10-year bonds payable. The bonds were issued to yield 6%. The company uses effective-interest amortization for the discount.

Due to an increase in general interest rates, these bonds were selling in the market at the end of June 20X5 at an effective rate of 8%. Because the company had available cash, $1,200,000 (face amount) of the bonds were purchased in the market and retired on 1 July 20X5. This repurchase took place after the 30 June interest payment was made and recorded.

Required:

1. Give the entry by Buoy Metals Corporation to record issuance of the bonds on 1 July 20X2.
2. Give the entry by Buoy Metals Corporation to record the retirement of $1,200,000 of the debt on 1 July 20X5. How should the gain or loss be reported on the 20X5 financial statements of Buoy Metals Corporation?
3. Was the retirement economically favourable to the issuer, investor, or neither?

★★ **A13-21 Debt Retirement:** The following cases are independent:

Case A On 1 January 20X5, Radar Company issued $200,000 of bonds payable with a stated interest rate of 12%, payable annually each 31 December. The bonds matured in 20 years and had a call price of 103, exercisable by Radar Company at any time after the fifth year. The bonds originally sold to yield 10%.

On 31 December 20X16, after interest was paid, the company called the bonds. Radar Company uses effective-interest amortization; its accounting period ends 31 December.

Required:

Give the entry for retirement of the debt.

Case B On 1 January 20X2, Nue Corporation issued $200,000 of 10%, 10-year bonds to yield 11%. Interest is paid each 31 December, which also is the end of the accounting period. The company uses effective-interest amortization. On 1 July 20X5, the company purchased all of the bonds at 101 plus accrued interest.

Required:

1. Give the issuance entry.
2. Give all entries on 1 July 20X5.

★★ **A13-22 Debt Retirement:** The following two cases are independent.

Case A At 31 December 20X3, QML Ltd reports the following on its statement of financial position:

Bonds payable, due 30 June 20X16, 6%, interest payable annually on 30 June	$15,000,000
Discount on bonds payable	186,750
Deferred upfront costs	53,550

Accrued interest payable of $450,000 was recorded on 31 December 20X3 ($15 million × 6% × 6/12) and the bond discount was correctly amortized to 31 December 20X3. On 1 March 20X4, 60% of the bond issue was bought back in the open market and retired at 98 plus accrued interest.

Required:

Provide the entries to record the interest and the retirement. Record interest and amortization only on the portion of the bond that is retired on 1 March 20X4; amortization of $429 must be recorded for the upfront costs and $1,494 on the discount.

Case B On 31 December 20X7, Dartmouth Company has the following bond on the statement of financial position:

Bond payable, 8%, interest due semi-annually on 31 March and 30 September; maturity date, 30 September 20X10	$12,000,000
Discount on bonds payable	88,000
	$11,912,000

Accrued interest payable of $240,000 was recorded on 31 December 20X7 ($12 million × 8% × 3/12) and the bond discount was correctly amortized to 31 December 20X7. On 31 March 20X8, semi-annual interest was paid and the bond discount was amortized by a further $8,000. Then, 30% of the bond was retired at a cost of $3,515,000 (exclusive of interest).

Required:

Provide the entries to record the bond interest and retirement on 31 March 20X8.

★★ connect

A13-23 Debt Retirement: At 31 December 20X8, Northern Resources Ltd. reports the following on its statement of financial position:

Bonds payable, 5%, interest payable semi-annually on 30 June and 30 December	$9,000,000
Discount on bonds payable	448,000
	$8,552,000

The effective interest rate, or market interest rate, was 6% on issuance. On 1 March 20X9, 30% of the bond issue was bought back in the open market and retired at 101 plus accrued interest. The following table relates to 20X9 (numbers have been rounded):

Amortization Schedule, Effective-Interest Method

Interest Period	Cash Interest	Interest Expense	Discount Amortization	Balance Unamortized Discount	Carrying Amount of Bonds
reporting date (above)				$448,000	$8,552,000
1	$225,000	$256,565	$31,565	416,435	8,583,565
2	225,000	257,505	32,505	383,930	8,616,070

Required:

Provide the entries to record:

1. Interest paid to the date of retirement on the 30% of bond retired.
2. Bond retirement.
3. Interest on 30 June 20X9 for the portion of the bond still outstanding.

★★★ excel

A13-24 Debt Issuance and Retirement—Accrued Interest: On 1 June 20X5, Bridle Corp. issued $40,000,000 of 7.5% bonds, with interest paid semi-annually on 30 April and 31 October. The bonds were originally dated 1 November 20X4, and were 15-year bonds. The bonds were issued to yield 8%; accrued interest was received on issuance. The company uses the effective-interest method to amortize the discount. On 31 December 20X5, 10% of the bond issue was retired for 99 plus accrued interest.

Required:

1. Calculate the issue proceeds and the accrued interest. (*Note:* Begin by calculating the present value of the bond at 1 May and 1 November 20X5.)
2. Provide the journal entry for 1 June 20X5.
3. Provide the journal entry at 31 October 20X5.
4. Provide the journal entry(ies) at 31 December 20X5.

★★ **A13-25 Debt Issuance—Defeasance:** Computer Medic Limited issues $800,000 of 9.5% bonds on 1 July 20X1. Additional information on the bond issue is as follows:

Bond date	1 January 20X1
Maturity date	1 January 20X11
Yield rate	12%
Interest payment dates	30 June, 31 December

Required:

1. Record the bond issue and the first interest payment under the effective-interest method.
2. On 1 August 20X6, the company defeased 30% of the bonds for the market price of 103 plus accrued interest. Record the entries necessary to update the portion of the bond issue defeased (interest from 30 June 20X6) and to record the defeasance.
3. What critical element of a defeasance allows it to be recorded with derecognition of the bond? Contrast this to in-substance defeasance.
4. Have interest rates risen or fallen between the issuance of the bonds and the defeasance? (Assume no significant change in the company's risk.)
5. Discuss the nature of the gain or loss recorded in (2).
6. Record the entry to accrue interest expense on 31 December 20X6, on the remaining bonds.

★★★ **A13-26 Partial Statement of Cash Flows:** The following balances are from the statement of financial position of Merit Ltd.

Account	20X9	20X8
Bonds payable, 7%	$17,000,000	$20,000,000
Discount on bonds payable	116,800	152,500
Bonds payable, 6.5%	4,000,000	10,000,000
Discount on bonds payable	21,300	61,500
Bonds payable, 7.25%	5,000,000	0
Discount on bonds payable	132,000	0

Additional information:

a. A portion of the 7% bond payable was retired at 101. Discount amortization of $14,700 was recorded during the year.
b. A portion of the 6.5% bond payable was retired at 97.5. Discount amortization of $5,200 was recorded during the year.
c. The 7.25% bond was issued in 20X9 in exchange for land. Discount amortization of $17,200 has been recorded during the year.
d. Interest expense was $2,110,000 for the year.

Required:

1. Prepare statement of cash flows items in financing activities related to the bond issuance and retirement.

2. Calculate the cash paid for interest in 20X9.
3. Calculate the gain or loss on bond retirements in 20X9.

★★ **A13-27 Partial Statement of Cash Flows:** Comparative SFP balances from Forsythe Solutions Corp.:

connect

	20X2	20X1
Interest payable	$ 62,500	$ 49,000
Bonds payable, 5%	8,000,000	0
Discount on bonds payable	196,000	0
Bonds payable, 6%	0	20,000,000
Discount on bonds payable	0	603,000

Additional information:

- The 5% bonds were issued for $7,800,000.
- The 6% bonds were retired for 102. Discount amortization prior to retirement was $54,000.
- Interest expense in 20X2 on both bonds was $625,000, including discount amortization.

Required:

1. Prepare statement of cash flows items in financing activities related to the bond issuance and retirement.
2. Calculate the amount of cash paid for interest in 20X2.
3. Calculate the gain or loss on bond retirement in 20X2.

★★ **A13-28 ASPE—Straight-line Amortization:** Return to the facts of Assignment 13-6.

eXcel

connect

Required:

1. Calculate the proceeds that would be raised on bond issuance.
2. Prepare an amortization table using the straight-line method of amortization, permitted under ASPE standards. Complete the first four payments *only*.
3. Prepare journal entries for 20X4 and 20X5, using the straight-line method. ABC has a 31 December fiscal year-end.
4. Why is the effective-interest method preferable to the straight-line method? What is the advantage of the straight-line method? Why does ASPE allow the straight-line method?

★★ **A13-29 ASPE—Straight-Line Amortization:** Return to the facts of Assignment 13-9.

Required:

1. Prepare a bond amortization table, as provided in Assignment 13-9, using the straight-line method, permitted under ASPE standards. Include only seven payments in the table.
2. Assume that the bond was issued on 1 April 20X1. Prepare all entries for 20X1 and 20X2. The fiscal year ends on 31 December.
3. Show how the bond would be reported on the statement of financial position as of 31 December 20X2, consistent with the entries in requirement 2.
4. Calculate, for period 1 and 7, interest expense as a percentage of the opening bond liability. Explain why this is not the yield rate of 5%.

★★★ **A13-30 ASPE—Comprehensive, Straight-line Amortization** Fast Transportation Company sold $1,500,000 of five-year, 12% bonds on 1 August 20X2. Additional information on the bond issue is as follows:

eXcel

Bond date	1 February 20X2
Maturity date	31 January 20X7
Yield rate	10%
Interest payment dates	31 July and 31 January
Bond discount/premium amortization	Straight-line method
Proceeds on issuance	$1,606,617

Required:

1. Record the bond issuance on 1 August 20X2.
2. Prepare the adjusting journal entry on 31 December 20X2.
3. Give the entry to record the interest payment on 31 January 20X3.
4. On 31 July 20X5, after interest is paid, Fast purchases and retires 40% of the bond issue at 98. Record the bond retirement.
5. What item(s) will appear on the statement of cash flows with respect to the retirement? Indicate the amount and the section.
6. How will the remaining bond appear on the statement of financial position directly after the retirement?

connect LEARNSMART SMARTBOOK

For more information on the resources available from McGraw-Hill Ryerson, go to www.mcgrawhill.ca/he/solutions.

CHAPTER 14

Shareholders' Equity

INTRODUCTION

Shareholders' equity represents the difference between the assets and liabilities of an entity. Equity is the *residual interest* in net assets because it is what is left when liabilities are subtracted from assets—the residual. Equity is therefore sometimes referred to as **net assets**. Equity has various components, or sources. Generally, shareholders' equity includes the *net contribution to the firm by the owners*, called *contributed capital*, plus the firm's *cumulative earnings retained* in the business.

Inmet Mining Company is a Canadian-based mining company involved in exploration, development, and mining of base metals, primarily copper and zinc. The company owns and operates mining operations in Turkey, Finland, Spain, and Panama. The company reported total assets of $6.6 billion in 2012, and approximately $2.6 billion in debt (39% of assets). The balance, 61% of assets, is financed through equity. Equity of Inmet Mining has several components. Equity includes over $1.6 billion of share capital, contributed surplus from stock-based compensation totalling $22 million; ($85) million in reserves that are unrealized losses from foreign exchange and investments, and $2.2 billion of retained earnings. The notes disclose that the share capital relates entirely to common shares, although the company is authorized to issue preferred shares and subordinate voting participating shares if it wishes. Retained earnings represents cumulative net earnings less dividends.

This chapter examines accounting issues related to contributed capital, particularly issuance and retirement of share capital. Accounting and disclosure for retained earnings is covered, including accounting for dividends. Other components of shareholders' equity are also discussed, with special attention given to reserves.

THE CORPORATE FORM OF ORGANIZATION

The whole topic of accounting for shareholders' equity applies specifically to corporations; only corporations can have shareholders and shareholders' equity. Partnerships and sole proprietorships have ownership interests but not share capital. A corporation may be formed either provincially or federally, and there is legislation governing the rights and responsibilities associated with incorporation. The discussion in this text is based on the federal *Canada Business Corporations Act (CBCA)*, with occasional references to provincial legislation.

Private versus Public Corporations

Private Companies Corporate entities may be either private or public. The vast majority of corporations in Canada are private, many of which are quite small. However, approximately half of the corporations on the *Financial Post*'s list of the 500 largest Canadian corporations are private. **Private companies** have a limited number of shareholders (generally limited to a maximum of 50 by the provincial securities acts). Shares cannot be traded on public markets. Private companies often have a **shareholders' agreement** that describes the ways in which shareholders can transfer their shares as well as other rights and responsibilities of the shareholders.

Private companies in Canada may choose to adopt Accounting Standards for Private Enterprise (ASPE), avoiding the more complex IFRS standards. Such a choice is based on the users of financial information and their needs.

Public Companies **Public companies** are those whose securities, either debt or equity, are traded on stock exchanges. Public companies must, in addition to the reporting requirements required by IFRS (or FASB), comply with the extensive reporting requirements of the particular stock exchange or exchanges on which the companies' securities trade.

Share Capital

Share capital, represented by share certificates, represents ownership in a corporation. Shares may be bought, sold, or otherwise transferred by the shareholders without the consent of the corporation unless there is an enforceable agreement to the contrary.

Common Shares A corporation may be authorized to issue several different **classes of shares**, each with distinctive rights. That is, different types of shares may be created, each with differing rights and privileges. Dividend entitlements and voting rights are characteristics that might be altered among classes. At least one class of shares must be **common shares**, which have the right to vote and the right to receive the residual interest in the net assets of the company on dissolution. Voting rights include the power to vote for the members of the Board of Directors. Common shareholders are entitled to dividends *only as declared*, and they are at risk if the Board of Directors chooses to reduce or eliminate a dividend.

Preferred Shares **Preferred shares** are so designated because they confer certain preferences over common shares. Preferred shares are not always titled "preferred" and may have a variety of names (e.g., Class A shares). The most common feature of preferred shares is a priority claim on dividends declared, usually at a stated rate or amount. Characteristics of preferred shares often involve the following:

- *Limited or nonexistent voting rights.* Typically, preferred shares are nonvoting. They may be given voting rights in certain circumstances, such as when preferred dividends have not been paid or during a vote on a takeover bid.
- *Dividend priority.* A corporation generally has no obligation to declare any type of dividend. When the Board of Directors does declare a dividend, preferred shareholders may have preference, which means that they get their preferred dividend before any common dividend. The dividend rate on preferred shares must be specified, usually as a dollar amount per share, such as $1.20 per share. Alternatively, the dividend may be described as a percentage or rate, such as 8¼%, 6%, or floating rate (i.e., tied to prime interest rates). When the dividend rate is a percentage, it must refer to some sort of

stated principal or par value for the share, which is a reference price, such as $25. This reference value has no special economic significance.

- *Cumulative dividends.* Preferred shares may have the right to receive cumulative unpaid past dividends (called **dividends in arrears**) in the current year before any common dividends can be paid.
- *Participating dividends.* Preferred shares may have the right to share additional dividends with common shares once the annual dividend has been paid to the preferred shareholders and the common shareholders receive some kind of base return.
- *Assets upon liquidation.* In case of corporate dissolution, preferred shares may have a priority over the common shareholders on the assets of the corporation up to a stated amount per share.
- *Conversion.* Preferred shareholders may have the right to convert to common shares or to another class of preferred shares with different entitlements.
- *Guarantee.* Preferred shareholders may have a guaranteed return of their invested principal at some point in time through redemption or retraction provisions.

The accounting implications of these terms will be explored in later sections of this chapter and the next.

Special Terms and Conditions While "classic" common and preferred shares abound, so do more exotic examples. In Canada, preferred issues may be structured to look a lot like debt—they pay a dividend related to interest rates and provide for repayment at a specific point in time. These preferred shares are designed to be sold to investors who not only want the preferential tax treatment given to dividend (versus interest) payments but also want some of the security provided by debt. The result is not permanent equity investment. We will take a closer look at these types of preferred shares in the next chapter.

Some companies issue common shares that have *multiple* votes or, at the opposite end of the spectrum, *limited or no voting* rights. These shares are called **special shares** or **restricted shares**. For example, consider the Quebec-based Bombardier Inc. This company, reporting $23.9 billion in assets at the end of 2011, is a manufacturer of business and commercial aircraft as well as rail transportation equipment and systems. The company has two classes of common shares outstanding, with equal dividend rights and equal claim to net assets on dissolution. However, the 1.9 billion Class A shares each have 10 votes each, or voting power of 18.9 billion votes, and ownership is concentrated in the Bombardier family. In contrast, the 1.4 billion Class B shares have 1 vote each, or voting power of 1.4 billion votes. Combined, there are 20.3 billion votes, 93% attributable to the Class A shares. However, the Class A share can be converted at any time into Class B shares and, indeed, since Class A shares are not traded, must be converted if the shareholder wishes to divest. Class B shares are convertible into Class A shares in the event of a takeover bid that is first approved by the Bombardier family shareholders or if the Bombardier family shareholdings slip below 50% of total Class A shares.

Note that the multiple voting shares are designed to allow the holders to *exercise voting control* but only while the company is in steady state with respect to ownership.

Par Value versus No Par Value Shares

Par value shares have a designated dollar amount per share, as stated in the articles of incorporation and as printed on the face of the share certificates. Par value shares may be either common or preferred. The CBCA and most provincial business corporation acts *prohibit the use* of par value shares, but several provincial jurisdictions permit their issuance (e.g., Quebec, Nova Scotia, and British Columbia).

Par value shares issued initially above par are said to have been issued at a **premium**. Issuing shares below par is not permitted under legislation. When par value shares are issued at a premium, only the par value is assigned to the share account. Any excess is allocated to the premium on share capital account, which is a *separate component of contributed capital.* Par values are usually set very low, and thus a major portion of the proceeds on issuance is classified as the premium. The classification of issuance proceeds in two separate accounts within the equity section, instead of one, has no *economic significance.* The *legal significance* is that par value represents legal capital, which cannot be distributed back to shareholders unless creditors formally approve. Contributed capital, on the other hand, may be distributed with the approval of the Board of Directors.

No-par shares do not carry a designated or assigned value per share. This means that all consideration (or value) received on issuance of the securities is classified in the share capital account. This reflects the economic substance of the transaction; that is, the shares were issued for a specific value. All consideration received is therefore legal capital.

Terms Related to Share Capital

The following terms are used to describe important aspects of share capital:

- *Authorized share capital.* The maximum number of shares that can be legally issued. Under the CBCA, a corporation is entitled to issue an unlimited number of shares, so there is no legal maximum. However, the corporation may choose to place a limit on authorized shares. Such a limit must be stated in the articles of incorporation and can be changed at a later date by application to the appropriate ministry for an amendment to the corporation's articles of incorporation. Some provincial legislation establishes a maximum.
- *Issued share capital.* The number of shares that have been issued to shareholders to date.
- *Outstanding share capital.* The number of shares that have been issued and are currently owned by shareholders. *Issued shares will be higher than outstanding shares if there are treasury shares outstanding. Shares that have been repurchased from shareholders and retired are considered to be neither issued nor outstanding.*
- *Treasury shares.* Shares that are reacquired by the corporation, and held pending resale. Treasury shares are *issued* but not *outstanding.*
- *Subscribed shares.* Unissued shares set aside to meet subscription contracts (i.e., shares "sold" on credit and not yet paid for). Subscribed shares are usually not issued until the subscription price is paid in full in accordance with legislative requirements.

CONCEPT REVIEW

1. What is the essential difference between a public and a private corporation?
2. What is the most common preference right of preferred shares over common shares?
3. What are restricted shares?
4. What are treasury shares?

ISSUANCE OF SHARE CAPITAL

Accounting for shareholders' equity emphasizes source; therefore, if a corporation has more than one share class, separate accounts must be maintained for each. If there is only one share class, an account entitled *share capital* may be used. In cases where there are two or more classes, account titles associated with the shares are used, such as *Common Shares; Class A shares; Preferred Shares, $1.25*; The dollar amounts listed with no-par preferred shares indicate the dividend entitlement.

Authorization The CBCA or the articles of incorporation will authorize an unlimited (or, less frequently, a limited) number of shares. This authorization may be recorded as a *memo entry* in the general journal and in the ledger account by the following notation:

Common shares—No-par value (authorized: unlimited shares)		

Shares Issued for Cash When shares are issued, a share certificate, specifying the number of shares represented, is prepared for each shareholder. This may be done in electronic form, with a brokerage house acting as an intermediary/custodian for the investor. Companies keep track of the number of shares held by each shareholder in a shareholder ledger, a subsidiary ledger to the share capital account.

In most cases, shares are issued for cash. The issuance of 10,000 common shares, no-par, for cash of $10.20 per share would be recorded as follows:

Cash	102,000	
Common shares, no-par value (10,000 shares)		102,000

Note that the common share account is credited for the total proceeds received. Had the shares been assigned a $1 per share par value, the proceeds would be divided between par value and premium:

Cash	102,000	
Common shares, $1 par (10,000 shares)		10,000
Contributed capital: premium on common shares		92,000

The $10,000 common share amount and the premium on common shares are separate equity accounts.

Shares Issued on a Subscription Basis Prospective shareholders may sign a contract to purchase a specified number of shares on credit, with payment due at one or more specified future dates. Such contractual agreements are known as **stock subscriptions**, and the shares involved are called *subscribed share capital. Shares are not issued until fully paid, according to the terms of incorporation legislation.* Because financial statement elements have been created by a legal contract, accounting recognition is necessary. The purchase price is debited to stock subscriptions receivable, and share capital subscribed is credited.

To illustrate, assume that 120 no-par common shares of BT Corporation are subscribed for at $40 by J. Tan. The entry by BT Corporation would be as follows:

Stock subscriptions receivable—common shares (Tan)	4,800	
Common shares subscribed, no-par (120 shares)		4,800

The receivable will be paid in three $1,600 instalments. Assume the third and last collection on the above subscription is received. The entries would be as follows:

To record the collection		
Cash	1,600	
Stock subscriptions receivable—common shares (Tan)		1,600
To record issuance of shares		
Common shares subscribed, no-par (120 shares)	4,800	
Common shares, no-par (120 shares)		4,800

A credit balance in common shares subscribed reflects the corporation's obligation to issue the 120 shares on fulfilment of the terms of the agreement by the subscriber. This account is reported in shareholders' equity on the statement of financial position along with the related share capital account.

There are two alternative ways to present stock subscriptions receivable. Some argue it should be classified as an asset: a current asset if the corporation expects current collection; otherwise, a noncurrent asset under the category *other assets*. Others argue it should be offset against the common shares subscribed account in the shareholders' equity section of the statement of financial position. That is, the amount receivable is shown as a contra account in equity. This presentation ensures that the *net* equity balances reflect only paid-in amounts as capital; promises of future payment are recorded but netted out. *Presentation as a contra account is the preferred approach,* as it maintains the integrity of the equity elements of financial statements.

Default on Subscriptions When a subscriber defaults after partial fulfillment of the subscription contract, certain complexities arise.[1] In case of default, the corporation may decide to (1) return all payments received to the subscriber; (2) issue shares equivalent to the number paid for in full, rather than the total number subscribed; or (3) keep the money received with no shares issued. The first two options involve no disadvantage to the subscriber, although the corporation may incur an economic loss if share prices have dropped. The third option is not common, although legislation generally does not prevent it. The first two options are illustrated below, using the J. Tan example, above. Assume that Tan made the first payment but subsequently defaulted on the arrangement.

Alternative 1—return all payments

To record the collection		
Cash	1,600	
Stock subscriptions receivable—common shares (Tan)		1,600
To record cash payment and reversal of commitment		
Common shares subscribed, no-par (120 shares)	4,800	
Stock subscriptions receivable—common shares (Tan)		3,200
Cash		1,600

Alternative 2—issue pro-rata shares

To record the collection		
Cash	1,600	
Stock subscriptions receivable—common shares (Tan)		1,600
To record share issuance and reversal of balance of commitment		
Common shares subscribed, no-par (120 shares)	4,800	
Stock subscriptions receivable—common shares (Tan)		3,200
Common shares, no-par (40 shares)		1,600

Non-Cash Issuance of Share Capital Corporations sometimes issue share capital for non-cash consideration. These transactions are also called *share-based payments*. Companies may pay for goods or services with shares, or acquire long-term assets. For example, the 2011 annual report of Argentium Resources Inc. discloses that 4,500,000 common shares were issued in 2011, valued at $1,575,000, issued as part of a transaction to acquire mining properties.

[1] A subscription agreement is a legal contract. The corporation may choose to take the subscriber to court to enforce payment and thus avoid default. This section deals with the treatment if the corporation allows the subscriber to avoid the contract commitment.

When shares are issued for non-cash assets or services or to settle debt, the transaction should be recorded at the *fair value of the assets received*, assuming that this value can be reliably determined. The fair value of the equity shares issued cannot be used to value the transaction unless the fair value of the assets *cannot be determined*. This should be a rare occurrence. Logically, though, all evidence should be considered, including the value of shares in recent similar transactions.

To illustrate, assume that Bronex Corporation issued 136,000 Class A no-par shares in exchange for land. The land was appraised at $420,000, while the shares, based on several prior transactions in the shares, were valued at $450,000. The transaction would be valued at $420,000, which is the more conservative value, but in the range of the implied value of the shares. The entry is:

Land	420,000	
Share capital, Class A no-par value (136,000 shares)		420,000

Basket Sale of Share Capital A corporation usually issues each class of its share capital separately. However, a corporation may issue two or more classes for one lump-sum amount (often referred to as a *basket sale*).

When two or more classes of securities are issued for a single lump sum, the total proceeds must be allocated logically among the several classes of securities. The two methods used in such situations are (1) the *proportional method*, in which the lump sum received is allocated proportionately among the classes of shares on the basis of the relative fair value of each security, and (2) the *incremental method*, in which the fair value of one security is used as a basis for that security and the remainder of the lump sum is allocated to the other class of security. When there is no fair value for any of the issued securities, proceeds may be allocated arbitrarily.

To illustrate, assume Vax Corporation issued 1,000 no-par common shares, and 500 no-par preferred shares, in three different situations:

Situation 1—Proportional method The common shares were selling at $40 per share and the preferred at $20. Assume the total cash received is $48,000, which has been approved by the Board of Directors. Because reliable fair values are available for both share classes, the proportional method is preferable as a basis for allocating the lump-sum amount, as follows:

Proportional allocation	
Fair value of common (1,000 shares × $40)	$40,000 = 4/5 of total
Fair value of preferred (500 shares × $20)	10,000 = 1/5
Total fair value	$50,000 = 5/5

Allocation of the lump-sum sale price of $48,000	
Common ($48,000 × 4/5)	$38,400
Preferred ($48,000 × 1/5)	9,600
Total	$48,000

The journal entry to record the issuance:

Cash	48,000	
Common shares, no-par (1,000 shares)		38,400
Preferred shares, no-par (500 shares)		9,600

Situation 2—Incremental method The common shares were selling at $40; a market for the preferred has not been established. Because there is no market for the preferred shares, the fair value of the common ($40,000) must be used as a basis for the entry:

Cash	48,000	
Common shares, no-par (1,000 shares)		40,000
Preferred shares, no-par (500 shares)		8,000

Situation 3—Arbitrary allocation When there is no established market for either class of shares, an arbitrary allocation is used. In the absence of any other logical basis, a temporary allocation may be made by the Board of Directors. If a fair value is established for one of the securities within a year, a correcting entry based on such value would be made.

Share Issue Costs Corporations often incur substantial expenditures when they issue shares in a public offering. These expenditures include registration fees, underwriter commissions, legal and accounting fees, printing costs, clerical costs, and promotional costs. These expenditures are called **share issue costs**. If the share issuance is planned but then abandoned, the costs are expensed. The costs of a successful share issuance are included "in equity"; they are not expensed. Two methods of accounting for share issue costs are found in practice:

1. *Offset method.* Under this method, share issue costs are treated as a reduction of the amount received from the issuance of the related share capital. The rationale to support this method is that these are one-time costs that cannot be reasonably assigned to future periodic revenues and that the net cash received is the actual appropriate measure of capital raised. Therefore, under this method, share issue costs are debited to the share capital account.
2. *Retained earnings method.* Companies will charge share issue costs directly to retained earnings. Retained earnings are reduced as a result. This reduces common equity but records the gross proceeds received from the issuance of shares to the share capital account.

   Both methods are found in practice, although the offset method is more common.

RETIREMENT OF SHARE CAPITAL

A company can buy back any of its shares, preferred or common, at any time, if they are offered for sale. Such a sale can be a private transaction, or a public (stock market) transaction. Legislation provides conditions (typically solvency tests that must be met subsequent to the purchase) for the purchase and cancellation of outstanding shares. Corporations that intend to buy back their own shares must file their plans with the relevant securities commissions; the plan is known as a **normal course issuer bid**.

Shares may also be bought back according to the terms of the shares themselves. Some preferred shares are *retractable*, which means that at the option of the shareholder and at a contractually arranged price, a company is required to buy back its shares. Other preferred shares are **callable**, or *redeemable*, which means that there are specific buyback provisions at the option of the company. In either of these transactions, the company deals directly with the shareholder.

Reasons for Share Retirement Why is repurchase of shares a good strategy for the company? The company may want to:

- *Increase earnings per share* (EPS). EPS is the ratio obtained by dividing earnings by outstanding shares. EPS is considered a critical indication of a company's earning performance and future prospects and is closely watched by financial markets. Idle cash, earning minimal interest income, can be spent to retire shares that will reduce the denominator (number of shares outstanding) of the EPS ratio. Because of the negligible return given up, this will not hurt the numerator (earnings) in a proportional fashion. Accordingly, EPS will rise, and the market price per share should rise as well.

- *Provide cash flow to shareholders in lieu of dividends.* A repurchase offer enables those shareholders who want to receive cash to do so through offering all or part of their holdings for redemption. There may be tax advantages of this form of payout because the recipient will pay taxes on capital gains on the shares rather than tax on ordinary dividend income. Those shareholders who do not wish to receive cash at the time can continue to hold their shares.
- *Acquire shares when they appear to be undervalued.* A corporation with excess cash may feel that buying undervalued shares for cancellation will benefit the remaining shareholders. These transactions also help make a market (i.e., provide a buyer) for the shares.
- *Buy out one or more particular shareholders and thwart takeover bids.*
- *Reduce future dividend payments by reducing the shares outstanding.*

ETHICAL ISSUES

Companies must exercise extreme caution in transactions involving their own shares because of the opportunity that the corporation has to use insider information to the detriment of a selling shareholder. For example, an oil company with inside knowledge of a profitable oil discovery could withhold the good news and acquire shares at an artificially low market price. This would unfairly deprive the selling shareholder of true fair value. For these reasons, security laws prohibit corporations from engaging in deceptive conduct, including acts related to transactions involving their own shares. Continuous disclosure of information is also required. Companies require regulatory approval to repurchase shares, often through a *normal course issuer bid,* which establishes the extent and the intent for share repurchase and retirement.

Accounting for Retirement There are no standards issued by the IASB that describe appropriate policy to follow when a company purchases and retires its own shares. Legislation dictates accounting treatment. Existing Canadian practice is described below.

When shares are purchased and immediately retired, *contributed capital* allocated to the shares is removed from the accounts. Where the reacquisition cost of the acquired shares is different from the average original issuance price (i.e., the *paid-in* capital), the cost is allocated as follows for no-par shares:

Condition	First, DEBIT	Then	
		CREDIT	DEBIT
When the reacquisition cost is *lower* than the average price per share issued to date	Share capital, at the *average paid-in value* per issued share	Other contributed capital from share retirement	n/a
When the reacquisition cost is *higher* than the average price per share issued to date	Share capital, at the *average paid-in value* per issued share	n/a	1. Other contributed capital that was created by earlier cancellation or resale transactions *in the same class of shares,* if any; then 2. Retained earnings.

The effect of this approach is to ensure that a corporation records *no change in earnings* (i.e., no gain or loss in earnings) from buying back its own shares. If a company could record gains and losses from transactions in its own shares, the potential for income manipulation is obvious.

Illustration: Case 1 Assume that Sicon Corporation has 200,000 no-par common shares outstanding. There is $1 million in the common share account, the result of an average issuance price per share of $5. The contributed capital account from previous retirement transactions of common shares has a $7,200 credit balance. The corporation acquired and retired 10,000 shares at a price of $6.25 per share. The specific shareholder who sold these shares back to Sicon Corporation had originally paid $4 per share. The transaction would be recorded as follows:

Common shares (10,000 shares)		
[($1,000,000 ÷ 200,000) × 10,000]	50,000	
Contributed capital, common share retirement	7,200	
Retained earnings ($62,500 – $50,000 – $7,200)	5,300	
Cash (10,000 × $6.25)		62,500

The first step in constructing this journal entry is to compare the cash paid to retire the shares ($62,500) with the *average* initial issuance price to date ($50,000). The specific issue price of these shares ($4) is irrelevant. The corporation paid $12,500 more to retire these shares than the average original proceeds. The $12,500 is debited first to contributed capital from prior common share retirements until that account is exhausted. *This contributed capital account may never have a debit balance.* Retained earnings is debited for the remainder. The effect of this transaction is to reduce paid-in capital by $57,200, retained earnings by $5,300, and total shareholders' equity by $62,500. *No loss is recorded in earnings.* Assets are reduced by $62,500.

Illustration: Case 2 If the shares were reacquired for $4.25 per share, the entry to record the transaction would be:

Common shares (10,000 shares)		
[($1,000,000 ÷ 200,000) × 10,000]	50,000	
Contributed capital, common share retirement ($50,000 – $42,500)		7,500
Cash (10,000 × $4.25)		42,500

Total shareholders' equity and paid-in capital go down by $42,500 ($50,000 less $7,500), reflecting the fact that the corporation paid less to repurchase the shares than the average issuance price to date. No gain is recorded. Assets are reduced by $42,500.

The price paid for the shares may be the current market price or a price agreed on when the shares were originally issued, as is the case for redeemable or retractable shares. In all cases, the entries follow the same pattern: Retirement price is compared with the average issuance price to date, and the difference is a capital amount.

Note that the contributed capital account involved in the above example was identified as contributed capital, common share retirement. Subsequent common share retirements will increase or decrease this account. However, if there are retirements of any other class of shares (e.g., preferred shares), then a *separate contributed capital account* would have to be set up. These contributed capital accounts are used only for transactions involving the *same class of shares.*

Reporting Example Cangene Corporation provides an example of the repurchase and cancellation of shares in its 2011 financial statements. In this example, Cangene reduced common shares by $836 (thousand) in 2011 ($680 in 2010), and retained earnings by $2,464 ($3,108 in 2010), meaning that the company paid $3,300 ($3,788 in 2010) to retire the shares.

Consolidated Statements of Changes in Equity

in thousands of U.S. dollars	Stated share capital	Retained earnings	Total
Balance at August 1, 2009	$52,376	$159,936	$212,312
Net income for the year ended July 31, 2010	—	16,467	16,467
Common shares purchased and cancelled under Normal Course Issuer Bids ("NCIB")	(680)	(3,108)	(3,788)
Balance at July 31, 2010	$51,696	$173,295	$224,991
Net income for the year ended July 31, 2011	$ —	$ 1,509	$ 1,509
Common shares purchased and cancelled under NCIB	(836)	(2,464)	(3,300)
Balance at July 31, 2011	$50,860	$172,340	$223,200

[Disclosure notes have been omitted.]

Source: Cangene Corporation, 2011 Annual Financial Statements, www.sedar.com, posted 25 October 2011.

Conversion of Shares

Shares of any class may include the provision that they may be converted, at particular times and/or in particular quantities, into shares of another class. For example, preferred shares may be convertible into common shares. Conversions are accounted for at *book value,* with an equal decrease to one share class and increase to another. For example, if 20,000 no-par preferred shares, issued for an average of $36.70 per share, were to convert according to pre-established terms to 60,000 no-par common shares (i.e., 3-for-1):

Preferred shares (no-par, 20,000 shares) (20,000 × $36.70)	734,000	
Common shares (no-par, 60,000 shares)		734,000

TREASURY STOCK

A firm may buy its own shares and hold them for eventual resale. This is called **treasury stock**. *Such shares may not vote at shareholder meetings or receive dividends.* The CBCA (and provincial legislation modelled after the act) provides that corporations that reacquire their own shares must immediately retire those shares. Thus, corporations may not engage in treasury stock transactions in most Canadian jurisdictions. However, there are some circumstances where shares may be purchased and held in trust before they are distributed to an employee under a share compensation arrangement. Some provincial legislation also allows companies to hold treasury stock. Treasury shares are far more common in other countries, where corporations regularly engage in treasury stock transactions, subject to the insider trading rules of the various stock exchanges.

The key to a treasury stock acquisition is that reacquired shares may be reissued. The company may eventually reissue the shares to raise additional capital—a process far faster/simpler through the issuance of treasury stock than a new share issue. The shares may also be used for stock dividends, employee stock option plans, and so on. A corporation that is permitted to engage in treasury stock transactions may have additional flexibility over one not so permitted. However, the importance of this aspect of treasury shares has decreased in recent years due to the prevalence of **shelf registration**, which is a standing approval from the securities commissions to issue more shares as needed.

Accounting for Treasury Stock Canadian practice regarding policy for the acquisition and resale of treasury stock is presented in this discussion because there are no standards issued by the IASB in this area.

When a company buys treasury stock, the cost of the shares acquired is debited to a treasury stock account, which appears as a *deduction* at the end of the shareholders' equity section. When the shares are resold, the treasury stock account is credited for the average cost, and the difference, which is the "gain or loss," affects various equity accounts. The "gain or loss" is not reported in earnings; a firm cannot improve reported earnings by engaging in capital transactions with its own shareholders.

When treasury stock is reissued at a price in excess of its cost, the excess should be recorded as contributed capital in a separate contributed capital account. Where the shares are reissued at less than their cost, the deficiency should be charged to contributed capital, if any, then retained earnings. The rules are as follows:

Condition	First, CREDIT	Then	
		CREDIT	DEBIT
When the reissue price is *higher* than the average price per share	Treasury stock, at the *average price per share*	Other contributed capital from treasury stock transactions	n/a
When the reissue price is *lower* than the average price per share	Treasury stock, at the *average price per share*	n/a	1. Other contributed capital from treasury stock transactions, if any; then 2. Retained earnings.

This method of accounting for treasury stock is called the **single-transaction method**. The treatment is the same as that used for share retirement. An example will illustrate the sequence of entries.

1. To record the initial sale and issuance of 10,000 common shares at $26 per share:

Cash (10,000 shares × $26)	260,000	
Common shares (10,000 shares)		260,000

2. To record the acquisition of 2,000 common treasury shares at $28 per share:

Treasury stock, common (2,000 shares × $28)	56,000	
Cash		56,000

Note: The cash price paid is always the amount debited to the treasury stock account.

3. To record reissuance of 500 treasury shares at $30 per share (above cost):

Cash (500 shares × $30)	15,000	
Treasury stock, common (500 shares at cost, $28)		14,000
Contributed capital from treasury stock transactions		1,000

Note: Had this reissuance been at cost ($28 per share), no amount would have been entered in the contributed capital account. If treasury shares are bought in a series of acquisitions at different prices, weighted average cost is used on disposition.

4. To record the acquisition of 1,000 common treasury shares at $35 per share:

Treasury stock, common (1,000 shares × $35)	35,000	
Cash		35,000

Acquisition changes the average cost in treasury stock: There is now $77,000 ($56,000 – $14,000 + $35,000) in the treasury stock account for 2,500 shares; this is a weighted average of $30.80 per share.

5. To record the reissuance of another 500 treasury shares at $19 per share (below cost):

Cash (500 shares × $19)	9,500	
Contributed capital from treasury stock transactions*	1,000	
Retained earnings	4,900	
Treasury stock, common (500 shares at average cost, $30.80)		15,400

*The debit is limited to the current balance in this account (see entry [3]); any remainder is allocated to retained earnings.

Assuming entries (1) through (5), and a beginning balance in retained earnings of $40,000, the statement of financial position will reflect the following:

Shareholders' Equity	
Contributed capital	
Common shares, 10,000 shares issued, and 8,000 shares outstanding; 2,000 shares are held as treasury stock	$260,000
Retained earnings ($40,000 – $4,900)	35,100
Total contributed capital and retained earnings	$295,100
Less: Treasury stock, 2,000 shares at cost	61,600
Total shareholders' equity	$233,500

CONCEPT REVIEW

1. What value is given to shares when they are issued in exchange for non-cash assets?
2. How can the separate classes of shares be valued when shares are issued as a basket?
3. When shares are redeemed and retired, how should the cost of the redemption be charged to the shareholders' equity accounts?

RETAINED EARNINGS

Retained earnings represents accumulated net earnings or net loss, error corrections, and retrospective changes in accounting policy, if any, less accumulated cash dividends, stock dividends, and other amounts transferred to contributed capital accounts. If the accumulated losses and distributions exceed the accumulated gains, a **deficit** will exist (i.e., a debit balance in retained earnings).

The following items directly affect retained earnings:

Decreases (debits)

- Cash and other dividends;
- Stock dividends;
- Share retirement and treasury stock transactions;
- Share issue costs;
- Spinoff of investment to shareholders;
- Adjustments related to complex financial instruments, such as hybrid financial instruments (see Chapter 15);
- Error correction (may also be a credit) (see Chapter 21); and
- Effect of a change in accounting policy applied retrospectively (may also be a credit) (see Chapter 21).

Increases (credits)

- Earnings (will be a debit if a net loss); and
- Removal of deficit in a financial reorganization.

Appropriations and Restrictions of Retained Earnings

Appropriated retained earnings and restricted retained earnings formally constrain a specified portion of accumulated earnings for a specified reason. Retained earnings are appropriated and restricted primarily to reduce the amount of retained earnings that financial statement readers might otherwise consider available to support a dividend declaration. Constrained retained earnings are sometimes called a *reserve*. **Appropriated retained earnings** are the result of discretionary management action. **Restricted retained earnings** are the result of a legal contract or corporate law.

The following are examples of some of the ways in which appropriations and restrictions of retained earnings may arise:

- To fulfill a contractual agreement, as in the case of a debt covenant restricting the use of retained earnings for dividends that would result in the disbursement of assets;
- To report a discretionary appropriation of a specified portion of retained earnings in anticipation of possible future losses; or
- To fulfill a legal requirement, as in the case of a provincial corporate law requiring a restriction on retained earnings equivalent to the cost of treasury stock held.

An appropriation of retained earnings *does not involve any segregation of assets.* Retained earnings appropriations are just accounting entries that divide existing retained earnings into multiple accounts. If management actually sets aside funds for a specific purpose, restricted cash investments will be reported as an asset.

Appropriation or restriction of retained earnings is formally made by transferring (debiting) an amount from retained earnings to (crediting) an appropriated retained earnings account. The entry has no effect on assets, liabilities, or total shareholders' equity. When the need for an appropriation or restriction no longer exists, the appropriated balance is returned to the unappropriated retained earnings account. Both appropriations and restrictions are rarely seen in practice; it is far more common to have a covenant in a lending arrangement specifying that the company must maintain a certain level of retained earnings.

DIVIDENDS

Nature of Dividends

A dividend is a distribution of earnings to shareholders in the form of assets or shares. A dividend typically results in a credit to the account that represents the item distributed (cash, non-cash asset, or share capital) and a debit to retained earnings.

Some corporate legislation and bond covenants place restrictions on the amount of assets and/or retained earnings that may be used for dividends. These constraints recognize the effects of dividends; that is, dividends require (1) a disbursement of assets and (2) a reduction in retained earnings, by the same amount. The company must have both assets and retained earnings to be eligible to declare/distribute dividends. Under the CBCA, a liquidity test must also be met: Dividends may not be declared or paid if the result would be that the corporation became unable to meet its liabilities as they came due or if the dividend resulted in the realizable value of assets being less than liabilities plus stated capital. In addition, dividends may not be paid from *legal capital (share capital)* without specific creditor approval.

Relevant Dividend Dates

Four dates have legal significance for dividends:

Declaration Date On the **declaration date**, the corporation's Board of Directors formally announces the dividend declaration. The courts have held that formal declaration of a cash or property dividend constitutes an enforceable contract between the corporation and its shareholders. Therefore, on the dividend declaration date, such dividends are recorded and a liability (i.e., dividends payable) is recognized.

Record Date The **record date** is the date on which the list of *shareholders of record,* who will receive the dividend, is prepared. Usually, the record date follows the declaration date by two to three weeks, to allow for changes in share ownership to be recorded. No entry is made in the accounts on the record date, but the shareholder list will determine the names on the eventual dividend cheques.

Ex-Dividend Date An investor who holds (buys) shares on or after the **ex-dividend date** *does not* receive the dividend. Technically, the ex-dividend date is the day following the record date, but, to provide time to record the transfer of shares, the effective ex-dividend date is usually several days prior to the date of record. Thus, the investor who holds shares on the day prior to the stipulated ex-dividend date receives the dividend.

Payment Date This date is determined by the Board of Directors and is usually stated in the declaration. It is the date on which dividends are paid or distributed to the shareholders of record. The **payment date** typically follows the declaration date by four to six weeks. At the date of payment, the liability recorded at date of declaration is debited, and the appropriate asset account is credited.

Note that of these four dates, the only ones that affect the accounting records of the company that declares the dividend are (1) the declaration date and (2) the payment date. The other two dates are significant for investors but not for accounting.

Cash Dividends

Assume the Board of Directors of Bass Company, at its meeting on 20 January 20X2, declares a dividend of $0.50 per common share, payable 20 March 20X2, to shareholders of record on 1 March 20X2. Assume that 10,000 no-par common shares are outstanding.

At declaration date—20 January 20X2		
Common dividends declared* (10,000 shares × $0.50)	5,000	
Cash dividends payable		5,000
*Later closed to retained earnings; alternatively, retained earnings may be debited directly		
At payment date—20 March 20X2		
Cash dividends payable	5,000	
Cash		5,000

Cash dividends payable is reported as a current liability.

Preferred shares typically have first preference on amounts declared as dividends. Assume that Bass Company, in addition to the 10,000 common shares mentioned above, also has 5,000 $1.20 preferred shares outstanding. The Board of Directors declared dividends totalling $10,000, with the same declaration and payment dates as in the previous example. The first $6,000 will go to the preferred shareholders (5,000 shares × $1.20 per share); the remaining $4,000 will be distributed to the common shareholders at the rate of $0.40 per share ($4,000 ÷ 10,000 shares). Entries will be as follows:

At declaration date—20 January 20X2		
Preferred dividends declared*	6,000	
Common dividends declared*	4,000	
Cash dividends payable, preferred (5,000 × $1.20)		6,000
Cash dividends payable, common (10,000 × $0.40)		4,000
*Later closed to retained earnings; alternatively, retained earnings may be debited directly		
At payment date—20 March 20X2		
Cash dividends payable, preferred	6,000	
Cash dividends payable, common	4,000	
Cash		10,000

If Bass Company were to have declared $5,000 of dividends, the preferred shareholders would have received it all. They have preference for the first $6,000 each year.

In corporate reporting, it is important to distinguish the portion of the dividend attributable to the preferred shares versus the common. Accordingly, these are recorded separately in the accounts.

Cumulative Dividends on Preferred Shares

Cumulative preferred shares provide that dividends not declared in a given year accumulate at the specified rate on such shares. This accumulated amount must be paid in full if and when dividends are declared in a later year *before any dividends can be paid on the common shares.* If cumulative preference dividends are not declared in a given year, they are said to have been *passed* and are called *dividends in arrears* on the cumulative preferred shares.

If only a part of the preferred dividend is met for any year, the remainder of the cumulative dividend is in arrears. Cumulative preferred shares carry the right, on dissolution of the corporation, to dividends in arrears to the extent that the corporation has retained earnings. However, different provisions for dividends in arrears may be stipulated in the articles of incorporation and bylaws.

Dividends in arrears are not liabilities. Since preferred shareholders cannot force the Board of Directors to declare dividends, dividends in arrears do not meet the definition of a liability. Dividends in arrears for cumulative preference shares must be disclosed in the notes to the financial statements.

Participating Dividends on Preferred Shares

Participating preferred shares provide that the preferred shareholders participate above the stated preferential rate on a pro rata basis in dividend declarations with the common shareholders. This works as follows:

- First, the preferred shareholders receive their preference rate.
- Second, the common shareholders receive a specified matching dividend *if the amount declared is high enough.*
- *If the total declared dividend is larger than these two amounts,* the excess is divided on a pro rata basis between the two share classes.

The pro rata distribution may be based simply on the respective number of shares outstanding, the two classes' *total* base level dividends, or the respective *total* capital balances.

Participation terms often reflect relative capital invested and must be specified in the articles of incorporation and stated on the share certificates.

Reporting Example An example of a company that has participating shares is the Power Corporation of Canada, a diversified international management and holding company active in financial services, communications, and a variety of other business sectors. Total assets are $256 billion. In its capital structure, the Power Corporation reports subordinated voting shares, which are common shares, and participating preferred shares with the following terms:

> Entitled to ten votes per share; entitled to a non-cumulative dividend of 0.9375¢ per share before dividends on the Subordinated Voting Shares and having the right to participate, share and share alike, with the holders of the Subordinated Voting Shares in any dividends in any year after payment of a dividend of 0.9375¢ per share on the subordinate voting shares.

The preferred shares are noncumulative but participate in dividends with common shares after both classes receive a base dividend.

Partially versus Fully Participating Shares may be *partially participating* or *fully participating*. If partially participating, preferred shares may participate in dividend declarations in excess of their preference rate, but the participation is capped at a certain level. Dividends above this level accrue solely to the common shareholders. Fully participating shares, on the other hand, share in the full extent of dividend declarations.

For example, a corporation may issue preferred shares entitled to a dividend of $0.50, with participation up to $0.70 after common shareholders receive $0.25 per share. The $0.25 dividend to the common shareholder is the matching dividend, and it is specified in the articles of incorporation. It is meant to provide a certain rate of return on the common shares in the initial allocation and acknowledges that the share classes are of different relative size and value. In this case, participation with the common shareholders is limited to the additional $0.20 above the regular $0.50 rate.

Example The following three cases, A, B, and C, illustrate various combinations of cumulative versus noncumulative rights and of participating versus non-participating rights. Assume that Mann Corporation has the following share capital outstanding:

Preferred shares, no-par, dividend entitlement, $0.50 per share; 10,000 shares outstanding	$250,000
Common shares, no-par, 40,000 shares outstanding	200,000

Case A Preferred shares are non-cumulative and non-participating; dividends have not been paid for two years; dividends declared, $28,000.

	Preferred	Common	Total
Step 1—Preferred, current ($0.50 × 10,000)	$5,000		$ 5,000
Step 2—Common (balance)		$23,000	23,000
Total	$5,000	$23,000	$28,000

Because the preferred shares are non-cumulative, preferred shares may receive dividends only for the current year regardless of the fact that dividends were missed in two previous years.

Case B Preferred shares are *cumulative* and *non-participating;* dividends are two years in arrears; total dividends declared, $28,000.

	Preferred	Common	Total
Step 1—Preferred in arrears ($0.50 × 10,000 × 2)	$10,000		$10,000
Step 2—Preferred, current ($0.50 × 10,000)	5,000		5,000
Step 3—Common (balance)		$13,000	13,000
Total	$15,000	$13,000	$28,000

Preferred shares receive their dividends in arrears and the current dividend before the common shares receive any dividend.

Case C Preferred shares are cumulative, two years in arrears and fully participating after common shares have received $0.25 per share. *Participation is based on the respective total base dividend for one year.* Total dividends declared in this case are $37,000. Participation is based on one year's dividends: Preferred shares are entitled to $0.50 per share ($5,000 total), and common will receive $0.25 per share ($10,000 total). The base dividend is $15,000 (i.e., $5,000 + $10,000). Payment of dividends in arrears does not affect this calculation, which is based on *one* year's base dividend. Participation is 1/3 ($5,000/$15,000) for the preferred and 2/3 ($10,000/$15,000) for the common.

	Preferred	Common	Total
Step 1—Preferred, in arrears ($5,000 × 2)	$10,000		$10,000
Step 2a—Preferred, current (10,000 × $0.50)	5,000		5,000
b—Common, matching (40,000 × $0.25)		$10,000	10,000
c—Extra dividend, participating 1/3 : 2/3	4,000	8,000	12,000*
Totals	$19,000	$18,000	$37,000

*Extra dividend available: $37,000 – $10,000 – $5,000 – $10,000 = $12,000.

Had the preferred shares been *partially* participating, say, to a *total* of $0.75 per share, then the current year (excluding arrears) preferred dividend would have been limited to $7,500, and participation would have been a maximum of $2,500 ($7,500 – $5,000). The common shares would then have received more of the final $12,000 layer of dividends ($9,500, or $12,000 – $2,500).

In the absence of an explicit stipulation in the articles of incorporation or bylaws, preferred shareholders have no right to participate in dividends with common shares beyond their stated dividend rate.

Property Dividends

Corporations occasionally pay dividends with non-cash assets. Such dividends are called **property dividends**, or *dividends in kind.* The property may be an investment in the securities of other companies held by the corporation, real estate, merchandise, or any other non-cash asset designated by the Board of Directors. The dividend is recorded at the fair value of the assets distributed, and a gain (or loss) is recorded for the difference between book value and fair value of the asset.

Liquidating Dividends

Liquidating dividends are distributions that are a return of the amount received when shares were issued, rather than assets acquired through earnings. Owners' equity accounts *other than retained earnings* are debited. Since such dividends reduce contributed capital, they typically require creditor approval.

Liquidating dividends are appropriate when there is no intention or opportunity to conserve resources for asset replacement. A mining company might pay such a liquidating dividend when it is exploiting a nonreplaceable asset. Mining companies sometimes pay dividends on the basis of "earnings plus the amount of the deduction for depletion." Shareholders must be informed of the portion of any dividend that represents a return of capital, since the liquidation portion of the dividend is not income to the investor and is usually not taxable as income; it reduces the cost basis of the shares.

When accounting for a liquidating dividend, the debit would not go to retained earnings. For example, share capital might be debited. However, any other contributed capital accounts would be debited and eliminated before share capital would be reduced.

Scrip Dividends

A corporation that has a temporary cash shortage might declare a dividend to maintain a continuing dividend policy by issuing a **scrip dividend**. The dividend takes the form of a certificate issued. This certificate is essentially a form of a promissory note, which will be repaid in cash on its due date. This form of dividend is also called a *liability dividend*.

Stock Dividends

A stock dividend is a proportional distribution to shareholders of additional shares of the corporation. A stock dividend does not change the assets, liabilities, or total shareholders' equity of the issuing corporation. It does not change the proportionate ownership of any shareholder. It simply increases the number of shares outstanding.

For instance, assume that Early Broadcasting Limited has 120,000 common shares outstanding. One shareholder, J.S. Brown, owns 12,000 shares, or one-tenth of the shares. The corporation declares and issues a 10% stock dividend. This has the following effect on share capital:

	Before Dividend		After Dividend*	
Total shares outstanding	120,000	*100%*	132,000	*100%*
Brown's shareholding	12,000	*10%*	13,200	*10%*

*Previous outstanding total × 110%.

Brown's relative ownership percentage has not changed. If the shares sold for $20 per share before the dividend, what will happen to that market value after the split? Logically, it should decline.

	Before	After	
A. Total market value of the company (120,000 × $20)	$2,400,000	$2,400,000	(i.e., no change)
B. Shares outstanding	120,000	132,000	
Price per share (A ÷ B)	$20	$18.18	
Brown's total market value			
12,000 × $20.00	$ 240,000		
13,200 × $18.18		$ 240,000	

What will really happen to the market price of the shares in this situation? The answer is unclear. Often, there is a smaller decrease in market price than the size of the stock dividend would seem to dictate. That is, market value might fall to $18.50 rather than $18.18. Some believe that this is a market reaction to other factors (e.g., an anticipated increase in cash dividends that historically follows a stock dividend). Because of the complexity and sophistication of the stock markets, it is very difficult to determine why a share price does or does not change on a given day. However, it is generally recognized that if a company doubles its outstanding shares through a stock dividend, the market price will reduce by approximately one-half.

In the books, a stock dividend can cause the transfer of an amount from retained earnings to the contributed, or paid-in, capital accounts (i.e., share capital). Therefore, it changes only the internal account balances of shareholders' equity and not the total shareholders' equity.

Reasons for a Stock Dividend Numerous reasons exist for a company to issue a stock dividend:

- To reveal that the firm plans to permanently retain a portion of earnings in the business. The effect of a stock dividend, through a debit to retained earnings and offsetting credits to permanent capital accounts, is to raise contributed capital and reduce retained earnings. This will shelter this amount from expectations of future declaration of cash or property dividends.
- To increase the number of shares outstanding, which reduces the market price per share and, in turn, tends to increase trading of shares in the market. Theoretically, a broader range of investors can afford investments in equity securities if the unit cost is low.
- To signal a planned future increase in cash dividends. As stated above, such a sequence of events has been historically validated, and the expectation of improved future cash flow tends to lift share price.

Dividend Reinvestment Plan A **dividend reinvestment plan (DRIP)** allows shareholders to choose between a cash dividend and a stock dividend. The terms of this might appear as follows:

Common shareholders may elect to have their cash dividends reinvested in common shares of the Company in accordance with the Company's Shareholder Dividend Reinvestment and Share Purchase Plan. Under the Plan, the Board of Directors determines whether the common shares will be purchased on the stock market or issued by the Company from treasury shares.

For example, Pengrowth Energy Company reported dividends declared of $280,198 in 2011. Of this amount, $54,698 is recorded as an increase to share capital, as part of the company DRIP program, and the remaining $225,500 would have been paid in cash. Such stock dividends are recorded at a market-related value.

Accounting Issues Related to Stock Dividends

One major issue in accounting for stock dividends is the value that should be recognized. The shares issued for the dividend could be recorded at fair value, at stated (or par) value, or at some other value.

There are no specific accounting standards on these issues, but the CBCA requires shares to be issued at fair market value. In Ontario, on the other hand, legislation specifically permits the Board of Directors to capitalize any amount it desires. In the United States, small stock dividends (i.e., less than 20% to 25% of the outstanding shares) *must* be recorded at fair value, while large stock dividends are recorded only as a memo entry (i.e., no value).

When the shareholder has the choice between cash and shares, it seems most logical to record the full fair value of the dividend. We will examine three alternatives: fair value, stated value, and memo entry.

Fair Value Method The Board of Directors would require capitalization of the current fair value of the additional shares issued. The fair value of the stock dividend should be measured on the basis of the market price per share on the declaration date.

Assume that Markholme Corporation has 464,000 common shares outstanding, originally issued for $2,784,000. The company declares and distributes a 5% common stock dividend on 1 July 20X2 and determines that an appropriate fair value is $7.25 per share. The following entry will be recorded:

Stock dividend (or, retained earnings) (464,000 × 5% = 23,200 × $7.25)	168,200	
Common shares, no-par (23,200 shares)		168,200

Stated Value Method The Board of Directors in certain jurisdictions may decide to capitalize a stated amount per share—average paid in per share to date, or par value, if applicable. Strong arguments can be made for some sort of stated value (i.e., not fair value) because (1) the corporation's assets, liabilities, and total shareholders' equity are not changed; and (2) the shareholders' proportionate ownership is not changed. If the market price per share is proportionately reduced by the stock dividend, then it is clear that the shareholders have received nothing of value and should not be encouraged to believe that they have. In these circumstances, capitalization should be limited to legal requirements.

If Markholme Corporation, explained above, declares the same 5% stock dividend but the Board of Directors determines that the average amount paid in to date for the outstanding common shares is to be used, then $6 ($2,784,000 ÷ 464,000) will be used to determine the capitalization amount. The entry will be identical, except the amount recognized will be $139,200 (464,000 × 5% × $6).

Memo Entry Since a large stock dividend may be issued for the primary purpose of reducing market price per share, it is obvious at least in this case that the shareholder has received nothing of value. A memo entry may be recorded to identify the number of shares issued, outstanding, and subscribed. No change is made in any capital account. This parallels the treatment of a stock split, to be discussed later in this chapter. Large stock dividends are often called *stock splits effected as a stock dividend*. For example, in March 2006, the Royal Bank of Canada announced a 100% stock dividend. If a shareholder owned 100 shares before the dividend, the shareholder had 200 shares afterward. The stock dividend was accounted for with a memo entry. However, this treatment may also be used for small stock dividends. Markholme Corporation, above, could record a memo entry documenting the distribution of 23,200 (464,000 × 5%) shares.

Timing of Recognition

Fundamentally, a stock dividend is recorded as a debit to retained earnings and a credit to the share capital account. However, unlike a cash dividend, a stock dividend *can be revoked prior to the issuance date*. As a result, many companies do not record the dividend on the declaration date but instead record it on the issuance date. Either recording approach can be used.

Example Marvel Corporation, which has 100,000 common shares outstanding, declares a 10% common stock dividend. The Board of Directors directs that the dividend be recorded at fair value. A total of 10,000 no-par common shares are issued. The fair value is $5 per share. The entries are as follows:

Alternative 1: Originating Entry at Declaration		
Declaration date		
Stock dividends (or, retained earnings)	50,000	
Stock dividends distributable*		50,000
*Reported as a credit in shareholders' equity until issuance.		
Issuance date		
Stock dividends distributable	50,000	
Common shares, no-par (5,000 shares)		50,000

Alternative 2: Originating Entry at Issuance		
Declaration date		
No entry		
Issuance date		
Stock dividends (or, retained earnings)	50,000	
Common shares, no-par (5,000 shares)		50,000

The differences between these two approaches are trivial. The stock dividends distributable account is not a liability because it does not involve settlement by the future transfer of assets (cash etc.) It is an obligation to issue equity and is properly classified in shareholders' equity. Note disclosure would accompany both alternatives.

Special Stock Dividends

When a stock dividend is of the same class as that held by the recipients, it is called an *ordinary stock dividend* (e.g., common shares issued to the owners of common). When a class of share capital other than the one already held by the recipients is issued, such a dividend is called a *special stock dividend* (e.g., preferred shares issued to the owners of common). In this case, the fair value of the preferred shares issued as a dividend should be recorded.

Fractional Share Rights

When a stock dividend is issued, many shareholders will own an "odd" number of shares and will be entitled to a fraction of a share. For example, when a firm issues a 5% stock dividend and a shareholder owns 30 shares, the shareholder is entitled to 1.5 shares (30 × 5%). When this happens, the firm may issue *fractional share rights* for portions of shares to which individual shareholders are entitled. It is also quite common for the company to write a cheque for the fair value of the fractional entitlement.

To demonstrate, suppose Moon Company has 1,000,000 outstanding no-par common shares. Moon issues a 5% stock dividend. The fair value of the common shares is $80 per share, and this value will be used to record the stock dividend. The number of shares to be issued is 5% of the number of shares outstanding (1,000,000 × 5%), or 50,000 shares.

Assume the distribution of existing shares is such that 42,000 whole or complete shares can be issued. The firm will issue fractional share rights for the remaining 8,000 shares. Each fractional share right will entitle the holder to acquire 5%, or 1/20, of a share. Since there are 8,000 shares yet to be issued, there will be 8,000 × 20, or 160,000 fractional share rights issued. A market will develop for the fractional share rights, with each having a fair value of approximately 1/20 of a whole share ($80 ÷ 20), or $4. Shareholders can buy or sell fractional share rights to the point where whole shares can be acquired. A holder will have to turn in 20 fractional share rights to receive one common share.

The entry for recording the issuance of the stock dividend and fractional share rights is as follows:

Stock dividends (or, retained earnings) (50,000 × $80)	4,000,000	
Common shares, no-par (42,000 shares × $80)		3,360,000
Common share fractional share rights (8,000 shares; 160,000 rights) (8,000 × $80)		640,000

When rights are turned in for redemption in common shares, the common share fractional share rights account is debited and common shares are credited. Suppose, for example, that 150,000 fractional share rights are turned in for 7,500 common shares (150,000 ÷ 20). The entry to record the transaction would be:

Common share fractional share rights	600,000	
Common shares, no-par (7,500 shares × $80)		600,000

If the remaining rights are allowed to lapse, the corporation would record contributed capital:

Common share fractional share rights	40,000	
Contributed capital, lapse of share rights (500 × $80)		40,000

Cash Alternative An alternative to the issuance of fractional share rights is to make a cash payment to shareholders for any fractional shares to which they are entitled. The shareholder above who owns 30 shares and is entitled to 1.5 shares will receive one share from the firm and a cash payment of $40 ($80 per share × .5 shares), representing the value of the one-half share at current fair value. The entry to record the cash payment is a debit to retained earnings and a credit to cash. This procedure is simpler for the shareholder because there is no need to buy or sell fractional shares.

If cash were offered for fractional shares, the stock dividend would be recorded, in summary form, as follows:

Stock dividends (or retained earnings) (50,000 × $80)	4,000,000	
Common shares, no-par (42,000 shares)		3,360,000
Cash (8,000 shares × $80)		640,000

This alternative clearly has cash flow implications for the company, but it avoids the complications of dealing with fractional shares for all concerned.

Summary Dividends and distributions are summarized as follows:

Type	Shareholder Receives	Recorded At	Watch Out For
Cash	Cash	Exchange amount; cash	Amount allocated to common versus preferred shares
Property	Some company asset as designated by the Board of Directors: inventory, investments, etc.	Fair value; gain or loss recorded on declaration	—
Scrip	Promissory note	Exchange amount; as stated	Shareholders get a receivable; company sets up a liability
Stock	Shares	May be recorded at fair value, book value, or an arbitrary value May also be recorded as a memo entry only	May issue fractional shares for part shares or May issue cash for part shares
Stock split (see next section)	Shares	n/a	Memo entry only; not recorded

CONCEPT REVIEW

1. Of the four dates pertaining to cash dividends, which dates require accounting entries? What are the entries?
2. What effect does a cash dividend have on shareholders' equity? How does the effect of a stock dividend differ from that of a cash dividend?
3. What is a participating preferred dividend?

STOCK SPLITS

A **stock split** is a change in the number of shares outstanding with no change in the recorded capital accounts. A stock split usually increases the number of shares outstanding by a significant amount, such as doubling or tripling the number of outstanding shares. Shares that sell at high market values are perceived to be less marketable, especially to smaller investors. Therefore, the primary purpose of a stock split is to increase the number of shares outstanding and decrease the market price per share. In turn, this may increase the market activity of the shares. By increasing the number of shares outstanding, a stock split also reduces earnings per share.

For example, Bell Canada Enterprises have split its shares three times since the company's inception:

- 1 October 1948, 4-for-1
- 26 April 1979, 3-for-1
- 15 May 1997, 2-for-1

An investor who owned 100 shares in 1948 would own 2,400 shares [([100 × 4] × 3) × 2] after the third split. These shares represent the same proportional share of the total company.

In contrast, a **reverse split** decreases the number of shares. It results in a proportional *reduction* in the number of shares issued and outstanding and an increase in the average book value per share. Reverse splits may be used to increase the market price of shares with a low market value per share. For example, Domtar Paper (Canada) Inc. implemented a 1-for-12 reverse split in 2009, with fractional shares distributed in cash:

As a result of the reverse stock split, every 12 shares of the Company's issued and outstanding exchangeable shares at the Effective Time have been automatically combined into one issued and outstanding exchangeable share, without any change in the par value of such shares, subject to the elimination of fractional shares resulting from the reverse stock split which have been aggregated and sold into whole shares on the open market by the Company's transfer agent with proceeds of such sales allocated to the record holders' respective accounts pro rata in lieu of fractional shares.

Accounting for Stock Splits

In a stock split, *a memo entry is recorded.* No consideration has been received by the corporation for the issued shares. Shares issued, outstanding, and subscribed are changed, as is par value, if any. The following dollar amounts are *not* changed:

1. Share capital account;
2. Additional contributed capital accounts;
3. Retained earnings; and
4. Total shareholders' equity.

Consider a 200%, or 2-for-1, stock split (two new shares for each old share), and compare it with a 100% stock dividend (one additional share for each share already outstanding). For example, assume Technology Corporation has 40,000 shares outstanding, which were issued initially at $10 per share. The current balance of retained earnings is $450,000. A 100% stock dividend and a 200% stock split accomplish the same things in economic terms in that they double the outstanding shares but halve the market value per share. However, the two transactions can appear differently on the books if the dividend is recorded but the split is reflected through a memo only. The difference is shown in Exhibit 14-1, where the stock dividend is recorded at $10 per share, and the split is accorded memo treatment.

In Exhibit 14-1, note that the stock dividend, recorded at $10 per share, changes both share capital and retained earnings. The stock split, however, changes neither of these amounts. *Total* shareholders' equity is unchanged by both the stock dividend and the stock split.

Commentary Remember that the shareholder is left in the same position whether there is a 200% stock split or a 100% stock dividend—two shares will be owned for every one share previously held. Similarly, the market price of the shares should be the same whether the transaction is described as a split or a dividend.

This similarity of results makes the different accounting methods suspect, since there are alternatives available for transactions that are basically the same. This hardly seems to promote the idea of *substance over form.* Accordingly, *memo treatment* of a large stock dividend is the preferable approach because it produces the same result as the memo treatment for a stock split.

Adjustments Required for Stock Splits When a stock is split, the per-share values all change. For example, in a 2-for-1 split, the paid-in value per share is halved. If Sincon Corporation has 40,000 outstanding shares and total contributed capital of $800,000, the average issue price is $20. After a 2-for-1 split, the company will have 80,000 shares, and the average issue price drops to $10 per share.

EXHIBIT 14-1

TECHNOLOGY CORPORATION

Stock Dividend and Stock Split Compared

	Total Prior to Share Issue	Total After 100% Stock Dividend	Total After 2-for-1 Stock Split
Initial issue 40,000 × $10 =	$400,000		
100% stock dividend: (40,000 + 40,000) × $10 =		$800,000*	
Two-for-one stock split: 80,000 × $5			$400,000
Share capital	$400,000	$800,000*	$400,000
Retained earnings	450,000	50,000*	450,000
Total shareholders' equity	$850,000	$850,000*	$850,000

*Retained earnings capitalized: 40,000 shares × $10 = $400,000 (entry: debit retained earnings, $400,000; credit share capital accounts, $400,000.) After the stock dividend, share capital equals $800,000, which is $400,000 + $400,000. Retained earnings is $450,000 – $400,000, or $50,000.

Similarly, other per-share amounts, such as earnings per share (EPS), will change. Suppose that Sincon had EPS of $3 before the split and paid dividends of $2 per share. The equivalent EPS after the split will be $1.50. To pay dividends after the split that are equivalent to the dividend rate before the split, Sincon needs to pay only $1—but on twice as many shares.

Because of the change in number of shares in a stock split (or a reverse split), the company must recalculate all prior years' per-share amounts so that they will be comparable with post-split per-share amounts. Earnings per share and dividends per share must be restated.

Conversion rights for senior securities must also be adjusted. If preferred shares are convertible into three common shares prior to a 2-for-1 common share split, the preferred shares will be convertible into six common shares after the split.

Implementation A stock split is implemented by either:

1. Calling in all of the old shares and concurrently issuing the split shares, or,
2. Issuing the additional split shares with notification to shareholders of the change in outstanding shares.

It is more common simply to issue additional shares. If the shares have an assigned par value, share certificates must be replaced to reflect revised par value.

ADDITIONAL CONTRIBUTED CAPITAL

Contributed capital is created by a number of events that involve the corporation and its shareholders. Several accounts for additional contributed (paid-in) capital were introduced in this chapter, such as contributed capital on share repurchase.

Donated Capital Sometimes a corporation will receive a donation of assets, which creates **donated capital**. An example would be a donation of land from a shareholder. In this case, the corporation records the donated asset at its fair market value, with a corresponding credit to donated capital. The donation is viewed by the accounting profession as a capital contribution rather than as an earnings item (i.e., it is not a gain.) Donated capital appears in shareholders' equity as additional contributed capital. It must be described as to source.

Other Shares may also be donated back to a company. Corporate legislation typically requires that such shares be retired, and the retirement entry is similar to the examples given earlier, except that there is no cash consideration given—the entire paid-in value of the shares (at average cost) is transferred to an additional contributed capital account. If the shares can be legally held and reissued, the shares may be accounted for as treasury shares.

Exhibit 14-2 summarizes some of the transactions that may cause increases or decreases in additional contributed capital.

EXHIBIT 14-2

TRANSACTIONS THAT MAY CHANGE ADDITIONAL CONTRIBUTED CAPITAL

Increase

1. Receipt of donated assets
2. Retirement of shares at a price less than average issue price to date
3. Issue of par value shares at a price or assigned value higher than par
4. Treasury stock transactions, shares reissued above cost
5. Stock option transactions (see Chapter 15)

Decrease

1. Retirement of shares at a price greater than average issue price to date, when previous contributed capital has been recorded
2. Treasury stock transactions, shares issued below cost, when previous contributed capital has been recorded
3. Financial restructuring

RESERVES

Reserves are equity accounts that accumulate gains and losses that are part of *other comprehensive income* but not part of *earnings*. The reserves are also called *accumulated other comprehensive income*. The reserves reflect the *cumulative amounts* of the items that are added to or subtracted from earnings to arrive at comprehensive income. These cumulative gains and losses are often *unrealized* but may also be *realized* amounts. Reserves are a component of shareholders' equity, usually presented below retained earnings.

Example Assume the following facts for AgriCorp Limited, a company with investments carried at fair value, with unrealized gains and losses recorded in other comprehensive income (OCI). That is, the company holds investments classified as fair-value-through-other-comprehensive-income (FVTOCI) investments:

	20X2	20X3	20X4
FVTOCI investments			
Cost; purchased in January 20X2	$100,000		
Fair value, end of year	$130,000	$110,000	$160,000
Earnings	$345,000	$287,000	$371,000

Based on this information, comprehensive income is as follows:

	20X2	20X3	20X4
Earnings	$345,000	$287,000	$371,000
Other Comprehensive Income:			
Change in fair value			
($130,000 – $100,000)	30,000		
($110,000 – $130,000)		(20,000)	
($160,000 – $110,000)			50,000
Comprehensive income	$375,000	$267,000	$421,000

The cumulative reserve (also called *accumulated other comprehensive income*) would be:

	20X2	20X3	20X4
Shareholders' equity			
Reserve caused by FVTOCI investments			
($130,000 – $100,000)	$30,000		
($110,000 – $100,000), or ($30,000 – $20,000)		$10,000	
($160,000 – $100,000), or ($10,000 + $50,000)			$60,000

This example has ignored income tax implications. Elements that are taxable, either in the current period or in the future, have tax assigned to them when recognized and are reported net of tax in other comprehensive income and in the reserve. Reporting issues related to income tax are explored in later chapters of this text.

Sources of Reserves Standard setters dictate the items that create *other comprehensive income* and thus cause reserves. There are a limited number of items at present, although the list seems to keep growing:

- Gains and losses on FVTOCI financial instruments (see Chapter 11);
- Revaluation reserves caused by revaluing property, plant, and equipment to fair value (see Chapter 10);
- Gains and losses on certain hedging instruments (see Chapters 13 and 15);
- Actuarial revaluations and certain experience gains and losses related to defined benefit pensions (see Chapter 19); and
- Translation gains and losses on foreign operations whose functional currency is a foreign currency rather than the presentation currency.

Standards require these amounts to be shown separately in reserves.

Translation Gains and Losses on Foreign Operations The final equity reserve listed above is the **cumulative foreign currency translation account**. This item represents unrealized gains and losses that arise from a certain type of foreign currency exposure.

In Chapter 13, accounting for a liability denominated in a foreign currency was reviewed; gains and losses caused by changes in foreign exchange rates are included in earnings as they arise, and no reserve is involved. However, many corporations have subsidiaries in one or more foreign countries. The basic operations of these foreign subsidiaries are carried out in a currency other than the Canadian dollar, and their separate entity financial statements are reported in the host country foreign currency. For the parent company to prepare consolidated financial statements, the foreign operation's *foreign currency* financial statements must be translated into the parent's *presentation currency*. The process of translation is a topic for advanced accounting courses and is not discussed here.

However, in general terms, translation of foreign operations gives rise to an overall exchange gain or loss. If the foreign operation has revenues and expenses primarily in the foreign currency, the subsidiary has a **functional currency** that is the foreign currency. The exchange gains and losses that arise from translating the financial statements of such foreign operations do not flow through earnings, but instead, the annual amounts are included in other comprehensive income. The cumulative amount is a reserve. Alternatively, if the foreign subsidiary's cash flows are dominated by sales and expenses that are not in the subsidiary's domestic currency, then remeasurement is required and exchange gains and losses are part of earnings.

STATEMENT OF CHANGES IN EQUITY, DISCLOSURE AND SCF

The details of the components of equity can be shown on the face of the statement of financial position, in a statement of changes in equity, or in the disclosure notes. That is, it is possible to show only a single line for equity in the SFP, with the break-down shown in the notes or on a statement of changes in equity.

Statement of Changes in Equity

Exhibit 14-3 illustrates the general format of a statement of changes in equity. Numbers have been assumed. Each company will tailor this statement to its own shareholders' equity accounts and transactions. There are columns for each account within equity. The statement starts with opening dollar balances, and has a line item for each source of change to an account, resulting in the end-of-year balance.

Note that *comprehensive income* affects retained earnings (for the amount of earnings) *and a reserve* (for the unrealized amounts that are part of other comprehensive income but not earnings, here assumed to be caused by FVTOCI investments). Some companies will add extra columns to include the *number of shares* for common and preferred shares, in addition to the dollar amount.

EXHIBIT 14-3

STATEMENT OF CHANGES IN EQUITY—GENERAL FORMAT

(in thousands) (numbers assumed)	Preferred Shares	Common Shares	Retained Earnings	Accumulated OCI (Reserve) FVTOCI Investments	Total Equity
Balance at 1 January 20X1	$2,000	$4,800	$13,600	$700	$21,100
Comprehensive income	—	—	2,300	150	2,450
Shares issued for cash	500	900	—	—	1,400
Share buyback	—	(350)	(200)	—	(550)
Share issue costs	—	—	(100)	—	(100)
Dividends to shareholders		—	(600)	—	(600)
Shares issued under DRIP program*	—	250	—	—	250
Balance at 31 December 20X1	$2,500	$5,600	$15,000	$850	$23,950

*Since there were $600 of dividends, and $250 of shares issued under a DRIP program, cash dividends must be $350.

Other Disclosure

For each class of share capital, the legal rights, preferences, and restrictions must be described in the disclosure notes. This includes all authorized share classes, whether shares are issued or not. The number of shares issued and fully paid at year-end must be disclosed, as well as shares issued and not fully paid (shares subscribed). The *number of shares* issued, repurchased, and retired during the year must be disclosed, if this information is not in the statement of changes in equity.

Companies must disclose their objectives, policies, and processes for *managing capital.* This includes their definition of capital, which obviously includes equity but also may include some forms of debt. If there are externally imposed capital requirements, these requirements and compliance with the requirements must be disclosed.

SCF

Transactions affecting equity accounts must be reflected on the statement of cash flows. However, non-cash transactions are excluded from the SCF and separately listed in the disclosure notes. The following items are common on the SCF:

- Net earnings, which increase retained earnings, are listed as the first item in operating activities, assuming that the indirect method is used to present operating activities.
- Dividends are a cash outflow, adjusted for any change in dividends payable. Dividends may be classified in financing activities or in operating activities, a policy choice to be made by the company.
- Stock dividends and stock splits are non-cash transactions.
- Shares issued for cash are listed as an inflow in financing activities. This may be shown net of share issuance costs or share issuance costs may be listed as a separate outflow, also as a financing item.
- Cash collected on subscriptions receivable are listed in financing activities.
- Purchase and sale of treasury stock creates cash flow, listed in financing activities as an outflow or an inflow.
- Shares bought back and retired are listed as an outflow in financing activities at their total cash amount, whether recorded in share capital, contributed capital, or retained earnings.
- Non-cash transactions include shares issued for assets other than cash, many changes in reserves that are based on unrealized changes in fair value, appropriations, and the like. These items are disclosed rather than listed on the SCF.

In all cases, the transaction affecting equity accounts should be recreated, and the cash impact determined. This cash flow is then listed on the SCF.

Example Return to the statement of changes in equity shown in Exhibit 14-3. Based on the information shown, the following items would be included on an SCF:

- In operating activities, earnings, $2,300
- In financing activities, issued common shares for cash, $900
- In financing activities, issued preferred shares for cash, $500
- In financing activities, paid share issue costs, ($100)
- In financing activities, bought back shares, ($550)
- In financing activities, or operating activities, paid dividends, $(350) ($600 – $250)

Non-cash transaction: issued shares of $250 under a dividend reinvestment program.

Reporting Example Exhibit 14-4 shows the statement of changes in shareholders' equity for ClubLink Enterprises Ltd., a Canadian public company engaged in golf clubs and resort operations. ClubLink has 44 golf locations, primarily in Ontario, Quebec and Florida, as well as rail, tourism, and port operations in Alaska.

EXHIBIT 14-4

CLUBLINK ENTERPRISES LIMITED

Consolidated Statements of Changes in Shareholders' Equity

(thousands of Canadian dollars)	Common Shares	Share Capital	Retained Earnings	Accumulated Other Comprehensive Earnings (Loss)	Total Shareholders' Equity
Balance, December 31, 2010	27,902,618	105,613	78,445	(3,347)	180,711
Activity during 2011					
Comprehensive earnings	—	—	16,388	1,756	18,144
Dividends	—	—	(8,355)	—	(8,355)
Shares repurchased and cancelled through normal course issuer bid which expired on September 19, 2011	(164,100)	(621)	(515)	—	(1,136)
Shares repurchased and cancelled through normal course issuer bid which expires on September 19, 2012	(39,100)	(148)	(103)	—	(251)
Exercise of stock options	90,000	405	—	—	405
Shares issued pursuant to dividend reinvestment plan	3,560	24	—	—	24
Balance, December 31, 2011	27,792,978	$105,273	$85,860	$(1,591)	$189,542

Source: ClubLink Enterprises Inc., 2011 Annual Financial Statements, www.sedar.com, posted 30 March 2012.

The statement begins with a column for the number of common shares. In the share capital account column, the statement shows that shares were issued during the period for $405 (all amounts in thousands) under the terms of stock options and that shares were repurchased. Because of the repurchases, share capital declined by $621 and $148, and retained earnings declined by $515 and $103, indicating that shares were repurchased for prices higher than their original issuance price. Comprehensive income is $18,144, which is distributed to retained earnings and to accumulated OCI. That is, $16,388 represents net earnings, which increases retained earnings. Another $1,756 is a foreign exchange gain on subsidiaries whose functional currency is the U.S. dollar. Gains from this source are allocated to accumulated OCI. This reserve is in a cumulative loss position at the beginning of the year, so the gain reduces the loss to date. Finally, dividends to shareholders of $8,355 reduced retained earnings, but some shareholders took advantage of a DRIP program, and common share account increased by $24.

CONCEPT REVIEW

1. How do a stock split and a stock dividend differ in their impact on the shareholders' equity accounts?
2. Identify at least two ways in which a corporation can obtain contributed capital other than by the issuance of new shares.
3. What items create unrealized gains and losses that give rise to reserves (AOCI) reported in equity?

Looking Ahead

Shareholders' equity issues are not now on the agenda of either the IASB or the Canadian AcSB. However, the definition of *accumulated other comprehensive income* and the circumstances under which it is recognized and derecognized are being deliberated as part of a review of the conceptual framework.

ACCOUNTING STANDARDS FOR PRIVATE ENTERPRISES

There are very few differences between public and private companies in the area of accounting for equity interests. However, private companies are *required* to follow the standards governing share retirement and treasury stock transactions as described. The IASB has no standards in this area; the chapter material is presented as a logical approach, but not the required approach, for public companies.

Shares with special terms and conditions are frequently encountered in private companies. This is caused by opportunities for tax planning, the need to balance competing shareholder interests, and various succession and incentive plans. Disclosure of the terms and conditions of shares is just as important for private companies as for public companies.

When shares are issued for non-cash consideration, a private company will value the transaction at the fair value of the shares given up, unless the valuation of the shares is problematic. If the fair value of the assets is more clearly determinable, then this value should be used. The IASB standards *require that the fair value of the assets received* be used to value the transaction.

For private companies, net income is reported, but there is no reporting of comprehensive income. There are no unrealized amounts that must be included in such a measure. For example, the investment category FVTOCI does not exist for private companies. If there are specific unrealized amounts that are excluded from net income, such as unrealized gains and losses from a foreign subsidiary, they are allocated directly to a separate equity account and are not channelled first through comprehensive income.

The approach to classifying foreign subsidiaries is different under ASPE. While IFRS relies on identification of a functional currency, ASPE requires foreign subsidiaries to be classified as self-sustaining or integrated, based on the nature and extent of parent company relations and transactions. Self-sustaining subsidiaries cause unrealized exchange gains and losses in equity, while integrated operations cause exchange gains and losses recorded in earnings.

Finally, a private company has no requirement to prepare a comprehensive statement of changes in equity. Only a retained earnings statement is included with the financial statements. The changes in other equity accounts may be included in the disclosure notes.

RELEVANT STANDARDS

CPA Canada Handbook, Part I (IASB):

- IAS 1, Presentation of Financial Statements
- IAS 32, Financial Instruments; Presentation
- IFRS 2, Share-Based Payments
- IFRIC 17, Distributions of Non-cash Assets to Owners

CPA Canada Handbook, Part II (ASPE):

- Section 1535, Capital Disclosures
- Section 3240, Share Capital
- Section 3251, Equity
- Section 3260, Reserves
- Section 3831, Non-monetary Transactions

SUMMARY OF KEY POINTS

1. Equity is a residual amount on the statement of financial position but has various component elements. The major sources are contributed capital from shareholders and earnings.
2. Ownership claims are represented by shares. Different share classes have different contractual rights; the two basic types of shares are common and preferred. Preferred shares have one or more contractually specified preferences over common shares, while common shares generally are voting and have a residual claim to the firm's assets.
3. In conformity with legislative requirements, most shares issued are no-par shares. The entire amount of consideration received on the issuance of no-par shares is recorded in the share capital account.
4. Authorized capital represents the total number of shares that legally can be issued. Issued shares are the number of shares that have been issued to shareholders to date. Treasury stock exists when outstanding shares are reacquired by the corporation and are held pending resale. Outstanding shares are those currently held by shareholders. Subscribed shares are unissued shares that must be used to meet subscription contracts.
5. When a corporation issues shares for assets or for services, the fair value of the goods or services received is used to value the transaction. If shares are issued as a basket, the proportional or incremental method could be used to value the transaction, based on information available.
6. Share issue costs are either offset against the proceeds received, resulting in the net proceeds being recorded in share capital, or deducted from retained earnings.
7. When shares are retired, an amount of share capital relating to the shares is first removed at average cost. If the remaining balance is a credit, it is used to increase a contributed capital account on share retirement. If the remaining balance is a debit, it is debited to existing contributed capital account from prior retirements in this class of shares, if any, and any remaining balance is debited to retained earnings.
8. Treasury stock is debited to a contra shareholders' equity account titled "treasury stock," at cost. When the stock is resold, the difference between the acquisition price and the resale price is accounted for using the same rules as retirements.
9. Retained earnings represents the accumulated profit or loss, less dividends declared since the inception of the corporation, and certain adjustments arising from share retirement, error correction, and changes in accounting policy.
10. Dividends are distributions to shareholders and may be in the form of cash, non-cash assets, debt, or the corporation's own shares.
11. Dividends are allocated to the various share classes based on their respective contractual claims. If preferred shares are cumulative and dividends are not paid in full in a

given year, dividends declared in a later year are first paid to the preferred shares for the amount in arrears (plus their current dividend) before any amount is allocated to common shares. If preferred shares are participating, they receive a base dividend, then the common shares receive a base dividend; any dividend declared over the base is allocated between the two share classes.

12. Stock dividends are proportional issuances of additional shares. Stock dividends may be recorded at fair value, at a stated amount, or in a memo entry. In general, small stock dividends are recorded at fair value, while large dividends are recorded in a memo entry.

13. Fractional shares are issued when a shareholder would receive a portion of a share as a result of a stock dividend. Fractional shares are recorded in a shareholders' equity account that may lapse and create contributed capital or may be turned in for whole shares, creating share capital. Alternatively, the company may pay out money in lieu of fractional shares.

14. A stock split is a change in the number of shares outstanding accompanied by an offsetting change in value per share. A memo entry reflects the changed number of outstanding shares.

15. Reserves within equity are caused by cumulative amounts designated by standard setters as part of other comprehensive income. Examples are fair value changes in FVTOCI investments, exchange gains and losses from certain foreign subsidiaries, and gains and losses on hedging transactions.

16. Companies are required to disclose the components of shareholders' equity, along with a statement that shows the change in each account within shareholders' equity during the year. Complete disclosure of the terms of shares is also required.

KEY TERMS

appropriated retained earnings
callable
classes of shares
common shares
cumulative foreign currency translation account
declaration date
deficit
dividend reinvestment plan (DRIP)
dividends in arrears
donated capital
ex-dividend date
functional currency
net assets
no-par shares
normal course issuer bid
par value shares
payment date
preferred shares
premium
private companies
property dividends
public companies
record date
reserve
restricted retained earnings
restricted shares
reverse split
scrip dividend
share issue costs
shareholders' agreement
shelf registration
single-transaction method
special shares
stock split
stock subscriptions
treasury stock

REVIEW PROBLEM 14-1

On 2 January 20X1, Greene Corporation was incorporated in the province of Ontario. It was authorized to issue an unlimited number of no-par value common shares, and 10,000 shares of no-par, $8, cumulative and non-participating preferred shares. During 20X1, the firm completed the following transactions:

8 Jan.	Accepted subscriptions for 40,000 common shares at $12 per share. Down payment on the subscribed shares totalled $150,000.
30 Jan.	Issued 4,000 preferred shares in exchange for the following assets: machinery with a fair market value of $35,000, a factory with a fair market value of $110,000, and land with an appraised value of $295,000.
15 Mar.	Machinery with a fair market value of $55,000 was donated to the company.
25 Apr.	Collected the balance of the subscriptions receivable and issued common shares.
30 June	Purchased 2,200 common shares at $18 per share. The shares were retired.
31 Dec.	Closed the income summary to retained earnings. The income for the period was $198,000.
31 Dec.	Declared sufficient cash dividends to allow a $1 per share dividend for outstanding common shares. The dividend is payable on 10 January 20X2 to shareholders of record on 5 January 20X2.

Required:

1. Prepare the journal entries to record the above transactions.
2. Prepare a multicolumn statement of changes in equity that explains the change in each equity account.
3. Prepare the shareholders' equity section of the SFP for Greene Corporation at 31 December 20X1.

REVIEW PROBLEM 14-1—SOLUTION

Account for subscription of common shares		
Cash	150,000	
Stock subscription receivable	330,000	
Common shares subscribed (40,000 shares)		480,000
Issue preferred shares in exchange for assets; recorded at fair market value of the assets		
Machinery	35,000	
Factory	110,000	
Land	295,000	
Preferred shares (4,000 shares)		440,000
Record receipt of donated assets		
Machinery	55,000	
Contributed capital—donations		55,000
Record receipt of cash for subscribed shares and issuance of shares		
Cash	330,000	
Stock subscription receivable		330,000
Common shares subscribed (40,000 shares)	480,000	
Common shares (40,000 shares)		480,000

continued on next page

Record acquisition and retirement of common shares		
Common shares ($480,000 ÷ 40,000) × 2,200	26,400	
Retained earnings	13,200	
Cash ($18 × 2,200)		39,600
Close the income summary		
Income summary	198,000	
Retained earnings		198,000
Record dividends declared		
Preferred dividends declared (or retained earnings)	32,000	
Common dividends declared (or retained earnings)	37,800	
Dividends payable, preferred shares		32,000
Dividends payable, common shares		37,800
Preferred dividend: 4,000 shares × $8		
Common dividend: 37,800 shares × $1		

GREENE CORPORATION

Changes in Shareholders' Equity for the Year Ended 31 December 20X1

	Preferred shares	Common shares	Common shares subscribed	Donated capital	Retained earnings	Total equity
Balance at 1 January 20X1	$ —	$ —	$ —	$ —	$ —	$ —
Earnings and comprehensive income					198,000	198,000
Shares subscribed			480,000			480,000
Shares issued	440,000	480,000	(480,000)			440,000
Share buyback		(26,400)			(13,200)	(39,600)
Donation of assets				55,000		55,000
Dividends to preferred shareholders					(32,000)	(32,000)
Dividends to common shareholders					(37,800)	(37,800)
Balance at 31 December 20X1	$440,000	$453,600	—	$55,000	$115,000	$1,063,600

GREENE CORPORATION

Shareholders' Equity at 31 December 20X1

Contributed capital	
Share capital	
Preferred shares, no-par, $8, cumulative and non-participating (10,000 shares authorized, 4,000 shares issued)	$ 440,000
Common shares, no-par (unlimited shares authorized, 37,800 shares issued and outstanding)	453,600
Other contributed capital	
Donation of machinery	55,000
Total contributed capital	$ 948,600
Retained earnings	115,000
Total shareholders' equity	$1,063,600

QUESTIONS

Q14-1 Describe the main categories of shareholders' equity.

Q14-2 If common shares are issued for a fixed asset, how is a value determined for the transaction?

Q14-3 What is the difference, from an accounting perspective, between par and no-par shares?

Q14-4 Briefly explain the alternatives for accounting for share issue costs.

Q14-5 When a company has 100,000 shares issued, and 10,000 shares held as treasury shares, how many shares are outstanding? If a cash dividend of $2 per share were declared, how much total dividend would be paid?

Q14-6 How can shares that are not callable be reacquired by a company? Why must corporations exercise caution in these transactions?

Q14-7 Why will EPS increase when shares are retired?

Q14-8 Identify and explain a transaction that causes *other contributed capital* to increase but does not result in any increase in assets or decrease in the liabilities of a corporation.

Q14-9 Explain how the purchase price is allocated when shares are reacquired and retired at a cash amount lower than average issuance price to date. What changes if average issuance price is lower?

Q14-10 When shares are retired, is the original issue price of those individual shares relevant? Why, or why not?

Q14-11 Is treasury stock an asset? Explain.

Q14-12 What is the effect on assets, liabilities, and shareholders' equity of the (a) purchase of treasury stock and (b) reissuance of treasury stock?

Q14-13 Explain the difference between cumulative and non-cumulative preferred shares, and the difference among non-participating, partially participating, and fully participating preferred shares.

Q14-14 Contrast the effects of a stock dividend (declared and issued) versus a cash dividend (declared and paid) on assets, liabilities, and total shareholders' equity.

Q14-15 What are fractional share rights, and why are they sometimes issued in connection with a stock dividend?

Q14-16 How is the entry to record a (cash) liquidating dividend different from the entry to record a normal cash dividend?

Q14-17 What do shareholders receive when a scrip dividend is declared?

Q14-18 Compare a stock split, both its substance and accounting recognition, with a large stock dividend. In what ways are the two the same or different?

Q14-19 If a shareholder donates a valuable piece of art to a company, to be displayed in the company boardroom, does the company record a gain on the transaction?

Q14-20 What are the common sources of reserves in equity?

CASE 14-1

CONSTANCE INC.

Constance Inc. (CI) is a small private company located in Miramichi, New Brunswick. CI was incorporated in late 20X0 and has 10 common shareholders, consisting of two founders and eight of the founders' friends and relatives. At the time of CI's incorporation, each shareholder was issued 200,000 common shares. In 20X1, CI completed development of technology that has the potential to revolutionize online clothing shopping. The technology, patented in 20X1 as *Check Me Out*, was sold to one major online clothing retailer in 20X1. During fiscal 20X2, an additional seven online clothing retailers purchased the technology. However, now, in early 20X3, cash is tight at CI. Current investors do not have the personal resources to invest further, yet CI desperately needs more cash to market and sell *Check Me Out* to clothing retailers. Bank loans are not an option for financing because of the perceived risk of CI. CI's founders believe that a takeover by a large technology company or on-line retailer is the best outcome for all.

Check Me Out enables a shopper to upload personal photographs to a clothing retailer's website, once the retailer is a client of *Check Me Out*. These photographs are translated into a 3-D image of the shopper. The shoppers can then virtually "try on" the retailer's clothing and view the resulting images from almost one hundred different angles. The technology has received positive feedback, and CI's owners are confident that CI will be a success. Large technology firms have started to show interest in CI as a takeover target. Shareholders are hoping that something firms up in this regard in the next 6 to 12 months.

The founders of CI are not knowledgeable in the area of financial accounting. They realize the importance of understandable financial statements and want to make sure all applicable accounting standards are followed. For this reason, they engage the firm of Martin and Leaves Public Accountants to advise on accounting transactions in the 20X3 fiscal year. You are a co-op student working at Martin and Leaves, with a strong handle on intermediate accounting topics. For this reason, you have been asked to evaluate several issues raised by CI and prepare a memo detailing your analysis, additional information needed, and your recommendations. CI prepares its financial statements in accordance with IFRS. You know that potential purchasers of CI will be very interested in reported EBITDA (earnings before interest, tax, depreciation, and amortization).

Issue 1: In January 20X3, CI's founders attended several trade shows to promote *Check Me Out.* The cost to attend these trade shows was quite high. Since CI did not have the cash to pay for these trips, a CI shareholder cashed in several hundred thousand loyalty points earned through a credit card to cover the flights and hotels. In exchange, CI issued 10,000 common shares to the shareholder. CI is unsure as to how to record this transaction. The shares issued might be worth $25,000, based on informal discussions with a technology company that has expressed interest in acquiring CI.

Issue 2: CI is currently engaged in a legal case over the patent for *Check Me Out*. Mark Ramsey, the ex-boyfriend of one of CI's founders, has filed suit against CI. Ramsey claims that *Check Me Out* was his idea. He is suing CI for $2,500,000. CI claims that the suit is preposterous and completely impossible to prove. Nothing has been recorded in the financial statements with respect to this lawsuit. Legal advice has yet to be sought.

Issue 3: On 1 March 20X3, CI declared a 10% stock dividend. The purpose of this was to appease the shareholders while they wait for a return on their investments. The stock dividend has yet to be issued.

Issue 4: In an effort to further market *Check Me Out* and create an additional revenue stream, CI developed an app for mobile phones during the first quarter of 20X3. This app is called *Check Me Out Mobile.* The most unique feature of this app is that it allows shoppers to virtually try on clothing while in a physical storefront. The app can display virtual images of the shopper wearing items on display in the store. The app can combine items from the store, other stores where the shopper has uploaded data, and the shopper's own closet. The app will be promoted with the slogan, "It's like having a stylist living in your phone," because of the variety of outfit alternatives that can be displayed.

A retailer does not have to be a *Check Me Out* client for shoppers to use the app in their store. However, functionality is greatly enhanced when the retailer is a client. For example, a retailer that is *Check Me Out* enabled will have codes displayed on clothing tags that can be scanned and quickly "tried on" by customers. If a retailer is not *Check Me Out* enabled, a shopper will have to take a picture of the clothing item to enter the item in their virtual wardrobe.

Costs of $150,000 were incurred to create the app. The breakdown of these costs, which are reported under intangible assets on CI's balance sheet, is as follows:

Market research	$25,000
Design of prototype	$35,000
Testing and refinement	$40,000
Advertising	$50,000

The app will go on sale on 1 April 20X3. Based on market research conducted, and the positive word of mouth that has been generated through various social media marketing campaigns, it is expected that initial sales of this product will be strong. CI forecasts sales of approximately $100,000 during fiscal 20X3. Beyond that, it is difficult to speculate what will happen. CI suspects that the long-term success of the app is dependent on whether clothing retailers continue to adopt *Check Me Out.*

Required:

Prepare the report requested.

(Laura Cumming, used with permission)

CASE 14-2

FRESH FUN INC.

Fresh Fun Inc. (FF) is a private Canadian company operating in eastern Newfoundland. The company offers kayak lessons, camping expeditions, children's camps, corporate team building events, and wilderness adventures. FF owns several camping sites and has an inventory of hiking equipment, camping equipment, snowshoes, and hiking poles that clients can rent or buy, as well as their line of wildly popular T-shirts. FF has experienced considerable growth since its formation six years ago, and the three owners, all active in the business, have recently agreed to sell a 25% interest to a nonactive investor. They are interested in taking on additional shareholders, including FF's current controller. They plan to use the money raised for additional expansion and are interested in taking the company public if they have sufficient growth.

It is now 14 March 20X2. You are an employee with Doyle Republic, public accountants. Your firm has been engaged by FF to assist with financial accounting for its 31 January 20X2 year-end. Draft financial statements have been prepared by Liam Hanlon, the company controller. Extracts from the draft financial statements is presented in Exhibit 1.

Kevin Maclean, one of the three original shareholders, has given you instructions as follows:

> "The terms of our bank loan require us to provide the bank with financial statements prepared in accordance with Canadian Generally Accepted Accounting Principles (GAAP). We plan to continue using Accounting Standards for Private Enterprises

(ASPE) for our 20X2 fiscal year but are also curious about the potential impact of International Financial Reporting Standards (IFRS) on our statements, particularly given our desire to raise additional capital. Therefore, we need you to analyze the attached information. Make any changes you feel are needed, and prepare a revised balance sheet. Also, if there are issues that would be treated differently under IFRS, explain these and create a second balance sheet so that we can see the magnitude of the changes. You may ignore all income tax issues."

Required:

Prepare a report that addresses Kevin's requests.

(Judy Cumby, used with permission)

EXHIBIT 1

FRESH FUN INC.
DRAFT FINANCIAL STATEMENTS (EXTRACTS)
(prepared by Liam Hanlon)

	31 January	
Balance Sheet (ASPE-Based)	**20X2**	**20X1**
	Draft	
Current assets	$275,000	$ 47,000
Property, plant, and equipment (net)	375,000	450,000
Goodwill	37,500	—
Total assets	$687,500	$497,000
Current liabilities	$ 42,000	$ 39,000
Constructive commitment	36,000	
Other long-term liabilities, interest rates 5%–10%	75,000	151,000
Total liabilities	$153,000	$190,000
Common shares	$150,003	$ 3
Contributed capital	37,500	—
Retained earnings	346,997	306,997
Total shareholders' equity	$534,500	$307,000
	$687,500	$497,000
Retained Earnings Statement		
Retained earnings, beginning	$306,997	$264,997
Net income for the year	64,000	72,000
Adjustment re: Labrador cabins	(5,000)	—
Dividends paid	(19,000)	(30,000)
Retained earnings, ending	$346,997	$306,997

Notes on the Draft Financial Statements

1. Golden Pond Getaway

The Golden Pond Getaway (Getaway) was purchased three years ago, at the bargain price of $350,000. The sellers were in a liquidity crunch due to equity market problems. This remote recreation facility includes two rustic but spacious cabins, furniture, a fire pit, a BBQ, and a storage shed. Getaway is located in an idyllic wooded setting along a pond occupied by several other cabin owners.

The land occupied by Golden Pond Getaway is owned by the Golden Pond Cabin Owners' Association. Golden Pond has a long-term land lease. (This arrangement is common in some cottage areas; the land is a permanent asset of the Association, and leases are renewed continuously. The cottage itself is an asset of the cottage owner and land tenant.)

FF has stated that their plan is to use the Getaway until January 20X7, at which time the facilities will likely be sold. After depreciation, the net book value of Getaway is $284,375 on 31 January 20X2. At 31 January 20X2, the fair value of the property, net of selling costs, is probably only $250,000. Accordingly, an impairment loss of $34,375 was recorded at 31 January 20X2.

In early February 20X1, FF's three shareholders attended a meeting of the Golden Pond Cabin Owners' Association. FF's shareholders promised that the company will donate $36,000 to the cabin owners' association in 20X7, prior to the sale of the property, for restoration or the area and common property as the Association sees fit. Although FF did not sign any legal agreement to this effect, past practice indicates that FF is reliable in living up to its public statements. In 20X2, $36,000 has been charged to promotion expense, and there is a long-term liability recorded.

Annual net cash flows from Getaway of $24,000 are expected to continue for the next five years. It is estimated that the facilities can then be sold for at least $175,000 around the end of January 20X7.

2. Labrador Cabins

In early August 20X1, FF struck a deal with Walk Among Us Limited (Walk), a Labrador-based company owned by two of FF's shareholders. FF transferred inventory of sporting equipment to Walk. These goods normally sell for $56,000, and that cost FF $27,000. In exchange, FF received two cabins located in northern Labrador. The land on which the cabins sit is still owned by Walk. The cabins had cost Walk $22,000 to construct several years ago. These cabins were fair valued at $52,000 by a qualified and independent appraiser, and this was the agreed-upon exchange value for the trade for FF's inventory.

The Labrador cabins have been recorded by FF at their original cost of $22,000. An adjustment of $5,000, the difference between the cost of the cabins and the inventory given up, was debited to retained earnings. FF has rented the cabins, in a four-year agreement for $9,500 per year, to an independent Labrador fishing and hunting guide company. This contract is expected to be renewed. Based on this estimated eight-year useful life, depreciation expense of $1,375 has been recorded in fiscal 20X2 (half-year in the first year of operation.)

3. Share Issuance

In January 20X2, an agreement was reached with an angel investor, who agreed to pay $150,000 for 25% of the company. This money will be paid to FF in July 20X2, at which time the shares will be issued. Since there is an agreement now, the amount has been recorded as share capital and an account receivable.

Because this purchase price indicates that the company is worth more than recorded net asset values, goodwill of $37,500 has been recorded, with contributed capital set up for this amount.

CASE 14-3

TOPSAIL LTD.

Topsail Ltd. (Topsail) was founded 10 years ago by Dave Jetson, a carpenter and entrepreneur. Topsail is a growing construction company, building houses and doing major renovations for residential customers throughout the greater Moncton area. Dave is the president and sole common shareholder of the company.

Topsail approached its credit union in early 20X1 to increase its long-term debt to finance the purchase of equipment. A great deal of Topsail's equipment had been showing the strain of increased use and its efficiency was slipping. The credit union agreed to finance this purchase using the new equipment as collateral but has imposed a reasonably stringent debt-to-equity covenant. They also require audited financial statements. In the fall of 20X1, Dave met Carlie Smith, a partner with Morash and Bruce, Professional Accountants LLP (MB), at a mutual friend's dinner party. He phoned her a week later because he decided to hire MB to help him out on various matters. You work as a staff accountant at MB.

Topsail has a fiscal year-end of 31 December 20X1. The credit union will require an audit. Prior statements have not been audited and have been prepared solely for preparation of Topsail's tax return. Earnings in recent years have averaged $300,000. Dave has already appointed another public accounting firm as Topsail's auditor; he wants advice from MB on identifying and setting accounting policy issues. Carlie took notes on the call and has turned the notes over to you for analysis (Exhibit 1).

Required:

Prepare a report for Carlie to use as the basis for advice to Dave on financial reporting issues.

EXHIBIT 1

Notes from Phone Conversation with Dave Jetson

Topsail received an order from a recurring customer, Skyline, for custom-built cabinets for its new large retail store in Dieppe. Topsail completed the cabinets on 30 November, well ahead of the contract delivery date of 9 December. Topsail had received a $100,000 deposit for the cabinets in early October, with the balance of the contract of $150,000 to be paid upon delivery and acceptance of the cabinets by Skyline. In early December, Skyline notified Topsail that it could not take delivery of the cabinets until 15 January 20X2 due to the unexpected delay in the opening of the company's new store. Dave has heard a rumour that the reason for the delay in opening was because of Skyline's inability to arrange financing for inventory.

Over the years, Topsail has acquired an extensive range of machinery and equipment, ranging from small hand-held pieces to its most costly piece of equipment, a top-of-the-line insulation blowing machine, purchased five years ago for $45,000. It now has a net book value of $30,000. A similar but more efficient machine will become available in February 20X2. Topsail plans to replace the aging equipment when this new product comes out on the market. Dave anticipates being able to sell the existing piece of equipment for $10,000.

In March 20X1, Dave spent $20,000 on an extensive advertising and marketing campaign to generate additional business for Topsail. This expenditure was set up as an intangible asset.

Dave mentioned that a former Topsail client, Bob Swaine, is suing the company for failure to finish the basement in his new home, which was purchased from

Topsail. Despite there being no mention of completion of a basement in the sale contract, Bob thought all new homes came totally finished. Topsail's lawyer is quite certain the case will be thrown out of court.

Dave recently issued Topsail preferred shares in the amount of $25,000 to one of his key employees, Doug Smith. The shares have a rate of return of 7% per annum and are cumulative, redeemable and retractable in two years' time at face value plus dividends in arrears, if any.

Dave used this money to help finance a $120,000 acquisition of common shares in Abel Electricity Ltd., owned by a group of electricians providing electrical services to Topsail and a number of other contractors in the Moncton area. Abel is the sole provider of electrical services to Topsail. Dave explained "Thank goodness I have pull with Abel, since I use their services all the time, especially now that my business is growing! I would have paid about $10,000 more for the work the company did this year if I had dealt with any other electrical company. Plus we did that swap, which is a big help with cash flow."

Dave reported that he swapped a used van that still worked but was no longer being used by Topsail in exchange for 100 hours of electrician time from Abel. Abel was all too happy to offer this service, since its cash flow has been sporadic and the bank had been threatening to cut its line of credit. Abel's income has continued to grow but the company seems to have trouble collecting receivables from customers on a timely basis. Dave said "I sure hope this investment pans out. I figure the initial $120,000 I paid for the shares will be worthwhile in the future. After all, Abel had income of over $200,000 last year, and it's only Abel's fourth year of operation!" Dave owns 25% of the shares of Abel.

Dave has not declared any dividends this year but usually takes out a mix of salary and common share dividends as recommended by his tax advisor. He will declare the common dividend soon but plans to wait for all the dividends on the preferred shares when they come due in two years' time. He has cleared this with Doug Smith, who agreed, because Doug figures that he can avoid paying income tax on the dividends for a couple of years under this scheme.

(Tammy Crowell, used with permission)

TECHNICAL REVIEW

TR14-1 Share Retirement: On 1 January 20X5, AlbaCore Ltd. reported the following in shareholders' equity:

Preferred shares, no-par value; authorized, unlimited shares; issued, 100,000 shares	$2,500,000
Common shares, no-par value; authorized, unlimited shares; issued, 620,000 shares	4,960,000
Contributed capital on retirement of preferred shares	30,000
Retained earnings	3,850,000

The company acquired and retired shares in the following sequence during 20X5:

1. Retired 20,000 common shares at $12 per share.
2. Retired 30,000 common shares at $6 per share.
3. Retired 10,000 preferred shares at $30 per share.
4. Retired 5,000 preferred shares at $22 per share.

Required:

1. Prepare journal entries for the share retirement transactions.
2. Calculate the balances in each equity account, after the effects of the transactions in requirement 1.

connect

TR14-2 Treasury Stock: At the end of 20X8, Minnow Reserves Corp. reported the following in shareholders' equity:

Preferred shares, no-par value; authorized, unlimited shares; issued, 50,000 shares	$1,250,000
Common shares, no-par value; authorized, unlimited shares; issued, 1,500,000 shares, outstanding, 1,450,000 shares	3,000,000
Contributed capital on treasury stock transactions	10,000
Retained earnings	2,600,000
Treasury stock, 50,000 common shares	(250,000)

The company had treasury stock transactions in the following sequence during 20X9:

1. Purchased 100,000 common shares as treasury stock at $8 per share.
2. Reissued 40,000 treasury shares at $9 per share.
3. Reissued 50,000 treasury shares at $4 per share.

Required:

1. Prepare journal entries for the treasury stock transactions.
2. Calculate the balances in each equity account, after the effects of the transactions in requirement 1.

connect

TR14-3 Dividends: On 31 December 20X5, Watercress Properties Ltd. reported the following in shareholders' equity:

Preferred shares, no-par value; $1.00 dividend, authorized, unlimited shares; issued, 75,000 shares	$1,875,000
Common shares, no-par value; authorized, unlimited shares; issued, 300,000 shares	3,900,000
Retained earnings	6,100,000

Dividends of $405,000 are declared in 20X6. Consider the following three cases:

	Preferred Cumulative?	Dividends Last Paid in	Preferred Participating?
Case A	No	20X2	No
Case B	Yes	20X3	No
Case C	Yes	20X5	Yes, after common receive $0.50 per share; participation base on relative dividends at base level

Required:

Calculate dividends to be paid to preferred and common shares in each case.

connect

TR14-4 Stock Dividends: On 1 January 20X5, Dolphin Operations Ltd. reported the following in shareholders' equity:

Common shares, no-par value; authorized, unlimited shares; issued, 2,400,000 shares	$ 7,200,000
Retained earnings	24,900,000
	$32,100,000

In 20X5, the company declared and issued a 10% stock dividend. The stock dividend was to be valued at $5 per share. The dividend resulted in a number of full shares being issued, but also there were 8,000 shares to be issued as fractional shares.

Required:

1. Prepare all journal entries for the stock dividend in 20X5. The dividend is recorded when issued. Fractional share rights are issued for fractional shares. One month after issuance, 60% of the rights are exercised and 40% lapse.
2. Repeat requirement 1, assuming cash is distributed in lieu of fractional shares.
3. Calculate the balances in the equity accounts, after the effects of the transactions in requirement 1. What do you notice about the total?

connect

TR14-5 Reserves (AOCI): On 31 December 20X6, Wave Exploration Ltd. reported the following in shareholders' equity:

Retained earnings	900,000
Reserve: Accumulated other comprehensive income re: FVTOCI investments	50,000
Reserve: Accumulated other comprehensive income re: foreign currency	(230,000)

Comprehensive income for 20X7 is as follows:

Earnings	$287,000
Other Comprehensive Income:	
Change in fair value of FVTOCI investments	(35,000)
Foreign exchange gain on foreign subsidiary	20,000
Comprehensive income	$272,000

Required:

1. Calculate the balance in each equity account, reflecting disposition of 20X7 comprehensive income.
2. Explain the meaning of each reserve account. What would make each account increase or decrease?

ASSIGNMENTS

★★ **A14-1 Corporate Accounts:** The following accounts are taken from the general ledger of GRL Trading Limited on 31 December 20X1:

Preferred shares, no-par value, $2, unlimited number authorized, cumulative and fully participating; 27,000 shares issued and outstanding	$ 168,000
Bonds payable, 7%	500,000
Stock subscriptions receivable, common shares	3,000
Common shares, no-par, unlimited number authorized; 45,000 shares issued and 44,900 outstanding	1,350,000
Discount on bonds payable	6,000
Retained earnings	653,000
Treasury shares, 100 common shares	8,600
Unrealized exchange gain on translation of foreign subsidiary's financial statements	150,500
Fractional common share rights	9,200
Contributed capital on common share retirement	18,900
Common shares subscribed, 100 shares	9,000

Required:

1. Prepare the shareholders' equity section of the SFP at year-end. Assume accounts have normal (i.e., debit or credit) balances.
2. Explain the meaning of each account in equity.

★ **A14-2 Share Issuance:** Lake Simcoe Limited (LSL) has unlimited no-par common shares authorized. The following transactions took place in the first year:

connect

a. To record authorization (memorandum).
b. Issued 120,000 shares at $32; collected cash in full and issued the shares. Share issue costs amounted to $71,100. Treat this amount as a reduction of the common share account.
c. Received subscriptions for 45,000 shares at $34 per share; collected 70% of the subscription price. The shares will not be issued until collection of cash in full.
d. Issued 500 shares to a lawyer in payment for legal fees related to trademark registration. The lawyer estimates that the legal services provided would have been worth $15,000.
e. Issued 10,000 shares and assumed an $80,000 mortgage in total payment for a building with a fair value of $310,000.
f. Collected balance on subscriptions receivable in (c).

Required:

Journalize the above transactions.

★★ **A14-3 Share Issuance:** Combine Enterprises Ltd. (Combine) was incorporated in 20X6. Unlimited no-par common shares were authorized. IFRS was chosen for external reporting. During the first week, the company had the following share transactions:

a. The company issued 100,000 shares to the group of four people who were instrumental in organizing the company and who will sit of the Board of Directors. Bill Jones, David Fong, Esther Emilio, and Vishal Jain each received 25,000 shares.
b. Esther Emilio will be the Chair of the Board. In exchange for 375,000 shares, she contributed land, appraised at $350,000, and a building that is appraised at $1,450,000 to $1,650,000. This will be the site of the operations of Combine.
c. David Fong signed a subscriptions agreement to pay $1,067,500 to the company in exchange for 175,000 shares. He will pay the money in equal instalments over the next five years.
d. Bill Jones received 350,000 shares for the assets of the company he was running prior to the incorporation of Combine; this company will now be part of Combine operations. Machinery was estimated to be worth $300,000 to $400,000, customer lists were estimated to be worth $1,200,000 to $1,500,000, but there was also goodwill implicit in the number of shares issued.
e. Vishal Jain invested $250,000 cash in exchange for 50,000 shares.

Required:

Discuss the valuation of each of the share transactions. Include a recommendation for each transaction.

★★ **A14-4 Share Issuance; Subscriptions:** Furrow Inc. reported the following in shareholders' equity at the end of 20X6:

connect

Common shares, no-par value; authorized, unlimited shares; issued, 1,220,000 shares	$ 5,612,000
Retained earnings	7,900,000
	$13,512,000

The company signed an agreement with Chemical Ltd. (Chemical) in early 20X7, wherein Chemical agreed to purchase 535,000 common shares for $2,140,000. Chemical paid

$140,000 on signing the contract, and agreed to pay $500,000 per year in each of the following four years. No shares were to be issued until all money was paid.

Required:

1. Journalize the share subscription agreement, and the initial payment. Then, calculate the balances in all equity accounts, reflecting the entries. Subscriptions receivable is a contra account in equity.
2. Justify treating subscriptions receivable as a contra equity account.
3. In each of the three cases described below, journalize all transactions. Then, calculate the balances in all equity accounts, reflecting the entries.
   a. Chemical Ltd. makes all payments on schedule and shares are issued after the final payment.
   b. Chemical makes the initial payment and the first annual payment and then cancels the agreement, with the permission of Furrow. Furrow issues no shares but is entitled to keep the money paid to date as part of the cancellation agreement.
   c. Chemical makes the initial payment and the first annual payment and then cancels the agreement, with the permission of Furrow. Furrow issues shares for the cash paid to date.

★ **A14-5 Share Retirement:** During 20X5, Walter Ltd. retired 4,000 common shares and 2,000 preferred shares, respectively. Earnings was $100,000 in 20X5, and dividends declared, $40,000. The comparative equity accounts for 20X4 and 20X5:

Balances 31 December	20X5	20X4
Preferred shares	360,000	460,000
Common shares	$1,200,000	$1,400,000
Contributed capital, retirement of preferred shares	54,000	0
Retained earnings	270,000	240,000

Required:

1. What was the original issue price of the common shares? The preferred?
2. What amount was paid for the common shares retired? The preferred? (*Hint:* Reconstruct the journal entries to record the retirement.)

★★ **A14-6 Share Retirement:** At the beginning of 20X1, the accounting records of Farhad Corporation reported the following:

Preferred shares, 3,000 shares outstanding, no-par	$ 75,000
Common shares, 90,000 shares outstanding, no-par	184,500
Contributed capital on common share retirement	55,000
Retained earnings	275,000

During the year, the company acquired and retired shares, while other shares were issued:

15 March	12,000 common shares bought and retired at $6 per share
16 March	1,500 preferred shares bought and retired at $27 per share
20 May	4,000 common shares bought and retired at $1 per share
25 May	300 preferred shares bought and retired at $24 per share
30 May	5,000 common shares issued at $12.32 per share
15 Nov.	2,000 common shares bought and retired at $14 per share

Required:

1. Give journal entries to record each share retirement transaction.
2. Calculate the closing balance in each account in shareholders' equity.

★★★ **A14-7 Share Retirement:** On 1 January 20X5, BC Ventures Corporation reported the following in shareholders' equity:

Preferred shares, no-par value; $0.70, cumulative; authorized, unlimited shares; issued, 80,000 shares	$ 386,000
Common shares, no-par value; authorized, unlimited shares; issued, 80,000 shares	642,000
Contributed capital on retirement of common shares	14,000
Retained earnings	1,250,000
Reserve for foreign exchange gains on foreign subsidiary	38,000

During 20X5, certain shares were reacquired. In accordance with the regulations in BC Ventures' incorporating legislation, all reacquired shares were retired. Transactions were as follows:

15 January	Bought 7,000 preferred shares for $5.20 per share
12 February	Bought 2,000 common shares for $11 per share
25 February	Bought 4,000 preferred shares for $4.00 per share
26 April	Bought 5,000 preferred shares for $6.00 per share
16 July	Bought 8,000 common shares for $7.50 per share

Other transactions during the year:

30 July	Stock dividend on common shares, 5%, declared and distributed. The Board of Directors agreed to capitalize the dividend at the market value of $7.75 per share.
30 November	The Board of Directors declared a dividend adequate to pay $1 per share to all common shareholders. This meant that they also had to declare the preferred dividend.

Required:

1. Prepare journal entries to reflect the above transactions. Show the split between common and preferred dividends in the dividend entries, as appropriate.
2. Prepare the shareholders' equity section of the SFP after reflecting the above transactions. Earnings were $308,200, and total comprehensive income was $351,000, reflecting earnings plus an additional gain of $42,800 on foreign exchange caused by a foreign subsidiary.

★ **A14-8 Treasury Stock:** On 1 January 20X1, Grand Prairie Corporation issued 750,000 no-par common shares at $8 per share. In 20X5, there were treasury stock transactions. On 15 January 20X5, the company purchased 8,400 of its own common shares at $6 per share to be held as treasury stock. On 1 March, 1,500 of the treasury shares were resold at $9. On 15 March, 1,000 shares were purchased for $2.84. On 31 March, 1,700 of the treasury shares were sold for $3.50. The remaining shares were cancelled and retired on 1 June. The balance in retained earnings was $1,925,000 prior to these transactions.

Required:

1. Provide all 20X5 entries.
2. Calculate the resulting balance in each of the shareholders' equity accounts.

★ **A14-9 Treasury Stock:** At the end of 20X2, Provoe Products Limited had 222,000 common shares outstanding, with a recorded value in the common share account of $875,000. Retained earnings was $673,500.

During 20X3, the following transactions affecting shareholders' equity were recorded:

a. Split common shares 3-for-1.
b. Purchased 8,000 shares of treasury stock at $4.25 per share.
c. Purchased 6,000 shares of treasury stock at $5 per share.

d. Issued 5,000 shares of treasury stock at $9.25.
e. Issued 6,000 shares of treasury stock at $3.
f. Retired 500 shares of treasury stock.
g. Declared and paid a dividend of $0.25 per common share.

Required:

1. Give entries for each of the above transactions.
2. Give the resulting balances in each capital account. Earnings for 20X3 was $472,000.

★★ connect

A14-10 Treasury Stock: Wolf Products Ltd. has treasury stock transactions in 20X9 as follows:

a. Feb. 27	Purchased 70,000 common shares as treasury stock at $6.50 per share.
b. March 15	Purchased 32,000 common shares as treasury stock for $5.50 per share.
c. April 30	Reissued 50,000 shares of treasury stock for $4.25 per share.
d. May 16	Purchased 27,000 common shares as treasury stock for $6.05 per share.
e. Nov. 26	Reissued 134,000 shares of treasury stock for $4 per share.

At the end of 20X8, Wolf had reported the following in shareholders' equity:

Common shares, no-par value; authorized, unlimited shares; issued, 2,900,000 shares, outstanding, 2,750,000 shares	10,585,000
Contributed capital on treasury stock transactions	66,800
Retained earnings	7,420,000
Treasury stock, 150,000 common shares	(630,000)

Required:

1. Prepare journal entries for the treasury stock transactions.
2. Calculate the balances in the equity accounts, after the effects of the transactions in requirement 1.

★ excel connect

A14-11 Dividends: In 20X3, Burney Services Limited had the following share capital outstanding:

Preferred shares, no-par value; $1.20 dividend: authorized, unlimited shares; issued, 50,000 shares	$1,250,000
Common shares, no-par value; authorized, unlimited shares; issued, 240,000 shares	642,000

No dividends were declared in 20X1 or 20X2, but $500,000 of dividends were declared in 20X3.

Required:

Calculate the amount of dividends that would be paid in 20X3 to each share class under the following separate cases:

Case A Preferred shares are cumulative and non-participating.
Case B Preferred shares are cumulative and participating with common shares after the common shares receive a $1 per share dividend. Participation is based on relative annual total base dividends.

★★ excel connect

A14-12 Dividends: Mountain Construction Corporation is authorized to issue unlimited $0.40 no-par preferred shares and unlimited no-par common shares. There are 15,000 preferred and 45,000 common shares outstanding. In a five-year period, annual dividends paid were $1,000, $4,000, $32,000, $5,000, and $90,000, respectively.

Required:

Calculate the amount of dividends that would be paid to each share class for each year under the following separate cases. Where applicable, the matching dividend per common share is $0.50.

Case A Preferred shares are cumulative and non-participating.
Case B Preferred shares are non-cumulative and non-participating.
Case C Preferred shares are non-cumulative and fully participating. Participation is based on the relative number of shares outstanding.
Case D Preferred shares are non-cumulative and partially participating up to an additional $0.40 per share. Participation is based on relative annual total base dividends.

★★ **A14-13 Dividends:** Western Horizons Limited has the following shares outstanding:

eXcel

Common, no-par	54,000 shares
Preferred, no-par, $0.75	18,000 shares

The matching dividend, if applicable, is $1 per share.

Required:

Compute the amount of dividends payable in total and per share on the common and preferred shares for each separate case:

Case A Preferred is cumulative and non-participating; dividends declared, $64,800. Dividends have not been paid for the last three years prior to this year.
Case B Preferred is non-cumulative and non-participating; no dividends have been paid for the last three years prior to this year; dividends declared, $40,500.
Case C Preferred is cumulative and fully participating after the common shares receive a matching dividend; no dividends have been paid in the last two years prior to this year; dividends declared, $120,000. Participation is based on relative annual total base dividends.
Case D Preferred is cumulative and partially participating up to an additional $0.90 after the common shares receive a matching dividend. Dividends have been paid in all prior years; dividends declared, $160,000. Participation is based on relative annual total base dividends.

★★ **A14-14 Stock Dividend:** Gupta Corporation was authorized to issue unlimited common shares and had 452,000 common shares outstanding on 8 March 20X2, with a recorded value of $1,367,000. On this date, the Board of Directors declared a 5% stock dividend, valued at the fair value of shares, $4.50 per share.

Required:

Prepare journal entry(ies) for each of the following independent circumstances:

1. The stock dividend is declared and issued on 8 March, and all shares are distributed on this date.
2. The stock dividend is declared and issued on 8 March, resulting in the issuance of a number of whole shares but also entitlement to the sum of 1,600 shares as fractional shares. These shares were outstanding until 30 April, at which time 70% were redeemed for whole shares and 30% expired.
3. The stock dividend is declared and issued on 8 March, resulting in the issuance of a number of whole shares but also involving entitlement to the sum of 1,600 shares as fractional shares. Cash was distributed to shareholders in lieu of fractional shares.
4. The stock dividend is declared on 8 March, and distributed on 8 April. The dividend is recorded on 8 March. On distribution on 8 April, whole shares are issued as well as entitlement to the sum of 1,600 shares as fractional shares. These fractional shares were outstanding until 30 April, at which time 70% were redeemed for whole shares and 30% expired.
5. Comment on the differences between requirements 2 and 3. What might be the advantages and disadvantages of issuing cash instead of fractional shares?

★★ **A14-15 Stock Dividend:** The records of Victoria Corporation showed the following balances on 1 November 20X5:

Solution

Share capital, no-par, 40,000 shares	$344,300
Retained earnings	592,100

On 5 November 20X5, the Board of Directors declared a stock dividend to the shareholders of record as of 20 December 20X5. The dividend was one additional share for each five shares already outstanding; issue date, 10 January 20X6. The appropriate market value of the shares was $12.50 per share. The annual accounting period ends 31 December. The stock dividend was recorded on the declaration date with a memo entry only.

Required:

1. Give entries in parallel columns for the stock dividend on the issue date assuming:

   Case A Fair value is capitalized.
   Case B $10 per share is capitalized.
   Case C Average paid in is capitalized.

2. Explain when each value is most likely to be used.
3. With respect to the stock dividend, what should be reported on the statement of financial position at 31 December 20X5?
4. Explain how the financial statements as of 31 December 20X5 would be different if the stock dividend were recognized on the declaration date.

★ **A14-16 Stock Dividend and Stock Split:** At the end of 20X6, Hiltz Industries Ltd. reported the following in shareholders' equity:

connect

Common shares, no-par value; authorized, unlimited shares; issued, 7,200,000 shares	$ 9,400,000
Retained earnings	26,420,000
	$35,820,000

At this time, the shares were trading in the range of $4 to $6 per share on public stock markets. The company's Board of Directors is contemplating two alternative courses of action:

1. Declaring a 50% stock dividend, or
2. Executing a 3-for-2 stock split.

Required:

1. Prepare the shareholders' equity section for each alternative, assuming that market value is used to capitalize the stock dividend.
2. What would the expected share price be in each case?
3. Which alternative would shareholders prefer? Explain.
4. Which alternative would the company prefer? Explain.

★ **A14-17 Stock Split:** Altheum Corporation Limited had the following shareholders' equity on 31 December 20X8:

$2 Preferred shares (75,000 shares issued and outstanding; cumulative, non-participating, and convertible into two common shares for each preferred share)	$1,050,000
Common shares (240,000 shares issued and outstanding)	648,000
Retained earnings	2,020,000
Reserve: OCI: unrealized gains from investments	160,000
Total shareholders' equity	$3,878,000

Earnings for 20X8 had been $432,000 and comprehensive income, which also included a $27,000 unrealized gain on an investment, was $459,000. Basic earnings per share was calculated as $1.18:

Net earnings	$432,000
Preferred dividend entitlement (75,000 shares × $2)	150,000
Earnings attributable to common	$282,000
Earnings per share ($282,000 ÷ 240,000 shares)	$ 1.18

During 20X8, the company paid the $2 per share preferred dividends and also paid $180,000, or $0.75 per share, in dividends to common shareholders. Dividends are reported in total and per share in the financial statements.

On 1 April 20X9, Altheum executed a 3-for-1 split of its common shares. All share contracts were revised to reflect this split. On 15 July 20X9, the company repurchased and retired 18,000 common shares at $11 per share.

Required:

1. Prepare the journal entry to record the 20X9 share repurchase.
2. Post-split, how many common shares would the holder of 8,000 preferred shares receive on conversion?
3. When the company prepares its comparative financial statements for 20X9, what amount will be reported for 20X8 earnings per share? What amount would be reported for 20X8 cash dividends per common share?
4. Explain any other ways, in addition to the recalculation of earnings per share, that the 20X8 comparative amounts and disclosures would be changed, when presented in the 20X9 financial statements.

★★ connect

A14-18 Stock Dividend and Stock Split: At the end of the 20X4 fiscal year, the shareholders' equity section of the statement of financial position of Chomney Corporation was as follows:

Shareholders' Equity	
Contributed Capital:	
Share capital:	
Preferred shares, no-par value, $1.25, cumulative and non-participating, unlimited shares authorized, 40,000 shares issued and outstanding	$ 1,000,000
Common shares, no-par value, unlimited shares authorized, 366,000 shares issued and outstanding	2,675,000
Other contributed capital: common share retirement	45,900
Total contributed capital	3,720,900
Retained earnings	12,001,000
Reserve for unrealized exchange gain on translation of foreign subsidiary	90,500
Total Shareholders' Equity	$15,812,400

The Board of Directors was considering three alternatives:

1. A 200% stock dividend for common shares, to be recorded as a memo entry.
2. A 200% stock dividend to be recorded at the fair value of the common shares, or $11 per share.
3. A 3-for-1 common stock split.

Required:

1. Prepare the shareholders' equity section, in three columns, with each column reflecting one of the alternatives above.
2. Evaluate the alternatives, and indicate what course of action you would recommend to the Board of Directors.

★★ **A14-19 Retained Earnings and Equity Accounts:** Below are selected accounts from O'Hara Oil Corp. at 31 December 20X1. The accounts have not been closed for the year but transactions have been correctly recorded.

Treasury stock, common	$ 106,000
Contributed capital on preferred share retirement	23,100
Fractional common share rights outstanding	9,200
Excess on common share retirement (shares retired for $401,000 while average issuance price was $316,000)	85,000
Increase in unrealized FVTOCI investment fair value in 20X1	24,000
20X1 earnings	890,400
Common shares	9,411,200
Class A preferred shares	2,500,000
Cash dividends, common shares	94,500
Change in accounting policy, net of tax (increases prior earnings)	64,900
Reserve re: FVTOCI investments, 1 January 20X1	44,700
Cash dividends, preferred shares	125,000
Retained earnings, 1 January 20X1	8,216,700
Stock dividend, common shares	116,500

Required:

1. Calculate comprehensive income.
2. Calculate the closing balance in retained earnings and the reserve re: FVTOCI investments.
3. Prepare the shareholders' equity section of the SFP as of 31 December 20X1.

★★ **A14-20 Reserves; Accumulated Other Comprehensive Income:** During 20X7, Greenwave Productions Limited reported the following:

a. FVTOCI investments with a recorded fair value of $455,700 were sold for $502,500. The original cost of these investments had been $216,000 in 20X5. Realized gains are transferred to retained earnings but are not a component of income or comprehensive income.
b. An exchange loss of $166,200 was recorded on the translation of the financial statements of a foreign subsidiary; this exchange loss is not included in earnings but is an element of comprehensive income and a reserve account.
c. Recorded earnings were $607,200.
d. Treasury stock, on the books for $345,000, was reissued for $333,000.
e. A second FVTOCI investment, held at year-end, had a fair value of $507,000 at the beginning of the year and $478,200 at the end of the year.
f. A stock dividend was recorded during the year, involving 146,000 shares to be issued, valued at $3.75 per share. Of these shares, 140,000 were issued in the form of full shares and 6,000 fractional shares for which cash was issued.

On 1 January 20X7, Greenwave reported the following in shareholders' equity:

Common shares	1,875,600
Retained earnings	3,004,200
Reserve: Accumulated other comprehensive income re: FVTOCI investments	429,500
Reserve: Accumulated other comprehensive income (loss) re: foreign currency	(620,000)
Treasury stock	(345,000)

Required:

1. Calculate comprehensive income.
2. Calculate the balances in all equity accounts, reflecting disposition of 20X7 comprehensive income and the transactions of the year.
3. Explain the meaning of each reserve account. What would make each account increase or decrease?

★ **A14-21 Statement of Changes in Equity, Comprehensive:** The following statement of changes in shareholders' equity summarizes various equity transactions that occurred during 20X2:

MORGAN CORPORATION

Changes in Shareholders' Equity for the Year Ended 31 December 20X2 (in thousands)

	Preferred shares	Common shares	Contributed capital from Common share retirement	Retained earnings	Total equity
Balance at 1 January 20X2	$210	$500	$70	$910	$1,690
Net earnings and comprehensive income				330	330
Shares issued	360	380			740
Share issue costs				(15)	(15)
Share buyback	(80)			(26)	(106)
Share buyback		(41)	11		(30)
Stock dividend to shareholders		107		(107)	—
Cash dividends to shareholders				(34)	(34)
Balance at 31 December 20X2	$490	$946	$81	$1,058	$2,575

Required:

Journalize the transactions in the statement of shareholders' equity. For earnings, close the income summary to retained earnings.

★★ **A14-22 Statement of Changes in Equity, Comprehensive:** Below is a partially completed statement of changes in equity for Torino Capital Limited (in thousands of dollars).

Solution

	Preferred shares	Common shares	Fractional shares outstanding	Retained earnings	Reserve for foreign exchange gains of foreign subsidiary	Total equity
Balance at 1 January 20X1	$3,000	$7,400	$240	$6,780	$451	$17,871
Comprehensive income, including earnings of $871 and foreign exchange on subsidiary, a gain of $39						
Common shares issued for cash of $788						
Preferred shares bought back; 10% of opening balance bought back for cash; paid $85 more than average issue price						
Cash dividends to shareholders; $170 to preferred and $367 to common						
Fractional shares turned in for common (80% of fractional rights); remainder are still outstanding						
Balance at 31 December 20X1						

Required:

Complete the statement of changes in equity to reflect the transactions and events described.

★ **A14-23 Statement of Changes in Equity, Comprehensive:** Robinson Industries reported the following statement of shareholders' equity for the year ended 31 December 20X7:

excel

connect

	Common share capital	Preferred share capital	Other contributed capital (all sources)	Retained earnings	Reserve re: unrealized gains, investments
Balance, January 1, 20X7	$ 5,992	$3,500	$1,202	$ 775	$48
Issuance of common shares for cash	7,650				
Retirement of common shares	(1,005)		(356)		
Costs associated with equity issue				(124)	
Stock dividend	247			(247)	
Comprehensive income				1,980	13
Retirement of preferred shares		(630)	(116)	(35)	
Balance, 31 December 20X7	$12,884	$2,870	$ 730	$2,349	$61

Required:

Answer the questions below:

1. What is the nature of the reserve? Where does it appear in the financial statements?
2. Earnings were $1,980. How much is comprehensive income?
3. What amount was paid to retire common shares during the year?
4. What amount was paid to retire preferred shares during the period? Why is there a deduction from contributed capital and also from retained earnings?
5. Costs associated with share issuance have been deducted from retained earnings. What other alternative could the company have considered?
6. What is the nature of the stock dividend? What are the alternatives for recording such a dividend?

★★ **A14-24 Statement of Changes in Equity, Comprehensive:** Green Energy Limited began 20X2 with shareholders' equity as follows:

excel

Preferred shares; $1 dividend, 240,000 shares issued and outstanding	$ 6,000,000
Common shares; 1,200,000 issued and 1,000,000 shares outstanding	7,500,000
Contributed capital on retirement of preferred shares	40,000
Retained earnings	2,165,000
Reserve for foreign exchange on foreign subsidiary	(320,000)
	$15,385,000
Treasury stock; 200,000 common shares	(2,200,000)
	$13,185,000

The company's tax rate is 40%. In 20X2, the company reported transactions that affected equity accounts:

1. Common shares, 2-for-1 stock split.
2. Common shares, 182,000 shares post-split, were repurchased and retired for $879,050.
3. All of the treasury shares were reissued for $2,175,400.
4. Green reported earnings of $421,800, including an after-tax discontinued operation loss amount of $34,600. There was an after-tax foreign exchange gain of $131,000 related to the foreign subsidiary.
5. Cash dividends of $326,500 were paid. This represented the required dividend on the preferred shares plus some common share dividend.
6. After the dividend was paid, 60,000 preferred shares were repurchased and retired for $23.50 per share.

7. Share retirement costs, legal fees relating to both preferred and common shares, amounted to $133,000 for the year.
8. The company recorded an error correction during the year, resulting in a $90,000 pretax increase to prior year's earnings.

Required:

Complete a columnar statement of changes in equity that reflects the transactions and events described. Use one column for each individual equity account, and show preferred dividends separately from common dividends.

★★ **A14-25 Transactions, Comprehensive:** Howard Corporation is a publicly owned company whose shares are traded on the TSX. At 31 December 20X4, Howard had unlimited shares of no-par value common shares authorized, of which 15,000,000 shares were issued. The shareholders' equity accounts at 31 December 20X4 had the following balances:

Solution

Common shares (15,000,000 shares)	$230,000,000
Retained earnings	50,000,000

During 20X5, Howard had the following transactions:

a. On 1 February, a distribution of 2,000,000 common shares was completed. The shares were sold for $18 per share.
b. On 15 February, Howard issued, at $110 per share, 100,000 of no-par value, $8, cumulative preferred shares.
c. On 1 March, Howard reacquired and retired 20,000 common shares for $14.50 per share.
d. On 15 March, Howard reacquired and retired 10,000 common shares for $20 per share.
e. On 31 March, Howard declared a semi-annual cash dividend on common shares of $0.10 per share, payable on 30 April 20X5, to shareholders of record on 10 April 20X5. (Record the dividend declaration *and* payment.) The preferred share dividend will be paid on schedule in October.
f. On 15 April, 18,000 common shares were acquired for $17.50 per share and held as treasury stock.
g. On 30 April, 12,500 of the treasury shares were resold for $19.25 per share.
h. On 31 May, when the market price of the common was $23 per share, Howard declared a 5% stock dividend distributable on 1 July 20X5, to common shareholders of record on 1 June 20X5. Treasury shares were not given the stock dividend. The stock dividend was recorded at market value only on distribution. The dividend resulted in fractional share rights issued, that, when exercised, would result in the issuance of 2,300 common shares.
i. On 6 July, Howard issued 300,000 common shares. The selling price was $25 per share.
j. On 30 September, Howard declared a semi-annual cash dividend on common shares of $0.10 per share and the yearly dividend on preferred shares, both payable on 30 October 20X5, to shareholders of record on 10 October 20X5. (Record the dividend declaration and payment.)
k. On 31 December, holders of fractional rights exercised those rights, resulting in the issuance of 1,850 shares. The remaining rights expired.
l. Earnings for 20X5 was $25 million.

Required:

Prepare journal entries to record the listed transactions. Round per-share amounts to two decimal places.

Copyright © 1990–2000 by the American Institute of Certified Public Accountants, Inc. All rights reserved. Reprinted with permission.

★★ **A14-26 Transactions, Comprehensive:** The following transactions may change an account in shareholders' equity in some way:

a. Declare and issue a 3-for-1 stock split.
b. Record donated land.
c. Acquire treasury shares.

d. Record an increase in the value (an unrealized gain) of FVTOCI investments carried at fair market value.
e. Declare dividends on preferred shares.
f. Declare a stock dividend, to be issued in four weeks' time.
g. Issue the stock dividend in (f), resulting in the issuance of common shares and fractional share rights.
h. Fractional shares issued in (g) are exchanged for common shares (75%) and the rest lapse (25%).
i. Retire common shares for cash at a price higher than the average issuance price to date. This is the first time common shares have been retired.
j. Reissue treasury shares for cash at a price higher than average acquisition cost. This is the first time treasury shares have been reissued.
k. After the transaction in (j), reissue treasury shares for cash at a price lower than average acquisition cost.
l. Record earnings for the year.

Required:

In the table below, indicate the effect of each transaction on the accounts listed. Use I = Increase, D = Decrease, and NE = No effect. The first one is done as an example.

Item	Share Capital	Fractional Share Rights	Other Contributed Capital	Retained Earnings	Reserve: Unrealized Gains on Investments	Treasury Stock
a.	NE	NE	NE	NE	NE	NE
b.						
c.						
d.						
e.						
f.						
g.						
h.						
i.						
j.						
k.						
l.						

★★ **A14-27 Balances, Comprehensive:** Zu Corp. has the following items in shareholders' equity at 31 December 20X8:

Preferred shares, $0.60 cumulative dividend, participating with common shares after the common shares have received $0.30 per share, 15,000 shares authorized and 4,000 shares issued and outstanding. Participation is based on the relative annual total base dividends.	$ 360,000
Common shares, unlimited shares issued, 93,000 shares issued and 92,000 shares outstanding	1,080,000
Contributed capital on preferred share retirement	17,000
Retained earnings	4,356,900
Treasury stock, common, 1,000 shares	18,000

The following transactions and events happened in 20X9, in chronological order:

a. A cash dividend of $38,000 was declared and paid.
b. 4,000 additional common shares were issued for land. The land was valued at $50,000, while recent transactions in common shares indicated a share value of $75,000.
c. Treasury shares (common), 500 shares were bought at $12,500.
d. Preferred shares, 500 shares, were purchased and retired for $130 per share.
e. Treasury shares, 600 shares were reissued at $15 per share.
f. A common stock dividend of 10% was issued. Treasury shares were considered ineligible for the stock dividend, by order of the Board of Directors. The stock dividend resulted in a number of whole shares issued, but 350 shares had to be issued in the form of fractional share rights, still outstanding at year-end. The dividend was valued at $40 per share.
g. Earnings for the year were $1,450,000.

Required:

1. From (a), specify the amount of cash dividend to the preferred shareholders, and the dividend to the common shareholders.
2. Calculate the final balance in each shareholders' equity account.
3. From (b), justify the value used to record the common shares issued.

★★ **A14-28 Statement of Cash Flows:** The following data relates to Ottawa Limited:

31 December	20X5	20X4
Preferred shares, no-par	$ 520,000	$ 460,000
Common shares, no-par	8,438,350	6,840,000
Common share fractional rights	8,750	—
Contributed capital on preferred share retirement	29,000	22,000
Contributed capital on common share retirement	—	96,000
Retained earnings	3,867,000	3,911,500

Transactions during the year:

1. Preferred shares were issued for $100,000 during the year. Share issue costs of $2,000 were charged directly to retained earnings. Other preferred shares were retired.
2. On 31 December 20X4, there were 570,000 common shares outstanding.
3. A total of 20,000 common shares were retired on 2 January 20X5 for $18 per share.
4. There was a 10% stock dividend on 1 April 20X5. This dividend was capitalized at $17.50, the fair value of common shares. The stock dividend resulted in the issuance of fractional rights for 3,200 whole shares. Of these, 2,700 whole shares were subsequently issued and fractional rights for a remaining 500 shares are still outstanding at the end of the year.
5. Cash dividends were declared during the year.
6. Common shares were issued in June 20X5 for land. The transaction involved issuing 3,000 common shares for land valued at $52,000.
7. Common shares (46,000 shares) were issued for cash on 30 December 20X5.
8. Earnings were $1,200,000 in 20X5.

Required:

Prepare the financing activities section of the SCF, including dividends paid, based on the above information.

★ **A14-29 Statement of Cash Flows:** Refer to the facts of A14-24.

Required:

Prepare the financing activities section of the SCF, including dividends paid, based on the information in A14-24.

★★ **A14-30 Transactions, Statement of Cash Flows:** The following data is related to Cold Brook Resources Ltd.:

	20X9	20X8
Preferred shares, no-par	$ 2,000,000	$ 3,000,000
Common shares, no-par	45,000,000	36,000,000
Preferred shares subscribed	4,000,000	0
Common share fractional rights	0	574,000
Contributed capital on lapse of rights	114,800	0
Contributed capital on preferred share retirement	122,000	0
Retained earnings	8,005,000	5,940,000
Subscriptions receivable, preferred shares	(700,000)	0

During the year, the following transactions took place:

a. Earnings were $2,600,000.
b. Cash dividends were paid.
c. The common share fractional rights converted into common shares (80%), and the remainder (20%) lapsed.
d. Common shares plus $2 million cash were issued to acquire a patent that was valued at $6,500,000.
e. Contracts were signed to issue preferred shares with a total consideration of $4,000,000. The prospective shareholders paid $3,300,000 and will pay the balance within 12 months.
f. Preferred shares were retired for cash.
g. Additional common shares were issued for cash.
h. Retained earnings was reduced by $200,300 as the result of share issue costs.

Required:

1. Show the retained earnings T-account, beginning with the opening balance and going to the closing balance. Label all items that caused the change in the account.
2. Prepare the investing and financing sections of the SCF, in as much detail as possible with the information given. Dividends paid are included in financing activities.

connect LEARNSMART SMARTBOOK

For more information on the resources available from McGraw-Hill Ryerson, go to www.mcgrawhill.ca/he/solutions.

CHAPTER 15

Financial Instruments: Complex Debt and Equity

INTRODUCTION

When accountants prepare financial statements, a major task is to classify and organize the accounts into categories. Unfortunately, some things are hard to classify. For example, RONA Inc. issued $4 million in Class D *preferred share capital*, entitled to a 4% cumulative dividend. Is it equity? The company is required to buy back $1 million in shares, at book value, every year. These shares do not seem to be a permanent, residual equity interest: since the company is required to repay the investor, RONA classifies these preferred shares as debt. Criteria will be reviewed in this chapter that help determine whether a security is debt or equity *in substance*.

Financial instruments that have elements of *both debt and equity* are called *compound financial instruments*. In this chapter, recognition and measurement of convertible debt will be used to illustrate accounting for compound financial instruments.

Another topic in this chapter is accounting for share-based payments, whether the contract is equity-settled or cash-settled, with the cash payment based on the value of shares. Share-based payments may be made to employees or provided to suppliers or to existing shareholders. The cost of share-based payments to employees (employee stock options) can be considerable. TD Bank, for example, has options for approximately 15.9 million shares outstanding, primarily with employees, which allow the purchase of shares at an average price in the range of $58 per share. Since market value is around $80 per share, the option holders are receiving something of value. Representational faithfulness dictates that this commitment, and its related cost, must be reflected in the financial statements.

This chapter also examines the use of derivative financial instruments to mitigate financial risk, specifically the use of hedges and swaps. The use of derivatives significantly alters the risk profile of a company, and they are recognized at fair value to ensure that the SFP reflects the complete financial position of the company.

In the Appendix to this chapter, posted on Connect, the various forms of *financial restructuring* are reviewed. When a company is in financial distress, debt may be settled for less than the amount owing, in cash or other assets, or lenders may accept share capital instead of their existing claims and become the residual risk takers. These arrangements pose many challenges for accountants.

FINANCIAL INSTRUMENTS—CLASSIFICATION

The Debt-to-Equity Continuum

Throughout most of the 20th century, the distinction between debt and equity financing instruments was clear. Debt financing was an amount borrowed, at some specific interest rate, payable at a fixed time in the future or at the option of the lender. Shareholders' equity was represented by share capital, plus residual interests accruing through retained earnings or capital transactions. The legal form of debt versus equity was unmistakable, and substance generally followed legal form.

Accountants traditionally relied on the legal nature of capital instruments for classification. If there was a stock certificate, the instrument was accounted for as equity; if there was a loan contract or agreement, the instrument was accounted for as a liability.

However, there came to be many forms of financing where the legal description did not seem to correspond with the parties' rights and obligations. Financial markets support a continuum of investments, with features that range from pure debt to pure equity, with a lot of grey in the middle. Many financial instruments do not comfortably fit into two simple categories.

For example, perpetual debt is a liability that pays annual interest, but the principal *never* has to be repaid. An **income bond** pays interest and principal, but interest is paid *only when the corporation has reported a certain level of earnings or operating cash flow* in the year. Then there are preferred **redeemable shares**, as reported by RONA, that have to be retired for cash at a certain time.

Some **hybrid financial instruments** have elements of both debt and equity. They are also called **compound financial instruments**. **Convertible debt**, convertible into a fixed number of shares at the investor's option, is an example. The issuing company allows the investor to convert the principal portion of the bond into a specific number of common shares on a certain date. The issuing company usually hopes that the bond will be converted to avoid paying out cash. Investors will convert if the shares are worth more money than the face value of the bond. Perhaps the company will avoid having to repay the principal, if share prices increase, but perhaps the company will have to repay the debt, if share prices are soft. This is an uncertain outcome and obviously hard to place into a pure debt or pure equity slot.

Classification by Substance

Reporting standards require that financial instruments must be classified as liability or equity in accordance with the *substance* of the contractual arrangement. If the financial instrument is part debt and part equity, it is a *compound financial instrument,* and *the component parts are classified separately.*

These requirements are an important application of the qualitative characteristic of *substance over form*: if it looks like a duck and it quacks like a duck, then it should be classified as a duck, even when it has a sign around its neck that says it is a moose! That is, classification depends on the nature of the instrument as debt or equity and not on its name or label.

Furthermore, payments to investors for the use of capital should be presented in accordance with the nature of the financial instrument as a liability or as equity. Payments that are associated with financial liabilities are an expense and should be presented in earnings, and payments associated with equity instruments should be presented in the statement of changes in equity. Gains and losses associated with debt retirement are reported in earnings. Gains and losses associated with equity are capital transactions and are *not* reported in earnings but, rather, affect equity accounts.

Tax Status Unaffected It is important to remember that the accounting classification *will not change the tax classification of an investment vehicle* because the tax classification is established by the Canada Revenue Agency rulings. Thus, "interest" payments on instruments that legally are debt but in substance are equity will be tax deductible as "interest," *even if the interest is reported as a deduction from retained earnings.*[1]

[1] An exception is that the interest paid on income bonds generally is not tax deductible. This is a specific provision of the Income Tax Act, and the tax treatment is not affected by the accounting treatment.

Similarly, if an "equity" item is classified as debt in the financial statements, and the "dividend" payment is reported as an expense in earnings, the "dividend" *will not be a tax-deductible expense.* The "dividend" in earnings will be adjusted in order to reconcile from accounting income to taxable income. This process is discussed in Chapter 16.

Debt versus Equity Classification Implications

Assume that a company raises $100,000 by issuing a financial instrument that will pay $6,000 per year to the investor. At the end of the fifth year, the company retires the financial instrument in a transaction in the open market, buying it back at market value of $109,500. The financial statements are affected by whether the instrument is classified as debt or equity. The impact of each classification can be summarized as follows:

Event	Liability Classification	Equity Classification
Issuance	Increases long-term liabilities	Increases shareholders' equity
Annual $6,000 payment	Increases interest expense; decreases earnings and thus decreases retained earnings	Reduces retained earnings as a dividend distribution; no impact on earnings
Annual $6,000 payment on SCF	In operating or financing section; company's choice of classification	In operating or financing section; company's choice of classification
Classification of $9,500 amount higher than book value at retirement	Recorded as a loss in earnings	Reduces shareholders' equity directly; no impact on earnings
$100,000 "repayment" of initial investment	Decreases long-term liabilities	Decreases shareholders' equity

There are two major differences between these alternative classifications:

1. Reported earnings is affected by interest expense and gains and losses on retirement when the classification is a liability. In contrast, these items bypass earnings if the classification is equity. For firms that jealously guard reported earnings and related trends, this distinction is important.
2. The classification of the element itself (i.e., as debt or equity) may be crucial to some corporations. The debt-to-equity ratio is often used in loan covenants to help control a major risk to lenders: the amount of debt outstanding. If debt-to-equity ratios are close to their contractually agreed maximums, then a new financial instrument issued and classified as equity is good news, indeed; one classified as a liability is not. The classification rules attempt to ensure that classification follows substance, not form, to limit the potential for manipulation.

Classification Factors

To classify a financial instrument, it is essential to look at the payment arrangements. A basic characteristic of debt is that *creditors have an enforceable legal right to receive payment.* In most ordinary debt arrangements, the debtor is obligated both to pay regular interest amounts and to repay the principal amount at a fixed and known time. There is no fixed maturity for some debt instruments, such as demand loans or lines of credit from a financial institution. In these cases, the lenders have the option of demanding repayment. The crucial aspect of debt is that *the creditors can demand payment.* Equity investors, on the other hand, cannot demand payment; any payment of dividends and the redemption or repayment of the amount invested is a voluntary action of the company.

Therefore, to determine whether a financial instrument is debt or equity *in substance*, and whether component parts must be separated, the following factors must be considered:

Factor	Debt	Equity	Comment
Cash payment of the periodic return on capital (i.e., the cash "interest" or "dividend' payment)	Must be paid or Must be paid if the investor wishes	Paid if the company wishes	Any cash payment that is mandatory or is made at the investor's option is a liability.
Cash principal repayment	Must be paid or Must be paid if the investor wishes (i.e., at the investor's option)	Paid if the company wishes	Any cash payment that is mandatory or is made at at the investor's option is a liability.
Unconditional right/ Ability to indefinitely defer cash payments by the (issuer) company	Cash payments cannot be deferred or Cash payments can be deferred for a limited period of time	Cash payments can be deferred forever if company wishes	Classic dividends are payable only if the company declares them and thus can be deferred indefinitely by simply not having any declaration; they represent equity. *If deferral is only for a period of time, then the element is a liability.*
Cash payment dependent on the outcome of an uncertain future event beyond the control of both the investor and the (issuer) company	Future event possible or *controllable by (issuer) company or the investor*	Future event *abnormal* or *highly unlikely and uncontrollable*	If a financial instrument has to be repaid only on the dissolution of the company, this is deemed abnormal, and the element is equity. If the financial instrument must be repaid only if a covenant is violated, this is within the control of the company at some level, and the element is a liability.
Contract allows periodic return and/or the principal be settled in the (issuer) company's own shares; contract must specify how the number of shares to be issued is determined	Number of shares issued *is based on the market value of shares at the time of distribution*	Number of shares issued *is fixed by contract*	If the number of shares to be issued is fixed, then the risk of share price fluctuation rests with the investor, and *the element is equity.* If shares to be issued are calculated based on the share price on the date of payment, then the company has to issue shares with a cash value equal to the amount owing, and the element is a liability. In this latter case, risk of share price fluctuation rests with the issuer.

Classification Example—Retractable Preferred Shares

Most preferred shares have a call provision, whereby the corporation can call in the shares and redeem them at a given price *if the company wishes.* The call price is specified in the corporate articles governing that class of share. Preferred share *call provisions* give management more flexibility in managing the corporation's capital structure than would be the case without a call provision. These shares *do not have to be repaid*; they are equity.

Some preferred shares include the provision that the shares *must* be redeemed on or before a specified date (**term preferred shares**) or an option to redeem that can be exercised *at the option of the shareholder* (retractable shares). When redemption is required or is at the option of the holder, then the mandatory final cash payout effectively makes the preferred shares a liability. The key is that cash repayment must either be contractually required or is at the option of the *investor*.

Effect of Escalation Clause Sometimes, a preferred share issue will not have a direct or explicit requirement for the company to repay. Instead, the repayment obligation may be established indirectly through its terms and conditions. For example, suppose that a redeemable preferred share contract requires the company to triple the dividend rate after five years or double the redemption price after five years. No prudent Board of Directors would leave the shares outstanding past year five at their significantly higher cost. The escalation clause clearly indicates that the shares will be redeemed before escalation. These shares will be classified as debt.

Classification of Dividends When preferred shares are classified as debt, *their dividends are reported as a financing expense*, a *deduction from earnings*, and are not reported on the statement of changes in equity as a reduction of retained earnings.

Recording dividends Normally, dividends are a legal liability *only when declared,* and the classification of preferred shares as a liability does not alter this. Dividends on preferred shares are normally recorded as declared. However, if dividends are *mandatory*, then their status changes. Mandatory dividends are a liability. Dividends are recorded annually whether declared or not. For example, if dividends are mandatory *and must be paid in cash at redemption*, then dividends are accrued as time passes.

Required Redemption at a Premium If preferred shares *must be redeemed at a value higher than book value*, the redemption premium should be accrued over the life of the shares using the effective interest method. For instance, assume that redeemable preferred shares were issued at $100 but have to be bought back for $110 at the end of five years. Each year, the company must accrue a portion of the $10 premium and expense it as a cost of financing.

Reporting Example BAM Investments Corp. is an investment holding company with total assets of just over $1.7 billion. The company reports approximately $487 million of retractable preferred shares as a liability, signalling that preferred shareholders can trigger cash repayment at any time. Terms are described in the disclosure notes as follows (emphasis added):

---

8. RETRACTABLE PREFERRED SHARES

. . .

Holders of .....[four classes of] Preferred Shares are entitled to receive cumulative quarterly dividends of $0.309375, $0.271875, $0.453125 and $0.303125 per share respectively, payable on the 7th day of March, June, September and December in each year.

Class AA Series I Preferred Shares may be surrendered for retraction at any time. The Class AA Series I Preferred Share Retraction Price will be paid in cash equal to the lesser of (i) 95% of Net Asset Value per Unit of BAM Split; and (ii) $25.00 less 5% of the Net Asset Value per Unit of BAM Split, in either case, less $1.00.

. . . The "Net Asset Value per Unit" is defined as the fair value of the Portfolio shares held by BAM Split plus (minus) the amount by which the value of the other assets of BAM Split exceed (are less than) the liabilities (including any extraordinary liabilities) of BAM Split and the redemption value of the preferred shares, divided by the total number of Units outstanding....

Source: BAM Investments Corp., 2011 Annual Financial Statements, www.sedar.com, posted 24 April 2012. (Emphasis added)

Classification Example—Other Redeemable Shares

"Redeemable" does not automatically mean that shares are liabilities. Shares that are redeemable *at the company's option* are not a liability. The company cannot be forced to pay cash, since redemption is voluntary; redemptions that can be avoided do not create a liability. Also, any senior shares that are *convertible into common shares* are clearly equity.

Classification Example—Mutual Funds

In some open-ended mutual funds, all shares are redeemable in cash at the option of the investors, who also have the legal right to cash payouts for accumulated earnings. These entities accordingly have no equity at all, since all ownership interests have the characteristics of debt and are classified as liabilities.

Classification Example—Perpetual Debt

Perpetual debt provides the holder with a contractual right to receive cash interest, but the principal (1) never has to be repaid, (2) has to be repaid only in the indefinite future, or (3) has to be repaid only in highly unlikely situations, such as upon liquidation of the company. For example, the ING Group has outstanding perpetual debt of over €8.8 billion, at interest rates from 4.2% to 9%.

Reporting *Perpetual debt is reported entirely as a liability.* This is a compound instrument with both debt and equity components, but the equity portion is valued at zero. All that remains is the liability. The principal amount of perpetual debt is equity in that it is an obligation due only on liquidation. What is the value of a payment that has a due date in the infinite future? *The present value of such an indefinite payment is zero.* However, the interest payments are a liability because they represent an obligation at fixed dates. The lender will be willing to pay for the interest stream, and it is the interest stream that generates loan proceeds. Only a liability is recorded, which is valued at the present value of the stream of future interest payments.

For example, assume that a $1,000,000, 10% perpetual debt instrument is sold to yield 10%. The present value of the principal, which never has to be repaid, is zero. The present value of the interest, $100,000 a year in perpetuity, is $1,000,000 (i.e., $100,000 ÷ 0.10). Thus, the bond sells for the value of the interest stream only. The interest stream is clearly a liability because it must be paid. Therefore, the $1,000,000 is classified as a liability. The principal portion certainly exists, as equity, but is valued at zero.

Classification Example—Compound Instrument: Convertible Debt

Convertible debt is a common example of a *compound instrument*, classified in the financial statements as part debt and part equity. These bonds often are issued by a corporation with the provision that they may be converted by the holder into shares (usually, common shares) at a specified price or ratio of exchange.

The conversion date might be the bond's maturity date, or at various points prior to maturity (e.g., for the last four years of the bond's life). There might be different conversion rights during different conversion windows. For example, an investor might be entitled to 10 common shares for every $1,000 bond if converted within the first five years of a 15-year bond, 7.5 shares for conversion in the sixth through tenth year, but only five common shares during years 11 through 15.

The conversion ratio is expressed either in the number of shares per bond, or in a price per share. For example, a bond that is convertible into 20 common shares per $1,000 bond is the same as one that is convertible at a price of $50 ($1,000 ÷ $20).

For example, Paladin Energy Ltd. issued US$300 million of unsecured convertible bonds in 2010. The bonds mature on 5 November 2015, and have a conversion price of US$5.67 per share, which means that 52,910,000 shares ($300 million ÷ $5.67) would be issued if the investors took shares instead of cash at maturity.

Characteristics of Convertible Debt A key element of convertible bonds is that in issuing the bonds, management fully expects (or hopes) that the conversion privilege will be attractive to the investors: The investors will, in fact, convert to common shares, and therefore the company will never have to repay the principal amount of the bonds in cash.

Conversion of a bond becomes attractive when the market price of the share entitlement rises above the conversion price. For example, suppose that an investor has a $1,000 bond (purchased at par) that is convertible into 25 common shares (i.e., the conversion price is $40). If the market price of the common shares is $46, the investor can make a profit of $6 per share, less any transaction costs, by converting the bonds and then selling the shares on the open market:

Market value of shares obtained on conversion ($46 × 25)	$1,150
Less: cost of bond	1,000
Profit for investor from conversion	$ 150

The market recognizes this reality, and therefore the market price of the bonds will increase to follow the conversion value of the shares. Therefore, once the market price of the shares rises above the conversion price, the bonds will sell at a price that is related to the value of the conversion privilege rather than at a price related to the merits of the debt instrument. In the eyes of the market, the bond ceases to trade as debt, and effectively is traded as equity.

Forced Conversion A convertible debenture can often be called for *cash redemption* by the company prior to maturity. The point of the cash redemption option is that management can *force conversion* before maturity if the market price is higher than the conversion price of the shares. The company calls the bond for *cash redemption*, knowing that the shares are worth more, and the investor opts for the higher value of shares. By forcing early conversion, the company makes sure that the share conversion takes place and cash repayment will not be necessary.

Convertible Debt with a Floating Conversion Price per Share Convertible debt may be issued where the *number of shares to be issued on conversion is not fixed by contract* but, rather, is based on the market value of the shares on the conversion date. If this is the case, the conversion option has *no intrinsic value to the investor* because the investor has no upside benefit. For example, if a $1,000,000 bond were convertible into shares at the market value of shares on the conversion date and this value was $80, then 12,500 shares would be issued. If the market value were $82, then 12,195 shares would be issued. *This type of bond has no equity component and is all debt.*

The reason for this conclusion is that if the conversion price is not fixed, the risks and rewards of changing share prices stays with the company. The investor has no upside potential or downside risk. The bond will always trade in financial markets as a pure liability, with no option attached. Essentially, when the price is based on the fair value of the day of conversion, the investor could just as well take cash and use this cash to purchase shares in the market. The conversion option at a floating conversion price simply allows transaction costs to be minimized.

Accounting Treatment of Convertible Debt A convertible bond with a fixed conversion price per share has elements of both debt and equity. The liability and the equity component are recognized separately when the bond is first recorded and then are accounted for separately to maturity. Refer to the next two sections.

CONCEPT REVIEW

1. What is a compound financial instrument?
2. What classification factors must be considered to aid in classifying a financial instrument as debt or equity?
3. What is the distinguishing characteristic that causes retractable preferred shares to be reported as debt rather than as shareholders' equity?
4. Under what circumstances will the fair value of a convertible bond reflect the fair value of the shares that would be obtained on conversion?

CONVERTIBLE DEBT—CONVERSION AT THE INVESTOR'S OPTION

Convertible debt that is convertible at the option of the investor at a fixed conversion price is initially recognized as a compound instrument, where *proceeds from issuance are divided between the liability and the equity element. The equity element represents the value of the option on common shares. The debt element represents principal plus interest.*

Initial Recognition Assume that Tollen Corporation sells $100,000 of 8% convertible bonds for $106,000. The market interest rate on the day of issuance is 10%.[2] Each $10,000 bond is convertible into 100 common shares on any interest date after the end of the second year from the date of issuance. Conversion is at the option of the investor. Also assume that it is appropriate to assign a value of $92,418 to the bond and $13,582 to the conversion privilege. (Measurement of these amounts will be analyzed in the next section.) The issuance will be recorded as follows:

Cash	106,000	
Bonds payable		92,418
Contributed capital: common share conversion rights		13,582

To simplify subsequent accounting for interest expense on the liability portion of the convertible bond, it is helpful to separately record the discount on initial recognition. A discount of $7,582 is recorded: the difference between the $92,418 net proceeds attributable to the bond and its $100,000 face value. The entry is now:

Cash	106,000	
Discount on bonds payable ($100,000 – $92,418)	7,582	
Bonds payable		100,000
Contributed capital: common share conversion rights		13,582

(The highlighted section is the only difference.)

The account, *common share conversion rights*, is an equity account that will be reported as contributed capital. In later years, *the amount in that account will be transferred to share*

[2] As is discussed in a later section, this interest rate is established by determining an interest rate for non-convertible debt with the same term and risk.

equity if and when the conversion rights are exercised or transferred to other contributed capital if the conversion rights lapse.

Using this approach, *the substance of the transaction* is recognized. Both a bond *and* an option were issued, and both are now reflected in the financial statements. Accounting for the debt will reflect an effective interest rate that approaches the true interest rate on the debt alone. Finally, the proceeds received for the equity portion of the instrument are reflected in equity.

Conversion When convertible bonds are submitted for conversion, the first task is to update any accounts relating to bond premium or discount, accrued interest, and foreign exchange gains and losses on foreign currency–denominated debt. Following these routine adjustments, the balance of the liability account (and related unamortized premium or discount) that pertains to the converted bonds must be transferred to the share account. *As well, the proportionate balance of the common share conversion rights account must be transferred to the share equity account.*

The conversion is recorded using the **book value method**, and the book value, or carrying value, of the debt is simply transferred to equity. For example, assume that all of the $100,000 Tollen bonds payable are converted to 1,000 common shares on an interest date. Assume that on this date, the stock price is $140 per share, and calculations show that $4,550 of discount remains unamortized after updating the discount account. The entry to record the conversion is:

Bonds payable	100,000	
Contributed capital: common share conversion rights	13,582	
Discount on bonds payable		4,550
Common shares		109,032

The market value of the common shares is not recorded. The value assigned to common shares ($109,032) is the carrying value of the bond ($100,000 – $4,550) plus the option value ($13,582).

Repayment at Maturity If the market value of underlying shares is less than face value at maturity, investors will request repayment, and the conversion rights will expire. Since this happens *at maturity*, all discount or premium accounts will be zero. The option value remains in equity, but its description should be changed to indicate that the option is no longer outstanding. This is done in a reclassification entry. The entries on cash repayment of the Tollen bonds would be:

Bonds payable	100,000	
Cash		100,000
Contributed capital: common share conversion rights	13,582	
Contributed capital: lapse of rights		13,582

Repayment Prior to Maturity If the bond is repaid prior to maturity, the amount paid for early retirement is allocated between the debt and equity components, using the incremental method. Any gain or loss on the liability retirement is recorded in earnings, while the retirement of equity results in adjustments to equity accounts, as illustrated in Chapter 14.

For example, return to the prior example of the Tollen bonds. Assume that the $100,000 Tollen bond is retired for $104,000 on an interest date prior to maturity. On this date, $4,550 of discount remains unamortized. Valuation models indicate that $97,000 of the $104,000 price paid represents the present value of the bond at current interest rates, and the remaining $7,000 relates to the equity portion. The entry to record the retirement is:

Bonds payable	100,000	
Contributed capital: common share conversion rights	13,582	
Loss on retirement of bonds [($100,000 – $4,550) – $97,000]	1,550	
Discount on bonds payable		4,550
Contributed capital: retirement of common share conversion rights ($13,582 – $7,000)		6,582
Cash		104,000

The loss on retirement of bonds is caused by the difference between the carrying value of the bonds ($95,450) and the portion of the retirement price assigned to debt ($97,000). The contributed capital amount is caused by the difference between the carrying value of the equity component ($13,582) and the portion of the retirement price assigned to equity ($7,000).

Measurement

When fair values must be estimated, the **fair value hierarchy** is consulted.

In Level 1, there are quoted market prices for *this exact financial instrument* in an active market, and the result is objectively verifiable.

If the financial instrument is not actively traded, a Level 2 estimate might be made. In Level 2, observable values from similar financial instruments are used to imply value. Adjustments must be made for differences, such as credit risk, term, or conditions. For example, if the company's bonds do not trade in active markets, there are no separate objective prices provided by arm's-length market transactions. However, the fair value of another fairly similar bond might be verified. The second bond fair value could be used as a reference point, adjusted for interest rate differentials, or credit rating, and so on. The resulting fair value is less reliable than a Level 1 directly observable value.

Finally, at Level 3 in the fair value hierarchy, there are observable fair values, but multiple or significant adjustments have to be made to infer a fair value, including a company's own data or estimation of unobservable factors. The resulting fair value is used for reporting but is correspondingly less reliable.

Measurement of the fair value of debt versus equity components of convertible debt can be especially problematic because the component elements *do not separately trade* in financial markets. In the fair value hierarchy, this moves the valuation to at least a Level 2 estimate.

To value the *liability portion of the compound instrument,* the present value of the bond must be calculated. The interest rate used for discounting is the critical variable that must be measured. The conversion option is valued at the residual: issuance price less the present value of a comparable *non-convertible* bond. This is called the **incremental method of valuation**.

For example, for the Tollen Corporation bond above, assume that the market interest rate for a similar, non-convertible was established to be 10%. The present value of the cash flows of an 8%, five-year, $100,000 bond (assuming annual interest payments) at an effective interest rate of 10%, can be calculated as $92,418. This is a Level 2 estimation because the interest rate is estimated. Subtracting $92,418 from the net proceeds of $106,000 leaves $13,582 attributable to the conversion option.

The key to this method is *to establish an appropriate discount rate,* with reference to financial markets and established, observable prices. Ten percent should represent the market interest rate for a (non-convertible) bond of similar term, security, and credit risk; this may be straightforward to establish, or not, depending on the activity in the bond market and the presence of similar companies.

Example Assume that Easy Company issues $1,000,000 of $1,000 bonds dated 1 January 20X2, due 31 December 20X4 (i.e., three years later), for $1,002,000. Interest at 6% is payable annually, and each bond is convertible at any time up to maturity into 250 common shares. When the bonds are issued, the prevailing interest rate for similar debt without a conversion option is 9%.

Using the incremental method, the amount of the proceeds that is attributable to the liability is measured as the present value of the cash flow, using the market rate of interest of 9%:

Face value [$1,000,000 × (P/F, 9%, 3)]	$772,180
Interest [($1,000,000 × 6%) × (P/A, 9%, 3)]	151,877
Total liability component	$924,057

The issuance of the convertible bonds will be recorded as follows:

Cash	1,002,000	
Discount on convertible bonds ($1,000,000 – $924,057)	75,943	
Bonds payable		1,000,000
Contributed capital: common share conversion rights ($1,002,000 – $924,057)		77,943

Impact on Earnings Interest expense is affected by the allocation of bond proceeds between debt and equity. In the entries above, a discount is recorded. The discount is amortized over the life of the bond, using the effective interest method, as illustrated in Chapter 12. Interest expense will decrease earnings.

Remember that the higher the value that is allocated to the option, the higher is the discount. The higher the discount, the more interest expense is recognized, and the lower earnings will be. This effect may influence the valuation adopted by management when the bond proceeds are initially recorded. For example, if there is a corporate bias to maximize earnings, a valuation that minimizes the amount allocated to the common share conversion rights and the discount will likely be chosen.

Note also that the amount allocated to the common share conversion rights remains in the contributed capital section of shareholders' equity permanently and never has an impact on earnings. The conversion rights account is *either folded into the common share account, if the option is exercised, or is part of other contributed capital, if the option is not exercised.*

Convertible Debt with a Floating Conversion Price per Share The previous example involved a bond with a fixed conversion price per share. If the conversion option was based on the market value of the common shares on the conversion date, then the option has no value to the investor. Such a convertible bond is classified entirely as debt.

Reporting Example

Pinetree Capital Limited is a diversified investment and merchant banking firm focused on the small cap market. Refer to the sample financial statements excerpts in Exhibit 15-1. The statement of financial position shows a 8% convertible debenture, a liability, valued at $67.8 million, and an equity account of $2.8 million related to the equity component of the convertible debenture. The disclosure notes indicate that the bonds are convertible into common shares and that the option was valued at a residual amount on initial recognition, after reflecting a 9.47% effective interest rate. Issuance costs have been separately netted with the liability and the equity component.

EXHIBIT 15-1

PINETREE CAPITAL LTD.

Selected Financial Statement Disclosures

From Disclosure Note 3

Convertible debentures have been classified as debt, net of the fair value of the conversion feature at the date of issue which has been classified as part of equity. The fair value of the conversion feature is recognized initially as the difference between fair value of the convertible debentures as a whole and the fair value of its liability component. The convertible debentures are separated into their liability and equity components using the effective interest rate method. Transaction costs related to the issue of the convertible debentures are allocated to the liability and equity components in proportion to their allocation of proceeds on initial recognition.

From Disclosure Note 9c

On May 17, 2011, the Company issued $75,000 principal amount of 8% convertible unsecured subordinated debentures maturing May 31, 2016. The convertible debentures are convertible into common shares of the Company on the basis of a conversion price of $4.25 per share ("Conversion Price"), subject to adjustment under certain circumstances. In connection with the convertible debentures, the Company paid cash commissions, legal costs and other expenses of $4,088 (issue costs).

For accounting purposes, the convertible debentures are separated into their liability and equity components using the effective interest rate method. The fair value of the liability component at the time of issue was calculated as the discounted cash flows for the debentures assuming a 9.47% effective interest rate which was the estimated rate for the debentures without the conversion feature. The fair value of the equity component (the conversion feature) was determined at the time of issue as the difference between the face value of the convertible debentures and the fair value of the liability component.

The following table summarizes the movement in the convertible debentures:

Principal	
Opening principal balance, December 31, 2010	$ —
Issued	75,000
Ending principal balance, December 31, 2011	75,000
Liability	
Opening liability balance, December 31, 2010	—
Issued—fair value of the convertible debentures	70,916
Finance expense (issue costs) allocated to the liability portion	(3,865)
Accretion of discount on convertible debentures	310
Amortization of the finance expenses on convertible debentures	478
Ending liability balance, December 31, 2011	67,839
Equity component	
Opening equity component balance, December 31, 2010	$ —
Issued	4,084
Finance expense (issue costs) allocated to the equity component	(223)
Net deferred income tax	(979)
Ending equity component balance, December 31, 2011	$ 2,882

Source: Pinetree Capital Ltd., 2011 Annual Financial Statements, www.sedar.com, posted 8 March 2012.

CONCEPT REVIEW

1. Why might a convertible bond issued at a price above par result in a discount on bonds payable recorded on the books?
2. Where is the account *common share conversion rights* reported in the SFP? What happens to this account on bond conversion? Repayment?
3. What is the key valuation measurement in determining the amount of issuance proceeds from a convertible bond to be allocated to debt?

CONVERTIBLE DEBT—CONVERSION MANDATORY

The preceding discussion dealt exclusively with debt that is convertible at the investor's option. Corporations may also issue convertible debt that pays interest in cash, but principal *must be settled by issuance of a specific number of shares on maturity.* This is again a *compound financial instrument*; however, this time the obligation to pay cash interest is a liability, and the *entire* principal portion is equity. As long as shares can be forced on an investor *at a price set in advance*, a bond falls in this category. *If the company has the right to repay principal in cash or shares, the bond is still classified as "conversion mandatory."* This is because the company cannot be forced to pay cash.

Measurement Using the *incremental method*, the liability portion of the compound instrument is valued based on present value of interest payments using an appropriate market yield rate, which reflects similar term, security, and credit risk. This is a Level 2 approximation of fair value. The equity portion of the bond is then the residual amount, the difference between issuance proceeds and the liability present value. Over the life of the bond, interest expense is recorded on the interest portion *only*, and cash payments are applied against the interest liability *only*, reducing it to zero by maturity. At maturity, the equity portion of the bond is transferred to share capital.

Example Suppose that Gagnon Ltd. issues a $100,000, 6%, four-year debenture for $103,500, repayable at maturity through the issuance of a fixed number of common shares (fixed conversion price). Interest is payable annually, in cash. A similar bond that was not convertible would have carried an interest rate of 8%. Since conversion is mandatory, and the number of shares to be issued is fixed, principal is equity. The interest must be paid in cash, so it is a liability. The issuance price is disaggregated as follows:

Issuance proceeds	$103,500
Interest present value [$6,000 × (P/A, 8%, 4)]	19,873
Equity portion	$ 83,627

When the bond is issued, the entry will be:

Cash	103,500	
Interest liability on debenture		19,873
Share equity—debenture		83,627

Note how different this is from the treatment of a bond that is convertible at the investor's option. There, the only equity portion was an option amount, and principal and interest were both included in the liability amount. When conversion is mandatory, the bond has been cleanly split into the interest portion (a liability) and the principal portion (equity).

As time passes, interest will be accounted for by the effective interest method, calculated only on the *outstanding balance of the interest liability*. The carrying amount of the interest liability will be increased by 8% each year, and the $6,000 annual payment of interest will reduce the liability. At the end of the first year, Gagnon will make the following entries to record the interest expense and the annual payment:

Interest expense ($19,873 × 8%)	1,590	
Interest liability on debenture		1,590
Interest liability on debenture	6,000	
Cash		6,000

Note that the amount that is paid as "interest," the $6,000, is treated as the reduction of the liability and interest expense is a far different number, based only on the recognized liability. The amortization of the interest liability over the four-year period is shown in Exhibit 15-2. At maturity, the interest liability will be zero by virtue of the payments made over the four years. The balance in the debenture equity account will be transferred to common share equity when the shares are issued at maturity:

Share equity—debenture	83,627	
Common shares		83,627

Share Equity Alternatives Some companies have chosen to increase the recorded value of the share equity account from the initial assigned value, *up to par value*, through a **capital charge** to retained earnings. This can be accomplished in one lump-sum entry at maturity, or gradually over the life of the bond. At maturity, *par value* would then be transferred to the common share account.

In the example above, this would involve increasing the $83,627 share equity-debenture account to $100,000, an increase of $16,373. This might be done gradually over the four years to maturity by decreasing retained earnings for a capital charge and increasing the share equity-debenture account annually. Alternatively, the $16,373 amount could be recorded in one year, at maturity. *There is variation in practice in this area.* An example of the lump sum approach is:

Capital charge (retained earnings)	16,373	
Share equity—debenture		16,373

Share equity—debenture	100,000	
Common shares		100,000

EXHIBIT 15-2

CONVERTIBLE DEBT—CONVERSION MANDATORY

Amortization of Interest Liability

Year	Beginning Balance of Interest Liability	Interest Expense at 8%	Payment	Ending Balance of Interest Liability
1	$19,873	$1,590	$6,000	$15,463
2	15,463	1,237	6,000	10,700
3	10,700	856	6,000	5,556
4	5,556	444	6,000	0

The capital charge would be reported as a line item in retained earnings and reduce the earnings available to common shareholders.

Interest Obligation Payment Variations If the company *must* pay interest in cash, the interest portion of the issue proceeds is a liability, as seen above. If the company is permitted, at the company's option, to issue shares at their current fair value in full payment of interest, the interest is still a liability and is recorded as such. However, if the bond agreement allows the company to issue shares at a *fixed price* in payment of interest, then this interest portion of the debt *is equity*. Risk falls on the debenture holder when the price per share is set because the holder's ultimate benefit from interest payments will depend on the market value of the shares and is not on a fixed monetary amount. To summarize:

Bond Terms—Interest Arrangement	Classification
Interest that must be paid in cash	Debt (as above)
Interest that the company has the option of paying in a fixed number of shares or by using a fixed price per share	Equity; the entire bond is equity, since principal is also equity
Interest that the company has the option of paying in a variable number of shares, using current market prices to establish value	Debt (as above)

Debt Principal with a Floating Conversion Price per Share Standard setters have determined that when the number of shares (price per share) required to settle the obligation is fixed, then the principal is equity, as illustrated above. If the number of shares is not fixed but, rather, is based on the current fair value of shares, the principal is a *financial liability* of the entity, and the bond is accounted for as a straightforward bond liability, as illustrated in Chapter 13. Remember that if the conversion price is the current share price, there is no transfer of risk, and the price risk stays with company.

CONCEPT REVIEW

1. If a bond must be converted to a fixed number of shares at maturity, how is the equity portion of the compound instrument measured?
2. If a bond must be converted to a fixed number of shares at maturity, will reported annual interest expense be higher or lower than the contractual interest paid?

STOCK OPTIONS

Stock options or **stock rights** are financial instruments that give the holder the right, but not the obligation, to buy shares at a fixed price at a certain point in time, called the **exercise date**. When an option is first issued, it usually has an exercise price that is equal to or higher than the current market price of the shares. The option has an **intrinsic value** only when the current share price rises above the exercise price. An option term can be lengthy, and share prices can be volatile; so an option has a **fair value**, depending on market expectations about the *eventual share price on the exercise date*, combined with the time value of money.

Stock options are a form of **derivative instrument**. They are derivative because their value arises or is *derived* solely from the value of the primary equity shares that they can be used to buy. Derivative instruments are designed to transfer risk by setting the conditions of an exchange of financial instruments at a particular time at fixed terms.

Suppose that Mercurial Limited issues 10,000 stock options to investors. Each option permits the investor to buy one Mercurial common share for $5 in four years' time. When the options are issued, the market price of Mercurial's shares is $4. These options are said to be **under water** when they are first issued because the exercise price is higher than the fair value of the shares. If the current market price of the shares rises to $8, the option then has an *intrinsic value* of $3. The option is also described as being **in-the-money** when it has an intrinsic value. However, the fair value of the option may still be zero, if the market price is expected to decline below $5 by the exercise date. If the market price of the common shares is below $5 on the expiration date, the rights will expire unexercised.

Logically, the fair value of the option is *the risk-adjusted present value of any expected positive difference between the market value and the option price on the day the rights are exercised.* For the Mercurial Limited options, the "perfect" valuation would be to predict the market price—accurately—in four years' time and discount the gain to today's dollars at an appropriate discount rate. Assume that the market price would be $18 in the future. The option would be worth $130,000 at exercise (i.e., 10,000 shares × ($18 – $5). If the appropriate discount rate were 8%, the present value of this option would be $95,554 (i.e., $130,000 × (P/F, 8%, 4)). Unfortunately, there is no crystal ball available to predict the future stock market price or the risk-adjusted four-year discount rate.

The fair value of options can be established by use of an option pricing model, such as the Black-Scholes or binomial pricing models. Option pricing models price an option based on certain factors, including the share price of the option contract, length of the option, current market value of the stock, volatility of stock price, expected dividends, and the risk-free interest rate.

When options trade in financial markets, option prices reflect Level 1 values; these fair values reflect the practical application of option pricing models. In other cases, if options are not traded or are thinly traded, option pricing models are the only valuation alternative available. Use of option pricing models to account for some options is contentious because these models were not developed to price long-term options. Furthermore, the results are a Level 2 (or perhaps Level 3) measurement in the fair value hierarchy and have no Level 1 measurement validity. That is, these options might never be separately traded and any suggested fair value is an educated guess. Standard setters feel, though, that it is better to be imprecise than to give up, and valuation based on these models is becoming increasingly entrenched in the financial reporting model.

Recording Assume that a corporation issues rights allowing the holder(s) to acquire common shares in four years' time at an acquisition price of $20 per share, which is the now-current market price of the common shares. The corporation issues 100,000 rights and specifies that it takes five rights to acquire a share, so 20,000 shares could be issued if all rights are exercised. The corporation receives $18,000 for the rights. Valuation in this case is straightforward because there is a market transaction, which is presumably based on the investor's assessment of option pricing.

The relevant dates are the (1) announcement date; (2) issuance date, or grant date; (3) exercise date; and (4) expiration date. Consider the following entries:

Announcement date:		
Memorandum: 100,000 stock rights approved, allowing purchase of 20,000 shares at $20 in four years' time.		
Issuance date; rights sold for a total of $18,000:		
Cash	18,000	
Contributed capital: stock rights outstanding		18,000

At exercise, assuming that the current market price of the common shares was $28, and all rights were exercised:

Exercise date:		
Cash (20,000 shares × $20)	400,000	
Contributed capital: stock rights outstanding	18,000	
Common shares		418,000

Alternatively, assuming that the current market price of common shares was $14, and all rights expired:

Expiry date:		
Contributed capital: stock rights outstanding	18,000	
Contributed capital, lapse of stock rights		18,000

Note that the stock rights outstanding account ends up in one of two places: *either folded into the common share account, if the rights are exercised, or as part of other contributed capital, if the rights are not exercised.* Both of these accounts are equity accounts, and both are elements of contributed capital.

Note also that *the current fair value of the shares on the exercise date, $28, is not reflected in the entry that records exercise of the options.* Financial statement users would often like to judge the terms of the rights offering, as approved by the Board of Directors. Details of all options are disclosed in the financial statements so that anyone can make these calculations. But comparison of issuance price versus fair value requires some digging!

Options Not Recognized

It will occasionally be appropriate to simply disclose the presence of outstanding stock options. For example, corporations trying to make themselves less attractive as a takeover target will sometimes issue rights or options that would make it far more expensive for an outsider to gain control. These are known as **poison pill** options. They are issued to existing shareholders for no consideration and are recorded by memorandum only because they have no fair value. If the rights were allowed to expire, a further memorandum entry would be recorded.

In the event of a hostile takeover bid, the current shareholders *not involved* in the takeover bid and hold poison pill options would be allowed to buy shares at significantly reduced prices. This would greatly increase the shares outstanding and severely dilute the value of the shares held by the parties that back the takeover bid and have no right to exercise their options.

Poison pill rights are recorded only as a memo in the books. Disclosure is prominent, to scare off the wolves!

WARRANTS

Stock rights that are issued as a *detachable contract* with another security (usually bonds) are called **stock warrants**. Stock warrants will trade separately from the bond to which they were originally attached and have a Level 1 fair value because of this separate market. Like rights, stock warrants may be exercised to acquire additional shares from the corporation or allowed to lapse on the expiration date (if any).

Stock warrants issued in conjunction with debt have three important characteristics that differentiate the "package" from regular convertible debt:

1. The warrants usually are *detachable*, which means that they can be bought and sold separately from the debt to which they were originally attached;
2. The warrants can be exercised without having to trade in or redeem the debt; and
3. The exercise of warrants results in cash paid for shares, which is not the case for convertible bonds.

On issuance, a portion of the bond price is allocated to the warrants. The allocation is credited to a contributed capital (shareholders' equity) account, calculated based on the market values of the two securities on the date of issuance (a **proportional method**). The fair value of debt is based on present value at the market interest rate, and warrants are valued based on trading values as soon as they begin to trade.

Example Embassy Corporation issues $100,000 of 8%, 10-year, non-convertible bonds with detachable stock purchase warrants. Nuvolari Corporation purchases the entire issue for 105 exclusive of accrued interest. Each $1,000 bond carries 10 warrants. Each warrant entitles Nuvolari to purchase one common share for $15. The bond issue therefore includes 1,000 warrants (100 bonds × 10 warrants per bond). Shortly after issuance, the warrants trade for $4 each ($4,000 in total) and the bonds were trading at 103 ex-warrants (i.e., without warrants attached) ($103,000 in total).

These fair values total to $107,000, $2,000 higher than the $105,000 issuance price. This implies market inefficiencies or changed market conditions in the short gap between issuance and active trading. However, the $105,000 value is factual and must be accounted for using all information present. An allocation of the $105,000 issuance proceeds is therefore based proportionally on both values:

Market value of bonds ($100,000 × 1.03)	$103,000
Market value of warrants ($4 × 1,000)	4,000
Total market value of bonds and warrants	$107,000
Allocation of proceeds to bonds [$105,000 × ($103,000 ÷ $107,000)]	$101,075
Allocation of proceeds to warrants [$105,000 × ($4,000 ÷ $107,000)]	3,925
Total proceeds allocated	$105,000

Issuance entry		
Cash	105,000	
Bonds payable		100,000
Contributed capital: detachable stock warrants		3,925
Premium on bonds payable ($101,075 – $100,000)		1,075

If the warrants are exercised when the market value of shares is $22:

Contributed capital: detachable stock warrants	3,925	
Cash ($15 × 1,000)	15,000	
Common shares		18,925

If the warrants expire:

Contributed capital: detachable stock warrants	3,925	
Contributed capital: lapse of warrants		3,925

The contributed capital account either rolls into the common share account on exercise, or remains in contributed capital with a different description on lapse. *This is the same pattern* as established for the contributed capital account created for the conversion option for bonds convertible at the investor's option and that used for options.

Reporting Example Pinetree Capital Ltd. reports $66.5 million in the equity section of the SFP for warrants and discloses that there are three warrant contracts outstanding.

The following table summarizes the warrants outstanding as at 31 December 2011:

Number of Warrants	Exercise Price	Expiry Date	Warrants Value
5,000,000	$15.00	April 16, 2012	$37,100
6,875,000	6.50	October 23, 2012	19,662
8,638,650	3.50	July 11, 2013	9,762
20,513,650			$66,524

Source: Pinetree Capital Ltd, 2011 Annual Financial Statements, www.sedar.com, posted 8 March 2012.

CONCEPT REVIEW

1. When does an option have an intrinsic value? How is this different from fair value?
2. When options are exercised, is the value assigned to the common shares issued equal to the fair value of the shares? Explain.
3. What are poison pill options?
4. Past Limited issues common stock warrants as part of an issue of debentures. The exercise price for common shares under the warrants is higher than the market price of the common shares when the bonds are issued. Should any part of the proceeds of the bond issue be credited to shareholders' equity? Explain.

SHARE-BASED PAYMENTS

Share-based payments result from transactions in which an entity acquires or receives goods or services, where the consideration is in the form of shares or referenced to (based on) the price of shares. This includes transactions where share options are granted for goods and services. Long-term compensation to employees is a common example of a share-based transaction, but shares or options may also be used to compensate suppliers. These share-based arrangements may be **equity-settled plans** (the recipient receives shares) or **cash-settled plans** (the recipient receives cash based on the value of shares.) Alternatively, the arrangement may allow the recipient or the issuer to choose between cash and share considerations.

Share-Based Payment to Nonemployees

Transactions involving equity-settled share-based payments with *nonemployees* are recognized when the service is rendered or the goods are received. Such transactions are valued at the fair value of the goods or services acquired. In the rare circumstances that fair value *cannot be measured*, then the fair value of the share rights granted must be estimated and recorded.

Example Assume that Terry Technologies Ltd. issues 500 no-par common shares to Vilt Holdings Limited for October 20X2 rent, which has been set in the lease agreement at $1,000 per month. The shares are currently trading at $2.10 per share. The entry is:

1 October 20X2		
Rent expense	1,000	
Common shares, no-par (500 shares)		1,000

The transaction is valued at the contractually set rent amount. The market value of the common shares is in the same range ($1,050; 500 shares × $2.10) but is not used to value the transaction. The Board of Directors, who must authorize this transaction, would consider this information, though, because they have a legislative duty to issue shares at fair value.

Example Assume that GT Ltd. issues 500 stock rights to Laura Brown as a director's fee. Two rights entitle Brown to purchase one common share for $30. The rights were issued on 1 March 20X2, expire on 31 December 20X2, and are exercised by Brown on 1 July 20X2 when the shares are trading for $36.50. Other directors were paid $800 cash. The entries to record issuance and exercise are:

1 March 20X2—issuance date		
Administrative expense (director's fees)	800	
Contributed capital: stock rights outstanding		800
1 July 20X2—exercise date		
Cash (250 shares × $30)	7,500	
Contributed capital: stock rights outstanding	800	
Common shares, no-par (250 shares)		8,300

The market value of the shares on the date the common shares were issued, $36.50, is not recognized. If the options were to expire, the entry would be:

Contributed capital: stock rights outstanding	800	
Contributed capital: lapse of stock rights		800

Note the pattern established: The contributed capital account either is folded into the common share account on exercise or remains in contributed capital with a different description on lapse.

Valuation Valuation may not be as simple as presented in these examples. For example, if all GT directors[3] were compensated through options, no cash reference price would exist. Could the directors' fees of other companies be used as a reference price? There might be no comparable companies, or the companies might have different compensation practices. In the *fair value hierarchy,* adjustments to comparative amounts would move the fair value to Level 2 or perhaps Level 3 equivalents. In the rare circumstances that no fair value is obtainable, the stock option would be valued using an option pricing model—also a Level 2 or Level 3 equivalent.

For example, read the following note from Belo Sun Mining, where the agent responsible for a private placement of shares was partially compensated through share warrants; these warrants were valued using an option pricing model because the fair value of services received could not be determined.

(i) On March 3, 2010, the Company closed a private placement offering for gross proceeds of $6,000,000 through the issuance of 24,000,000 units comprised of one common share and one purchase warrant. Each warrant is exercisable for one common share of Belo Sun at a price of $0.50 per share until March 3, 2012. In connection with this private placement, the Company issued 1,200,000 common shares to D&D Securities and Delano Capital Corp. (the "Agents") and issued 1,200,000 agent unit options that will entitle the Agents to acquire the same number of units of the Company at a price of $0.25 until March 3, 2012. The fair value of the agent unit options was estimated at $303,813 on the date of grant using the Black Scholes option pricing model with the following assumptions: expected dividend yield of 0%; expected volatility of 127%; risk free interest rate of 2.25% and an expected life of two years. The agent unit options have been valued based on the equity instruments granted, as the fair value of the services received is not reliably determinable.

Source: Belo Sun Mining Ltd., 2011 Annual Financial Statements, www.sedar.com, posted 29 March 2012.

[3] Directors are considered employees under the terms of IFRS 2.

Cash-Settled Payment to Nonemployees

Suppliers and other nonemployees might also be granted entitlements under a *cash-settled plan,* where they would be entitled to money rather than shares. In this case, a liability would be established and measurement would be adjusted annually. Cash-settled plans are illustrated for employees in the following section.

Share-Based Payment to Employees

Share-based payments are a common form of long-term compensation granted to employees, senior management in particular. *Plans may be equity settled or cash settled.* There are many alternative structures, including **stock option plans**, **stock appreciation rights** (SARs), **phantom stock plans**, and **restricted share units**. The range of these alternatives reflects certain tax strategies and also the understanding that employees might prefer to have cash rather than company shares. It can be complicated, under insider trading rules, for managers to buy shares under an option plan and then sell them to raise cash.

Also, volatility in stock price may make classic option programs unpopular. For instance, when stock prices go down, instead of going up, employees may be disappointed and leave the company. When stock prices shoot up, stakeholders may be concerned with the generous returns granted to employees. For example, one executive of Potash Corporation of Saskatchewan was estimated to be holding options that were in-the-money to the tune of $338 million at the end of 2010; this is an extremely high level of compensation.

Some of the more common long-term compensation arrangements are summarized in the table below:

Share-Based Arrangement	Employee Receives	Description
Stock option	Shares	Employee has right to buy shares at a set price during a particular period.
SARs—cash-settled	Cash	Employee receives positive difference between set reference price of shares and (later) fair value of shares; share price is expected to increase over a period of time; value paid in cash.
SARs—equity-settled	Shares	As above, only value is distributed in shares.
SARs—employee option	Cash or perhaps shares (at the employee's option)	As above, only value may be taken in cash or shares at the employee's choice.
SARs—employer option	Cash or perhaps shares (at the company's option)	As above, only it is the company's choice as to whether cash or shares are distributed.
Phantom stock plan—cash	Cash	Employee receives cash award equal to the fair value of a certain number of shares at a certain point in time.
Phantom stock plan—employee option—cash or shares	Employee has choice of cash or shares; often higher value of shares is offered as incentive to take shares	Employee receives cash award equal to the fair value of a certain number of shares at a certain point in time. Payment is in cash or shares.
Restricted share units	Cash	Depending on terms, employee is awarded units and is paid cash after certain performance standards are met or time passes. Amount is based on the value of the *increase in underlying share value* or the *total value* of underlying shares.

Summary of Characteristics of Share-Based Arrangements

The vesting period for share-based arrangements is important for accounting purposes. **Vesting** is achieved when the employee is entitled to the compensation, regardless of other conditions. Once vested, rights irrevocably pass to the recipient. For example, if an option vests after three years of employment and is exercisable after Year 5, an individual who leaves the company in Year 4 would still be able to exercise the option, while one who left in Year 3 would **forfeit**, or give up, the option.

Accounting Patterns Accounting for the share-based arrangements with employees can follow several patterns:

1. If the plan is *equity settled,* then the fair value is estimated *once, and once only,* when the equity rights are granted; this value is accrued over the *vesting period.* Expected forfeiture rates are estimated annually and the amounts are adjusted to actual forfeiture rates each period and at maturity (i.e., the plan is **trued up** annually, or brought to the correct final amount). If the plan vests immediately, the fair value is immediately recorded in full. Accrual increases an equity account and results in an expense that decreases earnings. The expense and equity accounts are recorded/adjusted annually.
2. If the plan is *cash settled,* then the *fair value* is *recalculated annually.* Fair value is based on a valuation model, which would include certain factors, such as share price volatility, plan duration, and so on. The yearly accrual represents the current year amount plus a correction of the prior cumulative estimate, reflecting cumulative accrual over the vesting period. Expected forfeiture rates are estimated annually and the amounts are adjusted to actual forfeiture rates each period and at maturity. That is, a cash-settled plan is *trued up for both fair value and forfeiture.* The accrual increases a liability account and results in an expense that decreases earnings.
3. If the plan allows employees to choose between cash and shares at maturity, then the plan is a compound instrument. The equity portion is recorded as in (1), above, while the liability portion reflects the treatment in (2).

In summary:

Classification	Amount	Remeasure for	Elements	Comment
Equity-settled plan	Fair value set by option pricing model on date of grant, adjusted for forfeitures	Forfeitures	Expense and equity	Recorded over period to vesting; no adjustment of initial fair value estimate; Remeasured annually for estimated forfeitures
Cash-settled plan	Cash to be paid estimated at fair value each year-end, adjusted for forfeitures	Fair value and forfeitures	Expense and liability	Recorded over period to vesting; Remeasured annually for estimated fair value and forfeitures
Compound instrument	Initial recognition of both liability and equity component	Equity—forfeitures only; Liability—fair value and forfeitures	Expense and equity and liability	Liability element measured as above; Equity element measured as above

Equity-Settled Plans

Equity-settled plans all follow the same accounting pattern and will be demonstrated through employee stock option plans.

Employee Stock Options Suppose that 20 employees are granted options for 250 shares each, a total of 5,000 common shares, at an exercise price of $20 per share. The options *vest* immediately, meaning that the employees can exercise the options whether employment continues or not. The options are exercisable after five years and expire after eight years, which means that there is a three-year exercise window starting after five years.

The company must determine the fair value of the option *on the date it is granted*, using an option pricing model. Assume that this total value is $48,000 for all 5,000 shares. Recognition of this amount is over the vesting period; it is recognized *all up front* if the options vest immediately or *over a period of years* if vesting spans more than one year. For this example, vesting is immediate, so the cost of the option is recognized as follows:

On the vesting date:		
Compensation expense	48,000	
Contributed capital: common share options outstanding		48,000

Now assume that the options do not vest until four years after they have been granted, and there is no risk of the employees forfeiting the options (i.e., all employees will stay with the company through the vesting period). In that case, one-quarter of the expense is recorded in each year:

Annual entry:		
Compensation expense ($48,000 ÷ 4)	12,000	
Contributed capital: common share options outstanding		12,000

Note that this amortization period is the *vesting period*, not the period of time before the options may be exercised (five years) or the window during which the options can be exercised (three years). The vesting period often coincides with the period before the options can first be exercised (five years), but this is not always the case.

After this entry is made annually for four years, $48,000 of total compensation expense is recorded and there is a $48,000 balance in the contributed capital account. The $48,000 estimate is not revisited; this fair value is *not subsequently adjusted for changes in option pricing variables.*

When the options are exercised, the contributed capital amount is moved into the common share account along with cash paid:

At exercise:		
Cash (5,000 shares × $20)	100,000	
Contributed capital: common share options outstanding	48,000	
Common shares		148,000

Options may *lapse* because the exercise price is higher than the common share price. If the options lapse, the amount recorded as contributed capital remains, but its classification is changed to indicate that the options have expired:

If the options lapse:		
Contributed capital: common share options outstanding	48,000	
Contributed capital: share options expired		48,000

The ironic part of a "lapsed options" situation is that the company has recorded an expense for an option plan, which has turned out to be of no value to the employee. Expired options would have been *under water* on the maturity date. However, the accounting valuation is based on the initial assessment of fair value on the date the options are granted. *The intrinsic value of the option on the exercise date, or the lack thereof, is not recognized in any circumstances.*

Measurement with forfeiture estimated Forfeiture during the vesting period must be estimated annually, and the amounts *trued up* at the end of the vesting period. For example, assume that the company *initially* estimates that only 16 of the 20 employees covered by the option agreement illustrated above are expected to stay until vesting. Three leave in the first year, one in the second, two in the third, and none in the fourth. By the end of the vesting period, six have forfeited and 14 receive options. Estimates of forfeitures are updated at the end of each period, and actual turnover is instructive in this estimate. Data are as follows:

Year	1	2	3	4
Estimates made by management:*				
Employees expected to remain until vesting	16 (80%)	14 (70%)	13 (65%)	—
Employees expected to forfeit	4 (20%)	6 (30%)	7 (35%)	—
Factual history:				
Employees actually forfeiting in the year (6 in total)	3	1	2	0
Employees actually receiving options (20 – 6)				14 (70%)

*These estimates are prepared by the company annually.

The expense for each period is as follows:

Time Period	1	2	3	4
Fair value	$48,000	$48,000	$48,000	$48,000
× *Cumulative* vested fraction	1/4	2/4	3/4	4/4
× Estimate of retention (above)	80%	70%	65%	70%*
= Required balance in the equity account at year-end	$ 9,600	$16,800	$23,400	$33,600
Opening balance	0	9,600	16,800	23,400
Expense for the period (Debit expense, credit contributed capital)	$ 9,600	$ 7,200	$ 6,600	$10,200

*Actual; 14/20

The annual expense is no longer an equal $12,000 amount, even though it is still based on the initial measure of $48,000 of fair value. Each year, the accrual is adjusted to the appropriate level of expected take-up, *on a cumulative basis*. In the first year, the expense of $9,600 is simply the $12,000 one-quarter fair value allocation multiplied by the expected 80% retention rate.

The Year 1 entry is:

Compensation expense	9,600	
Contributed capital: common share options outstanding		9,600

In the second year, however, the expected retention rate has declined to 70%. There is an annual expense of $12,000 multiplied by the new retention rate of 70% ($8,400) *combined with* an adjustment to the first-year expense to bring it down to the now-expected 70% retention rate (10% of $12,000, a recovery of $1,200.) The result is an expense of $7,200.

The Year 2 entry is:

Compensation expense	7,200	
Contributed capital: common share options outstanding		7,200

Fortunately, since cumulative adjustments are tedious, all adjustments are included on one line on the table shown above and do not have to be separately calculated. By the end of the fourth year, the equity account reflects the balance for the employees who actually receive vested options, and the cumulative expense is *trued up* at $33,600, or $48,000 × 14/20 employees.

Entries in Years 3 and 4 are:

Compensation expense	6,600	
Contributed capital: common share options outstanding		6,600

Compensation expense	10,200	
Contributed capital: common share options outstanding		10,200

When the options are exercised or lapse, entries follow the pattern that has been established in prior examples.

ETHICAL ISSUES

Management must use *best estimates* in estimating compensation cost accruals. There are many estimates required by the option pricing models that are used to establish fair value. In addition, though, retention rates are critical. If retention rates decline, the expense is lower not only because the annual portion of the expense is lower but also because the cumulative correction reduces expense in the current year. The expense could even be a *recovery* if retention estimates are significantly lowered and the company is well into the vesting period. Evidence to support retention must be gathered, but trends may be difficult to predict, making this area high risk for manipulation and misstatement.

Reporting example An example of accounting policies for share-based payments and stock option activity for Stantec Inc. follows.

From Disclosure Note 4

o) Share-based payment transactions

Under the Company's share option plan, the board of directors may grant to officers and employees remuneration in the form of share-based payment transactions, whereby officers and employees render services as consideration for equity instruments (equity-settled transactions).

Under the Company's deferred share unit plan, the chief executive officer and directors of the board of the Company may receive deferred share units equal to one common share. Under the Company's restricted share unit plan, senior vice presidents are granted share units that are to be settled after a two-year period. The deferred share units and restricted share units are share appreciation rights that can only be settled in cash (i.e., cash-settled transactions).

Equity-settled transactions

The cost of equity-settled transactions awards is measured by reference to the fair value at the grant date using a Black-Scholes option-pricing model. The cost of equity-settled transactions is recognized, together with a corresponding increase in equity, over the period in which the service conditions are fulfilled (the vesting period). The cumulative expense recognized for equity-settled transactions at each reporting date until the vesting date reflects the extent to which the vesting period has expired and the Company's best estimate of the number of equity instruments that will ultimately vest. The expense or credit to income for a period represents the movement in cumulative expense recognized as at the beginning and end of that period and is recorded in administrative and marketing expenses. No expense is recognized for awards that do not ultimately vest.

Cash-settled transactions

The cost of cash-settled transactions is measured initially at fair value at the grant date using a Black-Scholes option-pricing model. This fair value is expensed upon issue with the recognition of a corresponding liability. The liability is remeasured to fair value at each reporting date, up to and including the settlement date, with changes in fair value recognized in administrative and marketing expenses.

From Disclosure Note 24

Share options

Under the Company's share option plan, options to purchase common shares may be granted by the board of directors to officers and employees. Options are granted at exercise prices equal to or greater than fair market value at the issue date, generally vest evenly over a three-year period, and have contractual lives of 7 years. The aggregate number of common shares reserved for issuance that may be purchased upon the exercise of options granted pursuant to the plan shall not exceed 4,487,026 common shares. At December 31, 2012, 1,165,400 (2011—1,523,232) options were available for issue.

The Company has granted share options to officers and employees to purchase 1,475,823 shares at prices between $20.37 and $30.61 per share. These options expire on dates between August 18, 2013, and February 28, 2019.

December 31, 2012	**Shares #**	**Weighted Average Exercise Price $**
Share options, beginning of the year	1,578,300	26.64
Granted	375,500	29.75
Exercised	(460,309)	22.17
Forfeited	(17,668)	28.90
Share options, end of the year	1,475,823	28.79

...

Comparative figures have been excluded.

Source: Stantec Inc., 2012 Annual Financial Statements, www.sedar.com, posted 21 February 2013.

Cash-Settled Plans

Cash-settled plans all follow the same accounting pattern, and will be demonstrated through a cash-settled SARs plan.

Cash-Settled SARs Forty employees are awarded a total of 10,000 units of SARs at the beginning of 20X5. Each employee receives 250 units in a program that entitles him or her to a cash payment equal to the appreciation in stock price over the life of the SARs contract. The employees will receive cash at the end of the 20X7 year, if still with the employer at that time. The cash to be distributed is calculated as the fair value of company shares in 20X7, less a $10 *reference price*, which the company has chosen because it is the fair value of company shares when the SARs were granted in 20X5. These terms are set by contract and are different for every SARs arrangement. Each of these SARs units has an *intrinsic value* at any point in time, which is the difference between $10 and the current market price of the shares. Each SARs unit also has a fair value, which is the *expected time-adjusted value of the SARs unit at maturity.* Fair value is not just intrinsic value.

Data are as follows:

End of Year	20X5	20X6	20X7
Intrinsic value:			
Market value per share	$18	$12	$19
Reference price per share	10	10	10
Intrinsic value per share	$ 8	$ 2	$ 9
Fair value:			
Estimated fair value per share *(provided by a valuation model)*	$ 8.70	$ 3.00	n/a
Total fair value (for 10,000 units)	$87,000	$30,000	n/a
Cash payout:			
Total intrinsic value ($9 × 10,000 units)			$90,000

No forfeitures are expected. The entries make an annual accrual *with an adjustment for the cumulative balance, referenced to the new fair value.* Unlike the share-settled pattern, these entries are based on a new fair value each period, and are trued up to intrinsic value when the cash payout is made. These calculations can be done with or without the structure of the table that was illustrated for options.

20X5 entry:		
Compensation expense [($87,000) × (1 year ÷ 3 years)]	29,000	
Long-term compensation liability		29,000

20X6 entry:		
Long-term compensation liability [($30,000) × (2 years ÷ 3 years) = $20,000 versus $29,000 recorded]	9,000	
Compensation expense (recovery)		9,000

20X7 entry; adjustment and employees paid cash:		
Compensation expense [($90,000 Intrinsic value) × (3 years ÷ 3 years)] = $90,000 versus $20,000 recorded	70,000	
Long-term compensation liability		70,000
Long-term compensation liability	90,000	
Cash		90,000

Compensation expense can be a recovery, as shown in the 20X6 entry. *Cumulative* compensation expense recorded cannot fall below zero. If the *fair value* of the SARs units falls to zero, the balance in the liability account is then zero, and compensation expense recorded to date is reversed.

Measurement with forfeiture estimated Once expected forfeiture is incorporated, the calculations get one step more complicated, as illustrated below. The approach is the same as for options, but cash-settled plans *refer to a new fair value each period*, and so the approach is conceptually much different. Similar to the approach for options, forfeiture during the vesting period must be estimated annually, and the amounts *trued up* at the end of the vesting period to the real retention level *and the real cash cost*.

The cumulative actual level of forfeiture during the vesting period should be the base level of forfeiture rates but is also predictive evidence. In this example, the company initially estimates that 10 employees will leave and 30 will remain, for 75% retention. Seven actually leave, and 33 are paid under the SARs contract in 20X7, a retention level of 82.5%.

End of Year	20X5	20X6	20X7
Estimates made by management:*			
Employees expected to remain until vesting	30 (75%)	32 (80%)	n/a
Employees expected to forfeit	10 (25%)	8 (20%)	n/a
Factual history:			
Employees actually forfeiting in the year	6	1	0
Employees actually receiving SARs (40 – 7)			33 (82.5%)

*These estimates are prepared by the company annually.

The expense for each period is as follows:

End of Year	20X5	20X6	20X7
Fair value	$87,000	$30,000	$90,000
× *Cumulative* vesting fraction	1/3	2/3	3/3
× Estimate of retention (above)	75%	80%	82.5%*
= Required balance in the liability account at year-end	$21,750	$16,000	$74,250
Opening balance	0	21,750	16,000
Expense for the period (recovery) (debit expense, credit liability, or the opposite for the recovery year)	$21,750	($ 5,750)	$58,250

*Actual; 33/40

Similar to the approach used for options, the annual expense is the combination of the new layer of expense and a correction of old estimates. This time, both the fair value and the retention rate are corrected, which makes compensation cost even more volatile. Annual entries are:

20X5 entry:		
Compensation expense	21,750	
Long-term compensation liability		21,750

20X6 entry:		
Long-term compensation liability	5,750	
Compensation expense (recovery)		5,750

At the end of 20X7, the liability is trued up, and money is paid to the 33 employees who are still with the company:

20X7 entry; adjustment and employees paid cash:		
Compensation expense	58,250	
Long-term compensation liability		58,250
Long-term compensation liability	74,250	
Cash (33 employees × 250 units × $9 intrinsic value)		74,250

Compound Plans

If a plan allows employees the choice of taking cash or shares at the exercise date, then the plan is a compound financial instrument and represents both a financial liability *and* an option on shares. The liability is valued on initial recognition, and a residual value is assigned to equity rights. Established patterns are then used to account for each element. Compound plans will be demonstrated through phantom stock plans.

Phantom Stock Plan with Employee Payment Option Assume that an employee is awarded units in a phantom stock plan, where, after two years of employment, the employee is entitled to receive *either* 22,000 common shares *or* the right to a cash payment equal to the then-market value of 18,000 shares. The choice is up to the employee. This employee is expected to remain with the company for this period, so retention is not an issue. The shares are worth $8 each when the plan is established, at the beginning of Year 1, and share price increases to $9 and then $12 at the end of Years 1 and 2.

The equity portion is valued when the plan is established. At the beginning of Year 1, *valuation models* indicate that the fair value of the share alternative is $7 per share, or $154,000 ($7 × 22,000) in total. Initially, the cash alternative appears to be worth $144,000 ($8 × 18,000). Therefore, the option is valued at the residual, or $10,000 ($154,000 – $144,000.)

That is:

Equity alternative fair value, plan initiation, from valuation model	$154,000
Cash alternative fair value, plan initiation	144,000
Equity portion	$ 10,000

The equity portion is accrued over the two-year vesting period, or $5,000 per year. *The fair value of the option is recognized over the vesting period but is not subject to new estimates of fair value.*

The liability is revalued each period and is also recorded over the two-year vesting period. A valuation model is consulted, as for a cash-based SARs plan. In this example, the intrinsic value of the shares is used as the best estimate of the fair value of the liability. Note that the first time recognition is required is at *the end of the first year*, at which time the entry is based on a calculation that relies on the end-of-year $9 share value, or a total of $162,000 ($9 × 18,000). *The initial value of $144,000 is not used for this period but was used to establish the $10,000 equity portion.*

If there were forfeitures expected, these would be *re-estimated each year for both elements.*

Year 1 entry:		
Compensation expense	86,000	
Contributed capital: common share options outstanding [($10,000) × (1 year ÷ 2 years)]		5,000
Long-term compensation liability [($162,000) × (1 year ÷ 2 years)]		81,000

The liability is then *trued up* to the cumulative value with a calculation at the end of Year 2, $216,000 ($12 × 18,000). If there were forfeitures expected, these would be re-established each year for both elements.

Year 2 entry:		
Compensation expense	140,000	
Contributed capital: common share options outstanding [($10,000) × (1 year ÷ 2 years)]		5,000
Long-term compensation liability [($216,000) × (2 year ÷ 2 years), less $81,000]		135,000

This second entry updates the accounts at the end of Year 2. The employee may then elect to receive shares:

Year 2 entry; employee receives shares:		
Contributed capital: common share options outstanding	10,000	
Long-term compensation liability	216,000	
Common shares		226,000

Alternatively, the employee may take cash:

Year 2 entry; employee receives cash, and the option expires:		
Contributed capital: common share options outstanding	10,000	
Contributed capital: share options expired		10,000
Long-term compensation liability	216,000	
Cash		216,000

These entries reflect the pattern for equity-settled plans in that the value of the option is recorded over time and then is either folded into common shares (issuance) or contributed capital (lapse). It also reflects the pattern for liability-settled plans in that the liability fair value is remeasured annually and trued up to annual estimates of fair value.

Additional Complications Compensation plans are complex, and the accounting standards that govern their measurement, recognition, and disclosure are equally complex. There are rules that deal with performance conditions, market conditions, award restrictions, and changes after vesting, as well as rules that address indexed plans, combination plans, plan modifications, and so on. This section has looked at the overall patterns rather than the detailed rules for the many possible situations.

CONCEPT REVIEW

1. What do employees receive under a SARs compensation plan?
2. When there is a long-term compensation plan, under what circumstances is a liability recorded? A contributed capital account?
3. If a plan is equity settled, what will change if the fair value of the compensation contract increases? How would your response change if the plan were cash settled?

DERIVATIVES

General Nature of Derivatives

Corporations issue certain types of securities that are neither debt nor equity in themselves but that set terms and conditions for future exchange of financial instruments. There are many types of such derivative instruments, which have value because of shifts in value of the underlying security or index. Stock options are one example. By themselves, stock options represent neither an obligation of the corporation nor a share interest in the corporation; their *value is derived* from the value of the underlying security (shares) that can be acquired by exercising the option.

Accounting standards define a *derivative* as a financial instrument that has three characteristics:

1. The value of the derivative changes in response to the change in the underlying primary instrument or index;
2. It requires no initial net investment, or a very small investment; and
3. It is settled at a future date.

There are three main types of derivatives:

1. Options;
2. Forward contracts; and
3. Futures contracts.

Options An option is the right to buy or sell something in the future. A **call option** is the right to buy something at a given price in the future, and a **put option** is the right to sell something at a given price in the future. Options may be for commodities or financial instruments. For example, a company may issue a call option to buy 20,000 tonnes of coal at a given price at a given time. Alternatively, the company may be party to a put option to sell 1,000 shares of another company, now held as an investment, at a given price at a given time, if the company wishes.

Forward Contracts A **forward contract** is an obligation to buy or sell something in the future. Both the price and the time period are specified, and there is no way to avoid the transaction. For example, if a company agrees to sell 12,000 shares (now held as an investment) at $60 per share in 60 days, with no ability to avoid the transaction, this is a forward contract. If the transaction would take place only if the company wanted, then it would be an option.

Futures Contracts A **futures contract** is also an obligation to buy or sell something in the future. Both the price and the time period are specified, and there is no way to avoid the transaction. Futures contracts differ from forward contracts, though, in that they are traded on stock markets, brokers act as collection and delivery agents, and the company usually has to put some money up front, which is collateral, in the form of a **margin**. For example, if a company agrees to buy US$1,000 for Cdn$1,200 in 60 days through a financial institution that requires an initial payment of $120, this would be a futures contract and $120 is the margin.

Embedded Derivatives Some financial instruments are compound financial instruments and include both a **host contract** and an **embedded derivative** contract. The embedded derivative is not related to the economic risks and characteristics of the host contract and changes the cash flows of the contract over the life of the contract in some fashion, consistent with the presence of the derivative. If the derivative could be detached and transferred separately, it would be a *stand-alone derivative* and accounted for as such. *Embedded derivatives* cannot be detached from the host contract but also must be *separated on initial recognition* to allow the host contract and the derivative to be accounted for separately.

For example, assume that Brava Limited enters into a loan agreement, where the interest rate is changed each year, based on the price of silver. The host contract is the loan, and the embedded derivative is the adjustment of interest based on the silver commodity price. The loan and the embedded derivative are separately accounted for when the loan is signed. The derivative is valued at fair value and remeasured to fair value on each reporting date.

Accounting Recognition

Accounting standards require that companies:

- Recognize derivatives on the statement of financial position when the company becomes a party to the contract;
- Recognize the derivative instrument at fair value on initial recognition;
- At each reporting date, *remeasure* derivative assets or liabilities at their fair values; and
- Recognize gains and losses from the changed fair value, and gains and losses at settlement, in profit and loss in the period in which they arise, unless the derivative is designated as a hedge.

Although a derivative should be recorded when it is acquired (i.e., the company becomes a party to the contract), it often has no cost and a zero fair value at that time. Therefore, no entry is made. Adjustments to fair value are made on reporting dates and when the contract matures. The *fair value* of the derivative changes as underlying values change and is based on a valuation model that incorporates certain factors, such as duration, volatility, and risk. This change in fair value is recognized in earnings.

Example Assume that Bent Limited agrees to a forward contract to buy 4,000 shares of Resto Limited for $30 per share in 60 days. The current fair value of the shares is $30, so the initial fair value of this derivative is zero. This contract is not a hedge; accounting for hedges is explained below. There is no broker, and no margin payment is needed. The contract is recorded as a memorandum entry:

Memorandum entry: agreed to buy 4,000 Resto shares for $30 per share in 60 days.		

The shares of Resto are trading at $34 after 30 days, and the company has a gain because it can buy shares that are worth $136,000 for $120,000. The gain on the contract is recorded to reflect fair value.

Derivative instrument [($34 – $30) × 4,000]	16,000	
Gain on derivative instrument		16,000

When the shares are purchased, they have a fair value of $31 per share. A loss of $3 ($34 – $31) per share on the derivative contract is recorded, and then the contract is closed out:

Loss on derivative instrument	12,000	
Derivative instrument [($31 – $34) × 4,000]		12,000
Investment—Resto Ltd. shares ($31 × 4,000 shares)	124,000	
Cash ($30 × 4,000 shares)		120,000
Derivative instrument ($16,000 – $12,000)		4,000

Hedges

If an investor speculates in derivatives, the risk is *high* because derivatives essentially bet on future price changes. However, the usual purpose of derivatives in the corporate environment is to *reduce risk*. Derivatives often are used as **hedges**—as a way to offset a risk to which the company would otherwise be exposed. Hedged risks can include changes in exchange rates, interest rates, securities, and commodities (e.g., fuel, grain, nickel, silver, gold). For an item to be a hedge, the company must first *have risk* in an area and then put a hedge in place to *counter the risk*. That is, a loss on a primary instrument will offset a gain on a hedge instrument, and vice versa. The related gains and losses must be recognized in earnings concurrently.

Hedge accounting is complex and is a subject dealt with in advanced accounting courses. This discussion will focus on a brief look at the outcome in financial statements.

Hedge Example Suppose that Clix Incorporated sells goods to a U.S. customer. The selling price is stated in U.S. dollars. Assume that the amount of the sale is US$100,000 and that the U.S. dollar is worth Cdn$1.10 at the date of sale. Clix now has an account receivable (a primary financial asset) for US$100,000. On Clix's books, the receivable will be translated into Canadian dollars at the current exchange rate and reported at Cdn$110,000. Now, suppose that while Clix is waiting for the customer to pay, the exchange rate changes to US$1.00 = Cdn$1.02. The value of the receivable drops to Cdn$102,000; Clix has suffered a loss of $8,000 due to the exchange rate change.

Clix can protect itself from unpredictable exchange gains and losses by creating an offsetting financial liability for US$100,000. Any loss on the receivable will be exactly offset by a gain on the liability. It is possible that in the normal course of business, the company will incur U.S. dollar–denominated liabilities. For example, assume that Clix buys inventory from a U.S. supplier and agrees to pay in U.S. dollars. Even if the offset is not exactly $100,000, gains and losses will tend to cancel out.

That is:

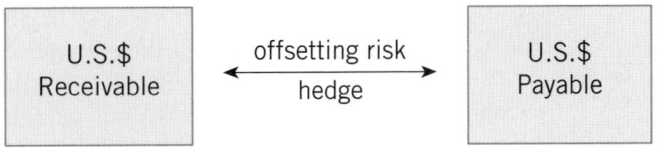

More commonly, however, a company will go to a financial institution and arrange a *forward contract*. As the result of such a contract, when the company receives US$100,000 from the customer, it will immediately turn the U.S. currency over to the bank. The bank agrees up front to the value (the price the bank will pay) for the U.S. dollars. For example, assume the *forward price* is $1.04. Clix is willing to "firm up" its future cash flow at $104,000. At maturity, Clix receives $104,000 from the bank and turns over US$100,000.

A forward contract is a common type of hedge. The bank will charge a small fee for this service, but the contract is akin to an insurance policy—the expense of the contract will eliminate the risk of a large loss. The contract also eliminates the possibility of a gain. However, *most companies prefer to deal with known cash flows*. Hedging is widely practised by companies that have exchange risk as a result of a transaction or proposed transaction.

Criteria for Hedge Accounting *Hedge accounting* is a set of accounting policies that dictate measurement and recognition of the hedge and its related transaction. *Hedge accounting* is voluntary and happens only after an element is designated as a hedge. The substance of a hedge is that the company is protected from gains or losses on the risk being hedged. Since there are so many ways to hedge, the designation of a hedge is largely left to management. Under hedge accounting, hedges may be identified as *cash flow hedges* or *fair value hedges,* and accounting treatment is dictated by the classification. A financial statement element, such as a derivative, will qualify for hedge accounting when a company has:

1. An established strategy for risk management that involves hedging;
2. Formal designation and documentation of the specific hedging relationship. This includes the requirement that the hedging relationship includes only eligible hedging instruments and hedged items; and
3. Expectation that the hedge will be highly effective, and the hedge is assessed each period. This includes the requirement that the fair value of the hedge be reliably measured.

Accounting Implications of Hedge Accounting Once the element has been designated as a hedge, accounting standards require that the gain or loss on a hedge be recorded in earnings *at the same time* that the gain or loss on the item being hedged is recognized. This simultaneous recognition of gains and losses allows for *offset*, and therefore the substance of the hedge is reflected in the financial statements.

Accounting mismatch Sometimes it will happen that the primary financial statement element (the result of a transaction that creates exchange risk) is hedged by an item that does not generate accounting gains or losses. The *offset accounting treatment* must then be *created.* For example, assume that Clix had the US$100,000 receivable and also had firm plans to buy inventory in U.S. dollars. Clix designates the planned inventory purchase as a hedge of the receivable, since Clix plans to use the US$100,000 receivable to pay for the inventory, and the timing of collection and payment coincide.

If there is an $8,000 loss on the account receivable because of exchange rate change, there will be *no offsetting gain on the planned inventory purchase because the payable is not recorded until the inventory is delivered.* The hedge is effective, but the accounting records do not reflect it. This is called an *accounting mismatch.* To fix this mismatch, the $8,000 loss on the receivable is not recorded in earnings. Instead, it is recorded in *other comprehensive income (OCI)* and flows to an equity account, an accumulated OCI *reserve for hedging.* This remains as an element in shareholders' equity until the transaction takes place.

In other circumstances, the hedge item may be on the books but valued at amortized cost and thus no gains and losses would be recorded to offset those of the primary financial instrument. To avoid this mismatch situation, the company may reclassify the hedge as an element that will be carried at fair value, so that it will be measured at fair value, and generate recognized gains and losses for the purpose of offset.

However accomplished, the objective of hedge accounting is to *arrange valuation and recording so that the gains on one side will offset losses on the other side of the hedge relationship*, reflecting the economic reality of the hedge relationship.

CONCEPT REVIEW

1. Explain the difference between a derivative financial instrument and a primary financial instrument.
2. What is an embedded derivative?
3. How should an existing derivative financial liability be measured at each reporting date?

STATEMENT OF CASH FLOWS AND DISCLOSURE

Statement of Cash Flows

The cash flows relating to complex financial instruments must be reported in the statement of cash flows (SCF) in a manner that is consistent with their substance. The net proceeds from the issuance of any financial instrument will be reported as a financing activity, with the nature of the instrument disclosed in the notes to the financial statements. If an instrument is a compound instrument that consists of both equity and liability components, then the individual components are reported *together* on the SCF—one line, not two, because one financial instrument was issued. Since conversions do not involve cash flow, they are not reported on the SCF. Non-cash transactions must be separately explained in the disclosure notes. Cash flows for interest and dividends may be presented in operating or financing sections, as determined by company policy.

As an example, consider the following liability and equity accounts of YTR Limited:

	20X5	20X4
Term preferred shares (liability)	—	$ 3,000,000
Convertible bonds payable	$ 8,000,000	—
Discount on bonds payable	245,000	—
Contributed capital: common share conversion rights	457,000	—
Contributed capital: stock rights outstanding	—	55,000
Common shares	13,800,000	13,645,000

Convertible bonds were issued in 20X5. Discount amortization in 20X5 was $15,000. The term preferred shares were redeemed during the year, at par. Stock rights had been issued to a law firm for legal services performed in 20X4 and were exercised in 20X5. There were no other common share transactions. Interest expense is $525,000, and the company classifies interest paid as a separate line item in the operating activities section of the SCF.

As a result of these transactions, the SCF would report:

1. In financing, as a source of funds, proceeds on issuance of convertible bonds, $8,197,000. The bonds were originally allocated $7,740,000 of the original proceeds (i.e., $8,000,000 – $260,000; the original discount before this year's amortization.) In addition, proceeds of $457,000 were allocated to the contributed capital equity account, $7,740,000 + $457,000 = $8,197,000.
2. In financing, as a use of funds, redemption of preferred shares, $3,000,000.
3. In financing, as a source of funds, issuance of common shares, $100,000. The common shares account has actually increased by $155,000 (or $13,800,000 – $13,645,000). However, this represents not only the cash received on the sale of shares but also the stock rights account, $55,000, that was transferred to common shares. Only the cash portion is shown on the SCF.
4. In operating activities, add-back of the non-cash interest expense caused by discount amortization, $15,000. Interest expense of $525,000 would be added back in operating activities and replaced with an outflow of $510,000 ($525,000 – $15,000) for interest paid.

The key to preparing an SCF is to reconstruct the changes to the various accounts, looking for cash flow. This cash flow is reportable. In operating activities, one must examine sources of revenue and expense that *do not reflect the underlying cash flow*. Discount and premium amortization and gains and losses from retirements must be adjusted.

Disclosure

The financial instruments described in this chapter are subject to common disclosure requirements. Financial instrument disclosure is extensive but should be limited to material areas to avoid overwhelming financial statement users. The objectives of disclosure are to ensure that information is available to *assess the significance of financial instruments for the company's financial position and performance,* the nature and extent of risks associated with financial instruments, and how those risks are managed. Some of the disclosures include:

1. The important components of each financial statement category (e.g., various loans);
2. Information related to fair value for liabilities. Methods used to assess fair value must be explained. When a financial instrument has been valued at fair value, detail about the change in fair value is required;
3. Information related to the legal terms of the financial instrument, including maturity dates, interest rates, collateral, and so on;
4. Various revenue and expense amounts and OCI reserve amounts must be disclosed separately, including interest expense, changes in equity reserve accounts, and so on;
5. Information on exposure to various sources of risk, as appropriate. Risks might include credit risk, liquidity risk, and market risk. Objectives, policies, and processes for managing risk must be disclosed. Such disclosure is extensive, and includes both qualitative and quantitative elements; and
6. Accounting policy information required as a matter of course for all financial statement elements.

Critical to these general disclosure categories is the requirement that *financial instruments be completely described.* This would include the carrying amount, principal amount, amounts issued or retired, options issued and retired, maturity dates, share prices, early settlement options, futures contracts, forward contracts, scheduled future cash commitments, stated interest rate, effective interest rate, repricing dates, collateral, currency, payment dates, interest rates, security, conditions, changes in valuation allowances, and any breach of conditions or covenants.

To say that these disclosures are extensive is an understatement. The more complex the situation, the more extensive is the disclosure. The emphasis is on terms and conditions and also on analyzing the risk associated with recognized and unrecognized financial instruments.

Reporting Example A portion of the financial risk management note for Shoppers Drug Mart Corporation is shown in Exhibit 15-3. Note that the company identifies and evaluates various sources of financial risk, and its policy/process to manage these risks. This information deals with interest rate risk, credit risk, and liquidity risk. Note that interest rate derivatives may be used to hedge interest rate risk. Liquidity risk is defined, risk management processes are described, and obligations are specifically classified as to timing.

EXHIBIT 15-3

SHOPPERS DRUG MART CORPORATION

Financial Risk Management Disclosures

5. FINANCIAL RISK MANAGEMENT OBJECTIVES AND POLICIES RELATED TO FINANCIAL INSTRUMENTS

Financial Risk Management Objectives and Policies

In the normal course of business, the Company is exposed to financial risks that have the potential to negatively impact its financial performance. The Company may use derivative financial instruments to manage certain of these risks. The Company does not use derivative financial instruments for trading or speculative purposes. These risks are discussed in more detail below.

Interest Rate Risk

Interest rate risk is the risk that fair value or future cash flows associated with the Company's financial assets or liabilities will fluctuate due to changes in market interest rates. The Company, including its Associate-

continued on next page

EXHIBIT 15-3 (*cont'd*)

owned store network, is exposed to fluctuations in interest rates by virtue of its borrowings under its bank credit facilities, commercial paper program and financing programs available to its Associates. Increases or decreases in interest rates will negatively or positively impact the financial performance of the Company.

The Company monitors market conditions and the impact of interest rate fluctuations on its fixed and floating rate debt instruments on an ongoing basis and may use interest rate derivatives to manage this exposure. From time to time, the Company may use interest rate derivatives to manage the interest rate risk on its commercial paper or other floating rate debt.

As at December 29, 2012, the Company had $423,372 (2011: $166,592) of unhedged floating rate debt. During the current financial year, the Company's average outstanding unhedged floating rate debt was $619,979 (2011: $386,193). Had interest rates been higher or lower by 50 basis points during the current financial year, net earnings for the financial year would have decreased or increased, respectively, by approximately $2,285 (2011: $1,396) as a result of the Company's exposure to interest rate fluctuations on its unhedged floating rate debt.

Credit Risk

Credit risk is the risk that the Company's counterparties will fail to meet their financial obligations to the Company, causing a financial loss.

Accounts receivable arise primarily in respect of prescription sales billed to governments and third-party drug plans and, as a result, collection risk is low. There is no concentration of balances with debtors in the remaining accounts receivable. The Company does not consider its exposure to credit risk to be material.

Liquidity Risk

Liquidity risk is the risk that the Company will be unable to meet its obligations relating to its financial liabilities.

The Company prepares cash flow budgets and forecasts to ensure that it has sufficient funds through operations, access to bank facilities and access to debt and capital markets to meet its financial obligations, capital investment program requirements and fund new investment opportunities or other unanticipated requirements as they arise. The Company manages its liquidity risk as it relates to financial liabilities by monitoring its cash flow from operating activities to meet its short-term financial liability obligations and planning for the repayment of its long-term financial liability obligations through cash flow from operating activities and/or the issuance of new debt or equity.

The contractual maturities of the Company's financial liabilities in the consolidated balance sheet as at December 29, 2012, are as follows:

	Carrying Amount	Payments Due in the Next 90 Days	Payments Due Between 90 Days and Less Than a Year	Payments Due Between 1 Year and Less Than 2 Years	Payments Due After 2 Years	Total Contractual Cash Flows
Bank indebtedness	$ 170,927	$ 170,927	$ —	$ —	$ —	$ 170,927
Commercial paper	250,000	250,000	—	—	—	250,000
Accounts payable and accrued liabilities	1,115,306	1,093,953	21,353	—	—	1,115,306
Dividends payable	54,180	54,180	—	—	—	54,180
Medium-term notes	696,807	17,715	467,715	256,487	—	741,917
Revolving-term debt	—	—	—	—	—	—
Other long-term liabilities	236,803	—	—	20,840	215,963	236,803
Total	**$2,524,023**	**$1,586,775**	**$489,068**	**$277,327**	**$215,963**	**$2,569,133**

Comparative figures have been excluded.

Source: Shoppers Drug Mart Corp., 2012 Annual Financial Statements, www.sedar.com, posted 28 February 2013.

Looking Ahead

Financial instrument issues have been on the agenda of the IASB continuously over the past decade. The focus of current projects is on the classification of financial assets rather than on liabilities and equity instruments. Hedging is also on the agenda.

Refinements to the financial instruments reporting structure model are almost annual, but are not directly related to the skeleton of the accounting approach that has been explained in this chapter.

ACCOUNTING STANDARDS FOR PRIVATE ENTERPRISES

One might expect that a private company would have significantly different (simpler) capital structure and that complex financial instruments, including options and hedges, would be rare. However, uniquely tailored debt and equity instruments flourish in private companies, and foreign exchange contracts are common risk management tools. The accounting standards governing these elements are reasonably similar under IFRS and ASPE, but there are several important differences:

1. Private companies sometimes issue preferred shares, redeemable in cash at the shareholder's option as part of tax-planning structures (so-called *high-low shares*). However, the clear intent is to retain an equity investment and not to redeem for cash. Under ASPE, these shares will be classified as equity, and can be recorded at par, stated, or assigned value. Conversely, *shareholder loans*, which many shareholders and lenders alike consider to be part of equity in a private company, are classified in the liability section regardless of intent.
2. Convertible debt must still be treated as a compound financial instrument, but the standard allows the company to record the equity element (the conversion option), at zero, which effectively makes the convertible debt entirely a liability.

Example Return to the Tollen Corporation example, earlier in the chapter, where Tollen issues a $100,000 8% convertible bonds for $106,000. The market interest rate on the day of issuance is higher than 8%, but cannot be determined with certainty for this ASPE company. Each $10,000 bond is convertible into 100 common shares on any interest date after the end of the second year from the date of issuance. Conversion is at the option of the investor. Under IFRS, a value was assigned to the conversion rights, and there was a bond discount. Under ASPE, the bond is entirely debt, and there is a $6,000 premium:

Cash	106,000	
Bonds payable		100,000
Premium on bands payable		6,000

Subsequent measurement of interest expense will include amortization of the premium, using either effective interest or straight-line approach, reducing the reported interest rate below 8% and not reflecting the expected higher market interest rate. This reporting is considered appropriate for ASPE companies due to the difficulty in measuring the appropriate yield rate and, thus, the value of the equity interest granted.

3. The stock-based compensation structure is largely the same, in that expense and equity elements are recognized for an equity-settled plan over the vesting period. Volatility measures used as an input for option pricing models are a challenge, since they are typically not observable for a private company. To alleviate this problem, ASPE allows a company to measure stock price volatility using a *calculated value* method. Following the calculated value method, the company would measure volatility using an industry-specific index or, if the industry were unique, a general stock price volatility index.

In addition, ASPE models allow a company *account for forfeiture when it occurs; no estimates are made of forfeiture when making accruals.* The company can estimate forfeiture as per the IFRS standard, but it is not required.

Example Return again to the example from earlier in the chapter where 20 employees are granted options for 250 shares each, a total of 5,000 common shares, at an exercise price of $20 per share. The options vest after four years and are estimated to have a fair value of $48,000. The company does not estimate forfeiture. Assume now that there is no forfeiture in the first year, four employees forfeit in Year 2 and one forfeits in Year 4:

First-year entry:		
Compensation expense ($48,000/4)	12,000	
Contributed capital: common share options outstanding		12,000
Second-year entries:		
Contributed capital: common share options outstanding	2,400	
Compensation expense (recovery) ($12,000 recorded to date × 4/20)		2,400
Compensation expense ($12,000 annual × 16/20 remaining)	9,600	
Contributed capital: common share options outstanding		9,600
Third-year entry:		
Compensation expense ($12,000 × 16/20 remaining)	9,600	
Contributed capital: common share options outstanding		9,600
Fourth-year entries:		
Contributed capital: common share options outstanding	1,800	
Compensation expense (recovery) ($28,800 to date × 1/16)		1,800
Compensation expense ($12,000 annual × 15/20 remaining)	9,000	
Contributed capital: common share options outstanding		9,000

Using this approach, the cumulative balance recorded to date for the forfeit options is reversed when the forfeiture happens. (This is the $2,400 in the second year and the $1,800 in the fourth year, above.) In Years 2 and 4, two entries are used to highlight the reversal for the employees who forfeit in the year. The two entries may be combined in one entry; the end result is identical.

4. Standards established for share-based payments have a narrower scope, which may affect reporting of any such distributions to suppliers or others. In addition, measurement is often based on the fair value of the consideration given up or the fair value of what is received, *whichever is the more reliable measure.* IFRS measurements rest on the fair value of goods and services received, except in rare circumstances.

5. Hedge accounting follows a different approach, as does accounting for embedded derivatives. For example, since *other comprehensive income* does not exist under ASPE, standards cannot allow for recognition of cash flow hedge amounts in OCI with the cumulative amount set in an equity reserve. Hedge accounting is available, bypassing net income, only when the critical terms of the hedge match the hedged instrument.

6. Disclosures in all areas are less onerous under ASPE.

RELEVANT STANDARDS

CPA Canada Handbook, Part I (IASB):

- IAS 32, Financial Instruments: Presentation
- IAS 39, Financial Instruments: Recognition and Measurement
- IFRS 2, Share-Based Payments
- IFRS 7, Financial Instruments: Disclosure
- IFRS 9, Financial Instruments
- IFRS 13, Fair Value Measurement

CPA Canada Handbook, Part II (ASPE):

- Section 3856, Financial Instruments
- Section 3865, Hedges
- Section 3870, Stock-Based Compensation and Other Stock-Based Payments

SUMMARY OF KEY POINTS

1. Financial instruments must be classified as debt or equity in accordance with their substance, not necessarily their legal form. If there are two component parts to a financial instrument, the two components are separately recognized on issuance.
2. Annual payments associated with a financial instrument that is classified as debt are classified as an expense; annual payments associated with a financial instrument classified as an equity instrument are not an expense and are classified on the statement of changes in equity.
3. Classification factors for a liability include whether the company can be forced to pay cash for principal and/or interest, whether payments can be deferred indefinitely, whether payment is required only if a highly unlikely event outside management control occurs, and whether payments that can be made in shares have a fixed or variable value.
4. Bonds that are convertible into a fixed number of common shares at the *investor's* option embody two financial instruments: a liability and an option contract on common shares, each of which are recognized separately on issuance.
5. Bonds that are mandatorily redeemable in a fixed number of shares will be classified as a compound instrument: a liability as to their annual cash interest component, and the residual, which is assigned to equity.
6. Stock options of various kinds are recognized on issuance and recorded as an element of shareholders' equity. On issuance of the underlying shares, the options account is folded into the share account. If the options lapse, the options account becomes contributed capital.
7. Share-based payments to suppliers are recognized when goods and services are received and measured at the fair value of those goods or services.
8. Share-based payments with employees that are equity-settled result in recognition of an expense and an equity element. The options are valued using an option pricing model. Compensation is recognized over the vesting period, with forfeiture estimated; forfeitures are *trued up* annually but fair value is not re-estimated.
9. Share-based payments with employees that are cash-settled result in recognition of an expense and a liability, accrued over the vesting period. Fair value and forfeiture are estimated over this period, and both estimates are *trued up* annually.

10. Share-based payments with employees where the employee has the choice between cash and equity settlement are compound instruments, with both an equity and liability element recognized.

11. Derivatives are contracts that specify an exchange of financial instruments at a specified price. Derivatives include options, forward contracts, and futures contracts. They can be used to hedge various types of risk, including exchange risk.

12. Derivative contracts are recorded at fair value. Gains and losses from changes in fair value are reported in earnings.

13. If a financial instrument is designated as a hedge, then gains and losses on the hedge will be recognized in earnings at the same time as gains and losses on the risk being hedged, so they offset each other. Under certain conditions, gains and losses on hedges are recorded in other comprehensive income and accumulated in equity reserve accounts.

14. The cash inflows relating to issuance of financial instruments are classified on the SCF as financing transactions. Cash outflows are classified in a manner that is consistent with the substance of the payments, both for payments *on* capital (i.e., interest and dividends) and repayments *of* capital (i.e., principal and share buybacks).

15. A company must disclose extensive information with respect to accounting policies used for financial instruments, fair values, significance of financial instruments, and nature and extent of risks. Financial instruments must be fully described in the disclosure notes.

16. ASPE is different from IFRS in the way certain redeemable preferred shares are classified, in valuation of the equity component of a convertible bond, in the measurement of the fair value of stock options, and in the approach to forfeiture related to stock options. ASPE also has a narrower scope for share-based payments, a narrower scope for hedge accounting, and less required disclosure.

KEY TERMS

book value method
call option
capital charge
cash-settled plan
compound financial instrument
convertible debt
derivative instruments
embedded derivative
equity-settled plans
exercise date
fair value
fair value hierarchy
forfeit
forward contract
futures contract
hedges
host contract
hybrid financial instrument
intrinsic value
in-the-money
income bond
incremental method of valuation
margin
perpetual debt
phantom stock plan
poison pill
proportional method
put option
redeemable shares
restricted share units
share-based payment
stock appreciation rights
stock options
stock option plan
stock rights
stock warrants
term preferred shares
trued up
under water
vesting

REVIEW PROBLEM 15-1

On 1 January 20X1, Amershi Limited issues $1,000,000 face amount of 8%, five-year, convertible debentures. Interest is payable semi-annually on 30 June and 31 December. The debentures are convertible at the investor's option at the rate of 20 common shares for each $1,000 bond at any time after 31 December 20X3. The market rate of interest for non-convertible bonds of similar risk and maturity is 6%. The net proceeds received by Amershi amounted to $1,250,000.

Required:

1. Record the issuance of the bonds on 1 January 20X1.
2. Prepare the journal entries for interest expense on 30 June 20X1 and 31 December 20X1. Amershi uses effective interest amortization for bond premium and discount.
3. Indicate how all amounts relating to the bonds will be shown on Amershi's statement of financial position and statement of comprehensive income for the year ending 31 December 20X1.
4. Assume that the holders of $300,000 face value bonds exercise their conversion privilege on 1 January 20X4, when the market value of the common shares is $65. Prepare the journal entry to record the conversion.

REVIEW PROBLEM 15-1—SOLUTION

1. The first step is to calculate the present value of the cash flows at the market rate of 6%, using semi-annual interest periods:

Principal [$1,000,000 × (P/A, 3%,10)]	$ 744,090
Interest [$40,000 × (P/F, 3%,10)]	341,208
	$1,085,298

Journal entry to record issuance

Cash	1,250,000	
Bonds payable		1,000,000
Premium on bonds payable		85,298
Contributed capital: common share conversion rights		164,702

2. Entries for interest expense during 20X1:

30 June 20X1

Interest expense ($1,085,298 × 3%)	32,559	
Premium on bonds payable	7,441	
Cash		40,000

Liability balance: $1,085,298 – $7,441 = $1,077,857

31 December 20X1

Interest expense ($1,077,857 × 3%)	32,336	
Premium on bonds payable	7,664	
Cash		40,000

3. Bond-related items on 20X1 financial statements:

Statement of comprehensive income	
Interest expense	$ 64,895
Statement of financial position	
Long-term debt	
Bonds payable	$1,000,000
Premium on bonds payable	70,193
	$1,070,193
Shareholders' equity	
Contributed capital: common share conversion rights	$ 164,702

4. Conversion of $300,000 face value bonds into 6,000 common shares on 1 January 20X4:

The present value of the converted bond on 1 January 20X4:

Principal [$300,000 × (P/A, 3%,4)]	$266,547
Interest [$12,000 × (P/F, 3%,4)]	44,605
	$311,152

Bonds payable	300,000	
Premium on bonds payable	11,152	
Contributed capital: common share conversion rights ($164,702 × 3/10)	49,411	
Common shares		360,563

REVIEW PROBLEM 15-2

On 1 January 20X5, Bateau Incorporated issued $10,000,000 face amount of 4%, 10-year, subordinated convertible debentures for $10,500,000 in a private placement. The debentures pay interest annually, in cash, on 31 December. At maturity, the principal must be paid through the issuance of 50 common shares for each $1,000 of the bonds' face value. A market rate of interest for financial instruments with similar risk, security, and term is 8%.

Required:

1. Record the issuance of the bonds on 1 January 20X5.
2. Record the interest expense and payment on the first interest date of 31 December 20X5.

REVIEW PROBLEM 15-2—SOLUTION

1. Interest:

These debentures pay interest annually, in cash; the present value of this cash flow is recorded by Bateau as a liability, using the market rate of interest:

$$\$400{,}000 \times (P/A, 8\%, 10) = \$2{,}684{,}032$$

Principal:

The bond must be settled though the issuance of common shares, so the remainder of the issuance price is equity:

Cash	10,500,000	
Interest liability—subordinated debentures		2,684,032
Share equity—subordinated debentures		7,815,968

2. *Entry to record interest expense on 31 December 20X5:*

Interest expense ($2,684,032 × 8%)	214,723	
Interest liability on subordinated debentures		214,723

Entry to record interest payment on 31 December 20X5:

Interest liability on subordinated debentures	400,000	
Cash ($10,000,000 × 4%)		400,000

QUESTIONS

Q15-1 Historically, what factors have dictated classification of a financial instrument as debt or equity? How is the classification made when based on the financial instruments rules?

Q15-2 What is a compound financial instrument? Give an example.

Q15-3 What is the distinguishing feature of debt?

Q15-4 Assume a company issues a financial instrument for $50,000 in 20X2 and retires it through an open market purchase for $56,000 in 20X5. In each of the intervening years, an annual payment of $2,500 was paid to the investor. How will the financial instrument affect earnings in each of the years if it is classified as debt? As equity?

Q15-5 Explain appropriate financial statement classification of retractable preferred shares, which have a required maturity date or are to be repaid at the option of the investor.

Q15-6 How is convertible debt classified if it is mandatorily convertible into a fixed number of shares? If it is convertible at the investor's option into a fixed number of shares?

Q15-7 Explain how to classify convertible debt if the conversion option specifies that the number of shares to be issued depends on the fair value of shares at the conversion date.

Q15-8 What happens to the common share conversion rights account created when convertible debt is issued and when the bond is actually converted? What if the bond is repaid in cash instead?

Q15-9 If a $400,000, 8% mandatorily convertible bond is issued at par and $76,400 of the issuance price is attributable to the interest obligation, how much interest expense will be recorded in the first year? The effective yield is 8%. How much is paid to the investor each year?

Q15-10 What is the distinction between stock options and stock warrants?

Q15-11 How is a share-based payment to a supplier measured in the financial statements?

Q15-12 If share rights are recognized on issuance, what happens to the share rights account if the share rights are exercised? Allowed to lapse? Compare this with the treatment of the common share conversion option account associated with convertible bonds.

Q15-13 When would a share-based compensation contract, payable after three years, result in an equity account being recognized in the first year? A liability? Both equity and a liability?

Q15-14 Assume that a cash-settled share-based payment scheme is established for an employee group. It will vest over five years and be paid at the end of the fifth year. The total fair value of the plan is estimated to be $400,000 at the end of Year 1, $175,000 at the end of Year 2, and $400,000 at the end of Year 3. No forfeiture is expected. How much compensation expense is recognized in the third year?

Q15-15 Repeat question 14, assuming that retention rates are estimated to be 80% at the end of Year 1, 75% at the end of Year 2, and 60% at the end of Year 3. How much compensation expense recognized in the third year?

Q15-16 Share-based payments to employees are trued up by the end of the vesting period. If the plan is cash-settled, for what factors is the plan trued up? If it is equity-settled?

Q15-17 Explain the terms of a SARs program for employees.

Q15-18 Define a derivative and a hedge.

Q15-19 Assume that a Canadian company sells a product to a U.S. customer and that the sale is denominated in U.S. dollars. What kind of a derivative instrument will eliminate the exchange risk? How will the transaction balance and the derivative instrument be reflected in the financial statements?

Q15-20 What areas of disclosure are required for financial instruments?

CASE 15-1

ZEBO LIMITED

"Amy, I need you to put your other projects on hold and do a little work on these financials for me."

With a sinking heart, you follow Jon Wong, your boss and Special Projects Manager for Holdings Ltd, into his office. It is mid-January, 20X3. You catch the pile of documents he tosses at you. The movie you were going to see tonight is now a dream—you have done "a little work" for Jon many times, and it is usually time consuming.

While Jon deals with several urgent phone calls, you flip through the documents and see that you have the draft SFP for Zebo, a subsidiary of Holdings (Exhibit 1). You also discover information on the retractable preferred shares of Zebo (Exhibit 2), several financing alternatives (Exhibit 3), stock option information (Exhibit 4) and an existing debt covenant arrangement (Exhibit 5).

"Right, Amy. Thanks. These draft financials do not include the statement of changes in equity—I'm sure you can deal with that. Don't forget—we comply with IFRS! I also know the statements do not include two major areas—the retractable preferred transaction and all the stock option transactions. You have the information you need. Please get these things taken care of. Then I want you to take a look at the two financing alternatives we have on the table. We need this money to pay down the current debt of this company. Both the bond alternatives are much cheaper. We will be making a decision on these alternatives in the next week or two, and the transaction will happen next quarter. Let me know what you think, but back that up with numbers, will you? We will meet tomorrow."

"Sure, Jon." You glumly return to your desk. It might be a long night. No Bourne for you!

Required:

Prepare for your meeting with Jon tomorrow.

EXHIBIT 1

ZEBO LIMITED

DRAFT Statement of Financial Position

As of 31 December (in thousands)

	20X2	20X1
Assets		
Current assets		
Cash	$ 2,200	$ 1,300
Accounts receivable, net	5,150	6,200
Inventory	14,450	12,220
Prepaid expenses and deposits	1,120	1,340
	22,920	21,060
Property, plant, and equipment (net)	40,500	31,230
Goodwill	5,500	5,500
	$68,920	$57,790
Liabilities		
Current liabilities		
Operating loan	$16,200	$ 7,900
Accounts payable and accrued liabilities	7,900	8,300
Deferred revenue	1,050	1,210
Provisions	2,640	2,050
	27,790	19,460

continued on next page

	20X2	20X1
Long-term liabilities		
Bonds payable, net	9,300	9,250
Deferred tax	3,210	3,960
Shareholders' equity		
Preferred share capital	2,700	2,700
Common share capital	18,320	18,320
Contributed capital—options	1,200	1,200
Retained earnings	5,840	2,495
Accumulated OCI—hedging	560	405
	28,620	25,120
	$68,920	$57,790

EXHIBIT 2

ZEBO LIMITED

Retractable Preferred Shares

On 7 March 20X2, the company's Board of Directors approved the cash redemption at par plus 10%, of all of the $2.7 million of mandatorily redeemable convertible preferred shares at 15 June 20X2. After this announcement, but before the cash redemption date, holders of $2.1 million of the preferred shares elected to convert their shares to common shares, according to the share agreement. These common shares had a fair value of $2.4 million at 15 June. The remaining $0.6 preferred shares were redeemed for cash on 15 June 20X2.

EXHIBIT 3

ZEBO LIMITED

Financing Options

Objective: Raise $10 million on the bond market and retire $10 million in operating loans to reduce interest costs.

Note: Alternatives are priced to sell at par.

	Alternative 1	Alternative 2
Principal	$10 million	$10 million
Interest rate	4%, semi-annual payments	6%, semi-annual payments
Maturity date	Ten years	Ten years
Security	Second charge on tangible fixed assets	Second charge on tangible fixed assets
Other terms	Convertible to 500,000 shares at maturity at issuer's option	Convertible to common shares at market price per share at maturity at investor's option

EXHIBIT 4

ZEBO LIMITED

Stock Option Information, 20X2

Stock option activity in 20X2 is as follows:

(in millions)	Number of Options	Weighted Average Exercise Price
31 December 20X1	650	$27.76
Grants	22	$20.00
Exercise	(34)	$18.50
Forfeits	(42)	$30.00
31 December 20X2	596	$27.70

The Black-Scholes option pricing model is used to estimate the fair value of options granted under the equity incentive plan. Fair value is recognized over the vesting period and is adjusted for expected retention. Cumulative contributed capital related to share-based compensation should be $1,620 at the end of 20X2, *after all transactions*, but then adjusted for new retention levels (expected to be 92%). Options exercised in 20X2 are associated with $165 of accrued cumulative compensation.

Note: No entries have been made for exercise or compensation cost in 20X2.

EXHIBIT 5

ZEBO LIMITED

Operating Loan Covenants

As part of the operating loan arrangement, Zebo must satisfy the following covenants on an annual basis. Annual financial statements must be audited.

1. A ratio of Current Assets to Current Liabilities of not less than 1:1; and
2. A ratio of Total Liabilities to Tangible Net Worth of not greater than 1.5:1.

"Tangible Net Worth" means the total of equity less intangibles, deferred charges, leasehold improvements, deferred tax debits, and unsecured advances to related parties. For the purpose hereof, intangibles are assets lacking physical substance.

"Total Liabilities" means all liabilities, exclusive of deferred tax liabilities and postponed debt.

CASE 15-2

ON-THE-CREST LTD.

On-the-Crest Ltd. (OCL) is a company operating in the used-vehicle industry. OCL derives its revenue from selling, licensing, and servicing software products for car dealers, from the sale of products to car dealers, and from the sale of used vehicles. Both through internal growth and acquisitions, OCL revenue has grown at the rate of 25% per year for each of the last five years. An initial public offering is planned in the next fiscal year.

Ida Wong, the audit partner, is seeking a summary memo from the senior in charge of the audit (see Exhibit 1). Ida has a meeting scheduled with Bill Valarian, CFO of OCL, tomorrow and needs to be aware of major reporting issues.

Required:

Review the notes and prepare a memo outlining accounting and reporting issues and alternatives. This memo will be the basis for the meeting with Bill Valarian.

EXHIBIT 1

ON-THE-CREST LTD.

Notes

From: Audit Senior
To: File
Re: Potential accounting issues—On-the-Crest Ltd. (OCL)

The following issues have come to light during the audit and may impact on the financial statements of OCL:

Convertible Debt

At the beginning of the current year, OCL issued $7 million of 7.25% debt with interest payable semi-annually on 30 June and 31 December. Bond issue costs were $300,000, which are being amortized over 10 years. The maturity date is 10 years from issuance unless either of the following options is exercised:

a. On the date of the IPO, the lender can submit the bond for cash repayment. OCL may, at that time, choose to repay the liability in cash or in OCL shares. The number of OCL shares to be issued is based on the chosen IPO price.

b. After the debt has been outstanding for 36 months, there is a 2-week period during which the lender can submit the bond for repayment in cash.

The $7 million proceeds on issuance of debt were recorded in a long-term liability account.

Options Granted to a Supplier

OCL issued options to Software Supply Limited (SSL) for 40,000 OCL shares. The options were issued to ensure that SSL made OCL a priority customer for the coming period, as SSL's services are critical for modifications to software that OCL provides to car dealers. The options are nonrevocable and are exercisable six months after any IPO. If there is no IPO, the options are to be repurchased and retired at a price based on a set formula. The presence of these options has been disclosed in the financial statements.

Exchange Rate Hedge

OCL placed an order with a Japanese supplier during the year when the exchange rate was ¥1 = $0.0095. On the delivery date, the exchange rate was ¥1 = $0.0090. OCL paid for the merchandise 90 days later when the exchange rate was ¥1 = $0.0104. However, OCL had hedged the account payable at a rate of ¥1 = $0.0085 and accordingly paid $161,500 to the exchange broker for the required yen. The inventory was recorded at the cash cost of $161,500.

Convertible Preferred Shares

Late in the fourth quarter of the current fiscal year, OCL issued $1.7 million of convertible preferred shares in a private placement. Under the terms of the share agreement, the $1.7 million investment will automatically be converted into 600,000 common shares of OCL on the commencement of trading of OCL common shares on the TSX. Investors may choose a cash payout instead, when trading commences, and would receive $1.7 million. There are no provisions for alternative arrangements if common shares are not traded on the TSX; the preferred shares would remain as preferred shares if OCL did not go public. The preferred shares have no preference rights to assets on the dissolution of the company but have a stated cash dividend of $100,000 per year. The dividend is paid quarterly, and on conversion, OCL must pay the dividend up to date in cash including arrears, if any, whether declared or not. All the $1.7 million proceeds are recorded in the equity account, preferred shares. No dividend was due; none was declared or recorded in the current fiscal year.

Pricing Agreement

For the first time, OCL provided certain price and payment incentives to customers to spur demand. OCL extended payment terms from the current 30 days to 60 days and specified that if pre-agreed list prices to *end consumers* are not realized, OCL would provide rebates. For example, assume OCL sold a product to a customer for $100 and expected it to be resold to the final customer for $165. If the final sale were to be priced at $155, OCL has agreed to accept $90 [$100 – ($165 – $155)]. OCL has accrued an allowance for all amounts expected to be lost under the guarantee, based on market research.

CASE 15-3

TECHNO WIZARD LTD.

Omni Services Ltd., a Canadian public company, is a conglomerate involved in publication of newspapers, media services, and information technology consulting. It recently entered into an agreement to purchase Techno Wizard Limited (TWL), which operates a printing business in Manitoba. Omni assumed control on 1 November 20X7.

It is now 14 November 20X7, and Omni has just received the 31 October 20X7 financial statements of TWL. Omni is now concerned that the price to be paid is excessive and is looking for advice leading up to its preclosing negotiations, scheduled for next week. Accordingly, you have been approached, as an outside accounting advisor, for your advice and expert opinion. The purchase agreement is described in Exhibit 1 and financial statement extracts are in Exhibit 2.

Required

Prepare a report that identifies potential issues. Include quantification of issues where possible.

EXHIBIT 1

PURCHASE AND SALE AGREEMENT EXTRACTS

Omni Services Ltd. (Purchaser) and Techno Wizard Ltd. (Vendor)

7.0 Purchase Price

7.1 The purchase price shall be $7.0 million Canadian dollars ($15 per share) subject to adjustment, if any, (see section 7.3), to be established two weeks after the reporting date in section 7.4.

7.2 The purchase price shall be payable $2 million in cash plus $2 million in Omni shares on 1 November 20X7, with the balance paid in cash on 15 December 20X7. Issued shares are valued using quoted prices for Omni shares on the TSX on 1 November 20X7.

7.3 The purchase price will be increased dollar-for-dollar for any excess over $7 million obtained as the product of two times the assets less liabilities of TWL on the SFP dated 31 October 20X7. Assets and liabilities are to be calculated as defined under IFRS standards.

7.4 TWL will provide 31 October 20X7 financial statements before the reporting date of 21 November 20X7.

EXHIBIT 2

EXTRACTS FROM TECHNO WIZARD LTD. FINANCIAL STATEMENTS

31 October 20X7

Statement of Financial Position (in thousands)

Assets	
Current Assets	
Cash	$ 1,420
Receivables	2,690
Inventory	3,700
Prepaid expenses	290
	8,100
Non-current Assets	
Capital assets, net	3,100
	$11,200
Liabilities	
Current Liabilities	
Bank indebtedness	$ 860
Accounts payable	2,100
Deferred revenue	1,740
	4,700
Non-current liabilities	
Bonds payable	2,100
Deferred income tax	162
Other	230
	$ 7,192

continued on next page

Equity	
Preferred shares	500
Print shop equity—bond	300
Contributed capital—share plan	320
Common shares	1,080
Retained earnings	1,808
	$ 4,008
	$11,200

Disclosure Notes Extracts

1. Foreign exchange losses are part of "prepaid expenses" in the amount of $160. All gains are included in earnings.
2. Bonds payable consists of $2.4 million face value of 10-year debentures issued on 1 December 20X6. The debentures were issued at par, and require annual interest of 3.5% payable each 31 May.

   Debentures of similar term and risk were issued by another company at par, carrying an interest rate of 8% within a month of this transaction.

   The debenture holders are entitled to the use of 1,000 hours of print shop capacity at any time after 1 June 20X7. Print shop usage is to be negotiated with a 30-day lead time, and TWL is responsible for all overhead and direct labour. Paper product used in printing is the responsibility of the debenture holder. No print shop capacity has been used to date under the agreement.
3. Included in accounts receivable is a $710 two-year delayed-payment arrangement set on 1 January 20X7. The customer will pay $710 on 31 December 20X8, plus 3% interest each 31 December. Interest rates for a comparable term are in the range of 7%. No interest has been accrued to date.
4. Preferred shares are held by the founding family of TWL and carry a cumulative dividend of 4% annually. Omni did not acquire these shares but has the right to redeem them for cash at book value.
5. Deferred revenue includes various advance payments made by customers under long-term contracts. Some contracts involve upfront fees that are recognized in revenue when received. Other contracts allow a final year of free service or stipulate that a renewal contract will include a free year of average usage covered under the expiring contract. The average length of a contract is three years.
6. TWL has a SARs plan that allows eight managers a cash payment based on the value of 10,000 shares each. The plan was set up in 20X6, and payment will be made in 20X8 for any increase in share value above $10 per share to any manager still employed with TWL at that time. Share value was to be determined using a formula, since TWL is not a public company. The valuation model used placed a value at $6 per unit as the expected payout when the plan was established in 20X6. To date, $320,000 of cost has been recognized. Two of the eight managers have left the firm, but all others are expected to continue through 20X8.
7. TWL has entered into a foreign currency exchange contract with respect to $200,000 of U.S. dollar long-term debt at 31 October 20X7. The company has recorded an asset and a gain of $76 in relation to this arrangement, based on its expectations regarding currency movements over the period to maturity.

TECHNICAL REVIEW

connect

TR15-1 Convertible Debt, Investor's Option: Closed Tech Ltd. issued convertible bonds on 1 July 20X8. The 15-year, 5% $10,000,000 bonds pay interest semi-annually each 30 June and 31 December. At the investor's option, each $1,000 bond is convertible into 50 common shares on the bond's maturity date.

Bond market analysts indicated that if the bonds had not been convertible, they would likely have sold to yield 6%, and have raised $9,020,000. They were, in fact, issued for $10,350,000.

Required:

1. Provide the journal entry to record the initial issuance of the bond.
2. Provide the entry to record interest at 31 December 20X8.
3. Prove that the $9,020,000 reference price provides a yield of 6% by establishing the present value of the bond. Allow for rounding.

connect

TR15-2 Convertible Debt, Mandatory Conversion: Mecca Energy Corp. issued a convertible bond on 1 August 20X9. The 10-year, 4% $12,000,000 bond pays interest semi-annually each 31 July and 31 January. At maturity, each $1,000 bond is convertible into 120 common shares, with conversion at Mecca's option; the company may also choose to repay the bond in cash. The bond was issued for $12,500,000. Market interest rates were approximately 5%.

Required:

1. Provide the journal entry to record the initial issuance of the bond.
2. Assume instead that the bond was convertible into common shares at the maturity date into common shares based on the market value of common shares at that time. Repeat requirement 1. Explain.

connect

TR15-3 Options and Warrants: Pont Chemical Remediation Ltd. had the following transactions in 20X6:

a. Options were issued allowing the holder to acquire 50,000 common shares in five years' time at an acquisition price of $20 per share, Using an option pricing model, the options are valued at $120,000. The options were issued for consulting and promotion work done, tasks that are not easily valued.
b. $5,000,000 8%, 10-year, non-convertible bonds with detachable stock purchase warrants were issued for $5,100,000. Shortly after issuance, the warrants trade for $300,000 in total, and the bonds were trading at 99, or $4,950,000, ex-warrants (i.e., without warrants attached).

Required:

1. Provide the journal entry to record the transactions above.
2. Assume that the options in (a) were exercised when the market price of common shares is $44. Provide the entry for exercise.
3. Alternately, assume that the options in (a) were allowed to lapse when the price of common shares is $16. Provide the entry for the lapse.

connect

TR15-4 Share-Based Compensation; Equity Settled: Darling Petrol Corp. granted stock options to executives in early 20X1. The stock options vest over five years and are exerciseable after six years; they expire after eight years. In total, the options allow the purchase of 400,000 shares at $2 per share. Option pricing models indicate that the options have a total value of $1,400,000. Estimates of retention are 82% at the end of 20X1 and 80% at the end of 20X2.

Required:

1. Provide the journal entry to be recorded with respect to the options at the end of 20X1 and 20X2.
2. What would the balance be in the equity account for stock rights at the end of the fifth year if retention remained at 80%?
3. Assume that retention was 80%, and the options were exercised at the end of the sixth year when the market price of common shares is $29. Provide the entry for exercise.
4. Alternatively, assume that retention was 80% but the options were allowed to lapse after eight years when the price of common shares is $1.25. Provide the entry for the lapse.

connect

TR15-5 Share-Based Compensation; Cash Settled: IT Solutions Limited has a cash-settled SARs program for employees. These employees will receive a cash payment after five years of service, calculated as the excess of share price over $7.50. In early 20X1, employees in total are granted 60,000 units in the program.

The fair value of one SARs unit is estimated at $1 at the end of 20X1, $3 at the end of 20X2, and $2 at the end of 20X3. Estimated retention is 90% at the end of 20X1, 88% at the end of 20X2, and 75% at the end of 20X3. The payment is made at the end of 20X5.

Required:

Provide the journal entry to be recorded with respect to the SARS program at the end of 20X1, 20X2, and 20X3.

ASSIGNMENTS

★ **A15-1 Classification; Impact of Debt versus Equity:** Laffoley Corporation needs to raise $7,000,000 to finance a planned capital expansion. The company has investigated two alternatives:

1. Issue $7 million of preferred shares at par. The shares can be redeemed at the company's option at the end of 10 years for a price estimated to be in the region of $7,200,000. Annual (cumulative) dividends would amount to $420,000.
2. Issue bonds, which the company can buy back on the open market at the end of 10 years; analysts estimate that it would cost $7,200,000 to reacquire the $7,000,000 issue. Annual interest would amount to $600,000.

Required:

1. Assume Laffoley's tax rate is 30%. What is the *after-tax* annual cost of the two alternatives?
2. Provide journal entries to record issuance, annual dividends or interest (for one year only), and retirement of both the shares and debt.
3. Assume that earnings, before interest and tax, in Year 10 was $2,000,000. The tax rate was 30%. Calculate earnings if equity were outstanding in Year 10, and retired at the end of the year. Calculate earnings if debt were outstanding in Year 10 and retired at the end of the year.

★ **A15-2 Classification:** Description of several financial instruments follows:

connect

Case 1 Convertible subordinated bonds payable, entitled to annual cash interest at 5%, paid semi-annually. At maturity, the bonds may be settled at the investor's option through the issuance of common shares using an exchange price of $5 per share. Alternatively, the investor may choose to be repaid in cash.

Case 2 Convertible subordinated bonds payable, entitled to annual cash interest at 5%, paid semi-annually. At maturity, the bonds may be settled at the issuer's option through the issuance of common shares using an exchange price of $5 per share. Alternatively, the issuer may choose to repay principal in cash.

Case 3 Convertible subordinated bonds payable, entitled to annual cash interest at 5%, paid semi-annually. At maturity, the bonds may be settled at the issuer's option through the issuance of common shares using the current market price of the shares. Alternatively, the issuer may choose to repay principal in cash.

Case 4 Convertible subordinated bonds payable, entitled to annual cash interest at 5%, paid semi-annually. At maturity, the bonds may be settled at the investor's option through the issuance of common shares using the current market price of the shares. Alternatively, the investor may choose to be repaid in cash.

Case 5 Series F second preferred shares, carrying a fixed cumulative dividend of $1 per share. The shares must be redeemed by the company at a price of $50 per share, plus dividends in arrears, if any, on 31 December 20X1.

Required:

Classify each of the above items as a financial liability, equity instrument, or compound instrument (part debt and part equity).

★ **A15-3 Classification:** Description of several financial instruments follows:

Solution

Case 1 Class D Series 2 shares, carrying a dividend entitlement equal to $5 per share or an amount equal to common share dividends, whichever is higher, redeemable at the investor's option at $62 per share. The company may, at its option, redeem the shares with class A common shares instead of cash, valued at their current market value.

Case 2 Convertible subordinated bonds payable, entitled to annual cash interest at 3.2%. At maturity, the bonds will be settled through the issuance of shares using an exchange price of $14 per share. Interest may also be paid in shares valued at $14 per share at the company's option.

Case 3 Series F second preferred shares, carrying a fixed cumulative dividend of $1 per share. The shares must be redeemed by the company at a price of $21 per share, plus dividends in arrears, if any, in 20X4.

Case 4 Convertible subordinated debentures payable, entitled to annual interest at 3.2%. At maturity, the debentures may, at the company's option, be paid out in cash or converted into common shares using an exchange ratio governed by the market value of shares at the conversion date.

Case 5 Series C first preferred shares, carrying a fixed cumulative dividend of $1.25 per share per annum, redeemable at the company's option at $25 per share.

Case 6 Series II preferred shares, carrying a fixed cumulative dividend of $1.75 per share increasing to $6.10 in 20X8. The shares are redeemable at the company's option at a price of $28 per share until 31 December 20X7 and at a price of $62 thereafter.

Case 7 Convertible subordinated 6% notes payable. At maturity, the debentures may, at the company's option, be paid out in cash or converted into common shares at the set exchange price of $30 per share.

Required:

Classify each of the above items as a financial liability, equity instrument, or compound instrument (part debt and part equity).

★★ **A15-4 Classification:** Value Production Corp. currently has a debt-to-equity ratio of 3.2-to-1, based on $16 million of debt and $5 million of equity. The company is looking to raise $2 million in new financing for an expansion plan. There is a debt covenant that requires the debt-to-equity ratio to be no higher than 3.5-to-1, and this is a major factor as the company looks at several financing alternatives.

Alternative 1: Issuance of $2 million of 5% preferred shares, redeemable in cash at the option of the investor.

Alternative 2: Issuance of $2 million of 6% preferred shares, redeemable in cash at the option of Value.

Alternative 3: Issuance of $2 million of 7% secured bonds, convertible into common shares at the option of Value, with conversion based on the market price of common shares at the conversion date.

Alternative 4: Issuance of $2 million of 6.5% unsecured bonds, convertible into common shares at the option of the investor, with conversion at $20 per share. This conversion option is estimated to be worth $250,000.

Required:

1. Calculate and comment on the relative annual cost of each alternative from Value's perspective. The company has a 35% tax rate. For the investor, what are the attractive elements of each investment?
2. Classify each alternative as debt or equity, and recalculate the debt-to-equity ratio.
3. Which alternative would you recommend to Value? Explain.

★★ **A15-5 Classification:** Glamour Mining Ltd. currently has a debt-to-equity ratio of 2.5-to-1, based on $50 million of debt and $20 million of equity. The company is looking to raise $10 million in new financing and must choose one of the following:

A. Convertible debt, unsecured, with a 6% interest rate, where conversion is mandatory in 20 years for 500,000 voting common shares. Interest is paid in cash annually.
B. Convertible debt, secured with company land and buildings, with a 5% interest rate, where conversion is at the investor's options in 20 years for 500,000 voting common shares. Interest is paid in cash annually. This conversion option is estimated to be worth $1,147,000.
C. Preferred shares, carrying an annual dividend of 4%, where the investor has the choice of cash repayment or 500,000 common shares in 20 years.

There is a debt covenant that requires the debt-to-equity ratio to be no higher than 3-to-1.

Required:

1. Calculate and comment on the relative annual cost of each alternative from the company's perspective. The company has a 40% tax rate. For the investor, what are the attractive elements of each investment?
2. Classify each alternative as debt or equity and re-calculate the debt-to-equity ratio. Use 6% as a market yield rate if present value calculations are needed.
3. Which alternative would you recommend to Glamour? Explain.

★ **A15-6 Classification:** A description of several financial instruments follows:

Case A Subordinated 8% debentures payable, interest payable semi-annually, due in the year 20X8. At maturity, the face value of the debentures may be converted, at the company's option, into common shares at the market price at that time. Interest may also be paid in shares using the market value of shares at the interest payment date.

Case B Series B shares, nonvoting, annual $1.25 cumulative dividend, convertible at the investor's option into 10 common shares in 20X6.

Case C Subordinated 4% debentures payable, interest payable in cash semi-annually, due in 20X9. At maturity, the face value of the debentures must be converted into common shares at a price of $22 per share.

Case D Series C shares, nonvoting, annual $1.25 noncumulative dividend, redeemable at the investor's option for $29 per share at any time.

Case E Subordinated bonds payable, bearing an interest rate of 5%, interest reset every five years with reference to market rates; principal due to be repaid only on the dissolution of the company, if ever, although may be repaid at the company's option on interest repricing dates.

Case F Series B preferred shares, annual $6 cumulative dividend, convertible into four common shares for every $100 preferred share at the investor's option, redeemable at $32 per share at the company's option in 20X10.

Required:

Classify each financial instrument as debt, equity, or compound (part debt and part equity). Explain your reasoning.

★★ Solution

A15-7 Convertible Debt: Marjorie Manufacturing Limited issued a convertible bond on 2 July 20X5. The $5 million bond pays annual interest of 8% each 30 June. Each $1,000 bond is convertible into 50 shares of common stock, at the investor's option, on 1 July 20X10 until 1 July 20X15, after which time each $1,000 bond may be converted into 45.6 shares until bond maturity on 30 June 20X20. Market analysts have indicated that had the bond not been convertible, it would have sold for $4,240,000, reflecting a market interest rate of 10% annually. In fact, it was issued for $5,325,000.

Required:

1. Provide the journal entry to record the initial issuance of the bond. Justify the amount allocated to the conversion privilege.
2. Verify the $4,240,000 price of the bond.
3. Calculate the interest expense that would be recorded in the first 12 months of the bond.
4. Would more or less interest expense have been recorded in requirement 3 if the conversion option were not recognized and the proceeds above par value ($325,000) were assigned to a premium account? Explain, but do not calculate.

★★ connect

A15-8 Convertible Debt; Investor's Option: Nero Solutions Company issued an $800,000, 6%, three-year bond for $806,000. The bond pays interest annually, at each year-end. At maturity, the bond can be repaid in cash or converted to 60,000 common shares at the investor's option. The market interest rate for bonds of similar term and risk, but that are not convertible, is in the range of 7%.

Required:

1. Calculate the portion of the bond to be recorded as a liability.
2. Provide the entry to record issuance of the bond.
3. Provide the entries to record interest expense and the annual cash payment each year over the bond's three-year life.
4. Provide the entry to record the maturity of the bond, assuming that shares were issued.
5. Provide the entry to record the maturity of the bond, assuming that cash is paid.
6. Provide the entry to record early repayment of the bond, assuming that it was repaid in cash in an open market transaction after two complete years. Cash of $810,000 was paid, of which $802,000 related to the liability and $8,000 related to the conversion option.

★★ connect

A15-9 Convertible Debt; Investor's Option: Blue Cliff Ltd. issued subordinated bonds payable on 1 January 20X1, when the market interest rate was 6%. The company received $10,760,000 for the bonds. The bonds were $10,000,000 of 4% subordinated convertible debentures payable, with interest payable semi-annually. These bonds were convertible at the investor's option in 15 years' time into common shares of the company at the rate of 25 shares for each $1,000 bond issued.

Required:

1. At what price would the bonds be issued if they were not convertible?
2. Explain the method used to value the conversion option.
3. Provide the entry to record issuance of the bond on 1 January 20X1.
4. Provide the journal entry to record interest on 30 June 20X1. Use the effective interest method to record discount amortization.
5. Provide the entry to record bond conversion to common shares at maturity, on 31 December 20X10. Common shares had a fair value of $44 per share at this time.
6. Assume instead that the bond was repaid in cash at maturity. Provide all entries to record the repayment/bond maturity. If repayment is in cash, what fair value for common shares is implied?

★★★ **A15-10 Convertible Debt; Three Cases:** The following cases are independent:

Case A

On 1 January 20X1, Wilson Products Limited issued a bond when market interest rates were 6%.

> Bonds payable, $10,000,000, 5%, due in 15 years' time. The bonds pay interest semi-annually each 30 June and 31 December. The bonds were issued at 104. The bonds are mandatorily convertible at the company's discretion into common shares at the fixed rate of 20 shares for each $100 bond at maturity. The company may, at its discretion, repay the bond for cash in lieu of shares.

Required:

Prepare the journal entry at 1 January 20X1, to record issuance of the bond. Also calculate interest expense for the year ended 31 December 20X1.

Case B

On 1 December 20X4, XBL Communications Limited issued a convertible bond that was convertible in 10 years' time into 604,000 common shares at the investor's option. The bond had a $5,000,000 par value, and 4.5% interest was paid semi-annually on 30 November and 31 May.

The bond sold for $5,700,000 when the market interest rate was 5%.

Required:

Provide entries on issuance and on 31 December 20X1, the fiscal year-end.

Case C

On the 31 October 20X1 SFP, Argon Mining Limited reported the following:

Debt		
Convertible bond payable, 3%, due 31 October 20X2, convertible into 500,000 shares	$8,000,000	
Less: discount	(299,000)	
		$7,701,000
Equity		
Contributed capital: common share conversion rights		$ 232,000

Interest is paid *annually* on 31 October, and the bonds were originally valued to yield 7%.

Required:

Provide entries on 31 October 20X2 to record the interest expense and payment, and show the conversion of the bonds to common shares on this date. The market price of common shares was $39 per share on 31 October 20X2.

★★★ **A15-11 Convertible Debt; Investor Option versus Conversion Mandatory:** AMC Limited issued five-year, 5% bonds for their par value of $900,000 on 1 January 20X1. Interest is paid annually. The bonds are convertible to common shares at a rate of 50 common shares for every $1,000 bond.

excel

connect

Required:

1. Assume that the bonds were convertible at the investor's option and that the conversion option was valued at $73,800.
   a. Provide the journal entry on issuance.
   b. Calculate interest expense for each year of the bond's five-year life. Use an interest rate of 7% for this requirement.
   c. Provide the journal entry to record maturity of the bond assuming shareholders convert their bonds to common shares.
   d. Assume instead that the bonds were repaid for $940,000 after interest was paid in Year 3. Provide the journal entry for retirement, assuming $68,000 of the payment related to the option and the rest related to the bond.
2. Assume that the bonds were mandatorily convertible at maturity.
   a. Calculate the portion of the original proceeds relating to interest and the equity portion. Use a discount rate of 6%.
   b. Provide the journal entry on issuance.
   c. Explain the financial statement elements that change when the bond is converted at maturity.

★ **A15-12 Convertible Debt; Mandatory Conversion:** Canada Resources Ltd. issued a 10-year, $10,000,000 debenture with an interest rate of 4.5%; cash interest is paid semi-annually. The market rate of interest for debt of similar size, risk, and term is 6%. The obligation can be satisfied at maturity either by cash or by issuing common shares valued at $14 per share, at the option of Canada Resources Ltd. The debenture was issued for $10,100,000.

Required:

1. Classify this debenture as debt, equity, or a compound instrument. Explain your reasoning.
2. Provide the entry to record issuance of the debenture.
3. What is the value of the liability amount(s) relating to the debenture that will be shown on the SFP at the end of the second year (after adjustments)?
4. Explain the financial statement elements that change when the bond is converted at maturity.
5. Suppose instead that the $10,000,000 debenture was convertible into common shares using a value of 101% of the average market value of common shares in the five trading days prior to conversion. Explain how this difference would affect your treatment of the debenture. Calculations are not necessary.

★★ **A15-13 Convertible Debt; Mandatory Conversion:** Twixt Corporation issued $5,000,000 of convertible bonds on 1 January for $4,790,000 cash. The bond had the following terms:

excel

connect

- Bonds mature in five years' time.
- Annual interest, 5%, is paid each 31 December.
- Bonds are convertible to 400,000 common shares at maturity or can be repaid in cash. This choice is up to Twixt Corp.

Current market interest rates are 6%.

Required:

1. Assign a value to the liability and the equity portions of the bond.
2. Provide the journal entry to record issuance of the bond.

3. Provide a schedule to show interest expense and amortization of the liability over the life of the bond.
4. What financial statement elements would be changed when common shares are issued at maturity? Explain.

★ **A15-14 Share Rights—Recognition:** Agmore Breakthrough Corp. is a small biotech company listed on the TSX. To conserve cash, the company frequently settles obligations through the issuance of rights and options. Shares are now trading for $5 per share but have fluctuated between $2 and $19 in the last year. Selected transactions:

a. Issued rights to the company lawyer for legal work done to date. These options allow purchase of 50,000 shares at $2 per share at any time over the next three years. The lawyer had billed $216,000, but the company felt it could have negotiated this down slightly—perhaps 10%—for cash payment.
b. Issued rights that allow purchase of 200,000 common shares at $5 per share at any time over the next two years. The options were issued for $144,200 cash.
c. Issued rights to a customer allowing the customer to receive 40,000 common shares in three years' time, for no cash cost. The rights have been granted based on the long service relationship between the two companies, are fully vested, and are unconditional.
d. Options in (a) and (c) above were exercised when the shares were trading at $11 per share. Options in (b) later expired.

Required:

Provide journal entries to record the transactions listed above. Justify the values used.

★ **A15-15 Share Rights—Recognition:** Maritime Corp. is a junior mining company listed on the TSX. The common share price of Maritime fluctuates in value. Recent swings went from a high of $16 to a low of $0.30. Maritime issued stock rights on 1 September 20X5 to a consultant, in exchange for a project completed over the last year. The consultant estimated her time was worth $37,000, but the company estimated that it could have had the necessary work done for about $31,000 cash. The rights specified that 4,000 common shares could be bought for $0.20 per share at any time over the next 10 years. The market price of common shares was $1.50 on the day the rights were issued. At the same time options were issued to the consultant, identical rights were issued to the company lawyer for work done to date. An option pricing model valued each set of stock rights at $35,000.

connect

Required:

1. Provide journal entries to record issuance of the two sets of rights. Justify values used.
2. Assume that two years after issuance, when the market price of the shares was $14, the consultant exercised her rights. Provide the appropriate entry.
3. Assume that 10 years after issuance, when the market price of the shares was $0.10, the lawyer's rights expired. Provide the entry, if any.

★★★ **A15-16 Share Rights and Warrants:** On 31 December 20X2, the shareholders' equity section of Sersa Corporation's statement of financial position was as follows:

excel

Common shares, no-par, unlimited shares authorized, issued and outstanding, 4,543,400 shares	$16,876,400
Contributed capital: common share warrants outstanding, 12,300 warrants allowing purchase of three shares each at a price of $26 per share	110,000
Share options outstanding	161,000
Retained earnings	34,560,900
Total shareholders' equity	$51,708,300

There were 46,000 share options outstanding, issued for legal services, valued at $161,000. These allow purchase of one share each for $19 cash; the options are exercisable over several years.

Transactions during the year:

a. Options were issued to existing shareholders as a poison pill in the case of a hostile takeover. These options allow purchase of two shares for each existing share held at a price of $1 each, to be exercisable only under certain limited conditions.
b. Warrants outstanding at the beginning of the year were exercised in full. The market value of the shares was $40.
c. Some outstanding $19 share options were exercised and 10,000 shares were issued. Remaining share options were not exercised in the current year. The market value of the shares was $40.
d. Options were issued that allow purchase of a total of 2,000 shares at a price of $32 per share, beginning in 20X4. The options were issued for four months of 20X3 rent, which was set by contract at $4,000 per month.
e. Options were issued for proceeds of $45,000, allowing purchase of 40,000 shares at a price of $35 per share.
f. One-quarter of the options issued in (e), above, were exercised. The market value of the shares was $48.

Required:

1. Provide journal entries for each of the transactions listed above.
2. Prepare the shareholders' equity section of the statement of financial position, reflecting the transactions recorded in requirement 1.
3. What items would appear on the statement of cash flows in the financing activities section as a result of the changes in the equity accounts documented in requirement 2?

★★ connect

A15-17 Share-Based Compensation; Cash-Settled: Just In Co. issues 500,000 SARs units to its eight-member top management group. These SARs allow the managers to receive a cash payment after holding the SARs for five years. The SARs vest on the payment date. The value of the SARs is calculated as the difference between the $34 per share fair market value of common shares on the date the SARs were issued and the fair market value on the date of payment. The company estimates that six of eight managers will remain with the company over the five-year period. This estimate remains unchanged over the first four years. One manager leaves after Year 2, one after Year 3, and one in Year 5, so that only five managers were paid at the end of Year 5.

The fair value of one SARs unit was estimated using a valuation model and was, at the end of Year 1, $4; Year 2, $1; Year 3, $2; Year 4, $17; and in Year 5, the actual market price of common shares was $53.

Required:

1. Why are SARs issued instead of common stock options?
2. How much compensation expense would be recorded in each of Years 1 to 5?
3. What would appear on the SFP at the end of each of Years 1 to 4?
4. What entry would be made on the maturity (payment) of the SARs?
5. Describe how the accounting for this compensation scheme would be different if the employees could choose between cash and shares at settlement.

★★ excel connect

A15-18 Share-Based Compensation; Cash-Settled: Pine Resources Ltd. has a SARs program for managers. These individuals receive a cash payment after four years of service, calculated as the excess of share price over $5. In early 20X1, individuals in the 25-member management team are granted a total of 100,000 SARs units. The payment is made at the end of 20X4. Data on estimated and actual retention are:

End of Year	20X1	20X2	20X3	20X4
Employees expected to remain until vesting	15 (60%)	20 (80%)	22 (88%)	n/a
Employees expected to forfeit	10 (40%)	5 (20%)	3 (12%)	n/a
Employees actually forfeiting in the year	2	0	1	1
Employees actually receiving SARs (25 – 4)				21 (84%)

The fair value of the entire 100,000 units was estimated to be $100,000 at the end of 20X1, $300,000 at the end of 20X2, and $120,000 at the end of 20X3. The actual share price was $7.40 at the end of 20X4.

Required:

1. Calculate compensation expense in each year of the SARs plan and the balance of the SARs liability at the end of each year.
2. What evidence suggests that the level of retention must be revised after 20X1 and 20X2?
3. Explain why compensation expense is volatile.

★★

Solution

A15-19 Share-Based Compensation; Cash-Settled: Pacific Trading Company has a SARs program for managers. These individuals receive a cash payment after three years of service, calculated as the excess of share price over $10. In early 20X3, the 30 members of the management team in total are granted 25,000 units in the program. The payment is made at the end of 20X5. Data on estimated and actual retention are:

End of Year	20X3	20X4	20X5
Employees expected to remain until vesting	25 (83%)	24 (80%)	n/a
Employees expected to forfeit	5 (17%)	6 (20%)	n/a
Employees actually forfeiting in the year	1	4	3
Employees actually receiving SARs (30 – 8)			22 (73.3%)

The fair value of one SARs unit is estimated at $3 at the end of 20X3 and $12 at the end of 20X4. The actual share price is $19 at the end of 20X5.

Required:

1. Provide the entry to record compensation expense in each year of the SARs plan, including the entry for cash payment in 20X5.
2. What evidence suggests that the level of retention must be revised for 20X4?
3. Describe how the accounting for this compensation scheme would be different if the employees could choose between cash and shares at settlement.

★★

A15-20 Share-Based Compensation; Equity-Settled: Wolmore Resources Limited is authorized to issue unlimited numbers of common shares, of which 40,500,000 have been issued at an average price of $22 per share. On 1 January 20X3, when shares were trading for $30 per share, the company granted stock options to each of its 42 senior executives. The stock options provide that each individual will be eligible to purchase, no earlier than 31 December 20X7, 3,000 common shares at a base option price of $30 per share. The options are nontransferable, vest on 31 December 20X7, and expire on 31 December 20X8. Option pricing models indicate that the options have a total value of $480,000. Estimates of retention are:

Year	20X3	20X4	20X5	20X6	20X7
Employees expected to remain until vesting	32 (76%)	30 (71%)	35 (83%)	34 (81%)	n/a
Employees expected to forfeit	10 (24%)	12 (29%)	7 (17%)	8 (19%)	n/a
Employees actually forfeiting in the year	0	5	2	0	0
Employees actually receiving options (42 – 7)					35 (83%)

Twenty-five individuals who received the options exercised on 31 December 20X7, when the share price was $54. The remaining individuals did not exercise the options. The share price fell to $24 in 20X8, and the remaining options lapsed.

Required:

1. Prepare the entries to record the granting of the options, annual expense, exercise, and lapse.
2. Why is the compensation expense not an equal amount each year? Be specific.
3. What intrinsic value was received when the options were exercised? Is this reflected in the financial statements? Explain.

★ **A15-21 Share-Based Compensation:** Smith Minerals Ltd. had compensation plans in effect for senior managers that included two long-term compensation elements. SFP accounts at the end of 20X4 are:

Liability—SARs plan 120,000 units are under SARs agreement, where the reference market price is $16 per common share, one share per SARs unit; valuation models indicate a fair value of $1.25 per SARs unit; the SARs have been outstanding for two years and must be held for a total of five years before vesting.	$ 54,000
Contributed capital—employee share options outstanding 106,000 shares are under option at an exercise price of $18. Common shares are now trading at $23. The options were valued using a binomial valuation model and determined to be worth $520,000. The options have been outstanding for three years and must be held for a total of five years before they can be exercised.	$280,800

Retention levels were estimated to be 90% at the end of 20X4.

Required:

1. Describe the likely features of the two kinds of compensation plans above. Provide the calculation to support the balances recorded.
2. Assume no new compensation entitlements were offered in 20X5. At year-end, the common share price was $31 and the fair value of a SARs unit was estimated to be worth $1.40. Retention is now assumed to be 85%. Give the entries to record compensation expense related to the above plans.

★★ **A15-22 Share-Based Compensation; Compound Plan:** Five vice presidents of Spinner Entertainment Limited are awarded units in a phantom stock plan at the beginning of 20X2. At the end of 20X4, after three years of employment, each vice president is entitled to receive *either*

- 5,000 common shares; or
- Cash equal to the market value of 3,500 shares.

When the rights were granted, the shares had a market value of $20, and valuation models indicated that the share alternative was worth $21.20 per share. Based on this information, the equity portion of the plan was valued at $180,000 for accounting purposes. The share price was $19 at the end of 20X2, $23 at the end of 20X3, and $20 at the end of 20X4. The fair value of the cash alternative is to be based on the intrinsic value of the plan on each reporting date. All vice-presidents were expected to stay with the company, and all did. Four of the five executives elected to take cash in 20X4, and the remaining vice-president took shares.

Required:

1. Verify the $180,000 option value at the inception of the plan.
2. Prepare the entries to record the annual expense entries and disbursement in 20X4.

★ **A15-23 Derivatives:** Moon Pacific Limited reported the following amounts on the 31 December 20X2 SFP (in thousands):

Assets		**Liabilities**	
Derivative asset	$1,455	Derivative obligation	$2,101
		Equity	
		Reserve: hedge gain	$ 134

Moon Pacific has material accounts receivable and purchase orders from customers that are denominated in euros. The company follows a policy of hedging all exchange exposure with futures contracts.

Required:

1. Explain the conditions that cause a derivative instrument to be an asset or a liability.
2. Explain the use of derivatives to hedge exchange exposure caused by U.S. dollar accounts receivable.
3. Are gains and losses from derivatives included in earnings? Explain.
4. What conditions must be met for hedge accounting to be invoked?
5. What is the most likely explanation for the presence of the $134 hedge reserve?

★ **A15-24 Derivatives:** Starco Corp. wishes to purchase 5,000 shares of Gertrom Ltd., a publicly traded company. Starco contracts to buy the shares from a related party, Unit Ltd., for $62 per share in 90 days' time. The fair value was $62 per share on this day. One month later, at year-end, the fair value of the Gertrom shares is $54 per share, and it is $55 per share at the end of 90 days. At that time, the shares are bought, and the contract is closed out.

Required:

1. Is this a forward contract or a futures contract? Explain.
2. What risk is the company hedging?
3. Prepare journal entries to record the inception of the contract, the change in its fair value at year-end, and its maturity.

★ **A15-25 Derivatives:** Dauphinee DL Corp. plans to purchase 100,000 shares of Santos Technology Ltd., a publicly traded company. Dauphinee has signed a contract to acquire the shares from Holding Company in 90 days, after certain approvals are obtained; these approvals are routine but time consuming. The agreed-upon price per share is $22.50, which is the fair value of the shares on the day the contract was signed. Santos shares have traded between $5 and $35 over the last year; the industry has been volatile. Sixty days after signing this agreement, it is Dauphinee's year-end, and Santos shares are trading for $28. At the time the contract matured, and the shares are purchased; the shares are trading for $16.

connect

Required:

1. Is this a forward contract or a futures contract? Explain.
2. What risk is the company hedging?
3. Prepare journal entries to record the inception of the contract, the change in its fair value at year-end, and its maturity.

★ **A15-26 ASPE; Classification:** Eldon Limited is a private company that complies with ASPE. Eldon issued the following financial instruments in 20X4:

1. *Convertible debentures* issued at 103. The debentures require interest to be paid semi-annually at a nominal rate of 7% per annum. The debentures are convertible by the holder at any time up to final maturity at a ratio of 10 common shares for each $1,000 principal amount.
2. *Shareholder loans*, 3%, due on demand, issued at par. The shareholders do not intend to request repayment unless the company is dissolved. This money was advanced as a loan but is considered equity by the shareholder and the lenders.
3. *Redeemable preferred shares* issued to Eldon's founding family. The shares carry an annual cash dividend at the rate of $12 per share and have a repurchase option at the choice of the investor. The shares were issued as a tax planning mechanism and are high/low shares.

Required:

With reference to ASPE, discuss the appropriate financial statement classification of each of these financial instruments.

★ **A15-27 ASPE; Convertible Debt:** On 1 January 20X6, Cedar Limited issues $5,000,000 face amount of 4%, five-year, convertible debentures. Interest is payable annually on 31 December. The debentures are convertible at the investor's option at an exchange price of $10 per share. The market rate of interest for non-convertible bonds of similar risk and maturity is 5%. The net proceeds received by Cedar amounted to $5,700,000.

Required:

1. Cedar is a public company. Record the issuance of the bonds on 1 January 20X6, and the journal entry for interest expense on 31 December 20X6. Cedar uses effective interest amortization for bond premium and discount.
2. Cedar is a private company and complies with ASPE. Record the issuance of the bonds on 1 January 20X6 and the journal entry for interest expense on 31 December 20X6. Cedar uses straight-line interest amortization for bond premium and discount.
3. Comment on the differences between requirements 1 and 2. Comment on the impact on the financial statements, and suggest a justification for the ASPE treatment.

★ **A15-28 ASPE, Share-Based Compensation; Equity-Settled:** Lucky Enterprises Limited has an executive stock option plan as follows: Each qualified manager will receive, on 1 January, an option for the computed number of common shares at a computed price. The number of option shares and the option price are determined by the Board of Directors, with advice from the compensation committee. The options are nontransferable. The vesting period is three years. Options can be exercised after they vest but expire six years after the date of issuance.

On 1 January 20X3, executives were granted options. An options pricing model was used to value the options, and a value of $450,000 was estimated. The options allow 100,000 shares to be issued for $5 per share. Retention estimates were 70% and 85% at the end of 20X3 and 20X4. In fact, the options were in-the-money on the vesting date, and 92,000 shares were issued at the end of 20X5 when the shares were trading for $16 per share. The remaining options were forfeit: 5,000 in 20X4 and 3,000 in 20X5. All forfeits were caused by turnover.

Required:

1. Lucky is a public company. Record the entry for compensation associated with options at the end of 20X3, 20X4, and 20X5 and also the entries for share issuance under options.

2. Lucky is a private company and complies with ASPE. Repeat requirement 1, including entries for forfeit options. The company does not estimate forfeiture in advance.
3. Comment on the differences between requirements 1 and 2. Comment on the impact on the financial statements, and suggest a justification for the ASPE treatment.

★★★ **A15-29 Statement of Cash Flows—Individual Transactions:** The following cases are independent:

Case A

Information from the 31 December 20X5 SFP of Holdco Limited:

	20X5	20X4
Bonds payable	$5,000,000	$ —
Discount on bonds payable	234,000	—
Common stock conversion rights	695,000	—

Convertible bonds were issued during the year. Discount amortization was $14,000 in 20X5.

Case B

Information from the 31 December 20X5 SFP of Sellco Limited:

	20X5	20X4
Bonds payable	$ 5,000,000	$10,000,000
Discount on bonds payable	160,000	346,000
Common stock conversion rights	695,000	1,390,000
Common shares	17,000,000	7,100,000

One-half of the bonds converted to common shares during the period. Other common shares were issued for cash. Discount amortization during the year was $26,000.

Case C

Information from the 31 December 20X5 SFP of Buyco Limited:

	20X5	20X4
Stock rights outstanding	$ 240,000	$ 295,000
Common shares	9,000,000	6,550,000

During the year, 10,000 stock rights originally valued at a price of $5.50 were exercised, and 10,000 common shares were issued for the exercise price of $14. One million stock rights, allowing qualified shareholders to acquire common shares at one-tenth the then-current fair value in the event of hostile takeover, were also issued during the year. Other common shares were sold for cash.

Case D

Information from the 31 December 20X5 SFP of Bothco Limited:

	20X5	20X4
Bonds payable	$ —	$10,000,000
Discount on bonds payable	—	26,450
Common stock conversion rights	—	1,390,000
Contributed capital, lapse of conversion right	1,390,000	—

Bonds payable matured in the year but were redeemed in cash at par and not converted.

Required:

For each case, list the appropriate items on the statement of cash flows caused by issuance, conversion, or derecognition of financial instruments. Do not include disclosure of interest or accounts related to interest expense (e.g., do not list discount amortization).

★★★ **A15-30 Statement of Cash Flows—Comprehensive Equity:** The following data are related to Eli Products Ltd.:

	20X9	20X8
Bonds payable, 7%	$10,000,000	$ 0
Discount on bonds payable	(690,000)	0
6% Preferred share liability, due 20X11	500,000	500,000
5% Preferred shares, no-par	2,600,000	2,600,000
Common shares, no-par	8,000,000	5,000,000
Common share fractional rights	68,000	0
Contributed capital: common stock conversion rights	525,000	0
Contributed capital: common share retirement	150,000	0
Contributed capital: employee stock options outstanding	387,500	160,000
Contributed capital on treasury stock transactions	165,000	0
Retained earnings	7,005,000	6,940,000
Treasury stock, 5% preferred shares	(500,000)	0

During the year, the following transactions took place and have been correctly recorded:

a. Reported earnings and comprehensive income was $3,200,000. Cash dividends were paid at the end of the year.
b. Retained earnings was reduced by $175,000 as the result of share issue costs.
c. Earnings includes $400,000 of compensation expense recorded for options to employees and also an amount for the 6% preferred share dividends.
d. There was a common share stock dividend during the year that resulted in a reduction to retained earnings of $710,000. Most of the shares were issued as whole shares, but some were issued in the form of fractional rights. All these rights are still outstanding at year-end.
e. Common shares with an average original issuance price of $500,000 were retired during the year.
f. 5% preferred shares with an original average book value of $900,000 were purchased as treasury shares early in the fiscal year. Half were resold almost immediately, and half were kept.
g. Additional common shares were issued for cash, as a stock dividend, and for the options in (i).
h. Convertible bonds were issued during the year. Discount amortization of $41,500 was recorded by the end of the year.
i. Employee stock options, along with $100,000 of cash, were exchanged for common shares during the year.
j. Any remaining change in accounts should be assumed to flow from a logical transaction.

Required:

1. List the items and amounts that caused the retained earnings account to change from its opening to closing balance. For the dividend through retained earnings, specify the amount to each share class.
2. List the items and amounts that caused the common share account to change from its opening to closing balance.
3. List the items that would appear in the financing activities section of the SCF. The company classifies dividends in the operating activities section.

★★★ **A15-31 Comprehensive Equity:** Acer Corporation reported the following balances at 1 January 20X1:

Solution

Interest liability—8% bond ($10,000,000 par value). Conversion into 76,000 common shares at maturity is mandatory	$ 4,997,000
Share equity—8% bond	5,102,000

Convertible $8, no-par preferred shares, 60,000 shares outstanding; convertible into 8 common shares for every 3 preferred shares outstanding	6,060,000
Class A no-par common shares, unlimited shares authorized, 915,000 issued and 899,000 outstanding	32,940,000
Common share warrants, allowing purchase of 90,000 shares at $32.50	660,000
Contributed capital: employee share options outstanding*	160,000
Contributed capital on preferred share retirement	55,000
Retained earnings	116,300,000
Less: Treasury shares, 16,000 common shares	(512,000)

*Forty thousand common stock options are outstanding to certain employees allowing purchase of one share for every two options held at a price of $27.50 per share. These options are vested and expire in 20X4.

The following events took place in 20X1:

a. Common shares were issued to employees under the terms of existing outstanding share options. 16,000 options were exercised when the share market value was $45.
b. Options were issued in exchange for a piece of land, appraised at $75,000. The options allow purchase of 100,000 shares at $15 each in five years' time. The market value of the shares was $46 on this date. The option was valued at $81,000 using the Black-Scholes option pricing model.
c. 40,000 common shares were acquired and retired at a price of $47 each.
d. 10,000 common treasury shares were acquired at a price of $44 per share.
e. A cash dividend was declared and paid. The annual dividend for the preferred shares and $1 per share for the common shares were both declared and paid.
f. 24,000 preferred shares were converted to common shares.
g. The annual interest expense was accrued on the 8% bonds, using the effective rate of 7.8%. The annual payment was made.
h. Two-thirds of the common share warrants outstanding at the beginning of the year were exercised when the market value of the shares was $49.50; the remainder lapsed.
i. Options were granted to employees at the beginning of the year, allowing purchase of one share for every two options held at a price of $35. Fifty thousand options were issued. These options become vested at the beginning of 20X5. The fair value of the options was $720,000 and the retention rate for the employee groups covered was estimated at 90%.
j. 10,000 preferred shares were retired for $107 each.
k. 20,000 treasury shares were sold for $32 each.
l. A 10% stock dividend was declared and issued. Treasury shares were not eligible for the stock dividend. The Board of Directors decided that the stock dividend should be valued at $30 per share. Most of the dividend was issued in whole shares; however, 41,000 fractional shares allowing acquisition of 4,100 whole shares were issued.

Required:

1. Provide journal entries (or memo entries) for the events listed.
2. Calculate the closing balance in each of the listed accounts at 31 December 20X1, reflecting the entries in requirement 1. Earnings for the year were $6,200,000, including interest in (g) and stock option expense in (i).

connect LEARNSMART SMARTBOOK™

For more information on the resources available from McGraw-Hill Ryerson, go to www.mcgrawhill.ca/he/solutions.

CHAPTER 16

Accounting for Corporate Income Tax

INTRODUCTION

Bombardier Inc. reported 2011 pre-tax income of $1,040 million. The company paid $137 million to the government in income taxes. Yet the income statement showed income tax expense of $203 million. On Bombardier's statement of financial position (SFP) is a long-term *deferred income tax* liability (included in other liabilities) of $67 million. How did Bombardier avoid paying income tax in 2011 and instead report $67 million in deferred tax liabilities?

Armtec Infrastructure Inc. reported in 2011 a pre-tax loss of $320 million. The company paid no income taxes in the period, but its loss after taxes was lower at $269 million. How can you have a lower loss when there are no taxes paid?

Accounting for corporate income tax might seem rather straightforward. After all, the exact amount of income tax for each year is computed on the corporation's income tax return. Why is income tax expense usually different (and sometimes vastly different) from the actual taxes paid in a year?

In fact, Bombardier paid the income taxes that it owed to the government for 2011; the company did not "avoid" paying income taxes at all. The difference arises from an accounting practice known as *interperiod income tax allocation*. For Armtec, like Bombardier, interperiod tax allocation or deferred taxes is the answer.

At any point in time, many individual assets (and liabilities) will have an *accounting carrying value* that differs from its *tax basis*. That difference will have an impact on the income taxes that will be due in a future period when the asset is used or disposed of. Accountants recognize that future tax liability in the accounts as deferred income tax. Deferred income tax liabilities are not amounts that are actually owed to the government. The subject of this chapter is the method of accounting for the future tax effects of differences between the tax basis and the accounting carrying value.

A second aspect of interperiod income tax allocation pertains to the recognition of future benefits of tax loss carryforwards. This is the topic of discussion in Chapter 17.

One other aspect of accounting for income taxation is the *investment tax credit*, a special tax provision intended to encourage certain types of capital investment by businesses. This specialized topic is discussed in the Appendix to this chapter.

One important note about the chapter title: only corporations are subject to income tax because only corporations are recognized as legal entities. The profits of partnerships and proprietorships are taxed as income of the owners. Income tax expense does not appear on the financial statements of either partnerships or proprietorships.

INCOME TAX PROVISION VERSUS EXPENSE

It is common in practice for companies to label income tax expense in the income statement as the **provision for income tax**. This is a somewhat confusing label because we usually use "provision" to indicate an estimated liability, such as "Provision for Warranty Costs."

Companies use the term "provision" for income tax expense because when a company has a loss for tax purposes, the income statement entry for income tax may be a credit rather than a debit. Rather than switch the income statement label from "expense" to "benefit," companies use the vague term "provision" to fit all circumstances. This practice might be viewed as sloppy terminology, but it is not apt to cause confusion to readers, and it is easier to use.

In this book, to avoid confusion between the income statement item and the tax liability, we henceforth will typically use the title "income tax expense," even when the expense is a credit (i.e., a recovery of previously paid income taxes). IFRS does not apply the word "provision" to income tax expense or recovery, although the word is used in practice.

INTERPERIOD TAX ALLOCATION—INTRODUCTION

Interperiod tax allocation deals with allocating tax expense to an appropriate year, regardless of when it is actually paid. A company adopts those accounting policies that management perceives will best satisfy the objectives of financial statement users and preparers. One broad objective of accounting standards and accounting policies is to measure net income, which usually is the result of many accruals, interperiod allocations, and estimates. In contrast, the major objective of the *Income Tax Act* and Regulations is to generate revenue for the government.

Because it is easier and more objective to assess tax when cash is flowing, tax policy generally favours taxing revenues and expenses on the basis of cash flows rather than coping with the results of accounting allocations. Some important exceptions relate primarily to inventories, capital assets, and multiperiod earnings processes (e.g., revenue from long-term contracts), but cash flows are crucial. In addition, the *Income Tax Act* exempts certain types of income from taxation and prohibits the deduction of certain types of expenses.

Differences between Taxable and Accounting Income

Both accounting income and taxable income are the net result of matching revenues and expenses (and gains and losses) of a period. Most items of revenue and expense are recognized in the same period for both accounting and tax purposes. But there are some differences. These differences can be categorized as:

- Permanent differences; or
- Temporary differences.

Permanent Differences A **permanent difference** arises when an income statement element—a revenue, gain, expense, or loss—enters the computation of either taxable income or pre-tax accounting income but never enters into the computation of the other. For example, dividend income received from another tax-paying Canadian corporation is included in accounting income but is not included in taxable income. Such dividends are tax-exempt revenue. They are a nonreversing or *permanent* difference because they are not subject to taxation.

Similarly, a company may sell land that it has held for a long time. Since land is a capital asset, the gain from selling the land is known as a *capital gain* for tax purposes. The full amount of the gain will be recognized on the company's income statement, but only 50% of a capital gain is included in taxable income. Therefore, the 50% of a capital gain that is *not* taxed is a permanent difference.

Certain types of expenses are not deductible for tax purposes. A common example is golf club dues paid by a corporation. The *Income Tax Act* specifically identifies golf club dues as non-deductible for tax purposes, but they are a legitimate expense if the corporation believes they should be part of, say, a sales or marketing effort. Therefore, the difference between pre-tax accounting income and taxable income that arises from golf club dues is a permanent difference. Or a company may forget to make a tax payment (e.g., for payroll) and is charged interest and a penalty. The *Income Tax Act* does not allow this as a deduction, but it is an expense on the income statement.

There also may be deductions that are allowed in computing taxable income that have no equivalent for accounting income. In some years, for example, companies have been permitted to deduct tax depreciation, called *capital cost allowance*, or CCA, based on an amount higher than the cost basis of the assets (e.g., the CCA rate could be based on 150% of the specified asset's cost). Since accounting depreciation expense can never exceed 100% of an asset's cost, the excess CCA is a permanent difference.

Accounting standards do not discuss permanent differences at all, because they are specific to each nation and have no counterpart in accounting. We will continue to use this terminology in the chapter.

Temporary Differences A **temporary difference** arises when the tax basis of an asset or liability differs from its accounting carrying value.

A temporary difference *originates* in the period in which it first enters the computation of either taxable income or accounting income and *reverses* in the subsequent period when that item enters into the computation of the other measure. An item can either:

- Be included in accounting income first and then included in taxable income in a subsequent period; or
- Enter into the calculation of taxable income first and then be included in accounting income in a later period.

A temporary difference can either be a taxable temporary difference or a deductible temporary difference. A taxable temporary difference will result in higher taxable income in the future, and a deductible temporary difference will result in lower taxable income in the future.

Origination and Reversal An estimated warranty liability (provision) is accrued for accounting purposes when revenue is recognized. For income tax purposes, the warranty costs are not allowed as a deduction until the warranty work is completed in the future, giving rise to an originating temporary difference. In the originating year, the expense is not allowed to reduce taxable income. In the following year, assuming that the warranty work has been completed, the costs incurred reduce taxable income and reverse the temporary difference:

- A temporary difference is said to *originate* when the difference between accounting recognition and tax treatment first arises or when a recurring temporary difference *increases* the accumulated balance of temporary differences.
- A temporary difference is said to *reverse* when the accumulated temporary differences are *reduced* by the "catch-up" recognition for tax and accounting.

Other Examples Another example is capitalized development costs. For income tax purposes, development costs can be deducted when incurred. For accounting purposes, capitalized development costs are recognized in determining net income only as amortization is expensed in later periods. The temporary difference relating to development costs originates when the costs are deducted on the tax return and reverses over several future years as the capitalized costs are amortized for accounting purposes.

Similarly, temporary differences arise from the difference between accounting depreciation and CCA deducted for tax purposes. This is the most complex example because the temporary difference arises from the fact that the historical cost of the capital assets is being allocated simultaneously for accounting and tax purposes but in different patterns. Straight-line depreciation is commonly used for reporting purposes by Canadian corporations, but CCA usually follows a declining-balance pattern of allocation.

The CCA/depreciation temporary difference does not arise from the fact that depreciation expense is deducted for tax purposes but not for accounting but rather from the fact that the depreciation expense usually is lower than CCA in the early years of an asset's life, giving rise to *originating* temporary differences. In later years, as CCA declines, the straight-line depreciation becomes larger than CCA, and the temporary difference *reverses*. The CCA/depreciation temporary difference is the most common type of temporary difference.

Exhibit 16-1 lists some of the more common types of permanent differences and temporary differences.

EXHIBIT 16-1

EXAMPLES OF PERMANENT AND TEMPORARY DIFFERENCES IN CANADA

Permanent Differences

- Dividends received by Canadian corporations from some other taxable Canadian corporations
- Equity in earnings of significantly influenced associate companies
- 50% of capital gains
- Golf club dues
- 50% of meals and entertainment expenses
- Interest and penalties on taxes
- Political contributions

Temporary Differences

- Depreciation for accounting purposes; CCA for tax
- Amortization of capitalized development costs for accounting; immediate deduction for tax
- Amortization of capitalized interest for accounting; deducted when paid for tax
- Writedown of inventories, investments, or tangible capital assets for accounting; loss recognized only when realized for tax
- Gains and losses on inventories valued at net realizable value for accounting; taxed when realized
- Instalment sales income recognized for accounting at time of sale; taxed when cash received
- Bad debt expenses recognized in year of sale for accounting; tax deductible when uncollectible
- Capital assets written up under the revaluation method; no taxable gain until asset class closed
- Fair value increases for investment properties or biological assets; gain taxable only when property is sold
- Warranty costs accrued for accounting in period of sale; tax deductible when paid
- Bond discount or premium, amortized for accounting but taxable expense or revenue only when the principal is settled at maturity

CONCEPT REVIEW

1. Explain why accounting income is different from taxable income.
2. What is a nonreversing or permanent difference? Give an example.
3. A company deducts warranty expense in 20X0 on the income statement but pays warranty claims in 20X1. In what year does this temporary difference originate? In what year does it reverse?

CONCEPTUAL ISSUES IN INTERPERIOD TAX ALLOCATION

Interperiod income tax allocation has been an area of controversy for a long time. Conceptually, there are three basic underlying issues:

1. The extent of allocation;
2. The measurement method; and
3. Discounting.

Before illustrating the mechanics of tax allocation, we will briefly address each of these three issues. Every accountant should have a basic understanding of these issues because tax allocation accounting standards have changed several times over the years, and different countries have used different methods. The fact that a single approach is now widespread with the adoption of international accounting standards by many countries does not mean that the issue is settled. There still is much dissatisfaction with current standards within the accounting profession; both accountants and financial statement users should have a basic understanding of the dimensions of the issue.

Furthermore, private enterprises using ASPE are not required to follow the liability method explained in this chapter. Private companies can choose whether or not to follow income tax allocation. Substantial numbers of bankers, financial analysts, and accountants believe that no allocation or the "taxes payable" method that is acceptable for private enterprises should be the standard for publicly accountable enterprises as well.

Extent of Allocation

Extent of allocation refers to the range of temporary differences to which interperiod tax allocation is applied. The two basic options are:

1. No allocation—the taxes payable method; and
2. Full allocation—the comprehensive tax allocation (liability) method.

An intermediate approach known as *partial allocation* was used in some countries in the past (notably, in the United Kingdom), but this method has largely been discarded.

Taxes Payable Method The **taxes payable method** recognizes the amount of taxes assessed in each year as the income tax expense for that year: income tax expense = current income tax. This is also known as the **flow-through method** because the actual taxes paid "flow through" to the income statement.

Advocates of the taxes payable method argue that income tax is an aggregate measure, applied to the overall operations of the company as a whole and that it is artificial to disaggregate the income tax amount. As well, the taxes payable method corresponds with the actual cash outflow for income tax. If cash flow prediction is a primary objective of financial reporting, the taxes payable method may be superior to earnings measured by using full allocation.

Viewed in the aggregate, temporary differences in a stable or growing company typically reverse and originate each year, with new originating temporary differences replacing those that are reversing. Taxes payable advocates argue that these aggregated temporary differences are "permanent" and will never result in a real cash flow. They also argue that the "future liability" that is created through tax allocation is not a genuine obligation—the government does not view the deferred tax "liability" as an amount owed to the government, and there certainly is no legal or constructive obligation to pay that amount.

The taxes payable method is currently permitted for private enterprises that have adopted ASPE but not for publicly accountable enterprises.

Comprehensive Tax Allocation Accountants who support **comprehensive tax allocation** (liability method) are in the clear majority, at least among standard setters. They argue that a future cash flow impact arises from all temporary differences, no matter how far in the future that impact occurs. Tax "saved" this year via an early tax deduction will have to be "paid" in a future year when the expense is recognized for accounting but cannot be deducted for tax. Furthermore, they argue that it is a serious violation of the matching concept to recognize a revenue or expense in net income without simultaneously recognizing its inevitable deferred income tax effect. And while aggregate temporary differences may not decline, the individual temporary differences that make up the aggregate do, in fact, reverse, even if they are replaced by new temporary differences.

Example The following example illustrates the two tax allocation bases: (1) the taxes payable method and (2) comprehensive tax allocation, both of which are used in Canada.

Suppose that Bowen Ltd. has pre-tax income in each of three years of $1,000,000. The first year's income includes a gain of $400,000 that will not be collected until 20X3. That is, there is a gain on the 20X1 income statement that will not be taxed until the money is collected in 20X3. Bowen's income tax rate is 35%.

In 20X1 and 20X2, Bowen's financial statements will show an account receivable of $400,000. So far as the Canada Revenue Agency is concerned, there is no receivable because Bowen owes nothing until the company actually collects the cash. The accounting basis of the receivable is $400,000, while the tax basis is zero. Bowen has a $400,000 temporary difference relating to the receivable, which has a future (or *deferred*) income tax impact of $140,000 (i.e., $400,000 × 35%).

If Bowen gives no recognition of the temporary difference, the company's taxable income will be $600,000 in 20X1, $1,000,000 in 20X2, and $1,400,000 in 20X3. Assuming an income tax rate of 35%, the taxes due for each period are $210,000 in 20X1, $350,000 in 20X2, and $490,000 in 20X3. This information is summarized as follows:

	20X1	20X2	20X3
Income before taxes (accounting basis)	$1,000,000	$1,000,000	$1,000,000
20X1 accounting gain that is taxable in 20X3	– 400,000		+ 400,000
Taxable income	$ 600,000	$1,000,000	$1,400,000
Tax rate	× 35%	× 35%	× 25%
Income tax assessed for the year	$ 210,000	$ 350,000	$ 490,000

Under the *taxes payable method*, each year's full tax assessment *flows through* to net income:

	20X1	20X2	20X3
Net income before income tax	$1,000,000	$1,000,000	$1,000,000
Income tax expense	210,000	350,000	490,000
Net income	$ 790,000	$ 650,000	$ 510,000

In the view of most accountants, reporting on a taxes payable basis "distorts" net income because the income tax relating to the $400,000 gain is reported in 20X3, while the gain itself is reported in 20X1. The corporation's apparent net income has declined significantly from 20X1 through 20X3, but the difference is due solely to the fact that income tax on part of 20X1's net income tax is included in income tax expense for 20X3.

When the *comprehensive tax allocation method* is used, the $140,000 income tax impact of the $400,000 gain is recognized in the same period (for accounting purposes) as the gain itself:

	20X1	20X2	20X3
Income before income tax	$1,000,000	$1,000,000	$1,000,000
Income tax expense:			
Current	210,000	350,000	490,000
Deferred	140,000	—	(140,000)
	350,000	350,000	350,000
Net income	$ 650,000	$ 650,000	$ 650,000

The entry to record the income tax expense in each year is:

20X1		
Income tax expense (I/S)	350,000	
Income tax payable (B/S)		210,000
Deferred income tax liability (B/S)		140,000

20X2		
Income tax expense (I/S)	350,000	
Income tax payable (B/S)		350,000
20X3		
Income tax expense (I/S)	350,000	
Deferred income tax liability (B/S)	140,000	
Income tax payable (B/S)		490,000

The deferred income tax liability will be shown on the statement of financial position at the end of 20X1 and 20X2, and then is *drawn down in* 20X3 when the temporary difference *reverses* and the tax is actually due. Note the distinction in terminology:

- A temporary difference *reverses*, while
- The deferred income tax liability/asset that relates to the temporary difference is *drawn down.*

CONCEPT REVIEW

1. What is the flow-through method of accounting for income tax expense?
2. Why does comprehensive tax allocation (liability method) result in better income reporting?

Measurement Method

When the effects of temporary differences are measured, should the tax rate be:

1. The rate in effect at the time that the temporary difference *first arises* (the deferral method), or
2. The rate that is *expected to be in effect* when the temporary difference reverses (the liability method)?

This is the *measurement method* issue.

Deferral Method The **deferral method** was used in Canadian GAAP a number of years ago. This method records the future tax impact by using the corporation's effective average tax rate in the year that the temporary difference first arises, or *originates*. Advocates of the deferral method argue that interperiod income tax allocation is simply a method of moving expense from one period to another and that the best measure of that expense is the effect that it had in the year that the temporary difference originated. The implication of the deferral method is that the SFP credit (or debit) for deferred income taxes is simply a deferred credit (or deferred debit) and should not be accorded the status of a liability (or asset). Deferred income tax credits and debits on the SFP are simply a necessary result of matching and improving income measurement. Conceptually, the focus is on the income statement.

Liability Method In contrast, the **liability method** uses the tax rate that will be in effect in the year of *reversal*. Proponents of this view argue that ultimate realization of the amount of the temporary difference depends on the tax rates in effect when the temporary differences reverse, and thus the amounts to be realized bear no relationship to the tax rates in effect when they originated. Conceptually, the emphasis is on measurement of the future cash flow impact, and the future amount to be paid (or received, if there is a net tax benefit) is viewed as a liability (or asset). The focus, therefore, is on the statement of financial position.

How can the tax rate in the year of reversal be projected? Prediction of future tax rates is a very tenuous proposition and might also tempt a company's management to use a high or low prediction that has a desired impact of increasing or decreasing net income. Therefore, the practical solution is that only *enacted* rates of tax will be used. If this year's tax rate is 30% and the tax rate for next year has already been enacted and is, say, 32%, then 32% is used to measure the balance in deferred income taxes.

Effect of Tax Rates In a world of stable tax rates, there would be no difference between the two methods. But tax rates are not always stable. Tax rates in Canada are subject to annual adjustment by the governments (federal and provincial), including the use of surtaxes (i.e., an extra tax calculated as a percentage of the basic income tax at the statutory rate).

What happens when tax rates change? Under the deferral method, no consequence for tax allocation arises from a change in tax rates. In contrast, the liability method requires that the liability (or asset) be adjusted to reflect each year's *best estimate* of the future tax liability (asset) arising from temporary differences. Therefore, every time there is a change in the corporate tax rate, companies must increase or decrease the amount for the deferred tax liability or asset. The offset to the adjustment is the income tax expense in the income statement.

Example In the earlier example, the tax rate was assumed to be constant throughout the three years. The problem becomes more interesting, however, if tax rates change while a temporary difference exists. We will illustrate the impact of the liability and deferral methods using the same example but with a modification in the tax rates:

- Net income before income taxes is $1,000,000 in each of 20X1, 20X2, and 20X3.
- A gain of $400,000 is included in accounting income in 20X1 but is not subject to tax until 20X3.
- The income tax rate in 20X1 is 35%; during 20X2, the rate is reduced by act of Parliament to 32%, which remains in effect for both 20X2 and 20X3.

The calculation of income tax payable under this revised scenario is as follows:

	20X1	20X2	20X3
Income before taxes (accounting basis)	$1,000,000	$1,000,000	$1,000,000
20X1 accounting gain that is taxable in 20X3	– 400,000		+ 400,000
Taxable income	$ 600,000	$1,000,000	$1,400,000
Tax rate	× 35%	× 32%	× 32%
Income tax payable	$ 210,000	$ 320,000	$ 448,000

Entries for the liability method are shown below. The 20X1 entry is identical to the earlier illustration:

20X1		
Income tax expense	350,000	
Income tax payable		210,000
Deferred income tax liability		140,000

In 20X2, using the liability method, the deferred income tax account must be adjusted to reflect the tax rate change. The temporary difference of $400,000 now will result in taxation of only $128,000 (i.e., the $400,000 temporary difference × 32%) instead of $140,000 ($400,000 × 35%). Therefore, we must reduce the balance of the deferred income tax liability by $12,000.

20X2		
Deferred income tax liability	12,000	
Income tax expense	308,000	
Income tax payable		320,000

The tax expense recorded is the net amount of the payable ($320,000) minus the reduction in deferred income tax ($12,000). The tax expense is now $308,000.

In 20X3, the temporary difference is *reversed* and the deferred tax liability is *drawn down* because the gain enters taxable income.

20X3		
Income tax expense	320,000	
Deferred income tax liability	128,000	
Income tax payable		448,000

Discounting

A final conceptual issue is whether deferred income tax balances should be discounted to present values. If the future tax consequence of a temporary difference is a liability, then the time value of money can be taken into account. If a corporation delays paying large amounts of income tax by taking advantage of completely legal provisions of the *Income Tax Act* (such as large CCA deductions), then the balance sheet credit represents, in effect, an interest-free loan from the government.[1]

In general, accounting standards require that non-current monetary assets and liabilities be shown at their discounted present value. Non-interest-bearing loans normally are discounted at an imputed rate of interest. Therefore, many accountants argue that income tax assets and liabilities also should be discounted to measure these monetary assets and liabilities in a manner that is consistent with the measurement of other monetary items.

Despite the strength of the theoretical arguments in favour of discounting, practical problems get in the way. There are difficulties in determining the interest rate to be used in discounting, and the timing of reversals is particularly problematic, as they depend on accounting policy, management judgements, and prediction of future years' taxable income.

Largely as the result of the many estimates that must be made to apply discounting, discounting is not applied to interperiod tax allocation. IAS 12 contains a single nine-word paragraph on this issue: "Deferred tax assets and liabilities shall not be discounted" [¶53].

[1] Bear in mind, however, that the government does not view the amount as owing to it. The liability is an accounting construct, not a "real" liability; the government cannot demand payment in the event of the company's financial distress.

CONCEPT REVIEW

1. What is the essential difference between the deferral method and the liability method of tax allocation?
2. A company records a deferred income tax liability in 20X1. In 20X2, the income tax rate changes. In 20X4, the deferred tax liability is drawn down and disappears. In what year is the impact of the rate change recognized, using the liability method?
3. Why aren't deferred income tax amounts discounted as are other long-term liabilities?

APPROACH TO INCOME TAX QUESTIONS

We will approach income tax questions in three steps:

Step 1—Calculate taxable income and income tax payable.

Step 2—Determine the change in deferred income tax.

Step 3—Combine income tax payable with the change in deferred income tax to determine tax expense for the year.

After finishing these three steps, we can determine the current year disclosure and account balances. Note that this approach is often called the *balance sheet approach*, as it is driven by balance sheet accounts—income tax payable and deferred income tax. This three-step approach provides a robust calculation methodology that also provides proof of balance sheet accounts.

We will look at a shortcut approach later in the chapter that can be used *only when tax rates have not changed*. However, in Canada, corporate tax rates (federal and provincial) tend to change rather frequently.

Step 1—Calculate Taxable Income and Income Tax Payable

To calculate taxable income, first adjust accounting income for temporary and permanent differences. Such differences are typically identified in the data and have to be sorted into permanent and temporary differences and those items that are added back versus subtracted. Start with accounting income, and identify the differences.

- An expense now on the income statement, but not tax deductible, must be added back (e.g., depreciation, fines, golf club dues).
- A revenue now on the income statement, but not taxable, is subtracted (e.g., dividend revenue).
- An expense not on the income statement, but allowable for tax purposes, is subtracted (e.g., CCA).
- A revenue that is taxable, but not on the income statement, is added (e.g., collections of accounts receivable that are taxable this year but were income statement revenue in a prior year).

After calculating taxable income, multiply by the current tax rate to obtain income tax payable.

Example The following facts pertain to accounting and taxable income for Mirage Limited in 20X1, Mirage's first year of operations:

- Net income before taxes is $825,000; there are no discontinued operations.
- In determining pre-tax accounting income, Mirage deducted the following expenses:
  - Political contribution $10,000;

- Golf club dues of $25,000;
- Accrued estimated warranty expense of $150,000; and
- Depreciation of $200,000 (Mirage owns capital assets of $1,600,000, which are being depreciated straight line over eight years).

• For tax purposes, Mirage deducts the following expenses:
- Actual warranty costs incurred of $100,000; and
- Capital cost allowance (CCA) of $300,000.

• The 20X1 tax rate is 30%.

The golf club dues and political contribution are permanent differences because this expense is not deductible for tax purposes. There are two types of temporary differences in this example: warranty costs and CCA/depreciation.

When accounting income is adjusted for permanent differences, the result is *accounting income subject to tax*. In this example, the result is $860,000. Temporary differences are then included, to yield taxable income of $810,000. Multiplying by the tax rate gives tax payable, $243,000.

Pre-tax accounting income		$825,000
Permanent differences		
Political contribution		+ 10,000
Golf club dues		+ 25,000
Accounting income subject to tax		860,000
Temporary differences		
Warranty expenses accrued, not tax deductible	+150,000	
Warranty costs incurred, tax deductible	−100,000	+ 50,000
Depreciation, not tax deductible	+200,000	
Capital cost allowance (CCA), tax deductible	−300,000	−100,000
Taxable income		$810,000
Tax rate		× 30%
Income tax payable		$243,000

Exhibit 16-2 summarizes the calculation of taxable income for each of the three years of our example: 20X1, 20X2, and 20X3. Assume that in 20X1, Parliament legislated a reduction in tax rates for the following two years, to 28% for 20X2 and then to 27% for 20X3. The other data shown in the exhibit for 20X2 and 20X3 are assumed. Each column shows the adjustments for the two types of temporary differences: warranty costs and CCA/depreciation. Income tax payable is then calculated from taxable income.

If the *taxes payable method* is used, analysis stops at this point. Tax expense is equal to tax payable, and no other financial statement elements are created.

Step 2—Determine the Change in Deferred Income Tax

The change in deferred income tax can be calculated in total for financial statement purposes. However, a total calculation is not quite adequate because individual types of temporary differences will reverse in different years. Thus, to determine the change in deferred income tax from year to year, we must calculate the required balance in deferred income tax for each source of temporary difference. We will then compare this required closing balance to the existing balance and get the adjustment needed.

To establish an appropriate format, we will use a table for this calculation. The following example table has some data filled in for a hypothetical capital asset example, which we will

EXHIBIT 16-2

MIRAGE LIMITED—CALCULATION OF TAXABLE INCOME

	20X1	20X2	20X3
Net income, before tax	$825,000	$900,000	$725,000
Permanent differences			
Political contributions	+ 10,000	0	0
Golf club dues	+ 25,000	+ 25,000	+ 30,000
Accounting income subject to tax	860,000	925,000	755,000
Timing differences			
Warranty expense	+150,000	+200,000	+160,000
Warranty claims paid	−100,000	−140,000	−230,000
Depreciation	+200,000	+200,000	+200,000
Capital cost allowance (CCA)	−300,000	−240,000	−180,000
Taxable income	$810,000	$945,000	$705,000
Enacted tax rate	30%	28%	27%
Income tax payable	$243,000	$264,600	$190,350

explain as we proceed. Assume that the enacted tax rates are 30% for Year 1 and 25% for Year 2:

	[1] Tax Basis	[2] − Accounting Basis	[3] = Year-End Temporary Difference	[4] × *t* = Deferred Tax Liability, Year-End Balance	[5] − Opening Balance	[6] = Adjustment
Year 1 (30% tax rate)						
Capital asset	$172,000	$190,000	$(18,000)	$(5,400)	0	$(5,400)
Year 2 (25% tax rate)						
Capital asset	$136,000	$160,000	$(24,000)	$(6,000)	$(5,400)	$ (600)

Deferred income tax is caused when the carrying value (book value) of an asset or liability is different for tax versus accounting. This table records *tax carrying values* (column 1), *accounting carrying values* (column 2), takes the difference between them (column 3), multiplies this difference by the tax rate to arrive at the closing balance (column 4). The closing balance (column 4) is compared with the existing balance in the deferred income tax account (column 5) and calculates the difference as the needed adjustment (column 6). The year-end balance (column 4) is the opening balance (column 5) plus or minus the adjustment (column 6) for the year. Looking at the table, column by column:

Column 1—If there were a set of books kept for tax purposes, this would be the balance in the capital assets account. In this example, a capital asset was bought for $200,000 at the beginning of Year 1, and $28,000 of CCA was charged for tax purposes in Year 1. CCA, of course, is the tax equivalent depreciation, so cost less accumulated CCA is $172,000. Looking vertically down this column, CCA was $36,000 in Year 2, bringing tax book value down to $136,000. These amounts are assets, so the numbers are not in parentheses.

Column 2—This is the net book value of capital assets on the books of the company. This $200,000 asset had $10,000 of depreciation in Year 1 and $30,000 in Year 2. Net book value is therefore $190,000 in Year 1 and $160,000 in Year 2. Again, the amounts are assets and are not in parentheses.

Column 3—Column 3 is calculated by subtracting column 2 from column 1. Note that the difference is negative because column 2 is the larger number; the column 3 amount is in parentheses because it is negative.

Column 4—Column 4 is calculated by multiplying column 3 by the enacted tax rate. This is $5,400 in Year 1 ($18,000 × 30%) and $6,000 in Year 2 ($24,000 × 25%). This is in parentheses; it keeps its character as a negative number, which means it will be a credit on the balance sheet. Column 4 is important—it is the *closing statement of financial position* of deferred income tax and thus reflects the correct balances for financial position.

Column 5—Column 5 is the opening balance in the deferred income tax account. In Year 1, it is zero, assuming that this is the first year of the temporary difference. In subsequent years, the opening balance is the closing balance of the prior year. That is, the $5,400 closing balance in Year 1 is the opening balance in Year 2. In our case, the Year 2 opening balance was a credit and, thus, is in parentheses.

Column 6—This is the adjustment column, and is the difference between the desired year-end balance (4) and the opening balance (5). It can be either a debit or a credit. In our example, the credit balance grows each time, so additional credits, in parentheses, are needed. *These amounts are part of the journal entries prepared.*

Observe that the adjustment in Year 2 automatically captures the two factors that affect the year-end closing balance of the deferred tax amount—(1) the change in tax rate from 30% to 25%, applied to the beginning balance of the temporary difference, and (2) the $6,000 increase in the temporary difference times the current tax rate:

(1) $(18,000) × –5% rate change	$ 900
(2) $(6,000) × 25% tax rate for Year 2	(1,500)
	$ (600)

Separate calculation of the impact of these two factors is not necessary for each item, but disclosure is required of the impact of each year's two changes for deferred tax liability as a whole, as we will discuss later.

Naturally, this analysis can be done without the table format. However, the information is logically organized in the table, and we will use this presentation in this text. Most of the table columns are mechanical, with no great computational challenge. The problematic columns are the first two—determining the tax basis and accounting basis of temporary differences.

Determining the Accounting Basis Think about the common sources of temporary differences listed in the first column below, and identify the related statement of financial position account that gives rise to each type of temporary difference:

Source of Temporary Difference	Related SFP Account
Depreciation and amortization	Net book value of capital assets, tangible and/or intangible
Inventory writedowns	Inventory
Fair value increases	Inventory
Revenue	Accounts receivable or deferred revenue
Warranty	Warranty provision
Bond discount and premium amortization	Net bond liability
Revaluation surplus	Capital assets

At this stage in your accounting studies, there should be little problem in establishing the accounting basis (or carrying value) of these types of accounts.

Determining the Tax Basis Determining the tax basis is not so obvious and needs some further analysis. We have already seen that for capital assets, the notional "tax balance sheet" would show cost less accumulated CCA charged. Cost less accumulated CCA is referred to as *undepreciated capital cost*, or UCC. As another example, assume that inventory is written down from cost of $400,000 to market value of $375,000 on the books. The accounting basis is $375,000, but the expense is not allowable for tax purposes, and therefore the inventory has a tax basis of $400,000 until sold.

With respect to assets:

- For monetary assets (i.e., receivables), the tax basis of a taxable asset is its accounting carrying value less any amount *that will be added to taxable income in future periods.*
- For non-monetary assets, the tax basis is the tax-deductible amount less all amounts *already deducted* in determining taxable income of the current and prior periods.

With respect to liabilities:

- For monetary liabilities, the tax basis is the accounting carrying value less any amount *that will be deductible for income tax in future periods.*
- For non-monetary liabilities (e.g., unearned revenue), the tax basis is its carrying amounts less any amount that *will not be taxable in future periods.*

An important aspect of these definitions of tax basis is that they all relate to future impacts on taxable income. That is, the tax bases are determined with respect to both the past and future impacts on taxable income.

Application The following examples apply these rules:

- Company A has a nonstrategic investment in the shares of Company Z. Company Z declares a dividend on 31 December 20X5, payable on 31 January 20X6 to shareholders of record on 15 January 20X6. Company A reports $15,000 dividend income in earnings for 20X5, but the dividend will be not be taxed until 20X6. The tax basis of the dividend receivable is zero: the carrying value of $15,000 less the amount that will be taxable in the future, which is the full $15,000.
- Company B has capital assets. The tax basis of this non-monetary asset is the tax-deductible amount, its full cost, less accumulated tax deductions to date, or accumulated CCA.
- Company C has a $45,000 warranty liability. The accounting liability is established because an expense is charged on the books, some of which is paid in the period but $45,000 of which will be paid in the future. For tax purposes, warranty claims are deducted when paid—in the future. The tax basis is the accounting carrying value, $45,000, less amounts that will be deducted in the future, the whole $45,000. Therefore, the tax basis is *zero*.
- Company D has a $75,000 unearned revenue account. The cash was received, and is taxable, in this period. It will be recognized on the income statement later, when earned. The tax basis is *zero*: the accounting carrying value of $75,000 less the amount already included in taxable income; it will therefore not be taxable again in the future.

You must carefully reason your way through these definitions, then do a reality check: *Nonzero for balance sheet items other than capital assets, the tax basis is often zero.* If there is a nonzero tax basis for an account related to a temporary difference, check your logic carefully! A nonzero result is plausible but relatively rare other than for capital assets and asset writedowns.

Permanent Differences By definition, permanent differences do not create deferred income tax. However, there may be statement of financial position accounts that relate to permanent differences (e.g., prepaid golf club dues). If this is the case, the tax basis is equal to the accounting basis.

For example, suppose that a company has been fined $2,000 for a building code infraction. The fine is not yet paid, and the company carries it as a current liability. Fines are not deductible for income tax purposes. Therefore, the tax basis of the fine is $2,000.

Clearly, the fine is a permanent difference and will have no tax impact. The fine has already been included in accounting income, since it has been accrued. For a monetary liability, the rule is that the tax basis is the accounting value ($2,000) less the amount that will be deductible for tax purposes (zero), so the tax basis is $2,000.

Since the tax basis is equal to the accounting basis for permanent differences, deferred income taxes are always zero for these items, and we simply exclude them from the table.

The equation becomes more complicated when an asset is partially tax deductible. For example, certain intangible assets, such as purchased goodwill and purchased subscription lists, are classified as eligible capital property for tax purposes, and 75% of the cost is subject to CCA at a declining-balance rate of 7%. The other 25% of the cost is not tax-deductible and therefore is a permanent difference. The tax basis is determined separately for the two components that make up the accounting carrying value. The cost of these assets must be broken down, with 75% included in calculations of deferred income tax and 25% excluded.

Example To illustrate the calculation of deferred income tax balances and adjustments, we will continue the Mirage Limited example.

At the end of 20X1, the tax bases and the accounting carrying values are as follows:

	Tax Basis dr. (cr.)	Carrying Value dr. (cr.)
Capital assets	$1,300,000	$1,400,000
Accrued warranty liability	0	(50,000)

The tax basis of the capital assets is the cost less accumulated CCA claimed: $1,600,000 – $300,000 = $1,300,000. Similarly, the carrying value of the capital assets is the cost less accumulated depreciation. Since 20X1 is the first year of operations and the year in which the assets were acquired, the carrying value is $1,600,000 – $200,000 = $1,400,000.

The carrying value of the warranty liability is the year-end balance in the accrual account: $150,000 – $100,000 = $50,000. The tax basis for a monetary liability is the accounting carrying value less the amounts that will be deducted for tax purposes in the future. Therefore, the tax basis of the warranty liability is $50,000 – $50,000 = $0.

These values are entered in the table in Exhibit 16-3, in columns 1 and 2. The difference between columns 1 and 2 is the temporary difference, shown in column 3. Columns 4 to 6 are completed by applying the tax rate, entering the zero opening balances for this first year of operation, and then subtracting.

Return to Exhibit 16-2, and note the facts assumed for 20X2 and 20X3. In 20X2, Mirage Limited claims CCA of $240,000 and $140,000 in warranty costs on its tax return while recognizing $200,000 in depreciation and $200,000 in accrued warranty expense on its income statement. Return to Exhibit 16-3, and note the tax and accounting bases. The carrying value of the capital assets declines to $1,200,000, while the tax basis declines by the amount of the 20X2 CCA, to $1,060,000. The difference is $140,000. At the 20X2 tax rate of 30%, the balance of the deferred tax liability relating to the CCA/depreciation temporary difference is $140,000 × 28% = $39,200 credit at 20X2 year-end.

For the warranty liability, the temporary difference is $110,000 at the end of 20X2. That is, the opening warranty liability on the books was $50,000. This is increased by 20X2 expense of $200,000 and decreased by payments of $140,000. The accounting liability is $110,000 at the end of 20X3. The tax basis is still zero. At 28%, the balance in the deferred income tax asset is $30,800. Opening balances are carried down from the closing balances of 20X1, totalled, and the required adjustment calculated.

We must calculate the ending deferred tax balance relating to *each type* of temporary difference because this information is needed for disclosure, as we will illustrate shortly.

However, it is not necessary to calculate the *adjustment* for each type of temporary difference; only the total adjustment need be calculated.

The year 20X3 continues, with the data included in calculating taxable income from Exhibit 16-2. CCA was $180,000, reducing the tax basis to $880,000. Depreciation was $200,000, and the accounting basis is now $1,000,000. The warranty liability on the books began at $110,000. It was increased by warranty expense of $160,000 and reduced by claims paid of $230,000 to end the year at $40,000. The tax basis is zero, since claims will be deducted when paid. Arithmetically, the row is extended, noting the tax rate is now 27%.

It is important to remember at this point that the adjustment for each year is the result of two factors:

1. *The effect of the change in the tax rate on opening temporary differences.* For example, the 20X2 tax rate decreased by 2%. The total opening temporary difference was $50,000, and thus the decrease in the tax rate decreases deferred income tax liability by $1,000 (i.e., $50,000 × 2%).
2. *The effect of current-year temporary differences.* In 20X2, the total temporary difference was reduced from a liability of $50,000 to a liability of $30,000. The impact of this is to *reduce* deferred income tax liability by $5,600—that is, ($50,000 – $30,000) × 28%.

The $6,600 debit adjustment in the table is the result of both factors. Both amounts need to be disclosed in the notes, as we will demonstrate shortly.

What Tax Rate? In the table, the tax rate that must be used is the enacted tax rate for the expected year of reversal. In our example, all rates were enacted in the year to which they pertain, as is normal practice in Canada. Thus, the 20X1 rate is used to measure deferred income tax at the end of 20X1, and so on. However, if the 20X2 rate were enacted in 20X1, then the 20X2 enacted rate would be used to measure deferred income tax at the end of 20X1.

EXHIBIT 16-3

MIRAGE LIMITED—DEFERRED INCOME TAX TABLE

	[1] Year-End Tax Basis dr. (cr.)	[2] Year-End Accounting Carrying Value dr. (cr.)	[3] = [1] – [2] Temporary Difference Deductible (Taxable)	[4] = [3] × *t* Deferred Tax Asset (Liability) at Year-End Rate	[5] = Previous Year Beginning Balance [4] dr. (cr.)	[6] = [4] – [5] Adjustment for Current Year dr. (cr.)
20X1—30%						
Capital assets	$1,300,000	$1,400,000	$(100,000)	$(30,000)	0	$(30,000)
Accrued warranty liability	0	(50,000)	50,000	15,000	0	15,000
Total	$1,300,000	$1,350,000	$ (50,000)	$(15,000)	0	$(15,000)
20X2—28%						
Capital assets	$1,060,000	$1,200,000	$(140,000)	$(39,200)	$(30,000)	$ (9,200)
Accrued warranty liability	0	(110,000)	110,000	30,800	15,000	15,800
Total	$1,060,000	$1,090,000	$ (30,000)	$ (8,400)	$(15,000)	$ 6,600
20X3—27%						
Capital assets	$ 880,000	$1,000,000	$(120,000)	$(32,400)	$(39,200)	$ 6,800
Accrued warranty liability	0	(40,000)	40,000	10,800	30,800	(20,000)
Total	$ 880,000	$ 960,000	$ (80,000)	$(21,600)	$ (8,400)	$(13,200)

After all, deferred income tax is an asset or liability, and if the temporary differences will reverse and cause income tax when the rate is 28%, then this is the most reliable measure of the future cash flow. Our prior comments on tax rates still stand—a future tax rate must be enacted to be used. This is to enhance reliability.

Also note that in 20X1, even if the 20X2 tax rates were enacted, only the 20X1 rates can be used to determine income tax payable in step 1. That is the whole meaning of the current-year tax rate—it dictates income tax payable!

Step 3—Combine Income Tax Payable with the Change in Deferred Income Tax to Determine Tax Expense for the Year

Our final step is to combine the calculation of tax payable with the change in the deferred income tax accounts to produce tax expense. This can be done in a schedule but is easily summarized in a journal entry, where there is:

1. A credit to tax payable, from step 1;
2. A debit or credit to deferred income tax asset/liability from step 2; and
3. A debit to tax expense, to balance.

Example Refer to the entries in Exhibit 16-4, based on the Mirage example. In each year, there is a credit to tax payable and a debit or credit to the deferred tax account, and tax expense is debited to balance the entry. The *balance* in the deferred income tax asset/liability account will be as follows in each year:

Year	Year-End Balance Asset/(Liability)
20X1	(15,000)
20X2	(8,400)
20X3	(21,600)

In this example, the balance is a credit in each year, and thus a net liability will be shown as a non-current liability on the statement of financial position.

STATEMENT OF FINANCIAL POSITION ELEMENTS

Deferred Income Tax Liabilities

Deferred income tax liabilities are created when tax paid is less than accounting accrual-based income tax expense. This occurs when revenue is recognized on the books but is not taxable until a later period. An accounting asset, such as an account receivable, exists, and its tax basis is zero. Deferred income tax liabilities are also created when tax expense deductions precede accounting expense deductions. For example, a declining-balance CCA results in higher expense in early years than straight-line accounting depreciation expense. As a result, UCC (unclaimed capital cost) is less than net book value. Deferred income tax liabilities result.

Deferred Income Tax Assets

Deferred income tax assets are created when tax is effectively prepaid. That is, tax on revenue is paid before the revenue is reflected on the income statement. For example, unearned revenue might appear on the accounting books, but deposits may be taxable when received. Tax is therefore paid before revenue is recognized for accounting purposes. A deferred tax asset is also created when expenses are on the accounting income statement before they are tax deductible, as for accrued warranty liabilities and the related expenses.

EXHIBIT 16-4

MIRAGE LIMITED—INCOME TAX JOURNAL ENTRIES

Income tax journal entry, 20X1		
Income tax expense	258,000	
Deferred income tax asset/liability		15,000
Income tax payable		243,000
Income tax journal entry, 20X2		
Income tax expense	258,000	
Deferred income tax asset/liability	6,600	
Income tax payable		264,600
Income tax journal entry, 20X3		
Income tax expense	203,550	
Deferred income tax asset/liability		13,200
Income tax payable		190,350

Asset Recognition Limit There are special concerns when deferred income tax is a debit balance. As you know, assets must represent future economic benefits, and those benefits must be probable. Deferred income tax assets will be realized only when future years come to pass and those temporary differences reverse in taxable income. If the company is in financial distress, there may not be sufficient taxable income in future years to benefit from the deferred income tax assets—if there is no taxable income and thus no tax due, the company cannot realize the benefit of lower taxes. Therefore, deferred income tax assets on the balance sheet can be recognized only to the extent that their realization is probable. *Probable* means a greater than 50% likelihood of the company generating enough taxable income to draw down the deferred tax asset. We will explore this issue in more depth in the next chapter.

Classification

On the face of the statement of financial position, income taxes currently receivable or payable must be shown separately. Current taxes cannot be combined with deferred income tax balances. Current income tax is a current item, while deferred income tax is always non-current. The classification of deferred tax balances is not affected by the nature of the asset or liability that gave rise to the deferred tax (i.e., current or non-current) and regardless of the time frame within which the temporary differences will reverse.

Netting The deferred income taxes relating to all assets and liabilities are lumped together and netted as a single amount if *for the same taxable company and the same taxing government.*

Since consolidated financial statements include several taxable entities, consolidated statements often show both a deferred tax *asset* and a deferred tax *liability*. For example, the company might have a net deferred tax liability relating to the parent company but a net deferred tax asset relating to a subsidiary.

Example Bombardier Incorporated operates internationally and has revenues and assets in many countries. The company reports in many different taxing jurisdictions. As a result of its multijurisdictional taxation, Bombardier shows two very substantial amounts for deferred income taxes in its 2011 statement of financial position (in millions):

Deferred income tax assets	$1,506
Deferred income tax liabilities	$67

CONCEPT REVIEW

1. What condition is necessary before a company can report a net deferred tax debit as an asset on its statement of financial position?
2. A corporation has two types of temporary differences. One type of temporary difference gives rise to a deferred tax liability, while the other gives rise to a deferred tax asset. Under what circumstances would the asset and liability be shown separately on the statement of financial position?

DISCLOSURE

General Recommendations

The general recommendations for disclosure of the components of the provision for income tax expense are as follows:

- The amount of income tax expense (or benefit) on earnings from continuing operations must be reported separately in the income statement; income tax expense should not be combined with other items of expense.
- The amount of income tax expense that is attributable to (1) current income taxes and (2) deferred income taxes should be disclosed, either on the face of the statement or in the notes.
- Discontinued operations and each component of OCI are reported net of income tax, but the amounts of income tax expense that relate to each item should be disclosed. Also, any income taxes relating to capital transactions should be disclosed.
- The change in deferred income taxes due to (1) changes in temporary differences and (2) tax rate changes (or imposition of new taxes) should be disclosed in the notes.

Example These disclosure standards, applied to the Mirage example, would result in the following disclosure on the income statement:

	20X1	20X2	20X3
Income before income tax	$825,000	$900,000	$725,000
Income tax expense:			
Current	243,000	264,600	190,350
Deferred	15,000	(6,600)	13,200
	258,000	258,000	203,550
Net income	$567,000	$642,000	$521,450

This disclosure breaks income tax expense down into the portion that is paid during the year, and the portion that relates to deferred income tax. This breakdown could also be shown in the disclosure notes.

In the notes, Mirage would break down the annual change in the deferred tax liability into the amounts caused by (1) tax rate changes and (2) changes in temporary differences:

	20X1	20X2	20X3
Increase (decrease) in deferred tax liability due to:			
Change in income tax rate applied to opening balance*	—	$(1,000)*	$ (300)**
Change in temporary differences	$15,000	(5,600)†	13,500††
Total change	$15,000	$(6,600)	$13,200

*$50,000 opening balance × 2% rate decrease = $(1,000)
**$30,000 opening balance × 1% rate decrease = $(300)
†$20,000 decrease in temporary differences × 28% = $(5,600)
††$50,000 increase in temporary differences × 27% = $13,500

Sources of Temporary Differences Publicly accountable enterprises also are required to disclose the types of temporary differences. For *each type*, an entity should disclose the amount of deferred tax recognized in the deferred tax balance on the statement of financial position. Obviously, materiality becomes an issue. Some companies have many different kinds of temporary differences. Some of these are substantial, while others may be quite small. Usually, the smaller ones are combined into an "other" category rather than being separately disclosed in detail.

Exhibit 16-5 presents the disclosure given by Bombardier Incorporated. Bombardier groups its temporary differences by asset versus liabilities. The company has a large number of items that are included in deferred tax assets and liabilities. Note that Bombardier also has a large amount of unrecognized deferred tax assets, since the probable provision is not met. We will discuss this in more detail in the following chapter. Note also that some of the deferred taxes relate to items in OCI.

Reconciliation of Effective Tax Rates The tax status of the corporation may not be obvious to the financial statement users. The reason is that the income tax expense (including both current and deferred taxes) reported by the company on its financial statements may appear to bear little resemblance to the expected level of taxes under the prevailing statutory tax rate. There is no way for an individual investor or creditor to know what factors caused the variation in the apparent tax rate for a public company.

Therefore, companies are required to provide a reconciliation between the statutory tax rate and the company's effective tax. The reconciliation can be either in percentages or in dollar terms.

As we have already seen, there are two general categories of causes for variations in the rate of tax:

1. Permanent differences, which cause items of income and/or expense to be reported in accounting income that is not included in taxable income, and
2. Differences in tax rates, due to:
   a. Different tax rates in different tax jurisdictions;
   b. Special taxes levied (and tax reductions permitted) by the taxation authorities; or
   c. Changes in tax rates relating to temporary differences that will reverse in future periods.

Temporary differences themselves are *not* a cause of effective tax *rate* variations. The "effective tax rate" is based on income tax expense and not on the amount of taxes a company actually paid. Therefore, deferred income tax expense is included in the apparent effective tax rate.

EXHIBIT 16-5

BOMBARDIER INCORPORATED—DISCLOSURE OF TEMPORARY DIFFERENCES

10. INCOME TAXES (CONTINUED)

Deferred income taxes

The significant components of the Corporation's deferred income tax asset and liability were as follows as at:

	December 31, 2011		January 31, 2011		February 1, 2010	
	Asset	Liability	Asset	Liability	Asset	Liability
Operating tax losses carried forward	$1,502	$ —	$1,261	$ —	$1,226	$ —
Retirement benefits	894	—	523	—	578	—
Advance and progress billings in excess of long-term contract inventories and advances on aerospace programs	847	—	412	—	400	—
Inventories	499	(67)	540	(53)	609	(65)
Provisions	463	—	461	—	370	—
Other financial assets and Other assets	(353)	—	(170)	—	(246)	—
PP&E	(273)	—	(108)	—	(77)	—
Other financial liabilities and Other liabilities	148	—	186	—	96	—
Intangible assets	(110)	—	(6)	—	48	—
Other	30	—	47	—	116	—
	3,647	(67)	3,146	(53)	3,120	(65)
Unrecognized deferred tax assets	(2,141)	—	(1,852)	—	(1,747)	—
	$1,506	$(67)	$1,294	$(53)	$1,373	$(65)

The details of changes of deferred income taxes were as follows for the fiscal years ended:

	December 31, 2011[1]	January 31, 2011
Balance at beginning of year, net	$1,241	$1,308
In net income	(66)	(67)
In OCI		
Retirement benefits	234	(40)
Cash flow hedges	54	17
Others[2]	(24)	23
Balance at end of year, net	$1,439	$1,241

[1]The fiscal year ended December 31, 2011 comprises 11 months of BA's results and 12 months of BT's results.
[2]Others mainly comprise foreign exchange rate effects.

Source: Bombardier Inc., or its subsidiaries, 2011 Annual Report, www.sedar.com, posted 1 March 2012.

Exhibit 16-6 shows an example of the tax rate reconciliation for Bombardier Incorporated. This company provides its reconciliation in dollars. The 2011 reconciliation begins by showing that the statutory rate that Bombardier normally would be expected to pay is 28.4%. However, the effective rate was reduced by the temporary and permanent differences. These differences appear to reduce Bombardier's effective tax rate to only 19.5%.

EXHIBIT 16-6

BOMBARDIER EFFECTIVE TAX RATE DISCLOSURE

The reconciliation of income taxes, computed at the Canadian statutory rates, to income tax expense was as follows for the fiscal years ended:

	December 31 2011[1]	January 31 2011
EBT	$1,040	$997
Canadian statutory rate	28.4%	30.0%
Income tax expense at statutory rate	295	299
Increase (decrease) resulting from:		
Recognition of previously unrecognized tax losses or temporary differences	(204)	(146)
Nonrecognition of tax benefits related to tax losses and temporary differences	98	53
Effect of substantively enacted income tax rate changes and tax status changes in certain entities	11	4
Permanent differences	(3)	7
Write down of deferred income tax assets	—	9
Other	6	(4)
Income tax expense	$ 203	$222
Effective tax rate	19.5%	22.3%

[1]The fiscal year ended December 31, 2011 comprises 11 months of BA's results and 12 months of BT's results.

The applicable statutory tax rates are 28.4% for the fiscal year ended December 31, 2011 and 30.0% for the fiscal year ended January 31, 2011. The Corporation's applicable tax rate is the Canadian combined rate applicable in the jurisdictions in which the Corporation operates. The decrease is mainly due to the reduction of the Federal income tax rate applicable to the Corporation for the fiscal year ended December 31, 2011 from 17.9% to 16.5%.

Source: Bombardier Inc., or its subsidiaries, 2011 Annual Report, www.sedar.com, posted 1 March 2012.

Accountant's versus Analyst's Concepts of Effective Tax Rate The definition of effective tax rate prescribed by accounting standards (e.g., 19.5% in Bombardier Incorporated's disclosure) includes deferred income tax. On the other hand, financial analysts usually view the effective tax rate as the amount of current taxes divided by pre-tax earnings, which is quite different from effective tax rate as defined by accounting standards.

For example, Bombardier had 2011 pre-tax earnings from continuing operations of $1,040 million. The breakdown of income tax expense is shown in Exhibit 16-7. Income tax expense was $203 million, composed of the following (in millions): current income taxes of $137 million and deferred income taxes of $66 million.

Under accounting standards, the effective tax rate is 19.5%, calculated as $203 ÷ $1,040 = 19.5%. In contrast, financial analysts would ignore the deferred income taxes and focus on the amount actually due to the government for the year, calculated as follows:

$$\$137 \div \$1{,}040 = 13\%$$

Financial analysts (and banks) are interested in what the company has to pay in cash, not what it might have to pay sometime in the future when the temporary differences all reverse

EXHIBIT 16-7

BOMBARDIER ANALYSIS OF INCOME TAX EXPENSE

ANALYSIS OF INCOME TAX EXPENSE

Details of income tax expense were as follows for the fiscal years ended:

	December 31, 2011[1]	January 31, 2011
Current income taxes	$137	$155
Deferred income taxes	66	67
	$203	$222

[1]The fiscal year ended December 31, 2011 comprises 11 months of BA's results and 12 months of BT's results.

Source: Bombardier Inc., or its subsidiaries, 2011 Annual Report, www.sedar.com, posted 1 March 2012.

(if ever). Comprehensive interperiod tax allocation is good at achieving matching but not so good at measuring the effect of income taxes on liquidity. That is why accounting standards insist that the income tax expense be disaggregated and that both current and deferred taxes be disclosed.

SHORTCUT APPROACH IF RATES HAVE NOT CHANGED

In some cases, a shorter computational approach may be used to account for income tax. This approach should be used *only if the income tax rate has not changed from the prior year*—if there is a change in tax rates, this simplified approach may give you the wrong answer. However, if the facts support the shortcut, it will save time.

The steps are as follows:

Step 1—Calculate taxable income and income tax payable.

Step 2—Determine the change in deferred income tax through a direct calculation.

Step 3—Combine income tax payable with the change in deferred income tax to determine tax expense for the year.

Only Step 2 has changed. A table such as that shown in Exhibit 16-3 need not be prepared; all that is needed is a direct calculation of the change in deferred income tax balances. Remember that the adjustment that flows from the table has two components—(1) a change to opening deferred income tax balances because of the tax rate change and (2) the current year increase. If the tax rate has not changed, there is no adjustment of opening deferred income tax balances, and the current-year increase (or decrease) is all that is needed. The balance in deferred income tax can be tracked with a simple T-account.

In Step 2, to determine the change in deferred income tax for the year, the calculation is:

Change in deferred income tax = the temporary difference during the year (accounting revenue or expense less the tax revenue or expense) × tax rate.

To illustrate the shortcut method, we will calculate the tax amounts for KelCo. Facts are as follows:

	20X2	20X3	20X4
Income before income tax	$242,000	$934,000	$1,361,000
Depreciation	230,000	230,000	230,000
CCA	287,000	197,000	312,000
Tax-free dividend revenue	—	75,000	—
Non-tax-deductible expenses	32,000	—	—
Tax rate	25%	25%	25%

The first step in the solution is to calculate taxable income and income tax payable for each year:

	20X2	20X3	20X4
Accounting income	$242,000	$934,000	$1,361,000
Permanent differences			
Dividend revenue	—	(75,000)	—
Non-tax-deductible expenses	32,000	—	—
Temporary differences			
Depreciation	230,000	230,000	230,000
CCA	(287,000)	(197,000)	(312,000)
Taxable income	217,000	892,000	1,279,000
Tax rate	25%	25%	25%
Income tax payable	$ 54,250	$223,000	$ 319,750

The second step is to determine the change in deferred income tax each year. There is only one source of deferred income tax, the depreciation/CCA on capital assets. In 20X2, CCA is $57,000 ($287,000 – $230,000) higher than depreciation. This translates into a $14,250 (i.e., $57,000 × 25%) increase (credit) in a deferred income tax liability. Since this is the first year, the balance in deferred income tax is also $14,250.

In 20X3, CCA is less than depreciation by $33,000 (i.e., $230,000 – $197,000). This will reduce the credit balance in the liability by $8,250: ($33,000 × 25%). The balance in deferred income tax liability is now $6,000: ($14,250 – $8,250). This $6,000 balance can be verified as being the cumulative temporary differences multiplied by the tax rate. In this example, we have total depreciation over the two years of $460,000, versus $484,000 of CCA, for a $24,000 cumulative difference, multiplied by the tax rate of 25% to again give $6,000.

In 20X4, CCA is larger than depreciation, this time by $82,000: ($312,000 – $230,000). This will increase the deferred income tax liability by $20,500: ($82,000 × 25%). The balance in deferred income tax liability is now $26,500: ($6,000 + $20,500). This can also be verified as $796,000 of cumulative CCA minus $690,000 of cumulative depreciation = $106,000 × 25% = $26,500.

The last step is to prepare the tax entries, which determine the tax expense for the year:

20X2		
Income tax expense	68,500	
Deferred income tax ($287,000 – $230,000) × 25%		14,250
Income tax payable		54,250
20X3		
Income tax expense	214,750	
Deferred income tax ($230,000 – $197,000) × 25%		8,250
Income tax payable		223,000
20X4		
Income tax expense	340,250	
Deferred income tax ($312,000 – $230,000) × 25%		20,500
Income tax payable		319,750

With this information, appropriate financial statement disclosure may be prepared.

Evaluation This method is far simpler. Remember, though, that it is to be used *only when the tax rate does not change*—and, in the Canadian business world, changing tax rates are a fact of life.

Actually, it is possible to use the shortcut method if the tax rate changes by also preparing a separate calculation of the effect of the tax rate change on opening deferred income tax. However, the possibility for error starts to become high, and the table approach is far more reliable. The other significant advantage of the table approach is that the deferred income tax account is proven each year, with the difference between tax and accounting basis backing up the integrity of this account. It is important to have such proof for all financial statement elements.

STATEMENT OF CASH FLOWS

The impact of income tax accounting on the statement of cash flows is clear: All tax allocation amounts must be reversed out of transactions reported on the statement of cash flows. The statement of cash flows must include only the actual taxes paid. When a company uses the direct method of presenting cash flow from operations, the amount of tax paid (recovered) during the year is a deduction (addition).

When the indirect method of presentation is used for operating cash flow, the deferred tax liability (and/or asset) that has been charged (or credited) to earnings must be added back to (or subtracted from) net income. That is, the change in deferred income tax is an add-back or deduction in operating activities. The change in income tax payable is another adjustment in operating activities.

Companies are required to disclose the amount of income taxes paid on the face of the statement of cash flows. The indirect approach described above does not accomplish this result because only the deferred tax add-back is displayed on the face of the statement. Therefore, companies that use the indirect approach take one of two approaches:

1. The reconciliation starts with earnings before taxes so that the amount of taxes paid (recovered) is disclosed directly as a disbursement (receipt) of cash; or
2. The reconciliation starts with net earnings, adds back the income tax expense, and shows the income taxes paid as a separate item.

Either approach is satisfactory.

CONCEPT REVIEW

1. What breakdown of tax expense must be provided?
2. What is the purpose of the reconciliation of the effective tax rate?
3. What amounts relating to income tax should appear in the operating activities section of the statement of cash flows?

IS DEFERRED INCOME TAX A LIABILITY?

It is possible to raise many questions about the validity of the deferred income tax concept. Deferred income tax is an allocation of an amount that arises largely from other allocations. It seems firmly grounded on the income statement concepts of revenue–expense recognition and matching, even though the FASB and IASB have strained mightily to justify income tax allocation under the asset-liability definitional approach. Even the name of the basic concept, income tax *allocation*, is derived from an income statement approach rather than a balance sheet approach.

The most important question, however, is the validity of viewing deferred income tax credits as a true liability when they arise as the result of major recurring temporary differences. We observed earlier in this chapter that the major single cause of temporary differences is the difference between two other allocations: depreciation for accounting versus CCA for tax. In aggregate, these temporary differences will not reverse as long as the company continues to invest in replacing its physical assets.

One important aspect of the liability definition is that *a liability represents an existing obligation*. But to whom is this obligation owed? Supporters of tax allocation argue that deferred income tax is similar to a warranty liability—the obligation is real, even though the specific parties to whom the liability will be fulfilled cannot be specifically identified. It is true that a warranty requires a cash outflow to as-yet-unknown parties. However, any income tax liability must be owed to specific known government jurisdictions. The other party is known precisely, but there is no current obligation for future taxes. The government does not consider the amount that we show as deferred income tax liabilities to be owing.

The reality of having to pay out cash in the future as recurring temporary differences (e.g., depreciation-CCA differences) are reversed depends on the joint occurrence of two conditions:

1. The asset basis of the temporary differences (i.e., the capital assets being depreciated) must shrink before there can be a net reversal, precipitating an actual cash outflow; and
2. The company must be earning taxable income while the net reversals are occurring.

While it is *possible* for these two conditions to co-exist, co-existence is unlikely. Asset bases contract when old assets are not being replaced, and that usually happens when the company is in decline. If a company is in decline it is unlikely to be generating taxable income.

Accounting standards call for recognizing a contingent liability when a cash flow *probably* will be realized. It can be argued that, at best, deferred income tax liabilities relating to recurring temporary differences should be disclosed as a contingent liability because the conditions necessary to precipitate a cash flow are not likely to occur—the liability is neither likely to occur, nor is the amount of future cash flow measurable.

Looking Ahead

Income taxes are not now on the agenda of either the IASB or the Canadian AcSB.

ACCOUNTING STANDARDS FOR PRIVATE ENTERPRISES

Accounting Method Private enterprises may elect to use either the *taxes payable method* of accounting for income taxes or the *comprehensive allocation* (liability method).

Under the taxes payable method, income tax expense is simply the amount of current income tax paid (or payable) to the government. There is no interperiod allocation of income taxes, and there are no deferred income tax amounts reported on the statement of financial position. This method was demonstrated earlier in the chapter.

Intraperiod allocation is still applied, however. Income tax expense must be allocated to:

- Earnings from continuing operations;
- Discontinued operations;
- Gains and losses recorded directly in retained earnings; and
- Gains and losses recorded directly in share capital.

The choice of accounting for income taxes is an all-or-nothing affair. A company cannot decide to use deferred income tax accounting for some types of temporary differences while using the taxes payable basis for other types.

Terminology The *CPA Canada Handbook, Part II* (ASPE), uses the term *future* income tax instead of *deferred* income tax. This is a carryover from the pre-2011 Canadian standard. However, there is no *requirement* to use that particular terminology—the two terms are used interchangeably. Many companies use "deferred" instead of "future."

Classification ASPE requires companies to classify deferred/future income tax liabilities and assets as either current or long-term. This is in contrast to the IFRS (which prohibits a "current" classification for any deferred tax amounts).

Deferred tax amounts are classified as current or non-current on the basis of the assets or liabilities that generated the temporary differences. For example, in the Mirage example used in this chapter, the deferred tax relating to the warranty temporary difference would be classified as current because the deferred tax relates to a current liability. Similarly, deferred taxes relating to inventory would be classified as current. The deferred taxes related to the capital assets would be classified as non-current. The expected period of time before the temporary difference reverses is irrelevant for the current–noncurrent classification.

Disclosure There is less disclosure required for private enterprises. In the accounting policies note, a company should disclose the fact that it is using the taxes payable method.

In addition, the company should reconcile its income tax expense to the average statutory income tax rate. This disclosure is similar to that described above for public companies. The reconciliation would include items such as:

- Large corporations' tax;
- Nondeductible expenses;
- Nontaxable gains, including the non-taxable portion of capital gains; and
- The amount of deductible temporary differences for which a future tax asset has not been recorded.

RELEVANT STANDARDS

CPA Canada Handbook, Part I (IFRS):

- IAS 12, Income Taxes

CPA Canada Handbook, Part II (ASPE):

- Section 3465, Income Taxes

SUMMARY OF KEY POINTS

1. The amount of taxable income often differs from the amount of pre-tax net income reported for accounting purposes.
2. The difference between taxable income and accounting income arises from two types of sources: nonreversing or *permanent* differences and *temporary* differences.
3. Permanent differences are items of revenue, expense, gains, or losses that are reported for accounting purposes but never enter into the computation of taxable income. Permanent differences also include those rare items that enter into taxable income but are never included in accounting income.
4. Temporary differences arise when the tax basis of an asset or liability is different from its carrying value (i.e., its accounting basis) in the financial statements.
5. The objective of *comprehensive interperiod income tax allocation* (liability method) is to recognize the income tax effect of every item when that item is recognized in accounting net income. The alternative to comprehensive allocation is the *taxes payable method.*
6. When the item of revenue, expense, gain, or loss first enters the calculation of *either* taxable income or accounting income, it is an *originating* temporary difference.
7. A temporary difference *reverses* when it is recognized in the other measure of income. For example, if an item is recognized first for tax purposes and later for accounting purposes, the temporary difference originates when the item is included in the tax calculation and reverses when the item is recognized for accounting.
8. Under the liability method of tax allocation, the tax effect is recorded at the currently enacted rate that will apply in the period that the temporary difference is expected to reverse. The current rate is used if no future years' tax rates are enacted.
9. Under the liability method, the balance of deferred income tax assets and liabilities must be adjusted to reflect changes in the tax rate as they are enacted. Deferred income taxes are not discounted.
10. Accounting for income tax involves calculating tax payable, calculating the change in the deferred income tax accounts, and then combining all elements to determine tax expense. Deferred income tax is calculated as the difference between the tax basis and the accounting carrying value of related balance sheet accounts, multiplied by the enacted tax rate.
11. Deferred income tax assets and liabilities are classified as non-current assets or liabilities. Deferred income tax balances relating to the same taxing jurisdiction and the same taxable entity are netted and reported as a single amount. Deferred taxes relating to different taxing jurisdictions cannot be offset against each other.

12. A reporting enterprise must explain in a note the difference between its effective tax rate and the statutory rate. In this context, the effective tax rate is the income tax expense (including deferred taxes) divided by the pre-tax net income. Entities must also disclose the sources of temporary differences.
13. The statement of cash flows must disclose the amounts of taxes actually paid or received for the year as part of cash flow from operations.
14. Private enterprises may choose to use the taxes payable method for income tax, in which case no deferred income tax is recorded, and tax expense equals tax paid.

KEY TERMS

comprehensive tax allocation
deferral method
flow-through method
interperiod tax allocation
liability method
permanent difference
provision for income tax
taxes payable method
temporary difference

REVIEW PROBLEM 16-1

The following information pertains to Suda Corporation at the end of 20X1:

	Tax Basis	Accounting Basis
Equipment	$400,000 UCC	$500,000
Capitalized development costs	0	$200,000

At the end of 20X1, Suda had a balance in its deferred income tax liability account of $105,000, pertaining to both the amounts above. That is, there is $35,000 related to equipment and $70,000 to the capitalized development costs. The enacted income tax rate (combined federal and provincial) at the end of 20X1 was 35%.

The following information pertains to the next three years:

	20X2	20X3	20X4
Net income	$200,000	$160,000	$100,000
New equipment acquired	—	100,000	—
Depreciation expense on equipment	65,000	70,000	75,000
CCA claimed	80,000	74,000	69,000
Amortization of development costs	40,000	50,000	45,000
Development costs incurred (deductible for tax purposes)	50,000	30,000	70,000
Income tax rate (enacted in each year)	35%	38%	38%

Required:

For each of 20X2, 20X3 and 20X4, calculate:

1. The income tax expense that would appear on Suda's income statement.
2. The balance of the deferred income tax liability or asset account(s) that would appear on Suda's statement of financial position.

REVIEW PROBLEM 16-1—SOLUTION

Calculation of taxable income and tax payable:

	20X2	20X3	20X4
Net income	$200,000	$160,000	$100,000
Plus depreciation on equipment	65,000	70,000	75,000
Less: CCA	(80,000)	(74,000)	(69,000)
Plus amortization of development costs	40,000	50,000	45,000
Less: Development costs incurred	(50,000)	(30,000)	(70,000)
Taxable income	$175,000	$176,000	$ 81,000
Tax rate	35%	38%	38%
Tax payable	$ 61,250	$ 66,880	$ 30,780

Calculation of tax basis and carrying value:

	Equipment		Development Costs	
	Tax Basis	Carrying Value	Tax Basis	Carrying Value
20X1 ending balances	$400,000	$500,000	0	$200,000
Additions	—	—		+ 50,000
CCA & depreciation/ amortization	(80,000)	(65,000)		(40,000)
20X2 ending balances	320,000	435,000	0	210,000
Additions	+100,000	+100,000		+ 30,000
Depreciation/amortization	(74,000)	(70,000)		(50,000)
20X3 ending balances	346,000	465,000	0	190,000
Additions				+ 70,000
Depreciation/amortization	(69,000)	(75,000)		(45,000)
20X4 ending balances	$277,000	$390,000	0	$215,000

Calculation of changes in deferred income tax liability:

	Year-End Tax Basis dr. (cr.)	Carrying Value dr. (cr.)	Temporary Difference Deductible (taxable)	Deferred Tax Asset (Liability) at Yr.-End Rate	Less Beginning Balance dr. (cr.)	Adjustment for Current Year dr. (cr.)
20X2—35%						
Equipment	320,000	435,000	(115,000)	(40,250)		
Development costs	0	210,000	(210,000)	(73,500)		
				(113,750)	(105,000)	(8,750)
20X3—38%						
Equipment	346,000	465,000	(119,000)	(45,220)		
Development costs	0	190,000	(190,000)	(72,200)		
				(117,420)	(113,750)	(3,670)
20X4—38%						
Equipment	277,000	390,000	(113,000)	(42,940)		
Development costs	0	215,000	(215,000)	(81,700)		
				(124,640)	(117,420)	(7,220)

Tax entries:

20X2		
Tax expense	70,000	
Tax payable		61,250
Deferred income tax liability		8,750
20X3		
Tax expense	70,550	
Deferred income tax liability		3,670
Tax payable		66,880
20X4		
Tax expense	38,000	
Deferred income tax liability		7,220
Tax payable		30,780

1. *Income tax expense*

	20X2	**20X3**	**20X4**
Current	$61,250	$66,880	$30,780
Deferred	8,750	3,670	7,220
Income tax expense	$70,000	$70,550	$38,000

2. *Deferred income tax liability balance*
Per table, column [4] above. Each year's balance will be reported as a single long-term credit amount, as follows:

20X2	$113,750
20X3	$117,420
20X4	$124,640

APPENDIX

THE INVESTMENT TAX CREDIT

General Nature

A *tax credit* is a direct, dollar-for-dollar offset against income taxes that otherwise are payable. The advantage of a tax *credit* (instead of a tax *deduction* for the expenditures) is that the amount of the tax credit is not affected by the tax rate being paid by the corporation. For example, if a $100,000 expenditure qualifies for a 7% tax credit, the tax reduction will be $7,000 regardless of whether the corporation is paying taxes at 20%, 30%, 40%, or any other rate.[2]

The Canadian *Income Tax Act* provides for *investment tax credits* (*ITC*) for (1) qualifying research and experimental development expenditures and (2) specified types of expenditures for capital investment. The expenditures that qualify for the investment tax credit are matters of government policy and change from time to time. By giving a tax credit, the government can influence companies to increase investments in certain types of facilities and in selected geographic areas by effectively reducing their cost. Qualifying expenditures can vary on three dimensions:

1. Type of expenditure;
2. Type of corporation; and
3. Geographic region.

To realize the benefit of a tax credit, it usually is necessary for the qualifying corporation to have taxable income and to generate income tax payable. If there is not sufficient tax payable in the year of the qualifying expenditures, the tax credit can be carried back three years and forward 20 years. Certain types of corporations may be eligible to receive the credit in cash, even if there is not enough tax due within the current and carryback periods to completely utilize the tax credit.

Accounting Treatment

In theory, there are two possible approaches to accounting for the investment tax credit (ITC):

1. The *flow-through approach*, whereby the ITC for which the corporation qualifies is reported as a direct reduction in the income tax expense for the year; or
2. The *cost-reduction approach*, in which the ITC is deducted from the expenditures that give rise to the ITC; the benefit of the ITC is thereby allocated to the years in which the expenditures are recognized as expenses.

International standards do not specifically discuss investment tax credits. However, *IAS* 20 does address the more general topic of government assistance, and tax credits clearly are a form of government assistance.

IAS 20 prescribes the *cost reduction approach*. The two categories of "cost" are:

- Costs recorded as expenses in the current period; and
- Costs that are recorded as assets.

The general approach for government grants, including ITCs, is to recognize them in profit or loss over the same periods in which the company recognizes the related costs as expenses. The following sections describe the accounting treatment for each type of cost.

Costs Reported as Current Expenses

The government often grants ITC for research and development expenditures. Some of those expenditures will not qualify for capitalization as development costs and will be charged to expense in the period in which they are incurred.

---

[2] Depending on the type of capital expenditure and the location of the enterprise, the investment tax credit may range from 7% to 35%.

Investment tax credits that relate to expenditures that are reported as expenses in the income statement are permitted to flow through to the income statement.

The ITC on current expenses may be reported in either of two ways:

1. As an item of "other income" in the profit and loss section of the statement of comprehensive income; or
2. As a reduction of (or offset against) the expense that gave rise to the ITC.

The second method may seem more consistent with the cost-reduction approach, but it is contrary to the general principle that revenues and expenses should not be shown net of taxes. Both treatments are acceptable under international standards.

Since the ITC will reduce the effective tax rate being paid by the corporation, a publicly accountable enterprise will treat the ITC as a tax rate reduction and will include it in its tax rate reconciliation.

Costs Capitalized

If the ITC qualifying expenditures are for a capital asset or are for development costs that can be capitalized and amortized, then the ITC itself is deferred and amortized on the same basis as the asset. This can be accomplished either by reducing the capitalized cost of the asset or by separately deferring and amortizing the ITC.

Investment tax credits related to the acquisition of assets would be either:

1. Deducted from the related assets with any amortization calculated on the net amount; or
2. Deferred and amortized to income on the same basis as the related assets.

The first option is to deduct the deferred ITC from the balance of the asset. The second approach is to recognize the ITC as *deferred income* on the balance sheet and then to amortize it along with the asset itself. The second approach seems more consistent with the cost-reduction theory than the first, but either may be used in practice.

For income tax purposes, the ITC is deducted from the tax basis of the asset.[3] The effect is as follows:

- For expenditures that are capitalized for accounting purposes but are deducted immediately for tax purposes (e.g., development costs), a temporary difference is created because the cost (net of ITC) is being deducted immediately but is charged to income via amortization over several years; and
- For capital assets, the tax basis and the accounting basis start out the same (i.e., both reduced by the amount of the ITC benefit), but temporary differences arise from any differences between CCA and depreciation.

Exhibits 16A-1 and 16A-2 demonstrate the relevant accounting procedures. Exhibit 16A-1 contains the basic data and illustrates the journal entries used to record the qualifying expenditure and the ITC. Exhibit 16A-2 shows the impacts on the financial statements. The exhibits assume that the deferred ITC is deducted from the asset on the balance sheet.

Disclosure of ITC and Other Government Grants

ITCs (and other types of government assistance) affect both the income/expense structure of the entity's operations and its cash flows. Therefore, the notes should disclose:

- The accounting policy and the method of presentation in the financial statements;
- The nature and extent of ITCs (and any government grants); and
- Any unfulfilled conditions or contingencies.

---

[3] Actually, it is a bit more complicated because the accounting deduction is made in the year of purchase, while the deduction from the tax base occurs only in the year(s) in which the ITC is *realized,* which is always at least one year later than the expenditure. We will ignore this additional temporary difference in this discussion.

RELEVANT STANDARDS

CPA Canada Handbook, Part I (IASB):

- IAS 20, Accounting for Government Grants and Disclosure of Government Assistance

CPA Canada Handbook, Part II (ASPE):

- Section 3805, Investment Tax Credits

EXHIBIT 16A-1

RECORDING THE INVESTMENT TAX CREDIT

Illustrative Data

1 *May 20X5*
Purchased eligible transportation equipment (30% CCA rate) costing $100,000, to be depreciated straight line over 10 years, no residual value, with a half-year's depreciation in the year of acquisition for both accounting and tax purposes.

31 *December 20X5*
Pre-tax income (after depreciation on new equipment), $150,000. Investment tax credit ($100,000 × 7%; not included in previous amounts), $7,000. The tax rate is 30%.

Entries for 20X5

a. *1 May—purchase qualified equipment*		
Equipment	100,000	
Cash		100,000
b. *31 December—record ITC*		
Income tax payable	7,000	
Deferred investment tax credit		7,000
c. *31 December—record depreciation expense*		
Depreciation expense ($100,000 × 1/10 × ½)	5,000	
Accumulated depreciation		5,000
d. *31 December—record amortization of investment tax credit for 20X5*		
Deferred investment tax credit ($7,000 × 1/10 × ½)	350	
Amortization expense		350
e. *31 December—record income tax on 20X5 earnings**		
Income tax expense ($150,000 × 30%)	45,000	
Deferred income tax liability ($13,950 – $4,650) × 30%		2,790
Income tax payable		42,210

*See Exhibit 16A-2 for the calculation of these amounts.

EXHIBIT 16A-2

REPORTING THE INVESTMENT TAX CREDIT

Calculation of Income Tax Expense

Tax and accounting cost of asset:	
Capital cost of equipment	$100,000
Less: Investment tax credit of 7%	7,000
Net capital cost	$ 93,000
Accounting income	$150,000
Depreciation	
[($100,000 × 1/10 × 1/2 year) – ($7,000 × 1/10 × ½)]	+ 4,650
CCA ($93,000 × 30% × ½ year*)	– 13,950
Taxable income	$140,700
Tax rate	× 30%
Current tax due before ITC	$ 42,210
Less: Investment tax credit ($100,000 × 7%)	7,000
Income tax payable	$ 35,210
Current income tax	$ 42,210
Deferred income tax liability [($13,950 – $4,650) × 30%]	2,790
Income tax expense	$ 45,000

*Assuming that only a half-year's deduction for CCA is claimable in the first year, as is usual.

Income Statement Reporting, Year Ended 31 December 20X5

Depreciation expense ($5,000 – $350 amortization of ITC)		$ 4,650
Pre-tax income		$150,000
Income tax expense—current (from above)	$42,210	
—deferred (from above)	2,790	45,000
Net income		$ 90,000

Statement of Financial Position Reporting, 31 December 20X5

Equipment (at cost)		$100,000
Accumulated depreciation	$ 5,000	
Deferred investment tax credit ($7,000 – $350)	6,650	11,650
Reported carrying value		$ 88,350
Income tax payable (from above)		$ 35,210
Deferred income tax liability (from above)		$ 2,790

SUMMARY OF KEY POINTS

1. The investment tax credit (ITC) is a direct reduction of income taxes that is granted to enterprises that invest in certain types of assets or in research and development costs.
2. There are two possible approaches to accounting for ITCs: (1) the flow-through approach and (2) the cost reduction approach.
3. IFRS recommends using the cost reduction approach, wherein the ITC is deducted (either directly or indirectly) from the asset or expense that gave rise to the ITC.
4. ITCs on expenditures that are reported as current expenses can be shown as an item of "other income" or deducted from the investment expense.

5. When qualifying expenditures are made to acquire an asset (including capitalized development costs), the ITC can either be (1) deducted from the asset's carrying value, with depreciation based on the net amount or (2) deferred separately as "deferred income" and amortized on the same basis as the asset itself.
6. The nature and amount of ITCs should be disclosed in the notes, as well as the company's accounting policy for ITCs, the method of presentation, and any unfulfilled conditions or contingencies.

QUESTIONS

Q16-1 Why is it common for companies to label income tax expense as a *provision* for income taxes?

Q16-2 How can differences between accounting and taxable income be classified? Define each classification.

Q16-3 XTE Corporation (a) uses straight-line depreciation for its financial accounting and accelerated depreciation on its income tax return and (b) expenses golf club dues for its top management. What kind of tax difference is caused by each of these items? Explain.

Q16-4 Temporary differences are said to "originate" and "reverse." What do these terms mean?

Q16-5 Give three examples of a permanent difference and three examples of a temporary difference.

Q16-6 Explain the two acceptable alternative options for the extent of allocation possible in dealing with interperiod tax allocation.

Q16-7 Why is the balance in a deferred income tax liability account not discounted?

Q16-8 Thertot Limited reported $100,000 of income in 20X4, $300,000 of income in 20X5, and $500,000 of income in 20X6. Included in 20X4 income is an expense, $50,000, that cannot be deducted for tax purposes until 20X6. Assume a 40% tax rate. How much income tax is payable in each year? How much income tax expense will be reported? Why are the total three-year payable and total three-year expense equal?

Q16-9 ATW Corporation has completed an analysis of its accounting income, taxable income, and the temporary differences. Taxable income is $200,000, and there are two temporary differences, which result in (a) a deferred income tax asset of $15,000 and (b) a deferred income tax liability of $20,000. The income tax rate for the current period and all future periods is 40%. There were no deferred income tax assets or deferred income tax liabilities as of the beginning of the current year. Give the journal entry to record income tax.

Q16-10 A company has $200,000 in originating temporary differences in 20X6, its first year of operation. The temporary differences give rise to a deferred income tax liability. The tax rate is 34% in 20X6. In 20X7, there were no new temporary differences, but the tax rate increases to 40%. If the liability method is used, at what amount will deferred income taxes be shown on the 20X7 statement of financial position?

Q16-11 A company reports a $1,000,000 revenue (long-term receivable and associated revenue) in accounting income in Year 1. It is taxable income when collected in Year 4. What is the accounting carrying value of the receivable at the end of Year 1? The tax basis? Assuming that the tax rate is 40% in Years 1 and 2, and 35% in Years 3 and 4, what will be the balance in the deferred income tax account at the end of each year?

Q16-12 A company bought $1,000,000 of equipment at the beginning of Year 1. Year 1 depreciation was $200,000 and CCA was $100,000. What is the tax basis of the assets at the end of Year 1? The accounting carrying value? If the tax rate is 20%, what is the balance in the deferred income tax account at the end of Year 1?

Q16-13 When do items on the statement of financial position have a different accounting carrying value and tax basis?

Q16-14 Do permanent differences cause the accounting carrying value and tax basis of the related item on the statement of financial position to differ?

Q16-15 On the statement of financial position, are deferred income taxes debits or credits? Explain. Is a debit to a deferred income tax account always a decrease and a credit always an increase? Explain.

Q16-16 Assume that a company reports a deferred income tax liability of $500,000. The enacted tax rate goes down. How will the account on the statement of financial position change if the liability method is used?

Q16-17 What kinds of differences cause a company to report taxes at a rate different from the statutory rate?

Q16-18 What is an investment tax credit?

Q16-19 Explain two different approaches to account for an investment tax credit for a capital asset.

Q16-20 How might an ITC received because of qualifying expenditures for capital assets be reported on the statement of financial position?

CASE 16-1

RINGO INCORPORATED

Ringo Incorporated is a small private company that is located in Northern Ontario. The company is a well-known player in the golfing industry. Ringo began operations several years ago by manufacturing and selling golf drivers (a specific type of golf club) and today offers a full range of golf clubs. During this current year, the company has decided that they would like to expand their operations into the United States.

As the existing warehouse does not provide sufficient capacity to meet the demands of the expansion, Ringo has leased a large warehouse down the street from the existing warehouse. The lease does not qualify for a capital lease under the current accounting standards for private entities. During the year, the company purchased several new capital assets and performed a comprehensive analysis of useful lives, residual values, and salvage values (Exhibit 1).

To finance the expansion, the company has approached the bank to lend Ringo a significant amount of money. The bank has agreed to lend Ringo the money but had several conditions that must be met before the loan will be finalized. One of the conditions is that the company prepares a comprehensive review of the estimates made surrounding their existing capital assets. A second condition involves the way that the company accounts for its income taxes. The bank will require the company to use the liability method as opposed to the taxes payable method. The company's tax rate is 40%.

At the time of the review, it was determined that some of the useful lives and residual values of the existing equipment had changed. It is now 4 January 20X14 and the accountant who works for Ringo is a bit confused about how to account for the new capital assets and the old capital assets with respect to the future tax amounts and also what impact the changes will have on the 31 December 20X13 financial statements. The accountant has solicited your input as a financial reporting consultant. You have accepted the offer and asked the accountant to provide you with all of the new and revised estimates (see Exhibit 1).

Required:

Prepare an analysis of the capital assets at Ringo.

EXHIBIT 1

New Capital Assets

Item	Date of Purchase	Purchase Price	Residual Value	Useful Life
Manufacturing Equipment #4	15 February 20X13	$562,350	$51,340	12 Years
Manufacturing Equipment #5	15 February 20X13	$678,900	$5,550	10 Years
Manufacturing Equipment #6	15 February 20X13	$110,000	$4,300	5 Years

Existing Capital Assets

Item	Date of Purchase	Purchase Price	Residual Value—Original	Residual Value—Revised	Useful Life—Original	Useful Life—Revised
Manufacturing Machine #1	15 February 20X9	$498,645	$24,500	Nil	10 Years	8 Years
Manufacturing Machine #2	15 February 20X9	$368,950	$8,250	$2,250	10 Years	12 Years
Manufacturing Machine #3	1 November 20X9	$156,000	$3,000	$8,000	10 Years	No Change
Office Furniture	15 February 20X9	$17,800	Nil	No Change	10 Years	No Change
Lap Top Computers	15 February 20X9	$10,560	Nil	No Change	6 Years	4 Years
Building	15 February 20X9	$797,000	Nil	No Change	30 Years	45 Years

Note: Ringo does not use the half-year rule for accounting for depreciation.

(Sara Stonehouse)

CASE 16-2

SOFTWARE INCORPORATED

Software Incorporated (SI) is a private corporation formed in the 1990s. SI develops and sells software for many purposes; theft recovery, geomapping, data and device security, and IT asset management. To help motivate management, SI has a stock option plan.

To help fund continued software development, SI has a bank loan with a major bank. The bank requires annual audited financial statements and has a financial covenant that stipulates a minimum current ratio.

SI has an expected taxable loss of $10,000,000 in 20X9. For the last three years the company has had taxable profits of $2,000,000 in 20X6; $5,000,000 in 20X7, and $1,000,000 in

20X8. SI's taxable loss this year was due to intensive development of new software for security over personal data. SI anticipates sales of this product to be significant due to concerns over identity theft.

You have recently been hired to develop new accounting policies for SI's 31 December year-end. You have been asked by the owners to discuss alternatives and provide recommendations on the appropriate accounting policies for events below that have occurred during 20X9. Where possible, you have been asked to quantify the impact of the accounting policies. SI is seriously considering going public next year and would like to know how your recommendations would be different if it was a public company. The incremental borrowing rate for SI is 10%. The tax rates for the last few years were 20X6 (38%), 20X7 (39%), and both 20X8 and 20X9 (40%).

1. SI offers computer theft recovery and secure asset-tracking services. These services are provided for a period of one to five years. The customer pays a fee that includes software, monitoring, and maintenance. The fee is due 30 days after installation of the software. Sales staff are paid a commission based on the number of service contracts they sell.
2. SI offers a warranty with its theft recovery software. If a computer equipped with the software is stolen and SI is unable to recover the stolen software using its software or delete data on the stolen computer, then the customer is eligible for a warranty of up to $1,000. To qualify, customers must file a police report. The amount of the warranty depends on the value of the stolen computer. Estimated warranty liabilities on the balance sheet at the end of 20X8 were $8 million. During 20X9, the estimated warranty costs based on a percentage of sales will be an additional $5 million. Actual warranty costs during 20X9 were $1 million.
3. SI currently uses the taxes payable method of accounting for income taxes. In 20X8, SI changed its method of accounting for software development from expensing to capitalizing as an intangible asset.
4. SI entered into a forward contract for the purchase of new equipment that the company is purchasing from Germany in 20X9 to protect itself against changes in the value of the euro. SI often enters into forward contracts, interest rate swaps, and foreign currency swaps to protect the company from risks. SI also has shares in a number of companies for the purposes solely of earning money. It has an investment department that manages this portfolio of investments. These investments are traded on a frequent basis.
5. SI has installed a series of satellite towers as part of its software-tracking services at a cost of $15 million. There is a regulatory obligation to dismantle these satellite towers in 20 years. The anticipated cost at that time is $2.5 million.
6. SI issued $15,000,000 convertible bonds, 8% semi-annual dividend on 1 January 20X9. The bonds were issued for net proceeds (cash) of $14,800,000. The bonds are convertible at the bondholders' option in 10 years into Class A common shares at the rate of 70 shares for each $1,000 bond.
7. SI uses the Black-Scholes method for estimating its stock option expense. During 20X9, SI estimated an expense of $15 million using the following assumptions:

	20X8	20X9
Expected life of options	4	3
Expected stock price volatility	71%	60%
Risk free interest rate	4%	3%

Required:

Prepare the requested report.

CASE 16-3

DEEP HARBOUR LIMITED

Deep Harbour Limited (DHL) is a private company owned by Daniel Lalande. Lalande started the company in 20X1, and DHL has reported reasonably consistent growth in profits from fiscal 20X1 to 20X7. The company is in the plastic moulding business and makes everything from toys to dashboards.

The year ended 30 November 20X8 has been challenging for DHL. The company invested $8.2 million in new injection moulding machinery in February 20X8. This meant a two-week scheduled production shutdown to allow for installation and training. The two weeks stretched to five weeks when last-minute replacement parts were delayed at the U.S. border. The machinery was fully operational in late March 20X8; however, additional costs were incurred.

DHL has used the taxes payable method, using accounting standards for private enterprises to account for corporate income taxes but now has to adopt the liability method for its bank. The Chartered Bank of Canada (CBC) provided a $7 million 10-year term loan for the new equipment but insisted that certain covenants be met with financial results measured using specific required policies. DHL has no differences from required accounting policies except for the tax accounting policy.

DHL must meet the following two balance sheet ratios under the terms of debt covenants:

1. The current ratio must exceed 1-to-1.
2. The total debt-to-equity ratio must be less than 4-to-1 (all non-equity credit accounts included in the numerator).

If covenants are breached, the loan may be called for repayment with 30 business days' notice. In practical terms, it is likely that a breach would result in higher financing costs, now prime plus ½%.

DHL has asked you, a public accountant, to review the financial statements and adjust the statement of financial position for the effects of the new income tax policy. DHL is aware that this policy will be applied retrospectively, and thus will affect comparative retained earnings statements.

For now, though, DHL would like the statement of financial implications quantified. Management understands that any change to deferred income tax changes the retained earnings balance.

The draft statement of financial position is shown in Exhibit 1, calculation of taxable income is in Exhibit 2, and other information is in Exhibit 3.

DHL has also asked you to evaluate (and make changes for) any other accounting policies that might concern you. DHL has no wish to fall afoul of CBC's judgements in any credit review process.

Required:

Prepare a report that responds to the concerns raised.

EXHIBIT 1

DEEP HARBOUR LIMITED STATEMENT OF FINANCIAL POSITION

As of 30 November 20X8

(in thousands)

Assets	
Current	
Accounts receivable	$ 2,690
Inventory, at lower-of-cost-or-market	513
Prepaid expenses	219
Investment tax credit receivable	1,200
	4,622
Property, plant, and equipment, net of depreciation	12,850
	$17,472
Current Liabilities	
Bank operating line of credit	$ 295
Accounts payable and accrued liabilities	3,071
Deferred investment tax credit, net of amortization (written off straight line over 4 years)	900
	4,266
Long-term debt	7,500
Shareholders' equity	5,706
	$17,472

EXHIBIT 2

DEEP HARBOUR LIMITED TAXABLE INCOME

Year Ended 30 November 20X8

(in thousands)

Accounting income	$2,252
Depreciation (including $3.5 on capitalized interest)	1,306
Capital Cost Allowance[1]	(404)
Inventory writedown to LCM[2]	40
Interest capitalized	(35)
Non-deductible entertainment and marketing expenses	84
Amortization of deferred investment tax credit	(300)
Taxable income	2,943
Income tax payable (@ 42%)	1,236
Less: Investment tax credit	1,200
Net tax payable	$ 36

[1]UCC at the end of 20X8, correctly calculated, was $9,100. This includes the new machinery net of the investment tax credit.
[2]Tax deductible when inventory is sold.

EXHIBIT 3

DHL OTHER INFORMATION

1. DHL has paid $120,000 of tax instalments in 20X8, recorded as prepaid expenses on the 30 November 20X8 statement of financial position.
2. No tax expense or liability has been recorded for 20X8 as yet. Accounting income was closed to retained earnings on a pre-tax basis to prepare the statement of financial position in Exhibit 3.
3. DHL offers a six-month warranty on certain products. In past years, warranty expense had been expensed when claims were paid, since the warranty was new and not easily estimable. However, DHL has now had three years' experience with the warranty program and can safely estimate that the warranty liability at the end of 20X8 is in the $60,000 to $80,000 range.
4. DHL capitalized $35,000 of interest on the bank loan for the period that the new equipment was being installed. Capitalized interest is deductible for tax purposes when paid.
5. A full year's depreciation was charged on all assets, including the new machinery. This machinery is being depreciated straight line over its expected life of 10 years. A full year's depreciation is charged in the first year.

TECHNICAL REVIEW

TR16-1 Temporary versus Permanent Difference: Listed below are a number of items that are required to adjust net income before income taxes to taxable income.

Item	Add or Subtract
a. Golf club dues, $20,000	_____
b. Depreciation expense, $60,000	_____
c. Costs incurred during year development, $100,000	_____
d. Warranty costs accrued during year, $30,000	_____
e. Interest and penalty for late payment payroll taxes, $25,000	_____
d. CCA, $180,000	_____
e. Amortization capitalized development costs, $10,000	_____
f. Costs incurred during year for warranty work completed, $22,000	_____

Required:

1. For each item, indicate if it will be added or subtracted from net income before income taxes.
2. For each item, indicate if it is a permanent difference or a temporary difference.

TR16-2 Calculation Taxes Payable: Hendrie Incorporated had net income before income taxes of $2,200,000 in 20X9. The tax rate for this year is 40%.

Required:

1. Use the information from TR16-1. After adjusting for all of the items listed above, what is the taxable income?
2. What is the amount of income taxes payable?

connect

TR16-3 Temporary Differences: Listed below are six independent sources of deferred income tax. For each item, indicate whether the deferred income tax account on the balance sheet would be a debit or a credit.

Item	Debit or Credit
a. Accelerated amortization (CCA) for income tax and straight-line depreciation for accounting	_____
b. Estimated warranty costs: cash basis for income tax and accrual basis for accounting	_____
c. Sales revenue when payment is deferred: cash basis for tax purposes but recognized on delivery for accounting	_____
d. Development costs: cash basis for income tax and capitalization and amortization for accounting	_____
e. Unrealized loss: loss recognized only on later disposal of the asset for income tax but market value (LCM) recognized for accounting	_____
f. Rent revenue collected in advance: cash basis for income tax, accrual basis for accounting	_____

connect

TR16-4 Deferred Tax Balances and Income Tax Expense: Hendrie Incorporated had net income before income taxes of $2,200,000 in 20X9. This is the first year of operations. The tax rate for this year is 40%.

Required:

1. Use the information from TR16-1. For each temporary difference identified, what is the deferred tax balance? Indicate if it is a deferred tax asset or a deferred tax liability.
2. Provide the entry to record income tax expense for 20X9. Identify the amount of income tax that is current and the amount that is deferred.

connect

TR16-5 CCA-Depreciation Differences: Parry Corporation acquired new equipment for $1,200,000 in 20X6. For accounting purposes, the equipment will be depreciated over five years, straight line, with a full year's depreciation in the first year. For income tax purposes, Parry can take CCA over the next three years of $120,000 in 20X6, $216,000 in 20X7, and $175,000 in 20X8. Parry's income tax rate is 34%.

Required:

For each 31 December, 20X6 through 20X8, determine:

1. The tax basis for the equipment.
2. The accounting basis for the equipment.
3. The amount of the temporary difference relating to the equipment.
4. The amount of the deferred income tax expense.
5. The balance of deferred income tax asset or liability that would be shown on the statement of financial position.

ASSIGNMENTS

★ **A16-1 Income Tax Allocation—Two-Year Period:** Miller Corporation provided the following data related to accounting and taxable income:

connect

	20X8	20X9
Pre-tax accounting income (financial statements)	$800,000	$ 880,000
Taxable income (tax return)	480,000	1,200,000
Income tax rate	38%	38%

There are no existing temporary differences other than those reflected in these data. There are no permanent differences.

Required:

1. How much tax expense would be reported in each year if the taxes payable method was used? What is potentially misleading with this presentation of tax expense?
2. How much tax expense and deferred income tax would be reported using comprehensive tax allocation (liability method) and the liability method? Why is the two-year total tax expense the same in requirements 1 and 2?

★ **A16-2 Deferred Tax Balances:** MacMillan Incorporated started operations in 20X6. The company provided the following information for its warranty balances for the past four years:

connect

	20X6	20X7	20X8	20X9
Warranty costs accrued	30,000	40,000	55,000	80,000
Costs incurred warranty work	25,000	35,000	60,000	55,000
Costs incurred development costs	90,000	100,000	120,000	50,000
Amortization development costs	0	18,000	38,000	50,000
Tax rate	40%	38%	38%	36%

Required:

1. What is the tax basis for development costs and the provision for warranty costs?
2. What is the accounting basis for development costs and the provision for warranty costs?
3. What is the deferred tax balance in each year?
4. Is the balance as asset or a liability?

★ **A16-3 Income Tax Allocation—Two-Year Period:** Verity Limited, a public company, reported the following information (in thousands) for 20X8 and 20X9:

	20X8	20X9
Income from continuing operations, before unusual item, discontinued operation, and income tax	$600,000	$500,000
Unusual item—gain on sale of capital assets (before income tax)	20,000	
Gain from discontinued operations, before income tax		44,000

Verity's income tax rate is 40%. The 20X8 unusual gain is not taxable until 20X9. The 20X9 gain on discontinued operations is fully taxable in 20X9.

Required:

Prepare a partial statement of profit and loss in good form for 20X8 and 20X9, starting with "Income from continuing operations, before unusual item and discontinued operations, and income tax."

★★ **A16-4 Income Tax Allocation; Alternatives:** The financial statements of Dakar Corporation for a four-year period reflected the following pre-tax amounts:

Solution

	20X4	20X5	20X6	20X7
Statement Profit and Loss (summarized)				
Revenues	$110,000	$124,000	$144,000	$164,000
Expenses other than depreciation	(80,000)	(92,000)	(95,000)	(128,000)
Depreciation expense (straight line)	(10,000)	(10,000)	(10,000)	(10,000)
Pre-tax accounting income	$ 20,000	$ 22,000	$ 39,000	$ 26,000
Statement of Financial Position (partial)				
Machine (four-year life, no residual value), at cost	$ 40,000	$ 40,000	$ 40,000	$ 40,000
Less: Accumulated Depreciation	(10,000)	(20,000)	(30,000)	(40,000)
	$ 30,000	$ 20,000	$ 10,000	$ 0

Dakar has a tax rate of 40% each year and claimed CCA for income tax purposes as follows: 20X4, $16,000; 20X5, $12,000; 20X6, $8,000; and 20X7, $4,000. There were no deferred income tax balances at 1 January 20X4.

Required:

For each year, calculate the deferred income tax balance on the statement of financial position at the end of the year using the liability method of tax allocation. Also calculate net income using the liability method of tax allocation.

★★ **A16-5 Cumulative CCA-Depreciation Differences:** McQuinn Corporation started operations in 20X5. The company acquired equipment in the first year for a price of $180,000. The equipment will be depreciated for accounting purposes over three years on a straight-line basis (with a full year's depreciation in the year of acquisition). For determining income tax payable, the company can deduct one-half of the purchase cost as CCA in the first year, one-third in the second year, and one-sixth in the third year.

connect

The company's 20X5 startup was successful, and in 20X6 the company bought identical equipment for $192,000. In 20X7, a third set of equipment was acquired for $198,000. The pattern of depreciation and CCA is proportionately the same for each acquisition. McQuinn's tax rate is 40%.

The company's management plans to continue the same level of investment for the foreseeable future, as long as the company remains profitable.

Required:

1. Determine the temporary difference relating to the tax versus accounting bases of the equipment (i.e., CCA versus accounting depreciation) for each of 20X5 through 20X7. What is the accumulated balance of the temporary difference at the end of each year?
2. What is the balance of the *deferred income tax* account at the end of each year?
3. What will happen to the accumulated temporary differences and deferred income tax if McQuinn continues to maintain its current level of investment in equipment, replacing each asset as it comes to the end of its useful life?
4. What conditions will be necessary to cause the timing difference balance to decline in future years?
5. Under what conditions will reversal of the accumulated timing differences cause a cash outflow?

★★ connect

A16-6 Cumulative Temporary Differences: At the end of 20X8, Carter Limited's statement of financial position showed equipment at total cost of $4,000,000. The equipment was being amortized at 10% per year, straight line, and was 40% depreciated at the end of 20X8. The income tax files showed unclaimed capital cost (UCC) for the equipment of $1,100,000. Carter's statement of financial position also showed an asset of $600,000 for unamortized development costs. The development costs had been incurred in previous years and had been deducted for income tax purposes in those prior years.

In 20X9, Carter acquired an additional $600,000 in equipment while scrapping equipment that originally cost $250,000. The CCA rate for Carter's equipment is 20%. Total CCA claimed for 20X9 was $230,000. Carter amortized $100,000 of the development costs.

Carter pays income tax at a rate of 38%.

Required:

1. Determine the cumulative temporary differences relating to equipment and development costs at the end of each of 20X8 and 20X9.
2. What is the balance of the *deferred income tax* account at the end of each year?
3. What are the accounting basis and the tax basis of the equipment and of the development cost at the end of each of 20X8 and 20X9?
4. If Carter maintains its capital asset base by reinvestment and renewal in future years, when will the deferred income tax balance begin to decline? Explain.

★ connect

A16-7 Tax Calculations: The following is selected information from the accounting records of Ross Incorporated for 20X9 its first year of operations:

Net income before income taxes	$980,000

In determining pre-tax accounting income, the following deductions were made:

a. Golf club dues	25,000
b. Accrued warranty costs	80,000
c. Depreciation	125,000

For tax purposes, the following deductions were made:

a. Warranty costs incurred	65,000
b. CCA	250,000

The capital assets, originally costing $1,250,000, are depreciated on a straight-line basis over 10 years, zero residual value, with a full year depreciation taken in Year 1. The tax rate is 36%.

Required:

Prepare the journal entry to record income tax at the end of 20X9.

★

A16-8 Tax Calculations: The records of Verity Corporation, in its first year of operation, at the end of 20X8, provided the following data related to income taxes:

a. Golf club dues expense in 20X8, $20,000, properly recorded for accounting purposes but not tax deductible at any time.
b. Investment income in 20X8, $650,000, properly recorded for accounting purposes but not taxable at any time.
c. Estimated expense for warranty costs, $140,000; accrued for accounting purposes at the end of 20X8; to be reported for income tax purposes when paid. There were no warranty costs incurred in 20X8.
d. Gain on disposal of land, $480,000; recorded for accounting purposes at the end of 20X8; to be reported as a capital gain for income tax purposes at the end of 20X10.
e. Costs incurred for development costs, $100,000; deducted for income tax purposes; recognized as depreciated. No depreciation of development costs in 20X8.

f. Equipment purchased in 20X8, $3,000,000; depreciation $200,000 recorded for accounting purposes in 20X8; CCA $300,000 deducted for income tax purposes in 20X8.

Accounting income (from the financial statements) for 20X8 was $2,400,000; the income tax rate is 38%. There were no deferred tax amounts as of the beginning of 20X8.

Required:

1. Are the individual differences listed above permanent differences or temporary differences? Explain why.
2. Prepare the journal entry to record income tax at the end of 20X8.
3. Show the amounts that will be reported on (a) the statement of financial position and (b) the statement of profit and loss for 20X8.

★ **A16-9 Tax Calculations:** Scarlett Corporation reported accounting income before taxes as follows: 20X6, $450,000; 20X7, $38,000. Taxable income for each year would have been the same as pre-tax accounting income except for the tax effects, arising for the first time in 20X6, of $4,800 in rent revenue, representing $800 per month rent revenue collected in advance on 1 October 20X6, for the six months ending 31 March 20X7. Rent revenue is taxable in the year collected. The tax rate for 20X6 and 20X7 is 40%, and the year-end for both accounting and tax purposes is 31 December. The rent revenue collected in advance is the only difference, and it is not repeated in October 20X7.

Required:

1. Is this a temporary difference? Why, or why not?
2. What is the accounting carrying value for the unearned rent at the end of 20X6? The tax basis? Explain.
3. Calculate taxable income and income tax payable, and prepare journal entries for each year-end.
4. Prepare a partial statement of profit and loss for each year, starting with pre-tax accounting income.
5. What amount of deferred income tax would be reported on the 20X6 and 20X7 statements of financial position?

★ **A16-10 Tax Calculations:** The pre-tax income statements for Lusch Corporation for two years (summarized) were as follows:

	20X8	20X9
Revenues	$660,000	$820,000
Expenses	450,000	590,000
Pre-tax income	$210,000	$230,000

For tax purposes, the following income tax differences existed:

a. Revenues on the 20X9 statement of profit and loss include $90,000 rent, which is taxable in 20X8 but was unearned at the end of 20X8 for accounting purposes.
b. Expenses on the 20X9 statement of profit and loss include political contributions of $30,000, which are not deductible for income tax purposes.
c. Expenses on the 20X8 statement of profit and loss include $52,000 of estimated warranty costs, which are not deductible for income tax purposes until 20X9.

Required:

1. What was the accounting carrying value and tax basis for unearned revenue and the warranty liability at the end of 20X8 and 20X9?
2. Compute (a) income tax payable, (b) deferred income tax, and (c) income tax expense for each period. Assume an average tax rate of 40%.

3. Give the entry to record income taxes for each period.
4. Complete statements of profit and loss to include income taxes as allocated.
5. What amount of deferred income tax will be reported on the statement of financial position at each year-end?

★ connect

A16-11 Tax Calculations: Arbuckle Incorporated recorded instalment sales revenue of $120,000 in 20X1 and $420,000 in 20X2. The revenue is not taxable until collected. Of the year 20X1 revenue, $80,000 was collected in 20X2 and the remaining $40,000 collected in 20X3. Of the year 20X2 revenue, $150,000 was collected in 20X3 and the rest in 20X4. Arbuckle's accounting earnings before income tax for the three years was as follows:

20X1	$800,000
20X2	980,000
20X3	660,000

On 1 January 20X1, the enacted rate for all years was 38%. During 20X3, the rate was revised to 40%.

Required:

Prepare the necessary journal entries to record income tax for the years 20X1, 20X2, and 20X3.

(Source: [Adapted] © CGA-Canada. Reproduced with permission.)

★ connect

A16-12 Tax Calculations: Fellows Incorporated started operations on 1 January 20X8 and purchased $2,000,000 of equipment. The income tax rate was 40% in 20X8 and 38% in 20X9. The following is information related to 20X8 and 20X9:

	20X8	20X9
Accounting income before income tax	$550,000	$820,000
Golf club dues	10,000	12,000
Accrued warranty costs	50,000	120,000
Warranty costs	40,000	90,000
Depreciation expense on equipment	200,000	200,000
Capital cost allowance	300,000	250,000

Required:

1. Prepare all income tax journal entries for 20X8 and 20X9.
2. What are the deferred tax balances on the statement of financial position in 20X8 and 20X9?

★ Solution

A16-13 Deferred Income Tax; Change in Tax Rates: DCM Metals Limited has a 31 December year-end. The tax rate is 30% in 20X4, 35% in 20X5, and 42% in 20X6. The company reports income as follows:

20X4	$550,000
20X5	123,000
20X6	310,000

Taxable income and accounting income are identical except for a $300,000 revenue reported for accounting purposes in 20X4, with one-half reported in 20X5 and one-half in 20X6 for tax purposes. The revenue is related to a long-term account receivable, taxable only when collected.

Required:

Compute tax expense and deferred income tax on the statement of financial position for 20X4, 20X5, and 20X6.

★★ **A16-14 Deferred Income Tax; Change in Tax Rates:** Stacy Corporation would have had identical income before tax on both its income tax returns and statements of profit and loss for the years 20X4 through 20X7, except for equipment that cost $120,000. The equipment has a four-year estimated life and no residual value. The equipment was depreciated for income tax purposes using the following amounts: 20X4, $48,000; 20X5, $36,000; 20X6, $24,000; and 20X7, $12,000. However, for accounting purposes, the straight-line method was used (i.e., $30,000 per year). The accounting and tax periods both end on 31 December. Income amounts before depreciation expense and income tax for each of the four years were as follows:

	20X4	20X5	20X6	20X7
Accounting income before tax and depreciation	$60,000	$80,000	$70,000	$70,000
Tax rate	30%	30%	40%	40%

Required:

1. Explain why this is a temporary difference.
2. Calculate the accounting carrying value and tax basis of the equipment at the end of each year.
3. Reconcile pre-tax accounting and taxable income, calculate income tax payable and tax expense, compute the balance in the deferred income tax account, and prepare journal entries for each year-end.

★★ **A16-15 Deferred Income Tax; Change in Tax Rates:** Buck Company has a deferred income tax liability in the amount of $320,000 at 31 December 20X7, relating to a $800,000 receivable. This sale was recorded for accounting purposes in 20X7 but is not taxable until the cash is collected. In 20X8, $600,000 is collected. Warranty expense in 20X8 included in the determination of pre-tax accounting income is $220,000, with the entire amount expected to be spent and deductible for tax purposes in 20X9. Pre-tax accounting income is $980,000 in 20X8. The tax rate is 38% in 20X8.

Required:

1. What is the accounting carrying value, the tax basis of the account receivable, and the warranty liability, at the end of 20X7 and 20X8? What was the enacted tax rate at 31 December 20X7?
2. Calculate taxable income and income tax payable, compute the balance in the deferred income tax accounts, and prepare journal entries for year-end 20X8.
3. Calculate the deferred income tax that would be reported on the statement of financial position at the end of 20X8.

★★ **A16-16 Tax Calculations; Change in Tax Rates:** On 1 January 20X3, Highmark Corporation reported the following amounts on the statement of financial position:

Deferred income tax asset related to warranty	$ 16,000
Deferred income tax liability related to capital assets	$120,000

On this date, the net book value of capital assets was $1,750,000 and undepreciated capital cost was $1,450,000. There was a warranty liability of $40,000. Taxable income of $500,000 (in total) in 20X1 and 20X2 had resulted in the payment of $195,000 of income tax.

In 20X3, accounting income was $170,000. This included non-tax-deductible expenses of $42,000, dividend revenue (non-taxable) of $12,000, depreciation of $75,000, and a warranty expense of $39,000. Warranty claims paid were $51,000 and CCA was $99,000.

Required:

Provide the journal entry to record tax expense in 20X3. The enacted tax rate was 41% in 20X3.

★★ **A16-17 Tax Calculations; Change in Tax Rates:** On 31 December 20X6, North Corporation reported the following amounts on the statement of financial position:

Deferred income tax asset related to warranty	$ 19,000
Deferred income tax liability related to capital assets	$304,000
Deferred income tax liability related to development costs	$456,000

On this date, the net book value of capital assets was $2,760,000 and undepreciated capital cost was $1,960,000. There was an estimated warranty liability of $50,000. Development costs capitalized as an asset were $1,200,000.

In 20X7, accounting income was $2,200,000. This included penalties related to late payment of payroll taxes of $50,000, depreciation of capital assets of $350,000, depreciation of development costs of $400,000, and a warranty expense of $180,000. Warranty claims paid were $130,000 and CCA was $550,000.

Required:

1. Provide the journal entry to record tax expense in 20X7. The enacted tax rate was 40% in 20X7.
2. Identify the following balances for 31 December 20X7:
   a. Deferred income tax asset
   b. Deferred income tax liability
   c. Estimated warranty liability
   d. Net book value of capital assets
   e. Development costs
   f. Undepreciated capital cost

★★ **A16-18 Tax Calculations—Tax Rate Change:** The statements of profit and loss for Gardner Corporation for two years (summarized) were as follows:

	20X8	20X9
Revenues	$800,000	$720,000
Expenses	724,000	608,000
Pre-tax accounting income	$ 76,000	$112,000
Taxable income (per tax return)	$188,000	$112,000

The income tax rate is 38% in 20X8 and 40% in 20X9. The 20X9 tax rate was enacted in 20X9. For tax purposes, the following differences existed:

a. Expenses (given above) on the 20X8 and 20X9 statements of profit and loss include golf club dues of $40,000 annually, which are not deductible for income tax purposes.
b. Revenues (given above) on the 20X9 statement of profit and loss include $40,000 rent revenue, which was taxable in 20X8 but was unearned for accounting purposes until 20X9.
c. Expenses (given above) on the 20X8 statement of profit and loss include $32,000 of estimated warranty costs, which are not deductible for income tax purposes until paid at a later date.

Required:

1. Explain whether each difference is a permanent or temporary difference.
2. Calculate income tax payable for each year.
3. Calculate income tax expense for each of 20X8 and 20X9. Also calculate the balance in the deferred income tax account at the end of 20X8 and 20X9.

★★ **A16-19 Tax Calculations—Tax Rate Change:** The records of Morgan Corporation provided the following data at the end of Years 1 through 4 relating to income tax allocation:

	Year 1	Year 2	Year 3	Year 4
Pre-tax accounting income	$58,000	$70,000	$80,000	$88,000
Taxable income (tax return)	28,000	80,000	90,000	98,000
Tax rate	36%	38%	40%	40%

The above amounts include only one temporary difference; no other changes occurred. At the end of Year 1, the company prepaid an expense of $30,000, which was then amortized for accounting purposes over the next three years (straight line). The full amount was included as a deduction in Year 1 for income tax purposes. Each year's tax rate was enacted in each specific year—that is, the Year 2 tax rate was enacted in Year 2 and so on.

Required:

1. Calculate income tax payable for each year.
2. Calculate income tax expense.
3. Comment on the effect that use of the liability method has on income tax expense when the income tax rate changes.

★★ **A16-20 Tax Rate Change; Two-Stage:** At the end of 20X6, Fawcett Ltd. had accumulated temporary differences of $1,000,000 arising from CCA/depreciation on capital assets. The balance of the deferred income tax liability account was $400,000. Over the next three years, Fawcett experienced the following:

	20X7	20X8	20X9
Accounting income, before income taxes	$400,000	$440,000	$500,000
Expenses not deductible for computing income tax	16,000	20,000	12,000
Temporary differences*	88,000	100,000	104,000

*Excess of tax-deductible expenses over expenses recognized in accounting income.

The tax rate was 40% for taxation years 20X6 and 20X7, 36% for 20X8, and 34% for 20X9.

Required:

1. Calculate income tax expense for each year, 20X7, 20X8, and 20X9. Assume that the rates for 20X8 and 20X9 were enacted year by year. Distinguish between current income tax expense and deferred income tax expense. State any additional assumptions that you make.
2. Assume instead that the rates for 20X8 and 20X9 were enacted in 20X7. How, if at all, would this affect income tax expense in each of the three years?

★★ **A16-21 Tax Calculations:** Martin Limited, in the first year of its operations, reported the following information regarding its operations:

a. Income before tax for the year was $2,500,000 and the tax rate was 38%.
b. Depreciation was $240,000, and CCA was $134,000. Net book value at year-end was $1,680,000, while UCC was $1,786,000.
c. The warranty program generated an estimated cost (expense) on the statement of profit and loss of $514,000 but the cash paid out was $348,000. The $166,000 liability resulting from this was shown as a current liability. On the income tax return, the cash paid is the amount deductible.
d. Golf club dues of $30,000 were included in the statement of profit and loss but were not allowed to be deducted for tax purposes.

In the second year of its operations, Martin Limited reported the following information:

a. Income before income tax for the year was $2,750,000, and the tax rate was 40%.

b. Depreciation was $240,000, and the CCA was $740,000. Net book value at year-end was $1,440,000, while UCC was $1,046,000.
c. The estimated costs of the warranty program were $574,000, and the cash paid out was $484,000. The liability had a balance of $256,000.

Required:
Prepare the journal entry to record income tax expense in the first and second years of operations. The second-year tax rate was not enacted until the second year.

(Source: [Adapted] © CGA-Canada. Reproduced with permission.)

★★ **A16-22 Tax Calculations; Rate Change:** In its first year of operations, Quan Corporation reported the following information:

a. Income before income taxes was $2,200,000.
b. The company acquired capital assets costing $3,600,000; depreciation was $240,000, and CCA was $180,000.
c. The company recorded an expense of $500,000 for the one-year warranty on the company's products; cash disbursements amounted to $380,000.
d. The company incurred development costs of $200,000 that met the criteria for capitalization. Development work was still ongoing at year-end.
e. The company made a political contribution of $20,000 to a local politician.
f. The income tax rate was 38%.

In the second year, Quan reported the following:

a. Legislation was enacted that changed the tax rate to 40%.
b. Income before income tax was $4,500,000.
c. Depreciation was $240,000; CCA was $342,000.
d. The estimated warranty costs were $600,000, while the cash expenditure was $550,000.
e. Additional development costs of $150,000 were incurred to complete the project. Amortization of $58,000 was recorded.
f. Golf club memberships for top executives cost $50,000.

Required:
Prepare the journal entries to record income tax expense for the first and second years of operation.

★★ **A16-23 Tax Calculations; Rate Change:** Golf Incorporated, which began operations in 20X3, uses the same policies for financial accounting and tax purposes with the exception of warranty costs and franchise fee revenue. Information about the $60,000 of warranty expenses and $90,000 franchise revenue accrued for book purposes is provided below:

Solution

	20X3	20X4	20X5
Warranty cost for book purposes	$60,000	—	—
Warranty cost for tax purposes (claims paid)	15,000	$20,000	$25,000
Franchise fee revenue, book, on account	90,000	—	—
Franchise fee revenue, tax, cash received	9,000	51,000	30,000
Effective tax rate	38%	40%	45%
Income before tax	$75,000	$90,000	$80,000

Required:
Prepare journal entries to record taxes for 20X3 to 20X5. The company uses the liability method. Separate deferred income tax accounts are used for each source of temporary differences. The tax rate for a given year is not enacted until that specific year.

(Source: [Adapted] © CGA-Canada. Reproduced with permission.)

★★ **A16-24 Tax Calculations:** Diversified Limited (DI) is a public company that started operations in 20X4. It opened a number of locations across Canada. In fiscal 20X4, the company had net income before tax of $290,000. The tax rate for 20X4 was 30%. DI has a 31 December year-end. The following occurred during 20X4.

a. DI purchased assets with an original cost of $780,000. The total depreciation for 20X4 was $52,000. For tax purposes, DI had $15,600 CCA deducted.
b. For sales during 20X4 DI recognized warranty expenses of $44,000. Actual warranty work completed during 20X4 was $30,000.
c. DI capitalized development costs of $200,000 for new product innovations. Amortization of this asset has not occurred yet, since the development work will continue in 20X5. These costs are deductible for tax purposes in the year.
d. DI contributed $5,000 to a local political campaign and expensed these costs during the year.
e. DI recognized revenues of $500,000 in 20X4. Only $440,000 of these revenues were collected and taxed during the year. The remainder will not be taxed until they are due and collected next year.

Required:

1. Provide the journal entry to record income tax expense during 20X4. Show all supporting calculations.
2. Identify the amount of income tax expense that is current and the amount that is deferred.
3. Identify the relevant amounts, if any, that will be shown on the December 31 year-end statement of financial position for a–f above.

★★ **A16-25 Tax Expense; Comprehensive:** At the end of 20X8, Anderson Corporation, a public company, reported the following items in the financial statements:

Deferred income tax liability related to accounts receivable	198,000
Deferred income tax liability related to capital assets	432,000
Deferred income tax asset related to warranties	54,000

In 20X8, the company reported $1,350,000 of taxable income. It also reported a $550,000 long-term receivable, taxable when collected. At the end of 20X8, capital assets had a net book value of $4,800,000 and a UCC balance of $3,600,000. Estimated warranty liabilities were $150,000.

In 20X9, Anderson reported accounting income of $2,250,000. Collections on the long-term receivable amounted to $420,000. There were non-deductible golf club dues of $32,000. Depreciation was $200,000 and CCA was $300,000. The tax rate was 38%.

Required:

1. Prepare a journal entry to record tax expense in 20X9. Tax rates were enacted in the year to which they pertain:
2. Identify the following balances at the end of 2X09:
   a. Deferred income tax asset
   b. Deferred income tax liability
   c. Estimated warranty liability
   d. Net book value of capital assets
   e. Accounts receivable
   f. Undepreciated capital cost

★★★ **A16-26 Tax Expense; Comprehensive:** Nu Limited reported income before income tax of $280,000 in 20X9. The tax rate for 20X9 was 40% and was enacted during the year. The enacted tax rate at the end of the previous year was 38%.

At the end of 20X8, the balance sheet of Nu included the net book value of equipment of $1,590,000, long-term accounts receivable of $240,000, and a warranty liability of $98,000. Long-term receivables represent taxable income when collected.

In 20X9, dividends (tax-free) received from taxable Canadian corporations were $32,000. Political contributions were $40,000. UCC was $960,000 at the beginning of the year. In 20X9, CCA was $100,000, and depreciation expense was $126,000.

During 20X9, long-term receivables of $80,000 were collected. There were no new long-term receivables. The warranty expense of $92,000 was equal to the warranty claims paid.

Required:

Calculate income tax expense for 20X9.

★★★ **A16-27 Tax Calculations; Comprehensive:** Crandall Corporation was formed in 20X1. Relevant information pertaining to 20X1, 20X2, and 20X3 is as follows:

excel

	20X1	20X2	20X3
Income before income tax	$100,000	$100,000	$100,000
Accounting income includes the following:			
Depreciation (assets have a cost of $120,000)	10,000	10,000	12,000
Pension expense*	5,000	7,000	10,000
Warranty expense	3,000	3,000	3,000
Dividend income (nontaxable)	2,000	2,000	3,000
Taxable income includes the following:			
Capital cost allowance	25,000	15,000	7,000
Pension funding (amount paid)	7,000	8,000	9,000
Warranty costs paid	1,000	4,000	3,000
Tax rate—enacted in each year	40%	44%	48%

*Pension amounts are tax deductible when paid, not when expensed. Over the long term, payments will equal total expense. The tax basis for the pension will always be zero. For accounting purposes, there will be a statement of financial position asset account asset called "deferred pension cost" for the difference between the amount paid and the expense, since the amount paid is higher.

Required:

Prepare the journal entry to record income tax expense for each year.

★★★ **A16-28 Investment Tax Credit (Appendix):** Pegasus Printing began operations in 20X4 and has bought equipment for use in its printing operations in each of the last three years. This equipment qualifies for an investment tax credit of 14%. Information relating to the three years is shown below:

	20X4	20X5	20X6
Income before income tax	$165,000	$456,000	$468,000
Income tax rate	25%	25%	25%
Equipment eligible for ITC	$ 40,000	$689,000	$450,000
Estimated life of equipment	10 years	13 years	12 years

a. Income before tax includes nondeductible advertising expenditures of $20,000 each year.
b. Equipment is depreciated straight line over its useful life for accounting purposes, assuming zero salvage value. A full year of depreciation is charged in the year of acquisition. CCA claims in 20X4 were $12,000; 20X5, $135,000; and 20X6, $216,000.

Required:

1. Calculate the depreciation expense in each of the three years, net of the investment tax credit amortization.
2. Calculate taxes payable in each of the three years. Note that depreciation added back is net depreciation, as calculated in requirement 1.
3. Calculate tax expense for each year, using Canadian standards (cost reduction) to account for the investment tax credit.
4. Calculate tax expense, using the flow-through approach for all tax amounts.
5. Why is the cost reduction approach preferable?
6. Show how capital assets, and the deferred investment tax credit, would be presented on the statement of financial position at the end of 20X4.

★★ **A16-29 Tax Calculations, Rate Change (ASPE):** Refer to the facts in A16-22.

Required:

Prepare the journal entries to record income tax expense for the first and second years of operation, assuming it is a private company that uses the taxes payable method.

★★ **A16-30 Tax Calculations (ASPE):** Refer to the case facts in A16-24.

Required:

Provide the journal entry to record income tax expense during 20X4 operation, assuming it is a private company that uses the taxes payable method. Show all supporting calculations.

connect LEARNSMART SMARTBOOK™

For more information on the resources available from McGraw-Hill Ryerson, go to www.mcgrawhill.ca/he/solutions.

CHAPTER 17

Accounting for Tax Losses

INTRODUCTION

In 2011, Armtec Infrastructure Incorporated recognized deferred income tax assets of $11 million. The deferred tax assets were created by recognizing the probable *future* tax benefit of *past* years' losses. By recognizing these deferred tax assets in 2011, Armtec Infrastructure Incorporated went from a loss of almost $321 million before income taxes to a loss of almost $270 million from continuing operations.

On the other hand, In-Touch Survey Systems Limited had Canadian taxable losses of $1.45 million available and recognized a benefit of only $54,440 related to loss carry-forwards. The remaining losses were not recorded, since it was not considered probable they would be used before they expire.

When a corporation's taxable "income" is actually a loss, the corporation can use that loss to reduce past and future income taxes. A loss will normally have tax benefits, but the benefits might not be *realized* in the period of the loss. Should future benefits be *recognized* in the year of the loss in order to achieve matching, or should the recognition be delayed, since the benefit may not be realized?

This chapter begins with an explanation of the income tax benefits that arise from a loss. Then we will discuss the issue of when and how to recognize those benefits.

RECOGNIZING THE TAX BENEFITS OF A LOSS

Accounting income is converted to taxable income by making appropriate adjustments for all temporary and permanent differences. This is true whether the accounting records report a net income or a net loss. Accounting income may become a taxable loss, and an accounting loss may become taxable income, depending on the nature of the permanent and temporary differences. When a corporation prepares its tax return and finds it has a taxable loss, the corporation is entitled to offset the loss against past and future taxable income as follows:

- The loss can be *carried back* for three years for a refund of tax previously paid.
- Any remaining loss can be *carried forward* for up to 20 years to reduce taxes that would otherwise be payable.

If the sum of the previous three years' plus the next 20 years' taxable income turns out to be less than the loss, any remaining potential benefit is lost.

It is simple to account for the tax benefits of the loss *carrybacks*; the taxes recovered are recognized on the income statement as a tax recovery in the loss year, and the refund receivable is shown on the statement of financial position as a current asset. Recognition occurs in the period of the loss because there is no uncertainty about whether or not the company will actually receive the benefit. Accounting for loss carrybacks will be demonstrated in the next section.

However, if the carrybacks do not fully utilize the loss, a recognition problem arises. Income taxes can be reduced in *future* periods as a result of the tax **loss carryforward**. Should the benefit of reduced future taxes be recognized in the period of the loss or only in the period in which the benefits are realized?

Looking at the definition of an asset in the framework, the loss should not be recognized unless it has probable future benefit. The general principle, therefore, is that the tax benefits of tax losses should be recognized in the period of the loss, *to the extent that they are probable.*

The actual amount of the benefit can be *measured* with reasonable assurance. If a company has a tax loss of $1 million and the tax rate is 35%, the potential benefit of the tax loss is that past and future income taxes will be reduced by $350,000 (i.e., $1 million × 35%). Tax rate changes may cause some variation, but the potential benefit is readily estimable.

What is not certain is whether the benefits of any carryforwards will actually be *realized.* In order to realize the benefit, the company must have enough taxable income during the carryforward period to use up the loss carryforward. Basically, the carryforward benefit is a contingent gain—a benefit will be realized only *if* something happens in the future. Contingent gains are not recognized, since this means income may be recognized and never realized. It is only in the event of virtual certainty where in reality there is an asset and recognition occurs. However, with loss carryforwards, there is much earlier recognition. Recognition of the carryforward benefit occurs whenever management decides that it is *probable* (i.e., greater than 50% probability) that the future tax benefits will be realized, which is a much lower threshold than virtual certainty.

Tax Loss versus Tax Benefits

To avoid confusion, it is necessary to keep track separately of the amount of the tax *loss* and the amount of the tax *benefit*. The **tax loss** is the final amount of taxable loss on the tax return. The **tax benefit** is the total present and future benefit that the company will be able to realize from the tax loss through a reduction of income taxes paid or payable to governments. Basically, the tax benefit is equal to the tax loss multiplied by the tax rate. Put another way, *the tax loss is the gross amount, and the tax benefit is the tax savings.* Since tax rates can change, keeping track of the gross amount is essential for calculating the tax savings.

TAX LOSS CARRYBACKS

A tax **loss carryback** entitles the corporation to recover income tax actually paid in the previous three years. For example, assume that Fabian Corporation was established in 20X1.

For the first four years, the company was moderately successful, but in the fifth year, it suffered a tax loss of $500,000. Fabian's taxable income for the first five years was as follows:

Year	Taxable Income	Tax Rate	Income Tax Paid
20X1	$100,000	40%	$ 40,000
20X2	240,000	40	96,000
20X3	160,000	35	56,000
20X4	300,000	37	111,000
20X5	(500,000)	38	—

The loss will be carried back to the preceding three years to recover tax previously paid. Normally, the loss is carried back to the earliest (oldest) year first, and then applied to succeeding years until the loss is used up. The year 20X1 is outside the three-year carryback period, and therefore the loss can be carried back only as far as 20X2. The tax recovery will be as follows:

Year	Carryback	Tax Rate	Tax Recovery
20X2	$240,000	40%	$ 96,000
20X3	160,000	35	56,000
20X4	100,000	37	37,000
Totals	$500,000		$189,000

In this example, the carryback completely utilizes the 20X5 tax loss of $500,000. Note that the tax is recovered at the rate at which it was originally paid, since Fabian is recovering taxes previously paid. The tax rate in the year of the loss (i.e., 38% for 20X5) is irrelevant for determining the amount of tax recoverable via the carryback. Fabian will record the benefit of that carryback as follows:

Income tax receivable (SFP)	189,000	
Income tax expense (recovery) (I/S)		189,000

The *credit* to income tax expense reflects the fact that it is a recovery of taxes paid in earlier years. A company will usually label this amount as "provision for income tax" or "income tax recovery" in its income statement. If any part of the tax loss is attributable to discontinued operations, the recovery must be allocated to the relevant components of income, as we described in Chapter 3 for *intraperiod* allocation.

In 20X3, the tax rate was 35%; in 20X4 it had increased to 37%. The company could maximize its recovery by applying more of the carryback to 20X4 instead of 20X3; there is no requirement in the *Income Tax Act* to apply the carryback sequentially. If the company follows a recovery maximization strategy, the carryback would be applied as follows:

Year	Carryback	Tax Rate	Tax Recovery
20X2	$240,000	40%	$ 96,000
20X4	260,000	37	96,200
Totals	$500,000		$192,200

Maximizing the carryback tax recovery is a viable strategy, but it is a bit of a gamble because if the company has a loss in 20X7, the 20X4 carryback potential will have already been used up, and the 20X3 tax is then out of reach because it is no longer within the allowable carryback period of three years. Therefore, companies usually apply the carryback sequentially, even if there may be an advantage of a higher income tax receivable if the carryback is applied nonsequentially to the years that had the highest tax rate.

TEMPORARY AND PERMANENT DIFFERENCES IN A LOSS YEAR

Step 1: Calculate Taxable Income (Loss)

The first step in doing a tax question is always to calculate taxable income. This involves adjusting accounting income for permanent and temporary differences. Temporary differences continue to originate and/or reverse regardless of whether the company is experiencing profits or losses. Permanent differences are likewise the same, whether accounting and/or taxable income are positive or negative. Indeed, it is quite possible for temporary differences and permanent differences to convert a pre-tax accounting profit to a tax loss. For example, assume the following facts for Michelle Limited for the fiscal year ending 31 December 20X8:

- Net income before taxes of $90,000, after deducting depreciation expense of $150,000;
- CCA totalling $280,000 deducted on the tax return;
- Net book value of property, plant, and equipment of $1,700,000 and unclaimed capital cost (UCC) of $1,200,000 on 1 January 20X8, a temporary difference of $500,000 that is reflected in an accumulated deferred income tax liability balance of $200,000 at 1 January 20X8;
- Non-deductible golf club dues of $10,000;
- Taxable income in the three-year carryback period of $360,000; and
- Tax rate of 40% in the current and previous years.

Michelle Limited's taxable income for 20X8 will be computed as follows:

Accounting income	$ 90,000
Permanent difference:	
Golf club dues	+ 10,000
Temporary difference:	
Depreciation	+150,000
CCA	–280,000
Taxable income (loss)	$ (30,000)

Step 2: Determine Deferred Income Tax

The next step is to determine the change to deferred income tax caused by current-year temporary differences and/or any change in the tax rate. This is normally done with a table, such as Exhibit 16-3, but since the tax rate did not change this year, the shortcut approach can be used.

The difference between CCA and depreciation yields a temporary difference of ($130,000) (i.e., $150,000 – $280,000). This temporary difference increases the deferred income tax liability by $52,000 (i.e., $130,000 × 40%).

The $30,000 tax loss creates a potential tax benefit of $12,000 (at 40%).

Step 3: Journal Entries

The third step is to prepare the journal entries. These entries reflect temporary differences, income tax receivable, and the impact on income tax expense.

The $52,000 of deferred income tax arising from temporary differences is recorded as follows:

Income tax expense (I/S)	52,000	
Deferred income tax liability—capital assets (SFP)		52,000

The $30,000 tax loss is carried back, which results in a tax recovery (at 40%) of $12,000:

Income tax receivable—carryback benefit (SFP)	12,000	
Income tax expense (I/S)		12,000

If these two entries are combined, the summary entry to record the provision for income tax will be:

Income tax expense	40,000	
Income tax receivable—carryback benefit	12,000	
Deferred income tax liability—capital assets (SFP)		52,000

The bottom of the income statement will show:

Income before income tax		$90,000
Income tax expense (Note 1)		40,000
Net income		$50,000
Note 1:		
Deferred income tax	$52,000	
Recovery of amounts paid in prior years	(12,000)	
Income tax expense	$40,000	

Tax Planning—Adjusting Temporary Differences

In the Michelle Limited example above, the temporary difference created a tax loss of $30,000. Since the company had available taxable income in the carryback period against which the loss can be offset, good tax strategy calls for taking the maximum allowable CCA in 20X8 in order to obtain a refund of taxes previously paid.

Suppose instead that the company did not have taxable income in the preceding three years. A tax loss in 20X8 would not permit the company to realize any tax benefit in 20X8 because there would be no possibility of receiving a tax refund. In a sense, the tax loss would go to waste unless the company generates profits in the carryforward period, never a sure thing.

Instead of having a tax loss, the company can simply reduce the amount of CCA that it deducts on its tax return for 20X8 by $30,000, from $280,000 to $250,000. CCA is an *optional* deduction; in any year, a company can deduct anywhere from zero to the maximum percentage allowed by tax regulations. A company will have a higher amount of unclaimed capital cost (and CCA) in *future years* if it claims less CCA in the *current year.* Companies make these decisions based on advice from their tax-planning advisors.

CONCEPT REVIEW

1. How many years can a tax loss be carried back? How many years into the future can it be carried forward?
2. What is the difference between the tax loss in a particular year and the tax benefit of the loss?
3. Why do companies usually apply a loss carryback sequentially (i.e., to the earliest year first), even if the tax refund might be slightly larger if they applied it to the carryback year that had the highest tax rate?

TAX LOSS CARRYFORWARDS

In the Fabian Corporation example earlier in the chapter, the tax benefit of the $500,000 tax loss in 20X5 was fully realized through the carryback. But suppose instead that the loss in 20X5 was $1,000,000. Then the carryback could utilize only $700,000 of the loss:

Year	Carryback	Tax Rate	Tax Recovery
20X2	$240,000	40%	$ 96,000
20X3	160,000	35	56,000
20X4	300,000	37	111,000
Totals	$700,000		$263,000

The tax benefit ($263,000) relating to $700,000 of the $1 million tax loss is realized through the carryback; the tax benefit is both *recognized* and *realized* in 20X5. After the carryback, there is a carryforward of $300,000 remaining. The tax benefit of the loss carryforward cannot be realized until future years, when the carryforward is applied against otherwise taxable income.

The accounting question is whether the future tax benefit of the carryforward can be *recognized* in 20X5, the period of the loss. Companies often want to recognize the benefits of a loss carryforward because that recognition decreases the apparent accounting loss. The income tax recovery is a credit entry in the income statement, reducing the amount of the reported loss. Recognition will also either (1) reduce the deferred tax liability or (2) create an asset on the SFP if there is no future tax liability to offset it against.

Basic Probability Principle—"More Likely Than Not"

The criterion for recognizing the future benefits is simply a matter of probability. If it is probable that the carryforward will be realized, then the benefit is recognized. On the other hand, if realization is unlikely, or not probable, then the potential benefit should not be recognized.

Conceptually, it is simple: A 51% probability of realization requires recognition; 49% probability means no recognition. In practice, estimation is more difficult and requires the use of professional judgement.

In deciding whether the probability is greater than 50%, management may consider possible tax-planning strategies, including actions such as:

- Reducing or eliminating CCA in the year of the loss and future years;
- Amending prior years' tax returns to reduce or eliminate CCA; or
- Recognizing taxable revenues in the carryforward period that might ordinarily be recognized in later periods.

Whether or not the over 50% criterion has been met is obviously a matter of professional judgement. In theory, there should be objective evidence as to the likelihood of realization.

Evidence of Probability

IAS 12 provides some guidelines to help managers (and auditors) decide whether the probability threshold has been met. Favourable evidence to support recognition includes the following:

- Earnings history that indicates future taxable profits;
- Loss was the result of an unusual event not likely reoccur (e.g., long strike);
- Enough accumulated taxable temporary differences to absorb the unrealized loss as the temporary differences reverse; or
- The existence of tax-planning opportunities that will create taxable profit in the carryforward period.

Another factor that can contribute to a positive probability assessment is the existence of contracts or back orders that are likely to generate more than enough taxable income to absorb the loss carryforward.

On the other hand, the probability criterion will *not* be met if:

- The company has a history of tax losses expiring without being used;
- A change in the company's economic prospects indicates that losses may continue for the next few years; and
- There are pending circumstances that, if not resolved in the company's favour, will impair the company's ability to operate profitably (e.g., significant patent infringement lawsuits or potential major environmental impacts caused by the company's operations).

When a company's management decides that the probability criterion for recognition of any part of the benefit of a tax loss carryforward has been met, the "nature of evidence supporting its recognition" must be disclosed in the notes.

Reducing Capital Cost Allowance

Two tax-planning strategies by which a company can increase the likelihood of realizing the benefits of a carryforward are (1) reducing or eliminating capital cost allowance deductions in the current and future years and (2) amending prior years' tax returns to reduce or eliminate CCA.

Earlier in this chapter, we pointed out that a company can reduce its tax loss by reducing or eliminating CCA in a loss year. The lower the loss, the more likely that its tax benefits can be realized. The key to this strategy is that CCA not claimed is not lost. CCA is an *optional deduction* for tax purposes. It is limited to a maximum, but there is no minimum. If a company chooses not to claim CCA in a year, the unclaimed capital cost (UCC) remains unchanged—except for additions to and retirements from the class—and CCA on the undiminished balance remains available as a deduction in future years.

One way of increasing the likelihood that a company will fully utilize a carryforward is to eliminate CCA in the carryforward years. In capital-intensive industries, CCA is very large, both in absolute amount and in relation to net income. Not claiming CCA has the effect of increasing taxable income, against which the carryforward can be used. After the carryforward benefits have all been realized, the company can resume deducting full CCA to reduce its taxable income in the following years.

A further strategy is to *amend prior years' returns* to reduce or eliminate CCA. The relevant time frame is the three previous years, those to which carrybacks apply. If CCA is reduced in those years, taxable income increases. If taxable income increases, more of the carryback can be used. Indeed, it may be possible to reduce prior years' CCA enough to completely use up the tax loss as a carryback. The CCA that is removed from prior-year tax returns is restored to the balance of UCC and available for deduction in future years.

The *Income Tax Act* imposes various restrictions on the amendment of prior years' returns, and these need not concern us here. But "playing around" with CCA is a fully legitimate way of either reducing a tax loss or using it up in prior and subsequent years.

Reassessment in Years Subsequent to the Loss Year

Once the future tax benefit of a tax loss carryforward has been recognized as an asset, the asset is subject to review at each reporting date. If the probability of realization drops to 50% or less, the deferred income tax asset should be reduced. There is nothing unusual about this requirement; assets are generally subject to review and to writedown if their value has been impaired. If an asset is unlikely to recover its carrying value, either through use or through sale, it should be written down.

The potential benefit of a tax loss carryforward may be recognized not only in the year of the loss but also in years subsequent to the loss year. Management may decide that the 50% probability threshold is not attained in the year of the loss and therefore will not recognize the tax loss carryforward benefits. In any subsequent year (i.e., prior to actually realizing the benefits), management may decide that the probability of realization has increased to over 50%. When the probability is judged to have become greater than 50%, the future benefit of a prior year's tax loss carryforward should be recognized in that year. Previous years are not restated.

Examples of Recognition Scenarios—Direct Recognition

We can illustrate the various basic recognition points by means of a simple illustration. Suppose that Parravano Limited has been in business for five years and incurs a loss of $500,000 in 20X5. The company has no temporary or permanent differences, and therefore the pre-tax accounting loss is the same as the loss for income tax purposes. The history of the company's earnings since the company began operations is as follows:

Year	Taxable Income (Loss)	Taxes Paid (Recovered)
20X1	$100,000	$40,000
20X2	(60,000)	(24,000)
20X3	140,000	56,000
20X4	30,000	12,000

The tax rate has been constant at 40% from 20X1 through 20X5.

In 20X5, Parravano incurs a loss of $500,000. A further loss of $100,000 occurs in 20X6.

In 20X5, Parravano can carry back $170,000 of the loss to recover taxes paid in 20X3 and 20X4, a total of $68,000. A carryforward of $330,000 remains, the potential tax benefit of which is $132,000 ($330,000 × 40%). Recognition of the future benefits of the carryforward depends on management's conclusions regarding the likelihood of realizing the benefits. The following scenarios illustrate recognition of the benefits of tax loss carryforwards under various possible assumptions concerning the likelihood of realization. The entries under each scenario are summarized in the "Direct Recognition" columns of Exhibit 17-1.

Scenario 1: Assuming future realization is judged to be probable in each year of the losses. If the probability of realizing the future tax benefit of the carryforward is judged to be more than 50%, the potential $132,000 benefit of the $330,000 20X5 carryforward is recognized in the year of the loss. The entry to record taxes for 20X5 will be as follows, assuming a 40% tax rate:

Entry in loss year 20X5		
Income tax receivable—carryback benefit (SFP)	68,000	
Deferred income tax asset—carryforward benefit (SFP)[1]	132,000	
Income tax expense (recovery) (I/S)		200,000
[1]$330,000 × 40% = $132,000		

EXHIBIT 17-1

COMPARISON OF METHODS FOR RECORDING TAX LOSS CARRYFORWARD BENEFITS

Scenario	Year	Direct Recognition			Using Valuation Account		
1a. C/B + full recognition of 20X5 C/F benefit	**20X5**	IT rec.—C/B	68,000		IT rec.—C/B	68,000	
		DIT asset—C/F	132,000		DIT asset—C/F	132,000	
		IT exp. (recovery)		200,000	IT exp. (recovery)		200,000
1b. Full recognition of 20X6 C/F benefit	**20X6**	DIT asset—C/F	40,000		DIT asset—C/F	40,000	
		IT exp. (recovery)		40,000	IT exp. (recovery)		40,000
2a. C/B, but no recognition of C/F benefit	**20X5**	IT rec.—C/B	68,000		IT rec.—C/B	68,000	
		IT exp. (recovery)		68,000	DIT asset—C/F	132,000	
					IT exp. (recovery)		200,000
					IT exp. (recovery)	132,000	
					Val. allow.—DIT asset		132,000
2b. Recognize full 20X5 + 20X6 C/F benefit	**20X6**	DIT asset—C/F	172,000		DIT asset—C/F	40,000	
		IT exp. (recovery)		172,000	IT exp. (recovery)		40,000
					Val. allow.—DIT asset	132,000	
					IT exp. (recovery)		132,000
3a. C/B but no recognition of C/F benefit	**20X5**	IT rec.—C/B	68,000		IT rec.—C/B	68,000	
		IT exp. (recovery)		68,000	DIT asset—C/F	132,000	
					IT exp. (recovery)		200,000
					IT exp. (recovery)	132,000	
					Val. allow.—DIT asset		132,000
3b. Partial recognition of C/F benefit	**20X6**	DIT asset—C/F	80,000		DIT asset—C/F	40,000	
		IT exp. (recovery)		80,000	IT exp. (recovery)		40,000
					Val. allow.—DIT asset	40,000	
					IT exp. (recovery)		40,000
4a. Same as scenario 1, above —full recognition	**20X5**	IT rec.—C/B	68,000		IT rec.—C/B	68,000	
		DIT asset—C/F	132,000		DIT asset—C/F	132,000	
		IT exp. (recovery)		200,000	IT exp. (recovery)		200,000
4b. Only $200,000 of total C/F benefit is now deemed probable	**20X6**	IT expense	52,000		DIT asset—C/F	40,000	
		DIT asset—C/F		52,000	IT exp. (recovery)		40,000
					IT expense	92,000	
					Val. allow.—DIT asset		92,000

Legend: IT = income tax; DIT = deferred income tax; C/B = carryback; C/F = carryforward

The total income tax expense (recovery) account on the 20X5 income statement (i.e., $68,000 + $132,000 = $200,000) is equal to 40% of the tax loss for 20X5 ($500,000 × 40%). The full potential tax benefit of the loss has been *recognized*, although only $68,000 will be *realized* in the current year.

In 20X6, the $40,000 potential tax benefit of the $100,000 loss will also be recognized, if management believes that the loss carryforwards from both years are likely to be realized within the carryforward period:

Entry in loss year 20X6		
Deferred income tax asset—carryforward benefit (SFP)[1]	40,000	
Income tax expense (recovery) (I/S)		40,000
[1]$100,000 × 40% = $40,000		

Scenario 2: Assuming future realization is judged to be improbable in 20X5 but becomes probable in 20X6. Now, suppose instead that due to Parravano's erratic earnings history, realization of the benefit of the carryforward is judged to be unlikely. The entry to record the tax benefit in 20X5 would then be limited to the amount of tax recovered through the carryback:

Entry in loss year 20X5		
Income tax receivable—carryback benefit (SFP)	68,000	
Income tax expense (recovery) (I/S)		68,000

In the following year, 20X6, Parravano Limited has a loss for both accounting and tax purposes of $100,000. Since there is no available taxable income in the carryback period, the $100,000 tax loss will be carried forward. The loss is still available to reduce future taxable income. The difference here is that there is no deferred income tax asset. The company now has two carryforwards that have been neither realized nor recognized:

- $330,000 from 20X5, expiring in 20X25; and
- $100,000 from 20X6, expiring in 20X26.

The total carryforward is $430,000.

However, suppose that Parravano obtained a large contract late in 20X6. The 20X6 operating results do not yet reflect the profit that will be generated by the contract, but the contract is expected to boost earnings considerably in 20X7 and the next several years. Therefore, management decides when preparing the 20X6 financial statements that it is probable that the full benefit of tax loss carryforwards from both 20X5 and 20X6 will be realized within the carryforward period.

Assuming a continuing tax rate of 40%, the future tax benefit of the total $430,000 carryforward is $172,000. Since, in management's judgement, the probability criterion has now been satisfied, the future benefit is recorded as an asset:

Recognition in 20X6 of future benefits		
Deferred income tax asset—carryforward benefit (SFP)[1]	172,000	
Income tax expense (recovery) (I/S)		172,000
[1]$430,000 × 40% = $172,000		

When the future benefit of $172,000 is recognized in the income statement, the 20X6 pre-tax loss of $100,000 will be converted into a net *income* of $72,000 simply as the result of recognizing the still-unrealized tax loss carryforward benefit:

Net income (loss) before income tax	$(100,000)
Income tax expense (recovery)	(172,000)
Net income (loss)	$ 72,000

Scenario 3: Partial recognition. In Scenario 2, we assumed that Parravano recognized all of the accumulated tax benefits in 20X6. It is possible, however, that management may decide that realization of only part of the benefit is probable. Suppose, for example, that Parravano management decided in 20X6 that the benefits from only $200,000 of the accumulated tax loss carryforwards had a probability of greater than 50% of being realized. At a tax rate of 40%, the entry to record the recognition in 20X6 will be:

Recognition in 20X6 of future benefits		
Deferred income tax asset—carryforward benefit (SFP)[1]	80,000	
Income tax expense (recovery) (I/S)		80,000
[1]$200,000 × 40% = $80,000		

The benefits from the remaining $230,000 tax loss carryforward can be recognized in a later period (within the carryforward period), if the probability of realization becomes greater than 50%.

Scenario 4: Reduction of previously recognized benefit. Like any other asset, the deferred income tax asset that arises from recognizing the future benefit of a tax loss carryforward must continue to have probable future benefit. If an asset no longer is likely to be recoverable or realizable, it must be written down to its probable future benefit. If the probable future benefit is zero, the asset must be completely written off. If the probable future benefit is greater than zero but less than the originally recorded amount, the balance should be reduced accordingly.

For example, return to the Scenario 1 entry for 20X5, when Parravano recorded a $132,000 deferred income tax asset because of a loss carryforward in 20X5:

Income tax receivable—carryback benefit (SFP)	68,000	
Deferred income tax asset—carryforward benefit (SFP)	132,000	
Income tax expense (recovery) (I/S)		200,000

But suppose that in 20X6, Parravano experiences an additional loss of $100,000. The total tax loss carryforward is now $430,000: $330,000 from 20X5 plus $100,000 from 20X6. When preparing the 20X6 financial statements, Parravano's management decides that realization of the future benefit of only $200,000 of the tax loss carryforward is probable within the carryforward period. The deferred income tax asset of $132,000 must be reduced to the lower amount of probable recovery: $200,000 × 40% = $80,000. The entry to reduce the balance of the deferred income tax asset is $52,000, the amount necessary to reduce the balance from $132,000 to $80,000:

Income tax expense (I/S)	52,000	
Deferred income tax asset—carryforward benefit (SFP)		52,000

There is nothing final about the estimate of future recovery. The probability of realizing the benefit is evaluated at each reporting date until the carryforward expires. In future years within the carryforward period, Parravano may decide that the probability of realization of the full carryforward benefit has become probable. If that happens, then the deferred income tax asset can be increased to reflect the higher probable amount.

Impact of Recognition Assumption on Net Income

The only difference between these four scenarios is the estimated probability of realizing the loss carryforward benefits. The earnings impacts of these different scenarios are summarized in Exhibit 17-2. Depending on management's realization estimates, the after-tax net loss in 20X5 varies from $(300,000) to $(432,000). In 20X6, the bottom line varies from a loss of $(152,000) to a net income of $72,000. Indeed, the potential net loss in 20X6 could be as high as $(192,000) if all of the previously recognized carryforward benefits were deemed improbable of realization.

These scenarios demonstrate two points: (1) the importance of management's estimates of the probability of recognition, and (2) the potential range of earnings management that is

EXHIBIT 17-2

COMPARISON OF NET INCOME UNDER DIFFERENT RECOGNITION SCENARIOS

Scenario		20X5	20X6
1	Income (loss) before income taxes	$(500,000)	$(100,000)
	Income tax expense (recovery)	(200,000)	(40,000)
	Net income (loss)	$(300,000)	$ (60,000)
2	Income (loss) before income taxes	$(500,000)	$(100,000)
	Income tax expense (recovery)	(68,000)	(172,000)
	Net income (loss)	$(432,000)	$ 72,000
3	Income (loss) before income taxes	$(500,000)	$(100,000)
	Income tax expense (recovery)	(68,000)	(80,000)
	Net income (loss)	$(432,000)	$ (20,000)
4	Income (loss) before income taxes	$(500,000)	$(100,000)
	Income tax expense (recovery)	(200,000)	52,000
	Net income (loss)	$(300,000)	$(152,000)

possible under the probability criterion for recognition. Financial statement readers should be wary of income tax "recoveries" that are recognized but not realized. These recoveries may well be reversed in future years, with resulting impacts on reported net earnings. They also are subject to manipulation if management is tempted to "manage" reported earnings—this is a potential ethical issue that professional accountants must be sensitive to.

USING A VALUATION ALLOWANCE

In the example above, we increased or decreased the balance of the deferred income tax asset directly. An alternative approach is to record the full amount of the potential future benefit and then use a **valuation allowance** to adjust for the probability of realization. The entries, using a valuation allowance, are summarized in the final columns of Exhibit 17-1.

As an analogy, think of accounts receivable. The full amount of accounts receivable is always recorded in the accounts, and then an allowance for doubtful accounts is used to reduce the balance to its estimated realizable value. The same principle can be applied to potential tax benefits of tax loss carryforwards. Return to the Parravano example. In every scenario, the full amount of the future tax benefit is recorded in 20X5, the loss year:

Deferred income tax asset—carryforward benefit[1]	132,000	
Income tax expense (recovery)		132,000
[1]$330,000 × 40%		

A valuation account is then considered, depending on the amount of recovery that is *probable.*

Scenario 1: Full recovery is probable. No valuation allowance is needed in this situation because management estimates that the company probably can realize the full benefit of the tax loss carryforward.

Scenario 2: Recovery is improbable at first, becoming probable in a later year. The full amount of the future benefit is recorded, as shown in the entry above. However, in 20X5, management believes that the probability of recovery is less than 50%. None of the future benefit should appear on the 20X5 SFP. An allowance for the full amount is required:

Income tax expense (recovery)	132,000	
Valuation allowance—deferred income tax (DIT) asset		132,000

When the company prepares a statement of financial position for 20X5, the valuation allowance will completely offset the DIT asset, and none of the asset will appear on the statement of financial position.

In 20X6, none of the 20X5 loss carryforward is used, and the company has an additional loss carryforward of $100,000. The full future benefit of the 20X6 loss is recorded (at 40%):

Deferred income tax asset—carryforward benefit	40,000	
Income tax expense (recovery)		40,000

The deferred income tax asset and its related valuation account now appear as follows:

Deferred income tax benefit relating to 20X5	$132,000
Deferred income tax benefit relating to 20X6	40,000
Total potential future benefits	172,000
Less: Valuation allowance	(132,000)
Balance prior to year-end 20X6 adjustment	$ 40,000

At the end of 20X6, management decides that full realization of the benefits now is probable. Therefore, the valuation allowance is reduced to zero in order to permit the full future value of the asset (i.e., $172,000) to appear on the 20X6 statement of financial position:

Valuation allowance—DIT asset	132,000	
Income tax expense (recovery)		132,000

Scenario 3: Partial recognition. In 20X5, a potential future tax benefit of $132,000 is recorded, which then is completely offset by a valuation account for $132,000:

Income tax receivable—tax loss carryback	68,000	
Deferred income tax asset—carryforward benefit	132,000	
Income tax expense (recovery)		200,000

Income tax expense (recovery)	132,000	
Valuation allowance—deferred income tax (DIT) asset		132,000

In 20X6, an additional $40,000 tax benefit is recorded for the 20X6 loss carryforward of $100,000:

Deferred income tax asset—carryforward benefit	40,000	
Income tax expense (recovery)		40,000

After this additional entry, there is a debit of $172,000 in the DIT asset account and $132,000 in the valuation allowance—a *net* balance of $40,000. Management decides that $200,000 of the carryforward is likely to be utilized. Therefore, the valuation account must be *reduced* by $40,000 to show the probable recovery of $80,000 as the net balance. The adjustment is:

Valuation allowance—DIT asset	40,000	
Income tax expense (recovery)		40,000

Only the net amount of $80,000 will be reported on the 20X6 statement of financial position:

Deferred income tax asset—carryforward benefit	$172,000
Valuation allowance—DIT asset	(92,000)
Balance reported on 31 December 20X6 statement of financial position	$ 80,000

Scenario 4: Reduction of previously recognized benefit. In this scenario, the benefit is fully recognized (at $132,000) in the year of the loss, 20X5. No valuation allowance is created because management feels that realization of the benefits is likely.

In 20X6, the company has another loss of $100,000. The potential future benefit of this loss is recognized:

Deferred income tax asset—carryforward benefit	40,000	
Income tax expense (recovery)		40,000

The gross accumulated tax loss carryforward is now $430,000 (i.e., $330,000 + $100,000) and the total recorded deferred income tax asset is $172,000 (i.e., $132,000 + $40,000).

At this point, management decides that the company probably will realize the benefits of only $200,000 of the total carryforward. The benefit is $200,000 × 40% = $80,000. Therefore, the valuation allowance is credited for $92,000 to bring the reported DIT asset balance down from $172,000 to the estimated probable realizable value of $80,000:

Income tax expense	92,000	
Valuation allowance—DIT asset		92,000

Write-off of Expired Carryforward Benefits When a company reaches the end of the carryforward period for any tax loss, any remaining DIT asset balance must be written off. When an allowance account is used, the expired portion of both the DIT asset and the valuation account must be written off.

For example, suppose that Parravano has not been able to utilize any of the tax loss carryforwards from 20X5 and 20X6. Assume that in recognition of this fact, the company had already credited the valuation account for the full amount of the benefits relating to those two years, $172,000. The carryforward period for the 20X5 loss ends 20 years later, in 20X25. At the end of 20X25, the 20X5 potential benefit of $132,000 must be eliminated:

Valuation allowance—DIT asset	132,000	
Deferred income tax asset—carryforward benefit		132,000

Both accounts will still contain the $40,000 balance relating to 20X6, but that amount will have to be eliminated in the following year (20X26) when the carryforward period for the 20X6 loss expires assuming that the losses are not realized.

Use of the Valuation Allowance Method The valuation allowance method may seem more cumbersome than simply recognizing or not recognizing the deferred income tax asset represented by a tax loss carryforward. However, many companies prefer the valuation allowance method because it keeps track of the full tax loss carryforward benefits. They are comfortable with the valuation allowance method because it is consistent with the approach used for other financial statement elements, such as accounts receivable and inventory net realizable amount valuations.

Of course, one reason for its popularity is that U.S. standards *require* use of the valuation allowance method. Therefore, any Canadian companies that report in the United States necessarily will use a valuation allowance.

Bear in mind that a valuation allowance is simply a bookkeeping convenience. Using a valuation method is *not a choice of accounting policy* because it has no effect on the numbers reported in the financial statements. The amount of future tax benefit that is reported on the SFP and in profit or loss will not be affected by the bookkeeping method the company chooses.

WHICH TAX RATE?

IFRS requires deferred tax assets and liabilities to be recognized at the rate(s) that are expected to be in effect when the temporary differences reverse or the tax loss carryforward benefits are realized. In most instances, that will be the rate that is enacted at the reporting date. However, if Parliament has approved a rate change that will take effect in one or more future years, the future benefits of tax loss carryforwards should be measured at the substantially enacted rates for those future years in which the benefits are expected to be realized. Given the difficulty of estimating exactly which year the benefits will be realized, companies may need to make adjustments to the recorded DIT asset for the carryforwards.

Tax Rate Changes

Once a deferred income tax asset has been recorded for a tax loss carryforward, the balance of that account must be maintained at the tax rate that is expected to be in effect when the carryforward is utilized. As noted above, the usual presumption is that the **substantially enacted tax rate** will be used.

In Scenario 1, above, Parravano recorded the full amount of the tax benefit from its $330,000 accumulated tax loss carryforwards in 19X5. Parravano will have a deferred income tax asset of $132,000 on its statement of financial position, recorded at a 40% tax rate.

Suppose that the tax rate goes down to 38% before Parravano actually uses any of the carryforward. The asset will have to be revalued to $330,000 × 38%, or $125,400. This change will be included as part of the annual re-evaluation of the DIT asset or liability. If the carryforward benefit is the only component of Parravano's DIT asset, the writedown would be recorded as follows:

Income tax expense ($132,000 – $125,400) (I/S)	6,600	
Deferred income tax asset—carryforward benefit (SFP)		6,600

If, instead, the tax rate goes up, the increase in the asset account will be *credited* to income tax expense.

CONCEPT REVIEW

1. What is the basic criterion for recognizing the benefit of a tax loss carryforward prior to its realization?
2. What tax rate should be used to recognize the future benefits of a tax loss carryforward?
3. Is it possible to recognize the future benefits of tax loss carryforwards in years subsequent to the loss year? If so, explain the necessary circumstances. If not, explain why not.
4. Once the future benefit of a tax loss carryforward has been recognized, does the asset always remain on the statement of financial position until the benefit has been realized?

BASIC ILLUSTRATION

To illustrate the recognition of tax loss carryforward benefits over a series of years, we will start with a fairly simple example that has no other types of temporary differences. To keep things interesting, however, we will include tax rate changes.

Assume the following information for Dutoit Limited:

	20X1	20X2	20X3	20X4
Net income before tax	$100,000	$(300,000)	$150,000	$250,000
Taxable income*	100,000	(300,000)	150,000	250,000
Tax rate	45%	40%	42%	43%

*Prior to including any tax loss carrybacks or carryforwards.

The first year of operations for Dutoit was 20X1. Assume that the tax rate for each year is determined during that year. For example, we do not know in 20X2 that the tax rate for 20X3 will be 42%. Dutoit does not use a valuation allowance.

Assuming Realization Is Not Probable

We will first assume that at no point does management believe that there is greater than a 50% probability that the company will be able to realize the benefits of any unused tax loss carryforward. This is a pessimistic assumption, of course, but in an uncertain environment, management may really not know if the company will have a profitable year until it is well underway.

20X1 The income tax is simply the taxable income times the tax rate:

Income tax expense ($100,000 × 45%)	45,000	
Income tax payable		45,000

20X2 $100,000 of the loss can be carried back to 20X1, to recover the prior year's taxes paid:

Income tax receivable—carryback benefit	45,000	
Income tax expense (recovery)		45,000

There is an unrecognized tax loss carryforward of $200,000.

20X3 Taxable income prior to deducting the tax loss carryforward is $150,000. The tax loss carryforward of $200,000 more than offsets the otherwise-taxable income for 20X3. No taxes will be due, and no income tax expense will be recorded or reported. There is a tax loss of $50,000 still unused.

For the sake of clarity, two entries can be made in a year where a loss carryforward is used. The first entry records income tax as though there were no loss carryforward:

Income tax expense ($150,000 × 42%)	63,000	
Income tax payable		63,000

Of course, the income tax payable does not have to be paid, so the second entry eliminates it, recording the use of the loss carryforward:

Income tax payable	63,000	
Income tax expense (recovery)		63,000

The company should show the offsetting effects of the two opposite income tax expenses on 20X3 earnings. The disclosure could be either on the face of the income statement or in the notes. If income statement presentation is used:

Net income		$150,000
Income tax expense (recovery):		
Income tax on current year's earnings	$63,000	
Tax reduction from tax loss carryforward	(63,000)	—
Net income		$150,000

20X4 There is $250,000 of taxable income, on which $250,000 × 43%, or $107,500, of tax would be payable. The remaining $50,000 carryforward is used, reducing the taxes otherwise due by $50,000 × 43%, or $21,500. The net amount owing is $86,000:

Income tax expense	107,500	
Income tax payable		107,500
Income tax payable	21,500	
Income tax expense (recovery)		21,500

The breakdown of income tax expense may be included in the notes or in the income statement. The income statement will show:

Income before income tax		$250,000
Income tax expense (recovery)		
Tax on current earnings	$107,500	
Recovered through loss carryforward	(21,500)	86,000
Net income		$164,000

Note that in each year, the carryforward is applied against taxable income in that year at the current rate. *The tax rate in the year of the loss is irrelevant.*

Assuming Realization Becomes Probable

Now, let us re-examine the situation assuming instead that in 20X3, Dutoit's management judges that it is probable that the benefits of the remaining carryforward will be realized.

The entries in 20X1 and 20X2 will not change. In 20X3, however, $150,000 of the carryforward is used to reduce 20X3 taxable income to zero. The remaining $50,000 carryforward is also recognized. The benefit of the full $200,000 carryforward is *recognized*, even though the benefit of only $150,000 is *realized* in that year by applying it against the taxable income in that year. The entries for 20X3 now are:

Income tax expense	63,000	
Income tax payable (unchanged)		63,000
Deferred income tax asset—carryforward benefit ($50,000 × 42%)	21,000	
Income tax payable	63,000	
Income tax expense (recovery)		84,000

The full benefit of the $200,000 carryforward has been *recognized* in 20X3. Income tax expense is a net credit on the income statement of $21,000, the unrealized portion of the carryforward.

Income before income tax		$150,000
Income tax expense (recovery):		
Income tax on current earnings	$63,000	
Recovery from tax loss carryforward ($200,000 × 42%)	(84,000)	(21,000)
Net income		$171,000

The income statement may simply show the $21,000 net recovery, but the detail should be disclosed in the notes.

In 20X4, the remaining $50,000 of tax loss carryforward is used, but it has already been *recognized*. The result, therefore, is that the balance of the deferred income tax (DIT) asset goes from $21,000 at the beginning of 20X4 to zero at the end of the year. The entries are:

Income tax expense	107,500	
Income tax payable ($250,000 × 43%)		107,500
Income tax payable ($50,000 × 43%)	21,500	
Deferred income tax asset—carryforward benefit		21,000
Income tax expense (recovery)		500

In the entry above, the credit to the DIT asset is the amount recorded. The change in the tax rate has made the loss carryforward worth an extra $500 ($50,000 × 1% = $500), which is credited to income tax expense.

EXTENDED ILLUSTRATION

In this illustration of accounting for the tax benefits of tax losses, we will assume that (1) the company has one type of temporary difference relating to property, plant, and equipment; (2) a loss arises in the second year; and (3) the income tax rate changes in the third and fourth years. The facts for Birchall Incorporated are as follows:

- In 20X1, Birchall begins operations and acquires equipment costing $1 million.
- The equipment is being depreciated straight line at 10% (i.e., at $100,000 per year), and the company's policy is to expense a full year's depreciation in the year of acquisition.

- Birchall claims CCA of $350,000 in 20X1, $200,000 in 20X2, $150,000 in 20X3, and $100,000 in 20X4.
- The tax rate is 40% in 20X1 and 20X2. During 20X3, Parliament increases the tax rate to 42%, applicable to 20X3 and following years, and, in 20X4, the rate is changed to 43%.
- Birchall's earnings before income tax for 20X1 through 20X4 are as follows:

20X1	$ 300,000
20X2	$(600,000) (loss)
20X3	$ 200,000
20X4	$ 600,000

The first step is to calculate taxable income, shown in Exhibit 17-3. In 20X1, taxable income is $50,000. At 40%, the current tax payable is $20,000.

Next, the change in deferred income tax is calculated. This is done in table format, as shown in Exhibit 17-4. The initial cost of the equipment was $1,000,000. In 20X1, Birchall deducts CCA of $350,000 on its tax return and depreciation of $100,000 on its income statement. As a result, the *tax basis* of the equipment at the end of 20X1 is $650,000 (i.e., $1,000,000 – $350,000) while the accounting carrying value is $900,000; a temporary difference of $250,000 exists. At the 40% enacted tax rate, the deferred income tax (DIT) liability for the equipment is $100,000. Combining these two elements gives Birchall's 20X1 income tax expense of $120,000:

Income tax expense	120,000	
Income tax payable		20,000
Deferred income tax liability—equipment		100,000

In 20X2, Birchall has a loss. The accounting loss (pre-tax) is $600,000, but the loss for tax purposes is $700,000 after adding back depreciation and deducting CCA (see Exhibit 17-3). Of the tax loss, $50,000 can be carried back to 20X1 to claim a refund of the $20,000 paid in that year. The remaining $650,000 of the tax loss will be carried forward.

At the end of 20X2, the tax basis of the equipment declines to $450,000 (after the 20X2 CCA of $200,000), while the carrying value declines to $800,000 (after deducting another $100,000 of depreciation). The temporary difference relating to the equipment therefore is

EXHIBIT 17-3

EXTENDED ILLUSTRATION—CALCULATION OF TAXABLE INCOME, INCOME TAX PAYABLE, AND DEFERRED INCOME TAX

	20X1	20X2	20X3	20X4
Tax Rate (t)	**40%**	**40%**	**42%**	**43%**
Accounting income (loss) subject to tax	$300,000	$(600,000)	$200,000	$600,000
Temporary difference:				
+ Depreciation	100,000	100,000	100,000	100,000
– CCA	(350,000)	(200,000)	(150,000)	(100,000)
Taxable income (loss) for current year	$ 50,000	$(700,000)	$150,000	$600,000
Income tax payable (before using the loss carryforward)	$ 20,000		$ 63,000	$258,000

EXHIBIT 17-4

EXTENDED ILLUSTRATION—DEFERRED INCOME TAX TABLE

	[1] Year-End Tax Basis dr. (cr.)	[2] Year-End Carrying Value dr. (cr.)	[3] = [1] – [2] Temporary Difference Deductible (Taxable)	[4] = [3] ×t Deferred Tax Asset (Liability) at Yr.-End Rate	[5] = prev.[4] Less Beginning Balance dr. (cr.)	[6] = [4] – [5] Adjustment for Current Year dr. (cr.)
20X1 *[t = 40%]:*						
Equipment	$650,000	$900,000	(250,000)	$(100,000)	0	$(100,000)
20X2 *[t = 40%]:*						
Equipment	450,000	800,000	(350,000)	(140,000)	$(100,000)	(40,000)
20X3 *[t = 42%]:*						
Equipment	300,000	700,000	(400,000)	(168,000)	(140,000)	(28,000)
20X4 *[t = 43%]:*						
Equipment	200,000	600,000	(400,000)	(172,000)	(168,000)	(4,000)

$350,000, resulting in a DIT liability of $140,000 at the end of 20X2. The year-end DIT liability adjustment is an increase of $40,000 over the previous year.

The 20X2 components related to the income taxes can be summarized as follows:

- Tax loss is $700,000, of which $50,000 is carried back and $650,000 is carried forward.
- DIT liability relating to equipment increases by $40,000.
- Birchall has a receivable for tax recovery (carryback) of $20,000.

From this point on, we must make assumptions about the probability of realizing the benefits of the $650,000 carryforward.

Situation 1: Assuming Probability of Realization is ≤50%

20X2

If realization is *not* probable, the components already identified above are recorded as follows for 20X2:

Income tax expense	20,000	
Income tax receivable—carryback benefit	20,000	
Deferred income tax liability—equipment		40,000

Exhibit 17-5 shows the journal entries to record income tax expense for 20X1 to 20X4.

20X3

In 20X3, taxable income is $150,000, as is shown in the third numeric column of Exhibit 17-3. This permits Birchall to use some of the tax loss carryforward to offset the otherwise taxable income. The entries to record income tax expense can be condensed into a single entry, but it may be more helpful to present them as two separate entries so we can see what is going on:

1. Without the carryforward, the income tax expense for 20X3 would be the tax payable on taxable income of $150,000 plus the change in the DIT liability. The tax basis of the equipment is $300,000, and the carrying value is $700,000, which yields a temporary difference of $400,000. The tax rate is changed to 42% in 20X3, which means that the ending balance

EXHIBIT 17-5

EXTENDED ILLUSTRATION—SITUATION 1 CARRYFORWARD

Realization Probability ≤50%
Income Tax Journal Entries

Income tax journal entry, 20X1		
Income tax expense	120,000	
Deferred income tax liability—equipment		100,000
Income tax payable		20,000
Income tax journal entry, 20X2		
Income tax expense	20,000	
Income taxes receivable—carryback benefit	20,000	
Deferred income tax liability—equipment		40,000
Income tax journal entries, 20X3		
Income tax expense	91,000	
Deferred income tax liability—equipment		28,000
Income tax payable ($150,000 × 0.42)		63,000
Income tax payable	63,000	
Income tax expense—carryforward benefit		63,000
Income tax journal entries, 20X4		
Income tax expense	262,000	
Deferred income tax liability—equipment		4,000
Income tax payable ($600,000 × 0.43)		258,000
Income tax payable	215,000	
Income tax expense—carryforward benefit ($500,000 × 43%)		215,000

of the DIT liability should be $168,000 (i.e., $400,000 × 42%). The entry to record the income tax expense *without* the carryforward is:

Income tax expense	91,000	
Deferred income tax liability—equipment ($168,000 – $140,000)		28,000
Income tax payable ($150,000 × 42%)		63,000

2. Applying $150,000 of the carryforward against the taxable income eliminates the amount of tax payable and reduces income tax expense:

Income tax payable ($150,000 × 42%)	63,000	
Income tax expense—carryforward benefit		63,000

The result for 20X3 is that net income tax expense of only $28,000 is recognized. At the end of 20X3, Birchall has an unused gross tax loss carryforward of $500,000:

20X2 tax loss	$700,000
Carryback to 20X1	– 50,000
Carryforward used in 20X3	–150,000
Remaining carryforward at end of 20X3	$500,000

20X4

For 20X4, taxable income is $600,000. In this year, CCA is equal to depreciation, and therefore there is no change in the amount of temporary difference relating to the equipment. However, there is a change in the tax rate, from 42% to 43%, and there is a change in the DIT liability. The DIT liability is $400,000 × 43% = $172,000, an increase of $4,000 over the 20X3 year-end DIT liability. The $500,000 loss carryforward is used to reduce income tax payable. The entries to record income tax expense are:

Income tax expense	262,000	
Income tax payable ($600,000 × 43%)		258,000
Deferred income tax liability—equipment		4,000
Income tax payable	215,000	
Income tax expense—carryforward benefit ($500,000 × 43%)		215,000

As the result of these three entries, the net income tax expense reported on the income statement is $47,000: ($262,000 – $215,000). The series of entries for this scenario is summarized in Exhibit 17-5.

Situation 2: Assuming Probability of Realization is >50%

20X1

No change from the prior example. See Exhibit 17-6 for a summary of the entries for this situation.

20X2

If realization is probable, then a tax asset will be recognized for the carryforward. In 20X2, the future benefit of the carryforward of $650,000 is recognized at the then-enacted rate of 40%. The income tax entry is:

Income tax receivable—carryback benefit	20,000	
Deferred income tax asset—carryforward benefit ($650,000 × 40%)	260,000	
Deferred income tax liability—equipment		40,000
Income tax expense (recovery)		240,000

This entry reflects that three things are going on:

1. Recognition of carryback benefits of $20,000 (debit);
2. Recognition of the future benefits of the carryforward of $260,000 (debit); and
3. Change in the temporary difference for equipment of $40,000 (credit).

The balancing amount is the income tax recovery for 20X2 that will be shown on the income statement.

The loss carryforward can be included in the deferred income tax table, as shown in Exhibit 17-6. Refer to 20X2. The loss carryforward is included as a positive number in column 3; the first two columns are left blank. Each year the *remaining* gross tax loss carryforward is entered in column 3 and the rest of the table is completed as usual. Equipment data is included in Exhibit 17-6 for the sake of completeness. Note that column 4 shows the SFP position at year-end. The statement of financial position at the end of 20X2 will show a single amount, a noncurrent deferred income tax *asset* of $120,000:

DIT asset—carryforward benefit	$260,000
DIT liability—equipment	(140,000)
DIT asset (non-current, net)	$120,000

EXHIBIT 17-6

EXTENDED ILLUSTRATION—SITUATION 2 CARRYFORWARD

Realization Probability >50%

Deferred Income Tax Table:

	Year-End Tax Basis dr. (cr.)	Year-End Carrying Value dr. (cr.)	Temporary Difference Deductible (Taxable)	Deferred Tax Asset (Liability) at Yr.-End Rate	Less Beginning Balance dr. (cr.)	Adjustment for Current Year dr. (cr.)
20X1 *[t = 40%]:*						
Equipment	$650,000	$900,000	(250,000)	$(100,000)	0	$(100,000)
20X2 *[t = 40%]:*						
Equipment	450,000	800,000	(350,000)	(140,000)	$(100,000)	(40,000)
Carryforward benefit	n/a	n/a	650,000	260,000	0	260,000
				120,000		
20X3 *[t = 42%]:*						
Equipment	300,000	700,000	(400,000)	(168,000)	(140,000)	(28,000)
Carryforward benefit	n/a	n/a	500,000	210,000	260,000	(50,000)
				42,000		
20X4 *[t = 43%]:*						
Equipment	200,000	600,000	(400,000)	(172,000)	(168,000)	(4,000)
Carryforward benefit	n/a	n/a	0	0	210,000	(210,000)
				(172,000)		

Income Tax Entries:

20X1

Income tax expense	120,000	
Deferred income tax liability—equipment		100,000
Income tax payable		20,000

20X2

Deferred income tax asset—carryforward benefit	260,000	
Income tax receivable—carryback benefit	20,000	
Deferred income tax liability—equipment		40,000
Income tax expense (recovery)		240,000

20X3

Income tax expense	91,000	
Deferred income tax liability—equipment		28,000
Income tax payable		63,000
Income tax payable ($150,000 × 42%)	63,000	
Deferred income tax asset—carryforward benefit		50,000
Income tax expense (recovery) [$650,000 × (42% – 40%)]		13,000

20X4

Income tax expense	262,000	
Deferred income tax liability—equipment		4,000
Income tax payable ($600,000 × 43%)		258,000
Income tax payable ($500,000 × 43%)	215,000	
Deferred tax asset—carryforward benefit		210,000
Tax expense (recovery) [$500,000 × (43% – 42%)]		5,000

20X3

In 20X3, there is initial taxable income of $150,000, after adjusting accounting income for the additional $50,000 temporary difference relating to equipment but before applying the tax loss carryforward. There is a net change in the DIT—equipment of $28,000 (see Exhibit 17-6). Applying $150,000 of the tax loss carryforward against the $150,000 taxable income reduces the tax loss carryforward to $500,000 (column 3) and the recorded amount to $210,000 (column 4). This is an adjustment of $50,000 (column 6). Again, we will record the results as two separate entries—the first as though there were no loss carryforward and the second recording loss usage.

20X3		
Income tax expense	91,000	
Income tax payable		63,000
Deferred income tax liability— equipment		28,000
Income tax payable ($150,000 × 42%)	63,000	
Income tax expense (recovery) [$650,000 × (42% – 40%)]		13,000
Deferred income tax asset—carryforward benefit		50,000

The second entry reflects the impact of the change in tax rates on the opening loss carryforward. Use of $150,000 of the loss carryforward clearly eliminates $63,000 of tax payable. This is the debit. The table tells us to credit the loss carryforward DIT asset by $50,000, to arrive at the correct closing balance. To make the journal entry balance, a further $13,000 credit to tax expense is needed. This amount can be proven as the change in the tax rate (2%, or 42% – 40%) multiplied by the *opening* tax loss of $650,000. In other words, the tax loss carryforward is more valuable because the tax rate increased, and tax expense is credited to reflect this.

20X4

In 20X4, there is taxable income of $600,000, tax payable (before any loss carryforward is used) of $258,000, and an increase in the DIT—equipment account of $4,000, as is shown in Exhibit 17-6. The entire remaining tax loss carryforward of $500,000 is used. Therefore, the entries to record income tax expense for 20X4 are:

Income tax expense	262,000	
Income tax payable ($600,000 × 43%)		258,000
Deferred income tax liability—equipment		4,000
Income tax payable ($500,000 × 43%)	215,000	
Tax expense (recovery) [$500,000 × (43% – 42%)]		5,000
Deferred tax asset—carryforward benefit		210,000

The DIT table shows no remaining loss carryforward at the end of 20X4, and this account must be reduced by $210,000 to zero. Again, the increase in tax rate has caused an adjustment to tax expense because of the higher value of the opening tax less carryforward. This is the $5,000 remaining credit.

On the statement of financial position at the end of 20X4, only the DIT—equipment remains, at a credit balance of $172,000: $400,000 accumulated temporary differences at a tax rate of 43%.

Comparison of Results The earnings impact of the above scenarios is summarized in the partial income statements shown in Exhibit 17-7. When the probability of realization is less than or equal to 50%, matching is not achieved. The income tax expense in each year has no

EXHIBIT 17-7

COMPARISON OF RESULTS
IMPROBABLE VERSUS PROBABLE REALIZATION OF TAX LOSS CARRYFORWARD BENEFITS

Probability ≤50% (see Exhibit 17-5):	**20X1**	**20X2**	**20X3**	**20X4**
Earnings (loss) before income tax	$300,000	$(600,000)	$200,000	$600,000
Less: Income tax expense (recovery)	120,000	(20,000)	28,000	47,000
Net income (loss)	$180,000	$(580,000)	$172,000	$553,000
Probability >50% (see Exhibit 17-6):				
Earnings before income tax	$300,000	$(600,000)	$200,000	$600,000
Less: Income tax expense (recovery)	120,000	(240,000)	78,000	257,000
Net income (loss)	$180,000	$(360,000)	$122,000	$343,000

relationship to the pre-tax earnings, except in the first year. Instead of matching, the adjustments are driven by the need to show an asset when the probability of realization is greater than 50%.

When the initial probability of realization is greater than 50%, however, the full benefits of the tax loss are recognized in the year of the loss, thereby matching the benefits in the year that the loss arose. Of course, it may seem a little odd to be talking about the "benefits" of a loss. A loss itself is not beneficial, but at least it can have some favourable consequences if the company is able to utilize the tax loss carryforward to reduce taxes payable.

Reporting Objectives

We have already pointed out that the matching doctrine is well served if the benefit of a loss carryforward is reported in the loss year. For example, assume that a company had an accounting and taxable loss of $100,000 in 20X2 and then accounting and taxable income of $100,000 in 20X3. The tax rate is 40%. It seems appropriate reporting to show both years net of $40,000 tax and report an after-tax net loss of $60,000 in 20X2 and an after-tax net income of $60,000 in 20X3. It is understood that the $40,000 benefit of the loss carryforward can be recorded in 20X2 before it is realized in 20X3 as long as realization is probable.

However, what if realization is not probable? In this case, the 20X2 net loss would be reported as $100,000, and the benefit of the loss carryforward would be recorded in 20X3. This would result in net tax expense of zero in 20X3, and reported net income would be $100,000. While the $100,000 loss is greater in 20X2 than the after-tax $60,000 alternative, the $100,000 20X3 reported results are greater as well. Management may prefer the "bounce" and be prepared to take a "big bath" in 20X2.

The swing caused by recognition may be even more pronounced. For example, assume that the $100,000 loss in 20X2 is followed by two years of breakeven results. If the probability of loss carryforward use shifts to "probable" in one of these years, $40,000 of net income will be reported, reflecting recognition of the loss carryforward deferred income tax asset. In this case, a positive trend in earnings can be manufactured by reassessment of probability. Alternatively, two or three years of loss carryforward may be recognized in one particular year, increasing results materially.

The reporting decision is based on the probability of realization. Probability is assessed by management, with the decision reviewed by external auditors. Accounting standards provide some guidance for evaluating probability, but auditors must proceed with great caution, given the magnitude of tax expense.

DISCLOSURE

Income tax expense relating to continuing operations should be shown on the face of the income statement. The amount of income tax expense may include benefits from either carrybacks or carryforwards, but there is not a requirement that those benefits be disclosed on the face of the income statement. Information on tax losses is confined to the disclosure notes and generally focused on *unrecognized* tax loss carryforwards rather than on amounts *realized* during the period. Disclosure is recommended for:

- The amount of benefit arising from a *previously unrecognized* tax loss that is used to either:
  1. Reduce current income tax expense by using the carryforward in the current period *if* it had not been recognized as a deferred tax asset in prior periods; or
  2. Reduce current deferred tax expense, such as by reducing CCA in prior periods and thereby reducing the amount of temporary differences relating to property, plant, and equipment (as well as the remaining tax loss carryforward).
- The amount of deferred tax expense arising from the writedown or reversal of a previous writedown of deferred tax assets.
- The amount and expiry date of *unused* tax losses for which no deferred tax asset has been recognized in the SFP.

Companies usually do disclose the amounts of tax loss carrybacks and carryforwards that were used during the year, whether or not they had been previously recognized as a deferred tax asset.

The problem with most disclosures is that it is very difficult, and often impossible, for a reader to figure out whether an income tax recovery has been *realized* or merely *recognized*. Recourse to the notes, to the effective tax rate disclosure, and to the statement of cash flows may provide clues, but often the information relating to income tax assets and liabilities is so summarized that it is impossible to figure out the details.

Disclosure Example

In Exhibits 16-5 to 16-7, we examined portions of Bombardier Inc. note disclosure for income taxes. In exhibit 17-8 we look a little further. In Exhibit 16-5, we see that Bombardier recognized tax losses of $1.502 million as an asset. Note that Bombardier Inc. has not recognized $7.825 million of their tax losses as an asset in 2011. This means the "probable" provision was not met for these losses.

EVALUATION OF FUTURE BENEFIT ACCOUNTING

The supporters of early recognition believe that, conceptually, future tax benefits should be matched to the loss that gave rise to those benefits. They argue that if benefits are recognized only when realized, net income in those future periods will be distorted.

However, many observers are troubled by the recognition of tax loss carryforward benefits before their realization. The principal concern is that future tax assets do not satisfy the basic definition of an asset. There has been no transaction that establishes the corporation's right to receive the future benefit; realization of the benefits is contingent on generating sufficient taxable income in the future. And, clearly, the government does not consider that it owes any money to the company.

The recognition of unrealized tax assets for tax loss carryforwards has the effect of reducing the apparent accounting loss. The effect of an operating loss is softened by this practice and gives financial statement users the perception that the loss is not as bad as it really is, even though the benefit of a carryforward has not been realized and there may be no more than a marginal probability (i.e., 51%) that the benefit will ever be realized.

EXHIBIT 17-8

BOMBARDIER INCORPORATED—DISCLOSURE OF OPERATING LOSSES

The net operating losses carried forward and deductible temporary differences for which deferred tax assets have not been recognized amounted to $7,825 million as at December 31, 2011 of which $2,208 million relates to retirement benefits that will reverse through OCI ($6,698 million as at January 31, 2011 of which $1,518 million relates to retirement benefits that will reverse through OCI and $6,400 million as at February 1, 2010 of which $1,607 million relates to retirement benefits that will reverse through OCI). Of these amounts, approximately $7,792 million as at December 31, 2011 have no expiration date ($6,670 million as at January 31, 2011 and $6,383 million as at February 1, 2010) and approximately $964 million relate to the Corporation's operations in Germany where a minimum income tax is payable on 40% of taxable income ($1,167 million as at January 31, 2011 and $1,160 million as at February 1, 2010).

In addition, the Corporation has $206 million of unused investment tax credits, most of which can be carried forward for 20 years and $48 million of net capital losses carried forward for which deferred tax assets have not been recognized ($128 million and $66 million as at January 31, 2011). Net capital losses can be carried forward indefinitely and can only be used against future taxable capital gains.

No deferred tax liabilities have been recognized on undistributed earnings of the Corporation's foreign subsidiaries and joint ventures when they are considered to be indefinitely reinvested. Upon distribution of these earnings in the form of dividends or otherwise, the Corporation may be subject to corporation and/or withholding taxes. Taxable temporary differences for which a deferred tax liability was not recognized amount to approximately $225 million.

Source: Bombardier Inc., or its subsidiaries, December 31, 2011 Annual Report, www.sedar.com, posted March 1, 2012.

ETHICAL ISSUES

Management must estimate the probability of realizing future tax benefits. There is a lot of management discretion involved. Although auditors may challenge management's probability estimates, accounting standards give few effective levers to the auditor. If the likelihood of realization is arguable, management may prefer to delay recognition to one or more periods following the loss. This will enhance net income in those future periods.

Management has discretion over the probability estimates and thus the timing of recognition of tax assets. Management also has the ability to remeasure those benefits at any time within the 20-year carryforward period. Thus, the recognition of unrealized tax loss carryforwards can become an ethical morass.

INTERNATIONAL CONSISTENCY?

The primary purpose of international standards is to harmonize financial reporting across financial markets so that all companies can report in financial markets other than that of their home country. Thus, it would appear that all international reporting would have to use the methods described in this chapter in order to conform to international standards.

While that may be true on the surface, the fact is that companies in some countries will be more conservative in their appraisal of realization probabilities, depending on the prevailing ethos in their home country. In a country that has very conservative accounting practices and a strong tradition of prudence in financial reporting (e.g., Germany and France), companies generally will view the probability of future recognition as being low. Thus, the future benefit of the carryforwards will not be recognized, even though they might have been recognized in similar circumstances if the reporting company were based in the United States or in Canada. The influence of the accounting and business environments of a company's home country can be very powerful.

Looking Ahead

Income taxes are not currently on the agenda of either the IASB or the Canadian AcSB.

ACCOUNTING STANDARDS FOR PRIVATE ENTERPRISES

Accounting Method As we said at the end of Chapter 16, private companies can choose between the taxes payable method and the comprehensive allocation method of accounting for income taxes. If the enterprise chooses to use comprehensive income tax allocation, everything in the preceding sections applies.

Tax Loss Carryforwards If an entity is using the taxes payable method, the company will not be able to recognize *future tax assets* arising from tax loss carryforwards. However, tax loss carryforwards will still be used to reduce income taxes in future years, but the benefit will be *recognized* only when *realized* via actual reductions in the company's tax bill when the carryforwards are used in future years. The company's accounting method does not affect the carryforwards themselves or the way that a company can use them to reduce taxes.

Section 3465 uses the phrase "more likely than not" instead of "probable" for assessing recognition of tax loss carryforwards. There is no difference in meaning, however. *Likely*, *probable*, and *more likely than not* all have the same meaning—a greater than 50% probability.

The ASPE specifically refers to use of a valuation allowance in conjunction with tax loss carryforwards. In contrast, *IAS* 12 makes no specific reference to valuation allowances. However, any company can use a valuation allowance instead of direct writedown. A valuation allowance is simply a bookkeeping convenience that does not affect the net amount shown in the financial statements.

RELEVANT STANDARDS

CPA Canada Handbook, Part I (IFRS):

- IAS 12, Income Taxes

CPA Canada Handbook, Part II (ASPE):

- Section 3465, Income Taxes

SUMMARY OF KEY POINTS

1. In Canada, tax losses may be carried back and offset against taxable income in the three previous years. The company is entitled to recover tax paid in those years. The tax recovery is based on the tax actually paid and not on the tax rate in the year of the loss.
2. If the three-year carryback does not completely use up the tax loss, a company is permitted to carry the remaining loss forward and apply it against taxable income over the next 20 years.
3. The future benefits of tax loss carryforwards should be recognized in the year of the loss if there is a greater than 50% probability that the benefits will be realized.
4. The likelihood of realizing the tax benefits of a loss carryforward can be increased by reducing the corporation's claim for CCA on its tax return in the carryback and carryforward years.

5. Future benefits of unrecognized tax loss carryforwards may be recognized in years following the loss if the probability of realization becomes greater than 50%.
6. Management reporting objectives may bias the probability assessment to allow loss carryforward recognition in particular years to emphasize an earnings recovery or other favourable trends.

KEY TERMS

loss carryback
loss carryforward
substantially enacted tax rate
tax benefit
tax loss
valuation allowance

REVIEW PROBLEM 17-1

Dezso Development Limited is a Canadian-controlled public company. The company has a 31 December fiscal year-end. Data concerning the earnings of the company for 20X6 and 20X7 are as follows:

	20X6	20X7
Income (loss) before income taxes	$(90,000)	$30,000
Amounts included in income		
Investment income	$ 1,000	$ 2,000
Depreciation expense—equipment	30,000	30,000
Depreciation expense—development costs	20,000	22,000
Amounts deducted for income tax		
Capital cost allowance	nil	35,000
Development expenditures	25,000	15,000
Income tax rate	38%	37%

Other information:

- Taxable income and the income tax rates for 20X2 through 20X5 are as follows:

Year	Taxable Income (loss)	Tax Rate
20X2	$ 7,000	40%
20X3	13,000	40
20X4	9,000	40
20X5	(12,000)	41

- At 31 December 20X5, equipment had net book value of $570,000, and unclaimed capital cost of $310,000.
- At 31 December 20X5, the statement of financial position showed an unamortized balance of development costs of $200,000 under "Other Assets."
- The investment income consists of dividends from taxable Canadian corporations.

Required:

1. For each of 20X6 and 20X7, prepare the journal entry or entries to record income tax expense. Assume that management judges that it is probable that the full benefit of any tax loss carryforward will be realized within the carryforward.
2. Show how the deferred income tax amounts would appear on the 20X6 year-end statement of financial position.

3. Suppose that management decided that it was probable that the company would use only $10,000 of the remaining gross tax loss carryforward.
   a. Show the entry that would be made to reduce the carryforward benefit. Use a valuation account.
   b. What impact would this entry have on the 20X8 financial statements for Dezso Development Limited?

REVIEW PROBLEM 17-1—SOLUTION

1. (a) 20X6 Tax Expense

The taxable income or loss can be calculated as follows:

	20X6	20X7
Accounting income (loss) before tax	$(90,000)	$30,000
Permanent difference: investment income	(1,000)	(2,000)
Accounting income (loss) subject to tax	(91,000)	28,000
Depreciation	30,000	30,000
CCA	nil	(35,000)
Depreciation of development costs	20,000	22,000
Development cost expenditures	(25,000)	(15,000)
Taxable income (loss)	$(66,000)	$30,000

The 20X5 tax loss will have been carried back to 20X2 ($7,000) and 20X3 ($5,000). After the 20X5 tax loss has been carried back, there remains $17,000 taxable income in the carryback period for the 20X6 loss:

Year	Taxable Income	Used in 20X5	Available in 20X6	Tax Receivable at 40%
20X2	$ 7,000	$ (7,000)	—	—
20X3	13,000	(5,000)	$ 8,000	$3,200
20X4	9,000	—	9,000	3,600
20X5	(12,000)	12,000	—	—
			$17,000	$6,800

The gross carryforward that remains after the carryback is $66,000 – $17,000 = $49,000. Assuming that realization of these benefits is probable and that the enacted tax rate remains at 38% when the 20X6 statements are being prepared, the carryforward benefit is $49,000 × 38% = $18,620.

The adjustments for the temporary differences for both years are summarized in the table below:

	Year-End Tax Basis dr. (cr.)	Year-End Carrying Value dr. (cr.)	Temporary Difference Deductible (Taxable)	Deferred Tax Asset (Liability) at Yr.-End Rate	Less Beginning Balance dr. (cr.)	Adjustment for Current Year dr. (cr.)
20X6 [t = 38%]:						
Equipment	310,000	540,000	(230,000)	$(87,400)	$(106,600)[1]	$19,200
Development costs	0	205,000[3]	(205,000)	(77,900)	(82,000)[2]	4,100
Carryforward benefit	—	—	49,000	18,620	0	18,620

[1]($570,000 – $310,000) × 0.41
[2]($200,000) × 0.41
[3]$200,000 + $25,000 – $20,000

20X7 [t = 37%]:						
Equipment	275,000	510,000	(235,000)	$(86,950)	$(87,400)	450
Development costs	0	198,000	(198,000)	(73,260)	(77,900)	4,640
Carryforward benefit	—	—	19,000	7,030	18,620	(11,590)

Putting all of these elements together gives us the following 20X6 summary of income tax expense:

Income tax receivable—carryback benefit	6,800	
Deferred income tax asset—carryforward benefit	18,620	
Deferred income tax liability—equipment	19,200	
Deferred income tax liability—deferred development costs	4,100	
Income tax expense (recovery)		48,720

(b) 20X7 Tax Expense

The taxable income for 20X7 is $30,000, as calculated previously. No tax is due for 20X7 because there is an available tax loss carryforward of $49,000. After applying $30,000 of the carryforward against 20X7 taxable income, a carryforward of $19,000 remains. At the newly enacted tax rate of 37%, the DIT asset related to the carryforward is $7,030. In recording the income tax expense for 20X7, the balance of the DIT carryforward account must be reduced from its beginning balance of $18,620 (debit) to an ending balance of $7,030 (debit), a credit adjustment of $11,590.

The adjustments for all types of temporary differences are summarized in the preceding table. The entry to record income tax expense, exclusive of the loss carryforward, is:

Income tax expense	6,010	
Deferred income tax liability—equipment	450	
Deferred income tax liability—deferred development costs	4,640	
Income tax payable ($30,000 × 0.37)		11,100

The entry to record loss carryforward use:

Income tax expense[1]	490	
Income tax payable ($30,000 × 0.37)	11,100	
Deferred income tax asset—carryforward benefit (per table)		11,590

[1]This is the reduction in value of the opening tax loss because of a 1% decline in the tax rate; ($49,000 × 1%).

2. 20X6 Statement of Financial Position Presentation

All three of the 20X6 temporary differences are non-current. Therefore, they will be combined into a single net amount when the SFP is prepared. The net amount is:

DIT asset—carryforward benefit	$ 18,620 (dr.)
DIT liability—equipment	(87,400) (cr.)
DIT liability—deferred development costs	(77,900) (cr.)
DIT liability, non-current	$(146,680) (cr.)

3. (a) Adjustment to DIT-carryforward benefit

The remaining carryforward at the beginning of 20X8 is $19,000, as determined in the answer to 1(b), above. At the enacted rate of 37% (assuming no change), the remaining carryforward benefit is $7,030 (i.e., $19,000 × 37%). A valuation account must be created to reduce the *reported* balance of the benefit to $3,700 (i.e., $10,000 × 37%), an adjustment of $3,330:

Income tax expense ($7,030 – $3,700)	3,330	
Valuation allowance—DIT asset		3,330

Note that the amount of the gross *recorded* benefit (before the valuation allowance) will remain at $7,030.

(b) Financial Statement Impact

There will be two effects:

- Income tax expense will be increased by $3,330.
- The deferred income tax asset relating to the tax loss carryforward benefit will be reduced to $3,700 on the statement of financial position.

Deferred income tax asset—carryforward benefit	$7,030
Less valuation allowance	3,330
Net asset	$3,700

QUESTIONS

Q17-1 What is the benefit that arises as a result of a tax loss?

Q17-2 Over what period can a tax loss be used as an offset against taxable income?

Q17-3 Why do companies usually use tax losses as carrybacks before using them as carryforwards?

Q17-4 When do *recognition* and *realization* coincide for tax losses?

Q17-5 Why is it desirable to recognize the benefit of a tax loss carryforward in the period of the accounting loss? Under what circumstances would such a benefit be *realized*?

Q17-6 What criteria must be met to *recognize* the benefit of a tax loss carryforward in the period of the accounting loss?

Q17-7 ABC Company has a taxable loss of $200,000. The tax rate is 40%. What is the potential benefit of the tax loss?

Q17-8 A company reports an accounting loss of $75,000. Depreciation for the year was $216,000, and CCA was $321,000. The company wishes to maximize its tax loss. How much is the tax loss?

Q17-9 Refer again to the data in Q17-8. Assume instead that the company wishes to minimize its taxable loss/maximize taxable income. How much is the taxable income (loss)? Explain.

Q17-10 Explain why a company might choose not to claim CCA when it reports (a) accounting income and (b) an accounting loss.

Q17-11 Define the term "probable."

Q17-12 What strategies can be used to increase the likelihood that a tax loss carryforward will be used?

Q17-13 Provide three examples of favourable evidence in assessing the likelihood that a tax loss carryforward will be used in the carryforward period.

Q17-14 A company has a tax loss of $577,000 in 20X4, when the tax rate was 40%. The tax loss is expected to be used in 20X6. At present, there is an enacted tax rate of 42% for 20X5. The government intends to increase the tax rate to 45% in 20X6, but no legislation concerning tax rates has yet been drafted. At what amount should the tax loss carryforward be recorded, if it meets the appropriate criteria to be recorded?

Q17-15 A company recorded the benefit of a tax loss carryforward in the year of the loss. Two years later, the balance of probability shifts, and it appears that it is not probable the loss will be used in the carryforward period. What accounting entry is required if a direct adjustment is made (i.e., not to a valuation account)?

Q17-16 A company did not recognize the benefit of a tax loss carryforward in the year of the loss. Two years later, the balance of probability shifts, and it appears probable that the loss will be used in the carryforward period. What accounting entries are required in each year if a valuation account is used?

Q17-17 How will income change if a tax loss carryforward, previously recognized, is now considered not probable to be used in the future?

Q17-18 A company has recorded a $40,000 benefit in relation to a $100,000 tax loss carryforward. The tax rate changes to 35%. What entry is appropriate?

Q17-19 Give three objections to the practice of recording a tax loss carryforward prior to realization.

Q17-20 What disclosure is required in relation to tax loss carryforwards?

CASE 17-1

SOCCER INCORPORATED

Soccer Incorporated (SI) is a public corporation incorporated in 20X2. SI operates a professional soccer team as well as other related activities. New bank financing was obtained in 20X9 for the construction of a new stadium. The bank requires annual audited financial statements and RI has a covenant with a maximum debt-to-equity ratio.

SI's players have an agreement with SI that entitles them to a bonus if SI exceeds net income of $25 million in the year. They agreed to this new bonus arrangement in 20X9 instead of a salary increase. Net income before any adjustments on 31 December 20X9 was $24 million. The players are upset, since the games have been well attended and they anticipated a substantial bonus payment. Management has stated that they have invested in the future which will provide healthy bonuses in later years. Exhibit 1 includes the income statement.

You have been hired by the players to review the accounting policies for SI's 31 December year-end. Exhibit 2 provides the notes to the accounting policies. You have been asked by the players to analyze the current accounting, discuss alternatives, where possible, and provide recommendations on the appropriate accounting policies for events that have occurred during 20X9. The incremental borrowing rate for SI is 10%. The tax rate for SI is 30%.

EXHIBIT 1

STATEMENT OF COMPREHENSIVE INCOME

Soccer Incorporated
Income Statement

(unaudited)

Year Ended Dec. 31, 20X9 (in millions)		
Revenues	$ 50	
Operating expenses	(22)	
Operating profit		28
Finance costs	(7)	
Finance income	3	
Net income		$24
Other Comprehensive Income		
Unrealized gain on investments recorded—FVTOCI	5	
Fair value changes on cash flow hedge	(1)	
Foreign exchange gain subsidiary	2	
Actuarial gain pension plan	3	
Comprehensive Income		$33

EXHIBIT 2

NOTES TO FINANCIAL STATEMENTS

1. Tickets can be purchased on-line through SI's new website or at the box office at the stadium. Customers using a credit card can purchase on-line tickets up to a year in advance. Revenue for on-line sales is recognized when the ticket is used. To increase sales of season tickets for the 20X10 season, when tickets are purchased, customers received a $50 gift card for use in the souvenir shop. Many customers used the gift card for holiday shopping in December. Revenue for season tickets is recognized as games are played.
2. SI provided 100,000 coupons for $2 off the game food combination at local grocery stores and pharmacies. The $200,000 was expensed as an advertising cost.
3. SI received a $100 million loan from the bank for the construction of the new stadium. Transaction costs of $2 million were expensed during the year as a finance cost. In 20X9, SI invested cash from the bank loan until needed for construction in shares of High Tech Incorporated. SI purchased 2% of the shares and will sell them when cash is needed over the next year and a half. These shares were classified as FVTOCI.
4. SI started construction of the new sports stadium in March 20X9. The estimated completion date was December 20X11. Costs capitalized in 20X9 were $15 million and included materials, labour, and variable overhead. Costs expensed in 20X9 were $2 million in interest. In July 20X9, a strike occurred that shut down construction for two months and will delay the opening of the new stadium.
5. SI issued $1,000,000 of term preferred shares to two of the owners. These shares have a cumulative dividend of 10% and a mandatory repayment date in 10 years. Any unpaid dividends must be repaid at that date. These shares were recorded on the statement of financial position as debt, and dividends were recorded as a finance cost.
6. SI issued common shares during the year. Share issue costs of $1 million were expensed as a financing cost.
7. SI has $10 million of unused losses. It has decided that the future is too uncertain to recognize the benefit of these losses. This industry has a history of strikes.
8. SI's uses the Black Scholes model to determine fair value. Since SI's shares are not frequently traded, it does not measure stock price volatility. SI's stock option plan vests annually over a five-year period. The entire stock option expense recognized in period stock option is granted. Any forfeitures are recognized when they occur.

CASE 17-2

DOWNHILL SKI COMPANY

Downhill Ski Company is experiencing financial difficulties. Earnings have been declining sharply over the past several years. The company has barely maintained profits over the last four years. In the current year, the company is expected to suffer a substantial loss for the first time in 10 years. A taxable loss will also be reported. The losses are expected to be significantly greater than the profits reported in the previous three years.

Downhill Ski Company is a manufacturer specializing in downhill racing skis and boots. The company supplies the Canadian National ski team but competition from larger manufacturers has forced Downhill Ski Company to keep its prices low when its expenses have been increasing. Also, the popularity of snowboarding has had a negative impact on sales. However, it has been found that many older adults who switch to snowboarding go back to skiing.

North Johnston, the sales and marketing manager, left the company last year to join Rossignol, a large multinational company. Cathy Thomas, former ski champion, was hired earlier this year as the new sales and marketing manager.

The owner of Downhill Ski Company, Wendy Hogarth, is not overly concerned with the loss for the current year and has the following comments to make:

> "With the hiring of Cathy Thomas as sales and marketing manager we will develop relationships with the National Ski Team and work on improving sponsorship of events. This should increase our sales.
>
> "Downhill Ski Company is developing a new type of ski that is not on the market yet. Some of the national ski team members tested the prototype of the ski and were thrilled with its performance. We are sure sales of the new ski will give us solid sales. We have already lined up buyers across Canada and the United States for this ski. Our financial forecast for next year is to make a profit.
>
> "We have a new large piece of equipment acquired at the end of last year. This manufacturing equipment is more efficient and will save us money on maintenance and repairs."

You have been hired by Wendy to provide accounting advice. She wants to know if she can recognize the loss this year as an asset on the statement of financial position. She would also like to know the impact on the financial statements of recognizing versus not recognizing the loss and if there are any tax-planning strategies the company should use in respect to recognition of the loss.

Required:

Write the report to Wendy.

CASE 17-3

SIGMA AUTO PARTS LTD.

Sigma Auto Parts Ltd. is an Ontario-based manufacturer of automobile parts. The Canadian operations supply automotive components and parts to three U.S. states and two Japanese auto manufacturers. Approximately 30% of Sigma's worldwide sales is generated by its Canadian operations.

The company has large operating subsidiaries in the United States, Mexico, Germany, and the Czech Republic. Sigma has recently established an operating subsidiary in the People's Republic of China to supply both international and domestic manufacturers in that country.

Sigma is a Canadian private company. However, the German subsidiary does have an outstanding public issue of nonvoting common shares that are traded on the Frankfurt exchange. Generally, financing is obtained through a combination of retained earnings, debt, and private equity placements in each subsidiary's home country, with the exception of China (as explained below). The company reports using international accounting standards, using U.S. dollars as the reporting currency.

Angelo Zhang has recently been promoted to the position of chief accountant at the Sigma head office in Windsor, Ontario. The newly appointed chief financial officer, Jean Adams, has asked Mr. Zhang to review several reporting issues and advise her on appropriate treatments. The specific issues are as follows:

1. Earlier in the year, a Canadian supplier claimed the right to terminate its obligations to supply Sigma with certain stainless steel products at the prices stated in two standing supply contracts with Sigma. The supplier has continued to supply the products but

invoiced Sigma at market prices rather than at the contracted prices. Sigma has continued to pay the supplier, but only at the contract prices. The accumulated differential between the invoiced market prices and the contract prices has been accumulating for several months and now amounts to about $30 million. Sigma and the supplier have agreed to submit their disagreement to binding arbitration. The arbitration hearing is expected to be held late in the following fiscal year.

2. Sigma is building new manufacturing facilities in the Czech Republic to replace some older facilities that have become obsolete. The new facilities should be ready within two years, whereupon operations will be transferred to the new facilities and the old site will be abandoned. Recent legislation in the Czech Republic makes Sigma responsible for demolition and site restoration costs in the event that the old facilities cannot be sold to a buyer that is willing to bear the costs of demolition or rebuilding. The currently estimated costs are $25 million for demolition and $10 million for site restoration (at the current exchange rate).
3. The U.S. operations have experienced profitability problems over the past several years. The decline of some of the U.S. auto manufacturers has taken its toll on the auto parts industry. The auto companies have been forcing suppliers' prices down, a situation that has led to the bankruptcy of one major U.S.–based auto parts manufacturer. For a while, Sigma U.S. was just about breaking even on an accounting basis but was in an operating loss position for tax purposes. However, for each of the most recent two years, Sigma's U.S. subsidiary has reported a significant loss for both accounting and tax purposes. In view of the basic strength of Sigma's cutting-edge operations and the strength of its worldwide operations, Jean Adams's predecessor felt confident in fully recognizing the income tax benefits that will be derived from any tax loss carryforwards. Now, however, the situation is not so clear-cut. It may be quite a while before the industry settles and Sigma is able to return the U.S. operations to profitability.
4. Generally, the subsidiaries in each country are financed locally rather than through significant direct investment from Canada. An exception is the new subsidiary in China; substantial direct foreign investment was necessary in order to quickly establish the company and also to obtain certain government approvals and tax benefits. Total direct investment in China currently is $103 million and is likely to increase over the next couple of years. The new Chinese yuan is tied to a basket of foreign currencies, of which the U.S. dollar represents the largest proportion. Due to the weakening of the U.S. dollar, the yuan has been gradually increasing in value.
5. During the current year, Sigma's German division issued €150 million of 7% unsecured subordinated debentures on a private placement basis. The debentures mature in five years and are not redeemable prior to maturity. Upon maturity, Sigma has the option of issuing nonvoting common shares, the number of shares dependent on their market value at the time.

Required:

Assume that you are Angelo Zhang. Prepare the report to Ms. Adams.

TECHNICAL REVIEW

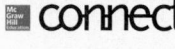

TR17-1 Loss Carryback: Burgher Limited had a taxable loss of $500,000 in 20X7. The tax rate in 20X7 is 36%. In the past three years, they had the following taxable income and tax rates:

	20X4	20X5	20X6
Taxable income	$200,000	$120,000	$80,000
Tax rate	40%	38%	36%

There are no temporary differences other than those created by income tax losses. The loss was caused by a strike, which was extremely unusual in this industry and not expected to occur again in the foreseeable future.

Required:

1. What is the amount of taxes that will be recovered in each year? Provide the journal entry for income tax receivable in 20X7.
2. Repeat requirement 1, assuming that the tax rates were 40% in 20X6, 38% in 20X5, and 36% in 20X4.

connect

TR17-2 Loss Carryback/Carryforward: Colavecchia Limited had a taxable loss of $1,500,000 in 20X8. The tax rate in 20X8 is 40%. In the past three years, the company had the following taxable income and tax rates:

	20X5	20X6	20X7
Taxable income	$420,000	$300,000	$210,000
Tax rate	36%	38%	40%

There are no temporary differences other than those created by income tax losses. The loss was triggered by a downturn in the economy.

Required:

1. What is the amount of taxes that will be recovered in each year? Provide the journal entry for income tax receivable in 20X8.
2. What is the amount of the loss carryforward?
3. Assuming the probable provision is met, since the economy is showing signs of recovery, what is the impact, if any, on the journal entry in requirement 1?
4. Assuming the probable provision is not met, since the economy remains sluggish, what is the impact, if any, on the journal entry in requirement 1?

connect

TR17-3 Loss Carryback/Carryforward: Petrilli Limited had a taxable loss of $2,500,000 in 20X8 and a $1,000,000 taxable loss in 20X9. The tax rate in 20X8 and 20X9 is 40%. In the three years before the losses, the company had the following taxable income and tax rates:

	20X5	20X6	20X7
Taxable income	$880,000	$950,000	$770,000
Tax rate	36%	38%	40%

There are no temporary differences other than those created by income tax losses. The company was struggling due to a competitor entering the market.

Required:

1. What is the amount of taxes that will be recovered in each year for the 20X8 loss? Provide the journal entry for income tax receivable in 20X8.
2. What is the amount of taxes that will be recovered in each year for the 20X9 loss? Provide the journal entry for income tax receivable in 20X9.
3. What is the amount of the loss carryforward in 20X9?
4. Assuming the probable provision is met, what is the impact, if any, on the journal entry in requirement 2?
5. Assuming the probable provision is not met, what is the impact, if any, on the journal entry in requirement 2?

connect

TR17-4 Benefits of Carryback and Carryforward: Maines Limited began operations in 20X3. For the first six years of operations, the company had the following pre-tax net income (loss):

Year	Taxable Income	Tax Rate
20X3	$ (120,000)	40%
20X4	720,000	39%
20X5	880,000	38%
20X6	(2,600,000)	37%
20X7	280,000	36%
20X8	600,000	38%

There have been no temporary differences between pre-tax accounting income and taxable income.

In 20X6, management was less than 50% certain that any tax carryforward would be realized. Management decided in 20X7 that full realization of carryforward benefits was probable and did not change that opinion in 20X8.

Required:

For each year, determine:

1. Income tax currently payable (receivable);
2. Income tax expense (recovery); and
3. Net income (loss).

connect

TR17-5 Carrybacks and Carryforwards in Successive Years: Qu Enterprises Limited was founded at the beginning of 20X0. For the first 10 years, the company had the following record of taxable income and loss (before considering any tax loss carryforwards or carrybacks):

Year	Taxable Income (Loss)
20X0	$ 75,000
20X1	40,000
20X2	15,000
20X3	(120,000)
20X4	10,000
20X5	(245,000)
20X6	(25,000)
20X7	45,000
20X8	75,000
20X9	360,000

The company had no temporary differences in any of the 10 years. The income tax rate was 40% from 20X0 through 20X5. In 20X6, the government enacted new legislation that called for reducing the rate to 38% for 20X6 and to 36% for 20X7 and beyond. In each year, management believed that it was probable to realize the benefit of any tax loss carryforwards.

Required:

Calculate income tax expense for each year, 20X0 through 20X9.

ASSIGNMENTS

★★ **A17-1 Income Tax Explanation:** Kong Corporation reported the following items with respect to income tax in the 20X6 financial statements:

Deferred income tax asset	$ 10,400
Deferred income tax liability	328,400

The 20X6 statement of comprehensive income shows the following income tax expense:

Income tax expense:	
Current	$75,000
Deferred	68,500
Impact of loss carryforward	(82,600)
	$60,900

The disclosure notes indicate that there is an unrecognized loss carryforward in the amount of $406,400. No tax loss carryforwards have been recorded as assets. The tax rate is 40%.

Required:

1. Explain the components of the 20X6 income tax expense. Why is there income tax expense if there is a loss carryforward?
2. Give an example of a statement of financial position account that could have caused a deferred income tax asset and a deferred income tax liability.
3. Why would the loss carryforward not have been recognized in its entirety in 20X6? What amounts and accounts would change if it could be recognized?
4. How much tax is currently payable? How much tax would have been payable if there had been no loss carryforward?

★ **A17-2 Probable Provision:** After utilizing any carrybacks, Nu Incorporated had a taxable loss of $1 million in 20X9. The company is trying to determine if the probable provision has been met and if it should record a deferred tax asset or not. For the past five years, Nu has had declining profits since investing in research of new products. The company has recently acquired one of its competitors, which had research in progress for a new product. Work has been completed on the project, and a patent was filed by the end of 20X9. Marketing studies show that this product, if successful, will have huge sales potential for a number of years. The company has initiated an advertising campaign to promote the product, which is expected to be launched 14 February 20X10. Unfortunately, in January 20X10 a lawsuit was launched, indicating patent infringement. Lawyers for the Nu Corporation do not think there is merit in the lawsuit. The company plans to go ahead with the launch of the product. The tax rate for the company is 38%.

Required:

1. Has the probable provision been met? Provide support for both sides.
2. What is the amount that would be recorded as a deferred tax asset if probable?
3. What is the impact of the tax losses if it is determined the probable provisions has not been met? Could a deferred tax asset be recorded in the future?

★★ **A17-3 Loss Carryback/Carryforward:** Kenmark Corporation started operations in 20X6. The statements of comprehensive income for the first four years of operations reflected the following pre-tax amounts:

connect

	20X4	20X5	20X6	20X7
Pre-tax income (loss)	$50,000	$(120,000)	$10,000	$20,000

There are no temporary differences other than those created by income tax losses. Kenmark has had a constant income tax rate of 38% for all four years.

Required:

1. Give entries to record income tax expense for each year, assuming that management has assessed that the probable provision has been met. Show computations.
2. Give entries to record income tax expense for each year, assuming that management has assessed that the probable provision has not been met. Show computations.
3. Give entries to record income tax expense for each year, assuming that management has assessed that the probable provision was met but on reassessment determined in 20X6 that it was not met. Show computations.

★ **A17-4 Loss Carryback; Entries and Reporting:** Graham Corporation reported pre-tax income from operations in 20X7 of $350,000 (the first year of operations). In 20X8, the corporation experienced a $130,000 pre-tax loss from operations. Future operations are highly uncertain. Assume an income tax rate of 38%. Graham has no temporary differences.

Required:

1. Assess Graham's income tax situation for 20X7 and 20X8. How should Graham elect to handle the loss in 20X8?
2. Based on your assessments in requirement 1, give the 20X7 and 20X8 income tax entries.
3. Show how all tax-related items would be reported on the 20X7 and 20X8 statement of comprehensive income and statement of financial position.

★ **A17-5 Loss Carryforward; Valuation Allowance:** The pre-tax income of Barrows Limited for the first three years was as follows:

connect

	20X6	20X7	20X8
Revenues	$276,000	$300,000	$325,000
Expenses	333,000	286,000	306,000
Earnings (loss) before income taxes	$ (57,000)	$ 14,000	$ 19,000

The company had no temporary differences in any of the three years. The income tax rate was constant at 36%.

In 20X6 and 20X7, the prospect for future earnings was highly uncertain. In 20X8, management decided that the future outlook for the company was quite good and that significant earnings would be generated in the near future.

Required:

1. Restate the above statements of comprehensive income to reflect income tax effects for each year.
2. Show any amounts relating to income taxes that would be reported on Barrows' statement of financial position in each of the three years.
3. Prepare journal entries to record income taxes in each year. The company's accountant has recommended using the valuation allowance approach to recording tax loss carryforward benefits.

★★ **A17-6 Loss Carryforward; Valuation Allowance; Rate Change:** Fellows Corporation had the following taxable and pre-tax accounting income:

connect

	20X6	20X7	20X8	20X9
Income (loss) before taxes	$(200,000)	$(40,000)	$60,000	$100,000
Tax rate	40%	40%	38%	38%

The income tax rate, which had gradually increased over several years to 40% in 20X3, remained at 40% for 20X4 taxable income. In 20X4, Parliament enacted legislation to reduce the income tax rate to 36% for 20X5 and the following years.

In management's judgement, it is probable that any tax loss carryforward will be fully utilized in the carryforward period.

Required:

Show the journal entry to record income taxes. Prepare the lower part of the CTC statement of profit and loss for 20X4, starting with "earnings before income tax."

★★ **A17-27 Explain Impact of Temporary Differences; Tax Losses:** You are the new accountant for Evanoff Limited (EL). You have been asked to explain the impact of income tax on the financial statements for the year ended 31 December 20X5. You discover the following:

- EL's product development expenses of $2 million have been deferred, to be amortized over the anticipated product life of four years starting two years from now.
- EL had depreciation expense of $780,000 in 20X5 but claimed no CCA. In the past, CCA charges have been significantly higher than depreciation, resulting in a $460,000 deferred income tax liability on the statement of financial position.
- In 20X5, EL had a loss for tax purposes of $3 million. The company's tax rate is 40%, constant since incorporation 10 years ago.
- In the past several years, accounting and taxable income have been steady but unimpressive in the range of $250,000 to $450,000. EL is aware that management has to make significant strategic changes to combat disastrous operating results this year. In particular, EL is faced with the need to upgrade capital assets to remain competitive. However, raising money for this venture will be very difficult.

Required:

Explain the income tax impacts of the above, and describe how results would be reported on the company's financial statements.

(ICAO, adapted)

★★ **A17-28 Tax Losses; Temporary Differences:** The 20X6 records of Laredo Incorporated show the following reconciliation of accounting and taxable income:

Net income per the financial statements	$124,000
Plus (minus)	
Dividend revenue	(2,900)
CCA in excess of depreciation	(42,300)
Warranty payments in excess of expense	(500)
Non-tax-deductible expenses	2,900
Taxable income	$ 81,200

In 20X5, Laredo Inc. had reported an operating loss, the tax benefit of which was fully recognized in 20X5 through loss carryback and recognition of a deferred tax asset.

Selected SFP accounts at the end of 20X5:

Deferred income taxes (regarding warranty amounts)	$ 320
Income tax receivable	16,400
Deferred income tax (asset: loss carryforward)	20,000
Deferred income tax (liability)	48,000
Warranty liability	1,000
Net book value of capital assets, after depreciation of $41,000	618,000

UCC at the end of 20X5 was $468,000. Depreciation expense in 20X6 was $41,000. The enacted tax rate in 20X5 was 32%. The enacted tax rate in 20X6 was 38%.

Required:

Present the lower portion of the 20X6 statement of profit and loss. Also include the tax entries for 20X6.

(Source: Atlantic School of Chartered Accountancy, © 2010)

★★ **A17-29 Tax Losses; Temporary Differences (ASPE):** Refer to case facts in A17-10.

Required:

Prepare the journal entries for income taxes for each of the four years. Assume the company uses the taxes payable method and that it is concerned it might have another significant loss in 20X9.

★★ **A17-30 Tax Losses; Temporary Differences (ASPE):** Refer to case facts in A17-20.

Required:

Prepare the journal entries for income taxes for 20X7, 20X8, and 20X9. Assume the company uses the taxes payable method.

connect LEARNSMART SMARTBOOK™

For more information on the resources available from McGraw-Hill Ryerson, go to www.mcgrawhill.ca/he/solutions.

CHAPTER 18

Leases

INTRODUCTION

In its 2012 financial statements, Canadian National Railway (CNR) discloses total lease commitments for its rolling stock of $1,908 million. Of this total, $1,232 million relates to finance lease obligations while $676 million relates to operating leases. In the disclosure notes, CNR explains: "During 2012, the Company recorded $94 million in assets it acquired through equipment leases ($87 million in 2011), for which an equivalent amount was recorded in debt."

In another part of the transportation industry, Air Canada (AC) operated 205 aircraft in its mainline fleet at the end of 2012. AC entered 2012 with 19 aircraft under finance leases and 77 under operating leases. Year-end debt for aircraft financing totalled $2.1 billion, of which less than $0.4 billion was for finance leases.

What is the difference between an operating lease and a finance lease? Why does CNR mainly use finance leases, while AC uses mostly operating leases?

Accounting for a lease may not appear to be a big problem. After all, the lessee is paying rent to the lessor, so on the surface it would appear that the lessee simply recognizes rent expense on the income statement, while the lessor reports rent revenue. However, things are not always what they seem.

The purpose of this chapter is to explain the circumstances under which a lease is treated as a form of financing, instead of a simple rental agreement, and how operating and financing leases should be reported by both lessees and lessors under current accounting standards. In the appendix to this chapter, we also will explain forthcoming changes in lease accounting that will have a profound impact on many corporations' financial statements.

DEFINITION OF A LEASE

A **lease** is a contract that gives the rights to use an asset in return for the payment of rent. In the commonly used sense of the term, a lease is a fee-for-usage contract between an owner of property and a renter. The asset's owner is the **lessor**, and the renter is the **lessee**. The lease specifies the terms under which the lessee has the right to use the owner's property and the compensation to be paid to the lessor in exchange.

Leased assets can include both real property and personal property. **Real property** means real estate: land and buildings. **Personal property** includes much more than the property that belongs to a person; it is any property that is not real property and includes both tangible assets (e.g., machinery, equipment, or transportation vehicles) and certain intangibles (e.g., patents).

THE LEASING CONTINUUM

Every lease contract is individual. Some types of leases are more or less standard, such as long-term automobile leases. Nevertheless, every lease requires separate negotiation, and the lease contract must be signed by both the lessor and the lessee.

In the process of negotiation, the parties reach agreement on many contractual facets, such as the length of the lease (the *lease term*); the amount and timing of lease payments; each party's responsibility for maintenance, insurance, and property taxes (for real property leases); cancellation terms; upgrading responsibilities; and so on.

As the lease term lengthens—in relationship to an asset's economic life—more and more of the risks and rewards pass from the lessor to the lessee. Suppose you want to rent a car. If you rent a car for one hour, you will pay a very high rate. If you rent for one day, you will pay a high rate, but the rate will be considerably less than the hourly rate times 24. If you rent for a month, the rate per day will be much lower than the rate to rent for one day. And if you rent for four years, a very low rental rate per day can be obtained. As the rental term lengthens, the daily rent goes down because more and more of the risk of ownership is transferred to the lessee.

At some point in this sliding scale of automobile rental payments, the lessee essentially agrees to pay the full value of the car via the rent payments. As the lease term grows longer, you bear a greater risk of obsolescence and of declining usefulness, but you also get the rewards of using the car at minimal cost per day.

Thus, lease contracts cannot easily be categorized into neat slots; each one is different. The leasing continuum is from very short-term leases to very long-term leases, with many leases in the middle.

To cope with this continuum, the accounting profession has, for more than 40 years, used two classifications for leases:

- Finance leases, wherein the lessor transfers substantially all of the risks and rewards of ownership to the lessee; and
- Operating leases, wherein the lessor does *not* transfer substantially all of the risks and rewards of ownership to the lessee.

Note the relationship between these two classifications. An operating lease is not defined directly. Essentially, an operating lease is defined as a lease that does not fit the definition of a finance lease.

Often, the motivation for the lessee's management is to negotiate a lease that has the appearance of an operating lease while still transferring most of the risks and rewards of ownership to the lessee. We will explain the reasons for this motivation later in the chapter, as well as the IFRS's forthcoming move to eliminate such motivation. Accountants must be able to exercise their professional judgement and discern *substance over form*.

Operating Leases

A lessee enters into an **operating lease** to obtain temporary use of an asset without having to buy it. This is appropriate when there is no long-term need for an asset or when the lessee's business is volatile and there is not a continuous need for the asset. The key to designating a lease as *operating* is not the actual length of the lease in time—it is the length of the lease in relation to the asset's economic life. An operating lease term covers a *relatively small proportion of the asset's economic life.*

Because an operating lease provides only a relatively short-term return to the lessor, the lessor bears the risk of ownership. If the lessee returns the asset after the rental period and the lessor cannot find another lessee, then the lessor incurs the costs not only of maintaining the asset but also of watching it sink slowly into obsolescence. Consequently, the longer the lease term, the lower is the per-period rental cost.

Finance Leases

At the other end of the leasing continuum, a finance lease gives the lessee substantially all of the benefits of ownership. The lessee also has to bear most of the risks of ownership. For example, the lessee is committed to the lease contract, even if the lessee has no further use for the asset.

When a lease transfers substantially all of the benefits and risks of ownership to the lessee, the lessee might as well have purchased the asset outright. Indeed, purchasing the asset would give more flexibility—there are no restrictions on what the owner does with an owned asset.

A little later in this chapter, we will explain the criteria for deciding whether a lease is a finance lease. First, however, we will look at operating lease accounting.

OPERATING LEASES

An operating lease is one that gives the lessee the right to use the asset for only a relatively short period of its useful life, such as renting a car or truck for a day, a month, or a year. Accounting for operating leases is not complicated. It is important to remember that lease terms—short-term versus long-term—are relative to the asset's economic life; 10 years is short term when applied to a building that may be useful for 60 years.

Overview of Operating Lease Accounting

Lessee Accounting The lessee makes periodic lease payments that are accounted for as operating expenses by the lessee. If a lessee rents a piece of construction equipment (e.g., a crane) for $20,000 a month, the lessee's entry will be as follows for each month's rental:

Rent expense—crane	20,000	
Cash		20,000

The crane itself does not appear on the lessee's books.

Lessor Accounting On the other side of the transaction, the lessor receives the periodic rent payment and credits rental income or lease income. The lessor credits the cash receipts to an income account, such as *rent revenue* (or *other income* if leasing is not one of the company's mainstream business activities):

Cash	20,000	
Rent revenue—crane		20,000

However, the lessor must acquire a piece of equipment before it can be leased out. Suppose that the crane cost $1,500,000 to purchase and is expected to be useful for 10 years. The crane will appear on the lessor's SFP as "equipment available for lease" and will be depreciated over its estimated useful life.

Example Exhibit 18-1 illustrates the operating lease accounting for both the lessee and the lessor. In this example, assume the following:

- Empire Equipment Ltd. (EEL) buys a crane on 6 January for $1,580,000. The crane has an estimated useful life of 10 years and an estimated residual value of $260,000.
- On 25 January, EEL enters into 10-month lease contract with Builders Inc. The monthly rent is $20,000. The crane will be delivered to Builders Inc. on 1 February.
- After Builders Inc. returns the crane at the end of November, the crane is idle for the remainder of the year.
- EEL is charging a standard fee of $15,000 for the cost of the crane's assembly, disassembly, and transport cost.
- EEL uses straight-line depreciation, taking a full year's depreciation in the year of acquisition.
- EEL's fiscal year ends on 31 December.

Note that there are two dates for each lease:

- The *inception of the lease*, which is the date at which the lessor and lessee commit to the principal provisions of the lease; this usually coincides with the signing of the lease agreement but could be earlier, such as in a *memorandum of agreement*; and
- The *commencement of the lease term*, which is the date upon which the lessee is entitled to use the asset.

For the lease with Builders Inc., the *inception* of the lease is 25 January, while the *commencement* of the lease term is 1 February.

The *date of inception* is the date when the accounting treatment of the lease as either an operating lease or a finance lease is determined. A substantial period of time can elapse between inception and commencement, such as when the asset must be constructed before the lease can commence (e.g., aircraft ordered under lease agreement that will not be delivered for several years). However, no formal entries are made in the accounting records until the lease commences.

Executory Costs Many operating leases require the lessee to pay specified costs relating to the leased asset during the lease term. These are known as **executory costs**. In this example, the lessee is required to pay $15,000 for the lessor's delivery and construction of the crane. For the lessee, this is just part of the cost of renting the crane and is charged to rent expense. For the lessor, the payment is reimbursement for labour and transportation costs that the lessor incurs to make sure that the crane is handled and assembled safely. Therefore, the lessor will not normally treat this cost as additional income; instead, the cash received is credited to a contra account to offset the costs incurred.

Uneven Payments Sometimes the operating lease payments are uneven. For example, when office rental space is very scarce, the lessee may be required to make an initial lump-sum payment to the landlord to obtain space.[1] If there is a large payment at the beginning (or inception) of the lease, the special payment is amortized over the period of time that the lessee is required to make lease payments. This period of time is called the **initial lease term**. The lease may be renewable, but since there is no obligation on the part of the lessee to renew the lease, the amortization must end with the initial term.

An alternative arrangement that also occurs, particularly for real property rentals, is that the lessor will "forgive" lease payments (or operating cost payments) for a limited period of time at the beginning of the lease. For example, in a market that has excess supply, a lessor may attract a lessee by agreeing that lease payments will not begin until six months after the lease starts. These forgiven payments also are amortized over the initial term of the lease by charging the contractual monthly lease payments to expense and amortizing the forgiven amounts over the full initial lease term.

---

[1] Such payments sometimes are known as *key money* and may be prohibited in some jurisdictions, particularly in those with rent controls on residential properties.

For example, assume that F212 Limited leases space in an office building for five years for an annual rental of $100,000. Because the office rental market is "soft," the lessor agrees that F212 need not begin paying rent until the second year; the first year's rent is forgiven. The substance of this deal is that F212 agrees to pay a total of $400,000 for five years; this averages out to an effective rental rate of $80,000 per year. For the first year, there is no cash flow for rent, but F212 will record an expense of $80,000, which is offset by a deferred credit:

Rent expense	80,000	
Deferred rent liability		80,000

For each of the next four years, the $80,000 will be amortized to rent expense, thereby reducing rent expense from the cash outflow of $100,000 to the average annual expense of $80,000. The annual entry on F212's books will be:

Rent expense	80,000	
Deferred rent liability	20,000	
Cash		100,000

The deferred rent will be reported as a current liability on the SFP, allocated between short-term and long-term liabilities, and usually combined with other deferred credits and accrued liabilities.

EXHIBIT 18-1

OPERATING LEASES COMPARISON OF LESSEE AND LESSOR ACCOUNTING

Lessee Accounting—Builders Inc.

1 February—payment of installation fee:		
Rental expense—crane	15,000	
Cash		15,000
Summary entry—payment of monthly rent		
Rent expense ($20,000 × 10 months)	200,000	
Cash		200,000

Lessor Accounting—Empire Equipment Ltd.

6 January—purchase of crane:		
Equipment for available for lease	1,580,000	
Cash		1,580,000
1 February—receipt of installation fee:		
Cash	15,000	
Crane delivery expenses		15,000
Summary entry—receipt of rent:		
Cash	200,000	
Lease income ($20,000 × 10 months)		200,000
31 December—depreciation of crane		
Depreciation expense*	132,000	
Accum. Depreciation—crane		132,000

*$1,580,000 – $260,000 ÷ 10 years = $132,000

Definition of an Operating Lease

The preceding sections explained, in general terms, the accounting for an operating lease. However, a fundamental question remains: *When is a lease an operating lease*? Current accounting standards answer this question only indirectly—an operating lease is *a lease that is not a finance lease*. Therefore, to understand the rather fuzzy distinction between an operating lease and a finance lease, we must examine the guidelines for designating a lease as a finance lease.

FINANCE LEASES

For accountants, the more challenging type of lease is one in which the lessor agrees to purchase an asset and lease it immediately to a lessee for substantially all of the economic life of the asset. When that happens, the lessor is not interested in using the asset, even though the lessor will hold legal title.

This type of lease is called a *finance lease* in accounting because, in substance, the lessor is providing an asset to the lessee in return for a cash flow stream that enables the lessor to recover its investment in the asset as well as earn a reasonable rate of return on the investment. A finance lease is a form of financing because the lessee acquires essentially full benefits of the leased asset without actually having to buy it.[2]

Thus, in accounting, a **finance lease** is defined as *any lease that transfers substantially all of the risks and rewards of ownership from the lessor to the lessee.*

A finance lease is reported in accordance with its substance as a financing instrument rather than as a simple rental. Most of the rest of this chapter will deal with accounting and financial statement reporting for finance leases.

Classification as a Finance Lease

A fundamental point is that classification of a lease as *finance* or *operating* depends on the substance of the lease rather than its legal form. This is a clear application of the qualitative characteristic of *substance over form*.

Thus, IAS 17, Leases, avoids using any quantitative guidelines. The basis for designating a lease as a finance lease is judgemental: *Do the terms of the lease transfer substantially all of the benefits and risks of ownership from the lessor to the lessee?* The exercise of professional judgement requires criteria or guidelines. To fill this obvious need, IAS 17 identifies circumstances that individually or in combination would indicate that substantially all of the risks and rewards of ownership are being passed to the lessee. If any of the following guidelines is satisfied, the lease should be classified as a finance lease:

1. *Is there reasonable certainty that the lessee will obtain ownership of the leased property at the end of the lease term?* This occurs (1) if the lease provides for automatic transfer of title to the lessee at the end of the lease, or (2) if the lessee is entitled to buy the asset at the end of the lease term at a price significantly lower than the expected fair value (often called a *bargain purchase option*).[3]
2. *Will the lessee receive substantially all of the economic benefits expected to be derived through use of the leased property?* This normally is indicated by a lease term that covers most of the asset's useful life. Since the economic benefit of assets goes down over time (through deterioration and obsolescence), substantially all of the economic benefit can be derived during a lease term that falls significantly short of the full physical life of the asset.

---

[2] Finance leases may also be called "capital leases," which is the term used by the FASB in the United States as well as in the *CPA Canada Handbook, Part II*, for private enterprises. The term "financial leases" is used in the finance industry.

[3] IAS 17 splits this into two separate situations—automatic transfer of title versus a bargain purchase. The outcome is the same either way.

3. *Will the lessor be assured of recovering substantially all of the investment in the leased property, plus a return on the investment, over the lease term?* This is determined on the basis of the present value of the lease payments.
4. *Is the leased asset so highly specialized that only the lessee can obtain the benefit without substantial modification?* This is particularly true of assets that are fixed in place and cannot be moved without incurring costs that probably would exceed the asset's remaining benefits.

Definitions To exercise our professional judgement in applying these guidelines, we need to define the measurement rules. The following definitions apply to both lessees and lessors:

- A **bargain purchase option** exists when there is a stated or determinable price given in the lease that is sufficiently lower than the expected fair value of the leased asset at the option's exercise date to make it likely that the lessee will exercise the option. Even if the lessee does not really want the asset after the end of the lease term, it would be advantageous to exercise the option and then resell the asset at its higher fair value. "Bargain purchase option" is not an explicit term in IAS 17, but it is a useful shorthand expression that is well used in practice.
- A **bargain renewal term** is one or more periods for which the *lessee* has the option of extending the lease at lease payments that are substantially less than would normally be expected for an asset of that age and type. "Bargain renewal term" also is a term not explicitly used in IAS 17 but used in practice because it captures the essence of renewal terms that would strongly entice a lessee to renew.
- The **lease term** includes:
  - All terms prior to the exercise date of a bargain purchase option;
  - All bargain renewal terms; and
  - All renewal terms at the *lessor's* option.
- A **guaranteed residual value** is an amount that the lessee promises the lessor can receive for the asset by selling it to a third party at the end of the lease term. If there is any deficiency in the sales proceeds when the lessor sells the asset, the lessee must make up the difference. The guaranteed residual value is decided when the lease contract is negotiated. A high guaranteed residual value will effectively reduce the periodic lease payments, while a low guarantee will increase the lease payments that a lessor will require to recover the lessor's investment in the asset.
- In contrast, the lessor may not guarantee the residual value, in which instance there is an **unguaranteed residual value**. The lessee has no liability for such an amount, but the size of the lessor's expected residual value will have a direct impact on the size of the lease payments.
- The lessee's **minimum net lease payments** are all payments that the lessee is required to make over the *lease term*, as described above (i.e., including bargain renewal terms), *net* of any operating or executory costs that are implicitly included in the lease payment, *plus* any guaranteed residual value. A bargain purchase price (if any) also is included.

It is important to deduct operating costs from the lease payments to find the **net lease payments**. For example, if the lessor pays insurance on the asset, the lessor includes an estimate of the cost of insurance premiums when setting the lease payments. The insurance is not a cost of *acquiring* the asset; however, it is a cost of *using* the asset. Therefore, any operating costs that are implicitly included in the lease payments must be estimated and subtracted to find the present value of the payments that represent, in substance, the cost of acquiring the asset.

The lessee's minimum net lease payments also do not include any amounts for **contingent lease payments**, which are additional lease payments that are based on subsequent events, such as payments calculated on a percentage of a lessee's gross sales revenue.

- **Initial direct costs** are the costs incurred when negotiating and arranging a lease. For a lessor, these costs may include not only negotiations with the lessee but also negotiations with the vendor or manufacturer from whom the lessor will obtain the asset to be leased.

- The **implicit lease interest rate** is the interest rate that equates (1) the minimum net lease payments, the initial direct costs, and the residual value (whether guaranteed or not) to (2) the fair value of the leased property at the beginning of the lease. This rate is calculated from the *lessor*'s point of view—the lessor's estimated cash flows over the minimum lease term (as defined above).
- The lessee's **incremental borrowing rate (IBR)** is the interest rate that the lessee would have to pay to obtain financing through the bank (or other credit sources) to buy the asset and is determinable with reasonable assurance.[4]

The interest rate used for discounting the net lease payments is the *lessor's* interest rate implicit in the lease, *if known by the lessee*. The lessor's implicit rate usually is *not* known by the lessee because:

- The lessee will not know the lessor's direct costs of the lease;
- The lessee does not know the lessor's estimated unguaranteed residual value;
- The lessor undoubtedly takes into account the expected value of any contingent rent when negotiating the lease terms, but those expected amounts are not included in any calculation from the lessee's point of view; and
- The lessor normally calculates the lease with an eye to obtaining an *after-tax rate of return*, which is not at all relevant to the lessee's accounting (which must be without the effect of income taxes).

When the lessee does not know the lessor's interest rate implicit in the lease, the lessee's incremental borrowing rate is used. In practice, the lessee's IBR is almost always the rate used for the lessee's accounting.

Contingent Rent **Contingent rent** is rent that depends on specified future events. Leases for retail space offer a common example of contingent rent—in addition to basic rent, the lessee (i.e., a retailer) usually agrees to pay a percentage of the store's gross sales to the lessor. Contingent rent may also be based on an asset's volume of use, on variations in the lessor's operating expenses (including property taxes) in connection with the lease, on price indices, or on market interest rates, to name a few.

Contingent rent is excluded from accounting lease calculations for both lessor and lessee. However, they are a very important part of decision analysis for both the lessor and the lessee. Indeed, some lease agreements, especially for retail space, depend on achieving a certain volume of activity; if that volume is not achieved, the lessor may have the right to terminate the lease.

Contingent rents are reported as operating expenses in the period that they are *incurred* rather than when they are *paid*. Sometimes this will require the lessee to accrue estimated contingent rent payments on a quarterly or monthly basis, even though the exact amount will not be known until after the end of the lease year.

Economic versus Useful Life The **economic life** of an asset is the maximum number of years that it can be economically productive. The **useful life** to a particular company may be shorter. For example, desktop computers may be useful for six years, but a company may choose to keep its desktop computers no more than four years to stay up to date. The economic life is six years, while the useful life is four years. Useful life can never be longer than economic life.

Fair Value Ceiling In no case should the asset be recorded at higher than its fair value. Consider a simple example. Suppose that a lessee agrees to pay the lessor $100,000 at the end of each year for four years. The fair value of the asset being leased is $300,000, and the asset

[4] In finance literature, the incremental borrowing rate is often called the *borrowing opportunity rate*, or *BOR*.

has a four-year useful life. The lessor's implicit rate of return is unknown, and therefore the lessee's IBR of 10% is used. At 10%, the present value of the lease payments is $316,987:

$$PV = \$100{,}000 \times (P/A,\ 10\%,\ 4) = \$316{,}987$$

If the lessee uses its IBR, the book value of the asset will be higher than the fair value of the asset. In such a case, the lessee must use a rate that discounts the lease payments to the $300,000 fair value of the asset. The equation is:

$$\$300{,}000 = \$100{,}000 \times (P/A,\ i,\ 4)$$

and must be solved for the value of i. The interest rate that solves this equation is 12.6%.[5]

An Informal Guideline While accounting standards provide criteria for lease classification that are based on the nature of the lease contract itself, professional judgement still is required. The basic issue is whether, in substance, the risks and benefits have been transferred from the lessor to the lessee.

One criterion that is not explicitly cited by the standard setters but that is very useful in practice is to look at the *nature of the lessor*. The nature of the lessor may be key to determining whether the lease is finance or operating.

For example, if the lessor is the leasing subsidiary of a bank, it should be clear that the lease is not an operating lease. Financial institutions have financial assets, not operating assets (except for their own tangible operating assets, of course) on their SFPs. A bank's leasing division will not assume the risks of owning an asset, even though it has legal title to many thousands of them through lease contracts. One can be assured that from the point of view of the bank, the lease is a finance lease, no matter how ingenious the drafting may have been to try to avoid the accounting finance lease criteria.

To fully realize the tax advantages that often are the driving force behind finance leases, a lessor must qualify as a lessor under the income tax regulations. That means that a lessor must derive at least 90% of its revenues from lease transactions. Any company that meets this criterion is a **financial intermediary**. Any lease that such a financial institution enters into can be assumed to be a finance lease, even if financial lease classification is not clear when the four finance lease guidelines have been applied.

CONCEPT REVIEW

1. What is the basic criterion that determines whether a lease is a finance lease?
2. When are operating lease rental payments allocated (as expense) to periods other than those in which the payments are made?
3. List the four guidelines that help financial statement preparers decide whether a lease is a finance lease.
4. Define the following terms:
   - Bargain renewal options;
   - Incremental borrowing rate; and
   - Lease term.
5. How can the nature of the lessor influence the lessee's accounting for a lease?

[5] The implicit rate can quickly be calculated with a financial calculator or with an Excel spreadsheet. An explanation of present value calculations can be found on Connect.

ACCOUNTING FOR FINANCE LEASES—LESSEE

If a long-term lease qualifies as a finance lease for accounting purposes, the asset is recorded on the lessee's books as though it had been purchased and financed by instalment debt. An outline of the accounting is described briefly below:

- The present value of the lease payments is determined by using:
  - The lessor's implicit rate, if known, and otherwise the lessee's IBR.
  - *Net* lease payments for the initial term, plus net lease payments for any bargain renewal terms, plus any renewal terms at the *lessor's* option, plus any *guaranteed* residual value or any bargain purchase price.
- The present value is recorded as the cost of the asset and is classified as a tangible or intangible capital asset. *The recorded cost cannot be higher than the asset's fair value.*
- The offsetting credit is to a *lease liability* account.
- Interest is accrued for each period, charged to interest expense, and credited to the lease liability account.
- Lease payments are debited to the lease liability account.
- The asset is depreciated or amortized by following the company's normal depreciation or amortization policy for that type of asset. However, the depreciation or amortization period cannot exceed the lease term unless the lease contains a bargain purchase option or automatic transfer of title at the end of the lease. Otherwise, the asset will be depreciated or amortized over the lease term (including bargain renewal terms).

The leased asset is accounted for as though it was owned, and the payments are treated as payments on an instalment loan. Once the present value is recorded as an asset and a liability, *there is no connection between the asset and the lease liability in the subsequent accounting.*

FINANCE LEASE ILLUSTRATION—BASIC EXAMPLE

We will begin our illustration of accounting for finance leases with a fairly simple example that focuses on the most significant aspects of lease accounting.

Assume that Lessee Limited wishes to acquire equipment that has an expected economic life of eight years and a fair value of $66,000. Instead of buying the asset outright, the company enters into a lease with Borat Corp., a Canadian finance company that specializes in asset-based financing. The facts are shown in Exhibit 18-2.

EXHIBIT 18-2

LEASE TERMS—BASIC EXAMPLE

- The fair value of the asset is $66,000.
- The lease begins on 1 January 20X2.
- The initial lease term is three years.
- Payments over the initial lease term are $20,000 per year, payable at the beginning of each lease year (i.e., on 1 January 20X2, 20X3, and 20X4).
- At the end of the initial lease term, the lease is renewable for another two years *at Lessee Limited's option* for $5,000 per year. Assume that the normal rental cost of three-year-old equipment of this type is almost $10,000 per year.
- Lessee Limited is responsible for insuring and maintaining the equipment.
- The asset reverts to the lessor at the end of the lease; the lease agreement contains no obligation for Lessee Limited to *guarantee* the residual value. However, the lessor estimates that the asset will have an *unguaranteed* residual value of $15,000 at the end of five years.
- Lessee Limited does not know the lessor's implicit rate of interest in the lease. Lessee's incremental borrowing rate is 8%.

In this example, the important elements for analysis are as follows:

- The *lease term* is five years—the initial lease term of three years plus the bargain renewal term of two years. Five years is 63% of the asset's estimated economic life of eight years.
- The *minimum net lease payments* are $20,000 for each of the first three years and $5,000 per year for the fourth and fifth years, for a total of $70,000. The present value of the minimum lease payments is $63,310:

PV = $20,000 (P/AD, 8%, 3) + $5,000 (P/AD, 8%, 2) (P/F, 8%, 3)
PV = $55,666 + $7,644
PV = $63,310

Note: P/AD means "present value of an annuity due," which has payments at the beginning of each period rather than at the end (which is P/A).

Applying the Lease Guidelines

Does this lease qualify for classification as a finance lease? Exhibit 18-3 applies the four finance lease guidelines to this example. The first and fourth guidelines clearly do not apply. Looking at the lease term relative to the asset's economic life, we can see that the lease covers *most* of the asset's economic life, but clearly not the full life. However, the lease clearly meets the third guideline, and thus Lessee Limited should classify the lease as a finance lease.

LESSEE ACCOUNTING—BASIC EXAMPLE

The general approach is, first, to find the discounted present value of the lessee's cash flows over the lease term, as defined above. Then, that present value is recorded as:

- A capital asset (debit), and
- The principal amount of a long-term liability (credit) (which contains a current component).

EXHIBIT 18-3

APPLYING THE FINANCE LEASE GUIDELINES—BASIC EXAMPLE

Guideline	Analysis
1. Does the lease transfer ownership to the lessee at the end of the lease, either automatically or by provision for a bargain purchase option?	**No.** The lease contains no purchase option and ownership of the asset will not transfer to the lessee at any time.
2. Is the lease term for the major part of the economic life of the asset?	**Perhaps.** The lease covers 5/8 of the asset's economic life, which is a majority of the years. Assets decline in economic value as they age. Lessee Limited may estimate that the asset's *useful* life is five years.
3. Does the PV of the minimum lease payments amount to substantially all of the asset's fair value?	**Yes.** The PV of lease payments is 96% of the asset's fair value.
4. Is the leased asset highly specialized to the lessee?	**No.** The lessor estimates a significant residual value, which would not be the case if the asset were highly specialized to the lessee's use.

The asset and liability are identical only when first recorded at the commencement of the lease. Subsequently, there is no parallel between accounting for the asset and the liability. In each year of the lease, the asset and the liability are remeasured individually:

- The leased asset is accounted for exactly as though it had been *purchased* by the lessee, except for some limitation on the depreciable life, if the asset is depreciable (which we will explain shortly).
- The liability is accounted for by the effective interest method, with each payment recorded first as interest on the outstanding balance for the preceding accounting period. The residual of the payment is recorded as a reduction of the principal amount.

The principal amount at the inception of the lease, 2 January 20X2, is the full present value of $63,310. The lease will be recorded as follows:

Asset under finance lease	63,310	
Lease liability		63,310

Amortization Table

Before accounting for the annual cash lease payments, we need to construct a *debt amortization table.* A lease amortization table is similar to the amortization tables illustrated in Chapter 13 for amortizing discount or premium on long-term debt. For leases, the purpose of a *lease amortization table* (or *amortization schedule*) is to determine how much of each year's cash lease payment goes to (1) interest expense and (2) reduction of principal.

An amortization table for this lease example is shown in Exhibit 18-4. The beginning-of-year cash flows are placed in the fourth column, and the net lease present value (at 8%) is placed at the beginning of the second column ("outstanding balance").

The first payment is made at the commencement of the lease, 1 January 20X2. Since this is the first day of the lease, there has been no elapsed time and therefore no accrued interest. The full amount of the net lease payment reduces the outstanding balance:

1 January 20X2:		
Lease liability	20,000	
Cash		20,000

Interest

On 1 January 20X3, the payment must be divided between interest and principal payment. Exhibit 18-4 shows that interest is $3,465 (i.e., $43,310 × 8%), which means that of the second $20,000 lease payment (1 January 20X3), $3,465 is charged to interest, and the remaining $16,535 of the lease payment will go to reducing the outstanding principal balance.

EXHIBIT 18-4

LEASE AMORTIZATION TABLE

1 January	Outstanding Balance	Interest at 8%	Net Lease Payment 1 January	Decrease in Balance	31 December Balance
20X2	$63,310	$ —	$20,000	$(20,000)	$43,310
20X3	43,310	3,465	20,000	(16,535)	26,775
20X4	26,775	2,142	20,000	(17,858)	8,917
20X5	8,917	713	5,000	(4,287)	4,630
20X6	4,630	370	5,000	(4,630)	0
Totals		$6,690	$70,000	$(63,310)	

The interest that has accrued through 20X2 must be recorded at year-end:

31 December 20X2:		
Interest expense	3,465	
Lease liability		3,465

On 1 January 20X3, Lessee Limited makes the second lease payment:

1 January 20X3:		
Lease liability	20,000	
Cash		20,000

Note that the 31 December 20X2 interest accrual is credited directly to the lease liability account. Alternatively, the accrued interest could have been credited to *accrued interest payable*, in which case the credit for the cash payment would need to be broken down between interest and principal. In practice, it is much simpler just to credit accrued interest directly to the lease liability account—then the cash payments can be credited to the lease liability without having to figure out how much of the payment gets credited to which account.

Exhibit 18-5 shows all of Lessee Limited's entries for the liability. The final column of the exhibit shows the accumulated balance of the total lease liability account. The year-end interest accruals increase the balance, while the lease payments reduce the balance. The final lease payment, on 1 January 20X6, reduces the balance to zero.

Observe that the lease liability balance after each lease payment is exactly the same amount as shown in the final column (year-end balance) of Exhibit 18-4. These amounts are highlighted in both exhibits.

Depreciating Leased Assets

Exhibit 18-5 illustrates only the entries for the liability. In addition, Lessee Limited must depreciate the asset. Depreciation is based on the discounted present value of the asset, as recorded, minus any guaranteed residual value.

IAS 17 identifies the depreciation period as being the shorter of (1) the asset's useful life or (2) the lease term (including bargain renewal terms). In practice, it is extremely unlikely that an asset's useful life will be less than the lease term *when the lease is being negotiated.* After all, why agree to pay for an asset after it has stopped being useful? However, things happen. Perhaps an asset becomes obsolete during its lease term, or the lessee changes the nature of its business and no longer needs that asset. In any case, the lessee needs to change the useful-life estimate for depreciation and shorten the depreciation period.

The economic life of an asset usually exceeds the lease term. The really important point is that the depreciation period can never be *longer* than the lease term unless the lessee will obtain title to the asset at the end of the lease, either automatically or by exercising a bargain purchase option.

If we assume that Lessee Limited's accounting policy for this type of asset is to amortize it on the straight-line basis with a full year's depreciation taken in the first year, then the depreciation of the leased equipment on 31 December 20X2 will be $12,662 (i.e., $63,310 ÷ 5). The entry at the end of each year, 20X2 through 20X6, will be:

Depreciation expense	12,662	
Accumulated depreciation – asset under lease		12,662

At the end of the lease term, when the asset is returned to the lessor, Lessee Limited must write off the fully depreciated asset:

Accumulated depreciation – asset under lease	63,310	
Asset under finance lease		63,310

EXHIBIT 18-5

LESSEE'S RECORDING OF FINANCE LEASE LIABILITY—BASIC EXAMPLE

	Dr.	Cr.	Lease Liability Balance
1 January 20X2			
Asset under finance lease	63,310		
Lease liability		63,310	63,310
Lease liability	20,000		**43,310**
Cash		20,000	
31 December 20X2			
Interest expense	3,465		
Lease liability		3,465	46,775
1 January 20X3			
Lease liability	20,000		**26,775**
Cash		20,000	
31 December 20X3			
Interest expense	2,142		
Lease liability		2,142	28,917
1 January 20X4			
Lease liability	20,000		**8,917**
Cash		20,000	
31 December 20X4			
Interest expense	713		
Lease liability		713	9,630
1 January 20X5			
Lease liability	5,000		**4,630**
Cash		5,000	
31 December 20X5			
Interest expense	370		
Lease liability		370	5,000
1 January 20X6			
Lease liability	5,000		**0**
Cash		5,000	

Financial Statement Impacts—Lessee

Statement of Financial Position At the end of 20X2, the outstanding principal balance in the lease liability account is $43,310 (before any accrued interest), as shown in both Exhibits 18-4 and 18-5. This liability must be shown as a long-term liability on Lessee Limited's SFP, except for the portion that will be paid within the next year. In our example, the next payment is at the start of the next fiscal year, and therefore the entire payment will be classified as a current liability. The total balance of $46,775, representing the principal balance of $43,310 plus accrued interest of $3,465, will be classified on the SFP as follows:

Current liability	$20,000
Long-term liability	26,775
Total	$46,775

Although the full amount of the next payment is classified as current in this simple example, that situation will arise only when the payment is due *immediately* after the reporting date. The current liability is not normally the amount of the next payment due. The current liability is not the amount of cash that will be paid in the next year, but rather *how much of the year-end liability balance* will be paid in the next year. We will illustrate this point a little later in the chapter.

On the asset side, the leased equipment will be shown either separately (if material) or as a part of the general equipment account. Similarly, the accumulated depreciation will be shown either separately or combined with the accumulated depreciation of similar assets. If the leased asset and its accumulated depreciation are shown on the face of the SFP as part of property, plant, and equipment, the company should disclose the amounts pertaining to leased assets in a disclosure note.

As usual, of course, the equipment can be shown net of accumulated depreciation on the face of the SFP with the gross amount and accumulated depreciation shown in a note.

Statement of Comprehensive Income The net earnings section of the SCI will include depreciation expense and interest expense. For 20X2, the amounts relating to the lease are:

Depreciation expense	$12,662
Interest expense	3,465

Each of these expenses can be combined with similar costs; the expenses relating to leased assets need not be reported separately. The interest expense for the lease will, however, be included with other long-term interest, which is reported separately from interest on short-term obligations.

Statement of Cash Flows If the indirect approach to operating cash flow is used, depreciation expense ($12,662) will be added back as an adjustment to net income for determining the cash flow from operations. As well, the principal component of the lease payment (for 20X2: $20,000 – $3,465 interest = $16,535 principal) is shown in the financing activities section as an outflow. Similarly, net income includes $3,465 in interest expense that was not a cash outflow in 20X2.

The only cash flow relating to the lease was the $20,000 payment at the beginning of the lease term. This amount will be shown as a financial outflow. The total amount of the finance liability will not enter the statement of cash flows because the offset to the lease liability was the leased asset, not cash. However, note disclosure of this non-cash transaction, if material, will be required.

Notes to Financial Statements The notes should disclose the commitment for future finance lease payments, both in total and individually for each of the next five years. The payments due under all of the reporting enterprise's finance leases can be added together and reported in the aggregate, of course.

Deferred Income Taxes

In Canada, leases normally are taxed in accordance with their legal form. The tax deduction is the amount of lease payments made during the tax year. The fact that a lease may be accounted for as a finance lease is of no interest to the Canada Revenue Agency.

Therefore, leases that are accounted for as finance leases are generally taxed by CRA as an operating lease. This difference in treatment will give rise to a *temporary difference*. Accounting for deferred income taxes and temporary differences was explained in Chapter 16.

CONCEPT REVIEW

1. Why must operating and executory costs be subtracted from finance lease payments before the lease payments are capitalized?
2. What impact does lease capitalization have on a company's total assets and on its debt-to-equity ratio?
3. Over what period should the lessee depreciate a leased asset?

Accounting by Lessees—Modified Example

The basic example was fairly simple because (1) the lease year coincided with the lessee's reporting year, (2) there was no guaranteed residual value, and (3) the lease included no provisions for operating costs. To explore lessee accounting a little more realistically, we will use an example that removes those simplifying assumptions.

The terms of the lease are given in Exhibit 18-6. In this example, the net lease payments are $180,000 per year—the $200,000 annual lease payment minus the annual insurance cost included therein. The present value of the lease includes both the net lease payments and the guaranteed residual value, even though the likelihood of having to pay that full guaranteed residual value is unlikely. The present value calculation is:

$$PV = \$180{,}000(P/AD, 8\%, 5) + \$75{,}000(P/F, 8\%, 5)$$
$$PV = \$776{,}183 + \$51{,}044 = \$827{,}227$$

Observe that the guaranteed residual value increases the PV by about 7%, even though the lessee may not have to pay all or any of this amount. This additional amount will affect the implicit interest cost implicit in the annual payments. This causes the lessee's PV to be higher than the asset's fair value.

Fair Value Cap and Implicit Interest Rate The fair value of the asset is the upper limit. In this example, the lessee's IBR yields a PV higher than the fair value. Therefore, the lessee

EXHIBIT 18-6

LEASE TERMS—MODIFIED EXAMPLE

- The fair value of the equipment is $800,000 at the inception of the lease.
- The lease term is five years. The lease commences on 1 April 20X2.
- There is no renewal option.
- Annual lease payments are $200,000 per year. Payments are due at the beginning of each lease year.
- The lease payments include the cost of insurance, estimated at $20,000 per year.
- The lessee guarantees a residual value of $75,000; the lessor promises to exercise due diligence to get the highest residual value on the open market at the end of the lease.
- The lessee does not know the lessor's implicit rate of interest in the lease. The lessee's incremental borrowing rate is 8%.
- The lessee's fiscal year ends on 31 December.

must calculate the implicit interest rate that equates the lease payments (plus residual value) to the $800,000 fair value:[6]

$$\$800{,}000 = \$180{,}000(P/AD,\ i,\ 5) + \$75{,}000(P/F,\ i,\ 5)$$
$$i = 9.8034\%$$

Implicit interest rates seldom work out to nice round numbers.

Amortization Table Exhibit 18-7 shows the amortization table for this lease, using the rate implicit in the lease. The entry at the commencement of the lease will be:

Asset under finance lease	800,000	
Lease liability		800,000

Executory Costs Lease payments often include implicit operating costs that will be paid by the lessor. Examples include insurance, maintenance, property taxes, and other continuing costs of using the asset. Implicit costs, such as these, are especially common in real property leases. These costs are known as executory costs. Executory costs must be excluded from the discounted cash flows. Estimated executory costs included in the lease payments must be charged to the relevant expense accounts (e.g., insurance, taxes) when the lease payment is made.

In this example, the annual lease payment includes an amount for insurance. When the lessee makes the lease payment, the insurance cost is debited to an expense account. For the initial payment on 1 April 20X2:

Insurance expense	20,000	
Lease liability	180,000	
Cash		200,000

Note that the insurance expense debit is for the originally *estimated* amount and not for the actual amount, even if the lessor actually pays a different amount for insurance. The

EXHIBIT 18-7

LESSEE AMORTIZATION TABLE—MODIFIED EXAMPLE

Lease Year Ending 31 March	Outstanding Balance	Interest at 9.8034%	Net Lease Payment 31 March	Change (Decrease) in Balance	Ending Balance
20X2	$800,000	$ —	$180,000	$(180,000)	$620,000
20X3	620,000	60,781	180,000	(119,219)	500,781
20X4	500,781	49,094	180,000	(130,906)	369,875
20X5	369,875	36,260	180,000	(143,740)	226,135
20X6	226,135	22,169	180,000	(157,831)	68,304
20X7	68,304	6,696	75,000	(68,304)	0
Totals		$175,000	$975,000	$(800,000)	

[6] The implicit interest rate was determined by entering the cash flows in an Excel worksheet and letting the computer find the implicit rate. This approach is highly recommended.

reason is that the estimate was used to determine the net lease payments, which then were discounted to find the present value. The only way that the liability accounting will work out is to stick to the predetermined *net lease* payments, even though the actual cost to the lessor may be different.

If the actual cost of the insurance is different from the estimate, and if the lease agreement requires (or permits) the lessor to refund any difference between the estimate and the actual cost, the lessee will credit the refund to the insurance expense account. Similarly, if the lessee is responsible for paying any additional amount, that extra payment will be charged to insurance expense. The basic PV and interest calculations are not affected.

Interest Expense In the basic example, interest was easy to deal with because the lease year coincided with the lessee's fiscal year. In the modified example, however, the lease year starts in April while the fiscal year starts in January. This is normal, of course—leases are not arranged for accountants' convenience.

At the end of 20X2, the lessee must accrue interest. The outstanding balance from 1 April to 31 December is $620,000. Interest at 9.8034% for 9 months is $45,586. The entry on 31 December 20X2 is:

Interest expense ($620,000 × 9.8034% × 9/12)	45,586	
Lease liability		45,586

After this interest accrual, the balance of the lease liability is $620,000 + $45,586 = $665,586.

On 1 April 20X3, the interest expense must be updated:

Interest expense ($620,000 × 9.8034% × 3/12)	15,195	
Lease liability		15,195

Observe that the 1 April 20X3 accrual is based on the outstanding amount of $620,000 as shown in the amortization table. The 31 December balance is *not* the basis for the final lease quarter's accrual because the PV calculation was based on annual payments, not quarterly. The interest period must coincide with the lease period used for calculating the implicit interest rate. Exhibit 18-8 shows the interest allocation that will occur over the five-year lease term, which affects six fiscal periods because of the overlap between lease year and fiscal year.

On 1 April 20X3, the $200,000 payment includes insurance cost of $20,000. This cost must be treated as a period expense. The entry is as follows:

Insurance expense	20,000	
Lease liability	180,000	
Cash		200,000

Depreciation The example contains a guaranteed residual value of $75,000. When determining the asset's depreciable cost, this guaranteed amount must be treated in exactly the same manner as though the asset had been purchased rather than leased. Remember that if any asset reaches the end of its useful life, any difference between the remaining undepreciated cost and the actual salvage value of the asset is reported as a gain or loss.

Thus, the depreciable cost of the leased asset is $725,000 (i.e., $800,000 – $75,000). Annual depreciation will be $145,000 *per lease year* instead of $160,000 as in the previous simpler example.

Cost Allocation Interest is not the only cost that must be allocated to fiscal years. Depreciation also must be allocated to fiscal years. Any operating costs that are included in the gross lease payment would be allocated, if they are material. In this example, those costs consist of the estimated insurance cost. Each cost must be allocated at 31 December of each year.

EXHIBIT 18-8

ALLOCATION OF INTEREST EXPENSE TO FISCAL YEARS

Lease Payment	Implicit Interest*		Allocation for Accounting		Fiscal Year: Interest Expense	Fiscal Year: Year-End
1 April 20X2	$ 0	=	$ 0	=	$ 45,586	31 Dec. 20X2
			45,586			
1 April 20X3	60,781	=	15,195	=	52,016	31 Dec. 20X3
			36,821			
1 April 20X4	49,094	=	12,273	=	39,468	31 Dec. 20X4
			27,195			
1 April 20X5	36,260	=	9,065	=	25,692	31 Dec. 20X5
			16,627			
1 April 20X6	22,169	=	5,542	=	10,564	31 Dec. 20X6
			5,022			
1 April 20X7	6,696	=	1,674	=	1,674	31 Dec. 20X7
Total interest	$175,000		$175,000		$175,000	

*From Exhibit 18-7.

Actual versus Guaranteed Residual Value After five years, the accumulated depreciation will be $145,000 × 5 = $725,000. The remaining book value is $75,000, which is the amount of the guaranteed residual value.

However, suppose that at the end of the lease, the lessor is able to sell the asset to a third party for only $50,000. The lessee will have to pay the $25,000 difference between the guarantee and the actual value. This amount must be recorded as a loss because the lease has ended—there is no future benefit to be gained from this payment. The entry will be as follows:

The entries to record the return of the asset to the lessor and this loss will be as follows:

Lease Liability	75,000	
Accumulated depreciation—leased asset	725,000	
Asset under finance lease		800,000

Loss on lease termination	25,000	
Cash		25,000

Full Set of Entries All of the journal entries to record both the leased asset and the lease liability over the entire five-year lease term are shown in Exhibit 18-9. The last column shows the lease liability balance at each date. The amounts highlighted in **blue** show the balance after each payment; these amounts match the ending lease-year balances shown on the amortization table in Exhibit 18-7. The amounts highlighted in **green** show the liability balance at the end of each fiscal year.

The liability balance at the end of each fiscal year is the *total* liability; on the SFP, the total will be divided into current and long-term portions, as described above.

EXHIBIT 18-9

LESSEE'S RECORDING OF FINANCE LEASE—MODIFIED EXAMPLE

	Dr.	Cr.	Lease Liability Balance
1 April 20X2			
Asset under finance lease	800,000		
Lease liability		800,000	
Insurance expense	20,000		
Lease liability	180,000		**620,000**
Cash		200,000	
31 December 20X2			
Interest expense	45,586		
Lease liability		45,586	**665,586**
Depreciation expense (9 months)	108,750		
Accumulated depreciation		108,750	
Prepaid insurance	5,000		
Insurance expense		5,000	
1 April 20X3			
Interest expense	15,195		
Lease liability		15,195	
Insurance expense	20,000		
Lease liability	180,000		**500,781**
Cash		200,000	
31 December 20X3			
Interest expense	36,821		
Lease liability		36,821	**537,602**
Depreciation expense	145,000		
Accumulated depreciation		145,000	
1 April 20X4			
Interest expense	12,273		
Lease liability		12,273	
Insurance expense	20,000		
Lease liability	180,000		**369,875**
Cash		200,000	

continued on next page

EXHIBIT 18-9 (*cont'd*)

LESSEE'S RECORDING OF FINANCE LEASE—MODIFIED EXAMPLE

	Dr.	Cr.	Lease Liability Balance
31 December 20X4			
Interest expense	27,195		
Lease liability		27,195	**397,070**
Depreciation expense	145,000		
Accumulated depreciation		145,000	
1 April 20X5			
Interest expense	9,065		
Lease liability		9,065	
Insurance expense	20,000		
Lease liability	180,000		**226,135**
Cash		200,000	
31 December 20X5			
Interest expense	16,627		
Lease liability		16,627	**242,762**
Depreciation expense	145,000		
Accumulated depreciation		145,000	
1 April 20X6			
Interest expense	5,542		
Lease liability		5,542	
Insurance expense	20,000		
Lease liability	180,000		**68,304**
Cash		200,000	
31 December 20X6			
Interest expense	5,022		
Lease liability		5,022	**73,326**
Depreciation expense	145,000		
Accumulated depreciation		145,000	
1 April 20X7			
Interest expense	1,674		
Lease liability		1,674	
Depreciation expense (3 months)	36,250		
Accumulated depreciation		36,250	
Insurance expense	5,000		
Prepaid expenses		5,000	
Lease liability	75,000		**0**
Accumulated depreciation	725,000		
Asset under finance lease (return of asset)		800,000	
Loss on lease termination	25,000		
Cash		25,000	

Calculating the Lease Liability Balance—Short-Cut Method

Suppose that your business colleague (or your instructor) asks for the balance of a lease liability at a specific point in time, mid-lease. One way to calculate the information is to prepare an amortization table. That is simple enough if the lease is straightforward and has a short term, but it is time consuming (especially in an examination) to make those calculations for a long and complex lease.

There is a quicker way of doing it. The trick is to remember that at any point during the lease term, *the balance of the lease liability account* is:

1. The present value of the remaining cash flows discounted to the date of the most recent payment, plus
2. Interest accrued since that last payment, if any.

For example, what is the lease liability of the previous example at 31 December 20X4? We can see from Exhibit 18-9 that the balance at that date is $397,070. The balance consists of two components:

PV of the remaining lease payments at 31 March 20X4 (see Exhibit 18-7)	$369,875
Accrued interest from 1 April through 31 December 20X4 (see Exhibit 18-8)	27,195
Lease liability, 31 December 20X4 (see Exhibit 18-9)	$397,070

To calculate this balance directly, all we need to know are (1) the remaining cash flows and (2) the interest rate:

$$PV = [\$180{,}000(P/F, 9.8034\%, 1) + \$180{,}000(P/F, 9.8034\%, 2) + \$75{,}000(P/F, 9.8034\%, 3)] \times [1 + (0.098034 \times 9/12)]$$

$$PV = [\$163{,}929 + \$149{,}294 + \$56{,}652] \times 1.0735255$$

$$PV = \$369{,}875 \times 1.0735255 = \$397{,}070$$

This is the same as the balance shown in Exhibit 18-9, obtained without calculating an amortization table. If you are asked to determine the liability balance at the end of Year 34 of a 40-year lease, this method is definitely a time-saver!

CONCEPT REVIEW

1. How should the current portion of the lease liability be determined?
2. When lease payment dates do not coincide with the company's reporting periods, how is interest expense calculated?
3. How does a guaranteed residual value affect the lessee's accounting for the lease?

SALE AND LEASEBACK

A **sale and leaseback** is a linked arrangement wherein a company sells an asset and simultaneously leases it back. Sale and leasebacks are most common for buildings. The transaction changes the asset from an *owned* asset to a *leased* asset.

A sale and leaseback gives an immediate cash inflow to the seller. The cash can be used to retire debt (particularly any outstanding debt on the asset, such as a mortgage or a collateral loan), used for operating purposes, or used for any other purpose that management wishes (e.g., paying a dividend).

The seller must evaluate the lease and identify it as being either a finance lease or an operating lease. The criteria for this judgement are exactly as described in earlier sections of this chapter.

The sale portion of the deal is initially recorded just like any other sale, with a gain or loss recorded for the difference between the net proceeds from the sale and the asset's net book value. The gain or loss might not be recognized in income in the year of the sale, however.

If the lease part of the sale-and-leaseback arrangement is a finance lease, *any gain or loss is deferred and amortized over the lease term.*

If the lease is an *operating lease*, the treatment of the gain or loss depends on the relationship between the selling price of the asset and its fair value at the date of sale:

- If the sale price is *equal* to the fair value, the gain or loss is recognized immediately.
- If the sale price is *greater* than fair value, the excess over fair value is deferred and amortized over the term that the asset is expected to be used (i.e., the lease term).
- If the sale price is *less* than the asset's fair value, any gain or loss is recognized in earnings immediately *unless* the lease payments are less than market lease terms, in which case the gain or loss is deferred and amortized over the lease term.

Bear in mind that the gain or loss is determined by the relationship between (1) the selling price and (2) the asset's carrying value. Fair value does not come into it—it is quite possible for the sales price to be below fair value and still trigger a gain.

The objective of deferring the gain is to prevent income manipulation. Without this restriction, a company could sell property at an inflated amount and then lease it back under a finance lease, thereby recognizing a gain in the period of the sale. In fact, what the company really would be doing is using the property as collateral for a loan that is hidden as a lease. Therefore, any gain (except as noted above for an operating lease) must be deferred and amortized in proportion to the lease payments over the lease term.

Interestingly, the requirement for deferring a gain can still result in the enhancement of reporting income over a period of years. This opportunity arises when a company enters into a sale and leaseback arrangement for a building that it owns but only partially occupies. Suppose, for example, that a company occupies only 10% of a building. If the company sells the building at a profit and then leases back just the portion that it occupies under a finance lease, the full gain can be deferred and amortized. The amortized gain may more than offset the lease payments, thereby enhancing reported net income over the lease period.

Recording a Sale and Leaseback

Assume that Vendeur Limited owns a building in central Montreal. Vendeur enters into an agreement with Bailleur Incorporated, whereby Vendeur sells the building to Bailleur and simultaneously leases it back. The details are as follows:

- The original cost of the building was $10,000,000; it is 60% depreciated on Vendeur's books.
- Bailleur agrees to pay Vendeur $8,500,000 for the building, which is the fair value at the time of the sale.
- Bailleur agrees to lease the building to Vendeur for 20 years. The annual lease payment is $850,000, payable at the *end* of each lease year.
- There is no guaranteed residual value.
- Vendeur will pay all of the building's operating and maintenance costs, including property taxes and insurance.
- The effective date of the agreement is 1 January 20X1.
- Vendeur's incremental borrowing rate is 9%.
- Bailleur's interest rate implicit in the lease is computed after tax and is not disclosed to Vendeur.

- Vendeur uses straight-line depreciation for its buildings, with full-year depreciation in the year of acquisition.

The building has a net book value, after accumulated depreciation, of $4,000,000. Since the selling price is $8,500,000, Vendeur realizes a gain of $4,500,000 on the transaction. The treatment of the gain depends on *whether the lease qualifies as a finance lease or as an operating lease.*

Finance Lease If the lease qualifies as a finance lease, the gain must be deferred and amortized over the lease term. Applying the four tests:

1. Is it likely that the lessee will obtain ownership of the leased property at the end of the lease? *No.*
2. Will the lessee receive substantially all of the economic benefits of the building? *Uncertain.* The building was 60% depreciated at the time of the sale, indicating that it is not a new building. The 20-year lease term could well be a major part of the remaining economic life of the building.
3. Is the lessor assured of recovering the investment in the leased property, plus a return on the investment, over the lease term? *Probably, because the present value of the lease payments is $7,759,264 at 9%, which is more than 90% of the sales price of the building.*
4. Is the leased asset highly specialized to the lessee? *No, there is no indication to that effect.*

Since at least one of the guidelines for classifying the lease as a finance lease is satisfied, the leaseback should be recorded as a finance lease. As a result, the gain must be deferred and amortized over the 20-year lease term.

The journal entry to record this sale on 1 January 20X1 is:

Cash	8,500,000	
Accumulated depreciation, building	6,000,000	
Building		10,000,000
Deferred gain on sale and leaseback of building		4,500,000

Using Vendeur's IBR of 9% yields a present value of the 20-year stream of end-of-year payments equal to $7,759,264. The lease is recorded as follows:

Building under finance lease	7,759,264	
Lease liability		7,759,264

At the end of 20X1, Vendeur will:

- Record the interest expense (at 9%);
- Pay the $850,000 annual lease payment to Bailleur;
- Depreciate the asset; and
- Amortize the deferred gain.

On 31 December 20X1, the interest expense and the lease payment will be recorded as follows:

Interest expense (7,759,264 × 9%)	698,334	
Lease liability		698,334
Lease liability	850,000	
Cash		850,000

Vendeur uses straight-line depreciation with a full years' depreciation in the year of acquisition. Since the lease term is 20 years, the straight-line rate is 5%. The entry to record depreciation of the leased building will be as follows, assuming no residual value:

Depreciation expense, building under finance lease	387,963	
Accumulated depreciation, building under finance lease		387,963

Finally, the deferred gain on the sale must be amortized. The gain should be amortized over the lease term in proportion to the lease payments. Since the payments are straight line over 20 years, the gain must similarly be amortized straight line over 20 years:

Deferred gain on sale and leaseback of building	225,000	
Depreciation expense, leased building ($4,500,000 ÷ 20)		225,000

The amortization of the gain is *credited* to the depreciation expense charged for the asset. The reason is that the sale and leaseback transaction had the effect of taking a building with a $4,000,000 book value and re-recording it on Vendeur's books at $7,759,264, close to its fair value. By offsetting the gain against the asset depreciation, the depreciation expense is reduced to $162,963, which is closer to the amount the building depreciation would have been if it had not been sold.

Operating Lease If the lease does not qualify as a finance lease, then by default it must be an operating lease. When the lease is an operating lease, the treatment of the gain or loss depends on the relationships between (1) the *carrying value* (or carrying value) of the asset being sold, (2) the *fair value* of the asset sold, and (3) the *transaction price* assigned to the asset in the sale and leaseback:

- If the transaction is *at fair value*, any gain or loss would be recognized immediately and not deferred.
- If the transaction price is *above fair value*, the difference between carrying value and the transaction price would be treated in two segments:
  - The difference between carrying value and fair value would be recognized immediately as a gain or loss; and
  - The difference between fair value and the transaction price would be deferred and amortized over the period during which the asset is expected to be used.
- If the transaction price is *below fair value*, the difference between carrying value and fair value is recognized immediately, *except* when the lease has sub-market lease payments that compensate the lessee for the loss. In that case, the difference between the transaction price and the carrying value is deferred and amortized over the period of expected use of the asset.

The first situation—a fair value transaction—is highly likely to occur in arms-length transactions. Other types of deals are likely to occur only between related parties, thereby raising many questions concerning accounting manipulation and tax avoidance, as well as potential ethics issues.

Thus, you will be happy to know that we will not go any further into the matter of operating leasebacks in this book. It is more important for you to understand the more common sale and leaseback agreement that results in a finance lease.

Leases for Land plus Buildings

A single long-term lease may cover the lease of a building as well as the land it is on. In accounting for such a lease, IAS 17 requires that the minimum lease payments be allocated between the land and building on the basis of "relative fair values of the leasehold interests in the land element and buildings element of the lease." This statement is easily misunderstood. It does *not* mean that the fair values of the land and building are the basis for the allocation. Instead, it means the fair value of each asset's *benefits* are being transferred to the lessee.

Perhaps the simplest way of grasping this concept is look at the land first. Land does not normally lose its economic value over time. There is no need for the lessor to be compensated for land deterioration, provided that the land is not being polluted and thereby becoming less valuable during the lease term. The lessor simply needs to earn a return on the investment in the land.

Buildings are different. Over the course of a long lease term, there is bound to be significant deterioration in a building, as well as obsolescence. For example, old multi-floor industrial buildings are largely obsolete now. Modern production generally requires vast floor spaces on a single level. Thus, those old buildings end up either getting torn down, or (if they are in good locations), they are converted for residential use, which has far less value. A long-term lease for a building, therefore, must compensate the lessor for significant loss of economic value.

Once the lease cash flows have been allocated to land and buildings, each component is accounted for separately. Usually, the land lease is reported as an operating lease, since the lease does not cover the major part of the land's life (being infinite) nor do the land-related portion of the lease payments cover most of the land's value.

The building, however, may be reported as either an operating lease or a finance lease. The guidelines for that reporting decision are the same as we have discussed above.

IAS 17 recognizes that the land portion of the lease may be immaterial. In that case, or if there is no basis on which to allocate the land and building portions, the lease can be accounted for as a whole without separate regard for the land portion.

CONCEPT REVIEW

1. Why may a company attempt to structure a lease to avoid having it classified as a finance lease for financial reporting purposes?
2. If a company sells an asset at a gain and then leases the asset back, how should the gain be recognized for financial reporting purposes?

LESSEE DISCLOSURE

Operating Leases

In the notes to the financial statements, lessees should give a general description of their significant leasing arrangements, including the basis on which contingent rent (if any) is determined and whether there are any renewal and/or purchase options. If any lessor has imposed financial restrictions on the lessee, such as limitations on additional debt or on dividend distributions, those should be disclosed.

Quantitatively, lessees should disclose lease payments recognized as expense in the current period, separated into (1) minimum lease payments and (2) contingent rents. Lessees should also disclose the company's obligation for operating lease payments (1) for the next year, (2) in total for the next four years, and (3) in total for all later years.

Operating leases that are on a year-by-year basis usually are not included in the disclosure because there is no obligation beyond the current year.

Finance Leases

A company's rights to leased assets are different from its rights to owned assets. A company can sell, modify, or otherwise dispose of owned assets without restriction. Owned assets can also be used as collateral for a loan. Leased assets, on the other hand, belong to the lessor.

The lessee does not have the same rights of ownership, even though the lessee bears substantially all of the risks and benefits of ownership and reports the lease as an asset.

To clarify that some assets shown on the balance sheet have been obtained through finance leases, both the leased assets and the related lease obligations should be reported separately, either on the face of the balance sheet or in a note.

Of course, the current portion of the lease liability should be shown separately, as has been described earlier in this chapter, *if* the lessee's reporting practice is to use a current–noncurrent classification in the SFP.

Other recommended disclosures are:

- A general description of the lessee's significant finance lease arrangements, including:
  - The basis for contingent rent, if any;
  - Any renewal terms, purchase options, or escalation clauses; and
  - Any financial restrictions imposed by the lessor, such as limits on dividend payments, additional debt, or additional leasing.
- The amount of any contingent rents recognized as expense during the period.
- For each class of leased asset, the net carrying value at the reporting date.
- The total of future minimum lease payments *and their present value* for:
  - The coming year;
  - Future years 2 through 5; and
  - All years (in aggregate) after year 5.
- A reconciliation between total future minimum lease payments and their present value.

Leases are financial instruments. Therefore, leases must conform to the general disclosure requirements for financial instruments, as discussed in Chapter 13.

Disclosure Example

An example of a finance lease disclosure note is shown in Exhibit 18-10. BCE Inc. has finance leases for two types of assets—communication satellites and office space. The disclosure shows that the company is committed to total future payments of $2,865 million on the year-end 2011 leases. The present value of that commitment is $1,959 million.

LONG-TERM LEASES: PROS AND CONS

Transfer of Income Tax Benefits

The transfer of income tax benefits from the lessee to the lessor is the driving force behind the bulk of finance leases. The legal owner of an asset can deduct CCA on the tax return. But the owner may not be able to use the CCA deduction or the full benefit of that deduction. Some examples of such a situation are:

- The owner is a nonprofit organization, such as a school, hospital, or charity.
- The owner is a for-profit business but either is losing money or is not earning enough to use the full amount of the available CCA.
- The owner is profitable but pays taxes at a lower rate than potential lessors.

If any of these conditions exist, then the CCA is more valuable to a lessor than to the potential user of the asset. Lessors calculate their return on investment on an after-tax basis, and lease industry competition forces the lessor to pass the benefit of any tax reduction on to the lessee in the form of lower lease payments. Therefore, the asset can often be leased for a cash flow present value that is less than the amount the lessee would pay to buy the asset.

Long-term leasing has several other potential advantages over buying an asset. However, the perceived advantages to the lessee also have offsetting disadvantages. For each purported advantage we will look at the apparent benefits first (**Pro**), and then at the related disadvantages (**Con**).

EXHIBIT 18-10

BCE INC. LEASE DISCLOSURE

Finance Leases

BCE's significant finance leases are for office premises and satellites. The office and campus leases have a typical lease term of 15 years. The leases for satellites, used to provide programming to our Bell TV customers, have lease terms ranging from 12 to 15 years. The satellite leases are non-cancellable.

The following table shows additions to and the net carrying amount of assets under finance leases.

	Additions		Net Carrying Amount	
At December 31	**2011**	**2010**	**2011**	**2010**
Network infrastructure and equipment	**263**	187	**913**	889
Land and buildings	**5**	79	**634**	725
Total	**268**	266	**1,547**	1,614

The following table provides a reconciliation of our minimum lease payments to their present value for our finance lease obligations.

At December 31, 2011	2012	2013	2014	2015	2016	Thereafter	Total
Minimum future lease payments	417	381	239	186	174	1,468	2,865
Less:							
Future finance costs	(124)	(111)	(100)	(91)	(84)	(396)	(906)
Present value of future lease payments	293	270	139	95	90	1,072	1,959

Source: BCE Inc. Annual Report 2011, Note 13, page 100. Used with permission from BCE Inc.

Off-Balance-Sheet Financing

Pro If a company enters a long-term lease and that lease does not qualify as a finance lease for accounting purposes, the company effectively has obtained financing for an asset without having to show the asset (and any related liability) on its SFP. For example, airlines often use leasing in this manner by entering into operating leases that last for several years but do not last long enough for the lease to qualify as a finance lease. Lessees may view "off-balance-sheet" financing as an advantage because they effectively incur debt that does not appear on the SFP.

Con The shorter the lease, the greater is the cost to the lessee. In shorter leases, more of the risk remains with the lessor. The lessor does not accept this risk out of generosity. The cost is passed back to the lessee in the form of higher annual lease payments and/or heavy cancellation penalties if the lessee does not renew. Therefore, a lessee may obtain off-balance-sheet financing, but at a real economic cost in higher expenses and operating cash flow expenditures.

100% Financing

Pro No financial institution will lend a buyer the full amount of the purchase price. Normally, financing can be obtained for no more than 75% or 80% of the cost of the asset. In contrast, a lease can effectively provide full financing, since there is no substantial down payment to be made at the inception of the lease.

Con This advantage exists only for assets that are readily transferable if the lessee defaults (e.g., automobiles, airplanes) and only to lessees that have high credit ratings. For other assets and less creditworthy lessees, the lessor covers the risk by forward-weighting the lease payments; that is, most of the cash flow for lease payments is in the early years of the lease. Also, since lease payments are payable at the beginning of each period, the first payment is, in effect, a down payment.

Protection against Obsolescence

Pro The shorter the lease term, the easier it is for the lessee to stay up to date with the latest technology. If a new product or process becomes available, the lessee can refuse to renew the existing lease and move to the newer product instead. An alternative is for the lessor to provide upgrade privileges in the lease. For example, an existing leased photocopier may be replaced by a newer model, or a leased automobile may be "rolled over" to a new model every second or third year. Such lease arrangements do help the lessee guard against obsolescence.

Con Flexibility comes at a price. The risk of obsolescence falls on the lessor, and the lessor will compensate for the added risk by charging higher lease payments. Lessor-provided upgrades can help provide flexibility, but they do lock the lessee into the lessor's product. As well, automatic upgrades are expensive. Many companies find it much less costly to skip a product generation unless it is crucial to be on the cutting edge of technology (e.g., many companies running Windows XP skipped Windows Vista and later installed Windows 7, thereby saving on both software costs and training costs with little or no loss of productivity; many are now skipping Windows 8).

Protection against Interest Rate Changes

Pro Lease payments are always determined on the basis of fixed interest rates, even when the lease contains escalation clauses or contingent payments. Therefore, a long-term or finance lease can protect the lessee from interest rate fluctuations.

Con If the lessee's business fluctuates in response to economic conditions, it may be better to use variable-rate loans from financial institutions to finance the assets. When the economy is down, interest rates are down, thereby not locking the company into a high implicit interest rate.

CONCEPT REVIEW

1. What is meant by off-balance-sheet financing?
2. Who holds legal title to a leased asset?
3. How can a lease be used to transfer CCA tax benefits from the lessee to the lessor?

AVOIDING LEASE CAPITALIZATION

IAS 17 (and its predecessor standards from the FASB and the CICA) has led to a number of capitalization-avoidance techniques and to the development of a whole industry dedicated to devising ways of leasing assets to companies while avoiding the capitalization criteria. Three common methods of avoiding capitalization are discussed below.

Use Contingent Rent Base a large part of the lease payment on contingent rent. Contingent rent is an amount that is dependent on future events, such as the sales volume for the retail occupant in a shopping mall. Contingent rent is ignored when the lease is being evaluated as a possible finance lease. Therefore, the larger the amount of rental that can be made dependent on future events, the lower the minimum net lease payments will be.

Insert a Third Party The true nature of a lease can be disguised by inserting a third party between the lessee and the lessor. The most common approach is for the lessee to form a separate company, the purpose of which is to lease assets to the operating company. The separate company enters into the formal lease agreement with the lessor, obligating itself to pay for the full cost of the asset over the lease term, and then enters into a year-by-year lease with the operating lessee.

Impose a Substantial Penalty for Non-renewal Corporations may lease major and crucial operating assets under lease agreements that provide for a year-by-year renewal (at the lessee's option) or for lease terms that are considerably shorter than the economic life of the asset. The lessor's offset for assuming higher risk is to insert very high cancellation or non-renewal clauses. Operating leases can be the result of a well-thought-out strategic positioning, but quite often they are deliberate attempts to obtain assets through off-balance-sheet financing. This approach is probably the most common method of avoiding lease capitalization.

LESSOR ACCOUNTING

Now that we have seen how lessees account for a finance lease, we can turn our attention to the other party in the transaction—the lessor.

Lessors: A Finance Industry

Any company can be a lessee. In theory, any company could also be a lessor. In practice, however, lessors constitute a highly concentrated specialized industry. In accounting textbooks, we do not normally examine specialized industries. Banks, insurance companies, mutual funds, regulated public utilities, real estate development companies, and private investment companies are all examples of specialized industries. Lessors fit into that same general category.

In Canada, not just any company can be an effective lessor. The specialized nature of leasing is the result of the *Income Tax Act*. Only companies that derive at least 90% of their revenue from leasing are permitted to deduct CCA in excess of rental revenue—a crucial aspect of successful lessor activity. Lessors are financial intermediaries. Often, they are subsidiaries of broader financial institutions, such as chartered banks or asset-based lending institutions. There are no publicly listed lessors in Canada.

An example of a major lessor is International Lease Financing Corporation (ILFC), a U.S.–based company that leases aircraft and related equipment. In 2011, ILFC had 927 aircraft leased to 177 different airline companies in 78 countries. The company is an indirect wholly owned subsidiary of AIG. AIG is primarily an insurance company. ILFC operates mainly through operating leases, although the company does engage in some finance lease activity.

Captive Finance Companies A finance company may also be a finance subsidiary of a manufacturer that was set up to facilitate sales of the manufacturer's products. These subsidiaries are known as **captive leasing companies**. For example, private-company Daimler Chrysler Financial Services Inc. offers sales financing through its subsidiaries, Chrysler Financial Canada, Mercedes-Benz Credit Canada, and Truck Finance Canada.

A manufacturing company also may carry out leasing services by incorporating a special-purpose entity (SPE) that is then consolidated into the parent company's financial statements. For example, Bombardier Inc. states in its 2011 financial statement notes that the company has "certain SPEs created solely to provide financing related to the sale of commercial aircraft." Further, the company explains:

> Typically, these SPEs are financed by third-party long-term debt and by third-party equity investors who benefit from tax incentives. The aircraft serve as collateral for the SPEs long-term debt.[7]

[7] From the Bombardier Inc. 2011 Annual Report, page 195, Note 34; www.sedar.com, posted 1 March 2012.

We will return to this topic of manufacturer's "sales-type leases" later in the chapter.

Differences between Lessee's and Lessor's Net Cash Flows

The lessor will work with the same basic set of lease terms, except that there is no prescribed interest rate. Instead, the lessor must use the rate of return that equates the PV of the lease payments to the cost of acquiring the asset, including any direct costs incurred in negotiations and any incidental costs to acquire the asset (e.g., transportation, commissions, etc.). There are some aspects of the lease that do not apply to the lessee and that therefore differentiate the lessor's net cash flow from that of the lessee. The three most important differences are:

1. *The initial cost of the asset.* The lessor may obtain a more favourable price on the asset, often by bulk buying. For example, lessors that deal in aircraft leasing usually buy a large number of planes from the manufacturer and then lease them in smaller quantities to a several individual airlines. By bulk buying, the lessor can negotiate especially favourable prices that would not be available to individual airlines. Therefore, an asset's cost to the lessor may be significantly less than the asset's fair value as perceived by the lessee.
2. *Residual value.* The lessor may expect a significant residual value. For example, when an airplane's lease with a mainline carrier ends, the residual value of the plane may still be quite high because smaller carriers, charter airlines, and cargo lines can use older planes.
3. *Tax shield.* The lessor can gain a significant tax shield from the aircraft's depreciation. The early tax cash flow savings from deducting depreciation (CCA, in Canada) will increase the after-tax cash flow from the lease, especially in the early years, greatly affecting the internal rate of return (IRR) on the lease.

As we continue with our basic example, we will take the first two differences into account, but leave the third aside because it is a specialized topic that analysts must be aware of but do not need to calculate.

Internal Rate of Return

The lessor accounts for the lease by the effective interest method. It may seem apparent that the lessor would automatically know the interest rate that it is charging the lessee. However, leases are *negotiated*, and since the lessor's cash flows will not be exact mirrors of the lessee's cash flow, the lessor's effective interest rate may not be obvious. Therefore, we must first determine the interest rate implicit in the lease, which represents the **internal rate of return (IRR)** that a lessor is earning (before tax) in this lease.

Our lessor in the basic example, Borat Corp., will base its accounting on the lease cash flows shown in Exhibit 18-2, plus these additional factors:

- Borat Corp. negotiated a purchase price of $60,000 for the asset. Additional direct costs amounted to $1,500.
- The expected unguaranteed residual value at the end of the lease term (i.e., five years) is $4,300.

To find the internal rate of return, we find the value of i in the following equation:

$$\$60{,}000 + \$1{,}500 = \$20{,}000\ (P/AD,\ i,\ 3) + \$5{,}000\ (P/AD,\ i,\ 2)\ (P/F,\ i,\ 3) + \$4{,}300(P/F,\ i,\ 5)$$

This equation can be solved by using a financial calculator or an Excel spreadsheet or by trial-and-error using present value tables.

The value of i that satisfies this equation is 14%. The lessor's rate of return is significantly higher than the 8% cost to Lessee Limited. The higher rate is due to the lower purchase price that the lessor was able to negotiate, plus (to a lesser extent) the unguaranteed residual value. This phenomenon is what can make leasing quite attractive in the right circumstances.

Guaranteed versus Unguaranteed Residual Values It is important to understand the different roles of guaranteed and unguaranteed residual values in finance lease accounting:

- A *guaranteed* residual value is part of the definition of *net lease payments* for both the lessee and the lessor.
- The lessee uses only the *guaranteed* residual value as part of its discounted cash flow because the lessee is committed to pay it if the lessor is not able to recover that amount by disposal of the asset at the end of the lease.
- The lessor, however, uses the lessor's estimate of residual value when determining the lease's implicit interest rate, regardless of whether it is guaranteed or unguaranteed by the lessee.

If the lessee guarantees a specified residual value, that guaranteed amount is the *minimum* residual value that the lessor would assume, but the lessor may well anticipate an even higher *unguaranteed* residual value, which is used in the lessor's analysis.

Lessor Accounting—Net Lease Basis

Initial Recording As we discussed previously, finance leasing companies almost always are financial institutions or financial intermediaries. Their business is to provide financing for an entity's asset acquisition, financing that is in the form of a lease rather than purchase financing, such as a direct loan. The lessor does not want any physical assets—the lessor's assets are *financial* assets. Thus, when a lessor acquires an asset on behalf of a lessee, the asset is delivered directly to the lessee.

Instead of recording the physical asset, the lessor records the *net lease receivable*. The **net lease receivable** is the amount that the lessor spent (or owes) for the asset and associated direct costs. The lessor negotiates a lease agreement with the lessee that will enable the lessor to recover the investment in the leased asset as well as earn interest. Thus, the net lease receivable is, by definition, equal to the costs incurred by the lessor. The entry for Borat would appear as follows:

Net lease receivable	61,500	
Cash (and/or accounts payable)		61,500

After initially recording the lease, Borat will account for each lease payment as a combination of (1) interest income and (2) principal payments to reduce the outstanding lease receivable. This is the reverse of the lessee's lease liability, but the amounts usually will be different because the lessor has a somewhat different cash flow. An amortization table can clarify the lessor's accounting.

Amortization Table The amortization table for Borat Corp. is shown in Exhibit 18-11. The first lease payment occurs at the commencement of the lease and immediately reduces the net lease receivable:

Cash	20,000	
Net lease receivable		20,000

This leaves $41,500 as the lease receivable throughout 20X2. At the end of 20X2, Borat must record the accrued interest, which is $41,500 × 14%, or $5,810, as indicated in the amortization table. The remaining amount of the payment, $14,190, reduces the net lease receivable.

Recording by the Net Method The entire series of entries for Borat is shown in Exhibit 18-12. These entries are essentially the reverse of the lessee's entries, except that Borat makes no entries concerning the asset because the physical asset is not on Borat's books.

The first two entries are to record the lease at its commencement and to record receipt of the first lease payment. At the end of 20X2, Borat must accrue the finance income earned on

EXHIBIT 18-11

LESSOR AMORTIZATION TABLE—BASIC EXAMPLE

1 January	Lease Receivable Before Payment	Interest at 14%	Payment Received, 1 January	Lease Receivable Change	Lease Receivable After Payment
20X2	$61,500	$ —	$20,000	$(20,000)	**$41,500**
20X3	41,500	5,810	20,000	(14,190)	**27,310**
20X4	27,310	3,823	20,000	(16,177)	**11,133**
20X5	11,133	1,559	5,000	(3,441)	**7,692**
20X6	7,692	1,077	5,000	(3,923)	**3,769**
20X7	3,769	531*	4,300	(3,769)	**0**
Totals		$12,800	$74,300	$(61,500)	

*Rounded up by $3 to balance.

the principal balance of $41,500 that was outstanding throughout 20X2, computed by the implicit interest rate of 14%. The accrued income is debited to the lease receivable balance rather than being recorded as accrued finance income. Receipt of the 1 January 20X3 lease payment is then credited in its entirety to the lease receivable.

Throughout the life of lease, Borat records the lease payments and accrues interest on the outstanding balance. The net lease receivable balances are shown in the final column of Exhibit 18-12. The balances shown in boldface type are those at the end of the lease year, and correspond directly to the end-of-year balances shown in Exhibit 18-11. The nonbolded amounts are the lease balances that will be shown on Borat's balance sheet at the end of each fiscal year.

Current–Noncurrent Distinction As we have discussed above, companies that negotiate leases are financial intermediaries. Financial institutions do not classify their assets on a current/noncurrent basis—the classification usually is in order of liquidity. Therefore, we do not need to worry about how much of the receivable will be collected within the next year.

Lessor Accounting—Gross Lease Basis

It is easy to see that lessor accounting is essentially just the reverse of lessee accounting, *if* the net lease basis is used. However, lessors usually *record* their lease receivables on a **gross lease basis**. Under the gross lease basis, the lessor records not just the PV of the future cash flows. Instead, the lessor records the undiscounted cash flows offset by a contra account for unearned finance income. At each reporting date, the lessor calculates the amount of finance income that has been earned for the reporting period. Instead of adding the accrued income to the lease receivable, it is deducted from the unearned finance income.

For *reporting*, the lessor will show only the net amount on the SFP. That is, the net asset is the remaining undiscounted lease payments minus the remaining unearned finance income.

Example Using the example above, the beginning net lease receivable consists of two amounts—(1) the total undiscounted cash flows that the lessor expects to receive, reduced by (2) the amount of interest that the lessor will recognize over the lease term:

Lease payments receivable	$70,000
Estimated residual value	4,300
Gross lease receivable (1)	74,300
Less: Unearned finance income (i.e., interest) (2)	12,800
Net lease receivable	$61,500

EXHIBIT 18-12

LESSOR RECORDING OF FINANCE LEASE—BASIC EXAMPLE

	Dr.	Cr.	Net Lease Receivable Balance—Dr.
31 December 20X1			
Lease receivable	61,500		
Cash, accounts payable		61,500	$61,500
[Delivery of equipment and commencement of the lease]			
1 January 20X2			
Cash	20,000		
Lease receivable		20,000	**$41,500**
31 December 20X2			
Lease receivable	5,810		$47,310
Finance income—leases ($41,500 × 14%)		5,810	
1 January 20X3			
Cash	20,000		
Lease receivable		20,000	**$27,310**
31 December 20X3			
Lease receivable	3,823		$31,133
Finance income—leases ($27,310 × 14%)		3,823	
1 January 20X4			
Cash	20,000		
Lease receivable		20,000	**$11,133**
31 December 20X4			
Lease receivable	1,559		
Finance income—leases ($11,133 × 14%)		1,559	$12,692
1 January 20X5			
Cash	5,000		
Lease receivable		5,000	**$ 7,692**
31 December 20X5			
Lease receivable	1,077		$ 8,769
Finance income—leases ($7,692 × 14%)		1,077	
1 January 20X6			
Cash	5,000		
Lease receivable		5,000	**$ 3,769**
31 December 20X6			
Lease receivable	531		$ 4,300
Finance income—leases ($3,769 × 14%)		531	
1 January 20X7			
Cash	4,300		
Lease receivable (to record the receipt of the residual value)*		4,300	**$ 0**

*The actual value received would be recorded, not the estimate. Any gain or loss is reported in earnings.

Using the basic example, the entry made at the commencement of the lease is as follows under each of the two different methods:

1. *Net lease method* (as in Exhibit 18-12):

31 December 20X1		
Lease receivable	61,500	
Cash, accounts payable		61,500

2. *Gross lease method*:

31 December 20X1		
Lease receivable	74,300	
Unrealized finance income		12,800
Cash, accounts payable		61,500

Under the gross method, the next three entries will be as follows (from Exhibit 18-12):

1 January 20X2		
Cash	20,000	
Lease receivable		20,000

31 December 20X2		
Unrealized finance income	5,810	
Finance income		5,810

1 January 20X3		
Cash	20,000	
Lease receivable		20,000

At the end of 20X2, the net balance of the lease receivable will be as follows:

Lease receivable ($74,300 – $20,000)	$54,300
Less unearned finance income ($12,800 – $5,810)	6,990
Net lease receivable	$47,310

This is the same amount shown in Exhibit 18-12 as the net lease receivable on 31 December 20X2. After the second $20,000 lease payment is made, the net balance drops to $27,310, which also can be verified by referring to Exhibit 18-12.

Why Use the Gross Method?

The gross and net methods yield the same results for the lessor's financial reporting. The net method is simpler and corresponds to the method normally used by lessees, and thus one might wonder why lessors use the gross method for recording.

Like all of the accounts shown on any company's SFP, the leases receivable account is a *control account*. The SFP amount is a total; underlying that total is a large number of individual leases. For good internal control, an important characteristic of a control account is that it can easily be reconciled to the underlying subsidiary records. For leases receivable, that means that the receivables for the individual leases can be added up to verify the balance in the control account. The gross method makes that reconciliation easier.

Lessors will have thousands, perhaps tens of thousands, of individual leases. Since the amounts in the lease payments receivable account are gross amounts, the balance can be verified by adding the remaining gross payments shown on all of the individual leases.

In contrast, under the net method it is necessary to compute the present value of each lease at a particular point of time to perform the reconciliation. Some of the leases may be in arrears, and the present values may not correspond with their planned amortization schedules. Reconciliation on the net method would be a major headache, even in computerized systems. Therefore, the gross method is used. The gross method has the additional advantage of separating the control account function (via the lease payments receivable) from the revenue recognition function (via the unearned finance revenue).

Lessees are likely to have relatively few leases, and those leases are incidental to their principal operations. Therefore, maintaining balances by the net method is no great problem for most lessees. Every lease that is reported as a finance lease will have its own amortization table, and summing the present values is fairly straightforward.

Disclosure for Lessors

Lessors should disclose the following:

- A general description of the lessor's leasing arrangements;
- The aggregate future minimum lease payments receivable (i.e., the gross amount) and the total amount of unearned finance income, reconciled to the present value of leases as shown on the SFP;
- The gross lease payments and PV of future minimum lease payments for each of the following periods:
  - Within the next year;
  - The total for years two through five; and
  - Later than the fifth year, in total.
- Any contingent rentals that have been taken into income;
- The estimated amount of unguaranteed residual values; and
- The accumulated allowance for uncollectible lease payments.

Exhibit 18-13 shows an example of lessor disclosure. Aastra Technologies Limited is a Canadian company that provides an extensive portfolio of enterprise communications products, system, and applications through a global network that reaches into more than 100 countries. As you can see from this description, Aastra is a producer, not a financial intermediary. However, the company enters into leases for its products, and those leases can be either operating or finance leases. The finance leases are reported on the gross method.

CONCEPT REVIEW

1. Why do lessors use the gross method rather than the net method of accounting for finance leases?
2. Where does the *unearned finance revenue* account appear on the statement of financial position?

Leases by Manufacturers and Dealers

Basic Nature Manufacturers and dealers may use leasing as a way of making sales. We all are familiar with the automobile advertising that prominently features interest rates for leasing cars, sometimes as low as 0%. But automobiles are not the only products sold heavily

EXHIBIT 18-13

EXAMPLE OF LEASE DISCLOSURE
AASTRA TECHNOLOGIES

Years Ending January 1

(in thousands of Canadian dollars)

8. Finance lease receivables

The Company's finance lease receivables include the following:

	2011	2010	January 1, 2010
Gross investment in finance leases	**$48,731**	$45,236	$44,646
Unearned finance income	**(3,926)**	(3,486)	(4,218)
Net investment in finance leases	**44,805**	41,750	40,428
Current portion	**(21,336)**	(17,426)	(11,831)
	$23,469	$24,324	$28,597

The future receipts of gross investment in finance lease receivables are as follows:

	2011	2010	January 1, 2010
Less than one year	**$23,297**	$19,397	$13,991
Between one and five years	**24,876**	25,804	30,608
More than five years	**558**	35	47
	$48,731	$45,236	$44,646

The future receipts of net investment in finance lease receivables are as follows:

	2011	2010	January 1, 2010
Less than one year	**$21,336**	$17,426	$11,831
Between one and five years	**22,951**	24,291	28,559
More than five years	**518**	33	38
	$44,805	$41,750	$40,428

Source: Aastra Technologies Limited, Annual Report 2011, www.sedar.com, posted 29 March 2012.

via leases. Other examples include computer equipment, office equipment, many types of industrial equipment, and business jets.

This type of lease is commonly known as a **sales-type lease** because the real point of it is to "move" the product. IFRS refers to this as a **manufacturer's lease**, although it can be used by dealers as well as by manufacturers. A sales-type or manufacturer's lease is a finance lease that, from the lessor's point of view, represents the sale of an item of inventory.

For the *lessee's* financial reporting, it does not matter whether the lessor is the producer of the product or is simply a financial intermediary. For the *lessor's* financial reporting, however, the distinction matters because a sales-type lease is viewed as two distinct (but linked) transactions:

1. The sale of the product, with recognition of a profit or loss on the sale; and
2. The financing of the sale through a finance lease, with finance income recognized over the lease term.

There is absolutely nothing new in recording or reporting a sales-type lease, once the transaction has been recognized as being two separate but related transactions. The sale is recorded at the fair value of the asset being sold, with the asset received in return being the present value of the lease payments. The lease is then accounted for as a **direct-financing lease.**

Example—Sales-Type Lease Assume that on 31 December 20X1, Binary Corporation, a computer manufacturer, leases a large computer to a local university for five years at $200,000 per year, payable at the beginning of each lease year. The normal cash sales price of the computer is $820,000. The computer cost Binary Corporation (BC) $500,000 to build. The lease states that the computer will revert to BC at the end of the lease term, but a *side letter* from BC to the university states BC's intention not to actually reclaim the computer at the end of the lease.

The implicit interest rate that discounts the lease payments to the $820,000 fair value of the computer is 11.04%. Unless the cost of financing is well in excess of this rate, the lease can be assumed to be a finance lease. Because the lessor is the manufacturer of the product and because the computer is carried on BC's books at a value that is less than fair value, the lease clearly is a sales-type lease.

The sale component of the transaction will be recorded as follows, using the net method:

31 December 20X1		
Lease payments receivable	820,000	
Sales revenue		820,000
Cost of goods sold	500,000	
Computer inventory		500,000

The first payment (at the inception of the lease) will be recorded as:

31 December 20X1		
Cash	200,000	
Lease payments receivable		200,000

The income statement for 20X1 will include a gross profit of $320,000 relating to the lease transaction, which is the profit on the sale. The statement of financial position on 31 December 20X1 will show a net lease receivable of $620,000: the gross lease payments of $1 million, minus the unearned finance revenue of $180,000, minus the first payment of $200,000.

In 20X2 and following years, the lease will be accounted for exactly as illustrated above for direct financing leases. Finance revenue (or interest income) will be accrued each reporting period at the rate of 11.04% on the net balance of the receivable and charged against the unearned finance revenue, while payments will be credited directly to the lease payments receivable account. The statement of financial position will include the *net* balance of the receivable.

Manufacturers and suppliers normally establish an incorporated subsidiary (an SPE) to handle the leases. These subsidiaries use the gross method of recording, as illustrated in Exhibit 18-13 for Aastra Technologies.

Estimating the Selling Price In the example above, the implicit interest rate was obtained by finding the rate that discounted the lease payments to the cash selling price of $820,000. But, in practice, the fair value or "cash price" may not be so obvious. The problem arises because many products that are sold via sales-type leases are subject to discounts or special "deals" wherein the actual price is less than the stated list price. In theory, the lease payments should be discounted to equal the actual price rather than the list price. In practice, this is harder to do because the actual price is often hidden in the transaction.

Sometimes, the "true" selling price can be approximated by looking at the appropriateness of the implicit interest rate. For example, a common tactic in long-term automobile leasing is to advertise a very low rate of interest (e.g., 0.9%), a rate that clearly is below the market rate of interest. A super-low rate really represents a decrease in the price of the car. A potential lessee can see what price he or she is getting by discounting the lease payments at whatever rate the bank would be willing to finance the car (i.e., at the borrower's incremental borrowing rate).

This essentially is the solution offered by IAS 17— the sales revenue should be measured as the lower of:

- The selling price as recorded for outright sales; or
- The present value of the minimum lease payments accruing to the lessor, discounted at the market rate of interest.

The actual determination of the revenue split (and profit split) between the sale and the lease components of the transaction is a matter of considerable judgement. The split will affect (1) gross profit on the sale in the current period and (2) interest revenue in future periods. Management is likely to define the sales price in a way that best suits its reporting needs. If the statements are audited, the auditor must test the reasonableness of management's sales price definition.

CONCEPT REVIEW

1. What is the basic difference between a sales-type lease and a finance lease?
2. In a sales-type lease, why is it often difficult to determine objectively the sales price of the item being "sold"?

LEASES IN THE STATEMENT OF CASH FLOWS

Lease capitalization has an interesting impact on the statement of cash flows. If a lease is reported as an operating lease, the lease payments are deducted as an expense in determining net income. Since the expense does represent a cash flow, the impact of the lease payments stays in the cash flow from operations.

The only exception arises when the cash flows are uneven or differ from the pattern of rent expense recognition. If lease payments in a year are different from the amount expensed, the difference will be an adjustment to cash flow from operations (if the indirect approach is used) or excluded from operating cash flows (if the direct approach is used).

If a lease is capitalized, on the other hand, the effects on the statement of cash flows are quite different:

- Although the initial lease agreement is viewed, in substance, as a purchase, the transaction is not shown on the statement of cash flows as an investing activity because it is a non-cash transaction—a lease obligation is exchanged for a leased asset. This non-cash transaction must be disclosed in the notes.
- All expenses relating to the leased asset are removed from net income when determining cash flow from operations:
  - Depreciation expense relating to the leased asset is added back to net income; and
  - The implicit interest expense is segregated on the statement of cash flows as part of interest expense relating to long-term obligations; the interest paid can be classified as either operating or financing.
- The principal repayment portion of the lease payments is shown as a financing activity (i.e., as a reduction of a liability).

The overall effect of lease capitalization is that the lessee can remove the lease payments from operating cash flow and reclassify them as financing activities. Over the life of the lease, the full amount of the net present value of the net lease payments is lifted out of operations (by adding back the depreciation) and instead is classified as a reduction of debt.

ETHICAL ISSUES

Under IAS 17, leasing offers multiple opportunities for managers to commit actions to deliberately mislead financial statement users. The most obvious and widespread is the simple expedient of leasing long-term assets through a series of relatively short-term leases. Accounting standards were not intended to make lease reporting an *option*. The intent was to *require* companies to report leases according to their substance.

In practice, though, managers often choose the reporting method for long-term leased assets and then negotiate the lease to accomplish that reporting goal. By carefully structuring lease provisions, management (with the encouragement of the leasing industry) can obtain long-term use of assets while still reporting the leases as operating leases.

For managers who are trying to meet short-term profit goals, this practice has two primary advantages. When leases are classified as operating leases:

- Both the leased assets and the related liabilities are kept off the balance sheet; and
- The lease-related expenses flowing onto the income statement will be lower in the early years of the lease contracts.

This is a practice known as "window dressing"—making the financial position of the company look better than it really is. Since the intent is to mislead financial statement readers, it clearly is an unethical practice.

Leasing also provides an opportunity for unethical behaviour through the use of related parties. Leasing through a related third party, such as through a company controlled by an officer or shareholder of the lessee, provides an opportunity for the third party to skim off profits through inflated lease payments. The requirements for consolidating *special purpose entities* (called *variable interest entities* in the United States) are intended to keep a company from hiding leases off-balance-sheet, but this intent can be circumvented by unethical managers.

Finally, sale-and-leaseback arrangements provide an opportunity to manipulate earnings. This can be done by (1) either selling an entire asset and then leasing only part of it back, or (2) leasing it via a series of operating leases that permit the selling company to recognize gains from the transaction in net income.

Looking Forward

The accounting profession's method of accounting for leases has always been unsatisfactory. The practice of financing assets through long-term leases has been an increasingly widespread practice (i.e., outside the railroad industry) for at least 60 years. Although the finance industry always differentiated between a financial lease and an operating lease, the accounting practice had been to base accounting on where legal title rested. Since the lessor had title to the asset, all lease payments were reported as current expenses.

The traditional practice led to vast amounts of off-balance-sheet financing, and eventually the then-new FASB in the United States decided to issue a new accounting standard on the topic. As the result of its deliberations, the FASB issued the accounting standard that has, with little change, governed lease accounting for 40 years, classifying the continuum of leases into two categories—*operating* leases and *capital* leases (which are called *finance* leases in IFRS, and *financial* leases in the finance industry). The IASB took the same general approach as the FASB, requiring differentiation between the two substantively different types of leases.

As a result of the requirement for capitalization, a whole new industry sprouted, one that was dedicated to devising leases that were finance leases in substance but that avoided classification under the FASB and IASB guidelines.

In recent years, a widespread dissatisfaction with lease accounting has led accounting standard setters to reconsider lease accounting. The approach has been to eliminate the operating-finance distinction and to treat all lease commitments in the same way, reporting them on the SFP at the present value of the lease commitment.

In May 2013, the IASB issued a re-exposure draft on a new lease accounting standard to replace IAS 17. The new standard is expected to be issued in 2014, with a probable effective date of 2017. The appendix to this chapter will explain the forthcoming changes, based on the May 2013 exposure draft.

ACCOUNTING STANDARDS FOR PRIVATE ENTERPRISES

The leasing standards for private enterprises are, in substance, the same as for publicly accountable enterprises. However, there are some differences in detail. One detail is that the *CPA Canada Handbook, Part II*, uses the term **capital lease** rather than the current IASB term *finance lease*. This is not a substantive difference in the terms *capital lease*, *finance lease*, and *financial lease* (the term used in the finance industry); all mean the same thing and are interchangeable. The standards do not require the use of only one term.

LESSEES

Criteria for Lease Capitalization

The basic guidelines (or criteria) for classifying a lease as a capital lease are essentially the same as in IAS 17 except:

- The *CPA Canada Handbook* rejects the criterion of "specialized use" that is contained in IAS 17. The AcSB states that not only is "special purpose" difficult to define but also that "special purpose" does not, in itself, indicate that substantially all of the risks and rewards of ownership have been transferred to the lessee.
- The guidelines contain quantitative "bright lines" that have been carried over from earlier leasing standards in the United States and Canada:
  - For deciding whether the lease term is equal to a major portion of the asset's economic life, major portion is "usually 75% or more."
  - For comparing the present value of minimum lease payments to the fair value of the asset, the guideline is "usually 90% or more."

Although IAS 17 deliberately avoids specifying quantitative bright lines, those thresholds continue to be used in practice in most entities, public and private, because they provide a target of "reasonableness" that tends to promote consistency. Nevertheless, the intended overall guiding principle for capital/finance leases continues to be whether the lease transfers substantially all of the risks and rewards of ownership to the lessee.

Interest Rate for Discounting

IAS 17 states that the interest rate should be the lessor's rate implicit in the lease, if known, and otherwise the lessee's IBR. In contrast, the *CPA Canada Handbook, Part II,* requires that the *lower* of the two rates be used. Since the lessor's implicit pretax rate of return is seldom known, the distinction may have little significance in general practice.

Leases of Land and Buildings

When a lease involves land *and* buildings, the lease payments are segregated between the land and buildings on the basis of the fair values of the underlying properties. This differs from IAS 17, in which the allocation is based on the *fair values of the leasehold rights*, not on the land and buildings themselves.

Disclosure

The disclosure requirements are relatively modest:

Operating Leases For leases lasting more than one year, disclose the future minimum lease payments (1) for each of the next five years and (2) in total.

Capital Leases
For capital leases, the following should be disclosed:

- The total amount of payments required for each of the next five years;
- The interest rate, maturity date, and amount outstanding for capital leases;
- The aggregate amount of interest expense, disclosed either separately or as part of interest on long-term debt;
- Whether leases are secured (e.g., by other assets of the entity); and
- For the leased asset(s), the cost (i.e., initial discounted present value), the depreciation method being used, and the amount of accumulated depreciation.

LESSORS

Classification

Whereas IAS 17 uses the same criteria for both lessees and lessors, the *CPA Canada Handbook, Part II*, imposes additional requirements before the lessor can capitalize a lease:

- The lessor's credit risk relating to the lease and the lessee is normal and is compared with the collectibility of similar receivables; and
- The lessor's unreimbursable costs can be reasonably estimated.

Both of these additional requirements must be satisfied. If not, then the lease is reported as an operating lease rather than a capital lease.

An interesting result of this additional requirement is that the lease can end up being reported asymmetrically. If the lessee reports the lease as a finance lease while the lessor reports it as an operating lease, the asset will be reported on the SFP of *both* the lessee and the lessor.

If the criteria for capitalization are met, a lessor then must classify the lease as either a direct financing lease or as a sale-type lease. A direct financing lease is essentially the same as a finance lease under IAS 17.

Initial Direct Costs

Under IAS 17, the lessor's initial direct costs (e.g., commissions or legal fees) for finance leases are capitalized as part of the lessor's cash flow and amortized over the lease period. In contrast, the *CPA Canada Handbook, Part II*, says that the lessor's initial direct costs should be expensed, both for a direct financing lease and a sales-type lease. However, the *CPA Canada Handbook, Part II*, also requires that an equivalent amount of the unearned lease income be recognized. The net effect is that there is no difference in the impact on net income.

For operating leases, initial direct costs are deferred and amortized over the lease term.

Impairment

At the end of each reporting period, a private enterprise lessor should assess the collectibility of the future cash flows from each lease. If future payments appear to be in doubt, such as by financial failure of the lessee, the lease should be written down to the highest estimated recoverable value, as either (1) the present value of the likely future cash flows or (2) the amount that can be realized by selling or releasing the asset.

Sale and Leaseback

The ASPE requirements for reporting any gain or loss arising from the sale in a sale and leaseback transactions differ from those of IAS 17 as follows:

- If the asset's fair value is less than its carrying value at the time of the sale, the loss should be recognized immediately because the asset was impaired at the date of sale.
- If the lease is an operating lease, any gain or loss from the sale transaction should be capitalized and amortized proportionate to the rental payments over the lease term (i.e., *not* immediately recognized as allowed by IAS 17 under most circumstances).
- If the lease is a capital lease, any gain or loss from the sale transaction should be capitalized and amortized proportionate to the depreciation on the leased asset (i.e., *not* over the term of the lease as required by IAS 17).

RELEVANT STANDARDS

CPA Canada Handbook, Part I (IASB):

- IAS 17, Leases

CPA Canada Handbook, Part II (ASPE):

- Section 3065, Leases

SUMMARY OF KEY POINTS

1. A lease is an agreement that conveys from a lessor to a lessee the right to use real property, plant, or equipment for a contracted price per period.
2. A lease for a relatively short period of an asset's useful life and that does not transfer substantially all of the asset's risks and benefits to the lessee is classified as an *operating lease*. Under an operating lease, rent payments are reported by the lessee as a current expense as the asset is used. For the lessor, the asset remains on the books and the rent payments are recorded as rent income.
3. A lease that transfers substantially all of the risks and benefits of ownership to the lessee is called a *finance lease*. There are four guidelines used to determine whether a lease is a finance lease: (1) Do the terms of the lease make it highly likely that title to the asset will transfer to the lessee at the end of the lease; (2) does the lessee enjoy the use of the asset over the major part of its economic life; (3) is the lessee committing to lease payments that will return substantially all of the lessor's investment in the leased asset plus a return on the investment; or (4) is the asset so special purpose for the lessee that it would have little benefit to others?
4. Finance leases are recorded by the lessee as though the asset had been purchased. For the lessee, the net lease payments over the lease term are discounted, usually at the lessee's incremental borrowing rate (assuming that the lessor's rate is not known), and the present value is recorded as both an asset and a liability. Once recorded, the asset and the liability are accounted for independently.
5. The asset is depreciated in accordance with the lessee's policy for assets of that type except that the depreciation period is limited to the minimum lease term (including bargain renewal terms) unless there is a bargain purchase option or other transfer of title to the lessee at the end of the lease term.

6. The lessee's lease liability is accounted for as an instalment loan with blended payments. Interest expense is calculated at the same rate as was used for discounting the payments; the excess of payments over interest expense reduces the outstanding liability balance.
7. The current portion of the lessee's lease liability consists of (1) accrued interest to the SFP date plus (2) the amount of principal that will be paid over the next year.
8. Finance leases are usually *taxed* as operating leases. As a result, temporary differences usually result in deferred income tax liabilities for the lessee.
9. A sale and leaseback arrangement is an agreement in which the owner of an asset sells it to a lessor and simultaneously leases it back. The subsequent lease is accounted for as either finance or operating, as for other leases. For a finance lease, any gain or loss on the sale is deferred and amortized over the lease term. For an operating lease, the accounting treatment of the gain or loss depends on the relationship between the selling price of the asset and its fair value at the date of sale.
10. The amount of finance lease obligations and assets held under finance leases should be separately disclosed by both lessees and lessors. Lessees should also disclose their commitments under operating leases and under finance leases for the next year, for the next four years in total, and then the aggregate amount for all remaining years.
11. A sales-type lease has two profit components for the lessor: (1) the profit or loss from the sale and (2) interest revenue from the lease financing.
12. The interest rate used in lessor accounting for a finance lease is the rate implicit in the lease. The net method and the gross method give the same results in the financial statements. Lessors normally use the gross method of recording finance leases to make it easier to reconcile the portfolio of leases to the summary amount in the SFP control account.
13. Under ASPE, a lessor treats a lease as a capital lease if, in addition to transferring substantially all of the risks and rewards of ownership to the lessee, two other criteria are met: (1) the credit risk is normal and (2) all executory and operating costs included in the lease payments can be reasonably estimated.
14. Under ASPE, a lessor must classify a capital lease as either a direct-financing lease or a sales-type lease. A direct financing lease arises when a lessor acts purely as a financial intermediary. A sales-type lease arises when a manufacturer or dealer uses leasing as a means of selling a product.

KEY TERMS

bargain purchase option
bargain renewal terms
capital lease
captive leasing companies
contingent lease payments
contingent rent
direct-financing lease
economic life
executory costs
financial intermediary
finance lease
gross lease basis
guaranteed residual value
implicit lease interest rate
incremental borrowing rate (IBR)
internal rate of return (IRR)
initial direct costs
initial lease term
lease
lessee
lessor
lease term
manufacturer's lease
minimum net lease payments
net lease receivable
net lease payments
operating lease
personal property
real property
sale and leaseback
sales-type lease
unguaranteed residual value
useful life

REVIEW PROBLEM 18-1

Orion leased a computer to Lenox Silver Inc. on 1 April 20X5. The terms of the lease are as follows:

• Lease term (fixed and noncancellable)	3 years
• Estimated economic life of the computer	5 years
• Fair market value of the asset at lease inception	$5,000
• Bargain purchase offer	None
• Transfer of title	None
• Guaranteed residual value by lessee, 1 April 20X8	$1,000
• Lessee's normal depreciation method*	straight line
• Lessee's incremental borrowing rate	11%
• Executory costs included in lease payments	None
• Initial direct costs	None
• Annual lease payment, beginning of each lease year	$1,620
• Lessor's implicit interest rate	10%
• Lessee's fiscal year-end	31 December

*Lenox Silver Inc. charges a half-year depreciation in the year of acquisition and a half-year in the year of disposition, regardless of the actual dates of acquisition and disposal.

Required:

1. Classify the lease from the perspective of the lessee.
2. Provide entries for the lease from 1 April 20X5 through 31 December 20X6.
3. Show how the leased asset and the lease obligation will be shown on the lessee's SFP at 31 December 20X6.
4. Suppose that at the end of the lease, the lessor tells the lessee to dispose of the asset, and to keep any proceeds in excess of the guaranteed residual value. Provide entries for the lessee on 1 April 20X8, assuming that the lessee sells the asset for $1,200 and remits the required $1,000 payment to the lessor.

REVIEW PROBLEM 18-1—SOLUTION

1. The lessor's implicit rate is known. Under IAS 17, the lessor's rate must be used if known. Under ASPE, the lessee uses the lower of the lessor's implicit rate or the lessee's incremental borrowing rate, IBR. Under either scenario, the discount rate will be 10%. Discounting the minimum lease payments, including the guaranteed residual value of $1,000, yields:

   P = $1,620 (P/A due, 10%, 3) + $1,000(P/F, 10%, 3)
   = $4,432 + $751 = $5,183

   Clearly, the lease is a finance lease because the present value of the minimum lease payments, $5,183, is greater than the $5,000 fair value of the leased property.

2. The asset and the offsetting liability must be capitalized. The capitalized value of the leased asset cannot be greater than the asset's fair value, and therefore the fair value of $5,000 must be used instead of the present value of $5,183. The entries at the inception of the lease will be:

1 April 20X5—commencement of the lease		
Asset under finance lease	5,000	
Lease liability		5,000
1 April 20X5—first payment		
Lease liability	1,620	
Cash		1,620

Since the lessee's IBR yields a present value that is higher than the fair value of the asset, it cannot be used for further accounting for the lease. Instead, the implicit rate *to the lessee* must be calculated by solving the following equation for *i*, the implicit interest rate:

$5,000 = $1,620 (P/A due, *i*, 3) + $1,000 (P/F, *i*, 3)

By using a computer spreadsheet, a financial calculator, or trial and error, we can find the implicit rate of 13.29%. This rate must then be used to accrue the interest and to record the components of the annual lease payments. The amortization table for the lease obligation is as follows:

Year	Beginning Balance	Interest Expense at 13.29%	Cash Payment	Reduction of Principal	Ending Balance
20X5	$5,000	$ 0	$1,620	$1,620	$3,380
20X6	3,380	449	1,620	1,171	2,209
20X7	2,209	294	1,620	1,326	883
20X8	883	117	1,000	883	0

The entries to record the depreciation, interest accrual, and payments through 31 December 20X6 are shown below.

31 December 20X5—adjusting entries

Depreciation expense	667	
Accumulated depreciation		667
[($5,000 – $1000) ÷ 3 × 1/2 = $500]		
Interest expense	337	
Lease liability		337
[($5,000 – $1,620) × 13.29% = $449 × 9/12 = $337]		

1 April 20X6—interest accrual

Interest expense	112	
Lease liability		112
[($5,000 – $1,620) × 13.29% = $449 × 3/12 = $112]		

1 April 20X6—second payment

Lease liability	1,620	
Cash		1,620

31 December 20X6—adjusting entries

Depreciation expense	1,333	
Accumulated depreciation		1,333
[($5,000 – $1000) ÷ 3]		
Interest expense	221	
Lease liability		221
[$294 (from amortization table) × 9/12]		

3. The lessee's SFP at 31 December 20X6 will include the following amounts:

Capital assets	
Asset under finance lease	$5,000
Less accumulated depreciation	(2,000)
	$3,000
Current liabilities	
Current portion of finance lease liability	$1,547
[$221 accrued interest at 31 December 20X6, plus $1,326 principal portion of the next payment (from amortization table)]	
Long-term liabilities	
Obligation under finance lease (from amortization table)	$ 883

4. 1 April 20X8—sale of asset

Cash (received from sale)	1,200	
Lease liability	1,000	
Accumulated depreciation	4,000	
Asset under finance lease		5,000
Cash (paid to lessor)		1,000
Gain on disposal of leased asset		200

This entry assumes that adjustments have already been made to (1) accrue the last of the interest and (2) record depreciation for 20X8.

REVIEW PROBLEM 18-2

Orion leased a computer to the Lenox Silver Company on 1 January 20X5. The terms of the lease and other related information are as follows:

- Lease term (fixed and noncancellable) — 3 years
- Estimated economic life of the equipment — 4 years
- Fair market value of the computer at lease inception — $5,000
- Lessor's cost of asset — $5,000
- Bargain purchase price — none
- Transfer of title — none
- Guaranteed residual value by lessee (excess to lessee) 1 January 20X8 — $1,000
- Collectibility of rental payments — assured
- Annual rental (first payment 1 January 20X5) — $1,620

Required:

1. Provide entries for the lessor from 1 January 20X5 through 1 January 20X6, using the net method of recording.
2. Provide the lessor's journal entry at the termination of the lease on 1 January 20X8, assuming that the asset is sold by the lessee on that date for $1,200.
3. Prepare the entries at the commencement of the lease (i.e., 1 January 20X5), assuming that the gross method is used instead.

REVIEW PROBLEM 18-2—SOLUTION

The lease is a finance lease because the lease term (three years) is a major part of the economic life of the asset. The lessor must account for the lease by using the interest rate implicit in the lease. The interest rate that discounts the lease cash flows to $5,000 is 13.29% (before tax) (solved by spreadsheet).

1. Lease entries, net method:

1 January 20X5—commencement of lease		
Lease receivable	5,000	
Cash, Inventory, etc.		5,000
1 January 20X5—first payment		
Cash	1,620	
Lease receivable		1,620
31 December 20X5—interest accrual		
Lease receivable	449	
Finance income		449
($5,000 – $1,620) × 13.29% = $449		

1 January 20X6—second payment

Cash	1,620	
Lease receivable		1,620

2. Termination of lease

1 January 20X8—receipt of guaranteed residual value from lessee

Cash	1,000	
Lease receivable		1,000

The fact that the lessee was able to sell the asset for $1,200 is irrelevant. The lessee gets to keep the extra $200.

3. Lease commencement, gross method:

1 January 20X5—commencement of lease

Lease receivable [($1,620 × 3) + $1,000]	5,860	
Unearned finance revenue		860
Cash, Inventory, etc.		5,000

1 January 20X5—first payment

Cash	1,620	
Lease receivable		1,620

APPENDIX

FORTHCOMING CHANGES IN LEASE ACCOUNTING

OVERVIEW

The issue of leasing has been under consideration jointly by the IASB and the FASB since 2006. There has been widespread dissatisfaction with the current operating/finance lease distinction. In particular, financial statement users (and many accountants) have been dissatisfied with preparers' practice of acquiring long-term use of major assets by entering into leases that are disguised as operating leases. This use of operating leases avoids showing the lease obligations as a liability, even when the operating lease has a very large nonrenewal penalty attached.

The IASB will issue a new standard on lease accounting in 2014 or 2015. Since IASB intends to give preparers time to accumulate two years of comparative data, the earliest possible effective date would be 2017. This standard has incorporated changes that have been under consideration for several years and have been discussed with the FASB so that both standard setters can issue new harmonized standards for lease accounting

The most significant changes are that it will eliminate two of the key aspects of current lease accounting under IAS17: (1) the distinction between operating leases and finance leases, and (2) the concept of sales-type leases. Instead, there will be two classifications:

- Short-term versus long-term for both lessees and lessors; and
- A *performance obligation* approach versus *derecognition approach* for lessors.

We will focus on lessee accounting in this brief appendix, as that is the main focus of this textbook and also is the area in which the changes will have the greatest consequences.

SHORT-TERM LEASES

Definition

A short-term lease is one that has a maximum term of no more than 12 months. The maximum term includes any period of time that gives the lessee economic incentive to exercise renewal or purchase options. This definition excludes leases that have no financial commitment beyond a year but may be repeatedly renewed at market rates. Thus, "short term" refers to the maximum term over which the lessee has made a binding commitment. It does not include continuing monthly or annual rental renewals (e.g., for office space) because the lessee has no binding commitment until the renewal actually happens. However, if the lessee has strong economic incentive to extend the term of a lease beyond 12, such as by onerous nonrenewal penalties built into the lease, the lease automatically becomes a long-term lease for accounting purposes.

Accounting—Lessees and Lessors

Lessees will account for short-term leases by recognizing the lease payments in net income, normally allocated on a straight-line basis. The lessee does not recognize any liability or asset relating to the lease. This is no change from current practice.

Similarly, the lessor recognizes lease revenue in net income over the term of the lease. The leased asset is depreciated as appropriate for its nature and intended life cycle.

The proposed accounting for short-term leases is essentially the same as the accounting for operating leases under IAS 17, as described in the main body of this chapter.

LONG-TERM LEASES—LESSEE

Basic Concept

The basic rule is simple—at the commencement of a lease, the lessee recognizes two amounts on the statement of financial position:

- A "right-of-use" asset; and
- A liability for the lease payments, including any initial direct costs.

The two amounts are the same—the present value of the cash flow stream. The discount rate is the pre-tax rate the lessor charges the lessee if it is known; otherwise it is the lessee's incremental borrowing rate. This is no different from current accounting for finance leases except for a wider definition of what is included in the cash flow stream.

Over the term of the lease, the lessee will:

- Amortize or depreciate the asset as appropriate for that type of asset; and
- Account for the liability by the effective interest method.

In other words, *all* leases will be reported on essentially the same basis as we have already described for finance leases in the main body of this chapter. There will be no need to determine whether or not the lease transfers substantially all of the asset's risks and rewards to the lessee.

A necessary element for designating a continuing contractual obligation as a lease is that the lessee must have control over the asset's use. For example, if a corporation contracts for a computer server to be used specifically and exclusively by that corporation, the contract is a lease because the corporation controls the server's use. In contrast, if the corporation contracts to use a server that also is serving other clients, the owner of the server controls the allocation of *space*; this contract is not a lease but is simply a supply of-services contract.

End-of-Lease Options

Leases often have some sort of option at the end of the lease. These are the same options as we discussed in the main body of this chapter: (1) purchase options and (2) renewal options.

Options that are more-or-less "irresistible" to the lessee are included in the minimum lease term and in the lease cash flow for determining the present value. However, the basis for deciding whether or not to include options in the discounted cash flow is being broadened. Options will be included in the discounted lease payments if they have *significant economic incentive for an entity to exercise the option.*

Significant economic incentive can be the result of any one of four types of factors or a combination thereof:

1. *Contract-based factors* written into the lease, such as substantial penalties for nonrenewal;
2. *Asset-based factors*, such as significant leasehold improvements installed by the lessee that will still have substantial future benefit at the end of the lease term;
3. *Entity-specific factors*, such as common industry practice; or
4. *Market-based factors*, such as potential fluctuations in asset market values or rental costs.

Thus, the forthcoming standard will go beyond the bargain purchase and bargain renewal options that now exist, both of which are contract-based factors, when deciding what potential cash flows should be included in the present value of the lease payments.

Long-Term Lease Classification

Long-term leases will be classified into two types:

- Type A: property; and
- Type B: other, or not property (i.e., leases for assets other than property).

Property is what we traditionally refer to as "real property": land and buildings. Everything else falls into the "other" category. Leases of property include parts of a building, such as a whole floor, and not just the entire building.

Type A Nonproperty will be accounted for by using a method called the *interest and amortization (I&A) approach.* Interest is accrued on the basis of the outstanding amount of the liability, and the asset is depreciated on the appropriate method for that type of asset. However, if the term of the lease is an insignificant part of the total economic life of the asset, or if the present value of the lease payments is insignificant relative to the asset's fair value, then the asset will be accounted for as Type B.

This approach establishes that assets that are not land and/or buildings (e.g., equipment) will be accounted for in essentially the same manner as we have explained in the main body of this chapter.

Type B In contrast, property will be accounted for by using one of two methods:

- The I&A approach (as described for finance leases in this chapter), but only *if* the lease is for the major part of the asset's life or the present value of the lease payments is for substantially all of the fair value of the asset. The I&A approach is essentially the same as the current requirement for finance leases.
- Otherwise, the *single lease expense* (*SLE*) *approach.*

The SLE approach is new. The idea is to achieve an even, straight-line expense on the lessee's SCI, as though they were paying regular rent on an operating lease basis, even though both the asset and the liability are reported on the lessee's SFP. It works like this:

1. Interest expense is determined on the basis of an amortization table.
2. The total amount to be charged to profit and loss over the life of the lease is determined as the sum of the present value of the lease payments (i.e., the amount recorded as the right-to-use asset) plus the total interest over the life of the lease.
3. Then, the total amount to be charged to P&L is divided by the number of periods in the lease term to determine the straight-line amount that should be charged to net income in each lease period.
4. Depreciation is calculated as the difference between total straight-line expense and the interest expense in each period.

Example of SLE Approach

Suppose that Speedy Ltd., a courier company, leases a storage building for a five-year period at $10,000 per year, payable at the beginning of each year. The lease commences on 2 January 20X1. The company is required to pay for adapting the building for its purposes, a cost of $5,000.

Let us assume that the appropriate interest rate is 6%. The present value of a $10,000, five-year annuity-due at 6% is $44,651. Adding the initial direct cost of $5,000 yields $49,651. The amortization table in Exhibit 18-A1 tells us that interest expense will total **$5,349**. Adding these two amounts together gives us $55,000. Dividing by the five-year term, the straight-line amount is $11,000 per year. This is the *total* amount that will appear on Speedy's income statement each year. This $11,000 is exactly equal to the annual payment of $10,000 plus the annual amortization of the initial $5,000 payment over the lease term of $1,000 ($5,000 ÷ 5). This is the same amount as would have been reported for an operating lease under IAS 17.

At commencement, Speedy would record the lease as follows:

2 January 20X1—commencement of the lease		
Asset under finance lease—delivery van	49,651	
Lease liability		49,651

2 January 20X1—first payment of $10,000 plus initial direct cost of $5,000		
Lease liability	15,000	
Cash		15,000

The lease liability declines to $34,651 after the initial payment. At the end of 20X1, interest will have accrued on that outstanding balance:

31 December 20X1—interest accrual		
Interest expense	2,079	
Lease liability		2,079
($34,651 × 6% = $2,079)		
31 December 20X6—asset amortization		
Depreciation expense	8,921	
Accumulated depreciation		8,921
($11,000 – $2,079 = $8,921)		

In following years, as the interest declines, the annual depreciation goes up. In the final year, the full amount of $11,000 will be for depreciation because there is no interest expense in the final year, since the last payment was made at the *beginning* of Year 5. The annual computation is shown in Exhibit 18-A2.

On Speedy's income statement, only the total annual amount of $11,000 will appear. In the statement of cash flows, the amounts will be included in operating activities section, not in the financing or investing activities sections.

EXHIBIT 18-A1

LESSEE AMORTIZATION TABLE—SPEEDY LTD.

1 January	Lease Liability Before Payment	Interest at 6%	Payments, 2 January	Lease Liability After Payment
20X1	$49,651	$ —	$15,000	**$34,651**
20X2	34,651	2,079	10,000	**26,730**
20X3	26,730	1,604	10,000	**18,334**
20X4	18,334	1,100	10,000	**9,434**
20X5	9,434	566	10,000	**0**
Totals		$5,349	$55,000	

EXHIBIT 18-A2

APPLICATION OF THE SINGLE LEASE EXPENSE APPROACH

Lease Year	Total Lease Expense	Interest (from Exhibit 18-A1)	Allocation for Depreciation
20X1	$11,000	$ 2,079	$ 8,921
20X2	11,000	1,604	9,396
20X3	11,000	1,100	9,900
20X4	11,000	566	10,434
20X5	11,000	—	11,000
Totals	$55,000	$ 5,349	$49,651

Reassessment of the Lease Liability

An important aspect of the proposed new standard is that it specifically provides for the possibility that economic circumstances will change and either the lease payments or the discount rate will change. For example:

- Market factors concerning the leased asset (e.g., changing technology) may make a bargain purchase option or renewal option no longer favourable. The lessee can then remeasure the value imputed to the right-of-use asset by reassessing the lease without the additional purchase or renewal payments originally envisioned.
- Similarly, market interest rates may have changed so that the lessee no longer has incentive to exercise a purchase option or renewal option.

The lessee reports the amount by which the right-of-use asset's value changes due to circumstances in the reporting period (i.e., gain or loss) as a component of profit or loss.

OTHER ISSUES

Lessor Accounting for Long-Term Leases

Lessor accounting also will undergo changes. For Type A leases, lessors will continue to "recognize" the leased asset by capitalizing the present value of the future lease payments (and related items, such as initial direct costs and residual values). This implies a net lease basis of recording.

However, the proposals call for recording a leased asset at the total of (1) the discounted present value of the residual value of the asset and (2) the total amount of the deferred profit. On the SFP, the two amounts would be presented net so that the result is very similar to current practice using the gross method of reporting.

There are quite a number of other proposed tentative changes relating to lessors, but as we have made clear earlier, lessors are a specialized industry (i.e., a type of financial intermediary), and thus we will not discuss these changes here.

Sale and Leaseback

A transaction will be accounted for as a sale and leaseback only if the seller (who also is the subsequent lessee) has retained control of the asset following the sale. This would apply only to the "whole asset."

If an owner sells a building and then leases back only part of it, then control of the whole asset is no longer in the hands of the seller/lessee. The transaction would be treated as a sale, recognizing any profit or loss on the sale. The subsequent lease will accounted for as described above, independent of the lessee's previous ownership.

Looking Forward

At the time of preparing this edition, the changes described above are somewhat tentative. However, they are the result of several years of joint study and discussion by the IASB and FASB boards and are a clear indication of what the forthcoming new standard will require.

One thing is abundantly clear—the dichotomy of operating versus capital leases that has existed for more than 40 years will disappear. For any lease term longer than one year, all lease payments (plus the amounts of any end-of-lease payments and/or renewals) will be discounted to present value, and the resulting lease liability will accounted for in the way that we now associate with finance leases.

This change is intended to eliminate the temptation for managers to enter into "operating" leases that really are disguised finance leases. This practice, while not exactly unethical (since it is within existing accounting standards), is largely intended to fool financial statement users into thinking the company has less debt than it really has. Such a practice comes with a cost—lessors do not enter into such arrangements on the same basis as they would for a straight capital lease. Therefore, the result should be to improve financial reporting by creating a "level playing field" that eliminates the temptation for manipulation and simultaneously reduces the genuine extra cost of carrying an operating lease when the lessee really seeks long-term use of the asset.

Stay tuned for future developments. More information will be posted on the book's website when it becomes known.

QUESTIONS

Q18-1 At the beginning of the fiscal year, a tenant signs a three-year lease to rent office space at the rate of $1,000 per month. The first six months are free. How much rent expense should be recognized in the first year of the lease?

Q18-2 Under what circumstances is a lease normally considered a finance lease? What role does judgement play?

Q18-3 Give three reasons that a company might enter into a long-term lease instead of buying an asset outright.

Q18-4 A car dealer advertises a new car lease with the following terms:

- $3,500 cash paid by the customer at the beginning of the lease;
- Monthly payments of $229 for 48 months; and
- A mandatory fee of $2,650 at the end of the lease; the lessee then owns the vehicle.

What is the substance of the lease contract?

Q18-5 Under what circumstances would a deferred rent liability appear on the SFP of a lessee company in an operating lease?

Q18-6 Define the following terms as used in lease accounting standards:

- Bargain purchase option (BPO)
- Lease term
- Minimum net lease payments
- Contingent lease payments
- Bargain renewal term
- Guaranteed residual value
- Incremental borrowing rate
- Interest rate implicit in the lease

Q18-7 A lessee signs a lease for a three-year term for $1,000 per year that has a renewal option at the lessee's option for a further three years for $1,000 per year. How long is the lease term, as defined by lease accounting standards?

Q18-8 How would your answer to Q18-7 change if the renewal was at the lessor's option? If rental during the second term was $1 per year instead of $1,000?

Q18-9 A lessee signs a lease for a two-year term that requires a yearly payment of $14,000, which includes $2,500 for insurance and maintenance cost. At the end of the two-year term, there is a $1,000 BPO. What is the total amount (undiscounted) of the minimum net lease payments?

Q18-10 Assume an asset has a fair market value of $48,500 and is leased for $10,000 per year for six years. Payments are made at the end of each year. Insurance costs included in this amount are $1,000, and there is a $6,000 guaranteed residual. What is the interest rate implicit in the lease for the lessee? Why is this not also the interest rate implicit in the lease for the lessor?

Q18-11 Assume a nonprofit organization wishes to acquire a particular asset. Why might it be cheaper to lease rather than buy the asset?

Q18-12 Assume a lease involves payments of $20,000 per year and is properly capitalized on the lessee's books at a 10% interest rate for $135,180. How much interest would be recognized in the first year of the lease if the payments were made at the beginning of the period? How much interest expense in the second year?

Q18-13 A lessee enters into a five-year finance lease with a five-year bargain renewal option, after which the asset is returned to the lessor. The asset is expected to have a 12-year useful life. Over what period should the lessee depreciate the asset?

Q18-14 How is the current portion of the lease liability determined if the lease payments are due and payable at the end of the fiscal year? How would your answer change if the payments were due at the beginning of the period?

Q18-15 What is a sale and leaseback? How are such transactions accounted for?

Q18-16 Suppose that a company owns a building. The company enters into a sale and leaseback arrangement to sell the building and then lease it back. The company makes a substantial profit on the sale. How should the gain from the sale be accounted for under IFRS? Under ASPE?

Q18-17 Suppose that a lessor is a private Canadian corporation reporting under ASPE. How does its status as a private corporation affect the classification of a lease, as compared with a public corporation?

Q18-18 What interest rate does the lessor use for discounting calculations associated with a lease?

Q18-19 Describe the nature of a sales-type lease. What kinds of entities offer such leases?

Q18-20 In a sales-type lease, how does separation of the sale component from the lease component affect revenue recognition in the current and future years?

CASE 18-1

BRING-IT-HOME INC.

Bring-It-Home Inc. (BIHI) is a Canadian corporation based and operating in Nova Scotia. BIHI's wide-ranging products and services are targeted at enhancing customers' quality of living, not only in their own homes but also within their communities. The company has enjoyed considerable growth due to the insight of its management team and creative talents of some key employees. BIHI is majority-owned by Flanagan's Inc., a Nova Scotia-based holding company. Flanagan's prepares its financial statements in accordance with International Financial Reporting Standards (IFRS), as does BIHI.

It is 15 February 20X5, and you, as a professional accountant with the accounting firm Mansbridge & Lang, have been asked by BIHI's president, Steve Power, to fill in as acting controller at BIHI. The current controller, Sidney Crosby, has gone on extended leave from BIHI for medical reasons. Mr. Crosby only joined BIHI part way through the current fiscal year, replacing the former controller who moved to another province with her family.

The one constant in BIHI's accounting department has been the assistant controller, Rory McIlroy. Although Rory is not a professional accountant, he is very energetic and willing to work extra hours when needed. Rory feels that the head office staff's bonus based on pre-tax income is a nice perk and he wants to make sure he is doing his best to help out his co-workers.

Mr. Power wants you to review the draft condensed financial statement for 31 December 20X4 (Exhibit 1). You also have reviewed the accounting for certain transactions underlying the draft statement (Exhibit 2). If you feel that any adjustments are needed, you are to explain the reason(s) and draft any necessary adjusting journal entries. You should then prepare a revised statement of financial position.

The public accounting firm of Doyle Republic is continuing as BIHI's auditors this year and observed the year-end inventory count.

Required

Prepare the information requested by Mr. Power. BIHI's combined federal and provincial tax rate is 20%.

EXHIBIT 1

BRING-IT-HOME INC.

Condensed Draft Financial Statement (*unaudited*)
31 December 20X4

(prepared by Rory McIlroy)

	31 December 20X4
Statement of Financial Position	
Current assets	$ 44,725
Greenhouse, net	81,000
Other property plant, and equipment (net)	143,365
Total assets	$269,090
Current liabilities	$ 8,250
Loan payable, government agency	90,000
Other long-term liabilities	67,000
Total liabilities	165,250
Common shares	7,000
Retained earnings	96,840
Total shareholders' equity	103,840
Total liabilities and shareholders' equity	$269,090

EXHIBIT 2

NOTES ON THE DRAFT FINANCIAL STATEMENTS

1. Bank Indebtedness

BIHI has a $60,000 long-term loan payable to Canadiana Bank. BIHI is to provide Canadiana with its audited financial statements, prepared in accordance with IFRS, within 90 days of its year-end. The loan bears interest at 10% and is callable if the company's debt-to-equity ratio exceeds 3:1.

The 10% interest rate Canadiana charged BIHI on its own credit-worthiness exceeds the 7% that Flanagan normally pays on its bank loans because BIHI's parent company deals with an international consortium of banks and thus is able to negotiate a better rate than BIHI.

2. Lease

On 2 January 20X4, BIHI acquired equipment via a five-year lease that requires annual payments of $25,000, due at the beginning of each year. The first payment was made on 2 January 20X4 and was charged to rent expense. The present value of the five payments, based on the 10% rate implicit in the lease, was $104,250 while the fair value of the equipment at the inception of the lease was $132,000. Because the equipment was custom-made for BIHI's needs, there is no residual value at the end of the five-year lease. The lease only covers five of the equipment's estimated physical life of eight years and is, therefore, being recorded as an operating lease.

3. Community Vegetable Greenhouse

On 1 July 20X4, BIHI acquired ownership of a large community greenhouse through a provincial government lending agency. To facilitate acquisition of the greenhouse, BIHI signed an agreement that requires the company to pay $90,000 to the lending agency on 30 June 20X9. As well, BIHI must pay simple interest of 3% on the loan, or $2,700 per year, on each of 30 June 20X5 through 30 June 20X9.

Acquisition of the greenhouse qualified for federal government assistance as the greenhouse was located in an economically challenged area of the province. After signing the paperwork to acquire the greenhouse on 1 July 20X4, BIHI received $15,000 from a federal government agency. The company expects to use the greenhouse for five years after which it should be almost worthless. Rory diligently made the following related entries during the current fiscal year:

1 July 20X4		
Greenhouse	90,000	
Loan payable		90,000
To record acquisition of the greenhouse		
Cash	15,000	
Head office expenses		15,000
To record receipt of government grant		
31 December 20X4		
Depreciation expense	9,000	
Accumulated depreciation, greenhouse		9,000
To record six months of depreciation under the straight-line method		
Interest expense	1,350	
Interest payable		1,350
To accrue six months of interest owing		

4. Sales

Until late 20X4, BIHI had an arrangement with Crafty Cabinets Ltd. (Crafty) to design kitchen cabinets requested by BIHI's customers. Crafty manufactures the cabinets as specified by BIHI. BIHI asks Crafty to hold these products in its warehouse for delivery to BIHI or to BIHI's customers, as specified. There is a fixed schedule for delivery of the goods to BIHI or its customers. Crafty notifies BIHI of all shipments from Crafty to BIHI or any of BIHI's customers.

In December, Rory recorded sales of $10,000 and a related cost of goods sold of $7,360 for goods manufactured by Crafty for one of BIHI's customers, Jake Doyle. BIHI had ordered the goods on behalf of Doyle. In mid-December, Jake emailed BIHI and copied Crafty, asking that the goods not be shipped until January 20X5. Jake will still pay BIHI according to the original schedule and terms but, due to unforeseen circumstances, will not be available to receive the goods in December.

5. Patent

BIHI is interested in expanding its manufacturing of customized kitchen cabinets and counter tops. In mid-December 20X4, BIHI was approached by Skerwink Designs Ltd., which holds a patent on an innovative process. Skerwink had paid $12,000 in legal fees to register the patent; that cost had been capitalized by Skerwink. In November, Skerwink had received an offer from another company to purchase the patent for $14,400. Skerwink was in need of some office equipment and instead of accepting the other company's offer, Skerwink proposed trading its patent to BIHI in exchange for some office equipment that BIHI no longer needed. BIHI's equipment's original cost was $21,000, had a net book value of $15,125 and had recently been professionally appraised at $18,750. The exchange was completed on 29 December 20X4. Rory recorded the trade by capitalizing the patent at $18,750 and recording a gain on the trade of $3,625.

(Provided courtesy of Judy Cumby; adapted)

CASE 18-2

WARMTH HOME COMFORT LIMITED

Warmth Home Comfort Limited (WHCL) is a Canadian manufacturer of furnaces and air-conditioning units. The company was acquired by a group of 15 investors eight years ago. Three of the investors are senior managers with the company, including Jacob Kovacs, who is president and chief executive officer.

Over the years WHCL had been quite successful, but it has struggled in the face of increasing competition from overseas competitors. The owners believe that three years from now WHCL will be poised to be a major player in the Canadian and the U.S. heating and cooling markets and may consider going public. Summary financial statements are provided in Exhibit 1. Kovacs points out that the company's financial performance seems to be improving, given the smaller loss in 20X7 and the increasing revenues after two years of falling sales.

Your firm has been auditor of WHCL since its first audit in 20X0. It is now January 20X8. This is the first year you are in charge of the audit. Yesterday, you visited WHCL and met with key personnel to discuss the forthcoming audit engagement. You obtained the following information.

1. In early fiscal 20X7, the company increased its debt load significantly by borrowing $300,000 from Colo Investors Ltd. Excerpts from the loan agreement are as follows:

   Warmth Home Comfort Limited (the borrower) covenants that:

   a. A current ratio of 1.2 or higher will be maintained; and
   b. The debt-to-equity ratio will not exceed 2:1. Debt is defined as all liabilities of the company.

2. In 20X1, WHCL introduced a new model of gas furnace that is popular with consumers because its reduced gas consumption results in lower heating bills. The furnace design has remained virtually unchanged since it was introduced. The furnaces are sold with 10-year warranties on parts and labour. Historically, claims have been minimal.

   In the summer of 20X7, several warranty claims were made against WHCL. Routine inspections by gas-company employees revealed cracked heat exchangers, which could leak gases that might cause health problems when mixed with warm air inside the house. Thirty claims were made, and WHCL paid for repairs. The cost of repairing each furnace was $150, which was expensed by WHCL.

   Jacob Kovacs believes that the furnaces were damaged because of poor installation by contractors. He cannot see more than an additional 40 or 50 units being damaged. The 30 repaired furnaces were manufactured in 20X5 and 20X6. Over 10,000 units of this model have been sold over the past seven years.

   Later, in a discussion with the chief engineer, you learn that she had examined the heat exchanger used in the gas-furnace model in question and saw no evidence of a design flaw. However, she expressed concern that the problem might be due to heavy use of the furnace. She noted that the 30 reported problems were in northern locations where the demands on the equipment are considerable. Between 1,500 and 2,000 furnaces were installed in houses in those locations.

3. In January 20X7, WHCL bid on and won a $1.05 million contract to supply heating and air conditioning equipment for a large commercial and residential project. Construction on the project began in March 20X7.

   The fixed-price contract calls for WHCL to start delivering and installing the equipment in early September 20X7. In addition, WHCL has agreed to pay a penalty if the project is delayed because WHCL is unable to meet the agreed-to timetable. A brief strike by its factory employees has caused production and delivery to lag about two weeks behind schedule, so WHCL is shipping units as soon as they are produced. According to the agreement, half of the equipment has to be shipped and installed at the project site by the end of February 20X8. Jacob Kovacs is confident that WHCL will be able to catch up to the promised timetable.

   In 20X7, WHCL recognized $350,000 of revenue based on the number of units shipped to year-end. WHCL has received $50,000 for the units that have been installed by year-end.

4. Starting in February 20X8, WHCL will begin offering customers the option of paying a monthly fee for the use of a furnace. At the end of a certain number of years, the customer can purchase the unit for a nominal amount or ask for a replacement furnace and continue with the monthly payments. WHCL will do all maintenance at no cost until a customer purchases the unit. This scheme is intended to help WHCL remain competitive. The terms for such arrangements have not been finalized, but Jacob Kovacs is confident that they will increase sales revenue. Jacob has asked for advice on how to account for them.

Your partner asks you to prepare a memo for him outlining the accounting issues that came to your attention as a result of your visit, applying IFRS.

Required:

Prepare the memo.

(Source: The Canadian Institute of Chartered Accountants, © 2010)

EXHIBIT 1

WARMTH HOME COMFORT LIMITED

Extracts from the Draft Financial Statements
Balance Sheet

As at December 31 (in thousands of dollars)

	20X7 (Unaudited)	20X6 (Audited)
Assets		
Current:		
Cash	$ 15	$ 100
Accounts receivable	875	587
Inventory	500	540
Other current assets	56	120
	1,446	1,347
Capital assets	2,606	2,256
Accumulated depreciation	(1,071)	(926)
	1,535	1,330
Total assets	$2,981	$2,677

continued on next page

EXHIBIT I (*cont'd*)

	20X7 (Unaudited)	20X6 (Audited)
Liabilities		
Current:		
Bank indebtedness	$ 450	$ 400
Accounts payable	581	395
Other current liabilities	118	100
	1,149	895
Long-term debt	825	525
	1,974	1,420
Shareholders' equity:		
Share capital	100	100
Retained earnings	907	1,157
	1,007	1,257
Total liabilities and shareholders' equity	$2,981	$2,677

CASE 18-3

SANDSUPPORT CORPORATION

Sandsupport Corporation (SC) is a privately owned company based in Alberta. The company provides support services for the oil and gas industry, especially for new exploration not only in Canada but also in other countries, such as Venezuela and Mexico.

Due to the ever-increasing worldwide demand for energy and the resultant increase in exploration activity, SC is planning a major expansion of its operational capacity. As part of this expansion, the company needs to acquire a significant amount of new equipment. In the past, the company has obtained external financing only through debt, mainly via private placements of secured first-mortgage debentures with pension funds and other institutional investors.

Additional financing will be needed to acquire the new equipment. However, management is hesitant about obtaining more straight debt financing due to restrictive covenants (e.g., on debt-to-equity ratio) that are in place for some of SC's existing debt. Therefore, management is considering three alternatives.

Leasing is the first possibility that management is considering. SC leases quite a lot of equipment to its clients on short-term leases for specific projects, and it had seemed logical to look into leasing as a way for SC to acquire the equipment. Management has been in contact with GWC Finance Corporation about negotiating a lease. Under the potential lease arrangements, GWC would purchase the equipment from its German manufacturer; the manufacturer would deliver the machinery directly to SC. SC would agree to a lease contract that would enable GWC to classify the lease as a finance lease, in accordance with its status as a tax-qualifying lessor. Since the equipment is quite specialized, the lease payments would be "front-loaded," with most of the total lease payments payable in the first five years. GWC has suggested that SC may be able to enter into an agreement with one of SC's major clients (e.g., Suncor or PetroCanada) for the client to guarantee a substantial residual value—enough to reduce the minimum lease payments to less than 90% of the equipment's fair value. SC would unofficially compensate the client through reduced fees for SC's services.

The second possibility would also involve leasing, but the lease would not be an obligation of SC. Instead, two SC shareholders would form a separate corporation and that corporation would enter into the lease with GWC. The new corporation would then lease the equipment to SC with an initial lease term of five years. After the first five years, the lease would continue on a year-to-year basis automatically until the GWC lease expired. At that point, GWC would transfer title to the new corporation, which, in turn, would sell the equipment to SC for nominal consideration.

The third option involves the issuance of convertible preferred shares to the Alberta Teachers' Pension Plan (ATPP). The proceeds of the share issue would be used to buy the equipment. SC has never previously used outside equity financing, but preferred shares seems to be a logical answer to the financing problem faced by SC. SC would be obligated to pay dividends annually at 8% of the paid-in value of the shares. Any time after five years, ATPP could convert to common shares (for whatever number of common shares will amount to a current market value equal to the preferred shares' original paid-in value). As well, SC would be able to call the shares for redemption at any time after five years.

Management is very experienced at being a lessor but not at all experienced at being a lessee. Therefore, the CFO has come to you for advice on the best route to take for the new financing. In particular, the CFO is concerned about the financial statement impact of these three alternatives.

Required:

Analyze the consequences of each of the above alternatives in a memo to your superior. Explain which one you would recommend for SC.

TECHNICAL REVIEW

★ connect

TR18-1 Operating Lease—Lessee: Argyle Ltd. signed a 36-month lease to rent a computer system for $5,000 per month. The value of the computer equipment is $400,000. The lease will commence on 1 November 20X1. As encouragement to lease the space, the lessor waived the first four months' rent. The remaining 32 payments will be due at the beginning of each month, starting on 1 March 20X2. Argyle Ltd.'s fiscal year-end is 31 December.

Required:

Prepare summary journal entries for Argyle for 20X1 and 20X2.

★ connect

TR18-2 Operating Lease—Lessor: Basil Ltd. leased computer equipment to a customer for 12 quarters (i.e., 36 months) for $15,000 per quarter; the first quarter's rent is payable at the start of the lease and then quarterly thereafter. The rate implicit in the lease is 8%. The lease commenced on 1 November 20X1. The carrying value of the equipment is $360,000. Basil Ltd. depreciates its equipment by the declining-balance method at a rate of 20%. Basil Ltd.'s year-end is 31 December.

Required:

Prepare journal entries for Basil for 20X1 and, in summary form, for 20X2.

★★ connect

TR18-3 Amortization Table—Lessee: Peridis Inc. has entered into a contract with an asset-based finance company to acquire some specialized equipment. The lease payments are $20,000 per year for eight years. At the end of the lease, Peridis guarantees to either (1) acquire the equipment from the lessor for $10,000 or (2) pay for the lessor's cost of removing the equipment, which also is estimated at $10,000. Peridis's incremental borrowing rate for this amount and term is estimated to be 8%. Peridis's fiscal year ends on 31 December.

Required:

1. Determine the present value of the lease payments.
2. Prepare an amortization table for this lease for Peridis.
3. Assume that the lease starts on 1 January 20X1. How much interest expense will Peridis report for each of 20X1 and 20X2?
4. Assume instead that the lease starts on 1 October 20X1. How much interest should the company record for each of 20X1 and 20X2?

★ connect

TR18-4 Finance Lease Fundamentals: Niko Limited signed a lease for a five-year term that requires yearly, beginning-of-year payments of $104,000, including $9,600 of annual maintenance and property taxes. Niko guarantees a residual value of $26,500 at the end of the lease term, although both parties expect the asset to be sold as used equipment for approximately $35,000 at that time.

Required:

1. How much are Niko's minimum lease payments, as defined for lease accounting purposes?
2. If Niko's IBR is 10%, what amount will Niko record as an asset?
3. How much will Niko record as an asset if the residual value is *unguaranteed*?
4. Suppose that the fair value of the leased asset is $375,000 at the inception of the lease. How would this fact affect the amount recorded for the leased asset?

★★ connect

TR18-5 Finance Lease—Lessor: On 1 January 20X1, Canada Leasing Inc. acquired an asset on behalf of Magnum Ltd. for $100,000. Canada Leasing and Magnum enter into a six-year lease for the asset, effective 1 January 20X1, with equal payments at the beginning of each lease year. Canada Leasing will earn 8% (before taxes) on the lease. Canada Lease has a 31 December fiscal year-end. Canada Leasing Inc. uses the gross method of recording finance leases.

Required:

1. Determine the amount of each lease payment.
2. Make the journal entries that would appear in Canada Leasing Inc.'s accounts for 20X1, 20X2, and 20X3, using the net method of recording.
3. Repeat requirement 2, but use the gross method of recording the lease.
4. What amount(s) relating to the lease will be shown on Canada Leasing Inc.'s SFP on 31 December 20X3?

ASSIGNMENTS

★★ **A18-1 Classify Two Leases:** Belangier Corporation has signed two leases in the past year. One lease is for handling equipment, the other for a truck.

HANDLING EQUIPMENT:

The handling equipment has a fair market value of $274,000. Lease payments are made each 2 January, the date the lease was signed. The lease is for four years and requires payments of $55,000 per year on each 2 January and can be renewed at the lessee's option for subsequent one-year terms up to three times, at a cost of $23,000 per year. At the end of any lease term, the equipment reverts to the lessor if Belangier does not exercise its renewal option. Annual maintenance and insurance costs are paid by the lessor and are estimated to be $5,000 per year for the first four years and $3,000 per year thereafter. These costs are included in the lease payments. Belangier estimates that the equipment has an economic life of eight to 10 years before it becomes obsolete.

TRUCK:
The truck has a list price of $135,000 but could be purchased by cash for 10% less. The truck lease runs for four years and has a quarterly lease payment of $5,000, due at the beginning of each quarter. The lease commences on 1 January. If the truck is used for more than 50,000 kilometres in any 12-month period, a payment of $0.25 per extra kilometre must be paid in addition to the annual rental. Belangier is responsible for all operating and maintenance costs.

At the end of the four-year lease agreement, Belangier may, at its option, renew the lease for an additional period; term and payments to be negotiated at that time.

Belangier has an 8% per annum incremental borrowing rate. The company uses straight-line depreciation for all of its tangible capital assets, using the half-year convention (i.e., a half-year depreciation in the first and last years). The truck has an estimated useful life of 10 years.

Required:
Classify each lease as a finance or operating lease. Justify your response.

★ **A18-2 Terminology; Classification; Entries:** Burrill Limited has a 6% incremental borrowing rate. On 1 January 20X1, Burrill signed the following lease agreement for a piece of equipment. The equipment has a fair value of $190,000 and a 12-year economic life. Other information is as follows:

- The noncancellable lease is for eight years.
- The lease payment is $24,000 annually, payable at the beginning of each lease year.
- Lease payments include $3,600 of maintenance expense annually.
- At the end of the lease term, the leased asset reverts to the lessor.

Other information:

- Burrill has a fiscal year that ends on 31 December.
- Burrill uses straight-line depreciation for similar capital assets.

Required:
1. For this lease, provide the:
   a. Lease term;
   b. Guaranteed residual value;
   c. Unguaranteed residual value;
   d. Bargain purchase option; and
   e. Minimum net lease payment.

   If these amounts do not exist in the above lease, enter "none" as your response. State any assumptions.
2. Is this lease an operating lease or a finance lease for the lessee? Explain your reasoning.
3. Prepare the journal entries for the first year of the lease on Burrill's books.
4. Would your answer to requirement 2 change if the lease contained a guaranteed residual value of $50,000? Explain.

★★ **A18-3 Terminology; Classification; Entries:** Canadian Leasing Inc. leased a piece of machinery to Ornamental Concrete Limited, with the following terms:

Solution

- The lease is for five years; Ornamental cannot cancel the lease during this period.
- The lease payment is $79,600 per year. Included in this is $7,900 in estimated insurance costs.
- At the end of the five-year initial lease term, Ornamental can elect to renew the lease for one additional five-year term at a price of $29,500, including $2,500 of estimated insurance costs. Market rentals are approximately twice as expensive.

- At the end of the first or second lease term, the leased asset reverts to the lessor.
- Lease payments are due at the beginning of each lease year.

Other information:

- Ornamental could borrow money to buy this asset at an interest rate of 8%.
- The equipment has a fair market value of $430,000 at the beginning of the lease term and a useful life of approximately 12 years.
- The lease term corresponds to the fiscal year.
- Ornamental uses straight-line depreciation for all capital assets.

Required:

1. For this lease, provide the:
   a. Lease term;
   b. Guaranteed residual value;
   c. Unguaranteed residual value;
   d. Bargain purchase option;
   e. Bargain renewal terms;
   f. Minimum net lease payment; and
   g. Incremental borrowing rate.

   If these amounts do not exist in the above lease, enter "none" as your response. State any assumptions.
2. Is this lease an operating lease or a finance lease for the lessee? Why?
3. Prepare journal entries for the first year of the lease on Ornamental's books.

★ connect

A18-4 Operating Lease—Lessee Inducement: The Association of Western Agricultural Producers leases space in an office complex and has recently signed a new, four-year lease, at the rate of $4,600 per month. However, the lessor offered six months "free" rent at the beginning of the lease as an inducement for the Association to sign the lease agreement.

The lease agreement was signed on 1 October 20X1; the lease will commence on 1 November 20X1. The Association has a 31 December fiscal year-end. Rent is due on the first day of each month.

Required:

1. Prepare journal entries for the first, sixth, and seventh months of the lease. Assume that financial statements are prepared monthly.
2. What amounts would be shown on the association's income statement and statement of financial position for this lease as of 31 December 20X2?

★★ connect

A18-5 Amortization Table; Interest: ExFed Limited has leased a vehicle from Essex Lease Corporation. Lease payments are $20,000 per year for five years, commencing 1 April 20X1. The lease contract provides for a purchase option of $25,000 at the end of the lease term, which is the estimated value of the vehicle after five years. ExFed's incremental borrowing rate is 5%. Essex's implicit rate of interest in the lease contract is 7%, and ExFed's chief financial officer is aware of it.

Required:

1. Prepare an amortization table for this lessee.
2. Determine the interest expense that ExFed Limited will report on its statement of comprehensive income for each of the years ending 31 December 20X1 and 20X2.

★★ connect

A18-6 Finance Lease—Lessee Amortization Table and Entries On 31 December 20X0, See Inc. entered into an agreement with Sor Ltd. to lease equipment. See Inc. will make four equal payments of $100,000 at the beginning of each lease year. Sor Ltd. anticipates that the equipment will have a residual value of $80,000 at the end of the lease, net of removal costs. See Inc. has the option of (1) paying $80,000 to retain the equipment or (2) allowing Sor Ltd. to remove it.

Sor Ltd.'s implicit interest rate in this lease is 7%. See Inc.'s incremental borrowing rate is 8%. See Inc. will depreciate the leased equipment on a straight-line basis over four years. The lease commences on 1 January 20X1. Assume that the fair value of the equipment on the open market is greater than the present value of the lease payments.

Required:

1. Prepare an amortization table for this lease for See Inc.
2. Prepare all entries that See Inc. will record for this lease and the leased equipment for 20X1 and 20X2.
3. Assume that See Inc. prepares quarterly financial statements. What is the amount of the outstanding lease liability that See Inc. should report as a *current* liability on its SFP on 30 June 20X2?

★★ **A18-7 Finance Lease—Lessor; Amortization Table; Net Method Entries** Refer to the information in A18-6.

Required:

1. Prepare an amortization table for this lease for Sor Ltd.
2. Prepare all entries that Sor Ltd. will record for this lease over its full term. Use the net method. Assume that the lessee exercises the purchase option.
3. If you also have solved A18-6, explain the reason(s) for any difference in the discounted present value of the lease payments, recorded by See Inc. and Sor Ltd.

★ **A18-8 Finance Lease—Lessor; Gross Method Entries** Refer to the information in A18-6.

Required:

1. Prepare all entries that Sor Ltd. will record for this lease over its full term, using the gross method.
2. On Sor Ltd.'s 31 December 20X2 SFP, what amount will appear for the lease receivable?

★★ **A18-9 Lessee Amortization Table; Entries:** Hui Corporation has negotiated a lease for new machinery. The machinery has a fair value of $825,000 and an expected economic life of seven years. The lease has a five-year term. Annual rental is paid at the beginning of the lease year, in the amount of $156,450. Insurance and operating costs, approximately $30,000, are paid directly by Hui Corporation and are not included in the lease payments. At the end of the lease term, the machinery will revert to the lessor, which will sell it for an expected $112,500. If the lessor does not realize $112,500 in the sale, then Hui has agreed to make up the difference. Hui does not know the lessor's implicit interest rate.

Required:

1. Prepare an amortization table for the lease. Hui's IBR is 10%.
2. Assume that the lease was entered into on 1 January 20X2. Hui Corporation has a 31 December fiscal year-end. Prepare journal entries for the lease for 20X2, including depreciation.
3. Assume that at the end of the lease, the lessor is able to sell the asset for $90,000 and that Hui Corporation makes up the shortfall. Prepare Hui's entry to record the lease termination (after first recording interest to the date of the transaction).

★★ **A18-10 Lessee Amortization Table; Entries:** Lu Limited is expanding and needs more manufacturing equipment. The company has been offered a lease contract for equipment with a fair value of $130,000. The lease has a five-year term, with beginning-of-year

payments. The lease is renewable for a further two years at the option of the lessee. Annual rental for the first term is $28,600, for the second, $11,500. Payments are made each 31 December. The first term rental includes $2,600 for maintenance and insurance, the second, $1,500. Lease payments are close to market lease rates for both the first and second terms. At the end of the second term, Lu can buy the asset for $1. The machinery has an expected life of 10 years. Lu Limited has an incremental borrowing rate of 10%. Lu has been told that the interest rate implicit in Lease 1 is 8%.

Required:

1. Prepare an amortization table for the lease.
2. Assume that the lease was entered into on 1 January 20X2. Lu has a 31 December fiscal year-end. Prepare journal entries for the lease for 20X2, including any entries relating to the asset.
3. Prepare the entry or entries necessary on 31 December 20X9, assuming Lu Limited exercises the bargain purchase option.

★★ Solution connect

A18-11 Finance Lease—Lease Year; Fiscal Year: On 17 August 20X1, Renfrew Corporation negotiated a lease agreement with National Leasing Limited (NLL) for computer equipment. The equipment has an expected economic life of 7 years and a fair market value of $72,000. The lease term is for five years, beginning on 1 October 20X1. Lease payments are $15,000 per year, payable at the beginning of each lease year. At the end of the lease term, the equipment reverts to NLL.

Renfrew has an incremental borrowing rate of 8% and does not know NLL's interest rate implicit in the lease. Renfrew uses straight-line depreciation calculated on a monthly basis. The company's fiscal year-end is 31 December.

Required:

1. Prepare an amortization table.
2. Prepare Renfrew's journal entries for 20X1 and 20X2.
3. Renfrew uses current–noncurrent classification. How much of the year-end 20X2 lease liability will be shown as a current liability and how much as a long-term liability?

★★ Solution connect

A18-12 Finance Lease—Lessee: On 2 January 20X4, Yvan Ltd., a public company, entered into a five-year equipment lease with Jeffery Leasing Inc. The lease calls for annual lease payments of $150,000, payable at the beginning of each lease year. Yvan's IBR is 7%. Yvan Ltd. does not know the lessor's interest rate. The fair value of the equipment is $675,000. Yvan Ltd. depreciates equipment on a straight-line basis, taking a full year's depreciation in the year of acquisition.

Required:

1. Prepare the lease liability amortization schedule for Yvan Ltd.
2. What amounts will appear on Yvan Ltd.'s statement of financial position, statement of comprehensive income, and statement of cash flows as of 31 December 20X4?
3. Prepare the journal entries relating to the leased asset and the lease liability for 20X4 and 20X5 for Yvan Ltd.

★★ Solution connect

A18-13 Finance Lease—Lessor: Refer to the information in A18-12. Jeffrey Leasing Inc. is a public company. Jeffrey Leasing's implicit interest rate in the Yvan lease is 6%.

Required:

1. Prepare the lease liability amortization schedule for Jeffrey Leasing Inc.
2. Prepare the journal entries relating to the lease for Jeffrey Leasing Inc. for 20X4 and 20X5, using the net method of recording the leased asset.
3. Repeat requirement 2, but use the gross method instead.

★★ connect

A18-14 Finance Lease—Lessee and Lessor: Sondheim Limited entered into a direct financing lease with New Age Leasing Corporation. Both companies report under IFRS. The lease is for new specialized factory equipment that has a fair value of $3,200,000. The expected useful life of the equipment is 15 years, although its physical life is far greater. The initial lease term begins on 1 April 20X2 and runs for 10 years. Annual lease payments are $400,000, payable at the beginning of each lease year. After the initial lease term, Sondheim has the option of renewing the lease on a year-by-year basis for as long as Sondheim wishes. Since the equipment will be obsolete by that time, the renewal is set at $10,000 per year, which is expected to be a fair rental value for equipment of that age. Other information is as follows:

- The interest rate implicit in the lease is 7%; Sondheim's incremental borrowing rate is 6%.
- Sondheim will amortize the equipment on a straight-line basis over the lease term.
- The fiscal year of both companies ends on 31 December.

Required:

1. Prepare the journal entries relating to the lease liability and the leased equipment for Sondheim for 20X2, including all appropriate adjusting entries.
2. What amounts will appear on Sondheim's statement of financial position and statement of cash flows at 31 December 20X2? Assume that Sondheim uses the indirect approach to determining cash flow from operating activities.
3. Prepare the journal entries relating to the lease for New Age for 20X2. Use the gross method of recording. What is the net amount of lease receivable that will appear on New Age's statement of financial position on 31 December 20X2?

★★ connect

A18-15 Finance Lease—Lessee; Guaranteed Residual; Future Balance: On 24 February 20X1, Ready Distributing Ltd., a public company, signed a lease for conveyor equipment. The equipment is intended to help Ready cope with an increased volume of business until the company is able to finance and build new facilities. The fair value of the leased equipment is $720,000.

The lease will commence on 1 October 20X1. The lease is for four years with lease payments of $30,000 per quarter (i.e., each three months), due at the beginning of each quarter. The lease is renewable for an additional four-year period at the same cost. If Ready does not renew after the initial lease term, the company must guarantee the lessor a residual value of $300,000. The lessor does not require a residual value guarantee at the end of the renewal period. The equipment's estimated economic life is 10 years.

Ready's incremental borrowing rate is a nominal 8% per annum, compounded quarterly.

Required:

1. Show the entry or entries that Ready should make for the fiscal year ending 31 December 20X1. The company uses straight-line depreciation for its equipment, with a full year's depreciation in the year of acquisition.
2. What amounts relating to the *lease liability* will appear on Ready's SFP for the year ending 31 December 20X3? Use the short-cut method, not an amortization table. [*Hint*: What is the PV of the remaining cash flows at that date? How does that compare to the PV of the future cash flows one year later?]

★★ connect

A18-16 Finance Lease—Lessee; Quarterly Payments; Current/Noncurrent: Packard Limited is planning on leasing 150 desktop computers from Hewlett Corporation. The list price for the computers is $2,000 each, or $300,000 in total. The lease will be for three years, starting on 1 October 20X4. The lease payments are $26,000 at the beginning of each quarter. Packard's incremental borrowing rate is 8% per annum. Packard's fiscal year ends on 31 December. The computers have an expected useful life of four years but will almost certainly have no market value at the end of the lease. Although it is not specified in the lease agreement, Packard's customary practice with such leases is to simply convey title to the computers at the end of the lease term, at a nominal payment by the lessee.

Required:

1. Prepare the journal entries to record the lease and lease payments for Packard's fiscal year ending 31 December 20X4.
2. What amounts relating to the lease liability will appear on Packard's 31 December 20X4 statement of financial position?

★★★

Solution

connect

A18-17 Finance Lease—Lessee Reporting: Videos-to-Go signed a lease for a vehicle that had an expected economic life of eight years and a fair value of $18,000. The lessor is the leasing subsidiary of a national car manufacturer. The terms of the lease are as follows:

- The lease term begins on 1 January 20X2 and runs for five years.
- The lease requires payments of $5,800 each 1 January, including $1,700 for maintenance and insurance costs.
- At the end of the lease term, the lease is renewable for three one-year periods, for $2,600 per year, including $2,100 for maintenance and insurance. The normal rental costs for a similar used vehicle would be approximately double this amount.
- At the end of any lease term, if Videos-to-Go does not renew the contract, the vehicle reverts to the lessor. The lessor may choose to leave the vehicle with Videos-to-Go if its value is low.

Videos-to-Go does not know the interest rate implicit in the lease from the lessor's perspective but has an incremental borrowing rate of 12%. Videos-to-Go has a 31 December year-end and uses straight-line depreciation for all assets.

Required:

1. Prepare a lease amortization schedule.
2. Prepare journal entries for 20X2 and 20X3.
3. Show how the lease would be reflected on the statement of financial position, income statement, and statement of cash flows for 20X2 and 20X3. Segregate debt between its current and noncurrent components. Assume the indirect method for operating activities in the statement of cash flows.
4. How much interest expense would be reported on the income statement in each year from 20X2 to 20X10 if Videos-to-Go has a 31 May fiscal year-end?

★★★

excel

A18-18 Finance Lease; Guaranteed Residual: Lessee Limited agreed to a noncancellable lease for which the following information is available:

a. The asset is new at the inception of the lease term and is worth $32,000.
b. Lease term is four years, starting 1 January 20X1.
c. Estimated useful life of the leased asset is six years.
d. The residual value of the leased asset will be $6,000 at the end of the lease term. The residual value is guaranteed by Lessee Limited.
e. The declining-balance depreciation method is used for the leased asset, at a rate of 30% per year.
f. Lessee's incremental borrowing rate is 10%.
g. Four annual lease payments will be made each 1 January during the lease term, and the first payment, due at inception of the lease term, is $8,626, including $1,100 of maintenance costs.
h. Lessee has a 31 December fiscal year-end.

Required:

1. Is this an operating lease or a finance lease? Explain.
2. Prepare a table showing how the lease liability reduces over the lease term.

3. Record the entries for 20X1.
4. Prepare the financial statement presentation of all lease-related accounts as they would appear in the financial statements of the lessee at 31 December 20X1. Include note disclosure.

★★★ excel connect

A18-19 Finance Lease; Fair Value Cap: On 31 December 20X1, Lessee Limited entered into a lease agreement by which Lessee leased a jutling machine for six years. Annual lease payments are $20,000, payable at the beginning of each lease year (31 December). At the end of the lease, possession of the machine will revert to the lessor. The normal economic life for this type of machine is 8 to 10 years.

At the time of the lease agreement, jutling machines could be purchased for approximately $90,000 cash. Equivalent financing for the machine could have been obtained from Lessee's bank at 14%.

Lessee's fiscal year coincides with the calendar year. Lessee uses straight-line depreciation for its jutling machines.

Required:

1. Prepare an amortization table for the lease, assuming that Lessee accounts for it as a finance lease.
2. Prepare all journal entries relating to the lease and the leased asset for 20X1, 20X2, and 20X3.
3. How would the amounts relating to the leased asset and lease liability be shown on Lessee's statement of financial position at 31 December 20X4?
4. Repeat requirement 2 assuming that the fair market value of the equipment was $77,273 at the inception of the lease.

★★★ Solution connect

A18-20 Sale and Leaseback: On 31 March 20X2, Supergrocery Inc. sold its major distribution facility, with a 30-year remaining life, to a real estate investment trust (REIT) for $9,000,000 cash. The facility had an original cost of $10,400,000 and accumulated depreciation of $3,600,000 on the date of sale.

Also on 31 March 20X2, Supergrocery signed a 20-year lease agreement with the REIT, leasing the property back. At the end of the 20-year lease term, legal title to the facility will be transferred to Supergrocery. Annual payments, beginning on 31 March 20X2, are $875,000. Maintenance and repair costs are the responsibility of Supergrocery. Supergrocery has an incremental interest rate of 9%. The company uses straight-line depreciation and has a 31 December year-end. Supergrocery records a part-year's depreciation, based on the date of acquisition, whenever it buys finance assets.

Required:

1. Give the 20X2 entries that Supergrocery Incorporated would make to record the sale and the lease.
2. Give the entries Supergrocery would make in 20X3 and 20X4 in relation to this transaction.
3. Show how the statement of financial position and income statement would reflect the transactions at the end of 20X2, 20X3, and 20X4. Do not segregate statement of financial position items between current and noncurrent items.

★★ connect

A18-21 Sale and Leaseback: Central Purchasing Limited (CPL) owns the building it uses; it had an original cost of $825,000 and a net book value of $450,000 as of 1 January 20X2. On this date, the building was sold to a real estate investment trust (REIT) for $500,000, which also was the building's fair value, and simultaneously leased back to CPL.

The lease has a guaranteed, 12-year term and required payments on 31 December of each year. The payments are $76,500, and the lease allows the property to revert to the lessee at the end of the lease. CPL could have mortgaged this property under similar terms at an interest rate of 9%. The REIT will pay property taxes estimated to be $6,200 per year. These costs are included in the lease payment. CPL will pay maintenance and operating costs. The building is being depreciated straight line, with an estimated remaining life of 16 years.

Required:

1. Prepare entries to record the sale and leaseback of the building.
2. Prepare year-end adjusting entries for 20X2.
3. Show how all amounts related to the sale and leaseback will be presented on the statement of financial position and statement of comprehensive income in 20X2.

★★ **A18-22 Sale and Leaseback:** Sportco Limited is suffering temporary cash flow difficulties due to poor economic conditions. To raise sufficient finance to allow operations to continue until economic conditions improve, Sportco entered into an agreement with a major lease corporation, Leaseco Limited. On 1 January 20X2, Sportco sold its largest manufacturing property to Leaseco at its fair market value, $1,750,000. The property had a net book value of $250,000 at the time of the sale.

Sportco, in turn, leased back the property from Leaseco for 15 years. The annual rent was $175,000, due each year starting on 1 January 20X2. Sportco can repurchase the property from Leaseco at the end of the lease term. The repurchase price (stated in the lease contract) is $2,500,000, based on projected fair values for the property. The land value is estimated to be 40% of the total fair market value of the property, while the building represents the other 60%. Sportco amortizes its buildings at a declining-balance rate of 10%.

Sportco's incremental borrowing rate is 7%. Its financial statements are prepared in accordance with generally accepted accounting principles.

Required:

How should Sportco account for this transaction in its financial statements for the year ending 31 December 20X2? Be specific, and explain the approach that you have chosen. Ignore any income tax issues and disclosure issues.

(Source: The Canadian Institute of Chartered Accountants, © 2010)

★★★ **A18-23 Sales-Type Lease—Lessor:** Jordin Limited is an equipment dealer that occasionally uses leasing as a means of selling its products. On 1 January 20X1, Jordin leased equipment to Easten Corporation. The lease term was four years with annual lease payments of $5,769 to be paid on each 31 December. The equipment has an estimated zero residual value at the end of the lease term. The equipment was carried in Jordin's accounts at a cost of $15,000. Jordin expects to collect all rentals from Easten, and there were no material cost uncertainties at the inception of the lease. The implicit interest rate in the lease was 11%.

Required:

1. Why is this a sales-type lease for Jordin?
2. How much is the gross profit or loss recognized by Jordin? The finance revenue recognized over the life of the lease?
3. Assume that the implicit interest rate is 4% (not 11%). How much is the gross profit or loss recognized by Jordin? The finance revenue recognized over the life of the lease?
4. Give the entries made by Jordin Limited (based on the 11% rate) at the inception of the lease. Use the gross method.
5. Show all lease-related accounts as they would appear in the statement of financial position and income statement of the lessee and the lessor at 31 December 20X3, for the year then ended. The lessor's statement of financial position is unclassified.

★★ **A18-24 Sales-Type Lease—Lessor:** On 14 June 20X1, Bruckner Corporation entered into an agreement to lease materials-handling equipment from Mahler Inc. The five-year lease commences on 1 July 20X1. Bruckner will pay lease payments of $100,000 at the beginning of each lease year. Bruckner also guarantees a residual value of $50,000.

Mahler Inc. is the manufacturer of the equipment Bruckner is leasing. The standard cost of manufacture is $350,000. The leased equipment normally sells for $480,000. When Mahler negotiates a lease with a customer, the company's expected rate of return varies with economic conditions and the cost of capital; currently, Mahler negotiates leases to obtain a return of 8%.

Required:

Prepare the appropriate entries for Mahler Inc. for 20X1 and 20X2 to record this lease, including the receipt of payments and the recognition of any revenue and expense. Mahler Inc. has a 31 December fiscal year-end.

★★ **A18-25 Statement of Cash Flows—Review:** Each of the following items must be considered in preparing a statement of cash flows for Phillie Fashions Inc. for the year ended 31 December 20X6:

1. Finance assets that had a cost of $10,000 6½ years before and were being depreciated straight line on a 10-year basis, with no estimated scrap value, were sold for $3,125.
2. Phillie Company leased an asset to a customer, as a way of selling it, on 31 December 20X6. Phillie recognized a net receivable of $23,456, after the first payment of $8,700. The $8,700 payment was collected on 31 December. The gross profit on the sale was $5,670. There was unearned finance revenue of $6,200 over the lease term, which lasts four years.
3. During the year, goodwill of $5,000 was completely written off to expense.
4. During the year, 250 shares of common stock were issued for $32 per share.
5. Finance asset amortization amounted to $1,000 and patent amortization to $200.
6. Bonds payable with a par value of $12,000, on which there was an unamortized bond premium of $360, were redeemed at 103.
7. Phillie Fashions Inc., as lessee, reported a net lease liability of $14,678 at the end of 20X6. In 20X5, the liability had been $15,766. The current portion of the liability was $2,410 each year.

Required:

For each item, state what would be included in the statement of cash flows, whether it is an inflow or outflow, and the amount(s). Assume that correct entries were made for all transactions as they took place and that the indirect method is to be used to disclose cash flow from operations. In your response, use a three-column format as follows:

Operating/Investing/Financing	Inflow/Outflow	Amount

★★ **A18-26 ASPE—Lessee:** Refer to the information in A18-14. Assume that Sondheim is a private enterprise that has chosen to use ASPE.

Required:

1. Determine the present value of Sondheim Limited's lease payments.
2. What amounts relating to the lease (and the leased asset) will Sondheim report in the company's statement of financial position and its statement of comprehensive income for the year ending 31 December 20X2?
3. If A18-14 has been solved, explain the relative impact of using ASPE, as compared with IFRS.

★ **A18-27 ASPE—Lessor:** Refer to the information in A18-12. Assume that Yvan Ltd. is a public company in receivership but needs the equipment to continue operating efficiently until the company completes the receivership process. Yvan Ltd.'s successful emergence from receivership is not assured. Jeffrey Leasing Inc.'s implicit interest rate in the Yvan lease is 6%. Jeffrey Leasing Inc. is a private company that uses ASPE.

Required:

1. Explain how Jeffrey Leasing Inc. should account for the Yvan lease.
2. Prepare the journal entries relating to the lease for Jeffrey Leasing Inc. for 20X5.

★★ connect

A18-28 ASPE—Lessee and Lessor: On 10 December 20X0, Noel Inc. entered into a six-year equipment lease with Williams Ltd. The terms of the lease are as follows:

- The lease will term begin on 1 January 20X1.
- The fair value of the equipment at the inception of the lease is $480,000. The equipment's expected useful life is six or seven years.
- Noel Inc.'s incremental borrowing rate is 11%.
- Lease payments are $100,000 per year, payable no later than the 31 December prior to each new lease year. That is, the first payment will be due by 31 December 20X0.
- Because of Noel Inc.'s shaky financial condition, Williams Ltd. determined the lease payments based on a 12% return, which is higher than Williams Ltd.' normal return, Noel Inc. is aware of Williams Ltd.'s rate.

Required:

1. Should Noel account for this lease as a finance lease or an operating lease? Explain fully.
2. How should Williams Ltd. report this lease? Explain fully.
3. What anomaly arises under ASPE when the lessor is bearing a higher-than-normal risk of default by the lessee?

★ connect

A18-29 Appendix—Equipment; Lessee: On 18 December 20X1, Kushner Construction Ltd. leased equipment from Schultz Equipment Inc. for use in building a new condominium project in downtown Calgary. The lease is for three years. The lease commences on 1 January 20X2. Annual lease payments are $100,000, payable at the beginning of each year. In addition, Schultz must pay $30,000 for delivery and set-up of the equipment (e.g., cranes) and another $30,000 at the end of the lease term for deconstruction and removal of the equipment. The lease is not renewable because Schultz will lease the equipment to other construction companies after Kushner's project is finished. Kushner's incremental borrowing rate is 8%. June.

Required:

1. Determine the amounts relating to this lease that Kushner should report on its statement of financial position at the end of 20X2 and 20X3.
2. What amounts relating to this lease will be reflected in Kushner's earnings for each of 20X2 and 20X3?

★ connect

A18-30 Appendix—Real Property; Lessee: Mackenzie Ltd. leased a small building from Brooklong Inc. The lease term was four years; the annual rent was $500,000 due at the start of each lease year. The lease commenced on 1 January 20X1. Mackenzie's incremental borrowing rate is 6%.

Required:

For each year, 20X1 through 20X4, determine the amounts for (1) interest expense and (2) amortization of the right-of-use asset (i.e., for the building).

connect LEARNSMART SMARTBOOK™

For more information on the resources available from McGraw-Hill Ryerson, go to www.mcgrawhill.ca/he/solutions.

CHAPTER 19

Post-Employment Benefits

INTRODUCTION

Many companies promise to provide their employees benefits after they retire. The most common form of *post-employment benefit* is a pension. However, a company may also provide other post-employment benefits, such as extended health care. These benefits are provided as compensation for employees' services during their working lives. Therefore, post-employment benefits are a form of deferred compensation, and the cost must be recognized during the employee's working life.

A pension may take the form of a *defined contribution plan*, where the employer's commitment and cost is limited to defined contributions. Alternatively, the plan might be a *defined benefit plan,* where the employer's commitment is to provide benefits, making the cost difficult to estimate because future events must be projected. Some of these projections are retention rates, mortality rates, retirement trends, and future interest rates. Accounting for defined benefit plans is complex.

To make matters more complicated, there are several different *actuarial cost methods* used to measure and allocate the annual cost of a defined benefit pension plan. Every actuarial cost method allocates the future estimated cost of pension benefits to the years of an employee's service in an effort to determine appropriate funding. Each actuarial cost method provides a different funding pattern. For those who want a better understanding of actuarial methodology, a unit on Connect illustrates the three basic actuarial methods.

Pension plans are big business and can affect an assessment of the solvency of the sponsoring company. For example, Air Canada reports total assets of $9.6 billion at the end of 2011, liabilities of $13.6 billion, and a shareholders' *deficit* of $4 billion. The disclosure notes show that the pension plan, whose assets and liabilities are not separately recorded by Air Canada, has assets of $11.9 billion and obligations of $14.5 billion, making the pension plan larger than the book value of the entire employer company. The pension plan is underfunded by $2.6 billion.

This chapter focuses primarily on accounting for pension plans but includes an example of other post-employment benefits. The general structure of pension calculations and assumptions are analyzed, various components of pension expense are explored, and a spreadsheet is introduced that helps to organize the data. The extensive disclosure requirements for post-employment benefits are reviewed. This chapter is based on the IFRS standard effective in 2013, and the ASPE standard effective in 2014. Accounting for post-employment benefits has changed significantly in the last few years, to ensure that the status of the pension plan is reflected on the company's SFP.

TYPES OF PENSION PLANS

Pension plans are typically *formal agreements* and part of contractual terms of employment. Pension plans may also be *legislative* or *industry based*, for example, if companies are required to contribute to national, provincial, or industry-specific plans. Pensions may also be represented by *constructive obligations,* based on informal practice. Informal practice gives rise to a constructive obligation when the company has no realistic choice but to pay employee benefits because of reputation or competitive forces.

There are two general types of pension plans:

1. Defined contribution plans, and
2. Defined benefit plans.

A **defined contribution plan** is one in which the employer makes agreed-upon (or *defined*) cash contributions to the plan each period, which are invested by a trustee on behalf of the employee. The employer has no legal or constructive liability to pay further contributions. For example, an employer may agree to contribute 6% of an employee's salary to a separate pension fund each year. The pension that the employee eventually receives as a result of those contributions is a function of the fund's investment success; the pension annuity is determined by the amount of accumulated contributions plus earnings on contributions at the time that the employee retires. The employee accepts both *actuarial risk* (benefits will be less than expected) and *investment risk* (assets invested will not completely fund the expected pension.)

A **defined benefit plan** is one in which the eventual *benefits* to the employee are stated in the pension plan. It is the employer's responsibility to fund this pension, and thus all risk stays with the employer. The benefits are normally calculated on the basis of the employee's salary at or near retirement and the length of her employment with the company. However, the defined benefit may also be a flat amount per year or a lump sum benefit on retirement. The estimate of the present value of cumulative pension benefits, adjusted for expected life expectancy, turnover, and a myriad of other factors, is called the *defined benefit obligation* and is estimated by an actuary.

The essential difference between the two types of plans can be summarized as follows:

Type of Plan	Contributions	Benefits	Risk
Defined contribution	Fixed	Variable	Employee has risk of low pension benefits
Defined benefit	Variable	Fixed	Employer has risk of high pension contributions

Classification of a Pension Plan

Classification of a plan as defined contribution or defined benefit rests on the *economic substance* of the plan, based on its terms and conditions. If the benefit formula is based on *anything more than* the contributions and the investment history to date or if the employer guarantees some specific level of pension or plan earnings, then the plan is a *defined benefit plan.*

PENSION TERMS

Contributory versus Noncontributory

A **contributory pension plan** is one in which the *employee* makes contributions to the plan, in addition to those made by the employer. Both defined contribution plans and defined benefit plans can be contributory, which acts to enforce some level of retirement savings. The other alternative is that the pension plan is **noncontributory**; in this case, the pension assets are contributed entirely by the employer.

Vesting

Pension plan benefits are said to be *vested* when the employee has the right to receive his or her pension entitlement even if he or she leaves the employer before retirement age. The pension is not actually paid until retirement, of course, but the funds in the pension plan are "earmarked" for that individual or rolled into the individual's RRSP. Some provinces require that benefits are immediately vested. Others require vesting after two years of service. Other jurisdictions apply the 10 + 45 rule; contributions become vested when the employee has worked for the same employer for 10 years *and* has reached age 45. Of course, employers may voluntarily commit themselves to faster vesting than legislation requires. Note that any contributions to a pension plan made by an *employee* are automatically vested.

Trustee

Most pension plans are trusteed, which means that there is an independent **trustee** that receives the pension contributions from the employer (and, if appropriate, from the employee), invests the contributions in accordance with provincial regulations and agreed-upon guidelines, and pays out benefits to pensioners. Trustees of pension funds are often financial institutions, such as trust companies and banks; a pension trustee is not an individual person. Most plans are trusteed because:

- Trusteeship is required for a plan to be registered.
- From an accounting perspective, if a pension plan is not trusteed and instead is administered by the company, the company must report both the pension plan assets and the defined benefit obligation separately on its SFP because the assets are under the control of the company. When a plan is administered by a trustee, however, the plan assets are beyond control of the company's managers and accounting recognition is based on the net pension plan position.

Trusteeship does not absolve the employer of responsibility to ensure that a defined benefit pension plan is solvent and able to pay pension benefits when they come due.

Registered

Pension plans normally are **registered** with the pension commissioner in the province of jurisdiction. The commissioner's office is responsible for seeing that the pension plan abides by pension legislation, including requirements for funding, reporting, trusteeship, actuarial valuation, and control over surpluses.

An important benefit of registration is that it enables the company to deduct from taxable income amounts contributed to the plan. If the plan is not registered, the employer *cannot deduct the pension contributions;* tax deductions will come only when the pension is actually paid to the employee or when a pension annuity is purchased on behalf of the employee at the retirement date. Since pension contributions are material, this would delay the tax deduction for the company and would be highly undesirable!

Actuarial Cost Methods

Since defined benefit plans entitle the employee to a specified (or *defined*) pension, the challenge for the employer is to make payments into the plan that will eventually provide enough money to pay the pension.

The task of determining an appropriate funding amount is the task of the **actuary**. An *actuary* is an expert who calculates statistical risks, life expectancy, payout probabilities, and so on. Actuaries are typically employed by insurance agencies and other financial institutions. Actuarial science is a well-established profession, with a rigorous multi-stage qualification process.

There are several different methods of measuring and allocating the pension amounts, known as **actuarial cost methods**. Every actuarial cost method allocates the future estimated cost of such post-employment benefits to the years of an employee's service in an effort to determine appropriate funding. The actuarial cost methods must also determine the present value of the defined benefit obligation to employees at the measurement date.

Actuarial Gains and Losses

Actuarial gains and losses exist in defined benefit plans. There are two sources of actuarial gains and losses:

1. A change in the present value of the defined benefit obligation to employees, *resulting from the experience of the plan to date, as compared with predicted amounts.* This is a retrospective measurement, based on experience to date and is sometimes referred to as an *experience gain or loss.*
2. Changes in the present value of the defined benefit obligation to employees, *resulting from a change in an assumption about the future.*

For example, assume that employee turnover was projected to be 2% in 20X1. The actual turnover was 5%, which means that the cumulative defined benefit obligation to the end of the 20X1 is now lower and an experience gain is measured. However, the 5% turnover rate for 20X1 is also used as evidence to lower retention projections for the next 20 years. This causes a prospective re-measurement and a further actuarial gain.

Pension legislation usually requires an employer to have an **actuarial revaluation** done at least once every three years. The actuary looks at the actual performance factors since the preceding revaluation (causing experience gains and losses) and at factors affecting future outlook (causing further actuarial gains and losses), and restates the defined benefit obligation accordingly. If the defined benefit obligation increases as the result of a revaluation, a loss occurs; if the defined benefit obligation decreases, a gain occurs.

Plan Settlement and Curtailment

On occasion, an employer may end its legal liability under an existing defined benefit pension plan, or end a portion of the benefits under a plan. This is called a **pension plan settlement**; the obligation to the pensionable group is settled by transferring assets to a trustee, purchasing specified annuities for employees, or otherwise terminating the financial commitments of the employer.

A **pension plan curtailment** takes place when there is a significant reduction in the number of employees covered by a plan, or some significant element of future service that will no longer qualify for benefits. This may happen when a company closes down a division or otherwise restructures or downsizes operations. It may also happen when workers agree to a major change in benefits, perhaps to preserve competitiveness.

In these circumstances, there is likely to be a substantial gain. Other times, a curtailment or settlement agreement may include special pension benefits that will increase the company's obligation and thereby result in a loss. It depends on the situational variables. *The gain or loss is the sum of the change in the defined benefit obligation and the change in pension assets.*

CONCEPT REVIEW

1. Explain the difference between a defined contribution pension plan and a defined benefit pension plan.
2. Why is trusteeship critical when accounting for pensions?
3. What is the risk to an employee if pension rights are not vested?
4. Who makes contributions to the pension plan if it is noncontributory?
5. What is a curtailment?

DEFINED CONTRIBUTION PLANS

The trend over the last 30 years, both in Canada and around the world, has been for more and more private sector companies that grant pensions to do so through defined contribution plans. Over 80% of the private company pension plans in Canada are defined contribution plans. Many companies with defined benefit pension plans are curtailing these plans and/or enrolling new employees in defined contribution plans. Defined contribution plans have lower financial risk for the employer because the cost of the program is known with certainty.

Current Service Cost

Accounting for defined contribution pension plans is straightforward because the obligation for each period is determined by the contribution for that period. The required payment equals the expense. The employer's required contribution for services rendered during the period is known as the *current service cost* for the period. No actuarial assumptions are required, and there is accordingly no possibility of an actuarial gain or loss from a change in assumptions.

Note that:

- The amount recorded is undiscounted unless the payment to the pension fund is delayed for more than 12 months after the end of the fiscal year. If discounting is required, the discount rate is based on the market yield of high-quality corporate bonds with similar term and currency as the pension payment stream.
- If there is an overpayment in a given year, the overpayment is recorded as a prepaid pension amount as long as the prepayment will lead to a reduction in future payments, or a cash refund, to the employer.

Example Suppose that Enterprise Fourchu Limité (EFL) pays $60,000 into the pension plan at the end of 20X1 as required under its pension plan for 20X1 services rendered. The entry is:

Pension expense	60,000	
Cash		60,000

Be careful to expense only amounts relating to the *current* year's service; there may well be an agreement covering 20X2, but it would not be recorded as a liability in 20X1.

Example—Delayed Payment Assume that EFL (above) has agreed to pay $60,000 at the end of 20X1 and *also* agrees to make another payment of $40,000 *relating to employees' 20X1 services* at the end of 20X4. Assuming an interest rate of 6%, the present value of the future payment is $40,000 × (P/F, 6%, 3) = $33,585. The entry to record 20X1 pension expense will be:

Pension expense	93,585	
Cash		60,000
Defined contribution pension liability		33,585

The defined contribution pension liability must have interest at 6% recorded each year. Interest is always calculated using the same rate that was used in discounting the obligation in the first place. Interest is an expense in earnings. It may be part of pension expense or recorded as interest expense; presentation is up to the company. In our examples, we will include the amount in pension expense.

Note the $33,585 pension liability recognized by EFL, above. In 20X2, EFL will record interest of $33,585 × 6% = $2,015. The liability will grow to $35,600 ($33,585 + $2,015) at the end of 20X2.

Example—Prepaid Amounts Assume EFL (above) contributes $80,000 to a plan for 20X1, and then discovers that its 20X1 payroll was less than expected for the year and the contribution should have been only $60,000. If the excess $20,000 can be used toward the 20X2 required payment or can be obtained as a cash refund, then a prepaid pension asset (or account receivable) is recorded and pension expense is $60,000. The entry is:

Pension expense	60,000	
Prepaid pension asset	20,000	
Cash		80,000

If no relief is offered for the overpayment, then pension expense is $80,000, and no asset exists.

Past Service Cost

An employer with a defined contribution plan may make an additional payment to a pension fund in recognition of past years' service, in essence improving the plan for employees. This amount is expensed in the period in which the payment is made. No deferrals are permitted.

DEFINED BENEFIT PLANS—INTRODUCTION

A defined benefit plan is a post-retirement benefit plan where the financial risk remains with the employer, as we have seen. Before examining the accounting approach for such plans, we will analyze plan structure, variables to be estimated, and actuarial cost methods.

Note that in defined benefit pension plans, the pension paid to a retiree must be based on some specific formula. Pensions that are based on a specific percentage of final year's salary are called **final pay pension plans**. However, pension benefits could alternatively be based on:

- **Flat benefit** per year of service, with no entitlement related to salary;
- Career average pay—that is, an average of the employee's earnings over the entire time spent with the employer;
- The best year's earnings (which permits employees to phase out toward the end of their careers); or
- An average of the last three (or five) years' earnings.

For example, a company may provide that an employee will receive an annual pension that is equal to 2% of the employee's final year's salary for each year of service. If the employee is earning $100,000 in the year before retirement and has worked for the company for 35 years, the annual pension will be:

Annual pension annuity = $100,000 × 2% × 35 years = $70,000

Alternatively, the pension agreement may provide a flat benefit of a life annuity of $1,000 per year for every year of service, regardless of salary, in which case the annual pension is:

Annual pension annuity = $1,000 × 35 years = $35,000.

Defined Benefit Plans—Structure

A defined benefit pension plan consists of pension fund assets, placed with a trustee, and the post-employment defined benefit obligation to employees.

Pension Plan Assets The assets of a pension fund are the assets held in a separate long-term employee benefit fund. This must be a separate legal entity. The sole purpose of the fund must be to pay employee benefits, and *the assets must not be available* to pay other liabilities of the employer, even if the employer is bankrupt.

Fund assets increase when the employer or the employee makes contributions to the fund, and when the assets generate return. The assets can decline if the plan generates a negative return. Assets also decline when benefits are paid to pensioners.

Assets are valued at *fair value,* the amount for which assets could be exchanged in a transaction between knowledgeable willing parties in an arms-length transaction. If fair values are not readily available, valuation models, such as adjusted reference prices or discounted cash flow, must be used to approximate fair value.

Defined Benefit Obligation The defined benefit obligation of a pension plan to its members is measured as the *present value* of *expected future payments* resulting from employee service in current and prior periods. It is a cumulative amount that increases each year that the employee works and earns a higher pension. The obligation also increases annually for an interest component because of the time value of money. It can increase or decrease because of actuarial gains or losses: when experience to date is different from the original estimate and/or when there are changed future estimates regarding retention, mortality, future salary levels, and so on. The obligation will decrease when benefits are paid to retirees.

Net Defined Benefit Pension Liability (Asset) The **net defined benefit pension liability (asset)** is the net overall funded status of the pension plan; the pension plan assets netted with the defined benefit obligation. If the defined benefit obligation is $4,500,000, and the plan assets are $3,700,000, then the plan has a net defined benefit pension liability status of $800,000. If the assets were $4,800,000 and the defined benefit obligation was $4,500,000, then the plan has a net defined benefit asset status of $300,000.

Ceiling Test for a Net Defined Benefit Asset If the pension plan assets are greater than the obligation, companies must evaluate an asset ceiling before declaring their asset status. The **asset ceiling** is a test to see if the "excess" assets in the plan *can be used to benefit the employer* in the future: This benefit must be in the form of a reduction of future contributions, or perhaps a cash refund. If the time span is greater than one year, the ceiling is a discounted value. Sometimes such future recoveries are realized through a **pension holiday,** whereby the employer in an overfunded plan is permitted to temporarily reduce or eliminate payments for the current service funding requirements.

Consider the example above, where assets were $4,800,000 and the defined benefit obligation was $4,500,000. These values are both present values. If future contributions could be reduced because the plan was overfunded, then the fund is genuinely in a $300,000 asset position. If no such relief is permitted under the terms of the plan and/or pension legislation, then the asset ceiling is invoked, and the plan is at a zero net position: $4,500,000 of liabilities and assets capped by the ceiling at $4,500,000 for reporting purposes.

Defined Benefit Plans—Variables to Be Estimated

Estimates must be made to calculate the defined benefit obligation, and the annual funding amount. *It is the actuary's responsibility to suggest the estimates necessary for the measurement of pension funding amounts and to make required calculations*; these are reviewed by the company to ensure they are appropriate.

ETHICAL ISSUES

The estimates used by management for pension measurements must be *unbiased* and *mutually compatible.* For example, since inflation rates and salary increases are related over the long run, it would make little sense to use a high estimated discount rate (which would include a high future inflation rate) while also assuming a very low rate of increase in salaries (which would imply a low future inflation rate).

There is always risk of bias in estimates, and there may be a corporate motive to minimize or maximize pension amounts. Unbiased estimates are neither imprudent nor excessively conservative. Care must be taken when looking at the quality of estimates; *best estimates* are required.

Major categories of assumptions can be described as follows:

1. Demographic assumptions—decisions that relate to the characteristics of the employees eligible for benefits:
   - *Employee turnover, disability, and early retirement.* Vesting may not occur immediately in defined benefit plans. Therefore, it is usually necessary to estimate what proportion of employees will stay long enough for vesting to occur. It is also necessary to establish how many will qualify for disability benefits prior to retirement, or elect to take a reduced, early retirement.
   - *Mortality rates.* Mortality determines the term of the eventual pension and is an important variable. Most plans provide minimum guarantees; the pensioner's estate receives a lump-sum payment if the pension is not paid for a certain number of years. A pension plan may specify **death benefits** or **survivor benefits** that give lump-sum or continuing benefits to a surviving spouse, partner, and/or child. The mortality rate and the extent of any trailing entitlements must be estimated. *Best estimates* assumptions in this category generally involve adjusting population mortality statistics for the characteristics of the specific employee group.
2. Financial assumptions—decisions that deal with economic variables:
   - *Future salary increases.* Since pension benefits are often tied to the employee's future earnings, it is necessary to estimate (or *project*) future salary increases. Salary increases are related, in part, to inflation rates. Therefore, it is necessary to estimate future inflation rates. Other variables include supply and demand in the labour force, seniority, and promotion. Costs of other benefits, such as medical services, may also need to be projected.
   - *Discount rates.* The discount rate is established with reference to market yield at the end of the fiscal year on high-quality corporate bonds. Again, inflation rates must be projected. Currency and term should be consistent with the pension obligation. If the market for these bonds is not deep, then the yield on government bonds is used as a reference point.

Defined Benefit Plans—Actuarial Cost Methods

Understanding *pension accounting* requires understanding *pension funding* because they interact. **Funding** is the manner in which the actuary, in consultation with the employer, sets the necessary contributions to the plan. The accounting measurements determine pension expense and do not have to be equal to funding. Similar factors and the same family of actuarial methods may be used for both—or not.

There are several actuarial cost methods that are used by the actuary to calculate the cash contributions that a company must make. It is important to emphasize that no one method is "better" than another; all methods provide full funding of benefits.

However, there is a significant difference between various actuarial cost methods in the *pattern* of payments made to the trustee over an employee's working life. If one particular actuarial cost method requires higher cash contributions in the early years of an employee's tenure with the company, it could be viewed as more fiscally conservative. Other actuarial cost methods require the bulk of funding to occur later in the employee's working life. All methods are acceptable for funding under pension legislation, and all are used in practice.

The three basic actuarial cost methods that can be used for funding can be described briefly as follows:

1. The **accumulated benefit method** calculates the contributions that an employer must make in order to fund the pension to which the employee currently is entitled, based on the *actual* years of service to date and on the *current* salary.
2. The **projected unit credit method** calculates the required funding based on the *actual* years of service to date but on a *projected* estimate of the employee's salary at the retirement date.
3. The **level contribution method** projects both the *final salary* and the *total* years of service and then allocates the cost evenly over the years of service.

Clearly, the level contribution method involves *more projections*, and the accumulated benefit method involves *fewer projections*.

Actuarial Cost Methods Comparison To illustrate the three actuarial cost methods, consider a basic illustration of a defined benefit pension. Assume that an employee named Chris begins working for Celebrities Limited at age 30. Assume the following:

- Chris's starting salary is $25,000 per year.
- The normal retirement age at Celebrities is 65.
- The pension plan provides that an employee will receive an annual pension of 2% of the final year's salary for each year of service.
- The pension is fully vested from the date of employment.

Some additional estimates are needed, which are provided by the actuary:

- The estimated life expectancy after retirement is 14 years.
- The expected return on the investment in pension plan assets will be 6%.
- Chris's salary will increase by a compound average annual rate of 3%.
- Chris will work for Celebrities for 35 years, until normal retirement age.

Comparison The computation details for each of the three methods are explained in a unit on Connect. *These calculations (for a group of employees) are performed by the actuary; the accountant should understand the approach and the estimates to which the calculations are sensitive.* Exhibit 19-1 summarizes the funding required for Chris' pension under each of the actuarial cost methods at selected ages. Remember, a company may use any actuarial cost method to determine funding.

EXHIBIT 19-1

COMPARISON OF FUNDING REQUIREMENTS FOR CURRENT SERVICE USING DIFFERENT ACTUARIAL COST METHODS

	Allocated Funding under Each Method		
Chris's Age	Accumulated Benefit	Projected Unit Credit	Level Contribution
30	$ 679	$ 1,856	$4,227
35	1,207	2,484	4,227
40	2,111	3,324	4,227
45	3,645	4,448	4,227
50	6,228	5,953	4,227
55	10,551	7,966	4,227
60	17,748	10,660	4,227
64	26,786	13,458	4,227

The allocation patterns are very different, and yet each method results in *full funding over the years of service.* The accumulated benefit method and the projected unit credit method both start with low payments and end with high payments. This pattern is most extreme with the accumulated benefit method. The level contribution method, as the name states, requires the same funding each year.

Bear in mind that the calculation is for just one employee, which is unrealistic. *A company's overall pension funding requirement is calculated for the employee group as a whole.* Employees just entering the workforce may have low pension amounts attributable to their service, which will offset the apparently dramatic increase in amounts for older employees. For an employee group as a whole, the relative difference in pension amounts between methods will level out *if the employee group is stable and has an even age composition.* However, the age and length-of-employment composition of employee groups are often unstable; there are usually more employees at the lower-experience levels of employment than at the senior levels.

Sensitivity to Assumptions The calculations are extremely sensitive to all basic assumptions within methods: turnover, early retirement and disability, mortality, salary increase, and discount rate. If the assumed rate of salary increase is changed from 3% to 4%, for example, all of the costs in the table above would *increase by almost 40%.* The discount rate sensitivity is also worthy of note. If the assumed discount rate were increased from 6% to 8% in the preceding example, the required contributions at age 35 would change as shown below for the three methods:

Interest Rate Assumed	At 6%	At 8%
Accumulated benefit method	$1,207	$ 635
Projected unit credit method	2,484	1,305
Level contribution method	4,227	2,470

This highlights the need to use appropriate assumptions. As previously stated, the accounting standard requires use of unbiased and mutually compatible assumptions.

Actuarial Cost Method for Accounting Measurement Accounting standards require the use of the *projected unit credit method* for pension measurements. Companies are all required to use the same actuarial cost method to ensure that a common measurement tool is used, and thus comparability is preserved. Generally, this method is felt to best measure the cost of entitlements earned during the period, and standard setters have been consistent in their preference for this method.

Companies do not have to use this method for funding, however. Many do because it is costly to have the calculations done twice by the actuarial consultants. If the projected unit credit method is used for accounting and another method is used for funding, a long-term accrual—either an asset or a liability—will result.

CONCEPT REVIEW

1. What events or transactions cause pension fund assets to change?
2. Identify two major demographic assumptions that must be made to project the cost of a pension.
3. Name three actuarial cost methods, and specify what projections, if any, are involved for each one.
4. Which actuarial method is required for accounting measurements for a defined benefit plan?

DEFINED BENEFIT PLAN PENSION ACCOUNTING—THREE ELEMENTS

Accounting for a defined benefit pension plan requires measuring and recording three different elements:

1. **Service cost**, which is the total of current service cost, any past service cost, and any gain or loss on plan settlement. This amount is expensed.
2. Net interest on the *net defined benefit pension liability* (i.e., net interest on the defined benefit obligation less pension plan assets). The net defined benefit pension liability is multiplied by the discount rate, and the resulting expense is included in earnings. If the plan is overfunded, the net status is an asset, and this is a revenue item.
3. Re-measurement of the *net defined benefit pension liability*, whether caused by actuarial gains or losses, a difference between plan assets' earnings and the discount rate applied in item 2, or other measurement issues. This amount is recorded in *other comprehensive income* (OCI) and *accumulated other comprehensive income* (accumulated OCI). *It is never recycled to earnings.* Amounts in accumulated OCI can be reassigned to other equity accounts, particularly retained earnings.

The following sections explain these three elements.

Element 1: Service Cost

Service cost is an expense. It comprises:

1. Current service cost,
2. Past service cost, and
3. A gain or loss on plan settlement.

Current service cost (CSC) is the annual measurement of the cost of the pension earned for work done during the year. Accounting standards require that current service cost be measured using the *projected unit credit method.* The actuary determines this figure and provides it in an actuarial report. It is an *expected present value* calculation based on numerous assumptions, as we have seen.

Past service cost (PSC) is the actuarial present value of pension benefits granted (or reduced) in an amended (or brand new) pension plan *for years of service already rendered* by current employees. Changes caused by a *curtailment,* which is the significant reduction in the number of employees covered by a plan, are also included in PSC. PSC will increase pension expense if benefits are increased and decrease pension expense if benefits are decreased.

PSC may arise when a plan is first initiated. At that time, employees *may* be given pension entitlements for their employment period prior to the initiation of the plan. From time to time, a company will amend its pension plan, often to increase benefits but sometimes to decrease benefits. PSC is created whenever an existing plan is amended to change benefits *based on years of service to date.* This involves a retrospective change in the defined benefit obligation that relates to prior service.

PSC is not amortized, and is not expensed over any potential funding period. It is expensed in its entirety when granted. (This is a departure from common historical practice, which, for decades, rested on an amortization scheme.)

The final element of service cost is any gain or loss caused by a plan settlement, a transaction that winds up a plan. The gain or loss on settlement is the difference between plan obligations and assets, recalculated to the date of settlement and reflecting the terms of the settlement.

Alternative Classification of Settlement, Curtailment, and Termination

A gain or loss on settlement or curtailment is normally part of service cost. If the plan settlement or curtailment arises when a company restructures or discontinues some aspect(s) of its operations, the costs would be presented separately in earnings, as *discontinued operations*, or as a *restructuring*, depending on the facts.

An employer sometimes offers special incentives to induce employees to retire, or to take early retirement. Enhanced retirement offers are called **termination benefits** and may include lump-sum payments, continuation of salary, and enhanced pension benefits. With respect to enhanced pension benefits, these special termination benefits are in addition to the benefits normally offered to employees. Therefore, the cost of providing these special benefits has not been included in the actuarial calculations for the employee group, either for funding or for accounting purposes. Consequently, special termination benefits require separate recognition of extra cost.

The costs of special termination benefits are accrued in the financial statements as an expense and a liability, once a company is demonstrably committed to the termination, as explained in Chapter 12. This commitment must take the form of a formal and detailed plan. The cost is recognized as a lump sum. Since the employees are leaving the company, amortization of the cost over future periods is not appropriate.

The cost of pension benefits included in termination benefits may be part of service cost, if the termination is in the ordinary course of business. Alternatively, if the facts dictate, the cost of pension benefits included in termination benefits may be part of discontinued operations or restructuring.

Example Refer to Exhibit 19-2 for data for Walker Corporation; this example will be extended for the remaining two elements of pension accounting in the following sections.

EXHIBIT 19-2

PENSION EXAMPLE

Walker Corporation has a defined benefit pension plan. It is now 31 December 20X5. The following data apply to the plan:

Current service cost for 20X5, measured using the projected unit credit method	$ 456,200
New past service cost granted in 20X5; defined benefit obligation increases	910,000
Amount paid to pension fund trustee	1,700,000
Actuarial gain in 20X5, caused by lower anticipated future retention rates; defined benefit obligation decreases	(124,000)
Actual earnings in the fund, reported by the pension fund trustee, including interest, dividends, and change in fair value	398,200
Benefits paid to pensioners from pension fund assets	134,800
Balances:	
Defined benefit obligation, end of 20X4	$11,675,000
Pension plan assets, fair value, end of 20X4	10,010,000
SFP Net defined benefit pension liability, end of 20X4	$ 1,665,000 cr.
SFP Accumulated OCI, pension, end of 20X4	288,400 dr.
Retained earnings, end of 20X4	23,688,100 cr.
20X5 Earnings, prior to any pension expense	8,842,500 cr.

Service cost is a straightforward combination of current and past service cost. However, sifting through the data can be challenging! The calculation is as follows:

1. Current service cost, measured using the projected unit credit method	$ 456,200
2. Past service cost granted in 20X5	910,000
	$1,366,200

The entry to record service cost:

Pension expense	1,366,200	
Net defined benefit pension liability		1,366,200

The $1,700,000 contribution to the pension fund trustee is also recorded. It is not an expense but affects the SFP pension account:

Net defined benefit pension liability	1,700,000	
Cash		1,700,000

The SFP account, here labelled a net defined benefit pension liability, is affected by all three elements of pension accounting. At the end of the day, it will be equal to the pension assets less the defined benefit obligation. If it has a credit balance, it is a liability and is reported as a long-term liability on the SFP. If it has a debit balance, it is an asset and is reported as a long-term asset. In this example, the account now has a credit balance of $1,331,200 (opening balance of $1,665,000 credit, plus $1,366,200, less $1,700,000), but more adjustments are to come.

In this example, the pension fund has paid $134,800 to pensioners during the year. This amount is not recorded by the employer; it reduces both the defined benefit obligation and the pension fund assets. It thus has no effect on the net position of the pension fund. *Payments to pensioners are not a component of pension expense.*

Element 2: Net Interest on the Net Defined Benefit Pension Liability (Asset)

Net interest on the net defined benefit pension liability is a change caused by the passage of time. It is, in essence, the combination of expected investment earnings on pension plan assets and accrued interest on the defined benefit obligation, all at the same discount rate. *The discount rate is the yield rate on high-quality corporate bonds. Terms and currency must match the pension liability terms and currency.*

In order to calculate this interest amount, the net balance should be *determined over the course of the year*, a weighted average that acknowledges the timing of fund contributions and payments to pensioners. The net interest calculation may be done by the actuary and provided in the actuarial report.

The accounting standard also encourages use of shortcuts and approximations in calculations, and thus we will avoid weighted averages in the interest of simplicity. The *opening balance* of the defined benefit obligation and the fund assets will be used as surrogates for the *balance during the year* in this calculation. The following steps are required:

1. Calculate the defined benefit obligation at the beginning of the year.
2. Determine the fair value of pension plan assets at the beginning of the year.
3. Determine the net defined benefit pension liability or asset by combining #1 and #2.

4. If the result is an asset, ensure that the asset ceiling does not restrict the value of the asset. If it is restricted, reduce the asset value to the ceiling, and recalculate the net balance.
5. Multiply the net position by the appropriate discount rate, the yield rate on high-quality corporate bonds with matching term and currency.

The resulting expense (or revenue) item may be presented as part of pension expense or shown separately as a financing expense. This presentation decision is left to the company, and diversity is expected in practice. In our examples, we will include the amount in pension expense.

Example Refer to Exhibit 19-2 for data for Walker Corporation; this example will now be used to demonstrate net interest. The market yield rate for high-quality corporate bonds of similar term and identical currency is 6%.

Net interest:

Defined benefit obligation, beginning of the year	$11,675,000
Pension plan assets, fair value, end of 20X4	10,010,000
Net defined benefit pension liability (not an asset, so the ceiling test is not needed)	$ 1,665,000
Net interest, at 6% ($700,500 – $600,600)	$ 99,900

Note that this $99,900 is, in essence, $600,600 ($10,010,000 × 6%) *of expected earnings on pension fund assets and* $700,500 ($11,675,000 × 6%) *on the defined benefit obligation. These two net out to $99,900.* The entry is:

Pension expense (or Interest expense) ($700,500 – $600,600)	99,900	
Net defined benefit pension liability		99,900

Asset Ceiling Example Had the assets been $12,000,000, then the net defined benefit *asset* would have been $325,000 ($11,675,000 of obligation versus $12,000,000 of assets), and interest at 6% would be $19,500, a revenue item in earnings. If the ceiling test for the $12,000,000 asset indicated that the highest asset value that could be used was only $11,700,000, then the net defined benefit asset would have been $25,000, and net interest would be $1,500, again a revenue item in earnings.

Element 3: Re-measurement of the Net Defined Benefit Pension Liability (Asset)

Re-measurement of the net defined benefit pension liability (asset) is recorded in OCI. It is not **recycled** to earnings but may be reclassified to another equity account, such as retained earnings. Re-measurement has three components:

1. Actuarial gains and losses;
2. The difference between expected earnings on pension plan assets, included in element 2, above, and actual fund earnings or loss; and
3. Any change dictated by the effect of invoking the asset ceiling rule.

Actuarial Gains and Losses Previous sections of this chapter have stressed that assumptions and estimates have a major impact on the measurement of pension amounts. An inevitable aspect of these estimates is that they will be wrong. Re-estimates will give rise to changes in the present value of the defined benefit obligation, changes that represent actuarial gains and losses. The two sources of changes in the present value of the defined benefit obligation are:

1. *Experience gains and losses,* caused by actual experience that shows that *what has actually occurred* is different from the assumptions made; and
2. *Changes in assumptions,* increases or decreases to pension amounts caused by changes in the assumptions *about the future* that underlie calculation of the defined benefit obligation.

Actuarial gains and losses are calculated by the actuary.

The impact on the SFP is as follows:

- Actuarial losses increase the net defined benefit pension liability on the SFP and are recorded as a debit to OCI.
- Actuarial gains reduce the net defined benefit pension liability on the SFP and are recorded as a credit to OCI.

For example, if there was a $46,000 experience loss, the following entry would be made:

OCI: pension	46,000	
Net defined benefit pension liability		46,000

The debit creates a (negative; contra) accumulated element of shareholders' equity on the SFP that accumulates over time. The recorded amount each year is reported in OCI, and earnings are combined with this OCI adjustment to arrive at comprehensive income. The amounts recorded to OCI are not part of earnings. For example, if earnings for this year were $100,000 in the example above, then comprehensive income would be $54,000 ($100,000 – $46,000) and an accumulated debit OCI reserve of $46,000 is reported on the SFP.

Expected versus Actual Return on Pension Plan Assets The expected return on plan assets is an estimate based on the corporate bond yield and will be incorrect, both over the long run and year-by-year. Actual return is reported by the fund trustee and includes all forms of return, including the change in fair value. Expected return is part of the net interest calculated in the second element of pension accounting, illustrated above. The difference between actual and expected return is calculated and recorded in accumulated OCI. That is, calculations may have assumed a 4% average return, but the actual return this year might have been +13% or –20%. This difference creates a gain or loss, which is recorded in accumulated OCI.

For example, if the expected returns were $42,000, and actual investment performance was $60,000, there is an $18,000 experience gain, and the following entry would be made:

Net defined benefit pension liability	18,000	
OCI: pension		18,000

The recorded OCI pension amounts are netted in one accumulated OCI pension account, whether they are positive or negative, and regardless of cause in the pension analysis. That is, the accumulated OCI account for pensions includes all the required element 3 adjustments: actuarial gains and losses *and* expected versus actual return.

Effect of the Asset Ceiling As we have seen, pension assets sometimes exist and are subject to a validity check to ensure that the pension asset is not overvalued and *that the enterprise will obtain value from that asset in the future.* There are complex rules and definitions in this area to establish the recoverable asset ceiling amount. In very simple terms, if a company has a net defined benefit pension asset and if it is limited by the asset ceiling, a loss amount is recorded to OCI as a result. Valuations are done yearly and may reverse if the ceiling is revalued.

For example, recall a prior example, where pension fund assets were $4,800,000 and the defined benefit obligation was $4,500,000. This implies a $300,000 asset position. If the asset ceiling is invoked, capping the asset at $4,500,000, then the plan is at a zero net position:

$4,500,000 of liabilities and assets capped by the ceiling at $4,500,000. The following entry would be made to record the asset ceiling limitation:

OCI: pension ($4,800,000 assets – $4,500,000 ceiling)	300,000	
Net defined benefit pension liability		300,000

This is a complex area and more specific examples are beyond the scope of this chapter.

Example Refer back to Exhibit 19-2 for data for Walker Corporation; this example will now be used to demonstrate actuarial gains and losses.

There is an actuarial gain during 20X5, caused by a change in assumptions. It is recorded as follows:

Net defined benefit pension liability	124,000	
OCI: pension		124,000

Assets were expected to earn 6%, which translates to $600,600 ($10,010,000 × 6%). This was recorded as one component of the second element of pension accounting. Actual earnings were $398,200. The difference is a loss of $202,400 ($600,600 – $398,200). This is recorded:

OCI: pension	202,400	
Net defined benefit pension liability		202,400

The net balance in the accumulated OCI account is now a debit of $366,800 ($288,400 dr. opening balance + $202,400 dr. – $124,000 cr.).

SFP Net Defined Benefit Pension Liability (Asset) Recognition

When all pension adjustments are recorded, the *net defined benefit pension liability* on the SFP will equal the difference between the plan assets and the defined benefit obligation. That is, the net overfunded or underfunded status of the plan will be recorded as an asset (overfunded) or a liability (underfunded) This is a highly desirable reporting result because it reflects reality. The pension adjustments are summarized as follows:

Pension Element	Normal Effect on Net Defined Benefit Pension Liability (SFP)	Comment
Contributions to the plan	Debit net defined benefit pension liability (credit cash)	
Service cost	Credit net defined benefit pension liability (debit expense)	Applies to current and past service, also plan settlements and curtailments.
Net interest cost	Credit net defined benefit pension liability (debit expense) (opposite if net position is an asset)	Calculated based on net balance of pension fund at the beginning of the year; this is a shortcut in lieu of the average over the period. The expense may be classified as a pension expense or a financing expense, at the company's option.
Actuarial gains and losses	For a loss: Credit net defined benefit pension liability (debit accumulated OCI) For a gain: Debit net defined benefit pension liability (credit accumulated OCI)	Applies to actuarial gains and losses, the difference between plan earnings and expected earnings, effect of asset ceiling test, and other measurement issues.

Example Refer to Exhibit 19-2 for data for Walker Corporation; this example will now be used to demonstrate the net defined benefit pension liability on the SFP. The new balance of this account is a liability $1,509,500, calculated as follows:

Opening balance (given)	$1,665,000 cr.
Payment to pension fund trustee	1,700,000 dr.
Service cost	1,366,200 cr.
Net interest	99,900 cr.
Actuarial gains and losses	124,000 dr.
	202,400 cr.
Closing balance	$1,509,500 cr.

It is possible to derive the closing balances in the pension benefit obligation and pension fund assets. The net amount of these two accounts provides proof for the $1,509,500 net defined benefit pension liability account.

Defined benefit obligation	
Opening balance—credit	$11,675,000 cr.
Increase due to current service cost	456,200 cr.
Increase due to interest accrued (6% of opening balance)	700,500 cr.
Increase due to new past service granted	910,000 cr.
Decrease due to change in actuarial assumptions	124,000 dr.
Decrease due to pension benefits paid to pensioners	134,800 dr.
Closing balance	$13,482,900 cr.
Pension fund assets	
Opening balance—debit	$10,010,000 dr.
Increase due to actual investment income earned	398,200 dr.
Decrease due to pension benefits paid to pensioners	134,800 cr.
Increase due to contributions during the year	1,700,000 dr.
Closing balance	$11,973,400 dr.
Net defined benefit pension plan ($13,482,900 – $11,973,400)	$ 1,509,500 cr.

Reporting The three elements that comprise pension accounting are now completely accounted for in the Walker Corporation example. Reporting is as follows, disregarding income tax considerations:

On the SCI:

Earnings (given, excluding pension expense)	$8,842,500 cr.
Pension expense ($1,366,200 + $99,900)	1,466,100 dr.
Earnings	$7,376,400 cr.
Other comprehensive income:	
Pension adjustments ($202,400 dr. and $124,000 cr.)	78,400 dr.
Comprehensive income	$7,298,000 cr.

On the Statement of changes in equity:

	Retained Earnings	Accumulated OCI, Pension
Opening balance (given)	$23,688,100 cr.	$288,400 dr.
Comprehensive income	7,376,400 cr.	78,400 dr.
Closing balance	$31,064,500 cr.	$366,800 dr.

On the SFP:

Long-term liability:	
Net defined benefit pension liability	$ 1,509,500 cr.
Equity:	
Retained earnings	31,064,500 cr.
Accumulated OCI, pension	366,800 dr.

Disposition of Accumulated OCI Amounts

Accumulated OCI may be reclassified into another equity account, most likely retained earnings. *Accumulated OCI amounts may not be included in earnings and thus are never recycled out of accumulated OCI as a revenue or an expense item.* If accumulated OCI were reclassified to retained earnings, the entry is straightforward. Refer again to the Walker Corporation example above. The cumulative balance in accumulated OCI is now a debit of $366,800. To reclassify to retained earnings:

Retained earnings	366,800	
OCI: pension		366,800

EVALUATION

As demonstrated, the net defined benefit pension liability or asset on the SFP represents the *net status* of the pension plan. That is:

	Defined benefit obligation (credit)
Less:	Pension fund assets (debit)
=	Net defined benefit pension asset/liability (debit or credit)

Netting financial statement elements is usually not permitted in financial statements unless certain stringent conditions are met. In the case of a pension plan, the company has both *the legal right* and *the intent* to meet pension obligations through the use of segregated pension assets. Thus, netting is justified.

Up until 2013, companies had many alternatives for slow and/or minimal recognition of actuarial gains and losses and past service cost, with the result that the net defined benefit pension asset/liability on the SFP did not reflect the actual net status of the plan. In particular, use of the *10% corridor method* to establish the need to amortize actuarial gains or losses resulted in minimal recognition of persistent cumulative actuarial amounts. These unrecognized amounts included the material experience losses on pension fund earnings that were a worldwide phenomenon after the financial market declines of 2008–2009. The resulting pension reporting on the SFP was widely criticized as misleading. Thus, the 2013 IFRS standard appears superior in this respect.

However, some financial statement users are troubled with the netting permitted on the SFP for pension plans and would prefer that pension assets be listed separately as an asset, with the pension obligation listed separately as a liability. Given the size of pension plans with respect to their sponsoring employers, this would have a radical effect on the SFP. However, since the company does not control the assets, and they are not available for any use other than pension payments, netting seems appropriate to most.

Another troubling aspect of the 2013 IFRS standard is the use of accumulated OCI for actuarial gains and losses, with no recycling to earnings. Such amounts are never recorded as an expense or revenue item and therefore are never reported in earnings. In particular, using a corporate borrowing yield rate to establish expected earnings for pension fund assets ensures that experience gains and losses will persist annually, since borrowing and investment yield rates diverge.

If the earnings figure is meant to reflect the company's results in dealing with business risks, then eliminating the continuing item of experience and other actuarial gains and losses from the calculation of pension expense is curious. The earnings figure is incomplete. Standard setters may have allowed this treatment on the basis that the standard at least deals with the SFP issue, without stirring up significant resistance among constituents. Note, however, that the U.S. FASB approach requires amounts to be (eventually) recycled out of OCI and into pension expense, so the 2013 IASB standard represents a step backward in creating harmonized standards.

ETHICAL ISSUES

The exclusion of actuarial gains and losses from earnings establishes some motive to shade initial estimates of fund earnings on the optimistic side, if earnings maximization is a reporting objective. Subsequent correction of these estimates, creating losses, will never impact earnings. Evaluation of reasonable estimates is particularly important in this context.

CONCEPT REVIEW

1. List the three elements that must be considered to account for a defined benefit pension plan.
2. What are the components of service cost?
3. How is net interest on the net defined benefit pension liability calculated?
4. What types of adjustments are recorded to accumulated OCI with respect to a defined benefit pension plan?
5. What entries affect the SFP account related to a defined benefit pension plan? What will this account equal, after all adjustments have been made?

SPREADSHEET APPROACH

One of the practical problems in pension accounting is simply keeping track of all of the different amounts that are involved, and a spreadsheet helps.

Example—First Year Data To begin the spreadsheet illustration, we will assume that the company, St. Mark Spas Limited (SMS), establishes a pension plan effective 1 January 20X1. The employees will receive pension entitlements for past years' service. The plan will be accounted for by the projected unit credit method, using unbiased assumptions. Additional information is obtained from the pension plan trustee and the actuary.

- The interest rate on corporate bonds with similar term and currency is 8%.
- At 1 January, 20X1, the present value of the defined benefit obligation for past service is $100,000 (at the 8% rate).
- Current service cost for the year 20X1 is $30,000, using the projected unit credit method.
- To adequately *fund* the current service cost and part of the past service cost, the company is required to make a cash contribution of $65,000 to the plan at the end of 20X1.

Element 1: Service cost for 20X1 is:

Current service cost	$ 30,000
PSC	100,000
Service cost, 20X1	$130,000

Element 2: Net interest cost for 20X1:

Defined benefit obligation, *beginning of the year*	$100,000
Pension fund assets, *beginning of the year*	0
Net defined benefit pension	$100,000
Net interest, 20X1, at 8%	$ 8,000

Element 3: Not applicable for 20X1

Since $65,000 was paid to the pension fund trustee, there will be a $73,000 ($65,000 – $130,000 – $8,000) net defined benefit pension liability reported as a long-term liability at year-end.

Spreadsheet Organization Exhibit 19-3 shows the pension accounting spreadsheet. Refer to this exhibit as the explanation proceeds, below. The columnar arrangement is as follows:

- The first two numerical columns keep track of the amount of the defined benefit obligation (credit) and the pension fund assets (debit). These are memorandum accounts and are not recorded directly on the company's books.
- The third column is used for summarizing pension expense, including both service cost and net interest cost. Once complete, pension expense is closed out to the (following) net defined benefit pension liability column, increasing the liability.
- Finally, there are two columns for the SFP accounts: the net defined benefit pension liability (or asset), and the accumulated OCI account.

Note that when the spreadsheet is completed each period, *the first two columns cross-add to equal the fourth column*. That is, the *net defined benefit pension* (first two columns) is equal to the *SFP liability* account (fourth column). Brackets in the spreadsheet are used to denote credits. Unbracketed numbers are debits.

First Year When the pension is initiated in 20X1, the $100,000 defined benefit obligation (credit, in brackets) and pension past service cost (debit) are entered.

Current service cost of $30,000 increases the defined benefit obligation (first column) and pension expense (third column), as does the $8,000 net interest on the net liability. The $65,000 funding contribution increases fund assets (second column) and is a decrease to the net defined benefit pension liability account. Pension expense, once complete, is transferred to the net defined benefit pension liability account. The columns are then added. Note that the first two columns add to equal the fourth column at this point. This is the reconciliation of the SFP net defined benefit pension liability account and proves that the spreadsheet is complete.

The entries for amounts are as follows:

Pension expense ($100,000 + $30,000)	130,000	
Net defined benefit pension liability		130,000

Net defined benefit pension liability	65,000	
Cash		65,000

Pension expense	8,000	
Net defined benefit pension liability		8,000

Second Year For 20X2, there will be another calculation of service cost. There now will be some earnings on the plan assets. SMS will receive a report from the pension plan trustee that explains the investment activity and investment results. Assume the following:

- Current service cost is $35,000.
- The *actual* return on the plan assets was $7,200 (a return of approximately 11% on the $65,000 in the plan at the *beginning* of 20X2).
- SMS contributes $68,000 cash to the plan at the end of 20X2, in accordance with the actuary's calculations for funding.
- The fair value of the plan assets at the end of 20X2 is $140,200.

Element 1: Service cost for 20X2 is:

Current service cost	$35,000

Element 2: Net interest cost for 20X2:

Defined benefit obligation, beginning of the year	$138,000
Pension fund assets, beginning of the year	65,000
Net defined benefit pension	$ 73,000
Net interest, 20X2 at 8% (8% of the obligation is $11,040 and 8% of the asset is $5,200; $11,040 – $5,200 = $5,840)	$ 5,840

Element 3: The *expected* return on the plan assets for 20X2 was 8% of the beginning-of-year plan assets of $65,000, or $5,200. The actual return was $7,200. The extra return of $2,000 above the expected return is an *experience gain*, which is one type of actuarial gain and is recorded in OCI.

EXHIBIT 19-3

PENSION ACCOUNTING SPREADSHEET

	Defined Benefit Obligation Decrease/ (Increase)	Plan Assets Decrease/ (Increase)	SCI Account Pension Expense	SFP Account Net Defined Benefit Pension (Liability)/Asset	SFP Account Accumulated OCI
20X1					
Initial PSC	$(100,000)		$100,000 dr.		
Current service cost	(30,000)		30,000 dr.		
Net interest on net pension	(8,000)		8,000 dr.		
			$138,000 dr.	$(138,000) cr.	
Funding contribution		$ 65,000		65,000 dr.	
Ending balance	**$(138,000) cr.**	**$ 65,000 dr.**		**$ (73,000) cr.**	—
20X2					
Current service cost	(35,000)		35,000 dr.		
Net interest on net pension	(11,040)	5,200	5,840 dr.		
Actuarial gain re: assets		2,000		2,000 dr.	(2,000) cr.
			$ 40,840 dr.	(40,840) cr.	
Funding contribution		68,000		68,000 dr.	
Ending balance	**$(184,040) cr.**	**$140,200 dr.**		**$ (43,840) cr.**	**$ (2,000) cr.**
20X3					
Current service cost	(32,000)		32,000 dr.		
Net interest on net pension	(14,723)	11,216	3,507 dr.		
Actuarial loss re: assets		(916)		(916) cr.	916 dr.
Actuarial revaluation	22,000			22,000 dr.	(22,000) cr.
			$ 35,507 dr.	(35,507) cr.	
Benefits paid	18,000	(18,000)			
Funding contribution		37,000		37,000 dr.	
Ending balance	**$(190,763)**	**$169,500**		**$ (21,263) cr.**	**$(23,084) cr.**

The entries for the 20X2 expenses, actuarial gain and funding payment are as follows:

Pension expense	35,000	
Net defined benefit pension liability		35,000
Net defined benefit pension liability	68,000	
Cash		68,000
Pension expense (components are $11,040 less $5,200)	5,840	
Net defined benefit pension liability		5,840
Net defined benefit pension liability ($7,200 – $5,200)	2,000	
OCI: pension		2,000

Refer again to the spreadsheet in Exhibit 19-3. Find the following items:

- Service cost of $35,000 increases the defined benefit obligation and pension expense.
- Net interest on the net pension obligation of $5,840 increases pension expense, and the two components of $11,040 (cr.) and $5,200 (dr.) are entered, increasing the defined benefit obligation and fund assets, respectively. See the row highlighted in yellow.
- The actuarial gain of $2,000 is entered in the pension fund asset column; this increases the return in column two to $7,200 ($5,200 expected plus the extra $2,000 of earnings). The $2,000 actuarial gain must be entered *twice more* in the spreadsheet; in the net defined benefit pension liability column and in accumulated OCI. It increases accumulated OCI because it is a gain, and decreases the accrued liability account. See the row highlighted in blue.
- Funding contributions of $68,000 increase fund assets and are also entered as a debit in column four.
- To complete the spreadsheet, pension expense is totalled and entered as a credit in column four. The columns are totalled and cross-added. Again, the total of the first two columns equals the fourth column, the net defined benefit pension liability account.

Third Year Assume the following additional facts for 20X3:

- Current service cost is $32,000, as calculated by the actuary;
- Actual return on the plan assets is $10,300;
- The first actuarial revaluation occurs. Due to changes in mortality assumptions, the defined benefit obligation is *decreased* by $22,000;
- Benefits of $18,000 are paid to retirees by the pension plan trustee; and
- SMS contributes $37,000 cash to the plan at the end of 20X3.

Element 1: Service cost for 20X3 is:

Current service cost	$32,000

Element 2: Net interest cost for 20X3:

Defined benefit obligation, beginning of the year	$184,040
Pension fund assets, beginning of the year	140,200
Net defined benefit pension	$ 43,840
Net interest, 20X3 at 8% (8% of the obligation is $14,723 and 8% of the asset is $11,216; $14,723 – $11,216 = $3,507)	$ 3,507

Element 3: The *expected* return on plan assets for 20X3 was 8% of the beginning-of-year plan assets of $140,200, or $11,216. The actual return was $10,300. The shortfall of $916 below the expected return is an actuarial loss. There is a $22,000 actuarial gain on the change in assumptions that triggered a recalculation of the pension benefit obligation.

The entries for the 20X3 expenses, actuarial gains and losses and funding payment are as follows:

Pension expense	32,000	
Net defined benefit pension liability		32,000
Net defined benefit pension liability	37,000	
Cash		37,000
Pension expense (components are $14,723 less $11,216)	3,507	
Net defined benefit pension liability		3,507
Net defined benefit pension liability	22,000	
OCI: pension		22,000
OCI: pension ($11,216 – $10,300)	916	
Net defined benefit pension asset/liability		916

Spreadsheet Refer to Exhibit 19-3. The following items are entered on the spreadsheet:

- The current service cost of $32,000 is added to the pension benefit obligation and pension expense.
- Net interest on the net defined benefit obligation of $3,507 is added to pension expense and the components of $14,723 interest on the obligation and $11,216 expected earnings on pension fund assets are included in the appropriate columns. See the row highlighted in yellow.
- The $916 ($11,216 – $10,300) shortfall in actual earnings is a deduction from pension assets; the combination of positive $11,216 and negative $916 in this column is equal to the actual earnings of $10,300. The $916 affects *both* the net defined benefit pension liability and accumulated OCI; since it is a loss, it is a debit in accumulated OCI and increases (credits) the SFP liability.
- The $22,000 gain from the actuarial revaluation *reduces* the defined benefit obligation in the first column, and it also is entered *twice more*. It decreases the net defined benefit pension liability and is a credit in accumulated OCI because it is a gain. See the row highlighted in blue.
- Benefits of $18,000 paid to retirees reduce pension plan assets and the defined benefit obligation but have no impact on financial statement accounts.
- Total pension expense is transferred to the net defined benefit pension asset/liability, in the fourth column.
- The funding contribution of $37,000 is added to the pension plan assets and is debited to the net defined benefit pension asset/liability.

Once more, the proof of accuracy is that the first two columns are equal to the fourth column. The pension is underfunded by $21,263, and this is the accrued liability that appears on the SFP. The projected benefit liability is $190,763, and pension fund assets are $169,500, a net of ($21,263.)

Summary of Spreadsheet Adjustments

The following table provides a summary of spreadsheet items caused by pension elements:

Column	Normal Balance	Increase	Decrease	Either Increase or Decrease
Defined benefit obligation	Credit	• Current service cost • Interest on obligation • New past service cost	• Benefit payments to retirees	• Actuarial revaluation • Credit this column if liability increases and debit this column if liability decreases
Pension plan assets	Debit	• Annual funding contribution • Expected earnings	• Benefit payments to retirees	• Actuarial gain or loss, the difference between expected and actual earnings • Credit if actual earnings are lower and debit if actual earnings are higher

Pension expense[1]	Debit	• Service cost		• Net interest on net pension liability/asset
				  • Debit if net interest cost on net liability
				  • Credit if net interest revenue on net asset

Net defined benefit pension asset/ liability	Debit if an asset Credit if a liability			• Credit for the expense amount • Debit for the funding amount • Debit or credit for actuarial gains (debit) or losses (credit)
Accumulated OCI	Credit if accumulated gains Debit if accumulated losses			• Debit or credit for actuarial gains (credit) or losses (debit) • Debit or credit for the effect of the asset ceiling, if needed.

[1]Pension expense also includes gains and losses from nonroutine settlements.

CONCEPT REVIEW

1. How does expected return on pension plan assets affect pension expense?
2. What two spreadsheet accounts change for service cost?
3. What two spreadsheet accounts are changed by benefits paid to employees?
4. What three spreadsheet accounts are changed by newly arising actuarial losses?

OTHER POST-EMPLOYMENT BENEFITS

Post-employment benefits typically involve more than pensions. **Other post-employment benefits** (OPEBs) include supplementary health care, prescription drug plans, dental benefits, and various insurance plans for retirees. Because of universal health care in Canada, the cost of these benefits is less than in some other countries, such as the United States. However, the cost of OPEBs can still be substantial.

There are some practical differences between pensions and other post-employment benefits, summarized as follows:

	Pensions	Other Post-Employment Benefits
Use	Regular monthly payments with predictable or estimable increases until entitlements cease.	Sporadic use from employee to employee and unpredictable cost increases.
Beneficiary	Retired employee usually with some survivor rights.	Retired employee and family members, as specified in the plan.
Funding	Plans are typically registered; likely to be fully or mostly funded during the working life of the employee.	*Plans are typically unregistered. Likely to be substantially unfunded because contributions to unregistered plans are not tax deductible for the employer.*
Revaluations	Periodic as required by legislation.	Likely frequent, to reflect changed cost estimates.

The differences in usage of the plans, in particular, make cost estimation even more uncertain than the already-uncertain pension estimates. Nonetheless, the relevance of the information dictates that reliability be sacrificed, with appropriate disclosure of variables used.

For many years, the cost of OPEBs was accounted for on a *pay-as-you-go* basis. That is, when the benefits were actually paid out or health care premiums paid for employees after retirement, the amount would be expensed at that time. This method was obviously flawed because the benefit was earned by the employee during employment, and *the company had an obligation prior to the retirement period.* Therefore, accounting standards now require that OPEBs be accounted for in a similar manner as pensions. That is, the annual analysis includes three elements:

1. Service cost, both OPEB current service and past service, plus plan settlements and curtailments;
2. Net interest cost on the net OPEB plan liability or asset; and
3. Recognition of OPEB actuarial gains or losses in accumulated other comprehensive income.

From an accounting/economic perspective, the most significant difference between OPEB and pension situations is that there are unlikely to be segregated asset balances for OPEBs because these plans are rarely registered. For an unregistered plan, contributions are not tax deductible by the employer until eventual benefits are paid; accordingly, there is little incentive to fund these plans.

Example Review the spreadsheet in Exhibit 19-4, which reflects the following data for 20X8:

Opening OPEB liability	$175,000	Contribution paid to other post-employment health care fund	$22,000
Opening plan assets	$10,000	Benefits paid by other post-employment health care fund to retirees during the period	$24,000
Actuarial revaluation during the period, OPEB liability increases because future health care costs are expected to rise	$16,000	Actual return on plan assets	$250
Current service cost	$29,000	Yield for corporate bonds	6%

EXHIBIT 19-4

OBEB ACCOUNTING SPREADSHEET

			SCI Account	SFP Account	SFP Account
	OPEB Obligation	**OPEB Plan Assets**	**OPEB Expense**	**Net OPEB (Liability) Asset**	**Accumulated OCI**
20X8					
Opening	$(175,000)	$10,000		$(165,000) cr.*	
Current service cost	(29,000)		$29,000 dr.		
Net interest expense (6%)	(10,500)	600	9,900 dr.		
			$38,900 dr.	(38,900) cr.	
Actuarial loss		(350)		(350) cr.	350 dr.
Actuarial loss	(16,000)			(16,000) cr.	16,000 dr.
Contribution		22,000		22,000 dr.	
Benefits paid	24,000	(24,000)			
Total	**$(206,500)**	**$ 8,250**		**$(198,250)***	**$16,350 dr.**

*$175,000 obligation, less $10,000 fund assets. For the closing balance, $206,500 less $8,250.

This spreadsheet follows the now-familiar pattern. Current service cost of $29,000 increases the obligation and the expense, as does the $9,900 net interest calculated on the opening net OPEB balance, that is, interest expense of $10,500 ($175,000 × 6%) on the OPEB obligation less earnings of $600 ($10,000 × 6%) on fund assets. The difference between expected return of $600 and actual return on $250 is a $350 actuarial loss recorded in assets, and also posted to accumulated OCI and the SFP net OPEB liability. The actuarial revaluation is a loss of $16,000, and is recorded in the OPEB obligation, SFP net OPEB liability, and accumulated OCI. Finally, cash paid to the fund increases the asset balance and affects the SFP liability account, and benefits paid reduce assets and the OPEB obligation.

STATEMENT OF CASH FLOWS

The cash flows relating to pensions and other OPEBs are almost certainly different from the accounting expense. On the statement of cash flows, the difference between expense and contributions to the fund is an adjustment in operating activities. Cash paid to the fund during the year is required disclosure in the pension note.

Example Return to the Walker Corporation example earlier in the chapter. Recall that the reporting was as follows:

On the SCI:

Earnings (given, excluding pension expense)	$8,842,500 cr.
Pension expense ($1,366,200 + $99,900)	1,466,100 dr.
Earnings	$7,376,400 cr.
Other comprehensive income:	
Pension adjustments ($202,400 dr. and $124,000 cr.)	78,400 dr.
Comprehensive income	$7,298,000 cr.

On the statement of changes in equity:

	Retained Earnings	Accumulated OCI, Pension
Opening balance (given)	$23,688,100 cr.	$288,400 dr.
Comprehensive income	7,376,400 cr.	78,400 dr.
Closing balance	$31,064,500 cr.	$366,800 dr.

On the SFP:

Long-term liability:	
Net defined benefit pension liability	$ 1,509,500 cr.
Equity:	
Retained earnings	$31,064,500 cr.
Accumulated OCI, pension	$ 366,800 dr.

On the SCF, the following items would be found:

In operating activities, earnings	$7,376,400
Changes in balance sheet accounts:	
Decrease in net defined benefit pension liability[1]	(233,900)

[1]Opening balance = $1,665,000 + $78,400 non-cash net actuarial losses = $1,743,400. The balance reported is $1,509,500, a further difference of $233,900. This is the remaining difference, and it is the difference between the $1,700,000 amount paid and the $1,466,100 pension expense, or $233,900. The amount paid is higher than the expense.

There are no other changes with respect to the pension reported on the SCF. Note that the change in accumulated OCI is a non-cash item, changing accumulated OCI and the net defined benefit pension liability. However, if the second element of pension expense is segregated and termed a financing expense ($99,900 in this case), it will be excluded from operating activities and classified as a financing cash outflow. This is a policy choice that is open to the company.

DISCLOSURE REQUIREMENTS

The disclosure requirements for post-employment benefits are unusually extensive. The financial statements themselves include the three elements relating to pensions and other post-employment benefits:

1. On the statement of comprehensive income, the amount of *expense* relating to providing post-employment benefits;
2. On the statement of comprehensive income, and the statement of financial position, the amount of *re-measurement* recorded (element 3 in our examples);
3. On the statement of financial position, the *net defined benefit pension asset or liability* that reflects the funded status of the pension plan; the defined benefit obligation netted with plan assets;
4. On the statement of cash flows, the change in the SFP pension liability *not* caused by accumulated OCI changes.

These amounts provide little direct information about the nature of post-employment benefits and the major underlying risks. Therefore, disclosure is the only viable way to assist users. Disclosure is required in three broad areas:

1. The characteristics of, and risks associated with, defined benefit plans;
2. Identification and explanation of recognized amounts; and
3. A description of how such plans might affect the amount, timing, and uncertainty of future cash flows.

Selected Disclosures

A narrative description of the plan is required, along with the legislative and governance framework for the plan. Disclosure includes important information about changes in the plan, risks, and also measurements used for accounting. Measurement disclosures are extensive, and all calculations and assumptions must be disclosed. Assumptions may reflect biases and will affect comparability, and so they are especially important disclosures.

Some major items:

1. A reconciliation of relevant pension amounts to the SFP asset or liability account over the year (i.e., all components that explain the change in the first two spreadsheet columns, to equal the SFP asset or liability account);
2. Amount of expense recognized for the period, and the components of the expense;
3. Changes in reserves and other comprehensive income, with each component shown separately;
4. Numerical disclosure separating plan assets into various asset categories;
5. Actual return on assets during the year;
6. Information about funding commitments, including contributions to the plan for coming years and information about the maturity profile of the defined benefit obligation;
7. Significant actuarial assumptions used to measure the defined benefit obligation; and
8. Sensitivity analysis, including the effect of changing significant actuarial assumptions.

The extensive array of disclosures represents an attempt to converge the disclosures required in many jurisdictions.

Refer to Exhibit 19-5, which shows the line-by-line disclosure of the changes in the defined benefit obligation and pension fund assets. At the 2011 year-end, there is a defined benefit obligation of $49.6 million, and pension fund assets of $48.5 million. The reconciliation to the SFP figure has been omitted, as has other extensive disclosure in this area. For OPEBs, there is a $1.6 million obligation and no segregated assets, as is standard practice in this area. The listed items that cause change in the obligation and assets should be largely familiar from the spreadsheet examples.

EXHIBIT 19-5

INTERNATIONAL FOREST PRODUCTS LIMITED

Extracts from Disclosure Note 22, Employee Future Benefits and Other Post-Retirement Plans

	Pension Benefits		Other Post-Retirement Benefits	
(C$ in thousands)	2011	2010	2011	2010
Defined benefit obligation:				
Beginning of year	$34,065	$30,593	$1,169	$1,025
Acquisitions	12,223	—	326	—
Service cost	580	368	29	21
Employee contributions	283	219	—	—
Interest cost	2,495	2,046	80	64
Benefit payments	(2,505)	(2,113)	(95)	(54)
Settlements	(290)	—	—	—
Actuarial loss	2,794	2,952	118	113
End of year	$49,645	$34,065	$1,627	$1,169
Plan assets:				
Beginning of year	$33,536	$30,457	$ —	$ —
Acquisitions	13,882	—	—	—
Expected return on plan assets	2,899	2,145	—	—
Employer contributions	2,231	2,253	95	54
Employee contributions	283	219	—	—
Benefit payments	(2,505)	(2,113)	(95)	(54)
Settlements	(343)	—	—	—
Actuarial gain (loss)	(1,467)	575	—	—
End of year	$48,516	$33,536	$ —	$ —

[References to disclosure notes deleted.]

Source: International Forest Products Ltd., Annual Financial Statements, year ended December 31, 2011, www.sedar.com, posted 17 February 2012.

CONCEPT REVIEW

1. What are the components of service cost, for both pension plans and OPEBs?
2. Why are most OPEBs underfunded, as compared with pension plans?
3. What is the likely intent of requiring extensive disclosures for pension assumptions?

Looking Forward

Post-employment benefit issues are not now on the agenda of either the IASB or the Canadian AcSB. Both groups have had recent new standards in this area—effective 2013 (IFRS) and 2014 (ASPE). As a result, further changes in the near future should not be expected. However, this is an area where IASB and FASB standards are different, and pressure for harmonization may lead to change in the future.

FASB Approach to Accounting for Post-Employment Benefits Under IASB rules, accumulated OCI amounts are never recognized in earnings. Accumulated OCI amounts may be transferred directly to retained earnings or another equity account. Under FASB rules, however, accumulated OCI amounts related to pensions are recycled to earnings; that is, actuarial amounts are recycled out of OCI and expensed over time.

This is a fundamental difference in the way accumulated OCI is treated, and resolution of this difference will likely only come about after there is a conceptual framework that governs accumulated OCI. At the moment, this account is largely unstructured and is subject to some considerable inconsistencies in the hands of standard setters.

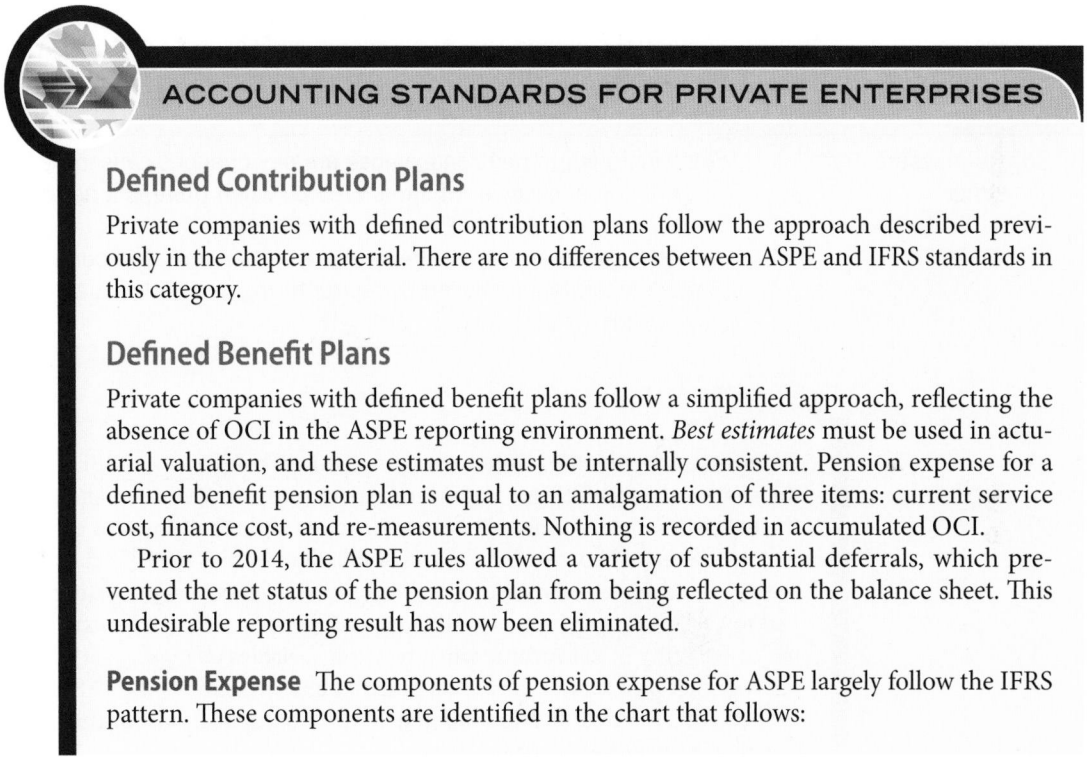

ACCOUNTING STANDARDS FOR PRIVATE ENTERPRISES

Defined Contribution Plans

Private companies with defined contribution plans follow the approach described previously in the chapter material. There are no differences between ASPE and IFRS standards in this category.

Defined Benefit Plans

Private companies with defined benefit plans follow a simplified approach, reflecting the absence of OCI in the ASPE reporting environment. *Best estimates* must be used in actuarial valuation, and these estimates must be internally consistent. Pension expense for a defined benefit pension plan is equal to an amalgamation of three items: current service cost, finance cost, and re-measurements. Nothing is recorded in accumulated OCI.

Prior to 2014, the ASPE rules allowed a variety of substantial deferrals, which prevented the net status of the pension plan from being reflected on the balance sheet. This undesirable reporting result has now been eliminated.

Pension Expense The components of pension expense for ASPE largely follow the IFRS pattern. These components are identified in the chart that follows:

ASPE Pension Expense Components	Comment
1. Current service cost	Measured using projected benefit method; identical to projected unit credit method.
2. Finance cost	Appropriate discount rate multiplied by the net defined benefit liability (asset) on the *opening balance sheet.* This net amount is the defined benefit obligation less plan assets at fair value. The discount rate is the market interest rate on high-quality debt instruments with timing and amounts that match the pension outflows. If the plan could be settled by means of an insurance or annuity contract with a third party, the interest rate inherent in this arrangement can be used as a discount rate.

continued on next page

Pension Expense Components	Comment
3a. Re-measurement: Actual versus expected return	The difference between expected return on assets included in item 2 and actual return is included immediately in pension expense. This has the effect of recognizing *actual return* in pension expense. Actual return may be volatile. Actual return includes annual payments, such as interest or dividends, and also the realized and unrealized gains and losses on the fair value of plan assets during the year.
3b. Re-measurement: Past service cost	Past service cost is the change in the defined benefit obligation caused by introduction, withdrawal or amendment of plan benefits with reference to prior service. The amount is expensed immediately; no deferral or amortization is permitted.
3c. Re-measurement: Actuarial gains and losses	Actuarial gains and losses are caused by revaluing the defined benefit obligation because of changes in assumptions. Actuarial gain and losses are immediately expensed. Under ASPE, nothing is recorded in accumulated OCI; this financial statement element does not exist in ASPE financial statements.
3d. Re-measurement: Other	Also included in pension expense are any changes caused by the presence of a valuation allowance, which is created when there is a net defined benefit pension *asset*, but there are limits on its use. Another cause of re-measurement are settlements and curtailments; if these latter elements are caused by restructuring or discontinued operations, any gain or loss is classified accordingly.

Comparison with IASB Rules As compared with IFRS, the ASPE approach has much the same look and feel. An important aspect of this is that the balance sheet will reflect the net defined pension liability or asset, which is the net status of the pension plan. The major difference between IFRS and ASPE is that there is no OCI classification. Amounts are expensed in the re-measurement (element 3) classification, rather than being classified to OCI. As compared with IFRS, the ASPE approach can be expected to cause some major volatility in net income when pension variables change.

Note that past service cost is classified as a *re-measurement* in ASPE and a *service cost* in IFRS; this is a classification difference with no implications for the treatment of PSC; it is expensed in either scheme.

There are many, many minor differences between IFRS and ASPE, related to plan curtailment and settlement, multi-employer plans, disclosure, and the like.

Example Refer to Exhibit 19-6 for data for Newmarket Limited. Corporate borrowing rates for high-quality bonds are in the range of 6%. These bonds have a term similar to anticipated pension payments.

EXHIBIT 19-6

ASPE PENSION EXAMPLE

Balances:	
Defined benefit obligation, end of 20X7	$2,472,900
Pension plan assets, fair value, end of 20X7	2,332,100
SFP Net defined benefit pension liability, end of 20X7	$ 140,800 cr.
Information relating to 20X8:	
Current service cost for 20X8, measured using the projected benefit method	$ 76,800
New past service cost granted in 20X8; defined benefit obligation increases	110,700
Amount paid to pension fund trustee	98,000
Actuarial loss in 20X8, caused by anticipated longer lifespan of retirees; defined benefit obligation increases	109,400
Actual earnings in the fund, reported by the pension fund trustee, including interest, dividends, and change in fair value	45,500

Pension expense is calculated as follows:

1.	Current service cost	$ 76,800
2.	Interest cost ($140,800 × 6%), or [$2,472,900 × 6% ($148,374) – $2,332,100 × 6% ($139,926)]	8,448
3.a	Re-measurement: Past service cost granted in 20X5	110,700
3.b	Re-measurement: Actual versus expected return ($139,926 expected versus $45,500 actual)	94,426
3.c	Re-measurement: Actuarial loss	109,400
		$399,774

The same total would be obtained by including interest on the entire PBO, *actual return on assets*, and omitting *category 3b*:

1.	Current service cost	$ 76,800
2.a	Interest cost ($2,472,900 × 6%)	148,374
2.b	Actual return	(45,500)
3.a	Re-measurement: Past service cost granted in 20X5	110,700
3.b	n/a	—
3.c	Re-measurement: Actuarial loss	109,400
		$399,774

The entry to record pension expense:

Pension expense	399,774	
Net defined benefit pension liability		399,774

The $98,000 contribution to the pension fund trustee is also recorded:

Net defined benefit pension liability	98,000	
Cash		98,000

RELEVANT STANDARDS

CPA Canada Handbook, Part I (IFRS):

- IAS 19, Employee Benefits, as amended, effective 2013

CPA Canada Handbook, Part II (ASPE):

- Section 3462, Employee Future Benefits, effective 2014

SUMMARY OF KEY POINTS

1. In a defined contribution pension plan, the amounts to be paid into the pension plan fund are determined, and the eventual pension is a function of the amounts paid in plus the earnings accumulated in the pension fund. Risk rests with the employee. The annual expense is normally equal to the contribution made to the plan.
2. In a defined benefit pension plan, the retirement benefits are defined as a function of either years of service or employee earnings, or both. The employer is responsible for contributing enough into the fund that, combined with investment earnings, will pay the pension to which the employee is entitled. Risk rests with the employer.
3. Pension plans are contributory if the employee pays into the plan. An employee has ownership of pension assets when rights have vested. Vesting is governed by pension legislation and pension contracts.
4. An employer's annual contribution to a defined benefit pension plan is calculated using an actuarial cost method. Alternatives exist with respect to the variables that are projected and the funding patterns. The projected unit credit method must be used for external reporting. This actuarial cost method projects salary levels but does not project years of service.
5. Because of the long time span involved in pension estimates, pension amounts are sensitive to the underlying assumptions used. These include demographic and financial assumptions. Estimates that are unbiased and mutually compatible must be used for accounting purposes.

6. A defined benefit pension plan consists of pension plan assets, segregated in a separate legal entity and managed by a trustee, and a defined benefit obligation, measured using the projected unit credit method. The net of these two numbers is the net funded position and the SFP net defined benefit pension liability or asset.

7. For a defined benefit pension plan, pension accounting involves examining three elements: (1) service cost measured using the projected unit credit actuarial cost method, (2) net interest on the net defined benefit pension liability or asset, and (3) re-measurement (through accumulated OCI) of the net defined benefit pension liability, including experience gains or losses and actuarial revaluations.

8. Service cost is an expense, and includes current service cost, past service cost, and gains and losses on plan settlements. Current service cost is an estimate of the cost of providing the pension entitlement that the employee has earned in the current year of employment. Past service cost is an estimate of the expected present value of retrospective pension entitlements relating to previous years' service when a new pension plan is instituted or when an existing plan is amended.

9. Net interest is an expense. It is measured by using the market yield for high-grade corporate bonds at the end of the year—bonds with similar term and currency as the net benefit obligation. Interest is measured on the net pension liability or asset, which is the net amount of pension plan assets and the defined benefit obligation. Net interest essentially has two elements: expected earnings on pension plan assets and accrued interest on the defined benefit obligation.

10. Re-measurements are included in accumulated OCI and are never recycled to earnings. Accumulated OCI amounts may be transferred to another equity amount, most likely retained earnings. Re-measurements include actuarial gains, which arise either because actual experience is different from expectations or because assumptions about the future are changed, or both. The difference between expected earnings on plan assets and actual return is a common source of re-measurement gain or loss.

11. Benefits paid to retirees reduce the value of the plan assets and reduce the defined benefit obligation. Benefits paid do not enter directly into the calculation of pension expense.

12. The SFP net defined benefit pension asset/liability account is equal to the net status of the pension plan. This is the overfunded or underfunded status of the plan–pension fund assets less the defined benefit obligation.

13. A spreadsheet is a useful way to organize data needed for pension plan accounting. The spreadsheet tracks the defined benefit obligation, pension plan assets, pension expense, the SFP asset or liability pension account, and accumulated OCI.

14. Other post-employment benefits (OPEB) include supplementary medical and dental plans for retirees. These benefits are accounted for in a similar fashion as pensions, with the cost accrued over the working life of the employee.

15. Companies must provide extensive disclosures for pensions and OPEB with respect to accounting policies and measurement of estimates. Disclosures include all changes during the year for plan assets and the defined benefit obligation, with these two accounts reconciled to the recorded net defined benefit pension asset or liability.

16. Under ASPE, defined benefit pension plans are accounted for by expensing all elements of pension cost—service cost, interest cost, and re-measurements. There are no deferrals, and no items are recorded in accumulated OCI.

KEY TERMS

accumulated benefit method
actuarial cost methods
actuarial gains and losses
actuarial revaluation
actuary
asset ceiling
contributory pension plan
current service cost
death benefits
defined benefit obligation
defined benefit plan
defined contribution plan
final pay pension plan
flat benefit pension plan
funding
level contribution method
net defined benefit pension liability (asset)
noncontributory pension plan
other post-employment benefits
past service cost (PSC)
pension holiday
pension plan curtailment
pension plan settlement
projected unit credit method
recycled
registered pension plan
service cost
survivor benefits
termination benefits
trustee

REVIEW PROBLEM 19-1

The following data relate to a defined benefit pension plan:

Defined benefit obligation, 31 December 20X5	$25,000
Long-term interest rate on corporate bonds	10%
Past service cost from amendment dated 31 December 20X6, liability is reduced because benefits were reduced	$ (1,200)
Actuarial revaluation dated 31 December 20X6; increase to liability because of changed mortality assumptions	$ 600
Actual return on plan assets for 20X6	$ 2,100
Fair value of plan assets, 31 December 20X5	$16,000
Funding payment at year-end 20X6	$ 4,000
Benefits paid to retirees in 20X6	$ 2,000
Current service cost for 20X6	$ 1,900

There is no balance in accumulated OCI on 31 December 20X5.

Required:

1. Calculate the SFP net defined benefit pension liability as of 31 December 20X5.
2. Compute the defined benefit obligation at 31 December 20X6 and the fair value of plan assets on the same date. Also calculate the net defined benefit pension.
3. Analyze the three elements of pension accounting for 20X6: service cost, net interest, and revaluations. Prepare entries and also an entry for the contribution to the fund during 20X6.
4. Calculate the SFP net defined benefit pension liability as of 31 December 20X6, and prove that this represents the net defined benefit position.
5. Assume instead that this pension plan is sponsored by a private company and ASPE applies. Prepare all entries for 20X6. Calculate the SFP net defined benefit pension liability as of 31 December 20X6.

REVIEW PROBLEM 19-1—SOLUTION

1. Net defined benefit pension liability, 31 December 20X5

Defined benefit obligation, 31 December 20X5	$25,000 cr.
Pension plan assets, 31 December 20X5	16,000 dr.
Net defined benefit pension liability, 31 December 20X5	$ 9,000 cr.

2. Defined benefit obligation, 31 December 20X6

Obligation, 1 January 20X6	$25,000
Current service cost, 20X6	1,900
Interest (10% of opening balance)	2,500
PSC	(1,200)
Actuarial revaluation	600
Benefits paid	(2,000)
	$26,800 cr.

Fair value of plan assets, 31 December 20X6	
Value at 1 January 20X6	$16,000
Actual return on plan assets	2,100
Funding contributions	4,000
Benefits paid	(2,000)
	$20,100 dr.

Net defined benefit pension, 31 December 20X6 ($26,800 – $20,100)	$ 6,700 cr.

3. Entries for three elements, and fund contribution

Service cost:		
Pension expense ($1,900 – $1,200)	700	
Net defined benefit pension asset/liability		700
Net interest:		
Pension expense ($9,000 × 10%) (components are $2,500 – $1,600)	900	
Net defined benefit pension asset/liability		900
Revaluation:		
Net defined benefit pension asset/liability (Experience gain on assets: $2,100 – $1,600)	500	
OCI: pension		500
OCI: pension (Revaluation)	600	
Net defined benefit pension asset/liability		600
Contribution:		
Net defined benefit pension asset/liability	4,000	
Cash		4,000

4. Net defined benefit pension liability, 31 December 20X6

($9,000 cr. Op. balance + $700 cr. + $900 cr. – $500 dr. + $600 cr. – $4,000 dr.)	$ 6,700 cr.

Proof: Equal to the net defined benefit pension as calculated in requirement 2

5. Pension expense, 20X6, under ASPE

Current service cost	$1,900
Finance cost ($9,000 × 10%), or $25,000 × 10% ($2,500) – $16,000 × 10% ($1,600)	900
Re-measurement: Past service cost; benefits reduced	(1,200)
Re-measurement: Actual versus expected return ($1,600 expected versus $2,100 actual) (gain)	(500)
Re-measurement: Actuarial loss	600
	$1,700

Entries:

Expense:

Pension expense	1,700	
Net defined benefit pension asset/liability		1,700

Contribution:

Net defined benefit pension asset/liability	4,000	
Cash		4,000

Net defined benefit pension liability, 31 December 20X6 ($6,700 cr.
($9,000 cr. Op. balance + $1,700cr. – $4,000 dr.)

QUESTIONS

Q19-1 Distinguish between a defined contribution pension plan and a defined benefit pension plan. Why are defined contribution plans attractive to employers?

Q19-2 Distinguish between a contributory pension plan and a noncontributory pension plan.

Q19-3 Why is it logical that contributions made by an employee to a pension plan vest immediately, while an employer's contributions may vest only after a certain period of time?

Q19-4 What is the incentive to the company for registering a pension plan?

Q19-5 What is the difference between an experience gain or loss and a gain or loss caused by a change in assumptions?

Q19-6 What causes a gain or loss related to a pension plan settlement or curtailment?

Q19-7 What causes an asset to be recorded when a company has a defined contribution pension plan?

Q19-8 What are the two components of the SFP net defined benefit pension liability (asset) related to a defined benefit pension plan?

Q19-9 What limit is placed on assets used in calculating a net defined benefit asset?

Q19-10 Identify the two major classifications of assumptions or estimates that must be established to estimate the funding required for a given defined benefit pension plan. What does it mean to have these assumptions internally consistent?

Q19-11 Identify three different actuarial cost methods and the major projections that differentiate the methods.

Q19-12 List and define the three elements required to account for a defined benefit pension plan.

Q19-13 What is a past service cost? How is it accounted for as part of pension expense?

Q19-14 How is net interest on the net defined benefit pension liability measured?

Q19-15 What amounts are recorded in accumulated OCI in relation to a defined benefit pension plan?

Q19-16 If the actual return on pension plan assets is a $42,000 loss and expected return is a positive $106,000, what is the actuarial amount recorded to accumulated OCI? If earnings are $500,000, how much is comprehensive income?

Q19-17 If a pension has a benefit obligation of $400,000 and pension fund assets of $250,000, what will be the resulting recognized SFP net defined benefit asset or liability pension account?

Q19-18 If a pension has a benefit obligation of $400,000 and pension fund assets of $450,000, under what circumstances will an asset of $50,000 *not* appear on the SFP?

Q19-19 Why are post-employment benefits other than pensions less likely to be fully funded? What difference will this make in financial statement treatment?

Q19-20 Are there accumulated OCI amounts on a balance sheet prepared in compliance with ASPE? Where are re-measurements classified under ASPE? What is the effect on total equity of this difference between ASPE and IFRS? What is the effect on net income?

Q19-21 Actual earnings on pension fund assets are $2,000, and expected earnings are $10,000. Show two ways this aspect of pension expense could be calculated under ASPE. Why is the total for both approaches identical?

CASE 19-1

PROPULSION XT LIMITED

Propulsion XT Limited (PXTL) is a manufacturer of personal and commercial transportation solutions, including train engines and train cars. The company is one of the largest private companies in Canada and complies with ASPE. A transition to IFRS has been discussed for some time but has never been implemented because of the more onerous disclosure requirements. The company does not prepare a classified balance sheet because inventories and unearned revenues would have to be split very arbitrarily into current and long-term amounts; there are many customer contracts outstanding that span multiple years. The company must comply with total debt-to-equity covenants for long-term debt arrangements, and there is an additional covenant on the maximum level of common share dividends.

The company reflects the $1,743 million unfunded status of its defined benefit pension plan as a long-term liability. The plan recorded large investment losses in 20X1, consistent with a sharp plunge in the stock market. Actuarial losses followed, caused by a decline in discount rates. Experience and actuarial losses are approximately $2,011 as at 31 December 20X5.

Both the audit committee and the risk management committee of the Board of Directors have pensions on the agenda. The audit committee of PXTL would like to more fully understand how the balance sheet would differ if IFRS standards were used. Restatement would be most helpful.

The risk management committee is concerned about the ongoing risk to PXTL of sponsoring this defined benefit plan. The committee would like to understand what leeway they have, if any, to reduce the underfunded status of the plan and annual expense, through re-examining the assumptions used. They are also wondering what the implication would be of switching to a defined contribution plan, as many companies in their industry have done. This might be a major issue in upcoming labour negotiations. Preliminary negotiations indicate that workers might be offered existing assets, plus $200 million, rolled to a separate trust in relation to existing claims. Premiums under a defined contribution plan are likely to be 120% of the $51 annual amount now transferred to the plan. Additional funding of $100 million per year, designed to address the underfunded status, would be eliminated.

You are an analyst in the financial reporting area, and you have been asked to redraft the financial statements and prepare a report that addresses the questions and alternatives raised to reflect IFRS for pension accounting. The report should include an explanation of your changes and any related concerns.

Required:

Prepare the suggested report.

EXHIBIT 1

PROPULSION XT LIMITED

Extracts from Balance Sheet
31 December 20X5

(in millions of dollars)

Liabilities	
Accounts payable and accrued liabilities	$ 5,540
Unearned revenue	2,126
Long-term debt	3,642
Net defined benefit liability	1,743
Deferred income tax	345
Derivative financial instruments	230
	$13,626
Equity	
Preferred shares	350
Common shares	1,235
Contributed surplus	116
Retained earnings	1,810
	3,511
	$17,137

PROPULSION XT LIMITED

Pension Information
31 December 20X5

(in millions of dollars)

	31 December 20X5
Fair value of plan assets	$ 5,020
Defined benefit obligation	6,763
Funded status—deficit	$ 1,743
Weighted average assumptions:	
Discount rate	5.25%
Rate of increase in future compensation	3.30%

Key assumptions: All future expected benefit payment cash flows at the measurement date are discounted at spot rates for AA corporate debt securities, as a surrogate for 30-year rates.

Sensitivity:
A 0.25% change in the discount rate would change the obligation by 3.4% and the pension expense by 7.5%.
A 0.25% change in future compensation expense would change the obligation by 0.2% and the pension expense by 1%.

CASE 19-2

CANDIDA LIMITED

Candida Limited is a Canadian public company in the business of exploration, production, and marketing of natural gas. It also has power generation operations. Earnings in 20X5 were $2.4 billion, and total assets were $24.1 billion.

You have recently begun work in the finance and accounting department. Your immediate task is to analyze and report on the pension information (see Exhibit 1) included in the last annual report. Your supervisor provided this information with a request:

> We have to prepare for an upcoming meeting of the audit committee. We have several new members of the committee, and the chairperson has suggested that we provide a brief report on Candida's pension issues to get everyone up to speed. It has been several years since we have discussed this issue in depth; this is the opportunity.
>
> Your report should include an explanation of defined benefit versus contribution plans (we have both but are curtailing the former), and the financial statement elements that relate to each plan. It will be necessary to explain the nature of the defined benefit obligation for the defined benefit plans and the pension plan asset balances and relate these amounts to the $115 million net defined benefit pension liability we include on the statement of financial position.
>
> We are particularly concerned about our potential pension position for 20X6, the coming year. We will see an increase in compensation cost of about 5%, which will accordingly increase pension cost. On top of the large investment losses we experienced in 20X5, this may mean serious increases in pension amounts. Your report should review the accounting treatment of the investment loss but also project our 20X6 pension expense. Finally, since our pension expense is likely going to be problematic next year, you should identify some key assumptions that Candida can consider to help reduce pension expense.

Required:

Prepare the report.

EXHIBIT 1

CANDIDA LIMITED

Selected Pension Information (in millions)

Statement of Comprehensive Income	**20X5**	**20X4**	**20X3**
Total expense for defined contribution plans	$ 12	$ 9	$ 6
Total expense for defined benefit plans	$ 12	$ 6	$10
Statement of Financial Position			
Net defined benefit pension liability	$115	$75	$20
Accumulated OCI, pension	53	20	17

Disclosure Notes

For Defined Benefit Plans	**20X5**
Defined benefit obligation	$228
Fair value of plan assets	113

Current service cost was $7 in 20X5 and $3 in 20X4.
The company contributed $50 to all pension plans in total during 20X5.

continued on next page

Included in the above defined benefit obligation of $228 is $14 of unfunded benefit obligation related to the Company's other post-employment benefits.

Assumptions are as follows:	20X5	20X4
Corporate bond yield rate	6.0%	6.5%
Rate of compensation increase	4.75%	3.0%
Health care costs trend rate for next year	+10%	

TECHNICAL REVIEW

connect

TR19-1 Defined Benefit Plan; Assets and Defined Benefit Obligation: The following data are to be used for TR19-1 to TR19-5. Goodday Limited has a defined benefit pension plan. The following information relates to the plan:

Balances:	
Defined benefit obligation, end of 20X7	$5,215,000
Pension plan assets, fair value, end of 20X7	4,810,000
SFP net defined benefit pension liability, end of 20X7	405,000 cr.
SFP accumulated OCI, pension, end of 20X7	69,200 dr.
Retained earnings, end of 20X7	8,601,400 cr.
20X8 earnings, prior to any pension expense	4,200,000 cr.
Current service cost for 20X8, measured using the projected unit credit method	601,900
New past service cost granted in 20X8, negative because benefits were reduced and the liability has declined	(356,000)
Amount paid to pension fund trustee	450,000
Actuarial gain in 20X8, negative because caused by higher anticipated future mortality rates and the liability has declined	(106,000)
Actual earnings in the fund, reported by the pension fund trustee, including interest, dividends, and change in fair value	144,800
Benefits paid to pensioners from pension fund assets	67,900
Interest rate on long-term corporate bonds, end of 20X8	5%

Required:

Calculate the balances of the defined benefit obligation and the pension plan assets at the end of 20X8. Use these values to calculate the SFP net defined benefit pension plan element for Goodday Limited at the end of 20X8.

connect

TR19-2 Defined Benefit Plan; Element 1: Refer to the data in TR19-1.

Required:

Calculate and record the first element of pension accounting for the defined benefit plan. That is, calculate service cost and prepare the entry to record service cost. Also record the payment to the pension fund trustee.

connect

TR19-3 Defined Benefit Plan; Element 2: Refer to the data in TR19-1.

Required:

Calculate and record the second element of pension accounting for the defined benefit plan. That is, calculate net interest cost, and prepare the entry to record interest cost. Calculate the two components of net interest: interest on the defined benefit obligation and expected earnings on fund assets.

connect

TR19-4 Defined Benefit Plan; Element 3: Refer to the data in TR19-1 and your response to TR19-3.

Required:
Calculate and record the third element of pension accounting for the defined benefit plan. That is, calculate revaluation(s), and prepare the entry(ies) to record these revaluation(s).

connect

TR19-5 Defined Benefit Plan; Reporting: Refer to the data in TR19-1 and solutions to TR19-2 to TR19-4.

Required:
1. Show the presentation of earnings and comprehensive income, reflecting the entries made to record the three elements of pension accounting. Also prepare the statement of changes in equity for retained earnings and accumulated OCI, and list the pension-related SFP account.
2. Prove that the SFP balance is equal to the net defined benefit pension liability/asset for the pension plan.

ASSIGNMENTS

★ **A19-1 Pension Terms:** Complete the sentences below:

1. The actuarial cost method that must be used to determine current service cost is the _____.
2. A pension plan where the risk of the level of eventual pension payments rests with the employee is called _____.
3. A contributory pension plan is a plan in which _____.
4. The asset ceiling is a limiting factor in pension accounting when _____.
5. Pension plans are usually registered because _____.
6. The actuarial cost method that projects years of service, and final salary, is called the _____.
7. Past service cost will be a negative number (reduces the projected benefit liability) when _____.
8. An experience gain or loss related to annual return on plan assets is the difference between _____ and _____.
9. The costs of pension benefit changes caused by _____ and _____ are often included in discontinued operations rather than in pension expense.
10. The expected present value of future pension benefits, evaluated using present value and actuarial expectations, including mortality, turnover, and the effects of current and future compensation levels, is called _____.
11. Two examples of demographic assumptions that must be made to project pension variables are _____ and _____.

★ **A19-2 Defined Contribution Plan:** TGY Limited has a defined contribution pension plan for its 160 employees. The plan is trusteed, and each year the company makes an annual contribution, matching employee contributions to the plan to a certain maximum. The funds are invested for the employees by the pension fund trustee using predetermined parameters.

The pension plan was established to target roughly 60% of final pay to employees as a pension, with survivor benefits or a minimum 10-year payout. None of these targets is guaranteed. Calculations were done based on mortality assumptions and an expected 5% yield. Contributions are re-evaluated every three years. Based on these assumptions, TGY paid $234,000 to the fund in 20X7. At the end of 20X7, plan assets total $2,890,000.

Required:

1. What are the employees of TGY entitled to as a result of this pension? How is this different from a defined benefit pension plan?
2. What difference would it make if the targets established above were guaranteed by the company?
3. What amount of pension expense would TGY report in 20X7?
4. If fund earnings were to be 8% in 20X8, instead of the 5% predicted, who would benefit? Explain.

★ **A19-3 Defined Contribution Plan:** A market analyst was quoted as saying:

> Defined benefit pension plans are really dead. Within 20 years, no companies in the private sector will be offering these plans—and the public sector is just daft if they don't follow suit. Why, in the first four months of this year, I know of dozens of companies that have frozen or closed their defined benefit plans. They allow new employees access to only defined contribution plans. Many of these companies just make end-of-year grants to employees directly into their personal RRSP accounts, and allow—force—the employees to make their own investment decisions. Of course, with employees more mobile between companies and less likely to stay with one employer all their lives, it can be attractive. Some people just like to get their hands on the money!

Required:

1. What factors associated with defined benefit plans have led to the trend toward defined contribution plans?
2. Evaluate the attractiveness of defined contribution plans for employees.

★ **A19-4 Defined Contribution Plan:** Zio Ltd. established a defined contribution pension plan at the beginning of 20X9. The company will contribute 3% of each employee's salary annually. Total salaries in 20X9 were expected to be $7.3 million. Accordingly, Zio paid $219,000 into the fund. After the year-end, it was determined that actual salaries were $6.5 million. Interest rates are in the range of 6%.

Required:

1. Is pension expense $219,000 or a lesser number? Explain.
2. Assume instead that Zio has agreed to pay $165,000 into the fund in 20X9. During the year, an employee left the company, forfeiting $35,000 of unvested pension benefits earmarked in the pension fund. Calculate the payment to the fund and the pension expense.
3. Assume instead that Zio agreed to pay $150,000 to the pension trustee in 20X9 but, because of cash flow issues, paid only $100,000. Zio agrees to pay the shortfall at the end of 20X11. In 20X10, the company makes a scheduled $150,000 payment to the pension fund for normal 20X10 pension entitlements. The same annual scheduled payment is made in 2011, plus the $50,000 arrears from 20X9. How much is pension expense and cash paid in each of 20X9, 20X10, and 20X11?

★ **A19-5 Defined Benefit Plan; Variables:** Belfiori Limited reports the following data for 20X8:

Plan assets, at fair value	
Balance, 1 January	$342,800
Balance, 31 December	344,100
Defined benefit obligation	
Balance, 1 January	$599,690
Balance, 31 December	704,200

The company has a contributory defined benefit pension plan covering all employees over the age of 30.

Required:

1. How much did the pension plan assets change during the year? Name three items that would cause plan assets to change.
2. How much did the defined benefit obligation increase during the year? Name five items that would cause this amount to change.
3. Compute the amount of the underfunded (overfunded) net position of the pension plan for accounting purposes at the beginning and the end of the year. Explain what these amounts mean.

★ **A19-6 Defined Benefit Plan; Actuarial Cost Methods:** There are three major approaches to measure and allocate pension amounts to given fiscal years. These approaches are used by actuaries to determine funding amounts and by accountants to determine amounts to be recorded in financial statements. Holo Company has a defined benefit pension plan that has been in existence for five years since 20X2. The company is reviewing its funding approach and has three different funding amounts for 20X7, each based on a different actuarial cost method:

#1 $5,000
#2 $2,500
#3 $3,900

Required:

1. Identify three actuarial cost methods, and specify the projections that differentiate these three methods.
2. Suggest which funding amount, above, is associated with which actuarial cost method. Explain.
3. Which actuarial cost method is required for external reporting? What will be the outcome if this method is not used for funding?
4. In each of the following circumstances, identify the funding method that Holo would likely find most appealing:
   a. Holo is experiencing a cash shortage and therefore is trying to conserve current cash balances.
   b. Holo would prefer to have cash payments stable from year to year.
   c. Holo would prefer to use a funding pattern that could also be used to measure the pension expense.

★ **A19-7 Defined Benefit Plan; Actuarial Cost Methods:** Ivan Resources Corp. sponsors a defined benefit pension plan for its unionized labour force. The company disclosed the following in its annual financial statements:

Solution

(in thousands)	31 December 20X5
Fair value of plan assets	$422,400
Defined benefit obligation	590,200
Funded status—deficit	$167,800

The company is considering the impact that changes in assumptions will have on its pension situation. In specific, the following:

a. Lower employee mortality rates
b. Higher than expected employee turnover
c. A rollback of wages by 3%
d. Higher borrowing rates

Required:

Separately for each suggested change in assumption, identify the impact on annual pension expense, the funded status of the pension, and accumulated OCI. Explain your conclusions.

★★ connect

A19-8 Defined Benefit Plan; Three Elements: Security Services Limited sponsors a defined benefit pension plan for its employees. It is now the 20X9 fiscal year. An appropriate interest rate for long-term debt is 7%. Information with respect to the plan is as follows:

Fair value of plan assets, 31 December 20X8	$6,258,000
Defined benefit obligation, 31 December 20X8	7,299,000
Actual return on plan assets for 20X9	61,100
Past service cost from amendment dated 31 December 20X9, liability is reduced because benefits were reduced	(203,200)
Actuarial revaluation dated 31 December 20X9; liability is reduced because of changed mortality assumptions	(603,700)
Funding payment at year-end 20X9	250,000
Benefits paid to retirees in 20X9	105,000
Current service cost for 20X9	233,400

Required:

1. Calculate the SFP net defined benefit pension liability as of 31 December 20X8.
2. Calculate the net defined benefit pension liability as of 31 December 20X9 by calculating the defined benefit obligation and the fair value of plan assets at 31 December 20X9.
3. Analyze the three elements of pension accounting for 20X9: service cost, net interest, and revaluations. Prepare entries, and also an entry for the contribution to the fund during 20X9.
4. Calculate the SFP net defined benefit pension liability as of 31 December 20X9, reflecting requirement 1 and the entries in requirement 3, and compare this with the net result in requirement 2.

★★ connect

A19-9 Defined Benefit Plan; Three Elements: Edmonton Trucking Limited sponsors a defined benefit pension plan for its employees. It is now the 20X2 fiscal year. Long-term corporate borrowing rates for companies with this risk profile are 6%. Information with respect to the pension plan is as follows:

Current service cost for 20X2	$ 175,200
Fair value of plan assets, 31 December 20X1	2,435,000
Benefits paid to retirees in 20X2	234,900
Funding payment at year-end 20X2	190,000
Defined benefit obligation, 31 December 20X1	2,988,000
Past service cost from amendment dated 31 December 20X2; liability is reduced because benefits were reduced	(116,500)

Actuarial revaluation dated 31 December 20X2; liability is increased because of changed salary increase assumptions	355,700
Actual return on plan assets for 20X2 (loss)	(104,800)

Required:

1. Calculate the SFP net defined benefit pension liability as of 31 December 20X1.
2. Calculate the net defined benefit pension liability as of 31 December 20X2 by calculating the defined benefit obligation and the fair value of plan assets at 31 December 20X2.
3. Analyze the three elements of pension accounting for 20X2: service cost, net interest, and revaluations. Prepare entries, and also an entry for the contribution to the fund during 20X2.
4. Calculate the SFP net defined benefit pension liability as of 31 December 20X2, reflecting requirement 1 and the entries in requirement 3, and compare this with the net result in requirement 2.

★★ **A19-10 Defined Benefit Plan; Three Elements:** The following data relate to a defined benefit pension plan:

excel

connect

Defined benefit obligation, 31 December 20X1	$106,000
Benefits paid to retirees in 20X2	14,000
Current service cost for 20X2	6,700
Actual return on plan assets for 20X2	3,200
Fair value of plan assets, 31 December 20X1	78,000
Funding payment at year-end 20X2	7,000
Past service cost from amendment dated 31 December 20X2; liability is increased because benefits were increased on a retrospective basis	3,700
Actuarial revaluation dated 31 December 20X2; decrease to liability because of changed mortality assumptions	(2,500)
Long-term interest rate on corporate bonds	7%

Required:

1. Calculate the SFP net defined benefit pension liability as of 31 December 20X1.
2. Compute the defined benefit obligation at 31 December 20X2 and the fair value of plan assets on the same date.
3. Analyze the three elements of pension accounting for 20X2: service cost, net interest, and revaluations. Prepare entries and also an entry for the contribution to the fund during 20X2.
4. Calculate the SFP net defined benefit pension liability as of 31 December 20X2, and prove that this represents the net defined benefit position of the pension plan.

★★ **A19-11 Defined Benefit Plan; Three Elements:** The following data relate to a defined benefit pension plan:

Solution

Defined benefit obligation, 31 December 20X8	$299,000
Fair value of plan assets, 31 December 20X8	302,000
Past service cost from amendment dated 31 December 20X9; liability is increased because benefits were increased on a retrospective basis	16,000
Benefits paid to retirees in 20X9	7,200
Current service cost for 20X9	9,100
Funding payment at year-end 20X9	6,000
Actuarial revaluation dated 31 December 20X9; decrease to liability because of changed mortality assumptions	(12,000)
Actual return (loss) on plan assets for 20X9	(4,700)
Long-term yield on corporate bonds	5%

Required:

1. Calculate the SFP net defined benefit pension asset as of 31 December 20X8. The asset ceiling does not limit the amount of the pension asset.
2. Compute the defined benefit obligation at 31 December 20X9 and the fair value of plan assets on the same date.
3. Analyze the three elements of pension accounting for 20X9: service cost, net interest, and revaluations. Prepare entries and also an entry for the contribution to the fund during 20X9.
4. Calculate the SFP net defined benefit pension liability as of 31 December 20X9, and prove that this represents the net defined benefit position of the pension plan.

★★ **A19-12 Defined Benefit Plan; Three Elements:** Scharp Limited has a defined benefit pension plan. The following information relates to this plan:

connect

excel

SFP net defined pension liability, 1 January 20X1	$52,500
Defined benefit pension obligation, 1 January 20X1	??
Actuarial loss on change in assumptions, arising during 20X1	15,000
Actual return on plan assets for 20X1—loss	2,000
Fair value of plan assets, 1 January	244,000
Current service cost for 20X1	19,200
Plan contribution for 20X1	24,000
Benefits paid in 20X1	7,500
Yield on long-term corporate bonds	4.5%
SFP Accumulated OCI, pension, 1 January 20X1	80,400 dr.
Retained earnings, 1 January 20X1	5,500,000 cr.
20X1 Earnings, prior to any pension expense	4,000,000 cr.

Required:

1. Compute the defined benefit obligation at 31 December 20X1 and the fair value of plan assets on the same date.
2. Analyze the three elements of pension accounting for 20X1: service cost, net interest, and revaluations. Prepare entries and also an entry for the contribution to the fund during 20X1.
3. Calculate 20X1 earnings after pension expense is recorded. Ignore any income tax. Also calculate comprehensive income, the closing balance of retained earnings, accumulated OCI, and the SFP net defined benefit pension liability as of 31 December 20X1. Prove that the SFP liability account represents the net defined benefit position of the pension plan.

★★ **A19-13 Defined Benefit Plan; Three Elements:** Computer Imaging Ltd. (CIL) established a formal pension plan 10 years ago to provide retirement benefits for all employees. The plan is noncontributory and is funded through a trustee that invests all funds and pays all benefits as they become due. Vesting occurs when the employee reaches age 45 and has been employed by CIL 10 years.

At the inception of the plan, past service cost (PSC) amounted to $300,000. The past service cost is being funded over 10 years by level annual end-of-year payments calculated at 5%, which is a reasonable approximation of long-term borrowing rates (see below actuarial report for the funding amount). Each year, the company also funds an amount equal to current service cost less any new actuarial gains or plus any new actuarial losses on the pension obligation. The yield rate on corporate bonds with an appropriate currency and term is 6%.

At the beginning of 20X8, the defined benefit obligation was $1,400,200. The fair value of investments was $1,075,790, and the net defined benefit pension liability on the SFP was $324,410.

The independent actuary's biennial revaluation report follows:

COMPUTER IMAGING LIMITED

Noncontributory Defined Benefit Pension Plan
Actuarial Report, 31 December 20X8

Current service cost		
Computed by the projected unit credit method		$ 85,375
Actuarial revaluation, effective 31 December 20X8		
Experience gains for		
Mortality	$ 7,875	
Employee turnover	12,625	
Decrease in defined benefit obligation due to increase in bond yield rate	49,500	
Net actuarial gains		$ 70,000
20X8 funding		
Current service cost	$85,375	
Past service cost	38,853	
Less: Revaluation gains of 20X8	(70,000)	
Total cash contribution to plan		$ 54,228
Pension plan asset portfolio		
Market value, 1 January 20X8		$1,075,790
Contributions		54,228
Portfolio performance, 20X8		
Interest, dividends, and capital gains		151,685
Market value, 31 December 20X8		$1,281,703
Other information:		
SFP Accumulated OCI, pension, 1 January 20X8		$ 100,900 dr.
Retained earnings, 1 January 20X8		$7,800,000 cr.
20X8 Earnings, prior to any pension expense		$5,850,000 cr.

Required:

1. Analyze the three elements of pension accounting for 20X8: service cost, net interest, and revaluations. Prepare entries and also an entry for the contribution to the fund during 20X8.
2. Calculate 20X8 earnings after pension expense is recorded. Ignore any income tax. Also calculate comprehensive income, the closing balance of retained earnings, accumulated OCI, and the SFP net defined benefit pension liability as of 31 December 20X8. Prove that the SFP liability account represents the net defined benefit position of the pension fund.

★★ **A19-14 Defined Benefit Plan; Three Elements:** In late 20X0, Urbo Valves Limited established a defined benefit pension plan for its employees. At the inception of the plan, the actuary determined the present value of the defined benefit obligation relating to employees' past services to be $1 million, as of the beginning of 20X1. This amount vests over 10 years.

In each year following inception of the plan, the actuary measured the defined benefit obligation arising from employees' services in that year. These current service costs amounted to $80,000 in 20X1, $82,000 in 20X2, and $85,000 in 20X3. The costs were determined by using an actuarial cost method based on employees' projected earnings.

All actuarial obligations and funding payments were determined by assuming an interest rate of 6%, which was the long-term borrowing yield. In accordance with provincial legislation, the past service cost was to be funded over 15 years, the maximum period allowed. Current service costs were to be fully funded at the end of each year.

In 20X4, the actuary conducted the mandatory triennial revaluation. The revaluation revealed that the plan assets at the end of 20X3 were $611,500. The defined benefit obligation at the end of 20X3 was $1,452,800. There was a balance of accumulated OCI of $21,600 (debit) in relation to the pension at the end of 20X3. The actuary also determined that the current service cost for 20X4 was $87,500. There was an experience gain of $21,870 on the pension plan obligation, arising in 20X4, as a result of higher mortality rates. The actual plan earnings for 20X4 were $55,055. At the end of 20X4, there was a curtailment of the pension plan, resulting in a reduction in the pension obligation of $75,000 and a reduction in assets of $34,000.

Required:

Determine the amount of pension expense for 20X4 and the change in accumulated OCI for the year.

★★ **A19-15 Defined Benefit Plan; Three Elements, Asset Ceiling:** Morocco Corporation initiated a defined benefit pension plan on 1 January 20X5. The plan does not provide past service benefits for existing employees. The pension funding payment is made to the trustee on 31 December of each year. The following information is available for 20X5 and 20X6:

	20X5	20X6
Current service cost, measured as of the beginning of the year	$150,000	$145,000
Funding payment	200,000	185,000
Net interest, as calculated by the actuary at 10%	15,000	11,000

Required:

1. Prepare the journal entries to record pension expense for 20X5 and 20X6. Net interest in 20X6 is the combination of interest on the defined benefit obligation and expected return on plan assets. Also record the funding payment. (Note that actual return is equal to expected return.)
2. What is the amount of the net defined benefit pension asset on the 31 December 20X6 statement of financial position? Prove that this is equal to the net position of fund assets and the defined benefit obligation.
3. What limits are there on the net defined benefit pension asset on the statement of financial position?
4. Prepare the necessary additional entry that would be made if there was an asset ceiling of $351,500 in 20X6. What would be the amount of the resulting net defined benefit pension asset on the 31 December 20X6 statement of financial position?

★ **A19-16 Pension Spreadsheet:** Jones Manufacturing Inc. sponsored a defined benefit pension plan effective 1 January 20X7. The company uses the projected unit credit actuarial cost method for funding and accounting. Long-term corporate bonds have a yield of 4%. Employees were granted partial credit for past service. The past service obligation has been measured at $1,640,000 as of 1 January 20X7. The company will pay $200,000 (for past service) plus all current service cost to the pension plan trustee each 31 December beginning 31 December 20X7. This funding arrangement will continue for five years and then be re-evaluated.

connect

excel

Data for 20X7 and 20X8

	20X7	20X8
Current service cost	$117,000	$157,000
Actual return on fund assets	—	6,800
Decrease in defined benefit obligation at year-end due to change in assumptions	—	37,000
Payments to pensioners	—	41,400

Required:
Prepare a spreadsheet containing all relevant pension information for 20X7 and 20X8.

★★ **A19-17 Pension Spreadsheet:** Maple Construction Corp. has a defined benefit pension plan. Information concerning the 20X7 and 20X8 fiscal years is presented below:

connect

excel

From the Plan Actuary:

- Current service cost in 20X7 is $430,000 and in 20X8 is $488,000.
- Defined benefit obligation is $4,975,000 at the beginning of 20X7.
- New past service cost in 20X8 is $45,000, a reduction in benefits.
- Accumulated OCI amounts are losses at the beginning of 20X7, amounting to $787,000.
- Benefits paid to retirees, $235,000 in 20X7 and $295,000 in 20X8.
- Actuarial revaluation in 20X7 showed a $406,000 increase in the obligation due to changes in mortality. Revaluations take place every four years.

From the Plan Trustee:

- Plan assets at market value at the beginning of 20X7 were $3,705,000.
- 20X7 contributions were $510,000 and in 20X8, $525,000.
- Actual earnings were $276,000 in 20X7 and $80,000 in 20X8.

Other Information:

- Yield on long-term debt, stable in 20X7 and 20X8, 6%.
- The opening net defined benefit pension liability on the SFP is the opening net amount of the defined benefit obligation and opening fund assets.

Required:
Prepare a spreadsheet for 20X7 and 20X8 that determines pension expense and also the closing net defined benefit pension asset or liability account and accumulated OCI.

★★ **A19-18 Pension Spreadsheet:** Gurung Company has a noncontributory, defined benefit pension plan adopted on 1 January 20X5. On 31 December 20X5, the following information is available:

connect

excel

For accounting purposes

- Interest rate used for pension amounts, 5%.
- Past service cost, granted as of 1 January 20X5, $200,000. This is also the defined benefit obligation on 1 January.
- Current service cost for 20X5, appropriately measured for accounting purposes, $67,000.

For funding purposes

- Funding was $99,500 in 20X5 for all pension amounts. The payment was made on 31 December.
- Actual earnings on fund assets, zero.

Required:

1. Prepare a pension spreadsheet that summarizes relevant pension data for 20X5.
2. Prepare a pension spreadsheet that summarizes relevant pension data for 20X6. The following facts relate to 20X6:
   - Current service cost for accounting was $96,000.
   - A plan amendment resulted in a past service cost of $40,000 being granted.
   - Total funding of the pension plan was $118,000, on 31 December 20X6.
   - Actual return on fund assets was $8,900.
   - An actuarial revaluation was done to reflect new information about expected turnover rates in the employee population. This resulted in a $35,000 increase in the defined benefit obligation, as of 31 December 20X6.

★★ **A19-19 Pension Spreadsheet:** Solutions Limited sponsors a defined benefit pension plan for its employees. At the beginning of 20X3, there is an accrued SFP pension liability of $152,800, as follows:

excel

Defined benefit obligation	$(509,100)
Plan assets (fair value)	356,300
Net defined benefit pension liability	$(152,800)

There are also actuarial losses of $72,700 in accumulated OCI with respect to the pension plan. The following data relate to the operation of the plan for the years 20X3 and 20X4:

	20X3	20X4
Current service cost	49,000	$ 42,000
Yield rate on long-term corporate bonds	5%	5%
Actual return (loss) on plan assets	(17,000)	21,000
Annual funding contributions, at year-end	65,000	82,000
Benefits paid to retirees	45,500	106,000
Increase in defined benefit obligation due to changes in actuarial assumptions as of 31 December each year	86,000	34,000

Required:

Prepare a spreadsheet that summarizes relevant pension data for 20X3 and 20X4. As part of the spreadsheet, calculate pension expense, the net defined benefit pension accrued benefit asset/liability, and accumulated OCI for 20X3 and 20X4.

★★ **A19-20 Pension Spreadsheet:** HDD Consultants Limited began a pension fund in the year 20X3, effective 1 January 20X4. Terms of the pension plan follow:

Solution

- The yield rate on long-term high-grade corporate bonds is 6%.
- Employees will receive partial credit for past service. The past service obligation, valued using the projected unit credit actuarial cost method and a discount rate of 6%, is $216,000 as of 1 January 20X4.
- Past service cost will be funded over roughly 15 years. The initial payment, on 1 January 20X4, is $20,000. This will earn interest in 20X4. After that, another $20,000 will be added to the 31 December funding payment each year for past service, including the 31 December 20X4 payment. The amount of funding will be reviewed every five years to ensure its adequacy.
- Current service cost will be fully funded each 31 December, plus actuarial losses or minus actuarial gains of the year, if those actuarial gains or losses are related to the defined benefit obligation. Experience gains and losses related to the difference between actual and expected earnings on fund assets will not affect plan funding in the short run, as they are expected to offset over time.

Data for 20X4 and 20X5

	20X4	20X5
Current service cost	$51,000	$57,000
Funding amount, 1 January 20X4	20,000	
Funding amount, 31 December	??	??
Actual return on fund assets	1,000	6,800
Increase in defined benefit obligation at year-end due to change in assumptions	—	16,000

Required:

Prepare a spreadsheet containing all relevant pension information for 20X4 and 20X5.

★★ **A19-21 Other Post-Employment Benefits:** Hruska Corp. provides post-employment benefits to its retirees for dental and supplementary health care. The following information relates to these benefits:

connect

Benefit obligation, 1 January 20X6	$56,000
Current service cost for 20X6	16,000
SFP accrued net OPEB liability, 1 January, 20X6	49,000
Accumulated OCI, OPEBs, 1 January 20X6, loss	23,000
Fund assets, 1 January 20X6	7,000
Contributions to the benefit fund for 20X6	9,000
Benefit payments to retired employees for 20X6	12,000
Actual return on fund assets	350
Yield rate on long-term corporate bonds	7%

Required:

1. Compute the benefit obligation for post-employment benefits at 31 December 20X6 and plan assets at 31 December 20X6.
2. Compute the appropriate expense for post-employment benefits for the year ended 31 December 20X6.
3. Compute the closing balances on related SFP accounts at 31 December 20X6.

Note: The solution to this question is based on an optional spreadsheet.

★★ **A19-22 Other Post-Employment Benefits:** Financial Metrics Ltd. provides life insurance and dental coverage to retirees. The yield rate on long-term debt is 5%. The following information relates to these benefits:

Fund assets, 1 January 20X2	0
Benefit obligation, 1 January 20X2	$1,282,000
Benefit payments to retired employees for 20X2	177,000
Service cost for 20X2	211,000
Accumulated OCI, OPEBs, 1 January 20X2, loss	186,000
Actuarial revaluation, performed at the end of 20X2; liability reduced due to change in mortality assumption	(300,000)
Contributions to the benefit fund for 20X2	178,000
Actual return on fund assets	0

Required:

1. Compute the benefit obligation for post-employment benefits and plan assets at 31 December 20X2.
2. Compute the appropriate expense for post-employment benefits for the year ended 31 December 20X2.
3. Compute the closing balances in SFP accounts related to these benefits as at 31 December 20X2.

Note: The solution to this question is based on an optional spreadsheet.

★★ **A19-23 Other Post-Employment Benefits; Spreadsheet:** Lin Developments Ltd. provides post-employment benefits to its retirees for supplementary health care, including prescription medication. Lin had an accumulated OCI loss amount related to OPEBs of $45,000 at the beginning of the year, an experience loss related primarily to unexpected cost increases in prescription medication.

Lin does not fund health care benefits to any great extent. As a result, there was only $21,500 in the fund asset account at the beginning of the year, while the estimated obligation for supplementary health care benefits was $566,300. Actual earnings of the fund this year were $600. Contributions of $46,400 were made to the fund and benefits paid out were

$43,900. In the current year, actuarial estimates indicate that current service cost is $67,800, and there is a new actuarial loss of $35,000 related to further increases in health care costs.

Required:

Prepare a spreadsheet for the current year that determines the expense for post-employment benefits, accumulated OCI, and also the closing accrued asset or liability with respect to the benefits. Begin by calculating the opening SFP OPEB liability balance. The long-term bond yield rate is 5%.

★ **A19-24 Defined Benefit Plan; Disclosure:** Extracts from the pension disclosures of Blue Pony Limited are shown below.

Pension Benefits

The estimated present value of accrued plan benefits and the estimated market value of the net assets available to provide for these benefits are as follows:

	20X2	20X1
Plan assets, at fair value	$545	$484
Defined benefit obligation	612	575
Deficiency	$ (67)	$ (91)

Actuarial assumptions:

	20X2	20X1
Yield rate for defined benefit obligation	5.25%	5.3%
Weighted average rate of compensation increase for defined benefit obligation	3.50%	4.00%
Retention rate	84%	88%

Accumulated OCI:

	20X2	20X1
Opening; accumulated losses	$ 94	$91
Actuarial and experience losses	16	3
Closing	$110	$94

Required:

1. With respect to the actuarial assumptions listed, explain how each assumption would be developed. Indicate whether the trend in each assumption would lead to higher or lower pension expense.
2. Explain the amount that would be recorded as an SFP pension liability.
3. Explain the nature of amounts that are recorded in OCI. Are these amounts recycled to earnings?

★ **A19-25 ASPE; Defined Benefit Plan:** Return to the facts of A19-8. Assume instead that this pension plan is sponsored by a private company and ASPE applies.

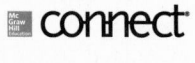

Required:

1. Prepare an entry to record pension expense and an entry to record the contribution to the pension fund for 20X9. *Note:* The solution to this assignment is based on one calculation of pension expense, followed by one entry for pension expense, rather than a series of entries for separate components.
2. Based on the entries in requirement 1, calculate the SFP net defined benefit pension liability as of 31 December 20X9, and prove this number based on the closing balances of the defined benefit liability and pension plan assets.

★ **A19-26 ASPE; Defined Benefit Plan:** Return to the facts of A19-9. Assume instead that this pension plan is sponsored by a private company and ASPE applies.

connect

Required:

1. Prepare an entry to record pension expense and an entry to record the contribution to the pension fund for 20X2. *Note:* The solution to this assignment is based on one calculation of pension expense, followed by one entry for pension expense, rather than a series of entries for separate components.
2. Based on the entries in requirement 1, calculate the SFP net defined benefit pension liability as of 31 December 20X2, and prove this number based on the closing balances of the defined benefit liability and pension plan assets.

★ **A19-27 ASPE; Defined Benefit Plan:** Return to the facts of A19-10. Assume instead that this pension plan is sponsored by a private company and ASPE applies.

Required:

1. Prepare an entry to record pension expense and an entry to record the contribution to the pension fund for 20X2. *Note:* The solution to this assignment is based on one calculation of pension expense, followed by one entry for pension expense, rather than a series of entries for separate components.
2. Based on the entries in requirement 1, calculate the SFP net defined benefit pension liability as of 31 December 20X2, and prove this number based on the closing balances of the defined benefit liability and pension plan assets.

★ **A19-28 ASPE; Defined Benefit Plan:** Return to the facts of A19-11. Assume instead that this pension plan is sponsored by a private company and ASPE applies.

Solution

Required:

1. Prepare all entries for 20X9.
2. Based on the entries based on requirement 1, calculate the SFP net defined benefit pension liability as of 31 December 20X9, and prove this number based on the closing balances of the defined benefit liability and pension plan assets.

★ **A19-29 ASPE; Defined Benefit Plan:** Return to the facts of A19-16. Assume instead that this pension plan is sponsored by a private company and ASPE applies.

Required:

Prepare a spreadsheet containing all relevant pension information for 20X7 and 20X8.

★★★ **A19-30 Comprehensive; Chapters 12, 13, 14, 15, 18, 19:** Oilfield Multiservices Ltd. (OML) offers oilfield operation services to the oil and gas industry in Alberta and Texas. OML owns no natural resource properties itself but assists in exploration activities through cementing and stimulation services. OML complies with ASPE. The company has prepared draft financial statements (Exhibit 1). However, some transactions during the year have not been properly reflected in the financial statements (Exhibit 2). Additional information on financial statement elements are provided in Exhibit 3. OML is required, as part of its bond agreement, to maintain a minimum level of retained earnings of $30 million, and a maximum debt-to-equity ratio of 1.5. In the debt-to-equity ratio, the numerator is "total liabilities." Since a number of the transactions that have not been processed affect debt and/or equity, the CFO is concerned that these key financial targets continue to be met.

Required:

1. Provide journal entries to account for the information provided in Exhibits 2 and 3. None of the adjustments mentioned alters income tax expense, income tax payable, or future

income tax. Round all adjustments to the nearest thousand. All amounts are given in thousands, except share volumes and per share amounts.

2. Prepare a revised statement of financial position, statement of comprehensive income, and statement of retained earnings.
3. Evaluate the key financial targets and suggest action for the coming year if there are concerns.

EXHIBIT 1

OILFIELD MULTISERVICES LTD.—DRAFT FINANCIAL STATEMENTS FOR THE YEAR ENDED 31 DECEMBER 20X7 (IN THOUSANDS)

STATEMENT OF FINANCIAL POSITION

Assets		
Cash		$ 14,960
Accounts receivable		30,497
Inventory		1,958
Prepaid expenses and deposits		930
Current assets		48,345
Fixed assets, net		78,441
Intangible assets		890
Suspense		8,338
Total assets		**$136,014**
Liabilities		
Accounts payable and accrued liabilities		$ 19,511
Income tax payable		1,600
Current bank loan		12,100
Current liabilities		33,211
Lease liability		3,985
Long-term debt	30,000	
Premium	1,210	31,210
Deferred income tax		6,900
Defined benefit obligation		620
Total liabilities		75,926
Shareholders' equity		
Preferred shares		5,100
Common shares		11,050
Contributed capital on common stock retirement		788
Stock options outstanding		450
Retained earnings		42,700
Total shareholders' equity		60,088
Total liabilities and shareholders' equity		**$136,014**

STATEMENT OF EARNINGS; YEAR ENDED 31 DECEMBER 20X7

Sales	$146,560
Expenses	
Operating	103,490
Selling, general, and administration	8,385
Interest	2,355
Depreciation	8,420
	122,650
Income before tax	23,910
Income tax	5,950
Net income	**$ 17,960**

STATEMENT OF RETAINED EARNINGS; YEAR ENDED 31 DECEMBER 20X7

Retained earnings, beginning of year	$ 27,965
Common share retirement	0
Dividends:	
Preferred dividends	0
Common share dividends	(3,225)
Stock dividends	0
Net income	17,960
Retained earnings, end of year	$ 42,700

EXHIBIT 2

OILFIELD MULTISERVICES LTD.—OUTSTANDING TRANSACTIONS

Note: Amounts are in thousands, except share volumes and per share amounts.

1. Preferred dividends were declared but not paid. They have not yet been recorded. They should be included in "Accounts payable and accrued liabilities."
2. On 1 October 20X7, 865,000 common shares were reacquired from a shareholder and retired. The $6,240 payment was debited to the "suspense" account, which now appears as an asset.
3. No premium amortization on the bond has been recorded for 20X7.
4. No adjustment has been made for compensation expense inherent in stock option plans.
5. The $2,098 payment made to the pension trustee was debited to the "suspense" account. No pension expense has been recorded in the 20X7 financial statements. The pension plan covers operating employees (85%) and administrative staff (15%).
6. A stock dividend of 10% was declared and distributed on 31 December on common shares. The Board of Directors agreed that this was to be capitalized at a value of $8 per share. The stock dividend has not yet been recorded.
7. The lease liability must be adjusted for interest and the current portion, which will be classified as part of the current liability "Current bank loan."

EXHIBIT 3

OILFIELD MULTISERVICES LTD.—ADDITIONAL INFORMATION

Note: Amounts are in thousands, except share volumes and per share amounts.

1. *Lease obligation*

   The lease obligation is the remaining portion of a 20-year capital lease with annual payments each 1 January of $612. The 1 January 20X7 payment was properly recorded. The interest rate used for lease capitalization was 7%. No interest has been recorded in 20X7, nor has the current portion of the lease liability been recorded.

2. *Share information*

   Preferred shares—$6 cumulative no-par preferred shares outstanding, 51,000 shares outstanding during the entire year in 20X7.

   Common shares—No-par common shares outstanding at the beginning of 20X7, 6,210,000 shares. During the year, 865,000 shares were retired on 1 October, and a 10% stock dividend was declared and distributed on 31 December.

3. *Bonds payable*

   Long-term debt consists of:
   Bonds payable, 6 1/4%, due 30 June 20X21 $30,000
   Premium amortization of $83 has yet to be recorded for the year.

4. *Outstanding stock options*

   Stock options have been outstanding during 20X7 for 265,000 shares. These options are held by senior administrative employees. They may be exercised for the first time on 1 January 20X9, and the related cost is being amortized over four years. The options were originally valued at $900 using the binomial option pricing model.

5. *Pension information*

   At the beginning of the year, the defined benefit pension plan had $9,096 in assets and $9,716 of defined benefit obligation. The actual return on assets was $435. Current service cost in 20X7 was $1,700 using the projected benefit actuarial cost method. A long-term interest rate of 6% was considered appropriate. Benefits paid to pensioners were $500. There were no re-measurements or new past service during the year.

(Source: [Adapted] © CGA-Canada. Reproduced with permission.)

connect LEARNSMART SMARTBOOK™

For more information on the resources available from McGraw-Hill Ryerson, go to www.mcgrawhill.ca/he/solutions.

CHAPTER 20

Earnings per Share

INTRODUCTION

References to earnings data expressed as earnings per share (EPS) are common in the financial press. Public companies report their EPS numbers quarterly and use the statistic to benchmark results and communicate targets. For example, Tim Hortons reported 2012 basic EPS of $2.60 (and diluted EPS of $2.59). In comparison, 2011 EPS was $2.36 ($2.35 diluted). 2012 EPS was 9.9% higher the previous year, which is slightly higher than earnings growth due because 4.3% fewer shares were outstanding during 2012. The company announced 2013 performance targets of diluted EPS of $2.87 to $2.97 for 2013.

All publicly listed enterprises must report earnings per share. EPS is calculated in order to indicate the proportionate per share interest in the company's earnings. An absolute increase in earnings is not, in itself, an adequate indicator because earnings may go up as a result of increased equity investment. For example, a company may issue more shares for cash. The increased investment should generate additional earnings for the company. For an individual shareholder, the real question is whether total net income increased enough to compensate for the increased number of shares outstanding. If the proportionate increase in earnings is higher than the proportionate increase in outstanding shares, then earnings attributable to each share will increase. Note that EPS is based on net income, not on comprehensive income.

This chapter demonstrates how to calculate earnings per share and its several subcomponents. We will deal first with basic EPS, which is defined as the profit or loss attributable to each outstanding share of common or "ordinary" shares. We will then deal with the intricacies of diluted EPS. Finally, we explore the uses and limitations of earnings per share data.

EPS FIGURES

Public companies must report both basic EPS and diluted EPS on the statement of comprehensive income. EPS is calculated based on:

1. Profit or loss from continuing operations, if presented; and then
2. Profit or loss (including discontinued operations).

Basic earnings per share is calculated as profit or loss attributable to common shareholders (net profit or loss minus preferred share claims and other prior claims) divided by the weighted-average ordinary (common) shares outstanding. The per-share amount of discontinued operations on their own must also be disclosed, but this may be in a disclosure note rather than on the face of the SCI. If there are no discontinued operations, then only EPS based on profit and loss is reported.

Some companies have securities in their capital structure that commit the company to issue potentially significant amount of common or "ordinary" shares in the future. As we discussed extensively in Chapter 15, these commitments can cause substantial change in the corporation's capital structure. Examples include convertible securities, stock options, and contingent commitments to issue ordinary (common) shares.

Diluted earnings per share is calculated in order to provide a basis for forward predictions. Diluted EPS shows the maximum reduction to EPS that could occur if all dilutive potential ordinary shares were issued—that is, if all dilutive stock options were exercised, all contingently issuable shares were issued, and all dilutive convertible debt and convertible preferred shares were converted to common shares.

Like basic EPS, diluted EPS must be calculated both on (1) profit or loss from continuing operations, if presented, and then (2) profit or loss.

INTERPRETING EPS

EPS numbers can be used as follows:

- *Basic EPS.* This is an historical amount that is based on the actual number of shares outstanding during the earnings period. Current EPS can be compared with EPS numbers from prior years to see whether the company is earning more or less for its common shareholders. It is a common way to communicate earnings information to shareholders. Basic EPS may indicate a trend to assist in forecasting, but it essentially tells us what has happened in the past.
- *Diluted EPS.* This is a forward-looking measurement. Diluted EPS gives an indication of the potential future impact that conversions (and options) will have on the earnings attributable to common shares. Companies usually issue convertible securities with the hope and expectation that they will convert to common shares and become part of the permanent capital of the company. If the company is successful in its financing strategy, the convertible senior securities will be converted rather than repaid. Thus, diluted EPS is not just a hypothetical figure—it reflects an impact that is likely to occur if and when the company is successful.

One important aspect of EPS numbers is that they mean nothing by themselves. Like all economic indices, they are meaningful only as part of a series. Trend over time is important. The EPS trend may be easier to interpret than the trend in earnings because EPS is adjusted for changes in capital structure. This removes the normal earnings expansion effect that arises through additional share capital and reinvested earnings.

By definition, discontinued operations will wind down and cease to be a factor in operating results. Therefore, EPS numbers based on earnings from continuing operations are more relevant for future projections than are EPS that includes discontinued operations.

When comparing companies, the absolute level of EPS is meaningless. The fact that one company has EPS of $4 per share while another has EPS of $28 per share does not demonstrate that the company with the higher number is more profitable. It all depends on the number of shares outstanding. Therefore, one company's EPS cannot be compared with another's. EPS numbers are meaningful only as part of the statistical series of that reporting company's historical and projected earnings per share.

Because EPS encapsulates a company's entire reported results for the year in a single number, EPS hides much more than it shows. If you place strong reliance on EPS as an indicator of a company's performance, you are blindly accepting management's selection of accounting policies, estimates, and measurements. EPS should be used only as a rough guide; it is no substitute for an informed analysis of the company's reporting practices.

ETHICAL ISSUES

EPS calculations are complex, and their meaning is sufficiently uncertain that many accountants believe the level of reliance on them is unwarranted. Using EPS as an important element in a company's goal structure can contribute to a short-term management attitude. This can lead to decisions that are detrimental to the long-term productivity and financial health of the company. For example, rather than investing cash in productive activities that enhance the company's earnings, management may engage in share buybacks in order to decrease the denominator of the EPS calculation. Indeed, managers have been known to issue debt to get cash for share buybacks, a strategy that increases leverage and thus exposes shareholders to greater risk.

Nevertheless, EPS computations continue to be reported by companies and anticipated by shareholders, analysts, and management. Knowledge of how EPS amounts are calculated is essential if intelligent use is to be made of the resulting figures.

BASIC EARNINGS PER SHARE

The basic EPS calculation is as follows:

$$\frac{\text{Net profit or loss available to ordinary shareholders}}{\text{Weighted-average number of ordinary shares outstanding}}$$

The following sections explain more fully both the numerator and denominator of the basic EPS calculation.

Ordinary (Common) Shares

EPS is calculated on the basis of ordinary shares. **Ordinary shares** are defined as equity instruments that are subordinate to all other classes of equity instruments. A company may also have **senior shares,** which are any shares that have claims with higher priority than ordinary shares. It is possible for a company to have more than one class of ordinary share, often with different voting rights. Typically, ordinary shares are common shares and senior shares are preferred shares.

If preferred shares participate fully in dividends with common shares, then they are not considered to be senior shares for the purpose of EPS calculation, regardless of whether the corporation calls them "preferred shares" or "senior shares."

Net Profit or Loss Available to Ordinary Shareholders

The numerator, *net profit or loss available to ordinary shareholders*, is net earnings of the company minus claims to earnings that take precedence over the ordinary share claim. The most usual prior claim to earnings is the dividend entitlement of senior (preferred) shares. The dividend rights of senior shares are deducted from earnings when calculating EPS as follows:

- For *noncumulative* senior shares, only those dividends actually declared during the period are subtracted in determining the EPS numerator.

- For *cumulative* senior shares, the annual dividend is subtracted from earnings *regardless of whether it has been declared for the year*; any future dividend distributions to ordinary shareholders can be made only after senior shares' dividends in arrears have been paid.

What happens if cumulative preferred share dividends are in arrears, and, say, three years' dividends are paid in Year 3 to clear up the arrears and bring the shares up to date? In Years 1 and 2, when no dividends were paid, the annual dividend entitlement would have been deducted from earnings in order to calculate basic EPS. In the third year, three years' dividends are paid, but *only the current-year dividend is deducted* when calculating basic EPS. It would be double counting (or double deducting!) to take Year 1 and Year 2 dividends off *again*.

So, for cumulative shares, the maximum deduction is one year's dividend. If shares are noncumulative, a deduction is made for any and all dividends declared in the period. This represents their maximum claim to earnings.

In Chapter 15, we discussed a type of preferred shares that are classified as debt because they have fixed repayment terms, or other characteristics that, in substance, render the shares debt rather than equity. "Dividends" on these preferred shares are similar to interest and are deducted to arrive at earnings rather than as a deduction from retained earnings. *As a result, earnings will already be net of these preferred dividends.* Be sure to understand the starting point; preferred dividends are deducted only once!

Other Adjustments While dividends on preferred shares are the most frequent adjustment to the earnings line in basic EPS, more adjustments may be needed. For example:

- If preferred shares are retired during the period, a "loss" will be recorded directly in shareholders' equity, if the price paid is higher than the average issuance price to date. This was described in Chapter 14. This loss is not included in net earnings but is included (subtracted) in the numerator of basic EPS.
- If there is a *capital charge* on a convertible bond that is recorded as a direct deduction from retained earnings, this amount is also subtracted in the numerator of basic EPS.

The important question is always *what are the earnings available to ordinary shareholders?* Increases or decreases to all equity accounts should be carefully reviewed before EPS is calculated.

Weighted Average Number of Shares

The denominator of the EPS calculation reflects the number of ordinary shares, *on a weighted average basis*, that were outstanding during the year. The denominator will include all classes of shares that have residual claim (last call) on dividends, whether or not they are called "ordinary" or "common" shares in the corporate or accounting records. The result is **weighted average ordinary shares (WAOS)** outstanding.

In this calculation, shares are weighted by the length of time they are outstanding during the period. If a corporation issues additional shares during the year, additional capital invested in the business should increase earnings proportionately. If the increase in outstanding shares does not result in a proportionate increase in earnings, then the company's use of that capital was inefficient and the new shares diluted the interests of the prior-existing shareholders.

Similarly, if the number of shares outstanding during the year is reduced through a share buy-back program, withdrawal of capital from the business can be expected to reduce earnings. The intent of the EPS calculation is to reflect the relative effect on earnings after including the change in shares outstanding.

Daily averaging is the most accurate method, and technically is required. However, *calculations done by full month are permitted* (8/12, 4/12, etc.), as an expedient and reasonable way to approximate the result that a more detailed daily analysis would provide. Calculations may have to be done more precisely if the approximation is not adequate in the circumstances. For example, if a new issue of shares doubles the number of shares outstanding, then rounding to the nearest month would be inappropriate.

Mandatorily Convertible Instruments On occasion, a company will issue a limited-term convertible security, (e.g., preferred shares or debt) that *must* be converted at the end of the term—conversion is not optional. This type of security usually arises in the context of venture capital. In order to raise capital during the early stages of a company's development or expansion, the company may issue preferred shares (or debentures) to an investor that contains a fairly generous dividend preference (or high interest). In return, the investor agrees to convert the preferred shares or debentures to ordinary (common) shares at the end of a specified period.

Since the additional **mandatorily convertible shares** will definitely be issued in the future (assuming the company survives to that point), those shares *must be included in basic EPS*. Since they already have been included in basic EPS, they are *not* again added in for the diluted EPS calculation—doing so would double-count them. The shares are included from the date that the company and the investor enter into the contract for the mandatorily convertible instrument.

Example Assume that a company has 9,000,000 common shares outstanding at the beginning of the year. The fiscal year for this company is the calendar year. An additional 3,000,000 shares are issued on 1 September. There will have been 9,000,000 shares outstanding for the first eight months of the year, followed by 12,000,000 for the last four months. The weighted-average number of shares outstanding is 10,000,000. This can be calculated using a number of approaches. For example,

Method 1

9,000,000 shares outstanding for eight months:	
9,000,000 × 8/12	= 6,000,000
12,000,000 shares outstanding for four months:	
12,000,000 × 4/12	= 4,000,000
WAOS	= 10,000,000

Method 2	Number of Shares	×	Months Outstanding	=	Weighted No. of Shares
	9,000,000		8		72,000,000
	12,000,000		4		48,000,000
	Total				120,000,000

WAOS = 120,000,000 ÷ 12 months = 10,000,000

Method 3

9,000,000 shares outstanding for the full year:	
9,000,000 × 12/12	= 9,000,000
3,000,000 shares outstanding for four months:	
3,000,000 × 4/12	= 1,000,000
WAOS	= 10,000,000

Each of these methods generates the same correct answer and all are acceptable approaches. All illustrations in this chapter will use the first method.

ETHICAL ISSUES

The EPS calculation immediately incorporates the effect of a new issue of shares into the denominator. However, it is unrealistic to expect earnings (the numerator of EPS) to respond instantly to increased capital if the shares were issued to obtain capital for increasing productive capacity. Investing in production is highly worthwhile, but it takes a while to pay off. Until earnings rise in the future from the new investment, EPS is lower than before the share issue (hopefully temporarily) and management risks derision from investors who demand instant pay-off.

One situation in which EPS may not decline in response to a substantial new issue of ordinary shares is when the new shares are used to buy another company. This is called a **business combination** in accounting, but usually is called a **merger** in conversation. When new shares are used to acquire another company, the earnings of the acquired company appear in the buying company's earnings (and EPS) immediately, from the date of the acquisition.

Since EPS is the most-watched number by the majority of investors, many corporate mergers are motivated by managers' desire to demonstrate their success at increasing EPS. They can do this without making any additional investment in productive capital if the current earnings of the acquired company are high enough to offset the impact of the new shares on EPS. This is a practice known as **buying earnings**. Some company managers are quite adept at this; they often can manage to cover up declining internal profitability of the parent company through a "buying spree"—a series of acquisitions of other companies that creates the illusion of great growth and lots of "synergies" (that usually fail to materialize) but that often makes no real contribution to the intrinsic earnings ability of the buying company.

For example, suppose that Edgar Limited has one million shares outstanding and net earnings of $10 million—an EPS of $10. Now, suppose Edgar found a profitable but relatively underpriced company, Monica Inc., which Edgar could acquire by giving Monica shareholders 100,000 Edgar shares in exchange for all of the Monica shares. Monica would then be a wholly owned subsidiary of Edgar. As such, Monica's earnings would be included in Edgar's consolidated earnings. Suppose that in the next year, Edgar continued to earn $10,000,000 and Monica earned $2,000,000. Edgar's consolidated earnings would rise to $12,000,000 while the outstanding shares would be 1,100,000. Thus, Edgar's EPS would rise to $10.91 simply because they bought another company instead of increasing Edgar's profitability or productivity.

Contingently Issuable Shares

Contingently issuable ordinary shares are ordinary shares that are issuable for little or no cash, upon the satisfaction of specific conditions in a contingent share agreement. For example, a company may agree to issue common shares to a stakeholder if a licence for a new product is granted or issue shares to the former shareholders of an acquisition target company if the acquired operation achieves a certain level of post-acquisition profit. Contingently issuable shares are included as outstanding in WAOS *from the date that the necessary conditions have been met.* This applies even if the shares are not issued until a later date.

For example, assume that Chairot Limited signed an agreement as part of a business acquisition that committed Chairot to issue 10,000 common shares for no cash consideration if the target company produced 500,000 units of a subassembly in the first quarter after acquisition. This goal was met at the end of March 20X0 and the shares were issued in July 20X0. For the purposes of WAOS calculation, the shares would be treated as though they were issued when the contingency was met, at the end of March 20X0.

Stock Splits and Stock Dividends

An entity may issue or reduce shares outstanding without a corresponding change in resources, that is, for no consideration. If shares are issued under such circumstances, they are sometimes called **bonus shares**. Two common examples of this situation are in the case of a **stock dividend** or a **stock split**. A stock dividend is a dividend payable by issuing shares of the company's own common stock. Such shares *are not weight-averaged*. Instead, the stock dividend or stock split is treated as though it had been in effect for the whole period. It is also *adjusted through all prior years* that are reported as comparative data. That is, dividend shares and split shares are treated as though they had always been outstanding.

Remember, when a share dividend or split occurs, common share equity is not changed, nor is the composition of the broader capital structure affected (i.e., no change to long-term debt or other elements). There is no substantive change to the corporation's net asset structure. Splits and stock dividends do not bring new assets into the corporation and therefore cannot be expected to generate additional earnings. Earnings are simply split up into pieces of different size.

In order to ensure comparability of EPS, *all* reported prior years' EPS numbers are restated to reflect splits and dividends. In the case of a 2-for-1 split, all prior EPS figures will be divided by two because one share outstanding in previous years is equivalent to two shares outstanding after the split. The denominator of the fraction doubles, so the product is halved.

Example The following example illustrates the calculation of WAOS when there are bonus shares.

- A corporation has 5,000 common shares outstanding on 1 January, the beginning of the fiscal year.
- On 31 March, the conversion privilege on convertible bonds is exercised by the bondholders, resulting in an additional 2,400 shares being issued.
- On 1 September, the shares are split 2-for-1.
- On 1 October, an additional 3,000 shares are issued for cash.

In this example, each share outstanding prior to 1 September is equivalent to two shares outstanding after that date. The denominator of the EPS calculation must be adjusted to reflect the shares outstanding at the end of the year, after the stock split. The discontinuity that occurs as the result of the stock split must be adjusted by multiplying the pre-September outstanding shares by the split factor (in this example, × **2**) as follows:

WAOS calculation:		
1 January–31 March (pre-split)	5,000 × **2** × 3/12	2,500
1 April–31 August (pre-split)	7,400 × **2** × 5/12	6,167
1 September–30 September	14,800 × 1/12	1,233
1 October–31 December	17,800 × 3/12	4,450
WAOS		14,350

The 5,000 shares outstanding for the first three months are equivalent to 10,000 (5,000 × 2) shares after the split. Similarly, the 7,400 shares are multiplied by two to arrive at 14,800 post-split shares. Shares issued after the date of the split are *not* multiplied by two because they are stated in post-split shares.

Post-Year-End Split or Dividend If there is a stock dividend or stock split *after the end of the year* (in the next fiscal period), it is factored into the weighted-average calculation of the *current year*. This applies to stock dividends and splits that take place before the audit report is signed.

Assume a company's fiscal year ends on 31 December 20X5. Thirty thousand common shares have been outstanding for the entire period. On 15 January 20X6, before the audit is complete and the financial statements issued, the company executes a 1-for-3 reverse split. The 30,000 shares become 10,000 shares. This 10,000 figure will be used for EPS calculations, even though the reverse split happened after the end of the year. After all, by the time the financial statements are released, the shareholders will be holding their new, smaller shares, and all data should be applicable to this new capital arrangement.

Indirect Effects of a Split or Dividend A split or dividend will change the terms of all outstanding share commitment contracts. That is, when there is a stock split or stock dividend, the number of shares into which each senior security is convertible is adjusted accordingly. For example, if a $1,000 bond was convertible into four common shares prior to a 2-for-1 split (i.e., a conversion price of $250), then it will automatically be convertible into eight shares (a conversion price of $125) after the split. There is *always* an anti-dilution provision to protect the holders of convertible securities and options. Option contracts will also change, increasing the number of shares offered and decreasing the option price.

Example: Basic EPS

Exhibit 20-1 shows the computation of basic EPS in a situation involving a simple capital structure that has nonconvertible preferred shares. It is based on the following facts:

1. Capital structure:	
Common shares, no-par, outstanding on 1 January	90,000 shares
Common shares, issued 1 May for cash	6,000 shares
Preferred shares, no-par, $1.20 (cumulative, nonconvertible) outstanding on 1 January	5,000 shares
2. Earnings data for the year ending 31 December:	
Net earnings from continuing operations	$147,000
Discontinued operations, net of tax	30,000
Net earnings and comprehensive income	$177,000

Exhibit 20-1 presents the computation of the weighted-average number of common shares outstanding during the year. The numerator for basic EPS is adjusted for preferred dividends. Remember that earnings is *before* these dividends, and an adjustment is needed.

The two EPS figures of $1.50 and $1.82 must be reported on the face of the statement of comprehensive income. The $0.32 EPS figure for discontinued operations may be reported either on the statement of comprehensive income or in the disclosure notes.

Multiple Classes of Common Shares

As we saw in Chapter 14, Canadian corporations may have multiple classes of common, or ordinary, shares outstanding. These share classes *participate* in dividends. A primary reason for having two or more classes of common shares is to vary the voting rights between the different classes, normally in order to prevent the controlling shareholders from losing control to hostile investors. So-called "preferred shares" that participate fully in dividends also qualify as *ordinary shares*.

When evaluating a company with multiple classes of shares, it is important to evaluate their dividend privileges. If the dividend privileges are *different*, then EPS calculations must be done for each class. *If two or more classes share dividends equally, share for share, then they are all ordinary shares and are lumped together in the denominator of the EPS calculation.*

For example, assume that a corporation has two classes of ordinary voting shares, Class 1 and Class 2. The shares have equal dividend rights. If there were 100,000 Class 1 shares with 10 votes each and 400,000 Class 2 shares with one vote each outstanding throughout the year, then 500,000 shares would be used for WAOS. The *voting* differential does not matter for EPS; it is only the *dividend* differential that matters.

EXHIBIT 20-1

BASIC EPS CALCULATION

	Earnings Available to Common Shares	Weighted-Average Number of Shares	Earnings per Share
Earnings:			
Net earnings from continuing operations	$147,000		
Less: Preferred dividend cumulative entitlement: 5,000 shares × $1.20	(6,000)		
Earnings available to common, continuing operations	$141,000		
Net earnings	$177,000		
Less: Preferred dividend cumulative entitlement: 5,000 shares × $1.20	(6,000)		
Earnings available to common, net earnings	$171,000		
Shares outstanding:			
90,000 × 4/12		30,000	
96,000 × 8/12		64,000	
Weighted average		94,000	
Basic EPS:			
Earnings from continuing operations	$141,000	94,000	$1.50
Discontinued operations*	30,000	94,000	0.32
Net earnings	$171,000	94,000	$1.82

*This per share amount may be included in a disclosure note.

Unequal Dividend Entitlements If the sharing of dividends is *unequal*, more than one basic EPS statistic will be calculated.

For example, assume that a corporation has net income of $280,000. The company also has 20,000 Class A shares and 80,000 Class B shares outstanding throughout the year. Class A shares receive three times the dividend declared on Class B shares. In this case, WAOS would amount to 140,000 shares—[(20,000 Class A shares × 3) plus 80,000 Class B shares]. Dividing $280,000 by 140,000 WAOS gives us $2 per share. Therefore, basic EPS is $6 per share for Class A and $2 per share for Class B.

Complex/Unequal Dividend Entitlements Dividend arrangements may provide a base dividend, followed by participation in any remaining dividends declared. For example, assume now that both Class A and Class B ordinary shares are entitled to receive a $1 per share dividend. After this amount, Class A shares are entitled to receive $2 per share in dividends for every $1 per share paid to Class B. Profit for the year was $220,000. As in the previous example, there were 20,000 Class A shares and 80,000 Class B shares outstanding throughout the year.

To keep it simple, also assume that there are no preferred shares, no shares issued or retired during the year, and no discontinued operations included in earnings.

To calculate basic EPS when the two share classes participate differently in dividend declarations, profit is assigned to the classes according to the base dividend, and then *all* of the remaining profit is allocated according to the sharing arrangement. This allocation is based on a ratio, which is a combination of the number of shares outstanding in each class and their relative dividend entitlement.

The result is two earnings pools, which are then divided by the number of shares for each respective pool. Finally, EPS for each pool is the additive sum of the base dividend and the entitlement to undistributed earnings. The calculations are as follows:

Step 1—Calculate earnings minus the base dividend

Profit is $220,000, and the base dividend is $100,000
[$1 × (20,000 Class A shares plus 80,000 Class B shares)]
Unallocated profit: $220,000 – $100,000 = $120,000

Step 2—Allocate undistributed earnings to the share classes

Class A receives $120,000 ×1/3* = $40,000
Class B receives $120,000 × 2/3* = $80,000

*Class A share dividend entitlement, in equivalent Class B shares = 60,000 [i.e., (20,000 × 2)**]

There are 80,000 Class B shares outstanding = 80,000
Fractions: A: 40 ÷ (40 + 80) = 1/3; B: 80 ÷ (40 + 80) = 2/3

**The 20,000 Class A shares are entitled to two times the Class B dividend.

Step 3—Determine per share amounts (from step 2)

Class A: $40,000 ÷ 20,000 shares = $2
Class B: $80,000 ÷ 80,000 shares = $1

Step 4—Add base dividend to the step 3 amounts

Class A: $1 + $2 = $3
Class B: $1 + $1 = $2

Basic EPS for each class reflects both the base dividend plus the dividend that would be received if *all earnings* were declared as dividends. If the number of shares outstanding had changed during the period, the denominator would be a weighted average for each class.

Declared or Not? This example assumes that the base dividend was declared. If the dividend is not declared, but is *cumulative*, then nothing changes. However, if the base dividend is *not cumulative*, then it is lost if it is not declared, and excess dividends over the base in future years would follow the (step 2) residual allocation. Therefore, if the base is not cumulative and is not declared, step 1 would not be required in the EPS calculation. In the vast majority of cases, the base dividend is cumulative, so all steps are needed.

CONCEPT REVIEW

1. What type of corporation is required to disclose earnings per share amounts?
2. What is the formula for basic earnings per share?
3. How does earnings available to ordinary shares differ from net earnings?
4. Asquith Corporation has 2,000 common shares outstanding on 1 January 20X0, issues another 400 shares on 1 July 20X0, and declares a 2-for-1 stock split on 31 December 20X0. What is the weighted-average number of shares outstanding for the year? What is the impact of the stock split on prior years' EPS amounts?
5. List the steps in calculating basic EPS when there are multiple common share classes.

DILUTED EARNINGS PER SHARE

Real Dilution

Earnings dilution occurs when additional shares are issued without a proportionate increase in the level of total earnings. This happens when, after the new shares are issued, the denominator of the EPS ratio increases proportionately more than the numerator. Thus EPS declines, or is diluted. We discussed this phenomenon earlier in the chapter; a company that issues additional shares to finance new productive capacity will most likely suffer decreased EPS in that year and quite possibly in several future years, until the additional capacity is paying off through increased sales or greater efficiency, or both. Of course, dilution can also occur if new shares are issued to finance poor investments.

Stock market investors tend to be an impatient lot. A company that experiences dilution usually sees its share value drop. That is one reason that so many companies are "taken private" by major investors, private equity firms, or management buy-outs—after becoming a private enterprise, the owners can invest major new capital into improved productivity without being harassed by impatient shareholders and investment advisors. If the new investment is successful, then the private investors can convert the private enterprise into a public company once again. If the private investors sell their own shares, they of course make a profit, but they also are leaving the company in much stronger position than it was. Everyone wins.

Diluted EPS

"Real" dilution is the result of issuing new shares without an instantly commensurate increase in earnings. Dilution also arises in the future, however, when investors and/or creditors exercise conversion options and/or stock options into ordinary shares. Since there is a predictable outcome based on current commitments, accounting standards require companies to quantify this future potential effect by computing not only basic EPS but also *fully diluted EPS*.

Diluted earnings per share is based on the *hypothetical situation* of complete share issuance for any contract that may entitle its holder to ordinary shares in the future. Diluted EPS is hypothetical in that it reflects the results of share transactions that have not taken place but are quite likely to take place in the future. It is often called a "what if?" number—that is, what happens *if and when the corporation satisfies all if its commitments to issue ordinary shares*?

Elements to Include Diluted EPS reflects the earnings dilution that would result from future share transactions in the following circumstances:

- Dilutive options to purchase shares are exercised, *and*
- Dilutive convertible senior securities outstanding are converted to common shares, *and*
- Dilutive *contingently issuable ordinary shares* are issued, *and*
- Any shares actually issued *during the year* because of (dilutive) convertible senior securities, share option contracts, or contingently issuable ordinary shares had been issued at *the beginning* of the fiscal year.

Convertible senior securities include debt and preferred shares, senior to common shares in their entitlement to interest or dividends. If these are convertible to common shares at some point in the future or have been converted to common shares during the period, they will enter into the calculation of diluted EPS.

A **stock option** gives the holder the right to acquire a share at a stated price. Options sometimes are issued as a part of a package offering of securities (i.e., as a sweetener to attract buyers to a bond issue) and also are widely used as a form of executive compensation. There are various types of options, including stock rights, warrants, and employee stock options. In this chapter, the word "options" will be used to encompass all alternatives. If options were exercised and/or are outstanding, they will be considered when calculating diluted EPS.

As previously discussed, *contingently issuable ordinary shares* are ordinary shares that are issuable for little or no cash, upon the satisfaction of specific conditions in a contingent share agreement. If these agreements are in place or such shares have been issued during the year, they will be a factor in diluted EPS.

Dilutive versus Anti-Dilutive Diluted EPS is meant to be a worst-case scenario. **Dilutive** elements are those that, when included in EPS calculations, cause a decrease in earnings per share (or an increase in a loss per share). **Anti-dilutive** elements are those that cause earnings per share to increase (or a loss per share to decrease). If share agreements are anti-dilutive contracts, they are *excluded* from the calculation of diluted EPS. This is a realistic assumption—the investors holding anti-dilutive elements would have no reason to convert to ordinary shares because they would be worse off after converting.

Diluted EPS Calculation

To calculate diluted EPS, we start with basic EPS and make adjustments for the potential issuance of dilutive ordinary shares.

Adjustment for Dilutive Options Options are dilutive when they are in-the-money. Options are said to be **in-the-money** *if the exercise price is lower than the market value of common shares.* For example, if an option contract specifies a share price of $34.50, and the share price is $50, then the options are in-the-money. If the share price is $20, the options are not in-the-money. *Options are included in diluted EPS calculations when dilutive, that is, only when they are in-the-money.* This reflects the fact that no sane investor would exercise an option if it were *not* in-the-money.

Treasury Stock Method Dilution adjustments for options are based on the **treasury stock method**. When option holders exercise their options, they must pay the option price to the corporation. Under the treasury stock method, those proceeds are assumed to be used to reacquire and retire common shares at the average market price during the period.

For example, assume that 1,000 options are outstanding with an exercise price of $10. The average price of common shares during the year was $40, so these options are in-the-money. If the options were exercised, another 1,000 shares would be outstanding for the period, and the company would receive $10,000 (i.e., $10 × 1,000).

In diluted EPS calculations, it is assumed that this $10,000 is used to repurchase and retire other common shares, also at the beginning of the year. Ten thousand dollars would buy 250 shares ($10,000 ÷ $40). The *denominator* of diluted EPS would be increased by 1,000 shares issued and decreased by 250 shares retired. The net adjustment is an increase of 750 shares.

These 750 shares are sometimes referred to as *bonus shares*. This is based on the reasoning that the whole transaction can be viewed as $10,000 ($10 × 1,000) raised for 250 shares at full price ($10,000 total proceeds ÷ $40) and 750 shares issued for no consideration. The 750 bonus shares can be directly calculated as 1,000 × ($40 – $10) ÷ $40.

Note that options are dilutive when the number of shares issued is greater than the shares retired; this occurs *only when options are in-the-money.*

Adjustment for Contingently Issuable Shares As previously described, contingently issuable shares involve little or no cash consideration and must be issued on the resolution of a specified contingency. If the contingency is resolved during the period and the shares become issuable, the shares are included in WAOS for basic EPS as of the date that the contingency was resolved. If not all of the necessary conditions have been satisfied, *the shares might have to be included when calculating diluted EPS.*

If the contingency period has ended, then there is nothing contingent—the outcome is known. Therefore, shares are included if the only unmet condition is that the date of the contingency period has not yet expired. Dilutive shares are included *based on the shares issuable as though the end of the reporting period were the end of the contingency period.* The shares are included in the denominator as of (1) the beginning of the reporting period or (2) the date of the contingent share agreement, whichever is later. Contingently issuable shares have no impact on earnings, and thus there is *no change to the numerator* of diluted EPS.

For example, assume that HyperForce Ltd. acquired GH Resources for $15 million early in 20X1. The purchase and sale agreement specified that if GH's core operations earned at least $4,000,000 per year for three years, the former shareholders of GH would be entitled to 100,000 ordinary shares in HyperForce. Assume the GH operation earned $5,800,000 during 20X1. If the contingency, earnings performance, were to have concluded at the end of 20X1 (i.e., been for one year only), the shares would be issuable. Therefore, the 100,000 common shares are included in the denominator of diluted EPS calculation for 20X1, backdated to the date in 20X1 when the acquisition became effective.

These shares are included in diluted EPS even though the agreement states that *three years* of earnings must be earned to satisfy the contingency. All that is required for inclusion in diluted EPS is that the necessary conditions are met *as if the contingency period ended at the end of 20X1*. If, on the other hand, the agreement were written to require *cumulative earnings of $12 million* before the shares were issuable, then the shares would not have been included in diluted EPS at the end of 20X1 because the condition had not yet been met.

Adjustment for Dilutive Senior Securities Bond and preferred share adjustments are based on the **if-converted method**. Under this method, the numerator and denominator of the EPS ratio are adjusted as though *the securities had been converted at the beginning of the period (or at the date of issue, if later)*.

The *numerator* of the EPS fraction is adjusted for dividends or after-tax interest that would have been saved if the bonds or preferred shares had been converted. In other words, how would the numerator be different if the convertible bonds did not exist? Interest expense would be eliminated. What if the preferred shares did not exist? No preferred dividends would have been paid. The effect to the denominator is straightforward in both cases. More shares would be outstanding!

Technicalities to note:

1. If there are a variety of conversion terms, perhaps depending on when the conversion were to take place, *the most dilutive alternative must be used.*
2. If convertible securities were issued during the year, the assumed conversion goes *back only to the date of issue*, not the beginning of the year.
3. If the conversion option lapsed during the year or if the security was redeemed or settled during the year, the conversion is still included (if dilutive) *up to the time at which it lapsed.*

Calculation Rules To summarize the potential adjustments:

Element	Change to Numerator	Change to Denominator
Options—treasury stock method	None	1. Increase by shares issued 2. Decrease by shares retired
Contingently issuable shares	None	Increase by shares issued
Convertible bonds—if-converted method	Increase by after-tax interest avoided	Increase by shares issued
Convertible preferred shares—if-converted method	Increase by dividend claim avoided*	Increase by shares issued

*If there were any other items recorded in the financial statements, such as gains or losses on preferred share retirement, these items would have been adjusted when calculating the basic EPS numerator and also included in the numerator adjustment here.

Individual Effect Note that convertible bonds and convertible preferred shares involve a change to the numerator *and* a change to the denominator. The **individual effect** of each convertible item is represented by this ratio. For instance, if there was $10,000 of after-tax interest on a bond that was convertible into 40,000 common shares, the individual effect would be $0.25 ($10,000 ÷ 40,000).

The *individual effect* must be calculated separately for each potentially dilutive element. It is the change to earnings entitlement divided by additional shares that would have to be issued, and it is used to establish dilution or anti-dilution and sequence for convertible senior securities.

Steps in Calculating Diluted EPS

The steps in calculating diluted EPS are listed in Exhibit 20-2. A flow chart of the process is shown in Exhibit 20-3. We will explain these steps in the example that follows; refer to the list as the example progresses.

EXHIBIT 20-2

STEPS IN CALCULATING DILUTED EPS

To Calculate Diluted EPS:

1. **Begin with the basic EPS numbers**, based on *earnings from continuing operations.* If there were no discontinued operations, begin with the only basic EPS number available, basic EPS based on net earnings.
2. If any options were **exercised** during the period, **determine if the options exercised were in-the-money**, and thus dilutive. **Adjust the denominator** as though these shares had been issued at the beginning of the period, using the **treasury stock method**.
3. **Identify options outstanding throughout the year**, the option price, and the average share price for the period. Determine if the options are in-the-money, and thus dilutive. **Adjust the denominator** as though these shares were issued at the beginning of the period, using the **treasury stock method**. If options were **issued during the year**, backdate only to the date of issue. Calculate a subtotal at this point.
4. If any contingently issuable shares were **issued** during the period, **adjust the denominator** as though these shares were issued at the beginning of the period. This moves the share issuance back to the beginning of the year.
5. **Identify contingently issuable shares outstanding at the end of the year**. Calculate the number of shares, if any, that would be issued if the contingency period were to end at the end of the current fiscal year. **Adjust the denominator** as though these shares were issued at the beginning of the period. *Calculate a subtotal at this point.*
6. **Identify any convertible senior debt or shares that actually converted** during the period. **Calculate the individual effect** of the converted securities, using the **if-converted method**. This adjustment moves the conversion back to the beginning of the year. The individual effect is after-tax interest or dividends divided by shares issued. Both the numerator and denominator reflect the number of months **before conversion** in the fiscal year.
7. **Identify the terms and conditions of convertible senior shares and debt outstanding throughout the year.** If there are various conversion alternatives at different dates, *use the most dilutive alternative.* If convertible securities were **issued during the year**, backdate only to the date of issue. **Calculate the individual effect** of the converted securities, using the if-converted method.
8. Compare the individual effects of the items identified in steps 6 and 7. **Rank the items,** from most dilutive (lowest individual effect) to least dilutive (highest individual effect).
9. Return to the subtotal taken in step 5. **Include the effects of actual and potential conversions** in cascading order, from most dilutive to least dilutive. Use the ranking from step 8. **Calculate a subtotal** after each item is added. Exclude anti-dilutive items.
10. Use the **lowest calculation** as diluted EPS.
11. **Repeat the process,** beginning with *basic EPS for net earnings.* Use exactly the same adjustments to the numerator and the denominator as in the first calculation. *No second test for anti-dilution is allowed.*

EXHIBIT 20-3

FLOW CHART OF STEPS FOR CALCULATING DILUTED EPS

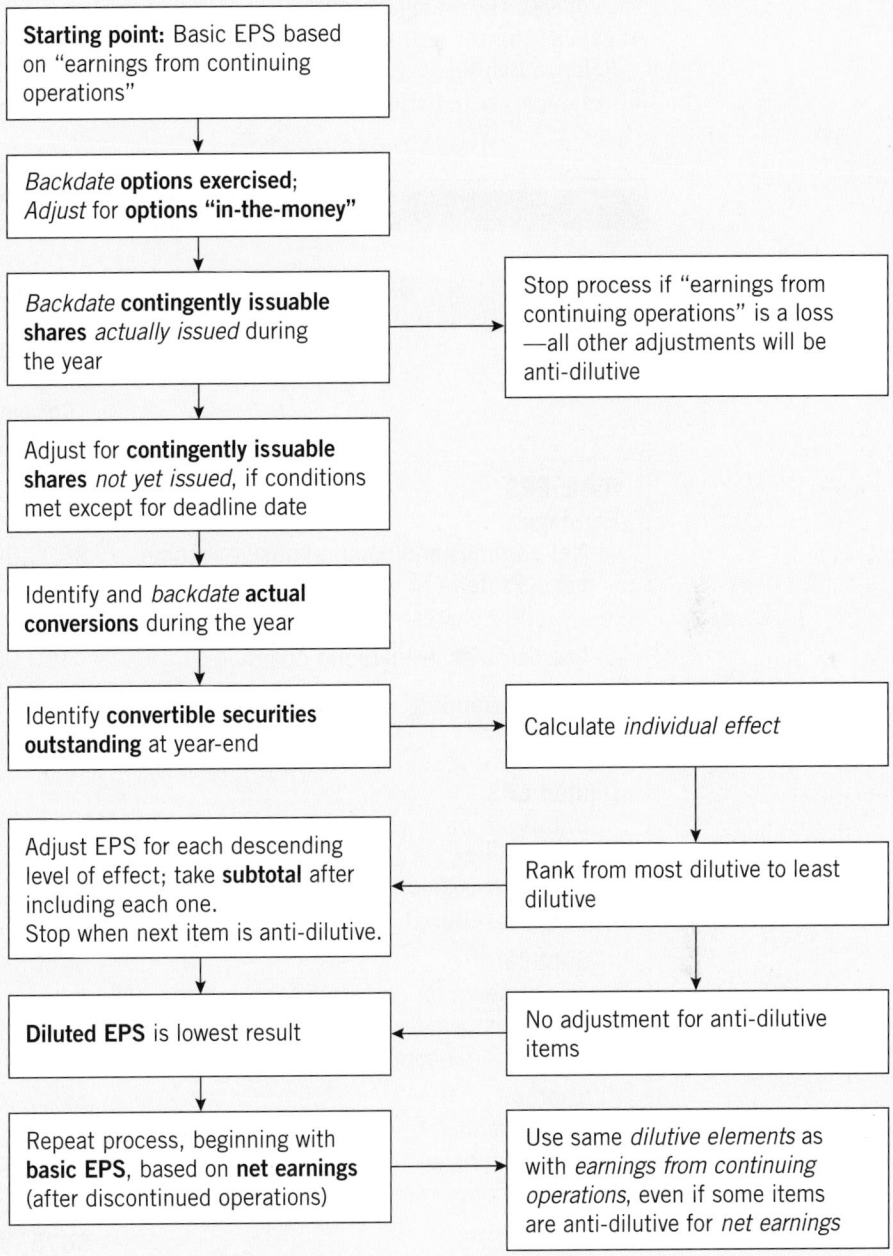

Diluted EPS Calculation: Example

Assume that a corporation has the following capital structure throughout all of 20X1:

- *Convertible debentures*: $1,000,000 maturity value, issued at 110; $100,000 of proceeds were attributable to the conversion option (and classified as shareholders' equity); 10% interest per annum, paid quarterly; convertible into 10 common shares for each $1,000 of bond maturity value at the option of the investor.
- *Convertible preferred shares*: 1,000 shares issued and outstanding; $150 annual per share dividend, cumulative; callable at $1,200 per share; convertible into common shares on a 5:1 basis until 20X5; convertible on a 10:1 basis thereafter.

- *Common shares*: 20,000 shares issued and outstanding all year.

Net earnings for 20X1 is $600,000 after income tax at a rate of 25%. There are no discontinued operations. There are no contingently issuable common shares. There are executive stock options outstanding all year, allowing purchase of 4,000 common shares at an option price of $50. The average market value of common shares during the period was $125. Interest expense for the year for the convertible bond was $120,000 ($1,000,000 × 12%).

Refer to Exhibit 20-2 to follow the steps for computing diluted EPS. The calculations for this example are in Exhibit 20-4.

EXHIBIT 20-4

BASIC AND DILUTED EPS CALCULATIONS

	Earnings Available to Common Shares	Weighted-Average Number of Shares	Earnings per Share
Basic EPS:			
Earnings:			
Net earnings and comprehensive income	$600,000		
Less: Preferred dividends:			
1,000 shares × $150	(150,000)		
Net earnings available to common	450,000		
Shares outstanding		20,000	
Basic EPS	**$450,000**	**20,000**	**$22.50**
Diluted EPS:			
Data from basic EPS, above	$450,000	20,000	$22.50
Adjustments for assumed options exercise:			
Shares issued		4,000	
Shares retired		(1,600)	
Subtotal	$450,000	22,400	$20.09
Adjustments for debenture conversion:			
Interest avoided (after-tax equivalent)	75,000		
Additional common shares issued		10,000	
Subtotal	$525,000	32,400	$16.20
Adjustments for preferred share conversion:			
Dividends avoided	150,000		
Additional common shares issued		10,000	
Diluted EPS	**$675,000**	**42,400**	**$15.92**

Starting Point The first step is to start with earnings before discontinued operations. Since this example has no discontinued operations, we can start with basic EPS of $22.50, as calculated at the top of Exhibit 20-4. Also, there are no shares issued under option contracts during the year, no contingently issuable common shares, and no actual conversions of senior securities during the period. Therefore, steps 2, 4, 5, 6, and 11 can be skipped. (A later comprehensive example will deal with these situations.)

Options Outstanding options are the next thing to consider (step 3). The company has outstanding options to issue 4,000 common shares at $50. The $50 option price is less than the $125 average market price of shares during the period, and therefore these options are *in-the-money* and dilutive. They must be included in diluted EPS.

If these shares had been issued at the beginning of the period, another 4,000 shares would have been outstanding for the whole period, increasing the denominator by 4,000 shares. The total proceeds would have been $200,000 (i.e., 4,000 × $50).

In the diluted EPS calculation, we assume that the proceeds would have been used to retire other common shares at the market price: 1,600 shares ($200,000 ÷ $125). The denominator increases by 2,400 shares (4,000 – 1,600) and the numerator does not change. We also can make this 2,400 share calculation directly: 4,000 × ($125 – $50) ÷ $125 = 2,400.

Convertible Securities In step 7, we calculate the individual effects of potential conversion of the two convertible securities. The numerator of the EPS fraction is adjusted by the amount of dividends or after-tax interest that will be saved if the senior securities are converted. The additional shares are added to the denominator.

Convertible debentures The debentures are convertible at the rate of 10 shares per $1,000. That works out to potential issuance of 10,000 additional shares that would be added to the denominator of the EPS ratio. Bond interest on the debentures is $100,000 before tax, which is $75,000 after 25% tax.

The *individual effect* of this convertible bond is $7.50 ($75,000 ÷ 10,000). When compared with the basic EPS of $22.50, we can readily see that this is dilutive (i.e., $7.50 is lower than $22.50).

Convertible preferred shares If the 1,000 shares of preferred shares had been converted at the beginning of the year, preferred dividends of $150,000 would have been avoided. Dividends are not tax deductible, and so we need no tax adjustment before adding this amount to the numerator.

The shares may be converted at the rate of 5:1 until the end of 20X5, and then the conversion ratio changes to 10:1. *The worst-case scenario, or more dilutive alternative, must be used in these calculations.* This is the 10:1 ratio. Thus, another 10,000 shares could potentially be issued. This gives us an *individual effect* of $15 (i.e., $150,000 ÷ 10,000 shares), which is dilutive in relation to basic EPS but is less dilutive than the *individual effect* of $7.50 for the bonds. This comparison is the step 8 ranking.

Ranking Now for step 9. The bonds' individual effect of $7.50 is more dilutive than the preferred shares' individual effect of $15, and the effect of the most dilutive is taken first. After the dilutive effect of the bonds is taken into account, a subtotal is taken before the convertible preferred shares are considered. Inclusion of the bonds reduces diluted EPS to $16.20.

Next, the preferred shares' individual affect of $15 is compared with this new EPS subtotal of $16.20, which shows that the preferred shares still are dilutive. The dilutive effects of the preferred shares are then added in.

Step 10 is the final determination of diluted EPS—$15.92.

Reporting Diluted EPS

Diluted EPS is reported on the face of the statement of comprehensive income, given equal prominence with basic EPS. Even if the two numbers are identical, they must both be disclosed. In the above example, the company would report:

Basic EPS	$22.50
Diluted EPS	$15.85

Diluted EPS Cascade

In Exhibit 20-4, we illustrated the **diluted EPS cascade** of adjustments, going from the most dilutive to the least dilutive. Note that options that are in-the-money (and any contingently issuable ordinary shares) are always dilutive because they involve no increase to the numerator. That is why they are *always done first* in diluted EPS calculations.

The *individual effect* tells us which other elements are potentially dilutive, but only in relation to unadjusted basic EPS. However, that is just at the first stage. An apparently dilutive element may turn out to be anti-dilutive when it gets its turn to be considered. The convertible securities with the *lowest individual EPS effect* are the most dilutive, and are entered first. If inclusion of a later item causes EPS to *increase*, it is *anti-dilutive and excluded.*

For instance, suppose that a company has $100,000 earnings available to common shareholders and 100,000 weighted-average ordinary shares. The company's basic EPS is $1. Two potentially dilutive securities are outstanding:

- Preferred shares, with a $45,000 dividend and a 100,000 share entitlement ($0.45 individual effect); and
- Bonds, with after-tax interest of $68,000, and a share entitlement of 75,000 shares ($0.91 individual effect).

Both elements look dilutive when compared to basic EPS of $1 but preferred shares are the more dilutive.

After the more dilutive preferred shares are included, diluted EPS is $0.73: ($100,000 + $45,000) ÷ (100,000 + 100,000). The bonds, with an individual effect of $0.91, are *no longer dilutive*. If they were included, diluted EPS would *increase* to $0.77: ($100,000 + $45,000 + $68,000) ÷ (100,000 + 100,000 + 75,000).

Diluted EPS is reported as $0.73, and the second security is omitted from the calculation. This is the cascade approach to diluted EPS calculations, and it results in diluted EPS being reported as the lowest possible number.

Actual Conversions During the Period

So far, we have illustrated diluted EPS giving effect to the year-end obligations to issue shares. Diluted EPS must also include calculations that reflect actual conversions, actual contingently issuable shares issued, and actual options exercised during the period. This adjustment is often called **backdating**: *adjusting the actual issuance as though it took place at the beginning of the period.* Backdating is done only if the result is dilutive.

The reason for backdating is to facilitate forward comparisons. In the years following the conversion, the full effects of the conversion will be reflected in basic EPS in that year, which will not be fully comparable with EPS in the year of the conversion because it included only a partial effect (i.e., following the date of actual conversion). Backdating puts actual conversions on the same footing as potential conversions, which are effectively backdated to the beginning of the fiscal period.

Steps 2, 4 and 6 in Exhibit 20-2 deal with backdating. The following examples demonstrate actual conversions of preferred shares, actual conversion of debt, and shares issued on the exercise of options.

Example 1—Converted Preferred Shares Assume that a corporation has two classes of shares outstanding:

- Class A preferred shares, 600 shares issued and outstanding at the beginning of the year; annual dividend rate of $1,000 per share, cumulative, dividend paid at the end of each quarter; each share is convertible into 50 shares of Class B common.
- Class B common shares, 50,000 shares issued and outstanding at the beginning of the year.

Also assume that:

- There are no other senior securities.
- Net earnings for 20X1, the year of the conversion, is $2,175,000; there are no discontinued operations.
- All 600 shares of Class A are converted into 30,000 Class B shares on 1 October 20X1; dividends for the first three quarters of the year were fully paid.

- Options are outstanding to issue 10,000 common shares to senior executives for $1 per share; the average share price during the year was $8. No options were exercised during the period. These options were outstanding during the whole year.

Basic earnings per share for 20X1 is $30, as calculated at the top of Exhibit 20-5. Diluted EPS begins with this figure, and then includes the effect of options. (Step 3 as listed in Exhibit 20-2). This reduces EPS to $26.04. Note that the options effect could be directly calculated as a reduction to the denominator of 8,750 shares [10,000 × ($8 – $1) ÷ $8]. The result is the same.

In 20X1, all 600 Class A shares were converted into 30,000 Class B shares (at 50 Class B shares per Class A share). For basic EPS, these newly issued shares would be multiplied by

EXHIBIT 20-5

BASIC AND DILUTED EPS CALCULATIONS

Actual Conversion of Preferred Shares

	Earnings Available to Common Shares	Weighted-Average Number of Shares	Earnings per Share
Basic EPS:			
Earnings:			
Net earnings	$2,175,000		
Less: Preferred dividends:			
600 shares × $250 per quarter × three quarters	(450,000)		
Earnings available to common	$1,725,000		
Shares outstanding			
50,000 × 9/12		37,500	
[50,000 + (600 Class A × 50 Class B)] × 3/12		20,000	
Basic EPS	**$1,725,000**	**57,500**	**$30.00**
Diluted EPS			
Data from basic EPS, above	$1,725,000	57,500	
Adjustments for assumed options exercise:			
Shares issued		10,000	
Shares retired (10,000 × $1) ÷ $8		(1,250)	
Subtotal	$1,725,000	66,250	$26.04
Adjustments for converted shares:			
Dividends on converted shares: 600 shares × $250 × three quarters	450,000		
Adjust shares for preceding three quarters: (600 Class A × 50 Class B) × 9/12		22,500	
Diluted EPS	**$2,175,000**	**88,750**	**$24.51**

the 3/12 of the year that they were outstanding and added to the *weighted-average* number of shares used in basic EPS. However, in future years there will be 30,000 additional Class B shares outstanding *all year*. Diluted EPS backdates the conversion (step 6). This is demonstrated in the highlighted section of Exhibit 20-5. There are two steps to the process of backdating:

- Profit available to common shareholders, the numerator, is adjusted for the dividends on the converted Class A shares that would not have been paid if the shares had converted at the beginning of the period. This is $450,000 ($250 per quarter × 600 shares × 3 quarters).
- The weighted-average number of shares is adjusted to reflect the full volume of additional Class B shares issued for the conversion, that is, 30,000 shares × 9/12, or 22,500 shares.

The *individual effect* of this conversion is $20 ($450,000 ÷ 22,500), which is dilutive in relation to the diluted EPS subtotal of $26.04. As a result, diluted EPS now drops to $24.51.

Example 2—Converted Debt Assume that a corporation has one class of shares outstanding but also has convertible bonds, some of which were converted during 20X1:

- 50,000 common shares are outstanding at the beginning of 20X1.
- Reported profit for 20X1 is $3,000,000; there are no discontinued operations.
- The corporation has $40 million principal amount of 10-year, 9%, convertible debentures that were issued five years previously. All are still outstanding at the beginning of 20X1. Each $1,000 face value of bonds is convertible into two shares of common stock at the investor's option, and thus the full $40 million would be convertible into 80,000 shares.
- Interest is paid semi-annually on 1 March and 1 September.
- The net proceeds from the bond issue amounted to $42 million. The present value of the liability cash flow at the date of issue was $40 million; the remaining $2 million was allocated to the conversion option. At the date of issuance, the market rate of interest for nonconvertible bonds of similar risk was 9%.
- On 30 June 20X1, one-quarter of the bonds are converted.
- The corporation's income tax rate is 25%.

The conversion of $10,000,000 principal amount of bonds results in an additional 20,000 shares issued. In the basic EPS calculation, the additional shares are outstanding for the second half of the year and are weighted proportionately in the denominator. The EPS numerator already includes, in earnings, a deduction for 9% (pretax) interest on $40,000,000 for the first half of the year and on $30,000,000 for the second half of the year following conversion. The calculation of basic EPS is shown at the top of Exhibit 20-6.

To calculate diluted EPS, the conversion must be backdated to the beginning of the year (step 6). The effect of the remaining unconverted bonds must be included (step 9). Both of these adjustments are made *only if dilutive*.

For backdating, the EPS numerator must be reduced by the six months' interest actually paid on the $10,000,000 principal amount of converted bonds. At 9% per annum and with a 25% income tax rate, the first six-months' interest on the converted bonds was:

$$\text{Interest expense} = \$10{,}000{,}000 \times 9\% \times (1.00 - 0.25) \times 6/12 = \$337{,}500$$

In general, the formula for computing the interest savings from conversion is:

Principal amount converted × interest rate × (1 − tax rate) × fraction of year *before* conversion.

For example, if the bonds had been retired after four months of the fiscal year, four months of interest would be added back.

The highlighted section of Exhibit 20-6 shows the add-back of $337,500 after-tax interest expense, and the weighted-average number of shares is increased to reflect the full amount of shares issued on conversion. Shares are calculated as 20,000 shares × 6/12. The EPS *individual effect* is $33.75 (i.e., $337,500 ÷ 10,000), which is dilutive, relative to basic EPS of $50.

Finally, the assumed conversion of the remaining dilutive convertible bonds must be considered. The interest expense for these still-outstanding bonds is:

Interest expense = $30,000,000 × 9% × (1.00 – 0.25 = $2,025,000

Shares to be issued would be 60,000 [($30,000,000 ÷ $1,000) × 2], and the *individual effect* of the bonds is $33.75 (i.e., $2,025,000 ÷ 60,000). These bonds are dilutive. The adjustment is included in Exhibit 20-6, resulting in final diluted EPS of $41.25.

EXHIBIT 20-6

BASIC AND DILUTED EPS CALCULATIONS

Partial Actual Conversion of Debt

	Earnings Available to Common Shares	Weighted-average Number of Shares	Earnings per Share
Basic EPS:			
Earnings:			
Net earnings	$3,000,000		
Earnings available to common	$3,000,000		
Shares outstanding:			
50,000 shares × 6/12		25,000	
70,000 shares × 6/12		35,000	
Basic EPS	**$3,000,000**	**60,000**	**$50.00**
Diluted EPS:			
Data from basic EPS, above	$3,000,000	60,000	
Adjustments for converted debt:			
Remove after-tax interest on converted debt: $10,000,000 × 9% × (1.00 – 0.25) × 6/12	337,500		
Adjust shares for first six months: 20,000 shares × 6/12		10,000	
Subtotal	$3,337,500	70,000	$46.68
Adjustment for remaining convertible debt:			
Removed after-tax interest on remaining debt: $30,000,000 × 9% × (1.00 – 0.25)	2,025,000		
Shares ($30,000,000 ÷ $1,000) × 2 shares per bond		60,000	
Diluted EPS	**$5,363,500**	**130,000**	**$41.25**

Note that the individual effect of the converted bonds and the unconverted bonds is identical—it does not matter which is done first in the cascade.

Example 3—Exercised Options If options had been exercised during the period, we would need to make an adjustment to backdate these shares to the beginning of the period *if they were dilutive*. Again, the treasury stock method would be applied for that portion of the year.

For example, suppose that a holder exercised options for 10,000 shares at $1 per share on 1 November, for a total consideration of $10,000. The average share price for the first 10 months of the year was $9. When calculating basic EPS, these shares would be weight-averaged in the denominator for two months.

For diluted EPS, as in step 2, the shares must be backdated to the start of the year. The denominator is increased by 8,333 (10,000 × 10/12) for shares issued. As always, the adjustment is made only if the options are in-the-money, and thus are dilutive.

Note that the $9 average market price used was the average for the first 10 months of the year, which is more applicable to this calculation than the average for the entire year.

CONCEPT REVIEW

1. What is the purpose of calculating diluted EPS?
2. Explain the difference between dilutive and anti-dilutive elements.
3. What is added to the numerator of diluted EPS for convertible bonds? For convertible preferred shares?
4. Assume basic EPS is $5. Two potentially dilutive elements exist, with an individual effect of $1 and $4.50, respectively. Under what circumstances would the $4.50 item be considered anti-dilutive?
5. How do actual conversions of senior securities affect the calculation of diluted EPS?
6. What assumption is made regarding the proceeds of option contracts when calculating diluted EPS? When are options dilutive?

COMPLICATING FACTORS

Convertible Securities and Options Issued During the Year

If convertible securities are issued during the year, the effect of a hypothetical conversion is backdated in the calculation of diluted EPS *only to the date of issue*. For example, suppose that DRV Corporation issued 8% convertible bonds payable on 1 November. When measuring interest expense, of course, only two months' interest would have been recorded. In calculating diluted EPS, two months' interest (not 12 months'!) is added to the numerator and two months of shares (not 12 months'!) are added to the denominator. That is, the bond is assumed to be converted on the date of issuance *if it was issued during the period*. Next year, when the bonds have been outstanding for a full year, the adjustments revert to normal—a full year.

The reason for not backdating new debt to the beginning of the year is that the additional capital introduced into the firm by issuing new debt has contributed to earnings only from the date of issue, not for the entire year. Remember that the numerator and denominator of the EPS ratio must always be consistent with each other.

Similarly, if options are issued during the year, they are backdated *only to the date of issuance* in diluted EPS calculations. Employee stock options are often issued at the end of a fiscal period, which means that they do not affect diluted EPS in their first year.

An illustration of this situation is included in the final example in the chapter.

Convertible Securities and Options Extinguished During the Year

What happens if a company has convertible securities or options during the year that are redeemed or settled in cash, or that expire during the year? Accounting standards specify that in that situation, the potential common shares, *if dilutive,* are included in the calculation of diluted EPS only up to the date of redemption, settlement, or expiry.

In practice, such securities or options would never be dilutive, and thus this is not something one really needs to worry about. If the holder of a convertible security accepts a cash repayment instead of converting, it is because the security is *not* in-the-money. If a security is in-the-money, issuers often call in the bonds for redemption in order to force holders to convert. This practice is called **forced conversion**.

The treatment of options is a little different. Suppose that options were outstanding until they expired on 30 September. The fact that they expired unexercised means that they were not in-the-money on the expiry date, but *theoretically* they may have been in-the-money earlier in the fiscal year. The options would be factored into diluted EPS for any period before 30 September during which they were in-the-money.

Reference Point for Diluted EPS

EPS on earnings from continuing operations always should be the yardstick used for assessing dilution versus anti-dilution. All decisions are made with this as the starting point. So, if an item is included for earnings from continuing operations, it is *also always included* for EPS based on net earnings.

For example, assume that earnings from continuing operations is $450,000. There is an after-tax loss from discontinued operations of $200,000, resulting in net earnings of $250,000. There are 10,000 common shares outstanding all year, and no preferred shares. Basic EPS is $45 based on earnings before the discontinued operation and $25 based on net earnings. Convertible debt, with after-tax interest of $70,000 and a share entitlement of 2,500 shares, is outstanding.

The individual dilutive effect of the convertible debt is $28 ($70,000 ÷ 2,500). This is dilutive to EPS calculated on earnings from continuing operations, but anti-dilutive to EPS calculated on net earnings. Nevertheless, the item must be included in diluted EPS for *both measures of diluted EPS.*

Diluted EPS will be as follows:

- For *earnings from continuing operations*:
  ($450,000 + $70,000) ÷ (10,000 + 2,500) = $41.60
- For *net earnings*:
  ($250,000 + $70,000) ÷ 12,500 = $25.60

Diluted EPS for net earnings, at $25.60, is higher than basic EPS of $25! But the bonds have to be included for both diluted EPS measures, since they were definitely dilutive for earnings from continuing operations.

Interest Expense or Interest Paid?

There are many situations in which a bond is offered at a discount or premium. When that happens, interest *expense* will include discount or premium amortization and will not coincide with amount of interest *paid.* In diluted EPS calculations, the adjustment to the numerator (i.e., earnings available to common shareholders) *must always be for interest expense.* A simple adjustment based on the nominal rate of interest will not work—discount or premium amortization must also be taken into account. Remember that we are adjusting earnings, and earnings reflect interest expense, not the amount of interest paid.

In the examples and problems in this chapter, we usually assume that the nominal interest rate is the same as the market rate to simplify calculations. But be aware that if this simplifying assumption is not in place, *the required adjustment is for interest expense, not interest paid.*

Measuring Share Price

Average share price is used to determine whether options are in-the-money and to calculate the share adjustment for the denominator of diluted EPS. Accounting standards state that a simple average of weekly or monthly prices is usually appropriate. If prices fluctuate widely over the period being used, an average of the high and low point for the period will usually be a more representative value than the closing price. If shares are thinly traded, an average of bid and asked price may be appropriate. Using average share price is justified because profit (the numerator for EPS) is generated *over the period,* and the denominator should also reflect the entire year.

However, use of averages can be problematic. Assume that share price on average was $40 for the period, but falls to $25 at the end of the fiscal year. Options are outstanding with a per-share price of $30. These options are in-the-money with respect to average share price, but not in relation to the closing price. If the closing market price is a good predictor of share price through the coming year, diluted EPS will imply an option exercise that would not be economically logical.[1] Average share price is used.

Diluted EPS in a Loss Year

When a company has reported a loss from continuing operations, adding *anything* positive to the numerator and/or increasing the number of common shares outstanding will *reduce the loss per share* and be anti-dilutive. Thus, diluted EPS is equal to basic EPS in a loss year because all potentially dilutive items will be anti-dilutive.

What if a company reported a loss of $100,000 from continuing operations but a gain of $500,000 from discontinued operations? Net earnings would be positive, at $400,000. Dilutive securities and options *are still classified as anti-dilutive* because the dilution test is performed with reference to earnings from continuing operations. If it is dilutive—or anti-dilutive—to the top line, it must be classified consistently thereafter.

Bonds Convertible at the Issuer's Option

Convertible bonds may be convertible at the option of either the investor or the issuer. The examples shown above have dealt with convertible bonds that are convertible at the option of the investor. *If it is the company's option to issue shares or cash on the maturity date, the bonds still must be considered for diluted EPS calculations.* The company cannot avoid inclusion by claiming that it intends to repay the bond with cash rather than shares. If the result is dilutive, the bond is included in diluted EPS calculations.

FVTPL Liabilities

Most liabilities are carried at amortized cost. Some, however, are classified as fair value through profit and loss (FVTPL) financial instruments. A company may designate a liability as FVTPL on initial recognition for a variety of reasons, including the need to avoid a mismatch if a related, hedged asset must be valued at fair value, if the liabilities are managed with reference to their fair value, or to simplify valuation if there is an embedded derivative in the liability.

FVTPL liabilities are valued at fair value, and changes in fair value are recorded as a component of earnings. If these liabilities are convertible bonds, then in the calculation of diluted EPS, their effect on net earnings includes fair value changes. Any gain or loss on the change in fair value that is included in net earnings must be adjusted on the numerator, after tax, and considered when evaluating whether the liability is dilutive or anti-dilutive.

---

[1] Several exposure drafts in this area have suggested the use of closing market values, but standard setters have not yet made any change.

CONCEPT REVIEW

1. What is the reference point for the dilution test?
2. When there is a difference between interest expense and interest paid, which number is used for convertible bonds in diluted EPS?
3. Why is diluted EPS generally equal to basic EPS in a loss year?

COMPREHENSIVE ILLUSTRATION

Having discussed all of the pieces of basic and diluted EPS, we'll now turn to a comprehensive illustration. Exhibit 20-7 contains the information for this example, and Exhibit 20-8 works through the EPS calculations.

This example uses data from FRM Corporation, a public corporation. The company has a complex capital structure that includes bonds and three classes of shares. At the beginning of the year, one class of convertible bond was outstanding, and a second class of convertible bonds was issued during the year. The Class A shares are publicly traded and are listed on the TSX. Each Class A share has one vote. The Class B common shares have 20 votes each. Class B shares are closely held by the company's founding family, as are the preferred shares. Although Class A and Class B have different voting rights, in all other respects the two classes of common shares are equal, including the rights to dividends and to assets upon dissolution.

As we can see in Exhibit 20-7, two of the bond issues are convertible (into Class A), as are the preferred shares (into Class B). In addition, there are contingently issuable Class A shares and employee stock options outstanding that give the holder the right to acquire one Class A share for each option held.

Before beginning the calculations, it is important to take notice of any changes in the capital structure that occurred during the year. Exhibit 20-7 shows the capital structure at the *end* of the fiscal year, but the *additional information* states that there was a partial conversion of the 10% debentures on 1 October. That piece of information is important for two reasons:

1. Shares were outstanding for only *part* of the year, which means that the weighted-average number of shares outstanding must be calculated for basic EPS, *and*
2. If dilutive, the conversion must be backdated when calculating diluted EPS.

The 8% convertible bonds were issued on 1 May. This is important because when the bonds are considered for diluted EPS calculation, they will be backdated only to the date of issue, or 8/12 of the year. Also note that the second set of options was issued on 31 December 20X1, at the end of the fiscal year. When backdating, these options are also backdated to the day of issue, giving them a weight of 0/12.

Basic EPS The top section of Exhibit 20-8 presents the calculation of basic EPS. The starting point is earnings from continuing operations, which is then reduced by the preferred dividends. Class A and Class B share *equally* in dividends, and therefore they are added together for the denominator without adjustment. The weighted-average number of shares reflects the new shares issued on 1 October. Basic EPS is $8.09 for earnings from continuing operations. The EPS effect of the discontinued operation is $1.80 ($200,000 ÷ 111,200) and EPS for net earnings is $9.89 [($1,200,000 – $100,000) ÷ 111,200].

Diluted EPS Diluted EPS must be calculated. The first item to evaluate is options, dilutive when the option price is less than market value. Refer back to the steps needed to calculate diluted EPS (see Exhibit 20-2). This is step 3; step 2 is not needed.

Only the first group of options, for 3,000 shares, must be evaluated. We should use lowest option price of $30 because it is the most dilutive and is in-the-money. Exercising the

EXHIBIT 20-7

FRM CORPORATION

Data for Comprehensive EPS Illustration

Year Ended 31 December 20X1

Capital Structure, 31 December 20X1:

Long-term debt:	
12% first mortgage bonds, due 1 July 20X9	$1,300,000
10% unsecured debentures, due 31 July 20X7, convertible into Class A common shares at $50 at any time prior to maturity	$ 960,000
8% unsecured debentures, due 15 April 20X20, convertible into 12,000 Class A common shares on or after 31 December 20X12	$1,500,000
Share capital:	
Preferred shares, dividend rate of $20 per share, cumulative and nonparticipating, convertible to Class B common shares at the rate of two shares of Class B for each share of preferred	5,000 shares
Class A common shares, one vote per share	104,800 shares
Class B common shares, 20 votes per share, sharing dividends equally with Class A common shares	10,000 shares

Options:
3,000 employee stock options issued on 31 December 20X0, each exchangeable for one Class A share as follows:

$30 per share prior to 1 January 20X4
$40 per share between 1 January 20X4 and 31 December 20X7
$55 per share between 1 January 20X8 and 31 December 20X10
The options expire at the close of business on 31 December 20X10

5,000 employee stock options, issued on 31 December 20X1, each exchangeable for one Class A share at a price of $25 per share prior to 31 December 20X11. The options expire at the close of business on 31 December 20X11.

Contingent shares:
FRM entered into a contingent share agreement in 20X0 when it acquired another company. FRM must issue 9,000 Class A shares in March of 20X4 if the acquired company's core operations earn $400,000 before tax each year from the acquisition date through 20X3. To date, earnings have surpassed this level.

Additional information:

- After-tax earnings for the year ended 31 December 20X1 were $1,200,000; this was after a $200,000 after-tax gain from discontinued operations.
- The income tax rate was 25%.
- The average market value of common shares during the period was $45.
- Dividends were paid quarterly on the preferred shares; there are no dividends in arrears.
- Dividends of $1 per quarter were declared on both Class A and Class B shares; the dividends were payable to shareholders of record at the end of each calendar quarter, and were paid five business days thereafter.
- On 1 October 20X1, 10% debentures with a principal amount of $240,000 were converted into 4,800 Class A shares (included in the outstanding shares listed above). At the beginning of the year, the total principal amount of the 10% debentures was $1,200,000.
- On 1 May 20X1, FRM issued $ 1,500,000 face value of 8% unsecured debentures, due 15 April 20X20, convertible into 12,000 Class A common shares on or after 31 December 20X12. The bonds were issued for $1,650,000, and $150,000 of the proceeds was classified in equity as the value of the conversion option.

options would raise additional capital of $90,000 (3,000 shares × $30). Retirement is calculated as $90,000 ÷ $45, or 2,000 shares. The net increase to the denominator is 1,000 shares (3,000 – 2,000). This can be directly calculated as [3,000 × ($45 – $30)] ÷ $45.

The second set of options was issued on 31 December 20X1. These options have no EPS effect because options are backdated only to the day of issue, which was the end of the current year. Now, let us move through the rest of the steps for this example.

Contingently issued shares Step 4—contingently issued shares actually issued during the year—is not needed because no new shares were actually issued during the period as the result of satisfying a contingency.

Contingently issuable shares Step 5 evaluates the 9,000 contingently issuable shares. These shares must be included in the denominator of diluted EPS because if the contingency period were to have ended at the end of 20X1, the shares would have to be issued because earnings targets have been met to date. There is no adjustment to the numerator for contingently issuable shares. These numbers are included in the calculation of diluted EPS, reducing the subtotal to $7.43.

Convertible debt or senior shares We now proceed to steps 6, 7, and 8 (refer to Exhibit 20-2.). The highlighted section of Exhibit 20-8 shows the calculation of individual effects for the preferred shares and convertible debt:

- *Preferred shares.* Each share of the convertible preferred has a dividend of $20. Each is convertible into two shares of Class B common. The individual effect is $20 ÷ 2 = $10. This is clearly anti-dilutive to basic EPS of $8.09. Preferred shares will be excluded from the diluted EPS calculation. (Note that the individual effect calculation can be based on the outstanding preferred share issue as a whole or on a per-share basis; the result is the same.)
- *10% debenture, actual conversion.* The conversion occurred on 1 October 20X1. This conversion must be backdated for 9/12 of the year, back to 1 January. Both after-tax interest and the number of shares are adjusted. Additional interest would be $24,000 ($240,000 × 10%) for a year, but is $13,500 after being multiplied by (1 – 25% tax rate) and by 9/12 of the year. Shares issued were 4,800, as used in the basic calculation, but are backdated by multiplying by 9/12 of the year. The *individual effect* is $3.75.
- *10% debentures.* Interest on the $960,000 principal amount is $96,000. Since the interest is deductible for income tax purposes, the effect of the interest on net earnings is $72,000, that is, $96,000 × (1 – 0.25). At a conversion price of $50, the $960,000 bonds can be converted into 19,200 Class A common shares ($960,000 ÷ $50). The *individual effect* is $3.75.
- *8% debentures.* These debentures carry interest of $120,000 pretax or $90,000 after-tax. They are convertible into 12,000 Class A common shares. The *individual effect* is $7.50. Both the interest and issuable shares are backdated from 31 December to the date of issuance, 1 May of the current year. This is a factor of 8/12 for both the numerator and the denominator.

The Cascade In steps 9 and 10 (see Exhibit 20-2), the securities are included in diluted EPS *in order of their dilutive effects:*

- First the 10% debentures, both the actual conversion and the assumed conversion. Their order does not matter, since their individual effects are the same. The subtotal is now $6.84.
- The 8% debentures, with an individual effect of $7.50, looked dilutive with respect to basic EPS of $8.09. However, they are anti-dilutive to the subtotal of $6.84. Thus they are excluded.
- The preferred shares, with an individual effect of $10, are also anti-dilutive and thus excluded.

The final result is diluted EPS of $6.84 for earnings from continuing operations.

EXHIBIT 20-8

FRM CORPORATION

Comprehensive EPS Illustration

(Based on Data in Exhibit 20-7)

	Earnings Available to Common Shares	Weighted-average Number of Shares	Earnings per Share
Basic EPS:			
Earnings from continuing operations after tax	$1,000,000		
Less: Preferred dividends: 5,000 shares × $20	(100,000)		
Shares outstanding:			
Class A			
100,000 × 9/12		75,000	
104,800 × 3/12		26,200	
Class B 10,000 × 12/12		10,000	
Basic EPS	**$ 900,000**	**111,200**	**$ 8.09**
Individual effect ratios:			
Preferred shares (per share)	$ 20	2	$10.00
Actual conversion of 10% debenture			
Interest saved: ($240,000 × 10%) × (1.00 – 0.25) × 9/12	13,500		
Additional shares: 4,800 × 9/12		3,600	3.75
10% debentures (remainder)			
Interest saved: ($960,000 × 10%) × (1.00 – 0.25)	72,000		
Additional shares: $960,000 ÷ $50		19,200	3.75
8% debentures			
Interest saved: ($1,500,000 × 8%) × (1.00 – 0.25) × 8/12	60,000		
Additional shares: given 12,000 × 8/12		8,000	7.50
Diluted EPS:			
Data from basic	$ 900,000	111,200	
Adjustment for assumed options exercise:			
Shares issued		3,000	
Shares retired		(2,000)	
Subtotal	900,000	112,200	$ 8.02
Adjustment for contingently issuable shares:		9,000	
Subtotal	900,000	121,200	$ 7.43
Actual conversion of 10% debenture:			
Interest saved	13,500		
Additional shares		3,600	
Subtotal	913,500	124,800	7.32
Adjustments for potential conversions:			
10% debenture:			
Interest avoided (after-tax equivalent)	72,000		
Additional shares		19,200	
Subtotal	985,500	144,000	6.84
8% debenture:			
Anti-dilutive since $7.50 is higher than $6.84	—		
Adjustment for preferred shares:			
Anti-dilutive since $10.00 is higher than $6.84		—	
Diluted EPS	**$ 985,500**	**144,000**	**$ 6.84**

EPS on Net Earnings So far, we have been dealing only with earnings from continuing operations. We also need to determine EPS on net earnings, including discontinued operations; this is step 11. We make no further dilution tests at this stage; the calculations are based on the dilutions arising from EPS on continuing operations, as follows:

- Basic EPS on net earnings: ($1,200,000 – $100,000) ÷ 111,200 shares = $9.89
- Diluted EPS on net earnings: ($1,200,000 – $100,000 + $13,500 + $72,000) ÷ 144,000 shares = $8.23

Basic EPS for discontinued operations is $1.80 (i.e., $200,000 ÷ 111,200 shares), which increases EPS on net earnings to $9.89 (i.e., $8.09 + $1.80). Diluted EPS for discontinued operations is $1.39 (i.e., $200,000 ÷ 144,000 shares).

Reporting EPS disclosure on the statement of comprehensive income would be as follows:

Earnings per share:

	Basic	Diluted
Earnings from continuing operations	$8.09	$6.84
Discontinued operations	1.80	1.39
Net earnings	$9.89	$8.23

Basic and diluted ESP for both earnings from continuing operations and for net earnings must be shown on the face of the statement of comprehensive income. However, the individual effect of the discontinued operations may be disclosed in the notes instead of being shown on the face of the SCI.

RESTATEMENT OF EARNINGS PER SHARE

Reported EPS is rarely revised. Once earnings are reported, they are retrospectively restated (i.e., changed) only in three circumstances:

- An error is discovered that would change earnings and EPS in one or more prior years; or
- The entity makes a change in accounting policy, either voluntarily or due to a change in accounting standards; or
- The entity has declared a stock dividend or stock split during the fiscal year (or after the fiscal year but before the financial statements are issued); EPS is retrospectively restated to reflect the different amount of shares that are now outstanding—all prior years' EPS numbers would be reduced by 50% after a 2-for-1 stock split, for example.

These retrospective changes improve the comparability of the financial statements. Needless to say, restatement is accompanied by extensive disclosure to ensure that financial statement users are adequately informed.

Changes in estimates, the most common classification of accounting change, affect only the current year and future years and thus do not require restatement. We will look at the matter of corrections and restatements more intensively in the next chapter, Chapter 21.

SUBSEQUENT CHANGES IN SHARE CAPITAL

Companies have special disclosures required for *subsequent events*—transactions or events that take place in the period between the end of the fiscal period and the date that financial statements are authorized for issue. If there have been common share transactions in this period, then the effects of these share transactions must be disclosed. That is, if a subsequent event would significantly change the number of common shares or the potential common shares used in basic or diluted EPS, the transaction must be disclosed and described. Companies have a relatively short period after their fiscal year in which to report; they obviously have added incentive to report quickly, to reduce the reporting burden by keeping this time period short.

Examples of transactions that would have to be disclosed include issuing common shares for cash on the exercise of options, or for cash with the proceeds used to pay out other sources of financing. For example, if common shares were issued after the end of the fiscal year and the proceeds were used to retire preferred shares or debt, disclosure would be required. Issuance of new options or convertible securities would introduce a new element into diluted EPS (potential shares) and also qualify for disclosure.

REQUIRED DISCLOSURE

Financial statements should include the following:

1. Basic and diluted EPS must be disclosed on the face of the statement of comprehensive income for both net earnings from continuing operations and net earnings. Basic and diluted EPS must both be reported, even if they are exactly the same amount. Materiality cannot be invoked to avoid disclosing diluted EPS! The EPS effect of the discontinued operation must also be disclosed, but this can be either on the SCI or in a disclosure note.
2. A disclosure note must include:
   - The amounts used as the numerator and denominator for both basic and diluted EPS.
   - A reconciliation of the numerators of both basic and diluted EPS to the profit or loss numbers reported. This includes an explanation of adjustments to the numerator of diluted EPS for each individual effect by class of instrument.
   - A reconciliation of the denominators of both basic and diluted EPS to the number of common shares outstanding.
   - Details of securities excluded from the calculation of diluted EPS because they were anti-dilutive.
   - Details of share transactions, in the period after the end of the fiscal year but before the financial statements are authorized for issue, including stock dividends or splits.
   - Details of convertible securities, options, and any other share contracts issued in the period after the end of the fiscal year but before the financial statements are authorized for issue.

Reporting Example Toronto-based Magna International Inc., one of the world's largest automobile parts manufacturer, reported earnings per share as follows on the company's 2011 statement of income (loss):

Earnings (loss) per Common Share or Class B Share:	2011	2010	2009
Basic	**$4.26**	$4.36	$(2.03)
Diluted	**$4.20**	$4.30	$(2.03)

Exhibit 20-9 shows Magna's note disclosure. Magna had no discontinued operations. The company shows an adjustment for stock options and restricted stock issued during the year; this would be a backdating for shares issued during the year. The company also points out that the convertibility of employee incentive stock options was not included in the diluted EPS calculation "because these options were not in-the-money."

EXHIBIT 20-9

MAGNA INTERNATIONAL INC.

Notes to Consolidated Financial Statements

[All amounts in U.S. dollars and all tabular amounts in millions, except per share figures, unless otherwise noted]

5. EARNINGS (LOSS) PER SHARE

Earnings (loss) per share are computed as follows:

	2011	2010	2009
Basic earnings (loss) per Common or Class B Share:			
Net income (loss) attributable to Magna International Inc.	**$1,018**	$1,003	$ (453)
Average number of Common and Class B Shares outstanding during the year	**239.3**	230.0	223.6
Basic earnings (loss) per Common or Class B Share	**$4.26**	$4.36	$ (2.03)
Diluted earnings (loss) per Common or Class B Share:			
Net income (loss) attributable to Magna International Inc.	**$1,018**	$1,003	$ (453)
Average number of Common and Class B Shares outstanding during the year	**239.3**	230.0	223.6
Adjustments			
Stock options and restricted stock [a]	**3.5**	3.0	—
	242.8	233.0	223.6
Diluted earnings (loss) per Common or Class B Share	**$ 4.20**	$ 4.30	$ (2.03)

[a] Diluted earnings (loss) per Common or Class B Share exclude 2.1 million [2010 – 3.9 million; 2009 – 5.2 million] Common Shares issuable under the Company's Incentive Stock Option Plan because these options were not "in-the-money."

Source: Magna International Inc. Audited Annual Financial Statements 2011, www.sedar.com, posted 12 March 2012.

OTHER PER SHARE AMOUNTS

EPS is not the only per share statistic that may be presented in the audited financial statements. Companies are permitted to disclose per share numbers other than basic and diluted figures in the disclosure notes. For example, a specific subcomponent of earnings may be reported on a per-share basis. The denominator must be calculated using WAOS as per basic and diluted requirements, and the company must disclose the basis on which the numerator is determined, including whether it is before or after tax.

Companies sometimes publish a statistic called **cash flow per share**, based on a subtotal in the SCF. Some companies use cash flow from operating activities as the basis for this calculation, and some use an intermediate subtotal such as earnings adjusted for non-cash items (e.g., depreciation expense and unusual gains and losses). Inclusion of cash flow per share is permitted under international standards, subject to the calculation and disclosure requirements described above.

However, securities regulators in Canada generally prefer that such disclosures be presented less prominently than the EPS. Presentation in the disclosure notes is considered to be more appropriate than showing them on the statement of cash flows or the statement of comprehensive income.

Looking Forward

The current international EPS standard has been in effect since 2005. The IASB has no plans to revise it in the foreseeable future. Since EPS is a very commonly used metric, it makes sense not to meddle with it too often—frequent revisions would have a negative effect on its perceived usefulness. However, bear in mind that as accounting standards change (which they do fairly regularly), historical EPS figures may not really be comparable with current amounts due to changes in measurement methods that cannot be applied retrospectively to more than one or two prior periods.

ACCOUNTING STANDARDS FOR PRIVATE ENTERPRISES

There is no private company Canadian GAAP with respect to EPS. Private companies may voluntarily decide to present EPS data, if they believe that it would useful to their financial statement users. Private companies with a larger shareholder group, such as co-operatives and employee-owned companies, might present EPS as a standard part of financial reporting. Private companies may look to IAS 33 for guidance, or they may design a statistic that meets their users' requirements. Disclosure of the calculation approach used is obviously important to improve understanding.

RELEVANT STANDARDS

CPA Canada Handbook, Part I (IFRS):

- IAS 33, Earnings per Share

CPA Canada Handbook, Part II (ASPE):

- None

SUMMARY OF KEY POINTS

1. Earnings per share provides information about the change in earnings as compared with changes (if any) in the common share base. Basic EPS is the basis for comparing the current period's earnings with that of prior periods, while diluted EPS gives an indication of the long-run impact that conversions and options could have on common earnings. Because it is computed on a *per share* basis, EPS removes the effect of increases in net earnings due to larger invested capital obtained through new share issues.
2. EPS figures are computed for (1) earnings from continuing operations and for (2) net earnings.
3. Basic EPS is calculated by dividing earnings available to common shareholders (e.g., earnings less preferred dividend claims) by the weighted-average number of shares outstanding.
4. Weighted-average ordinary shares (WAOS) is used in the denominator of basic EPS. WAOS is calculated by weighting shares for the number of months they are outstanding. However, if there was a stock dividend or stock split during the reporting period, these additional ordinary shares are not weight-averaged but treated as though they have always been outstanding.

5. If there are multiple classes of common shares with different dividend entitlements, separate basic EPS statistics must be calculated to reflect their claims.

6. When a company has dilutive senior securities, contingently issuable shares or options, diluted EPS must be calculated. The steps to calculate diluted EPS are shown in Exhibit 20-2. For the purposes of calculating diluted EPS, elements are included at their most unfavourable (lowest) price. Potentially dilutive items are included in diluted EPS calculations in a cascade, beginning with the most dilutive.

7. Diluted EPS excludes the effects of any convertible securities or options contracts that are anti-dilutive. Anti-dilutive items have the effect of *increasing* EPS in relation to basic EPS from continuing operations.

8. When calculating diluted EPS, in-the-money options are assumed to be issued at the beginning of the fiscal period and proceeds used to retire shares at average market values. This is called the *treasury stock method.*

9. Contingently issuable shares are included in diluted EPS if the shares would be issuable if the contingency period were to end at the end of the current fiscal year.

10. Convertible bonds and preferred shares are included in diluted EPS calculations using the *if-converted method*, whereby after-tax interest and preferred dividends are adjusted in the numerator and common shares issued for the denominator. This reflects a hypothetical conversion to common shares at the beginning of the year.

11. Diluted EPS includes an adjustment that backdates actual conversions of senior securities (convertible debt and preferred shares) and shares issued under option contracts to the beginning of the fiscal period, if dilutive.

12. Securities and options issued during the period are backdated only to the date of issue. Dilutive conversion privileges and options that expired or were extinguished during the period are included for the period during which they were outstanding.

13. All potentially dilutive elements are anti-dilutive in a loss year because they would *decrease* a loss per share; this means that diluted EPS is equal to basic EPS in a loss year.

14. Both basic and diluted EPS figures are reported on the statement of comprehensive income. This is the case even if there is no potential dilution. A disclosure note must include calculation details, including reconciliation of earnings and WAOS data, and details of excluded anti-dilutive elements. The amount of EPS that is attributable to discontinued operations also should be disclosed, either on the face of the SCI or in the notes.

KEY TERMS

anti-dilutive
backdating
basic earnings per share
bonus shares
business combination
buying earnings
cash flow per share
contingently issuable ordinary shares
convertible senior securities
diluted earnings per share
diluted EPS cascade
dilutive
earnings dilution
forced conversion
if-converted method
in-the-money
individual effect
mandatorily convertible shares
merger
ordinary shares
senior shares
stock dividend
stock option
stock split
treasury stock method
weighted average ordinary shares outstanding (WAOS)

REVIEW PROBLEM 20-1

Ice King Products Incorporated reported after-tax profit of $6.5 million in 20X5. Its capital structure included the following as of 31 December 20X5, the *end* of the company's fiscal year:

Long-term debt:	
Bonds payable, due 20X11, 12%	$ 5,000,000
Bonds payable, due 20X15, 9%, convertible into common shares at the rate of two shares per $100	$10,000,000
Shareholders' equity:	
Preferred shares, $4.50, no-par, cumulative, convertible into common shares at the rate of two common shares for each preferred share, shares outstanding, 150,000	
Preferred shares, $2.50, no-par, cumulative, convertible into common shares at the rate of one common share for each preferred share, shares outstanding, 400,000	
Common shares, shares outstanding, 1,500,000	

Options to purchase common shares (options have been outstanding all year):
- Purchase price, $20; expire 20X11, 100,000 options
- Purchase price, $52; expire 20X14, 200,000 options

Each option allows the purchase of one share.

Transactions during 20X5:
- On 1 July, 400,000 common shares were issued on the conversion of 200,000 of the $4.50 preferred shares.
- On 1 December, 100,000 common shares were issued for cash.

Additional information:
- Average common share price, stable during the year, $40
- Tax rate, 25%
- Quarterly dividends were declared on 31 March, 30 June, 30 September, and 31 December

Required:

Calculate basic and diluted earnings per share.

REVIEW PROBLEM 20-1—SOLUTION

	Earnings Available to Common Shares	Weighted-average Number of Shares	Earnings per Share
Basic EPS:			
Net profit	$6,500,000		
Less: Dividends on $4.50 preferred:			
($4.50 ÷ 4) × 350,000 shares × 2 quarters	(787,500)		
($4.50 ÷ 4) × 150,000 shares × 2 quarters	(337,500)		
Less: Dividends on $2.50 preferred:			
400,000 shares × $2.50	(1,000,000)		
WAOS:			
1,000,000 shares × 6/12		500,000	
1,400,000 shares × 5/12		583,333	
1,500,000 shares × 1/12		125,000	
Basic EPS	**$4,375,000**	**1,208,333**	**$3.62**

Individual effect; dilution test			
9% Bonds:			
Interest, ($10,000,000 × 9%) × (1.00 – 0.25)	$ 675,000		
Shares, ($10,000,000 ÷ $100) × 2		200,000	$3.38
$4.50 preferred actual conversion:			
Dividend adjustment:			
(4.50 ÷ 4) × 200,000 shares × 2 quarters	$ 450,000		
Additional weighted-average shares: 400,000 × 6/12		200,000	$2.25
$4.50 preferred			
Dividends, $4.50 × 150,000 shares	$ 675,000		
Shares, 150,000 × 2 common shares		300,000	$2.25
$2.50 preferred			
Dividends, $2.50 × 400,000	$1,000,000		
Shares, 400,000 × 1 share		400,000	$2.50
Diluted EPS			
Basic EPS	$4,375,000	1,208,333	$3.62
$20 options—shares issued		100,000	
—shares retired (100,000 × $20) ÷ $40		(50,000)	
$52 options—excluded, $52 > $40			
Subtotal	$4,375,000	1,258,333	$3.48
$4.50 preferred actual conversion:			
Dividend adjustment:			
(4.50 ÷ 4) × 200,000 shares × 2 quarters	450,000		
Additional weighted average shares 400,000 × 6/12		200,000	
$4.50 preferred:			
Dividends, $4.50 × 150,000 shares	675,000		
Shares, 150,000 preferred × 2 common shares		300,000	
Subtotal	5,500,000	1,758,333	3.13
$2.50 preferred shares: dividends, $2.50 × 400,000	1,000,000	400,000	
Subtotal	$6,500,000	2,158,333	3.01
9% Bonds			
Bonds, with an individual effect of $3.38, are anti-dilutive as their inclusion would increase diluted EPS above $3.01.	—	—	
Diluted EPS	**$6,500,000**	**2,158,333**	**$3.01**

QUESTIONS

Q20-1 Why are weighted-average ordinary shares used in EPS calculations?

Q20-2 Explain why and when dividends on noncumulative preferred shares must be subtracted from earnings to compute basic EPS.

Q20-3 What adjustments, in addition to preferred dividends, might be made to the numerator of basic EPS?

Q20-4 What is the purpose of diluted EPS?

Q20-5 What is the required EPS disclosure if discontinued operations are reported?

Q20-6 If common shares are issued during the year under a contract that involves meeting a contingent requirement, as of what date are the shares included in the weighted-average ordinary share calculation?

Q20-7 A company split its common shares 2-for-1 on 30 June of its fiscal year, which ends on 31 December. Before the split, 4,000 common shares were outstanding. How many weighted-average ordinary shares should be used in computing EPS? How many shares should be used in computing a comparative EPS amount for the preceding year?

Q20-8 Assume that a company has two classes of shares that both have voting rights and are entitled to the proceeds of net assets on dissolution. One class is entitled to receive 10 times the dividends of the other class. How would the two classes be treated in calculating basic EPS?

Q20-9 A company has basic EPS based on earnings from continuing operations of $4.50 and on net earnings, $3.50. A potentially dilutive element has an individual effect of $4. Is the element dilutive or anti-dilutive?

Q20-10 Specify the impact on both the numerator and denominator when calculating diluted EPS for dilutive (a) convertible preferred shares, (b) convertible debt, (c) contingently issuable shares, and (d) options.

Q20-11 Options are outstanding for 100,000 shares at $10. The average market price during the period is $25. What adjustment would be made to the denominator of diluted EPS?

Q20-12 What is the difference between a dilutive security and an anti-dilutive security? Why is the distinction important in EPS considerations?

Q20-13 What does it mean if options are said to be in-the-money? Are options dilutive when they are in-the-money? Explain.

Q20-14 A company has an agreement outstanding at the end of the fiscal year that requires it to issue common shares in the future for no additional cash consideration if certain conditions are met. How does the company decide whether to include the shares in diluted EPS or exclude them?

Q20-15 CH Holdings has basic EPS of $14. The individual effect of convertible preferred shares is $12, and the individual effect of convertible bonds is $6. In which order should the convertible elements be included in diluted calculations? In what circumstances would the convertible preferred shares be anti-dilutive in sequence?

Q20-16 ABC Company has a $14 million convertible bond outstanding that requires payment of $1.2 million in interest annually. Interest expense is $1.35 million. Why is interest expense different than the interest paid? For the purposes of diluted EPS, which interest figure is relevant?

Q20-17 Wilcorp Limited reported a loss of $610,000. There are 550,000 shares outstanding. The company has outstanding stock options for 100,000 common shares at $10 per share. The average common share price was $25 during the period. Calculate basic EPS and diluted EPS.

Q20-18 Under what circumstances would the EPS of prior years be restated?

Q20-19 A company with a 31 December year-end issues shares for cash and retires non-convertible bonds with the proceeds on 10 January of the next fiscal year. What disclosure is required in the 31 December financial statements? Why?

Q20-20 Barbaro Ltd. plans to disclose *cash flow per share from operating activities* in addition to EPS. What conditions must the company meet?

CASE 20-1

THURTECH LIMITED

ThurTech Limited (TTL) is a Canadian public company involved in network technology for mobility telecommunications. This network technology allows super-fast data services to be offered through mobile platforms at a premium rate as a strategy to increase revenue per user for the carriers. TTL's customers are mobility carriers in many North, Central, and South American countries.

In 20X2, TTL reported basic earnings per share of $2.27 and diluted EPS of $2.10. The company forecasted EPS growth of approximately 12% for 20X3.

Unfortunately, 20X3 revenues were relatively flat through the first three quarters. TTL reported an EPS growth rate of 8% during the first three quarters, an increase that had been generated largely through cost reduction rather than revenue growth. Internal projections indicated that this lower growth rate in EPS would likely be reported for the overall year if immediate action was not taken. Exhibit 1 shows the projected annual 20X3 EPS figures, reflecting the 8% improvement from operations.

Consequently, early in the fourth quarter, senior management began to discuss ways to "close the gap" between the 8% actual EPS growth rate and the 12% target. Mindful of the sluggish stock market share price, and with an eye on its own compensation and stock option packages, management expressed strong interest in making significant changes before the end of the 20X3 fiscal year.

TTL has 1.2 million common shares promised for future distribution under option contracts granted to senior management. Stock options are a substantial element of compensation. Additional options will be granted at the end of 20X3. The options granted will be at a price equal to the current share price and will vest immediately. They may be exercised in four years' time, as long as the manager is still with TTL. The number of shares granted under option depends on corporate performance and could range from zero to 400,000 shares.

A number of situations and/or opportunities that would potentially affect EPS for the year have been discussed internally. For example, management has proposed that 850,000 common shares be repurchased and retired in the fourth quarter. The required funding for this, $16,150,000, would have to be borrowed. Management is permitted to borrow up to $2 billion without further Board of Directors' approval; at the end of the third quarter, outstanding debt amounted to $1.8 billion.

TTL has idle land on the books at an historical cost of $695,000. The market value of this land is $1,180,000; sale would therefore generate a before-tax profit of $485,000. The land is adjacent to one of TTL's five manufacturing facilities and has been held for future expansion. Management is confident that when future expansion is necessary, land can be obtained at one or another of the existing locations for a reasonable sum. Therefore, senior management has proposed that this idle land be sold during the fourth quarter of 20X3.

One part of the company's debt financing is a bond payable carried on the books at $500 million, at a fixed interest rate of 6%. Since market interest rates are now in the range of 8%, the present value of this debt is $470 million. Management has suggested that this debt be recorded at its present value, recognizing the reduction in debt as a financing gain on the statement of comprehensive income.

TTL has several major orders for product that will be delivered in the first quarter of 20X4. Management is considering ways to expedite these orders to ensure that delivery is completed in the fourth quarter of 20X3. Management is confident that the company can complete production, although not installation at customers' sites. One customer has indicated willingness to accept early delivery of the product despite the fact that installation will not be possible in 20X3 due to technological issues. However, the customer is willing to accept delivery only on condition that payment can be delayed until the originally scheduled payment date. TTL is willing to accept this delayed payment condition and intends to offer early delivery to all customers without requiring expedited payment. If these orders are booked in 20X3, gross profit will increase in the range of between $800,000 and $1.2 million.

TTL expects to conclude a transaction with an Indian company, Bombay Telecom Limited (BTL), in the fourth quarter of 20X3. In this transaction, TTL network technology will be exchanged for manufacturing equipment procured by BTL. This equipment will be used to produce a component for TTL that will help establish TTL's leading-edge product. Valuation of the transaction is problematic, however. TTL knows that the technology it is shipping to BTL would sell in the range of $1.5 million, but sales of this line are not common and the product was specifically produced for BTL at a cost of $600,000. The equipment acquired does not have a readily established market value because it is unique. The product line that the equipment supports is projected to have a 10-year life, producing gross margins of 60%, but the eventual volume is highly speculative.

Required:

Prepare a report for management in which you explain the effects that the situations described above would have on earnings per share for the 20X3 fiscal year. Assume that TTL has a 25% marginal income tax rate. Also, point out any concerns that management should consider before undertaking these proposed solutions to the EPS situation.

EXHIBIT 1

PROJECTED EPS—20X3

Basic EPS:

$$\frac{\text{Net income} - \text{Preferred dividends}}{\text{Weighted-average ordinary shares}} = \frac{\$50{,}621{,}900 - \$2{,}000{,}000}{19{,}765{,}500}$$

$$= \frac{\$48{,}621{,}900}{19{,}765{,}500}$$

$$= \underline{\underline{\$2.46}}$$

Diluted EPS:

$$\frac{\text{Basic} + \text{preferred dividends}}{\text{Basic} + \text{common shares for preferred}} = \frac{(\$48{,}621{,}900 + \$2{,}000{,}000)}{(19{,}765{,}500 + 1{,}600{,}000)}$$

$$= \frac{(\$48{,}621{,}900 + \$2{,}000{,}000)}{(19{,}765{,}500 + 1{,}600{,}000) + (1{,}200{,}000 - 160{,}000)^*}$$

$$= \frac{\$50{,}621{,}900}{22{,}405{,}500}$$

$$= \underline{\underline{\$2.26}}$$

*Shares under stock options – shares retired with option proceeds

CASE 20-2

DEXLUX LTD.

Dexlux Ltd. (DL) is a vertically integrated manufacturer and retailer of moderately priced high-fashion footwear, leather goods, and accessories. DL's common shares are listed on the Toronto Stock Exchange. DL has stores in over 180 major Canadian shopping malls and operates over 50 "boutiques" in larger retail stores. Until the current year, DL had three retail stores in the United States. In general, operating results in 20X9 have been disappointing, with lower same-store sales trends and higher costs across the board.

Exhibit 1 shows preliminary operating results for 20X9. Exhibit 2 shows details of accounting issues that must be resolved before the financial statements can be finalized. No accounting recognition has been given to stock options outstanding or granted during the year, as valuation estimates were not complete when the draft financial statements were prepared. This information has recently been obtained.

Required:

Analyze the accounting issues as identified, and prepare revised draft statement of comprehensive income, including earnings per share.

EXHIBIT 1

DEXLUX LIMITED

Draft Statement of Comprehensive Income

(in thousands of Canadian dollars)

For year ended 31 December	20X9
Revenue	
Sales	$164,960
Investment and other revenue	4,320
	169,280
Expenses	
Cost of sales, selling, and administrative	142,860
Amortization	11,940
Closure costs, U.S. operations	1,450
Interest, net	2,230
	158,480
Operating earnings, before tax	10,800
Income tax	2,700
Net earnings and comprehensive income	$ 8,100

EXHIBIT 2

DEXLUX LIMITED

Additional Information

1. Outstanding share information:

	Number	Consideration (in thousands)
A. Multiple voting shares, 31 December 20X8 and 20X9	1,580,000	Nominal
B. Subordinate voting shares		
Balance, 31 December 20X8	5,225,000	$23,890
Shares repurchased 20 March 20X9	(816,000)	(3,730)
Shares issued on exercise of stock options 31 August 20X9	78,000	728
Balance, 31 December 20X9	4,487,000	$20,888

The multiple voting shares and subordinate voting shares have identical attributes except that the multiple voting shares entitle the holder to four votes per share and four times the dividend, if declared, on the subordinate voting shares. The multiple voting shares are held by the company founder and his family. Only the subordinated voting shares are publicly traded.

2. On 2 March 20X9, the company received permission from the Ontario Securities Commission for a Normal Course Issuer Bid that allows the company to repurchase up to 20% of its outstanding shares, or approximately 1,045,000 shares during the period from 2 March 20X9 to 2 March 20X10. The share transaction in March 20X9 was made pursuant to this bid agreement. Consideration of $6,840 (thousand) was paid for the shares, with the excess over average paid-in capital to date charged to retained earnings.
3. On 24 February 20X6, DL issued $40 million of convertible senior subordinated notes payable. The net proceeds after deducting offering expenses and underwriter's commissions were $37 million. The convertible debt was allocated between debt and equity elements, which are classified separately on the statement of financial position. The value of the debt element was based on the present value of the interest stream over the life of the note using an interest rate for a similar liability that did not have an associated conversion feature. The balance was recorded as equity.

   The notes are convertible at DL's option at various dates between 20X14 and the maturity date of the note, 24 February 20X17. The conversion price is set at $15 per share until 20X15 and then changes to $10 per share. In 20X9, there is a charge for interest expense amounting to $1,780 and a $590 after-tax reduction to retained earnings, representing accretion on the equity amount. When calculating basic EPS, the $590 must be deducted from the numerator.
4. DL maintains a stock option plan for the benefit of directors, officers, and senior management. The granting of options and the related vesting period are at the discretion of the Board of Directors. The option price is set as the five-day average of the trading price of the subordinated voting shares prior to the effective date of the grant. Options granted vest 36 months after the date of issuance, and can be exercised from the vesting date until 10 years after the date of grant. Options are granted on 31 December in the year of grant. The fair value of options granted was as follows:

Year of Grant	Per Share Value	Share Entitlements Originally Granted
Prior to 20X6	$4.785	404,000
20X6	4.270	210,000
20X7	6.473	176,000
20X8	5.540	206,000
20X9	7.180	25,000

The status of outstanding options is as follows:

	Shares Under Option	Weighted Average Exercise Price
Outstanding at the beginning of the year	695,000	$11.21
Granted, 31 December, 20X9	25,000	10.53
Exercised	(78,000)	6.62
Outstanding at the end of the year	642,000	11.10
Options exercisable at the end of the year	405,800	10.90

At the end of the year, the market price of subordinated voting shares was $11.25, and had been stable for most of the year. Any recorded compensation cost is a permanent difference for tax purposes and will not change recorded tax amounts.

5. In March 20X9, DL announced that it would close its U.S. retail operation, consisting of three retail stores. The stores had been a separate division of the company, reported separately with a dedicated retail manager. The stores were run using normal retail protocols established for other stores and relied on DL infrastructure. However, fashion trends appeared to be unique in these locations, and DL did not have adequate brand recognition to reach required sales targets. Two retail stores were closed at the end of March, with the third one closed at the end of April. Pretax information (in thousands) concerning these locations:

	20X9
Sales	$ 532
Operating loss	(467)
Writedown of capital assets	(1,045)
Lease and employee termination costs	(405)
Current assets	$ 23
Capital assets	—
Current liabilities	—

CASE 20-3

DECATUR HOLDINGS LIMITED

Decatur Holdings Limited (DHL) is a diversified Canadian company based in Winnipeg, Manitoba. DHL's primary business is the distribution and retailing of pharmaceutical and health care products. DHL's shares are traded on the Toronto Stock Exchange. Common shares traded in the $8–$14 range in 20X5. The primary holder of DDL's debt is the Amalgamated Public Sector Pension Plan. Extracts from DHL's draft 20X5 financial statements are shown in Exhibit 1; DHL's share capital disclosures are shown in Exhibit 2.

You are an accountant in the corporate reporting department of DHL. Financial statements are in the process of being finalized for the 20X5 fiscal year, which ended on 31 December 20X5. The audit committee will meet next week, with several accounting policy issues left to resolve. EPS calculations must also be completed.

DHL owns and operates distribution facilities in several locations across Canada. The company also operates a chain of retail health care stores. While the company operates stores in every province, DHL has the strongest presence in the western provinces. The company owns the real estate under all of its distribution centres and most of its standalone stores but also operates stores some in leased properties. When DHL stores are anchor tenants in small malls, DHL prefers to own the commercial real estate property and act as landlord to other tenants. Stores in large urban malls, however, are leased from the mall operator, which, in most cases, is Lincoln Property Investments Inc.

As an owner of 284 real estate parcels, DHL frequently engages in real estate transactions, frequently as seller when the company decides to close a store in an underperforming location. Each transaction results in a gain or loss, of course. DHL labels gains on sale of real estate as "capital gains" on the statement of comprehensive income. The term is not used in its income tax context; it is just DHL's term for gains and losses on sale.

In the late fall of 20X5, one major real estate property owned by DHL burned to the ground. DHL was the sole occupant of this building, which had a book value of $17 million. Inventory with a book value of $7.2 million was destroyed in the fire. A team of insurance adjustors is assessing the situation; the fire is thought to be electrical in origin. The fire investigators and the insurance adjustors have yet to file their reports.

DHL carries property and casualty insurance. Lawyers for DHL believe that DHL is entitled to insurance recovery for the fair value of the property destroyed. Consequently, DHL filed a claim for $32.2 million, of which $25 million is for the building, and $7.2 million for inventory. The expected payout is $31.2 million, after a $1 million deductable under the policy. Income tax triggered by the potential insurance proceeds is estimated to be $1.4 million in current taxes payable and another $0.7 million in deferred income tax. The property and inventory remain on DHL's books in the meantime.

Effective 31 December 20X5, DHL sold certain real estate properties to Sunne Real Estate Investment Trust (Sunne REIT). The properties had a book value of $239 million and were sold for $374 million gross cash proceeds. In addition, DHL received units in Sunne REIT estimated to be worth $50 million. There were brokerage and legal costs of $7 million associated with the sale. Income tax triggered by the sale amounted to $27 million in current taxes payable plus another $4 million in deferred income tax. The transfer has yet to be reflected in the 20X5 financial statements.

As part of the transaction with Sunne REIT, DHL entered into new lease agreements with respect to its occupancy in a portion of the real estate properties now owned by Sunne REIT. The leases have an expected total term of between 17 and 23 years; initial lease arrangements are established for five years, followed by renewal periods to the end of the term. Minimum rents range from $8 to $14 per square foot, plus a percentage of gross revenue, and there are planned base rental increases every five years.

DHL entered into a five-year referral contract during the year. Physiotherapy and chiropractic services represent a large and growing market in Canada, and pharmacists in DHL stores are often consulted by customers about appropriate action. Any retail customer who requests physiotherapy and chiropractic advice or services in a DHL store will be referred to Nature Force Limited, a national chain that is the Canadian leader in such services. The agreement specifies that in the first year of the agreement, DHL will be paid the higher of $1 million or 30% of client billings resulting from referrals. Revenues in the second year are 30% of billings, with no minimum, and then the percentage reduces from 30% to 25%, then 20% and 15% over the remaining three years of the contact. After the first year, either side can end the agreement with 60 days' notice. An appropriate information system has been established to ascertain the extent of billings Nature Force realizes from the referrals, subject to external verification.

To date, Nature Force has not made any payment to DHL for Year 1 minimum payment because the amount is not due until the 12-month anniversary of the agreement, which occurs in October 20X3. No revenue has been recorded by DHL in the 20X5 financial statements. The pharmacists report that referrals have been "quite strong," although there are regional differences.

The company regularly calculates and disseminates information on basic and diluted EPS numbers, before and after capital gains and income tax. Company management prefers to focus on results before capital gains and income tax when communicating to shareholders, as gains from sale of real estate are sporadic, and business units have operating targets on a pretax basis. In 20X4, the company recorded earnings before capital gains and income tax of $5.60 per share, and diluted EPS before capital gains and income tax of $5.56. After capital gains and income tax, the numbers were $5.03 and $4.99.

Required:

In preparation for the coming audit committee meeting, prepare a report that includes analysis of the accounting issues inherent in the transactions above and any other reporting issues. Recalculate net earnings, if appropriate, and prepare EPS calculations for 20X5.

EXHIBIT 1

DECATUR HOLDINGS LIMITED

Extracts from Financial Statements

31 December 20X5

(in millions of Canadian dollars)	20X5 Draft	20X4
Statement of comprehensive income		
Revenue	$15,015	$14,065
Operating earnings	$ 468	$ 473
Earnings before capital gains	$ 388	$ 368
Capital gains	—	89
Income tax	(116)	(126)
Net earnings and comprehensive income	$ 272	$ 331
Statement of financial position		
Capital stock	$ 365.7	$ 257.7
Contributed surplus	2	0.1
Retained earnings	2,405	2,207

EXHIBIT 2

DECATUR HOLDINGS LIMITED

Share Capital Information

31 December 20X5

(in millions of Canadian dollars)	20X5 Draft	20X4
Preferred shares, par value $25 each, Series 2 cumulative, redeemable at the company's option, dividend 3%, convertible 2-for-1 into Class A shares, unlimited shares authorized, 1,680,000 shares outstanding (20X4, 2,600,000 shares)	$ 42	$ 65
Class A shares, with no par value, entitled to dividends on an equal per share basis with Class B shares, voting, one vote per share, unlimited shares authorized, 34,000,000 shares outstanding (20X4, 31,300,000 shares)	316.1	185.1
Class B shares, voting, three votes per share, unlimited shares authorized, 34,000,000 shares outstanding, sharing dividends equally with Class A, share per share	7.6	7.6

In January 20X5, 190,000 options were issued. Options allow the holders to purchase 190,000 Class A shares at nil cost beginning in 20X14 and expiring in 20X18 and 20X19.

In late March 20X5, 1,200,000 Class A shares were purchased for cancellation at a cost of $60 million. Other shares were issued for cash in July 20X5. In late December 20X5, 920,000 Series 2 preferred shares were purchased for cancellation at a cost of $25 million.

TECHNICAL REVIEW

connect

TR20-1 Basic EPS: Angelo Ltd., a public company, had 600,000 common shares outstanding at the beginning of 20X4. On 1 March 20X4, Angelo Ltd. purchased and retired 120,000 shares that had been owned by one of the company founders. On 30 June, the company issued 60,000 shares to a venture capital firm upon maturity of a $100,000 10% mandatorily convertible debenture. On 30 September, the company issued 120,000 new shares for cash. Angelo Ltd.'s after-tax 20X4 earnings amounted to $1,200,000.

Required:
Compute basic EPS.

connect

TR20-2 Basic and Diluted EPS: Hominem Inc. has 100,000 common shares outstanding. Earnings from continuing operations amounted to $1,500,000 (after tax) for 20X4. Hominem's income tax rate is 25%. The company had no discontinued operations. At the end of 20X4, the market price of the company's common shares was $27. Hominem had these additional components in its capital structure at the end of the year:

- 15,000 cumulative preferred shares outstanding since 20X2; each share is entitled to an annual dividend of $20 per share and is convertible into five shares of common after 30 June 20X9.
- 6% debentures amounting to $500,000, of which $100,000 had been issued on 1 May 20X4. The debentures are convertible into 12 shares per $1,000.
- Outstanding options permitting the holder to buy 5,000 common shares in 20X6 or later for $35 per share.

Required:
1. Compute basic EPS.
2. Compute diluted EPS, using a cascade if appropriate.

connect

TR20-3 EPS with Loss from Discontinued Operations: Refer to the information in T20-2. Assume that Hominem Inc. had a loss on discontinued operations of $1,000,000 (after tax).

Required:
Compute diluted EPS.

connect

TR20-4 EPS—Complex Capital Structure: Kouk Corporation has the following capital structure at the end of 20X7:

- 100,000 Class A shares carrying five votes per share.
- 100,000 Class B shares, carring one vote per share.
- Dividends are shared on a 5:1 ratio—$5 to Class A for every dollar paid to Class B.

Additional information:

- Kouk Corporation's tax rate is 20%.
- Net earnings amounted to $2,100,000 for 20X7; there were no discontinued operations.
- Kouk paid $1,200,000 in dividends at the end of 20X7.

Required:
1. Determine the amount of dividends that were paid to Class A and Class B shares, both in total and per share for each class.
2. Calculate basic EPS.

connect

TR20-5 Basic and Diluted EPS—Conversions: During 20X1, Discolux Limited had two classes of shares outstanding:

- Class A preferred shares, 1,000 shares issued and outstanding at the beginning of the year; quarterly dividend rate of $200 per share, cumulative; each share is convertible into 40 shares of Class B common.
- Class B common shares, 141,000 shares issued and outstanding at the beginning of the year.

Also assume the following:

- Net income for the year is $3,000,000; there are no discontinued operations.
- 600 shares of Class A were converted into 24,000 Class B shares on 1 April 20X1; dividends for the first quarter of the year were paid on 30 March 20X1.
- Options to issue 10,000 common shares to senior executives for $3 per share were outstanding during the entire year. No options were exercised during the year. The average share price during the year was $10.

Required:

1. Determine the weighted-average number of shares outstanding during 20X1.
2. Determine basic EPS.
3. Determine diluted EPS.

ASSIGNMENTS

★ **A20-1 Weighted-Average Common Shares:** The following cases are independent.

excel

connect

Case A Jethrow Limited had 1,000,000 common shares outstanding on 1 January 20X2.

- On 27 February 200,000 shares were issued for $50 each.
- 300,000 shares were issued on 1 August.
- A 2-for-1 stock split was distributed on 30 August.

Case B On 1 January 20X7, Doomsday Corporation had 200,000 nonvoting Series A shares and 600,000 Series B voting shares outstanding. Series A shares have a $2 per share cumulative dividend paid quarterly and are convertible into two Series B shares at any time after 31 December 20X9.

- On 1 October 20X7, 30,000 Series A shares were converted to B shares.
- On 1 December 20X7, 72,000 Series B shares were retired for cash.

Required:

For each case, calculate the number of weighted-average ordinary shares to use in the calculation of basic EPS. Assume a 31 December year-end.

★ **A20-2 Weighted-Average Common Shares:** The following cases are independent:

Solution

Case A Halifax Limited had 2,500,000 common shares outstanding on 1 January 20X8. On 1 March, 600,000 common shares were issued for cash. On 1 July, 300,000 common shares were repurchased and retired. On 1 November, 560,000 common shares were issued as a stock dividend.

Case B Marvelex Limited had 6,000,000 common shares outstanding on 1 January 20X8. No shares were issued or retired during 20X8, which has a 31 December year-end. On 15 January 20X9, before the financial statements were finalized, a 1-for-4 reverse stock split took place.

Case C Redux Limited had 2,860,000 common shares outstanding on 1 January 20X8. On 1 March, 286,000 common shares were issued as a 10% stock dividend. On 1 June, 200,000 common shares were repurchased and retired. On 1 November, 400,000 shares were issued as part of a contingent share agreement. The contingency had been met on 1 August 20X8, but the shares were not issued until 1 November 20X8.

Required:

For each case, calculate the weighted-average number of common shares to use in the calculation of basic EPS in 20X8.

★ **A20-3 Dual Share Classes:** Murchie Limited earned $8,000,000 in 20X2 and paid dividends of $2,700,000. The company has two classes of voting shares. Class A shares have six votes per share, while Class B shares have one vote per share. Both participate in the distribution of net assets in the event of dissolution. There were 600,000 Class A shares outstanding all during 20X2, and 1,400,000 Class B shares.

Class A shares are entitled to dividends as declared, in the amount of $1 per share, before the Class B shares receive any dividends. After the Class A dividend, Class B shares will receive dividends as declared up to $1.50 per share. If any dividends are declared above this amount, both classes are to be allocated an identical per share dividend.

Required:

1. Determine basic EPS for each share class for 20X2.
2. Repeat requirement 1 assuming that there is no base dividend and dividends are split on a per-share basis between the two classes such that Class A shares receive 10 times the Class B entitlement per share.

★ **A20-4 Dual Share Classes:** Darlington Industries Limited reported earnings of $1,000,000 in 20X6; no dividends were declared. Darlington has two classes of ordinary shares—Class A and Class B. The characteristics of the two classes of shares are as follows:

connect

- 60,000 Class A shares and 750,000 Class B shares were outstanding throughout the year.
- Class A shares get 15 votes per share; Class B has one vote.
- If dividends are declared, Class A shares are entitled to a base dividend of $3 per share while Class B shares are entitled to a base dividend of $0.60 per share. Additional dividends beyond the base dividend are shared on an equal basis per share.

Required:

Calculate basic EPS for 20X6.

★ **A20-5 Basic EPS:** At the end of 20X6, the records of Security Systems Corporation showed the following:

Bonds payable, 7%, nonconvertible		$ 320,000
Preferred shares:		
Class A, no-par, $0.60, nonconvertible, noncumulative, outstanding 60,000 shares		300,000
Class B, no-par, $0.70, nonconvertible, cumulative, outstanding 30,000 shares		600,000
Common shares, no-par, authorized unlimited shares:		
Outstanding 1 January, 186,000 shares	$1,785,000	
Retired shares 1 May, 36,000 shares	(345,483)	
Issued a 300% stock dividend on 1 November, on outstanding shares (450,000 additional shares)	—	1,439,517
Retained earnings (no dividends declared)		1,710,000
Earnings from continuing operations, after income taxes		$ 160,500
Discontinued operations, net of tax		10,000
Net earnings		$ 170,500

Required:
Compute basic EPS. Show computations.

★ **A20-6 Basic EPS for Three Years; Restatement:** Ramca Corporation's accounting year ends on 31 December. During the three most recent years, its common shares outstanding changed as follows:

	20X7	20X6	20X5
Shares outstanding, 1 January	150,000	120,000	100,000
Shares sold, 1 April 20X5			20,000
25% stock dividend, 1 July 20X6		30,000	
2-for-1 stock split, 1 July 20X7	150,000		
Shares sold, 1 October 20X7	50,000		
Shares outstanding, 31 December	350,000	150,000	120,000
Net earnings and comprehensive income	$375,000	$330,000	$299,000

Required:

1. For purposes of calculating EPS at the end of each year, for each year independently, determine the weighted-average number of shares outstanding.
2. For purposes of calculating EPS at the end of 20X7, when comparative statements are being prepared on a three-year basis, determine the weighted-average number of shares outstanding for each year.
3. Compute EPS for each year based on computations in requirement 2. There were no preferred shares outstanding.

★ **A20-7 Contingently Issuable Shares:** On 1 January 20X1, Barnhill Information Technologies reported 3,650,000 common shares outstanding. During the prior year, 20X0, the company had acquired Semere Systems, a supplier company, in a cash and share transaction. The purchase agreement included the following provisions:

excel

1. Barnhill will issue an additional 250,000 common shares to the prior shareholders of Semere if the operating profit of the Semere business unit, as defined by agreement, was in excess of $1,000,000 for each of 20X0, 20X1, and 20X2;
2. Barnhill will issue an additional 100,000 shares to the prior shareholders of Semere if a new product under development by Semere is patented before year-end 20X4; and
3. Barnhill agreed to issue an additional 200,000 shares to the prior shareholders of Semere if a lawsuit outstanding in 20X0 against Semere were resolved for a net cost of less than $150,000, including legal fees.

In late March 20X1, the court dismissed the lawsuit against Semere. Consequently, 200,000 shares were issued to the prior shareholders of Semele on 31 October 20X1.

Barnhill reported earnings of $5,092,000 for 20X1. The Semere Systems business unit turned in strong operating results, with $1,500,000 profit earned, similar to its results in 20X0. The product under development had not advanced to the patent stage by the end of 20X1. Barnhill had no other share transactions in 20X1.

Required:
Calculate basic and diluted earnings per share figures for 20X1.

★ **A20-8 Contingently Issuable Shares:** On 1 January 20X1, Aker Aviation Services Ltd. entered into an agreement to purchase Moore Fuels Limited. The agreement included the following terms:

1. Aker agreed to issue an additional 2,000,000 shares to the prior shareholders of Moore if Aker retained 80% of the customers of Moore at the end of 20X3.
2. Aker agreed to issue 1,300,000 common shares to the prior shareholders of Moore if five key employees remained with Aker through the end of 20X5.

3. Aker agreed to issue an additional 500,000 shares to the prior shareholders of Moore if five new retail fuel units were opened before the end of 20X4.

Aker had 11,500,000 common shares outstanding at the beginning of 20X2. Net earnings were $1,445,000 in 20X2. To date, customer retention was in the range of 75%, and the key employees have remained in Aker's employment. Four new retail outlets were opened in 20X1, and one in early February 20X2. Accordingly, 500,000 common shares were issued to the prior shareholders of Moore, but not until 31 August 20X2. Aker had no other share transactions in 20X2.

Required:

Calculate basic and diluted earnings per share figures for 20X2.

★★ **A20-9 Basic EPS:** The Duckworth Ltd. 20X5 financial statements include the following:

excel

connect

Statement of comprehensive income		
Year ended 31 December 20X5		
Earnings from continuing operations		$ 3,336,000
Discontinued operations (net of tax)		432,000
Net earnings and comprehensive income		$ 3,768,000
Statement of financial position		
31 December 20X5		
Bonds payable, 5%, nonconvertible		$10,000,000
Preferred shares, no-par value, $0.90, nonconvertible, noncumulative, outstanding during year, 500,000 shares		10,000,000
Common shares, no-par value:		
Outstanding 1 Jan., 34,000,000 shares	$7,360,000	
Sold and issued 1 April, 3,240,000 shares	1,400,000	
Issued 10% stock dividend, 30 Sept., 3,724,000 shares	1,490,000	10,250,000
Retained earnings		7,910,000

The company declared and paid preferred dividends of $20,000 during the year and had an effective tax rate of 25%.

Required:

1. Compute basic EPS.
2. Repeat requirement 1, assuming that the preferred shares are cumulative.

★★ **A20-10 EPS—Loss on Discontinued Operation:** The following information pertains to Archibald Acquisitions Ltd. (AAL) for the year ended 31 December 20X3:

a. AAL had 100,000 common shares outstanding at the end of 20X3. Of that number, 10,000 had been issued on 30 March 20X3. No dividends were issued to common shares during the year.
b. The company had 20,000 $10 cumulative nonparticipating preferred shares outstanding throughout 20X3. Dividends of $6 were declared and paid during the year. The preferred shares are convertible into two common shares for each preferred share at any time.
c. AAL had $1,200,000 in 8% convertible debentures outstanding throughout the period. The debentures are convertible into 20 common shares per $1,000 principal amount. The company paid $96,000 in interest and recorded interest expense of $102,000 during 20X3.
d. In December 20X3, the company recorded a loss of $600,000 (after income tax) on a discontinued operation.
e. AAL is subject to an income tax rate of 25%.

Required:

1. Determine 20X3 basic EPS and diluted EPS, both before and after discontinued operations, assuming after-tax earnings from continuing operations of $1,500,000.
2. Repeat the calculations of basic and diluted EPS, but assuming instead that after-tax earnings from continuing operations were $640,000.

★★ **A20-11 EPS—Loss on Discontinued Operation:** Bolshevik Limited's statement of financial position at 31 December 20X2 reported the following:

connect

Long-term notes payable, 6%, due in 20X9	4,000,000
Bonds payable, par value $10,000,000, 5%, each $1,000 of face value is convertible into 30 common shares; bonds mature in 20X13, net of discount	8,200,000
Common stock conversion rights	590,000
Common shares, voting, 950,000 shares outstanding	26,000,000

Additional information:

a. 50,000 common shares were issued at $50 on 1 July 20X2.
b. Common share options are outstanding, entitling holders to acquire 150,000 common shares at $9 per share.
c. Interest expense on the convertible bonds was $420,000 in 20X2.
d. Income tax rate is 25%.
e. The average common share price over the year was $11.
f. Earnings from continuing operations for 20X2 was $250,000, after tax; the company had a loss on a discontinued operation of $200,000, net of income tax effects.

Required:

Compute the EPS amount(s) that Bolshevik Limited should report for 20X2.

★★ **A20-12 EPS, Individual Effect, Cascade:** The Birch Corporation has the following items in its capital structure at 31 December 20X7, the end of the fiscal year:

connect

a. Options to purchase 400,000 common shares were outstanding for the entire period. The exercise price is $17.50 per share. The average common share price during the period was $40.
b. Preferred shares, $2 per quarter, cumulative, no-par, convertible into common shares at the rate of five shares of common for each preferred share. Seven thousand shares were outstanding for the whole year.
c. $3 million par value of 9% debentures, outstanding for the entire year. Debentures are convertible into five common shares for each $100 bond. Interest expense of $285,000 was recognized during the year.
d. Preferred shares, $5, cumulative, no-par, convertible into common shares at the rate of three shares of common for each one preferred share. Four thousand shares were outstanding for the entire year. No dividends were declared in 20X7 on these shares.
e. $8 million par value of 11.5% debentures, outstanding for the entire year. Debentures are convertible into a total of 520,000 common shares. Interest expense of $660,000 was recognized during the year.

Required:

1. Calculate the individual effect for diluted EPS for each of the above items. The tax rate is 35%. For options, calculate shares issued and shares retired.
2. Assume Birch reported basic EPS from continuing operations items of $1.29 [($1,000,000 – $14,000 – $20,000) ÷ 750,000], discontinued operations gain of $1.00 ($750,000 ÷ 750,000) and EPS for net earnings of $2.29 [($1,750,000 – $14,000 – $20,000) ÷ 750,000]. Calculate diluted EPS, and show how it would be presented on the statement of comprehensive income.

★★ **A20-13 EPS Computations, Financial Instruments:** On 31 December 20X3, the capital structure of Victor Varieties Limited was as follows:

Solution

- $4,500,000 face value of 12% debentures, due 1 April 20X10, convertible into eight common shares per $1,000. Interest on the 12% debentures is paid on 1 April and 1 October of each year. On 2 April 20X3, 12% debentures with a face value of $1,500,000 had been converted. Interest expense on these bonds was $48,000 in 20X3. Interest expense on all the 12% bonds amounted to $624,000, including the $48,000.
- $3,000,000 face value of 12.4% debentures, due 30 June 20X15, convertible into eight common shares per $1,000 after 30 June 20X7. Interest expense related to these bonds was $450,000 in 20X3. Interest is paid on 30 June and 31 December of each year.
- 30,000 cumulative preferred shares issued and outstanding, $8 per share dividend, redeemable at the shareholder's option at $100 per share. These preferred shares are classified as debt. Dividends are reported as a financing expense in earnings.
- 100,000 options outstanding to senior management, exerciseable in 20X14. The options allow purchase of 100,000 at $25 per share. Average market price in 20X3 was $14.
- 60,000 common shares issued and outstanding.

Victor Varieties reported net earnings after tax of $600,000 for 20X3. The tax rate was 40%.

Required:
Compute EPS for 20X3.

★★ **A20-14 Basic and Diluted EPS:** The following information relates to Willowdale Limited's financial statements for the year ended 31 December 20X6:

connect

a. On 1 January 20X6, Willowdale's capital structure consisted of the following:
   - 450,000 common shares, issued for $5.75 million, were outstanding.
   - 50,000 preferred shares bearing cumulative dividend rights of $5 per year.
   - $1 million (par value) of 8% convertible bonds ($1,000 face value), with interest payable on 30 June and 31 December of each year. Each $1,000 bond is convertible into 65 common shares, at the option of the holder, at any time before 31 December 20X11.
   - Outstanding options for 50,000 common shares at a price of $5 per share. The average market value of common shares during the period was $20.

b. On 30 September 20X6, Willowdale issued an additional 100,000 common shares for $1.5 million cash.

c. Willowdale reported earnings of $1.5 million for the year ended 31 December 20X6 net of tax of 25%.

Required:
Calculate the basic and diluted earnings per share figures for 20X6.

★★ **A20-15 Basic and Diluted EPS:** At the end of 20X7, the records of Info Solutions Limited reflected the following:

Solution

Statement of financial position:

Bonds payable, 10%, $600,000 par value, issued 1 January 20X0; entirely converted to common shares on 1 December 20X7; each $1,000 bond was convertible to 110 common shares	$ 0
Preferred shares, $0.50, convertible 2-for-1 into common shares, cumulative, nonparticipating; shares issued and outstanding during year, 30,000 shares	390,000

Common shares, no-par value, authorized unlimited shares; issued and outstanding throughout the period to 1 July 20X7, 150,000 shares. 300,000 shares were sold for cash on 1 July 20X7, additional shares were also issued on 1 December when bondholders converted	2,820,000
Common stock conversion rights, related to 10% bonds payable, above	0
Retained earnings (no dividends declared during year)	1,710,000
Statement of comprehensive income:	
Net earnings (after $47,250 of interest expense to 1 December on convertible bonds, as above)	366,000

Average income tax rate, 30%.

Required:

Compute the required EPS amounts. Show computations, and round to two decimal places.

★★ **A20-16 Individual Effects:** For the year ended 31 December 20X3, Daffy Daisy Donut Corporation (DDD) had earnings from continuing operations of $2,300,000 before taxes and a loss on discontinued operations of $1,500,000 before tax. DDD pays income tax at an average rate of 30%. DDD had the following items and occurrences regarding its capital structure in 20X3:

a. 400,000 common shares issued and outstanding during the entire year; the shares carry one vote each.
b. 5,000 preferred shares issued to a private equity firm on 1 July for cash. The shares carry a cumulative dividend of $16 per share per year. These preferred shares carry five votes per share. On 31 December 20X8, the preferred shares mandatorily convert to four shares of common for each share of preferred.
c. $60,000 in 8% convertible bonds maturing in 20X9. The bonds are convertible into common shares at a conversion rate of $20 (that is, five shares per $100 or 50 shares per $1,000).
d. 1,000 options issued to senior managers, exercisable for common shares at $20. The average market price of the common shares was $12 during 20X3.

Required:

1. Determine the individual effect on EPS for each any of the potentially dilutive items in DDD's capital structure.
2. Determine all earnings per share amounts that DDD should report in its financial statements for 20X3.

★★ **A20-17 Individual Effects:** MacAfee Corporation has basic earnings per Class A common share of $2.61. MacAfee has a tax rate of 25%. The average share price during the year was $42. Review each of the following items:

connect

a. Class B nonvoting cumulative $1 shares, 75,000 shares outstanding all year, convertible into Class A shares at the rate of four Class B shares for one Class A share. Dividends of $0.50 were declared this year and basic EPS properly reflects the dividend entitlement of these preferred shares.
b. Class A common stock options outstanding all year for 30,000 shares at a price of $65.
c. Class A common stock options outstanding all year for 30,000 shares at a price of $35.
d. Class A common stock options granted at the end of the fiscal year for 10,000 shares at $32 per share.
e. 12%, eight-year $5,000,000 convertible bonds outstanding all year, convertible into 18 Class A common shares for every $1,000 bond. A bond discount was recorded when the

bond was originally issued and amortization of $43,750 was recorded on the discount this year. On issuance, $420,000 of common stock conversion rights were recorded in shareholders' equity.

f. 8%, 15-year, $9,000,000 convertible bonds outstanding all year, convertible into 24 Class A common shares for every $1,000 bond. A bond discount was recorded on issuance, and amortization of $19,200 was recorded on the discount this year. On issuance, $145,000 of common stock conversion rights were recorded in shareholders' equity.

Required:

Indicate whether each of the above items would be included or excluded in a calculation of diluted EPS, and why. The solution should include the individual effect of each item, as applicable. If the item is included, indicate the change to the numerator and denominator of diluted EPS.

★★ **A20-18 Basic and Diluted EPS:** The shareholders' equity of Cameron Corporation as of 31 December 20X6, the *end* of the current fiscal year, is as follows:

connect

$1 cumulative preferred shares, no-par, convertible at the rate of 4-for-1; 350,000 shares outstanding	$ 9,150,000
Common shares, no-par; 3,500,000 shares outstanding	15,000,000
Common stock conversion rights	231,000
Retained earnings	30,600,000

Additional information:

- On 1 July 20X6, 150,000 preferred shares were converted to common shares at the rate of 4-for-1.
- During 20X6, Cameron had convertible subordinated debentures outstanding with a face value of $4,000,000. The debentures are due in 20X12, at which time they may be converted to common shares or repaid at the option of the holder. The conversion rate is 12 common shares for each $100 debenture. Interest expense of $175,000 was recorded in 20X6.
- The convertible preferred shares had been issued in 20X0. Quarterly dividends, on 31 March, 30 June, 30 September, and 31 December, have been regularly declared.
- The company's 20X6 net earnings were $2,289,000, after tax at 30%. Common shares traded for an average price of $18, stable in each quarter of the year.
- Cameron had certain employee stock options outstanding all year. The options were to purchase 600,000 common shares at a price of $14 per share. The options become exercisable in 20X13.
- Cameron had another 100,000 employee stock options outstanding on 1 January 20X6, at an exercise price of $22. They expired on 30 June 20X6.

Required:

Show the EPS presentation that Cameron would include on its 20X6 statement of comprehensive income.

★★ **A20-19 Basic and Diluted EPS, Split:** Accounting staff at Linfei Corporation have gathered the following information:

- Common shares outstanding on 31 December 20X4, 300,000.
- A 3-for-1 stock split was distributed on 1 February 20X4.
- 280,000 common shares were sold for cash of $50 per share on 1 March 20X4.
- Linfei purchased and retired 40,000 common shares on 1 June 20X4.
- 50,000 Series II options were issued in 20X1, originally allowing the holder to buy one share at $25 for every option held beginning in 20X8. Terms of the options were adjusted for the split in February. (The shares were tripled and the price reduced to one-third.)

- Linfei has $4,000,000 par-value convertible bonds outstanding. There is $692,000 in a common stock conversion rights account with respect to the bonds. Each $1,000 bond was originally convertible into 30 common shares. Terms were adjusted for the split in February. Interest expense on the bond, including discount amortization of $48,000, was $420,000 in 20X4. The bonds are convertible at any time before their maturity date in 20X18.
- Net profit in 20X4 was $860,000.
- The tax rate was 40% and the average common share price in 20X4, after being adjusted for the split, was $20.

Required:
Calculate all EPS disclosures for 20X4. Note that there were 300,000 common shares outstanding at the end of the fiscal period and calculations must work backward from this date.

★★ **A20-20 Diluted EPS, Conversions:** Targeted Ltd. (TL) reports the following calculations for basic EPS, for the year ended 31 December 20X4:

Numerator:	Net earnings, $18,600,000, less preferred dividends of $1,500,000
Denominator:	Weighted-average ordinary shares outstanding, 6,240,000
Basic EPS:	$2.74 ($17,100,000 ÷ 6,240,000)

Assume two different scenarios for Targeted Ltd—Case A versus Case B as shown below:

Case A Assume that TL had 800,000 convertible preferred shares outstanding at the beginning of the year. Each share was entitled to a dividend of $2 per year, payable $0.50 each quarter. Each share is convertible into three common shares. After the third-quarter dividend was paid, 200,000 preferred shares converted to 600,000 common shares. The information above regarding dividends paid and the weighted-average ordinary shares outstanding properly reflects the conversion for the purposes of calculating basic EPS.

Case B Assume instead that TL had nonconvertible preferred shares outstanding in 20X4, on which dividends of $1,500,000 were paid. Also assume that TL had convertible bonds outstanding at the beginning of 20X4. On 1 November, the entire bond issue was converted to 2,400,000 common shares, per the bond agreement. The information above regarding earnings properly reflects interest expense of $2,803,317 from 1 January to 1 November. The weighted-average ordinary share figure also reflects the appropriate common shares for the conversion. The tax rate is 30%.

TL also had options outstanding at the end of the fiscal year, for 500,000 common shares at an option price of $15. The average common share price was $28 during the period.

Required:
Calculate diluted EPS for each of Case A and Case B, independently.

★★ **A20-21 EPS, Cascade:** Ashante Sports Collections Limited (ASCL) ended 20X5 with 700,000 common shares outstanding, after issuing 200,000 common shares for cash on 31 December. The tax rate is 40%. There were no other common share transactions during the period. Net earnings were $1,300,000. The following elements are part of ASCL's capital structure:

connect

a. ASCL had $5,000,000 (par value) of 8% bonds payable outstanding during the year. The bonds are convertible into 80 common shares for each $1,000 bond. Bond interest expense was $403,000 for the year.
b. ASCL had 40,000 options outstanding throughout 20X5 to purchase 120,000 common shares for $3 per share. The average share price during the year was $15. The options were not exercisable until 20X10.

c. ASCL had 70,000, $1.25 preferred shares outstanding. The shares were cumulative. No dividends were declared in 20X6. The shares were convertible into 50,000 common shares.
d. ASCL had a contingent share agreement outstanding to issue 50,000 common shares to the prior shareholders of a company that ASCL had acquired in 20X2. The shares become issuable if the acquired company's operations accumulate $5,000,000 of post-acquisition earnings before the end of 20X8. Earnings have been $3,500,000, to date, and the target is expected to be met in 20X7.
e. ASCL had $8,000,000 (par value) of 6% bonds payable, issued on 31 March 20X5. The bonds are convertible into 40 common shares for each $1,000 bond. Bond interest expense was $285,750 for the nine months of the year that the bond was outstanding.

Required:
Compute basic and diluted EPS for 20X5.

★★ **A20-22 EPS, Cascade; Stock Split:** Bytol Corp had the following common share transactions and balances during 20X8:

1 January—140,000 shares outstanding
30 April—55,000 shares issued on conversion of $5,000,000 bonds payable
30 September—25,000 shares issued on conversion of preferred shares
1 December—3-for-1 stock dividend

Bytol reported net earnings of $920,000 in the year. The bond that converted on 30 April had been a 6%, five-year $5,000,000 convertible bond. It converted at maturity. There had originally been a bond discount recorded, with a remaining balance of $8,333 at the beginning of the year. There was also a $216,000 common stock conversion option recorded in equity with respect to this bond. This was transferred to the common share account on bond conversion. There were preferred shares outstanding, $2.00 cumulative shares, convertible 5-for-1 prior to the split and 15-for-1 after the split. The preferred dividend was payable quarterly (that is, $0.50 per quarter) and 5,000 of the total 20,000 outstanding preferred shares converted after the dividend paid on 30 September. The tax rate was 40%.

Required:
Calculate basic and diluted EPS for 20X8.

★★ **A20-23 EPS—Stock Split, Discontinued Operations:** Sea Products Corporation (SPC) reported $6,080,000 of earnings from continuing operations for the 20X4 fiscal year, and an after-tax loss from discontinued operations of $7,610,000. Preferred dividends and a common dividend of $1 per share were declared in 20X4. The average common share price was $7 during the period (adjusted for the split; see below), and the tax rate was 35%.

SPC reported the following financial instruments as part of its capital structure at the end of 20X4:

1. 4,900,000 common shares outstanding. Of these, 2,450,000 had been issued as a 2-for-1 stock split on 1 October 20X4. The terms of all share contracts were adjusted to reflect the split, and adjusted values are given in the information that follows.
2. $5,000,000 of bonds payable, convertible into 120,000 common shares beginning in 20X12 at the option of the investor. The bonds are reported as a liability, with a discount, and as an element of equity. Interest paid this year was $240,000, and there was $50,600 of discount amortization recorded.
3. 600,000 preferred shares, with a $2 per share cumulative dividend. There had been 700,000 shares outstanding at the beginning of 20X3. In January, 100,000 shares, with an average issuance price of $625,000, were retired for $699,000.
4. Options outstanding: 150,000 shares at an option price of $10, exercisable beginning in 20X7; 500,000 shares at an option price of $5, exercisable beginning in 20X12; 200,000 shares at an option price of $4, exercisable beginning in 20X13.

Required:
Calculate required EPS disclosures.

★★ **A20-24 EPS—Contingent Shares, Conversions:** Information regarding Fujing Ltd:

- Common shares outstanding on 31 December 20X1: 100,000. The company had issued 40,000 shares under a contingent share agreement on 1 December 20X2. It had also issued 50,000 common shares when preferred shares converted on 30 September 20X2.
- The average price of common shares was $14.
- The 40,000 shares issued under a contingent share agreement were issued under an agreement with a previously acquired company. The agreement stated that if a lawsuit that had been filed against this acquired company (before it was acquired by Fujing) were to be dismissed in court action, then 40,000 shares would be issued. The court dismissed the lawsuit in late November, and shares were issued on 1 December.
- A second contingent share agreement related to profit levels of a target company. This contingent share agreement calls for an additional 50,000 common shares to be issued in 20X5 if 20X2, 20X3, and 20X4 earnings from the target company each reach a certain level. This level was attained in 20X2.
- Preferred shares, $3, cumulative: these shares were convertible 5-for-1. At the beginning of the year, 30,000 shares were outstanding and 10,000 shares converted on 30 September 20X2. The dividend is paid quarterly.
- Fujing Ltd. has $3,000,000 par value convertible bonds outstanding. There is $104,000 in a common stock conversion rights account with respect to the bonds. The bonds are convertible into 50,000 common shares. Interest paid on the bond was $180,000, and there was discount amortization of $17,000. The bonds are convertible at any time before their maturity date in 20X20.
- Net earnings in 20X2, $602,000.
- The tax rate was 20%.

Required:
Calculate basic and diluted EPS for 20X2.

★★ **A20-25 Two-Year Basic EPS, Interpretation:** Huron Resources is a public oil field services company. Selected information follows:

	20X4	20X3
Bonds payable, 7%, due 20X16	$ 6,000,000	$ 6,000,000
Preferred shares, $3 dividend, noncumulative, 100,000 shares outstanding	$ 1,600,000	$ 1,600,000
Preferred shares, $2 dividend, cumulative, 50,000 shares outstanding. Redemption price $20 per share plus dividends in arrears, if any	$ 2,100,000	$ 2,100,000
Common shares, 900,000 shares outstanding at the end of 20X4 after 300,000 shares were issued for cash on 31 October 20X4; no share transactions in 20X3	$16,200,000	$10,700,000
Dividends declared during the year	$ 540,000	0
Net earnings and comprehensive income	$ 700,000	$ 400,000

Required:

1. Calculate basic EPS for 20X4 and 20X3.
2. Interpret the trend in basic EPS.
3. Repeat requirement 1, assuming that the shares issued in 20X4 were issued as a result of a stock dividend.

★★ **A20-26 Two-Year Basic EPS, Interpretation:** Gannon Ltd. reported earnings as follows:

Year ended 31 December	20X2	20X1
Earnings from continuing operations (net of tax)	$993,000	1,019,000
Discontinued operations (net of tax)	(116,000)	77,000
Net earnings and comprehensive income	$877,000	$1,096,000

The capital structure of Gannon Ltd included the following :

31 December	20X2	20X1
Bonds payable, 5%, due 20X15	$5,000,000	$5,000,000
Class B Preferred shares, $0.70, cumulative, nonparticipating; shares issued and outstanding, 120,000 shares, issued 1 January 20X2	3,000,000	—
Class A Preferred shares, $1, noncumulative, nonparticipating; shares issued and outstanding, 50,000 shares	1,250,000	1,250,000
Common shares, no-par, authorized unlimited shares; issued and outstanding on 1 January 20X1, 150,000 shares. Retired for cash, on 1 November 20X1, 50,000 shares. Shares were split 3-for-1 on 30 November 20X2. Outstanding 31 December 20X2, 300,000 shares.	3,500,000	3,500,000
Retained earnings; no dividends declared in 20X2 or 20X1	2,570,000	1,693,000

Required:

1. Calculate 20X2 basic EPS, including the comparative 20X1 calculation.
2. Interpret the trend in basic EPS.

★★★ **A20-27 EPS—Complex Structure:** MacDonald Corporation had the following securities outstanding at its fiscal year-end 31 December 20X7:

excel

connect

Long-term debt:	
Notes payable, 14%	$4,500,000
8% convertible debentures, par value $2,500,000, net of discount	2,410,000
9.5% convertible debentures, par value $2,500,000, net of discount	2,452,000
Equity:	
Preferred shares, $5 dividend, payable as $1.25 per quarter, no-par, cumulative convertible shares; authorized, 100,000 shares; issued, 30,000 shares	4,700,000
Common shares, no-par; authorized, 5,000,000 shares; issued, 600,000 shares	2,000,000
Common share conversion rights	189,000

Additional information:

a. 20X7 net earnings were $790,000. There were no discontinued operations.
b. Interest expense was $216,000 on the 8% debentures, and $250,000 on the 9.5% debentures.
c. Options to purchase 200,000 common shares at $11 per share beginning in 20X15 were outstanding throughout the year.
d. Additional options were issued on 1 May 20X7 to purchase 50,000 common shares at $27 per share in 20X9. The price per share becomes $25 in 20X10 and $20 in 20X11. These options expire at the end of 20X11.
e. The preferred shares are convertible into common shares at a rate of 9-for-1. They were issued on 1 October 20X7.

f. The 8% convertible debentures are convertible at the rate of seven shares for each $100 bond. The 9.5% convertible debentures are convertible at the rate of six shares for each $100 bond.
g. The tax rate is 30%; common shares traded for an average of $40 during the year.
h. No common shares were issued or retired during the year.

Required:
Calculate all EPS disclosures.

★★★ **A20-28 EPS, Discontinued Operations; Interpretation:** Marcella Corporation reported 20X6 earnings from continuing operations of $2,022,800 and a loss from discontinued operations of $677,800 after tax. The tax rate was 30%.

Marcella reports the following information regarding its securities:

a. 400,000 $2 no-par cumulative preferred shares, issued 1 July 20X6. The shares are convertible into Class A common shares 6-for-1 at the option of the investor. The dividend was paid on a quarterly basis.
b. There are 175,000 $1.20 no-par cumulative preferred shares outstanding during 20X6. These shares were convertible into Class A common shares 4-for-1 at the option of the investor. All preferred shares converted to Class A common shares on 31 December 20X6 after the preferred dividend was paid.
c. There are $3,000,000 of convertible bonds payable outstanding during 20X6, convertible into Class A shares at the rate of 30 shares per $1,000 bond, at the option of the investor. This bond was recorded as a hybrid financial instrument. During the year, interest of $300,000 was paid; the company recorded interest expense of $281,000.
d. Marcella had 2,300,000 Class A common shares outstanding at the beginning of the year. On 1 February, the company repurchased and retired 750,000 Class A common shares on the open market for $18 per share. Marcella issued 50,000 common shares for $22 per share on 1 December.

At the beginning of the year, 200,000 options were outstanding, allowing senior management to purchase 200,000 Class A shares for $5 per share. On 1 September, 60,000 of these options were exercised, when the market value of the common shares was $19 per share. The average market value for the first eight months of the year was $15 per share. The remaining options are still outstanding and will expire in 20X10.

All preferred dividends, plus common dividends of $1 per share, were paid on schedule in 20X6.

At the end of 20X6, another 400,000 options, for 400,000 Class A shares at a price of $24, were issued to management. These options have an expiry date of 20X15. The average common share price for the entire year was $22 per share.

Required:
1. Calculate required EPS disclosures.
2. Interpret the EPS results

★★★ **A20-29 EPS—Complex Structure, Split:** At 31 December 20X1, Regina Realty Limited had the following items on the statement of financial position:

eXcel

Preferred shares, Class A, nonvoting, cumulative, par $10, $0.50 dividend per share, redeemable at the investor's option at par in 20X11; 200,000 authorized, 30,000 issued	$ 300,000
Preferred shares, Class B, voting, cumulative, par $15, $0.90 dividend per share, redeemable at the company's option at par plus 20%; convertible at the rate of one preferred share to two Class A common shares; 200,000 authorized, 90,000 issued	$1,350,000

Common shares, Class A, voting with one vote per share; unlimited shares authorized, 500,000 shares issued	$5,357,000
Common shares, Class B, voting with ten votes per share; entitled to two times the dividends of a Class A common share, unlimited shares authorized, 50,000 shares issued	$ 587,000
Retained earnings	$2,966,000

The Class A preferred shares are redeemable in 20X11 at the investors' option and are classified as a liability. Dividends on these shares are reported as interest expense and have been deducted from earnings.

At 31 December 20X1, there were two common share Class A stock options outstanding:

- $10 per share exercise price and 60,000 shares, able to be exercised after 1 July 20X1 and expiring on 1 July 20X3.
- $9 per share exercise price and 88,000 shares, able to be exercised after 1 July 20X18 and expiring on 1 July 20X20.

During 20X2, the following occurred:

a. Net earnings was $1,140,000, correctly calculated.
b. Class A common shares were issued on 1 March 20X2 when the $10 options described above were fully exercised.
c. The tax rate was 40%.
d. The average Class A common share price during the period was $12, after giving effect to the stock split described in (f). The adjusted average for January and February was $14.
e. No dividends were declared or paid to any of the shareholders.
f. There was a 3-for-1 stock split of the Class A and Class B common shares on 1 November. All outstanding shares, option contracts, and conversion terms were adjusted accordingly. (That is, the number of shares increased and the price per share decreased.)

Required:

Prepare the earnings per share disclosure for the year ended 31 December 20X2 in good form.

(Source: The Canadian Institute of Chartered Accountants, © 2010.)

★★★ **A20-30 EPS—Complex Structure:** The following data relate to Freeman Incorporation:

Solution

Year Ended 31 December 20X6	
From the statement of comprehensive income	
Net earnings and comprehensive income	$18,000,000
From the statement of financial position	
Long-term debt:	
10% convertible debentures, due 1 October 20X13	$ 9,000,000
Shareholders' equity	
Convertible, callable, voting preferred shares of no-par value, $0.20 cumulative dividend; authorized 600,000 shares; issued and outstanding 600,000 shares	10,600,000
Common shares, voting, no-par, authorized 5,000,000 shares; issued and outstanding, 3,320,000 shares	13,700,000
Common stock conversion rights	375,000

FROM THE DISCLOSURE NOTES:

- The $0.20 convertible preferred shares are callable by the company after 31 March 20X14, at $60 per share. Each share is convertible into one common share.
- Options to acquire 500,000 common shares at $53 per share were outstanding during 20X6.

Additional information:

a. Cash dividends of 12.5 cents per common share were declared and paid each quarter.
b. The 10% convertible debentures with a principal amount of $10,000,000 due 1 October 20X13, were issued 1 October 20X3. A discount was originally recorded, and discount amortization was $20,000 in the current year. Each $100 debenture is convertible into two common shares. On 31 December 20X6, ten thousand $100 debentures with a total face value of $1,000,000 were converted to common shares. Interest was paid to the date of conversion, but the newly issued common shares did not qualify for the 31 December common dividend.
c. The 600,000 convertible preferred shares were issued for assets in a purchase transaction in 20X4. The dividend was declared and paid on 15 December 20X6. Each share is convertible into one common share.
d. Options to buy 500,000 common shares at $53 per share for a period of five years were issued along with the convertible preferred shares mentioned in (c).
e. At the end of 20X5, 3,300,000 common shares were outstanding. On 31 December 20X6, 20,000 shares were issued on the conversion of bonds.
f. A tax rate of 40% is assumed.
g. Common shares traded at an average market price of $75 during the year.

Required:
Calculate all EPS disclosures.

connect LEARNSMART SMARTBOOK™

For more information on the resources available from McGraw-Hill Ryerson, go to www.mcgrawhill.ca/he/solutions.

CHAPTER 21

Accounting Changes

INTRODUCTION

Between 2007 and 2009, Bombardier Inc. reported a total of nine changes in accounting policies. All of the changes were required by new or revised accounting standards. There were no accounting policy changes in 2010—that was a "quiet" year because Canadian publicly accountable enterprises were preparing for the changeover to IFRS. Then the accounting change tsunami struck in 2011, necessitating a thorough revamping of accounting policies—Bombardier devoted 20 pages of its note disclosures to the change and its effects. The change reduced the opening comparative shareholders' equity by 75%, from US$3,769 million to US$960 million. In the 2012 financial statements, Bombardier cites seven forthcoming accounting policy changes by IFRS. Obviously, accounting policies are changing regularly and can have a big impact, which makes year-to-year comparisons of financial results very difficult to interpret.

Accounting attempts to deal with these changes by requiring retrospective application of accounting policy changes. That means that prior comparative financial statements and historical data series (e.g., earnings per share) should be restated as though the new policies have always been in effect.

While restatement is the ideal, it often is not possible. The detailed data that are needed to restate previous year's earnings, EPS, and net assets simply are not available. As accounting has moved to encompass more fair value reporting, the only information available from the past is historical cost information. Thus, most policy changes actually are not fully reflected in prior years' restated statements and statistics except for the most recent year or two.

This chapter will explore the ways that accounting policy changes can be reported and the circumstances that govern each approach. As well, we will look at changes in estimates and corrections of errors, which are other types of accounting changes.

TYPES OF ACCOUNTING CHANGES

There are three types of accounting changes:

1. Change in accounting estimate;
2. Change in accounting policy; and
3. Correction of an error in prior years' financial statements.

We will discuss the nature of each of these types of changes in the following sections. Some changes require adjustment to prior years' financial statements, known as **restatement**, but other changes do not. It is important to understand the differences between the different types of changes and the impact that each type has on the financial statements of prior, current, and future years.

CHANGES IN ACCOUNTING ESTIMATES

Changes in accounting estimates are very common. Many financial statement elements require estimates of future values or events, and estimates are frequently changed. Examples of significant accounting estimates include the following:

- Uncollectible accounts receivable;
- Inventory obsolescence;
- Fair values of financial assets; and
- Judgement concerning one or more of the criteria for capitalizing development costs.

A **change in accounting estimate** occurs when management decides that assumptions used for accounting measurements in the past should be revised in light of new information or new circumstances. Changes can occur for several reasons:

- New, reliable information is available.
- Experience has provided insights into operating factors such as usage patterns or benefits.
- The company's economic environment has changed, requiring a re-evaluation of the assumptions underlying management's accounting estimates.
- Probabilities underlying accounting estimates have changed.
- There has been a shift in the nature of the company's business operations, so past estimates may need adjustment to fit current business strategies.

Accounting for Changes in Estimates

Changes in accounting estimates are part of the accounting routine. They reflect the environmental changes that affect an organization on a continuing basis rather than reflecting substantive changes in the *way* that accounting is being done. Therefore, changes in accounting estimates are accounted for *prospectively*, by applying them only in the current and future periods.

Prospective application means that the new or revised estimate is used in the current and future periods, until new evidence or circumstances indicate that the estimate needs to be changed again. There is no revision of prior years' financial statements.

One example is depreciation policy. The choice of depreciation method is a policy choice. But all of the other factors underlying depreciation expense are estimates—(1) useful life, (2) residual value, and (3) pattern of asset usage. Any or all of these estimates may change over time as a company gains more experience with various types of assets or as changes in technology may alter the estimates.

When the underlying estimates are changed, the new estimates are used for current and future depreciation calculations—that is, they are applied *prospectively*. Prior years' financial statements are not restated.

Disclosure Requirements

Disclosure requirements for changes in estimates are minimal. IAS 8 requires only that a company disclose "the nature and amount of a change in an accounting estimate that has an effect in the current period or is expected to have an effect in future periods ..." On the surface, this seems to say that companies should disclose *all* changes in estimate.

However, it really has an impact only for estimates that are "fixed," such as the useful life estimates used for depreciation and amortization. Most estimates are "flexible" in the sense that they fluctuate over time, sometimes year-to-year, depending on the company's business environment. For example, the estimate of uncollectible accounts receivable is subject to annual (or even quarterly) adjustment with the rise and fall of the economy (or of the company's customers).

A single measurement often requires *multiple* estimates. For example, Montreal-based CAE Inc. (the world's principal manufacturer of flight simulators) devotes six paragraphs to describing the company's revenue recognition policies in its 2012 financial statements. One paragraph reads as follows:

> Revenue from construction contracts for the design, engineering and manufacturing of training devices is recognized using the percentage-of-completion method when the revenue, contract costs to complete and the stage of contract completion at the end of the reporting period can be measured reliably and when the contract costs can be clearly identified and measured reliably so that actual contract costs incurred can be compared with prior estimates, and the economic benefits associated with the transaction will flow to the Company.[1]

This paragraph alone suggests the substantial number of recurring estimates that are necessary for measuring just one component of the company's revenue. Changes in these individual estimates are not disclosed in the statements; the amount of detail would be overwhelming.

This is a typical disclosure for any company that produces under long-term contracts. Remember from Chapter 6 that recognition under percentage-of-completion always requires many estimates. These estimates are applied on a contract-by-contract basis and may change even for an individual contract from year to year.

Similarly, estimates for items such as uncollectible accounts receivable and warranty expense depend on year-by-year estimates. Therefore, disclosure of changes in estimates is rare—changes in estimates happen every year for most of the financial statement elements in every company.

Disclosure Example

One specific area in which IFRS requires disclosure of some changes in estimates is in post-employment benefits. Exhibit 21-1 illustrates CAE Inc.'s disclosure of interest assumption for 2012 as compared with 2011.

Since the company decreased its assumed discount rates on the pension obligation, the present value of those obligations will have increased from 2011 to 2012. On the other hand, the discount rate applied to the return on plan assets has not changed (for the Canadian plans); a commensurate decrease in the expected return would have increased the company's funding obligation.[2]

Toronto-based AAstra Technologies Limited provides an example of a voluntary disclosure of a change in estimate. In its 2011 financial statements, the company stated:

> During the year ended December 31, 2011, the Company recorded … a reversal of inventory previously written down of $348 (2010 – $1,390), due to the sale of the inventory previously written down.[3]

In other words, management's estimate of the nonrecoverable value of inventory had been overstated in both 2009 and 2010, necessitating a reversal of the writedowns in the following years (i.e., 2010 and 2011).

---

[1] CAE Inc. 2011 Annual Report, Note 1, page 93.

[2] Note that effective with fiscal years beginning on or after 1 January 2013, IAS 19 will require companies to use the same discount rate for both the pension obligation and the net pension cost.

[3] Aastra Technologies Limited Annual Report 2011, page 45.

EXHIBIT 21-1

CAE INC.

Changes in Significant Estimates for Post-Retirement Benefits

Significant assumptions (weighted average):

	Canadian		Foreign	
	2013	**2012**	**2013**	**2012**
Pension obligation as at March 31:				
Discount rate	**4.25%**	4.75%	**3.53%**	4.12%
Compensation rate increases	**3.50%**	3.50%	**2.98%**	2.98%
Net pension cost for years ended March 31:				
Expected return on plan assets	**6.0%**	7.00%	**4.19%**	5.20%
Discount rate	**5.75%**	5.75%	**4.05%**	5.13%
Compensation rate increases	**3.50%**	3.50%	**3.01%**	2.35%

Source: CAE Inc. Annual Report 2012, Note 15, p. 123, www.sedar.com, posted 28 June 2013.

Change in Policy or Estimate?

Accounting estimates are changed very often, sometimes annually, as a company accumulates new information and gains more experience. Normally, the financial statement effect is less dramatic with a change in estimate rather than a change in policy. Also, the application method is usually different—policy changes are applied retrospectively, while estimate changes are applied prospectively.

Therefore, it is important to distinguish between estimates and policies. When it is difficult to decide whether a change is a change in policy or estimate, *the change should be treated as a change in estimate.*

Example—Changes in Depreciation Method Companies occasionally change their depreciation or amortization methods for long-term tangible and intangible assets. A change in estimated residual value or in the estimated useful life of a tangible capital asset can easily be seen as a change in estimate. On the other hand, a change from declining balance to straight line may appear to be a change in policy because the depreciation *method* has changed, not just the estimates underlying application of the method. However, the choice of depreciation method reflects management's estimate of the expected pattern of use. If the pattern of use is different than expected, then the change in method is a change of estimate, not policy.

Therefore, a change in depreciation method should be reported as a change in accounting estimate rather than as a change in accounting policy. For example, Bombardier Inc. explains its approach to amortization methods and changes in the useful lives as follows:

> The amortization methods and estimated useful lives are reviewed on a regular basis, at least annually, and changes are accounted for prospectively. The amortization expense is recorded in cost of sales, SG&A or R&D expenses based on the function of the underlying assets.[4]

Bombardier properly treats the change in depreciation method the same way as it would treat changes in estimates, such as useful life or residual value.

[4] Bombardier Inc. Annual Report 2013, Note 2, page 143.

ETHICAL ISSUES

Many changes in accounting estimates are disclosed, but many others are not. This is one of the "unknowns" that make financial statement analysis a challenge. Is the company using essentially the same estimates this year as it did in prior years? There is no way of knowing without inside information. Even for the estimates that are disclosed, it can be quite a challenge to sift through all of the changes and make sense of their implications.

This lack of transparency leads to a potential ethical concern. Since estimates underlie virtually every amount in the balance sheet, fairly subtle simultaneous changes in many estimates can have a significant impact on reported earnings. Individual changes may be immaterial, but the cumulative effect of many changes can be quite material.

For example, if a company's senior management wants to increase reported earnings, they may decrease the estimate of uncollectible receivables, prolong depreciation and amortization, take "the benefit of the doubt" about inventory items of dubious salability, use relatively lower estimates of accrued liabilities, and so forth.

The changes wrought by each individual change in estimate may be relatively minor, but if the changes increase EPS by a few cents to meet the company's earnings projections, it is a successful management strategy (although deficient in ethics). Remember that net income is a residual number; if net income is 10% of revenue, then changing estimates to reduce total reported expense by 1% will increase net income by almost 10% as those expense reductions flow through to earnings. Variation in estimates is not trivial.

By definition, all estimates are just that—*estimates*, not known or verifiable amounts. There always is a feasible range of estimates. Managers and accountants should strive to base their judgements on reasonable estimates that do not push at the limits, high or low, of the feasible range.

CONCEPT REVIEW

1. A company has accounts receivable of $200,000 and an allowance for doubtful accounts of $40,000. Bad debts have been estimated in the past at 25% of accounts receivable but now are estimated to be 15%. How much is bad debt expense (recovery) this year?
2. Capital assets with a cost of $500,000 have been depreciated for three years, assuming a useful life of five years and no residual value. This year, revised estimates are a total of eight years of useful life with no residual value. What is the amount of depreciation expense for this year?

CHANGES IN ACCOUNTING POLICIES

A **change in accounting policy** is a change in the way that a company accounts for a particular type of transaction or event, or for the resulting asset or liability. Accounting policy changes can be mandatory or voluntary:

- A change is a **mandatory change** when the IASB issues a new accounting standard or revises an existing standard. There have been many changes in standards over the past decade, and more changes are on their way. GAAP-constrained companies must alter their policies to conform to the new recommendations.
- A change is a **voluntary change** when management switches from one acceptable method of accounting to another acceptable method to provide more reliable and relevant information to users.

Note that both types of changes *are from one policy to another*. This differentiates a *change* in accounting policy from adoption of a *new* policy. We will talk about adopting new accounting policies a little later in the chapter.

Mandatory Changes Mandatory changes in accounting policy have been pervasive in recent years as new accounting standards have been introduced and existing standards altered. Bombardier's 2012 financial statements explain seven changes in accounting standards, only two of which are expected to have no impact on the company's reported results.[5]

Voluntary Changes Voluntary accounting policy changes are allowed only if the new policy results in information that is both (1) reliable and (2) more relevant for financial statement users. This criterion is met when the change gives the users of financial statements better information about the effects of transactions, events, or conditions on the entity's financial position, financial performance or cash flows.

Clearly, information has to be *reliable* to be included in the financial statements. However, the new policy has to be *more relevant* than the old policy to be adopted. IFRS does not provide guidance for judging the relevance of resulting information. Relevancy is subjective, so this will be a difficult judgement in some circumstances, particularly since it is *management* making assumptions about what will be more relevant to *users*.

A voluntary change in accounting policy may occur in response to changes in an entity's reporting circumstances, such as:

- A change in reporting objectives;
- A change in the way of doing business—for example, a shift to higher-risk business strategies that make the prediction of future outcomes more difficult and less reliable; or
- A desire to conform to industry practice.

One of the most common reasons for changing one or more accounting policies is a change in reporting objectives. For example, when the ownership of a company changes, the priority of objectives often changes or new objectives that previously did not exist suddenly become important. Examples of changes in ownership include the following:

- A company that previously was privately held may decide to issue shares on the public market and will discontinue use of private enterprise reporting standards and adopt IFRS instead.
- Control of the reporting enterprise may be acquired by another corporation in a business combination, and the acquired company may need to change its accounting policies to be consistent with those used by its new parent company.
- A new investor may purchase shares in a private company and have the power to specify that certain reporting objectives, such as cash flow prediction, are adopted.

Some changes are precipitated by industry practice. Investors tend not to be kind to companies that use one or more significant accounting policies that differ from general practice in that industry. Financial analysts can be quite aggressive at pointing out accounting policies they would like to see changed. Analysts can give management a very good idea of how a change of accounting policy would make information more useful for analysis.

---

[5] Bombardier Annual Report 2013, Note 2, pages 145–146.

ETHICAL ISSUES

Although information should be more relevant to the users, an underlying motive for accounting changes may be management's desire to manage earnings. Management may wish to change accounting policies:

- To satisfy ratios specified in lending covenants;
- To meet the published expectations of financial analysts, feeding stock prices; or
- To maximize the value of stock options granted to management.

While these objectives may seem highly desirable to managers, they do not satisfy the IFRS requirement that new policies must be *more relevant* to financial statement users. Senior accountants and auditors must be alert to such "window dressing," which is exactly what the requirement for increased relevance is intended to discourage. All changes in accounting policy must be evaluated in an objective fashion before being approved by senior financial officers and/or auditors.

REPORTING ACCOUNTING CHANGES

General Methodology

Retrospective Application with Full Restatement The basic approach to accounting for changes in policy is **retrospective restatement**.[6] The process is as follows:

- The new accounting policy is applied to events and transactions from the date of origin of each event or transaction.
- The financial statements for each prior period that are presented for comparative purposes are restated to reflect the new policy.
- Opening retained earnings (or other component of share equity, as appropriate) for each comparative period is adjusted for the cumulative prior income effect.
- All summary financial information for earlier periods, such as net income, total assets, earnings per share, and so on, is restated as well. All reported financial results after the change look as though the new policy had always been in effect.

Retrospective application of an accounting policy change is intended to make *current and future* financial information comparable with reported results for comparative prior periods. Earnings trends and other analytical data that are based on historical comparisons are not valid unless the same accounting policies are used throughout the time series. The qualitative criteria of *consistency* and *comparability* are enhanced by restatement, at least in the short run.

Retrospective Application with Partial Restatement Often, it is impracticable to apply full retrospective restatement. Retrospective restatement is *impracticable* if:

- It is not possible or feasible to determine the effects of the new policy on previous period(s);
- Application would require assumptions about management's intent in prior period(s); or
- It is impossible to reliably know what the appropriate measurements and valuations would have been in the prior period(s).

If full restatement is impracticable, the next best approach is to restate as far back as possible with the data available. Sometimes, this is possible for the past five years (the normal

[6] The word "retrospective" is used in IAS 8. Previously, Canadian standards and companies used "retroactive." "Retrospective" and "retroactive" mean the same thing when used in accounting. Many companies continue to use "retroactive."

period that companies publish comparative series of financial performance indicators). To go back further is often impossible.

In practice, *partial restatement* usually means restating the opening balances of the prior and current years. The new policy is applied in full for both the current and prior years. Thus, both the financial position and the earnings for the two years are based on the new standard, thereby facilitating comparison of the current year with the previous year.

All retrospective application requires the company to restate balances as far back as possible. That means that at the date that the new policy is applied, the opening SFP balances should incorporate the effect of the new policy as though it had been applied throughout the life of the enterprise.

Prospective Application Even partial restatement is not always feasible. A company may not be able to measure the cumulative effect on opening SFP balances. If so, then prospective application may be used. Under *prospective application*, adjustments are made from the start of the current period. Indeed, it might be impracticable to measure the effect of an accounting policy change to *any* prior period, including the immediately preceding year. In that case, the policy is applied from the date of adoption forward, with no adjustment to restate opening SFP balances.

Comparability of Statistical Series—A Caution The objective of retrospective restatement is, as explained above, to promote interyear comparability. However, this works only in the short run. Long-run comparative series, such as net earnings, EPS, operating margin, and return on investment, are all compromised by frequent changes in accounting policies. It is impossible for a company to go back 10 or often even five years and restate those statistics in any meaningful way. The data simply are not there, and even if they were, it would be both a monumental task and very costly for a company to attempt full restatement of 10 prior years' results.

Such an extensive restatement of statistics (e.g., EPS) may have been feasible in years past when accounting standards were changed infrequently. However, the flurry of new and revised standards in recent years renders the task virtually impossible. Many analysts work with a five-to-ten-year series of earnings, EPS, and return-on-investment ratios, but frequent and significant changes in accounting standards have sharply reduced the feasibility of multiyear trend analysis.

More than 20 new or revised standards became effective between 2006 and 2013. Sometimes standards even affect the way an enterprise arranges its business affairs. We cannot be too confident that prior years' comparative data has been fully adjusted for all of the effects of those many changes. Normally, data going back more than five years will not be fully adjusted.

Almost certainly, any statistical series that have been compiled by analysts will not be adjusted for accounting policy changes because the analysts do not have access to the internal company data that are required to make the adjustments. Indeed, for many complex enterprises, it is virtually impossible to compare pre-2011 financial results with post-2011 financial results due to Canada's adoption of IFRS in 2011.

One might argue that the nature of a business's operations has also been changing over time and thus the ingredients of earnings are ever-changing. While that may well be true, applying changing measurement to changing conditions just makes the statistical series even less meaningful. It is like constructing a price index that prices a different set of goods each year—it will yield a statistical series of prices, but comparisons will not have much meaning because the measurement method is not consistent—garbage in, garbage out.

RETROSPECTIVE APPLICATION

The basic rule in adjusting for changes in accounting policy is really quite simple:

> Restate prior period reported amounts as far back as practicable; if you do not have the information to enable restatement, then apply the new policy in the current and future years.

This is no official IFRS terminology, but it is the essence. Now, let us go on to the application of this simple-seeming rule.

Guidelines The following guidelines apply to accounting policy changes that are applied by restating prior years. The same approach is used for correction of prior years' accounting errors, which we will discuss in more detail in the last major section of this chapter.

In the following list, note that the first guideline refers to *recording* the change in the company's books, while the next four guidelines refer to *reporting* in the financial statements and disclosure notes.

For *recording* in the entity's accounts:

1. The *cumulative* impact of the change on the *beginning* balances of the current year must be calculated. These changes are *recorded* in the accounts by means of a general journal entry. The cumulative impact of the accounting policy change on prior year's net income is recorded as an adjustment to the beginning balance of retained earnings or accumulated OCI, depending on the type of adjustment required.

For financial statement *presentation*:

2. The information necessary to make the change *in the current and prior periods* must be obtained from the underlying accounting records.
3. Account balances that affect the prior years' comparative financial statements must be recalculated using the new policy, including all affected balance sheet and income statement accounts. The comparative statements must be restated to reflect the changed amounts in the full financial statements.
4. Summary comparative information (e.g., earnings per share, total assets, shareholders' equity) that are presented publicly, such as in the annual report, must be recalculated using the new policy.
5. Opening retained earnings is restated to remove the effect of the accounting change from prior earnings. Opening retained earnings *as restated* is shown as a subtotal. This is done for all comparative years. The amount of the adjustment will change as the *number of prior years* declines.
6. If the adjustment was to other comprehensive income, then the opening accumulated OCI amounts would require restatement and be shown as a subtotal.

Under retrospective restatement, all prior-period data are restated for financial reporting purposes. However, the entry to record the cumulative effect of the change is made only in the current year. Prior years' books have been closed—the cumulative adjustment must be made to opening retained earnings (or accumulated OCI) of the current year.

Illustration

Exhibit 21-2 presents the data for an illustration of the retrospective approach with restatement. In this example, we assume that Sunset Corporation has decided to change its method of accounting for inventories from average cost (AC) to first-in, first-out (FIFO), in the fiscal year ending 31 December 20X5. To make the change, Sunset must not only recalculate its inventory balances for the end of 20X4 to determine net income for 20X5 but also recalculate its inventory balances for the beginning of 20X4 to restate the comparative results for 20X4.

The first step in restatement is to determine which balances will be affected by the change. For a change in inventory method, the following balances will be affected:

- Beginning inventory;
- Ending inventory;
- Cost of goods sold;
- Income tax expense;
- Deferred income tax (on the SFP); and
- Retained earnings.

The statement of comprehensive income, the statement of financial position, and the retained earnings section of the statement of changes in equity will all require restatement for 20X4. A change in accounting policy does not affect cash flows. However, if the company uses the indirect method of presenting cash from operations, a change in inventory method will affect the operations section of the statement of cash flows because:

- The policy change will alter both cost of goods sold and income tax expense, which affects net income, which is the starting point for determining cash flow from operations (using the indirect presentation approach); and
- The change in inventory and the change in deferred income tax are adjustments to convert net income to cash flow.

These two adjustments will net out, causing no change in the total reported cash from operations. Nevertheless, the changes must be made to maintain the articulation between the statement of cash flows and the other two statements.

In our inventory example, the following impacts of the accounting change must be calculated:

1. The cumulative effect on balances up to 1 January 20X5 (the year of the change);
2. The cumulative effect on balances up to 1 January 20X4; and
3. The specific impact on the accounts for the year 20X4, for comparative restatement purposes.

The new basis of accounting must then be used for the current year, 20X5. The calculations for Sunset Corporation are as follows, using the amounts presented in Exhibit 21-2.

EXHIBIT 21-2

SUNSET CORPORATION DATA FOR CHANGE IN ACCOUNTING POLICY

Change from Average Cost to FIFO for Inventory

1. During 20X5, Sunset Corporation decides to change its inventory cost method from average cost (AC) to first-in, first-out (FIFO) for accounting purposes, effective for fiscal year 20X5. The change will also be made for income tax purposes. The reporting year ends on 31 December, and the company's income tax rate is 30%.
2. From its records, the company determines the following information relating to the change:

	20X5		20X4	
	FIFO	**AC**	**FIFO**	**AC**
Statement of Financial Position				
a. Beginning inventory	$ 60,000	$ 50,000	$ 47,000	$ 45,000
b. Ending inventory	80,000	65,000	60,000	50,000
Statement of Changes in Equity				
c. Retained earnings, beginning balance	$201,000			$ 92,000
d. Net income (see below)	210,000			189,000
e. Dividends declared and paid	88,000			80,000
f. Retained earnings, ending balance	$323,000			$201,000
Statement of Comprehensive Income				
g. Income before income tax	300,000*			270,000
h. Income tax expense	90,000			81,000
i. Net income	$210,000			$189,000

*Reflects FIFO policy.

Recording—Impact to 1 January 20X5

The journal entry to record the effects of the change in policy is based on the cumulative effect at the beginning of 20X5:

a. 20X5 opening inventory increases by $10,000—from $50,000 under AC to $60,000 under FIFO;

b. The increase in 20X5 opening inventory means an increase of $10,000 in 20X4 ending inventory;

c. The increase in 20X4 ending inventory means 20X4 cost of goods sold should be lowered by $10,000;

d. The reduction of 20X4 cost of goods sold means that comparative 20X4 earnings must be increased by $10,000; and

e. The $10,000 in retrospective additional 20X5 earnings flows is credited to retained earnings.

For reporting purposes, the cumulative increase belongs to retained earnings from prior years. In contrast, the full impact of the restatement will flow through to taxable earnings in 20X5 because prior years' income tax returns cannot be changed retroactively. Therefore, the adjustment to retained earnings must take into account the additional taxes that will be due for 20X5. After tax (at 30%), the net increase in retained earnings is $7,000. The entry to restate prior years' earnings is:

Inventory	10,000	
Current income tax payable (30% tax rate)		3,000
Retained earnings		7,000
[cumulative effect of policy change prior to 20X5]		

This entry establishes the new accounting policy in the accounts as of the *beginning* of 20X5; all future entries will be made on the basis of the new accounting policy. No additional entries are necessary.

Reporting—Impact to 1 January 20X4

The cumulative impact of the change in policy for all years prior to 20X4 is captured in the change to 20X4 beginning inventory. The cost of goods adjustment is:

$47,000 (FIFO) – $45,000 (Average Cost) = $2,000; income is higher.

After income tax, assuming a 30% tax rate, the impact on accumulated earnings is:

$2,000 × (1 – 30%) = $1,400; income is higher.

This adjustment for pre-20X4 is not recorded in the books. The effect has already been captured in the retained earnings adjusting entry made in 20X5, as described just above.

Reporting—Effect on the Financial Statements of 20X4

Restatement of the 20X4 financial statements requires changing the beginning and ending inventory balance on the SFP and the cost of goods sold on the statement of comprehensive income. Changing the cost of goods sold has an impact on income tax expense, net income, and deferred income tax. The change in net income flows through to retained earnings and therefore to total shareholders' equity.

The ending 20X4 inventory under FIFO is $60,000, compared with the $50,000 originally reported in the 20X4 financial statements, as shown in Exhibit 21-2. Opening inventory is now $47,000, instead of $45,000. The effect on 20X4 net income is as follows:

- FIFO has a higher beginning inventory, increasing cost of goods sold and lowering pretax net income by $2,000.
- FIFO also has a higher ending inventory, lowering cost of the goods sold and increasing pretax net income by $10,000.
- The net effect of the changes in the beginning and ending inventories is to increase 20X4 income before tax by $8,000—the $10,000 increase due to the impact on ending inventory minus the $2,000 decrease caused by the change in beginning inventory.
- The income tax rate is 30%; the increase in income tax expense from the change in policy is $2,400: $8,000 × 30%.

The changes to the 20X4 statements can be summarized as follows:

Statement of Comprehensive Income

Cost of goods sold decreases by $8,000 (credit).
Income tax expense increases by $2,400 (debit).
Net income increases by $5,600 (credit).

Statement of Financial Position

Inventory (ending) increases by $10,000 (debit).
Current income tax payable changes by $3,000 (credit).
Retained earnings increases by $7,000 (credit).

Note that the changes in the statement of comprehensive income reflect the impact of the accounting policy change *only* for 20X4. The change in the SFP, however, reflects the *cumulative* impact of the changes up to the end of 20X4. The difference between the total adjustment of $7,000 and the 20X4-related adjustment is the amount related to periods *prior* to 20X4:

Total change in retained earnings	$7,000 credit
Less: Impact on the net income and retained earnings for 20X4, as calculated above	5,600 credit
Impact on retained earnings prior to the beginning of 20X4	$1,400 credit

Restated Financial Statements Exhibit 21-3 shows the relevant amounts from the 20X5 and restated 20X4 comparative statements. The figures in the statements are based on the amounts shown in Exhibit 21-2 except that the 20X4 statement amounts have been restated for the change to FIFO, based on the analysis above. The comparative 20X4 SFP includes inventory at FIFO instead of average cost. The deferred income tax amounts are also restated.

The retained earnings statement shows an adjustment for *both* years instead of just the single adjustment of $7,000 that was recorded. The adjustment is based on the amount of adjustment for *prior* years. Remember that it is the *beginning* balances that are being adjusted. The pre-20X4 adjustment is effective at the beginning of 20X4; the restatement adjustment relating to 20X4 affects the beginning balance for 20X5.

Observe that the restated beginning balance for 20X5 agrees with the restated ending balance for 20X4, as it should. These amounts are highlighted in Exhibit 21-3.

The note discloses the impact of the change on each of 20X4 and 20X5. The 20X4 impact is apparent from the adjustments. The 20X5 impact, however, is derived from Exhibit 21-2.

EXHIBIT 21-3

SUNSET CORPORATION

Selected Amounts from Comparative Financial Statements
Change from Average Cost to FIFO for Inventory—Retrospective Application

	20X5 (FIFO Basis)	(Restated) 20X4 (FIFO Basis)
Statement of Financial Position		
Ending inventory (FIFO)	$ 80,000	$ 60,000
Statement of Comprehensive Income—Earnings Section		
Income before income tax	$300,000	$278,000(1)
Income tax expense	90,000	83,400(2)
Net income	$210,000	$194,600
Earnings per share (100,000 shares assumed)	$ 2.10	$ 1.95
Statement of Changes in Equity—Retained Earnings Section		
Beginning balance, as previously reported	$201,000	$ 92,000
Add: Cumulative effect of inventory accounting policy change, net of tax of $3,000 in 20X5 (20X4—$600)	7,000	1,400
Beginning balance, restated	208,000	93,400
Add: Net income (from above)	210,000	194,600
Deduct: Dividends declared	(88,000)	(80,000)
Ending balance	$330,000	$208,000

(1) $278,000 = $270,000 + $8,000 (decrease in 20X4 CGS due to accounting change)
(2) $83,400 = $81,000 + $2,400 (income tax expense for 20X4 due to accounting change)

Note to Financial Statements
During 20X5, the Corporation changed its accounting policy for inventory from average cost to first in, first out. As a result, restated 20X4 net income was increased by $5,600 (5.6¢ per share). The change increased 20X5 net income by $3,500 (3.5¢ per share). The 20X4 statements have been restated to reflect the change in accounting policy.

Under average cost, the increase in inventory for 20X5 would have been $15,000. Under FIFO, the increase is $20,000. FIFO causes an additional $5,000 of cost to flow into inventory rather than into cost of goods sold; the after-tax impact is $3,500 (i.e., $5,000 × 70%).

Restating Statistical Series Assume that Sunset Corporation issues a five-year summary of prior years' results, such as total revenue, cost of goods sold, net earnings, and EPS. To apply full restatement, Sunset must restate that comparative information as well as restating the 20X4 financial statements. Revenue will not be affected by the change in inventory method, but CGS, net earnings, and EPS will be affected (although perhaps not by much).

To restate the years prior to 20X4 (i.e., 20X0 through 20X3), Sunset must have the prior years' inventory data in its computer archives. These data can be retrieved to make the restatement. The adjustment to restate will be quite straightforward as long as the inventory data are in sufficient detail to convert from average cost to FIFO.

There is no need to go through a full CGS analysis. The impact on those statistical series can be measured by calculating the effect of the change in policy on opening and ending inventories for each of the preceding five years:

- An increase in *opening* inventory will increase the year's CGS and decrease net earnings and EPS; a decrease in opening inventory will have the opposite effects.
- An increase in *ending* inventory will decrease that year's CGS and increase net earnings and EPS; a decrease in ending inventory will have the opposite effects.

Remember that *full restatement* requires all historical series to be restated, not simply the prior year's financial statements.

Disclosure Requirements

When a company changes an accounting policy, the company should explain in the company's disclosure notes:

- The nature of the change;
- The amount of the adjustment for the current and prior period for each financial line item that is affected by the change;
- The amount of adjustments for periods prior to those presented in the comparative statements, to the extent practicable; and
- If retrospective restatement is not applied or applied fully, the reason(s) that retrospective application is wholly or partially impracticable should be explained.

If the change is due to a new or revised accounting standard, the company should also disclose the title of the standard and its transition provisions.

If the change is *voluntary*, the company should explain why the new policy provides better and more useful (i.e., "reliable and more relevant") information for financial statement users.

CONCEPT REVIEW

1. A company changes from declining-balance to straight-line depreciation, resulting in a decrease to the accumulated depreciation account. Will the deferred income tax account be debited or credited as a result? Explain.
2. A company changes from FIFO to weighted-average cost flow assumptions regarding inventory. At the beginning of the year, the FIFO inventory was $120,000, while weighted average was $105,000. If the tax rate is 30%, what is the amount of the cumulative adjustment to opening retained earnings?
3. Refer to the data in question 2. Does retained earnings increase or decrease?

PROSPECTIVE APPLICATION

If a company cannot restate its prior year's financial results due to a lack of sufficiently detailed information, the company can use prospective application. In this situation, the effect of the change is reported as far back as possible. Usually, this means that the company makes a single catch-up adjustment in the year of the change, but prior years' comparative statements and summary information are not restated.

The prospective approach also is used for a change in accounting policy if it is permitted by a new accounting standard. The transition provisions in any new or revised accounting standard will say whether or not the prospective approach is permitted.

Guidelines The following guidelines apply to accounting policy changes that are reported by using the prospective approach:

1. The cumulative impact of the change on all of the relevant beginning balances for the current year is computed and *recorded*, including the change in retained earnings (or accumulated OCI).
2. The cumulative impact of the change is reported in the financial statements as an adjustment to opening retained earnings (or accumulated OCI) for the current year.
3. Prior years' financial statements included for comparative purposes remain unchanged. All summary information reported for earlier years also remains unchanged.

Comparative Illustration To illustrate the difference between retrospective and prospective application, assume the same facts as in the previous example for retrospective application (see Exhibit 21-2), *except* that Sunset Corporation does not have adequate information to determine the 20X4 beginning inventory on the FIFO basis.

If the opening 20X4 inventory at FIFO is not available, then it is not possible to restate the 20X4 financial statements; we can restate only the ending balance of 20X4 (which is the beginning balance of 20X5). The adjustment for 20X5 is exactly as was illustrated earlier:

Inventory	10,000	
Current income tax payable (30% tax rate)		3,000
Retained earnings		7,000
(cumulative effect of policy change prior to 20X5)		

Under prospective application, the $7,000 adjustment cannot be allocated between 20X4 and 20X5; the entire adjustment must be both *recorded* and *reported* in 20X5.

Selected comparative statement amounts are shown in Exhibit 21-4. Note that there are no adjustments to the original 20X4 amounts. Nevertheless, the year-end 20X5 amounts are identical to those in Exhibit 21-3 under retrospective application.

Use of Prospective Application Prospective application of accounting policy changes is quite restricted. If a company does not have the information necessary to restate at least the prior year's results, the change normally should be delayed for one year so that the necessary information can be accumulated to make a smooth transition. That is the reason that most new or revised accounting standards become effective more than one year after they have been issued—the delay gives companies time to adjust their information collection process. Sometimes, however, standard setters believe that it is more important to make significant and meaningful changes quickly than to delay implementation until sufficient comparative information can be accumulated.

The change in inventory method that we illustrated above is really a *voluntary* change because both inventory methods are acceptable under GAAP. Voluntary changes always should be made only after sufficient information has been obtained to restate comparative numbers. Otherwise, users may suspect that the company is trying to hide something during a changeover without restatement. We used this inventory example only to emphasize the difference between retrospective and prospective application. In the following section, we will look at two examples of prospective restatement in practice.

Disclosures When prospective application is used for changes in accounting policy, reporting requirements are reduced to the following disclosures:

1. The fact that the change has not been applied retrospectively;
2. The effect of the change on current and future financial statements; and
3. The reasons that retrospective application cannot be done.

EXHIBIT 21-4

SUNSET CORPORATION

Selected Amounts from Comparative Financial Statements
Change from Average Cost to FIFO for Inventory—Prospective Application

	20X5 (FIFO Basis)	20X4 (AC Basis)
Statement of Financial Position		
Ending inventory (FIFO)	$ 80,000	$ 50,000
Statement of Comprehensive Income—Earnings Section		
Income before income tax	$300,000	$270,000
Income tax expense	90,000	81,000
Net income	$210,000	$189,000
Earnings per share (100,000 shares assumed)	$ 2.10	$ 1.89
Statement of Changes in Equity—Retained Earnings Section		
Beginning balance, as previously reported	$201,000	$ 92,000
Add: Cumulative effect of inventory accounting policy change, net of tax of $3,000	7,000	—
Beginning balance, restated	208,000	92,000
Add: Net income (from above)	210,000	189,000
Deduct: Dividends declared	(88,000)	(80,000)
Ending balance	$330,000	$201,000

Note to Financial Statements
During 20X5, the Corporation changed its accounting policy for inventory from average cost to first in, first out. Insufficient information was available to adjust 20X4 opening inventories to FIFO. As a result, 20X4 financial statements have not been restated. All relevant adjustments have been recorded in 20X5.

Early Adoption **Early adoption** means that a company applies a new or revised standard prior to its mandatory effective date. Some new and revised standards permit early adoption—others prohibit it. There are two main reasons for prohibiting early adoption:

- *To promote comparability.* If the change is substantial and may significantly affect users' intercompany comparisons, it is best if all companies make the change in the same year.
- *To give time to collect data.* Early adoption usually means that a company will not restate (or not be able to restate) its prior-period data. By prohibiting early adoption, standard setters remove any excuse for not restating at least the most recent one or two prior years.

IFRS 9, *Financial Instruments,* is an example of a new standard that permitted early adoption and prospective application. The mandatory effective date was for fiscal periods beginning on or after 1 January 2013, with retrospective application. In addition, though, the standard explicitly stated that if the new standard were applied prior to 1 January 2012, the company "need not restate prior periods," which indicates that prospective application is permitted within a restricted period of time but not by companies that apply the standard on the mandatory adoption date.

When "New" Is Not a "Change"

Throughout our discussion of accounting policy changes, we have repeatedly referred to (1) mandatory implementation of new or revised standards and (2) voluntary changes in policy. However, there is one other instance in which a company adopts a "new" (to it) accounting policy. Adopting a *new accounting policy* must not be confused with a *change* in accounting policy. The following are not *changes* in accounting policy:

1. *Adopting an accounting policy for transactions or other events that differ in substance from those previously occurring.* An example would be a change in the method of generating revenue, such as by introducing instalment sales in addition to sales that require full payment. There is a substantive difference in the way that revenue will be realized, and this change may call for applying a different accounting policy from the one previously used.
2. *Adopting a new accounting policy for transactions or other events that did not occur previously or were immaterial.* For example, a company may have been expensing all product development costs without applying the criteria for capitalization because such costs were immaterial. If development costs become significant, the company then will begin applying deferral criteria. This is adoption of an accounting policy and is new to the company but is not a *change* of accounting policy because a material amount of development costs had not previously been incurred.

When a company adopts an accounting policy for the first time due to new types of contracts, transactions, or events, the new policy must be added to the company's accounting policy disclosure note with an explanation of why a new policy has been adopted. Obviously, there would be no question of restatement, either because (1) that type of transaction or event has not arisen in prior periods or (2) the transaction or event has not been materially significant in prior years—any adjustment would also be immaterial.

CONCEPT REVIEW

1. When is it appropriate to apply a new accounting standard on a *prospective basis*?
2. Why might prospective application of a revised accounting standard make it difficult to compare the current-year earnings with prior-year earnings?
3. If a company is uncertain about whether an accounting change is a change in policy or a change in estimate, how should it treat the change?

CORRECTION OF A PRIOR-PERIOD ERROR

Prior-period errors are omissions or mistakes that were made in the application of accounting principles in one or more earlier periods. Mistakes can be mathematical errors, oversights, misinterpretations of fact, or intentional fraud. Errors relate to information that:

1. Was available when the prior-period's financial statements were prepared; and
2. Could reasonably be expected to have been obtained and taken into account in the preparation and presentation of those financial statements.

An error correction is *not* an adjustment of an accounting estimate of a prior period. For example, suppose that in 20X1, a company uses past experience with existing products to estimate a warranty liability for a new product. In 20X2, that estimate turns out to be seriously inadequate. In 20X2, the company will adjust its warranty liability and the related expense to recognize the new reality—a *change in accounting estimate*. However, if it turns out that the company's managers overlooked clear evidence that the liability would be significantly higher, and the evidence was available in 20X1, then the misstatement calls for an error correction.

Again, hindsight is not permitted to dictate error classification, but hindsight can be very illuminating when evaluating facts. Sometimes errors are quite clear cut:

- Management discovers that a portion of inventory at the beginning of the year was overlooked when the physical count was taken.
- The company sells through agents; the company failed to accrue commission liabilities that had not been paid at the end of the fiscal year.
- Routine repairs to equipment were capitalized instead of expensed.

However, errors are not always simple. In particular, revenue recognition errors can be a nightmare to correct because so many different accounts are affected by erroneous revenue recognition practices—that is, inventories, accounts receivable, doubtful accounts, commissions, warranty liabilities, and so forth.

Events Not Reportable as Errors A vital aspect of errors is that they do not arise from a change in estimate or a change in policy. They are mistakes, whether accidental or intentional. Any item that is in error should have been recorded differently in the previous period given the accounting policies and accounting estimates at the time.

For example, a company may have followed a practice of capitalizing and amortizing development costs in earlier periods only to discover later that the company would receive no future benefit from the expenditures. The policy to capitalize and amortize may have been completely rational and justifiable on the evidence at the time, but later evidence alters the situation. The company would write off the development costs when it became clear that no future benefit would be derived, but that is a *change in estimate*, not an error.

Another example of an event that is *not* accounted for as an error correction is an income tax audit. The income tax reported for a year is considered to be an estimate until confirmed by a CRA audit. If, in 20X5, an audit results in $100,000 of extra tax paid, specifically relating to 20X2 and 20X3, restatement is not appropriate. Instead, 20X5 income tax expense is increased by $100,000.

Error Correction

The correction of an accounting error is accounted for retrospectively, with restatement. The error should not have happened, which means that the statements for one or more past periods were simply wrong. In many cases, the error will have reversed itself by the current period, requiring no adjustment to the current period's statements. In other cases, reversal is not complete and correction is needed.

For example, suppose that the inventory stored in a Cuban warehouse was accidentally not included in the ending inventory count for 20X1. As a result of this error, 20X1 ending inventory will be understated, cost of goods sold overstated, and net income understated. The resulting understatement of beginning inventory in 20X2 will cause an understatement of cost of goods sold and an overstatement of net income for 20X2. If the ending inventory for 20X2 is correctly stated (i.e., including the Cuban inventory), the cumulative error will wash out because the overstatement of 20X2 net income will offset the understatement of 20X1 net income—20X2 ending retained earnings will be correct.

If the error is discovered in 20X3, no adjustment needs to be made *on the books* because there are no misstated accounts (either SFP or SCI) for 20X3. But an error that self-corrects over time still causes misstatements for the earlier periods that were affected. The comparative statements must be changed.

Example of Error Correction An example of disclosed error correction is shown in Exhibit 21-5. In the fourth quarter of 20X3, Joseph Ventures Inc. discovered an error in its reporting of marketable securities that had occurred at its 31 December 20X1 year end. Exhibit 21-5 shows the company's disclosure of the correction.

The error had been in understating fair value of these instruments. The correction was to increase the fair value at the beginning of 20X2 by $22,717. This change increased the 20X1

EXHIBIT 21-5

JOSEPH VENTURES INC.

31 December 20X3
Example of Error Correction

Note J—Marketable securities

In the fourth quarter of 20X3, an error was discovered that understated marketable securities reported as investments at year-end 20X1. The fair value of marketable securities is adjusted at each reporting date and recorded as a fair value adjustment in the consolidated statement of comprehensive income. Accordingly, the error was corrected by restating the fair value of the securities by $22,717 at the start of 20X2 with a corresponding credit to 20X2 opening retained earnings. The adjustment resulted in an decrease in comparative earnings for 20X2 of $22,717, with no effect on the earnings for the year ended 31 December 20X3.

comprehensive earnings by the same amount, which was offset by an offsetting decrease in the comparative earnings for 20X2. The earnings for 20X3 were unaffected because the error had self-corrected by adjustments to the securities' fair value in 20X2.

Counterbalancing Errors

Most changes flow through retained earnings at some point in time. If and when the impact of the change has "washed through," no entry for the change is needed. For example, assume that an amortizable asset with a cost of $15,000 and a useful life of three years was expensed when it was purchased in early 20X1 instead of being capitalized and amortized over its three-year life. If the error is discovered in late 20X2, the following adjustment must be made, assuming there is no income tax:

Amortization expense [20X2 ($15,000 ÷ 3)]	5,000	
Capital assets	15,000	
Accumulated amortization		10,000
Retained earnings		
($15,000 – $5,000 20X1 amortization)		10,000

However, if this error is discovered in 20X4, no entry is needed. The asset would have been fully amortized by the end of 20X3 and removed from the books. The $15,000 amortization that should have been recorded in 20X1, 20X2, and 20X3 is fully offset by the $15,000 expense erroneously recorded in 20X1. Both retained earnings and net assets are correct without any entries. The comparative figures must be adjusted for *reporting*, but such a restatement does not require any book entry for *recording*.

Example: Inventory Errors Counterbalancing takes place in the course of one year for errors that are made in valuing inventory, since closing inventory for one year is opening inventory for the next year. Consider the data in Exhibit 21-6. Look first at the original data.

What will change if the 20X5 closing inventory is found to be overstated by $25,000? That is, assume that the correct closing inventory for 20X5 is $425,000, not $450,000. Refer to the corrected numbers in **boldface** in Exhibit 21-6. The error has made 20X5 income, assets, and retained earnings too high by $25,000, and they are corrected downward. However, 20X6 income was too low by $25,000, and it is corrected upward. By the end of 20X6, retained earnings and inventory are correctly stated. No entry is needed in 20X6 for this correction, although *comparative financial results must be changed.*

EXHIBIT 21-6

COUNTERBALANCING INVENTORY ERRORS

Income Statement:	*20X6—Original*	*20X6—Restated*	*20X5—Original*	*20X5—Restated*
Sales	$6,000,000	$6,000,000	$5,500,000	$5,500,000
Opening inventory	450,000	**425,000**	325,000	325,000
Purchases	3,520,000	3,520,000	3,400,000	3,400,000
Closing inventory	(345,000)	(345,000)	(450,000)	**(425,000)**
Cost of goods sold	3,625,000	**3,600,000**	3,275,000	**3,300,000**
Gross profit	$2,375,000	**$2,400,000**	$2,225,000	**$2,200,000**
Statement of Financial Position:				
Closing inventory	$ 345,000	$ 345,000	$ 450,000	**$ 425,000**
Retained earnings	$1,345,000	$1,345,000	$1,240,000	**$1,215,000**

Impractibility On rare occasion, restatement may be **impracticable**. This situation arises when the company does not have sufficient detail available in prior years to enable the company to restate prior years with sufficient accuracy. This may happen, for example, if fair values were incorrectly assigned to inventories (e.g., biological assets) or to investment properties over several years.

It may not always be feasible to determine the correct values in retrospect. When remeasuring the effect of the error in *all* prior years is impracticable, the error should be reported prospectively from the earliest date practicable, which usually will be the beginning of the year in which the error was discovered. If the error cannot be corrected even at the beginning of the current year, then no restatement of balances can be made and the correct accounting method and/or measurements must be applied completely prospectively.

CONCEPT REVIEW

1. A company has begun offering new products to its customers that provides the basic product, a right to upgrades at nominal cost, and a built-in service contract. The company has begun to use a new revenue recognition policy. Should this new policy be accounted for as a *change* in accounting policy? Explain.

2. An internal auditor has discovered that in the previous year, her company accidentally applied the estimation technique for doubtful accounts "upside-down," assigning the greatest risk of default to the newest accounts receivable and the lowest risk of default to the oldest accounts. This resulted in a very large charge of $5 million for doubtful accounts in that year instead of the $1.5 million that a proper estimate would have yielded. In the current year, the technique was applied correctly and the appropriate adjustment was made to the allowance account. What action should the company take, if any, to correct this estimation error?

SUMMARY OF APPROACHES FOR ACCOUNTING CHANGES

Exhibit 21-7 shows the decision process for applying the three kinds of accounting changes. Exhibit 21-8 summarizes the treatment of cumulative effects and prior-period restatements.

EXHIBIT 21-7

DECISION PROCESS FOR APPLYING ACCOUNTING CHANGES

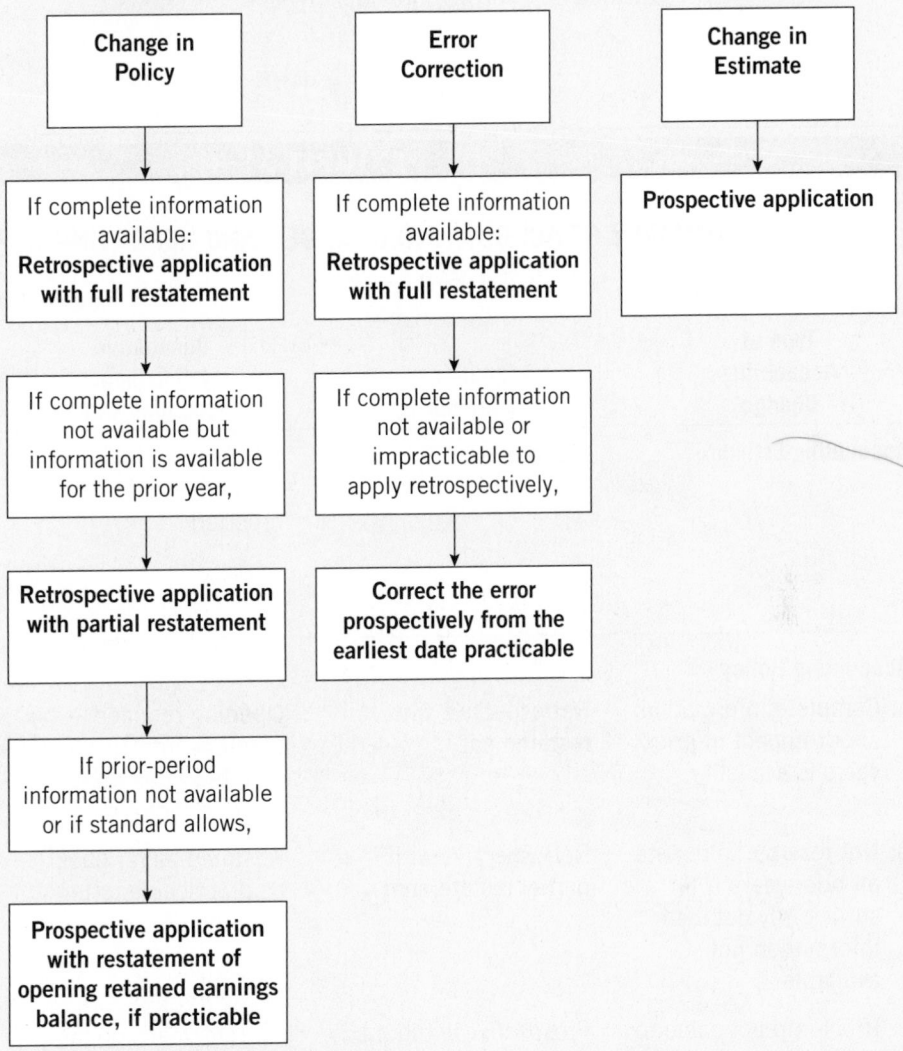

These two exhibits may be helpful when trying to conceptualize and remember the different approaches to accounting changes.

STATEMENT OF CASH FLOWS

Previous sections have shown that accounting changes affect the SFP, the retained earnings statement, and sometimes the SCI. It is not so obvious, however, that a new accounting policy may also affect the statement of cash flows. A change in accounting policy will not usually affect the net change in cash—the "bottom line" of the statement of cash flows. However, a new accounting policy may affect the classification of amounts in the statement of cash flows.

For example, a change from capitalizing to expensing of start-up costs will move the annual start-up cost from the investing section to the operations section. Cash inflow from operations will decrease because the expense is now included, while the cash outflow for investment in long-term assets (i.e., capitalized start-up costs) will also decrease. The long-term effect on the statement of cash flows, therefore, will be to shift the start-up costs from the *investment activities* section to the *operating activities* section of the statement of cash flows. The shift will decrease the apparent cash flow from operations, even though the overall cash flow is not affected.

Similarly, the *correction of prior-period errors* may affect the amounts shown in prior-periods' statement of cash flows if the error affects the amounts previously reported.

Changes in accounting estimates will not affect the classification of cash flows because such changes are applied prospectively. Changes in accounting estimates do not affect the method of reporting individual types of cash flows.

EXHIBIT 21-8

SUMMARY OF ACCOUNTING CHANGES AND REPORTING APPROACHES

Type of Accounting Change	Accounting Approach	Restatement Methodology: Cumulative Adjustment Identified with	Restatement Methodology: Comparative Statements and Results of Prior Years
Accounting Estimate	Prospective	Cumulative adjustment not computed or reported	Prior years' results remain unchanged; new estimates applied only to accounting for current and future periods
Accounting Policy			
a. Complete information about impact in prior years is available	Retrospective with full restatement	Opening retained earnings retrospectively restated in all affected prior periods	Comparative prior years' results and statistical series restated to new policy
b. Not feasible to restate all prior years—sufficiently detailed information not available	Retrospective with partial restatement	Restated as far back as practicable, often only the previous year	One or more recent years restated; earlier years and statistical summaries unchanged
c. If (1) impracticable to determine cumulative effect at beginning of current period or (2) specifically permitted by a new accounting standard	Prospective without restatement	Current year's opening retained earnings adjusted for cumulative effect of the change, if known; if effect not known, then no adjustment	Prior years' results remain unchanged; new policy applied only to current and future events and transactions
Accounting Error			
a. Complete information about impact in prior years is available	Retrospective with full restatement	Opening retained earnings restated (if the error has not self-corrected)	Prior years' results restated to correct the error
b. Not feasible to restate all prior years—sufficiently detailed information not available	Retrospective with partial restatement	Restated as far back as practicable, usually only the previous year	One or more recent years restated; earlier years and statistical summaries unchanged

ETHICAL ISSUES

Accounting changes present something of an ethical minefield for the unwary professional accountant. Management is, quite properly, always concerned about the perceptions of outsiders who use the financial statements. Managers can often feel tempted to alter accounting policies to mollify concerned statement users. However, the current standards on policy changes do make it rather difficult for a company to make voluntary accounting policy changes, especially in a public company. Very few voluntary changes are observable in public companies. Private companies, however, have more opportunities to make policy changes because they are subject to less scrutiny and because they are less tightly constrained by a requirement for GAAP compliance.

Sometimes, an accounting policy is changed effectively, though not technically, by a change in assumptions and estimates. For example, Canadian software companies usually followed the IFRS (and ASPE) requirement that companies capitalize and amortize development costs if certain criteria are satisfied. In doing so, however, the companies found themselves penalized in the U.S. stock market because they did not treat all development costs as an expense, as required by U.S. GAAP. To make themselves more comparable with their U.S. competitors, many companies simply decided that the criteria for deferral were no longer being met and therefore that the costs should be expensed immediately. This was not a change in accounting policy *per se*, but it had the same effect by means of a declared change in assumptions.

That particular example is fairly innocent in that the change had the effect of lowering reported earnings but improved investor perception of the transparency of financial reporting. The change did seem to provide more relevant information for the U.S. users, who felt that non-American standards were substandard and therefore discounted the companies' share value.

In other instances, however, voluntary policy changes may be driven primarily by management's desire to maximize earnings or to maximize its own compensation rather than by any demonstrable benefit to users. These changes lay a trap for the accountant who goes along with management's desires to manipulate earnings, and severe penalties may lie down the road.

Of course, we all are well aware of the subjectivity of accounting estimates. This subjectivity is unavoidable—it is the nature of estimates. But there is a fine line between reasonable estimates on one hand and earnings manipulation on the other hand. Manipulation leads to misstatement, and where the misstatement is deliberate, the accountant is guilty of fraud, even if the accountant is following instructions of his or her employer.

Looking Forward

The IASB has no plans to revisit the topic of accounting changes. It does not appear in the current (2013) work plan or discussion memoranda.

ACCOUNTING STANDARDS FOR PRIVATE ENTERPRISES

The requirements for all types of accounting changes are essentially the same in Section 1506 as in IAS 8. Section 1506 has been harmonized with IAS 8. However, two differences remain:

- As we discussed in Chapter 4, IFRS requires disclosure of new standards that have been issued but not yet effective; the potential effect should also be disclosed, even if the disclosure is that the new standard will have no effect.

In contrast, ASPE does not require disclosure of issued but not-yet-effective standards.

- When an entity makes restatements, IFRS requires the opening SFP of the comparative years to also be presented. For example, if the company is reporting a prior period adjustment for the year ended 31 December 20X5, then the SFPs for 31 December 20X5 *and* 20X4 are presented, along with the SFP at 1 January 20X4.

ASPE has no requirement to present the opening balance sheet as at 1 January 20X4.

RELEVANT STANDARDS

CPA Canada Handbook, Part I (IFRS):

- IAS 8, Accounting Policies, Changes in Accounting Estimates, and Errors

CPA Canada Handbook, Part II (ASPE):

- Section 1506, Accounting Changes

SUMMARY OF KEY POINTS

1. Changes in accounting *estimates* may be caused by new information or by recent experience that changes previous predictions or perceptions. Changes in accounting estimates must always be applied prospectively.
2. If there is doubt as to whether a change is a change in estimate or a change in policy, it should be assumed to be a change in estimate.
3. Changes in accounting policy may be *mandatory*, caused by a new or revised accounting standard.
4. Changes in accounting policy may be *voluntary*, but only if the change results in information that is both reliable and more relevant.
5. Changes in accounting policy must be accounted for *retrospectively* (also known as *retroactively*), with restatement of prior periods if practicable. Statistical series, such as earnings and return on equity, should also be restated to reflect the new policy.
6. If full restatement of prior periods is not practicable, then application should be retrospective as far back as possible, with an adjustment to retained earnings for any earlier cumulative effect of the change.
7. If restatement is impracticable, opening retained earnings for the current period should be adjusted for the cumulative effect of the policy change, and the effect of the change should be accounted for *prospectively* in the current period and future periods.
8. If it is not feasible to measure the cumulative effect of a policy change, the change can be applied prospectively in the current period without adjusting retained earnings.
9. Some new or revised accounting standards permit early adoption. When early adoption is permitted, the IASB *may* permit prospective application for specific standards.
10. Information must be disclosed to allow users to understand (1) why an accounting change has been made and (2) the effect of the accounting change.
11. On occasion, a company (or its auditors) discovers that there was an accounting error in a prior period. If the error was material, the error must be corrected in the

comparative figures, even if it has self-corrected over the long run. If it is impracticable to restate, the error must be corrected prospectively.

12. Accounting changes do not typically affect underlying cash flows, but they can affect the amounts presented on prior years' statement of cash flows by changing the section in which the cash flows are reported.

KEY TERMS

change in accounting estimate
change in accounting policy
early adoption
impracticable
mandatory changes
prior-period errors
prospective application
restatement
retrospective restatement
retrospective application
voluntary changes

REVIEW PROBLEM 21-1

Each of the following situations is independent:

1. *Change in estimated useful life and residual value.* Phelps Company purchases equipment on 1 January 20X6 for $36,000. The company uses the straight-line method of depreciation, taking a full year's depreciation in the year of acquisition. The equipment has an estimated residual value of $6,000 and an estimated useful life of three years. In 20X7, Phelps decides that the machine really has an original total life of four years and a residual value of $5,000.

   Required:
   What is the depreciation expense for 20X7?

2. *Retrospective change in accounting policy.* Rhein Inc. (a private enterprise) changes its method of accounting for long-term construction contracts from the percentage-of-completion method (PC) to the completed-contract method (CC) in 20X7. The years affected by the change, and incomes under both methods, appear below (ignore income tax):

Year	PC	CC
20X5	$400	$200
20X6	300	150
20X7	500	800

   Required:
   If the financial statements for 20X6 and 20X7 are shown comparatively, what is the amount of the accounting policy adjustment to the 1 January balance of retained earnings for 20X6 and 20X7?

3. *Error correction and retrospective adjustment.* Helms Limited purchases a delivery truck for $14,000 on 1 January 20X6. Helms expects to use the truck for only two years and then sell it for $4,000. The accountant is instructed to use straight-line depreciation but neglects to record any depreciation in 20X6. Rather, the accountant charges the entire cost to delivery expense in 20X6. The company's controller discovers the error late in 20X7.

   Required:
   Provide the 20X7 entries to record depreciation and the error correction, and indicate the amounts of the cumulative retrospective adjustment to opening retained earnings appearing in the 20X6 and 20X7 comparative retained earnings statements. Ignore income tax.

4. *Error correction, retrospective adjustment, and comparative statements.* On 1 July 20X7, a full year's insurance of $2,400, covering the period from 1 July 20X7 through 30 June 20X8, was paid and debited to insurance expense. Assume:
   - The company uses a calendar fiscal year.
   - Retained earnings at 1 January 20X7 is $20,000.
   - No adjusting entry for insurance is made on 31 December 20X7.
   - Reported net income for 20X7 (in error) is $22,800.
   - Net income for 20X8 is $30,000 (assuming that the error has not been discovered).
   - Net income for 20X9 is $40,000.
   - There is no income tax.

   Required:

   a. List the effect of the error on relevant accounts, and net income, in 20X7 and 20X8.
   b. Prepare the entry to record the error if it was discovered in 20X7.
   c. Prepare the entry to record the error if it was discovered in 20X8, and prepare the 20X7 and 20X8 comparative retained earnings statements. The amount is deemed material.
   d. Prepare the entry (if needed) to record the error if discovered in 20X9.

REVIEW PROBLEM 21-1—SOLUTION

1. Book value, 1 January 20X7 = $36,000 – [($36,000 – $6,000) × 1/3] = $26,000

   Depreciation for 20X7 = ($26,000 – $5,000) × 1/(4 – 1) = $7,000

2. The impact on the opening retained earnings is the cumulative difference in prior years' net income under the two methods:

   At 1 January 20X6: $200 dr. This is the $200 decline in 20X5 income from $400 under PC to $200 under CC.

   At 1 January 20X7: $350 dr. Also a decline in income, for 20X5 and 20X6: ($400 + $300) – ($200 + $150).

3. The purchase should have been debited to equipment, but instead was debited to delivery expense, which has since been closed to retained earnings. Therefore, retained earnings must be reduced (credited) by the difference between the (correct) depreciation expense and the (incorrect) recorded delivery expense. The 20X7 entry to record the error correction is:

Equipment	14,000	
Retained earnings, error correction		9,000
Accumulated depreciation—equipment		5,000

[20X6 depreciation = ($14,000 – $4,000) × 1/2 = $5,000]

In 20X7, depreciation expense is recorded for that year:

Depreciation expense	5,000	
Accumulated depreciation—equipment		5,000

The opening retained earnings adjustment would be $9,000 for 20X7. There is no adjustment to the opening retained earnings in 20X6, since the equipment did not exist prior to 20X6.

4. a. *Effect of error if not discovered* (– means understated; + means overstated)

Item	20X7	20X8
Insurance expense	+$1,200	–$1,200
Ending prepaid insurance	– 1,200	No effect
Net income	– 1,200	+ 1,200
Ending retained earnings	– 1,200	now correct

b. *If error discovered in 20X7:*

Prepaid insurance	1,200	
Insurance expense		1,200

c. *If error discovered in 20X8:*

Prepaid insurance	1,200	
Retained earnings, error correction		1,200

A second entry would be made to record 20X8 insurance expenses:

Insurance expense	1,200	
Prepaid insurance		1,200

Comparative retained earnings statement:

	20X8	20X7
Retained earnings, 1 January, as previously reported	$42,800*	$20,000
Error correction	1,200	0†
Retained earnings, 1 January, restated	44,000	20,000
Net income	28,800‡	24,000§
Retained earnings, 31 December	$72,800	$44,000

* This balance reflects erroneous 20X7 income: $42,800 = $20,000 + $22,800.
† No year prior to 20X7 was affected by the error.
‡ $30,000 erroneous income – $1,200 (20X8 income was overstated).
§ $22,800 + $1,200.

d. *If error discovered in 20X9:*

No entry is needed because the error has counterbalanced.

QUESTIONS

Q21-1 A company has always used the allowance method to value accounts receivable and establish a bad debt expense on the income statement. In the current year, it changed from using the aging method to the percentage of sales method to determine the extent of the required allowance. How would you classify the change?

Q21-2 Why are changes in estimates so prevalent?

Q21-3 How is a change in accounting estimate accounted for?

Q21-4 If there is doubt about whether a change is a change in policy or a change in estimate, how should it be treated? Why do you think accounting standards have this requirement?

Q21-5 Explain the difference between a voluntary and mandatory change in accounting policy.

Q21-6 What criteria must be met for a voluntary accounting policy change to be allowed? What difficulty is there in justifying a voluntary change?

Q21-7 What role do a company's reporting objectives play in changes in accounting policy?

Q21-8 Explain the difference between a change in estimate and an error correction.

Q21-9 Accounting changes involve (1) policies, (2) estimates, and (3) error corrections. For each of the following, identify the type of change:

a. A lessor discovers, while a long-term capital lease term is in progress, that an estimated material unguaranteed residual value of the leased property has probably become zero.

b. After five years of use, an asset originally estimated to have a 15-year total life is now to be depreciated on the basis of a 22-year total life.
c. Because of inability to estimate reliably, a contractor began business using the completed-contract method. Now that reliable estimates can be made, the percentage-of-completion method is adopted.
d. Office equipment purchased last year is discovered to have been debited to office expense when acquired. Appropriate accounting is to be applied at the discovery date.
e. A company that used 1% of sales to predict its bad debt expense discovers losses are running higher than expected and changes to 2%.

Q21-10 How is an accounting error accounted for?

Q21-11 What are the advantages of retrospective restatement for a change in accounting policy? Why is it not required for *all* changes in accounting policy?

Q21-12 Assume that a company had traditionally expensed development costs but now satisfies capitalization criteria and thus has changed its policy. Explain how the change in development cost accounting will affect the statement of cash flows.

CASE 21-1

COUTURE COQUET LIMITED

Couture Coquet Limited (CCL) is a privately held company headquartered in Montreal. The company operates a chain of retail clothing stores in major cities across Canada, although most of the company stores are in Ontario and Quebec. The stores in each province are owned by a separate wholly owned subsidiary—for example, Couture Coquet Ontario Ltd—for provincial taxation purposes as well as to limit liability in the event of financial difficulties within any particular province. Officially each provincial subsidiary is headed by a regional manager who is designated as the CEO. In practice, there are only five different individuals in that role because there is a single person as CEO of each of the prairie provinces and another for the maritime provinces.

The company has been quite successful. This success is largely due to engaging a small group of young adults whose task it is to detect fashion trends among young people well before the major fashion houses do—finding out what's "cool" among youth. Local manufacturing then makes it relatively easy for CCL to quickly design and manufacture new styles of clothing and deliver the merchandise to its stores.

CCL manufactures most of its apparel in its own facility in Montreal. The manufacturing facility is owned by CCL, the parent company. For provincial tax purposes, CCL sells the finished products to the provincial subsidiaries through a transfer-pricing mechanism.

Some manufacturing is also contracted out to other manufacturers, principally in Quebec. The company prides itself on getting the latest fashions to its stores in a very short time, usually within two weeks after a specific fashion trend has been detected. Due to the chain's quick response to emerging markets, the company has been able to serve the youth market quite well despite offering no major "name brand" clothing. The primary emphasis is on clothing and fashion for young women, but about 20% of sales are of young men's clothing, such as trendy jeans and pullovers.

No merchandise stays in the stores very long. The store managers are told that as soon as sales of a product begin to decline, the product should go on sale at increasing discounts until all is sold. CCL's fiscal year is the Saturday closest to January 31, as is normal in the industry. At the end of the fiscal year, there always is some merchandise in the stores that is priced to clear.

Eighty-five percent of the stores are in leased spaces in major shopping malls. The other 15% are street-front locations, which also are leased. CCL owns no real estate except for its manufacturing facilities, which also contain short-term storage space for fabrics and for finished goods prior to shipment to the stores.

The lease terms are normal for the industry. Initial leases are for a 10-year period, subject to five-year renewals. For the initial lease term, the lessor normally provides lease inducements, which include free rent for a limited period or leasehold improvements installed by the lessor at no cost to the lessee. Under the lease contract, rents increase by a predetermined amount each year. Lessees also pay contingent rent based on sales volume, in addition to the base amount. CCL recognizes contingent rent in the month that the sales occur. All leases are reported as operating leases.

New stores require several months of preparation before opening for business and also must be renovated periodically under the terms of the lease—normally every five years. Rental cost incurred during the preparation period (or subsequent renovation) is reported as rent expense.

The cost of leasehold improvements is capitalized and depreciated over their useful life. CCL is required to remove CCL-installed leasehold improvements when a lease is terminated; the space must be delivered back to the lessor in clean and clear condition.

The founder-owners of the company no longer take an active part in running the day-to-day business. A management team with significant front-line retailing experience is now in charge. Historically, financing has come mainly from retained earnings, although the SFP does show a significant amount of long-term debt at comparatively high interest rates, given the current (early 20X9) borrowing environment. That debt is mainly in the form of debentures held by a municipal employees' pension fund investment trust, secured by CCL's tangible capital assets.

Short-term financing is provided by a bank line of credit. The line of credit is secured by a proportion of accounts receivable and inventory. However, the accounts receivable are minimal, since the company's sales are mainly by cash or by debit or credit card. Therefore, inventory is the primary security.

Overall, the company has a pretax cost of capital of 10%.

Recently, CCL has begun to have difficulty in achieving the profit levels to which the owners have been accustomed, although the company is not in any financial distress. It now is nearing the 20X9 fiscal year-end and CCL's financial group is prepared for the year-end closing. CCL managers have decided to look more closely at certain aspects of the way CCL does business, as well as how the company reports the results of operations.

The senior managers also are concerned about a forthcoming change in accounting standards relating to leases, and need to know what implications this will have on CCL's reported financial condition. At the end of fiscal year 20X9, the minimum rent payable (including automatic rent escalation clauses, excluding contingent rents) are summarized as follows:

(in thousands of Canadian dollars)	**26 January 20X9**
Within one year	$ 45,300
After one year but not more than five years	132,000
More than five years	52,500
	$229,800

The CFO is concerned about the potential financial reporting aspects of the following situations:

1. In 20X7, CCL purchased 100% of the shares of a small clothing manufacturer in Montreal, which then became a subsidiary of CCL. CCL was one of its customers, as were several other retailers. CCL paid $5,000,000 for that company, of which $2,000,000 was allocated to goodwill. Within a year of the purchase, many of the subsidiary's other customers left because they were concerned that CCL might steal their clothing designs. CCL managers had not expected those defections, since CCL's designs were generally ahead of their competitors. As a result, the subsidiary has not been able to

stay profitable. CCL has been in talks to possibly sell the subsidiary to a U.S.–based clothing chain.

2. One of CCL's major stores suffered a sharp decline in sales volume in 20X9 due to the entry of a U.S.–based retail fashion competitor in a nearby location. This sharply reduced volume of sales is expected to persist throughout the remaining four-year term of the lease. CCL management predicts that the discounted net cash flow from this store will be less than the present value of the future lease payments and lease termination costs.
3. Another store is located in a shopping mall that is suffering a decline in overall sales volume. CCL's sales in that location remain strong. However, quite a few other tenants have left the mall. Due to the rise in vacancies, the mall owner has been offering steeply discounted lease rates to prospective new tenants. CCL has approached the owner and requested a reduction in its rent to equal that being offered to new tenants, but the owner has refused to reopen the terms of CCL's lease.
4. CCL has large electronic billboards mounted on the fronts and roofs of some buildings, space that is leased from the building owners. The lease contracts require CCL to restore the facades and roofs to the owner's satisfaction at expiry. The CCL financial manager has discovered that CCL completely overlooked one significant lease and has not accounted for that restoration cost. As well, due to a decline in interest rates in 20X9, the auditor recommends that CCL remeasure all of CCL's asset retirement obligations.
5. The company has been using the taxes payable method of accounting for income tax. CCL's financial manager is negotiating with a private equity fund for new financing to replace higher-cost existing debt capital. The private equity firm would prefer that CCL adhere to IFRS practice. Therefore, he has proposed that the company change to the taxes allocation approach effective for 20X9, the year just ended.
6. In 20X8, the company's designers had made a rare error in anticipating a fashion trend that failed to develop. As a result, the company ended the previous year with a severe overstock of that line of clothing. In retrospect, the company should have written down that portion of the inventory. Instead, the merchandise was sold for about 20% of its manufacturing cost to a clearance house in San Francisco. The merchandise manager has recommended that the opening inventory for 20X9 be restated to recognize the loss in value of those items.

Required:

Assume that you are Christopher Robins, an independent accounting consultant. The CFO of CCL has asked for a memo concerning changes that may be needed for CCL's accounting as it moves to implement IFRS. Prepare the memo.

CASE 21-2

MTC

Philip Roth is just finishing his first week as chief financial officer of MTC. He was recruited from Atkins Consulting to replace the former CFO who had been relieved of his duties when major errors and shortfalls in certain inventory and trading accounts were discovered.

MTC is the current corporate name of an enterprise once known as Midlands Telephone Corporation. Midlands had been providing landline telephone service to several midcountry provinces for most of the 20th century and into the 21st century. The company had been reorganized in the early 1980s to separate its regulated telephone service from its more adventurous, nonregulated endeavours. The company had grown to a billion-dollar enterprise with investments in several fields, acquired largely through purchases of other going concerns. The core of MTC's earnings, however, remained in the telephone business.

Early this year, the company lost an appeal to the regulatory agency to protect its base market. The agency had ruled that MTC would no longer have a protected monopoly for landline telephone service in its service region but that other companies (including TV cable companies and wireless companies) could compete for local telephone service. MTC had an enormous asset base, built up over the years to generate the highest possible earnings. As is typical in regulated industries, the company had been permitted to set rates that would enable it to earn a set rate of return on its asset base—the larger the asset base, the higher the earnings. The company capitalized all betterments and replacements, and used the longest possible depreciation periods for its capital assets. With the advent of deregulation, the company would no longer be able to generate such an attractive rate of return on its assets, which raised questions in the financial press about the "overvaluation" of its capital asset base.

This regulatory ruling was only one of several blows that the company had suffered in recent months. A previous loss of protection in the long-distance telephone market had caused MTC's earnings to drop sharply, with the result that MTC had the first loss of its history in its telephone business last year. The loss was expected to be even larger in the current year.

To make matters worse, rumours began to circulate in the financial community that MTC was covering up huge losses in one of its nontelephone divisions, one that manufactured copper wire and electrical switching devices. Copper is a world-traded commodity that has a very volatile price, and most companies that use copper engage in hedging operations to protect themselves. MTC's Board of Directors hired Atkins Consulting to find out if there was any truth to the rumours, and, unfortunately, there was. Managers and traders in the division had been speculating heavily in copper, and had covered up massive trading losses over the past three years, some of which were hidden in fictitious inventory records. MTC's copper inventory (and other accounts) turned out to be overstated by over $100 million.

The company's employees were also becoming restive. In its latest labour negotiations, just completed last month for the telephone operations, the company had to promise redundancy protection for employees if the company was required to downsize its telephone operations. The company agreed not to lay off any employees with more than 15 years of service, although the company would have the right to place them in a "redundancy pool" to be redeployed anywhere else in the company that they might be useful. Employees who are laid off will be given a severance package amounting to two months' salary plus one month's additional salary for each year of service. The severance would not be given as a lump sum but would be paid to the individual over a one-year period following the departure. Furthermore, the new labour agreement provided that pension benefits for any laid-off employee would automatically vest, even if the employee had not reached the point at which the benefits would normally become vested. The remaining employees would benefit from a significant enhancement of their defined benefit pension plan; employees' benefits would increase by between 10% and 20%, depending on the length of service.

The company had just served notice to the first 1,200 of its employees that they would be laid off, but the Board of Directors expected that at least 5,000 employees would be laid off over the next two years.

Philip Roth was one of the consultants who uncovered the rogue copper trading. He had been hired as CFO of MTC to "clean up the mess" in the financial reporting and control areas. One of his first responsibilities was to recommend to the audit committee of the Board of Directors how the company should report the impacts of its recent changes in fortune in its financial statements for the current year. Although the company was only midway through the fiscal year, the Board and CEO would have to discuss financial projections in a public forum, particularly with the investment analysts who closely followed the company's performance.

Required:

Assume that you are Philip Roth. Prepare a report to the audit committee.

CASE 21-3

MOUNTAIN MINES LUBRICATION LTD.

Mountain Mines Lubrication Ltd. (MML), a Canadian private company, supplies lubricant to mining operations in northern British Columbia and the Northwest Territories. MML commenced operations four years ago and is based in Prince George, B.C. MML has two lubricant products, "Slip Coat" and "Maximum Guard." MML's lubricants are used in large, expensive mining machines and are crucial to the operation of the machines. Without good lubrication, the machines will overheat and break down.

The mining industry has not performed well in recent years, but over the last summer the economy has picked up and, according to MML's owner, Max Mulholland, the B.C. mines are running at peak capacity. Customer service is key to the business. Max says that MML has been able to survive the hard times because it is more flexible and its products cost less than those of its competitors.

MML is a new client of your firm. You, the CA, have been assigned to conduct the review engagement. You have met with Max and with Nina Verhan, the bookkeeper. Your notes are in Exhibits 1 and 2. You have been working at the client's office for two days. The partner would like a memo analyzing the issues you have identified in the review.

Required:

Prepare the memo.

EXHIBIT 1

Excerpts from Your Discussion with Max Mulholland

"I do everything I can to keep costs down. Take the bank, for example. It had wanted audited financial statements, prepared in accordance with IFRS, before it would approve my new line of credit, but I know how much you guys charge for an audit. I've got product at remote locations, and it would cost a fortune just to fly you out there to look at my inventory. So I talked the bank down to accept a report based on a review engagement, for now.

"Minimizing costs is vital in our business. Take shipping costs. Some of my clients are in pretty remote areas, and it costs a lot to ship lubricant up there. So I send enough lubricant up there in one shipment to last them for a year. They put the stuff in their machines as they need it, and report to me how much they've used. When my salesman makes the annual delivery, he confirms the information they have provided. That way they are happy because they don't have to wait for lubricant to be delivered, and I keep my costs and my prices low.

"Of course, there are always problems. On August 30, the supervisor at Scorched Earth called to warn me they were really low on lubricant. That was a bit of a surprise to me because we shipped a lot up there in the spring, but I know they've been working hard in August and those older machines really go through the stuff.

"Flexibility is another strong point. You know things have been bad in the mining industry, but they have picked up this year, which means that our business has picked up as well. Some mines were experiencing cash flow problems, and even though lubricant is not their biggest expense, every little bit helps. So instead of charging them for product as they put it into their machines, I've arranged to have meters installed to read the number of hours a machine is in use, and they are charged based on hours of usage. It takes about four weeks before a machine needs to have its lubricant tanks refilled, if it is running at peak capacity."

EXHIBIT 2

Excerpts from Your Discussion with Nina Verhan, Bookkeeper

"Max is excited about this year. A lot of orders have come in since the mines started picking up. We were concerned about cash flows, but Max thinks they are going to be okay. Big Scar Mine, a new diamond mine in the Northwest Territories, has started operations, and we are its supplier.

"Max told you about our new charging plan, based on hourly usage. When the mine workers pour lubricant into the tank on one of their machines, they let me know by fax. I send them a "no charge" invoice, and at the same time I charge the cost of lubricant to cost of sales. Max thinks that it is a good reminder of the special deal we are giving them. Then, each week, they fax in their meter readings, and I charge them based on the hours of operation of the machine and record the revenue at that time. We just started doing it this way this year, for three of our four customers. Here is our inventory list for all our mines (see Exhibit 3).

"I've also prepared draft financial statements for you. Here are some excerpts (see Exhibit 4).

"Our three BC mine customers have really picked up over the summer. For July, August, and September they have been running at full capacity. The Scorched Earth Mine is the only one in BC not owned by Broken Wing Properties, and it has really been financially squeezed lately. Scorched Earth was pretty eager to switch to our new hourly usage billing because its cash flow was tight.

"Based on our average selling prices and costs, you will see that our percentage gross margins have increased over last year, and our volume of sales has also increased nicely. I would say we have had a pretty good year.

"The Big Scar Mine has a large amount of our inventory on site. That mine is owned and operated by North Canadian Developments Ltd., a subsidiary of Broken Wing Properties.

"We have received all the meter readings from our hourly usage customers, up to August 31. I noticed that the Scorched Earth Mine meter reading is low, so I will ask our salesman to recheck the meter when he makes another delivery this week. I have billed Scorched Earth for August on the hours that the mine has provided."

EXHIBIT 3

MOUNTAIN MINES LUBRICATION LTD.

Current Inventory List (Note 1)

As at 31 August, 20X9

	Slip Coat	Maximum Guard
Average sales price per kg		
20X9	$16.00	$22.50
20X8	15.00	21.00
Average cost per kg		
20X9	$13.50	$18.25
20X8	13.00	17.25
Prince George warehouse	3,000 kg	1,000 kg
Scorched Earth Mine (BC)		
On-site (Note 2)	0 kg	20 kg
Mining machine capacity	50 kg	50 kg
Date of last top-up	25 August	25 August
Moon Crater Mine (BC)		
On-site (Note 2)	300 kg	300 kg
Mining machine capacity	50 kg	50 kg
Date of last top-up	13 August	13 August
Dead Fish Mine (BC)		
On-site (Note 2)	800 kg	900 kg
Mining machine capacity	20 kg	20 kg
Date of last top-up	n/a	n/a
Big Scar Mine (NWT)		
On-site (Note 2)	3,500 kg	5,000 kg
Mining machine capacity	200 kg	300 kg
Date of last top-up	28 August	28 August

Notes:

1. Scorched Earth Mine, Moon Crater Mine, and Big Scar Mine are billed by hourly machine usage. Dead Fish Mine is billed for product when it is poured into the tanks.
2. On-site does not include lubricant contained in the machines.

EXHIBIT 4

MOUNTAIN MINES LUBRICATION LTD.

Excerpts from Draft Financial Statements

Income Statement

For the Years Ended 31 August

	20X9	20X8
Sales	$336,250	$276,390
Cost of sales	286,291	232,090
Gross margin	49,959	44,300
Other expenses	37,309	36,150
Income before taxes	12,650	8,150
Income tax expense	3,500	2,490
Net income	9,150	5,660
Retained earnings—opening	37,750	32,090
Retained earnings—closing	$ 46,900	$ 37,750

Balance Sheet

As at 31 August

	20X9	20X8
Cash	$ —	$ 8,790
Accounts receivable	67,540	57,423
Inventory	234,365	156,837
Property, plant, and equipment	146,600	113,600
	$448,505	$336,650
Bank overdraft	$ 37,929	$ —
Accounts payable	143,476	63,700
Current portion, long-term debt	60,000	20,000
Long-term debt	115,000	175,000
Common stock	45,200	40,200
Retained earnings	46,900	37,750
	$448,505	$336,650

Gross Margin per Product:

	Slip Coat	Maximum Guard	Total
20X9			
Sales	$136,000	$200,250	$336,250
Cost of sales	117,933	168,358	286,291
Gross margin	$ 18,067	$ 31,892	$ 49,959
Number of kg sold	8,500	8,900	17,400
20X8			
Sales	$111,750	$164,640	$276,390
Cost of sales	96,850	135,240	232,090
Gross margin	$ 14,900	$ 29,400	$ 44,300
Number of kg sold	7,450	7,840	15,290

(CICA)

TECHNICAL REVIEW

★ connect

TR21-1 Change of Estimate: Ludwig Corporation purchased a capital asset for $150,000 in early 20X1. Management estimated that the asset would have a 10-year life with an estimated residual value of $20,000 and would be depreciated on a straight-line basis with a full year's depreciation in the year of purchase. In 20X5, management decides that the asset's useful life will be twelve years. Management also decides to change the depreciation method to 20% declining balance.

Required:

1. Explain how these changes will affect the 20X5 year-end financial statements (including disclosure notes).
2. Prepare any journal entries that Ludwig Corporation should make in 20X6 to reflect these changes.

★ connect

TR21-2 Error Correction: In 20X7, after the 20X6 annual financial statements had been issued, Marcella Stores Inc. discovered that a significant transposition error had been made in recording the ending inventory for 20X5. The inventory had been recorded as $1,401,000 when it should have been $1,104,000. Marcella Stores' average income tax rate is 30%.

Required:

1. Explain how discovery of this error will affect Marcella Stores' comparative financial statements and financial reporting for 20X7.
2. Prepare any journal entries that would be necessary in 20X7 to correct this error.
3. Suppose that the error in the 20X5 ending inventory was not discovered until 20X8. How, if at all, would this change your answers to requirements 1 and 2?

★ connect

TR21-3 Error Correction: Tianan Corporation acquired equipment in 20X1 for $200,000. Management instructed the accounting staff to depreciate the equipment on a 20% declining balance rate. In 20X3, as the year-end financial statements are being prepared, the chief accountant discovers that the equipment had been depreciated over the previous two years at 25% instead of 20%. Tianan's income tax rate is 30%.

Required:

1. Indicate the amounts of the adjustments that should be made to opening retained earnings in the comparative statements of changes in equity for each of 20X2 and 20X3.
2. Provide the 20X3 entries to record 20X3 depreciation and to correct the previous years' error.

★ connect

TR21-4 Accounting Policy Change: Brockton Limited began applying international standards in 20X8. One of the necessary adjustments was to adjust past inventory records to remove warehousing expenses from the balances of the ending inventories for 20X5, 20X6, and 20X7, and restate earnings for 20X6 and 20X7. The pre-adjustment inventory balances and the warehousing costs contained therein were as follows:

Year	Balance, 31 December	Warehousing costs
20X7	$800,000	$ 30,000
20X6	680,000	18,000
20X5	720,000	25,000

Required:

1. Explain the impact this change will have on the company's earnings. Assume an income tax rate of 30%.

2. Prepare the adjusting entry (entries) that Brockton Limited will need to make on its books in 20X8 to reflect the above information.

★ connect

TR21-5 Accounting Policy Change: Plastics Limited (PL) had been a public company for the past 15 years. However this year, 20X6, PL's senior management acquired 90% of the shares outstanding in public hands and, as permitted by securities legislation, forced the redemption of the remaining minority shares and took the company private. Management then sought to simplify some of PL's accounting policies for the benefit of its bankers and creditors, with greater transparency regarding cash flows. One of the changes management wished to make was to report product development expense on the basis of costs incurred rather than by capitalizing and amortizing those costs. The company's records contain the following information regarding the deferred development cost account:

Year	Beginning Balance	Costs Incurred	Amortization	Ending Balance
20X5	$35,584	$ 6,000	$8,317	$33,267
20X4	28,480	16,000	8,896	35,584
20X3	25,600	10,000	7,120	28,480
20X2	12,000	20,000	6,400	25,600
20X1	0	15,000	3,000	12,000

Required:

Determine the restatements that PL will need to make to net earnings for each year, 20X1 through 20X5, as well as the necessary 20X6 adjusting entry. PL's income tax rate is 30%.

ASSIGNMENTS

★ **A21-1 Overview—Types of Accounting Changes:** Analyze each case and choose a letter code under each category (type and approach) to indicate the preferable accounting for each case.

Type of Change	Accounting Treatment
P = Policy	RFR = Retrospective with full restatement
E = Estimate	RPR = Retrospective with partial restatement
AE = Accounting error	PNR = Prospective with no restatement

a. Changed depreciation method from declining balance to straight line to conform with industry practice.
b. Changed from cost method to revaluation method for capital assets; prior years' valuations are obtainable.
c. Wrote off development costs accumulated and capitalized in two previous years due to serious doubts about the project's viability.
d. Changed from FIFO to average cost for inventory to reduce accounting costs. Only the previous year's opening balance can be reconstructed.
e. Changed residual value of an intangible capital asset to zero based on new economic circumstances.
f. Discovered that a $400,000 acquisition of machinery two years ago had been debited to the land account.
g. Discovered a transposition error in the previous year's opening inventory: $17,200; should have been $71,200.
h. A private company changed from the percentage-of-completion method to completed-contract method for all contracts currently in process and for all new contracts. All prior balances can be reconstructed.

i. Changed measurement method for asset retirement obligations to present value basis instead of undiscounted estimated costs.
j. Changed from historical cost to net realizable value for inventory valuation to comply with new accounting standards. The opening balance cannot be reconstructed.

★ **A21-2 Overview—Types of Accounting Changes:** Analyze each case and choose a letter code under each category (type and approach) to indicate the preferable accounting for each case.

Type	Approach
P = Policy	RWR = Retrospective with restatement
E = Estimate	RNR = Retrospective with no restatement
AE = Accounting error	P = Prospective

a. Changed the depreciation method for delivery vehicles from straight line to declining balance.
b. Discovered that a contract with a supplier had become an onerous contract in the previous year but the company had not recognized any associated loss.
c. Changed the method of estimating bad debts accrued from a percentage-of-sales to an aging methodology.
d. Changed from straight-line to accelerated depreciation to reflect the company's changing technological environment.
e. Recognized an impairment of $1.5 million in a capital asset group. An impairment of $1 million became apparent two years previously but had not been recorded until this year.
f. Switched from FIFO to average cost to conform to parent company preferences. Opening balances for the current and previous two years can be reconstructed.
g. Used the instalment sales method in the past five years; an internal audit revealed that use of this method was intended to delay revenue recognition, even though the customers were highly creditworthy.
h. Began capitalizing development costs because criteria for deferral were met this year for the first time; in the past, future markets had been too uncertain to justify capitalization.
i. Changed inventory cost method to exclude warehousing costs, as required by IFRS.
j. Incorrectly applied a 20% declining balance rate to equipment acquired three years previously when management had instructed that a 15% rate be used.

★ **A21-3 Overview—Types of Accounting Changes:** The following 10 situations all involve a change in accounting. For each situation, assume the company is public unless specified otherwise.

a. Straight-line depreciation for the past three years has been calculated with no deduction for residual value because none was expected; management now believes a residual value of 10% of original cost is appropriate.
b. Straight-line depreciation for the past three years has been calculated with no deduction for residual value because of an oversight.
c. A private company had been using full allocation for income taxes; the company changes to the taxes payable method for the current year.
d. Arithmetic error was made in calculating the closing inventory for 20X1; it now is 20X3.
e. A tree farm changed its inventory valuation method from historical cost to net realizable value to comply with the requirements of IAS 41. Past NRVs cannot be determined.
f. Investment property was reported at fair value in prior years but the measurement method was discovered to be flawed. A more accurate method has been adopted for the current year.
g. Changed from straight-line depreciation to units-of-production depreciation to conform to industry practice.
h. The unamortized balance of capitalized development costs is deemed worthless as a result of technological changes that occurred in the current year; all further development costs will be expensed.

i. A private company adopted percentage-of-completion for a long-term construction contract; all prior contracts were short term and used completed contract.
j. Changed from revenue recognition at cash collection to revenue recognition at point of delivery because of a marked improvement in the creditworthiness of the customer.

Required:

For each of these situations, briefly explain:

1. The type of accounting change.
2. The appropriate method for reporting the change, including a discussion of how amounts, if any, are determined.
3. The effect of the change on the financial statements, if any.

★ **A21-4 Change in Estimates:** The comparative statements of Luhou Limited, an outdoor advertising company, showed the following information:

	20X7	20X6
Retained earnings, 1 January 20X7	$3,635,000	$3,440,000
Net income	451,000	395,000
Dividends	(220,000)	(200,000)
Retained earnings, 31 December 20X7	$3,866,000	$3,635,000

In 20X8, it came to the attention of Luhou's newly hired financial vice-president that management had re-estimated the cost of removing roof-mounted billboards and restoring the roofs at the end of 20X7 but had made no adjustment in that year.

The cost estimates at the end of 20X7 had increased by close to 40%, from $320,000 to $450,000. The average remaining period of time before the roof leases expire (and the decommissioning costs are incurred) was eight years from the end of 20X7. Decommissioning costs (i.e., asset retirement obligations) are discounted at a rate of 6%.

Required:

1. Should the financial results for 20X7 be restated, or should the change in estimate be accounted for prospectively from 20X8? Explain fully.
2. Assume for the purposes of this requirement that 20X7 results should be restated. Prepare the journal entry (or entries) necessary to effect the restatement. Luhou's income tax rate is 25%.

★★ **A21-5 Accounting Changes:** Ng Holdings Limited had its first audit in 20X4. Its preliminary income figure, before tax, was $786,000. The following items were discovered:

a. Ng issued a bond payable at the beginning of 20X1 and received par value for its $1,000,000 convertible bond. The bond is convertible at the option of the investor. A value of $84,000 should have been assigned to the conversion option and classified in shareholders' equity. Any discount on the bond should be amortized over its 15-year life, straight line.
b. The company uses the aging method of estimating the required allowance for doubtful accounts. However, the method had been incorrectly applied in 20X4, with the result that the allowance was understated by $26,000 at the end of 20X4.
c. In April 20X4, a building site was swapped for another, similar property. No cash changed hands. The land had a book value of $233,000; the transaction was recorded at the appraised value of the property received, which was $325,000.
d. The company had accumulated tax loss carryforwards amounting to $400,000 at the end of 20X4. None of the deferred tax benefit of these carryforwards had previously been recognized. In January 20X5, however, company managers decided that for preparing the 20X4 financial statements, it now was probable that the benefits will be realized within the carryforward period.

Required:

1. Classify each of the changes described above, and identify the correct accounting treatment.
2. Calculate revised 20X4 net income. The tax rate is 25%.
3. If a retrospective adjustment to retained earnings is needed, calculate the retrospective adjustment. The tax rate is 25%.

★★

connect

A21-6 Accounting Corrections: Kushner Products Ltd. (KPL) experienced some turmoil among the staff in the accounting department during 20X7, with staff leaving and resultant vacancies for extended periods of time. As a result, the level of professionalism was not what it should have been. Stability was restored in early 20X8 when a new chief accountant was hired. However, the 20X7 statements had already been issued.

The new chief accountant put a thorough-going review process in place to test the reliability of the 20X7 accounting records. In addition to some immaterial errors, the review revealed some potentially more significant problems:

a. Vacation pay amounting to $260,000 had not been accrued at the end of 20X7.
b. The company had entered into a 10-year lease for equipment early in 20X6. The lease had been recorded as a finance lease, but the review process revealed that the lease did not qualify for finance lease treatment. The $100,000 beginning-of-year payments had been discounted at 8% and recorded as both a capital asset and a lease liability. The asset was being depreciated straight line over the lease term.
c. A major inventory purchase had been invoiced (and paid for) at $450,000. The goods acquired had been recorded at that value, of which 40% were still in inventory at 20X7 year-end. However, investigation revealed that the inventory had been fraudulently overpriced (with the cooperation of a KPL employee) at $50,000 above its true value.
d. In the previous year, KPL had recognized the tax benefit (at a rate of 30%) of $800,000 in tax loss carryforwards. The investigation revealed that the evidence to support the likelihood of realizing these carryforward benefits had been grossly exaggerated; the benefit should not have been recognized.

Required:

1. Prepare the necessary journal entries to correct or adjust the records for each of the above items. The income tax rate is 25%.
2. Determine the amount of restatement necessary for the 20X7 net income.

★★

Solution

A21-7 Change in Estimated Useful Life: Stacey Corporation has been depreciating equipment over a 10-year life on a straight-line basis. The equipment, which cost $24,000, was purchased on 1 January 20X1. It has an estimated residual value of $6,000. On the basis of experience since acquisition, management has decided in 20X5 to depreciate it over a total life of 14 years instead of 10 years, with no change in the estimated residual value. The change is to be effective on 1 January 20X5. The 20X5 financial statements are prepared on a comparative basis; 20X4 and 20X5 incomes before depreciation were $49,800 and $52,800, respectively. Disregard income tax considerations.

Required:

1. Identify the type of accounting change involved, and analyze the effects of the change. Which approach should be used—prospective without restatement, retrospective with partial restatement, or retrospective with full restatement? Explain.
2. Prepare the entry, or entries, to appropriately reflect the change (if any) and 20X5 depreciation in the accounts for 20X5, the year of the change.
3. Illustrate how the change, the equipment, and the related depreciation should be reported on the 20X5 financial statements, including comparative 20X4 results.

★ **A21-8 Change in Estimate:** Barker Corp., which has a calendar fiscal year, purchased its only depreciable capital asset on 1 January 20X3. Information related to the asset:

connect

Original cost	$560,000
Estimated residual value	48,000
Depreciation method	Declining balance
Depreciation rate	20%

In 20X5, Barker decreased the estimated residual value to $16,000, and increased the depreciation rate to 30%. Both changes are the result of experience with the asset and revised expectations about the pattern of usage.

Additional information:

	20X5	20X4
Revenue	$2,800,000	$2,240,000
Expenses other than depreciation and tax	1,680,000	1,534,400
Gain (loss) from discontinued operations, before tax	(40,000)	—
Tax rate	25%	25%

Required:

1. Calculate the ending 20X5 balance of accumulated depreciation, and show the 20X5 entry/entries for depreciation.
2. Provide the condensed comparative statement of comprehensive income for 20X5, including disclosures related to the accounting change.

★ **A21-9 Error Correction:** Shariff Ltd. signed an operating lease on 1 January 20X0. The lease was a 40-year term on a piece of land. The land reverts to the lessor at the end of the lease term. The lease requires annual payments, on each 1 January, of $45,000 for the first 10 years. Annual 1 January payments of $20,000 were required for the second 10 years, 1 January payments of $10,000 for the third 10 years, and 1 January payments of $2,000 for the final 10 years. The lease payments have all been made on schedule but have all been expensed as paid (i.e., it is now the end of 20X4 and the 20X3 rent has been paid and expensed, but the 20X4 books are still open). The lease should have been expensed evenly over the lease term, regardless of the payment scheme.

Required:

1. Provide the entry to correct the error.
2. Determine the amount by which pretax earnings must be adjusted for each prior year when Shariff prepares a five-year summary of financial results.

★ **A21-10 Error Correction:** In 20X6, Cathode Corporation, a calendar fiscal-year company, discovered that depreciation expense was erroneously overstated $40,000 in both 20X4 and 20X5 for financial reporting purposes. Net income in 20X6 is correct. The tax rate is 30%. The error was made only for financial reporting, affecting depreciation and deferred income tax accounts., CCA had been recorded correctly, and thus there will be no change in taxes payable.

connect

Additional information:

	20X6	20X5
Beginning retained earnings	$265,000	$180,000
Net income (includes error in 20X5)	125,000	145,000
Dividends declared	80,000	60,000

Required:

1. Record the entry in 20X6 to correct the error.
2. Provide the comparative retained earnings statement for 20X6, including any required note disclosure.

★★ **A21-11 Accounting Changes—Depreciable Assets:** Tech Manufacturing Corporation reports the following situations in 20X6 with respect to its high-tech manufacturing equipment:

a. Machine 1 was acquired at a cost of $872,000 in 20X3. The machine was depreciated on a straight-line basis over its expected six-year life. At the end of 20X6, management decided that this machine should have been depreciated over a total useful life of eight years. Salvage value, expected to be negligible, has not changed.
b. Machine 2 was acquired at a cost of $448,500 in 20X5. It was being depreciated on a declining-balance method using a rate of 40%. Salvage values were expected to be minimal. In 20X6, management decided that, based on the usage patterns seen to date, units-of-production would be a more appropriate method of depreciation. The machine is used sporadically and suffers from wear and tear only as used (i.e., obsolescence is not much of a factor in the loss of utility). Estimated units-of-production total 350,000, of which 75,000 units were produced in 20X5 and 30,000 units in 20X6.
c. Machine 3 was acquired in 20X3 at a cost of $325,000. Management discovered in 20X6 that the machine was expensed in 20X3, despite the fact that it had a useful life of 10 years, with a 10% salvage value. Straight-line depreciation should have been used for this asset.

For all depreciation methods, the company follows a policy of recording a full year of depreciation charged in the first year, but no depreciation is charged in the year of disposal.

Required:

1. Classify each of the changes described above, and identify the correct accounting treatment.
2. For each machine, calculate 20X6 depreciation.
3. If a retrospective adjustment is needed, calculate the retrospective adjustment in 20X6. The tax rate is 25%.

★★★ Solution

A21-12 Policy Change—Resource Exploration Costs: Gunnard Limited was formed in 20X4 and has a 31 December year-end. Gunnard Company changed from successful efforts (SE) to full costing (FC) for its resource exploration costs in 20X5. SE is still used for tax purposes. The change was made to reflect changed corporate reporting objectives; more stable net income was deemed desirable to support a more stable stock market share price. Under FC, all exploration costs are deferred; under SE, only a portion are deferred. Under both approaches, the deferred cost balance is amortized yearly.

Had FC been used in 20X4, a total of $3,200,000 of costs originally written off under SE would have been capitalized. A total of $4,700,000 of such costs were incurred in 20X5. Gunnard discloses 20X4 and 20X5 results comparatively in its annual financial statements. The tax rate is 30% in both years.

	SE	FC
Amortization of resource development costs:		
20X4	$ 40,000	$ 240,000
20X5	200,000	850,000
Resource development costs expensed:		
20X4	$3,200,000	—
20X5	4,700,000	—

Additional information for Gunnard:

	20X5	20X4
Revenues	$7,100,000	$4,400,000
Expenses other than resource development costs, amortization, and income tax	2,050,000	720,000

Required:

1. Prepare a 20X5 comparative statement of comprehensive income using the old policy, successful efforts.
2. Prepare the 20X5 entry/entries for FC amortization and the accounting change. Assume that no amortization has been recorded by Gunnard to date in 20X5.
3. Prepare the comparative statements of comprehensive income under FC, and include disclosures related to the accounting change.
4. Prepare the comparative retained earnings section of the statement of changes in shareholders' equity for 20X5, reflecting the change.
5. How will the classification of development costs on the statement of cash flows change as a result of the new policy?

★★ **A21-13 Error Correction—Leasing:** In early 20X1 Picton Ltd., a public company, entered into a capital lease that required Picton to make $100,000 beginning-of-year payments for six years. The interest rate implicit in the lease was 7%; Picton's IBR was 6%. For accounting purposes, Picton calculated the present value of the lease at 6%, obtaining a value of $521,236. This amount was used in 20X1 and 20X2 to account for the lease liability and for straight-line depreciation of the asset under lease. In 20X3, the chief accountant discovered that the company should have used the lessor's rate implicit in the lease, as required by IFRS.

connect

Required:

1. Determine the amounts relating to the lease that Picton would have included in its 20X1 and 20X2 SFP and SCI.
2. Determine the amounts that Picton should have reported instead.
3. Prepare journal entries necessary to retrospectively correct the errors. Assume a 20% income tax rate.

★★ **A21-14 Error Correction:** Excerpts from the 31 December financial statements of Simpson Limited, before any corrections.

	20X7	20X6	20X5
Income statement:			
Cost of goods sold	$790,000	$705,200	$676,800
Statement of financial position:			
Inventory	$ 34,500	$ 30,900	$ 19,700
Retained earnings:			
Opening retained earnings	$331,000	$260,800	$211,500
Net income	104,700	91,200	70,300
Dividends	(21,000)	(21,000)	(21,000)
Closing retained earnings	$414,700	$331,000	$260,800

After these financial statements were prepared, but before they were issued for 20X7, a routine review revealed a major mathematical error in calculating 20X5 closing inventory. Instead of $19,700, closing inventory should have been $16,100.

There is no income tax.

Required:

1. What entry is needed to correct the error in 20X7? Explain.
2. Restate all the above information, as appropriate, to retrospectively correct the error.
3. What disclosure of the error is needed?

★★ **A21-15 Error Correction:** Trelarkin Forpas Limited (TFL) reported the following in its 31 December financial statements:

	20X9	20X8	20X7
Income statement			
Depreciation expense (all assets)	$ 100,400	$ 91,600	$ 92,400
Balance sheet			
Capital assets (net)	$1,216,200	$1,147,600	$1,005,400
Retained earnings statement			
Opening retained earnings	$ 879,200	$ 905,800	$ 655,800
Net income (loss)	(135,700)	41,200	317,800
Dividends	(67,800)	(67,800)	(67,800)
Closing retained earnings	$ 675,700	$ 879,200	$ 905,800

After the draft 20X9 financial statements were prepared but before they were issued, TFL discovered that a capital asset was incorrectly accounted for in 20X5. A $200,000 capital asset was purchased early in 20X5, and it should have been depreciated on a straight-line basis over eight years with a $40,000 residual value. Instead, it was written off to expense.

The error was made on the books, but the capital asset was accounted for correctly for tax purposes. The tax rate was 25%.

Required:

1. What entry is needed to correct the error in 20X9?
2. Restate all the above information, as appropriate, to retrospectively correct the error.
3. What disclosure of the error is needed?

A21-16 Error Correction—Lease: On 4 July 20X2, Giovanni Ind. leased computer equipment through the leasing subsidiary of Giovanni's bank. The lease was for five years at $240,000 per year, payable at the beginning of each lease year. Giovanni recorded the initial lease payment as prepaid rent and amortized it to rent expense at the end of each month.

In April 20X4, the controller determined that the lease had been incorrectly reported as an operating lease; it should have been accounted for as a finance lease. Upon inquiry, the controller concluded that the bank subsidiary's implicit interest rate in the lease was 6%.

Giovanni uses straight-line depreciation for equipment. The company's income tax rate is 20%.

Required:

1. What effects will this correction have on the financial statements for 20X2 and 20X3?
2. Prepare the necessary journal entries to correct the lease accounting.

★ **A21-17 Policy Change—Investment:** Catherine Limited has an investment with an original cost of $400,000. The investment was accounted for using the cost method in 20X0, 20X1, and 20X2. This year, 20X3, the company must conform to new accounting standards and report the investment at fair value. Fair values were $390,000, $410,000, and $450,000 at the end of 20X0, 20X1, and 20X2, respectively. The investment had a fair value of $466,000 at the end of 20X3. The change is to be accounted for retrospectively with restatement of the prior year's statements. The company wishes to record the change in 20X3, and to adjust the investment account to fair value at the end of 20X3. *Note*: The change affects the shareholders' equity account, *unrealized holding gains* (a separate component of other comprehensive income), instead of retained earnings.

Required:

Prepare appropriate journal entries for this situation. The income tax rate is 25%.

★★ **A21-18 Policy Change—Bad Debts:** Betteroff Corporation was incorporated on 1 January 20X3. In the past, it has not provided an allowance for doubtful accounts. Instead, uncollectible accounts were expensed when written off and recoveries were credited to bad debt expense when collected. Accounts were written off if they were outstanding for more than four months.

In December 20X5, the company decided to change its accounting policy to account for bad debts as a percentage of credit sales, in compliance with GAAP and with industry practice. Statistics for the past three years are summarized as follows:

		Accounts Written Off and Year of Sale			Recoveries and Year of Sale	
Year	**Credit Sales**	**20X3**	**20X4**	**20X5**	**20X3**	**20X4**
20X3	$100,000	$550	—	—	$10	—
20X4	150,000	650	$750	—	30	$20
20X5	225,000	—	900	$950	—	40

Accounts receivable at 31 December 20X5 were $50,000 after write-offs but before any allowance for doubtful accounts.

Required:

1. How should the change in accounting policy be accounted for?
2. Prepare the journal entry to reflect the change in accounting policy and to adjust 20X5 bad debt expense. State your assumptions and show your supporting calculations, in arriving at a percentage rate for bad debts. Disregard income tax.

(Source: [Adapted] © CGA-Canada. Reproduced with permission.)

★★ **A21-19 Retrospective Policy Change:** Armstrong Limited has used the average cost (AC) method to determine inventory values since the company was first formed in 20X3. In 20X7, the company decided to switch to the FIFO method, to conform to industry practice. Armstrong will still use average cost for tax purposes. The tax rate is 30%. The following data have been assembled:

connect

	20X3	20X4	20X5	20X6	20X7
Net income, as reported, after tax	$56,000*	$65,000*	$216,000*	$255,000*	$125,000**
Closing inventory, AC	35,000	45,000	56,000	91,000	116,000
Closing inventory, FIFO	41,000	57,000	52,000	84,000	130,000
Dividends	5,000	7,000	7,000	10,000	14,000

*Using the old policy, average cost
**Using the new policy, FIFO.

Required:

Present the comparative retained earnings statement for 20X7, giving effect to the change in accounting policy.

★★ **A21-20 Inventory Policy Change:** On 1 January 20X5, Baker Limited decided to change the inventory costing method used from average cost (AC) to FIFO to conform to industry practice. The annual reporting period ends on 31 December. The average income tax rate is 30%. The following related data were developed:

	AC Basis	FIFO Basis
Beginning inventory, 20X4	$ 30,000	$30,000
Ending inventory		
20X4	40,000	70,000
20X5	44,000	76,000
Net income		
20X4: AC basis	80,000	
20X5: FIFO basis		82,000
Retained earnings		
20X4 beginning balance	120,000	
Dividends declared and paid		
20X4	64,000	
20X5		70,000
Common shares outstanding, 10,000		

Required:

1. Identify the type of accounting change involved. Which approach should be used—prospective, retrospective without restatement, or retrospective with restatement? Explain.
2. Give the entry to record the effect of the change, assuming the change was made only for accounting purposes, not for income tax purposes.
3. Complete the following schedule:

	FIFO Basis	
	20X5	20X4
Statement of financial position		
Inventory	$	$
Retained earnings		
Statement of comprehensive income		
Net income and comprehensive income		
Earnings per share		
Statement of changes in equity—retained earnings section		
Beginning balance, as previously reported		
Cumulative effect of accounting change		
Beginning balance restated		
Net income		
Dividends declared and paid		
Ending balance		

★★ **A21-21 Change in Policy; Error:** TXL Corporation has tentatively computed income before tax as $660,000 for 20X4. Retained earnings at the beginning of 20X4 had a balance of $3,600,000. Dividends of $270,000 were paid during 20X4. There were dividends payable of $60,000 at the end of 20X3 and $90,000 at the end of 20X4. The following information has been provided:

1. The company used FIFO for costing inventory in deriving net income of $660,000. It wishes to change to average cost to be comparable with other companies in the industry. Accordingly, the change in policy should be applied retrospectively. The comparable figures for ending inventory under the two methods are:

December 31	FIFO	Average
20X1	$408,000	$420,000
20X2	450,000	435,000
20X3	480,000	462,000
20X4	486,000	510,000

2. In January 20X3, the company acquired some equipment for $3,000,000. At that time, it estimated the equipment would have an estimated useful life of 12 years and a salvage value of $360,000. In 20X3, the company received a government grant of $480,000, which assisted in purchasing the equipment. The grant was credited to income in error. The company has been depreciating the equipment on a straight-line basis and has already provided for depreciation for 20X4 without considering the government grant. Management realizes that the company must account for the government grant by crediting it directly to the equipment account.

The income tax rate for the company is 30%. Assume that all of the stated items are fully taxable or deductible for income tax purposes.

Required:

1. Prepare a schedule to show the calculation of the correct net income for 20X4 in accordance with generally accepted accounting principles.
2. Prepare, in good form, the retained earnings section of TXL's statement of comprehensive income for the year ended 31 December 20X4. Comparative figures need not be provided.

(Source: [Adapted] © CGA-Canada. Reproduced with permission.)

★★ **A21-22 Change in Accounting for Natural Resources:** In 20X6, Black Oil Inc. changed its method of accounting for oil exploration costs from the successful efforts method (SE) to full costing (FC) for financial reporting because of a change in corporate reporting objectives. Black Oil has been in the oil exploration business since January 20X3; prior to that, the company was active in oil transportation.

	SE	FC
20X3	$ 15,000	$ 45,000
20X4	66,000	75,000
20X5	75,000	105,000
20X6	120,000	180,000

Black Oil reports the result of years 20X4 through 20X6 in its 20X6 annual report and has a calendar fiscal year. The tax rate is 30%. The change is made for accounting purposes but not for tax purposes. Thus, the deferred income tax account is changed.

Additional information:

	20X3	20X4	20X5	20X6
Ending retained earnings (SE basis)	$54,000	$69,000	$93,000	n/a
Dividends declared	27,000	31,200	28,500	$36,000

Required:

1. Prepare the entry in 20X6 to record the accounting change. Use "natural resources" as the depletable asset account.
2. Prepare the retained earnings section of the comparative SCE. Include three years: 20X6, 20X5, and 20X4.
3. Describe how the accounting policy change would affect the statement of cash flows.

★★★ **A21-23 Retrospective Policy Changes:** Linfei Limited has a 31 December year-end, and a tax rate of 25%. Management has asked you to respond to the following situations:

connect

1. The company has always used the FIFO method of determining inventory costs; starting in 20X7, it will now use weighted-average cost. Opening and closing inventories for 20X7 under FIFO are $2,655,000 and $3,300,000, respectively. Opening and closing inventories under weighted average are $2,100,000 and $2,600,000, respectively. Provide the journal entry to record the change.
2. Return to requirement 1. Additional information is as follows:
   - In 20X7, opening retained earnings was $4,365,000. Net income, before any adjustment due to the change in inventory method, was $1,600,000. Dividends were $235,000.
   - In 20X6, opening retained earnings was $4,010,000, net income was $565,000, and dividends were $210,000.
   - For 20X6, opening inventory was $2,400,000 under FIFO and $2,000,000 under weighted average.

   Prepare a comparative retained earnings section of the statement of changes in equity, giving retrospective effect to the change in accounting policy.
3. Return to your retained earnings statement in requirement 2. Prepare a comparative retained earnings statement assuming that comparative balances could not be restated; that is, the only information you have to work with, in addition to the income, retained earnings, and dividend information, is that provided about opening and closing inventory balances in requirement 1.
4. An asset was acquired in 20X4 at a cost of $400,000. The salvage value of $40,000 was estimated. The asset has been depreciated on the declining-balance method at a rate of 20% in each of 20X4, 20X5, and 20X6. On 1 October of this year, 20X7, management decided to change depreciation methods and will now use the straight-line method. This change is made on the basis of usage information that indicates that the asset is used about the same amount in each year of life. The new estimates are a *total* life of 12 years and a salvage value of $25,000. Depreciation expense has not yet been recorded for 20X7. Provide the appropriate journal entry/entries.

★★★ **A21-24 Multiple Accounting Changes:** Zealand News Ltd. made several financial accounting changes in 20X6:

First, the company changed the total useful life from 20 years to 14 years on a $350,000 asset purchased 1 January 20X2. The asset was originally expected to be sold for $50,000 at the end of its useful life, but that amount was also changed in 20X6, to $200,000. Zealand News Ltd. applies the straight-line method of depreciation to this asset. Depreciation has not yet been recorded in 20X6.

Second, the company decided to change inventory costing from FIFO to weighted average (WA) but is unable to accurately determine WA inventory in prior year-ends. The FIFO 20X6 beginning and ending inventories are $30,000 and $45,000. Under WA, the 20X6 ending inventory is $35,000. The company expects WA to render income numbers more useful for prediction, given inflation.

Third, the company changed its policy for accounting for certain staff training costs. Previously, the costs were capitalized and amortized straight line over three years, starting with the year of the expenditure. The new policy is to expense training costs as incurred, in compliance with revised accounting standards for intangible assets. A total of $100,000 was expended in 20X3, $0 in 20X4, $60,000 in 20X5, and $45,000 in 20X6.

Fourth, an error in amortizing patents was discovered in 20X6. Patents costing $510,000 on 1 January 20X4 have been amortized over their legal life (20 years). The accountant neglected to obtain an estimate of the patents' economic life, which totalled only five years.

Zealand News Ltd. is a calendar fiscal-year company and is subject to a 30% tax rate.

Additional information:

	20X6	20X5
Beginning retained earnings	$489,000	$319,000
Net income, after tax	335,000*	220,000
Dividends declared	70,000	50,000

*This is the correct reported amount and includes the appropriate amounts related to all the expenses affected by the accounting changes.

Required:

1. Record the 20X6 entries necessary to make the accounting changes. If the change cannot be made, explain why.
2. Prepare the 20X5 and 20X6 retained earnings section of the comparative statement of changes in equity, with note disclosures for the accounting changes.

★★★ connect

A21-25 Accounting Changes, Comprehensive: EC Construction Limited (EC) has 100,000 common shares outstanding in public hands. The balance of retained earnings at the beginning of 20X7 was $2,400,000. On 15 December 20X7 EC declared dividends of $3 per share payable on 5 January 20X8. Income before income tax was $600,000 based on the records of the company's accountant.

Additional information on selected transactions/events is provided below:

a. At the beginning of 20X6, EC purchased some equipment for $230,000 (salvage value of $30,000) that had a useful life of five years. The accountant used a 40% declining-balance method of depreciation but mistakenly deducted the salvage value in calculating depreciation expense in 20X6 and 20X7.
b. As a result of an income tax audit of 20X5 taxable income, $74,000 of expenses claimed as deductible expenses for tax purposes was disallowed by the CRA. This error cost the company $29,600 in additional tax. This amount was paid in 20X7 but has been debited to a prepaid expense account.
c. EC contracted to build an office building for RD Corporation. The construction began in 20X6 and will be completed in 20X8. The contract has a price of $30 million. The following data (in millions of dollars) relate to the construction period to date:

	20X6	20X7
Costs incurred to date	$ 8	$13
Estimated costs to complete	12	7
Progress billings during the year	6	10
Cash collected on billings during the year	5	8

The accountant used the completed-contract method in accounting for this contract, which is not permitted for a public company.

d. On 1 January 20X7, EC purchased, as a long-term investment, 19% of the common shares of One Limited for $50,000. On that date, the fair value of identifiable assets of One Limited was $220,000 and was equal to the book value of identifiable assets. Goodwill has not been impaired. No investment income has been recorded. One paid no dividends, but reported income of $25,000 in the year. EC has significant influence over One.
e. EC has an effective tax rate of 25%.

Required:

1. Calculate 20X7 net income for EC.
2. Prepare the 20X7 retained earnings statement in good form. Comparative numbers need not be shown.

★★ **A21-26 ASPE—Change from IFRS to ASPE:** Wuhan Corporation is a Vancouver-based company that engages in a large volume of international activities. The company has a largely independent wholly owned subsidiary in Hong Kong. Wuhan Corporation had been publicly traded on the TSX-V until mid-20X6, when a wealthy Vancouver tycoon purchased all of Wuhan's outstanding shares through his private investment company. As Wuhan is no longer public but still needs to be audited, management decided to change its financial reporting from IFRS to Canadian ASPE effective in 20X6. Selected financial information (as reported under IFRS) is shown below (in thousands of Canadian dollars):

	20X3	20X4	20X5
Balances, 31 December:			
Retained earnings	$44,000	$45,000	$41,000
Deferred income tax liability	11,000	8,000	9,000
OCI—accumulated translation gain (loss)	5,300	6,800	4,800
OCI—accumulated pension remeasurement	(8,000)	(11,000)	(9,600)
Year's translation gain (loss) on Vancouver subsidiary (OCI)	(2,700)	1,500	(2,000)
Year's actuarial gain (loss) on defined benefit pensions (OCI)	(1,500)	(3,000)	1,400
Net income for the year	7,000	7,500	2,000
Dividends declared and paid during the year	5,000	5,000	6,000

Wuhan's management, with the consent of the new owner, has elected to change to the taxes payable method.

Required:

1. Explain the impacts that the change to ASPE will have on Wuhan's restated comparative financial statements for 20X4 and 20X5.
2. Determine the restated net income for 20X4 and 20X5.

★ **A21-27 ASPE—Rationale for Accounting Changes:** Arctic Charm Corporation is a privately owned Canadian company. The company experienced poor operating results in the years 20X0 to 20X3, and, in 20X3, it reorganized and refinanced its operations. Creditors were asked to accept partial payment; shareholders invested additional capital. As part of the restructuring, Arctic Charm accepted covenants imposed by Spenser Venture Capital Corporation. Violation of these debt covenants would trigger a demand for immediate repayment of long-term debt and almost certainly mean that the company would be placed in receivership or bankruptcy. The covenants included minimum working capital requirements, and an upper limit on the overall debt-to-equity ratio.

The 20X4 pretax operating results were acceptable. The company wishes to make the following two accounting changes before issuing its financial statements for 20X4:

a. Change from comprehensive tax allocation to the taxes payable method.
b. Change depreciation policies from declining balance to straight line. Capital assets are fairly new but have been depreciated for three to five years under declining-balance rates. The company would adjust all capital asset balances to the amounts that would have existed had straight-line depreciation always been used. The company believes that straight-line depreciation is more indicative of the equipment's actual usage. The equipment is not subject to rapid technological obsolescence.

Arctic Charm's CFO met with officials from Spenser to obtain their consent to these changes. The officials accepted Arctic Charm's proposed changes as being in compliance with ASPE as required by the loan agreement.

Required:

Describe the impact of these changes on the financial statements and debt covenants. Consider the appropriateness of these changes in your response.

★★ **A21-28 ASPE—Accounting Changes:** Mohammed Limited, a private company, made the following changes to its accounting in 20X5:

connect

a. Increased the straight-line depreciation rate on the company's building from 5% per year to 8% per year. The building was acquired 8 years previous for $1,200,000. The company's tax rate is 25%.
b. Renewed a lease on a roof that the company has been using for a microwave transmission tower. In the current year, Mohammed Limited renewed the lease for an additional five years. The company is obligated to remove the tower and completely restore the roof when the lease expires; the estimated restoration cost is $200,000, which is double the original estimate.
c. Decided that it is more likely than not that the future benefits of tax loss carryforwards of $3 million will be realized.
d. Entered into a 10-year lease for equipment at the beginning of 20X4. The lease is for $20,000 per year, with beginning-of-year payments. The lease has a five-year bargain renewal option at the end of the 10 years. The 20X4 lease payment was recorded as lease expense. Mohammed Limited's incremental borrowing rate is 6%.

Required:

Describe the impact of these changes on the financial statements. As appropriate, make journal entries to record the financial statement impacts.

★★ **A21-29 Aspe—Accounting Changes, Inventory, and Revenue:** Late in 20X6, the management of Richter Minerals Inc., a Canadian private company, decided to change the company's inventory valuation method and, concurrently, its revenue recognition method. Historically, the company had used an average cost basis for all inventories and had recognized revenue when minerals were shipped to customers. Now, effective with the year beginning 1 January 20X7, Richter will recognize revenue when the minerals have been refined and are ready for sale, at which point the inventory will be adjusted to net realizable value at the end of each reporting period. Richter's minerals are easily sold at any time on the world market via electronic trading. Richter's shareholders and principal lenders have approved the change in policy.

At the end of 20X6, Richter had inventory (at cost of production) totalling $70 million. Of that total, $20 million was of unrefined ore, and $50 million was refined minerals. At NRV, Richter's refined minerals inventory was $72 million. The 20X6 opening inventory contained refined minerals of $44 million at cost; using market price indices, Richter's management was able to determine that the 20X6 opening inventory was worth $60 million at NRV. Richter's 20X6 sales revenue was $250 million.

During 20X7, Richter recognized revenue of $360 million, on the new reporting basis. Ending inventory of refined minerals amounted to $82 million; production cost was $55 million.

The income tax rate was 25% in both years.

Required:

1. How much will this change affect the previously reported net income for 20X6?
2. Can this change be applied retrospectively with restatement? Explain the difficulties that management might encounter when restating years prior to 20X6.
3. Prepare any journal entries that are necessary to record the change in accounting policies.

★★★ **A21-30 ASPE—Change Regarding Construction Contracts:** KLB Corporation, a private company, has used the completed-contract method to account for its long-term construction contracts since its inception in 20X3. On 1 January 20X7, management decided to change to the percentage-of-completion method to better reflect operating activities and conform to industry norms. Completed contract was used for income tax purposes and will continue to be used for income tax purposes in the future. The income tax rate is 25%. The following information has been assembled:

Solution

Year Ended 31 December	20X3	20X4	20X5	20X6	20X7
Net income, as reported	$100,000	$120,000	$150,000	$140,000	160,000*
CC income, included in above	0	60,000	0	120,000	0
PC income, as calculated	40,000	65,000	50,000	40,000	75,000
Opening retained earnings	0	90,000	190,000	320,000	440,000
Dividends	10,000	20,000	20,000	20,000	20,000
Closing retained earnings	90,000	190,000	320,000	440,000	580,000

*Includes PC income, not CC income, in earnings.

Required:

1. Identify the type of accounting change involved. Which approach should be used—retrospective with full restatement, retrospective with limited restatement, or prospective without restatement? Explain.
2. Give the entry to appropriately reflect the accounting change in 20X7, the year of the change.
3. Restate the 20X7 retained earnings section of the statement of changes in equity, including the 20X6 comparative figures.
4. Assume that only the opening balance in 20X7 can be restated and that the cumulative effect cannot be allocated to individual years. Recast the 20X7 comparative retained earnings section of the CSE accordingly.
5. Assume that no balances can be restated. Can the change be made in 20X7? Explain.

connect LEARNSMART SMARTBOOK™

For more information on the resources available from McGraw-Hill Ryerson, go to www.mcgrawhill.ca/he/solutions.

CHAPTER 22

Financial Statement Analysis

INTRODUCTION

Between 2007 and 2009, WestJet Airlines increased revenue by 30%, while net earnings declined by 15%. Between 2010 and 2011, revenue increased by 18% and net earnings by 64%. That sounds really impressive, but the percentages depend partially on the starting point—the denominator. What happened? Well, we can make some guesses—the company's revenues are mainly in Canadian dollars while its aircraft purchases, aircraft lease payments, and fuel costs are all in U.S. dollars. Changing fuel prices and exchange rates can add a lot of volatility to the company's net profits. On the financing side, WestJet's long-term debt load has been declining as a proportion of total assets, starting at over $1 billion on 1 January 2010 to $670 million by the end of fiscal 2012.

If you were a major lender to WestJet, or an investor, how would you go about analyzing the company's asset and liability structure, its earnings performance, its return on assets and equity, and its ability to service its large debt load? If you were an employee representative, how would you appraise a company's ability to increase wages or to meet pension funding obligations?

Financial statement analysis is a broad and complex field. Entire books (and whole university courses) are devoted to financial statement analysis. In this chapter, we touch only on the more general aspects of financial analysis. Any aspiring accountant should understand how to take financial statements apart and analyze their significance.

The emphasis in the chapter is on basic analytical techniques. However, it often is necessary to recast a company's financial statements in order to make them more useful for the analyst's specific needs. The appendix to this chapter contains an example of recasting. The example has been adapted from a real company (although disguised).

OVERVIEW OF STATEMENT ANALYSIS

Financial statement analysis can be broken down into the following steps:

1. *Determine why the analysis is being done and clarify the decision focus.* What questions does the analyst hope to answer by completing the analysis? A lender will have concerns different from an equity investor or supplier.
2. *Gather all available data.* This would include not only the most recent financial statements but also information on the company's business, its industry and competitors, and the economy. A complete analysis may be done only with an understanding of the environment within which the company conducts business.
3. *Apply the appropriate analytical techniques.* There is a large variety of ratios and other analytical tools to use; given the decision being made and the context, the "right" analytical tools must be chosen.
4. *Analyze and interpret the results.* This is the most important step of any financial statement analysis. It is easy to perform the calculations; it is much more difficult to understand how the results will impact the decisions being made.

We will now look at each of these steps in some detail.

Clarify the Decision Focus

The starting point is to be clear about what decision is to be made as a result of the financial statement analysis. A sample of possible decisions includes:

1. Equity investment decisions;
2. Lending decisions;
3. Contractual decisions, such as accepting employment, negotiating collective agreements, or entering into a joint ventures; and
4. Regulatory decisions, including the need for rate or price increases, or the impact of past regulatory decisions.

Each of these decisions will require a somewhat different approach to the analysis and a different set of priorities. For example, a prospective investor in common shares will be concerned primarily with the long-term profitability of the company while a trade creditor will be primarily interested in short-term liquidity. This difference in emphasis is illustrated by the fact that many creditors will continue to extend credit to a company with declining profitability in which no rational investor would buy shares.

There also is a difference between looking at a company as a new, prospective stakeholder or as an existing stakeholder who needs to decide whether to continue the relationship or to bail out. A prospective stakeholder (e.g., an investor, creditor, or contractor) is concerned about the future safety and profitability of a contemplated investment or contract. In contrast, an existing stakeholder is concerned with the financial and/or operational ramifications of terminating an existing investment or contract.

Therefore, it is crucial to know the nature of the decision in question.

This chapter describes several different techniques for analysis, but most of the discussion is devoted to traditional ratio analysis. It is possible to compute dozens of financial statement ratios, but an analyst should first determine what decisions need to be made and then select the relevant ratios that will assist with this assessment.

Gather the Data

Different types of data will be required to prepare and analyze ratios. The company's financial statements and notes are only the starting point. An analyst must also obtain an understanding of the company and the industry in which the company operates. Information that the analyst requires about the company itself might include:

- The mix of products and services sold;

- The geographic areas in which the company sells its products/services;
- Assets that are leased versus owned;
- Businesses acquired in the past few years;
- The company's strategy for growth; and
- Major shareholders.

The above information is vital to understanding profitability and efficiency ratios discussed later in the chapter.

The Environment

Company analysis must always be a forward-looking process interpreted within a broader context of:

- The general economic environment;
- The economic and competitive climate of the country or region in which the company operates; and
- The structure and outlook of the industry in which the company competes.

The company's financial outlook must be assessed in respect of the future trends of the industry and how competitors will react. Investors will also need to evaluate the market price of the company's shares. For lenders, the company's future must be evaluated with respect to its ability to service its debt without straining its current operations and its competitiveness.

We will give examples of how the environment impacts specific ratios later in the chapter.

The Financial Statements

The most important piece of data is the financial statements, including the notes, auditor's report, and other additional information. However, before the statements can be used for calculating the ratios, the analyst should review the accounting policies used in conjunction with the auditor's report to ensure the statements are in a format that is useful. Later in this chapter, we look at examples of recasting that might be required to make the statements more useful for analysis.

Examine the Auditor's Report

A public company must have an unqualified audit opinion to be traded on major stock exchanges. In cases where a private company has used non-GAAP accounting policies, the auditor will have to qualify their opinion. A qualification in an **auditor's report** should not *necessarily* be cause for concern. A company may choose to use accounting policies that are more in accordance with the interests of the primary users than IFRS or ASPE would be. A privately held company, for example, may report its capital assets at a restated value that reflects the value against which its lenders have extended loans.

Normally, an auditor will attempt to quantify the impact (i.e., on net income) of a deviation from GAAP and will either report the impact in the auditor's report or refer the reader to a financial statement note that discusses the deviation.

If a private company does not have an audit, a public accountant may nevertheless be retained for a **review engagement**, in which a full audit is not performed but a review of the financial statements for general consistency with GAAP (or with a disclosed basis of accounting) and for reasonableness of presentation is completed. Banks often rely on these review engagement reports as assurance that the company's accounting practices are worthy of belief and that the financial statements are therefore plausible.

Examine Accounting Policies

We have stressed throughout this book that managers' accounting policy choices are governed by the objectives of financial reporting in the particular circumstance.

The financial reporting objectives adopted by a company may not correspond with a specific user's preferred objectives. Therefore, the first task of an analyst is to determine the reporting objectives that are implicit in the financial statements. If the implicit objectives do not correspond with the user's objectives, then adjustments to the financial statements will probably be needed before they are of maximum use. Discerning the implicit objectives often is easier said than done.

Notes to Financial Statements To the extent that they exist, most of the clues to the implicit reporting objectives can be found in the notes to the financial statements.

The first note to financial statements is the accounting policy note in which the company describes the GAAP that is being followed and its accounting policy choices. In Canada, it will be important for the analyst to know which GAAP has been used: IFRS, ASPE or Accounting Standards for Not-for-profit Organizations (*Part III* of the *CPA Canada Handbook*) or accounting standards for the public sector (used by universities, governments, etc.)

An analyst looks in the notes to gain an understanding of how assets, liabilities, revenue, and expenses have been recognized. Exhibit 22-1 highlights examples of the type of information that an analyst would look for in reviewing the notes for each of the related statements.

Recast the Financial Statements Based on the results of her review of the company's financial statements and notes, an analyst may need to recast the financial statements to suit her needs before applying analytical approaches. Situations that suggest a needed restatement include the following examples:

- The SCI is revised to remove nonrecurring gains and losses.
- The SCI and SFP are revised to remove the effects of deferred income tax liabilities and assets.
- The SCI and SFP are revised to reflect a different policy on capitalization of certain costs:
  - Capitalized costs are shifted to the SCI in the year they occurred and depreciation/amortization is removed; or
  - Expenditures charged directly to the SCI are removed and capitalized instead with depreciation/amortization added.
- Loans to and from shareholders are reclassified as shareholders' equity.
- The securitization of accounts receivable is classified as debt on the SFP rather than as a sale of receivables (see Chapter 7).
- The estimated present value of assets under operating leases is added to capital assets and to liabilities to "put back on the balance sheet" the assets being used and the related obligations. (See Chapter 18.)

In recasting the statement to reflect different accounting policies, it is important to remember to adjust for both sides of transactions. For example, deleting deferred income tax expense must be accompanied by adding the balance of the deferred income tax liability to retained earnings and not by simply *ignoring* the balance.

An illustration of recasting financial statements is presented in the Appendix to this chapter.

Apply the Appropriate Techniques

Once the focus of the analyst's decision is clarified and the data has been gathered, the analyst then selects the appropriate ratios to use for her review. The key word here is "appropriate." As there are a large number of analytical tools to choose from, the analyst should select only those that will aid in her decision. Many ratios overlap in the input data and results. In this chapter, we have selected some of the more common analytical tools that are used in practice. There are many more ratios that analysts use, some of which are specific to certain industries. For example, in the retail industry, sales-per-square-foot is a key ratio that is used to assess how effectively and efficiently retail floor space is used. Later in the chapter, we will see how the techniques are applied.

EXHIBIT 22-1

INFORMATION TO GATHER FROM THE NOTES

Statement of Comprehensive Income	Statement of Financial Position	Statement of Cash Flows
What type of revenue recognition policy is being used: one that recognizes revenue early or more on a deferred basis?	What inventory costing policies are being used: FIFO, average cost?	If earnings (with depreciation/amortization added back) are significantly and repeatedly larger than operating cash flows, the company may be maximizing net income.
Are costs immediately expensed or capitalized and amortized in later periods?	Are accounts receivables securitized? Should the securitization be shown on the SFP as a form of financing?	If operating cash flow is significantly larger than earnings, the company may be very conservative in its accounting practices, reporting minimum net earnings (e.g., by anticipating future expenditures through current provisions), or may be trying to minimize its current tax bill.
If revenue recognition is deferred but all operating costs are expensed as incurred, income minimization may be the objective for income tax or political reasons.	What models are used for long-term assets—cost, fair value, or the revaluation model?	Does the cash flow from operations exclude important operating expenses (e.g., development costs) that management has capitalized and shifted to the investing section?
Are there any nonrecurring gains included in operating revenues?	What depreciation/amortization policies are used for the long-term assets?	How much of the investing cash flow is for replacement to maintain the level of current operations versus growth expenditures for expanding operations?
What is the extent of nonrecurring losses and where are these reported?	Are there significant off-balance sheet assets and liabilities due to operating leases being used?	

Analyze and Interpret the Results

Ratios do not give answers; they give clues on what is going on in the company. Analysts take these clues and make conclusions by putting together their knowledge of the company, the industry, and their experience. But ratios are useless unless they can be compared with something else. Below we examine what comparisons are made along with some precautions to be taken.

Comparative Information

There are two bases for comparison: (1) cross-sectional and (2) longitudinal.

Cross-sectional comparison analyzes a company in relation to other companies in the same year. Comparisons of this type frequently appear in business articles that compare the recent performance of one company with its competitors. Cross-sectional comparison is very useful, but caution must be exercised that similar measurements (i.e., ratios) are being used. If the comparison companies used significantly different accounting policies then no comparison can be valid unless the companies have all been adjusted to reflect similar accounting policies. Comparison of the return on assets for a company that owns all of its capital assets with one that uses operating leases for its capital assets will be invalid. Similar business models are also important for a proper comparison.

For example, in the grocery retail industry, some companies operate a franchise model, and others own their retail outlets directly. Let us look at an example. Company A operates a franchise model. All of its retail outlets are operated by franchisees who are independent entrepreneurs. Company A, the franchisor, sells product to the franchisees and owns large distribution centres from which the inventory is shipped. Revenue consists of franchise fees and sales of product to the franchisees. In this situation, the sales are all credit sales with terms requiring payment within 21 days. Inventory is held for fewer than 5 days in the distribution centres before it is shipped to the stores. In comparison, Company B operates a business model where it owns all of its own retail outlets. Revenue represents sales to the end consumers with no credit terms available. Inventory consists of product that is in distribution centres and in the stores. Although inventory is held for fewer than 5 days in the distribution centre, it has an average holding period of 18 days in the stores.

Given these operating policies, Company A and Company B will have different ratios for days in inventory and days in receivable. An analyst who did not properly gather data on these companies and did not understand these differences in the business models would end up making incorrect conclusions when comparing these ratios.

Longitudinal comparisons look at a company over time, comparing this year's performance with earlier years. A comparison is often made to other companies or to general economic returns during the same time span.

Some databases facilitate both types of comparison on an industry basis. These industry comparisons can be helpful but must be used with a great deal of caution. Industry statistics are constructed without attention to underlying reporting, accounting policy, or business model differences, and therefore it seldom is clear whether the comparisons are truly valid. In addition, it is tempting to decide that one company is a good investment (for example) because its profitability ratios are better than its competitors. It may well be, however, that the entire industry is sick, and that the company being analyzed is perhaps less sick.

Remember, ratio analysis can be useful, but can also be very misleading if inappropriate comparisons are made.

Other Limitations to Ratio Analysis

Other than choosing the right "comparables" and ensuring consistent accounting policies, there are other limitations for ratio analysis:

- *Universality.* Ratios with the same name can be calculated using different inputs. For example, some analysts calculate a debt-to-equity ratio using only market values, not book values. Others may use only interest-bearing long-term debt, while others may use total liabilities. There is no "right" calculation. The analyst will choose the inputs he wishes to use based on the information he is trying to obtain. The caution here is for the analyst to determine his own ratios and not rely on the calculations performed by others.
- *Size.* Ratios calculate relationships between one number and another and by definition remove the effect of size. For example, take two companies that manufacture the same product. Company A has sales of $500 million and gross profit of $175 million resulting in a gross profit margin of 35% ($175/$500). Company B has sales of only $7,000,000, and gross profit of $2,100,000, with a gross profit margin of 30% ($2,100/$7,000). Although Company A is more than 70 times larger than Company B, we still do the

comparison. The key question here is, could Company A have a better gross profit margin simply because it is larger? And the answer is maybe. If there are economies of scale and Company A can purchase inputs cheaper (e.g., due to volume discounts) and have lower unit manufacturing costs, then size does matter. In comparing these companies, the impact of size would be considered.

There are also some potential drawbacks to using ratios:

- Ratios are meaningful only if there is a clear understanding of the purpose of each relationship.
- Ratios are only as valid as the data from which they are derived.
- Ratios require a basis for comparison.
- Ratios are a clue to areas needing investigation—they rarely, if ever, supply answers.

Throughout this book, we have emphasized that different accounting policy decisions and different accounting estimates can yield dramatically different reported results. If the basic financial data are subject to variability, then ratios calculated from that data are unreliable.

Indeed, managers may deliberately select accounting policies and estimates with the intent of affecting certain ratios; we have repeatedly referred to this motivation throughout the book. For example, the decision to lease major operating assets through an operating lease rather than a finance lease often is motivated by management's desire to keep the implicit debt off the balance sheet. In using ratios, therefore, the rule most certainly must be, *analyst be wary*!

We are now ready to look at how ratios are calculated and used in practice.

RATIO ANALYSIS

Once the statements have been adjusted to suit the needs of the analyst (i.e., to facilitate making the decision at hand), the statements may be subject to numerical analysis or "number crunching." The basic tool of numerical analysis is ratios. A ratio is simply one number divided by another. Given the amount of numbers in a set of financial statements, especially over a series of years, an incredible number of ratios could be computed. The trick to avoiding overwork (and total confusion) is to identify which ratios have meaning for the analyst's purpose, and then focus just on those few instead of computing every possible ratio.

To demonstrate how these analytical techniques are applied and analyzed, we will be examining the same set of financial statements throughout the chapter. Exhibit 22-2 provides the statement of financial position and the statement of comprehensive income for our company, Grocery Retailer Inc. (GRI). GRI operates across Canada and has 630 owned retail outlets with total sales of $13 billion. It competes in the grocery retail sector, and competitors include smaller, locally owned stores, similar size domestic competitors, and larger global competitors. Some competitors use a franchise approach, others corporately own the retail outlets, and some even have a mix of both types of operating strategies. Since food is a staple product and the industry is mature, sales are constant, with small year-over-year growth rates due to inflation. Intense competition and changing customer preferences play a large role in companies gaining or losing market share. In this type of industry, growth primarily comes from acquisitions. Costs are impacted by fuel prices, labour relations, regulatory requirements, and logistics. During 2013, GRI acquired another company that retails specialty products to a new customer group. The bulk of the acquisition price was for property, plant, equipment, and intangible assets. GRI also owns investment property which is accounted for using the fair value model. Rental income and related costs were immaterial and included in revenue for the year.

Common-Size Analysis

Common-size analysis or *vertical analysis* takes each item on a financial statement and computes it as a percentage of a fixed base. On the SFP, the base is usually total assets. On the SCI, each line item would be calculated as a percentage of net sales. Vertical analysis is the simplest of a broader set of techniques known as *decomposition analysis*; the more complex approaches to decomposition analysis will not be discussed in this text.

EXHIBIT 22-2

GROCERY RETAILER INC. FINANCIAL STATEMENTS

Statement of Comprehensive Income for Years Ended December 31, 2013, 2012, and 2011

(in millions of dollars)

	2013 $	2012 $	2011 $
Sales	13,000	12,400	12,230
Cost of goods sold	10,400	10,150	10,020
Gross profit	2,600	2,250	2,210
Expenses			
Electricity and natural gas	120	110	110
Rent, taxes, and occupancy costs	270	250	240
Wages and benefits	710	645	690
Depreciation and amortization	260	260	270
Change in fair value of investment properties	10	5	—
Other	280	260	300
Total expenses	1,650	1,530	1,610
Operating income	950	720	600
Finance costs	120	130	150
Earnings before income taxes	830	590	450
Income taxes	210	150	130
Net earnings	620	440	320
Other comprehensive income			
Actuarial gains (losses)	(70)	(40)	20
Comprehensive income	550	400	340

Statement of Financial Position as at December 31, 2013, 2012, and 2011

(in millions of dollars)

	2013 $	2012 $	2011 $
ASSETS			
Current assets			
Cash and cash equivalents	70	100	90
Accounts receivable	350	300	320
Inventories	1,050	720	760
Prepaid expenses	10	10	10
	1,480	1,130	1,180
Noncurrent assets			
Property, plant and equipment	4,150	3,370	3,450
Investment properties	50	30	10
Intangible assets	1,250	650	670
Goodwill	900	700	700
Total assets	7,830	5,880	6,010

continued on next page

EXHIBIT 22-2 (*cont'd*)

	2013 $	2012 $	2011 $
LIABILITIES AND EQUITY			
Current liabilities			
Bank loans	340	380	400
Accounts payable and accrued liabilities	1,400	1,100	980
Provisions	230	20	30
Current portion of long term debt	280	280	280
	2,250	1,780	1,690
Noncurrent liabilities			
Long term debt	2,700	1,750	1,850
Defined benefit liabilities	150	120	130
Deferred taxes	130	110	80
Other liabilities	120	10	10
	5,350	3,770	3,760
Equity			
Common shares	680	680	980
Retained earnings	1,970	1,530	1,390
Accumulated other comprehensive income	(170)	(100)	(120)
Total shareholders' equity	2,480	2,110	2,250
Total liabilities and equity	7,830	5,880	6,010

Note 1—Dividends of $180 million were paid each year.

Note 2—Finance costs for 2013 includes interest on short-term debt of $15 million and interest on long-term debt of $105 million. For 2012, interest on short-term debt and long-term debt was $17 million and $113 million, respectively.

Note 3—The income tax rate for 2013 and 2012 was 25.3% and 25.4% respectively.

Note 4—The cash flow from operations was $1,010 million and $870 million for 2013 and 2012, respectively.

Vertical (common-size) analysis is useful for seeing the relative composition of the SFP or SCI. Analysts sometimes use these numbers for comparisons with industry norms or other competitors. For example, an analyst may want to compare the *gross margin* of one company with another by comparing the relative proportion of sales that is consumed by cost of goods sold. Similarly, an analyst may look at common-size numbers to see if a company's inventory is too large, in comparison with total assets, relative to others in the industry.

Managers sometimes are sensitive to the uses that analysts make of vertical analysis and adopt accounting policies accordingly. For example, managers who are aware that analysts look closely at the relative proportion of cost of goods sold may elect accounting policies that treat most overhead costs as period costs rather than as inventory costs. By reducing inventory costs, cost of goods sold is lower relative to sales because fewer costs are inventoried and the gross margin percentage appears to be higher.

Exhibit 22-3 shows the vertical analysis for GRI. On the SCI, sales are set at 100% and all other numbers are calculated as a proportion of sales.[1] This analysis shows that the cost of goods sold as a percentage of sales has declined from 81.9% to 80%. This would be seen

[1] The calculations for vertical and horizontal analysis are easy to do in a computer spreadsheet, since in each case the process is simply dividing all cells by a constant. The tedious part is entering the data in the worksheet in the first place.

EXHIBIT 22-3

VERTICAL ANALYSIS OF GRI

Grocery Retailer Inc.
Statement of Comprehensive Income
for Years Ended December 31, 2013, 2012, and 2011

	2013 $	2012 $	2011 $
Sales	100.0%	100.0%	100.0%
Cost of goods sold	80.0%	81.9%	81.9%
Gross profit	20.0%	18.1%	18.1%
Expenses			
Electricity and natural gas	0.9%	0.9%	0.9%
Rent, taxes, and occupancy costs	2.1%	2.0%	2.0%
Wages and benefits	5.5%	5.2%	5.6%
Depreciation and amortization	2.0%	2.1%	2.2%
Change in fair value of investment properties	0.1%	0.0%	0.0%
Other	2.2%	2.1%	2.5%
Total expenses	12.8%	12.3%	13.2%
Operating income	7.2%	5.8%	4.9%
Finance costs	0.9%	1.0%	1.2%
Earnings before income taxes	6.3%	4.8%	3.7%
Income taxes	1.6%	1.2%	1.1%
Net earnings	4.7%	3.6%	2.6%
Other comprehensive income			
Actuarial gains/losses	–0.5%	–0.3%	0.2%
Comprehensive income	4.2%	3.3%	2.8%

Note: There might be slight differences due to rounding.

Grocery Retailer Inc.
Statement of Financial Position
as at December 31, 2013, 2012, and 2011

	2013 $	2012 $	2011 $
ASSETS			
Current assets			
Cash and cash equivalents	0.9%	1.7%	1.5%
Accounts receivable	4.5%	5.1%	5.3%
Inventories	13.4%	12.2%	12.6%
Prepaid expenses	0.1%	0.2%	0.2%
	18.9%	19.2%	19.6%
Noncurrent assets			
Property, plant and equipment	53.0%	57.3%	57.4%
Investment properties	0.6%	0.5%	0.2%
Intangible assets	16.0%	11.1%	11.2%
Goodwill	11.5%	11.9%	11.6%
Total assets	100.0%	100.0%	100.0%

continued on next page

EXHIBIT 22-3 (*cont'd*)

	2013 $	2012 $	2011 $
LIABILITIES AND EQUITY			
Current liabilities			
Bank loans	4.3%	6.5%	6.7%
Accounts payable	17.9%	18.7%	16.3%
Provisions	2.9%	0.3%	0.5%
Current portion of long term debt	3.6%	4.8%	4.7%
	28.7%	30.3%	28.2%
Noncurrent liabilities			
Long term debt	34.5%	29.8%	30.8%
Defined benefit liabilities	1.9%	2.0%	2.1%
Deferred taxes	1.7%	1.8%	1.3%
Other liabilities	1.5%	0.2%	0.2%
	68.3%	64.1%	62.6%
Equity			
Common shares	8.7%	11.6%	16.3%
Retained earnings	25.2%	26.0%	23.1%
Accumulated other comprehensive income	−2.2%	−1.7%	−2.0%
Total shareholders' equity	31.7%	35.9%	37.4%
Total liabilities and equity	100.0%	100.0%	100.0%

as an improvement but the analyst would have to investigate what caused this to happen. Although most other costs have remained relatively constant over the three years, wages and income taxes have increased, while finance costs have decreased as a percentage of revenues. On the SFP, total assets is set at 100% and all other numbers are computed as a percentage of total assets. The analysis of the SFP indicates a lot more variation over the period with almost all elements on the statement changing as a percentage of total assets. Some of the more notable changes include: declines in cash and property, plant, and equipment; and increases in inventory, intangible assets, and long-term debt. The next step would be for the analyst to try to determine the cause of these changes and the impact on her decision. We will gather more information on this as we examine specific ratios.

Trend Analysis

Trend analysis or **horizontal analysis** looks at how the individual items on a financial statement have changed over time. The base year selected is set to 100 and other years' amounts are recomputed relative to the base amount. Obvious calculations include the trend of sales over time and the trend of net income over time. Analysts may construct special measures, such as EBIT (earnings before interest and taxes) or EBITDA (earnings before interest, taxes, depreciation, and amortization), and perform trend analysis on those measures. If the trend of sales is stronger than the trend of earnings, then the company is experiencing declining earnings relative to sales, even though earnings are increasing in absolute terms. That may be either good or bad (as will be explained in the following section), depending on other factors in the analysis.

Horizontal analysis is best used when the nature of the company's operations is relatively stable, with few changes in lines of business and without significant business combinations. Otherwise, it is difficult to discern whether significant changes in SFP and SCI amounts are the result of continuing business or of entering and leaving new lines of business.

Exhibit 22-4 shows the trend analysis for GRI. The base year is 2011 and each item on the statement is calculated as a percentage of the base year. One thing to note about horizontal

EXHIBIT 22-4

TREND ANALYSIS FOR GRI

Grocery Retailer Inc.
Statement of Comprehensive Income
for Years Ended December 31, 2013, 2012, and 2011

	2013 $	2012 $	2011 $
Sales	106.3%	101.4%	100.0%
Cost of goods sold	103.8%	101.3%	100.0%
Gross profit	117.6%	101.8%	100.0%
Expenses			
Electricity and natural gas	109.1%	100.0%	100.0%
Rent, taxes, and occupancy costs	112.5%	104.2%	100.0%
Wages and benefits	102.9%	93.5%	100.0%
Depreciation and amortization	96.3%	96.3%	100.0%
Other	93.3%	86.7%	100.0%
Total expenses	102.5%	95.0%	100.0%
Operating income	158.3%	120.0%	100.0%
Finance costs	80.0%	86.7%	100.0%
Earnings before income taxes	184.4%	131.1%	100.0%
Income taxes	161.5%	115.4%	100.0%
Net earnings	193.8%	137.5%	100.0%
Other comprehensive income			
Actuarial gains/losses	–350.0%	–200.0%	100.0%
Comprehensive income	161.8%	117.6%	100.0%

Grocery Retailer Inc.
Statement of Financial Position
as at December 31, 2013, 2012, and 2011

	2013 $	2012 $	2011 $
ASSETS			
Current assets			
Cash and cash equivalents	77.8%	111.1%	100.0%
Accounts receivable	109.4%	93.8%	100.0%
Inventories	138.2%	94.7%	100.0%
Prepaid expenses	100.0%	100.0%	100.0%
	125.4%	95.8%	100.0%
Noncurrent assets			
Property, plant and equipment	120.3%	97.7%	100.0%
Investment properties	500.0%	300.0%	100.0%
Intangible assets	186.6%	97.0%	100.0%
Goodwill	128.6%	100.0%	100.0%
Total assets	130.3%	97.8%	100.0%

continued on next page

EXHIBIT 22-4 (*cont'd*)

	2013 $	2012 $	2011 $
LIABILITIES AND EQUITY			
Current liabilities			
Bank loans	85.0%	95.0%	100.0%
Accounts payable	142.9%	112.2%	100.0%
Provisions	766.7%	66.7%	100.0%
Current portion of long term debt	100.0%	100.0%	100.0%
	133.1%	105.3%	100.0%
Noncurrent liabilities			
Long term debt	145.9%	94.6%	100.0%
Defined benefit liabilities	115.4%	92.3%	100.0%
Deferred taxes	162.5%	137.5%	100.0%
Other liabilities	1200.0%	100.0%	100.0%
	142.3%	100.3%	100.0%
Equity			
Common shares	69.4%	69.4%	100.0%
Retained earnings	141.7%	110.1%	100.0%
Accumulated other comprehensive income	141.7%	83.3%	100.0%
Total shareholders' equity	110.2%	93.8%	100.0%
Total liabilities and equity	130.3%	97.8%	100.0%

analysis is—you cannot add up the percentages in a given year to derive any totals. On examining the SCI, we see that sales increased 6% from 2011 to 2013. However, net income increased by 58%. Part of this difference is the lower cost of goods sold as we saw earlier. Although some costs increased more than the 6%, wages and benefits, depreciation, and finance costs all were less, contributing to the higher net income. The SFP analysis shows that most items grew more than 6%. Inventories, investment properties, and intangibles grew significantly as did many of the liabilities. One caution about using percentages is the absolute dollar amount of the starting base. Look at the investment properties, which grew 500% from 2011 to 2013. However, the base in 2011 was only $10 million, and the absolute growth was only $40 million to a closing amount of $50 million.

As we see, common-size and trend analyses are providing clues and indicators that will require further investigation by the analyst.

CONCEPT REVIEW

1. Why is it crucial to approach financial statement analysis with a clear understanding of the decision focus?
2. How can an analyst find out what accounting policies a company is using? What type of information should the analyst look for in the notes?
3. Why would a financial analyst want to recast a company's financial statements before performing ratio analysis or other analytical techniques?
4. What is the difference between *vertical* analysis and *horizontal* analysis of financial statement components?
5. What type of data, other than financial statements, is required to complete the analysis of a company?

Common-size (vertical) and trend (horizontal) analysis are systematic computations of index ratios, but the term **ratio analysis** is most commonly applied to a large family of ratios that compare the *proportional relationship* between two different account amounts in a single year's financial statements. Common-size ratios are strictly within a single financial statement, but other ratio analyses can be either between amounts within a single statement or between amounts in two different statements.

There are literally dozens of ratios that can be computed from a single year's financial statements. The important task for an analyst is to focus on the ratios that have primary meaning for the decision at hand. There are many ways of grouping ratios, but those that will be discussed in the following pages are grouped as follows:

- Profitability ratios measure the company's ability to generate a return on invested capital;
- Efficiency ratios measure how well the company manages its assets;
- Solvency ratios measure the company's ability to meet its debt commitments; and
- Liquidity ratios measure the company's ability to pay obligations coming due in the next 12 months.

Profitability Ratios

It is common for the press and individual investors to talk about the return on sales that a company is earning, such as "Canadian Tire had 2011 earnings of $467 million on revenues of $10,387 million, a return of only 4%."

Statements like this suggest that the most important profit relationship is between profit and revenue. However, the driving force in a capitalistic enterprise is to earn a return *on invested capital.* If you are going to put money into a savings account, you normally will want to put it in the bank that will give you the largest interest rate. You want to know how much you will make on your investment, *in percentage terms.* You will compare *rates* of interest, not absolute amounts, because the quantity of dollars or euros or yuan that you have in your savings account will vary over time.

The same principle is true for all investments. An enterprise's profitability is measured by the rate of return that it earns on its invested capital and not by the absolute dollar profit that it generates. A billion dollars in profit is high if it was earned on an investment of only $2 or $3 billion. But if it was the return on a $50 billion investment, then the investment is yielding only 2% ($1/$50); a very poor return, indeed.

Similarly, companies may proudly cite sharply increased profit figures, perhaps up 40% or even 100% over the preceding year, and attribute this increase to the managers' fiscal and business acumen. But if a 50% increase in profit was accompanied by a 100% increase in invested capital, then the return on investment has gone down, not up. For example, a company increased its profits from $4 million in 2012 to $6 million in 2013, representing a 50% increase. However, the total amount invested in the company increased from $40 million to $100 million resulting in a return of 10% ($4/$40) in 2012, but only 6% ($6/$100) in 2013.

Sometimes an increase in absolute profit is due to a takeover of another company; the current year's earnings are a reflection of *both* companies' performance, whereas the previous year's results included only the parent company. The return on the current combined company has to be compared to the return on the sum of both companies in the previous year to get any meaningful comparison. Extending this to the example above—suppose that the company acquired another company for $60 million, causing the investment to increase from $40 million to $100 million. If the acquired business should have generated a 10% yield then the combined profit in 2013 should have also been $10 million and not $6 million.

Profitability ratios fall into two categories. *Profitability on sales (return on sales profitability) ratios* assist in providing information on how much of each dollar of revenue is retained for profits (similar to the vertical analysis discussed above). *Return on investment profitability ratios* determine the yields on different types of investments. These ratios will consist of a numerator from the SCI and a denominator from the SFP.

Types of Profitability Ratios Some of the common return-on-sales profitability ratios are:

- Gross profit margin:

$$\frac{\text{Gross profit}}{\text{Total revenue}}$$

This ratio examines how much of the revenue is used to cover the cost of the goods and how much is left over to cover the other operating costs of the company.

- Operating margin:

$$\frac{\text{Net income + Interest expense + Income taxes (i.e., EBIT)}}{\text{Total revenue}}$$

This is a commonly used ratio. It tells us how much the company earns on each dollar (or euro, yuan, yen, peso, etc.) of revenue. Since the numerator is EBIT, it removes the effects of financing and income taxes and makes it easier to compare profitability between companies that use different proportions of debt versus equity and are subject to different tax rates.

However, both of these ratios should never be used in isolation as they only give us information on costs incurred and no indication of the return on *investment* that the company is achieving. Operating margin must be used in conjunction with asset turnover, a ratio that we discuss in the next section (and which is illustrated in Exhibit 22-5).

For the return-on-investment profitability ratios, the analyst has to view the investment from the appropriate standpoint for her decision. A common shareholder will be interested primarily in **return on common share equity**; a preferred shareholder will be interested in the return on total shareholders' equity; and a bond holder will be interested in the return on long-term capital (i.e., shareholders' equity plus long-term debt, often called **total capitalization**). All analysts will be interested in the underlying **return on total assets**. These are some of the possible denominators for a profitability ratio.

The numerator of any profitability ratio will reflect a return *over time* because it is derived from the SCI. In contrast, the denominator will reflect SFP values at a *point in time*. To make the numerator and denominator consistent, the denominator should be calculated as the *average* over the year.[2] Ideally, the denominator should be based on an average of monthly or quarterly investment, but a simpler and more common approach is to average the SFP numbers at the beginning and end of the year being analyzed. However, if there were major changes in the investment during the year (e.g., the acquisition of another company in the first quarter of the year), then a weighted average should be estimated.

The numerator of any ratio must be consistent with its denominator in substance as well as on the time dimension. The return to common shareholders is measured not by net earnings, but by *earnings available to common shareholders* (which basically is net earnings less preferred share dividends, as explained in Chapter 19).

[2] Note that this may differ between analysts. For example, some analysts may use the beginning balance of the investment only, rather than an average for the period.

Common profitably ratios are discussed below.

- Return on total long-term capital, after tax:

$$\frac{\text{Net income} + [\text{Interest expense on long-term debt} \times (1 - t)]}{\text{Average long-term debt} + \text{Average total shareholder's equity}}$$

The **return on long-term capital** measures the return on all types of capital invested in the company—both the equity and the interest-bearing debt. It must be calculated by dividing total capitalization into a profit measure that removes the effects of financing. Since interest expense is included in net income and since interest also affects income tax, the numerator must have the effects of interest on long-term debt by adding back the after-tax interest expense (by multiplying interest by $1 - t$, where t = average tax rate for the corporation).

- Return on total assets (ROA), before tax:

Return on *total assets* can be measured by dividing total assets into EBIT.

$$\frac{\text{Net income} + \text{Total interest expense} + \text{Income tax expense}}{\text{Average total assets}}$$

- Return on total assets (ROA), after tax:

Return on *total assets* can be measured by dividing total assets into net earnings:

$$\frac{\text{Net income} + [\text{Total interest expense} \times (1 - t)]}{\text{Average total assets}}$$

This ratio measures the return on the total investment made in assets. A higher ratio indicates a better return. However, the analyst should also examine why this is occurring. For example, does the company lease many of its assets, which cause the assets to be reported off-balance-sheet? Even when assets are reflected on the SFP, their values are hard to assess. Asset carrying values are normally at historical cost, which means that the equity values also implicitly reflect historical costs. If the assets are old and the profitability is compared with a company that has newer assets, the company with the older assets should appear to be more profitable because its asset base cost less (due to cheaper historical costs) and is more fully depreciated. The net income figure will reflect lower relative depreciation expenses, due to the relatively lower cost of older assets. The apparent profitability in such a company can be quite misleading; if new investments were made, the same return would not be earned. This higher ROA is likely not sustainable in the long run.

An analyst may elect to use ROA before tax, if taxes are volatile year-over-year, or he is comparing to competitors that have different income tax rates. Some analysts attempt to adjust for differing relative accumulated depreciation by basing the measurement on EBITDA, earnings before interest, taxes, depreciation, and amortization.[3]

[3] In the airline industry, aircraft rental payments usually are also added back, so the measure becomes EBITADAR: earnings before interest, tax, amortization, depreciation, and aircraft rental.

- Return on equity (ROE):

$$\text{Return on equity} = \frac{\text{Net income}}{\text{Average shareholder's equity}}$$

This ratio measures the return that the company has been able to earn on the shareholders' equity. Net income already includes interest expense (and its tax benefit). If we wanted to examine the return to the common shareholders only, then we would have to subtract the preferred dividends from the net income in the numerator to arrive at the amount of earnings left after all other claims are deducted and adjust the denominator to be average common shareholders' equity.

It is very useful to compare this ratio with the return on assets. If financial leverage is positive, the return on shareholder's equity will be higher than the return on assets. However, if after-tax interest on debt is higher than the return on assets, this ratio will be lower than the return on assets and may be negative.

Whatever profitability ratio(s) is (are) used, the effects of accounting policies (and of operating policies, where these create off-balance-sheet assets and liabilities) must be considered. Pay particular attention to assets that are reported at fair values versus historical costs as this will impact all of the investment profitability ratios. Asset balances may be volatile as fair values change year-over-year, as will be the equity balances.

Lessons to Remember When Evaluating Profitability The moral of this tale is:

- Profitability ratios must have a measure of investment in the denominator (based on the statement of financial position) and a measure of profitability in the numerator (based on the income statement, excluding other comprehensive income).
- The denominator and the numerator must be logically consistent.
- Both the denominator and the numerator are the product of many accounting policy choices and even more accounting estimates by management.
- Both components of the ratio may need adjustment both for accounting policies and for off-balance-sheet financing and investment.

Profitability ratios are summarized in Exhibit 22-5.

Profitability ratios do have one clear advantage over other measures of profitability (e.g., earnings per share or total net income). The advantage is that since profitability is expressed as a *percentage of investment* (except for operating margin and gross profit margin), it is possible to separate true increased profitability from normal growth. Most profitable companies pay out only a portion of their earnings as dividends. Some companies pay no dividends at all. The earnings retained by the company are reinvested in operations; since shareholders' equity increases, so must the net assets of the company. Since there is more invested capital, the company will have to generate a larger net income to maintain the same return on invested capital. This is normal growth.

The proper test of managerial competence is not whether management has been able to increase EPS or net income; in a profitable industry and good economic times, managers have to be truly incompetent *not* to enjoy increased profits. The proper test is whether management has been able to maintain or, preferably, increase the rate of return on the increasing investment base.

Using Total Comprehensive Income As the accounting standards move to recognize more items in other comprehensive income, there is some debate as to whether or not profitability ratios should use total comprehensive income (which includes OCI) as the numerator instead of net income. Supporters for using total comprehensive income suggest that because some items will never recycle back to profit or loss, any profitability measures should include these gains and losses. Items that will never recycle include gains and losses

EXHIBIT 22-5

SUMMARY OF PROFITABILITY RATIOS

Ratio Name	Computation	Significance and Difficulties
Gross profit margin	$\frac{\text{Gross profit}}{\text{Total revenue}}$	Indicates the gross profit margin earned on each dollar of sales. Should be used in conjunction with *operating margin* and *asset turnover.*
Operating margin	$\frac{\text{Net income + Interest expense + Income taxes}}{\text{Total revenue}}$	Indicates the profit margin (before taxes) earned on each dollar of sales. Should be used in conjunction with asset turnover.
Return on total long-term capital, after tax	$\frac{\text{Net income + [Interest expense on long-term debt} \times (1 - t)]}{\text{Average long-term debt + Average shareholder's equity}}$	Measures the return on long-term interest-bearing debt and equity.
Return on total assets, before tax	$\frac{\text{Net income + Total interest expense + Total income taxes}}{\text{Average total assets}}$	Indicates the overall return that the company is earning on its asset investment on a before-tax basis.
Return on total assets, after tax	$\frac{\text{Net income + [Total interest expense} \times (1 - t)]}{\text{Average total assets}}$	Indicates the overall return that the company is earning on its asset investment on an after-tax basis.
Return on equity	$\frac{\text{Net income}}{\text{Average total shareholders' equity}}$	Shows the historical after-tax return to all shareholders for the period.
Return on common shareholders' equity	$\frac{\text{Net income – Preferred dividends}}{\text{Average total shareholders' equity – Average preferred share equity}}$	Shows the historical after-tax return to just the common shareholders for the period.

arising from revaluations, actuarial adjustments and fair value changes for investments classified as FVTOCI. Once again, it will be up to the analyst to decide the level of inputs for profitability to be measured.

Components of Profitability Ratios The previous section discussed several overall measures of profitability. A key to profitability analysis, however, involves breaking profitability down to its basic components. For example, any company's return on total assets can be dissected into two components: asset turnover and operating margin. Recall that return on assets, before-tax is calculated as follows:

$$\textit{Return on assets before-tax} = \frac{\text{Earnings before interest and taxes (EBIT)}}{\text{Average total assets}}$$

This can be disaggregated into two other ratios:

1. EBIT ÷ Total revenue = *Operating margin*
2. Total revenue ÷ Average total assets = *Asset turnover*

Operating margin multiplied by asset turnover equals return on assets:

$$\frac{\text{EBIT}}{\text{Total revenue}} \times \frac{\text{Total revenue}}{\text{Average total assets}} = \frac{\text{EBIT}}{\text{Average total assets}}$$

Earlier, we pointed out that earnings as a proportion of revenues (i.e., **operating margin**) by itself is not a useful measure of profitability because it ignores the amount of investment that was employed to generate that level of sales and income. A valid and often successful strategy for a company is to increase its sales volume (i.e., its *asset turnover*) by cutting its profit margin. Although the profit margin goes down, the return on assets will rise if the increase in sales volume is enough to make up for the reduced profit margin.

Other companies may use a strategy of increasing the operating margin, even at the risk of a possible loss of sales volume. If the operating margin is very small, such as 4%, only a 2% increase in price will increase the operating margin by 50% (i.e., from 4% of sales to 6% of sales). The company will be better off unless sales volume drops by 33%; that will depend on the price elasticity of demand. In a highly competitive market, a small increase in price could easily cost the company more by a drop in sales volume than it gains in margin.

The point is that *judging profitability by using only the operating margin is always wrong.* Operating margin does not reflect the level of investment, and overall profitability can be judged only in relation to investment.

Exhibit 22-6 calculates profitability ratios for GRI and summarizes the findings.

Putting these ratios together, what conclusions can be reached? We see that earnings for GRI increased primarily due to a reduction in the costs of goods sold. We also know that the company acquired another company that resulted in increases in its tangible and intangible assets. The company uses the fair value for reporting its investment property and the amount of the fair value change added about 1% to the operating profit. We also have to see if the company has entered into any new operating leases that are reported off the balance sheet. Since the new business acquired is a specialty business, it may be that this business earns a higher margin, which would explain the increases in all of the profitably ratios. Before this analysis is complete, we need to compare to competitors to see if the returns were consistent with, above, or below peers in the same industry.

Efficiency Ratios

The objective of **efficiency ratios** is to analyze certain aspects of operational efficiency. Efficiency ratios are also known as **turnover ratios** because the two most commonly cited efficiency ratios are *accounts receivable turnover* and *inventory turnover.*

Accounts Receivable Turnover This ratio is intended to measure the average length of time it takes to collect accounts receivable. The turnover ratio is determined by dividing sales revenue by average accounts receivable.

Accounts receivable turnover = Revenue ÷ Average accounts receivable

EXHIBIT 22-6

PROFITABILITY RATIOS FOR GRI

Ratio	2013	2012	Discussion
Gross profit margin	2,600/13,000 = 20%	2,250/12,400 = 18.1%	The gross profit margin has improved. The question is why? The analyst would look to see whether or not selling prices had increased and/or costs of goods sold declined over the year due to cheaper products/costs.
Operating margin	950/13,000 = 7.3%	720/12,400 = 5.8%	The operating margin has also improved by 1.5%. However, we know 1.9% (20% – 18.1%) of this came from the gross profit margin. This means that other operating costs actually increased. From the common size and trend analysis, we saw that wages and benefits increased over the year.
Return on total long-term capital	620 + 105 (1 – 0.253)/ (2,700 + 1,750 + 2,480 + 2,110)/2 = 698/4,520 = 15.4% *Interest on long-term debt.	440 + 113 (1 – 0.254)/ (1,750 + 1,800 + 2,110 + 2,250)/2 = 524/3,955 = 13.2% *Interest on long-term debt.	The return on total long-term capital also increased from 13.2% to 15.4%, or 2.2%. This is an improvement. Although the absolute dollar value of the long-term debt increased, the company appears to have invested the new debt in assets that produce a higher return.
Return on assets, after tax	620 + 120 (1 – 0.253)/ [(7,830 + 5,880)/2] = 10.3%	440 + 130 (1 – 0.254) [(5,880 + 6,010)/2] = 9.0%	This ratio has also improved. GRI has made a significant increase in total assets, but the return has improved with this investment.
Return on equity	620/[(2,480 + 2,110)/2] = 27%	440/[(2,110 + 2,250)/2] = 20.2%	This also shows improvement for the year, increasing about 6.8%.

If the ratio is 4:1, for example, it indicates that, on average, the accounts receivable "turns over" four times a year, which implies that the average collection period is one quarter of a year, or three months.

This ratio is translated into a parallel ratio called the **average collection period of accounts receivable** by dividing the accounts receivable turnover into 365 days; a turnover of four yields an apparent collection period of 91(365/4) days.

The numerator should include only sales on account, but an external analyst of a retail enterprise will have no way of knowing how much of the revenue was on account. In these cases, total revenue is used. In some industries, however, it is rare to have cash sales and therefore the total sales can safely be assumed to be sales on account.

The **accounts receivable turnover ratio** is difficult to interpret. Presumably, a short collection period (a high turnover ratio) is better than a long one because it indicates that the company is able to realize cash from its sales in a shorter period of time. It also implies that there are very few long-outstanding accounts that may prove to be uncollectible. This might be true for companies in industries where there is a widespread customer base and essentially equal terms given by each company to its customers.

However, one is quite likely to encounter companies that have special relationships with major customers. The major customers may effectively dictate payment terms. For example, a company that derives most of its revenue from government contracts may show a very slow turnover, and yet the collectability of the accounts is assured despite the "age" of the accounts.

Another problem for an external analyst is that the accounts receivable shown on the SFP may not be typical throughout the year. The fiscal year of a business may be established on the basis of the *natural business year* and the report date may be the lowest period of activity in a seasonal business. The accounts receivable may be at their lowest level for the whole year. Bankers who use the turnover ratio may insist on monthly data. However, an even more likely scenario for such analysts is to request an **accounts receivable aging schedule**, in which the receivables are categorized by the length of time they have been outstanding (e.g., less than 30 days, 31–60 days, 61–90 days, and more than 90 days). Any special payment terms (such as extra-long payments for related companies) are specifically indicated.[4] Disclosure notes on credit risk included in the financial statements often provide this information for external users who do not have access to internal documents.

Because of the problems cited above, an analyst may be more interested in the *trend* of the ratio, as an indicator of whether the collection period is stable or getting longer or shorter. If the ratio changes year to year, it will not be easy for an external analyst to determine the cause of the change and whether the change is good or bad. Additional information, such as the type of customers and the economic trends, may be required to complete this analysis.

Inventory Turnover The **inventory turnover ratio** indicates the relationship between the cost of goods sold and the average inventory balance:

Inventory turnover = Cost of goods sold ÷ Average inventory

A high turnover ratio is often presumed to be better than a low ratio because a high ratio suggests that less investment in inventory is needed to generate sales. A low ratio, on the other hand, suggests that there may be excessive quantities of inventory on hand or that there are a lot of slow-moving or unsellable items in inventory.

The objective of inventory management is to maintain *optimum* inventory levels rather than *minimum* inventory levels. Maintaining too low an inventory may result in items not being available for sale when the customer requests them, and therefore sales are lost. Furthermore, with the advent of just-in-time inventory systems in many businesses, suppliers are sometimes left with the burden of maintaining inventories. This means that a supplier's finished goods inventory may be higher than in earlier years, and yet the ability to sell that inventory may be virtually guaranteed through the supplier arrangements. Therefore, a low inventory turnover may not necessarily be bad, and a high turnover may not necessarily be ideal.

The inventory turnover ratio can be converted to **days in inventory** by dividing 365 days by the turnover. So a turnover of 12 times indicates that the inventory is on hand for approximately 30 days. This ratio will be impacted by the nature of the inventory and how long the

[4] Some companies give different payment terms to different customers. In that case, aging schedules are usually based on the due date of payment and reflect the number of days past due.

process takes to convert raw materials into finished goods. Consider a winery, where wine is aged for years before it is ready for sale and therefore a significantly higher days in inventory (lower turnover ratio) is expected.

Accounts Payables Turnover This ratio is intended to indicate how long the company takes to pay its suppliers and is calculated as below:

Accounts Payables turnover = Cost of goods sold ÷ Average accounts payables

Similar to the above ratios, the **days in payables** can be determined by taking 365 days and dividing by the payables turnover ratio. This is a difficult ratio to interpret because on the one hand, the company should take as long as possible to pay its suppliers. This will free up cash to be used internally and give the company "free credit" from the supplier. On the other hand, if the company takes too long to pays its suppliers, this will jeopardize supplier relationships and force suppliers to require cash on delivery or refuse to ship to the company. How many days a company can take to pay its suppliers will often depend on how much "power" it has to dictate payment terms. For example, if the company represents a large percentage of the supplier's sales, then it is likely that the company will be able to take longer to pay.

Asset Turnover As we have seen, **asset turnover** is a major component of return on assets. It measures the sales dollars generated by all of the assets. The higher this ratio, the more efficient the company is at using its assets in its sales effort. This ratio is calculated as follows:

Total asset turnover = Total Revenue/Total assets

This ratio is impacted by the type of assets used by the company, the measurement bases used (i.e., fair value or historical cost) and whether or not there are substantial off-balance-sheet assets due to the use of operating leases.

The principal efficiency ratios are summarized in Exhibit 22-7. Exhibit 22-8 shows the calculations of the efficiency ratios for GRI.

Since ratios should never be analyzed in isolation, what do these efficiency ratios tell us? We can see that GRI is holding inventory longer. The asset turnover ratio has also worsened. We know that the company purchased another company during the year. This could cause the mix of inventory products to change, causing the turnover ratios to decline. However, we also saw under the profitability ratios that all ratios had improved, indicating that although there was an increase in the level of investment in various asset accounts, the company was earning higher profits from this investment. Additional information would be required to understand the inventory turnover results.

Solvency Ratios

The basic objective of **solvency ratios** is to assess the ability of the company to make both the interest and principal payments on its long-term obligations. These ratios stress the long-term financial and operating structure of the company. They can be further classified as follows:

- **Leverage ratios**, which measure the relative amount of the company's financing that was obtained through debt (versus equity); and
- **Debt service ratios**, which test the ability of the company to generate sufficient cash flow from operations to pay the required payments for debt interest and principal.

Solvency ratios interact with profitability ratios because a company's long-run solvency is in doubt if the company cannot generate enough profit to not only service the debt but also earn an adequate return for shareholders.

EXHIBIT 22-7

SUMMARY OF EFFICIENCY RATIOS

Ratio Name	Computation	Significance and Difficulties
Accounts receivable turnover	Sales revenue (on credit) / Average trade accounts receivable	Indicates efficiency of trade accounts receivable collection but is difficult to interpret without knowledge of the customer base. Average year-end accounts receivable balances may not be representative of seasonal variation.
Average collection period of accounts receivable	365 (days) / Accounts receivable turnover	Converts the accounts receivable turnover into the average collection period, in days. Has the same measurement problems as does the turnover ratio.
Inventory turnover	Cost of goods sold / Average inventory	Yields the number of times that the inventory "turns over" during a year. A low ratio may indicate possible overstocking, if valid comparative information is available. Year-end average inventory balances may not be representative of seasonal variation.
Average days in inventory	365 (days) / Inventory turnover	Converts the inventory turnover into the average days in inventory. Has the same measurement problems as does the turnover ratio.
Accounts payable turnover	Cost of goods sold / Average accounts payable	Yields the number of times that the accounts payables "turn over" during a year. A low ratio may indicate the company is taking too long to pay its suppliers. Year-end average payable balances may not be representative of seasonal variation.
Average days in payables	365 (days) / Accounts payable turnover	Converts the payables turnover into the average days in payables. Has the same measurement problems as does the turnover ratio.
Asset turnover	Total revenue / Average total assets	Shows the level of sales that are being generated per dollar of investment in assets. This is one component of return on assets, and should be used in conjunction with operating margin (see Exhibit 22-5).

EXHIBIT 22-8

EFFICIENCY RATIOS FOR GRI

Ratio	2013	2012	Discussion
Accounts receivable turnover	13,000/[(350 + 300)/2] = 40 times	12,400/[(300 + 320)/2] = 40 times	See discussion for average collection period below.
Average collection period of accounts receivable	365/40 = 9 days	365/40 = 9 days	The collection period for the accounts receivable remained consistent at 9 days. The reason this is very low is that a large portion of the sales will be cash sales and therefore paid immediately. Ideally, we would want to use just credit sales in this ratio, but this amount is not known.
Inventory turnover	10,400/[(1,050 + 720)/2] = 11.8 times	10,150/[(720 + 760)/2] = 13.7 times	See discussion below for days in inventory.
Days in inventory	365/11.8 = 31 days	365/13.7 = 27 days	The number of days that inventory is held has increased by 4 days from 27 to 31 days. Does the company have a different product mix now? What happens to the inventory that is spoiled, and are there any holding costs?
Accounts payable turnover	10,400/[(1,400 + 1,100)/2] = 8.3 times	10,150/[(1,100 + 980)/2] = 9.8 times	See discussion below for days in inventory.
Days in accounts payable	365/8.3 = 44 days	365/9.8 = 37days	GRI is taking about 44 days to pay its suppliers, and this has actually increased by 7 days over the year. Is this consistent within the industry? How many suppliers does the company deal with, and does GRI have some power with its suppliers to delay payments, or will this jeopardize supplier relationships?
Total asset turnover	13,000/[(7,830 + 5,880)/2] = 1.9 times	12,400/[(5,880 + 6,010)/2] = 2.1 times	The asset turnover ratio has worsened over the year. The company has increased its investment in assets by 33%, but revenues have increased by only 5%. Why have the assets increased, and what are the types of assets that have increased?

Leverage Ratios Leverage is the extent to which a company uses fixed-term interest-bearing obligations to finance its assets. In public companies, the focus is on long-term debt (including retractable preferred shares, if any). For analysis of a private company, the focus is on interest-bearing debt, primarily bank debt, perhaps both short term and long term; loans from shareholders are not included but are reclassified as owners' equity.[5]

The concept of **leverage** is that if a company can earn a rate of return on its assets that is higher than the rate it has to pay on debt, the shareholders will benefit because the surplus return (i.e., above the rate of interest on borrowings) will flow through to benefit the shareholders in the form of higher earnings per share. Of course, if a company earns *less* on its investment than the rate of interest, the shareholders' interests will suffer; this is known as **negative leverage**. The return on total assets, before tax (EBIT ÷ total assets) can be directly compared with the average interest rate on debt to see if leverage is positive or negative. The margin by which the return on assets exceeds the average interest rate is the **margin of safety**; the closer they get, the greater is the risk of negative leverage. Therefore, leverage plays an important role in the assessment of profitability because it affects the distribution of the earnings to the different providers of capital. Leverage also is a measure of solvency because it is one measure of risk.

If a company has a large amount of debt relative to its shareholders' equity, the company is said to be *highly levered* (or *highly leveraged*). Leverage increases the volatility of the residual earnings to the shareholders because the interest must always be paid, regardless of the amount of earnings. For example, a company has the following results:

(in thousands of dollars)	2013 $	2012 $	2011 $
Operating income before interest and taxes	2,000	1,000	1,500
Interest	(500)	(500)	(500)
Taxes	(450)	(150)	(300)
Net profit or loss	1,050	350	700

From the above table, we see that operating income decreased by 33% in 2012 and increased by 100% in 2013. However, the net profit or loss left for the shareholders decreased by 50% in 2012 and increased by 200% in 2013. The interest is fixed at $500 in all three years and as a result the fluctuations in earnings are amplified.

Some companies try to lessen this risk by entering into variable-rate loans instead of fixed-rate loans. If the company's earnings are responsive to the general economy, and if interest rates tend to decrease when the economy slows, then a decrease in earnings might be at least partially matched by a decrease in interest rates. Some companies that have substantial fixed-rate obligations effectively convert these to variable-rate obligations by entering into interest rate swaps.

The most basic measure of leverage is the **total debt-to-equity ratio**.

Debt-to-equity = Total debt* ÷ Total Shareholders' equity

*Total debt refers to all short-term and long-term interest-bearing debt.

[5] The concept of leverage is discussed more extensively in financial management texts. For example, see *Fundamentals of Corporate Finance, 5th Canadian Edition* by Richard Brealey, Elizabeth Maynes, et al. (McGraw-Hill Ryerson, 2012).

The numerator, in its simplest form, is the total interest-bearing debt including short-term debt, current portion of long-term debt and long-term debt. The denominator is the total shareholders' equity (excluding retractable preferred shares, which are classified as debt, but including shareholders' loans, if any).

This is one ratio where the numerator and denominator can be defined in a number of ways, depending on the nature of the company and the objectives of the analyst. When the ratio is computed for assessing solvency (and risk of insolvency), all monetary obligations, both short term and long term, are normally included (excluding deferred income taxes, unearned revenues, and other miscellaneous deferred credits).

There are many other adjustments that could be added to the numerator including:

- Estimated present value of operating lease obligations on assets essential to operations;
- All other monetary obligations, including trade accounts payable; and
- Liabilities related to pension obligations and long-term provisions (environmental and decommissioning liabilities, for example).

The key point here is that there is no one correct method to calculate this ratio and many variations are used in practice depending on the objectives of the analyst.

Variants to the basic debt-to-equity ratio use some measure of *invested capital* as the denominator, which includes both debt and equity. These ratios answer the question: *How much of the company's invested capital has been obtained through debt?* These can be defined as follows (in their simplest form):

Debt-to-total capitalization = Total debt* ÷ (Total debt* + Shareholders' equity)

Debt-to-total assets = (Total debt*) ÷ Total assets

*Total debt refers to all short-term and long-term interest-bearing debt.

As is the case with the basic debt-to-equity ratio, the numerator and denominator for the above ratios may vary somewhat, depending on the point of view of the analyst, and be adjusted for inclusions and exclusions as noted earlier. Also note how the debt-to-equity ratio relates to the debt to total capitalization ratio. The value for a debt-to-equity ratio will be higher than for a debt-to-total-assets ratio. A debt-to-equity ratio of 1:1 will be a debt-to-total capitalization ratio of 1:2. This arithmetic may seem obvious, but since all of these types of ratios are commonly referred to as debt-to-equity ratios, it is important to be clear on the definition of the ratio used in discussions.

The debt-to-equity ratio (and its variants) is a measure of **financial risk**. Because leverage increases the volatility of earnings, the increase in return to shareholders is a result of an increase in risk. A high debt-to-equity ratio is safest when a company has a high and steady level of earnings, particularly when the company can control its return on assets. High levels of financial risk can be most safely used in companies that have low levels of *operating risk*. **Operating risk** is the responsiveness of a company's earnings to fluctuations in its level of revenue. The more volatile operating earnings are, the less a company should rely on financial leverage.

For example, leverage is high in the financial services sector and in regulated public utilities. In financial institutions, the interest being paid on debt and the interest charged to borrowers are both responsive to money market conditions. As long as the debt portfolio is matched (in maturities) to the asset portfolio, net earnings can be relatively stable. In public utilities, rates are set to achieve a rate of return on assets that has been approved by the regulators; the permitted rate of return on assets is too low to attract share equity, but by levering up the earnings through lower-rate debt, utilities can provide an adequate return to attract share capital. In contrast, biotech companies that have a very high operating risk with volatile earnings and cash flows will likely have little leverage.

Debt-Service Ratios A traditional ratio used in solvency analysis is the **times-interest-earned**, or interest coverage, **ratio**, which is the ratio of interest expense to earnings before interest and taxes (EBIT). This is believed to indicate the relative amount by which earnings can decrease before there are not enough profits to pay the interest. In reality, the interest would be paid, since failure to do so would risk throwing the company into receivership and possibly bankruptcy.

Since interest expense is tax deductible, the numerator of the ratio normally is EBIT. Again, it may be appropriate to use net earnings adjusted for accounting policies, as described in earlier sections. Also, the numerator should include interest on all indebtedness, long term and short term, plus interest on finance leases. Default on any component of interest can have dire consequences. Remember that finance costs on the SCI may include gains and losses as well as interests costs; this ratio requires only interest expenses.

If a times-interest-earned ratio is approaching 1:1, the company already is suffering negative financial leverage. It is possible to estimate the number of times by which EBIT must exceed interest expense to avoid negative leverage. To avoid negative leverage, a company must earn an overall rate on its total capitalization that is at least equal to the interest being charged on the debt. Therefore, if the amount of shareholders' equity is three times the amount of debt, EBIT should be at least four times the total interest expense (i.e., the earnings on one part debt *plus* three parts owners' equity).

A broader debt-service ratio is **times-debt–service-earned ratio**. This ratio goes well beyond the times-interest-earned ratio to look not only at the amount of interest that must be paid, but also at the amount of principal payments that must be made. The times-interest-earned ratio implicitly assumes that debt can be refinanced, which may be a valid assumption in prosperous times. But if the company's fortunes decline, the financial markets freeze up, or interest rates soar, it may be difficult to obtain new financing to "roll over" the debt. The debt-service ratio attempts to look at the ability of a company to *service* its overall debt load.

The numerator of this ratio is *cash*, not earnings. The starting point is the cash flow from operations as reported on the statement of cash flows. This amount should be adjusted by adding back interest paid. Interest is tax deductible, and therefore the current income tax paid should also be added back to the cash flow from operations—$C_{op}BIT$ instead of EBIT.

The denominator should include not only interest paid but also the cash outflows for principal repayments and finance lease payments. The denominator is not always easy to measure and requires a careful reading of the notes. The cash flows relating to debt and finance leases for the next five years is disclosed in the notes to the financial statements.

Taxes raise a particular problem because interest is deductible for tax purposes, while principal payments are not. Since principal payments have to be paid in after-tax dollars, it takes a higher pre-tax cash flow from operations to generate enough cash to repay principal. On the other hand, finance lease payments usually are deductible in full, including both the capital portion and the implicit interest expense, thereby adding an additional complication. The easiest way around this problem is to divide the non-tax-deductible cash flows by 1 minus the company's average tax rate: $1 - t$. This converts the principal payments to pre-tax equivalents and then all amounts in the ratio are comparable.

Common solvency ratios are summarized in Exhibit 22-9.

Exhibit 22-10 shows the calculations of the solvency ratios for GRI.

Overall, we see that the company's level of debt increased, as well as its asset base. This indicates that the debt was used primarily to finance the purchase of the new assets. Even though there is more debt, the increased earnings and cash flows indicate that the company still has the ability to service the debt on an annual basis.

Liquidity Ratios

The general objective of **liquidity ratios** is to test the company's ability to meet its short-term financial obligations. Therefore, the focus is on the composition of current assets and current liabilities.

EXHIBIT 22-9

SUMMARY OF SOLVENCY RATIOS

Note: Below, "Total debt" refers to interest-bearing short-term and long-term debt. (In other cases, "Total debt" may refer to all liabilities. Similarly, "Long-term debt" may refer to just the long-term interest-bearing debt or all long-term liabilities.)

Ratio Name	Computation	Significance and Difficulties
Debt-to-equity	$\frac{\text{Total debt}}{\text{Total shareholders' equity}}$	Indicates the relative proportions by which the company is financed with total debt regardless of whether short-term or long-term. May vary if the level of short-term debt changes year by year. Inclusions may be necessary, as described earlier.
Long-term debt-to-equity	$\frac{\text{Long-term debt}}{\text{Total shareholders' equity}}$	Indicates the relative proportions by which "permanent" investment is financed through long-term debt versus shareholders' equity.
Total debt-to-total-capitalization	$\frac{\text{Total debt}}{\text{Total debt + Total shareholders' equity}}$	Indicates the proportion of total capital that is financed through debt.
Long-term debt-to-total-capitalization	$\frac{\text{Long-term debt}}{\text{Long-Term debt + Shareholders' equity}}$	Indicates the proportion of long-term capital that is financed through debt.
Debt to total assets	$\frac{\text{Total debt}}{\text{Total assets}}$	Indicates the proportion by which assets are financed through debt.
Times-interest-earned	$\frac{\text{Net income + Interest expense + Tax}}{\text{Interest expense}}$	Indicates the ability of the company to withstand a downturn in earnings and still be able to earn enough to pay interest (and avoid default). Reflects accounting earnings rather than cash flow.
Times-debt–service-earned	$\frac{\text{Cash flow from operations + Interest + Tax}}{\text{Interest + Finance lease payments + [(Projected annual principal payments) ÷ (1 − } t\text{)]}}$	Indicates the ability of the company to service its debt, including leases, from its pre-tax operating cash flow. Operating cash flow must include changes in current monetary items.

EXHIBIT 22-10

SOLVENCY RATIOS FOR GRI

Ratio	2013	2012	Discussion
Debt-to-equity	(340 + 280 + 2,700)/2,480 = 1.3 times	(380 + 280 + 1,750)/2,110 = 1.14 times	Debt has increased so the company has more total debt than in 2012.
Long-term debt-to- equity	2,700/2,480 = 1.1 times	1,750/2,110 = 0.83 times	Most of the increase in debt was in long-term debt.
Total debt-to-capitalization	(340 + 280 + 2,700)/(340 + 280 + 2,700 + 2,480) = 0.57	(380 + 280 + 1,750)/(380 + 280 + 1,750 + 2,110) = 0.53	As a result of the higher debt, we see that the proportion of debt used to finance the company has increased from 53% to 57%.
Total debt-to-assets	(340 + 280 + 2,700)/7,830 = 0.42	(380 + 280 + 1,750)/5,880 = 0.41	Even though debt increased significantly, there was little change in this ratio. This indicates that the debt was used for investment in assets.
Times-interest-earned	(620 + 120 + 210)/120 = 7.9 times	(440 + 130 + 150)/130 = 5.5 times	Even though the debt has increased, the company's ability to finance the debt has actually improved due to increases in its net earnings year-over-year. We do see that the finance costs were lower in 2013 compared with 2012, even though the debt was higher. This could be due to lower rates negotiated on the debt, and the timing of when the new debt was actually issued.
Times debt–service-earned	(1,010 + 120 + 210)/[120 + (280/(1 – 0.253))] = 2.7 times	(870 + 130 + 150)/[130 + (280/(1 – 0.254))] = 3.1 times	Even though there is a significant increase in the amount of debt, the company still generates enough operating cash flows to cover the annual payments required to service the debt (although the ratio has declined). It appears that the new debt has no annual repayments required and will be repaid at maturity.

Current Ratio The grandparent of all ratios is the **current ratio**. Use of this ratio has been traced back almost 100 years. It is a simple ratio to calculate:

Current ratio = Current assets ÷ Current liabilities

The current assets are the "reservoir" of assets from which the current liabilities will be paid. Therefore, this ratio suggests the margin of safety for creditors. A common rule of thumb is that current assets should be twice the current liabilities; the ratio should be 2:1. But like all rules of thumb, a ratio of 2:1 may not be appropriate for a particular company or a particular industry. If cash flows are steady and reliable, then there is no need for such a high ratio. On the other hand, a volatile cash inflow may require a higher average ratio to provide a margin of safety so that the company can continue to pay its payroll and other immediate cash expenses.

If the current ratio is used as a measure of liquidity, then the components of current assets must be "liquid" or realizable in the short run. Current assets include inventory and prepaid expenses. Prepaid expenses obviously are not convertible into cash, but they do indicate expenses that have already been paid and will not require an additional cash outflow in the next period.

Inventories are a bigger problem. If the inventories are readily sellable, then it is appropriate to include them as a liquid asset. But there is no way for an external analyst to tell whether the inventories are sellable or not; there is no disclosure that can help. In fact, inventories that are not very sellable will accumulate, increasing the current assets and improving the current ratio. If inventories are an important component of current assets, increasing inventory levels can be a danger sign.

Current liabilities may include unearned revenue. As with prepaid expenses, unearned revenue represents past cash flow. It does not represent a cash obligation of the company in the same way that accounts and notes payable do.

Quick Ratio The **quick ratio** is also called the **acid-test ratio.** It is intended to overcome the deficiencies of the current ratio by excluding inventories and other non-monetary current assets. To be consistent, non-monetary current liabilities (e.g., unearned revenue and other deferred credits) should also be excluded. Therefore, the ratio is determined as follows:

Quick ratio = Monetary current assets ÷ Monetary current liabilities

A ratio of less than 1:1 is generally undesirable. However, a low ratio is no cause for concern if the company's operating cash flow is steady and reliable. As with solvency ratios, liquidity ratios can be effectively interpreted only in reference to the *operating risk* and *financial risk* of the company. If cash inflows are stable, a low liquidity ratio should not be a cause for concern. But if cash flows are very volatile, even a high liquidity ratio should not make the analyst complacent. Cash can vanish from a high-risk operation very quickly.

Cash Conversion Cycle A measure known as the **cash conversion cycle** also gives us some idea of liquidity and how long cash is tied up in financing the accounts receivable and inventories. It is actually a combination of some earlier ratios as follows:

Cash conversion cycle = Average days in inventory + Average collection period for accounts receivable – Average days in payables

The cash conversion cycle starts with a company's investment in inventory. At the time, the inventory is sold (after the holding period of days in inventory), an accounts receivable will result. The payable to the supplier must be paid, and finally cash is collected from the accounts receivable and the cycle begins again. If the cash conversion cycle is positive, then a company must finance these numbers of days. If the cash conversion cycle is negative, this implies that the company has the use of cash before the suppliers must be paid. Consider the following two examples:

	Days in Inventory	Average Collections Period for Accounts Receivable	Average Days in Payable	Cash Conversion Cycle
Company A	10	30	45	–5
Company B	30	30	45	15

In both cases the suppliers are paid in 45 days and receivables are collected in 30 days. However, in the case of Company A, the days in inventory is only 10 days, which results in a negative cash cycle. Company B has 30 days for inventory, resulting in a positive cash conversion cycle. These results indicate that Company A likely has short-term investments on hand (for investing the excess cash on a short-term basis), and Company B may have to borrow short-term debt to finance the 15 days.

Defensive-Interval Ratio The current ratio and the quick ratio are static ratios in that they look at only the ability of the company to pay its short-term obligations with the short-term assets that exist at the SFP report date. Both ratios are flawed because they do not consider the rate at which expenditures are incurred. An alternative ratio is one that tests the number of days that the company could operate if the cash inflow were cut off, such as by a strike or an emergency shutdown. While many expenses are eliminated in a shutdown, others continue. For a company to survive a shutdown, it has to be able to pay its continuing operating costs. The intent of the **defensive-interval ratio** is to see how many days the company could pay its continuing expenses in the absence of an inflow of cash from operating revenue. The basic form of the ratio is as follows:

$$\frac{\text{Monetary current assets}}{\text{Annual operating expenditures} \div 365}$$

The difficulty with this ratio is in deciding what should be in the numerator and what should be in the denominator. The numerator clearly should be restricted to monetary assets (e.g., cash and cash equivalents, accounts receivable, and short-term investments).

The denominator would include only those cash expenses that will continue in the event of a shutdown. Many labour costs would be eliminated in a shutdown, as would acquisitions of new inventories and supplies. The problem for the external analyst, however, is that the financial statements seldom give enough detail to permit this analysis. Therefore, external analysts usually use short-term monetary assets (without deduction for monetary liabilities) as the numerator and operating expenses less non-cash charges (e.g., depreciation and amortization) in the denominator. The name of the ratio, by the way, comes from the concept of the short-term monetary assets as being *defensive assets*.

Common liquidity ratios are summarized in Exhibit 22-11.

EXHIBIT 22-11

SUMMARY OF LIQUIDITY RATIOS

Ratio Name	Computation	Significance and Difficulties
Current	$\frac{\text{Current assets}}{\text{Current liabilities}}$	Indicates ability to pay liabilities with current assets but includes inventories, prepaid expenses, and other deferred assets and liabilities.
Quick (acid-test)	$\frac{\text{Monetary current assets}}{\text{Monetary current liabilities}}$	A more refined test than the current ratio because it excludes non-monetary assets and liabilities.
Cash conversion cycle	Average days in inventory + Average collection period for accounts receivable – Average days in payables	A measure of how long cash is "tied up" in working capital and not available for use. How long it takes to convert working capital investments into cash.
Defensive interval	$\frac{\text{Monetary current assets}}{\text{Projected daily operating expenditures}}$	Indicates the approximate number of days that the company can continue to operate with the currently available liquid assets. Denominator is very difficult to estimate by an external analyst.

Exhibit 22-12 shows the calculations of the liquidity ratios for GRI.

Assessment of GRI's liquidity ratios indicates that the current ratio, quick ratio, and defensive interval measures are all very low. However, the cash conversion cycle is negative, indicating that excess cash is generated from the operations, and this is primarily due to most of its sales being cash sales. As a result, cash will steadily come in to pay for current obligations and liquidity should not suffer.

Consolidated Statements

Most Canadian corporations operate through a series of subsidiaries. This is true even of quite small companies. One small chain of three restaurants, for example, may have each restaurant set up as a separate corporation. A company that operates in more than one province almost certainly will have at least one subsidiary in each province. Therefore, the analyst must be aware of just what he or she is analyzing: an individual corporation or a corporate group?

IFRS requires that the primary set of statements for a public company with subsidiaries be the *consolidated* financial statements, wherein all of the assets, liabilities, revenues, and expenses of all of the companies in the group are combined. The statements will give no clue as to which items belong to which legal corporate entity within the corporate group. If the company is a private corporation using ASPE, consolidated statements are optional and not a requirement.

An investor who is considering purchasing the shares of a corporation usually will want to see statements that show the full resources under control of the corporation, including those held by subsidiaries. The prospective investor is investing in the *economic entity*, and the consolidated statements are the appropriate basis of analysis.

A creditor or lender is in a different position, however. A creditor or lender holds an obligation only of the *separate legal entity*, not of the corporate group. Therefore, creditors or

EXHIBIT 22-12

LIQUIDITY RATIOS FOR GRI

Ratio	2013	2012	Discussion
Current ratio	1,480/2,250 = 0.66	1,130/1,780 = 0.63	The current ratio has slightly increased, but it is still significantly below 1 (and even more below 2:1). Is this cause for concern? Likely not, since in this industry, most of the sales are cash sales and cash will be coming in daily and at a steady rate to cover the current obligations.
Quick ratio	(70 + 350)/ 2,250 = 0.19	(100 + 300)/ 1,780 = 0.22	The quick ratio is very low, but the same issues discussed above are still relevant.
Cash conversion cycle	31 + 9 – 44 = –4 days (From Exhibit 22-8)	27 + 9 – 37 = –1 days (From Exhibit 22-8)	The cash conversion cycle has improved. Although inventory days increased by 4 days, the company also lengthened its payment terms by 7 days. As long as the suppliers are in agreement with this, there should not be any concerns.
Defensive Interval	[(70 + 350)/ (10,400 + 120 + 270 + 710 + 280)/365] = 13 days (See Notes 1 and 2)	[(100 + 300)/ (10,150 + 110 + 250 + 645 + 260)/365] = 13 days (See Notes 1 and 2)	There has been no change in this, although it is very low.

Note 1—GRI has both cash sales and credit sales. The cash sales have an immediate collection period. If we calculated a weighted average of the cash and credit sales amounts, we would arrive at a better indicator for cash collection on sales.

Note 2—As discussed earlier, the specific numbers to use for the denominator and numerator are difficult to determine for external analysts. For GRI, we have estimated projected daily operating expenditures, using the sum of cash expenditures from the SCI as follows:

(COGS) + (Electricity + natural gas) + (Rent, taxes and occupancy costs) + (Other)/365 days

lenders must be careful to analyze the separate-entity statements of the specific corporation to which they are extending credit or granting loans.

The consolidated statements can give a very misleading view; lenders have been burnt in the past by lending money to a parent company on the basis of consolidated statements only to discover later that all of the cash flow is in the operating subsidiaries. Lenders may demand cross-company guarantees of debt, but trade creditors usually cannot demand such a guarantee. Cross-company guarantees may not be very effective anyway, since they are usually subordinated, and there may be legal impediments to their enforcement when they cross borders, especially national borders.

Therefore, financial statement analysis must be performed on the statements that are appropriate for the decision being made. Generally speaking, equity investors will use consolidated statements while creditors and lenders should use unconsolidated statements for their primary analysis.

Multi-industry Corporations

Many corporations engage in several lines of business. These corporations may be either publicly or privately owned. Because they have a broad spectrum of activities, they cannot be classified as being in a specific industry. Industry comparisons are a common aspect of financial statement analysis, particularly of ratio analysis. The inability to slot many corporations into a specific industry classification may appear to create a problem for the analyst. However, the inability to classify a corporation by industry should not, in itself, be of concern.

At the level of profitability analysis, the rate of return *on investment* should not vary by industry. The competition for capital is economy-wide and worldwide, so an investor should expect the same return on an investment *at a given level of risk* no matter what industry or industries a company is in.

Risk Assessment is also a function of risk and return—while companies in a certain industry often have similar capital structures because of an underlying commonality of operating risk, there also are significant differences between companies in an industry. Industry classification is not an adequate definition of risk. For example, there is a relatively low risk level inherent in the operations of established mobile phone companies in contrast to the high risk borne by new entrants to the market.

The key is *risk*; the analyst must be able to evaluate the risks to the company and its ability to survive downturns and benefit from upturns. Industry analysis is useful because the general *market risk* is broadly similar to all of the players in that market. When a company's participation in several different markets is summarized in annual financial statements, it is impossible to tell just what the company's exposure to different risks is in different markets. Therefore, public companies are required to provide **segment reporting** as supplementary information in their annual financial statements. The volume of activity is reported both by industry and by geographic region.

Segment reporting gives the analyst a better idea of the company's exposure to the risks inherent in different industries and in different parts of the world. However, it is not feasible to perform ratio analysis at the same level of detail as for the company as a whole because the numbers included in the segment data are distinctly "fuzzy." The revenues include revenues between segments at transfer prices; the costs include allocated amounts with no useful disclosure of the nature of the allocations, and the operating profits therefore are the net result of two approximations. Segment disclosures certainly are better than no disclosures at all, but they do need to be taken with a grain of salt.

Conclusion

The following are some concluding observations on ratio analysis:

- The apparent simplicity of ratio analysis is deceptive; ratios are only as good as the underlying data.
- The analyst must take care to analyze the correct set of financial statements: consolidated or separate legal entity.
- Financial statements often have to be adjusted to suit the analyst's needs before meaningful ratio analysis can be performed.
- Industry comparisons can be helpful, but there is no assurance that the industry averages are "right" or are based on similar accounting policies and measurements.
- Assessments of investment profitability, solvency, and liquidity are not really industry dependent, but they do depend to some extent on an analysis of risk for each line of business.

- There is no point in computing masses of ratios; it is more important to identify one or two key ratios in each category that are relevant to the analyst's decision needs and concentrate on those.
- Given the many estimates and approximations underlying both the numerator and denominator of *all* ratios, it is absurd to calculate them to more than two significant digits; computing to three or more digits gives ratios an appearance of precision that is completely unwarranted.
- Be careful in using ratios that have been calculated by others. As we have seen, ratios can have many variations where different analysts use different numbers in both the numerator and the denominator. Remember the variations of the debt-to-equity ratio that were available, depending on what was included and excluded in determining its components.

Finally, ratios can be very helpful when understood and used properly. Ratios provide clues and indicators; it is up to the analyst to use his or her expertise in analyzing all of the ratio results on an integrated basis to make the final conclusions.

CONCEPT REVIEW

1. What is the essential relationship between the numerator and denominator of any effective investment profitability ratio?
2. Is it necessarily a good thing for efficiency ratios to be very high?
3. Why do some analysts prefer to use debt-service ratios, such as times-debt-service-earned ratio, rather than the more common times-interest earned ratio?
4. Why should creditors and lenders be wary of basing their analyses on consolidated financial statements?

OTHER ANALYTICAL TECHNIQUES

In addition to basic ratio analysis, other more sophisticated analytical techniques can be applied to the amounts in the financial statements or to the ratios themselves. These techniques include the following:

- *Time-series analysis.* The purpose of time-series analysis is to predict the future values of the ratios. Time-series analysis can be applied to cross-sectional ratios themselves or to the underlying financial data. The data can be used "raw" or can be subjected to transformations, such as logarithmic transformation.
- *Residual analysis.* This is a time-series analysis based on the differences between computed ratios and industry (or economy) averages. The intent is to identify the extent to which changes in a company's ratios are common to the industry (or economy) as a whole. Such an analysis may help to discover when a company is performing better or worse than other companies over a period of time.
- *Statistical multivariate ratio analysis.* In this approach, ratios are not analyzed one by one but fitted into a statistical model in an attempt to predict some type of outcome, such as impending bankruptcy.

An implicit assumption of these approaches is that the underlying *economic processes* that generate the numbers and ratios are stable. Furthermore, there is an implicit assumption that the underlying *measurement methods* (i.e., accounting policies and accounting estimates) also are stable and remain unchanged over the period of analysis and into the period being predicted. Neither assumption should automatically be taken as correct in a rapidly changing economic environment, especially in light of the dozens of changes in accounting standards over the past decade. This book will not delve further into these sophisticated statistical approaches.

ACCOUNTING STANDARDS FOR PRIVATE ENTERPRISES

Analytical techniques described above can be used on any financial statements, regardless of the underlying accounting standards followed. In all cases, the analyst must first be aware if the statements are prepared under IFRS or ASPE and make adjustments in the ratios, accordingly.

SUMMARY OF KEY POINTS

1. There are four main steps to completing financial statement analysis: understanding the objective of the analysis; gathering the data required; calculating the ratios; and analyzing the results.
2. The auditor's report (if any) should be reviewed with an eye to opinion qualifications and to comments regarding accounting policies, if any. The auditor's report serves only as assurance that accounting policies meet current accounting standards.
3. The essential first step in statement analysis is to fully understand the financial statements. The statements cannot be meaningfully analyzed unless they are viewed within the framework of management's reporting objectives and accounting policies.
4. Clues to the accounting policies used by management are found in the notes to the financial statements. The policy note may give only sketchy information, but the notes relating to individual financial statement components may provide more useful information.
5. The accounting policies used by management may not be the most suitable for the purpose of the analyst's decision needs. The analyst may find it useful to recast the financial statements using different policies, such as by removing the effects of nonrecurring gains and losses from net income, or by treating as expense certain expenditures that the company has capitalized.
6. When the analyst recasts a company's financial statements, there may not be adequate information provided in the notes for an accurate restatement. Approximations often are necessary.
7. *Vertical analysis* (or *common-size analysis*) involves calculating financial statement components as a percentage of the total, such as SFP amounts as a percentage of total assets and SCI components as a percentage of total revenue.
8. Vertical analysis is useful for removing the effects of absolute changes in amounts; changes in the relative composition of SFP and SCI components may become more readily apparent.
9. *Horizontal analysis* (or *trend analysis*) involves calculating individual financial statement components over several years as an index number, with a base year set at 100. Horizontal analysis is used to determine the relative change in amounts between years.
10. *Ratio analysis* compares the proportional relationship between different items within a single year's financial statements. Often, it is necessary to adjust the numerator and denominator of a ratio by excluding or reclassifying certain components.
11. *Return on sales profitability ratios* measure how dollars of revenue are spent in costs required to earn those revenues. *Investment profitability ratios* are those that compare a measure of earnings (the numerator) with a measure of investment (the denominator). It is essential that the numerator and denominator be logically consistent.

12. *Efficiency ratios* attempt to measure selected aspects of the company's operations, such as inventory turnover or the accounts receivable collection period. Efficiency ratios must be used with great caution by an external analyst because the SFP amounts may not be typical of the balances throughout the period.

13. *Solvency ratios* reflect the ability of the company to meet its long-term obligations. Static solvency ratios include various forms of the debt-to-equity ratio; flow ratios examine the ability of the company to meet its debt financing obligations through its cash flows from operations.

14. *Liquidity ratios* test the company's ability to cover its short-term obligations with its existing monetary assets.

15. All ratios are based on accounting numbers that are the result of the company's accounting policies and which include the effects of many estimates made by management. Despite the fact that ratios can be computed to many decimals, they really are very approximate measures that must be interpreted with extreme caution.

KEY TERMS

accounts receivable aging schedule
accounts receivable turnover ratio
acid-test ratio
asset turnover
auditor's report
average collection period of accounts receivable
cash conversion cycle
cross-sectional comparison
current ratio
days in inventory
days in payables
debt service ratios
debt-to-equity
debt-to-total assets
debt-to-total-capitalization
defensive-interval ratio
efficiency ratios
financial risk
horizontal (trend) analysis
inventory turnover ratio
leverage
leverage ratios
liquidity ratios
longitudinal comparisons
margin of safety
negative leverage
operating margin
operating risk
profitability ratios
quick ratio
ratio analysis
return on common share equity
return on long-term capital
return on total assets
review engagement
segment reporting
solvency ratios
times-debt-service-earned ratio
times-interest-earned ratio
total capitalization
total debt-to-equity ratio
turnover ratios
vertical (common-size) analysis

REVIEW PROBLEM 22-1

Below are the financial statements of Gold Mining Inc. (GMI) for the years ended 20X11 to 20X13.

GOLD MINING INC.

Statement of Financial Position as at December 31

(in millions of Canadian dollars)

	20X13 $	20X12 $	20X11 $
Cash and cash equivalents	281	404	758
Accounts receivable	560	519	311
Inventory	487	509	304
Prepaid expenses	80	25	15
	1,408	1,457	1,388
Property, plant, and equipment	6,342	6,010	4,385
Mineral property costs	1,894	1,940	1,569
Total assets	9,644	9,407	7,342
Liabilities			
Accounts payable and accrued liabilities	403	465	325
Taxes payable	105	69	22
Total current liabilities	508	534	347
Long-term debt	1,775	2,408	1,249
Deferred income taxes	689	481	357
Asset retirement obligations	383	267	180
Total liabilities	3,355	3,690	2,133
Shareholders' equity			
Share capital	3,050	2,945	2,902
Retained earnings	3,239	2,772	2,307
Total shareholder's equity	6,289	5,717	5,209
Total liabilities and shareholder's equity	9,644	9,407	7,342

GOLD MINING INC.

Statement of Comprehensive Income for the Years Ended December 31

(in millions of Canadian dollars)

	20X13 $	20X12 $	20X11 $
Total net sales	4,240	4,232	2,616
Operating expenses			
Operating costs	1,659	1,726	936
Distribution costs	401	395	328
Royalty costs	275	279	242
Depreciation	510	502	305
Total operating costs (Cost of goods sold)	2,845	2,902	1,811
Profit from mining operations	1,395	1,330	805
Other expenses			
General and administration	223	210	189
Interest expense	179	115	130
Other	36	32	39
Total other expenses	438	357	358
Net earnings before taxes	957	973	447
Income taxes	240	244	112
Comprehensive income for the year	717	729	335

Required:

Calculate the following ratios for Gold Mining Inc. for 20X13 and 20X12:

- Operating margin
- Return on total long-term capital, after tax
- Return on assets, after tax
- Return on equity
- Average collection period of accounts receivable
- Average days in inventory
- Average days in payables
- Debt to equity
- Debt to total assets
- Times interest earned
- Current ratio
- Quick ratio

Comment on what the ratios reveal; that is, has the ratio improved or worsened from 20X12 to 20X13, and is there cause for concern? What additional information would you need to complete your analysis?

REVIEW PROBLEM 22-1 SOLUTION

	20X13	20X12	Discussion
Operating margin	(1,395 – 223 – 36)/4,240 = 26.8%	(1,330 – 210 – 32)/4,232 = 25.7%	Slight increase in margin
Return on total long-term capital, after tax	717 + 179 (1 – 0.25)/[(1,775 + 2,408 + 6,289 + 5,717)/2] = 10.5%	729 + 115 (1 – 0.25)/[(2,408 + 1,249 + 5,717 + 5,209)/2] = 11.2%	Decrease in return on capital
Return on assets, after tax	717 + 179 (1 – 0.25)/[(9,644 + 9,407)/2] = 8.9%	729 + 115 (1 – 0.25)/[(9,407 + 7,342)/2] = 9.7%	Decrease in return on assets
Return on equity	717/[(6,289 + 5,717)/2] = 11.9%	729/[(5,717 + 5,209)/2] = 13.3%	Decrease in return on equity
Average collection period of accounts receivable	365/[4,240/(560 + 519)/2] = 46 days	365/[4,232/(519 + 311)/2] = 36 days	Significant increase and cause for concern
Average days in inventory	365/[2,845/(487 + 509)/2] = 64 days	365/[2,902/(509 + 304)/2] = 51 days	Significant increase and cause for concern
Average days in payables	365/[(2,845 – 510*)/(403 + 465/2)] = 68 days	365/[(2,902 – 502*)/(465 + 325)/2] = 60 days	Significant increase and cause for concern
Debt-to-equity	1,775/6,289 = 0.28	2,408/5,717 = 0.42	Large reduction due to substantial increase in equity and reduction in debt
Debt-to-total assets	1,775/9,644 = 0.18	2,408/9,407 = 0.26	Large reduction due to reduction in debt
Times-interest-earned	(717 + 179 + 240)/179 = 6.3 times	(729 + 115 + 244)/115 = 9.5 times	Decreased due to decline in profits, but an increase in interest expense
Current ratio	1,408/508 = 2.8	1,457/534 = 2.7	Very slight improvement; no cause for concern
Quick ratio	(281 + 560)/508 = 1.7	(404 + 519)/534 = 1.7	Relatively stable year-over-year The only concern here is that the average collection period for receivables has increased, which may impact bad debts

Note 1—Tax rate is estimated as 25% (240/957) for 20X13 and 25% (244/973) for 20X12.

*Depreciation is subtracted, since this is not a cash cost and would not be part of payables.

Overall, the margins and profits have declined in 20X13 compared with 20X12. This has caused the profitability ratios to worsen. However, the solvency ratios have improved due to an increase in equity (due to a share capital issue) and a reduction in debt. Although the times-interest-earned has increased, with the reduction in debt, this may decline in the coming year. The most critical areas of concern are the efficiency ratios. The company's accounts receivable days collection period has increased 10 days, along with the company's days in inventory, which has increased 13 days. We see that the company is dragging its payables out to 68 days, likely to compensate for the amount of additional cash tied up in receivables and inventories. The current ratio and quick ratio have remained stable over the two-year period.

Examples of additional information required include:

- First of all, in the mining industry, we need to understand what the price of gold has done over the two year period and how this impacts revenues.
- Why have the operating margins declined? This could be due to lower selling prices and/or higher operating costs. In the case of GMI, why might operating costs have increased?
- Why has the average days in inventory increased? Is this an industry trend indicating that supply is greater than demand? Or has Gold Mining Inc. been producing too much inventory and is unable to sell it for some entity-specific reason?
- Why has the average days for collection of receivables increased? Is this a trend in the industry? Has Gold Mining Inc. changed its mix of customers and/or credit terms?
- What is the average days in payables for competitors? GMI's days has increased significantly and may hinder its relationships with suppliers.
- What is the leverage of competitors in the industry? GMI has reduced its leverage with an issue of equity and a reduction of debt. Why was this action taken by the company?

APPENDIX

RECASTING FINANCIAL STATEMENTS—DEMONSTRATION CASE

Introduction

This chapter has emphasized that it may be necessary for an analyst to recast a company's financial statements before any ratio analysis is undertaken. To illustrate the task of restatement, we have chosen the financial statements of a Canadian company, QDO Limited (not the real name). We will restate these financial statements to reflect different accounting policy choices. After the restatement, we will compare the results of ratio analysis before and after restatement.

The Company

QDO is a publicly traded software development company following IFRS. Its primary line of business is the design and development of large-scale custom software for specific large clients. Clients include several of the provinces, one Canadian bank, and two international insurance companies. Between 20X5 and 20X8, gross revenue tripled and net income increased from $262,725 to over $2 million. Operating margin, based on the published financial statements, increased from 0.26% in 20X5 to 7% in 20X8. The company's statement of comprehensive income for the most recent four years is shown in Exhibit 22A-1; the statement of financial position is shown in Exhibit 22A-2; the statement of cash flows is shown in Exhibit 22A-3.

EXHIBIT 22A-1

QDO LIMITED

Consolidated Statement of Comprehensive Income

For the Years Ended 31 December

(in thousands of Canadian dollars)	20X8	20X7	20X6	20X5
Gross revenue	$29,276	$19,305	$14,317	$10,231
Less: Cost of goods sold	4,497	2,519	1,519	1,407
Gross profit	24,779	16,786	12,798	8,824
Expenses				
Operating and administrative	22,390	15,108	11,718	8,323
Depreciation and amortization—PPE	203	49	22	6
Finance leases	143	85	23	1
Software development costs	513	67	—	—
Total expenses	23,249	15,309	11,763	8,330
Operating profit	1,530	1,477	1,035	494
Finance income (interest on cash deposits)	1,265	—	—	—
Finance costs	(164)	(224)	(238)	(95)
Income before income tax	2,631	1,253	797	399
Income tax expense (recovery)	569	(199)	(3)	137
Net profit or loss and comprehensive income	$ 2,062	$ 1,452	$ 800	$ 262

EXHIBIT 22A-2

QDO LIMITED

Consolidated Statement of Financial Position

As at 31 December

(in thousands of Canadian dollars)	20X8	20X7	20X6	20X5
ASSETS				
Current assets				
Cash and cash equivalents	$ 8,716	$ —	$ —	$ —
Accounts receivable	6,459	4,658	5,112	2,370
Work in progress	7,451	2,780	—	—
Hardware inventory	569	—	—	—
Prepaid expenses and supplies inventory	1,151	470	126	123
	24,346	7,908	5,238	2,493
Property, plant, and equipment				
Leasehold improvements	852	317	278	16
Furniture, fixtures, and computer equipment	624	121	138	16
Assets under finance lease	1,374	817	359	156
	2,850	1,255	775	188
Less: Accumulated depreciation	(293)	(90)	(38)	(11)
	2,557	1,165	737	177
Other assets				
Software development costs	15,233	5,157	1,580	112
Deferred income taxes	—	355	409	409
	15,233	5,512	1,989	521
Total assets	$42,136	$14,585	$7,964	$3,191
LIABILITIES AND SHAREHOLDERS' EQUITY				
Current liabilities				
Bank and other loans	$ 2,806	$ 3,371	$2,653	$ 900
Accounts payable and accrued liabilities	7,054	3,550	2,131	918
Deferred revenue	530	461	183	140
Current portion of finance lease obligations	281	161	85	23
	10,671	7,543	5,052	1,981
Noncurrent liabilities				
Finance lease obligations	1,488	1,101	662	134
Deferred income taxes	214	—	104	104
Total liabilities	12,373	8,644	5,818	2,219
Shareholders' equity				
Share capital	26,994	3,989	1,090	497
Retained earnings	2,769	1,952	1,056	475
	29,763	5,941	2,146	972
Total liabilities and shareholders' equity	$42,136	$14,585	$7,964	$3,191

EXHIBIT 22A-3

QDO LIMITED

Consolidated Statement of Cash Flows

For the Years Ended 31 December

(in thousands of Canadian dollars)	20X8	20X7	20X6	20X5
Operations				
Net profit or loss for the year	$ 2,062	$ 1,452	$ 800	$ 262
Add: Non-cash items				
Deferred income taxes	569	(50)	—	50
Depreciation and amortization	859	200	45	7
Deferred lease rent credits	—	82	142	—
Finance income	(1,265)			
Finance costs	164	224	238	95
Income taxes (recovery)	0	(149)	(3)	87
Net change in working capital items	(3,619)	(579)	(1,315)	(261)
	(1,230)	1,180	(93)	240
Interest paid	(178)	(230)	(257)	(105)
Interest received	1,202			
Income taxes paid	(150)	10	(90)	(110)
Cash provided by (used for) operating activities	(356)	960	(440)	25
Investment				
Investment in software products	(10,588)	(3,645)	(1,469)	(110)
Purchase of fixed assets	(1,034)	(36)	(162)	(89)
Proceeds from disposal of fixed assets	—	—	—	160
Cash provided by (used for) investment activities	(11,622)	(3,681)	(1,631)	(39)
Financing				
Net issue (repayments) of bank and other loans	(565)	718	1,753	(164)
Repayments of finance lease obligations	(325)	(161)	(55)	(24)
Issue of shares	21,858	2,525	2,138	244
Loss on sale of repurchased shares	(46)	—	—	—
Dividends declared	(14)	(295)	(176)	(33)
Shares purchased and cancelled	(214)	(66)	(1,589)	(9)
Cash provided by (used for) financing activities	20,694	2,721	2,071	14
Increase (decrease) in cash during year	$ 8,716	$ 0	$ 0	$ 0
Cash and cash equivalents, beginning of year	0	0	0	0
Cash and cash equivalents, end of year	$ 8,716	$ 0	$ 0	$ 0

In 20X7, the company's managers decided to develop some of its large-scale custom software designs into off-the-shelf turn-key proprietary products that would be adaptable to any prospective user. In addition, the company launched an ambitious sales expansion plan, establishing offices in 11 Canadian cities and 10 U.S. cities, plus one in Singapore. To help finance the expansion, the company raised approximately $22 million through a public issue of common shares early in 20X8. The company also increased its line of credit with a Canadian bank to $5 million.

The product development expenditures for the proprietary products were accounted for in accordance with accounting standards. Since, in management's judgement, all of the criteria for capitalization were satisfied, it was acceptable to capitalize the development expenditures. It is now 20X9. Over the first three months of the year, the company has completely used the cash and cash equivalents that are shown on the year-end 20X8 SFP and is near the limit on its line of credit. The company's CEO has approached the Canadian bank with a proposal to further extend the company's line of credit to enable the company to continue development of its proprietary software and to support the costs of the new sales offices until the offices become self-sufficient.

Task

You are an analyst for the Canadian bank. The bank's Credit Committee is interested in the sustainable operating cash flow of QDO. Investment in software development is considered by the bank to be an ongoing operating activity, crucial to the success of the company. Therefore, the chair of the Credit Committee has asked you to recast QDO's 20X7 and 20X8 financial statements as follows:

- Development costs incurred in each year should be shown as a current expense.
- All deferred income tax amounts should be reversed out of the statements.

Once the statements have been restated, the Credit Committee would like you to calculate a few ratios that relate to the company's ability to sustain increased borrowing. Specifically, the requested ratios are:

1. Return on total assets, before tax;
2. Total liabilities-to-shareholders' equity; and
3. Times-interest-earned.

Nonrecurring items of revenue or expense should be eliminated before calculating any ratios based on net income. The ratios should be calculated both on the original financial statements and on the restated amounts.

Additional Information

The following information is extracted from QDO's disclosure notes:

1. Summary of significant accounting policies

(c) Software product costs

Costs, including an allocation of interest and overhead, which relate to the development and acquisition of computer-based systems, where the systems are expected to be sold in substantially the same form in the future, are capitalized. It is the Company's policy to charge these costs to profit or loss, commencing in the year of development completion, based on projected-unit-sales over a period of no longer than three years or when it is determined that the costs will not be recovered from related future revenues.

5. Software product costs

The following is an analysis of software product costs:

	20X8	20X7
Net balance, beginning of year	$ 5,157,271	$1,579,174
Additions during the year	10,588,218	3,644,763
Less: Amortization for the year	(512,711)	(66,666)
Net Balance, end of year	$15,232,778	$5,157,271

Demonstration Case—Solution

Approach

The assignment from the Credit Committee is to recast the statements by making two changes:

- The accounting policy for development costs should be changed from capitalization to immediate expensing.
- The effects of income tax allocation are to be removed so that the statements reflect only the current income tax due.

To make these changes, we need to take the following steps:

1. *Statement of comprehensive income*
   - Add expenditures on development costs to expenses.
   - Remove amortization expense relating to development costs from expenses (to avoid double-counting).
   - Remove deferred income tax expense, if any.
2. *Statement of financial position*
   - Remove development costs from assets.
   - Reclassify deferred income tax balances—move from other assets and noncurrent liabilities to retained earnings.
   - Restate retained earnings.
3. *Statement of cash flows*
   - Reclassify development expenditures—move from investing activities to operations.
   - Remove development cost amortization addbacks.
   - Remove deferred income tax addbacks.

Statement of Comprehensive Income

The SCI shows "software development costs" of $513 for 20X8 and $67 for 20X7. These numbers tie in to Note 5, which shows the same amounts as amortization. Therefore, these amounts must be removed from the SCI. Expenditures on development costs of $10,588,218 for 20X8 and $3,644,763 for 20X7 are shown in Note 5. These must be added to expenses in the recast SCIs.

Since the bank wants to see the effects of using a "flow-through" approach for income tax, the deferred income tax expense must be removed. The 20X7 SFP shows an asset balance for deferred income taxes of $355. In 20X8, the balance is a liability of $214. The net change, therefore, is a credit of $569 on the SFP. To balance, the company must have charged $569 in deferred income tax to the income statement. This amount can be verified by referring to the statement of cash flows, which shows a non-cash addback of $569 for deferred income taxes. This is also the total amount of income tax expense shown in the income statement. The company had no current taxes due in 20X8.

For 20X7, the statement of cash flows shows a *negative* addback for deferred income tax of $50. This indicates that the amount was a *credit* to income. This can be verified by looking at the change in the net balance of deferred income taxes on the SFP. At the end of 20X6, there were two deferred income tax balances, a liability for $104 and an asset of $409, for a net debit balance of $305. In 20X7, the company recorded a net deferred income tax credit to income of $50. The net change can be reconciled in the form of a general journal entry:

Change in Deferred Tax Amounts, Year-End 20X6 to Year-End 20X7

Deferred income tax liability ($104 – $0)	104	
Deferred income tax asset ($409 – $355)		54
Income tax expense, deferred		50

The SFP effect of this change is to eliminate the liability balance of $104 and reduce the asset balance from $409 to $355.

In summary, the adjustments to net income for 20X8 and 20X7 are as follows:

	20X8	20X7
Net income, as reported	$ 2,062	$ 1,452
Plus: Amortization of software development costs	513	67
Less: Expenditures on software development costs	(10,588)	(3,645)
Plus (less): Deferred income tax expense (credit)	569	(50)
Restated net income (loss)	$ (7,444)	$(2,176)

These adjustments obviously will change retained earnings for both year-ends. However, there are two other adjustments that must be made to the 20X7 *beginning* balance of retained earnings:

1. The SFP at year-end 20X6 shows software development costs as an asset of $1,580. Using the bank's preferred policy of expensing development costs, these costs should have been charged to operations when incurred. Reclassifying this amount means removing it as an asset and charging it against year-end 20X6 retained earnings.
2. The change to flow-through reporting of income tax expense requires that the balances of the deferred tax balances at the beginning of 20X7 (i.e., at year-end 20X6) be eliminated. The net balance at the end of 20X6 is $409 asset minus $104 liability, for a further net reduction in retained earnings of $305.

Therefore, the 20X7 beginning retained earnings must be restated to a deficit of $829:

	20X6
Ending retained earnings, as reported	$1,056
Adjustment to reclassify capitalized software development costs	(1,580)
Adjustment to eliminate deferred income tax balances	(305)
Restated retained earnings (deficit), 31 December 20X6	$ (829)

The adjustments shown above for 20X6 retained earnings and for 20X7 and 20X8 net income can be used to restate the SFP and the SCI. The restated SCI's are shown in Exhibit 22A-4.

Statement of Financial Position

Adjustments to the restated SFP's shown in Exhibit 22A-5 are:

- The asset amounts shown for software development costs in the original SFPs are both removed.
- The deferred income tax balances are removed.
- The retained earnings is restated for the two above adjustments:

	20X8	20X7
Original balance in retained earnings	$2,769	1,952
Remove the software development costs balance	(15,233)	(5,157)
Remove the deferred income taxes balance	214	(355)
Restated balance in retained earnings	(12,250)	(3,560)

EXHIBIT 22A-4

QDO LIMITED

Consolidated Statement of Comprehensive Income

Years Ended 31 December

	As Reported		Restated	
(in thousands of Canadian dollars)	**20X8**	**20X7**	**20X8**	**20X7**
Gross revenue	$29,276	$19,305	$29,276	$19,305
Less: Cost of goods sold	4,497	2,519	4,497	2,519
Gross profit	24,779	16,786	24,779	16,786
Expenses				
Operating and administrative	22,390	15,108	22,390	15,108
Depreciation and amortization—PPE	203	49	203	49
Finance leases	143	85	143	85
Software development costs	513	67	10,588	3,645
Total expenses	23,249	15,309	33,324	18,887
Operating profit	1,530	1,477	(8,545)	(2,101)
Finance income (interest on cash deposits)	1,265	—	1,265	—
Finance costs	(164)	(224)	(164)	(224)
Income before income tax	2,631	1,253	(7,444)	(2,325)
Income tax expense (recovery)	569	(199)	0	(149)
Net profit or loss and comprehensive income	$ 2,062	$ 1,452	$ (7,444)	$ (2,176)

Statement of Cash Flows

On the statement of cash flows, the operations section begins with the restated net income for each year. The two amounts of amortization must be adjusted by the amounts of amortization included in the original statements but now eliminated in the restatement. Also, the addback for deferred income taxes is eliminated.

In the investment section, investment in software products must be eliminated. The total cash flows for each year do not change, of course, but the subtotals for operating and investment change considerably. The restated statement of cash flows are shown in Exhibit 22A-6.

Ratios

It is obvious that changing the development cost accounting has a major impact on QDO's financial statements. Instead of showing a profit, the restated amounts indicate a substantial loss. Assets are significantly reduced and retained earnings go into a deficit position.

The operating loss situation in 20X8 is actually even worse than stated, when nonrecurring items are considered, as requested. Net income for the most recent year includes investment income of $1,265,000. This investment income is the result of temporary investment of the proceeds of the common share issue. The case states that all of the cash and short-term investments were used in operations (and development) early in 20X9. Since there are

EXHIBIT 22A-5

QDO LIMITED

Consolidated Statement of Financial Position

Years Ended 31 December

	As Reported		Restated	
(in thousands of Canadian dollars)	**20X8**	**20X7**	**20X8**	**20X7**
ASSETS				
Current assets				
Cash and cash equivalents	$ 8,716	$ —	$ 8,716	$ —
Accounts receivable	6,459	4,658	6,459	4,658
Work in progress	7,451	2,780	7,451	2,780
Hardware inventory	569	—	569	—
Prepaid expenses and supplies inventory	1,151	470	1,151	470
	24,346	7,908	24,346	7,908
Property, plant, and equipment				
Leasehold improvements	852	317	852	317
Furniture, fixtures, and computer equipment	624	121	624	121
Assets under finance lease	1,374	817	1,374	817
	2,850	1,255	2,850	1,255
Less: Accumulated depreciation	(293)	(90)	(293)	(90)
	2,557	1,165	2,557	1,165
Other assets				
Software development costs	15,233	5,157	—	—
Deferred income taxes	—	355	—	—
	15,233	5,512	—	—
Total assets	$42,136	$14,585	$26,903	$9,073
LIABILITIES AND SHAREHOLDERS' EQUITY				
Current liabilities				
Bank and other loans	$ 2,806	$ 3,371	$ 2,806	$3,371
Accounts payable and accrued liabilities	7,054	3,550	7,054	3,550
Deferred revenue	530	461	530	461
Current portion of finance lease obligations	281	161	281	161
	10,671	7,543	10,671	7,543
Noncurrent liabilities				
Finance lease obligations	1,488	1,101	1,488	1,101
Deferred income taxes	214	—	—	—
Total liabilities	12,373	8,644	12,159	8,644
Shareholders' equity				
Share capital	26,994	3,989	26,994	3,989
Retained earnings (deficit)	2,769	1,952	(12,250)	(3,560)
	29,763	5,941	14,744	429
	$42,136	$14,585	$26,903	$9,073

EXHIBIT 22A-6

QDO LIMITED

Consolidated Statement of Cash Flows

Years Ended 31 December

	As Reported		Restated	
(in thousands of Canadian dollars)	**20X8**	**20X7**	**20X8**	**20X7**
Operations				
Net profit or loss for the year	$ 2,062	$ 1,452	$ (7,444)	$(2,176)
Add: Non-cash items				
Deferred income taxes	569	(50)	—	—
Depreciation and amortization	859	200	346	133
Deferred lease rent credits	—	82	—	82
Finance income	(1,265)		(1,265)	
Finance costs	164	224	164	224
Income taxes (recovery)	0	(149)	0	(149)
Net change in working capital items	(3,619)	(579)	(3,619)	(579)
	(1,230)	1,180	(11,818)	(2,465)
Interest paid	(178)	(230)	(178)	(230)
Interest received	1,202		1,202	
Income taxes paid	(150)	10	(150)	10
Cash provided by (used for) operating activities	(356)	960	(10,944)	(2,685)
Investment				
Investment in software products	(10,588)	(3,645)	—	—
Purchase of fixed assets	(1,034)	(36)	(1,034)	(36)
Proceeds from disposal of fixed assets	—	—	—	—
Cash provided by (used for) investment activities	(11,622)	(3,681)	(1,034)	(36)
Financing				
Net issue (repayments) of bank and other loans	(565)	718	(565)	718
Repayments of finance lease obligations	(325)	(161)	(325)	(161)
Issue of shares	21,858	2,525	21,858	2,525
Loss on sale of repurchased shares	(46)	—	(46)	—
Dividends declared	(14)	(295)	(14)	(295)
Shares purchased and cancelled	(214)	(66)	(214)	(66)
Cash provided by (used for) financing activities	20,694	2,721	20,694	2,721
Increase (decrease) in cash during year	$ 8,716	$ 0	$ 8,716	$ 0
Cash and cash equivalents, beginning of year	0	0	0	0
Cash and cash equivalents, end of year	$ 8,716	$ 0	$ 8,716	$ 0

no investments, there will be no investment income in 20X9. Removing the nonrecurring income increases the 20X8 loss:

	As Reported	Restated
Net income (loss)	$2,062	$(7,444)
Less: Non-recurring investment income	(1,265)	(1,265)
Income (loss) on continuing operations	$ 797	$(8,709)

The ratios requested, before and after restatement, are as follows:

1. Return on total assets, before tax, 20X8:

$$\frac{\text{Net income + Interest expense + Income tax expense}}{\text{Total assets (average)}}$$

Before restatement:
($2,062 + $164 + $569) ÷ [($14,585 + $42,136) ÷ 2] = $2,795 ÷ $28,361 = **9.9%**

After restatement:
(–$8,709 + $164) ÷ [($9,073 + $26,903) ÷2] = – $8,545 ÷ $17,988 = **–47.5%**

2. Total liabilities to shareholders' equity:

$$\frac{\text{Total liabilities}}{\text{Shareholders' equity}}$$

Before restatement: $12,373 ÷ $29,763 = **42%**
After restatement: $12,159 ÷$14,744 = **82%**

Times-interest-earned:

$$\frac{\text{Net income + Interest expense + Income tax expense}}{\text{Interest expense}}$$

Before restatement: ($2,062 + $164 + $569) ÷$164 = $2,795 ÷ $164 = **17.0**
After restatement: (–$8,709 + $164) ÷$164 = –$8,545 ÷ $164 = **–52.1**

Conclusion

This case demonstrates not only the process that must be followed for restatements but also the importance of ensuring that the financial statements reflect accounting policies that are consistent with the decisions to be made. If the bank looked at the financial condition of the company only as shown in the published statements, it would receive a much different picture of the financial health and profitability of the company than is presented in the recasted statements. Changing the underlying reporting objective to cash flow prediction results in using accounting policies that give a much more negative view of the company.

The moral of this story? It is foolish to undertake any ratio analysis without first examining the appropriateness of the underlying financial accounting policies of the company!

QUESTIONS

Q22-1 List three financial statement users and a decision for each that may rest on financial statement analysis.

Q22-2 Why is a potential investor's perspective different than an existing investor's perspective?

Q22-3 Explain why financial analysts and others, in analyzing financial statements, examine the summary of accounting policies.

Q22-4 Explain why the actual disclosure of accounting policies in financial statements might not be as helpful as analysts and other financial statement users might wish.

Q22-5 What does it mean to "recast" the financial statements? Why are financial statements recast?

Q22-6 Distinguish between vertical and horizontal analyses. Briefly explain the use of each.

Q22-7 Explain the two ratios that combine to form return-on-assets. What strategies can a company use to maximize return-on-assets?

Q22-8 Explain the return-on-assets ratio. Why is it a fundamental measure of profitability?

Q22-9 Moller Company's average collection period for accounts receivable is 24 days. Interpret this figure. What is the accounts receivable turnover ratio? What does it reveal?

Q22-10 Maddox Steel Company has an inventory turnover of 9; interpret this figure. What is the company's average days in inventory?

Q22-11 Explain the circumstances where a company has debt financing and (a) has negative leverage or (b) has positive leverage.

Q22-12 Current assets and current liabilities for two companies with the same amount of working capital are summarized below. Evaluate their relative liquidity positions.

	Co. X	Co. Y
Current assets	$300,000	$900,000
Current liabilities	100,000	700,000
Working capital	$200,000	$200,000

CASE 22-1

PLASTICS MOULDING CO.

Plastics Moulding Co. (PMC) is a plastics company that operates in Canada. PMC manufactures plastic bottles for customers in North America. The company is publicly traded and follows IFRS. PMC has recently renewed its bank loan and the bank requested stricter covenants due to a reduction in lower forecasted revenues and earnings. The new covenants for 20X13 are as follows:

- Total liabilities (all liabilities excluding deferred taxes) to equity to be a maximum of 1.0.
- Times-interest-earned to be a minimum of 5.0 times.
- Current ratio to be a minimum of 1.0.

The company also has stock options outstanding that can be exercised only once profitability ratios meet certain targets. For the executive management team, these targets are as follows:

- Return-on assets-to be greater than 6%.
- Net income as a percentage of revenue to be no less than 10%.

It is now early December 20X13, and the accounting department has just completed its expected results for 20X13.

PMC recently hired a new financial analyst, Eric Forman, who has been examining the company's accounting policies. Eric would like to make some changes in some of these policies, as he believes that the changes will provide more relevant information to PMC's users. You are the CFO and Eric has come to you with some of his ideas. For you to be able to make this decision, you have asked Eric to explain the changes for 20X13 and what they would have been in 20X12 reports, if these new accounting policies were adopted.

Below, is the summary of Eric's memo:

1. PMC should adopt the revaluation model for its land. The land was purchased about 30 years ago and has a cost of $50 million for 20X13 and 20X12. Eric has been able to determine that the fair value of the land at the end of 20X13, 20X12, and 20X11 to be $450 million, $400 million, and $425 million, respectively.

2. PMC currently uses the cost model for its investment properties. Eric suggests that the company adopt the fair value model for investment properties. During 20X13 and 20X12, the company recognized depreciation of $24.9 million and $32 million, respectively (included in Other operating expenses). The fair value of all of the investment properties is estimated to be $850 million, $880 million, and $790 million for 20X13, 20X12, and 20X11, respectively.
3. The bonds receivable are currently recognized at amortized cost. Eric would like to classify these at FVTPL as the selling price has been increasing on these bonds, and it has been mentioned that PMC might sell once the price reaches a certain level. The bonds' fair market value was $195.2 million for 20X11; was $205.2 million in 20X12; and is estimated to be $210.2 million in 20X13.

As CFO, you have decided that the financial statements for 20X12 and forecasted 20X13 should be recast showing the impact of adopting the three proposed accounting policy changes. The memo to the Board will have to include these restatements and a summary of the impact on the loan covenants and the share option targets. The memo should also discuss any possible volatility that these accounting policies may introduce on PMC's financial statements and ratios. A final recommendation will be required as to whether or not the company should adopt any of these changes. (The impact on deferred taxes is to be included using a rate of 30%.)

Required:

Prepare the memo for the Board.
Below are the current financial statements of PMC.

Additional information:
Total assets for 20X11 were $2,904.6 million. Of this amount, the land was $50 million, investment property was $630 million, and the bonds receivable were $163 million.

EXHIBIT 1

PLASTICS MOULDING CO.

Consolidated Statement of Financial Position 31 December

(in millions of Canadian dollars)	20X13 Forecasted	20X12 Actual
Assets		
Current assets:		
Cash and cash equivalents	$ 17.1	$ 88.8
Short-term investments	45.8	75.9
Accounts receivable	373.1	378.2
Inventories	136.3	130.9
	572.3	673.8
Long-term bond receivables	165.2	165.2
Property, plant, and equipment	1,245.7	1,165.7
Investment properties	625.9	650.8
Intangible assets	171.7	163.4
Goodwill	369.1	375.5
Total assets	$3,149.9	$3,194.4

continued on next page

(in millions of Canadian dollars)	20X13 Forecasted	20X12 Actual
Liabilities and shareholders' equity		
Current liabilities:		
Accounts payable and accrued liabilities	$ 514.5	$ 609.6
Long-term debt due within one year	55.8	87.9
	570.3	697.5
Long-term debt	987.6	962.7
Deferred income taxes	98.4	106.1
	1,656.3	1,766.3
Shareholders' equity		
Capital shares	190.5	186.8
Retained earnings	1,303.1	1,241.3
	1,493.6	1,428.1
Total liabilities and shareholders' equity	$3,149.9	$3,194.4

Consolidated Statement of Comprehensive Income

Years Ended 31 December

(in millions of Canadian dollars)	20X13 Forecasted	20X12 Actual
Revenue	$1,116.7	$1,127.6
Cost of sales	718.0	690.7
Other operating expenses	190.9	194.8
	908.9	885.5
Earnings before interest and taxes	207.8	242.1
Interest income	11.0	13.0
Interest on long-term debt	(41.4)	(35.7)
Earnings before taxes	177.4	219.4
Income tax at 30%	53.2	65.8
Net earnings and comprehensive income	$ 124.2	$ 153.6

CASE 22-2

PETERSON PRODUCTS LIMITED

You have just returned from a meeting with a friend who is considering an opportunity to invest in nonvoting shares of Peterson Products Limited (PPL). PPL is a private company following ASPE and is offering to issue this new class of shares to a select group of private investors. Your classmate was very enthusiastic about the company, pointing out the company's unusually high return on assets, its low debt-to-equity ratio, and its high operating margin, as compared with other companies of a similar nature. Your classmate is also impressed with the company's high positive cash flow, which has exceeded $1 million in each of the past two years.

PPL is a product development company. It contracts with other companies to develop product ideas to a state where they can be readily produced and marketed. The services offered by PPL range from lining up suppliers to provide the raw product, to packaging and distribution of a rather simple product at the most modest level of service, to full development and design work, manufacturing design, pilot plant construction, and product testing for complex industrial products.

The development of specific products is done under contract. The standard contract provides for PPL to be reimbursed for all direct costs plus a fixed percentage of direct costs to cover overhead and provide a profit. Most contracts contain an upper limit on costs that PPL cannot exceed without approval of the contracting party.

Some of the work on contracts is carried out directly by engineering and other product staff who are employed directly by PPL. Frequently, however, segments of contracts are subcontracted to specialist companies. The subcontracts usually are fixed-fee contracts, and since any cost overruns will have to be absorbed by the subcontractor, it is the practice of PPL to recognize all of PPL's profit on the subcontracted portion of the contract as soon as the subcontract is signed. About 50% (30% for 20X6) of PPL's contract revenue and related costs recognized in 20X7 (20X6) net income had not yet been completed by the subcontractors. Although specific product development is done under contract, PPL also engages in development work of its own in order to have a storehouse of development knowledge and expertise that it can apply to future contracts. The amortization of these development costs is over five years and is included in the overhead component of contracts.

While the company has been in existence for over 25 years, it has become much more aggressive in the last two years since Dale Peterson assumed the positions of president and CEO. Dale is the daughter of Ian Peterson, the founder of the company. She completed an MBA at Concordia University and took over management of the company when her father decided to retire to Australia.

The new president and CEO has altered the way in which PPL acquires its equipment. In previous years, PPL purchased the equipment and other fixed assets that it needed. Now the company owns only minor furniture with the bulk of assets leased on a month-to-month basis from IRS Ltd. IRS purchased $1,433,000 of equipment for PPL in 20X7 ($1,385,000 in 20X6). IRS rents the equipment to PPL for $29,500 per month. Ninety percent of the equipment that PPL owned three years ago has since been sold, much of it to IRS, at fair market values, with any resulting gains reported in current income. IRS finances purchase of the assets through bank loans. IRS is owned by Dale Peterson. Dale and other shareholders have personally guaranteed the IRS bank loans, but PPL is not a guarantor.

PPL's shares at present are owned equally by Ian, Dale, and Christopher, Dale's brother. Christopher does not participate in the management of the company nor take any active interest in its affairs aside from welcoming the dividends that he receives.

Dale has proposed issuing 100 shares of a new class of nonvoting shares to a limited number of new investors for $10,000 per share. The new shares would receive dividends equally with the voting common shares and would have the same rights as voting shares if the company is liquidated. The nonvoting shareholders would be able to sell their shares back to the company at any year-end at the net book value per share.

Your friend has left with you, for your perusal, the audited financial statements that follow. PPL currently pays tax at 40%. He also left some information that shows the following comparative ratios for product development companies:

Total Debt-to-equity	0.67
(Note that this industry average uses total liabilities, not just interest-bearing debt)	
Operating margin	6%
Return on assets, before tax	20%
(Note that this industry average uses the closing balance of assets, not the average.)	

Required:

Analyze the financial statements of Peterson Products Limited, and advise your friend as to the wisdom of investing in PPL nonvoting shares.

EXHIBIT 1

PETERSON PRODUCTS LIMITED

BALANCE SHEET

As at March 31

(all amounts in thousands of Canadian dollars)	20X7	20X6
Current assets		
Cash	$ 75	$ 58
Contract billings receivable	520	413
Unbilled contract receivables	417	110
Work in progress	541	736
	1,553	1,317
Equipment, furniture, and fixtures—net	350	1,750
Patents	1,512	917
Total assets	$3,415	$3,984
Current liabilities		
Accounts payable and accrued expenses	$ 487	$ 441
Bank overdraft	—	1,000
	487	1,441
Future income tax	915	615
	1,402	2,056
Shareholders' equity		
Common shares	600	600
Retained earnings	1,413	1,328
	2,013	1,928
Total liabilities and shareholders' equity	$3,415	$3,984

PETERSON PRODUCTS LIMITED

STATEMENT OF INCOME

Years Ending 31 March

(all amounts in thousands of Canadian dollars)	20X7	20X6
Revenue		
Contract revenue	$5,250	$4,640
Gain on disposal of fixed assets	340	104
	5,590	4,744
Expenses		
Contract costs	3,870	3,169
General selling and administrative expenses	805	670
Interest expense	70	175
Total expenses	4,745	4,014
Earnings before taxes	845	730
Income tax expense	410	355
Net income and comprehensive income	$ 435	$ 375

PETERSON PRODUCTS LIMITED

STATEMENT OF CASH FLOWS

Years Ended 31 March

(all amounts in thousands of Canadian dollars)	20X7	20X6
Operating activities:		
Net income	$ 435	$ 375
Depreciation	123	263
Patent amortization	183	121
Future income tax	300	230
Gain on sale of fixed assets	(340)	(104)
	701	885
Decrease (increase) in working capital balances	(173)	(244)
Cash provided by operations	528	641
Financing activities:		
Dividends paid	(350)	(450)
Investing activities:		
Patents	(778)	(432)
Proceeds from disposal of fixed assets	1,617	1,472
Increase (decrease) in cash and cash equivalents	$1,017	$1,231

CASE 22-3

FOREST INDUSTRY

You are evaluating two public companies in the forest industry. Both companies follow IFRS and are integrated companies that own or lease timber properties (biological assets), harvest trees, and make building supplies and paper products. This industry is very volatile. The profiles are as follows:

Canamora Forest Products Inc.

Canamora Forest Products Inc. (CFP) is a leading Canadian-integrated forest products company. The company employs approximately 6,800 people. The company has extensive production facilities in British Columbia and Alberta, and a lumber remanufacturing plant in the United States. The company is a major producer and supplier of lumber and bleached kraft pulp. It also produces semi-bleached and unbleached kraft pulp, bleached and unbleached kraft paper, plywood, remanufactured lumber products, hardboard panelling, and a range of specialized wood products, including baled fibre and fibremat. Products are sold in global markets.

Fallsview Building Materials Ltd.

Fallsview is a North American–based producer of building materials, including oriented strand board, medium-density fibreboard, hardwood plywood, lumber, I-joists, specialty papers, and pulp. The company is also the United Kingdom's largest producer of wood-based panels, including particleboard and value-added products. The company employs over 2,600 people in North America and 1,000 in the United Kingdom.

You have obtained some limited industry norms that relate to years prior to those presented for the two companies; industry norms are difficult to establish for the current years.

Selected ratios for the forest industry in Canada:

	20X5	20X4	20X3
Long-term interest-bearing debt-to-equity (%)	0.81	0.68	0.72
Operating profit margin	15.8	13.4	7.7
Return on assets (using year-end balance for denominator)	7.6	6	0.7
Return on equity (using year-end balance for denominator)	17.4	12.5	1.5
Current ratio	2.1	2.1	1.9

Summarized financial data for each company is shown in Exhibit 1. A standard financial statement analysis form is included.

The companies both have unqualified audit reports and have similar accounting policies except for the following:

1. Fallsview uses FIFO while Canamora uses weighted-average cost for inventory.
2. Both companies use a combination of straight-line and units-of-production depreciation methods for property, plant, and equipment, but Fallsview uses useful lives that are approximately 25% longer than those used by Canamora.

Required:

Provide an analysis that compares Fallsview and Canamora from the perspective of:

1. A potential short-term creditor.
2. A potential common stock investor.

Assume a tax rate of 30% for both companies.

EXHIBIT 1

COMPARATIVE FINANCIAL STATEMENTS (IN MILLIONS)

Statements of Finanical Position

	Fallsview		Canamora	
	20X6	20X5	20X6	20X5
Assets				
Cash and cash equivalents	$ 208	$ 17	$ 20	$ 67
Temporary investments	24	—	—	—
Accounts receivable	304	321	267	242
Inventory	325	381	515	530
Total current assets	861	719	802	839
Property, plant, and equipment	1,469	1,518	1,984	1,903
Biological assets	230	190	27	22
Total assets	$2,560	$2,427	$2,813	$2,764

continued on next page

	Fallsview		Canamora	
	20X6	20X5	20X6	20X5
Liabilities				
Current liabilities				
Accounts payable	$ 480	$ 364	$ 323	$ 316
Current portion of long-term debt	53	49	4	15
Total current liabilities	533	413	327	331
Long-term debt	556	384	1,077	921
Other liabilities	170	65	96	97
Deferred income tax	147	363	38	112
	873	812	1,211	1,130
Total liabilities	1,406	1,225	1,538	1,461
Shareholders' equity				
Preferred shares	—	—	60	60
Common shares	657	657	889	880
Retained earnings	497	545	326	363
	1,154	1,202	1,275	1,303
Total liabilities and equity	$2,560	$2,427	$2,813	$2,764

STATEMENTS OF COMPREHENSIVE INCOME

	Fallsview		Canamora	
	20X6	20X5	20X6	20X5
Net sales	$1,986	$2,265	$2,066	$2,134
Costs and expenses				
Manufacturing/product costs	1,809	1,642	1,803	1,730
Change in fair value of biological assets	(50)	(20)	(10)	(8)
Depreciation and depletion	106	113	148	144
Selling and administration	58	67	90	90
	1,923	1,802	2,031	1,956
Operating income	**63**	**463**	**35**	**178**
Interest expense	64	60	52	40
Other (income) expense	(9)	(6)	(62)	25
Income before income tax	8	409	45	113
Income tax expense (recovery)	(18)	84	26	(34)
Net income and comprehensive income	$ 26	$ 325	$ 19	$ 147
Dividends				
Preferred	—	—	$ 2	$ 2
Common	$ 74	$ 25	$ 54	$ 50

(Source: [Adapted] © CGA-Canada. Reproduced with permission.)

TECHNICAL REVIEW

connect

TR22-1 Accounts Receivable Turnover: PWX Inc. has the following information for its years ended June 30:

	20X3	20X2	20X1
Gross Sales	$567,800	$650,700	$589,200
Accounts receivable	$62,500	$67,500	$53,200

Required:
Calculate the accounts receivable turnover and average collection period for 20X3 and 20X2. Comment on the trend. What additional information would an analyst require to properly understand this trend?

connect

TR22-2 Return on Assets Before Tax: Below is selected information for XTM Inc. for the years ended December 31:

	20X9	20X8	20X7
Revenue	$12,700,200	$10,520,000	$8,900,500
EBIT	$1,040,000	$956,000	$875,000
Total assets	$16,800,000	$17,300,000	$18,600,000

Required:
Calculate the return on assets before tax using the two components for 20X9 and 20X8. Discuss what the ratios reveal about the company.

connect

TR22-3 Cash Conversion Cycle: Selected data is provided below for KLS Co.:

	20X5	20X4	20X3
Revenue	$12,700,200	$10,520,000	$8,900,500
Cost of goods sold	$10,922,000	$8,940,000	$7,743,000
Accounts receivable	$1,220,000	$1,070,000	$975,400
Inventories	$1,690,300	$1,326,800	$909,000
Accounts payable	$1,346,000	$1,090,600	$997,000

Required:
Calculate the cash conversion cycle for 20X5 and 20X4. Is it likely that the company has short-term investments or requires short-term bank financing?

connect

TR22-4 Current Ratio and Quick Ratio: Selected accounts from the SFP of SMI Limited at 31 December 20X8 and 20X7 are provided below:

(in thousands of dollars)	20X8	20X7
Current assets		
Cash and cash equivalents	$ 17,100	$ 88,900
Short-term investments	65,700	75,900
Accounts receivable	373,900	370,100
Inventories	156,900	126,700
Prepaid expenses	156,700	45,100
Total current assets	$770,300	$706,700
Total current liabilities	$451,000	$425,000

Required:
Calculate the current ratio and quick ratio for SMI for 20X8 and 20X7. Comment on what the ratios reveal.

connect

TR22-5 Debt-to-Equity Ratio: Selected accounts from the SFP of ARM Co. at August 31 20X3 and 20X2:

(in thousands of dollars)	20X8	20X7
Short-term bank loans	6,790	5,800
Current portion of long-term debt	560	720
Long-term debt	89,700	92,000
Total shareholders' equity	75,900	93,400

Required:
Calculate the debt-to-equity ratio for ARM. What has happened to the leverage of the company, and why?

ASSIGNMENTS

★ excel

A22-1 Horizontal and Vertical Analysis—Income Statement: Simard Trading Company's income statement (condensed) for two years is shown below:

31 December	20X4	20X5
Gross sales	$550,000	$606,000
Sales returns	(10,000)	(6,000)
	540,000	600,000
Cost of goods sold	(270,000)	(360,000)
Gross margin	270,000	240,000
Expenses		
Selling expenses	120,600	130,700
Administrative expenses	75,600	66,000
Restructuring	10,800	8,000
Interest	5,400	6,000
Income tax expense	14,400	7,300
	226,800	218,000
Net income and comprehensive income	$ 43,200	$ 22,000

Required:

1. Prepare vertical percentage analysis of the income statement. Round to the nearest percent. Comment on any particularly notable changes from 20X4 to 20X5.
2. Prepare a horizontal percentage analysis of the income statement. Use a single-step format. Round to the nearest percent. Comment on any significant changes from 20X4 to 20X5.

★ **A22-2 Horizontal and Vertical Analysis—SFP:** Bryant Company's statement of financial position (condensed and unclassified) for two years is shown below:

Solution

31 December	20X4	20X5
Cash	$ 60,000	$ 80,000
Accounts receivable (net)	120,000	116,000
Inventory (FIFO)	144,000	192,000
Prepaid expenses	8,000	4,000
Funds and investments (at cost)	60,000	88,000
Property, plant, and equipment	560,000	664,000
Accumulated depreciation	(104,000)	(196,000)
Intangible assets	12,000	60,000
Total	$860,000	$1,008,000
Accounts payable	$160,000	$ 100,000
Other current liabilities	40,000	40,000
Long-term mortgage payable	200,000	172,000
Common shares, no-par	340,000	520,000
Retained earnings	120,000	176,000
Total	$860,000	$1,008,000

Required:

1. Prepare a comparative SFP in good form, including vertical percentage analysis. Round to the nearest percent.
2. Prepare a horizontal percentage analysis of the comparative SFP in good form. Round to the nearest percent.

★★ **A22-3 Vertical and Horizontal Analyses—SFP:** The SFP for Heresy Limited is as follows:

	31 December		
Statement of Financial Position	**20X5**	**20X4**	**20X3**
Cash	$ 516,000	$ 330,000	$ 295,000
Marketable securities	420,000	570,000	630,000
Receivables, net	450,000	510,000	550,000
Inventory	1,725,000	1,494,000	934,000
Property, plant, and equipment	7,644,000	5,439,000	4,039,000
Less: Accumulated depreciation	(1,951,200)	(1,461,000)	(976,000)
Intangible capital assets	378,000	405,000	350,000
	$9,181,800	$7,287,000	$5,822,000
Current liabilities	$ 279,000	$ 258,000	$ 579,000
Debentures payable	1,978,500	2,022,000	800,000
Common shares	3,450,000	2,100,000	2,100,000
Retained earnings	3,474,300	2,907,000	2,343,000
	$9,181,800	$7,287,000	$5,822,000

Required:

1. Prepare a comparative vertical percentage analysis. Round to the nearest percent.
2. Prepare a horizontal percentage analysis of the comparative SFP. Round to the nearest percent.
3. What conclusions can you reach about the changes in the company's asset and liability structure between 20X3 and 20X5?

★★ **A22-4 Ratio Interpretation:** Simon Inc. had the following events occur during the year. Simon follows IFRS.

connect

1. Simon has a fleet of trucks. It was recently decided that the company would replace old trucks with operating leases rather than buying trucks as it had in the past using borrowed funds.
2. The company repurchased shares during the year, at prices higher than issue prices.
3. The company has equity investments that have been classified as FVOCI. During the year, the investments increased significantly in value.

Required:

For each of the above transactions, discuss the implication on the company's debt-to-equity ratio, return-on-assets and operating profit margin. (Treat each event in isolation.)

★★ **A22-5 Ratio Interpretation:** Sweets Inc., a candy manufacturer that follows IFRS, had the following events occur during the year:

1. Sweets decided to increase the number of years in depreciating its property and equipment from 30 to 40 years for the property, and from 10 to 15 years for its equipment. The company uses the straight-line depreciation method.
2. Sweets has taken on a new customer that will result in a 25% increase in sales. However, to obtain this contract, Sweets had to agree to extend credit terms to 45 days. For all other customers, credit terms have been consistently 30 days.
3. In the current year, Sweets determined that tax loss carryforward benefits were now probable and set up the benefit in the current year. The benefits were significant and represented more than 30% of net income.

Required:

For each of the above changes, discuss the implication on the company's debt-to-total asset, days in receivable, current ratio, and operating margin. Treat each change in isolation.

★ **A22-6 Ratio Interpretation:** Remox Co. has the following selected information from its financial statements:

connect

(in thousands of dollars)	20X9	20X8
Revenues	2,330	1,805
Cost of goods sold	2,056	1,538
Accounts receivable	210	215
Inventories	230	225
Accounts payable	281	275

Required:

1. Calculate the cash conversion cycle for 20X9 and 20X8. (Use closing balances, rather than average balances, in the calculations.)
2. The company would like to improve its cash conversion cycle by three days by changing its days in inventory for 20X9. What would the revised inventory balance have to be to accomplish this reduction?

★★ **A22-7 Ratio Interpretation:** Wilcox Limited has total assets of $35,000,000, and manufactures fine hand tools. Selected financial ratios for Wilcox and industry averages are as follows:

	Wilcox			Industry
	20X5	20X4	20X3	Average
Current ratio	2.41	2.12	2.04	2.28
Quick ratio	1.11	1.10	1.05	1.22
Inventory turnover	2.62	2.78	2.90	3.50
Return on equity	0.16	0.14	0.15	0.11
Debt-to-equity ratio	1.44	1.37	1.41	0.95
Return on assets	.12	.11	.11	.10
Asset turnover	3.14	3.01	3.00	3.70
Operating margin	.06	.05	.05	.05

Required:

Referring to the information presented above:

1. Identify two financial ratios of particular interest to:
   a. A financial institution that provides an operating line of credit for daily cash management needs. The line of credit is secured with a charge on inventory.
   b. A supplier, about to decide whether to sell to Wilcox on credit.
   c. An investment banker, consulting with Wilcox on a potential public offering of common shares.
2. Discuss what these financial ratios reveal about Wilcox.

★★ **A22-8 Vertical and Horizontal Analyses:** Four-year comparative statement of comprehensive income and SFP for Firenza Products Inc. (FPI) are shown below. FPI has been undergoing an extensive restructuring in which the company has discontinued or sold several divisions in order to concentrate on its core business. As a result, the size of the company has decreased considerably.

Statement of Comprehensive Income

Years ended 31 December	20X8	20X7	20X6	20X5
Net sales	$284.1	$949.6	$1,388.8	$2,153.9
Cost of products sold	369.2	793.5	1,045.9	1,649.0
Depreciation and amortization	38.4	94.8	88.7	146.9
Selling and administrative	46.4	49.0	53.4	82.7
Operating earnings (loss)	(169.9)	12.3	200.8	275.3
Interest expense	(1.7)	(14.8)	(16.2)	(40.5)
Other income (expense)	32.6	(0.5)	(5.3)	34.8
Earnings (loss) from continuing operations before income tax	(139.0)	(3.0)	179.3	269.6
Income tax (recovery)	(46.9)	(2.6)	79.7	115.4
Earnings (loss) from continuing operations	(92.1)	(0.4)	99.6	154.2
Earnings (loss) from discontinued operations	390.7	119.9	54.8	—
Net earnings and comprehensive income	$298.6	$119.5	$ 154.4	$ 154.2

Condensed Statement of Financial Position

31 December	20X8	20X7	20X6	20X5
Assets				
Current assets	$ 957.7	$ 407.6	$ 126.2	$ 197.7
Assets of discontinued operations	—	647.4	1,262.9	—
Investments and other	90.6	36.3	65.8	97.8
Property, plant, and equipment	1,289.2	1,286.5	1,318.2	2,200.3
Net assets	$2,337.5	$2,377.8	$2,773.1	$2,495.8

Liabilities and shareholders' equity				
Current liabilities	$ 736.5	$ 329.0	$ 157.3	$ 131.3
Liabilities of discontinued operations	—	174.5	438.3	—
Long-term debt	—	—	75.0	227.6
Deferred income taxes	161.8	202.8	136.7	190.0
Common shares	250.0	250.0	250.0	250.0
Retained earnings	1,189.2	1,421.5	1,539.6	1,488.1
Preferred shares issued by subsidiaries	—	—	—	34.3
Noncontrolling interest	—	—	176.2	174.5
Total liabilities and shareholders' equity	$2,337.5	$2,377.8	$2,773.1	$2,495.8

Required:

1. Prepare a vertical analysis of both the SCI and the SFP.
2. Prepare a horizontal analysis of the SCI and SFP. Use 20X5 as the base year.
3. What conclusions about the company and its financial practices can you discern from your analysis?

★ **A22-9 Ratio Interpretation:** The following ratios are available for a three-year period for Woolfrey Limited:

	20X6	20X7	20X8
Current ratio	1.7	1.8	1.9
Quick ratio	1.1	0.9	1.0
Average collection period of accounts receivable	51 days	57 days	66 days
Inventory turnover	4.5	4.0	3.3
Debt to total assets	51%	46%	41%
Long-term debt to shareholders' equity	52%	57%	62%
Sales as a percentage of 20X6 sales	100%	103%	107%
Gross profit percentage	36%	35%	35%
Operating margin	7%	7%	7%
Return on total assets	8%	8%	8%
Return on shareholders' equity	14%	13%	13%

Required:

1. Explain why the current ratio is increasing while the quick ratio is decreasing.
2. Comment on the company's use of financial leverage.

★★ **A22-10 Compute and Explain Profitability Ratios:** The 20X5 comparative financial statements for Thompson Corporation reported the following selected information:

connect

	20X3	20X4	20X5
Sales revenue	$18,000,000	$19,500,000	$20,250,000
Net income	150,000	180,000	142,500
Interest expense, long-term debt	15,000	18,000	27,000
Income tax expense	60,000	90,000	90,000
Long-term debt	1,200,000	1,500,000	1,650,000
Shareholders' equity, common and preferred*	2,100,000	2,175,000	2,190,000
Total assets	5,250,000	5,250,000	5,700,000
Preferred share dividends	9,000	15,000	18,000
Income tax rate	30%	35%	40%

*Preferred shares, $150,000 in all years.

Required:

1. Based on the above financial data, compute the following ratios for 20X4 and 20X5:
   a. Return on total assets, before tax
   b. Return on total assets, after tax
   c. Return on long-term capital, before tax
   d. Return on long-term capital, after tax
   e. Return on common shareholders' equity
   f. Operating margin
   g. Asset turnover
2. As an investor in the common shares of Thompson, which ratio would you prefer as a primary measure of profitability? Why?
3. Explain any significant trends that appear to be developing.

★★ **A22-11 Ratio Analysis:** The table below shows selected information reported by a Canadian retailer during a five-year period:

(in millions of dollars, except EPS)	20X5	20X4	20X3	20X2	20X1
Gross operating revenue	$ 8,687	$ 9,121	$ 8,606	$ 8,253	$ 7,714
Operating expenses	7,788	8,200	7,694	7,416	6,896
Depreciation and amortization	248	226	207	192	185
Interest expense	147	123	63	76	84
Income taxes	144	168	200	201	190
Net earnings	335	375	412	355	330
Current assets	5,113	3,979	3,138	2,541	2,973
Inventories	934	917	779	667	675
Property and equipment (net)	3,180	3,199	3,284	2,881	2,744
Total assets	8,790	7,784	6,765	5,805	5,956
Current liabilities	2,564	2,000	2,114	1,664	1,821
Long-term debt (excl. current)	1,102	1,374	1,342	1,168	1,171
Shareholders' equity	3,687	3,565	3,108	2,785	2,511
Basic EPS	$ 4.10	$ 4.60	$ 5.05	$ 4.35	$ 4.04
No. of common shares at year-end (000s)	78,178	78,178	78,048	78,047	78,033
No. of retail outlets	1,216	1,207	1,168	1,130	1,112

Required:

Based on the data above, analyze the changes that have occurred over this five-year period in terms of profitability and solvency.

★ **A22-12 Ratio Analysis; Liquidity and Efficiency:** The condensed financial information given below was taken from the annual financial statements of Conter Corporation:

	20X3	20X4	20X5
Current assets (including inventory)	$ 840,000	$1,008,000	$1,176,000
Current liabilities	630,000	672,000	588,000
Cash sales	3,360,000	3,276,000	3,444,000
Credit sales	840,000	1,176,000	1,050,000
Cost of goods sold	2,352,000	2,457,000	2,520,000
Inventory (ending)	504,000	588,000	420,000
Accounts receivable	252,000	268,800	256,200
Total assets (net)	4,200,000	5,040,000	5,880,000
Projected daily operating expenditures	12,600	13,020	12,180

Required:

1. Based on the above data, calculate the following ratios for 20X4 and 20X5. Briefly explain the significance of each ratio listed. Use the following format:

Ratio	20X4	20X5	Significance
Current			
Quick			
Defensive interval			
Asset turnover			
Accounts receivable turnover			
Average collection period of accounts receivable			
Inventory turnover			

2. Evaluate the overall results of the ratios, including trends.

★★ **A22-13 Compute and Summarize Significance of Ratios:** Fader Corporation's 20X4 and 20X5 SFP and 20X5 SCI are as follows (in millions of dollars, except per share amounts):

Solution

connect

Condensed Statement of Financial Position

31 December	20X5	20X4
ASSETS		
Cash	$ 11	$ 20
Investments (short-term)	3	4
Accounts receivable (net of allowance)	23	19
Inventory (FIFO)	31	37
Prepaid expenses	4	3
Investments, long-term	31	31
Property, plant, and equipment (net of accumulated depreciation of $29 (20X4), $37 (20X5)	81	72
Total assets	$184	$186
LIABILITIES AND SHAREHOLDERS' EQUITY		
Accounts payable	$ 22	$ 10
Accrued liabilities	2	2
Notes payable, long-term	41	45
Common shares, no par (60,000 shares outstanding)	76	76
Retained earnings (including 20X4 and 20X5 income)	43	53
Totals	$184	$186

Statement of Comprehensive Income, 20X5

Sales revenue (1/3 were credit sales)	$153
Investment revenue	4
Cost of goods sold	(70)
Distribution expense	(20)
Administrative expense (includes $8 of depreciation)	(15)
Interest expense	(4)
Income tax expense (the tax rate is 40%)	(20)
Net income and comprehensive income	$ 28
Additional information:	
Cash flow from operations	$ 22

Required:

Compute the 20X5 ratios that measure:

a. Profitability (after tax only)
b. Efficiency

c. Solvency
d. Liquidity

For each category, use a format similar to the following (example given for 20X4):

Ratio	Formula	Computation	Significance
Current ratio	$\frac{\text{Current assets}}{\text{Current liabilities}}$	$83 ÷$12 = 6.9	Short-term liquidity; adequacy of working capital

★ **A22-14 Selected Ratios:** The 20X9 condensed SCI and the 20X9 and 20X8 condensed SFP for Farrokh Limited are shown below. All sales are on credit.

Condensed Statement of Comprehensive Income

Year ended 31 December 20X9	
Sales revenue (all on credit)	$40,000
Cost of goods sold	22,500
Gross profit	17,500
Operating expenses	12,100
Operating income	5,400
Interest expense	1,500
Income before income taxes	3,900
Income tax expense	1,100
Net income and comprehensive income	$ 2,800

Condensed Statement of Financial Position

31 December	20X9	20X8
Cash	$ 5,500	$ 7,500
Accounts receivable (net)	13,500	14,500
Inventory	8,000	6,000
Plant and equipment	40,000	38,000
Accumulated depreciation	(18,000)	(22,500)
Land	35,000	30,500
Total	$84,000	$74,000
Accounts payable	$ 5,800	$ 6,000
Long-term notes payable	13,700	10,000
Common shares	20,000	15,000
Retained earnings	44,500	43,000
Total	$84,000	$74,000

Required:

Compute the following ratios for 20X9:

a. Return on assets before taxes
b. Asset turnover
c. Operating margin
d. Return on shareholders' equity
e. Inventory turnover
f. Average collection period of accounts receivable

(Source: [Adapted] © CGA-Canada. Reproduced with permission.)

★ **A22-15 Profitability and Solvency Ratios, Competing Companies:** Abacus Limited and Zandi Corporation are competing businesses. Abacus owns all of its operating assets, financed largely by secured loans. Zandi rents its operating assets from a major industrial leasing company. The 20X2 SCIs and SFPs for the two companies are shown below.

Statements of Comprehensive Income

Year ended 31 December 20X2	Abacus	Zandi
Sales revenue	$ 540,000	$270,000
Direct costs of providing services	300,000	150,000
Depreciation	100,000	10,000
Other expenses	60,000	87,000
Total operating expenses	460,000	247,000
Net operating earnings	80,000	23,000
Interest expense	24,000	—
Earnings before income taxes	56,000	23,000
Provision for income taxes	17,000	7,000
Net earnings and comprehensive income	$ 39,000	$ 16,000

Statements of Financial Position

31 December 20X2	Abacus	Zandi
Current assets	$ 260,000	$130,000
Property, plant, and equipment	1,000,000	50,000
Accumulated depreciation	(600,000)	(30,000)
Total assets	660,000	$150,000
Current liabilities	$ 120,000	$ 60,000
Long-term liabilities	360,000	—
Common shares	100,000	50,000
Retained earnings	80,000	40,000
Total liabilities and shareholders' equity	$ 660,000	$150,000

Required:

1. Compute the following ratios for both companies (for convenience, use 20X2 year-end balance sheet amounts instead of averages):
   a. Operating margin
   b. Asset turnover
   c. Return on assets
   d. Return on share equity
   e. Total debt-to-shareholder's equity
2. Evaluate the two companies, based on the ratios you have calculated. Which company do you think is more profitable?

★ **A22-16 Competing Companies, Continuation:** Refer to the information in A22-15; Zandi's financial statements contain the following note disclosure:

Commitments:
The Company has commitments for operating lease payments for the next five years as follows:

20X3	$53,000
20X4	49,000
20X5	45,000
20X6	40,000
20X7	35,000

Required:

Determine how this additional information would affect the ratios for Zandi that are required in A22-15. Assume that the disclosed lease payments are due at the end of each year and that Zandi's incremental borrowing rate is 8%. Ignore any income tax impact.

★★ **A22-17 Ratio Analysis—Segmented Information:** Drug Inc. has operating segments defined by geographic regions. Below is the information that was provided in the notes related to these segments:

connect

(in millions of Canadian dollars)	Canada	United States	Europe
Revenues	2,389	5,860	1,458
Gross margin	624	1,758	408
Operating expenses	(502)	(1,348)	(335)
Depreciation and amortization included in operating expenses	50	120	38
Total assets	3,689	7,900	1,690

Required:

1. What ratios can be calculated using the above information?
2. What do these ratios reveal? Why might any differences arise in these ratios?

★★ **A22-18 Leverage—Sell Share Capital versus Debt, Analysis:** Bui Limited is considering building a second plant at a cost of $7,600,000. Management has two alternatives to obtain the funds: (1) sell additional common shares or (2) issue $7,600,000, five-year bonds payable at 10% interest. Management believes that the bonds can be sold at par for $7,600,000 and the shares at $80 per share. The statements (before the new financing) show the following selected information:

Average net income for past several years (net of tax)	400,000
Long-term liabilities	$1,600,000
Common shares, no par (40,000 shares)	3,200,000
Retained earnings	1,300,000

The average income tax rate is 30%. Dividends per share have been $6 per share per year. Expected increase in pre-tax income (excluding interest expense) from the new plant is $1,500,000 per year.

Required:

1. Prepare an analysis to show, for each financing alternative,
   a. Expected total net income after the addition;
   b. After-tax cash flows from the company to prospective owners of the new capital; and
   c. The (leverage) advantage or disadvantage to the present shareholders of issuing the bonds to obtain the financing, as represented by comparing return-on-assets to return-on-equity.
2. What are the principal arguments for and against issuing the bonds, as opposed to selling the common shares?

★★ **A22-19 Comparative Analysis:** Frank Smythe, the owner of Cuppola Limited, has asked you to compare the operations and financial position of his company with those of Ling Limited, a large company in the same business and a company that Frank Smythe considers representative of the industry.

	Cuppola Limited		Ling Limited	
	20X1	**20X0**	**20X1**	**20X0**
Statements of Financial Position				
Assets				
Cash	$ 100,000	$ 20,000	$ 100,000	$ 125,000
Accounts receivable	70,000	60,000	800,000	750,000
Inventories	230,000	190,000	2,400,000	1,825,000
	400,000	270,000	3,300,000	2,700,000
Property, plant, and equipment	500,000	500,000	5,300,000	5,000,000
Accumulated depreciation	(300,000)	(270,000)	(2,600,000)	(2,300,000)
Goodwill	—	—	500,000	500,000
	200,000	230,000	3,200,000	3,200,000
	$ 600,000	$ 500,000	$6,500,000	$5,900,000
Liabilities and shareholders' equity				
Bank indebtedness	$ 40,000	$ 30,000	$ 500,000	$ 300,000
Trade accounts payable	135,000	100,000	1,300,000	650,000
Current portion of long-term debt	20,000	20,000	300,000	300,000
	195,000	150,000	2,100,000	1,250,000
Long-term debt	30,000	50,000	1,400,000	1,700,000
	225,000	200,000	3,500,000	2,950,000
Shares issued and outstanding				
—preferred	—	—	500,000	500,000
—common	50,000	50,000	1,500,000	1,500,000
Retained earnings	325,000	250,000	1,000,000	950,000
	375,000	300,000	3,000,000	2,950,000
	$ 600,000	$ 500,000	$6,500,000	$5,900,000
Statements of Comprehensive Income				
Sales	$1,300,000	$1,000,000	$9,000,000	$7,500,000
Cost of sales	(936,000)	(700,000)	(6,120,000)	(5,250,000)
Expenses, including income tax	(266,500)	(250,000)	(2,100,000)	(1,800,000)
Net income and comprehensive income	$ 97,500	$ 50,000	$ 780,000	$ 450,000

Required:

Compare the operations and financial positions of the two companies, supporting your comments with useful ratios and percentages.

★★ **A22-20 Investment Analysis:** Sandy Panchaud has come to you for some independent financial advice. He is considering investing some of his money in an operating company, and he wants to know which of the two alternatives he has identified is the better investment. They are both in the same industry, and Mr. Panchaud feels he could buy either for book value. The most recent statements for each company are provided below:

	Company A	Company B
Statements of Comprehensive Income		
Sales	$2,797,000	$2,454,000
Cost of goods sold	1,790,000	1,594,000
Gross margin	1,007,000	860,000
Operating expenses	807,000	663,000
Operating income	200,000	197,000
Interest expense	70,000	43,000
Income before income tax	130,000	154,000
Income tax expense	52,000	62,000
Net income and comprehensive income	$ 78,000	$ 92,000

	Company A	Company B
Statements of Financial Position		
Cash	$ 66,000	$ 27,000
Accounts receivable (net)	241,000	262,000
Merchandise inventory	87,000	110,000
Prepaid expenses	12,000	7,000
Plant and equipment (net)	792,000	704,000
	$1,198,000	$1,110,000
Accounts payable and accrued liabilities	$ 191,000	$ 173,000
Long-term debt	635,000	310,000
Common shares	50,000	200,000
Retained earnings	322,000	427,000
	$1,198,000	$1,110,000

Required:

Prepare a response to Mr. Panchaud. Your response should include an appropriate selection of ratios and a common-size (vertical analysis) income statement.

★★ **A22-21 Recasting, Selected Ratios (Appendix):** A loan officer for the Dominion Bank of Alberta wishes to recast her client's financial statements so that they reflect income tax expense on a taxes payable basis. The tax rate is 30%. One of her clients is Frobisher Bay Corporation (FBC). FBC's condensed year-end 20X4 statements are shown below:

Statement of Comprehensive Income

Year ended 31 December 20X4	
Sales revenue	$660,000
Cost of goods sold	360,000
Depreciation expense	72,000
Interest expense	12,000
Other expenses	96,000
	540,000
Earnings before income tax	120,000
Income tax:	
—current	14,400
—deferred	21,600
	36,000
Net earnings and comprehensive income	$ 84,000

Statement of Financial Position

31 December 20X4	
Current assets	$144,000
Capital assets:	
—Tangible (net)	624,000
—Identifiable intangible	168,000
Total assets	$936,000
Current liabilities:	
Accounts payable	96,000
Accrued liabilities	24,000
	120,000
Long-term debt	384,000
Deferred income tax	192,000
Total liabilities	696,000
Common shares	60,000
Retained earnings	180,000
Total shareholders' equity	240,000
Total liabilities and shareholders' equity	$936,000

Required:

1. Recast FBC's statements.
2. Compute the following ratios, both before and after recasting the statements:
   a. Operating margin
   b. Return on total assets (after tax)
   c. Total liabilities to shareholders' equity

★★ **A22-22 Integrative Problem, ASPE:** The following information is available for Davison Limited, a private company, for the year ended 31 December 20X6:

Solution

connect

Balance Sheet 31 December

	($ thousands)	
	20X6	**20X5**
Cash	$1,720	$1,110
Marketable securities	450	550
Receivables, net	1,150	1,170
Inventory	2,575	2,110
Property, plant, and equipment	3,984	3,396
Less: Accumulated amortization	(1,650)	(1,487)
Intangible assets	555	417
Goodwill	135	135
	$8,919	$7,401
Current liabilities	$2,190	$1,900
Convertible bond payable	833	834
Future income taxes	619	585
Preferred shares	500	500
Common stock conversion rights	166	166
Common shares	2,150	1,700
Retained earnings	2,461	1,716
	$8,919	$7,401

Statement of Earnings

Year ended 31 December	20X6
Sales (on account)	$10,450
Cost of goods sold	7,619
	2,831
Operating expenses	1,548
	1,283
Income tax	385
Net income	$ 898

Additional information:

- The company has a $1,000,000, 10% bond outstanding. Each $1,000 bond is convertible into 50 common shares at the investor's option. The bond proceeds were split between the debt and equity when the bond was issued. In 20X6, interest expense of $98 per bond was recognized.
- The tax rate is 30%.
- In 20X6, stock options were outstanding to key employees, allowing them to buy 40,000 common shares for $16 per share at any time after 1 January 20X18. The common shares were recently valued to be $20 for 20X6.
- 420,000 common shares were outstanding on 31 December 20X6; 40,000 of those shares had been issued for cash on 1 February 20X6.
- Preferred shares are cumulative and have a dividend of $4 per share; 10,000 shares are outstanding. Each share can be converted into four common shares at any time.
- Davidson Limited declared and paid dividends totalling $25,000 in 20X6.

Required:

Calculate the following ratios for 20X6 based on the financial statements above:

a. Debt-to-equity (total debt)
b. Inventory turnover
c. Quick ratio
d. Return on assets (after tax)
e. Return on common shareholders' equity
f. Accounts receivable turnover (all sales are on account)
g. Asset turnover
h. Return on long-term capital, after tax
i. Operating margin

connect LEARNSMART SMARTBOOK

For more information on the resources available from McGraw-Hill Ryerson, go to www.mcgrawhill.ca/he/solutions.

APPENDIX

Statement of Cash Flows

COMPREHENSIVE ILLUSTRATION

The statement of cash flows (SCF) was the subject of Chapter 5 of Volume One of this text. Subsequent chapters have reviewed the impact of various transactions and accounting policies on the SCF, when topics were covered. This appendix summarizes that material and reviews a comprehensive SCF example.

The SCF has three main sections—operating, investing, and financing activities. The *operating activities* section deals with cash generated, or used, from the primary revenue-producing activities of the enterprise, and the related expenditures. The operating activities section has two formats, the indirect method, which involves a reconciliation of earnings to cash flow, and the less common direct method, which shows cash inflows from customers, and cash outflows to suppliers, employees, and so on. When the indirect method of presentation is used, the adjustments for non-cash items are typically presented first, with a subtotal, and then the adjustments for changes in statement of financial position (SFP) elements, providing a two-step method of presentation.

The *investing activities* section deals with cash flows related to long-term assets (fixed assets), investments, and other assets, both purchase and sale. The *financing activities* section includes cash flow from or for borrowing, and transactions with shareholders.

Cash consists of cash balances, cash-equivalent investments with initial term of under 90 days, less bank overdrafts if those overdrafts regularly fluctuate during the period. Cash on the SCF must be reconciled to the balances reported on the SFP.

Non-cash transactions are omitted from the SCF, and *offsetting* (e.g., offsetting loan repayments with new loans) is not permitted.

Cash flow for/from income tax, cash received for dividend or interest income, and cash paid for interest must be shown separately. This should be accomplished on the SCF, but some companies use supplementary disclosure to convey this information.

The reporting standard allows some *policy choice* for classification:

- Cash paid for interest on borrowings can be classified in operating activities or in financing activities.
- Cash paid to shareholders for dividends may be classified in operating activities or in financing activities.
- Cash interest received and cash dividends received by the investor may be classified in operating activities or in investing activities.

The major points to remember about the SCF are summarized in Exhibit A-1.

EXHIBIT A-1

STATEMENT OF CASH FLOWS

Cash	• Cash is defined as cash plus cash-equivalent temporary investments (e.g., money market certificates; maximum original 90-day term) less bank overdrafts that regularly fluctuate.
Comprehensive income	• Begin SCF operating activities (indirect method) with earnings, not comprehensive income. Elements of OCI usually are non-cash items, but if they involve cash, they are classified according to their nature.
Discontinued operations	• Begin SCF with earnings before discontinued operations. • Show cash flow impact of discontinued operation separately in appropriate section.
Income tax	• Cash paid or received for income tax is usually classified in operating activities. Cash inflow or outflow must be separately disclosed. • If tax relates to a capital transaction (e.g., tax triggered by a dividend payment to shareholders), then it is included with that capital transaction in another section of the SCF. • The change in deferred income tax is a non-cash item and is an element in determining the amount paid.
SFP elements related to revenues and expenses	• Adjust earnings for the change in SFP elements items that relate to revenue or expense items. (e.g., accounts receivable and payable, inventory, prepaids, etc.) • If a SFP element item does not relate to earnings (e.g., dividends payable), adjust for the change in the appropriate section (e.g., financing).
Investments	• Purchase price is an outflow under investing activities; proceeds of sale are an inflow. • Recognized changes in fair value of FVTPL investments are non-cash items in earnings and are adjusted in the operating activities sections of the SCF. If the investment is a FVTOCI investment, changes in fair value are recorded to OCI, and are non-cash items that are excluded from the SCF. • Gains and losses on sale are adjusted in operating activities. • Cash inflow from interest or dividends may be classified in operating activities or in investing activities. Cash inflow must be separately disclosed in either case. • Equity-based investment revenue is backed out of earnings; dividends received from an associate are included in operating (or investing) activities.
Fixed assets	• Purchase price (if cash) is an outflow under investing activities; proceeds of sale are an inflow. • Non-cash transactions (e.g., swaps) excluded from the SCF. Transactions that are partially cash and partially non-cash are included on the SCF at the cash amount. • Depreciation is added back in operating activities as a non-cash expense. • Gains and losses on retirement are adjusted in operating activities. • Impairment writedowns are added back in operating activities. Impairment reversals are deducted.
Identifiable intangible assets	• Purchase price (if cash) is an outflow under investing activities; proceeds of sale are an inflow. • Amortization is added back in operating activities. • Impairment writedowns are added back as a non-cash charge in operating activities. Impairment reversals are deducted.

EXHIBIT A-1 (*cont'd*)

Goodwill	• Part of a larger purchase of a business unit; purchase price (if cash) is an outflow under investing activities; proceeds of sale are an inflow. • Impairment writedowns are added back in operating activities.
Borrowing	• Amount borrowed is an inflow under financing activities; repayments are outflows. • Netting new and old loans is not permitted. • Interest paid may be classified in operating activities or in financing activities. Cash outflow must be separately disclosed in either case. • Amortization of discount is a non-cash item and is an element in determining the amount of interest paid. • Gains and losses on retirement are adjusted in operating activities.
Equity	• Cash investment by shareholders is an inflow under financing activities. • Amount paid to retire shares is an outflow under financing activities. • The difference between the amount paid to retire shares and the average issuance price changes equity accounts and is not listed separately on the SCF.
Dividends	• Dividends paid may be classified in operating activities or in financing activities. • Stock dividends and splits are not cash flows and do not appear on the SCF.
Complex financial instruments	• Amount borrowed/invested is an inflow under financing activities; repayments are outflows. • If a hybrid instrument is issued, only one cash inflow is recorded on the SCF for both elements. • Amortization of discount is adjusted in operating activities and is an element of determining the amount of interest paid. • Conversion of a financial instrument into common shares is a non-cash transaction and is excluded from the SCF. • Gains and losses on retirement are adjusted in operating activities.
Stock options	• Expense is adjusted in operating activities; added back as a non-cash transaction. • Cash received for shares issued under options, if any, is recorded as an inflow in financing activities. The value of options recorded in common shares upon exercise is a non-cash transaction and is not recorded on the SCF. • If options are recorded on the receipt of non-cash assets, the transaction is a non-cash transaction and is excluded from the SCF.
Leases	• Increase in assets and liabilities because of a new finance lease for the lessee is a non-cash transaction and excluded from the SCF. • Reduction in lease liability is an outflow under financing activities. • Depreciation on leased assets is added back in operating activities. • Interest is classified and disclosed as per borrowing section.
Pensions	• Change in accrued benefit pension obligation on the SFP recorded in AOCI is non-cash and not included on the SCF. • Change in accrued benefit pension obligation on the SFP is adjusted in operating activities. • Amount paid to pension trustee is adjusted in operating activities.

COMPREHENSIVE SCF EXAMPLE

The data for a comprehensive example is found in Exhibit A-2 and includes the financial statements and additional information concerning critical transactions. To analyze the data, the changes in the transactions will be translated into journal entries, then entered into the T-accounts that support the SCF. The information may also be analyzed through journal entries alone or in a worksheet. All analysis alternatives will produce the same SCF.

EXHIBIT A-2

HUM ENTERPRISES LIMITED

The records of Hum Enterprises Limited show the following:

Statement of Earnings, for the Year Ended 31 December 20X8:

Sales		$1,402,300
Cost of goods sold		631,100
Gross profit		771,200
Operating expenses and other:		
Depreciation expense	$ 43,200	
Selling expenses	107,900	
Administrative expenses	119,900	
Interest expense	35,300	
Other expenses	43,200	
Investment revenue	(1,400)	
Loss on sale of machinery	16,000	
Total expenses		364,100
Earnings before income tax		407,100
Income tax expense		174,000
Earnings		$ 233,100

SCI, for the Year Ended 31 December 20X8:

Earnings	$ 233,100
Plus: Increase in fair value, FVTOCI investment	44,300
Less: Realized gain on sale of FVTOCI investment	(2,800)
Less: Actuarial loss on defined benefit pension	(20,000)
Comprehensive income	$ 254,600

Statement of Changes in Equity, for the Year Ended 31 December 20X8:

	Common shares	CSCR	CC: Options	Retained earnings	AOCI: Pension	AOCI: Investments
Opening balance	$ 930,000	$83,300	$60,000	$209,000	$(44,000)	$22,000
Comprehensive income:						
Earnings				233,100		
Pension and FVTOCI adjustments					(20,000)	44,300
FVTOCI transfer on realization				2,800		(2,800)
Dividends				(75,500)		
Share issuance; machinery	261,100					
Share issuance; bond	735,500	(83,300)				
Share issuance; options	51,400		(14,000)			
Options recorded			24,000			
Share retirement	(478,000)			(121,200)		
Closing balance	$1,500,000	$ 0	$70,000	$248,200	$(64,000)	$63,500

continued on next page

EXHIBIT A-2 (*cont'd*)

Statement of Financial Position, Year Ended

December 31	20X8	20X7
Assets:		
Cash	$ 40,000	$ 29,200
FVTOCI investments	226,300	70,700
Accounts receivable (net)	112,500	147,200
Inventory	179,100	187,300
Prepaid rent	4,700	—
Land	276,000	204,000
Machinery	1,899,000	1,743,900
Accumulated depreciation	(801,600)	(839,000)
Goodwill	890,400	890,400
Total	$2,826,400	$2,433,700
Liabilities and shareholders' equity:		
Accounts payable	$ 139,000	$ 215,200
Salaries payable	46,100	45,500
Taxes payable	21,000	29,000
Bonds payable; 6%	—	652,200
Bonds payable; 7.2%	600,000	—
Discount on 7.2% bonds payable	(11,200)	—
Deferred income tax	148,900	184,800
Accrued pension benefit liability	64,900	46,700
Common shares, no-par	1,500,000	930,000
Common stock conversion rights	—	83,300
Contributed capital: stock options	70,000	60,000
Retained earnings	248,200	209,000
AOCI: pension	(64,000)	(44,000)
AOCI: investments	63,500	22,000
Total	$2,826,400	$2,433,700

Analysis of selected accounts and transactions:

1. Issued additional 7.2% bonds payable for cash, $588,000.
2. Cash dividends were declared and paid.
3. A FVTOCI investment with an original cost of $47,200 was sold for $50,000 cash at the beginning of 20X8. This investment had a carrying value of $50,000 (fair value) at that time. Realized gains are transferred to retained earnings. FVTOCI investments with a cost of $161,300 were acquired during the year.
4. There is a stock option plan for senior administrative staff, accounted for using the fair value method. Stock options with a book value of $14,000 were exchanged, along with $37,400 cash, for common shares in 20X8. The remaining increase in the stock options account is explained by additional compensation expense recorded, using the fair value method.
5. The 6% bond payable was converted into common shares at the beginning of the fiscal year.
6. Land was acquired for cash.
7. Machinery with an original cost of $106,000 and a net book value of $25,400 was sold for a loss of $16,000. Additional machinery for other activities was acquired for common shares.

8. Common shares with an average original issue price of $478,000 were retired for $599,200.
9. The accrued pension benefit liability was increased by $20,000 due to an actuarial revaluation and $1,800 because of the difference between funding and the pension expense.

The entries that follow *re-create* the transactions for the year, reflecting (in summary) the company's entries for the year. The entries must be sufficient to change the opening balance to the closing balance, per the financial statements provided. In the re-creation of entries, the SCF amounts are represented by cash or operating activities items in an entry.

As a first step, earnings is entered as an increase to retained earnings and the first item in the operating activities sections:

a. *Cash: operating activities,* net earnings	233,100	
Retained earnings		233,100

Next, the changes in all non-cash working capital accounts that relate to revenue and expense items are adjusted to the operating activities section:

b. Cash: operating activities—decrease in accounts receivable	34,700	
Accounts receivable		34,700
c. *Cash: operating activities*—decrease in inventory	8,200	
Inventory		8,200
d. Prepaid rent	4,700	
Cash: operating activities—increase in prepaid rent		4,700
e. Accounts payable	76,200	
Cash: operating activities—decrease in accounts payable		76,200
f. *Cash: operating activities*—increase in salaries payable	600	
Salaries payable		600
g. Taxes payable	8,000	
Cash: operating activities—decrease in taxes payable		8,000

The obvious non-cash expenses are adjusted:

h. *Cash: operating activities*—depreciation expense	43,200	
Accumulated depreciation		43,200
i. Deferred income tax	35,900	
Cash: operating activities—deferred income tax		35,900
j. *Cash: operating activities*—discount amortization	800	
Discount on bonds payable ($12,000 – $11,200)		800

The original discount on the bond was $12,000 ($600,000 – $588,000). The discount appears as $11,200 on the SFP, implying discount amortization of $800 during the period.

The accrued pension benefit liability increased by $20,000 this period, caused by an actuarial revaluation that was recorded in AOCI. The amount does not change cash flow and is not recorded on the SCF. The remaining $1,800 change in the accrued pension benefit liability is caused by the difference between pension expense and pension funding, and is shown in the operating section of the SCF:

k. AOCI—pension	20,000	
Accrued pension benefit liability		20,000
l. Accrued pension benefit liability	1,800	
Cash: operating activities—pension liability		1,800

Remaining non-cash items, and gains and losses on various transactions will be adjusted as other accounts are analyzed.

FVTOCI investments were purchased during the period:

m. FVTOCI investments	161,300	
Cash: investing activities—purchased FVTOCI investments		161,300

A FVTOCI investment was sold for $50,000 cash, as the question states. The investment has a carrying value of $50,000 at the time of sale. The investment had been written up from cost of $47,200 through the recognition of an unrealized holding gain in accumulated other comprehensive income. This unrealized holding gain is reclassified to retained earnings when any actual sale takes place.

n. *Cash: investing activities*—sale of FVTOCI investments (fair value)	50,000	
FVTOCI investments		50,000
Accumulated other comprehensive income: investments ($50,000 – $47,200)	2,800	
Retained earnings		2,800

The remaining change in the investments account and accumulated other comprehensive income is explained by the revaluation of FVTOCI investments to fair value at year-end. There is no effect on the SCF.

o. FVTOCI investments ($70,700 – $50,000 + $161,300 = $182,000 vs. $226,300)	44,300	
Accumulated other comprehensive income: investments ($22,000 – $2,800 = $19,200 vs. $63,500)		44,300

Land was purchased during the period:

p. Land ($204,000 – $276,000)	72,000	
Cash: investing activities—purchase of land		72,000

Machinery was sold:

q. *Cash: investing activities*—sale of machinery ($25,400 – $16,000)	9,400	
Accumulated depreciation ($106,000 – $25,400)	80,600	
Cash: operating activities—loss on sale on machinery (as reported)	16,000	
Machinery		106,000

The accumulated depreciation account has been increased by current-year depreciation expense and decreased by the accumulated depreciation on the machinery sold. These two entries completely explain the change in the accumulated depreciation account.

Machinery was acquired for common shares. This transaction is assumed to explain the remaining change in the machinery account. The acquisition is a non-cash transaction that is not reflected on the SCF:

r. Machinery ($1,899,000 – ($1,743,900 – $106,000)	261,100	
Common shares		261,100

Bonds were converted into common shares, which explains the decrease in the 6% bond and the common stock conversion rights account. Again, this is a non-cash transaction that does not appear on the SCF.

s. Bonds payable, 6%	652,200	
Common stock conversion rights	83,300	
Common shares		735,500

Bonds were also issued in 20X8:

t. *Cash: financing activities*—issuance of bond	588,000	
Discount on bonds payable	12,000	
Bonds payable, 7.2%		600,000

The original discount was $12,000; it has already been amortized by $800, and thus the closing balance of $11,200 is fully explained in the entries.

Common shares were retired, at a price higher than average issuance price. The difference is a direct debit to retained earnings:

u. Common shares	478,000	
Retained earnings	121,200	
Cash: financing activities—retirement of common shares		599,200

Common shares were issued under the terms of stock options, which results in a cash inflow to the company:

v. *Cash: financing activities*—issued common shares	37,400	
Contributed capital: stock options	14,000	
Common stock		51,400

The common stock account has had many changes, but the entries now explain all the changes. The opening balance was $930,000, decreased by $478,000 because of the retirement and increased by common shares issued for machinery, $261,100; common shares issued on bond conversion, $735,500; and shares issued under option terms, $51,400. This equals the closing balance of $1,500,000.

Stock options were also recorded as compensation expense, which is a non-cash expense:

w. *Cash: operating activities*—non-cash compensation expense	24,000	
Contributed capital: stock options ($60,000 – $14,000 = $46,000 vs. $70,000)		24,000

Finally, there were cash dividends:

x. Retained earning ($209,000 + $233,100 + $2,800 – $121,200 = $323,700 – $248,200)	75,500	
Cash: financing activities—dividends		75,500

These entries retrace the effects of all transactions, isolating their impact on the SCF. The next step is to post them to T-accounts (Exhibit A-3), and then prepare the SCF itself (Exhibit A-4). In Exhibit A-4, it is assumed that Hum uses the two-step indirect method to present the operating activities, and separate disclosure of cash flow for interest, income tax, and cash received for dividends and/or interest is accomplished through a separate disclosure note. (Note that these cash flows should be shown on the face of the SCF, but there is variation in practice, and we will begin with this simple presentation that is supplemented with note disclosure.) Dividends paid to shareholders are classified in financing activities.

EXHIBIT A-3

HUM ENTERPRISES LIMITED

T-Account Analysis

Cash

Opening	**29,200**		
Operating activities			
a) Net earnings	233,100	d) Increase in prepaid rent	4,700
b) Decrease in accounts receivable	34,700	e) Decrease in accounts payable	76,200
c) Decrease in inventory	8,200	g) Decrease in taxes payable	8,000
f) Increase in salaries payable	600	i) Decrease in deferred tax	35,900
h) Depreciation expense	43,200	l) Decrease in pension liability	1,800
j) Discount amortization	800		
q) Loss on sale of machinery	16,000		
w) Compensation expense	24,000		
Investing activities			
n) Sold FVTOCI investments	50,000	m) Purchased FVTOCI investments	161,300
q) Sold machinery	9,400	p) Purchased land	72,000
Financing activities			
t) Issued bond	588,000	u) Retired shares	599,200
v) Issued shares	37,400	x) Dividends	75,500
Closing	**40,000**		

continued on next page

EXHIBIT A-3 (*cont'd*)

FVTOCI Investments

Op.	70,700		
m)	161,300	n)	50,000
o)	44,300		
Cl.	226,300		

Accounts receivable (net)

Op.	147,200		
		b)	34,700
Cl.	112,500		

Inventory

Op.	187,300		
		c)	8,200
Cl.	179,100		

Prepaid rent

Op.	—		
d)	4,700		
Cl.	4,700		

Land

Op.	204,000		
p)	72,000		
Cl.	276,000		

Machinery

Op.	1,743,900		
r)	261,100	q)	106,000
Cl.	1,899,000		

Accumulated depreciation

		Op.	839,000
q)	80,600	h)	43,200
		Cl.	801,600

Goodwill

Op.	890,400		
Cl.	890,400		

Accounts payable

		Op.	215,200
e)	76,200		
		Cl.	139,000

Salaries payable

		Op.	45,500
		f)	600
		Cl.	46,100

Taxes payable

		Op.	29,000
g)	8,000		
		Cl.	21,000

Bonds payable, 6%

		Op.	652,200
s)	652,200		
		Cl.	—

Bonds payable. 7.2%

		Op.	—
		t)	600,000
		Cl.	600,000

Discount on bonds payable

Op.	—		
t)	12,000	j)	800
Cl.	11,200		

Deferred income tax

		Op.	184,800
i)	35,900		
		Cl.	148,900

Accrued pension benefit liability

		Op.	46,700
		k)	20,000
l)	1,800		
		Cl.	64,900

Common shares

		Op.	930,000
u)	478,000	r)	261,100
		s)	735,500
		v)	51,400
		Cl.	1,500,000

CSCR

		Op.	83,300
s)	83,300		
		Cl.	—

CC: stock options

		Op.	60,000
v)	14,000	w)	24,000
		Cl.	70,000

Retained earnings

		Op.	209,000
u)	121,200	a)	233,100
x)	75,500	n)	2,800
		Cl.	248,200

AOCI: pension

Op.	44,000		
k)	20,000		
Cl.	64,000		

AOCI: investments

		Op.	22,000
n)	2,800	o)	44,300
		Cl.	63,500

Direct Method of Presentation for Operating Activities

The operating activities section for Hum Enterprises has been restated, using the direct method of presentation, in Exhibit A-5. The operating activities section now reflects cash received from customers and cash paid for various revenue and expense items. If a revenue or expense line item does not involve cash (e.g., depreciation) or does not reflect the actual cash flow (e.g., gains and losses on sale), it is excluded from the operating activities section.

To prepare the direct method disclosure, begin with the revenue or expense line item. For example, revenues imply an inflow of $1,402,300 in this example, which is sales revenue. Next, any adjustment from the indirect method reconciliation is included. In our case, this is a decrease in accounts receivable, increasing cash collected, by $34,700, so the cash collected is $1,437,000. For the expenses, the beginning point is an outflow, the expense reported. For example, interest expense was $35,300, implying a ($35,300) outflow of this amount. The

EXHIBIT A-4

HUM ENTERPRISES LIMITED

Statement of Cash Flows

Year Ended 31 December 20X8

Cash provided by (used in) operating activities		
Earnings	$233,100	
Add (deduct) items not involving cash:		
Depreciation	43,200	
Decrease in deferred income tax	(35,900)	
Compensation expense re: stock options	24,000	
Amortization of discount on long-term debt	800	
Loss on sale of machinery	16,000	
	281,200	
Changes in non-cash balance sheet accounts:		
Accounts receivable decrease	34,700	
Inventory decrease	8,200	
Prepaid rent increase	(4,700)	
Accounts payable decrease	(76,200)	
Salaries payable increase	600	
Taxes payable decrease	(8,000)	
Decrease in accrued pension benefit liability	(1,800)	
		$234,000
Cash provided by (used in) investing activities		
Investments purchased	(161,300)	
Sale of investments	50,000	
Sale of machinery	9,400	
Land purchased	(72,000)	
		(173,900)
Cash provided by (used in) financing activities		
Bonds issued	588,000	
Common shares retired	(599,200)	
Common shares issued	37,400	
Cash dividend paid	(75,500)	
		(49,300)
Increase in cash and cash equivalents		10,800
Cash, beginning of year		29,200
Cash, end of year		$ 40,000

Supplementary information:

Note disclosure of non-cash transactions:

1. Machinery was acquired for common shares $261,100.
2. The 6% bond converted to common shares during the year. The bond carrying value of $652,200 and common stock conversion rights of $83,300 were transferred to common shares, resulting in an increase in common shares of $735,500.
3. Shares were issued for $51,400, of which $14,000 was cash; the balance was related to stock options.

Cash flows for interest and/or dividends received, interest paid, and income tax paid:

1. Cash received for interest and/or dividends was $1,400.
2. Cash paid for interest was $ 34,500 ($35,300 – $800 discount amortization).
3. Cash paid for income tax was $217,900 ($174,000 + $8,000 + $35,900).

indirect method included an add-back (positive amount) of amortization of the discount of $800. When the negative and positive are combined, the outflow for interest is ($34,500). All adjustments used with the indirect method must be incorporated for the direct method and will eliminate the non-cash income statement lines.

Alternative Classification

The SCF for Hum Enterprises has been restated in Exhibit A-6. This presentation shows cash paid for income tax on the face of the SCF in operating activities. It also uses the alternative classification of interest or dividends received (in investing activities) and interest paid (in financing activities). Note the highlighted items in the exhibit. The operating activities section now shows adjustments for the recognized revenue or expenses, essentially backing them all out of earnings. This is achieved by subtracting investment revenue and adding back income tax expense and interest expense. The operating activities section also omits all adjustments (i.e., bond discount amortization, deferred tax, change in tax payable) related to these line items. Cash flow for these items is now separately listed, as for income tax, or it is listed in the alternative classification—an inflow of interest or dividends in the investing activities section, and cash paid for interest (the expense combined with the discount amortization) in financing activities. Because these items are now listed separately on the SCF, supplementary disclosure for their cash flow amount is no longer needed. Other supplementary information, for non-cash transactions, has not changed and is not repeated.

Remember also that dividends paid may be classified in financing activities or in operating activities.

EXHIBIT A-5

HUM ENTERPRISES LIMITED

Statement of Cash Flows
Direct Presentation of Operating Activities

Year Ended 31 December 20X8

Operating Activities—Direct Method	
Cash from customers ($1,402,300 + $34,700)	$1,437,000
Cash from investment revenue ($1,400)	1,400
Cash paid to suppliers (– $631,100 + $8,200 – $76,200)	(699,100)
Cash paid for salaries and other expenses (– $107,900 – $119,900 – $43,200 – $1,800 + $24,000 – $4,700 + $600)	(252,900)
Cash paid for interest (– $35,300 + $800)	(34,500)
Cash paid for income tax (– $174,000 – $8,000 – $35,900)	(217,900)
	$ 234,000

Note: Other sections of the SCF are identical.

EXHIBIT A-6

HUM ENTERPRISES LIMITED

Statement of Cash Flows
Alternative Presentation of Cash Flows: Income Tax, Interest, and Dividend/Interest

Year Ended 31 December 20X8

Cash provided by (used in) operating activities		
Earnings	$233,100	
Add (deduct) items not involving cash and nonoperating items:		
Depreciation	43,200	
Compensation expense re: stock options	24,000	
Loss on sale of machinery	16,000	
Income tax expense	174,000	
Interest expense	35,300	
Investment income	(1,400)	
	524,200	
Changes in non-cash balance sheet accounts:		
Accounts receivable decrease	34,700	
Inventory decrease	8,200	
Prepaid rent increase	(4,700)	
Accounts payable decrease	(76,200)	
Salaries payable increase	600	
Decrease in accrued pension benefit liability	(1,800)	
		485,000
Cash paid for income tax (– $174,000 – $8,000 – $35,900)		(217,900)
		$267,100
Cash provided by (used in) investing activities		
Investments purchased	(161,300)	
Sale of investments	50,000	
Interest/dividends received	1,400	
Sale of machinery	9,400	
Land purchased	(72,000)	
		(172,500)
Cash provided by (used in) financing activities		
Bonds issued	588,000	
Interest paid	(34,500)	
Common shares retired	(599,200)	
Common shares issued	37,400	
Cash dividend paid	(75,500)	
		(83,800)
Increase in cash and cash equivalents		10,800
Cash, beginning of year		29,200
Cash, end of year		$ 40,000

CONCEPT REVIEW

1. What are the three categories of cash flows that should be reported on a company's SCF?
2. What classification alternatives are permitted for dividends paid, cash from investment revenue, and interest paid?
3. What items must be adjusted to convert earnings to cash from operating activities?
4. How does the direct method of presentation differ from the indirect method in the operating activities section of the SCF?
5. Is a bond conversion included on the SCF? Explain.
6. What is reported on the SCF for the sale of a FVTOCI investment? Explain.

Looking Forward

SCF issues are not now on the agenda of either the IASB or the Canadian AcSB.

ACCOUNTING STANDARDS FOR PRIVATE ENTERPRISES

As stated in Chapter 5, a statement of cash flows is required under accounting standards for private enterprises (ASPE) as part of a set of complete financial statements. The ASPE requirements for this statement are very similar to the IFRS presentation requirements, with the following differences:

1. Dividends paid must be classified as a financing activity.
2. Interest received and paid and dividends received must be classified in operating activities. There is no choice of alternative classification.
3. There is no requirement to disclose separately the cash flow for interest paid, dividends and interest received, and cash paid for income tax.

RELEVANT STANDARDS

CPA Canada Handbook, Part I (IFRS):

- IAS 7, Statement of Cash Flows

CPA Canada Handbook, Part II (ASPE):

- Section 1540, Cash Flow Statement

SUMMARY OF KEY POINTS

1. The SCF classifies cash flows from operating activities, cash flows relating to investing activities, and cash flows relating to financing activities. In each category, cash flow includes both inflows and outflows.
3. Operating cash flows are related to the main revenue-producing activities of the business and are connected to the earnings process. Investing cash flows describe long-term asset acquisitions and the proceeds from sale of long-term assets. Financing cash flows describe the sources of debt and equity financing and repayments of liabilities and equities, excluding liabilities directly relating to operations, such as accounts payable.
4. The reporting basis for the SCF is the net cash position. The net cash position includes cash plus cash-equivalent investments, less bank overdrafts. Cash equivalents include short-term liquid investments that are held for current needs and that bear little risk of change in value (maximum 90-day term).
5. The SCF implications of major SFP elements have been summarized in Exhibit A-1.
6. Cash from operating activities can be presented though the indirect method or the direct method. When the indirect method is used, it is common to use a two-step approach, where first, non-cash and nonoperating items are added back, and then changes in SFP accounts related to revenue and expense are adjusted.
7. Gross cash flows are reported. Transactions are not offset, or netted, against other flows in the same category.
8. Cash paid for income tax, cash paid for interest, and cash received for interest or dividends must all be separately disclosed. This can be accomplished through add-backs and deductions using the indirect presentation method in operating activities. Some companies use supplementary note disclosure for this information.
9. Interest paid may be classified as an operating outflow or a financing outflow. The same two choices are available for dividends paid. Interest and dividends received may be classified as operating activities or investing activities.

TECHNICAL REVIEW

Note: In all assignment questions, unless directed otherwise, assume that dividends paid are financing activities, and assume that interest paid and received, and dividends received, are operating transactions.

TRApp2-1 SCF—Cash from Operating Activities: Selected accounts from the SFP of Ivan Limited at 31 December 20X5 and 20X4 are presented below, in thousands. Ivan reported earnings of $600 in 20X5, and depreciation expense was $110. Bonds of $100 par value were issued during the period for $90 and a discount of $10 was originally recorded.

As at 31 December	20X5	20X4
Accounts receivable	$300	$420
Inventory	250	175
Accounts payable	150	190
Interest payable	40	15
Deferred income tax liability	140	100
Bonds payable	500	400
Discount on bonds payable	(22)	(25)

Required:

1. Prepare the operating activities section of the SCF, using the indirect approach and the two-step presentation method.

2. Calculate cash paid for interest and income tax, assuming that interest expense is $90 and income tax expense is $120.
3. Repeat requirement 1, assuming that interest paid is classified in the financing activities section and cash paid for income tax is listed separately in operating activities.

connect

TRApp2-2 SCF—Cash from Operating Activities, Direct Method: Continuing from TR APP-1, the SCI for Ivan Limited follows:

Statement of Comprehensive Income, for the Year Ended 31 December, 20X5 (in thousands):

Sales		$2,500
Cost of goods sold		1,000
Gross profit		1,500
Depreciation expense	$110	
Selling and administrative expenses	580	
Interest expense	90	780
Earnings before income tax		720
Income tax expense		120
Earnings and comprehensive income		$ 600

Required:

Using the SCI and the facts from TR APP-1, prepare the operating section of the SCF. Cash paid for interest is included in the financing activities sections.

connect

TRApp2-3 SCF—Investing Activities: Selected accounts from the SFP of Pod Limited at 31 December 20X5 and 20X4, are presented below. Equipment with an original cost of $50,000 and net book value of $5,000 was sold for $12,000. Other equipment was sold for cash. FVTPL investments with a carrying value of $15,000 were sold for $15,000. There were no other purchases or sale of investments.

As at 31 December	20X5	20X4
Assets		
FVTOCI investments	$ 150,000	$ 120,000
FVTPL investments	300,000	200,000
Equipment, net	530,000	400,000
Accumulated amortization, equipment	(270,000)	(230,000)

Required:

List the items that would be included in the SCF from these accounts for 20X5. Include the appropriate section (operating, investing, or financing).

connect

TRApp2-4 SCF—Financing Activities: Selected accounts from the SFP of Operto Corporation at 31 December 20X5 and 20X4, are presented below (in thousands). Operto reported earnings of $500 in 20X5. Bonds payable were retired during the year at 105. Discount amortization for the year was $10. A financing lease with a present value of $180 was recorded in 20X5; payments had been made under the lease contract by the end of the fiscal year.

As at 31 December	20X5	20X4
Bonds payable, 7%	$450	$700
Discount on bonds payable	(30)	(70)
Lease liability	165	—
Common shares	300	230
Retained earnings	610	540

Required:
List the items that would be included in the SCF from these accounts for 20X5. Include the appropriate section (operating, investing, or financing). List the non-cash item disclosure. Make logical assumptions about unexplained changes in accounts.

connect

TRApp2-5 SCF—Transactions from Equity: The statement of changes in equity, from the financial statements of Forte Corporation, for the year ended 31 December 20X1, is as follows (in thousands):

	Common shares	Contributed capital: Options	Retained earnings	AOCI: Pension	AOCI: Investments
Opening balance	$1,000	$220	$6,500	$(1,200)	$300
Comprehensive income			500	(100)	200
			50		(50)
Cash dividends			(120)		
Stock dividend	440		(440)		
Share issuance; options	140	(60)			
Options recorded		90			
Share retirement	(30)		(210)		
Closing balance	$1,550	$250	$6,280	$(1,300)	$450

Required:
List the items that would be included in the SCF from these accounts for 20X1. Include the appropriate section (operating, investing, or financing). List the non-cash item disclosure. Assume that FVTOCI investments were sold for $75; carrying value was $75 on this date, but the original cost had been $25. The realized gain was transferred to retained earnings.

ASSIGNMENTS

Note: In all assignment questions, unless directed otherwise, assume that dividends paid are financing activities, and assume that interest paid and received and dividends received are operating transactions.

★★★

connect

AApp2-1 Statement of Cash Flows: The financial statements of Hanen Limited for the 20X1 fiscal year follow (in thousands):

Statement of Comprehensive Income, for the Year Ended 31 December 20X1:

Sales	$13,100
Cost of goods sold	6,500
Gross profit	6,600
Depreciation expense	860
Selling and administrative expenses	2,450
Goodwill impairment	2,000
Interest expense	440
Loss on sale of fixed assets	370
Earnings before income tax	480
Income tax expense	150
Earnings and comprehensive income	$ 330

Statement of Changes in Equity, for the Year Ended 31 December 20X1:

	Common shares	Preferred shares	Cont'd capital: Options	Cont'd capital: Preferred share retirement	Retained earnings
Opening balance	$ 500	$1,200	$320	400	$2,900
Comprehensive income					330
Dividends—cash					(75)
Dividends—stock	200				(200)
Share issuance; fixed assets	710				
Share issuance; options	50		(45)		
Options recorded			100		
Share retirement		(600)		100	
Share retirement	(400)				(180)
Closing balance	$1,060	$600	$375	$500	$2,775

Statement of Financial Position, Year Ended

December 31	20X1	20X0
Assets:		
Cash	$ 145	$ 200
Accounts receivable (net)	650	720
Inventory	1,615	820
Fixed assets	9,820	7,560
Accumulated depreciation	(4,120)	(3,500)
Goodwill	—	2,000
Total	$8,110	$7,800
Liabilities and shareholders' equity:		
Accounts payable and accrued liabilities	$ 625	$ 560
Income taxes payable	30	40
Notes payable	130	25
Bonds payable	700	700
Discount on bonds payable	(30)	(45)
Deferred income tax	1,345	1,200
Common shares, no-par	1,060	500
Preferred shares, no-par	600	1,200
Contributed capital: stock options	375	320
Contributed capital: preferred share retirement	500	400
Retained earnings	2,775	2,900
Total	$8,110	$7,800

Additional information:

1. There is a stock option plan for executives, on which $100 of expense was recorded. Options were exercised during the year.
2. Machinery was acquired in exchange for common shares during the year. Other fixed assets were acquired for cash.
3. Fixed assets with an original cost of $900 and a net book value of $660 were sold at a loss of $370.
4. Assume unexplained changes in accounts are from normal transactions.

Required:

1. Prepare the statement of cash flows, using the two-step indirect method in the operating activities section. Include a list of required note disclosure for non-cash transactions. Omit the separate disclosure of cash flow for interest, investment income, and income tax.
2. Explain the company's cash transactions for the year, based on the SCF.

★★★ **AApp2-2 Statement of Cash Flows:** The following data are provided regarding Tema Corporation:

Statement of Earnings and Comprehensive Income

For the Year Ended 31 December 20X8

Revenues		
Sales	$760,000	
Interest and dividends	30,500	
Gain on sale of land	7,000	
		$797,500
Expenses and losses		
Cost of goods sold	$350,000	
Selling expenses	40,200	
Depreciation expense	19,600	
Interest expense	8,300	
Loss on sale of fixed assets	2,100	
Income tax expense	113,200	533,400
Earnings and comprehensive income		$264,100

Statement of Financial Position

As at 31 December 20X8	**20X8**	**20X7**
Assets		
Cash and cash equivalents	$ 83,200	$ 53,100
Accounts receivable	209,000	240,000
Inventory	182,100	175,000
Land	—	8,900
Fixed assets (net)	814,200	695,000
	$1,288,500	$1,172,000
Liabilities and shareholders' equity		
Accounts payable	$ 89,900	$ 104,300
Income tax payable	75,700	47,100
Cash dividends payable	16,000	—
Bonds payable	200,000	—
Less: Unamortized discount	(44,000)	—
Preferred shares	90,000	50,000
Common shares	395,000	350,000
Common stock conversion rights	30,000	—
Retained earnings	435,900	620,600
	$1,288,500	$1,172,000

Additional information:

1. Fixed assets with an original cost of $45,200 were sold for $17,100. Land was also sold for cash.
2. A stock dividend valued at $25,000 was issued in June 20X8.
3. Fixed assets valued at $40,000 were acquired for preferred shares during the year.
4. Convertible bonds were issued for cash in January 20X8.
5. The bond discount was amortized by $4,000 during the year.
6. Assume other changes to SFP accounts represented normal events.

Required:

Prepare an SCF for the year ended 31 December 20X8. Use the indirect method for operations. Include a list of required note disclosure for non-cash transactions. Omit the separate disclosure of cash flow for interest, investment income, and income tax.

★★★ **AApp2-3 Statement of Cash Flows:** The following financial information is available for Crane Incorporated for the 20X3 fiscal year:

Statement of Financial Position

As at 31 December	20X3	20X2
Cash	$ 5,000	$ 20,000
Accounts receivable	270,000	180,000
FVTPL investments	190,000	230,000
Inventory	731,000	632,000
Land	330,000	410,000
Building	1,040,000	1,120,000
Accumulated depreciation, building	(470,000)	(380,000)
Machinery	1,080,000	875,000
Accumulated depreciation, machinery	(219,000)	(212,000)
Goodwill	50,000	110,000
	$3,007,000	$2,985,000
Current liabilities	$ 52,000	$ 90,000
Bonds payable	1,000,000	1,000,000
Discount on bonds	(10,000)	(15,000)
Deferred income tax	24,000	66,000
Preferred shares	1,048,000	843,000
Common stock conversion rights	190,000	190,000
Common shares	565,000	500,000
Retained earnings	138,000	311,000
	$3,007,000	$2,985,000

Statement of Earnings and Comprehensive Income

For the Year Ended 31 December 20X3

Sales	$1,684,000
Cost of goods sold	1,103,000
Gross profit	581,000
Depreciation	
Building	110,000
Machinery	75,000
Goodwill impairment	60,000
Interest	115,000
Other expenses	311,000
Investment loss: decrease in fair value of FVTPL investments	40,000
Gain on sale of land	(22,000)
Loss on sale of machine	27,000
	716,000
Earnings (loss) before income tax	(135,000)
Income tax recovery	54,000
Earnings (loss) and comprehensive loss	$ (81,000)

Additional information:

1. No FVTPL investments were purchased or sold. These investments are not cash equivalents.
2. A partially depreciated building was sold for an amount equal to its net book value.
3. Cash of $40,000 was received on the sale of a machine whose original cost was $135,000. Other machinery was purchased for cash.
4. Preferred shares were issued for cash on 1 March 20X3. Dividends of $50,000 were paid on these shares in 20X3.

5. On 1 September 20X3, 25,000 common shares were purchased and retired. The shares had an average issuance price of $55,000 and were repurchased for $57,000. On 1 November 20X3, 65,000 common shares were issued in exchange for machinery.
6. Bonds payable are convertible to common shares at the rate of 17 common shares per $1,000 bond after 1 July 20X5 at the investor's option.

Required:

Prepare a statement of cash flows, in good form. Include a list of required note disclosure for non-cash transactions. Use the direct method for cash flows from operating activities.

★★★ **AApp2-4 Statement of Cash Flows:** The financial statements of CWL Corporation for the 20X7 fiscal year follow (in thousands):

Solution

Statement of Comprehensive Income, for the Year Ended 31 December 20X7:

Sales	$5,100
Cost of goods sold	2,900
Gross profit	2,200
Depreciation expense	450
Selling and administrative expenses	970
Interest expense	345
Gain on sale of fixed assets	(140)
Earnings before income tax	575
Income tax expense	310
Earnings and comprehensive income	$ 265

Statement of Changes in Equity, for the Year Ended 31 December 20X7:

	Common shares	Preferred shares	Cont'd capital: Options	Common stock conversion rights	Cont'd capital: Preferred share retirement	Retained earnings
Opening balance	$3,100	$500	$220	$500	200	$1,400
Comprehensive income						265
Dividends—cash						(135)
Share issuance; options	200		(10)			
Options recorded			60			
Bond conversion	1,400			(500)		
Share retirement		(100)			(200)	(75)
Share retirement	(105)					(315)
Closing balance	$4,595	$400	$270	$ 0	$ 0	$1,140

Statement of Financial Position, Year Ended

December 31	20X7	20X6
Assets:		
Cash and cash equivalents	$ 650	$ 890
Accounts receivable (net)	1,340	1,420
Inventory	2,295	2,170
Fixed assets	7,160	7,300
Accumulated depreciation	(2,040)	(2,900)
Total	$9,405	$8,880

continued on next page

December 31	20X7	20X6
Liabilities and shareholders' equity:		
Accounts payable and accrued liabilities	$ 540	$ 610
Income taxes payable	130	250
Notes payable	1,840	400
Bonds payable	—	1,000
Discount on bonds payable	—	(120)
Deferred income tax	490	820
Common shares, no-par	4,595	3,100
Preferred shares, no-par	400	500
Contributed capital: stock options	270	220
Common stock conversion rights, convertible bond	—	500
Contributed capital: preferred share retirement	—	200
Retained earnings	1,140	1,400
Total	$9,405	$8,880

Additional information:

1. There is a stock option plan for executives, on which $60 of expense was recorded. Options were exercised during the year.
2. The bond payable was convertible and was converted during the year after discount amortization of $20 had been recorded.
3. Fixed assets with an original cost of $1,650 and a net book value of $340 were sold at a gain of $140.
4. Assume unexplained changes in accounts are from normal transactions.

Required:

1. Prepare the statement of cash flows, using the two-step indirect method. Include a list of required note disclosure for non-cash transactions.
2. Prepare the separate disclosure of cash flow for interest paid, and income tax.
3. Repeat the operating activities section of the SCF, using the direct method of presentation.

★★★ **AApp2-5 Statement of Cash Flows:** The financial statements of Erroll Limited for the 20X2 fiscal year follow (in thousands):

Statement of Earnings, for the Year Ended 31 December, 20X2:

Sales	$52,300
Cost of goods sold	35,600
Gross profit	16,700
Depreciation expense	4,620
Selling and administrative expenses	7,150
Investment revenue	(650)
Interest expense	1,140
Loss on impairment of goodwill	3,900
Earnings before income tax	540
Income tax expense	110
Earnings	$ 430

SCI, for the Year Ended 31 December 20X2:

Earnings	$430
Less: Actuarial revaluation of projected benefit obligation	(500)
Comprehensive income	$ (70)

Statement of Changes in Equity, for the Year Ended 31 December 20X2:

	Common shares	CC: Options	Common stock conversion rights	Retained earnings	AOCI: Pension
Opening balance	$10,500	$850	$350	$8,700	$(1,100)
Comprehensive income				430	(500)
Stock dividends	350			(350)	
Share issuance; bond conversion	980		(350)		
Share issuance; options	200	(185)			
Options recorded		215			
Share retirement	(100)			(620)	
Closing balance	$11,930	$880	$ 0	$8,160	$(1,600)

Statement of Financial Position, Year Ended

December 31	20X2	20X1
Assets:		
Cash	$ 1,165	$ 2,270
FVTPL investments	1,460	1,400
Accounts receivable (net)	5,050	6,330
Inventory	19,480	11,400
Fixed assets	31,125	28,800
Accumulated depreciation	(18,320)	(13,700)
Goodwill	3,760	7,660
Total	$43,720	$44,160
Liabilities and shareholders' equity:		
Accounts payable and accrued liabilities	$ 3,950	$ 3,900
Income taxes payable	65	40
Long-term debt	15,970	16,500
Bonds payable	—	700
Discount on bonds payable	—	(80)
Accrued pension benefit liability	3,750	3,100
Deferred income tax	615	700
Common shares, no-par	11,930	10,500
Contributed capital: stock options	880	850
Common stock conversion rights	—	350
Retained earnings	8,160	8,700
AOCI: pension	(1,600)	(1,100)
Total	$43,720	$44,160

Additional information:

1. The bond was convertible to common shares and was converted during the period after $10 of discount amortization had been recorded.
2. During the year, FVTPL investments had a $430 increase in value, included in earnings in the investment revenue category. Dividend revenue is also included in investment revenue. FVTPL investments were sold at $900 (their carrying value) and other FVTPL investments were purchased.
3. A fixed asset was acquired for $400 during the year, with the vendor issuing a long-term note for the full purchase price. Other fixed assets were acquired for cash.
4. There is a stock option plan for executives, on which $215 of expense was recorded. Options were exercised during the year.
5. Assume unexplained changes in accounts are from normal transactions.

Required:

1. Prepare the statement of cash flows, using the two-step indirect method. Include a list of required note disclosure for non-cash transactions. Omit the separate disclosure of cash flow for interest, investment income, and income tax.
2. Repeat requirement 1, assuming that cash flow for tax is shown separately in operating activities, cash flow for interest is classified in financing activities, and cash flow for investment income is included in investing activities.

★★ **AApp2-6 Statement of Cash Flows:** Presented below are selected financial statements of Alfa Company for the 20X4 fiscal year:

Solution

Statement of Financial Position

As at 31 December	20X4	20X3
Assets		
Cash	$ 5,200	$ 44,000
FVTOCI investments	8,000	16,000
Accounts receivable (net)	230,400	192,000
Inventories	360,400	316,000
Land	27,000	64,000
Fixed assets (net)	274,000	264,000
Total assets	$905,000	$896,000
Liabilities and shareholders' equity		
Bank overdraft	$ 88,600	$ 71,500
Accounts payable	91,700	93,000
Wages payable	26,000	24,000
Income tax payable	30,000	—
Cash dividends payable	6,000	—
Bonds payable, 10%	200,000	240,000
Convertible bonds payable	19,000	30,000
Discount on convertible bonds payable	(1,700)	(3,000)
Common share conversion rights	950	1,500
Common shares (no par)	277,450	277,000
Retained earnings	161,000	150,000
AOCI: investments	6,000	12,000
Total liabilities and equities	$905,000	$896,000

Statement of Earnings and Comprehensive Income

Year ended 31 December 20X4

Sales		$1,260,000
Investment revenue: interest and dividends on FVTOCI investments		5,600
Total revenues		$1,265,600
Cost of sales	$948,000	
Wages expense	124,000	
Interest expense	16,600	
Depreciation expense	28,000	
Other expenses	75,000	
Loss on sale of land	5,000	1,196,600
Earnings before income tax		$ 69,000
Income tax		30,000
Earnings		$ 39,000
Change in value of FVTOCI investments		6,000
Comprehensive income		$ 45,000

The following additional data have been provided:

- Early in the year, FVTOCI investments were sold for their fair value of $16,000. The realized increase in fair value, $12,000 was transferred to retained earnings. Other investments were purchased for $2,000, and their fair value has increased by year-end.
- Equipment costing $43,000 was purchased during 20X4, and used equipment was sold at its book value of $5,000.
- The 10% bonds are being retired at the rate of $40,000 per year and were retired at par value. A portion of the convertible bonds was exchanged for common shares during 20X4. The discount was amortized by $200 during the year.
- The company spent $17,000 to reacquire and retire its own common shares. These shares had an average issue price of $10,000.
- Alfa declared cash dividends during 20X4.

Required:

1. Prepare a statement of cash flows in good form. Use the indirect method to present the operating activities section. Also prepare separate disclosure of cash flow for dividends and interest received, interest paid, and income tax. Include a list of required note disclosure for non-cash transactions.
2. Provide an assessment of the company's cash transactions based on your SCF.

(Source: (Adapted) © CGA-Canada. Reproduced with permission.)

★★ **AApp2-7 Statement of Cash Flows:** Presented below are the financial statements of Maple Leaf Company for the year ending 31 December 20X3:

Statement of Financial Position

31 December	20X3	20X2
Assets		
Cash	$ 50,000	$ 45,000
Accounts receivable (net)	105,000	70,000
Inventories	130,000	110,000
Land	162,500	100,000
Plant and equipment (net)	245,000	266,500
Patents	15,000	16,500
	$707,500	$608,000
Liabilities and equities		
Accounts payable	$192,600	$133,700
Wages payable	36,400	45,000
Interest payable	6,700	15,800
Income tax payable	16,900	4,200
Deferred income tax liability	70,000	50,000
Bonds payable	65,000	100,000
Discount on bonds payable	(4,000)	(10,000)
Accrued pension benefit liability	26,700	22,500
Common shares (no par)	191,500	182,000
Contributed capital on retirement of common shares	16,000	—
Retained earnings	101,000	73,000
AOCI: pension	(11,300)	(8,200)
	$707,500	$608,000

Statement of Earnings and Comprehensive Income

Year ended 31 December 20X3

Sales		$600,000
Cost of sales		280,000
Gross margin		320,000
Expenses		
Wages expense	$185,000	
Depreciation expense	10,000	
Amortization of patents	1,500	
Interest expense	18,000	
Gain on retirement of bonds	(10,000)	
Miscellaneous expense	3,500	
Loss on sale of equipment	2,000	210,000
Income before income tax		110,000
Income tax		49,500
Earnings		$ 60,500
Revaluation of pension liability		(3,100)
Comprehensive income		$ 57,400

Additional information:

- Common shares issued and outstanding at 31 December 20X2 were 42,000.
- In March, the company issued a 10% stock dividend to shareholders of record on 16 February 20X3, valued at market price per share of $7.
- In April, Maple Leaf issued common stock for land, valued at $20,000. Other shares were issued for cash.
- The company sold equipment costing $26,500, with a net book value of $11,500.
- On 31 October 20X3, Maple Leaf declared and paid cash dividend to common shareholders.
- Common shares with an average issuance price of $90,000 were retired for cash in December 20X3.
- Discount amortization was $2,500 during the year. A portion of the bond payable was redeemed for cash.

Required:

1. Prepare a statement of cash flows in good form. Use the indirect method to present the operating activities section. Include separate disclosure of cash paid for interest and income tax paid in the operating activities section.
2. Provide an assessment of the company's cash transactions based on requirement 1.

(Source: [Adapted] © CGA-Canada. Reproduced with permission.)

★★ **AApp2-8 Statement of Cash Flows; Financing Activities:** Information for Fortune Limited follows:

SFP extracts:

	31 Dec. 20X5	31 Dec. 20X4
8% bonds payable	$ —	$2,000,000
Plus: Premium	—	45,600
	—	2,045,600
Convertible 6% bonds payable	3,000,000	—
Less: Discount	(57,000)	—
	2,943,000	—
Preferred shares	520,000	400,000
Common shares (500,000 shares as of 1 January 20X5)	8,678,000	6,800,000
Common share conversion rights	210,000	—
Contributed capital on common share retirement	—	52,000
$8.00 stock options outstanding	80,000	—
$11.50 stock warrants outstanding	400,000	605,000
Retained earnings	9,754,000	8,950,000

Additional information:

1. The 8% bonds payable were redeemed for cash at the beginning of the year at a redemption price of 102. There was no premium amortization prior to the redemption.
2. Convertible 6% bonds were issued during the period. Discount amortization of $3,000 was recorded in 20X5 after issuance.
3. On 1 January 20X5, 20,000 common shares were retired for $410,000.
4. Stock options, for 10,000 common shares at $8.00 each, were issued for land on 1 October 20X5.
5. Earnings and comprehensive income for the period, $1,450,000.
6. Some of the $11.50 options outstanding at the beginning of the year were exercised. This resulted in the issuance of 100,000 common shares at $11.50 each.
7. Additional common shares were issued for cash and cash dividends were declared and paid.

Required:

Prepare the financing activities section of the statement of cash flows, in good form, for the year ended 31 December 20X5. The change in accounts is explained by the "other information" and/or by a logical transaction.

★★ **AApp2-9 Statement of Cash Flows:** The financial statements of Clarion Limited for the 20X5 fiscal year follow (in thousands):

Statement of Earnings, for the Year Ended 31 December 20X5:

Sales	$3,620
Cost of goods sold	1,200
Gross profit	2,420
Depreciation and amortization expense	1,570
Selling and administrative expenses	750
Investment revenue	(240)
Interest expense	140
Gain on sale of fixed assets	(70)
Earnings before income tax	270
Income tax expense	80
Earnings	$ 190

SCI, for the Year Ended 31 December 20X5:

Earnings	$190
Plus: Increase in fair value, FVTOCI investment	310
Less: Realized gain on sale of FVTOCI investment	(160)
Comprehensive income	$340

Statement of Changes in Equity, for the Year Ended 31 December 20X5:

	Common shares	CC: Options	Retained earnings	AOCI: Investments
Opening balance	$2,700	$450	$3,900	$690
Comprehensive income			190	310
FVTOCI transfer on realization			160	(160)
Cash dividends			(100)	
Share issuance; patent	430			
Share issuance; options	150	(125)		
Options recorded		75		
Share retirement	(300)		(220)	
Closing balance	$2,980	$400	$3,930	$840

Statement of Financial Position, Year Ended

December 31	20X5	20X4
Assets:		
Cash	$ 75	$ 30
FVTPL investments	310	300
FVTOCI investments	1,900	1,200
Accounts receivable (net)	2,035	1,615
Inventory	1,480	2,100
Fixed assets	9,400	8,800
Accumulated depreciation	(4,250)	(3,200)
Patent (net)	390	—
Total	$11,340	$10,845
Liabilities and shareholders' equity:		
Accounts payable and accrued liabilities	$ 1,350	$ 1,800
Income taxes payable	15	40
Lease liability	540	—
Bonds payable	1,000	1,000
Discount on bonds payable	(30)	(35)
Deferred income tax	315	300
Common shares	2,980	2,700
Contributed capital: stock options	400	450
Retained earnings	3,930	3,900
AOCI: investments	840	690
Total	$11,340	$10,845

Additional information:

1. FVTOCI investments with an original cost of $300 were sold during the year. Their carrying value and fair value was $460. Unrealized gains were transferred to retained earnings when realized. Other FVTOCI investments with a cost of $850 were acquired during the year.
2. All the $10 change in the FVTPL investment account relates to unrealized changes in fair value of the investments, included in investment income. Investment income also includes $230 interest and dividend revenue on all investments and thus has totalled $240.
3. A financing lease for heavy machinery, with a present value of $600, was recorded in 20X5. Payments were made on the lease contract. The leased assets are included in fixed assets on the SFP.

4. There is a stock option plan for executives, on which $75 of expense was recorded. Options were exercised during the year.
5. A patent was acquired in exchange for common shares. Patent amortization expense of $40 is included in depreciation and amortization expense.
6. Fixed assets with an original cost of $700 and a net book value of $120 were sold for $290.
7. Assume unexplained changes in accounts are from normal transactions.

Required:

1. Prepare the statement of cash flows, using the two-step indirect method. Include a list of required note disclosure for non-cash transactions. Omit the separate disclosure of cash flow for interest, investment income, and income tax.
2. Explain the company's cash transactions for the year, based on the SCF.
3. Repeat the operating activities section of the SCF, using the direct method of presentation.

★★★ **AApp2-10 Statement of Cash Flows:** The financial statements of Simon Corporation for the 20X9 fiscal year follow (in thousands):

Statement of Earnings, for the Year Ended 31 December, 20X9:

Sales	$26,800
Cost of goods sold	14,700
Gross profit	12,100
Depreciation	2,290
Selling and administrative expenses	4,250
Investment revenue	(640)
Interest expense	1,980
Gain on sale of fixed assets	(320)
Earnings before income tax	4,540
Income tax expense	2,080
Earnings	$ 2,460

SCI, for the Year Ended 31 December 20X9:

Earnings	$2,460
Plus: Increase in fair value, FVTOCI investment	70
Less: Realized gain on sale of FVTOCI investment	(200)
Less: Actuarial revaluation of projected benefit obligation	(560)
Comprehensive income	$ 1,770

Statement of Changes in Equity, for the Year Ended 31 December 20X9:

	Common shares	CC: Options	Retained earnings	AOCI: Investments	AOCI: Pension
Opening balance	$1,100	$350	$23,900	$360	(2,470)
Comprehensive income			2,460	70	(560)
FVTOCI transfer on realization			200	(200)	
Dividends—cash			(225)		
Dividends—stock	450		(450)		
Share issuance; options	300	(270)			
Options recorded		175			
Share retirement	(20)		(320)		
Closing balance	$1,830	$255	$25,565	$230	$3,030

Statement of Financial Position, Year Ended

December 31	20X9	20X8
Assets:		
Cash	$ 1,155	$ 2,650
FVTPL investments	3,690	3,300
FVTOCI investments	250	430
Accounts receivable (net)	11,950	11,870
Inventory	7,910	7,310
Fixed assets	39,400	38,500
Accumulated depreciation	(14,700)	(13,950)
Goodwill	16,845	16,845
Total	$66,500	$66,955
Liabilities and shareholders' equity:		
Accounts payable and accrued liabilities	$ 7,240	$ 6,990
Income taxes payable	650	685
Short-term bank debt	3,905	8,405
Lease liability	1,060	—
Bonds payable	20,000	20,000
Discount on bonds payable	(225)	(285)
Deferred income tax	4,070	3,720
Accrued pension benefit liability	4,950	4,200
Common shares, no-par	1,830	1,100
Contributed capital: stock options	255	350
Retained earnings	25,565	23,900
AOCI: investments	230	360
AOCI: pension	(3,030)	(2,470)
Total	$66,500	$66,955

Additional information:

1. FVTOCI investments with an original cost of $50 and carrying (fair) value of $250 were sold during the year. Unrealized gains were transferred to retained earnings when realized. No FVTOCI investments were acquired during the year.
2. In the FVTPL category, there were no purchases or sales during the year. Investment income includes the recognized change in fair value.
3. A financing lease for earth-moving equipment, with a present value of $1,200, was recorded in 20X9. Payments were made on the lease contract. The leased assets are included in fixed assets on the SFP.
4. There is a stock option plan for executives, on which $175 of expense was recorded. Options were exercised during the year.
5. Fixed assets with an original cost of $4,240 and a net book value of $2,700 were sold for cash.
6. Assume unexplained changes in accounts are from normal transactions.

Required:

1. Prepare the statement of cash flows, using the two-step indirect method. Include a list of required note disclosure for non-cash transactions.
2. Prepare the separate disclosure of cash flow for interest, interest received, and income tax paid.
3. Repeat the operating activities section of the SCF, using the direct method of presentation.

connect LEARNSMART SMARTBOOK

For more information on the resources available from McGraw-Hill Ryerson, go to www.mcgrawhill.ca/he/solutions.

TABLE I-1: Present value of 1: (P/F, *i*, *n*)

$$P/F = \frac{1}{(1 + i)^n}$$

n	2%	2.5%	3%	4%	5%	6%	7%	8%	9%	10%	11%	12%	14%	15%
1	0.98039	0.97561	0.97087	0.96154	0.95238	0.94340	0.93458	0.92593	0.91743	0.90909	0.90090	0.89286	0.87719	0.86957
2	0.96117	0.95181	0.94260	0.92456	0.90703	0.89000	0.87344	0.85734	0.84168	0.82645	0.81162	0.79719	0.76947	0.75614
3	0.94232	0.92860	0.91514	0.88900	0.86384	0.83962	0.81630	0.79383	0.77218	0.75131	0.73119	0.71178	0.67497	0.65752
4	0.92385	0.90595	0.88849	0.85480	0.82270	0.79209	0.76290	0.73503	0.70843	0.68301	0.65873	0.63552	0.59208	0.57175
5	0.90573	0.88385	0.86261	0.82193	0.78353	0.74726	0.71299	0.68058	0.64993	0.62092	0.59345	0.56743	0.51937	0.49718
6	0.88797	0.86230	0.83748	0.79031	0.74622	0.70496	0.66634	0.63017	0.59627	0.56447	0.53464	0.50663	0.45559	0.43233
7	0.87056	0.84127	0.81309	0.75992	0.71068	0.66506	0.62275	0.58349	0.54703	0.51316	0.48166	0.45235	0.39964	0.37594
8	0.85349	0.82075	0.78941	0.73069	0.67684	0.62741	0.58201	0.54027	0.50187	0.46651	0.43393	0.40388	0.35056	0.32690
9	0.83676	0.80073	0.76642	0.70259	0.64461	0.59190	0.54393	0.50025	0.46043	0.42410	0.39092	0.36061	0.30751	0.28426
10	0.82035	0.78120	0.74409	0.67556	0.61391	0.55839	0.50835	0.46319	0.42241	0.38554	0.35218	0.32197	0.26974	0.24718
11	0.80426	0.76214	0.72242	0.64958	0.58468	0.52679	0.47509	0.42888	0.38753	0.35049	0.31728	0.28748	0.23662	0.21494
12	0.78849	0.74356	0.70138	0.62460	0.55684	0.49697	0.44401	0.39711	0.35553	0.31863	0.28584	0.25668	0.20756	0.18691
13	0.77303	0.72542	0.68095	0.60057	0.53032	0.46884	0.41496	0.36770	0.32618	0.28966	0.25751	0.22917	0.18207	0.16253
14	0.75788	0.70773	0.66112	0.57748	0.50507	0.44230	0.38782	0.34046	0.29925	0.26333	0.23199	0.20462	0.15971	0.14133
15	0.74301	0.69047	0.64186	0.55526	0.48102	0.41727	0.36245	0.31524	0.27454	0.23939	0.20900	0.18270	0.14010	0.12289
16	0.72845	0.67362	0.62317	0.53391	0.45811	0.39365	0.33873	0.29189	0.25187	0.21763	0.18829	0.16312	0.12289	0.10686
17	0.71416	0.65720	0.60502	0.51337	0.43630	0.37136	0.31657	0.27027	0.23107	0.19784	0.16963	0.14564	0.10780	0.09293
18	0.70016	0.64117	0.58739	0.49363	0.41552	0.35034	0.29586	0.25025	0.21199	0.17986	0.15282	0.13004	0.09456	0.08081
19	0.68643	0.62553	0.57029	0.47464	0.39573	0.33051	0.27651	0.23171	0.19449	0.16351	0.13768	0.11611	0.08295	0.07027
20	0.67297	0.61027	0.55368	0.45639	0.37689	0.31180	0.25842	0.21455	0.17843	0.14864	0.12403	0.10367	0.07276	0.06110
21	0.65978	0.59539	0.53755	0.43883	0.35894	0.29416	0.24151	0.19866	0.16370	0.13513	0.11174	0.09256	0.06383	0.05313
22	0.64684	0.58086	0.52189	0.42196	0.34185	0.27751	0.22571	0.18394	0.15018	0.12285	0.10067	0.08264	0.05599	0.04620
23	0.63416	0.56670	0.50669	0.40573	0.32557	0.26180	0.21095	0.17032	0.13778	0.11168	0.09069	0.07379	0.04911	0.04017
24	0.62172	0.55288	0.49193	0.39012	0.31007	0.24698	0.19715	0.15770	0.12640	0.10153	0.08170	0.06588	0.04308	0.03493
25	0.60953	0.53939	0.47761	0.37512	0.29530	0.23300	0.18425	0.14602	0.11597	0.09230	0.07361	0.05882	0.03779	0.03038
26	0.59758	0.52623	0.46369	0.36069	0.28124	0.21981	0.17220	0.13520	0.10639	0.08391	0.06631	0.05252	0.03315	0.02642
27	0.58586	0.51340	0.45019	0.34682	0.26785	0.20737	0.16093	0.12519	0.09761	0.07628	0.05974	0.04689	0.02908	0.02297
28	0.57437	0.50088	0.43708	0.33348	0.25509	0.19563	0.15040	0.11591	0.08955	0.06934	0.05382	0.04187	0.02551	0.01997
29	0.56311	0.48866	0.42435	0.32065	0.24295	0.18456	0.14056	0.10733	0.08215	0.06304	0.04849	0.03738	0.02237	0.01737
30	0.55207	0.47674	0.41199	0.30832	0.23138	0.17411	0.13137	0.09938	0.07537	0.05731	0.04368	0.03338	0.01963	0.01510
31	0.54125	0.46511	0.39999	0.29646	0.22036	0.16425	0.12277	0.09202	0.06915	0.05210	0.03935	0.02980	0.01722	0.01313
32	0.53063	0.45377	0.38834	0.28506	0.20987	0.15496	0.11474	0.08520	0.06344	0.04736	0.03545	0.02661	0.01510	0.01142
33	0.52023	0.44270	0.37703	0.27409	0.19987	0.14619	0.10723	0.07889	0.05820	0.04306	0.03194	0.02376	0.01325	0.00993
34	0.51003	0.43191	0.36604	0.26355	0.19035	0.13791	0.10022	0.07305	0.05339	0.03914	0.02878	0.02121	0.01162	0.00864
35	0.50003	0.42137	0.35538	0.25342	0.18129	0.13011	0.09366	0.06763	0.04899	0.03558	0.02592	0.01894	0.01019	0.00751
36	0.49022	0.41109	0.34503	0.24367	0.17266	0.12274	0.08754	0.06262	0.04494	0.03235	0.02335	0.01691	0.00894	0.00653
37	0.48061	0.40107	0.33498	0.23430	0.16444	0.11579	0.08181	0.05799	0.04123	0.02941	0.02104	0.01510	0.00784	0.00568
38	0.47119	0.39128	0.32523	0.22529	0.15661	0.10924	0.07646	0.05369	0.03783	0.02673	0.01896	0.01348	0.00688	0.00494
39	0.46195	0.38174	0.31575	0.21662	0.14915	0.10306	0.07146	0.04971	0.03470	0.02430	0.01708	0.01204	0.00604	0.00429
40	0.45289	0.37243	0.30656	0.20829	0.14205	0.09722	0.06678	0.04603	0.03184	0.02209	0.01538	0.01075	0.00529	0.00373
45	0.41020	0.32917	0.26444	0.17120	0.11130	0.07265	0.04761	0.03133	0.02069	0.01372	0.00913	0.00610	0.00275	0.00186
50	0.37153	0.29094	0.22811	0.14071	0.08720	0.05429	0.03395	0.02132	0.01345	0.00852	0.00542	0.00346	0.00143	0.00092

TABLE I-2: Present value of an ordinary annuity of *n* payments of 1: (P/A, *i*, *n*)

$$P/A = \frac{1 - \frac{1}{(1+i)^n}}{i}$$

n	2%	2.5%	3%	4%	5%	6%	7%	8%	9%	10%	11%	12%	14%	15%
1	0.98039	0.97561	0.97087	0.96154	0.95238	0.94340	0.93458	0.92593	0.91743	0.90909	0.90090	0.89286	0.87719	0.86957
2	1.94156	1.92742	1.91347	1.88609	1.85941	1.83339	1.80802	1.78326	1.75911	1.73554	1.71252	1.69005	1.64666	1.62571
3	2.88388	2.85602	2.82861	2.77509	2.72325	2.67301	2.62432	2.57710	2.53129	2.48685	2.44371	2.40183	2.32163	2.28323
4	3.80773	3.76197	3.71710	3.62990	3.54595	3.46511	3.38721	3.31213	3.23972	3.16987	3.10245	3.03735	2.91371	2.85498
5	4.71346	4.64583	4.57971	4.45182	4.32948	4.21236	4.10020	3.99271	3.88965	3.79079	3.69590	3.60478	3.43308	3.35216
6	5.60143	5.50813	5.41719	5.24214	5.07569	4.91732	4.76654	4.62288	4.48592	4.35526	4.23054	4.11141	3.88867	3.78448
7	6.47199	6.34939	6.23028	6.00205	5.78637	5.58238	5.38929	5.20637	5.03295	4.86842	4.71220	4.56376	4.28830	4.16042
8	7.32548	7.17014	7.01969	6.73274	6.46321	6.20979	5.97130	5.74664	5.53482	5.33493	5.14612	4.96764	4.63886	4.48732
9	8.16224	7.97087	7.78611	7.43533	7.10782	6.80169	6.51523	6.24689	5.99525	5.75902	5.53705	5.32825	4.94637	4.77158
10	8.98259	8.75206	8.53020	8.11090	7.72173	7.36009	7.02358	6.71008	6.41766	6.14457	5.88923	5.65022	5.21612	5.01877
11	9.78685	9.51421	9.25262	8.76048	8.30641	7.88687	7.49867	7.13896	6.80519	6.49506	6.20652	5.93770	5.45273	5.23371
12	10.57534	10.25776	9.95400	9.38507	8.86325	8.38384	7.94269	7.53608	7.16073	6.81369	6.49236	6.19437	5.66029	5.42062
13	11.34837	10.98318	10.63496	9.98565	9.39357	8.85268	8.35765	7.90378	7.48690	7.10336	6.74987	6.42355	5.84236	5.58315
14	12.10625	11.69091	11.29607	10.56312	9.89864	9.29498	8.74547	8.24424	7.78615	7.36669	6.98187	6.62817	6.00207	5.72448
15	12.84926	12.38138	11.93794	11.11839	10.37966	9.71225	9.10791	8.55948	8.06069	7.60608	7.19087	6.81086	6.14217	5.84737
16	13.57771	13.05500	12.56110	11.65230	10.83777	10.10590	9.44665	8.85137	8.31256	7.82371	7.37916	6.97399	6.26506	5.95423
17	14.29187	13.71220	13.16612	12.16567	11.27407	10.47726	9.76322	9.12164	8.54363	8.02155	7.54879	7.11963	6.37286	6.04716
18	14.99203	14.35336	13.75351	12.65930	11.68959	10.82760	10.05909	9.37189	8.75563	8.20141	7.70162	7.24967	6.46742	6.12797
19	15.67846	14.97889	14.32380	13.13394	12.08532	11.15812	10.33560	9.60360	8.95011	8.36492	7.83929	7.36578	6.55037	6.19823
20	16.35143	15.58916	14.87747	13.59033	12.46221	11.46992	10.59401	9.81815	9.12855	8.51356	7.96333	7.46944	6.62313	6.25933
21	17.01121	16.18455	15.41502	14.02916	12.82115	11.76408	10.83553	10.01680	9.29224	8.64869	8.07507	7.56200	6.68696	6.31246
22	17.65805	16.76541	15.93692	14.45112	13.16300	12.04158	11.06124	10.20074	9.44243	8.77154	8.17574	7.64465	6.74294	6.35866
23	18.29220	17.33211	16.44361	14.85684	13.48857	12.30338	11.27219	10.37106	9.58021	8.88322	8.26643	7.71843	6.79206	6.39884
24	18.91393	17.88499	16.93554	15.24696	13.79864	12.55036	11.46933	10.52876	9.70661	8.98474	8.34814	7.78432	6.83514	6.43377
25	19.52346	18.42438	17.41315	15.62208	14.09394	12.78336	11.65358	10.67478	9.82258	9.07704	8.42174	7.84314	6.87293	6.46415
26	20.12104	18.95061	17.87684	15.98277	14.37519	13.00317	11.82578	10.80998	9.92897	9.16095	8.48806	7.89566	6.90608	6.49056
27	20.70690	19.46401	18.32703	16.32959	14.64303	13.21053	11.98671	10.93516	10.02658	9.23722	8.54780	7.94255	6.93515	6.51353
28	21.28127	19.96489	18.76411	16.66306	14.89813	13.40616	12.13711	11.05108	10.11613	9.30657	8.60162	7.98442	6.96066	6.53351
29	21.84438	20.45355	19.18845	16.98371	15.14107	13.59072	12.27767	11.15841	10.19828	9.36961	8.65011	8.02181	6.98304	6.55088
30	22.39646	20.93029	19.60044	17.29203	15.37245	13.76483	12.40904	11.25778	10.27365	9.42691	8.69379	8.05518	7.00266	6.56598
31	22.93770	21.39541	20.00043	17.58849	15.59281	13.92909	12.53181	11.34980	10.34280	9.47901	8.73315	8.08499	7.01988	6.57911
32	23.46833	21.84918	20.38877	17.87355	15.80268	14.08404	12.64656	11.43500	10.40624	9.52638	8.76860	8.11159	7.03498	6.59053
33	23.98856	22.29188	20.76579	18.14765	16.00255	14.23023	12.75379	11.51389	10.46444	9.56943	8.80054	8.13535	7.04823	6.60046
34	24.49859	22.72379	21.13184	18.41120	16.19290	14.36814	12.85401	11.58693	10.51784	9.60857	8.82932	8.15656	7.05985	6.60910
35	24.99862	23.14516	21.48722	18.66461	16.37419	14.49825	12.94767	11.65457	10.56682	9.64416	8.85524	8.17550	7.07005	6.61661
36	25.48884	23.55625	21.83225	18.90828	16.54685	14.62099	13.03521	11.71719	10.61176	9.67651	8.87859	8.19241	7.07899	6.62314
37	25.96945	23.95732	22.16724	19.14258	16.71129	14.73678	13.11702	11.77518	10.65299	9.70592	8.89963	8.20751	7.08683	6.62881
38	26.44064	24.34860	22.49246	19.36786	16.86789	14.84602	13.19347	11.82887	10.69082	9.73265	8.91859	8.22099	7.09371	6.63375
39	26.90259	24.73034	22.80822	19.58448	17.01704	14.94907	13.26493	11.87858	10.72552	9.75696	8.93567	8.23303	7.09975	6.63805
40	27.35548	25.10278	23.11477	19.79277	17.15909	15.04630	13.33171	11.92461	10.75736	9.77905	8.95105	8.24378	7.10504	6.64178
45	29.49016	26.83302	24.51871	20.72004	17.77407	15.45583	13.60552	12.10840	10.88120	9.86281	9.00791	8.28252	7.12322	6.65429
50	31.42361	28.36231	25.72976	21.48218	18.25593	15.76186	13.80075	12.23348	10.96168	9.91481	9.04165	8.30450	7.13266	6.66051

TABLE I-3: Present value of an annuity due of *n* payments of 1: (P/AD, *i*, *n*)

$$P/AD = \left[\frac{1 - \frac{1}{(1+i)^n}}{i} \right] \times (1+i)$$

n	2%	2.5%	3%	4%	5%	6%	7%	8%	9%	10%	11%	12%	14%	15%
1	1.00000	1.00000	1.00000	1.00000	1.00000	1.00000	1.00000	1.00000	1.00000	1.00000	1.00000	1.00000	1.00000	1.00000
2	1.98039	1.97561	1.97087	1.96154	1.95238	1.94340	1.93458	1.92593	1.91743	1.90909	1.90090	1.89286	1.87719	1.86957
3	2.94156	2.92742	2.91347	2.88609	2.85941	2.83339	2.80802	2.78326	2.75911	2.73554	2.71252	2.69005	2.64666	2.62571
4	3.88388	3.85602	3.82861	3.77509	3.72325	3.67301	3.62432	3.57710	3.53129	3.48685	3.44371	3.40183	3.32163	3.28323
5	4.80773	4.76197	4.71710	4.62990	4.54595	4.46511	4.38721	4.31213	4.23972	4.16987	4.10245	4.03735	3.91371	3.85498
6	5.71346	5.64583	5.57971	5.45182	5.32948	5.21236	5.10020	4.99271	4.88965	4.79079	4.69590	4.60478	4.43308	4.35216
7	6.60143	6.50813	6.41719	6.24214	6.07569	5.91732	5.76654	5.62288	5.48592	5.35526	5.23054	5.11141	4.88867	4.78448
8	7.47199	7.34939	7.23028	7.00205	6.78637	6.58238	6.38929	6.20637	6.03295	5.86842	5.71220	5.56376	5.28830	5.16042
9	8.32548	8.17014	8.01969	7.73274	7.46321	7.20979	6.97130	6.74664	6.53482	6.33493	6.14612	5.96764	5.63886	5.48732
10	9.16224	8.97087	8.78611	8.43533	8.10782	7.80169	7.51523	7.24689	6.99525	6.75902	6.53705	6.32825	5.94637	5.77158
11	9.98259	9.75206	9.53020	9.11090	8.72173	8.36009	8.02358	7.71008	7.41766	7.14457	6.88923	6.65022	6.21612	6.01877
12	10.78685	10.51421	10.25262	9.76048	9.30641	8.88687	8.49867	8.13896	7.80519	7.49506	7.20652	6.93770	6.45273	6.23371
13	11.57534	11.25776	10.95400	10.38507	9.86325	9.38384	8.94269	8.53608	8.16073	7.81369	7.49236	7.19437	6.66029	6.42062
14	12.34837	11.98318	11.63496	10.98565	10.39357	9.85268	9.35765	8.90378	8.48690	8.10336	7.74987	7.42355	6.84236	6.58315
15	13.10625	12.69091	12.29607	11.56312	10.89864	10.29498	9.74547	9.24424	8.78615	8.36669	7.98187	7.62817	7.00207	6.72448
16	13.84926	13.38138	12.93794	12.11839	11.37966	10.71225	10.10791	9.55948	9.06069	8.60608	8.19087	7.81086	7.14217	6.84737
17	14.57771	14.05500	13.56110	12.65230	11.83777	11.10590	10.44665	9.85137	9.31256	8.82371	8.37916	7.97399	7.26506	6.95423
18	15.29187	14.71220	14.16612	13.16567	12.27407	11.47726	10.76322	10.12164	9.54363	9.02155	8.54879	8.11963	7.37286	7.04716
19	15.99203	15.35336	14.75351	13.65930	12.68959	11.82760	11.05909	10.37189	9.75563	9.20141	8.70162	8.24967	7.46742	7.12797
20	16.67846	15.97889	15.32380	14.13394	13.08532	12.15812	11.33560	10.60360	9.95011	9.36492	8.83929	8.36578	7.55037	7.19823
21	17.35143	16.58916	15.87747	14.59033	13.46221	12.46992	11.59401	10.81815	10.12855	9.51356	8.96333	8.46944	7.62313	7.25933
22	18.01121	17.18455	16.41502	15.02916	13.82115	12.76408	11.83553	11.01680	10.29224	9.64869	9.07507	8.56200	7.68696	7.31246
23	18.65805	17.76541	16.93692	15.45112	14.16300	13.04158	12.06124	11.20074	10.44243	9.77154	9.17574	8.64465	7.74294	7.35866
24	19.29220	18.33211	17.44361	15.85684	14.48857	13.30338	12.27219	11.37106	10.58021	9.88322	9.26643	8.71843	7.79206	7.39884
25	19.91393	18.88499	17.93554	16.24696	14.79864	13.55036	12.46933	11.52876	10.70661	9.98474	9.34814	8.78432	7.83514	7.43377
26	20.52346	19.42438	18.41315	16.62208	15.09394	13.78336	12.65358	11.67478	10.82258	10.07704	9.42174	8.84314	7.87293	7.46415
27	21.12104	19.95061	18.87684	16.98277	15.37519	14.00317	12.82578	11.80998	10.92897	10.16095	9.48806	8.89566	7.90608	7.49056
28	21.70690	20.46401	19.32703	17.32959	15.64303	14.21053	12.98671	11.93516	11.02658	10.23722	9.54780	8.94255	7.93515	7.51353
29	22.28127	20.96489	19.76411	17.66306	15.89813	14.40616	13.13711	12.05108	11.11613	10.30657	9.60162	8.98442	7.96066	7.53351
30	22.84438	21.45355	20.18845	17.98371	16.14107	14.59072	13.27767	12.15841	11.19828	10.36961	9.65011	9.02181	7.98304	7.55088
31	23.39646	21.93029	20.60044	18.29203	16.37245	14.76483	13.40904	12.25778	11.27365	10.42691	9.69379	9.05518	8.00266	7.56598
32	23.93770	22.39541	21.00043	18.58849	16.59281	14.92909	13.53181	12.34980	11.34280	10.47901	9.73315	9.08499	8.01988	7.57911
33	24.46833	22.84918	21.38877	18.87355	16.80268	15.08404	13.64656	12.43500	11.40624	10.52638	9.76860	9.11159	8.03498	7.59053
34	24.98856	23.29188	21.76579	19.14765	17.00255	15.23023	13.75379	12.51389	11.46444	10.56943	9.80054	9.13535	8.04823	7.60046
35	25.49859	23.72379	22.13184	19.41120	17.19290	15.36814	13.85401	12.58693	11.51784	10.60857	9.82932	9.15656	8.05985	7.60910
36	25.99862	24.14516	22.48722	19.66461	17.37419	15.49825	13.94767	12.65457	11.56682	10.64416	9.85524	9.17550	8.07005	7.61661
37	26.48884	24.55625	22.83225	19.90828	17.54685	15.62099	14.03521	12.71719	11.61176	10.67651	9.87859	9.19241	8.07899	7.62314
38	26.96945	24.95732	23.16724	20.14258	17.71129	15.73678	14.11702	12.77518	11.65299	10.70592	9.89963	9.20751	8.08683	7.62881
39	27.44064	25.34860	23.49246	20.36786	17.86789	15.84602	14.19347	12.82887	11.69082	10.73265	9.91859	9.22099	8.09371	7.63375
40	27.90259	25.73034	23.80822	20.58448	18.01704	15.94907	14.26493	12.87858	11.72552	10.75696	9.93567	9.23303	8.09975	7.63805
45	30.07996	27.50385	25.25427	21.54884	18.66277	16.38318	14.55791	13.07707	11.86051	10.84909	9.99878	9.27642	8.12047	7.65244
50	32.05208	29.07137	26.50166	22.34147	19.16872	16.70757	14.76680	13.21216	11.94823	10.90630	10.03624	9.30104	8.13123	7.65959

Index

A
Aastra Technologies Limited, 343, 347, 352, 370, 1094, 1095, 1251
abandoned asset, **94**
accelerated amortization methods, 533
accountability
  private corporations, 5–8
  public corporations, 4–5
accountants and ethics, 11
accounting
  accrual accounting, 12
  disclosed basis of accounting (DBA), **6–7**
  for exchange rate fluctuations, 788–790
  for finance leases, lessee, 1068
  for hedges, 918
  for long-term debt, 777
  professional judgement. *See* professional judgement
  for retirement, 833–835
  share-based payments, 906
  for stock splits, 849–850
  terminology changes, 60
  for treasury stock, 836–837
accounting carrying values, 964
accounting changes
  See also accounting policy changes
  Accounting Standards for Private Enterprise (ASPE), 1271–1272
  comparability of statistical series, 1256
  decision process for applying, 1269*f*
  disclosure requirements, 1262
  estimate changes, 1250–1253
  ethics, 1271
  leases, forthcoming changes, 1107–1112
  prior-period errors, 1265–1268
  prospective application, 1256, 1262–1265
  reporting, 1255–1256, 1270*f*
  retrospective application, 1256–1262
  retrospective application with full restatement, 1255
  retrospective application with partial restatement, 1255–1256
  statement of cash flows (SCF), 1269–1270
  summary, 1270*f*
  summary of approaches, 1268–1269
  types of, 1250
accounting choices. *See* accounting policy choices
accounting concepts, 36–38
accounting cycle
  accounting information system (AIS), 660–661, 661–678
  adjusted trial balance, 662*f*, 672
  financial statements preparation, 662*f*, 673–675
  identification of transactions or events, 661–662
  journalize and post adjusting journal entries, 662*f*, 666–672
  journalize and post closing entries, 662*f*, 675–676
  journalize and post reversing journal entries, 662*f*, 677–678
  journalize transactions and events, 662*f*, 663
  post from journal to ledger, 662*f*, 663–665
  post-closing trial balance, 662*f*, 676
  reversing journal entries (RJEs), **677**–678
  unadjusted trial balance, 662*f*, 665–666*f*
accounting estimates
  accounting policy changes, *vs.* change of, 1252
  amortization requirements, 535–536
  changes in, 153, 1250–1253
  depreciation requirements, 535–536
  disclosure, 1250–1251
  ethics and amortization, 558–559
  ethics and changes in, 1253, 1271
  ethics and compensation cost accruals, 909
  importance of, 57
  income smoothing, **16**–17
  of input measures, 292–293
  inventory estimation methods, 419–424
  measurement uncertainty, 157
  multiple, 1251
  revenue, 289–290, 293, 306–307
  in statement of financial position (SFP), 140–141
accounting fiction, 142
accounting identity, **659**
accounting income, **82**
accounting information system (AIS)
  accounting cycle. *See* accounting cycle
  accounts, 659
  cash disbursements journal, 681–682
  cash receipts journal, 681–682
  defined, **660**–661
  financial statements, 660
  general journal, 681
  purchases journal, 680–681
  recording transactions, 659–660
  sales journal, 679–680
  special journals, 679–683
  subsidiary ledgers, 678–679
  technology, impact of, 661
  worksheets, 684–686
accounting mismatch, 594, 918
accounting policies, 152–155, 156
  adopting new accounting policy, 1265
  financial statement analysis, 1303–1304
accounting policy changes
  See also accounting changes
  change in estimates, *vs.*, 1252
  compulsory change, 152
  defined, **1253**
  described, 152–155
  disclosure requirements, 1262
  mandatory change, 1253–1254
  new accounting policy, *vs.*, 1265
  presentation, 1257
  prospective application, 1262–1265
  recording, 1257
  reporting, 1257
  reporting objectives, 1254
  retrospective application, 1256–1262
  voluntary change, 1253–1254
accounting policy choices
  amortization, 533–537
  cash flow statements, 209
  depreciation, 533–537
  and ethics, 213
  expenditures, 472
  factors, 534–535
  financial statement concepts, 36–38, 37*f*
  qualitative criteria, 43–47
  revenue recognition, 305–307
  and SFP amounts, 140
  statement of cash flows (SCF), 212–213
  structure of accounting policy choice, 36–38, 37*f*
accounting policy convention approach, 543–544
accounting standards
  See also generally accepted accounting principles (GAAP); International Accounting Standards Board (IASB); International Financial Accounting Standards (IFAS)
  authoritative source of, 2
  for Canadian private enterprises, 5–7
  for Canadian publicly accountable enterprises, 4–5
  changes to, 152–155
  comparability issues, 7–8
  financial statement analysis, 1304
  international standards, 2–4, 1035
  leases, changes to, 1107–1112
  long-lived assets, 497*f*
  multiple sets of, 7
  new, 156–157
  pension measurements, 1140
  projected unit credit method, 1140
Accounting Standards Board (AcSB), **2,** 6, 21, **228,** 856
Accounting Standards for Private Enterprise (ASPE), 6
  accounting changes, 1271–1272
  accounts receivable, 371
  assets and liabilities, 62*f*
  balance sheet, 136, 162
  biological assets, 310
  borrowing costs, 801
  as Canadian accounting standard, 1–2
  capital lease, 1098–1099
  capitalization, 801
  carrying value, 164
  cash, 371
  CPA Canada Handbook, Part II (ASPE), 2, 21, 162, 163, 979
  completed-contract method, 308–309
  component depreciation, 559
  comprehensive income, 107
  comprehensive tax allocation, 979, 1036
  constructive liabilities, 748
  contingent liabilities, 163, 748–749
  convertible debt, 922
  corporate income tax, 979
  cost method, 631
  deferred income tax, 979
  defined benefit plans, 1161–1164
  defined contribution plans, 1161–1164
  disclosure, 310, 427, 923, 1100
  disclosure notes, 84, 163–164
  dividends, 223–224
  earnings per share, 109, 1220
  equity, 163
  equity method, 631
  and ethical professional judgement, 38
  financial liabilities, 748–750

financial statements, 21, 61–62, 686
foreign subsidiaries, 856
forfeiture, 923
format, 107
hedges, 923
held-for-sale assets, 108
impairment, 1100
impairment losses, 560
income tax, 223
initial direct costs, 1100
interest, 223
interest rate, 1099
inventory, 427
lease capitalization, 1099
leases, 1099–1101
leases of land and buildings, 1099
lessees, 1099–1100
lessor, 1100–1101
liability method, 979
line items, 108
long-lived assets, 497*f*
long-term liabilities, 801
minimum depreciation, 559–560
non-monetary transactions, 309–310
notes receivable, 371
onerous contracts, 427
operating lease, 1098–1099
passive investments, 630
pension expense, 1161–1162
pension plans, 1161–1164
post-employment benefits, 1161–1164
preferred shares, 922
private enterprises, 21, 61–62, 107–109, 826
proportionate consolidation, 631
and qualitative characteristics, 61*f*
related party transactions, 164
restructuring, 109
revaluation accounting, 560–561
revenue recognition, 308
sale and leaseback, 1101
segments, 163
share retirement, 856
share-based payments, 923
shareholder loans, 922
shareholders' equity, 856
statement of cash flows (SCF), 223–224, 228, 1388
straight-line measurement of interest expense/revenue, 366–367
straight-line (SL) method, 371–372, 749–750, 801–802
strategic investments, 630–631
tax loss carryforwards, 1036
taxes payable method, 979, 1036
transaction recording, 686
treasury stocks, 856
writedowns, 427
accounting-based covenants, 775
accounts
contra account, 670
control account, 665, 678
current accounts, 200
doubtful accounts, 350–351
nominal accounts, 659
non-cash accounts, 204, 206
permanent accounts, 659
real accounts, 659
subsidiary account, 665
T-account, 213–220, 659–660*f*
temporary accounts, 659
accounts payable, 718–719
accounts payable turnover, 1322
accounts receivable
Accounting Standards for Private Enterprise (ASPE), 371
aging method, 353–355
allowance for doubtful accounts, 350–351
amortized cost category, 348
average collection period of accounts receivable, 1320
cash discounts, 348–349
cash flows from sales, 356–357
classification of, 348
credit card transactions, 356
credit sales method, 353, 355
debit card transactions, 356–357
direct write-off of uncollectible accounts, 355–356
and disclosure, 369–370
foreign currency receivables, 368–369
FVTPL category, 348, 356
loans secured by, 357
maturity value, 363
notes receivable, 362–368
reporting, 352
sales returns and allowances, 349–350
special purpose entities (SPEs), 361–362
and statement of cash flows (SCF), 369–370
statement of financial position (SFP), 143
transfer of, 357–362
valuation allowances, 348–352
valuation of the allowance for doubtful accounts, 353–355
write-off and recovery, 351–352
accounts receivable aging schedule, **1321**
accounts receivable turnover ratio, **1321**
accounts/notes receivables, 344
accrual accounting, 12
accrual concept, 52
accruals
adjusting journal entries (AJEs), 666–667
defined, 52
expenses, 668
accrued expenses, **668**
accrued interest, 603–604, 737–738, 739, 784–785
accrued revenue, **669**
accumulated benefit method, **1139**
accumulated other comprehensive income, 856
acid-test ratio, **1330**
acquisition cost, 535, 593
acquisition transactions, 486
active market, 601
actuarial cost methods
for accounting measurement, 1140
accumulated benefit method, 1139
defined, **1133**
defined benefit plans, 1138–1140
level contribution method, 1139
projected unit credit method, 1139
sensitivity to assumptions, 1140
actuarial gains and losses, **1134,** 1144–1145, 1149
actuarial revaluation, **1134**
actuary, **1133**
ad hoc approach, 213, 234
adaptation of IFRS, 3
additional contributed capital, 850–851
additional markup, **422**
additional markup cancellation, **422**
additional paid-in capital, **146**
additions, **468**
adjusted trial balance, 672
adjusting comparative statements, 100–101
adjusting events, **161**
adjusting journal entries (AJEs)
accruals, 666–667
bad debt expense, 670
classification of, 666–672
cost of goods sold, 670–671
deferrals, 666–667
defined, **666**
depreciation expense, 669–670
expedient recording method, 667
income tax expense, 671–672
journalizing and posting, 666–672
periodic system, 670
perpetual system, 670
standard recording method, 667
adjustments
bank reconciliation, 377–379
equity method, 619
foreign currency translation adjustment, 147–148
stock splits, 849–850
adoption of IFRS, 3
advances, 720
agent, 267
aggregation, 413
aging method, **353**–355
aging schedule, 354*f*
agricultural produce, **294–295**
AIG, 1088
Air Canada, 1, 2, 81, 85, 86*f*, 89–90, 532, 1059, 1131
AIS. *See* accounting information system (AIS)
AJE. *See* adjusting journal entries (AJEs)
all-inclusive approach, 83
allocation
of impairment loss, 548–550
interperiod allocation, 12, 52
interperiod tax allocation, 957–959
partial allocation, 957
allocation of consideration, 285–286, 320
allowance for bad debts, 361
allowance for doubtful accounts, **350**–351
allowance for sales returns, 274
AltaGas Ltd., 776, 798–800
alternative accounting treatments, 357–358
alternative classification, 1386–1387
amortization
See also depreciation
10% corridor method, 1148
accounting policy choices, 533–537
acquisition cost, 535
amortization systems, 544
asset retirement obligations, 544
biological assets, 531
bond amortization tables, 780–783
bonds, 786
Capital Cost Allowance (CCA), 564–566
commercial mortgages, 774
conceptual analysis of, 534
conceptual basis of, 530–531
debt amortization table, 1070–1071
decommissioning costs, 544
defined, **530**
depreciation. *See* depreciation

amortization (*continued*)
disclosure requirements, 552–557*f*
discontinued operations, 98
discount, of, 604
effective-interest method, 363–366, 605–607*f*, 736
estimates required, 535–536
ethics, 558–559
expense, 531
factors influencing policy choice, 534–535
final-year convention, 544
finance leases, 1070–1071, 1075
fractional-year amortization, 542–544
full-first-year convention, 543–544
generally accepted accounting principles (GAAP), 669–670
group depreciation, 544–545
half-year convention, 543
held-for-sale, 536
held-for-sale capital assets, 531
investment property, 531
lease amortization table, 1070–1071, 1075, 1090–1091, 1110
nature of, 530–532
premium, 604
recognition of amortization expense, 531
residual value, 536
sale and leaseback, 1082–1083
spare parts, 537
standby equipment, 537
statement of cash flows (SCF), 558
straight-line (SL) method, 537–539*f*, 605–607*f*, 749–750
useful life, 535
amortization methods
accelerated amortization methods, 533
declining-balance (DB) method, 538*f*, 539*f*
decreasing charge, 533
diminishing-balance (DB) method, 541
double-declining balance (DDB), 541
estimates, 541
formulas, 538*f*
productive-output (PO) method, 538*f*, 539*f*, 540
service-hours (SH) method, 538*f*, 539*f*, 540
straight-line (SL) method, 537–539*f*, 605–607*f*
units of production method, 540
units of service, 540–541
variable charge, 533
amortization period, 536
amortization schedules, 539*f*, 1070–1071
amortization table for finance leases, 1070–1071, 1075
amortized cost (AC)
accounts receivable, 348
classification, 344
defined, **593**
portfolio, 593–594
amortized cost (AC) method for investments, 597–598, 603–609
analysis. *See* ratio analysis
Andrew Peller, 295–296
anti-dilutive elements, **1200**
appropriated retained earnings, **838**
appropriation, **147**
arbitrary allocation, 832
Argentium Resources Inc., 830–831
Armtec Infrastructure Inc., 101–102, 102*f*, 529, 552–557*f*, 953, 1009
ASPE. *See* Accounting Standards for Private Enterprise (ASPE)
assessment of cash flows, 12–13
asset ceiling, **1137,** 1144, 1145–1146
asset disposals, 93–97, 93*f*
asset retirement obligations, 544
asset turnover, **1322**
asset-backed commercial paper (ABCP), **345**
assets
abandoned asset, 94
Accounting Standards for Private Enterprise (ASPE), 62*f*
acquisition of, and historical costs, 54
agricultural produce, 294–298
on balance sheet, 142
biological assets, 137*f*, 144, 294–298, 310, 464, 487
capital assets, 472–473
contingent, 726
contract asset, 317
current, 94, 136, 137*f*, 142–143
deferred income tax assets, 969–970
defined, **50*f***
and discontinued operations, 101
disposals, 93–97, 93*f*
donated assets, 473–474
economic life, 1066
exploration and evaluation (E&E) assets, 481
financial assets, 137*f*, 143
in financial statements, 48
fixed assets, 144, 299–302
goodwill, 52, 464, 483–486
government assistance, 505–506
held-for-sale, 94–95, 137*f*
idle asset, 94
intangible assets. *See* intangible assets
investment property, 464
leased, 1080–1081
liquidation of, 827
long-lived asset. *See* long-lived assets
monetary assets, 298
net assets, 50*f*, 825
noncurrent assets, 94, 143–144
non-monetary assets, 298, 483
offsetting, 145
pension plan assets, 1137, 1145
property, plant, and equipment, 464
regional differences in, 137–138
return on assets, 140
return on total assets, 1315
self-constructed assets, 469
selling individual, 94
statement of financial position (SFP), not on, 141
statement of financial position (SFP), on, 137*f*, 142–144
tangible capital assets, 144
associates, **595**–596
Aston Hill Financial Inc., 626–627*f*
auditor's report, **1303**
authorization date, 778
authorized share capital, 828
Autonomy, 306
available information, 351
average collection period of accounts receivable, **1320**
average cost, 436–437

B
backdated, 305
backdating, **1206**
bad debt estimation, 353*f*
bad debt expense, **670**
bad debts allowance, 361
balance sheet, 21
See also statement of financial position (SFP)
Accounting Standards for Private Enterprise (ASPE), 136, 162–163
cash flows, 204
defined, **136**
BAM Investments Corp., 889
Bank Act, 4
bank debit and credit memos, **381**
bank loans
long-term bank financing, 774–775
short-term bank loans, 772–773
bank overdrafts, 200
bank reconciliation
adjusting entries, 380–381
balancing, 379–380
credit memo, 381
debit memo, 381
defined, 346–347
as internal control, 346–347
purpose of, 377
bank reconciliation adjustments, **347,** 377–379
bargain purchase option, **1065**
bargain renewal term, **1065**
barter, **298**
barter transactions, 298–299
basic earnings per share
See also diluted earnings per share; earnings per share (EPS)
adjustments, 1192
bonus shares, 1195
calculation, 1191
capital charge, 1192
contingently issuable ordinary shares, 1194
defined, **89, 1190**
disclosure, 1218–1219
illustration, 1213–1217
interpretation, 1190–1191
mandatorily convertible shares, 1193
multiple classes of common shares, 1196–1198
net profit or loss available to ordinary shareholders, 1191–1192
ordinary shares, 1191
senior shares, 1191
stock dividends, 1195–1196
stock splits, 1195–1196
weighted average ordinary shares (WAOS), 1192–1193
basket purchase, **466**
basket sale, 831
BCE Inc., 81, 153–155, 1085–1086*f*
Bell Canada Enterprises, 848–849
Belo Sun Mining, 904
betterment, **468**
bias, freedom from, 45
big bath, **17–18**
bill-and-hold arrangements, **277**–278
billings on contract, 290, 291
biological assets, 137*f*
Accounting Standards for Private Enterprise (ASPE), 310
amortization, 531
defined, **294–295, 464**

depreciation, 531
example, 295–298
presentation, 487
in statement of financial position (SFP), 144
blended payments, 367, 774
Bombardier Inc., 4–5, 85, 87*f*–88*f*, 89–92, 138, 139*f*, 140, 150, 151*f*, 157–160, 827, 953, 970, 972–974, 1034–1035, 1249, 1252
bond date, **778**
bond indenture, **775**
bond sinking funds, 142
bond valuation, 777–778
bonds
accrued interest, 784–785
amortization, 786
amortization tables, 780–783
bond date, 778
book value, 780
call option, 793
call price, 793
classification of, 777
convertible bonds, 1208–1209, 1212–1213
convertible debt, 891
defeasance, 795–796
defined, 775
delayed issuance, 784
face value, 778
fair value, 777–778, 786
foreign currency-denominated, 613–614
if-converted method, 1201
income bond, 886
initial discount amortization, 785
in-substance defeasance, 796–797
interest expense, 785–786
issuance, 784
maturity date, 778
nominal interest rate, 778
open-market extinguishment, 795
par value of, 778
payable, example, 778–783
payment dates different from statement dates, 783–784
redeemable bond, 793
retractable bond, 793
bonus shares, **1195**
bonuses, 723
book value, 299, 343
book value method
commercial substance, **300**–301
defined, **298, 893**
book value of the transferor, 164
borrowing, 358, 360–361
borrowing costs, 492*f*
Accounting Standards for Private Enterprise (ASPE), 801
capitalization of, 790–792
defined, 791
borrowing opportunity rate (BOR), 1066*n*
See also incremental borrowing rate (IBR)
brand names, 144, 477*f*
breakage, **731**
Brookfield Asset Management Incorporated, 463, 502–503*f*, 591
bundle of goods and/or services, 284, 320
business combination, **1194**
buying earnings, **1194**

C
CAE Inc., 135, 265, 1251–1252
call option, **793, 915**
call price, **793,** 888
callable shares, **832**
Canada Business Corporations Act (CBCA), 826
Canada Labour Code, 733
Canada Pension Plan (CPP), 722
Canada Revenue Agency (CRA), 13, 309, 564, 886, 1073
Canadian Business Corporations Act (CBCA), 2, 826
Canadian Institute of Chartered Accountants (CICA), 2
Canadian National Railway (CNR), 1059
Canadian Tire Corporation Limited, 715, 717–718, 745–746
Cangene Corporation, 199, 834–835
capital assets
equity securities, in exchange for, 473
financed with low-interest debt, 472–473
capital charge, **898,** 1192
Capital Cost Allowance (CCA), 13, 564–566, 955, 1015
capital gain, 954
capital lease
See also finance leases
Accounting Standards for Private Enterprise (ASPE), 1099
defined, **1099**
disclosure, 1100
operating lease, *vs.*, 1098–1099
capital maintenance, **42–43,** 44*f*
capital transactions, 153–155
capitalization
Accounting Standards for Private Enterprise (ASPE), 801
avoiding lease, 1087–1088
of borrowing costs, 790–792, 801
calculations, 791–792
capitalize, **213**
capitalized costs, 487
captive leasing companies, **1088**
carrying value, 164, 530
cash, 137*f*
Accounting Standards for Private Enterprise (ASPE), 371
classification of, 345
collection and revenue recognition, 279–281
defined, **142, 200**
delayed payment contracts, 283–284
as financial asset, 344
FVTPL category, 345
internal control over, 346–347
reporting, 347
statement of cash flows (SCF), 1375
T-account, 213–220
cash conversion cycle, **1330**–1331
cash disbursements journal, **681,** 682*f*
cash discounts, **348**–349, **409**
cash dividends payable, 720
cash equivalents, 137*f*
defined, **142, 200, 345, 592**
reporting, 347
statement of cash flows (SCF), 628
T-account, 213–220
cash flow from operating activities, 12
cash flow per share, 12, **1219**
cash flows
analysis, 204
assessment, 12–13
capitalized costs, reporting, 487
classification of, 223–224
discounted cash flows, 283
examples of, 201*f*
and policy choices, 212–213
predictions, 12–13
and realization, 53
and recognition, 53
separate disclosure items, 224–226
to shareholders, 833
speeding cash flows from sales, 356–357
cash receipts journal, **681**–682, 682*f*
cash redemption, 891
cash-generating unit (CGU), **98, 546,** 547, 548–549
cash-settled payment, 905
cash-settled plans
defined, **903**
forfeiture, 912–913
stock appreciation rights (SARs), 911–912
cash-to-cash cycle, 359
CCA. *See* Capital Cost Allowance (CCA)
changes in accounting estimates
defined, **1250**
described, 153
disclosure, 1250–1251
disclosure example, 1251–1252
ethics, 1253, 1271
prospective application, 1250
changes in accounting policy. *See* accounting policy changes
changes in net assets, 266, 272
changes in wealth, 82
chartered banks, 4
Chase Container Corporation, 436–439
cheque register, 681
cheques, 377–379
chief financial officer (CFO), 11
Chrysler Financial Canada, 1088
CPA Canada Handbook, Part I (IFRS), 2, 21
CPA Canada Handbook, Part II (ASPE), 2, 21, 162, 163, 979, 1099–1100
Clarification of Acceptable Methods of Depreciation and Amortization, 559
classes of items, 47
classes of shares, **826**
classification
accounts receivable, 348
alternative classification of statement of cash flows (SCF), 1386–1387
assets and liabilities on SFP, 136–138
cash, 345
cash flows, 223–224
compound instrument, 890–891
computer software, 479
convertible debt, 890–891
corporate income tax, 970
debt *vs.* equity, 887
derecognition, 359–361
equity *vs.* debt, 887
factors, 887–888
fair value through profit or loss (FVTPL), 356
finance leases, 1064–1067
financial assets, 344
of financial instruments, 886–892
lessor, 1100
long-term leases, 1108–1109
mutual funds, 890
other comprehensive income (OCI), 83
of pension plans, 1132
perpetual debt, 890

classification (*continued*)
redeemable shares, 890
retractable preferred shares, 888–889
statement of cash flows (SCF), 200, 223–224, 1375
by substance, 886–887
tax status of investment, 886–887
closing entries, 675–676
Clublink Enterprises Limited, 854
collateral security, **362, 719**
collectability, **319**
collection, 279–280
commercial mortgages, 774
commercial paper, **345**
commercial substance, **300**–301
commitments, **49**
common shares, **826, 1191**
common-size (vertical) analysis, 1307–1309, **1309**–1311, 1314
comparability, **45**
compensated-absence liabilities, 733–734
compensating balance, **345**
compensation plans, 914–915
completed-contract method, **308**–309, 319
completeness, **45**
complex financial instruments, and statement of cash flows (SCF), 919
compliance statement, **156**
component accounting, **465–466**
component depreciation accounting, **532**–533*f*, 542, 559
compound financial instruments, 885, **886,** 890–891
compound plans, 913–915
comprehensive income
and ASPE, 107
consolidated statements of, 88*f*
defined, **82**–83
net income, *vs.*, 91
comprehensive tax allocation, **957**–959, 979, 1036
computer software costs, 477*f*, 479–480
Conceptual Framework, 106–107, 162
Conceptual Framework for Financial Reporting (IFRS), 10, 43
conditional payments, 723
confirmatory value, **44**
consideration, **54, 269**
consignee, 278
consignment, **408**
consignment arrangements, **278**–279
consignor, 278
consistency, **45**
consolidated balance sheet, 488*f*–489*f*
consolidated financial statements, 1332–1334
consolidated income statement, 87*f*, 89
consolidated method, 600
consolidated statement of cash flows, 203*f*
consolidated statement of financial position, 139*f*
consolidated statement of operations, 86*f*
consolidated statements of changes in equity, 148, 149*f*, 150, 151*f*
consolidated statements of comprehensive income, 88*f*
consolidation, 362, **600,** 623–624
constant dollar capital maintenance, **42**
construction-in-progress inventory, **290**
constructive liability, 730
constructive obligation, **103–104,** 105*f*, **474, 716**
contingencies, 157
Accounting Standards for Private Enterprise (ASPE), 163–164
defined, **158, 724**
disclosures for, 745
and liabilities, 726
contingent, **278**
contingent assets, 726
contingent lease payments, **1065**
contingent rent, **1066,** 1087
contingently issuable ordinary shares, **1194**
continuity assumption, **41**
continuum of asset disposals, 93*f*
contra account, **670**
contract asset, **317**
contract liability, **317**
contract-based approach, **268**–269, 307, 317, 318–320
contracts
compliance, 14–15
customer loyalty programs, **286**–287
executory contract, **49**
franchise fees, **287**
long-term contracts, 288–291, 293–294, 321
multiple goods and service contracts, 284–287
onerous contract, **293**
contracts in progress, 407
contractual rate, 778
contractual right, 344
contributed capital, 146–147
contributed surplus, **146**
contributory pension plan, **1132**
control, 271, 272, 273, 278, 595
control account, 665, 678
control blocks, **11**
convention, **542**
convergence of IFRS, 3
convergence project, 20
conversion cost, **410**
conversion of preferred shares, 827
conversion of shares, 835
convertible bonds, 1208–1209, 1212–1213
convertible debt
Accounting Standards for Private Enterprise (ASPE), 922
accounting treatment of, 891
book value method, 893
capital charge, 898
cash redemption, 891
characteristics of, 891
classification, 890–891
conversion, 893
conversion at investor's option, 892–896
conversion mandatory, 897–899
debt principal, 899
defined, **886**
diluted earnings per share, 1208–1210
discount rate, 894
earnings, impact on, 895
fair value hierarchy, 894
floating conversion price per share, 891, 895, 899
forced conversion, 891
incremental method, 894, 897
initial recognition, 892–893
interest obligation, 899
measurement, 894–895, 897–898
repayment, 893–894
share equity alternatives, 898–899
convertible senior securities, **1199**
copyrights, 144, 477*f*, 536*f*
corporate income tax
See also interperiod tax allocation
Accounting Standards for Private Enterprise (ASPE), 979
approach to income tax questions, 962–969
Capital Cost Allowance (CCA), 955
capital gain, 954
classification, 970
deferred income tax, 963–969
deferred income tax assets, 969–970
deferred income tax liabilities, 969, 978–979
disclosures, 971–975, 979
discontinued operations, 971
income tax expense, 974–975
income tax payable, 962–963
interperiod tax allocation. *See* interperiod tax allocation
introduction, 953
investment tax credit, 984–987
netting, 970–971
provision for income tax, 954
shorter computational approach, 975–977
statement of cash flows (SCF), 977
statement of financial position elements, 969–971
tax expense for the year, 969
tax rates, 968–969, 973–974
taxable income, 962–963
taxes payable method, 957, 979
corporate reporting objectives, 534
corporations
See also private companies; public companies
Board of Directors, 826
dividends. *See* dividends
multi-industry corporations, 1334
share capital, 826
shareholders' equity, 826
corridor method, 1148
cost deferrals, 275–277, 729–730
cost flow methods, 435–439
cost investments, **595**
cost method, **599,** 609, 631
cost model, **465,** 482–483
cost of goods sold, 670–671
cost ratio, 421
cost recovery method, **280**–281, 288
cost to complete, 292
cost to date, 292
cost-based inventory. *See* inventory
cost/benefit effectiveness, **46**–47
cost-reduction approach, 984
costs
acquisition cost, 535, 593
average cost, 436–437
capitalization of borrowing costs, 790–792
capitalized costs, 487
computer software costs, 477*f*, 479–480
conversion cost, **410**
current service cost (CSC), 1141
debt issuance costs, 786–787
decommissioning costs, 544
deferred, 275–277
development costs, 478–479
direct costs, 292, 410

elements of, 469, 476
environmental, 466
executory costs, 1062, 1075–1076
future costs, 103
historical cost, 36, 141, 406*f*
ineligible costs, 479
interest cost, **469,** 471
inventory costs, 408–410
investment tax credit (ITC), 984–985
laid-down cost, **408,** 412
overhead costs, 410, **469**
research costs, 478–479
safety, 466
share issue costs, 832
site restoration costs, 474–475
subsequent costs, 467
website development costs, 477*f*
counter the risk, 917
counterbalancing errors, 1267–1268
coupon rate, 778
coupons, 731
covenants, **9,** 15, **775**–776
CPP (Canada pension plan), 722
CRA. *See* Canada Revenue Agency (CRA)
credit balances, 348
credit card transactions, 356
credit facility, **772**
credit memo, **381**
credit sales method, **353,** 355
credit unions, 4
critical estimates and decisions, 306–307
critical event, **269**
cash collection, 279–280
at delivery, 271, 284
cross-sectional comparisons, **1306**
crown corporations, **4**
CSC. *See* current service cost (CSC)
cumulative currency translation difference (CCTD), 91, 148
cumulative dividends, 827
cumulative foreign currency translation account, **852**
cumulative senior shares, 1192
currency
foreign currency, 344, 345–346
reporting, 4
stable dollar, 42
current accounts, 200
current assets
cash, 137*f*, 142
classification of, 137
defined, **94, 136**
in statement of financial position (SFP), 142–143
current cost, **54**
current exchange rate, 344, 346, 368
current income tax, 92
current liabilities, **136, 743**
current ratio, **1330**
current service cost (CSC), **1141**
current tax liabilities, 137*f*
current-noncurrent presentation, 136
customer lists, 477*f*
customer loyalty programs, **286**–287, 731–732
cut-off errors, **417**–418, 426

D

Daimler Chrysler Financial Services Inc., 1088
damaged inventory, 415–416
date of sale, 280
days in inventory, **1321**
days in payables, **1322**
death benefits, **1138**
debenture, **775**
debit card transactions, 356–357
debit memo, **381**
debit-credit convention, **659**
debt
classification factors, 887–888
convertible debt. *See* convertible debt
debt-to-equity continuum, 886
modification of, 797
perpetual debt, 886, 890
substitution of, 797
debt amortization table, 1070–1071
debt covenants, **775**–776
debt issuance costs, **786**–787
debt retirement
defeasance, 795–796
derecognition, 792
derecognition at maturity, 793
derecognition prior to maturity, 793–794
in-substance defeasance, 796–797
recording, 794–795
substitution or modification of debt, 797
debt service ratios, **1322,** 1327
debt transactions on cash flow statements, 211–212
debt-to-equity continuum, 886
debt-to-total assets, **1326**
debt-to-total capitalization, **1326**
declaration date, **839**
declassification as held-for-sale, 97
declining balance, 140
declining-balance (DB) method, 538*f*, 539*f*
decommissioning costs, 544
decommissioning obligation, **474**–475
decomposition analysis, 1307
defeasance, **795**–796
defensive-interval ratio, **1331**–1332
deferral method, **959**–961
deferrals
adjusting journal entries (AJEs), 666–667
cost deferral, 275–277
defined, **52**
expenses, 668
revenue deferrals, 275–277, 668
deferral-type entries, **666**–667
deferred corporate income tax, 963–969, 978
deferred expenses, **668**
deferred gross margin, 280
deferred income tax
corporate income tax, 963–969
leases, 1073
loss year, 1012
deferred income tax liabilities, 969, 978–979
deferred revenue, **668**
deferred tax liabilities, 137*f*
deferred taxes, 92–93
deficit, **837**
defined benefit obligation, **1137**
defined benefit plans
10% corridor method, 1148
Accounting Standards for Private Enterprise (ASPE), 1161–1164
actuarial cost methods, 1138–1140
asset ceiling, 1137, 1144
curtailment classification, 1141–1143
defined, **1132**
demographic assumptions, 1138
disposition of accumulated OCI amounts, 1148
evaluation, 1148–1149
example, 1142–1143
expected *vs.* actual return, 1145
final pay pension plans, 1136
financial assumptions, 1138
flat benefit pension plan, 1136
introduction, 1136–1140
net defined benefit pension liability (asset), 1137
net interest on the net defined benefit pension liability (asset), 1143–1144
netting, 1148–1149
obligation, 1137
pension holiday, 1137
pension plan assets, 1137, 1145
re-measurement of the net defined benefit pension liability (asset), 1144–1146
service cost element, 1141–1143
settlement classification, 1141–1143
statement of financial position (SFP), 1146–1148
structure, 1137
termination benefits, 1142
termination classification, 1141–1143
variables to be estimated, 1137–1138
defined contribution plans
Accounting Standards for Private Enterprise (ASPE), 1161–1164
current service cost, 1135–1136
defined, **1132**
delayed payment, 1135–1136
prepaid amounts, 1136
degree of completion, 291
delayed issuance, 784
delayed payment contracts, 283–284
delayed revenue recognition, 277
depletion, **530**
deposits, 377, 720
depreciable amount, **530**
depreciation
See also amortization
accounting policy choices, 533–537
asset retirement obligations, 544
biological assets, 531
Capital Cost Allowance (CCA), 564–566
conceptual analysis of, 534
conceptual basis of, 530–531
decommissioning costs, 544
defined, **530**
disclosure requirements, 552–557*f*
equity method, 620
estimates required, 535–536
ethics, 558–559
example, 552–557*f*
factors influencing policy choice, 534–535
finance leases, 1076
fractional-year amortization, 542–544
generally accepted accounting principles (GAAP), 669–670
group depreciation, 544–545
investment property, 531
nature of, 530–532
policy, 140
recognition of amortization expense, 531
spare parts, 537
standby equipment, 537
statement of cash flows (SCF), 558
depreciation expense, **669**–670

depreciation methods
changes, 1252
declining-balance (DB) method, 538*f*, 539*f*
diminishing-balance (DB) method, 541
productive-output (PO) method, 538*f*, 539*f*, 540
service-hours (SH) method, 538*f*, 539*f*, 540
straight-line (SL) method, 537–539*f*
depreciation period, 536
depreciation schedules, 539*f*
derecognition
See also recognition
classification, 359–361
debt retirement, 792
defined, **357**
ethics, 359
long-lived assets, 482–483
at maturity, 793
prior to maturity, 793–794
tests to allow, 359–360
derecognized, **792**
derivative instruments, **899**
derivatives
accounting recognition, 916–917
described, 899
embedded derivative, 916
forward contract, 915
futures contract, 915–916
hedges, 917–918
nature of, 915–916
options, 915
stand-alone derivatives, 916
detachable contract, 901
determinable amount of cash, 344
development, 478
different market and stated rates, 364–365
diluted earnings per share
See also basic earnings per share; earnings per share (EPS)
actual conversions during the period, 1206–1210
adjustment for contingently issuable shares, 1200–1201
adjustment for dilutive options, 1200
adjustment for dilutive senior securities, 1201
anti-dilutive elements, 1200
backdating, 1206
calculation, 1200–1205
calculation, example, 1203–1205
cascade, 1205–1206
contingently issuable ordinary shares, 1199
converted debt, 1208–1210
converted preferred shares, 1206–1208
convertible bonds at issuer's option, 1212
convertible securities and options extinguished during the year, 1211
convertible securities and options issued during the year, 1210
convertible senior securities, 1199
defined, **89, 1199**
dilutive elements, 1200
dilutive senior securities, 1201
dilutive *vs.* anti-dilutive, 1200
disclosure, required, 1218–1219
disclosure note, 1218–1219
earnings dilution, 1199
exercised options, 1210
flow chart of steps in calculating, 1203*f*
forced conversion, 1211
FVTPL liabilities, 1212
if-converted method, 1201
illustration, 1213–1217
individual effect, 1201–1202
interest expense, 1211
interpretation, 1190–1191
loss year, in, 1212
public companies, reporting, 1189–1190
reference point, 1211
reporting, 1205
share price measurement, 1212
steps in calculating, 1202*f*
stock option, 1199
treasury stock method, 1200
diluted earnings per share cascade, **1205**–1206
dilutive elements, **1200**
dilutive options, 1200
dilutive senior securities, 1201
diminishing-balance (DB) method, **541**
direct costs, 292, 410
direct inventory reduction method, 414–415
direct observation, **56**
direct presentation of operating activities, 208–209, 221–222, 307, 1384–1386
direct write-off, 355–356
direct-financing lease, **1096**
disclosed basis of accounting (DBA), **6–7**
disclosure
accounting estimates, changes in, 1250–1251
accounting policy changes, 1262
and accounting policy presentation, 306–307
Accounting Standards for Private Enterprise (ASPE), 84, 310, 923, 979, 1100
accounts receivable, 369–370
basic earnings per share, 1218–1219
capital lease, 1100
cash flows, 13, 223–224
constructive obligation, 103–104, 105*f*
contingencies, 745
corporate income tax, 971–975, 979
critical estimates and decisions, 306–307
diluted earnings per share, 1218–1219
discontinued operations, 100
earnings per share (EPS), 1218–1219
economic dependence, 161*f*
example of, 101–102, 102*f*, 626–627*f*
expanded disclosure, 18
finance lease, 1084–1085
financial instruments, 625–627, 919–920
for financial liabilities, 745
impairment loss, 550
information, 361
intangible assets, 488
International Financial Accounting Standards (IFRS), 1251
inventory, 424–425
investment tax credit (ITC), 987
investments, 625–629
lessee, 1084–1085
lessors, 1094
long-term liabilities, 798–800
loss carryforward, 1034
operating lease, 1084, 1100
other post-employment benefits, 1159–1160
pension plans, 1159–1160
poison pill, 901
previously unrecognized tax loss, 1034
property, plant, and equipment, 488
prospective application, 1263
provisions, 745–746
recognition *vs.*, 49
retrospective application, 1262
revenue recognition, 306–307
separate disclosure items, 224–226
share capital, 854
statement of cash flows (SCF), 919–920, 1384–1386
strategic investments, 627
tax losses, 1034
unrecognized tax loss carryforwards, 1034
disclosure notes, 21
accounting standards, 156–157
Accounting Standards for Private Enterprise (ASPE), 163–164
additional detail, 157
basic earnings per share, 1218–1219
compliance statement, 156
computer software, 480
contingencies, 157, 158
defined, **155**
diluted earnings per share, 1218–1219
earnings per share, 1218–1219
economic dependence, 160–161
general classification of, 155–156
goodwill, 490*f*, 492*f*–494*f*
guarantees, 157, 158
intangible assets, 492*f*–494*f*
long-lived assets, 489*f*–495*f*
measurement uncertainty, 157
non-cash transaction, 211
property, plant, and equipment, 489*f*–490*f*, 495*f*
related party transactions, 157, 160
research and development costs, 491*f*–492*f*
revaluation model, 568
segment disclosures, 159–160
subsequent events, 161–162
underlying assumptions, 157
discontinued operations, 90
amortization, 98
and asset groups, 101
defined, **98–99**
equity method, 619
example, 99
illustration of, 100–101
reporting, 99–102
statement of comprehensive income (SCI), 99
statement of financial position, 99–100
discount, 472, **604**
discount rate, 894, 1138
discounted cash flows, 283
discounting
defined, **717**
interperiod tax allocation, 961
present value calculation, 735
and provisions, 726
disposal groups, **97,** 137*f*
distinct performance obligations, **320**
distressed markets, 603
dividend reinvestment plan (DRIP), **844**
dividend revenue, 304–305
dividends
cash dividends, 839–840

classification of, 889
complex/unequal dividend entitlements, 1197–1198
cumulative dividends, 827
cumulative on preferred shares, 840
declaration date, 839
declared, 1198
disclosure of cash flows, 223–224
dividend reinvestment plan (DRIP), 844
ex-dividend date, 839
liquidating dividends, 843
liquidity test, 839
multiple classes of common shares, 1196–1198
nature of, 838–839
participating dividends, 827
participating on preferred shares, 840–842
payment date, 839
priority, 826–827
property dividends, 842
record date, 839
recording, 889
relevant dividend dates, 839
scrip dividend, 843
stock dividends, 843–847
summary, 848
unequal dividend entitlements, 1197
dividends in arrears, **827**
Domtar Paper (Canada) Inc., 849
donated assets, 473–474
donated capital, **850**–851
double-declining balance (DDB), **541**
double-entry system, **659**
doubtful accounts, 350–351
downstream, **623**

E
early adoption, **1264**
early retirement, 1138
earnings
See also income
big bath, 17–18
defined, 82
income smoothing, 16
maximization, 17
minimization, 17
revenue recognition, 306
volatility, 599
earnings before income taxes (EBT), 90
earnings before interest and taxes (EBIT), 90
earnings dilution, **1199**
earnings expectations, 57
earnings per share (EPS)
Accounting Standards for Private Enterprise (ASPE), 109, 1220
basic earnings per share. *See* basic earnings per share
cash flow per share, 1219
diluted earnings per share. *See* diluted earnings per share
disclosure, required, 1218–1219
disclosure note, 1218–1219
ethics, 1191, 1194
figures, 1190
illustration, 1213–1217
interpretation, 1190–1191
other per share amounts, 1219
public companies, reporting, 1189–1190
references in financial press, 1189
restatement of, 1217
share capital, subsequent changes in, 1217–1218
share retirement, 832
statement of comprehensive income (SCI), 89
earnings quality, 12
earnings statement. *See* income statement
earnings targets, **57–58**
earnings-based approach, **268,** 269–271
eBay Inc., 266–267
EBIT (earnings before interest and taxes), 1311
EBITDA (earnings before interest, tax, depreciation, and amortization), **775,** 1311
economic dependence, 160–161
economic entity, 1332
economic income, **82**
economic life, **1066**
economic service potential, 530
economic value added (EVA), **268**
effect of escalation clause, 889
effective interest rates, **735, 777**
effective-interest method, 363–366, **605**–607*f*, **736**
efficiency ratios
accounts payable turnover, 1322
accounts receivable aging schedule, 1321
accounts receivable turnover, 1319–1321
accounts receivable turnover ratio, 1321
asset turnover, 1322
average collection period of accounts receivable, 1320
defined, **1319**
for Grocery Retailer Inc., 1324*f*
inventory turnover ratio, 1321–1322
objective of, 1319
summary of, 1323*f*
EI (employment insurance), 722
elements, **47**
embedded derivative, **916**
embezzlement, 346
employee benefits, 722
employee disability, 1138
employee payment option, and phantom stock plans, 913
employee share-based arrangements, 905–906
employee stock options, 907–909
employee turnover, 1138
employment insurance (EI), 722
enacted tax rate, 1023, 1027
end-of-lease, 1108
Enron, 154
entity concept, **41**
entity-specific assumptions, **39,** 40–43
entry value, 55
environment, and financial statement analysis, 1303
environmental costs, 466
environmental obligations, 730
EPS. *See* earnings per share (EPS)
equity, 163, 887
equity components of debt instruments, 146
equity method
Accounting Standards for Private Enterprise (ASPE), 631
acquisition, 619
adjustments, 619
consolidation, 623–624
defined, **600**
discontinued operations, 619
downstream, 623
example, 619–622
fair values, 620–621
goodwill, 620–621
goodwill impairment, 623
illustrated, 618–619
investment revenue, 621–622
other comprehensive income (OCI), 619
reclassification, 624–625
subsequent depreciation, 620
unrealized profit elimination, 623
upstream profit, 623
equity-settled plans, **903,** 907–910
errors, 153, 154, 417–419, 1265–1268
See also prior-period errors
estimable returns, 349
estimates. *See* accounting estimates
ethical professional judgement, **38**
ethics
of accountants, 11
amortization estimates, 558–559
best estimates for compensation cost accruals, 909
buying earnings, 1194
capital assets, 472
capitalization policy, 487
changes in accounting estimates, 1253, 1271
changes in assumptions and estimates, 1271
choice of accounting policy, 213
consignment arrangements, 279
constructive liability, 716
depreciation estimates, 558–559
derecognition, 359
earnings manipulation, 1271
earnings per share (EPS), 1194
earnings per share (EPS) calculations, 1191
embezzlement, 346
errors, 154
exclusion of actuarial gains and losses, 1149
exercising professional judgement, 59–60
future tax benefits, 1035
held-for-sale classification, 95
insider information, 833
in-substance defeasance, 796
internal control system, 346
inventory accounting, 425–426
lawsuits, 727
lease reporting, 1098
management representations, 594
net realizable value (NRV), 415
pension plans and best estimates, 1138
relevancy of information, 1255
retirement transactions, 794
revenue recognition policy decision, 275, 278, 305–306
users objectives *vs.* managers' motivations, 19
window dressing, 1098, 1255
evaluation costs, 477*f*
evaluative decisions, 9
events, 661–662, 663
events approach, 82
exact calculation approach, 542–543
exception reporting, 14
exchange gain or loss, **369,** 724
exchange of dissimilar goods or services, 299

exchange of non-monetary assets, 483
exchange of similar goods or services, 298–299
exchange rates, 42, 368
fluctuations, 788–790
foreign currency, 344, 345–346
long-term debt, 788
spot rate, 723, 788
exchange value, 164
ex-dividend date, **839**
executory contracts, **49, 728**
executory costs, **1062,** 1075–1076
exercise date, **899**
exit value, 55
expanded disclosure, **18**
expected value, **725**
expedient recording method, **667**
expense recognition, and matching, 52–53
expenses
accrued expenses, **668**
bad debt expense, **670**
deferred expenses, **668**
defined, **49, 50*f*, 266**
gains and losses, *vs.,* 266
incidental expenses, **471**
income tax expense, **671**–672, 954
tax expense for the year, 969
exploration and evaluation (E&E) assets, 481
Exposure Draft, 559
external reporting of investments, 597*f*
external users, **11**
external-user objectives
cash flow assessment and predictions, 12–13
contract compliance, 14–15
income tax deferral, 13–14
managers' motivations, *vs.,* 19
performance evaluation, 15–16
stewardship, 15
Exxon Mobile Corporation, 160

F

face value, **363, 778**
factoring, 357
factors of production, 41
fair market value cap, **302**–303, 471–472
fair value
biological assets, 294
bonds, 777–778, 786
defined, **55**–57, **601, 899**
derivatives, 916
in distressed markets, 603
as financial asset, 344
financial liabilities, 800
fixed assets valuation, 299
hierarchy for measuring, 601–602
and impairment, 607–608
sources of, 301
unavailable, 286
undeterminable, 602–603
fair value ceiling, 1066–1067
fair value hierarchy, **894,** 904
fair value less costs of disposal, **546**
fair value less the cost to sell, **94**
fair value method
commercial substance, 300–301
comparison, 617
defined, **298, 599**
fixed assets, 301–302
stock dividends, 845
fair value model, **465**
fair-value-through-other-comprehensive-income (FVTOCI) investment
adjustment, 614
defined, **594**–595
earnings volatility, 599
example, 614
impairment, 617
reporting, 614–617
fair-value-through-profit-and-loss (FVTPL)
accounts receivable, 348
classification, 356
defined, **594**
example, 610–614
impairment, 613
investment, 594, 599
liability, 1212
other issues, 613–614
faithful representation, **44**–45, 47, 90
FASB. *See* Financial Accounting Standards Board (FASB)
feedback value, **44**
fee-for-usage contract, 1060
fiduciary enterprise, **4**
FIFO, **438**
final pay pension plans, **1136**
final-year convention, 544
finance industry, 1088
finance leases
See also leases
accounting for, lessee, 1068
amortization table, 1070–1071, 1075
applying the lease guidelines, 1069–1070
bargain purchase option, 1065
bargain renewal term, 1065
classification as, 1064–1067
contingent lease payments, 1065
contingent rent, 1066
cost allocation, 1076–1077
deferred income tax, 1073
defined, 1061, **1064**
depreciating leased assets, 1071
depreciation, 1076
disclosure, 1084–1085
disclosure note, 1085, 1086*f*
economic life, 1066
executory costs, 1075–1076
fair value cap, 1074–1075
fair value ceiling, 1066–1067
financial intermediary, 1067
financial statements, 1072–1073
guaranteed residual value, 1065
guidelines, 1064–1065, 1069–1070
illustration, basic, 1068–1069
implicit lease interest rate, 1066, 1074–1075
incremental borrowing rate (IBR), 1066
informal guideline, 1067
initial direct costs, 1065–1066
interest calculation, 1070–1071
interest expense, 1076–1077
International Accounting Standards Board (IASB), 1107
journal entries, full set, 1078
land and buildings, 1083–1084
lease term, 1065, 1068, 1074
lessee accounting, basic example, 1069–1074
lessee accounting, modified example, 1074–1080
liability balance calculation, 1080
minimum net lease payments, 1065
net lease payments, 1065
recording liability, lesee, 1072
recording of, by lessee, 1078–1079
recording of, by lessor, 1092*f*
residual value, 1077
sale and leaseback, 1082–1083
short-cut method of calculation, 1080
statement of cash flows (SCF), 1073
statement of comprehensive income (SCI), 1073
statement of financial position (SFP), 1072–1073
unguaranteed residual value, 1065
useful life, 1066
Financial Accounting Standards Board (FASB), 20, 38, 268
leases, 1098, 1107, 1111–1112
post-employment benefits, 1161
financial assets, 137*f*, 143
accounts/notes receivables as, 344
cash as, 344
classification, 344
defined, **344**
fair value, 344
foreign currency, 344, 345–346
International Accounting Standards Board (IASB), 922
transaction value, 344
financial flexibility, 138
financial instruments
See also investments
classification by substance, 886–887
classification factors, 887–888
classification of, 886–892
compound financial instruments, 885, 886
defined, **592,** 716
disclosure of, 625–627, 919–920
early adoption, 1264
fair values and classification of, 370
hybrid financial instruments, 886
long-term debt. *See* long-term debt
prospective application, 1264
under review, 371
statement of cash flows (SCF), 919
stock options, 899–901
financial intermediary, **1067**
financial lease, 1060, 1099
financial liabilities, 137*f*
See also liabilities
common, 718–723
defined, **716**
disclosure for, 745
fair value, recording, 800
other financial liabilities, 717
Financial Post, 11
financial reporting
cash flow objectives, 12–13
conflicting objectives, 18
and contract compliance, 14–15
evaluative decisions, 9
general purpose, 10–11
income tax reporting, *vs.,* 13–14
objectives of, 8–10, 10*f*, 21
and performance evaluation, 16
and stewardship, 15
user objectives, 11–16
financial risk, **1326**
financial statement analysis
accounting policies, examination of, 1303–1304
accounting standards, 1304

application of techniques, 1304
auditor's report, 1303
common-size (vertical) analysis, 1307–1309, 1309–1311, 1314
comparative information, 1306
consolidated financial statements, 1332–1334
data gathering, 1302–1304
decision focus, 1302
decomposition analysis, 1307
environment, 1303
horizontal analysis, 1311–1314
information from notes, 1305*f*
multi-industry corporations, 1334
other analytical techniques, 1335
ratio analysis. *See* ratio analysis
recasting, 1304
recasting, demonstration case, 1342–1351
residual analysis, 1335
restatement, demonstration case, 1342–1351
restatement of, 1304
result analysis and interpretation, 1305
review engagement, 1303
statistical multivariate ratio analysis, 1335
time-series analysis, 1335
trend analysis, 1311–1314
vertical (common-size) analysis, 1307–1309, 1309–1311, 1314
financial statements
and Accounting Standards for Private Enterprise (ASPE), 21
assets in, 48
balance sheet. *See* balance sheet
concepts of, 36–38
consolidated financial statements, 1332–1334
defined, **660**
direct economic impacts, 9
disclosure notes, 155–162
elements of, 47–53, 50*f*, 61
finance lease, 1072–1073
general purpose, 36
IFRS requirements, 19–21
income statement. *See* income statement
liabilities in, 48
limitations of concepts, 36
notes to financial statement, 1073
off-balance-sheet financing, 1086
preparation of, 673–675
presentation. *See* presentation formats
purpose of, 8
recognition, 49
restated financial statements, 1342–1351
statement of cash flows (SCF). *See* statement of cash flows (SCF)
statement of changes in equity (SCE). *See* statement of changes in equity (SCE)
statement of comprehensive income (SCI). *See* statement of comprehensive income (SCI)
statement of financial position (SFP). *See* statement of financial position (SFP)
financing
100% financing, 1086–1087
equity financing. *See* shareholders' equity
long-term, 773–777
off-balance-sheet financing, 1086
reporting example, 776
short-term, 772–773
sources of, 772–777
financing activities, **200,** 1375
finished goods, 410
first-in, first-out (FIFO), **438**
fixed assets
defined, **144**
exchanges of, 299–302
fair value method, 301–302
flat benefit pension plan, **1136**
flipping, **99**
flow-through approach, 984
flow-through method, **957**
FOB destination, 408
FOB shipping point, 407
forced conversion, 891, **1211**
Ford Motor Company, 268
foreign currency
and debt denomination, 788–790
exchange rates, 344, 345–346, 788–790
hedges, **788**
investments, 613
payables, 723–724
receivables, 368–369
foreign currency translation
adjustment, 147–148
defined, **5**
gains and losses, 852–853
foreign operations, 852–853
foreign subsidiaries, 91, 856
forfeit, **906**
forfeiture
Accounting Standards for Private Enterprise (ASPE), 923
cash-settled plans, 912–913
employee stock options, 908–909
forgivable loan, **505**
forward contract, **915**
fractional share rights, 846–847
fractional-year amortization, 542–544
fractional-year depreciation, 542–544
franchise fees, **287**
franchise rights, 477*f*
franchises, 144, 279, 536*f*
fraud, 405, 426
free on board (FOB), 407
freedom from bias, 45
freedom from material error, **45**
full periodic interest, 603
full-first-year convention, 543–544
fully diluted earnings per share, 1199
fully participating shares, 841–842
function within the enterprise, 85
functional currency, **4, 853**
funding, **1138**
future benefit, 48
future benefit accounting, 1034–1035
See also tax losses
future costs of restructuring, 103
future income tax, 979
future taxes, 92–93
futures contract, **915**–916
FVTOCI. *See* fair-value-through-other-comprehensive-income (FVTOCI) investment
FVTPL. *See* fair-value-through-profit-and-loss (FVTPL)

G

GAAP. *See* generally accepted accounting principles (GAAP)
gains
defined, **48,** 82, **266**
exchange gain, 369
holding gains, 599
long-lived assets, 487
realized holding gains, 599
revenue and expenses, *vs.,* 266
unrealized holding gains, 599
general journal, **663,** 664*f*, **681,** 683*f*
general ledgers, **664**–665
general presentation format, 84–91
general purpose financial reporting, **10**–11
general purpose financial statements, 36
general revenue recognition principle, 268–271
generally accepted accounting principles (GAAP)
amortization, 534, 564, 669–670
choice of, 4
deferral method, 959
depreciation, 534, 564, 669–670
inventory valuation, 412
limitations of applying GAAP, 140
market values, 141
private companies, 6–7
public corporations, 2, 4
types of, 1304
U.S. GAAP, 4, 5, 20
gift cards, 731
going-concern assumption, **41**
goods
barter, 298
exchange of dissimilar goods, 299
exchange of similar goods, 298–299
multiple goods and service contracts, 284–287
purchased and in transit, 407
purchased for resale, 408–409
transfer at a single point in time, 271–281
transfer over time, 282–283
goods and services tax (GST), **409**
goods purchased and in transit, 407
goods purchased for resale, 408–409
goodwill, 52
defined, **464, 483–484**
disclosure notes, 490*f*, 492*f*–494*f*
equity method, 620–621
example, 485–486
form of acquisition, 486
impairment, 550–551
measurement of, 484
negative goodwill, 486
reversal of, 551
useful life, 532
governance, EU approach, 41
government assistance, 474, 505–506
government business enterprises, 4
government grants, and investment tax credit (ITC), 987
Grocery Retailer Inc., 1307–1313, 1319–1322, 1324
gross basis, **267**
gross lease basis, **1091**–1094
gross lease basis leases, 1091–1093
gross margin method, **419**–421
gross margin rate, **419**
gross method, 1093–1094, 1096
gross revenue, 266–268
group accounts, 544
group asset, 550
group depreciation, **544**–545
group purchase, 466
GST (goods and services tax), 409
guarantee of preferred shares, 827

guaranteed investment certificates (GICs), **345**
guaranteed residual value, **1065,** 1090
guarantees, **158,** 719–720

H
half-year convention, 543
harmonized sales tax (HST), **409**
See also provincial sales tax (PST); sales taxes
hedges
accounting for, 918
accounting mismatch, 918
Accounting Standards for Private Enterprise (ASPE), 923
criteria, 918
defined, **788, 917**
example, 917
International Accounting Standards Board (IASB), 922
held-for-sale, **536**
held-for-sale assets
Accounting Standards for Private Enterprise (ASPE), 108
declassification, 97
defined, **94**–95
statement of financial position (SFP), 143
two-step, 95–97
held-for-sale capital assets, 531
held-to-maturity investments, 143
Hewlett-Packard (HP), 306
hidden entries, 219
hierarchy of fair value, 55–57
High Liner Foods Incorporated, 488–495
highest and best use, **56**
high-low shares, 922
high-quality earnings, **12**
historical cost, 36, 141, 406*f*
historical cost convention, **54**
holding gains and losses, **599**
horizontal (trend) analysis, **1311**–1314
host contract, **916**
hostile takeover bid, 901
HST, 409
hybrid financial instruments, **886**
Hydro One Inc., 771

I
IASB. *See* International Accounting Standards Board (IASB)
idle assets, **94**
idle cash, 592
if-converted method, **1201**
IFRS. *See* International Financial Accounting Standards (IFRS)
IFRS Foundation, 2–3
impairment, 368
defined, **530,** 613
and fair value, 607–608
fair-value-through-other-comprehensive-income (FVTOCI), 617
lessor, 1100
reversals, 608–609
impairment indicators, 547
impairment loss
defined, **546**
disclosure, 550
group of assets, 548–550
individual asset, 548, 549
measurement of, 547–548
reversal of, 549, 550, 551
impairment tests
defined, 144, **546**
goodwill, 550–551
of long-lived assets, 547–550
Imperial Oil Ltd., 160
implicit lease interest rate, **1066**
impracticable, **1268**
imputed interest, **791**
incidental expenses, **471**
incidental revenues, **471**
income
accounting income, 82
comprehensive income, 82–83
defined, **48, 50*f*, 82**–84
economic income, 82
maximization, 17
net income, 82
income bond, **886**
income smoothing, **16**–17
income statement
consolidated income statement, 87*f*, 89
discontinued operations, 98–102
earnings per share (EPS), 89
elements, 50*f*
financial statements, 21
income statement format
alternative formats, 85–88
general presentation format, 84–91
multiple-step statement, 90
single-step statement, 90
income tax
Capital Cost Allowance (CCA), 13, 564–566
cheating, 14
disclosure of cash flows, 223–224
expense, 671–672, 954
personal, 721–722
statement of cash flows (SCF), 1375
Income Tax Act, 13, 14, 564, 954, 961, 984, 1011, 1088
income tax allocation, **92**
income tax deferral, **13**–14
income tax expense, **671**–672
income tax minimization, 13
income tax payable, 723
income tax reporting *vs.* financial reporting, 13–14
incorporated subsidiary, 1096
incorrigible, 534
incremental borrowing rate (IBR), **777, 1066**
incremental method, 832
incremental method of valuation, **894**
indefinite life, **531**–532
indemnification, **158**
indirect observation, **56**
indirect presentation
cash reporting, 307
of operating activities, 208–209
separate disclosure items, 224–226
statement of cash flows, 220–221*f*
individual effect, **1201**–1202
industrial design registrations, 477*f*, 536*f*
industry norms, 534
ineligible costs, 479
inferred fair value, 601
inflation, 42
information
for bank reconciliation, 378*f*
disclosure of, 361
initial direct costs, **1065**–1066, 1100
initial lease term, **1062**
Inmet Mining Company, 825
input measures
estimation of, 292–293
output measures, *vs.,* 291–292
input methods, **282**
input tax credit, 409
instalment sales method, **280**
in-substance defeasance, **796**–797
insurance premiums, 722
intangible assets, 137*f*
defined, **144, 464**
disclosure, 488
disclosure notes, 491*f*, 492*f*–494*f*
elements of cost, 476
goodwill, 52, 464, 483–486
legal life of certain, 536*f*
property, plant, and equipment, 476–477*f*
specific, 478–481
statement of financial position (SFP), 144, 487
intangible capital assets, 531–532
intellectual property, 279
intercorporate investments, 592–596
interest
accrued interest, 603–604, 737–738, 739
disclosure of cash flows, 223–224
imputed interest, 791
market interest rate, 363
measurement of interest expense, 778
payment dates, 783–784
stated interest rate, 363
statement of cash flows (SCF), 223–224
straight-line measurement, 366–367
interest cost, **469,** 471
interest expense
bonds, 785–786
diluted earnings per share, 1211
discounted amortization, 604
effective-interest method, 363–366, 605–607*f*, 736
finance leases, 1076–1077
foreign currency debt denomination, 788–790
premium amortization, 604
straight-line (SL) method, 366–367, 749–750
interest income, 82, 1375
interest payment dates, **778**
interest rates
Accounting Standards for Private Enterprise (ASPE), 1099
effective interest rates, 735
incremental borrowing rate (IBR), 777, 1066
long-term leases, 1087
market interest rate, 363
nominal interest rates, 735
stated interest rate, 363
interest revenue, 304–305
interest-bearing notes, **363, 719**
internal control
bank reconciliation, 346–347
cash, 346
internal control system, **346**
internal rate of return (IRR), **1089**
internally developed intangibles, 477*f*, 478
internally generated computer software, 479–480*f*
International Accounting Standards (IAS)
disclosure of estimates, 1250–1251
leases, 1099–1101

International Accounting Standards Board (IASB)
accumulated other comprehensive income, 856
changes, forthcoming in lease accounting, 1107–1112
changes in accounting policy, 152–155, 162, 1253–1254
changes in revenue recognition, 265, 268, 307, 317–321
Conceptual Framework, 106–107, 162
defined, **2**–4, 20
finance leases, 1099, 1107
financial assets, 922
financial elements definition, 748
hedging, 922
investment categories, 628–629
leases, 1098–1099
liability definition, 748
operating leases, 1107
post-employment benefits, 1161
retirement of shares, 833
sales-type leases, 1107
statement of cash flows (SCF), 228
International Financial Accounting Standards (IFRS), 1, 36
changes in accounting policy, 152–155
comparability issues, 7–8
consolidated financial statements, 1332
cost flow assumptions, 411–412
described, 2–3
disclosure of estimates, 1251
financial assets, reporting, 343
financial liabilities, 748–750
financial statements required by, 19–21
income definition, 82
investment categories, 628–629
legal and regulatory requirements, 4
long-term liabilities, 801–802
pension plans, 1148–1149
post-employment benefits, 1161
and professional judgement, 38
statement of financial position (SFP) usage, 136
tax rates, 1023
International Forest Products Limited (Interfor), 11, 202, 203*f*, 210, 223, 224, 742–743, 1160
International Lease Financing Corporation (ILFC), 1088
interperiod allocation, 12, 52
interperiod tax allocation
See also corporate income tax
accounting and taxable income, differences, 954–956
capitalized development costs, 955–956
comprehensive tax allocation, 957–959, 979
conceptual issues in, 957–962
deferral method, 959–960
defined, **92, 954**
discounting, 961
extent of allocation, 957–959
flow-through method, 957
introduction, 954–956
liability method, 960, 979
measurement method, 959–961
origination, 955
partial allocation, 957
permanent differences, 954–956
reversal, 955
taxes payable method, 957, 979
temporary differences, 955–956
in-the-money, **900, 1200**
In-Touch Survey Systems Limited, 109
intraperiod tax allocation, **92,** 979
intrinsic value, **899**
inventory
aggregation, 413
average cost, 436–437
consignment arrangements, 279
contracts in progress, 407
cost elements, 408–410
cost flow assumptions, 411–412
cost flow methods, 435–439
damaged inventory, 415–416
decrease in, 424
direct inventory reduction method, 414–415
disclosures, 424–425
errors, 417–419, 1267–1268
estimation. *See* inventory estimation methods
ethical issues, 425–426
finished goods, 410
first-in, first-out (FIFO), 438
increase in, 424
inventory allowance method, 414–415
inventory costs, 408–410
items to include, 407–408
last-in, first-out (LIFO), 438
as line item on SFP, 137*f*
lower-of-cost-or-NRV valuation, 412–415
market value, 406*f*
nature of, 407
net realizable value (NRV), 143, 290, 412
obsolete inventory, 415–416
periodic inventory system, 432–435, 665
perpetual inventory system, 407, 432–435, 665
policy issues, 407
purchase commitments, losses on, 416–417
raw materials, 408–409, 410
reporting issues, 424–425
repurchase agreements, 408
shrinkage, 433
specific identification, 435–436
statement of cash flows (SCF), 424
in statement of financial position (SFP), 143
supplies inventory, 411
types of, 406*f*
work in progress, 407, 410
writedowns, 413–415
inventory allowance method, 414–415
inventory costs
elements of, 408–410
goods purchased for resale, 408–409
laid-down cost, 408
manufactured goods, 410–411
periodic inventory system, 411
perpetual inventory system, 411
raw materials, 408–409
sales taxes, 409–410
service contracts, 410
supplies inventory, 411
inventory estimation methods
gross margin method, 419–421
retail inventory method, 421–424
inventory turnover, 1319–1322
inventory turnover ratio, **1321**–1322
inventory valuation, 406
invested capital, **150,** 1314
investing activities, **200,** 213, 1375
investment funds, 4
investment property, 137*f*
amortization, 531
defined, **144, 464**
depreciation, 531
example, 502–503*f*
presentation, 487
investment tax credit (ITC)
corporate income tax, 984–987
cost-reduction approach, 984
costs capitalized, 985
current expenses, 984–985
disclosure, 987
flow-through approach, 984
general nature of, 984
government grants, 987
recording, 985–986
reporting, 986–987
investments
See also financial instruments
accounting for, 597–601
accounting methods, summary of, 598*f*
accounting mismatch, 594
acquisition cost, 593
active investment portfolio, 592
amortized cost (AC), 593–594
amortized cost (AC) method, 597–598, 603–609
associates, 595–596
bonds, 613–614
classification criteria, 592–596
consolidated method, 600
cost investments, 595
cost method, 599, 609
current *vs.* long-term, 625
disclosure, 625–629
equity method, 600, 618–623
external reporting, 597*f*
fair value, 593, 601–603
fair value method, 599
fair-value-through-other-comprehensive-income (FVTOCI), 594–595, 599, 614–617
fair-value-through-profit-and-loss (FVTPL), 594, 610–614
as financial asset, 143
foreign currency, 613
idle cash of, 592
impairment, 607–609, 613
joint arrangement, 596
legal framework, 592
long-term, 592
objectives, 592
passive investment, 592
reclassification, 624–626
recording *vs.* reporting, 600
reported on the equity basis, 137*f*
share investment, 609, 613
short-term investments, 143
special funds, 143
statement of financial position (SFP), 144
strategic alliances, 592
strategic investments, 144, 592
subsidiaries, 595
in tangible capital assets, 144
investors, 773
involuntary conversions, **482**

issuance
delayed, 784
between interest dates, 784
non-cash, 830–831
of share capital, 828–832
issuance price, **605**
items to be shown on SFP, 136–138

J
joint arrangement, **596**
joint operation (JO), **596**
joint venture (JV), **596,** 600
journal entry, **663,** 1013
journals
cash disbursements journal, 681, 682*f*
cash receipts journal, 681–682, 682*f*
defined, **663**
general journal, 663, 664*f*, 681, 683*f*
purchases journal, 680–681
sales journal, 679–680
judgement. *See* professional judgement

K
key money, 1062*f*

L
laid-down cost, **408,** 412
land, 531, 544
land and buildings
Accounting Standards for Private Enterprise (ASPE), 1099
sale and leaseback, 1083–1084
last-in, first-out (LIFO), **438**
lawsuits, 147, 158, 726–728, 739–740
lease amortization table, 1070–1071, 1075, 1090
lease arrangements, 141
lease term, 1060, **1065,** 1068*f*, 1074
leasehold improvements, 477*f*
leases
Accounting Standards for Private Enterprise (ASPE), 1099–1101
asset, initial cost, 1089
capital lease, 1099
capitalization, avoiding, 1087–1088
changes, forthcoming, 1107–1112
CPA Canada Handbook, Part II (ASPE), 1099
contingent rent, 1087
deferred income tax, 1073
defined, **1060**
direct-financing lease, 1096
disclosure, 1084–1085
ethics, 1098
executory costs, 1062
finance leases. *See* finance leases
Financial Accounting Standards Board (FASB), 1098
gross lease basis, 1091–1093
inception date, 1062
initial lease term, 1062
internal rate of return (IRR), 1089–1090
International Accounting Standards (IAS), 1099–1101
key money, 1062*f*
land and buildings, 1083–1084
lease term, 1065, 1068, 1074
leasing continuum, 1060–1061
lessee. *See* lessee
lessor. *See* lessor
liability reassessment, 1111
long-term leases. *See* long-term leases
looking forward, 1098–1099
manufacturers and dealers, 1094–1097
manufacturer's lease, 1095
memorandum of agreement, 1062
modified example, 1074–1080
net lease basis, 1090–1093
operating leases. *See* operating leases
penalty for non-renewal, 1088
personal property, 1060
real property, 1060
reporting, and ethics, 1098
residual value, 1089, 1090
sale and leaseback, 1080–1084
sales-type lease, 1095, 1096
short-term leases, 1107
statement of cash flows (SCF), 1097
substance over form, 1060
tax shield, 1089
third party, 1088
leasing continuum, 1060–1061
ledgers, 664–665, 678–679
legal capital, 839
legal obligations, **716**
legal title, 1098
lenders, 773
Leslie Corporation, 56
lessee
accounting, basic example, 1069–1074
accounting, modified example, 1074–1080
accounting for finance leases, 1068
Accounting Standards for Private Enterprise (ASPE), 1099–1100
amortization table, 1070–1071, 1110
defined, **1060**
depreciating leased assets, 1071
disclosure, 1084–1085
financial statements, 1072–1073
guidelines, 1069–1070
interest calculation, 1070–1071
long-term leases, 1107–1111
long-term leases, basic rule, 1107–1108
net cash flows, 1089
recording finance lease, 1078–1079
recording liability, 1072
short-term leases, 1107
lessor
accounting for, 1088–1097
Accounting Standards for Private Enterprise (ASPE), 1100–1101
amortization table, 1090–1091
captive leasing companies, 1088
classification, 1100
current-noncurrent distinction, 1091
defined, **1060**
direct-financing lease, 1096
disclosure for, 1094
finance industry, 1088
gross lease basis, 1091–1094
gross method, 1093–1094, 1096
impairment, 1100
internal rate of return (IRR), 1089–1090
long-term leases, 1111
manufacturers and dealers, 1094–1097
nature of, 1067
net cash flows, 1089
net lease basis, 1090–1093
net lease receivable, 1090
net method, recording, 1090–1091
recording, finance lease, 1092*f*
recording, initial, 1090
short-term leases, 1107
level contribution method, **1139**
leverage, **1325**
leverage ratios, **1322,** 1325–1326
liabilities
See also financial liabilities
Accounting Standards for Private Enterprise (ASPE), 62*f*
categories of, 716–718
classification of, 743–745, 887
common financial liabilities, 718–723
compensated-absence, 733–734
contingent liabilities, 163–164
contract liability, 317
current liability, 136, 144–146, 743
debt retirement, 792–797
decommissioning liabilities, 474–475
deferred income tax as, 978
deferred income tax liabilities, 969, 979
defined, **50*f*, 716**
discounting impact, 735–743
financial liabilities. *See* financial liabilities
in financial statements, 48
foreign currency payables, 723–724
IASB proposed definition, 748
lease liability, reassessment, 1111
long-term liabilities, 145, 743–744
no-interest note payable, 735–737
non-financial liabilities, 716, 724–735
not on the SFP, 141
note payable with different market and stated rate, 738–739
offsetting, 145
perpetual debt, 890
refund liability, 319
regional differences in, 137–138
reporting example, 717–718
short-cut method of lease, 1080
statement of cash flows (SCF), 747–748, 797–800
liability dividend, 843
liability method, 957, **960**–961, 979
licences, 144
licensing arrangements, **279**
licensing fees, 279
LIFO, **438**
limited lives, long-lived assets with, 546
limited votes, and shares, 827
line items to be shown on SFP, 136–138
line of credit, **201**
liquidating dividends, 843
liquidity
of assets and liabilities, 137
defined, **140**
liquidity ratios
acid-test ratio, 1330
cash conversion cycle, 1330–1331
current ratio, 1330
defensive-interval ratio, 1331–1332
defined, **1327**
for Grocery Retailer Inc., 1333*f*
quick ratio, 1330
summary of, 1332*f*
liquidity test, 839
Live Entertainment, 154
loan guarantees, 719–720
loans
forgivable loan, 505
line of credit, 201
long-term loans, 143, 773–774, 788–790
secured by accounts receivable, 357

shareholder loans, 922
short-term bank loans, 772–773
longitudinal comparisons, **1306**
long-lived assets, 52
accounting standards, 497*f*
biological assets, 137*f*, 294–298, 464
defined, **546**
derecognition of, 482–483
gains, 487
goodwill, 52, 464, 483–486
impairment, 546–551
impairment tests of, 547–550
intangible assets, 137*f*, 144, 464, 476–477*f*
investment property, 464
losses, 487
not depreciated or amortized, 531–532
property, plant, and equipment, 464
statement of cash flows (SCF), 486–487
valuation of, 464–465
long-term bank financing, 774–775
long-term contracts
bill-and-hold arrangements, 277–278
completed-contract method, 321
construction contracts, 282, 291*f*, 292*f*, 306
losses on, 293–294
percentage-of-completion method, 288–291, 321
service contracts, 282
long-term debt
accounting for, 777
bonds, 775
debentures payable, 775
debt covenants, 775–776
foreign currency, 788–790
measurement of interest expense, 778
other sources of, 775
statement of cash flows (SCF), 797–800
long-term financing, 773–774
long-term leases
100% financing, 1086–1087
basic rule, 1107–1108
classification, 1108–1109
end-of-lease, 1108
income tax benefit transfer, 1085
lessee, 1107–1111
lessor accounting for, 1111
off-balance-sheet financing, 1086
protection against interest rate changes, 1087
protection against obsolescence, 1087
single lease expense (SLE) approach, 1109–1110
long-term liabilities
Accounting Standards for Private Enterprise (ASPE), 801
defined, **145, 743**–744
disclosures for, 798–800
International Financial Accounting Standards (IFRS), 801–802
long-term loans, 143
bank financing, 774–775
defined, **773–774**
exchange rate fluctuations, 788–790
long-term receivables, 143
loss carryback
defined, **1010**
example, 1010–1012
loss carryforward
Capital Cost Allowance (CCA), 1015
comparison of recording methods, 1017*f*
defined, **1010**
disclosure, 1034
evidence of probability, 1015
future realization is improbable, 1018
future realization is judged probable, 1016–1017
illustration, basic, 1024–1026
illustration, extended, 1026–1033
improbable recovery becoming probable, 1020–1021
"more likely than not" principle, 1014–1015
partial recognition, 1018, 1021–1022
previously unrecognized tax loss, 1034
probable full recovery, 1020
realization becomes probable, 1026
realization is not probable, 1024–1025
realization of probability is greater than 50%, 1030–1033
realization of probability is less than or equal 50%, 1028–1030
reassessment in subsequent years, 1016
recognition assumption on net income, impact of, 1019–1020
recognition scenarios, examples, 1016–1019
reduction of capital cost allowance, 1015
reduction of previously recognized benefit, 1022
reporting objectives, 1033
tax benefits of, 1010
tax rates, 1023
unrecognized tax loss carryforwards, 1034
valuation allowance, 1020–1023
write-off of expired carryforward benefits, 1022–1023
losses
defined, **49, 50*f*, 266**
exchange loss, 369
holding gains and losses, 599
impairment loss, 548–550
long-lived assets, 487
on long-term contracts, 293–294
purchase commitments, 416–417
realized holding losses, 599
revenue and expenses, *vs.*, 266
tax benefits of, 1010
unrealized holding losses, 599
lower-of-cost-or-NRV valuation, 412–415
low-quality earnings, **12**
loyalty programs. *See* customer loyalty programs
lump-sum purchase, 466

M

Magna International Inc., 161, 1218–1219
maintenance, 467–468, 732
maintenance tests, **15,** 775
major inspections, **468**
major segment, 98*n*
maker, 363
management representations, 594
Management's Discussion and Analysis (MD&A), 141
mandatorily convertible shares, **1193**
mandatory change, **1253**–1254
manufactured goods, 410–411
manufacturer's lease, **1095**
Maple Leaf Foods Incorporated, 463
margin, **916**
margin of safety, **1325**
markdown, **422**
markdown cancellation, **422**
market interest rate, **363, 719**
market risk, 1334
market value, 141, 406*f*
markups, **422**
matching, **52**–53
material weaknesses, 418
materiality, **46,** 472
maturity date, **744, 778**
maturity value, **363**
maximization of net income, **17**
MD&A (Management's Discussion and Analysis), 141
measurability, 49
measurement
agricultural produce, 295
biological assets, 295
of consideration, 283–284
defined, **53**
of goodwill, 484
of impairment loss, 547–548
not possible, 293
percentage-of-completion method, 291–293
private enterprises, 62
of property, plant, and equipment, 469–475
remeasurement, 475
straight-line measurement of interest expense/revenue, 366–367
measurement methods
current cost, 54
defined, **36**
fair value, 55–57
historical cost convention, 54
interperiod tax allocation, 959–961
present value, 55
progress over time, 282–283
realizable value, 55
settlement value, 55
measurement uncertainty, 157
measurement variability, and professional judgement, 58
memo entry
stock dividends, 845
stock splits, 849
Mercedes-Benz Credit Canada, 1088
merger, **1194**
minimization of earnings, **17**
minimum compliance, **18**
minimum net lease payments, **1065**
minority interest, 89*n*, **148**
modification of debt, **797**
monetary accrued liabilities, 720
monetary assets, **298**
monetary items, **344**
money market funds, 345
money market instruments, **345**
mortality rates, 1138
mortgages, 774
most advantageous market, 56
most likely outcome, **725**
moving average, **436**
multi-industry corporations, 1334
multiperiod recognition, 282
See also percentage-of-completion method
multiple classes of common shares, 1196–1198
multiple deliverable contracts, 286–287

multiple deliverables, 271, **284**–285, 320
multiple goods and service contracts, 284–287, 320
multiple votes, and shares, 827
multiple-step statement, **90**
music licenses, 279
mutual funds, 4, 890

N
nature of expense, **85**
nature of the lessor, 1067
NCI. *See* non-controlling interest (NCI)
negative goodwill, **486**
negative leverage, **1325**
Nestlé Group, 727–728
net asset principle of revenue/expense recognition, **52,** 53, 272, 273*f*
net assets, **50*f*, 825**
net basis, **267**
net book value, **530,** 670
net cash flows
lessee, 1089
lessor, 1089
net defined benefit pension liability (asset)
asset ceiling, 1145–1146
defined, **1137**
expected *vs.* actual return, 1145
net interest, 1141, 1143–1144
re-measurement, 1141, 1144–1146
statement of financial position (SFP), 1146–1148
net income
and cash flow from operations, 212
comprehensive income, *vs.*, 91
defined, 82
unrealized holding gains or losses, 599
net lease basis leases, 1090–1091
net lease payments, **1065**
net lease receivable, **1090**
net method, 1090–1091
net of related tax, 92
net off, 358
net realizable value (NRV), 143, 290, **412**–415
net revenue, 266–268
net status, 1148
netting, 145, **970**–971, 1148–1149
neutrality, **45**
New Flyer Industries Inc., 81, 425
no-interest note payable, 735–737
nominal accounts, **659**
nominal dollars, **42**
nominal interest rates, **735**
nonadjusting events, **161**–162
non-cash accounts, 204, 206
non-cash consideration, 284
non-cash issuance of share capital, 830–831
non-cash transactions, 210–211, 1375
non-contributory pension plan, **1132**
non-controlling interest (NCI)
defined, **89, 148, 600**
as line item, 137*f*
in subsidiaries, 148–151
non-cumulative senior shares, 1191
noncurrent assets
defined, **94**
held-for-sale two-step, 95–97
statement of financial position (SFP), 143–144
noncurrent presentation, 136
non-financial liabilities, **716,** 724–735
non-interest-bearing notes, **363, 719**
non-monetary assets, **298,** 303–304
non-monetary transactions
Accounting Standards for Private Enterprise (ASPE), 309–310
barter transactions, 298–299
defined, **298, 483**
valuation alternatives, 298
non-notification basis, **357**
nonreciprocal transfers, 473, **661**
nonrefundable upfront fees, **283**
nontrade receivables, **348**
no-par shares, **828**
normal capacity, **411**
normal course issuer bid, **832,** 833
Nortel Networks Corp., 35, 58, 154
not distinct, **320**
not profitable, 293
note references, 138
notes payable
classification of, 744
as common financial liability, 719
discount, 472
valuation, 362
notes receivable
Accounting Standards for Private Enterprise (ASPE), 371
blended payments, 367
collateral security, 362
defined, **348**
different market and stated rates, 364–365
effective interest method, 363–366
face value, 363
impairment, 368
interest-bearing notes, 363
market interest rate, 363
maturity value, 363
non-interest-bearing notes, 363
stated interest rate, 363
straight-line measurement method, 366–367
straight-line method, 371–372
terminology, 363
transfer of, 368
valuation, 362
notes to financial statements. *See* disclosure notes
notification basis, **357**
NRV, 143, 290, 412–415

O
objective and reliable evidence, **285**
objectives of financial reporting, **8**–11, 10*f*, 60–61
objectivity, 60
obligating event, **716**
obsolescence, 531, 1087
obsolete inventory, 415–416
OCI. *See* other comprehensive income (OCI)
off-balance-sheet financing, 1086
offset method, 832, 918
offsetting, 145, 210, 1375
100% financing, 1086–1087
onerous contracts, **293, 416,** 427, **728**
Ontario Securities Commission (OSC), 4
operating activities
See also statement of cash flows (SCF)
defined, **200**
direct presentation of, 208–209, 221–222, 1384–1386
indirect presentation of, 208–209
summary of adjustments in, 227–228
operating cycle, **136**
operating expenses, 90
operating leases
accounting for lessee, 1061, 1063*f*
accounting for lessor, 1061–1062, 1063*f*
Accounting Standards for Private Enterprise (ASPE), 1098–1099
capital lease, *vs.*, 1098
capital leases, *vs.*, 1098–1099
classification, 1060
contingent rent, 1084
defined, **1060**–1061, 1064
disclosure, 1084, 1100
executory costs, 1062
initial lease term, 1062
International Accounting Standards Board (IASB), 1107
sale and leaseback, 1083
uneven payments, 1062–1063
operating line of credit, **772**
operating margin, **1319**
operating revenues, 90
operating risk, **1326**
operating segment, **159**
option pricing models, 900, 904, 909
options
bargain purchase option, **1065**
call option, 793, 915
derivatives, 915
dilutive options, 1200
option pricing models, 900, 904, 909
put option, 915
stock. *See* stock options
Ordeal Ltd., 56
orderly transaction, **55**
ordinary shares, **1191**
ordinary stock dividends, 846
original sales price, **422**
other comprehensive income (OCI)
as category of comprehensive income, 83
defined, **50*f*, 595**
described, 88*f*, 90–91
disposition of accumulated OCI amounts, 1148
equity method, 619
items of, 147–148
net defined benefit pension liability (asset), 1141, 1148
other financial liabilities, 717
other post-employment benefits (OPEBs)
accounting spreadsheet, 1157
Accounting Standards for Private Enterprise (ASPE), 1161–1164
defined, **1156**
disclosure, 1159–1160
Financial Accounting Standards Board (FASB), 1161
International Accounting Standards Board (IASB), 1161
International Financial Accounting Standards (IFRS), 1161
statement of cash flows (SCF), 1158–1159
output measures *vs.* input measures, 291–292
output methods, **282**
outstanding share capital, 828
overdrafts, **201, 345**
overhead costs, 410, **469**
owners' equity, 48, **50*f***

P
Paladin Energy Ltd., 890
par value of bonds, **778**
par value shares, 146, **827**
parent company, 142, **595**
parent company preferences, 534
Parmalat, 405
partial allocation, 957
partial cash transactions, 211
partial statement of cash flows, 222*f*
partially participating shares, 841–842
participating dividends, 827
passive investment, **592,** 630
past service cost (PSC), **1141**
past transaction, 48
patents, 144, 477*f*, 536*f*
pay-as-you-go, 1156
payee, 363
payment date, **839**
payroll deductions, 722
payroll taxes, 721–722
Pengrowth Energy Company, 844
pension accounting spreadsheet
  first year data, 1149–1151
  second year data, 1151–1153
  summary, 1154–1155
  third year data, 1153–1154
pension expense, 1161–1162
pension funds, 4
pension holiday, **1137**
pension plan curtailment, **1134**
pension plan settlement, **1134**
pension plans
  10% corridor method, 1148
  Accounting Standards for Private Enterprise (ASPE), 1161–1164
  accumulated benefit method, 1139
  actuarial cost methods, 1133, 1139–1140
  actuarial gains and losses, 1134
  classification of, 1132
  contributory pension plan, 1132
  current service cost (CSC), 1141
  curtailment, 1134, 1141–1143
  death benefits, 1138
  defined benefit plan. *See* defined benefit plans
  defined contribution plans, 1135–1136
  disclosure, 1159–1160
  discount rate, 1138
  disposition of accumulated OCI amounts, 1148
  ethics, 1138
  example, 1142
  funding, 1138–1139
  future salary increases, 1138
  International Financial Accounting Standards (IFRS), 1148–1149
  level contribution method, 1139
  net status, 1148
  netting, 1148–1149
  noncontributory pension plan, 1132
  other post-employment benefits (OPEBs), 1156–1157
  past service cost (PSC), 1141
  projected unit credit method, 1139
  registered, 1133
  service cost, 1141
  settlement, 1134, 1141–1143
  spreadsheet approach, 1149–1155
  statement of cash flows (SCF), 1158–1159
  statement of financial position (SFP), 1148–1149
  survivor benefits, 1138
  termination benefits, 1142
  terms, 1132–1134
  trustee, 1133
  types of, 1132
  vesting, 1133
percentage-of-completion method, **282,** 291*f*, 294*f*
performance evaluation, 15–16
performance guarantee, **158**
performance obligation, **269**
periodic inventory system, 411, **432**–435, **665**
periodic system, adjusting journal entries (AJEs), 670
peripheral events, 266
peripheral transactions, 266
permanent accounts, **659,** 660*f*
permanent differences, **954**–956, 966–967
perpetual debt, 886, **890**
perpetual inventory system, **407,** 411, **432**–435, **665**
perpetual system, adjusting journal entries (AJEs), 670
personal income taxes, 721–722
personal property, **1060**
Petro-Canada, 56
phantom stock plans, **905,** 913–915
Philip Services, 154
physical capital maintenance, **42**
Pinetree Capital Limited, 895–896, 902–903
poison pill, **901**
Porter Airlines Inc., 1
post-closing trial balance, 676
post-employment benefits
  Accounting Standards for Private Enterprise (ASPE), 1161–1164
  Financial Accounting Standards Board (FASB), 1161
  International Accounting Standards Board (IASB), 1161
  International Financial Accounting Standards (IFRS), 1161, 1251
  introduction, 1131
posting, **663–664**
Power Corporation of Canada, 841
precision, **150**
prediction of cash flows, 12
predictive value, **44**
preferred shares
  Accounting Standards for Private Enterprise (ASPE), 922
  assets upon liquidation, 827
  characteristics of, 826–827
  conversion, 827
  converted preferred shares, 1206–1208
  cumulative dividends, 827
  cumulative dividends on, 840
  defined, **826**–827
  dividend priority, 826–827
  effect of escalation clause, 889
  guarantee, 827
  if-converted method, 1201
  participating dividends, 827
  participating dividends on, 840–842
  redemption at a premium, 889
  reporting example, 889
  restricted shares, 827
  retractable preferred shares, 888–889
  special shares, 827
  term preferred shares, 888
  voting rights, 826
premium, **604, 827,** 889
preparer motivations
  earnings management, 16–18
  expanded disclosure, 18
  minimum compliance, 18
  users objectives, *vs.*, 19
preparers, **11**
prepayments, 143
present right, 48
present value, **55, 735**
presentation
  accounting policy changes, 1257
  goodwill, 487
  investment property, 487
  property, plant, and equipment, 487
presentation currency, **4,** 21
presentation formats
  current-noncurrent presentation, 136
  gains and losses, 266
  general, 84–91
  by liquidity, 137
  long-term contracts construction contracts, 291*f*, 292*f*
  order of, 137
  regional differences in, 137–138
  revenue, 306–307
principal, 268
principal market, 56
principal payments, 774
principal value, 778
prior-period errors
  corrections, 153, 1266–1267
  counterbalancing errors, 1267–1268
  defined, **1265**–1266
  events not reportable as errors, 1266
  impracticable, 1268
private companies
  See also private enterprises
  accountability, 5–8
  defined, **826**
  generally accepted accounting principles (GAAP), 6–7
  public companies, *vs.*, 826
private enterprises
  and Accounting Standards for Private Enterprise (ASPE), 6, 21, 61–62, 107–109, 826
  defined, **5**
  disclosed basis of accounting (DBA), **6–7**
  financial statement elements, 61–62
  IFRS, using, 5–6
  measurement, 62
  objectives and qualitative characteristics, 60–61
  private placements, **5–6**
private placements, **5–6**
privately owned banks, 4
probability, 49, 1015
product financing arrangements, **279**
product recall, 277
productive capacity capital maintenance, **42**
productive-output (PO) method, 538*f*, 539*f*, **540**
professional judgement
  company acting as agent, 268
  company acting as principal, 268
  defined, **38**
  dividends classification, 224

professional judgement (*continued*)
and ethics, 59–60
and expense recognition, 53
finance leases, 1065
impairment writedowns, 551
interest classification, 224
and International Financial Accounting Standards (IFRS), 38
and measurement variability, 58
and problem of earnings targets, 57–58
and reserves, 58–60
substance over form, 1060
profit elimination, unrealized, 623
profit or loss section, 84–85
profitability on sales ratios, 1314
profitability ratios
components of, 1318–1319
defined, **1314**
evaluation of, 1317
for Grocery Retailer Inc., 1320
operating margin, 1319
return on common share equity, 1315
return on long-term capital, 1316–1317
return on total assets, 1315
summary of, 1318*f*
total capitalization, 1315
total comprehensive income, 1317–1318
types of, 1315–1317
progress billings, **289**
prohibited internally developed intangibles, 478
projected unit credit method, **1139,** 1140
property, plant, and equipment, 137*f*
additions, 468
basket purchase, 466
betterment, 468
capitalization norms, 469–472
common capitalization practices, 470*f*
component accounting, 465–466
costs, safety or environmental, 466
defined, **464**
disclosure, 488
disclosure notes, 489*f*–490*f*, 495*f*
elements of cost, 469, 476
general criteria, 465
government assistance, 474, 505–506
intangible assets, 476–477*f*
maintenance, 467–468
major inspections, 468
measurement of, 469–475
ordinary repairs, 467–468
presentation, 487
recognition of, 465–468
repairs, 467–468
replacement of major part, 468
spare parts, 466
statement of financial position (SFP), 144
subsequent costs, 467
property dividends, **842**
property taxes, 722–723
proportional method, 466, 831, **902**
proportional relationship, 1314
proportionate consolidation, **631**
proprietary assumption, **40–41**
prospective application
comparative illustration, 1263, 1264*f*
defined, **1250**
described, 1262
disclosures, 1263
early adoption, 1264
financial instruments, 1264
guidelines, 1263
use of prospective application, 1263
prospective treatment, **153**
provincial sales tax (PST), **409**
See also harmonized sales tax (HST); sales taxes
provision for income tax, **954**
provisions
and Accounting Standards for Private Enterprise (ASPE), 164
classification of, 744–745
compensated-absence liabilities, 733–734
contingent assets, 726
coupons, 731
defined, **104, 716**
disclosure for, 745–746
environmental obligations, 730
estimate change, 740–742
examples of, 726–734, 742–743
executory contracts, 728
gift cards, 731
lawsuits, 726–728, 739–740
loyalty programs, 731–732
maintenance, 732
measurement of, 725–726
non-financial liabilities, 724–735
onerous contracts, 728
prohibited practices, 726
repairs, 732
reporting example, 727–728
and restoration, 730
for restructuring, 729
returns, 730–731
sales returns, 730–731
self-insurance, 732–733
on SFP, 137*f*
summary, 734
warranty, 729–780
PSC. *See* past service cost (PSC)
PST, 409
public companies, 141, 159
accountability, 4–5
defined, **826**
diluted earnings per share, reporting, 1189–1190
earnings per share (EPS), reporting, 1189–1190
generally accepted accounting principles (GAAP), 2, 4
private companies, *vs.*, 826
public enterprise, 4
publicly accountable enterprise (PAE), **4**–5
publishing rights, 477*f*
purchase at premium, 606–607
purchase commitments, losses on, 416–417
purchases journal, **680**–681
purchasing power, 42
purchasing power parity, **42**
purpose-bought subsidiaries, **99**
put option, **915**

Q
qualifying assets, **790**–791
qualitative criteria
and Accounting Standards for Private Enterprise (ASPE), 61*f*
defined, **36**
enhancing qualities, 44*f*, 45–46
fundamental qualities, 44–45, 44*f*
pervasive constraints, 44*f*, 46–47
and private enterprises, 60–61
trade-offs, 47
quality of earnings, **212**
Quebec Securities Commission, 2
quick ratio, **1330**

R
rates of return, **140**
ratio, **1327**
ratio analysis
common-size (vertical) analysis, 1307–1309, 1309–1311, 1314
conclusion, 1334–1335
consolidated statements, 1332–1334
decomposition analysis, 1307
defined, **1314**
efficiency ratios, 1319–1322
horizontal analysis, 1311–1314
limitations to, 1306–1307
liquidity ratios, 1327–1332
multi-industry corporations, 1334
profitability ratios, 1314–1319
proportional relationship, 1314
solvency ratios, 1322–1327
trend analysis, 1311–1314
vertical (common-size) analysis, 1307–1309, 1309–1311, 1314
raw materials, 408–409, 410
real accounts, **659**
real property, **1060**
realizable value, **55**
realization
and cash flows, 53
defined, **51**
recognition, *vs.*, 51–52
realized holding gains or losses, **599**
recasting financial statements, 1342–1351
receivables
See also accounts receivable; notes receivable
foreign currency receivables, 368–369
long-term receivables, 143
nontrade receivables, **348**
uncollectible receivables, 350
reciprocal transfers, **661**
reclassification, 91, 624–626
recognition
See also derecognition
amortization expense, 531
and cash flows, 53
commitments, 49
criteria, 51*f*
defined, **49**
derivatives, 916–917
disclosure, *vs.*, 49
internally developed intangibles, 478
net defined benefit pension liability (asset), 1146–1148
realization, *vs.*, 51–52
revenue. *See* revenue recognition
stock dividends, 845–846
reconciliation, **201,** 219
reconciliation method, 224–226
record date, **839**
recording
accounting policy changes, 1257
investment tax credit (ITC), 985–986
reporting investments, *vs.*, 600
stock options, 900–901
recording method, 600
recording transactions, 659–660
recourse, **357**

recoverable amount, **94, 546**
recycled, **147, 1144**
recycling, 91
redeemable bonds, **793**
redeemable shares, 832, **886,** 890
refund liability, **319**
regional differences in presentation, 137–138
registered pension plans, **1133**
related party transactions, 157, **160,** 164
relative fair value method, **285**–286, 320
relevance, **44,** 47, 282, 293, 309
reliability, 45, 47
remeasurement, 475, 1144–1145
repairs, 467–468, 732
replacement of major parts, 468, 483
reportable segment, **159**
reporting
  accounting changes, 1255–1256
  accounting policy changes, 1257
  accounts receivable, 352
  comparability of statistical series, 1256
  currency, 4–5
  investment tax credit (ITC), 986–987
  perpetual debt, 890
  preferred shares, 889
  prospective application, 1256
  retrospective application with full restatement, 1255
  retrospective application with partial restatement, 1255–1256
reporting method, 600
reporting periods, 486
repurchase agreements, **408**
research, 478
research and development (R&D) costs, 478–479, 491*f*–492*f*
reserves
  defined, **58**–60, **147**–148, **851**
  example, 851–852
  sources of, 852
residual analysis, 1335
residual interest, 825
residual value, **530,** 536, 1077, 1089
residual value method, **285,** 286, 320
resource exploration, 477*f*
restated financial statements, 1342–1351
restatement, **1255**
restoration, and provisions, 730
restricted actions, 775–776
restricted covenants, 775–776
restricted retained earnings, **838**
restricted share units, **905**
restricted shares, **11, 827**
restrictions (reserves), **147**
restructuring, 104–106, 106*f*, 109
  provisions for, 729
restructuring plan, **103**
retail inventory method, **421**–424
retained earnings, 146–147
  appropriations, 838
  restrictions, 838
  shareholders' equity, 837–838
retained earnings method, 832
retainer, 283
retirement of assets, 544
retirement of shares
  accounting for, 833–835
  conversion, 835
  reasons for, 832–833
retractable bonds, **793**
retractable preferred shares, 888–889
retractable shares, 832
retrospective application
  accounting policy changes, 1256–1262
  defined, **1255**
  disclosure, 1262
  financial statement presentation, 1257
  with full restatement, 1255
  illustration, 1257–1258
  with partial restatement, 1255–1256
  recording, 1257, 1259
  reporting, 1257, 1259–1262
retrospective restatement, **1255**
return on assets, **140**
return on common share equity, **1315**
return on equity (ROE), 1317
return on investment (ROI), **140,** 150
return on investment profitability ratios, 1314
return on long-term capital, **1316**–1317
return on sales ratios, 1314
return on total assets, **1315**
return rates, **140**
returnable deposits, 720
returns on sales
  not predictable, 274–275
  predictable, 272–274
  and provisions, 730–731
revaluation accounting, 560–561
revaluation approach, 144
revaluation model, **465,** 567–569*f*
revaluation surplus, 560–561, 567–569*f*
revenue
  accrued revenue, 669
  deferrals, 275–277
  deferred revenue, 668
  defined, **48,** 82, **266**
  dividend revenue, 304–305
  estimation of, 289–290, 293
  franchise fees, 287
  gains, *vs.,* 266
  gross revenue, 266–268
  interest revenue, 304–305
  losses, *vs.,* 266
  net assets, impact on, 52, 53, 272, 273*f*
  net revenue, 266–268
  over time, 282–283
  short-term service revenue, 272
  statement of cash flows (SCF), 307
  unearned revenue, 271, 307
Revenue from Contracts with Customers (IASB), 307, 317
revenue recognition
  2017 revenue recognition standard, 317–321
  Accounting Standards for Private Enterprise (ASPE), 308
  agricultural produce, 294–298
  bill-and-hold arrangements, 277–278
  biological assets, 294–298
  at cash collection, 279–281
  consignment arrangements, 278–279
  contract-based approach, 268–269, 318–320
  cost recovery method, 280–281, 288
  current standard, 268
  delayed, 277
  delayed payment contracts, 283–284
  at delivery, 271–272
  earnings-based approach, 268
  earnings-based requirements, 269–271
  economic value added (EVA), 268
  and ethics, 275, 278, 305–306
  instalment sales method, 280
  International Accounting Standards Board (IASB), changes in, 265, 268, 317–321
  licensing fees, 279
  long-term contracts, 288–298
  measuring progress over time, 282–283
  multiple deliverable contracts, 286–287
  multiple goods and service contracts, 284–287
  non-cash consideration, 284
  non-monetary transactions, 298–304
  policy, choice, 305–307
  process, 266, 267*f*
  quantity of revenue, 271
  revised standard, 268–269
  for sale of goods, 269, 270*f*
  for sale of services, 269–271
  sale with a right of return, 272–275
  transfer of goods at a single point in time, 271–281
  transfer of goods over time, 282–283
  transfer of services over time, 282–283
  transfer services at a single point in time, 271–281
revenue recognition process, 268
reversal of impairment loss, 549–551
reverse split, **849**
reversing journal entries (RJEs), **677**–678
review engagement, **1303**
rewards, 269, 271, 276, 278, 284, 360
right to recovery asset, **319**
risk
  assessment, 1334
  market risk, 1334
  operating risk, 1326
  of ownership, 360
  and reward, 269, 271, 276, 278, 284
risk profile, 138
RONA Inc., 885

S

safety costs, 466
sale and leaseback
  Accounting Standards for Private Enterprise (ASPE), 1101
  changes, forthcoming, 1111
  defined, **1080**–1081
  finance lease, 1082–1083
  land and buildings, 1083–1084
  operating lease, 1083
  recording a, 1081–1083
sale of goods, revenue recognition for, 269, 270*f*
sale/derecognition, 357–359, 360
sales
  original sales price, 422
  returns not predictable, 274–275
  returns predictable, 272–274
  revenue, 304
  with right of return, 319
  with service agreement, 275–277, 319
  with warranty, 275–277, 319
sales journal, **679**–680
sales returns and allowances, 349–350
sales returns and refunds, 730–731
sales taxes, **409**–410, 721
  See also harmonized sales tax (HST); provincial sales tax (PST)
sales-type leases, **1095,** 1096, 1107

SARs. *See* stock appreciation rights (SARs)
savings institutions, 4
SCF. *See* statement of cash flows (SCF)
SCI. *See* statement of comprehensive income (SCI)
scrip dividends, **843**
Securities Exchange Commission (SEC), 4
securitization, **357**
segment disclosures, **159**–160, 163
segment reporting, 98, **1334**
self-constructed assets, **469**
self-correcting errors, 418–419
self-insurance, 732–733
senior shares, **1191**
separate and distinct, **318**
separate legal entity, 1332–1333
separate-entity assumption, **39–40**
separately identifiable, 285
service agreements, 275–277, 319
service contracts, 410
service cost, **1141**
service-hours (SH) method, 538*f*, 539*f*, **540**
services
  barter, 298
  exchange of dissimilar services, 299
  exchange of similar services, 298–299
  multiple goods and service contracts, 284–287
  short-term service revenue, 272
  transfer at a single point in time, 271–281
  transfer over time, 282–283
settlement value, **55**
SFP. *See* statement of financial position (SFP)
share capital
  See also shares
  arbitrary allocation, 832
  authorization of, 828
  authorized share capital, 828
  basket sale of, 831–832
  classes of shares, 826
  and corporations, 826
  default on subscriptions, 830
  defined, **146**
  disclosures, 854
  dividends. *See* dividends
  earnings per share, 1217–1218
  issuance of, 828–832
  non-cash issuance, 830–831
  no-par shares, 828
  outstanding share capital, 828
  preferred shares, 826–827
  premium, issued at, 827–828
  retirement of, 832–835, 856
  share issue costs, 832
  shares issued for cash, 829
  special terms and conditions, 827
  stock splits, 848–850
  subscribed shares, 829
  terms related to, 828
  treasury stock, 835–837
  voting rights, 826–827
share conversion, 827
share investment, 609, 613
share issue costs, **832**
share-based payments
  accounting patterns, 906
  Accounting Standards for Private Enterprise (ASPE), 923
  defined, **903**
  to employees, 905
  to nonemployees, 903–904
  summary of characteristics, 906
shareholder loans, 922
shareholders' agreements, **15, 826**
shareholders' equity
  See also shares
  Accounting Standards for Private Enterprise (ASPE), 856
  and corporations, 826
  dividends, 838–848
  donated capital, 850–851
  reserves, 851–853
  retained earnings, 837–838
  share capital, 826
    See also share capital
  sources of, 145–146
  statement of cash flows (SCF), 854–855
  statement of changes in equity (SCE), 853–854
  stock splits, 848–850
  treasury stock, 835–837
shareholders of record, 839
shares, 11, 146
  See also share capital; shareholders' equity
  bonus shares, 1195
  callable, 832
  classes of, 826
  common, 826
  contingently issuable ordinary shares, 1194
  conversion of, 835
  floating conversion price per share, 891, 895
  high-low shares, 922
  issued for cash, 829
  mandatorily convertible shares, 1193
  multiple classes of common shares, 1196–1198
  no-par, 828
  ordinary shares, 1191
  par value, 827
  partially *vs.* fully participating, 841–842
  preferred, 826–827, 840–842, 922
  redeemable, 832
  restricted, 827
  retractable, 832, 888–889
  senior shares, 1191
  share-based payments, 903–906
  special, 827
  subscribed, 829
  weighted average ordinary shares (WAOS), 1192–1193
shelf registration, **836**
Shoppers Drug Mart Corp., 732, 920–921
short-term bank loans, 772–773
short-term financing, 772–773
short-term investments, 143
short-term leases, 1107
short-term service revenue, 272
shrinkage, **433**
significant deficiencies, 418
significant influence, **595**
single lease expense (SLE) approach, 1109–1110
single-step statement, **90**
single-transaction method, **836**–837
site restoration costs, **474**–475
small and medium-sized enterprises (SME), **5**
Softchoice Corporation, 148, 149*f*
software, 144, 279
software product development, 479–480*f*
solvency ratios
  debt service ratios, 1322, 1327
  defined, **1322**
  for Grocery Retailer Inc., 1329*f*
  leverage ratios, 1322, 1325–1326
  summary of, 1328*f*
  times-debt-service-earned ratio, 1327
  times-interest-earned ratio, 1327
sources of reserves, 852
spare parts, **466,** 537
special funds, 143
special journals
  accounting information system (AIS), 679–683
  cash disbursements journal, 681, 682*f*
  cash receipts journal, 681–682, 682*f*
  defined, **663**
  general journal, 681, 683*f*
  purchases journal, 680–681
  sales journal, 679–680
special purpose entities (SPEs), 359, **361,** 362, 1098
special purpose statements, 142
special shares, **827**
special stock dividends, 846
specific identification, **435**–436
specific intangible assets, 478–481
spot rate, **723, 788**
spreadsheet approach to pension accounting, 1149–1155
spreadsheet method, **234**–236
  See also T-account method
spreadsheet procedures, 234–236
stable currency assumption, **41–42**
stable dollar, 42
stand-alone derivatives, 916
stand-alone value, **285**
standard recording method, **667**
standards. *See* accounting standards
standby equipment, **537**
Stantec Inc., 910
stated interest rate, **363, 719**
stated value method, 845
stated value shares, 146
statement of cash flows (SCF), 20, 21
  See also operating activities
  accounting changes, 1269–1270
  accounting policy choices, 212–213
  Accounting Standards for Private Enterprise (ASPE), 223–224, 228, 1388
  and accounts receivable, 369–370
  alternative classification, 1386–1387
  amortization, 558
  cash, 200, 1375
  cash equivalents, 628
  cash paid for interest, 1375
  classification, 200, 223–224, 1375
  complex financial instruments, 919
  comprehensive illustration, 1375–1389
  corporate income tax, 977
  defined, **200**
  depreciation, 558
  direct presentation, 208–209, 221–222, 1384–1386
  disclosure, 919–920, 1384–1386
  dividends, 223–224, 1375
  evaluation, 211
  example, comprehensive, 1378–1384
  example of, 202, 203*f*, 204–208, 206*f*
  finance lease, 1073

financing activities, 1375
income tax, 223–224, 1375
indirect presentation, 208–209, 220–221*f*
interest, 223–224, 1375
interpretation issues, 212–213
interpretation of, 202
inventory costs, 424
investing activities, 1375
leases, 1097
liabilities, 747–748
long-lived assets, 486–487
long-term debt, 797–800
non-cash transactions, 210–211, 1375
note disclosure, 211
objectives of the, 200
offsetting transactions, 210, 1375
operating activities, 1375, 1384–1386
organization, 200
other post-employment benefits (OPEBs), 1158–1159
partial cash transactions, 211
pensions, 1158–1159
preparation of, 204
reporting example, 920–921
revenue reported, 307
shareholders' equity, 854–855
summary of major points, 1375–1377
supplementary disclosure, 1375
T-account method, 213–216
T-account procedures, 216–220
two-step indirect presentation, 210, 221*f*
worksheet, 234*f*–235*f*
statement of changes in equity (SCE), 20
additional paid-in capital, 146
appropriation, 147
contributed surplus, 146
defined, **145**
equity components of debt instruments, 146
example, 155*f*, 205*f*, 215*f*, 673*f*–674
par value shares, 146
reserves, 147
retained earnings, 146–147
share capital, 146
shareholders' equity, 853–854
stated value shares, 146
statement of changes in retained earnings, 21
statement of comprehensive income (SCI)
abbreviations, 87
Conceptual Framework, 106–107
defined, **83**
discontinued operations reporting, 99
earnings per share (EPS), 89
elements of, 48–49, 50*f*
example of, 205*f*, 214*f*–215*f*, 673*f*
finance lease, 1073
financial statement under IFRS, 19, 20, 21
revenue recognition, 317, 318*f*
revenue recognition process, 267*f*
statement of financial position (SFP)
See also balance sheet
accounting estimates in, 140–141
Accounting Standards for Private Enterprise (ASPE), 136
accounts receivable, 143
allowances, reporting, 352
assets, 142
balance sheet use in ASPE, 136
biological assets, 144, 487
cash, 142
cash equivalents, 142
classification, 136–138
consolidated statement, example, 139*f*
current assets, 142–143
current liabilities, 136
current-noncurrent presentation, 136
deferred income tax assets, 969–970
deferred income tax liabilities, 969
defined, **136**
discontinued operations reporting, 99–100
elements of, 48, 50*f*
example of, 205*f*, 214*f*, 674*f*
finance lease, 1072–1073
financial statement component, 19
goodwill, 487
held-for-sale assets, 143
historical cost-based, 141
intangible assets, 144
International Financial Accounting Standards (IFRS), 136
inventory, 143
investment property, 144, 487
items to be reported on, 136, 137*f*
liabilities, 144–145
limitations of, 140–142
liquidity, 137
net defined benefit pension liability (asset), 1146–1148
noncurrent assets, 143–144
note references, 138
offsetting assets and liabilities, 145
pension plans, 1148–1149
prepayments, 143
presentation, 136–138
property, plant, and equipment, 144, 487
purpose of, 138–140
revenue recognition, 306, 317
revenue recognition process, 267*f*
short-term investments, 143
strategic investments, 144
trade receivables, 143
statistical multivariate ratio analysis, 1335
stewardship, 15
stewardship reporting, **15**
stock appreciation rights (SARs), **905,** 911–912
stock dividends
accounting issues, 844–845
basic earnings per share, 1195–1196
defined, **1195**
described, 843–844
fair value method, 845
fractional share rights, 846–847
memo entry, 845
ordinary stock dividends, 846
reasons for, 844
recognition, timing, 845–846
special stock dividends, 846
stated value method, 845
timing of recognition, 845–846
stock option plans, **905**
stock options
defined, **899**–900, **1199**
employee stock options, 907–909
forfeiture, 908–909
in-the-money, 900
poison pill, 901
recording, 900–901
reporting example, 910
stock rights, 899
stock warrants, 901
unrecognized, 901
stock rights, **899**
See also stock options
stock splits
accounting for, 849–850
adjustments, 849–850
basic earnings per share, 1195–1196
defined, **848**–849, **1195**
implementation, 850
memo entry, 849
post-year-end split, 1195–1196
reverse split, 849
stock subscriptions, **829**
stock warrants, **901**
stock-keeping unit, 680
straight-line balance, 140
straight-line measurement of interest expense/revenue, 366–367
straight-line (SL) method
Accounting Standards for Private Enterprise (ASPE), 371–372, 749–750, 801–802
amortization, 605–607*f*
defined, **537**–539*f*, **749**–750
strategic alliances, 592
strategic investments, 144, **592,** 627, 630–631
subscribed share capital, 829
subscribed shares, 829
subscription lists, 144
subsequent events, **161**–162, 163, 1217
subsidiaries
consolidation, 141–142
control, 142
foreign, 91
investment, 595
non-controlling interest (NCI), in, 148–151
purpose-bought, 99
related party transactions, 160
translation gain/loss on foreign subsidiaries, 147–148
subsidiary account, 665
subsidiary company, **595**
subsidiary ledgers, 664–665, **678**–679
substance over form, **44,** 886, 1060
substantially enacted tax rate, **1023**
substitution of debt, **797**
successful efforts method, **481**
summary of adjustments in operating activities, 227–228
supplies inventory, 411
survivor benefits, **1138**
sustainable business enterprise, 41

T

T-account, **659**–660*f*
T-account analysis, 217*f*
T-account method, 213–216
See also spreadsheet method
T-account procedures, 216–220
tangible capital assets, **144**
tax allocation. *See* interperiod tax allocation
tax basis, 953
tax benefit, **1010**
tax carrying values, 964
tax credit, 984
tax deferral *vs.* tax evasion, 14
tax depreciation, 955
tax evasion *vs.* tax deferral, 14

tax losses
Accounting Standards for Private Enterprise (ASPE), 1036
benefits of, 1010
defined, **1010**
disclosure, 1034
ethics, 1035
future benefit accounting, 1034–1035
international standards, 1035
introduction, 1009
loss carryback, 1010–1012
loss carryforward, 1010, 1014–1020
permanent differences in loss year, 1012–1014
tax benefits, *vs.,* 1010
tax rates, 1023
temporary differences in loss year, 1012–1014
valuation allowance, 1020–1023
tax minimization, 13, 14
tax planning, 1013
tax rates
accountant's *vs.* analyst's concepts of, 974–975
corporate income tax, 968–969, 973–974
deferral method, 960–961
liability method, 960–961, 979
loss carryforward, 1023
substantially enacted tax rate, 1023
tax shield, 1089
taxable income
corporate income tax, 962–963
interperiod tax allocation, 954–956
loss calculation, 1012
tax-book conformity, **14**
taxes
goods and services tax (GST), 409
harmonized sales tax (HST), 409
payroll taxes, 721–722
property taxes, 722–723
provincial sales tax (PST), 409
sales taxes, 721
taxes payable method, **957,** 979, 1036
T-bills, **345**
TD Bank, 885
technology, impact of, 661
temporary accounts, **659,** 660*f*
temporary differences
See also interperiod tax allocation
defined, **955,** 956
sources of, 966, 972
term loans, **774**
term of commercial mortgages, 774–775
term preferred shares, **888**
termination benefits, **1142**
terminology changes, 60
10% corridor method, 1148
tests and derecognition, 359–360
Tim Hortons, 1189
timeliness, **46,** 293, 309
time-period assumption, **39**
times-debt-service-earned ratio, **1327**
time-series analysis, 1335
times-interest-earned ratio, **1327**
title transfer, **408**
Toronto Stock Exchange (TSX), 1, 2, 4
total capitalization, **1315**
total debt-to-equity ratio, **1325,** 1326
trade accounts payable, **718**–719
trade accounts receivable, **348**
trade and other payables, 137*f,* 144
trade and other receivables, 137*f*
trade credit, 772
trade names, 477*f*
trade receivables, 143
trademarks, 144, 279, 477*f,* 536*f*
trade-offs, 47
transaction value, 344
transactions, 661–**662,** 663, 686
transactions approach, 82
transfer, 343
transfer value, 625
transferee, **358**
transferor, **358,** 359
transfers
of accounts receivable, 357–362
nonreciprocal transfers, 473, 661
notes receivable, 368
reciprocal transfers, 661
risks and rewards, 360
translation gain/loss, 147–148
treasury bills (T-bills), **345**
treasury stock method, **1200**
treasury stocks
accounting for, 836–837
Accounting Standards for Private Enterprise (ASPE), 856
defined, **835**
trend analysis, 1311–1314
for Grocery Retailer Inc., 1312*f*–1313*f*
trend (horizontal) analysis, 1311–1314
Truck Finance Canada, 1088
trued up, **906**
trustee, **1133**
turnover ratios, **1319**
See also efficiency ratios
two-step indirect presentation, 210, 221*f*
Tyco, 154

U
unadjusted trial balance, 665–666*f*
uncollectible receivables, 350
under water, **900**
underlying assumptions
capital maintenance, 42–43, 44*f*
continuity assumption, 41
defined, **36, 38–39**
entity-specific assumptions, 39, 40–43
financial statements, 157
proprietary assumption, 40–41
separate-entity assumption, 39–40
stable currency assumption, 41–42
time-period assumption, 39
unit-of-measure assumption, 40
understandability, **46**
unearned revenue, 271, 307
unguaranteed residual value, **1065,** 1090
uniformity, **46**
union dues, 722
unit-of-measure assumption, **40**
units of production method, 540
units of service, 540–542
universal assumptions, **39**–40
unobservable values, **56**
unrealized holding gains or losses, **599**
unrealized profit elimination, 623
unremitted earnings, **600**
unusual items, **90**
unwinding, **737**
upstream profit, **623**
U.S. GAAP, 4, 5, 20
useful life, 535, **1066**
users. *See* external-user objectives

V
valuation, 362, 904
valuation allowance method, 1023
valuation allowances
accounts receivable, 348–352
defined, **1020**
example, 1020–1022
valuation allowance method, 1023
write-off of expired carryforward benefits, 1022–1023
valuation alternatives, 298, 300
valuation of the allowance for doubtful accounts, 353–355
value added, **41**
value added tax (VAT), **409**
value changes, 83 cd
value in use, **546**
variable interest entities, 1098
verifiability, 36, **46,** 282, 293, 309
vertical (common-size) analysis, 1307–1309, **1309**–1311, 1314
vesting, **906, 1133**
virtual certainty, **730**
volatility, 599
voluntary changes, **1253**–1254
voting rights
common shares, 826
limited or nonexistent, 826, 827
preferred shares, 826–827

W
warranties
as constructive liability, 730
cost deferral method, 729–730
sale with a warranty or service agreement, 275–277, 319
warrants, 901–903
website development costs, 477*f,* 480–481
weighted average number of shares, **89**
weighted average ordinary shares (WAOS), **1192**–1193
weighted average system, **436**
Westcast Industries Inc., 104, 106*f*
WestJet Airlines, 1301
window dressing, 1098, 1255
work in process, 407
work in progress inventory, 407, **410**
working capital loans, 772
worksheets
accounting information system (AIS), 684–686
defined, **684**
illustration, 684–686
writedowns, 99, 412, 413–415, 426, 427
write-off and recovery, **351**–352
write-off of expired carryforward benefits, 1022–1023
write-offs, 355–356, 1022–1023

Y
year-end, **369,** 724
yield, **735, 777**